Caribbean Islands

Debra Miller

Ginger Adams Otis, Conner Gorry, Jill Kirby, Michael Kohn,
Thomas Kohnstamm, Alex Leviton, Oda O'Carroll, Gary Prado Chandler,
Liza Prado Chandler, Michael Read, Ryan Ver Berkmoes

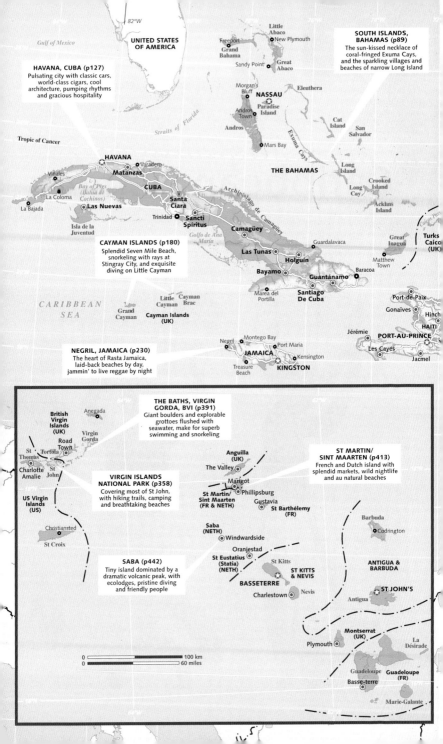

HAVANA, CUBA (p127)
Pulsating city with classic cars, world-class cigars, cool architecture, pumping rhythms and gracious hospitality

SOUTH ISLANDS, BAHAMAS (p89)
The sun-kissed necklace of coral-fringed Exuma Cays, and the sparkling villages and beaches of narrow Long Island

CAYMAN ISLANDS (p180)
Splendid Seven Mile Beach, snorkeling with rays at Stingray City, and exquisite diving on Little Cayman

NEGRIL, JAMAICA (p230)
The heart of Rasta Jamaica, laid-back beaches by day, jammin' to live reggae by night

THE BATHS, VIRGIN GORDA, BVI (p391)
Giant boulders and explorable grottoes flushed with seawater, make for superb swimming and snorkeling

ST MARTIN/ SINT MAARTEN (p413)
French and Dutch island with splendid markets, wild nightlife and au natural beaches

VIRGIN ISLANDS NATIONAL PARK (p358)
Covering most of St John, with hiking trails, camping and breathtaking beaches

SABA (p442)
Tiny island dominated by a dramatic volcanic peak, with ecolodges, pristine diving and friendly people

Gulf of Mexico

82°W

UNITED STATES OF AMERICA

Little Abaco
New Plymouth
Freeport
Grand Bahama
Sandy Point
Great Abaco

Morgan's Bluff
NASSAU
Andros Town
Paradise Island
Eleuthera
Cat Island
San Salvador

Straits of Florida

Tropic of Cancer

HAVANA Varadero
Matanzas
Viñales
La Coloma
Bay of Pigs (Bahía de Cochinos)
La Bajada
CUBA
Las Nuevas
Isla de la Juventud
Santa Clara
Trinidad **Sancti Spíritus**
Camagüey
Archipiélago de Camagüey

Andros
Mars Bay

THE BAHAMAS

Long Island
Long Cay
Crooked Island
Acklins Island

Great Inagua
Matthew Town
Turks & Caicos (UK)

Golfo de Ana María
Las Tunas
Guardalavaca
Holguín
Bayamo
Guantánamo
Baracoa

Marea del Portilla
Santiago De Cuba

Port-de-Paix
Gonaïves Hinch
HAITI

CARIBBEAN SEA

Little Cayman Cayman Brac
Grand Cayman
Cayman Islands (UK)

Jérémie
PORT-AU-PRINCE
Les Cayes
Jacmel

Negril Montego Bay
Port Maria
JAMAICA Kensington
Treasure Beach
KINGSTON

Anegada
British Virgin Islands (UK)
Virgin Gorda
Road Town
St Thomas Tortola
Charlotte Amalie St John
US Virgin Islands (US)

Christiansted
St Croix

Anguilla (UK)
The Valley
Marigot
St Martin/ Sint Maarten (FR & NETH) Phillipsburg
Gustavia
St Barthélemy (FR)

Saba (NETH)
Windwardside
Oranjestad
St Eustatius (Statia) (NETH)
St Kitts
ST KITTS & NEVIS
BASSETERRE
Charlestown Nevis

Barbuda
Codrington

ANTIGUA & BARBUDA
ST JOHN'S
Antigua

Montserrat (UK)
Plymouth
La Désirade

Guadeloupe **Guadeloupe (FR)**
Basse-terre
Marie-Galante

0 ───── 100 km
0 ───── 60 miles

ELEVATION

	2400m
	2100m
	1800m
	1500m
	1200m
	900m
	600m
	300m
	150m
	75m
	0

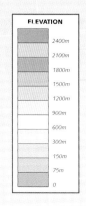

0 — 250 km
0 — 150 miles

ATLANTIC OCEAN

Tropic of Cancer

OLD SAN JUAN, PUERTO RICO (p315)
Colonial walled city at the heart of the capital, oozing with charm, fabulous restaurants and nightlife

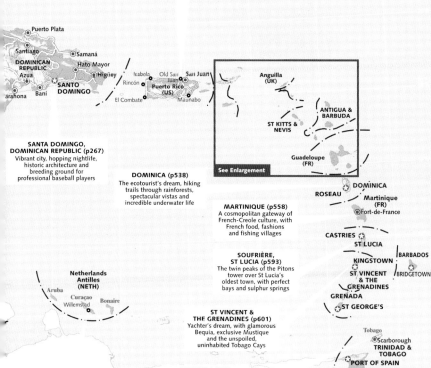

Cockburn Town

Puerto Plata

Santiago   Samaná

DOMINICAN REPUBLIC   Hato Mayor

Azua   Higüey   Ísabela   Old San   San Juan   Anguilla (UK)
    Rincón   Juan
arahona   Bani   **SANTO DOMINGO**   **Puerto Rico (US)**
            El Combate   Maunabo

ANTIGUA & BARBUDA

ST KITTS & NEVIS

SANTA DOMINGO, DOMINICAN REPUBLIC (p267)
Vibrant city, hopping nightlife, historic architecture and breeding ground for professional baseball players

DOMINICA (p538)
The ecotourist's dream, hiking trails through rainforests, spectacular vistas and incredible underwater life

Guadeloupe (FR)

See Enlargement

DOMINICA
ROSEAU   Martinique (FR)

MARTINIQUE (p558)
A cosmopolitan gateway of French-Creole culture, with French food, fashions and fishing villages

Fort-de-France

CASTRIES   **ST LUCIA**

BARBADOS

SOUFRIÈRE, ST LUCIA (p593)
The twin peaks of the Pitons tower over St Lucia's oldest town, with perfect bays and sulphur springs

KINGSTOWN   BRIDGETOWN
ST VINCENT & THE GRENADINES

Netherlands Antilles (NETH)

Aruba   Curaçao   Bonaire
Willemstad

GRENADA
ST GEORGE'S

ST VINCENT & THE GRENADINES (p601)
Yacht's dream, with glamorous Bequia, exclusive Mustique and the unspoiled, uninhabited Tobago Cays

Tobago

Scarborough
TRINIDAD & TOBAGO
PORT OF SPAIN
Trinidad

TOBAGO (p702)
Lightly developed, with gorgeous beaches, excellent coral and drift diving, affordable accommodations and welcoming locals

WILLEMSTAD, CURAÇAO (p745)
Colorful colonial architecture, cosmopolitan waterfront and embracing Dutch heritage

VENEZUELA

°W   68°W   66°W   64°W   62°W   60°W   GUYANA

Destination Caribbean Islands

Think of the Caribbean and inevitably you conjure up clichéd images of white-sand beaches and tropical drinks with little umbrellas. It's a pleasant thought, but we're here to tell you the islands offer *so* much more.

The contradictions hit you the moment you arrive. With a history built on piracy and sugar, slavery, revolt and colonial identity, the islands support a vibrant mix of cultures. There are cricket players and Rastas, Cuban rebels and lobster fishermen. The shifting sands on sheltered beaches come in impossible hues, from sugar white and salmon pink to coffee brown and charcoal black. While some islands shimmer just above sea level, others jut out like verdant icebergs.

It's an archipelago intimately tied to the sea and you'll fall under its spell the moment you taste salt on your skin. You'll forever remember seeing your first sea turtle float by and the sensation of grinning with a snorkel in your mouth. You'll climb high peaks whose forests redefine the word 'green,' where tropical birds flit about in flashes of color and fill the air with a symphony of squawks and song. You'll dance to rhythms of reggae, salsa and soca. You'll eat fresh seafood and spicy stews, and spend lazy afternoons snoozing in hammocks. And yes, you'll likely have some drinks garnished with little umbrellas as you watch the sunset from a beautiful white-sand beach.

WES WA

Beaches, Cays & Surf

MAURICIO HANDLER

Divers explore the boulders of the Baths (p391), Virgin Gorda, British Virgin Islands

MICHAEL LAWRENCE

Palm trees fringe Pigeon Point
(p705), Tobago, Trinidad & Tobago

OTHER HIGHLIGHTS

- Anguilla's Shoal Bay East (p408) confirms the picture-postcard image of a Caribbean beach.
- The uninhabited Tobago Cays (p619), St Vincent & the Grenadines, lure many yachts to their clear, turquoise waters.
- World Heritage–listed Bonaire Marine Park (p743), Bonaire, is tailored for superb diving and snorkeling.

JIM WARK

Yachts channel through the pristine waters of the Exumas (p90), the Bahamas

The Pitons (p585) rise dramatically from the shoreline of St Lucia

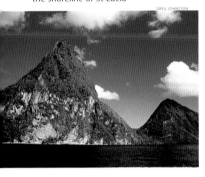

GREG JOHNSTON

GREG JOH

A diver mixes with the locals at Stingray City (p187), Grand Cayman, Cayman Islands

Windsurfing boards await the action at Cabarete (p296), Dominican Republic

SCOTT DO

Street Life

Bright, pastel-colored buildings line the streets of Old San Juan (p315), Puerto Rico

A stallholder in Nassau (p66), the Bahamas, offers a refreshing drink and a friendly smile

Customers prop up an open-air bar in Marigot (p416), St Martin

OTHER HIGHLIGHTS

- World Heritage–listed Habana Vieja (p129), in Cuba's City of Havana, is the best-preserved colonial complex in the Americas.
- With a maze of narrow streets set around its harbor, Grenada's capital, St George's (p657), is a quaint and colorful city.
- Step back in time exploring the stone-and-wood buildings of picturesque Roseau (p542), Dominica.

Festivals & Music

JEFF GREENBERG

Join the vibrant parades in Nassau's Junkanoo
(p72), the Bahamas

Marvel at the colorful costumes during
Carnival (p555), Dominica

MICHAEL LAW

RHONDA GUTENBERG

Cuban musicians (p126) perform on the
beach, City of Havana, Cuba

OTHER HIGHLIGHTS

- Along with mesmerizing sunsets, hip, laid-back
  Negril (p230), Jamaica, is famed for consistently
  high-quality reggae performances.
- Loud music and dancing fill the streets in Anse
  La Raye (p593), St Lucia, at the Friday-night
  jump-up parties.

Contents

Lonely Planet books provide independent advice. Lonely Planet does not accept advertising in guidebooks, nor do we accept payment in exchange for listing or endorsing any place or business. Lonely Planet writers do not accept discounts or payments in exchange for positive coverage of any sort.

Lonely Planet réalise ses guides en toute indépendance et les ouvrages ne contiennent aucune publicité. Les établissements et prestataires mentionnés dans ce guide ne le sont que sur la foi du jugement et des recherches des auteurs, qui n'acceptent aucune rétribution ou réduction de prix en échange de leurs commentaires.

Los libros de Lonely Planet ofrecen información independiente. La editorial no acepta ningún tipo de propaganda en las guías, así como tampoco endorsa ninguna entidad comercial o destino. Los escritores de Lonely Planet no aceptan descuentos o pagos de ningún tipo a cambio de comentarios favorables.

Regional Map Contents

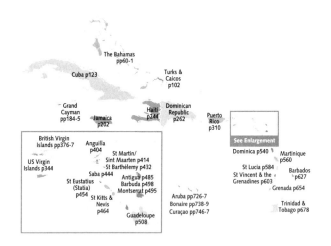

The Bahamas pp60-1
Cuba p123
Turks & Caicos p102
Grand Cayman pp184-5
Jamaica p202
Haiti p244
Dominican Republic p262
Puerto Rico p310
British Virgin Islands pp376-7
Anguilla p404
US Virgin Islands p344
St Martin/ Sint Maarten p414
St Barthélemy p432
Saba p444
St Eustatius (Statia) p454
St Kitts & Nevis p464
Antigua p485
Barbuda p498
Montserrat p495
Guadeloupe p508
Aruba pp726-7
Bonaire pp738-9
Curaçao pp746-7
See Enlargement
Dominica p540
Martinique p560
St Lucia p584
St Vincent & the Grenadines p603
Barbados p627
Grenada p654
Trinidad & Tobago p678

The Authors

DEBRA MILLER
Coordinating Author, Diving & Snorkeling, US Virgin Islands, British Virgin Islands, Trinidad & Tobago

Growing up dipping her toes in the Pacific Ocean along the British Columbia coast, Deb was a water baby from the get-go. In California, she worked as a senior editor for Lonely Planet's scuba diving and snorkeling guides, where she read about so many Caribbean destinations that she finally had to get to the bottom of it (literally). To date, she's logged hundreds of underwater hours and an equal amount of time topside, chatting with locals over a cold Carib. Today, Deb writes for several magazines; this is her eighth book for Lonely Planet.

My Favorite Trip

My husband came to meet me in St John (p357) when I was researching the US Virgin Islands. From the moment his plane arrived until he left a few days later, all it did was rain – hard. The first night, over rum cocktails, while the storm raged outside our condo at the Gallows Point Resort (p359), we decided we'd ignore the rain. The next day, we drove up to Trunk Bay (p361) with snorkeling gear and had a blast playing in the water. The beach, one of the world's truly great strands, was completely empty. That night, we ate seafood at Morgan's Mango (p360) and got drenched walking home in the rain. It was a good reminder that a tropical rain shower can be just as wonderful as tropical sun.

British Virgin Islands (UK)

Trunk Bay

St John

Cruz Bay

US Virgin Islands (US)

GINGER ADAMS OTIS
Puerto Rico

Ginger Adams Otis is a journalist living in New York City. She first saw Puerto Rico while on a Caribbean sailing trip with her parents at age 14 and has returned numerous times since to report on island politics. Ginger was in Old San Juan to write about the 500-year anniversary of Columbus' 'discovery,' and also covered the 2002 expulsion of the Navy from Vieques, a story she first started reporting in 1999. She recently worked on Lonely Planet's 3rd edition of *Puerto Rico*. Ginger also writes for the *Nation*, *Newsday*, *Village Voice*, *In These Times*, and other local and national publications.

LONELY PLANET AUTHORS

Why is our travel information the best in the world? It's simple: our authors are independent, dedicated travellers. They don't research using just the Internet or phone, and they don't take freebies in exchange for positive coverage. They travel widely, to all the popular spots and off the beaten track. They personally visit thousands of hotels, restaurants, cafés, bars, galleries, palaces, museums and more – and they take pride in getting all the details right, and telling it how it is. For more, see the authors section on www.lonelyplanet.com.

CONNER GORRY
Snapshots, Cuba

Conner's first foreign adventure was to Vieques, Puerto Rico, at age eight, partly explaining her attraction to Caribbean islands that subvert the dominant paradigm. In between getting a BA in Latin American Studies and an MA in International Policy (both with Cuba specialization), she volunteered in Cuba. Along the way, she has learned to 'resolver' as a tourist, TV talent scout, film festival juror, writer, reporter and food critic. Conner has written heaps of Lonely Planet guides to far-flung places in Latin America, most recently *Cuba* 3 and *Guatemala, Belize & Yucatán* 5. She also edits and writes for the monthly journal *MEDICC Review, Health & Medical News of Cuba*.

JILL KIRBY
Bahamas, Turks & Caicos

Having been lucky enough to travel through the Caribbean islands by fishing boat and ferry, Jill has taken time over the years to dance her way through the Reggae Sumfest in Jamaica, bask through Christmas on Barbados beaches and dive her way through New Year in St Vincent & the Grenadines, with just a bit of partying along the way. She continued diving across the Caribbean during an 18-month world trip, until reaching Australia, which is now her home. As a journalist and freelance writer, Jill jumped at the chance to cover the Bahamas and Turks & Caicos for this guide. She also updated Lonely Planet's 3rd edition of *Bahamas, Turks & Caicos*.

MICHAEL KOHN
Haiti

Born and raised in California, Michael had an early affection for sand and sea. He made first contact with the Caribbean during his student days, on various visits to St Martin, Martinique, Puerto Rico and Barbados, among other paradise spots. He probably would have ended up combing the Caribbean beaches forever had the twists of fate not led him to Asia, where he began a career in journalism, working mainly with the Associated Press and BBC radio. Michael spent three years based in Ulaan-baatar, with writing forays to south Asia. He is now full time with Lonely Planet and has worked on Lonely Planet guides to Central Asia, Tibet, Mongolia and the Middle East.

THOMAS KOHNSTAMM
St Vincent & the Grenadines, Barbados, Grenada

Thomas' first experience in the Caribbean was on the beaches and off-shore islands of Costa Rica and Panama in the mid-1990s. He was intrigued by the history and culture as much as by the beautiful scenery, and went on to study hybrid Caribbean languages as part of his degree. He has now visited islands from Cuba to Carriacou, surfed in Barbados, dived in the Tobago Cays, lived with former political prisoners in St George's and is convinced that, pound-for-pound, the Caribbean produces the best music in the world. He would live in the Caribbean full-time if only he could ski there.

ALEX LEVITON
Anguilla, St Martin/Sint Maarten, St Barthélemy, Saba, St Eustatius, St Kitts & Nevis

After growing up on a peninsula, Alex spent as much time as possible in slow-moving crafts on large bodies of water, from kayaks in northern California to *gulets* in Turkey. Especially because she's now land-locked in Durham, North Carolina, she was enthralled to return to the Eastern Caribbean where, just as she remembered, there is a tremendous amount of water. It was on this trip, while snorkeling in Saba, that she believes she saw her first sea turtle; her contact lenses had been stolen in St Martin (from a bag, not her person), so she's not quite sure.

ODA O'CARROLL
Antigua & Barbuda, Guadeloupe, Dominica, Martinique, St Lucia

From the far-flung reaches of midwest Ireland, Oda packed her kitbag at 17 and went to the big smoke to study Communications. She has lived in Dublin more or less ever since, with sporadic bouts of travel in between, and has worked as a TV researcher, screenwriter and director there for 15 years. She lives in the city with her husband and two daughters and has previously worked on Lonely Planet's *Britain, Ireland, Dublin, France* and *Corsica* guides.

GARY PRADO CHANDLER
Dominican Republic

Gary wrote the Dominican Republic chapter with wife and coauthor Liza. Gary's first trip to Dominican Republic was in 1998, when he joined a friend for a family visit and ended up staying for two months. This latest trip spanned Carnival, Independence Day and Semana Santa – the three main holidays – which made the research a bit of a challenge, but gave Gary plenty of opportunity to improve his merengue moves (unfortunately, it had no apparent effect). Gary is a graduate of UC Berkeley and Columbia Journalism School. This is his third assignment with Lonely Planet, after *Brazil* and *Central America*. He and Liza live in San Francisco.

LIZA PRADO CHANDLER
Dominican Republic

Liza coauthored the Dominican Republic chapter, joining husband Gary. A graduate of Brown University and Stanford Law School, Liza worked as a corporate attorney for three years before deciding she'd had quite enough of all that social standing, steady income and career advancement, and became a travel writer instead. She coauthored two books to another Caribbean destination – Cancún and the Yucatán Peninsula – before taking on one of her favorite places to travel, the Dominican Republic. This is her first assignment with Lonely Planet. After three years abroad and on the road, she and Gary now live in San Francisco.

MICHAEL READ
Cayman Islands, Jamaica

Michael, having finally figured out how to turn his proclivities for rum and vintage reggae into a paying gig, is an attentive student of Jamaica's school of life. When not chasing the horizon, Michael can be found in Oakland, California, where he has worked with LonelyPlanet.com and as an independent author, graphic designer, exhibitions curator and photographer. He contributed to the recent editions of *Mexico* and *USA & Canada on a Shoestring*, and was the main author of *Great Smoky Mountains & Shenandoah National Parks*. As this book went to press, Michael was back in the Caribbean, happily researching and writing the next edition of *Jamaica*.

RYAN VER BERKMOES
Aruba, Bonaire & Curaçao

Ryan Ver Berkmoes is fond of any place where his Dutch name raises nary an eyebrow. The ABCs excel in this department because folks there not only trill his name off their tongues, but give it a Papiamento lilt as well. He's been fond of the islands since he first wrote about them in 1993 and always welcomes a chance to return. His other activities include writing a range of Lonely Planet books to places that can never be too warm.

CONTRIBUTING AUTHOR

Dr David Goldberg, MD wrote the Health chapter (p784). David completed his training in internal medicine and infectious diseases at Columbia-Presbyterian Medical Center in New York City, where he has also served as voluntary faculty. He is an infectious diseases specialist in Scarsdale, New York, and is the editor-in-chief of the website www.mdtravelhealth.com.

Getting Started

It's always good to do a little advanced planning before any trip, and a vacation to the Caribbean Islands is no different. While it's hard to make generalizations about the region as a whole, the one thing the islands have in common is a relaxed, welcoming atmosphere. Travel around the Caribbean is relatively easy but it can be expensive, so making some plans ahead of time can really help.

WHEN TO GO

The busiest time for travel in the Caribbean Islands is mid-December to mid-April. Although this period does have drier and slightly cooler weather, the principal variable in making it the high season is the weather *elsewhere,* as the bulk of Caribbean tourists are 'snowbirds' escaping colder weather in North America and Europe.

You can enjoy dramatically discounted 'summer' hotel prices by visiting the islands in the low season, mid-April to mid-December. In addition, most airfares to the Caribbean are cheaper during this period, the beaches are less crowded, tourist areas have a more relaxed pace and last minute bookings for cars, flights and hotels are seldom a problem.

See p762 for climate charts.

On the minus side, the trade winds aren't as prevalent in summer, so the chance of encountering oppressively muggy weather is higher. Summer is also the hurricane season, particularly bad in August and September, when some hotels, restaurants and shops simply close for the month.

November and early December can be a pleasant time to visit, as long as you don't mind the odd rain shower beating down on your beach blanket. Hurricane season is over, and many hotels take a late-summer break to spruce up, so their rooms are at their preseason finest, the crowds are just beginning to show and the prices are still low.

COSTS & MONEY

In general, traveling in the Caribbean Islands is expensive, but costs can vary greatly depending on which islands you visit, the type of accommodations you choose and how you travel.

Accommodations will generally be the heftiest part of your budget. On islands such as Barbados, Trinidad and Tobago, a conventional hotel room or apartment can be quite reasonable; on pricier islands such as Antigua or Grand Cayman, a comparable room could easily cost twice

---

A HIGH WIND GONNA BLOW

The word 'hurricane,' denoting fierce cyclonic storms with winds in excess of 75mph (120km/h), comes from the language of Taíno Indians and their god of malevolence, Jurakán. Generally, the 'seeds' of these storms begin to grow off the west coast of Africa near the Cape Verde Islands. They migrate across the equatorial girdle of the Atlantic to the southern Caribbean as upper-atmospheric disturbances driven by the easterly trade winds. Here, they linger and pick up moisture and energy until the earth's spinning propels the growing storms north through the Caribbean. These storms have kicked the islands' asses in the past few years, and evidence of the devastation is everywhere. More evident, however, is the islanders' resilience. Somehow, board by board, they manage to rebuild their houses and lives, all the while bolstering their optimism that next year's storms won't be so bad.

DON'T LEAVE HOME WITHOUT...

In general, the Caribbean Islands are casual, so only bring clothes that will be comfortable in heat. Travel light: you'll likely spend most of your time in a bathing suit, T-shirt and shorts. Plus, many regional airlines charge extra for heavy baggage. If you're coming from winter in Helsinki or Montréal, don't be fooled into thinking you need a sweater. Trust us, you don't! One long-sleeve T-shirt to prevent sunburn or mosquito bites will be plenty. Flip-flops are ubiquitous and rarely inappropriate.

A few essentials you don't want to forget:

- basic medical kit
- mosquito repellent and sunscreen
- sun hat or baseball hat
- Swiss Army knife
- clothes washing detergent, plus a length of cord for drying laundry
- binoculars (especially for bird-watchers)
- mask, snorkel and fins (you can rent these, but having them along will save you money and free you up to jump in the water at whim)
- a small, quick-dry towel, for those times when the whim hits
- flashlight with batteries (blackouts are common)
- plastic resealable bags – essential for keeping things dry (use them to protect your camera, seal up airline tickets and passports, and store wet bathing suits)
- Lonely Planet's *French Phrasebook* (for Guadeloupe, Martinique, St Barth, St Martin and Haiti) and *Latin American Spanish Phrasebook* (for Cuba, Puerto Rico and Dominican Republic)
- a universal electrical current adapter.

as much. Of course the type of accommodations will also dictate cost – daily rates can vary from US$50 at a guesthouse to US$1000 at an exclusive resort. In this book, we've listed accommodations accordingly: budget US$75 or less; midrange US$76 to US$195; and top end US$196 and up.

Food can be relatively expensive, in part because much of it is imported. A great way to save money is to sample some of the local street food, which is usually both cheap and delicious. Seafood dinners in open-air seaside restaurants can be pricey, but savoring the same fare at a 'local' restaurant can cost half as much. Another good way to save costs is to rent a room or villa with a kitchen, buy local products and do your own cooking. In this book, we've listed meal prices accordingly: budget US$10 or less; midrange US$11 to US$25; and top end US$26 and up.

'Food can be relatively expensive, in part because much of it is imported.'

Transportation costs vary greatly. Car rentals generally cost between US$40 and US$80 a day. On the more developed islands, public buses provide a cheap way of getting around (plus a good dose of cultural immersion). On some islands, such as the US and British Virgin Islands, inexpensive passenger ferries connect the islands; in other areas, such as the Bahamas and most of the Dutch islands, regional airplanes provide the only method of interisland transportation. Air travel between islands can be expensive, but there are numerous deals floating around, including air passes with Leeward Island Air Transport (known only as LIAT; the main regional airline). See p770 for more.

Some little nagging costs can add up quickly, including local hotel taxes, departure taxes and hotel service charges (up to 25%).

READING UP
Books

The list of books written about Caribbean history, culture, flora, fauna and geography could fill an encyclopedia. Included here is a selection of recommended reads, chosen for their entertainment value, or the historical and cultural insights they give to the region. Books more relevant to the individual islands are listed under Books in the Directory of each chapter.

- *From Columbus to Castro: The History of the Caribbean 1492–1969* by Eric Williams. It's 35 years since this book was first published, but it remains an incredibly detailed account of the Caribbean's cruel and dramatic history, through colonialism, sugar, slavery and the search for cultural identity.
- *A Brief History of the Caribbean: From the Arawak and Carib to the Present* by Jan Rogozinski. A well-written book that checks in on recent developments in the islands' social, economic and political climate.
- *The Penguin Book of Caribbean Short Stories* by EA Markham (editor). Anyone looking for a good anthology of Caribbean writing ought to pick up this book, which includes stories from Jean Rhys, Jamaica Kincaid and VS Naipaul, as well as some expat writers.
- *Birds of the West Indies* by Herbert Raffaele, et al. The quintessential field guide, this book covers every species, including migrant and rare birds. Each species is identified by field marks, range, habitat and sound, along with color pictures.
- *Sailors Guide to the Windward Islands* and *Cruising Guide to the Leeward Islands* by Chris Doyle & Nancy Scott. Updated every couple of years, these books are thoroughly researched and packed with information from navigational approaches and entry regulations to where to pick up provisions and marine supplies.
- *Whispers from the Cotton Tree Root: Caribbean Fabulist Fiction* by Nalo Hopkinson (editor). This collection of 'Fabulist fiction' includes well-known and more contemporary Caribbean authors whose stories blend magical realism and ghost stories with old myths and fables.
- *The Ultimate Caribbean Quiz Book* by John Gilmore. A fun, brain-teasing read for anyone familiar with the entire Caribbean. There are 50 quizzes on everything from cricket to cuisine.

'The list of books written about the Caribbean could fill an encyclopedia.'

Websites

The Internet is a valuable research tool, but the barrage of information can be overwhelming. A good place to start is **Lonely Planet** (www.lonelyplanet.com), where you'll find succinct summaries of the islands, plus the Thorn Tree online forum, which has a special branch devoted to Caribbean travel, another devoted to Cuba and a special worldwide Diving & Snorkeling branch. For Caribbean vacation planning, we recommend the following:

A-Z Caribbean Islands (www.aguidetoparadise.com) A superb resource for pretrip planning.

Caribbean Hotel Association (www.caribbeanhotels.com) This site has links to the individual islands' hotel associations.

Caribbean Music (www.caribbeanmusic.com) An online resource and shop selling Caribbean music, including reggae calypso, salsa and steel pan.

Caribbean On-line (www.caribbean-on-line.com) An essential pretrip planning tool with maps, hotel and restaurant reviews, plus an active online discussion group.

Caribbean Travel & Life Magazine (www.caribbeantravelmag.com) The online version of this monthly magazine posts feature stories, planning tips and photos for post-trip daydreaming.

Caribseek (www.caribseek.com) A good search directory with links to sites throughout the Caribbean.

Cruise Critic (www.cruisecritic.com) Offers profiles and frank reviews of cruise ships, cruise industry news and analysis, plus last-minute deals.

RESPONSIBLE TRAVEL

Tourism pays the bills in most of the Caribbean, and the impact on the environment and the culture is huge. Here are a few pointers for minimizing your impact.

▪ Do not waste water. Fresh water is an extremely precious commodity on all of the islands, where desalination plants work overtime converting saltwater to fresh. Many islanders depend only on rainwater collected in cisterns, so keep in mind that winter – peak tourism time – is the driest time of year.

TOP SPOTS

Feature	Island	Page
Beaches		
Pink Sands	Harbour Island, Bahamas	p88
Les Salines	Martinique	p577
Grace Bay	Turks & Caicos	p108
Shoal Bay East	Anguilla	p408
Negril	Jamaica	p230
Shopping		
San Juan	Puerto Rico	p326
Nassau	New Providence, Bahamas	p75
George Town	Cayman Islands	p190
Charlotte Amalie	St Thomas, US Virgin Islands	p355
Marigot	St Martin	p418
Kid-Friendly		
Grand Cayman	Cayman Islands	p186
Nassau	New Providence, Bahamas	p66
Port Lucaya	Grand Bahama, Bahamas	p79
Eagle Beach	Aruba	p735
Culebra	Puerto Rico	p331
Mountains/Volcanoes		
The Pitons	St Lucia	p585
La Soufrière	St Vincent	p610
Mt Scenery	Saba	p449
Blue Mountains	Jamaica	p215
Pico Duarte	Dominican Republic	p300
Nightlife		
San Juan	Puerto Rico	p325
Port of Spain	Trinidad	p694
Casa de la Música	Cuba	p141
Pt Lucaya	Grand Bahama, Bahamas	p84
St Martin	St Martin	p415
Hiking		
Boiling Lake	Dominica	p552
El Yunque	Puerto Rico	p328
Lucayan National Park	Grand Bahama, Bahamas	p84
Pico Duarte	Dominican Republic	p300
Virgin Islands National Park	St John, US Virgin Islands	p358
Gay-Friendly		
San Juan	Puerto Rico	p314
Havana	Cuba	p174

▪ Never litter – sure, you'll see many locals do it, but you definitely shouldn't. Almost everything discarded on land makes its way to the sea, where it can wreak havoc on marine life. Carry your trash off beaches, trails and campsites. You can even haul out trash others have left behind.

▪ Travel globally; shop locally. Not only will buying local products infuse the local economy, it will also help to save you money. You will have plenty of opportunities to drink imported beers, but why not try one of the many beers brewed locally?

Feature	Island	Page
Saba	Saba	p450
St Barthélemy	St Barthélemy	p433
St Croix	US Virgin Islands	p367
Romance		
Old San Juan	Puerto Rico	p314
Eleuthera	Bahamas	p88
Owen Island	Little Cayman	p196
Nevis	Nevis	p472
Malecón	Cuba	p133
Waterfalls		
Trafalgar Falls	Dominica	p551
El Nicho	Cuba	p157
Bassins Bleu	Haiti	p254
Dunn's River Falls	Jamaica	p219
El Limón	Dominican Republic	p287
Bird-watching		
Asa Wright Nature Center	Trinidad	p697
Codrington Lagoon	Barbuda	p500
Bosque Estatal de Guánica	Puerto Rico	p336
Inagua National Park	Great Inagua, Bahamas	p92
Tobago Forest Reserve	Tobago	p713
Gardens		
Versailles Gardens	Nassau, Bahamas	p70
Jardín de las Hermanas Caridad	Cuba	p145
Botanical Gardens of Nevis	Nevis	p474
Andromeda Botanic Gardens	Barbados	p642
Mamiku Gardens	St Lucia	p596
Sailing		
Annual Spring Regatta & Sailing Festival	Tortola, British Virgin Islands	p382
Family Island Regatta	Exumas, Bahamas	p90
Atlantic Rally for Cruisers	St Lucia	p598
Easter Regatta	Bequia, the Grenadines	p621
Antigua Sailing Week	Antigua	p502
Wild Places		
Anegada	British Virgin Islands	p395
Northern Coast	Dominica	p549
Chutes du Carbet	Guadeloupe	p522
Soufrière Hills Volcano	Montserrat	p496
Grand Etang National Park	Grenada	p665

- When diving, snorkeling, boating or just playing in the water, remember that coral is a living organism that gets damaged with every touch, kick or step.
- Never, ever, buy any souvenirs made of coral, seashell or turtle shell. Because of tourist demand, coral is often pillaged from pristine reefs, which leaves the underwater ecosystem and its convoluted food chain at risk. Turtle hunting is a primary reason sea turtle populations continue to decline. Ask yourself if that pretty turtle-shell necklace is really worth it. Also keep in mind that turtle-shell jewelry, as well as sea-turtle taxidermy and food products, are prohibited entry into the USA, Canada, Australia and most other countries. The importation of black coral is likewise banned in more than 100 countries.
- When driving on the islands, keep an eye out for stray dogs, chickens and goats, all of which meander aimlessly through the island roads.
- Impatience will get you about as far as a toboggan in the Caribbean Islands, where time flows with the tides. Slow down, mon. Always start with 'Good day,' *'buenos días'* or *'bonjour'* before launching into a conversation or abruptly asking questions; you'll find that a smile and a courteous attitude go a long way.
- Many people, especially vendors in the marketplaces, do not like to be photographed; ask first, and respect the wishes of those who refuse. If someone asks you for cash in exchange for the photo-op, consider complying.

FAVORITE FESTIVALS & EVENTS

No matter what Caribbean island you land on, you'll quickly discover one thing: Caribbean Islanders love to party! No matter what time of year, come rain or shine, you'll find plenty of live music, dancing in the streets and countless reasons to celebrate. Here are a few of our favorites:

- **Port of Spain's Carnival** (p690) Trinidad spends all year gearing up for its legendary street party, with steel-pan bands, blasting soca and calypso music, and outrageous costumes.
- **Junkanoo** (p72) The Bahamas national festival takes over Nassau, starting in the twilight hours on Boxing Day (December 26). It's a frenzied party with marching 'shacks,' colorful costumes and music.
- **Carnaval, Santiago de Cuba** (p174) Cuba's oldest, biggest and wildest celebration is held in the last week of July.
- **Fiesta de Santiago Apostal** (p340) Puerto Ricans celebrate their mixed African and European ancestry during the last five days of July by donning colorful *vejigante* masks (colorful papier-mâché masks depicting often scary characters from African and European mythology) and parading through the streets of Aldea Loíza.
- **Crop-Over Festival** (p647) Barbados' big three-week festival marks the end of the sugarcane harvest. Festivities start in mid-July with calypso competitions and end with a big parade.
- **Santiago's Carnival** (p274) The Dominican Republic's most traditional Carnival celebration (and one of the largest), featuring two rival groups – La Joya and Los Pepines – each boasting fantastic handmade masks with huge horns and toting 'weapons' made of inflated cow bladders tied to long cords.
- **Carnival, Antigua** (p502) Antigua's annual carnival takes place at the end of July and culminates in a grand parade, with plenty of music and mayhem to get you in the festive mood.
- **Reggae Sumfest** (p224) Die-hard Rastafarians and Marley followers come from all over the world to jam with the masses at Jamaica's top reggae festival, held every July in Montego Bay.

Itineraries
CLASSIC ROUTES

VIEWING THE VIRGINS   Two Weeks

Some of the world's best sailing is in the protected US and British Virgin Islands, where a friendly port is always nearby and usually stocked with icy-cold beer. You can also tour the area by an excellent network of ferries. Start with a day of duty-free shopping in **Charlotte Amalie** (p355) and lunch on local cuisine at **Gladys' Cafe** (p354). Catch an island taxi to **Red Hook** (p355), and spend a couple of nights along the Atlantic at the **Sapphire Beach Resort & Marina** (p356). Next, hop on a ferry to **St John** (p357), where you can overnight in a tent at the ecoresort **Maho Bay Camps** (p362) or sleep to the sound of waves at **Gallows Point Resort** (p359) in Cruz Bay. Spend a few days snorkeling at pristine beaches like **Trunk Bay** (p361) or **Cinnamon Bay** (p361). Take a ferry to the British Virgin island of **Jost Van Dyke** (p393), where you can swill local brew at **Foxy's Tamarind Bar** (p394) in Great Harbour. Then, ferry to West End on **Tortola** (p384) and have dinner in Road Town at **Le Cabanon** (p383). Head to **Cane Garden Bay** (p385) for a couple of days of seafood eating and beachside lounging, or take a rainforest hike to the top of **Sage Mountain** (p385). Finally, take the lovely ferry ride to **Virgin Gorda** (p389), where you can snorkel among giant boulders at the **Baths** (p391).

Island hopping through the US and British Virgin Islands is easy. This itinerary takes you duty-free shopping on St Thomas, snorkeling on Virgin Gorda, and leaves plenty of time for sun worshipping as well.

KICKING AROUND THE CAYMANS   Three Weeks

On **Grand Cayman** (p183) spend a few days doing nothing at all on the exquisite **Seven Mile Beach** (p187). Ready for some activity? Hover weightless at one of the many celebrated **diving sites** (p187), or if you're not certified, get some diving instruction. Continue exploring the underwater realm: strap on a mask and visit the denizens of **Stingray City** (p187). Resurface to view sea turtles at the **Cayman Turtle Farm** (p191); don't forget to send a postcard home from **Hell** (p191). Next, enact your submarine scenario fantasies on a 1000ft (300m) dive with **Atlantis Adventures** (p188) in George Town. Visit **Rum Point** (p192) for snorkeling, sun worship and the quintessential mudslide. Next, track the elusive blue iguana in the **Queen Elizabeth II Botanic Park** (p192), then dip into island history at **Pedro St James Castle** (p191) and the **National Museum** (p187). For a change of scene, island-hop over to **Cayman Brac** (p192) and spend a day or more hiking to pirate caves or along the cliffs for stupendous views. Charter a boat and fish for yellowfin or marlin, or merely contemplate your navel on the peaceful public beach. Fly to **Little Cayman** (p195) for more fun in the sun: dive or snorkel off **Bloody Bay** (p196) and peer into the abyss, or have a close encounter with a booby at **Booby Pond Nature Reserve** (p195). Kayak – or swim – to tiny **Owen Island** (p196) for a Robinson Crusoe experience amongst the swaying palms.

This island-hopping expedition offers up the best of the Cayman Islands' gorgeous beaches, world-famous water sports and traditional Caribbean charm. It begins with a thorough exploration of Grand Cayman and concludes on the far-flung 'sister islands,' Cayman Brac and Little Cayman.

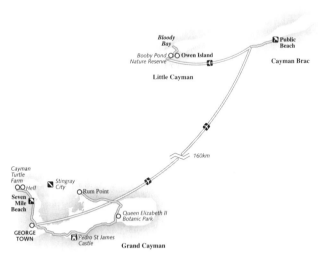

BASKING IN THE BAHAMAS   Two to Four Weeks

Spend three days in **Nassau** (p66) seeing the sights before taking a three-day trip to **Alice Town** (p85) on North Bimini to go bonefishing, or snorkel the mystical **Bimini Road** (p85) and sup at Hemingway's haunts.

Head to **Grand Bahama** (p76) for a few days of glorious beach-bumming and trips to see **dolphins** (p81) or to go kayaking in **Lucayan National Park** (p82). Fly to Marsh Harbour on **Great Abaco** (p86) and relax on **Treasure Cay's** (p87) exquisite beach before taking ferries to friendly **Green Turtle Cay** (p87) for a Goombay Smash, and Elbow Cay to wander lovely **Hope Town beach** (p87).

Fly to George Town on **Great Exuma** (p90) for some relaxing **houseboating** (p90) amongst the cays, a visit to **Stocking Island** (p90) and a snorkel around the entrancing **Thunderball Grotto** (p90). Then head over to pretty **Long Island** (p91) for the humbling churches of **Clarence Town** (p92) and the world's deepest blue hole at nearby **Turtle Cove** (p92). Take a dive off **Shark Reef** (p91) and regain your nerves on the beach at **Guana Key** (p92).

Finally, fly to **Eleuthera** (p88) to see the beautiful people on **Harbour Island** (p88). Now is the time to take your beloved's hand and stroll the rosy hue of **Pink Sands Beach** (p88) at sunset.

This 870-mile (1400km) run is definitely designed for water-babies who delight in exploring islands where dogs snooze in the shadows of pastel-colored cottages. Take a water-taxi, ferry or plane to destinations where some extra-ordinary snorkeling and diving await you, and sugar-soft empty beaches invite you to relax.

CUBAN CAVORT   Two Weeks to Two Months

With two weeks and a car you can see a lot of Cuba, but using public transport can give you a good (sometimes better!) taste too. With two months, you can travel the breadth in depth, exploring more remote locales and relaxing for a spell at your preferred beach.

After ogling the incredible architecture in **Havana** (p127), head to **Santa Clara** (p152) and the venerable **Monumento Ernesto Che Guevara** (p153), with its superb mausoleum. Push on from here to overnight in a seaside home in charming **Cienfuegos** (p157) before continuing to **Trinidad** (p159), a Unesco World Heritage site. You can easily spend a week in this colonial town hiking in **Topes de Collantes** (p160), horseback riding in **Valle de los Ingenios** (p160) or lazing at **Playa Ancón** (p160). Push east to **Santiago de Cuba** (p162) and its many attractions including the **Castillo de San Pedro del Morro** (p166), the **Cuartel Moncada** (p164) and, of course, the kicking nighttime music scene. Be sure to save at least two days for exploring in and around **Baracoa** (p169), one of Cuba's loveliest areas.

Most international flights take you into Havana or Santiago de Cuba, but you can easily start this adventure in **Varadero** (p148), another popular entry point, often with insanely cheap air and hotel deals on offer.

You can cover the 861km between Havana and Santiago de Cuba in 15 hours. If you're on the bus-train combo, add more time, but skip Topes de Collantes, as it's hard to reach with public transportation.

ROADS LESS TRAVELED

EASTERN CARIBBEAN ESCAPE   Two Weeks

Secluded white-sand beaches, gourmet seafood and French restaurants, breathtaking accommodation, stunning scenery – anyone can find a reason to tread deep off the beaten path in the Eastern Caribbean.

The hub of **St Martin/Sint Maarten** (p413), is the most animated…or over-crowded, depending on your point of view. Gorgeous beaches and classy restaurants rub elbows with high-rise hotels and gentlemen's clubs. Head to **Grand Case** (p420) to eat and **Marigot** (p418) to shop.

For quieter dining and beaches, ferry to English-speaking **Anguilla** (p402) and rent your own villa. Try one of the 80 restaurants, including the beachfront lobster shack **Palm Grove** (p408) at Junk's Hole Bay.

Fly a charter plane over to **St Barth** (p430) for a surprisingly laid-back, beachy vacation. Next head to **Saba** (p442), a volcanic iceberglike island shooting straight out of the Caribbean, with some of the best **hiking** (p449) around. Stay at the **Ecolodge Rendez Vous** (p446) or **El Momo Cottages** (p446), in Windwardside, to complete your oneness with nature. For some of the best diving on the planet, hop onto a 10-minute flight to **St Eustatius** (Statia; p459).

Move on to **St Kitts & Nevis** (p462), which have a plethora of palm tree–lined beaches and centuries-old **plantation inns** (p476). Both islands offer a good dose of culture, history and wild monkeys.

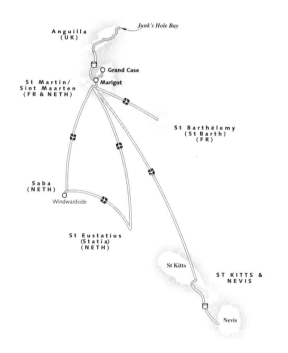

St Martin functions as the transportation hub to these tiny islands. It's just a ferry ride to the famous beaches on Anguilla and St Barth. Volcanic Saba and historic St Eustatius (Statia) offer fantastic underwater experiences. St Martin is famous for its nightlife, but St Kitts has casinos and beach bars that liven up considerably at night too.

THE ABCS BY ABC   Two Weeks

Great beaches, superb diving and tropical nightlife are yours on a tour of
Aruba, Bonaire and Curaçao. The catch is that each island offers something entirely different, so you'd better visit all three.

Aruba (p725) has the best beaches and is the easiest to reach from
North America, so this is the place to start banishing your pallor. Hit the
long crescent of sand at **Eagle Beach** (p735), which fronts the most relaxed
places to stay. Having nailed your base tan, venture further afield to
Dos Playa within **Arikok National Wildlife Park** (p736). It's rugged here and
you can enjoy the stark beauty of the cactus-covered landscape, sand
dunes and high surf.

Bonaire (p737) is a 45-minute flight from Aruba. With only a 10th of
the population, it feels remote and you won't have to fantasize hard that
you have finally gotten away. Reefs surround the island and the **diving**
(p743) is about the best in the world. You'll have your pick of spots that
line the roads and if you're not already certified, this is the place to do
it, as the island's inherent relaxed charm make for a stress-free learning
experience.

Curaçao (p744) feels like the most urban of the three. And although
you can escape to the rural beauty of the north, much activity centers on
the capital of **Willemstad** (p745). Here huge ships rumba along the channel that cleaves through the middle of the historic old town. Locals and
visitors alike make their own moves at the many nightclubs and bars;
the music is a manic mix of calypso, reggae, salsa and more.

Start reciting your
ABCs as you bask
along some of the
Caribbean's best
beaches, hike
through sand dunes
and experience
dazzling diving. You
can't help but
warm to the rich
history and Dutch-
Caribbean culture,
with plenty of
stellar nightlife
mixed in.

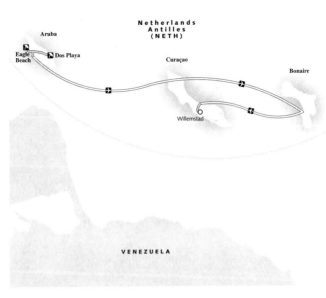

TAILORED TRIPS

GREATER MOUNTAINS

The islands of the Dominican Republic, Haiti, Puerto Rico and Jamaica are part of the Greater Antilles (along with Cuba and the Caymans) and among their few commonalities, they share some the Caribbean's most incredible mountains. On Puerto Rico, the 43-sq-mile (111-sq-km) Caribbean National Forest, more commonly known as **El Yunque** (p328) for its distinctive peak, has the island's only remaining virgin forest – some trees are more than 1000 years old. The Dominican Republic boasts a whopping 10 national parks, including **Parque Nacional Los Haitises** (p283) and **Parque Nacional José del Carmen Ramírez** (p300), which is the home to Pico Duarte, the Caribbean's tallest peak.

Sharing the island of Hispaniola, neighboring Haiti has two mountain parks, **Parc National La Visite** (p255) and **Parc National Macaya** (p255), in which grows the country's remaining cloud forest.

Head west to Jamaica and you'll find the legendary **Blue Mountains** (p215), home to more than 500 species of flowering plants.

The topography of the region is perfect for growing coffee beans, and the country's Blue Mountain coffee is often called the best in the world.

HOPPIN' AROUND

Rum gets most of the attention in the Caribbean, but you can't forget about the local brews. Heaven forbid you come to the islands and order an imported beer, especially when there are enough local suds to keep you satiated for a lifetime.

This is obviously…hicc…an informal itinerary, not really intended for a…hicc…single trip.

Start your tour of island suds on New Providence, Bahamas, and shuffle up to the bar and order a **Kalik** (p64); try the gold – it's the best. Zip over to the Caymans for some **Stingray Dark** (p183), then down to Jamaica for the ever-refreshing **Red Stripe** (p207). Jet over to the Virgin Islands for some **Blackbeard Ale** or **Foxy's Lager** (p348) and, just so you don't get thirsty, head south for a sample of Antigua's **Wadadli** (p486), a delicious pale lager. Continue your search for the perfect malt by heading to the pristine island of Dominica for a taste of **Kubuli** (p542), then float down to St Lucia for a bottle of **Piton Lager** (p586). Go southeast to Barbados for a bottle of **Banks beer** (p629), take a whack of the cricket bat, and then follow the ball down to Trinidad for the ubiquitous **Carib** (p683). Finish off drinking with the Dutch on Aruba, where you can try the tasty **Balashi beer** (p725). If you're still thirsty after all that, well then you probably need some help. Cheers!

WORLD CUP WANDER

Cricketers throughout the Caribbean got their whites covered in grass stains after hearing the Caribbean would host the 2007 Cricket World Cup. They dropped their bats, kicked their wickets and rolled around in the grass hooting for joy. On many islands, cricket is a big, big deal. Past and present members of the West Indies team achieve hero status in these parts, and hosting the World Cup is a little like hosting the Olympics. Massive preparations are underway. More seats will be added to **Queen's Park Oval** (p680), the Caribbean's oldest cricket ground in Port of Spain, Trinidad; Grenada's hurricane-wracked **Queen's Park** (p658) will have to be rebuilt; **Kensington Oval** (p644) in Bridgetown, Barbados, is undergoing massive renovations; the relatively new **Beausejour Stadium** (p591), St Lucia, is getting more seats; **Warner Park Stadium** (p466) in Basseterre, St Kitts, will more than double in size; the new **Sir Vivian Richards Stadium** (p484) is under construction in Antigua; and Jamaica's 30,000-seat **Sabina Park** (p213) is undergoing major upgrades.

Tickets are already on sale and tourism and cricket officials throughout the region are giddy as they scramble to get the cricket-obsessed Caribbean ready for her big performance; they are well aware that the event could significantly boost the local economies and that the entire British Commonwealth will be watching.

Jamaica

St Kitts ○ ○ Antigua

St Lucia ○
Barbados ○
Grenada ○

Trinidad

Snapshots

CURRENT EVENTS

There are some folks you don't want crashing the party: Charlie, Frances, Ivan and Jeanne, a deadly quartet of storms, walloped the Caribbean in August and September 2004, killing scores and leaving a multibillion dollar trail of destruction. While Jamaica, Grenada, the Cayman Islands, Cuba, the Dominican Republic and Haiti – the countries hardest hit – fought to right themselves, the damage highlighted inequities within the region. Haiti, the poorest nation in the western hemisphere, suffered particularly. Food shortages, public health threats and rioting following Tropical Storm Jeanne required an international relief effort that included UN aid workers, Cuban medical brigades and multimillion dollar aid packages from the US and EU; with thousands dead and tens of thousands homeless, pleas for risk reduction and disaster prevention rang around the region.

Taking people's minds off disaster were the feverish preparations for the World Cricket Cup, to be held in the Caribbean in 2007; host countries include Antigua, Jamaica, Barbados, Grenada, St Kitts, St Lucia and Trinidad.

Taking it twice on the chin, the **Bahamas** got hit by both Hurricane Frances and Tropical Storm Jeanne and while there were no deaths or serious injuries, roads were chewed up and coastal villages and properties suffered. Eleuthera took the brunt of it. Development issues continue to chaff as public access to beaches and land is restricted by new resorts. Drug trafficking and the violence it begets are other challenges facing the country.

A major shipwreck found near East Caicos is being hailed as the 'Plymouth Rock' of **Turks & Caicos**. Marine archaeologists surveyed a wooden wreck presumed to be *Trouvadore*, a slave ship that sank off the islands in 1841. All 193 Africans on board survived and, amazingly, were set free following the ordeal. These African survivors increased the island's population by 7% and all current residents share blood with them. The fascinating event is being made into a PBS documentary, *Trouvadore: Last Voyage of an African Slaver*.

All politics, all the time: welcome to the **Cuba** channel. The arrest of 75 dissidents in 2003 sparked a human-rights flap that saw the EU withdraw support from the island. Once some prisoners were released in 2004, the EU and Cuba were buddies anew. Not so the behemoth to the north: President George Bush's desire to rid the world of Fidel reached new heights with a strengthened US travel ban. Cuba has since discovered oil near Varadero. Stay tuned. In November 2004, the US dollar was withdrawn from circulation, but the famed double economy was maintained by substituting nationally produced *pesos convertibles* in their stead. In an 'only in Cuba' scenario, the new currency is abbreviated CUC – 'kooks' in local vernacular.

Houses were reduced to kindling and boats were beached after Hurricane Ivan hit the **Caymans** on September 13, 2004. An estimated quarter to a half of the island's 15,000 homes were damaged and elections to be held on November 17 were postponed until May 2005. At the time of research, travelers were required to show proof of air and land reservations to Cayman Islands' immigration officials before being permitted entry into the country. (For the latest updates on the effort to rebuild the Cayman Islands and how it affects travel, see www.cayman.org.)

The Island: Martinique, by John Edgar Wideman, is a stream-of-consciousness inspirational poetic-prose romp around Martinique, riffing on everything from slavery to guided tours.

The World Bank's Caribbean representative, Debrework Zewdie, stated that the World Bank is concerned that the current AIDS pandemic could lead to 'regional economic collapse.'

There's something about prison flicks…especially Jose Enrique 'Pinky' Pintor's *La Cárcel La Victoria El Cuatro Hombre,* filmed in the Dominican Republic's most over-crowded and terrifying prison, using inmate actors. The violent verité flavor stays with you.

The **Dominican Republic**, mired in economic crisis, elected Leonel Fernández in May 2004 on a platform of fiscal responsibility. This has been sorely lacking in the DR, which is still recovering from widespread bank fraud uncovered in 2003, amounting to over 20% of the country's GDP (ouch). The country sent troops to Iraq and signed on to the Central American Free Trade Agreement (CAFTA), bringing them deeper into the US fold. Meanwhile, the innovative government program called *Comer es Primero* (Eating Comes First), distributed debit cards to 6000 poor families who use the US$19 balance to buy food. Now, if they could only solve the blackouts – electricity shortages regularly plunge the country into darkness. Economic losses of about US$51 million from Tropical Storm Jeanne, don't help.

Things are much worse in neighboring **Haiti**, where the ouster of President Jean-Bertrand Aristide on February 29, 2004 and the 2004 hurricane season left the country in shambles. Tropical Storm Jeanne killed 3006 people, and hundreds more have died in random urban violence, including gruesome beheadings by gangs undertaking 'Operation Baghdad.' Police brutality and violent protests add to a cycle of crises the nearly 7000 UN peacekeepers can't snap. National elections set for November 2005 have attracted some 100 possible candidates, though it seems a thankless job. In October 2004, the US State Department issued a travel warning for Haiti; this warning is updated regularly and can be found at http://travel.state.gov/travel/cis_pa_tw/tw/tw_917.html.

In September 2004, Hurricane Ivan rode roughshod over **Jamaica**, causing an estimated US$362 million in damages. International aid organizations mobilized with food and medicine donations and the US promised nearly US$4 million in aid. Jamaica's economic woes spiraled downward due to the hurricane, tax hikes and unemployment sparking episodic violence in Kingston's poorer neighborhoods. Even Bob Marley couldn't rest in peace, as a row erupted when his widow Rita Marley pledged to move his remains to Ethiopia. Instead, what would have been Bob's 60th birthday on February 1, 2005 was celebrated with a memorial concert series in Addis Ababa.

Don't be surprised if your *café con leche* costs a little more on **Puerto Rico** these days: Tropical Storm Jeanne ripped out coffee plants and killed milking cows, though the majority of the estimated US$100 million in crop damage was to banana and plantain trees. President Bush has promised to look at the commonwealth's relation to the US and whether statehood or independence might not be a better solution.

On the nearby **US Virgin Islands**, the incumbent Virgin Islands Party (VIP) lost the 2004 elections after 17 years in power. Elections in **Anguilla** (rhymes with vanilla) were held on February 21, 2005, with incumbent Chief Minister Osbourne Fleming stumping on jobs created by the new $21 million international airport and multimillion dollar golf course.

There was big news out of **Antigua & Barbuda** as Prime Minister Lester Bird went down in the March 2004 elections, throwing the Bird family from its 50-year political nest. He was defeated by labor activist Baldwin Spencer of the United Progressive Party (UPP), who immediately extended the lease of the US Antigua Air Station to 2008, prompting a courtesy call from the biggest US congressional delegation ever to visit the islands. In 2004, Antiguan Rastafarians staged a protest calling for the legalization of marijuana, stating that their herbal sacrament presents 'great commercial potential'; legalization is highly unlikely, considering the US provides substantial aid to the island to fight drug trafficking.

Cricket is huge on **St Kitts & Nevis** and they, like most of the cricketing islands, hunger to host the World Cup in 2007. Not surprising then that

Cuba has the lowest infant mortality rate in the region (5.8 per 1000), Haiti has the highest (79 per 1000); Barbados has the highest life expectancy (77.2), Haiti the lowest (49.5); see the UNDP Report at http://hdr.undp.org /reports/global/2004 /pdf/hdr04_HDI.pdf.

On January 1, 1804, Haiti became the western hemisphere's second colony (after the USA) to declare independence, becoming the world's first Black republic.

Michele Wucker lends her keen journalistic style and sensibility in *Why the Cocks Fight: Dominicans, Haitians, and the Struggle for Hispaniola*, an informative and highly readable history of the island.

Warner Park Cricket Stadium is being upgraded and gussied up, thanks to a US$1.4 million grant from Taiwan; in 2004, China and Taiwan took their ideological battle to the Caribbean (see below). Nevis, forever hoping to secede from St Kitts, failed to pass a referendum in 2004.

Being a colony underlies the political discourse on many of the islands, including **Guadeloupe**, whose conservative party lost regional elections in 2004 – the first time in 12 years. The rout was interpreted as a mandate to maintain strong ties with France. Seems changes to the legislature the year before flirted too close to independence. On November 21, 2004, a magnitude 6.0 earthquake hit Guadeloupe, killing a boy and destroying several homes.

In March 2004, **Dominica** swung diplomatic recognition from Taiwan to China after the latter proffered US$112 million in aid. China has been busy in the region, having signed major trade and aid deals with Cuba, Trinidad & Tobago and Jamaica. Three churches in Dominica were damaged in the earthquake that also hit Guadeloupe.

The economy of **St Lucia**, already shaky as preferential EU terms for Caribbean bananas are phased out, looked even grimmer after Hurricane Ivan destroyed 30% of the banana crop, signifying an estimated US$3.7 million loss in revenue. Many homes and buildings were also damaged. St Lucian diplomat Edwin Laurent will argue on behalf of his country, St Vincent & the Grenadines and Dominica regarding the EU-banana issue. On a positive note, Unesco designated the Piton's Management Area a World Heritage site in 2004. The seaside double-volcano complex contains sulfur springs, fumaroles and extensive offshore coral reefs.

For **St Vincent & the Grenadines**, economic diversification tops the 'to do' list, as they too face losing preferential EU terms for their bananas by 2006. The matter took on urgency when Hurricane Ivan felled 20% of the banana crop and 50 homes. Luckily, extra revenue is coming from filthy-rich vacationers buying private islands nearby, and from Hollywood: all three of the *Pirates of the Caribbean* movies are set in St Vincent and the Tobago Cays, providing local employment and grist for the gossip mill. Star sightings will be possible through 2006. Johnny Depp, anyone?

Yup, Hurricane Ivan had his way with **Barbados** too, damaging over 370 homes, some completely. Though hurricanes are associated with high winds – and Ivan gusted at 160mph (257km/h) – flooding and ocean surges are often more dangerous and damaging. A Canadian woman drowned in floodwaters here during the hurricane.

The destruction wrought by Hurricane Ivan elsewhere is nowhere close to what **Grenada** suffered. Tourism installations and the nutmeg crop – the country's two top earners – were blown away, 39 people died and 8000 to 10,000 were made homeless; the storm completely destroyed 90% of the island's structures. Damage estimates are around US$900 million, more than double the country's GDP. Projections indicate that Grenada will not show economic growth for over a decade, and a moratorium on the country's foreign debt is a possibility. Another alternative being bandied about is a political union with St Vincent, which unfurled a huge safety net in the wake of the storm. Even former Prime Minister Nicholas Brathwaite (1990–95) couldn't escape the looting rampages in the post-storm melee: his house and car (even the spare tires!) were stripped clean.

In 2004, a Chinese delegation arrived in **Trinidad & Tobago** brandishing a silk purse with loans totaling US$152 million for export ventures and another US$7.6 million *gift* for projects to be decided later. The day before the aid package was proffered, Trinidad & Tobago (like Dominica)

The legacy of slavery and development of modern race relations are plot flashpoints for *Sugar Cane Alley*, an inspiring movie about a young Black orphan in 1930 Martinique.

In 1983 St Kitts & Nevis merged and declared independence from Britain, becoming the smallest nation in the western hemisphere.

For an articulate look at the complexities of the US–Puerto Rico relationship, check out *The Disenchanted Island: Puerto Rico and the United States in the 20th Century* by Ronald Fernández.

announced they were switching loyalties from Taiwan to China. China, the hosts of the 2008 Olympics, also discussed buying asphalt from Trinidad & Tobago, as the country will need lots of it for the construction frenzy leading up to the games.

Accused of a nasty corruption scandal involving a justice minister and shady political donations, the coalition governing **Curaçao**, led by the Frente Obrero Liberashon (FLO), took a tumble in April 2004. A new coalition, led by the Antillean Restructuring Party (PAR), emerged from the fray.

The **ABC Islands** made major political news in October 2004 when a joint Dutch–Netherlands Antillean commission issued the Jesurun Report, recommending that Curaçao and **Sint Maarten** become autonomous states within the Dutch kingdom (like Aruba's status since 1986), and that **Saba**, **St Eustatius** and **Bonaire** return to being governed by the Hague. (St Eustatius voted to remain a part of the Netherlands Antilles, effectively leaving it the only member.) Relations between the federated islands of the Netherlands Antilles have always been volatile. Curaçao – the governmental seat – feels it does the most work for the least reward and are self-sufficient enough to fly solo. The smaller islands complain that the government in Curaçao overlooks their concerns. Everyone agrees the current situation is too complicated, though the solution may be more complicated still: the soon-to-be independent islands need to ramp up their judiciary and police force, plus there's US$2 billion in Antillean debt for the Netherlands to assume. No timetable was offered for the change over, though it's likely to happen in 2006.

For a stark look at what International Monetary Fund (IMF) restructuring programs can do to a country's economic and social fabric, see the powerful documentary *Life & Debt* (2001), about Jamaica's plight.

HISTORY
In the Beginning

Where, exactly, did the first people of the Caribbean come from? When did they arrive and why? These are basic questions archaeologists, anthropologists and other '-ists' have been debating for decades and if you're after a career promising Caribbean travel, this puzzle might be the ticket. What is known definitively is that the first inhabitants arrived on the islands closest to South America around 4000 BC. These nomadic hunter-gatherers were followed by waves of Arawaks (a collective term for the Amerindian people believed to be from the Orinoco River Delta around Venezuela and Guyana) who moved north and west, beginning the great tradition of Caribbean island-hopping. Indeed, one of the Caribbean's recurrent themes, from pre-Colombian times until right now, has been movement of peoples.

Established in 1634, Curaçao's Jewish community is the western hemisphere's oldest.

Around AD 1200, the Arawaks were happily farming, fishing and making pottery when the Caribs from South America started fanning out over the Caribbean. The Caribs killed the Arawak men and enslaved the women, triggering another wave of migration that sent the Arawaks as far west as Cuba and as far north as the Bahamas. When the Spanish explorers arrived, they dubbed the warfaring people they encountered 'cannibals' (a derivation of the word 'caribal' or Carib), for their reputed penchant for eating their victims. Since the Arawaks had no written language, little of their culture survived, except – thankfully for weary travelers – the hammock.

1493	1651
Columbus returns on his second voyage, sighting and naming much of the Eastern Caribbean	Mass suicide by Caribs in Grenada who preferred to jump off a cliff than to be subjugated by the Spanish

Europeans in the Caribbean

Christopher Columbus led the European exploration of the region, making landfall at San Salvador in the Bahamas on October 12, 1492 – no matter that he thought he was in Asia. He too island-hopped, establishing the first settlement in the Americas on Hispaniola, today shared by the Dominican Republic and Haiti. Discovering new lands gives glory, but what Columbus and subsequent explorers wanted was gold. Funny, though: despite four trips during which Columbus named and claimed much of the region for the Spanish crown, from Trinidad in the south to the Virgin Islands in the north, he never found much gold.

That's not to say there weren't riches: the land was fertile, the seas bountiful and the native population, after initial resistance by the toughest of the remaining Caribs, forcibly pliant. The conquistadores set to exploiting it all, violently. Focusing on the biggest islands promising the highest returns, they grabbed land, pillaged and enslaved, settling towns in Cuba, the Dominican Republic, Puerto Rico and Jamaica.

Except for minerally-rich Trinidad taken early by the Spanish, the Eastern Caribbean was left largely to its own devices until the English alit on St Kitts in 1623, sparking domino-effect colonization of Barbados, Nevis, Antigua and Montserrat. Not to be outdone, the French followed, settling Martinique and Guadeloupe, while the Dutch lay claim to Saba, St Eustatius and St Martin. Over the next 200 years, the Europeans fought like children over these islands and possession changed hands so often that a sort of hybridized culture developed; some islands, like St Martin and St Kitts, were split between two colonial powers.

Columbus anointed the Cayman Islands 'Las Tortugas' for all the sea turtles swimming about (by 1790 the population was kaput); they were renamed for the cayman – a once ubiquitous crocodile-type animal, no longer found in this area.

Independence & Neocolonialism

The Caribbean colonial story is largely one of giant agricultural interests – most notably sugar, but also tobacco, cattle and bananas – fueled by greed and slavery that promoted power struggles between landowners, politicians and the pirates that robbed them. The Bahamas, with hundreds of cays, complex shoals and channels, provided the perfect base for pirates like Henry Jennings and 'Blackbeard' (Edward Teach) who ambushed treasure-laden boats headed for Europe. On the home front, Britain, Spain and France were embroiled in tiffs, scuffles and all-out war that allowed colonial holdings to change hands frequently. The English took Jamaica in 1655 and held Cuba momentarily in 1762, while the Spanish and French agreed to divide Hispaniola in 1731, creating the Dominican Republic and Haiti of today. The legacies of this period – the ramparts of Santo Domingo, the fortresses of Old San Juan and Havana and the vibrant mix of cultures – are among the most captivating attractions for travelers.

Except for the Eastern Caribbean, which has historically been more laidback and easily controlled by its European overseers, colonial infighting had locals plotting rebellion and independence. Haiti was way in front of the curve in declaring independence in 1804, followed by the Dominican Republic in 1844 and Cuba in 1902. For some smaller islands such as St Vincent and the Grenadines, and Barbuda and Antigua, the solution has been to band together. Other islands have opted to maintain strong, neocolonial ties to the parent country, as is the case with

Travel across the rocky emotional landscape of young immigrants navigating life between New York and the Dominican Republic in *Drown* (1997), the potent short story collection by Junot Diaz.

1834	1916–24
Britain abolishes slavery throughout its empire; Dutch follow suit in 1863	US occupation of the Dominican Republic; also occupies Haiti from 1915–34

the French protectorates of St Barthélemy, Martinique and Guadeloupe and the commonwealth situation between Puerto Rico and the US. Independence on the one hand and statehood on the other has always had its champions in Puerto Rico, with statehood narrowly losing plebiscites in 1993 and 1998.

A different, but tenuous, alternative was forged by the Dutch holdings of Aruba, Curaçao, Bonaire, Sint Maarten, St Eustatius and Saba. In 1954, these holdings became an autonomous federation under Dutch rule known as the Netherlands Antilles, though the charter stipulated that each was to eventually become independent. Only Aruba successfully detached from the group, in 1986, which sent the remaining Netherlands Antilles into a political economic tailspin that is still being worked out (see p40). For travelers, all this geopoliticking means close attention has to be paid to current visa requirements for the different islands (see p769).

Into the Future

The 20th century has been a mixed bag for the region. US intervention in countries seen as geostrategically important, particularly Haiti and Cuba, usually does more harm than good. Furthermore, monocrop agriculture – bananas in Jamaica, nutmeg in Grenada – means the islands are at the mercy of heavy weather and market fluctuations. At the same time, it polarizes societies into the rich who own the land and the poor who work it. This inevitably fosters socialist tendencies, including Fidel Castro, but also Maurice Bishop in Grenada (1979–83). Economic instability, especially, has given rise to dictators such as Rafael Leonidas Trujillo for 31 years in the Dominican Republic and the Duvaliers (Papa and Baby Doc) for 29 years in Haiti.

One thing all the islands have in common is tourism, which began taking hold when other sectors of the islands' economies began to crumble, particularly agriculture. Crop-leveling hurricanes (eg Gilbert in 1988, Hugo in 1989) spurred some islands to develop tourism industries, while the 1997 World Trade Organization ruling favoring Central American bananas over Caribbean ones forced St Vincent and Martinique to look at diversifying. Far from a panacea, unfettered tourism can wreak havoc on the environment (see p48) or give rise to societal woes like prostitution in Cuba. Furthermore, while tourism has saved the financial day for many islands, it too is beholden to outside forces like market fluctuations, weather and unpredictable events such as terrorist attacks; post-September 11 travel figures were down even in the Caribbean. The region – widely perceived as safe – rebounded from the terrorist slump, with tourism up by 7% in 2004, only to be hit by violent hurricanes.

The future, always foggy, is even cloudier in the Caribbean as economic stability is so dependent on outside forces, including US economic performance, weather, international trade rulings and International Monetary Fund (IMF) aid tied to austerity programs – some of which haven't gone down so well. Like anywhere, HIV/AIDS, drugs (especially trafficking and money laundering), crime, unemployment and immigration issues are problems confronting the Caribbean. Of course, each island's particular history is more complex than this summary can convey; see individual chapters for the full scoop.

Ten thousand of the 43,103 people who call the Cayman Islands home are US transplants.

The Caribbean suffers from 'brain drain.' For example, 75% of Jamaicans holding higher education degrees live in the US.

Providing a ray of hope, musician-producer Wyclef Jean launched Yéle Haiti in 2005, a nonprofit organization dedicated to promoting sustainable development programs in his native Haiti; get informed and involved at www.yelehaiti.org.

1959

Cuban Revolution triumphs

September 15–October 1, 1998

Hurricane Georges rips through the Caribbean, killing 602

TIPS ON MEETING LOCALS

The top strategy for meeting locals is to use the greetings and language of the host island. On the whole, Caribbean culture is much more personal (some say warmer) than those of the industrialized north and fast friends can be made or lost on a *buenos días* (good day). Whether it's Jamaican patois or ABC Island *papamiento*, get a phrasebook and go out on a linguistic limb. Managing a few useful phrases also makes it easier to hop on a bus or skiff, hire a local dive master or sniff out the neighborhood saloon. Baseball games, cricket matches and festivals are other fertile venues for meeting people. Finding a village or island you like and exploring it in depth exposes you to more of the local fabric than running around racking up destination points. Find a favorite Jamaican jerk pit or *boulangerie* in Martinique and bond over food. Oftentimes, making friends is as easy as cracking a bottle of rum over dominoes or gossiping at a Dominican or Puerto Rican *colmado* (convenience store).

On certain islands, it's not uncommon to meet extraordinarily friendly locals who eventually reveal themselves as the opportunists (or prostitutes) they really are, including 'rent-a-Rastas' in Jamaica and *jineteros/as* in Cuba. Stay savvy and keep your wits (or at least your sense of humor!) about you.

PEOPLE

The stereotypical island slacker, swinging in a hammock with joint in hand, couldn't be further from the truth in today's Caribbean. On most islands, economic necessity or outright hardship means working in the fields, factory or hotel in a constant effort to make ends meet. Family is the hub on which life turns and interpersonal relationships make the day-to-day fun and purposeful. Gossiping is a major hobby. Casual with time and commitments, many islanders prefer to converse with a friend over one last beer than rush to catch a bus.

Chivalrous at best, misogynistic at worst, machismo is a complex cultural phenomenon on many islands. Far from the simple domination of women – indeed, some social scientists argue, convincingly, that it's really the women holding the reins in these societies – machismo embraces many facets of the human condition including emotional vulnerability and virility. It can also manifest itself in homophobia, which has reached alarming, virulent proportions on some islands. In June 2004, gay activist Brian Williamson was stabbed to death in a hate crime in Jamaica, where gay sex is punishable by up to 10 years in jail. Abhorrent, antigay lyrics in popular dance hall songs fuel the culture of hate there. In 1997 the Cayman Islands refused a cruise ship carrying 910 gay passengers into port. At the opposite end of the rainbow, gay, lesbian and transgender people in Cuba are protected by antidiscrimination laws.

Health is a perennial challenge for the region. According to Unaids, the Caribbean has the second-highest rate of adult HIV infection (2.3%) after sub-Saharan Africa. Although some countries including Barbados, the Bahamas and Cuba have had success in lowering infection rates, in other places such as Jamaica, rates of infection are reaching crisis proportions. For more information, see p787.

Another simmering issue is immigration: Dominicans sailing to Puerto Rico, boatfuls of Haitians alighting in the Bahamas and Cubans floating around the Florida Straits are common CNN-fodder. Unfortunately, in searching for a better life, people often lose it: in 2001, a boat packed with illegal immigrants sank near St Martin, killing at least 20. The land of opportunity, of course, is the US, which maintains a politically driven immigration policy that grants disgruntled Cubans automatic residency, but regularly turns away desperate Haitians.

In 2004, Human Rights Watch issued the report 'Hated to Death,' describing the antigay culture and violence in Jamaica; to read it in full see www.hrw.org/reports /2004/jamaica1104.

You can read about growing up Bahamian in the autobiographies *The Measure of a Man* and *This Life* by Cat Island native Sidney Poitier; Sir Sid is now Bahamian ambassador to Japan.

Aside from the Carib reservation on Dominica of some 3000, little vestige of the original inhabitants remains in the Caribbean. Instead, there is the complex swirl of cultures and colors from all the people who came after: English, Spanish, French and Dutch mixed with Africans brought over as slaves. Once slavery was abolished, indentured laborers came from China, India and the Middle East, changing islands' identities. Regional immigration also adds to the mix: 'Bahatians' – Haitians born in the Bahamas – are recognized (and often discriminated against) as a separate group, and expats from the US have altered the makeup of some islands.

Done up on batsmen, bowlers and sticky wickets at www .windiescricket.com or www.caribbean cricket.com.

SPORTS

You need only ask 'cricket or baseball?' to get your finger on the pulse. Closest to the US, baseball rules in the Bahamas, Puerto Rico, the Dominican Republic and Cuba and the programs in the last three are so well developed, players regularly jump from there into the US big leagues. Indeed, Dominican ball is a two-way street, with American superstars like the Oakland A's' Eric Byrnes (aka 'Capitán América') filling out summer league rosters on the island. Catching a game in Cuba or the Dominican Republic is tons of fun.

Cricket may seem quaint to Americans, but it's serious business in the Caribbean, where rivalries (and fans) are rabid and the sport attracts major dollars. Islands where cricket rules include Jamaica, the Leeward and Windward Islands, Barbados and Trinidad & Tobago, and while there are no national clubs, the top players from these countries form the powerhouse West Indies team. Anxiety billows from the Cricket World Cup fumarole, as expectations for the 2007 showdown run high, and islands jockey to host the event.

The 2004 World Series Most Valuable Player was Boston Red Sox Manny Ramirez, and American League MVP was the Anaheim Angels' Vladimir Guerrero. Both hail from the Dominican Republic.

While volleyball (especially the beach variety) and soccer are big in the Caribbean, basketball just seems to grow in popularity. Puerto Rico and Cuba have leagues and though few cagers jump from Caribbean courts to the NBA, Adonal Foyle from St Vincent & the Grenadines, now of the Golden State Warriors, is an exception. He is a player, poet and hostel host; you can bunk down in his Canouan guesthouse (p616).

If you're at all tuned into the summer Olympics, you'll have noticed that folks from the Caribbean run *fast*. In the 2004 games in Athens, Bahamians Tonique Williams-Darling took gold in the women's 400m and Debbie Ferguson won bronze in the 200m. Furthermore, gold-medal sprinter Kim Collins, 'the Fastest Man on Earth,' hails from St Kitts, where you'll drive along Kim Collins Hwy.

Phil Jackson, co-architect of the Michael Jordan–Chicago Bulls dynasty, cut his teeth coaching in the Puerto Rican basketball league.

Sailing, swimming, free diving, windsurfing, water polo – whatever water-based sport – has its practitioners and stars in the Caribbean.

RELIGION

It's quite probable that every religion under the sun is practiced somewhere in the Caribbean. Nevertheless, Christian religions are still the classic forces on islands with a strong European heritage, as are Islam and Hinduism on islands with large East Indian populations such as Trinidad and Guadeloupe. Animist sects (obeah) have strongholds in Jamaica, the Bahamas and the Eastern Caribbean. Meanwhile evangelical sects are soaring in popularity as the promise of a peaceful afterlife appeals to those fed up with the violence and destruction of the here and now.

Yet the islands are most closely identified with Afro-Caribbean religions like Vodou in Haiti and Santería in Cuba. These religions trace their roots to Africa, but were overlain and mixed with Christian iconography and doctrine when the slaves were brought over. Masking tribal beliefs and traditions with those of the overseers ensured the survival and transmutation of these religions and you'll see evidence of them throughout your travels, such as small altars in homes and Santería initiates dressed all in white.

Rastafarianism was promulgated by Ethiopian Emperor Haile Selassie whom Rastas regarded as the Chosen One. The religion sprouted from Marcus Garvey's 'back to Africa' movement in the '30s, but gained worldwide exposure thanks to spliff-smoking, dreadlocked adherents like Bob Marley who believe that Africans are the 13th lost tribe of Israel and that they will be led from exile in Babylon (Jamaica) to Zion or the 'Promised Land' (Ethiopia) by Jah (God). To this end, Selassie gifted 500 acres (202 hectares) in Ethiopia to Jamaican Rastas in 1971 so that they might worship freely, as pacifists, Rasta-style – largely by smoking their marijuana sacrament as they pleased. From a high of about 2500 Jamaicans living in Ethiopia, only about 100 remain; in Jamaica, some 100,000 claim Rastafarianism as their religion.

For an initiate's look at Vodou, see Zora Neale Hurston's *Tell My Horse*. Though written in the 1930s, Ms Hurston's fluid, detailed prose keeps it fresh. Couple this with the fine *Divine Horsemen: The Living Gods of Haiti* by Maya Deren.

ARTS

The list of Caribbean literary giants is so long, your on-the-road reading could comprise only local writers. Try the prescient essays of Cuban apostle José Martí, or the lyrical poems by Alejandro Tapia y Rivera, the 'father of Puerto Rican literature.' Likewise, the poetry of Nobel Prize–winning author Derek Walcott from St Lucia and novels by VS Naipaul from Trinidad make great trip reading. Jamaica Kinkaid is Antigua's most famous writer, responsible for *A Small Place,* a frank indictment of tourism's adverse effects on Antigua.

The Caribbean diaspora has contributed immeasurably to the islands' literary catalog; check out Edwidge Danticat from Haiti (especially her beautifully crafted, but haunting novel *The Farming of Bones*) or *Tres Tristes Tigres* (Three Trapped Tigers), the masterwork by Cuban exile Guillermo Cabrera Infante.

No matter the medium, Cuba is an artistic powerhouse: the paintings of Wilfredo Lam, the films of Tomás Gutiérrez Alea (*Death of a Bureaucrat; Memories of Underdevelopment*), the National Ballet of Cuba and the indelible images shot by Korda – including the Che you see peddled worldwide – are testament to artistic achievement. The Dominican Republic and Puerto Rico, both with arts schools, have a rich arts scene as well. Perhaps the most celebrated Caribbean painter is impressionist Camille Pissarro, born on St Thomas in 1803 and known for his landscapes.

At the other end of the spectrum is the naive or primitive art for which Haiti is famous. Bold works that tackle simple themes – this naive style has a strong tradition in Haiti, where painters such as Hector Hyppolite have made their names nearly household. Bahamian Amos Ferguson and self-taught Jamaican artists Bishop Mallica 'Kapo' Reynolds and John Dunkley are in the same vein. Works in this style of varying quality can be found, from the finest galleries to the tackiest tourist fair.

Interestingly, the region also has its share of famous actors, most notably Oscar-winners Sidney Poitier from the Bahamas and Benicio Del Toro from Puerto Rico.

From Cuba's all-male secret societies to the ganja-puffing rituals of Rastafarians, *Creole Religions of the Caribbean* by Margarite Fernández Olmos and Lizabeth Paravisini-Gebert Is one of the most current and comprehensive treatments of the region's religions.

Hollywood loves the Bahamas under water. The first undersea motion picture, *Thirty Leagues under the Sea,* was shot here in 1914 by John Ernest Williamson, and 007 is a repeat visitor; check out *Dr No* or *Thunderball,* where Bond (Sean Connery) meets Domino (Claudine Auger) in a coral garden.

MUSIC

Even if you're clueless about socialists in Jamaica or volcanism in Montserrat, you surely know reggae from salsa and maybe even calypso from rumba. That's because Caribbean music has traveled far beyond its powdery shores en route to international chart success: Harry Belafonte's 'Banana Boat Song' was among the first, followed by many Bob Marley reggae anthems. More recently, the triple platinum trio The Fugees, led by Haitians Wyclef Jean and Pras Michel (with New Jersey–born Lauryn Hill), and the Ry Cooder Cuba project Buena Vista Social Club, have added Caribbean flavors to the global mix. Again, islanders emigrating to countries far and wide contribute to this global diffusion.

Cuba and Its Music: From the First Drums to the Mambo (2004) by ethnomusicologist Ned Sublette has been called magnificent for its detailed treatment of Cuban music up to 1952; African influences, race relations and politics in the musical context figure prominently.

Although each island has its own musical style, all Caribbean music is percussion-based, born as a lingua franca from Africans confronting their new, nightmarish reality where music became one of the only repositories for tribal traditions (religion was the other). It's unsurprising that European and North American styles eventually began to infuse Caribbean rhythms. Thematically, sociopolitical commentary/criticism has always dominated: one of the hottest songs in Cuba is *Dique No* (Just Say No), an antiwar rap criticizing the invasion of Iraq. Sex is another ubiquitous theme and you'll hear lots of salacious rhythms and raunchy rhymes permeating the Caribbean airwaves.

Calypso, born in 19th-century Trinidad & Tobago among field hands who sang in French Creole to obscure the lyrics' meaning from the landowners, continues to rely on clever wordplay (though now in English), and the Carnival competitions are a hot highlight. Calypso – too great a tradition to remain contained – eventually spawned soca, an eminently danceable mix of soul and calypso. These islands are also the birthplace of the steel drum, the distinct, resonant sounds of which ring out everywhere from empty lots in Port of Spain to the platforms of New York City subways.

Then there's reggae. With Jamaica as its fountainhead, this musical style, driven by a kicking drum bass afterbeat, drifts from every bar, bus and beach throughout the Caribbean. Reggae lyrics traditionally addressed problems facing Jamaica's urban poor, including discrimination and marginalization, while also projecting positive messages related to identity and self-affirmation. The reggae pantheon is huge, but deities you're sure to hear include Peter Tosh and Bunny Livingston (with Marley, the original Wailers), Jimmy Cliff, the legendary producer Lee 'Scratch' Perry, Toots and the Maytals, Black Uhuru and Burning Spear. Of course, reggae giant Bob Marley, who succumbed to brain cancer on May 11, 1981, is Jamaica's global cultural ambassador still.

The classic reggae drama is *The Harder They Come*, starring Jimmy Cliff, but fans shouldn't miss *The Reggae Movie*, chock-full of concert footage from Burning Spear, Inner Circle, Ziggy Marley and more.

Dancehall – a raw, cheap-to-produce genre that's like the bastard child of a Rasta and gangsta rapper – incorporates lewd lyrics with ghetto angst that created a whole new musical royalty in Jamaica including Yellowman, producers Sly & Robbie and Shabba Ranks (with his none-too-subtle hit 'Hard and Stiff').

If you're not hearing reggae and its hybrids, you're hearing salsa and its offshoots. Dance floors from San Juan to Santo Domingo sizzle with salsa's up-tempo beat, sassy brass and smoking rhythm sections. Born in New York City from the *son*-mambo-rumba fusion played by the Cuban and Puerto Rican diaspora in the '60s and '70s, salsa – both music and dance – have hit big with Puerto Rican superstars such as Eddie Palmieri and Cuban bands like Los Van Van and NG La Banda. The latter spearheaded the modern salsa style called *timba*, played by big orchestras heavy on the horns. Cuban Celia Cruz, who died in 2004, is known as the 'Queen of Salsa.' *Regguetón* is the Spanish-speaking Caribbean's dancehall, a salsa-rap amalgam featuring down-and-dirty lyrics designed to move your booty.

Rap pioneer and elder statesman Grandmaster Flash (Joseph Saddler) is from Barbados.

ENVIRONMENT
The Land

The Caribbean or West Indies circumscribes a 1490-mile (2397km) arc beginning with the Bahamas, followed by the Greater Antilles (Cuba, Jamaica, Hispaniola and Puerto Rico) and the US and British Virgin Islands. Next is the Leeward Islands (from Anguilla to Dominica), including the small islets of Saba and St Eustatius (Statia), and the Windward Islands (from Martinique to Grenada), that together with nearby Barbados, comprise the Lesser Antilles. At the arc's bottom, near Venezuela, are Trinidad & Tobago and the ABC Islands (Aruba, Bonaire and Curaçao).

Geologically, the islands split into those of volcanic origin and those created by coral forming on top of layers of limestone over millions of years. In the latter category are the Bahamas, the Greater Antilles, the Virgin Islands, Anguilla and Barbados, while the volcanic islands form a crescent from Saba to Grenada. But this is no 'Ring of Fire': most of the volcanoes here became dormant long ago; Martinique (Mt Pelée, 1902), St Vincent (Soufrière volcano, 1979) and Montserrat, whose Soufrière Hills volcano has been in episodic eruption since 1995, are exceptions. Trinidad & Tobago, in a unique geological category, didn't rise from the ocean, but split off from mainland South America. See the boxed text on p48.

> Well-written and chock-full of descriptions, color photos and illustrations, *The Nature of the Islands: Plants & Animals of the Eastern Caribbean*, by Virginia Barlow, is the best overall guide to the region's flora and fauna.

Wildlife
ANIMALS

Except for large iguana populations and tree rats on certain islands, land animals have largely been hunted to extinction. Responsibility is shared between humans and other introduced species including the mongoose, raccoons, cats, dogs and donkeys. Once again, Trinidad, home to 100 types of mammal, is the exception to the rule (see p682).

If you're anxious to behold the Caribbean's richest fauna, you're going to get wet. One of the world's most complex ecosystems is coral, a diminutive animal that lives in giant colonies that form over millennia. Many different types of coral make up a reef including orange gorgonians, finger coral, brain coral, sinewy sea fans and bunches of star coral, all found here. Fish pecking away at nutritious tidbits or hiding out in the reef include the iridescent Creole wrasse, groupers, kingfish, sergeant majors and angel fish. Hang around and you might see inflatable porcupine fish, barracudas, nurse sharks, octopus, moray eels and manta rays. See p51 for the region's best diving.

Other species you may see include pilot, sperm, blue and humpback whales, famous for their acrobatic breaching from January to March. Spinner, spotted and bottlenosed dolphins, and loggerhead, green, hawksbill and leatherback turtles are common sights for divers. Manatees or sea cows, herbivorous marine mammals so ugly they're cute, are found in waters around Cuba, the Dominican Republic, Jamaica and Puerto Rico. All of these animals are on the threatened or endangered species list – part of the reason the Bahamas is criticized for its captive dolphin facilities.

Hundreds of bird species, both endemic and migratory, frequent the Bahamas, Trinidad & Tobago and Cuba, the islands with the largest populations. The Bahamas is home to the endangered Bahama parrot, with its distinct red and green plumage and, at 50,000-strong, the hemisphere's largest flock of West Indian (Caribbean) flamingoes. Puerto Rico has a shrinking number of Puerto Rican parrots and is home to the

> Cuba is home to the both the world's smallest toad, the *ranita de Cuba* (Cuban tree toad; 0.4in or 1cm) and the world's smallest bird, the *zunzuncito* (bee hummingbird; 2.5in or 6.5cm).

> Get beyond the halyards with sailor Ann Vanderhoof in her sea yarn *An Embarrassment of Mangoes: A Caribbean Interlude* as she explores the secret islets and culinary delights of the West Indies.

endangered Puerto Rican nightjar. Common Caribbean seabirds include brown pelicans, white cattle egrets and herons. Hummingbirds and bananaquits are always around, searching for something sweet.

PLANTS

The Caribbean covers many vegetation zones collecting thousands of plant species. The tropics in bloom feel like an epiphany and you'll see flowering trees such as the orange flamboyant, crimson African tulip *(spathodea)*, white frangipani with its intoxicating scent and the dark-blue blossoms of the lignum vitae, the hardest of all known woods. Hundreds of orchid species bejewel damper areas (best January to March) and vermilion bougainvillea, exotic birds of paradise, hibiscus of all colors and spiky crimson ginger pop up everywhere.

Environmental Issues

The sheer popularity of the region as a destination creates or aggravates environmental problems. Specific sites suffering from overexposure include the reef around Tobago Cays off St Vincent & the Grenadines, a popular anchorage for sailors, and the reefs around the Virgin Islands, which have been damaged by careless snorkelers and divers.

CARIBBEAN GEOGRAPHY 101

You will often hear the Caribbean Islands referred to in numerous ways – the Leewards, the Windwards, the West Indies etc. It can get confusing, so here's a quick primer in Caribbean geography.

The Caribbean Islands form an archipelago of thousands of islands that stretch from the southeast coast of Florida in the USA to the northern coast of Venezuela. The largest island within the Caribbean Sea is Cuba, followed by the island of Hispaniola (shared by the nations of Haiti and the Dominican Republic), then Jamaica and Puerto Rico. These larger islands are often referred to as the Greater Antilles. The Greater Antilles also include the Cayman Islands, due to their western location. The Bahamas (officially the Commonwealth of the Bahamas), to the north, are technically outside of the Caribbean archipelago – although we have covered them in this book.

The **Les**ser Antilles is the archipelago that extends east and southeastward from the Virgin Islands down to Trinidad & Tobago, just off the northern coast of Venezuela. Also called the Eastern Caribbean Islands, the Lesser Antilles are further divided into the the Leeward Islands and the Windward Islands.

The Leeward Islands (from north to south) are the US Virgin Islands (USVI), the British Virgin Islands (BVI), Anguilla, St Martin/Sint Maarten, St Barth, Saba, St Eustatias (Statia), St Kitts & Nevis, Antigua & Barbuda, Montserrat and Guadeloupe.

The Windward Islands (from north to south) are Dominica, Martinique, St Lucia, St Vincent & the Grenadines and Grenada. Barbados and Trinidad & Tobago are often geographically considered part of the Windwards, but do not belong to the Windward Islands geopolitical group.

The islands are further classified by their national sovereignty. The British West Indies consists of Anguilla, Turks & Caicos, the Cayman Islands, Montserrat (an 'overseas territory') and BVI (a crown colony) due to their affiliation with the UK.

The French West Indies include Guadeloupe, St Martin, St Barth and Martinique due to their status as Départments d'Outre-Mer of France.

The Netherlands Antilles islands, all possessions of the Netherlands, are Aruba, Curaçao, Bonaire, St Maarten, Saba and St Eustatius. Aruba, Bonaire and Curaçao (often called the ABC Islands) are also known as the Leeward Netherlands Antilles. (A recent referendum has signalled the possible disbanding of the Netherlands Antilles; see p40.)

For our purposes, we've called the whole mess the Caribbean Islands, but you'll see the other terms peppered throughout the text.

Waste is a big problem. Mountains of garbage crowd Havana, acrid refuse burns from Vieques to Puerto Plata and sewerage needs somewhere to go – too often into the sea, unfortunately. St Barth is one island finding creative answers like converting burning trash into energy. One easy, effective measure for travelers is to carry their own water bottle, refilling it as needed instead of buying bottled water and contributing to landfill or illegal dumping.

In 1979 two tankers collided near Trinidad & Tobago, pouring 88 million gallons of crude oil into the sea, making it the worst spill in the world to date.

Larger islands, in particular, have had difficulty inculcating a culture of conservation. Despite deforestation laws, only 10% of the Dominican Republic is forested and neighboring Haiti is only 5% forested. Over-fishing is a major problem. The Bahamas outlawed long-line fishing in 1959, the first Caribbean island to do so, but now struggles with poachers; some communities have established marine preserves independently of the government to curb the abuse. In June 1997, an environmental scandal surfaced involving Grenada, St Kitts & Nevis, St Vincent, St Lucia and Dominica, accused of taking bribes from Japan in exchange for helping block protection measures for endangered species.

Nevertheless, no legislation or vigilance can stop the environmental destruction wrought by a hurricane which indiscriminately uproots trees and clogs reefs; scientists estimate it will take up to five years for Cuba's Parque Nacional Península de Guanahacabibes, a Unesco biosphere reserve, to recover from the effects of Hurricane Ivan.

FOOD & DRINK

There is this erroneous stereotype that Caribbean food is all exotic fruits and rice, seafood and spice. Indeed, you'll be surprised to find how bland Bahamian food can be, disappointed at the dearth of tropical fruits in Cuba (so vexing to travelers) and wondering why fish hardly figures in the Puerto Rican diet. But all Caribbean cuisine shares one characteristic: it's a hybrid, a mixture of all the cultures that have called these islands home. You'll find patisseries in Guadeloupe, fish-and-chips in Barbados, chutneys in Trinidad and stir-fries in Havana's Chinatown.

Grenada is known as 'The Isle of Spice,' since there are more spices per square mile than anywhere else on the planet. It's one of the biggest producers of nutmeg and also cultivates cloves, mace and cocoa.

Staples & Specialties

A fish still dripping with salt water, thrown on the grill and spritzed with lime has made many a Caribbean travel memory. Red snapper, mahimahi (dolphin fish), lobster, shrimp and crab are simply prepared like this, while on the French islands a more elaborate *colombo de poisson* (shark poached in a broth of onions, coconut cream, lime juice and dark rum – yum!) is the order of the day. Most islands have a pickled fish dish *(escovitched* or *escobeche)*, a jazzy marinade of vinegar, lime and spices with a complexity belied by the simple ingredients. In the Bahamas, conch (pronounced 'conk') is so popular any which way – pounded, marinated and frittered, deep fried, grilled, in salad, chowders and stews – the animal is headed towards the threatened species list.

As for meat, there's the ubiquitous chicken. 'Do they hatch fried?' you might ask once you get a look at all the fried chicken joints in the Caribbean. Bits of chicken mixed with rice make an occasional appearance as *arroz con pollo* in the Spanish-speaking islands and as chicken *pelau* in Trinidad and St Vincent. With a dash of lime juice and mustard, it's the Barbadian specialty called fowl down-in-rice. The other omnipresent staple is pork, which is the star protein in Cuban and Puerto Rican sandwiches *(lechón asado)*. Pigs are also roasted whole on a pit at big, boisterous celebrations and the skin is fried up in greasy, savory chunks as *chicharrones*. Beef is not eaten widely, except in Jamaica, where goat is also a staple.

Get your favorite F and help a good cause with the *Red Cross Cookbook* sold in the Turks & Caicos. It's a fabulous collection of Bahamian and Turks & Caicos' recipes – a bargain for US$10.

Dive Training & Certification

The Caribbean is an excellent place to begin or continue your dive training. If you want to experience diving for the first time, most dive operations offer a short beginner course for nondivers; commonly dubbed a 'resort course,' it includes brief instructions, followed by a shallow beach or boat dive. The cost generally ranges from US$75 to US$100, depending on the operation and whether a boat is used.

For those who want to jump into the sport wholeheartedly, a number of dive shops offer full open-water certification courses. The cost generally hovers around US$400, equipment included, and the entire course takes the better part of a week. If you already plan to be certified but don't want to spend your vacation in a classroom, consider a 'warm-water referral' program, where you take the classes at home, then complete your open-water dives in the Caribbean.

Two organizations are widely recognized as providing the best and most professional certification in the world. Most reputable dive operators are affiliated with either the Professional Association of Diving Instructors (PADI) or the National Association of Underwater Instructors (NAUI). Affiliation with either of these organizations means the dive shop adheres to high standards of safety and professionalism.

Dive Tours

Several companies offer dive trips that include all hotel and diving costs. Live-aboards are big yachts outfitted for a group of divers. Passengers sleep and eat meals on board, and spend days doing multiple dives. Both land-based dive tours and live-aboards offer a unique way to become immersed in the sport and meet other divers (who tend, incidentally, to be a social lot). Rates for week-long, land-based tours in the high season range from US$600 to US$1200. Live-aboard trips range from around US$1400 to US$2200 for seven nights. Prices are based on double occupancy and do not include airfare.

RESPONSIBLE DIVING

Please consider the following tips when diving and help preserve the ecology and beauty of reefs.

- Never use anchors on the reef and take care not to ground boats on coral.

- Avoid touching or standing on living marine organisms or dragging equipment across the reef. Polyps can be damaged by even the gentlest contact. If you must hold on to the reef, touch only exposed rock or dead coral.

- Be conscious of your fins. Even without contact, the surge from fin strokes near the reef can damage delicate organisms. Take care not to kick up clouds of sand, which can smother organisms.

- Practice and maintain proper buoyancy control. Major damage can be done by divers descending too fast and colliding with the reef.

- Resist the temptation to collect or buy corals or shells or to loot marine archaeological sites, such as shipwrecks.

- Ensure that you take home all your garbage and any litter you may find as well. Plastics in particular are a serious threat to marine life.

- Do not feed fish.

- Minimize your disturbance of marine animals. Never ride on the backs of turtles.

LAND-BASED TOURS

PADI Travel Network (☎ 800-729-7234; www.padi.com) The PADI organization runs dive package tours at a number of Caribbean destinations including Bonaire, Dominica, St Lucia, Bahamas and Cayman Islands, to name a few.

Scuba Voyages (☎ 800-544-7631; www.scubavoyages.com) These trips go to Tobago, ABC islands, St Vincent and St Lucia, among others.

World Dive Adventures (☎ 800-433-3483; www.worlddive.com) These trips usually include a week's worth of hotels, meals and two dives per day. Destinations include Dominica, Statia, Saba, Cayman Islands and Turks & Caicos.

LIVE-ABOARDS

Aggressor (☎ 800-348-2628; www.aggressor.com) With a fleet of live-aboards plying several of the world's waters, Aggressor has a great reputation. The 18-passenger *Cayman Aggressor IV* tours the Caymans and the 20-passenger *Turks & Caicos Aggressor II* tours – you guessed it – the Turks & Caicos.

Explorer Ventures (☎ 800-322-3577; www.explorerventures.com) These popular live-aboards include the MV *Caribbean Explorer*, which travels the Bahamas, and the MV *Caribbean Explorer II*, which cruises to Saba, St Kitts, Statia and Sint Maarten. The MV *Turks & Caicos Explorer* heads to those islands.

Peter Hughes Diving (☎ 800-932-6237; www.peterhughes.com) This long-respected company has week-long live-aboard tours of Tobago on the 18-passenger *Wind Dancer*.

Marine Conservation Organizations

Coral reefs and oceans face unprecedented environmental pressures. The following groups are actively involved in promoting responsible diving practices, publicizing environmental marine threats and lobbying for better policies:

Caribbean Environment Programme (www.cep.unep.org)
CORAL: The Coral Reef Alliance (www.coral.org)
Ocean Futures (www.oceanfutures.com)
Project AWARE Foundation (www.projectaware.org)
Reef Ecology Foundation (www.reefecologyfoundation.org)
Reef Environmental Education Foundation (REEF; www.reef.org)
Reef Keeper International (www.reefkeeper.org)

DREAM DIVE SITES

The following dive sites were picked as 'dream dives' for several reasons: they represent the wide diving variety the Caribbean has to offer, they are easily accessible with local dive operators, and they're all fantastic snorkeling sites to boot. The final attribute they share is that they are simply awesome dives.

Cayman Islands: Bloody Bay Wall, Little Cayman

Little Cayman has some of the finest Caribbean wall diving, where sheer cliffs drop so vertically they make you gasp in your regulator. Little Cayman's Bloody Bay Marine Park encompasses some 22 mooring sites spanning both Bloody and Jackson's Bays. The shallow tops of the walls – some just 20ft (6m) below the surface – are nearly as incredible as their depths. The snorkeling here can be fantastic. The drop-offs sink quickly along this mile plus–long stretch of the island's north shore. Coral and sponges of all types, colors and sizes cascade downward as you slowly descend along the wall. Most dives here range from 40ft to 100ft (12m to 30m) deep. Giant Nassau grouper, horse-eye jacks, triggerfish and many small tropicals make this area come alive.

- Dive type: wall
- Shore/boat: boat
- More info: www.divinglittlecayman.com

Of the world's 375 species of shark, only 30 have ever attacked humans. Since 1580, only 18 shark attacks have been reported in the Caribbean Islands. Most shark encounters in these waters occur with curious nurse and reef sharks that, unless provoked, will not attack humans.

Don t forget your C-card! If you are a certified diver, you ll be required to have proof before a reputable dive operator will rent you equipment or take you out on a dive. Your PADI, NAUI or other certification card will do the trick.

The stern with its propeller now lies in 20ft (6m) to 40ft (12m) of water. The forward half lies nearby and intact under about 80ft (24m) of water. Three years after the wreck, divers salvaged copper, cotton, liquor and US$20,000 worth of money and gold. Divers picked the wreck clean until the BVI National Parks Trust moved in to preserve the wreck in the 1970s. Today, it is one of the Caribbean's best wreck dives, offering lots to look at for snorkelers, and novice and experienced divers.

  ▢ Dive type: wreck
  ▢ Shore/boat: boat
  ▢ More info: www.bviscuba.com

Over time, sunken ships become hardy, artificial reefs that provide excellent habitats for marine creatures, no matter where they are in the food chain.

St Eustatius (Statia)

Hard-core divers will appreciate the focus in St Eustatius (Statia) on its underwater bounty and the sheer variety of its dive sites. The island's last volcanic eruption was 1600 years ago, but you can still see evidence of the hardened lava-flow on the seabed, providing deep trenches and fissures. Vestiges of the 18th-century colonial Statia are found beneath the surface, such as portions of quay wall that slipped into the sea, and old ballast stones, anchors, canons and ship remains have become vibrant coral reefs. A series of newly sunk wrecks add diving variety. Statia's waters are protected by the St Eustatius Marine Park.

  ▢ Dive type: reef and wreck
  ▢ Shore/boat: boat
  ▢ More info: www.statiatourism.com

St Vincent & the Grenadines

The 32 cays and islands that compose the Grenadines stretch out in a bracelet of tropical jewels between St Vincent and Grenada. Long known as a yachters' haven, the sparsely inhabited islands and pristine bays shelter thriving offshore reefs. You'll find steep walls decorated with black coral around St Vincent, giant schools of fish around Bequia, a coral wonderland around Canouan and pure bliss in the Tobago Cays. The five cays are palm-studded deserted islands surrounded by shallow reefs that are part of a protected marine sanctuary, and offer some of the most pristine reef diving in the Caribbean.

  ▢ Dive type: wall and reef
  ▢ Shore/boat: boat
  ▢ More info: www.svgtourism.com

St Lucia: The Keyhole Pinnacles

You wonder sometimes if Picasso came along with his paintbrush to coat St Lucia's corals with splashes of vibrant color. One of the best sites to see this display is the Keyhole Pinnacles, four underwater sea mountains that mimic the drama of St Lucia's famed Pitons. Rising up from 1000ft (305m) below sea level to just below the surface, the pinnacles are coated in colorful hard and soft corals, sea sponges and delightful fans. Underwater photographers flock here to snap brilliantly vivid shots.

  ▢ Dive type: pinnacle
  ▢ Shore/boat: boat
  ▢ More info: www.stlucia.org

SNORKELING

Donning a mask and snorkel allows you to turn the beach into an underwater aquarium. There are numerous sites throughout the Caribbean that offer splendid coral gardens, often teeming with colorful tropical

---

TOP SNORKELING SITES

The following is a list of some of the region's top snorkeling sites. Some are popular; others are off the beaten track. All of the dives listed in this chapter are great snorkeling sites too.

- Anse Chastanet Marine Reserve, St Lucia (p593)
- Buccoo Reef, Tobago (p706)
- Buck Island, St Croix, US Virgin Islands (p366)
- De Palm Island, Aruba (p730)
- Exhuma Cays Land & Sea Park, Bahamas (p90)
- Loblolly Bay, Anegada, British Virgin Islands (p396)
- Shoal Bay West, Anguilla (p406)
- The Baths, Virgin Gorda, British Virgin Islands (p391)
- Stingray City, Grand Cayman (p187)
- Wreck of the *Jettias*, Antigua (p501)

---

fish including many varieties of wrasses, damselfish, sergeant majors, large rainbow-colored parrotfish, angelfish, ballooning pufferfish and octopus. The best snorkeling is usually along rocky outcrops or on shallow reefs.

Some travelers bring along their own mask, snorkel and fins, but if you prefer to travel light you can usually rent equipment (US$7 to US$10 per day) at dive shops or beachside watersports shacks. Having your own equipment can be enormously liberating, letting you jump in the water wherever you want.

The Bahamas

The Bahamian islands may have tourism's footprints in their sands and millionaires hiding in their cays, but fishing is still the main livelihood for many and a gentle character prevails. Streets too narrow for cars fill with children playing after school, vibrant *goombay* rhythms drift across the bay while rows of sleeping workers nod their way home on the sunset ferries, and joyful gospel choirs fill the sky with unrestrained passion on Sundays.

A jigsaw past of British rule, African slave culture and American tourism has created a conservative, friendly and highly religious population, which embraces with equal fervor their beloved churches, the pagan exuberance of Junkanoo's carnival and the US dollar. Yet outside the bustling Straw Market and booming cruise ships of Nassau, hundreds of deserted cays and inhabited 'Family' islands quietly celebrate empty beaches of icing-sugar sand that dissolve into turquoise seas as clear as Venetian glass, described by astronauts as the most beautiful on earth.

Around these peaceful islands, where international poachers roam, fishing fans also drop anchor, and scuba divers explore vast drop-offs and mysterious blue holes, while giant rays drift across glistening shallows and fishing boats crisscross the horizon.

FAST FACTS

- **Area** Over 700 islands spread in a 750-mile (1206km) arc that add up to some 5363 sq miles (13,890 sq km) of land
- **Capital** Nassau, New Providence
- **Country code** ☎ 242
- **Departure tax** US$15, US$18 from Freeport. Normally included in ticket prices.
- **Famous for** Sir Sidney Poitier, James Bond films and spectacular diving
- **Language** Bahamian Standard English
- **Money** Bahamian dollar (B$$); B$$1= US$1 = €0.83 = UK£0.57
- **Official name** Independent Commonwealth of the Bahamas
- **People** Bahamians
- **Population** 299,697
- **Visa** North American, UK and most Western European travelers don't require a visa; other nationalities need to get one in advance; see p98

HIGHLIGHTS

- **Eleuthera** (p88) Relish the delicate hues of the island's pink beaches with a sunset stroll and your beloved by your side.
- **Nassau** (p66) Dance in the streets and hoot along with crowds at Junkanoo dancers and marching bands.
- **Long Island** (p91) Dive with the gentle giants, rays and groupers, in the virgin depths off this pretty island.
- **Friday Night Fish-Fry** (p70) Savor the tiny golden bubbles of a Kalik beer, peppery snapper and lively company at weekend get-togethers.
- **Green Turtle Cay** (p87) Take a boat trip to the cay and sip a Goombay Smash alongside the chatty regulars at Miss Emily's Blue Bee Bar.

HOW MUCH?

- **Jitney bus ride** US$1
- **Two-tank dive** US$80
- **Comfortable double room** US$130
- **Day-long snorkeling trip** US$90
- **Day's car hire** US$90

LONELY PLANET INDEX

- **Gallon (imperial) of gas** US$3.50
- **Liter of bottled water** US$1.80
- **Bottle of Kalik beer** US$3
- **Souvenir T-shirt** US$20 to US$30
- **Street snack: chicken and fries** US$8

ITINERARIES

- **Three days** Explore New Providence by *jitney* (private minibus), eat Bahamian breakfasts and laze on Cabbage Beach. Take a snorkeling day trip to Rose Island.
- **One week** Add a flight to Bimini for bonefishing or Abaco for cay-hopping.
- **Two weeks** Add trips to Eleuthera and the Exumas for beaches, boating and diving, Inagua for flamingos, or Cat Island and San Salvador for traditional living.

CLIMATE & WHEN TO GO

George Washington referred to the Bahamian archipelago as the 'Isles of Perpetual June.' George was not exaggerating; the Bahamas enjoy around 320 sunny days a year, and daytime temperatures during winter (December to April) average 70°F (21°C) and a perfect 80°F (26°C) in summer. In general, the islands are balmy year-round, with cooling, near-constant trade winds blowing by day from the east. See p762 for climate-chart information.

The so-called rainy season extends from late May to November, and humidity in the northern islands is relatively high year-round, but declines from northwest to southeast across the archipelago. Hurricanes normally skirt around the Bahamas. However, recent years have seen Floyd in 1999 and 2004's Frances and Jeanne strike some devastating blows.

The high season typically runs from mid-December to mid-April, when hotel prices are highest. Some hotels are booked solid around Christmas and Easter. In the low or off season (the remainder of the year), many hotels reduce their rates by as much as 60%. Some Family Island hotels close for the low season, but tourist accommodations are always available.

HISTORY

The original inhabitants of the Bahamas were the Lucayans, a tribe of Arawak Indians who arrived near the turn of the 9th century. Christopher Columbus and the Spanish arrived in 1492, yelling '*Tierras!*' on sighting the New World and almost immediately started shipping the Lucayans out from Cat Island as slaves.

Tales of Spanish treasure lured pirates and other adventurers, such as Francis Drake and Walter Raleigh. San Salvador became the base for Raleigh's colony at Roanoke Island, England's first settlement in America.

Pirates, such as Henry Jennings and 'Blackbeard' (Edward Teach), who terrorized his victims by wearing flaming fuses in his matted beard and hair, took over New Providence, establishing a lawless city that in 1666 was lined with brothels and taverns for 'common cheats, thieves and lewd persons.'

The British finally established order and an administration answerable to the English crown in 1718. In the 1760s Governor William Shirley, former governor of Massachusetts, upped the ante, draining swamps, surveying the land and laying Nassau's streets.

THE BAHAMAS

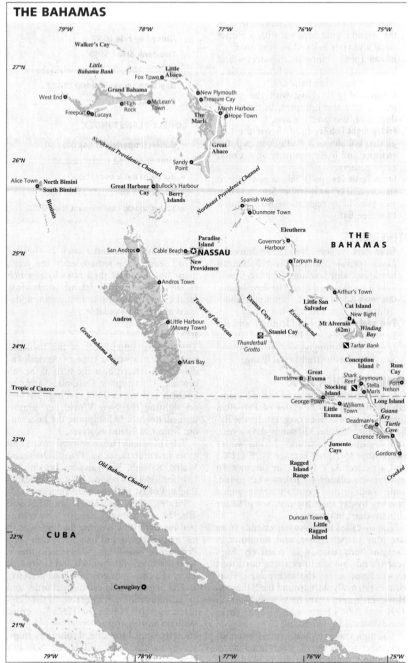

THE BAHAMAS

Walker's Cay

27°N

Little Bahama Bank

Fox Town

Little Abaco

Grand Bahama

West End

High Rock

McLean's Town

Freeport Lucaya

New Plymouth
Treasure Cay

Marsh Harbour
Hope Town

The Marls

Northwest Providence Channel

Great Abaco

Sandy Point

26°N

Alice Town

North Bimini
South Bimini

Biminis

Great Harbour Cay

Bullock's Harbour

Berry Islands

Spanish Wells

Dunmore Town

Northeast Providence Channel

Eleuthera

THE BAHAMAS

Paradise Island

Governor's Harbour

25°N

San Andros

Cable Beach

NASSAU

New Providence

Tarpum Bay

Andros Town

Tongue of the Ocean

Exuma Cays

Arthur's Town

Little San Salvador

Cat Island

New Bight

Andros

Little Harbour
(Moxey Town)

Staniel Cay

Exuma Sound

Mt Alvernia
(62m)

Winding Bay

Great Bahama Bank

24°N

Thunderball Grotto

Tartar Bank

Mars Bay

Conception Island

Rum Cay

Barreterre

Great Exuma

Shark Reef

Seymours

Stella Maris

Port Nelson

Tropic of Cancer

Stocking Island

George Town

Little Exuma

Williams Town

Long Island

Guana Key

Deadman's Cay

Turtle Cove

23°N

Clarence Town

Jumento Cays

Gordons

Crooked

Ragged Island Range

Old Bahama Channel

22°N

CUBA

Duncan Town

Little Ragged Island

Camagüey

21°N

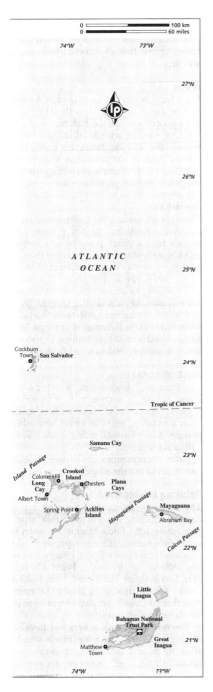

The American Revolution boosted the city's fortunes, as citizens took to rum-running. Meanwhile, Loyalist refugees – many quite rich or entrepreneurial – began arriving, giving new vigor to the city. These wealthy Whites lived well and kept many slaves until the British Empire abolished the slave trade in 1807. The British Navy liberated more men and women from illegal slavers crossing Bahamian seas, freeing them to join their emancipated brethren.

The Modern Era

While Nassauvians made hay by illicitly supplying liquor to the US during Prohibition, Yankees flocked to make merry in Nassau and her new casino. When Fidel Castro then spun Cuba into Soviet orbit in 1961, the subsequent US embargo forced revelers to seek their pleasures elsewhere; Nassau became *the* new hot spot.

Tourism and finance bloomed together. The government promoted the nascent banking industry, encouraging British investors escaping onerous taxes.

This upturn in fortunes coincided with (and perhaps helped spark) the evolution of party politics and festering ethnic tensions, as the White elite and a growing Black middle class reaped profits from the boom. Middle-class Blacks' aspirations for representation coalesced with the pent-up frustrations of their impoverished brothers. On July 10, 1973 the islands of the Bahamas officially became a new nation; the Independent Commonwealth of the Bahamas, ending 325 years of British rule.

Yet in 1984 it was revealed that Colombian drug barons had corrupted the new Bahamian government at its highest levels, and the country's drug-heavy reputation tarnished its image abroad. Tourism and financial investment declined, so the government belatedly launched a crackdown led by the US Drug Enforcement Agency (US DEA).

The electorate had had enough and voted in a conservative, business-focused government, the Free National Movement (FNM), in 1992.

In August 1999 Hurricane Dennis raked the Abacos and Grand Bahama. A month later Hurricane Floyd – a 600-mile (965km) wide whopper – pounded Cat, San Salvador, Abaco and Eleuthera with winds up to 155 mph (249km/h). In 2004, two more hurricanes, Frances and Jeanne, hit these same islands along with Grand Bahama in quick succession. Massive flooding and the destruction of many buildings again hit the tourism industry on these islands.

Despite the government's efforts to eradicate the trade, at the time of writing drug trafficking was still very much alive, pumping millions of black market dollars into the economy each year.

THE CULTURE

Contemporary Bahamian culture revolves around the family, the church and the sea. However, the proximity of North America and cable TV has had a profound influence on contemporary life and material values, although many British traditions and attitudes remain.

Many Bahamians also keep spirit beliefs held over from slave days, when African religions melded with Christianity. All kinds of practices have evolved to guard against evil spirits. Physicians are known to tie a black cord around a newborn baby's wrists to guard against evil spirits, and a Bible is often placed at the head of a sleeping child for the same reason.

In Nassau and Freeport most working people are employed in banking, tourism or government work and live a nine-to-five lifestyle. The maturation of the banking and finance industries has fostered the growth of a large professional class, many of whom have become extremely wealthy.

The folks of the inhabited islands outside of New Providence and Grand Bahamas, called the Family Islands or Out Islands, are altogether more at ease and neighborly, as well as more traditional. Thus the practice of obeah (a form of African-based ritual magic), bush medicine and folkloric songs and tales still infuse their daily lives. Tourism has barely touched many islands and poverty sits hand-in-hand with undeveloped local economies. Here people live a hand-to-mouth existence alleviated by the government's social security system, fishing, catching conch and lobster, and raising corn, bananas and other crops for the kitchen.

ARTS

Relative to its neighbors, the Bahamas' intellectual tradition is comparatively weak, and for a capital city, Nassau's visual and performance arts are surprisingly unsophisticated. Quintessential Bahamian styles have evolved though, especially in music and art.

Music

From hotel beach parties to the raw sound-system dance clubs of Over-the-Hill, Nassau's poorer quarter, the Bahamas rocks to the soul-riveting sounds of calypso, soca, reggae, and its own distinctive music that echoes African rhythms and synthesizes Caribbean calypso and soca and English folk songs into its own *goombay* beat.

GOOMBAY

This type of music – the name comes from an African word for 'rhythm' – derives its melody from a guitar, piano or horn instrument accompanied by any combination of goatskin *goombay* drums, maracas, rhythm sticks, rattles, conch-shell horns, fifes, flutes and cowbells to add a uniquely Bahamian *kalik-kalik-kalik* sound. It's typified by a fast-paced, sustained, infectious melody. *Goombay* is to the Bahamas what reggae is to Jamaica, and is most heard during Christmas and midsummer Junkanoo celebrations.

RAKE 'N' SCRAPE

The Bahamas' down-home, working-class music is rake 'n' scrape, usually featuring a guitar, an accordion and shakers made from the pods of poinciana trees, and other makeshift instruments, such as a saw played with a screwdriver.

Rake 'n' scrape music can be heard at local bars throughout the islands.

Painting & Literature

The so-called father of Bahamian art is Amos Ferguson, the foremost folk artist. Like fellow-artist Eddie Minnis, Ferguson is intensely spiritual. His naive palette-bright canvases focus upon religion, history, nature and folklore, or 'ol' story.' Brent Malone, Max Taylor, Rolph Harris and Alton Roland Lowe – the Bahamas' artist laureate for more than three decades – are also all writ large in the Bahamian art world.

The oils of seventh-generation Loyalist Abaconian Alton Lowe are much sought after by blue bloods and corporations. Eddie Minnis, also cartoonist, songwriter and musician, is inspired by his devotion to the church of Jehovah's Witnesses. His limited-edition prints are popular, and his original oils, works of intricate detail and vibrant color (he paints less than a dozen per year), command thousands of dollars.

Bahamian Anthology (College of the Bahamas) is a selection of poetry, stories and plays by Bahamian writers.

ENVIRONMENT
The Land
The Bahamian archipelago has beaches, but it also has bush. Virtually every island is a bird-watcher's haven, for the vegetation is relatively open.

The linear islands are strewn in a general northwest-southeast array. Several – Great Abaco, Eleuthera, Long Island, Andros – are as much as 100 miles (160km) long. Few, however, are more than a few miles wide. All are low-lying, the terrain either pancake-flat or gently undulating. Cat Island's Mt Alvernia, the highest point in the Bahamas, is only 206ft (62m) above sea level.

Virtually the entire length of these shores is lined by white- or pinkish-sand beaches – about 2200 miles (3540km) in all – shelving into turquoise shallows.

Most islands have barrier reefs along the length of their eastern shores, anywhere from 200yd to 2 miles (182m to 3.2km) out, that offer protection from Atlantic waves. Some islands are separated by great trenches, such as the Tongue of the Ocean, a Grand Canyon–scale crevasse more than 5 miles (8km) deep.

The islands are pocked by many giant sinkholes – water-filled, often fathomless circular pits that open to underground and submarine caves and descend as much as 600ft (182m).

Unique creatures have evolved to exist solely within the gloom of the underwater caverns, including blind, pigmentless fish. Local lore attributes deadly mermaids, mermen and sea monsters to many of the holes.

Wildlife
Apart from wandering donkeys, horses and raccoons, the archipelago's largest native land animals – iguanas – can reach 4ft (1.2m) in length. They are shy and harmless vegetarians that have been virtually wiped

out by humans, feral dogs and cats. Iguanas now inhabit some outlying isles and cays, and are protected.

Both bird-watchers and marine-life fans will exalt in the Bahamas. The Bahamas is a bird-watcher's paradise, with about 300 recorded species of birds. Only a few are endemic, including the Bahama swallow, endangered Bahama parrot and the Bahama woodstar hummingbird, which weighs less than a US nickel yet is a pugnacious little character.

The West Indian (Caribbean) flamingo – the national bird – inhabits Crooked Island, Long Cay and Great Inagua, a sanctuary with over 50,000 brethren.

The region's marine life is as varied as the islands and coral reefs themselves. Depending on whom you believe, the Bahamas has between 900 sq miles and 2700 sq miles (2330 sq km and 6992 sq km) of coral reef and countless species of fish, such as bonito, stingrays, sharks, kingfish, jewelfish and deep-blue Creole wrasse.

Humpback whales pass through the waters windward of the Bahamas and blue whales are also frequently sighted. Atlantic bottlenose dolphins frequent these waters, as do the less often seen Atlantic spotted dolphins.

Three species of marine turtles – green, loggerhead and, more rarely, hawksbill – use the islands' beaches as nesting sites. Turtles migrate thousands of miles to nest and lay the eggs for tomorrow's turtles, as they have for at least 150 million years. Unfortunately these creatures are endangered, yet still hunted.

The Bahamas has 22 national parks and reserves maintained by the Bahamas National Trust, including large sections of the barrier reef. The parks are used for both scientific research and for protecting endangered species, such as the Bahamian parrot, green turtles and the world's largest breeding colony of West Indian flamingos, as well as a myriad of native marine life.

Notably, the 175-sq-mile (453-sq-km) Exuma Cays Land & Sea Park, beginning 30 miles (48km) southeast of Nassau, was created in 1958 as the first marine fishery reserve in the world. The park now teems with prehistoric life forms, coral reefs, turtles, fish, the endangered rock iguana and the hutia.

Environmental Issues

Outside of the national park system, inappropriate development, pollution and overexploitation increasingly threaten wildlife and marine resources. Although the Bahamas was the first Caribbean nation to outlaw long-line fishing, a threat to the marine ecology, the islands' stocks of grouper, spiny lobster and conch all face the consequences of overfishing. Commercial poaching, mostly by Cuban-Americans from Florida in the west and by Dominicans in the east, has also been a significant problem. In the late 1970s the problem stirred several island communities to establish their own nongovernmental reserves.

Coral reefs have witnessed destruction by anchors, careless divers and snorkelers, as well as by Bahamian fishermen. The biggest culprit, however, is Mother Nature: hurricanes cause as much natural devastation as a minor war.

FOOD & DRINK
Food

Most food is imported, and vegetarians and vegans will have a really, really tough time. There are few fruit and vegetables around, while conch, meat, fish, chicken and carbohydrates rule (much of the food is fried or baked). Colonial cultural hangovers include steak and kidney, bangers and mash and shepherd's pie, while main courses are served with coleslaw, slices of fried plantain, baked macaroni cheese and the ubiquitous peas'n'rice.

Those with delicate stomachs should avoid meat souse (mutton boiled in saltwater), along with tongue, trotters, anything else grey and wobbly, lime juice and pepper.

Everyone eats conch (pronounced 'conk'). The tough snail-like mollusk is served pounded, minced and frittered; marinated and grilled; raw as a ceviche or in a conch salad (diced with onions, celery, pepper and cucumber and then soaked in lime juice); as a chowder or 'soused' (stewed); 'scorched' (scored in a salad); and 'cracked' (battered and deep-fried). However, if you are tempted to try either grouper or conch be aware that they are both increasingly scarce species. Fishermen bemoan the difficulty of finding them as easily as they used to, and everyone agrees that overfishing is the culprit. Grouper populations have collapsed in most of the

Caribbean, and the Nassau grouper is now classified as an endangered species in many areas. Similarly the conch has been listed one category below threatened status.

Drink

The Bahamian beer Kalik is fantastic; golden bubbles and a keen flavor. The national Bahamian cocktail could be the Goombay Smash, a lethally easy-to-drink fruit juice and rum cocktail, although the Bahama Mama is probably one of the better-known rum cocktails, with a coffee liqueur thrown into it for good measure.

The infamous rum that bottoms up all of these local cocktails is simply called 151. It's not allowed on planes as it's actually 151% proof and highly flammable!

There is an excellent range of quality rums available, including Bacardi's line, which has a factory on New Providence, and flavored rums, like coconut, banana, mango and pineapple.

NEW PROVIDENCE

pop 228,330

For one of the smallest islands in the Bahamian chain, New Providence's importance far outweighs its size. Around two-thirds of the nation's population live on this 21-mile (33km)-long isle, most within the bustling capital city Nassau, which covers the east of the island. The old colonial streets of downtown Nassau virtually spill over with busy residents, hedonistic holidaymakers, shopping cruise-ship tourists and besuited business types.

Outside of downtown Nassau, fun-filled Cable Beach's beachside resorts and the all-pervasive excitement of the Atlantis complex on adjoining Paradise Island, are a small collection of peaceful disparate communities and fishing villages. Here Bahamians gather to chat over conch salads and a chilled, golden Kalik beer on the dock, and children play on unspoilt beaches after school.

Although the glittering turquoise seas and white sugar-soft sands of Cable, Paradise and Cabbage Beaches are renowned, other smaller but equally idyllic spots surround this isle, such as Cave and Love Beaches, and the southern beaches where the snorkeling is grand and the diving superb.

NEW PROVIDENCE

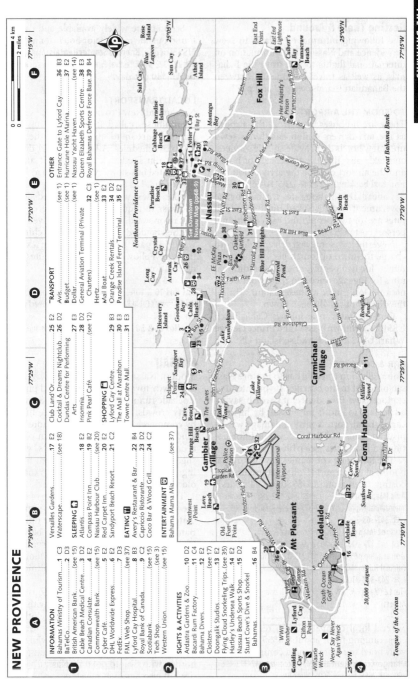

INFORMATION
Bahamas Ministry of Tourism	1 C3
BaTelCo	2 D3
British American Bank	(see 15)
Cable Beach Medical Centre	3 D2
Canadian Consulate	4 E2
Commonwealth Bank	(see 15)
Cyber Café	5 E2
DHL Worldwide Express	6 E2
FedEx	7 D3
FML Web Shop	8 B3
Lyford Cay Hospital	9 C2
Royal Bank of Canada	(see 15)
Scotiabank	(see 3)
Tech Shop	(see 15)
Western Union	(see 15)

SIGHTS & ACTIVITIES
Ardastra Gardens & Zoo	10 D2
Bacardi Rum Factory	11 C4
Bahama Divers	12 E2
Cloisters	(see 17)
Doongalik Studios	13 E2
Flying Cloud Snorkeling Trips	(see 35)
Hartley's Undersea Walk	14 E2
Nassau Beach Sports Shop	15 D2
Stuart Cove's Dive & Snorkel Bahamas	16 B4

Versailles Gardens	17 E2
Waterscape	(see 18)

SLEEPING
Atlantis	18 E2
Compass Point Inn	19 B2
Nassau Harbour Club	(see 20)
Red Carpet Inn	20 E2
Sandyport Beach Resort	21 C2

EATING
Avery's Restaurant & Bar	22 B4
Capriccio Ristorante	23 D2
Coco Bar & Wood Grill	24 C2

ENTERTAINMENT
Bahama Marina Mia	(see 37)

Club Land'Or	25 E2
Cocktail & Dreams Nightclub	26 D2
Dundas Centre for Performing Arts	27 E3
Insomnia	28 D2
Pink Pearl Café	(see 12)

SHOPPING
Lyford Cay Marathon	29 B3
The Mall at Marathon	30 D2
Towne Centre Mall	31 E3

TRANSPORT
Avis	(see 1)
Budget	(see 1)
Dollar	(see 1)
General Aviation Terminal (Private Charters)	32 C3
Hertz	(see 1)
Mail Boat	(see 1)
Orange Creek Rentals	34 D2
Paradise Island Ferry Terminal	35 E2

OTHER
Entrance Gate to Lyford Cay	36 B3
Hurricane Hole Marina	37 E2
Nassau Yacht Haven	(see 14)
Queen Elizabeth Sports Centre	38 E3
Royal Bahamas Defence Force Base	39 B4

Getting There & Around

The following information relates to New Providence and Nassau. For information on international flights to and from the Bahamas, as well as travel information between the Bahamian islands, see p98 and p773.

TO/FROM THE AIRPORT

There are no buses to or from the airport, as the taxi-drivers' union has things sewn up. A few hotels do provide shuttle services, and taxis also line the forecourts of hotels and the airport outside the arrivals lounge. For **taxi bookings** (☎ 242-323-5111/4555), call a day ahead. Destination rates are fixed by the government and displayed on the wall; all rates are for two people and each additional person costs US$3.

Nevertheless, some taxi drivers may try to charge the third or fourth person the same rate as for two people, or charge additional rates for luggage once you reach your destination. Don't agree to these blatant scams – the drivers normally back down.

One-way rates are as follows: Cable Beach US$15, downtown Nassau and Prince George Wharf US$22, and Paradise Island US$27.

CAR & SCOOTER

You really don't need a car to explore Nassau or to get to the beaches. If you intend to explore New Providence, it's worth saving a taxi fare to and from Nassau by hiring a car at the airport. Collision damage waiver insurance costs US$15 a day. For information on road rules, see p100.

The following companies have car-rental booths at the airport (Dollar is the cheapest, costing from around US$80 per 24 hours):

Avis (Map p65) Cable Beach (☎ 242-322-2889); Nassau International Airport (☎ 242-377-7121); Paradise Island (☎ 242-363-2061)

Budget (Map p65) Nassau International Airport (☎ 242-377-7405); Paradise Island (☎ 242-363-3095)

Dollar (Map p65) Nassau (☎ 242-325-3716; British Colonial Hilton Nassau); Nassau International Airport (☎ 242-377-8300)

Hertz (Map p65; ☎ 242-377-8684; Nassau International Airport)

Several local companies also rent cheaper cars, ranging from about US$55 daily. Ask your hotel to recommend a company or try **Orange Creek Rentals** (Map p65; ☎ 242-323-4967, 800-891-7655; fax 356-5005; West Bay St, Nassau).

Scooters are widely available and can be found outside most major hotels for around US$50 a day. **Knowles Scooter Rentals** (Map pp68-9; ☎ 242-322-3415; Festival Pl, Nassau) rents scooters for US$40 per day.

LOCAL TRANSPORT

Nassau and New Providence are well served by minibuses, called *jitneys,* which run constantly from 6am to 8pm, although there are no fixed schedules. All buses depart downtown from Frederick St at Bay St and at designated bus stops. No buses run to Paradise Island. Destinations are clearly marked on the buses, which can be waved down. Likewise to request a stop anywhere when you're onboard, simply ask the driver.

The standard bus fare is US$1 (children US$0.50) paid to the driver upon exiting the bus. Following are sample routes and destinations:

Bus No 6 Travels to South New Providence.

Bus Nos 10 & 10A Serve Cable Beach and Sandy Point.

No 38 Serves Cable Beach and Prince George Wharf via Over-the-Hill.

Bus Nos 24 & 30 Travel to the New Paradise Island Bridge.

NASSAU

Modern Nassau is not such a far cry from the rowdy town that once harbored pirates, stockade runners and Prohibition-avoiding party crowds. It's still a lively place fuelled by commerce and rum, just of a more legal kind! The small historic downtown core is a charming mix of narrow streets, grand sugar-pink neocolonial government buildings, and, dignified in their faded grandeur, old wooden and limestone buildings.

This pretty snapshot is also a hub of commerce and government, policed by immaculately dressed and starched police officers. Bankers in pinstriped shirts dodge between tourists toward a myriad of international banks, intent on manipulating billions of dollars to make the wealthy wealthier in this offshore banking haven.

The waterfront and Bay St shops (the heart of downtown) are packed with tax-free emeralds, spicy rums and silk clothing. Small restaurants serve chattering tourists fuelled by multicolored cocktails, while vast cruise ships loom overhead disgorging their hordes, who swamp not only Nassau's identity but also her cash registers.

Jitneys run constantly to the soft sands of Cable Beach and taxis honk for those heading for Paradise Island's snowy-white Cabbage Beach. Cable Beach and Paradise Island resorts offer great deals and a heap of fun and activities for families. From water sports to Kids Clubs and the wonders of Atlantis, kids of all ages have a ball here.

Low-income and middle-class residential suburbs extend inland for miles. Government ministries, modern shopping malls and colleges all lie south of downtown, while Over-the-Hill is a middle- and low-income area bounded by Prospect and Blue Hill Ridges to the north and south. This is the heart and soul of African-Bahamian life and a real display of Nassau's infinitely less-affluent residents.

Orientation

Historic downtown Nassau is 10 blocks long and four blocks wide, and faces north toward Paradise Island and Nassau Harbour. The town rises south to Prospect Ridge, a steep limestone scarp that parallels the entire north shore about 0.5 miles (800m) inland. A second, higher ridge – Blue Hill Heights – rises to 120ft (36m) and runs east to west along Nassau's southern border, 3 miles (4.8km) inland. The major residential areas lie between the ridges.

The main thoroughfare through town is Bay St, which runs east to the Paradise Island Bridge; beyond it follows the windward shore as Eastern Rd. West of downtown, Bay St becomes West Bay St, which runs west to Cable Beach, past Lyford Cay and joins Eastern Rd to complete an island loop.

Downtown, Bay St is one way, from west to east. The main westbound thoroughfare downtown is Shirley St, which begins at Eastern Rd.

Paradise Island is 4 miles (6km) long and 0.5 miles (800m) wide, tapering to the west. It is divided in two by a narrow manmade waterway linking Nassau Harbour to the Atlantis marina. Two road bridges (one to enter and the other to exit the island) link Paradise Island to New Providence. Both bridges have pedestrian walkways.

MAPS

Aside from this guide's own maps, the free tourist *Bahamas Trailblazer Map* and *Super Map* are available in shops and hotels.

Information

EMERGENCY

Air Sea Rescue Association (☎ 242-325-8864)
Ambulance (☎ 242-322-2221)
Fire (☎ 242-302-8404)
Med-Evac (☎ 242-322-2881)
Police (☎ 242-322-4444)
Red Cross (☎ 242-323-7370)
State Care Medical & Emergency Centre (☎ 242-328-5596)

INTERNET ACCESS

Expect to pay around US$10 per hour for Internet services with pretty good-quality computers and connections.
Bahamas Internet Cafe (Map pp68-9; ☎ 242-325-7458; Bay St, Nassau; ☺ 9am-5pm Mon-Sat)
Cyber Café (Map p65; ☎ 242-363-1253; cybercafé3@coralwave.com; Paradise Island Shopping Centre, Paradise Island; ☺ 9am-6pm Mon-Sat)
FML Web Shop (Map p65; ☎ 242-363-2241; Hurricane Hole Plaza, Paradise Island; ☺ 7am-7:30pm Mon-Sat, noon-7:30pm Sun)
Internet café (Map pp68-9; ☎ 242-323-1000; West Bay Hotel, West Bay St, Nassau; ☺ 9am-5pm Mon-Sat)
Tech Shop (Map p65; ☎ 242-327-0081; www.techshops.com; West Bay St, Cable Beach; ☺ 9am-7pm Mon-Fri, 10am-6:30pm Sat, 11am-4pm Sun) In the same row of shops as the Cable Beach Medical Centre.

MEDICAL SERVICES

Pharmacies are located in all shopping malls, but keep mainly standard hours.
Cable Beach Medical Centre (Map p65; ☎ 242-327-2886; West Bay St, Cable Beach) Located outside Sandals Royal Bahamian.
Doctor's Hospital (Map pp68-9; ☎ 242-322-8411, 242-302-4600; cnr Shirley St & Collins Ave) Privately owned full-service hospital, provides emergency services and acute care.
Princess Margaret Hospital (Map pp68-9; ☎ 242-322-2861; cnr Elizabeth Ave & Sands Rd) The main facility is this government-run, full-service hospital providing emergency services and acute care.

MONEY

There are plenty of banks clustered around Rawson Sq and Bay St. ATMs dispensing US and Bahamian dollars can be found easily throughout Nassau and at banks like the Royal Bank of Canada (E Hill St, Bay St and Cable Beach).

The Commonwealth Bank, Scotiabank, British American Bank and Western Union also have branches in Cable Beach.

DOWNTOWN NASSAU

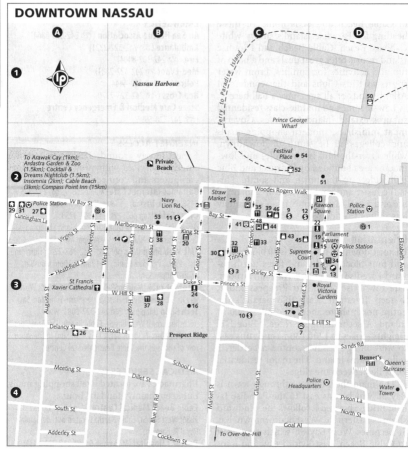

Central Bank of the Bahamas (☎ 242-302-2600; Market St, Nassau) Come here to change Bahamian currency.

Destinations (Map pp68-9; ☎ 242-322-2931; 303 Shirley St, Nassau) Represents Amex.

Scotiabank (Map pp68-9; ☎ 242-356-1400; Rawson Sq, Nassau) Has 24-hour ATM accepting Visa, MasterCard and Discover cards.

POST

DHL Worldwide Express (Map p65; ☎ 242-394-4040; East Bay St, Nassau)

FedEx (Map p65; ☎ 242-322-5656; www.fedex.com; EE McKay Plaza, Thompson Blvd, Nassau)

Main post office (Map pp68-9; ☎ 242-322-3025; cnr E Hill & Parliament Sts, Nassau; ⊗ 8:30am-5:30pm Mon-Fri, 8:30am-12:30pm Sat)

TELEPHONE

For telephone information and the services available in Nassau and New Providence, see p97.

BaTelCo East St (Map pp68-9; ☎ 242-323-6414; ⊗ 7am-10pm); John F Kennedy Dr (Map p65; ☎ 242-323-4911) Has public phone booths for international calls.

TOURIST INFORMATION

The Bahamas Ministry of Tourism is a government-run department with offices in Nassau and across the Bahamian islands (see p97). However, limited information is available. Your best bet is to access the official Bahamas website and others listed under Internet Resources on p96. Following a fire in the Ministry of Tourism HQ,

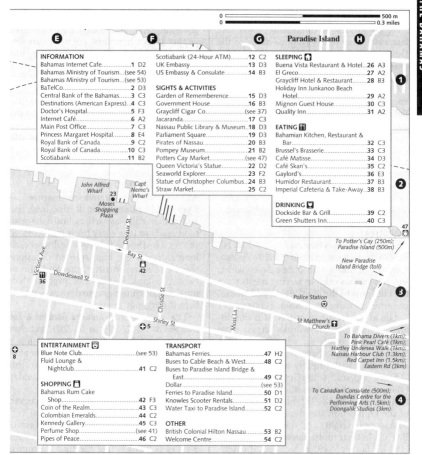

an office is located in the British Colonial Hilton (contact details can be found below). Tourist centers in Nassau can be located as follows:

Bahamas Ministry of Tourism (www.bahamas
.com; 9am-5pm Mon-Fri) British Colonial Hilton (Map pp68–9; 242-302-5000; Bay St, Nassau); Nassau International Airport (Map p65; 242-377-6806; Airport Arrivals Terminal); Welcome Centre (Map pp68-9; 242-326-9781; Festival Pl; 9am-5pm Mon-Fri) The Welcome Centre service is also available on weekends if a cruise ship is in port.

Dangers & Annoyances
Avoid Over-the-Hill at night, as this area suffers from some drug-related violence. Also use caution by day, as the area's down-at-heel quality is aggravated by the presence of 'Joneses' (drug users). You should also avoid walking alone downtown at night; stick to well-lit main streets.

Sights
DOWNTOWN NASSAU
The heart of downtown Nassau is a compact and colorful historic district, with many evocative museums and well-preserved buildings from the 18th and 19th century. An example is the interactive **Pirates of Nassau** (Map pp68-9; 242-356-3759; pirates@bahamas .net.bs; King St; adult/child US$12/6; 9am-6pm Mon-Fri, 8:30am-noon Sat), a hugely popular walk-through re-creation of hairy pirates and their violent lifestyle.

West & East Hill Streets

Here sit houses of diminished glory like **Jacaranda** (Map pp68–9), once home to the Duke of Windsor, and **Dunmore House** (Map pp68–9), beautifully refurbished as the National Art Gallery of the Bahamas.

The vast candy pink Georgian **Government House** (1737; Map pp68–9), residence to the Bahamas' Governor-General, displays a jauntily dressed **statue of Christopher Columbus** (Map pp68–9) on the steps overlooking Duke St.

Twenty Cubans at the **Graycliff Cigar Co** (Map pp68-9; ☎ 242-322-2795; West Hill St, Nassau; admission free; ⌚ 9am-5pm Mon-Fri) roll pounded sheets of aromatic tobacco, supervised by Avelino Lara, former personal roller for Fidel Castro. Visitors are always courteously welcomed.

Bay Street

The emotive **Pompey Museum** (Map pp68-9; ☎ 242-326-2566; Vendue House; adult/child US$1/0.50; ⌚ 10am-4:30pm Mon-Fri, 10am-1pm Sat), once a slave-auction site, has various exhibits tracing events from the Lucayans to the bootleggers, and vibrant paintings by naive artist Amos Ferguson.

Life at the west end of Bay St is dominated by possibly the world's largest **straw market** (Map pp68–9), where everything from straw hats to bags, dolls and T-shirts is decorated with brightly colored motifs.

Some pink-and-white Georgian buildings (1805–13) intimately nestle around **Parliament Sq** (Map pp68–9) housing the Leader of the Opposition (on the left), the House of Assembly (right) and the Senate (facing Bay St). In their midst, **Queen Victoria's Statue** (1905; Map pp68–9) reflects still-held allegiances dating back to her youth.

A few yards north is the small **Garden of Remembrance** (Map pp68–9), with a cenotaph honoring Bahamian soldiers who died in the two world wars.

Shirley Street

The **Nassau Public Library & Museum** (1797; Map pp68-9; ☎ 242-322-4907; admission free; ⌚ 10am-8pm Mon-Thu, 10am-5pm Fri, 10am-4pm Sat), an octagonal building, contains narrow jail cells, now crammed with books and dusty periodicals (the dungeon still exists below ground), and a museum upstairs.

EAST OF DOWNTOWN

Lively **Potter's Cay market** (Map pp68–9) sits beneath Paradise Island Bridge, welcoming fishing boats carrying their daily trade of glistening fish and conch shells. Searing pepper sauces, herbs and vegetables are also sold alongside the distressing sight of dismembered turtles. Yet this is a great place to hang out and watch the pandemonium whenever a boat arrives.

Alongside artists conjuring up dazzling Junkanoo masks, **Doongalik Studios** (Map p65; ☎ 242-393-6640; www.doongalikstudios.com; 18 Village Rd, Nassau; admission free; ⌚ 9am-5pm Mon-Fri) sells exuberant and vivid Bahamian paintings, exotic crafts, T-shirts and furniture.

WEST OF DOWNTOWN

At the entrance to **Arawak Cay** (Map p65) is a very lively village of small bars, fresh fish and conch stalls, as well as hot-Bahamian food ready to take away from multicolored shacks. Lunchtime fish sales and weekend-long fish-fries are high-spirited occasions worthy of a smoky fritter, chat and rum or two! Also Junkanoo 'shacks' practice their music and choreographed dance moves here throughout the year.

The well-stocked **Ardastra Gardens & Zoo** (Map p65; ☎ 242-323-5806; fax 323-7232; Chippingham Rd, Nassau; adult/child US$12/6; ⌚ 9am-5pm) has a few placid iguanas, and a small regiment of marching West Indian flamingos who strut their stuff at 11am, 2pm and 4pm Monday to Saturday.

Cable Beach (Map p65) is a long-curved stretch of white beach and sparkling turquoise sea. Linked to downtown Nassau, the coastal section of West Bay St travels for 3 miles (4.8km) before meeting the tourist complexes that make up this suburb. Named for the undersea telegraphic cable that came ashore here in 1892, Cable Beach's oversized resorts appear to also have been derived from the Floridian peninsular, and are beloved of families seeking simple seaside pleasures.

PARADISE ISLAND

The island is famous for the white sands of the 2-mile (3.2km)-long **Cabbage Beach**. Now lined with resorts, it is beloved by those who enjoy people-watching and water sports.

Paradise Island Dr runs through the **Versailles Gardens** (Map p65), which fall away on both sides. Developed as a hideaway by a wealthy Swedish industrialist in 1939, and modeled on Versailles, this lovely sweeping 35-acre (14-hectare) garden, stepped in tiers, is lined with fountains and classical statues depicting the millionaire's heroes: Hercules, Napoleon Bonaparte and Franklin D Roosevelt to name a few. At the crest is **Cloisters** (Map p65), a romantic gazebo where weddings are often held. This genuine 14th-century cloister was purchased by newspaper magnate William Randolph Hearst from an Augustine estate in France. Visitors are welcome.

No trip would be complete for families, or even big kids, without a visit to the 34-acre (14-hectare) **Waterscape** (Map p65; ☎ 242-363-3000 ext 28; www.atlantis.com) at the Atlantis resort (p74). A whole host of lagoons here are home to over 200 species of marine life, claimed as the world's largest open-air aquarium. Don't miss Predator Lagoon, which is full of sharks with refined tastes and elegant incisors. A **guided tour** (US$25; ☉ 9am-5pm) for nonguests takes in a number of attractions, built for kids of all ages.

Activities

DIVING & SNORKELING

New Providence offers superb diving close to its shores, including fantastic wall and wreck dives. The most noted sites lie off the southwest coast between Coral Harbour and Lyford Cay. Equipment can be hired from the following operators.

One of the Bahamas best outfits, **Stuart Cove's Dive & Snorkel Bahamas** (Map p65; ☎ 242-362-4171; www.stuartcove.com; PO Box CB-13137, Nassau) offers a mass of diving, Professional Association of Diving Instructors (PADI) certification and snorkeling choices, including a bone-rattling shark wall and shark-feeding dive (US$135); a two-tank dive trip (US$88); and wall-flying – a two-tank underwater scooter adventure (US$135). Snorkeling trips are available (adult/child US$48/24), and you can even pilot your own Scenic Underwater Bubble (SUB), a scooter with air wheels and a giant plastic bubble that envelops your shoulders and head (US$135).

Another good bunch, **Bahama Divers** (☎ 242-393-5644; www.bahamadivers.com; PO Box 5004, Nassau) has a variety of trips, including the Lost Blue Hole (famous for its sharks and schools of stingrays) and wrecks. A three-hour learn-to-dive course can be taken prior to PADI certification courses, which cost US$449. A two-tank dive costs US$130, and half-day snorkeling trips are also available (US$30).

BAHAMAS' 10 BEST BEACHES

- **Pink Sands Beach** Harbour Island (Eleuthera; p88)
- **Gordon's Beach** Long Island (p92)
- **Treasure Cay Beach** (Abaco; p87)
- **Churchill Beach** Grand Bahama (p81)
- **Pink Sand Beach** Governor's Harbour (Eleuthera; p89)
- **Hope Town Beach** Elbow Cay (Abaco; p87)
- **Taino Beach** Grand Bahama (p81)
- **Guana Key Beach** Long Island (p92)
- **Stocking Island Beach** Exumas (p90)
- **Cabbage Beach** Paradise Island (New Providence; opposite)

BOAT EXCURSIONS

Dozens of day trips are offered, with options for snorkeling, diving, beach time, island visits, partying, sunset and dinner cruises, and anything else you can think of! A few vessels depart the Nassau waterfront; most depart the dock immediately west of the Paradise Island Bridge.

Bahamas Ferries (Map pp68-9; ☎ 242-323-2166; www.bahamasferries.com) offers a 'Harbour Island Day Away' excursion to wonderful Eleuthera. It departs from Potter's Cay, takes two hours each way, and includes a tour of Harbour Island and lunch on idyllic Pink Sands Beach (adult/child US$159/99).

Flying Cloud Snorkeling Trips (Map pp68-9; ☎ 242-363-4430; flyingcloud@coralwave.com; Paradise Island Ferry Terminal) can arrange a day of fun, with a catamaran cruise, snorkeling around lovely little Rose Island and a chance to snooze in a hammock after a beach barbecue lunch with wine (adult/child US$90/45).

Hartley's Undersea Walk (Map pp68-9; ☎ 242-393-8234/7569; www.underseawalk.com; East Bay St, Nassau) offers a 3½-hour cruise that includes an escorted undersea adventure (adult US$125); you don't need snorkeling or diving experience to wear a roomy brass helmet with large glass windows for all-around viewing. Trips depart from Nassau Yacht Haven.

Seaworld Explorer (Map pp68-9; ☎ 242-356-2548; shorex@batelnet.bs; Moses Shopping Plaza, Bay St, Nassau), a 45-passenger semisubmarine with a

THE BAHAMAS

window-lined hull, has a great 90-minute excursion above the fish-filled coral reefs of the Sea Gardens Marine Park off the north shore (adult/child US$22/10).

SPORT FISHING

Nassau is a grand base for sport fishing, with sites just 20 minutes away. Charters can be arranged at most major hotels or by calling a charter company. The following recommended companies charge two to six people around US$400/700 per half/full day:

Born Free Charter Service (☎ 242-393-4144; Nassau)

Brown's Charter (☎ 242-324-2061; www.browns charter.com; Nassau)

Chubasco Charters (☎ 242-324-3474; Nassau)

WATER SPORTS

Water sports are available at all the resorts along Paradise and Cabbage Beaches. Most of the motorized sports are operated by local entrepreneurs. Typical prices include US$50 per person for 30 minutes of jet-skiing, US$20 per person for a 15-minute banana boat ride and US$35 per person for 10 minutes of parasailing.

Nassau Beach Sports Shop (Map p65; ☎ 242-327-7711 ext 6590; Nassau Beach Hotel, West Bay St, Cable Beach; ◷ 9am-5pm) rents sailboards for US$20 per hour.

Festivals & Events

For all the major Bahamian festivals, such as Boxing Day's brilliant Junkanoo, see p96. Otherwise you can contact the Bahamas Ministry of Tourism (p97) for events and dates. Following are a few fun-filled local proceedings:

Caribbean Muzik Fest This will make you shake something in June! Move to reggae, soca, calypso and dancehall at the Queen Elizabeth Sports Centre (Map p65) until dawn.

Emancipation Day Held on the first Monday of August. Fox Hill features an early morning 'Junkanoo Rush,' brilliant fun for all, as well as the emancipation celebrations.

Police Band Annual Christmas & Classical Concert The Royal Bahamas Police Force Band performs with vigor at the Atlantis Resort to welcome Christmas.

JUMPING AT JUNKANOO

You feel the music before you see it…a frenzied barrage of whistles and horns overriding the *ka-LICK-ka-LICK* of cowbells, the rumble of drums and the joyful blasts of conch shells. Then the costumed revelers stream into view, whirling and gyrating like a kaleidoscope in rhythm with the cacophony. This is Junkanoo, the national festival of the Bahamas, a mass of energy, color and partying that starts in the twilight hours of Boxing Day.

Junkanoo is fiercely competitive and many marchers belong to 'shacks,' groups who vie to produce the best performance, costume, dancing and music. The most elaborately costumed performers are one-person parade floats, whose costume can weigh over 200lb (90kg) and depict exotic scenes adorned with a myriad of glittering beads, foils and rhinestones. Many spend a year planning their costumes, keeping their designs a carefully guarded secret.

The name (junk-uh-*noo*) is thought to come from a West African term for 'deadly sorcerer.' Others say the festival is named for John Canoe, the tribal leader who demanded that his enslaved people be allowed to enjoy a festivity.

Junkanoo, which had its origins in West African secret societies, evolved on the plantations of the British Caribbean among slaves who were forbidden to observe their sacred rites. The all-male cast of masqueraders hid their identity, following West African mask-wearing tradition.

At first Junkanoos were suppressed by the Bahamian colonial government, which feared they might get out of hand and lead to slave uprisings. Creole elements found their way into the ceremony, along with British Morris dancing, polka and reels. On Jamaica and other islands, Junkanoo was suppressed to extinction, but in the Bahamas it became an integral part of the culture.

When Junkanoo parades flood down Bay and Shirley Sts in Nassau and erupt on the Family Islands, the energy is that of a joyous and frenetic explosion. In Nassau the first 'rush,' as the parade is known, takes place on Boxing Day (December 26); the second occurs on New Year's Day and the third in summer, when teams practice their game plans. Parades begin at about 3am and finish by noon in time for a big lunch!

Sleeping

Nassau isn't cheap or getting cheaper. Many hotels are outrageously overpriced, but there are a few bargains. Remember to ask about specials, and that low-season (April to mid-December) rates drop between 25% to 60%. Downtown hotels tend to be smaller generally and cheaper than those in Cable Beach. Quoted rates here do not include additional charges unless specified.

DOWNTOWN NASSAU
Budget
Buena Vista Restaurant & Hotel (Map pp68-9; ☎ 242-322-2811; stanbv2000@yahoo.com; Delancy St; r US$50; P ✗ ☒) This faded old mansion, acclaimed for its restaurant, still has much charm, and some great-value lodgings upstairs. The rooms are clean and furnished with lovely antique furniture, and come with TV, radio, IDD phones and private bath. The rates are inclusive, and it's only a 10-minute walk into town or to the city beach.

Mignon Guest House (Map pp68-9; ☎ 242-322-4771; 12 Market St, PO Box N-786, Nassau; s/d US$40/45; ✗) This is an outstanding bargain in the heart of downtown Nassau. Six pleasant and clean small rooms each come with a TV. Toilet and bath facilities, and a kitchenette, including microwave and fridge, are shared. Security is good and rates are inclusive.

Midrange
Holiday Inn Junkanoo Beach Hotel (Map pp68-9; ☎ 242-356-0000; www.basshotels.com/holiday-inn; West Bay & Nassau Sts; r US$135; P ✗ ☒ ⬛ ☒) Although things can be a little haphazard occasionally, this hotel has the best facilities of the midrange hotels in Nassau. Rooms are clean, light and comfortable, and decorated in bright tropical pastels. Each has a private bath, balcony, TV, safe, fridge, data port, hairdryer, iron and coffeemaker. Beds are firm and spacious. The hotel also has a guest laundry, gym, shop, business-service facilities, restaurant and bar.

Quality Inn (Map pp68-9; ☎ 242-322-1515; www.qualityinn.com; cnr West Bay & Nassau Sts, Nassau; r US$90; P ✗ ☒ ☒) This shiny new hotel sits next door to the Junkanoo, and all rooms face onto the sea, some with better views than others. The cheerfully decorated rooms are nearly as well equipped as their neighbors (no fridge, though), which will attract a similar business clientele as well as midrange travelers.

El Greco (Map pp68-9; ☎ 242-325-1121; fax 325-1124; cnr W Bay & Augusta Sts, PO Box N-4187, Nassau; s/d US$90/110; P ✗ ☒ ☒) At the west end of downtown, this compact family-run hotel, enhanced by Spanish decor, surrounds a small courtyard with pool and bougainvillea. The rooms can be gloomy and the fittings old, but the location is good and rates are inclusive. Upstairs rooms are larger, have balconies and a little more light.

Top End
Graycliff Hotel & Restaurant (Map pp68-9; ☎ 242-322-2796; www.graycliff.com; West Hill St, Nassau; r US$290; P ✗ ☒ ⬛ ☒) Nassau's most discreet and character-laden hotel is this fabulous 250-year-old Georgian home built by a wealthy pirate and hidden away above town on West Hill St. Nine lofty-ceilinged rooms and five romantic cottage suites in the garden have windows on all sides, and the baths are exquisite. The central rooms feature unique Cuban art, comfortably faded and eclectic furnishings, a smoking room and library resplendent with the rich aroma of Cuban cigars, an astonishing wine cellar, and a restaurant beloved of gourmets and regular themed evenings of South American cuisine. The tranquil garden contains a saltwater Olympic-length pool – one of three pools – in a stone courtyard that hosts intimate weddings. A history of celebrity guests include Sir Winston Churchill, the Beatles and LL Cool J.

WEST & EAST OF DOWNTOWN
Sandyport Beach Resort (Map p65; ☎ 242-327-4279; www.sandyport.com; West Bay St, Cable Beach; r US$210; P ✗ ☒ ☒) This snazzy new residential-resort complex at the west end of Cable Beach has a marina, fitness center, tennis courts and a church to keep you toned, spiritually and physically. Airy, modern and well-equipped town houses offer good value with week-long deals. Rates are for two adults and two children. The gardens are incomplete, but the beach is just across the road.

Red Carpet Inn (Map p65; ☎ 242-393-7981; www.redcarpetinnbahamas.com; East Bay St, Nassau; r US$120; P ✗ ☒ ☒) This contemporary 40-room hotel, with adequate but plain rooms, is a quiet and simple place, and the security is good. The rooms are clean, with double beds, fridges, microwaves, TV and phone. There's also a restaurant and guest laundry facilities.

check out prices at home before visiting the Bahamas). Most stores close at night and on Sunday, even when the cruise ships are in port.

Tourist shops sell warm buttery rum cakes in fancy sealed tins for around US$20. Or try one right now at the **Bahamas Rum Cake Shop** (Map pp8-9; ☎ 242-322-3444; Bay St; 7am-5pm Mon-Fri, 9am-noon some Sat) for US$6.

ARTWORK
Galleries abound, and many souvenir shops sell either cheap, original or hand-copied oil and acrylic Haitian paintings for as little as US$15.

Doongalik Studios (Map p65; ☎ 242-393-6640; www.doongalikstudios.com; 18 Village Rd, Nassau) For vibrant Junkanoo-inspired paintings, crafts and T-shirts; see also p70.

Kennedy Gallery (Map pp8-9; ☎ 242-325-7662; www.kennedygallerybahamas.com; Parliament St, Nassau)

CIGARS
Premium Cuban cigars can be bought for a song in Nassau, but remember, Uncle Sam prohibits US citizens from importing them. The good news is that Graycliff's cigars are not made with Cuban tobacco so are permitted by US customs.

Graycliff Cigar Co (Map pp68-9; ☎ 242-322-2795; West Hill St, Nassau; 9am-5pm Mon-Fri) Castro's own cigar roller, Avelino Lara, oversees fellow Cubans hand-rolling these award-winning cigars; see also p70.

Pipes of Peace (Map pp8-9; ☎ 242-322-3908; cnr Bay & Charlotte Sts) Has a fine selection of Cuban cigars.

DUTY-FREE GOODS & COLLECTIBLES
There are swathes of designer clothing, leather, linen and Bahamian goods as well as perfume outlets. Jewelry and watches are also big-ticket items here. The following should whet your appetite:

Coin of the Realm (Map pp8-9; ☎ 242-322-4497; Charlotte St, Nassau) Bahamian coins, stamps and semi-precious stones.

Colombian Emeralds (Map pp8-9; ☎ 242-322-2230; Bay St, Nassau) Bright sparkling emeralds and much more.

Perfume Shop (Map pp8-9; ☎ 242-322-2375; cnr Bay & Frederick Sts, Nassau) A vast collection of designer sniffs.

SOUTH NEW PROVIDENCE
Adelaide
Seventeen miles (27km) to the southwest of Nassau, Adelaide is a quiet village whose nostalgic lifestyle revolves around fishing.

Visually it isn't noteworthy, but it is about as close as you can get to traditional life on the island. The village dates back to 1832, when it was founded for slaves freed from a Portuguese slave trader, on a spit of land jutting into a navigable creek rich in conch, fish and lobster.

The village is fronted by narrow, white-sand **Adelaide Beach** (Map p65), extending between South Ocean and the village. Fishing boats are drawn up on the beach, and the wharf is lively at sunset when the day's work is done.

For yummy seafood and rum drinks, loiter at **Avery's Restaurant & Bar** (Map p65; ☎ 242-362-1547; Adelaide Village; mains US$10-20; lunch & dinner).

Bacardi Rum Factory
After Fidel Castro's expropriation of the Bacardi family's rum factories during the Cuban Revolution, the family set up its business in other locales, including this site east of Coral Harbour and southwest of Carmichael Village. This **factory** (Map p65; ☎ 242-362-1412; cnr Bacardi & Carmichael Rds) produces Bacardi rum (the family successfully sued the Castro regime for the Bacardi title) from sugar imported from other Caribbean islands. Free tours are held from 10am to 3pm Monday to Thursday.

GRAND BAHAMA

pop 46,570
Grand Bahama, lying 110 miles (177km) northwest of New Providence, is the second most popular tourist destination in the Bahamas. Nevertheless it isn't as sophisticated or wealthy as its neighbor and has a more relaxed vibe. With tourism centered on Freeport and Lucaya, and industry based around the port at the western end of the island, much of this flat and narrow 85-mile (136km)-long isle has been left in peace.

Blanketed by miles of upright Cuban pines and the glorious Lucayan National Park, the southern shore is lined with sugar-white beaches leading into warm, jewel-colored waters. Turtles occasionally slowly emerge from the sea to nest at Gold Rock, Hawksbill and High Rock Creeks.

The northern shores celebrate a bountiful and colorful birdlife that relishes its

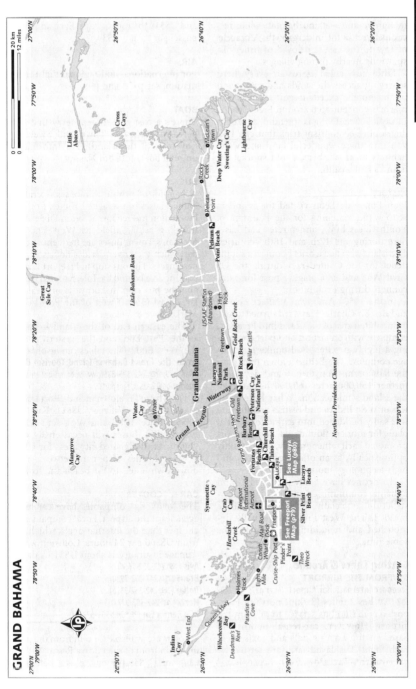

THE BAHAMAS

mangrove and wetland habitat, while raccoons ferret in the undergrowth. A bracelet of cays to the east is beloved of fisherfolk, spawning nearby fishing villages.

Little curly tailed lizards are everywhere, scurrying across the sands and pavements of the hotels, excellent golf courses and marinas concentrated around Freeport and Lucaya. Scuba diving is splendid, as are the developing ecotourism trips that can take you into these wonderful land and water habitats to kayak, bicycle and snorkel the island's real wealth.

History

Juan Ponce de León visited the island in 1513 while searching for the Fountain of Youth (bless him), and pirates had bases here during the 17th and 18th centuries. The island also had a brief boom as a supply depot for the Confederacy during the US Civil War and as a staging post for rum-runners during Prohibition.

In the 1950s American Wallace Groves and Brit Sir Charles Hayward turned a vast, uninhabited area of the island into Freeport; complete with an airport and port containing a highly profitable oil-bunkering storage complex. The British crown then gave the lads permission to buy and develop a further 150,000 acres (60,000 hectares) of the island's midsection. What little there was of West Indian and British architecture was sadly bulldozed into extinction. Initial plans for tourism floundered, and Freeport promoted itself rather grandly, and certainly optimistically, as an offshore financial and high-technology industrial center.

Hurricanes have badly damaged Grand Bahama communities and tourism infrastructure, especially Frances and Jeanne in 2004. The West End was virtually demolished and rebuilding is going to take some time.

Getting There & Around

TO/FROM THE AIRPORT
Freeport International Airport (Map p77; ☎ 242-352-6020) lies 2 miles (3.2km) north of Freeport. There's no bus service to or from the airport. However, car-rental booths are based in the arrivals hall and taxis meet each flight. Displayed fares are set by the government. Taxi rides for two people to/from the airport to Freeport are US$11,

and US$19 to/from Lucaya. Each additional passenger costs US$3.

AIR
For international and regional flight information, see p773 and p98.

BOAT
There's a free government ferry that runs between McLean's Town and Sweetings Cay (east of the island). For information on mail boats to/from Nassau, see p99.

BUS
A handful of private minibuses operate as 'public buses' on assigned routes from the bus station in Freeport at Winn Dixie Plaza, traveling as far afield as West End and McLean's Town. Buses are frequent and depart when the driver decides he has enough passengers. The bus stop in Freeport is at the parking area behind the International Bazaar, and the bus stop in Lucaya is on Seahorse Dr, 400yd (364m) west of the Port Lucaya Marketplace & Village.

The eastern end of the island is known as the 'East End' and the western part as the 'West End.' Timetables can be obtained from the **Grand Bahama Island Tourism Board** (Map p79; ☎ 242-325-8356; www.grand-bahama.com; International Bazaar, Freeport).

Fares from Freetown include Port Lucaya Marketplace & Village (US$1), East End (US$8, twice daily) and West End (US$4, twice daily). Buses will occasionally drop you in taxi-designated city areas for US$2.

Free shuttles also run between most downtown hotels to the beach and town.

CAR & SCOOTER
The following companies have car-rental agencies at the airport. Local companies are cheaper than the internationals, which cost from US$60 per 24 hours. Collision waiver damage insurance is about US$15 a day.
Avis (☎ 242-352-7666)
Brad$ (☎ 242-352-7930)
Dollar (☎ 242-352-9325)
Hertz (☎ 242-352-9277)
KSR Rent A Car (☎ 242-351-5737)

Scooters are available for rent from the parking lot in front of the Lucaya Resort & Yacht Club for US$40 per day, plus a hefty cash deposit.

TAXI

You'll find taxis at the airport and major hotels.

Fares are fixed by the government for short distances.

You can call for a radio-dispatched taxi from **Freeport Taxi** (☎ 242-352-6666) or **Grand Bahama Taxi Union** (☎ 242-352-7101).

FREEPORT & LUCAYA

pop 33,000

Grand Bahama is dominated by Freeport and its southeastern suburb Lucaya. Freeport is a planned city, with wide, grid-arranged streets and uninspired modern buildings. The strange, sprawling entity lacks both an easily definable character and an easily

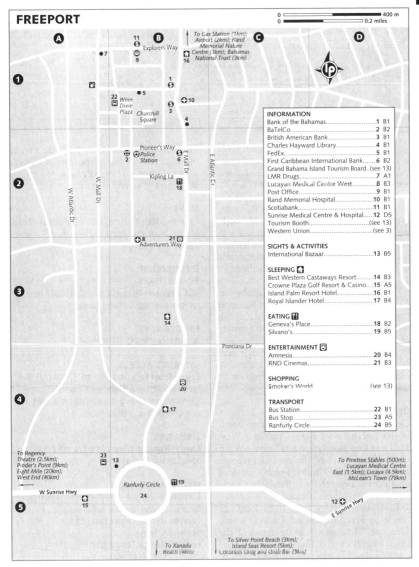

FREEPORT

0 _____ 400 m
0 _____ 0.2 miles

INFORMATION
Bank of the Bahamas............................**1** B1
BaTelCo...**2** B2
British American Bank..........................**3** B1
Charles Hayward Library......................**4** B1
FedEx..**5** B1
First Caribbean International Bank........**6** B2
Grand Bahama Island Tourism Board..(see **13**)
LMR Drugs...**7** A1
Lucayan Medical Centre West..............**8** B3
Post Office...**9** B1
Rand Memorial Hospital.....................**10** B1
Scotiabank...**11** B1
Sunrise Medical Centre & Hospital.....**12** D5
Tourism Booth...............................(see **13**)
Western Union.................................(see **3**)

SIGHTS & ACTIVITIES
International Bazaar............................**13** B5

SLEEPING 🛏
Best Western Castaways Resort..........**14** B3
Crowne Plaza Golf Resort & Casino....**15** A5
Island Palm Resort Hotel....................**16** B1
Royal Islander Hotel...........................**17** B4

EATING 🍽
Geneva's Place...................................**18** B2
Silvano's...**19** B5

ENTERTAINMENT 🎭
Amnesia...**20** B4
RND Cinemas.....................................**21** B3

SHOPPING
Smoker's World.............................(see **13**)

TRANSPORT
Bus Station..**22** B1
Bus Stop..**23** A5
Ranfurly Circle..................................**24** B5

THE BAHAMAS

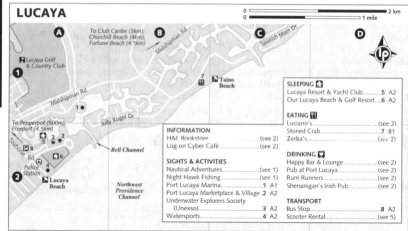

LUCAYA

SLEEPING
Lucaya Resort & Yacht Club..........**5** A2
Our Lucaya Beach & Golf Resort....**6** A2

EATING
Luciano's.....................................(see 2)
Stoned Crab.................................**7** B1
Zorba's......................................(see 2)

INFORMATION
H&L Bookstore ....(see 2)
Log on Cyber Café.....................(see 2)

SIGHTS & ACTIVITIES
Nautical Adventures..................(see 1)
Night Hawk Fishing...................(see 1)
Port Lucaya Marina.....................**1** A1
Port Lucaya Marketplace & Village.**2** A2
Underwater Explorers Society
    (Unexso)...............................**3** A2
Watersports................................**4** A2

DRINKING
Happy Bar & Lounge..................(see 2)
Pub at Port Lucaya.....................(see 2)
Rum Runners............................(see 2)
Shenanigan's Irish Pub...............(see 2)

TRANSPORT
Bus Stop.....................................**8** A2
Scooter Rental............................(see 5)

recognizable center. There *is* a center; however, it is lost amid copses of pine, and comprises a few banks, some stores and not a single building of historical interest.

Lucaya is a tourism oasis and is by far the nicer option for those on holiday. It is antiseptic, but sits on a great stretch of beach, and it's possible to walk easily and safely to all the bars and restaurants, of which there are few! Although Freeport has marginally cheaper accommodations, the facilities in Lucaya offer more choice.

The exception to the rule is the fabulous facilities of the Crowne Plaza Golf Resort & Casino (p82), which make life easy and fun for families. Many of the resorts run a variety of activities for children.

There's a fairly constant stream of *jitneys* traveling between Freeport and Lucaya. A car is necessary for exploring the rest of the island.

Orientation
Central Freeport lies 1 mile (1.6km) north of the International Bazaar between West Mall and East Mall Drs. At its heart is Winn Dixie Plaza. Most of the central Freeport hotels actually lie 1 mile (1.6km) south of downtown, centered on Ranfurly Circle and the International Bazaar.

East Sunrise Hwy runs from Ranfurly Circle in Freeport toward Lucaya, where Seahorse Rd turns off to the heart of the Lucaya hotel district. Taino, Churchill and Fortune Beaches extend east from Lucaya.

The Grand Bahama Hwy will take you to the east end of the island and McLean's Town. Queen's Hwy will take you to the West End of Grand Bahama.

MAPS
Free copies of the *Grand Bahamas Trailblazer Map* are piled high in hotel lobbies and tourist shops.

Information
BOOKSTORES
H&L Bookstore (Map p80; ☎ 242-373-8947; Port Lucaya Marketplace & Village, Lucaya)

EMERGENCY
Ambulance (☎ 242-352-2689)

INTERNET ACCESS
Log on Cyber Café (Map p80; ☎ 242-559-0111; Port Lucaya Marketplace & Village; per 15min US$5; ☻ 9am-10pm) For long-distance calls and Internet access, although rates are expensive.

LIBRARIES
Charles Hayward Library (Map p79; ☎ 242-352-7048; East Mall Dr, Freeport)

MEDICAL SERVICES
LMR Drugs (Map p79; ☎ 242-352-7327; 1 West Mall Dr, Freeport; ☻ 8am-9pm Mon-Sat)
Lucayan Medical Centre East (☎ 242-373-7400; East Sunrise Hwy, Freeport)
Lucayan Medical Centre West (Map p79; ☎ 242-352-7288; Adventurers Way, Lucaya)

TAXI

You'll find taxis at the airport and major hotels.

Fares are fixed by the government for short distances.

You can call for a radio-dispatched taxi from **Freeport Taxi** (☎ 242-352-6666) or **Grand Bahama Taxi Union** (☎ 242-352-7101).

FREEPORT & LUCAYA

pop 33,000

Grand Bahama is dominated by Freeport and its southeastern suburb Lucaya. Freeport is a planned city, with wide, grid-arranged streets and uninspired modern buildings. The strange, sprawling entity lacks both an easily definable character and an easily

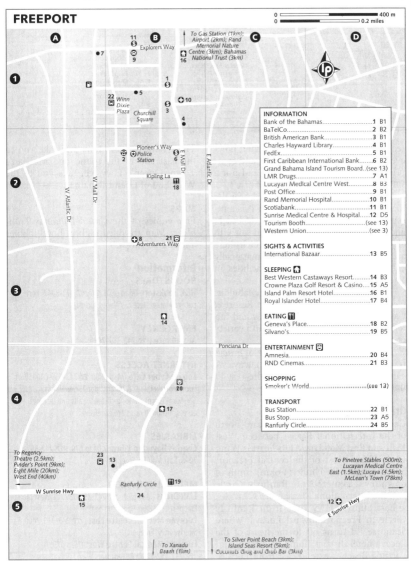

FREEPORT

0 ——————— 400 m
0 ——————— 0.2 miles

INFORMATION	
Bank of the Bahamas	**1** B1
BaTelCo	**2** B2
British American Bank	**3** B1
Charles Hayward Library	**4** B1
FedEx	**5** B1
First Caribbean International Bank	**6** B2
Grand Bahama Island Tourism Board	(see 13)
LMR Drugs	**7** A1
Lucayan Medical Centre West	**8** B3
Post Office	**9** B1
Rand Memorial Hospital	**10** B1
Scotiabank	**11** B1
Sunrise Medical Centre & Hospital	**12** D5
Tourism Booth	(see 13)
Western Union	(see 3)

SIGHTS & ACTIVITIES	
International Bazaar	**13** B5

SLEEPING	
Best Western Castaways Resort	**14** B3
Crowne Plaza Golf Resort & Casino	**15** A5
Island Palm Resort Hotel	**16** B1
Royal Islander Hotel	**17** B4

EATING	
Geneva's Place	**18** B2
Silvano's	**19** B5

ENTERTAINMENT	
Amnesia	**20** B4
RND Cinemas	**21** B3

SHOPPING	
Smoker's World	(see 13)

TRANSPORT	
Bus Station	**22** B1
Bus Stop	**23** A5
Ranfurly Circle	**24** B5

THE BAHAMAS

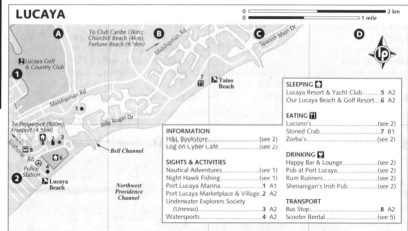

LUCAYA

INFORMATION
H&L Bookstore.............................(see 2)
Log on Cyber Café.....................(see 2)

SIGHTS & ACTIVITIES
Nautical Adventures...................(see 1)
Night Hawk Fishing....................(see 1)
Port Lucaya Marina.......................**1** A1
Port Lucaya Marketplace & Village.**2** A2
Underwater Explorers Society
  (Unexso)...................................**3** A2
Watersports...................................**4** A2

SLEEPING 🏠
Lucaya Resort & Yacht Club..........**5** A2
Our Lucaya Beach & Golf Resort....**6** A2

EATING 🍴
Luciano's..................................(see 2)
Stoned Crab...................................**7** B1
Zorba's......................................(see 2)

DRINKING 🍷
Happy Bar & Lounge...................(see 2)
Pub at Port Lucaya.....................(see 2)
Rum Runners..............................(see 2)
Shenanigan's Irish Pub................(see 2)

TRANSPORT
Bus Stop.......................................**8** A2
Scooter Rental............................(see 5)

recognizable center. There *is* a center; however, it is lost amid copses of pine, and comprises a few banks, some stores and not a single building of historical interest.

Lucaya is a tourism oasis and is by far the nicer option for those on holiday. It is antiseptic, but sits on a great stretch of beach, and it's possible to walk easily and safely to all the bars and restaurants, of which there are few! Although Freeport has marginally cheaper accommodations, the facilities in Lucaya offer more choice.

The exception to the rule is the fabulous facilities of the Crowne Plaza Golf Resort & Casino (p82), which make life easy and fun for families. Many of the resorts run a variety of activities for children.

There's a fairly constant stream of *jitneys* traveling between Freeport and Lucaya. A car is necessary for exploring the rest of the island.

Orientation

Central Freeport lies 1 mile (1.6km) north of the International Bazaar between West Mall and East Mall Drs. At its heart is Winn Dixie Plaza. Most of the central Freeport hotels actually lie 1 mile (1.6km) south of downtown, centered on Ranfurly Circle and the International Bazaar.

East Sunrise Hwy runs from Ranfurly Circle in Freeport toward Lucaya, where Seahorse Rd turns off to the heart of the Lucaya hotel district. Taino, Churchill and Fortune Beaches extend east from Lucaya.

The Grand Bahama Hwy will take you to the east end of the island and McLean's Town. Queen's Hwy will take you to the West End of Grand Bahama.

MAPS

Free copies of the *Grand Bahamas Trailblazer Map* are piled high in hotel lobbies and tourist shops.

Information

BOOKSTORES
H&L Bookstore (Map p80; ☎ 242-373-8947; Port Lucaya Marketplace & Village, Lucaya)

EMERGENCY
Ambulance (☎ 242-352-2689)

INTERNET ACCESS
Log on Cyber Café (Map p80; ☎ 242-559-0111; Port Lucaya Marketplace & Village; per 15min US$5; 🕑 9am-10pm) For long-distance calls and Internet access, although rates are expensive.

LIBRARIES
Charles Hayward Library (Map p79; ☎ 242-352-7048; East Mall Dr, Freeport)

MEDICAL SERVICES
LMR Drugs (Map p79; ☎ 242-352-7327; 1 West Mall Dr, Freeport; 🕑 8am-9pm Mon-Sat)
Lucayan Medical Centre East (☎ 242-373-7400; East Sunrise Hwy, Freeport)
Lucayan Medical Centre West (Map p79; ☎ 242-352-7288; Adventurers Way, Lucaya)

Rand Memorial Hospital (Map p79; ☎ 242-352-6735; East Atlantic Dr, Freeport) Entrance on East Mall Dr.
Sunrise Medical Centre & Hospital (Map p79; ☎ 242-373-3333; East Sunrise Hwy, Lucaya)

MONEY
Bank of the Bahamas (Map p79; ☎ 242-352-7483; cnr Bank Lane & Woodstock St, Freeport)
British American Bank (Map p79; ☎ 242-352-6676; East Mall Dr, Freeport)
First Caribbean International Bank (Map p79; ☎ 242-352-6651; East Mall Dr, Freeport)
Scotiabank (Map p79; ☎ 242-352-6774; Regent Centre, Explorers Way, Freeport)
Western Union (Map p79; ☎ 242-352-6676, East Mall Dr, Freeport) Based at the British American Bank.

POST
FedEx (Map p79; ☎ 242-352-3402; www.fedex.com; Seventeen Plaza, cnr Woodstock St & Bank Lane, Freeport)
Post office (Map p79; ☎ 242-352-9371; Explorers Way, Freeport)

TELEPHONE
BaTelCo (Map p79; ☎ 242-352-6220; Pioneer's Way, Freeport) Offers telephone and fax services.

TOURIST INFORMATION
Grand Bahama Island Tourism Board (Map p79; www.grand-bahama.com; International Bazaar, Freeport) Main office (☎ 242-352-8044); Tourism booth (☎ 242-352-8356)
Tourism booth (☎ 242-352-2052; Grand Bahama International Airport)

Dangers & Annoyances
At night use caution downtown near Winn Dixie Plaza, and west of Freeport at Pinder's Point and Eight Mile. Post-hurricanes, there have been problems with street lighting in some of these areas and there have been some reports of drug-related violence.

Sights & Activities
INTERNATIONAL BAZAAR
This compact, but overrated and disheveled marketplace (Map p79) on the northwest side of Ranfurly Circle is worth a browse. Beyond the Japanese *torii* gates, a maze of tight-knit lanes is lined with cafés and shops.

PORT LUCAYA MARKETPLACE & MARINA COMPLEX
A 12-acre (4.8-hectare) shopping, dining and entertainment area, **Port Lucaya Marketplace &**

Village (Map p80; ☎ 242-373-8446; www.portlucaya .com) fronts the Port Lucaya Marina. Together they form an integrated yacht basin and waterfront tourism area, much more appealing than the International Bazaar. At its heart beats **Count Basie Sq**, where everything from church choirs to Junkanoo bands perform on weekends.

BEACHES
The best beaches include **Silver Point** (Map p77) and **Lucaya Beach** (Map p77), near the hotels; **Taino Beach** (Map p77), a long beach with fine sand; **Churchill Beach** (Map p77) and **Fortune Beach** (Map p77), which extend several miles east of Taino Beach; and the stunning **Gold Rock Beach** (Map p77) at Lucayan National Park.

DIVING & SNORKELING
Diving is excellent off Grand Bahama. One prime site is the *Theo* wreck, a 240ft-long (73m) sunken freighter with safe swim-through areas, and East End Paradise, an underwater coral range. There are also two Spanish galleons – the *Santa Gertrude* and *San Ignacio* – which ran aground in 1682. Try the following diving outfits:
Fantasia Tours (☎ 242-373-8681; www.snorkeling bahamas.com) Offers half-day snorkeling trips (adult/child US$35/18) to a shallow coral reef on a catamaran. Book through your hotel or the contact details above.
Seaworld Explorer (☎ 242-373-7863) A two-hour trip (adult/child US$39/25) on a glass-bottom boat that saves your hairdo and brings you closer to the marine world. Phone for details or book through your hotel.
Underwater Explorers Society (Map p80; Unexso; ☎ 242-373-1244; www.unexso.com; Port Lucaya Marina) Offers a full range of dive programs, including a two-tank dive for US$70, and rents equipment for US$43. The Ocean Open Dolphin Experience allows interaction with trained dolphins in their natural element, the open sea, for US$199.

SPORT FISHING & BONEFISHING
The Gulf Stream, off the west coast of Grand Bahama, teems with game fish. The Northwest Providence Channel drops to 2000ft (609m) just 400yd (365m) off the south shore, where snapper and barracuda are prevalent. And bonefishing is superb on the flats of the Little Bahama Bank to the north and east of the island.
Night Hawk Fishing (Map p80; ☎ 242-373-7226; Port Lucaya Marina) offers half-day charter fishing trips from US$65. Other charter operators

include **Nautical Adventures** (Map p80; ☎ 242-373-7180), also at the Port Lucaya Marina.

HORSEBACK RIDING
Pinetree Stables (Map p79; ☎ 242-373-3600; www
.pinetree-stables.com; Beachway Dr, Freeport) offers
two-hour horseback rides (US$75) galloping through pine forests and along the south shore – yippee!

KAYAKING
Kayak Nature Tours (☎ 242-373-2485; www.grandbahamanaturetours.com) leads sea kayaking tours (US$69) from Freeport into Lucayan National Park, as well as biking tours (US$79) and kayaking/snorkeling trips (US$69). These wonderful trips allow you to relish the natural quiet and splendor of the park and its many scaled, furry and feathered inhabitants.

Festivals & Events
For information on these festivals and events, and many others, contact the **Grand Bahama Island Tourism Board** (☎ 242-325-8356; www.grand-bahama.com; International Bazaar, Freeport).
Conch Cracking Contest In October, sleepy McLean's Town, at the east end of the island, hosts this contest. It's not much fun for the conch, but a great day for the humans.
Grand Bahama Conchman Triathalon Held in November, this endurance feat tests amateur athletes to the limit.
Junkanoo Parade Held on Boxing Day and New Year's Day. The highlight of the social calendar kicks off at 5am downtown, with costumed revelers and a cacophony of sounds. The build-up starts in January of the year in which it is occurring – 11 months in advance – with practices downtown near the post office. For more details, see the boxed text, p72.
Sailing Regatta Held in June, with three days of racing and onshore partying.

Sleeping
Budget options are as scarce as hen's teeth. However, nearly all accommodations reviewed here offer great specials, even in high season. Expect heavy additional taxes and daily service charges nonetheless.

BUDGET
Island Palm Resort Hotel (Map p79; ☎ 242-352-6648; ispalm@batelnet.bs; East Mall Dr, Freeport; r US$70; Ⓟ ✗ ☼ ☎) Let's just say that 'resort' is an exaggeration, and that there are some dingy rooms. Nevertheless, it's very cheap

(specials in high season bring rooms down to US$56), there is a small pool, and a free daily bus goes to beaches and into town. The Safari Restaurant & Nightclub on-site keeps the resort lively at night, but good security keeps things from getting too rowdy.

MIDRANGE
Best Western Castaways Resort (Map p79; ☎ 242-352-6682; www.castaways-resort.com; East Mall Dr, Freeport; r US$110; Ⓟ ✗ ☼ ☎ ☎) This new hotel is spic-and-span, and offers large, light and modern rooms, well furnished, with cable TV and balconies. Facilities include a reasonably priced restaurant, full-sized pool and courtesy buses to two beaches. Security is great, and so are the staff.
Crowne Plaza Golf Resort & Casino (Map p79; ☎ 242-350-7000; www.theroyaloasis.com; cnr Mall Dr & East Atlantic Ave, Freeport; r US$100; Ⓟ ✗ ☼ ☎ ☎) This vast resort has been cleverly updated as a family-friendly complex, complete with tennis courts, water sports, beach lagoon and water park. Seven restaurants include the children-only 'Odie' (where kids can be left to eat with free hotel supervision for an hour). There's also the Fat Cat Beach Club (for kids aged three years and older, from 9am to 9pm) and babysitting facilities are available (from US$20). Two championship 18-hole courses will please golf fans, while those with twitchy fingers can enjoy the Casino's temptations.
Royal Islander Hotel (Map p79; ☎ 242-351-6000; www.royalislanderhotel.com; East Mall Dr, Freeport; r US$104; ✗ ☼ ☎) An attractive two-story property surrounds a courtyard with pool and shady palms. Rooms are large, cheerfully furnished with bright prints and there's heaps of light. All come with in-room safe, cable TV and phone, but unfortunately no tea- or coffee-making facilities. However, there's also a Jacuzzi, restaurant and children's playground.
Lucaya Resort & Yachtclub (Map p80; ☎ 242-373-6618; www.portlucayaresort.com; Bell Chanel Rd, Port Lucaya; r US$100; Ⓟ ✗ ☼ ☎) This is the best location for the most reasonable rates in Lucaya. Although 'resort' is stretching it a bit, 10 two-story units encircle lawn and a full-sized pool with Jacuzzi. The rooms are light, spacious and spotless, all with patios or balconies. Some look out over the full-service marina. Adjacent to the Port Lucaya Marketplace & Village's bars and

restaurants, the hotel is just over the road from the big Our Lucaya resort and that gorgeous beach!

Island Seas Resort (☎ 242-373-1271; iseas@batel net.bs; 123 Silver Point Dr, Silver Point Beach; r US$120; P 🗙 🔀 🛋) Tucked away on its own, this intimate resort sits on a small beach and is highly popular with families. One- and two-bedroom self-catering units surround the beachside Coconuts Grog and Grub Bar, and facilities include a pool with swim-up bar (lazy and lucky beggars), plus tennis, shuffleboard court and water sports. A complimentary bus runs into town.

TOP END

Our Lucaya Beach & Golf Resort (Map p80; ☎ 242-373-2396; www.ourlucaya.com; Seahorse Rd, Port Lucaya; r US$320; P 🗙 🔀 🛋 🛋) Incorporating two main accommodations, the pricier Westin and cheaper Sheraton hotels, this attractive open complex has been well designed and is a brilliant family location. The resort sits on 7 acres (2.8 hectares) of public beachfront, and incorporates numerous restaurants, bars (with dancing), a casino, three fabulous swimming pools with slides totaling 50,000 sq ft (4645 sq meters), kiddies' facilities, the Port Lucaya Marketplace & Village promenade of boutiques, cafés, bars and shops, and two 18-hole golf courses, all linked by a 0.75 mile (1.2km) boardwalk. Phew! Special deals bring rates right down (a high-season room costs US$200). If this place suits your bank balance, gambling mother-in-law, golf-fanatic partner and attention-span-challenged kids, book soon…

Eating & Drinking

There are a heap of informal and friendly choices in Freeport and the Port Lucaya Marketplace & Village, where you can often find live music and dancing on most Thursday nights and weekends.

FREEPORT

Freeport's International Bazaar has more than a dozen places to eat, but most are forgettable. Your best options are the eateries and bars found in Freeport's hotels, the selection we've provided here and some locations outside of town.

Silvano's (Map p79; ☎ 242-352-5110; Mall at Sunrise Hwy, Ranfurly Circle, Freeport; mains US$9-10; 🕑 lunch

& dinner Tue-Sun) Making the best coffee and gelato in town, this elegant restaurant also serves a good plate of pasta.

Geneva's Place (Map p79; ☎ 242-352-5085; cnr East Mall Dr & Kipling Lane; mains US$5-10; 🕑 breakfast & lunch) The place for good Bahamian food. The fish and peas'n'rice are great, and the guava duff (sweet dumpling with guava purée) is virtually drowned in a milky rum sauce.

Pepperpot (☎ 242-373-7655; 8 East Sunrise Hwy, Lucaya; mains US$6; 🕑 breakfast, lunch & dinner) This takeout eatery reputedly serves the island's best peas'n'rice and fried chicken. Stopping here at night is not recommended, though.

LUCAYA

The following eateries and bars are located in the Port Lucaya Marketplace & Village.

Zorba's (Map p80; ☎ 242-373-6137; mains US$8-15; 🕑 breakfast, lunch & dinner) Enjoy your meal alfresco beneath a canopy of grapevines and pink bougainvillea. Tasty reasonably priced breakfasts and Greek cuisine, such as moussaka and Greek salad for US$10, pull in the punters.

Luciano's (Map p80; ☎ 242-373-9100; mains US$20-40; 🕑 lunch & dinner Mon-Sat) Specializing in Italian and French fare, the food is very good. Try the superb grouper with almonds, and enjoy the balcony's harbor view.

Also recommended for food and/or the odd sundowner:

AUTHOR'S CHOICE

Club Caribe (☎ 242-373-6866; Mather Town off Midshipman Rd; mains US$8-12; 🕑 11am-6pm Sun & Tue, 11am-10pm Wed-Sat) As soon as you walk onto the wooden deck with a chilled beer in hand and look out over the wide blue ocean and deserted beach, you'll understand this recommendation. Hidden away from the madding crowds, this restaurant/bar is simple yet homey and a marvelously friendly place to hang out. Bahamians gather here for great peppery fish salads and Friday night pig roasts, as well as live Bahamian music on Friday and Saturday nights (hotel transfers are provided). Whether for a long tasty lunch, convivial dinner or rum-fuelled celebration of the sunset, you won't be disappointed with the ambience, food or surroundings. Enjoy!

Rum Runners (Map p80; ☎ 242-373-7233)
Happy Bar & Lounge (Map p80; ☎ 242-373-6852) A sports bar with TV.
Shenanigan's Irish Pub (Map p80; ☎ 242-373-4734)
Pub at Port Lucaya (Map p80; ☎ 242-373-8450) For great pub grub.

TAINO BEACH

Stoned Crab (☎ 242-373-1442; Taino Beach; mains US$22-30; ⊗ dinner) This classic serves its specialty to many amateur gourmets, namely the 'Seafood Platter': lobster, crab, *mahi-mahi* (a white-meat fish) and shrimp. Crabcake appetizers are also yum.

Entertainment

RND Cinemas (Map p79; ☎ 242-351-3456; RND Plaza, East Atlantic Mall Dr, Freeport; admission US$10) Five-screen cinema showing mainstream hits.

Amnesia (Map p79; ☎ 242-351-2582; East Mall Dr, Freeport; ⊗ 9pm-late Thu, Fri & Sat) This tropical-themed nightclub has a state-of-the-art light and sound system blending reggae, soca, *goombay* and hip-hop. Hours and admission fees vary, so check beforehand (if you can remember!). The resorts offer in-house entertainment, while the **Port Lucaya Marketplace & Village** (Map p80; ☎ 242-373-8446; www.portlucaya .com) hosts live music Thursday to Sunday. This is a great open-air setting, with a stage and dance floor surrounded by open bars and cafés. Head here for some rake'n'scrape, quadrille dancing and general fun.

Shopping

The duty-free shopping is unremarkable except for jewelry and perfumes, and even then it's hard to find a bargain. Your best bet is to head to Freeport's International Bazaar and Port Lucaya Marketplace & Village, clutching a price-comparison list from home.

CIGARS

Cuban cigars are a great buy. Most quality gift shops sell Cohibas (the Rolls-Royce of cigars), Montecristos and other notable brands at 50% or more off black-market US prices. We recommend **Smoker's World** (Map p79; ☎ 242-351-6899; International Bazaar, Freeport).

STRAW-WORK & NATIVE ITEMS

There are several straw markets behind the International Bazaar that sell all types of woven straw crafts, as well as T-shirts, carvings and ethnic jewelry.

Look for native woodcarvings, especially the simple yet dramatic works by Michael Hoyte, often hewn from ebony driftwood washed ashore from Africa.

EAST OF FREEPORT

East of the Grand Lucayan Waterway (a 7.5-mile, or 12km, canal), the Grand Bahama Hwy runs parallel to the shore to the east end of the island. Side roads lead to the south shore's talcum-powder soft beaches.

Water Cay

This tiny, simple settlement is on the cay of that name, 2 miles (3.2km) off the north shore. The community relies on fishing and is as unspoiled as it gets on Grand Bahama.

Old Free Town

The settlement of Old Free Town, 3 miles (4.8km) east of the Grand Lucayan Waterway, was forcibly abandoned in the 1960s when the Port Authority acquired the land. There are several blue holes (subaqueous caves), notably **Mermaid's Lair** and **Owl Hole**. Stalactites dangle from the roof of the bowl. And owls have nested on the sill as long as residents can remember – the blue holes are well hidden, so ask a local for directions.

Peterson Cay National Park

This 1.5-acre (0.6-hectare) park is the only cay on Grand Bahama's south shore. It is one of the Family Islands' most heavily used getaway spots, busy with locals' boats on weekends. Coral reefs provide splendid snorkeling and diving. You can hire a boat from any marina in Freeport and Lucaya. Take snorkel gear and a picnic.

Lucayan National Park

This 40-acre (16-hectare) park is Grand Bahama's finest treasure. There is a bat nursery in the underwater cave system, the longest in the world, with over 6 charted miles (9.6km) of tunnels and blue holes where you can find fish by throwing a little bread into the water.

Mangrove trails spill out onto the secluded and beautiful **Gold Rock Beach**.

For park entry conditions and further information contact the **Bahamas National Trust** (☎ 242-352-5438; Rand Memorial Nature Centre, E Settlers Way, Freeport).

WEST OF FREEPORT

West of Freeport, a slender, scrub-covered peninsula, separated from the 'mainland' by Freeport Harbour Channel, extends north-west to West End. There are few beaches until you reach Deadman's Reef.

The channel opens to **Hawksbill Creek**, named for the once-common marine turtles that now only infrequently come ashore. There's good diving offshore, especially at **Paradise Cove**.

West End

This fishing village, 25 miles (40km) west of Freeport, was a sleepy haven of tumble-down shacks, half-sunken boats and piles of sun-bleached conch shells. The West End was decimated by the 2004 hurricanes, Frances and Jeanne, which swooped in over Grand Bahama from this end of the island. Rebuilding the community will take some time.

Once the center of activity on the island, Prohibition rum-runners ruled the roost, and yachters with sterling surnames, like Kennedy, DuPont or Hearst, were callers to the Grand Bahama Resort & Country Club.

The village was also known for the stone-and-wood **Mary Magdalene Church** (1893), complete with three small yet beautiful stained-glass windows designed in contemporary style.

NORTH ISLANDS

These three groups of islands and their cays offer very different experiences. The Biminis are internationally renowned as much for Ernest Hemingway's *Islands in the Stream* as for their world-record–breaking bonefishing championships. Abaco has the history of the Bahamas alive and well running in the blood of her Loyalist descendants, who live in the loveliest cay townships anywhere in the Bahamas. The fashionably thin Eleuthera is a true-blue Caribbean dreamtime, promised by marketeers everywhere but rarely delivered.

BIMINIS

pop 1740

Big-game fishing devotees have headed to North and South Bimini for decades, and are a mainstay of the local Biminite economy;

as are the less-welcome rowdy college students whooping it up during spring break. Scuba divers are lured to the islands' sunken Spanish galleons and the wreck of a WWI freighter. Then there's the underwater Bimini Rd, acclaimed to be part of the 'lost city' of Atlantis, and a pretty unique opportunity to dive with wild Atlantic spotted dolphins in the open ocean.

Ernest Hemingway made the Biminis famous through his writing and hard-drinking years as a Bimini resident. However, a former Prohibition-era bar, the Bimini Big Game Fishing Club, can claim the crown to launching Biminis' fishing tourism.

Bimini has been featured in *Cocoon* and *Silence of the Lambs,* among other movies.

North Bimini's unpretentious **Alice Town** is the center of activities, with the most beautiful beach in Bimini Bay. The less-developed South Bimini has long been favored by US expats who fly or boat in for weekends.

Information

There are public telephone booths all along King's Hwy.

Bahamas Ministry of Tourism (☎ 242-347-3529; fax 242-347-3530; Government Bldg, Alice Town; ☯ 9am-5:30pm Mon-Fri)

Government Medical Clinic (☎ 242-347-2210)

Police North Bimini (☎ 242-347-3144); South Bimini (☎ 242-347-3424)

Post office (☎ 242-347-3546; Government Bldg, Alice Town)

Royal Bank of Canada (☎ 242-347-3031; King's Hwy, Alice Town; ☯ 9am-3pm Mon, Wed & Fri)

Sights

No visit to the Biminis is complete without raising a drink at the famous **Compleat Angler Hotel & Bar**, where Papa Hemingway duked it out every Sunday.

'**Bimini Road**' stretches along 1000ft (304m) and is named for the strange underwater formations resembling paving blocks of a giant aqua-highway, while local lore attributes the inspiration for Martin Luther King, Jr's 'I Have a Dream' speech to the mystical effect of the **Healing Hole**. The great man bathed in this freshwater sulfur spring, shortly before giving that memorable and moving speech.

Several restaurants, such as Captain Bob's, have **Fishing Halls of Fame** celebrating celebrity and the masses of more-memorable kills. A plethora of fishing festivals and world-record breakers add to these displays.

Activities
BONEFISHING & SPORT FISHING
Fishing charters typically cost US$400 to US$500 per half day and US$800 to US$900 per full day. North and South Bimini marinas offer charters, bonefishing and deep-sea adventures, including **Bimini Big Game Fishing Club & Marina** (☎ 242-347-3391; www.biminibiggame .com) and **Blue Water Marina** (☎ 242-347-3166; fax 242-347-3293).

For great bottom fishing, the world champ is **Bonefish Ansil Saunders** (☎ 242-347-2178), which charges around US$300/600 per half/full day.

DIVING & SNORKELING
Bimini Undersea Adventures (☎ 242-347-3089; www.biminiundersea.com; Bimini Big Game Resort & Marina, Alice Town) offers two-tank dives for US$90 and snorkel trips (adult/child US$40/20). Its wonderful 'Wild Dolphin Excursions' (adult/child US$120/100) leave the dolphins totally in charge.

Sleeping
All the hotels in Alice Town are strung along King's Hwy. Rooms are usually fully booked during big-fishing tournaments.

Compleat Angler Hotel (☎ 242-347-3122; fax 242-347-3293; PO Box 601, Alice Town; r US$90; P ✗ ☒) For atmosphere, the best bar in town and a look at Hemingway's old hangout, take a room and a drink here. Mr Hemingway's snoring could be heard from Room 1; you may prefer a sea view. Character-laden rooms are wood-paneled and imbued with the spirit of bar tales and Bahamas living. Weekly live music makes the joint jump. Who cares? You'll be downstairs dancing your socks off.

Sea Crest Hotel (☎ 242-347-3071; PO Box 654, Alice Town; r US$100; P ✗ ☒) Take a 3rd-floor room for views in this pleasant, modern and friendly place. Room facilities include cable TV and fridges.

Eating
Most hotels and pubs around town offer meals, as do the following options:

Captain Bob's (☎ 242-347-3260; Blue Harbour Marina, Alice Town; breakfast US$10; ✆ breakfast & lunch Wed-Mon) Bahamians pack in early for scrumptious corned-beef hash with eggs, French toast and omelettes.

Anchorage Restaurant & Bar (☎ 242-347-3166; Bimini Blue Water Resort, Alice Town; mains US$12-30; ✆ breakfast, lunch & dinner) Good reasonably priced food includes burgers, salads and tasty seafood dishes.

Getting There & Around
For more information on travel to and from the Biminis, see p99.

AIR
Many people arrive at the sea-plane landing on North Bimini or at South Bimini Airport.

BOAT
Water-taxi service between North and South Bimini departs near the Bimini mailboat dock (US$5).

GOLF CART
Most places are within walking distance. However, golf carts can be hired at both the North and South Bimini marinas for US$65 per day.

ABACOS
pop 14,815
The Abacos and yachting go together like wind and sail, earning the chain the nickname the 'Sailing Capital of the World.' The boomerang-shaped chain comprises the 130-mile (209km)-long Abaco, the nation's third-largest settlement, and a necklace of dozens of smaller cays. Most folks and businesses are based in Marsh Harbour, which has a quiet, small-town Floridian feel, or on the Loyalist Cays (named for the residents' forefathers, who fled here avoiding persecution during the American Revolution), east of Marsh Harbour: Elbow, Man O' War, Great Guana and Green Turtle Cays.

The Abacos' gaily painted, gingerbread clapboard houses are still framed by white picket fences, and set along narrow streets bordered by hibiscus and vivid bougainvillea. These unassuming cottages and inns sit on talcum-fine beaches or alongside the many marinas. Coral reef gardens fringing the Atlantic beckon; walk off the village beach at Great Guana Cay for great snorkeling, dive at Fowlers Cay, and don't miss the exuberant onshore fun of sailing regattas, searching Abacos National Park for the endangered Bahamian parrot or the fun-filled summer Goombay festivities.

Information

Public telephones are in central areas. The website www.go-abacos.com is very useful.

Bahamas Ministry of Tourism (☎ 242-367-3067; fax 367-3068; Memorial Plaza, Queen Elizabeth Dr, Marsh Harbour; ☺ 9am-5:30pm Mon-Fri)

Hospital clinic (☎ 242-366-4010; Marsh Harbour)

Police (☎ 242-367-3500)

Post office (☎ 242-367-2571; Marsh Harbour)

Royal Bank of Canada (☎ 242-365-6323; Marsh Harbour)

Sights & Activities

BEACHES

Do not miss the white-sand crescent and glowing turquoise shallows of **Treasure Cay Beach**, north of Marsh Harbour, one of the Bahamas' most beautiful beaches. Also lovely is **Hope Town Beach** at Elbow Cay.

DIVING & SNORKELING

Try the snorkeling at Mermaid Reef on the north side of Marsh Harbour.

Abaco Dive Adventures (☎ 242-367-2963; www .abacodiveadventures.com; Abaco Beach Resort, Marsh Harbour) has two-tank and wreck dives (US$110), night dives (US$126) and snorkel trips (US$50).

BOATING & SAILING

Sailboats and motorboats can be rented at most marinas. Demand often exceeds supply, so make reservations early.

Blue Wave Boat Rentals (☎ 242-367-3910; www .bluewaverentals.com; Harbour View Marina, Marsh Harbour) charges US$150 per day, US$375 for three days and US$700 per week for its boats.

Seahorse Boat Rentals (☎ 242-367-2513; www.sea horseboatrentals.com; Marsh Harbour) rents 20ft (6m) boats for US$190 a day, US$910 a week.

Captain Justin Sands (☎ 242-367-3526; www .bahamasvg.com/justfish.html) is a highly recommended bonefishing guide who will prepare and price tailor-made trips for you.

Sleeping

Few visitors tend to stay in Marsh Harbour or on the mainland for long, heading instead for the picturesque Abacos cays. For some wonderful rental cottages try the web-

sites www.abacobahamas.com and www .abacovacations.com.

Lofty Fig Villas (☎ 242-367-2681; loftyfig@mymail station.com; Bay St, Marsh Harbour; r US$110; P ☒ ☒ ☒) These canary-yellow units sit conveniently in the middle of town. They surround a small pool and each has a patio. The cottages need a little TLC, but are well equipped, light and pleasant.

Conch Inn Marina & Hotel (☎ 242-367-4000; www .go-abacos.com/conchinn; Bay St, Marsh Harbour; r US$130; ☒ ☒) Newly renovated, these rooms with cable TV are comfortable and convenient. The marina has a good restaurant, lively and convivial bar, and a small, refreshing freshwater pool.

Eating & Drinking

There's a good selection of cafés and bars on the Cays. The following Marsh Harbour restaurants host regular musical bashes.

Mangoes (☎ 242-367-2366; Bay St, Marsh Harbour; mains US$18-25; ☺ lunch & dinner) International dishes with a Bahamian twist are served on a shaded deck overlooking the marina. Fish and mango combinations are delicious, and desserts are simply wicked; a favorite among Bahamians and anyone with taste buds.

Sapodilly's Harbourside Bar & Grill (☎ 242-367-3498; Bay St, Marsh Harbour; mains US$12-25; ☺ lunch & dinner) The tree-shaded deck welcomes drinkers and diners throughout the day. Great burgers and crunchy fish appetizers satisfy, as do the pasta and fish dishes.

AUTHOR'S CHOICE

Miss Emily's Blue Bee Bar (☎ 242-365-4181; Victoria St; ☺ noon-10pm) Teetotaler Miss Emily invented the seductively lethal Goombay Smash at Green Turtle Cay's legendary bar; apparently the record is a whopping 22 of these in one night. The man was taken home in a wheelbarrow.

Getting There & Around

AIR

For information on air travel to the Abacos, see p98.

BOAT

Albury's Ferry Service (☎ 242-367-3147, 242-365-6010; www.oii.net/alburysferry) operates scheduled daily water taxis to Elbow (Hope Town), Man

THE BAHAMAS

O' War and Great Guana Cays (adult/child US$10/5). The dock for Elbow and Man O' War is at the east end of Bay St; the dock for Great Guana Cay is at Conch Inn Marina.

Getting Around

BICYCLE, MOTORCYCLE & CAR

Rental Wheels (☎ 242-367-4643; Bay St, Marsh Harbour; ☒ 8am-5pm Mon-Fri, 9am-1pm Sat & Sun) has cornered the market, with rental rates as follows: bicycles US$10/45 per day/week, motorbikes US$45/200 per day/week and cars US$65/300 per day/week.

GOLF CARTS

Golf carts can be hired on the cay docks for around US$50 per day.

TAXI

Fares are pre-established. A ride between Marsh Harbour's airport and most hotels costs US$10 for two people. Taxis run up and down Marsh Harbour and are easy to flag down.

ELEUTHERA

pop 8545

Eleuthera, a slender wisp of an island about 100 miles (160km) long yet barely a bowshot wide, is famous for its stunning blush-pink sands washed by Atlantic rollers. On the east coast dramatic cliffs, sheltered coves and offshore coral reefs add to the picture. Divers who 'collect' wrecks can explore the victims of the Devil's Backbone, while fishing fans hunt around the Bight of Eleuthera, west of the island. The island was put within easy reach of Nassau in 1999 when a high-speed ferry service was introduced, also carrying day-trippers to the haunt of the rich, famous and beautiful: Harbour Island, barely 3 miles (4.8km) long, and nominated as the prettiest island in the Caribbean.

While hotels across Eleuthera and Harbour Island are pricy, the self-catering accommodations in Eleuthera are generally excellent, which makes these truly idyllic beaches and sparkling turquoise waters accessible to us all.

Harbour Island

Amazingly, this isle, 2 miles (3.2km) from the mainland, still maintains an attractive Bahamian character, despite the laconic wealth displayed by expats and holidaymakers. An indescribably lovely coral-pink beach runs the length of the windward shore, and breakers are stopped by offshore coral reefs, guaranteeing superb bathing and snorkeling.

INFORMATION

Public telephone booths sit along Bay St.

Bahamas Ministry of Tourism (☎ 242-333-2621; Bay St; ☒ 9:30am-5pm Mon-Fri)

Harbour Island Medical Clinic (☎ 242-333-2227; Church St)

Police (☎ 242-333-2111)

Post office (☎ 242-333-2215; Goal Lane)

Royal Bank of Canada (☎ 242-333-2250; Murray St; ☒ 9am-1pm Mon-Fri)

SIGHTS

One of the finest examples of Loyalist architecture is the **Loyalist Cottage** (Bay St), west of Princess St, dating back to 1797.

The funky side of things is to be found at the corner of Dunmore and Clarence Sts, where a mish-mash of signs, international license plates and driftwood relics are displayed, painted with humorous limericks and aphorisms.

No exaggeration, the wide and stunning length of **Pink Sands Beach** is really pink; a faint blush by day, turning a rosy red when fired by the dawn or sunset.

ACTIVITIES

Harbour Island is surrounded by superb snorkeling and dive sites, highlighted by the Devil's Backbone. The pristine reefs are littered with ancient wrecks.

Valentine's Dive Centre (☎ 242-333-2080; www .valentinesdive.com; Bay St) offers a two-tank dive (US$70), underwater scooters (US$125) and snorkeling (US$30). Fishing fans can charter boats for US$400/650 per half/full day.

Fishing guides and boats cost around US$350/600 per half/full day. Recommended guides are **Patrick Roberts** (☎ 242-333-3014) or **Bonefish Stuart** (☎ 242-333-2072).

Horseback riding on Pink Sands Beach costs around US$20 per half-hour; wave down the gent strolling the sands with his untethered four-legged friends.

SLEEPING

There are great-value rental properties on the island; try **Bahama Sands Real Estate** (☎ 242-332-2662) and **Krataios Real Estate (Red Apple) Rentals** (☎ 242-333-2750; www.redapplebb.com).

AUTHOR'S CHOICE

Bahama House Inn (☎ 242-333-2201; www
.bahamahouseinn.com; cnr Dunmore & Hill Sts; r
US$140; ✗ ✗) A charming and subtly re-
stored colonial home, this is a super and
spacious B&B. Outdoor decking connects
cool and comfortable living areas (dining
and library/lounge), while the rooms are
furnished with eclectic colonial furniture,
some with draped four-poster beds. Rooms
have private baths and overlook a large
garden and patio deck; made for a quiet
read and glass of chilled rum and pineapple
juice. A studio apartment is also offered.
No children under 12 years are allowed.

Coral Sands Hotel (☎ 242-333-2350; pamela@
coralsands.com; Chapel St; r US$235; P ✗ ✗ ✗)
This classy and intimate beach resort extends over 14 acres (5.6 hectares). Rooms
blend Caribbean colors, wicker furniture
and artwork to create quite a homey feel.
Oceanfront rooms have French doors opening to balconies. A library, games room,
tennis court and water-sports facilities are
all on-site.Bicycles, scooters and golf carts
are also available for rent.

Pink Sands Resort (☎ 242-333-2030; www.pink
sandsresort.com; Chapel St; r US$655; P ✗ ✗ ✗ ✗)
The decor is superb in these luxurious cottages dotted throughout a tropical garden:
throw rugs on rough-cut marble-like floors,
and oversize Adirondack chairs with batik
fabrics set against a mellow wash of pastels.
Cottages contain a full sound and TV system, wet bar, private patio and exotic baths.
Rates include full breakfast and dinner in
the splendid Moroccan bar-lounge.

EATING & DRINKING
You won't go hungry and thirsty here, but
it may cost you.

Harbour Lounge (☎ 242-333-2031; King St; mains
US$15-38; ✗ lunch & dinner Tue-Sun) This cozy,
pink-and-mint-green restaurant serves up
such treats as curried pumpkin soup and
grilled fish with spicy sauces. An outside
terrace is perfect for people-watching.

Ma Ruby's (☎ 242-333-2161; Tingum Village Hotel
& Bar; mains US$10-20; ✗ lunch & dinner) Serving
native dishes, such as grouper fritter, the
outdoor/indoor café and bar are bright
and airy with an upbeat decor. Ma Ruby's

'Cheeseburgers in Paradise' featured in
Jimmy Buffett's *Parrothead Handbook*.

Vic Hum Club (☎ 242-333-2161; cnr Barrack & Mun-
nings Sts; ✗ 11am-late) This funky and sometimes fiery locale has a fine collection of
rums, a checkerboard court that doubles as
a dance floor, a busy pool table and live reggae music. Most importantly, the world's
largest coconut sits behind the bar.

GETTING THERE & AROUND
Air
For flights to Eleuthera, see p98.

Bicycle & Golf-Cart Rental
To get around most people walk or use a
bicycle (per day US$20) or golf cart (per
day US$50), which you can rent from taxi
drivers and rental agencies based at the
Government Dock.

Boat
For ferries to Eleuthera, see p99. There is
no scheduled mail-boat service between
Nassau and Harbour Island. On Harbour
Island, water taxis operate from the Gov-
ernment Dock to North Eleuthera (US$5).

Governor's Harbour
The sleepy island 'capital' surrounds a broad
harbor that runs west along a peninsula to
Cupid's Cay, apparently the original settle-
ment of the Eleutheran Adventurers. Ask for
directions to the gorgeous and rosy **Pink Sand
Beach** that lies over the hill away from town.
There is a branch of the **Bahamas Ministry of
Tourism** (☎ 242-332-2142; Queen's Hwy).

A 200-year-old colonial complex set amid
an orchid garden, **Duck Inn** (☎ 242-332-2608; www
.theduckinn.com; Queen's Hwy; d US$110; P ✗ ✗) in-
corporates the comfortable, fully equipped
Hunnie Pot, Flora and Cupid's Cottage.
Worth the trip alone, Cupid's Cottage overlooks the serene and beautiful bay waters.

SOUTH ISLANDS

The quiet and serene Long Island is made
for those who love exploring, with picturesque villages, beautiful coves and very
friendly people. The Exumas and their
cays meanwhile, are beloved of boaters and
kayakers. Both islands' sailing regattas are
also tremendous fun.

EXUMAS
pop 3540

The Exumas are a 100-mile (160km)-long necklace of 365 cays headed by Great Exuma and Little Exuma, the two largest islands. Most of the small cays are uninhabited, apart from sun-bathing iguanas.

The main settlement on Great Exuma stands on the west shore of Elizabeth Harbour sheltered from the Atlantic by Stocking Island, a tantalizing sliver of land lined by fine beaches almost its entire length.

George Town, Great Exuma's administrative center, is really a village, with only one main street. The Tropic of Cancer runs through town, hopefully correctly following the unsigned one-way system. George Town's **Family Island Regatta** is beloved of the local population, as well as traditional boatbuilders.

There are dozens of superb reef sites and wrecks. Dolphins, hammerhead and nurse sharks, and the occasional whale, cruise the deep waters. Kayaking is also superb in the Exumas, especially around the 175-sq-mile (453-sq-km) Exuma Cays Land & Sea Park (established 1958); the world's first marine 'replenishment nursery,' with outstanding anchorages and even more-outstanding dive sites.

Information

There are public telephone booths in all the main centers. The following services are all located in George Town.

Bahamas Ministry of Tourism (☎ 242-336-2430; fax 242-336-2431; Queen's Hwy)

Government Medical Clinic (☎ 242-336-2088; Queen's Hwy)

Police (☎ 242-336-2666)

Post office (☎ 242-347-3546; Government Bldg)

Scotiabank (☎ 242-336-2651; Queen's Hwy)

Sights

George Town's buildings include the serene white-stoned **St Andrew's Anglican Church**, which sits atop a bluff above Lake Victoria, while the sugar-pink and white neoclassical **Government Administration Building** houses everything from the post office to the jail.

Stocking Island is a 600-acre (240-hectare), pencil-thin island lined with beaches, about 1 mile (1.6km) offshore. With no roads on the island all access is by boat. Try snorkeling at the cuts between Stocking Island and Elizabeth Island, and between Elizabeth Island and Guana Cay.

A 400ft (121m)-deep **blue hole** on the Atlantic side is said to be one of only two living intertidal stromatolite reefs in the world; a living fossil, dating back three-and-a-half million years.

A highlight of any visit to **Staniel Cay** is a snorkel or dive trip into **Thunderball Grotto**. The exquisite cavern, named for its inclusion in the Bond movie *Thunderball,* was also used for scenes in *Splash* and another Bond movie *Never Say Never Again.* Please be careful of the current here!

Activities

DIVING & KAYAKING

The Exumas is an excellent area for sea kayaking and snorkeling.

Exuma Scuba Adventures (☎ 242-336-2893; www .exumascuba.com; Queen's Hwy, George Town) offers two-tank dives (US$75), one-tank nighttime dives (US$60) and day-long snorkeling adventures, which include lunch on a deserted cay (US$90).

Starfish (☎ 242-336-3033; www.kayakbahamas.com; George Town) hosts a variety of activities, including four-hour guided kayak trips (US$60), Castaway Getaways (US$125) and three-hour Eco Boat tours (adult/child US$55/44). Kayaks can be hired for US$40 a day.

BONEFISHING & SPORT FISHING

Bandits Bonefishing Lodge & Pirate's Den (☎ 242-358-8062; info@banditsbonefishing.com; George Town) offers angling (US$400 per day) and has accommodations/fishing packages, including three nights and two days of fishing for US$1450.

Sleeping

There are fabulous rental properties on the island. Try **Minn's Cottages** (☎ /fax 242-336-2033/242-336-2645) or more options from **Ocean View Realty** (☎ /fax 336-2443; Queen's Hwy, George Town).

Bahama Houseboats (☎ 242-336-2628; George Town; 🖳) Sleeping under the stars while moored on an uninhabited cay surrounded by emerald seas – now that *is* a dream! Good little kitchens, plus sundecks and comfortable furnishings, make this a thoroughly enjoyable getaway-from-it-all option. The 35ft (10m) one-bed houseboats at US$315/1895 per night/week, and 43ft (13m) two-bed houseboats for US$430/2600 per night/week make this dream an affordable reality.

Peace & Plenty Bonefish Lodge (☎ 242-345-5555; www.ppbonefishlodge.net; Queen's Hwy; 2-person r US$252; P ✗ ✗) This small attractive lodge overlooks the sea and a small beach. It's comfortable and friendly, and beloved of fishing fans. A great bar and restaurant will serve your catch, as well as seafood and steaks for dinner (mains US$20 to US$35).

Palm Bay Beach Club (☎ 242-336-2787; www.palm baybeachclub.com; Queen's Hwy, George Town; r US$149; P ✗ ✗ ✗) This intimate beach club sits on a small beach. Recommended.

Eating & Drinking

In George Town, the fish-fry area, down from the Peace & Plenty inn, has a plethora of great little outdoor bars and takeaway eateries that open at sunset and on weekends.

Chat n Chill Bar & Grill (☎ 242-336-2800; www.chatn chill.com; Stocking Island; mains US$6-11; ✗ lunch & dinner) A spirited and affable outdoor bar on Stocking Island's main beach, with customers' small boats and kayaks lined up alongside. It specializes in Island Daiquiris and barbecue dishes, while its Sunday pig roast (US$15) is one of the social highlights in George Town. Call for pickups from George Town dock, and rejoice in *the* perfect beach bar!

Cheaters Restaurant & Bar (☎ 242-336-2535; Queen's Hwy, South George Town; mains US$8-25; ✗ lunch & dinner Wed-Sat) Bahamian dishes served at this cool and simple eatery draw a crowd. The yummy sides of peas'n'rice, coleslaw and macaroni alone make it worth the trip. The bar livens up at night.

Getting There & Around

AIR

For air travel information to the Exumas, see p98. Taxis await the arrival of all flights to the airport, and cost US$28 to George Town. However, two good car-rental agencies are based at the airport (see right).

BICYCLE

Bike rental is available from **Starfish** (☎ 242-336-3033; www.kayakbahamas.com; George Town) for US$20/25 per half/full day.

BOAT

Ferries to Stocking Island depart from Peace & Plenty Bonefish Lodge's dock at 10:30am and 1:30pm daily (US$8 round-trip).

CAR & SCOOTER

Don's Rent A Car (☎ 242-345-0112; Exuma Airport; ✗ 7am-5pm Mon-Sun) rents excellent air-con vehicles from US$65 per day.

Prestige Scooter Rental (☎ 242-357-0066; George Town) rents scooters from US$50 per day.

TAXI

Both **Luther Rolle Taxis** (☎ 242-345-5003) and **Leslie Dames** (☎ 242-357-0015) offer taxi service around the island.

LONG ISLAND

pop 2980

This is one of the most attractive of the Family Islands; a narrow 2-mile (3.2km)-wide strip that stretches for 60 miles (96km). Follow the Queen's Hwy past stunning white and sky-blue Gothic churches, lush greenery, pretty villages brimming with bougainvillea, and pastel-colored schoolyards full of curious and happy children.

The solitary highway leads off to a myriad of magnificent bays, blue holes, and miles and miles of beach. The island's inhabitants are scattered among about 35 settlements, growing bananas and rows of corn, along with vegetables and pineapples.

On the eastern shore, Atlantic rollers crash against cliffs and offshore reefs, while the west coast consists of a string of shallow bays. In late spring hundreds of yellow butterflies appear, dancing to their own tune.

This pristine diving paradise has untapped treasures, while the wall dives and the fast-paced action of Shark Reef are acclaimed.

Deadman's Cay

Although many visitors fly to Stella Maris, an upscale residential community near the north end of the island, Deadman's Cay is Long Island's main settlement and the site of its second airport.

INFORMATION

Public phone booths can be found at all settlements.

BaTelCo (☎ 242-337-1337; Deadman's Cay)
Emergency (☎ 242-377-0999)
Medical clinic (☎ 242-337-1222; Deadman's Cay)
Police Deadman's Cay (☎ 242-337-0999); Stella Maris Airport (☎ 242-338-2222)
Post office (☎ 242-337-1064; Deadman's Cay)
Scotiabank (☎ 242-338-2057; Deadman's Cay; ✗ 9am-1pm Mon-Thu, 9am-5pm Fri)

THE BAHAMAS

SIGHTS

A terrible road leads to **Guana Key**, an exquisite cay and jade-colored shallow bay. In good weather you can snorkel over the wreck of an old freighter.

The **Columbus Memorial** and plaque dedicated to 'the peaceful aboriginal people of Long Island and to the arrival of Christopher Columbus' is at the northern tip of the island. The vivid sea here offers great snorkeling.

Turtle Cove, a 2-mile (3.2km)-wide bay near the small settlement of Deans, boasts a fabulous beach, turquoise shallows, and the world's deepest blue hole (660ft; 201m) leading to a vast underwater cavern and magnificent cove. Bring a picnic!

The peaceful harbor settlement of **Clarence Town** has a stupendous setting on a hillside overlooking the sparkling harbor waters. Gleaming from on high are the extraordinary **Paul's Anglican Church**, and the white- and blue-edged **St Peter's Catholic Church** replete with soaring spires.

East of town is Lochabar Bay, a dazzling cove that funnels to a vast blue hole and white-sand beach. Coral reefs lie offshore. At the southern end of the island is the isolated and startlingly beautiful **Gordon's Beach**.

The highlight of the island's festivities is May's **Long Island Regatta**, held at Salt Pond.

Max Conch Bar & Grill (opposite) is the center of liquid events.

ACTIVITIES

Reeldivers (☎ 242-338-0011; www.reeldivers.com; Salt Pond) has two-tank dives for US$125, three-hour snorkel trips for US$50, half-day kayaking/snorkeling for US$65 and underwater scooters from US$35. Dive-stay packages are also available with this professional and friendly bunch.

Typical fishing charter fees are US$350 per day, for two people.

Bonafide Bonefishing (☎ 242-338-2035; www.bonafidebonefishing.com; Stella Maris; ☺ 9am-7pm Mon-Fri) owner and guide Docky Smith also offers fishing lessons (per hour US$60).

Cape Santa Maria Beach Resort (☎ 242-338-5273; www.capesantamaria.com; Cape Santa Maria) can arrange bonefishing excursions (US$200/250 per half/full day) and deep-sea fishing (US$550/800 per half/full day). The resort has its own private airstrip and charters.

SLEEPING

There are some fabulous rental properties on the island. Try the following little beauty.

Bahamian Mood Vacation Rentals (☎ 242-337-0056; www.bahamianmood.com; Clarence Town; r US$90; P X X) This colorful two-story house

---

THE BEST OF THE REST

The heart of traditional Bahamian culture still beats on **Cat Island**, one of the islands least touched by tourism. Obeah (a form of African-based ritual magic) and bush medicine are still practiced. Cat has several interesting historic sites, including plantation ruins and the Mt Alvernia Hermitage.

The island's second-largest settlement is **Arthur's Town**, 30 miles (48km) north of New Bight. The hamlet's main claim to fame is that it was the boyhood home of Sir Sidney Poitier, the Academy Award–winning actor. Sadly his childhood home is now derelict.

On top of **Mt Alvernia** (206ft; 62m), or Como Hill, as it is called by locals, is a blanched-stone church, built by the hermit Father Jerome, with a bell tower that looks like something Merlin might have conjured up in the days of King Arthur. You can enter the small chapel, tiny cloister, and a guest cell the size of a large kennel. It's reached by a rock staircase hewn into the side of the hill. From the top, you can marvel at the spiritually reviving 360-degree view. Try to make it at sunrise or sunset.

The diving off the south shore is superb; a 12-mile (19km) front contains caves and coral canyons to explore. The prime dive site is **Tartar Bank**, a column-like plateau covered by coral, sponges and sea fans. **Winding Bay** offers fabulous gorgonians and black coral.

The biggest happening of the year is the **Cat Island Regatta** on Emancipation Day (the first Monday in August), when scores of Cat Islanders return from afar and the population quadruples. The highlight of this homecoming is the sailboat races, while fun events like dominoes tournaments and fashion shows play to the accompaniment of great rake 'n' scrape bands.

has four units, a wraparound sundeck and a startling white-sand beach.

Chez Pierre Bahamas (☎ 242-338-8809; www.baha mahouseinn.com; Simms; d US$130; P ⊠ ⊠) A hell-of-a-road leads you to a piece of heaven. A stretch of tucked-away beach contains chef Pierre's home, restaurant and dining room, and some modern and delightful wooden huts on stilts overlooking the ocean.

Who needs mod cons and TV? Dinner and breakfast for two are included in these excellent rates. Fall asleep following a delicious pasta dinner to the sound of the sea. Just blissful.

Seaview Lodge (☎ 242-333-0100; Salt Pond; r US$90; P ⊠ ⊠) For great value you don't need to go further than these modern, clean, white and spacious apartments. Fully equipped kitchens and comfy living areas in these one- and two-bedroom lodgings make these a bargain for couples or families.

EATING & DRINKING

Max Conch Bar & Grill (☎ 242-337-0056; www.max conchbar.com; Deadman's Cay; mains US$6-12; ⊙ lunch & dinner) *The* hot spot in town, everything you need to know and want to share can be told while sitting around this circular outdoor bar. A lively and convivial host is well matched by his customers and family.

Daily specials satisfy the appetite, while good humor enlivens and mends the soul.

Outer Edge Grill & Bar (☎ 242-337-3445; Flying Fish Marina, Clarence Town; mains US$8-18; ⊙ breakfast, lunch & dinner Wed & Fri-Mon) Not a bad setting for this outdoor harborside bar and restaurant. The food is quick and tasty, the rums are smooth, and the atmosphere is relaxing and calm.

King's Bake & Snack Shop (☎ 242-338-8916; Simms; ⊙ 7am-6pm) Simply the best bakery on the island, Bahamians start trooping in here early to grab daily specials like yummy pineapple tarts, pumpkin bread and hot savory patties.

GETTING THERE & AROUND

For information on air travel to Long Island, see p98.

Mr T Car Rentals (☎ 242-337-1054; Deadman's Cay Airport) rents good reliable air-con vehicles from US$60 per day. Remember to look left, right and up as you drive across the airport's runway to and from his residence!

Swift Car Rentals (☎ 242-338-8533; Queen's Hwy, Simms) also rents cars from its garage north of Deadman's Cay (from US$60 per day).

The airport is well served by taxis, although it's best to rent a car to get around yourself.

Somehow **Andros** escaped the relentless tourist development and population boom of New Providence, yet it's actually the largest of the Bahamian islands. Comprising three islands, with a reputation for superb bonefishing and diving, it still pulls in the punters.

While fishing fans can hire some excellent guides to search for **Lowe Sounds** lobsters, divers can savor the spectacle of the third-longest reef in the world, at the **Tongue of the Ocean Wall**, which drops off a scary 6000ft (1.8km). Among a myriad of blue holes, it is in the **Blue Hole** that large rays and sharks gather, while the **Barge** is now a condo for some friendly groupers.

Andros is smothered in pine forests, thick undergrowth and marshy wetlands, which harbor wild boars, dove, ducks and quail that try to outrun and outfly the seasonal hunters. Giant land crabs also run unwittingly toward the cooking pot when they go searching en masse for love in late spring and early summer.

Andros has a **Sailing Regatta** in June, while July sees a kickoff between Andros and the Berry Islands; the **All Andros & Berry Islands Independence Regatta**. This marathon is composed of a bonefishing tournament, sailboat races, volleyball matches, boatbuilding, crab cracking (don't ask) and the most competitive and electric of all – a dominoes tournament.

Semiarid, scrub-covered **Great Inagua** receives few tourists. Beaches, too, are few, but the island boasts the largest flock of flamingos in the western hemisphere. Over fifty thousand of these leggy birds parade in the relative splendor of **Bahamas National Trust Park**. A veritable haven for fans of the feathered friend, dozens of other bird species include roseate spoonbills, reddish pink egrets, avocets, cormorants and tricolored Louisiana herons. Best times to visit are in the early morning and late evening, and take plenty of bug spray with you! The island, which has meager tourist facilities, is still dominated by the salt industry.

THE BAHAMAS

DIRECTORY

Information listed in this directory is specific to the Bahamas Islands. For information pertaining to the entire region, check
the book's main directory (p757).

ACCOMMODATIONS

With a fantastic range of cheerful little
cottages, welcoming inns, stylish condos,
and super hotels and resorts, the Bahamian islands cater for most tastes, if not
all budgets. There are some excessive and
often unjustified accommodations rates. To
add insult to injury, a plethora of taxes and
imaginative surcharges are used by all lodgings to hike up your bill by around 20% to
30%. Check prior to booking that quoted

> **EMERGENCY NUMBERS**
>
> **Ambulance, Fire & Police** (☎ 911, 919)

---

rates are inclusive of all these creeping additional costs.

Nearly all hostelries also change their
rates at least twice a year between low and
high season. While this guide quotes high-
season rates, be aware that some hotels
charge even higher prices from Christmas
Eve through to New Year's Day. Now for
the good news: the low season (or summer)
extends for most of the year from mid-April
to mid-December.

During this period accommodations
prices drop between 20% and 60%, so although this region is pricy, it is possible
to avoid teeth-clenching charges and find
value-for-money lodgings.

Rates for all budgets are normally for two
people. In high season decent budget rooms
cost around US$70 a night, although bar-
gains are to be found. Midrange hotels will
ask for US$130 and above, while upscale
resorts will charge from US$200.

Your best bet is to contact the hotels directly by telephone or via their websites,
as many offer good discounts. These discounts and special offers can save up to 30%
on the published rate and are not available
to walk-in customers.

Camping

The Bahamas does not encourage campers.
Camping on the beaches is illegal and there
are no official campsites, even in wilderness areas.

Rental

The Bahamas boasts hundreds of private
houses for rent, from modest cottages to
lavish beachfront villas. These units can be
cost-effective if you're traveling with your
family or a group of friends. Rental rates
begin at US$1500 per week. The Bahamas
websites (see p96) link to real estate agencies, which manage a wealth of rental properties. Some agencies are also listed in this
chapter.

Resorts

All-inclusive resorts are cash-free, self-
contained hotels or village resorts; you pay

> **PRACTICALITIES**
>
> ▪ **Newspapers & Magazines** Daily New
> Providence newspapers include the
> morning's *Nassau Guardian* and the
> afternoon's *Tribune*, as well as the
> *Bahama Journal*. The tabloids *Punch*
> and *Confidential Source* are published
> weekly. Grand Bahama enjoys the
> daily *Freeport News* and twice-monthly
> *Freeport Times*, and Abaconians read the
> weekly *Abaconian* and *Abaco Journal*.
>
> ▪ **Radio & TV** The government-owned
> Bahamas Broadcasting Corporation
> operates TV Channel 13 (ZNS) and radio
> stations ZNS-1, ZNS-2, ZNS-FM and ZNS-
> 3. Commercial radio stations include
> Love 97FM, More 94.9FM and Jamz
> 100FM. Most hotels also offer American
> cable TV.
>
> ▪ **Video Systems** VHS is the standard,
> and tapes may be bought in photo-
> supply shops.
>
> ▪ **Electricity** Hotels operate on 11V (60
> cycles), as per the USA and Canada.
> Plug sockets are two- or three-pin US
> standard.
>
> ▪ **Weights & Measures** The imperial and
> metric systems are both in use. Liquids
> are generally measured in pints, quarts
> and gallons, and weight in grams,
> ounces and pounds.

a set price and (theoretically) pay nothing more once you set foot inside the resort. Caution is needed when choosing a resort, as many properties have jumped onto the 'all-inclusive' bandwagon for marketing purposes, but don't supply the goods to back the claims.

ACTIVITIES

Anything to do with these glorious warm brilliantly colored seas is a delight, and easy to arrange. All the islands have outfits to take you diving and snorkeling. Normally a two-tank dive costs around US$70 without gear, and snorkeling around US$40 for a half-day trip.

Many Bahamians do both regularly, and it's often possible to walk off a beach and be within yards of precious living coral teeming with fish.

Remember that just touching the coral is enough to kill it and destroy the fish life. And remember to bring your own snorkeling gear, as it costs US$10 per day if you rent it.

Boat excursions for all activities abound, whether your thing is fishing, sailing, kayaking, sightseeing or simply lazing on a boat sipping rum punch while someone else does all the hard work.

Day excursions cost from about US$60 to US$150 depending upon your activities. Fast ferry trips from Nassau are a cheap and quick way to get to a few of the Family Islands, and they make a great day out. Tickets start from US$60.

Likewise, all islands have facilities to hire or charter boats. Unless there's a few of you to share, it is pricey. Charters range from US$600 per day.

Bird-watchers should contact the **Bahamas National Trust** (☎ 242-393-1317), which has information on the hundreds of wonderful species that visit, holiday or live on these isles.

BOOKS

For a view of Bahamian society through the eyes of foreigners try *Out Island Doctor* by Evans Cottman, a Yankee teacher who fell for Crooked and Acklins Islands in the 1940s, or Ernest Hemingway's *Islands in the Stream*, a fictitious but accurate look at Bimini life and his own bohemian ways during WWII.

Actor Sidney Poitier tells of his upbringing on Cat Island in his autobiographies, *This Life* and *The Measure of a Man*.

Bush Medicine in the Bahamas by Leslie Higgs (Nassau Guardian) provides recipes for curing everything, from warts to a broken heart. *Bahamas Cookery; Cindy's Treasures* by Cindy Williams is a great collection of simple regional dishes, such as guava duff with a creamy rum sauce.

Obeah and other Bahamian folk religions are the subjects covered in *Ten, Ten, the Bible Ten – Obeah in the Bahamas,* by Timothy McCartney.

Telcine Turner's *Once Below a Time: Bahamian Stories* is an illustrated collection of short stories for children, while *An Evenin' in Guanima: A Treasury of Folktales from the Bahamas* by Patricia Glinton-Meicholas is a classic. *'Who Let the Dog Out?' Dottie's Story* by Carole Hughes tells the tale about a dalmatian born on Green Turtle Cay who heads off to explore the world.

Want to know more about drug trafficking in the Bahamas? Check out *The Cocaine Wars* by Paul Eddy, Hugo Sabogal and Sara Walden.

CHILDREN

The Bahamas pursues the family traveler aggressively, and the larger hotels compete by providing good facilities for children. Most hotels have a babysitter or nanny service. Large resorts, such as Atlantis, have a full range of activities for children. Children under 12 years normally room with their parents for free.

The Bahamas Ministry of Tourism's brilliant program **Children-to-Children** (☎ 242-322-7500; www.bahamas.com) links visiting children with local kids, who can participate in activities together.

DISABLED TRAVELERS

Disabled travelers will need to plan their vacation carefully, as few allowances have been made for them in the Bahamas. The tourist board can provide a list of hotels with wheelchair ramps, as can the **Bahamas Council for the Handicapped** (☎ 242-322-4260; Commonwealth Blvd, Elizabeth Estates, Nassau) and the **Bahamas Association for the Physically Disabled** (☎ 242-322-2393; fax 322-7984; Dolphin Dr, Nassau, PO Box N-4252, Nassau). The latter are also able to rent a van and portable ramps for those with wheelchairs.

EMBASSIES & CONSULATES

Bahamian Embassies & Consulates

Canada (☎ 613-232-1724; ottawa-mission@bahighco
.com; 50 O'Connor St, Ste 1313, Ottawa, ON K1P 6L2)
China (☎ 852-2147-0202; fax-852-2893-3917; Ste
704-705 A Sino Plaza 7F, 255-257 Gloucester Rd, Causeway
Bay, Hong Kong)
UK (☎ 0207-408-4488; fax 207-499-9937; 10 Chesterfield St, London W1X 8AH)
USA Florida (☎ 305-373-6295; fax 305-373-6312; Bahamas Consulate General, 25 SE 2nd Ave, Ste 818, Miami,
FL 33131); Washington DC (☎ 202-319-2660;
bahemb@aol.doc; 2220 Massachusetts Ave NW, Washington, DC 20008)

Embassies & Consulates in the Bahamas

Most countries are represented by honor-
ary consuls.
Canada (☎ 242-393-2123/4; fax 242-393-1305; Shirley
St Plaza, Nassau, New Providence)
UK (Map pp68-9; ☎ 242-325-7471; fax 242-323-3871;
Bitco Bldg, East St, Nassau, New Providence)
USA (Map pp68-9; ☎ 242-322-1181/2/3; embnas@state
.gov; Mosmar Bldg, Queen St, Nassau, New Providence)

FESTIVALS & EVENTS

No traditional African festivals were retained in the Bahamas. Nonetheless, several
folk festivals evolved from the brief slave
era, notably **Junkanoo** and **Emancipation Day**.
On these days Bahamians go from church
to church and end the day in merrymaking
and traditional dancing. Nassau also hosts
a midyear Junkanoo in June.

The main Junkanoo Festival is held in
Nassau, beginning before sunrise on Boxing Day. In Grand Bahama and in the
Family Islands they start the festivities at
around 3am on Boxing Day. For more details on the Junkanoo Festival, see the boxed
text, p72.

There's a wealth of festivals in the Family Islands involving bonefishing championships, as well as cultural and sporting
celebrations.

Information for these festivals can be
found through the Bahamas Ministry of
Tourism website listed under Internet Resources (right) and via visitor information
centers. The more famous regattas, the **Family Island Regatta** (April) in the Exumas and
the **Long Island Regatta** (May) are fabulous
fun, when locally made sailing craft compete for prizes and partying abounds.

HOLIDAYS

Bahamian national holidays that fall on Sat-
urday or Sunday are usually observed on
the following Monday. The Bahamas has
the following national holidays:
New Year's Day January 1
Good Friday Friday before Easter
Easter Monday Monday after Easter
Whit Monday Seven weeks after Easter
Labour Day First Friday in June
Independence Day July 10
Emancipation Day First Monday in August
Discovery Day October 12
Christmas Day December 25
Boxing Day December 26

INTERNET RESOURCES

www.bahamas.com The official tourism website of the
Bahamas contains some travel packages but little hard
information.
www.bahamas.net.com The official website of the
company that produces all the local tourist information and
free maps has some restaurant and accommodations listings.
www.bahama-out-islands.com This usefully
promotes the inhabited islands outside of New Providence
and Grand Bahama.
www.geographia.com/bahama Information about
the country, its history and present culture.
www.thenassauguardian.com The newspaper's site
is a good starting point to find out about issues key to the
country.

MONEY

The Bahamian dollar (BS$) is linked one-
to-one with the US dollar, so you can use
US currency everywhere. Note that the
only bank permitted to exchange amounts
of more than BS$70 is the Central Bank of
the Bahamas (p67) in Nassau. Hence, it's a
good idea to spend all your Bahamian dollars prior to departure.

The major commercial banks maintain
branches throughout the islands, although
in the Family Islands they are thin on the
ground.

ATMs

There are ATMs in the leading tourist
centers. Most accept Visa, MasterCard and
Amex via international networks, such as
Cirrus and Visa/PLUS.

Credit Cards

Major credit cards are widely accepted
throughout the islands. Credit cards are *not*

widely accepted for general transactions in the more remote Family Islands. You can use your credit card to get cash advances at most commercial banks. Companies that accept credit cards may add an additional charge of up to 5%.

Traveler's Checks

Traveler's checks are widely accepted throughout the Bahamas, except on the more remote Family Islands, although some hotels, restaurants and exchange bureaus charge a hefty fee for cashing traveler's checks.

To report lost Amex traveler's checks in the Bahamas, contact **Destinations** (☎ 242-322-2931; 303 Shirley St, Nassau).

TELEPHONE

The government-owned **Bahamas Telecommunications Corporation** (BaTelCo; Map p65; ☎ 242-302-7000; John F Kennedy Dr, Nassau, New Providence) has an office on most Bahamian islands. Even the smallest settlement usually has at least one public phone. Many booths require phone cards, issued in denominations of US$5, US$10 and US$20.

Hotel rates are expensive and should be avoided when possible. Many hotels also charge for an unanswered call after the receiving phone has rung five times.

Cell (Mobile) Phones

You can bring your own cell phone into the Bahamas, but you may be charged a customs fee upon entry (refunded upon exit). Your phone will not operate on BaTelCo's cellular system unless you rent temporary use of a 'roaming' cellular line.

Domestic Calls

Local calls are free of charge, although hotels will charge US$0.75 to US$1 per call. Some useful numbers:

Current Time & Temperature (☎ 917)
Directory Assistance (☎ 916)
International Operator Assistance (☎ 0)

International Calls

Many Bahamian phone booths and all BaTelCo offices permit direct dial to overseas numbers. It is far cheaper to call direct from a phone booth than to call from your hotel via an operator. For example, assisted calls to the USA cost around US$1.80 per

three-minute minimum, then US$0.90 per minute. Calls to Canada cost around US$1.30, then US$1.30 per minute, to Europe it costs US$2.90, then US$2.15 per minute, while call charges to Australia and New Zealand are just frightening.

Many national companies offer a service for their subscribers, issuing international charge cards and a code number. Costs for calling home are then billed directly to your home number. The following companies provide such cards:

AT&T USA Direct (☎ 1-800-225-5288)
British Telecom (☎ 0-800-345-144)
Canada Direct (☎ 1-800-389-0004)
MCI (☎ 1-800-888-8000)
Sprint (☎ 1-800-389-2111)
Telstra Australia (☎ 1-800-038-000)

Phone Cards

The majority of Bahamian public telephones accept only prepaid phone cards issued by **BaTelCo** (☎ 242-302-7827), available at stores and other accredited outlets near phone-card booths. The phone cards are sold in denominations of US$5, US$10, US$20 and US$50.

Phone Codes

The Bahamian country code is ☎ 242. You need to dial this when making interisland calls. When dialing within an island, you just need to dial the seven-digit local number. The country code has been included in the Bahamian phone listings in this chapter.

To call the Bahamas from the US and Canada, dial ☎ 1-242 + the local number. From elsewhere, dial your country's international access code + ☎ 242 + the local number.

TOURIST INFORMATION
Local Tourist Offices

Abacos (☎ 242-367-3067; Memorial Plaza, Queen Elizabeth Dr, Marsh Harbour)
Eleuthera Governor's Harbour (☎ 242-332-2142; Queen's Hwy); Harbour Island (☎ 242-333-2621; Bay St)
Exumas (☎ 242-336-2430; Queen's Hwy, George Town)
Freeport (Map p79; ☎ 242-352-8044; International Bazaar)
Nassau British Colonial Hilton (Map pp68–9; ☎ 242-302-5000; Bay St, Nassau); Nassau International Airport (Map p65; ☎ 242-377-6806; Airport Arrivals Terminal); Welcome Centre (Map pp68–9; ☎ 242-326-9781; Festival Pl; ☻ 9am-5pm Mon-Fri)

THE BAHAMAS

Tourist Offices Abroad
Canada (☎ 416-968-2999; bmotca@bahamas.com; 121 Bloor St E, No 1101, Toronto, Ontario, M4W 3M5)
France (☎ 01-45-26-62-62; info@bahamas-tourisme.fr; 113-115 rue du Cherche Midi, 75006 Paris)
Italy (☎ 02-481-94-39-02; info@vertexic.com; Corso Magenta 54, 20123 Milan)
UK (☎ 0207-355-0800; info@bahamas.co.uk; Bahamas House, 10 Chesterfield St, London W1J 5JL)
USA California (☎ 800-439-6993, 310-312-9544; gjohnson@bahamas.com; 11400 West Olympic Blvd, suite 204, Los Angeles, CA 90064); Florida (☎ 954-236-9292; bmotfl@bahamas.com; 1200 South Pine Island Rd, Suite 750, Plantation, FL 33324); Illinois (☎ 773-693-1500; bmotch@bahamas.com; 8600 W Bryn Mawr Ave, No 820, Chicago, IL 60631); New York (☎ 212-758-2777; bmotny@bahamas.com; 150 E 52nd St, 28th fl, New York, NY 10022)

Also in the US is the **Bahamas Out Islands Promotion Board** (☎ 954-475-8315; www.boipb.com; 1200 South Pine Island Rd, Suite 750, Plantation, FL 33324).

VISAS
Citizens from many countries, including the US, Canada, the EU and Commonwealth countries, do not require a visa for stays up to three months. Citizens of most Central and South American countries, including Mexico, do not require a visa for stays up to 14 days. Visas are required for longer stays.

Citizens from the following countries require passports and visas for stays of any duration: Dominican Republic, Haiti, South Africa and all communist countries. Citizens from all other countries should check the current entry requirements at the nearest Bahamian embassy or with the **Immigration Department** (☎ 242-322-7530; fax 242-326-0977; PO Box N-831, Hawkins Hill, Nassau). There are also offices for Immigration at Nassau International Airport and at Prince George Wharf.

TRANSPORTATION

GETTING THERE & AWAY
Entering the Bahamas
All visitors need to carry valid passport and a return or onward ticket. From December 31, 2005, all US travelers need to carry a passport when traveling to the Caribbean, including the Bahamas, or they will not be granted permission to re-enter the US (see the boxed text, p772).

Air
The Bahamas has six international airports, including two major hubs:
Exuma International Airport (GGT; ☎ 242-345-0095; George Town, Exuma)
Freeport International Airport (FPO; ☎ 242-352-6020; Freeport, Grand Bahama)
Marsh Harbour International Airport (MHH; ☎ 242-367-3039; Marsh Harbour, Abacos)
Moss Town Exuma International Airport (MWX; ☎ 242-345-0030; Moss Town, Exuma)
Nassau International Airport (NAS; ☎ 242-377-7281; Nassau, New Providence)
North Eleuthera International Airport (ELH; ☎ 242-335-1242; North Eleuthera)

The national airline **Bahamasair** (☎ 242-377-5505, in Freeport 242-352-8341; www.bahamasair.com) has an unblemished safety record and its pilots have an excellent reputation (see www.airsafe.com for details). However, delays and lost luggage are regular occurrences. Bahamians say 'If you have time to spare, fly Bahamasair.' You are warned.

For flights to the Bahamas from outside the Caribbean, see p773. The following airlines fly to and from the Bahamas from within the Caribbean:
Air Jamaica (☎ 242-377-3301, 1-800-523-5585; www.airjamaica.com; hub Montego Bay)
Bahamasair (☎ 242-377-5505, in Freeport ☎ 242-352-8341; www.bahamasair.com; hub Nassau)
Skyking (☎ 649-941-5464; www.skyking.tc; hub Provenciales)

GETTING AROUND
Perusing a map, you may be tempted to think that island-hopping down the chain is easy. It ain't, unless you have your own boat or plane. Interisland air is centered on Nassau. Getting between the islands without constantly backtracking is a bit of a feat. Even the mail boats are Nassau-centric.

Air
Interisland flights offer the only quick and convenient way to travel within the Bahamas, and islanders ride airplanes like Londoners use buses. Private charter flights could be considered if you are traveling in a group. They fly to/from the General Aviation Terminal.

Bahamasair (☎ 242-377-5505, in Freeport ☎ 242-352-8341; www.bahamasair.com; hub Nassau) The dominant airline in the Bahamas. Operates on a hub-and-spoke system, so if you want to fly between adjacent islands, such as Cat and Long Islands, you will have to first return to Nassau. If you do a lot of island-hopping, you'll begin to feel like a yo-yo and may need to overnight in Nassau between flights; budget accordingly. Flies from Nassau to Marsh Harbour, Abaco three times daily, Andros twice daily, Cat Island once daily, Crooked Island twice weekly, Eleuthera twice daily, Exumas three times per day, Freeport six times per day, Inagua three times per week, Long Island daily and San Salvador three times per week.

Cat Island Air (☎ 242-377-3318; fax 242-377-3723; hub Nassau) Flies from Nassau to Cat Island twice daily and from Nassau to San Salvador three times a week.

Major's Air Services (☎ 242-352-5778; www .thebahamasguide.com/majorair; hubs Grand Bahama & Eleuthera) Flies from Freeport to Marsh Harbour daily, Biminis daily and Andros twice weekly.

Southern Air (☎ 242-367-2498; www.southernaircharter .com; hub Nassau) Flies from Nassau to George Town, Exumas daily, and from Long Island to the Exumas twice weekly.

Western Air (☎ 242-329-4000; fax 242-329-3167; hubs Andros & Nassau) Flies from Nassau to Bimini twice daily, Andros twice daily and Freeport six times daily.

Bicycle

Cycling is a cheap, convenient, healthy, environmentally sound and above all *fun* way to travel. Major resort hotels rent bicycles for US$20 daily. Unfortunately, the bikes are heavy, have only one gear and are virtually guaranteed to give you a sore bum.

Boat
FERRY & WATER TAXI

The only ferry operation in the islands is **Bahamas Ferries** (Map pp68-9; ☎ 242-323-2166/8; www .bahamasferries.com), a high speed ferry linking Nassau, Andros, Abacos, Eleuthera and the Exumas.

Water taxis ply between Nassau and Paradise Island. Several other offshore islands and their neighboring cays are served by private water taxis.

Government-run water taxis link islands that are a short distance apart, such as North Bimini and South Bimini, Mangrove Cay and South Andros, and Crooked and Acklins Islands.

MAIL BOAT

Around 30 mail boats sail under government contract to most inhabited islands. They regularly depart Potter's Cay in Nassau for Grand Bahama and all the Family Islands. Traditionally sailing overnight, boat journeys last five to 24 hours. You can call the **Dockmaster's Office** (☎ 242-394-1237) and check the **Bahamas Ministry of Tourism** (www.bahamas.com) website for the latest schedules and prices.

Bus

Nassau and Freeport have dozens of *jitneys* (private minibuses), licensed to operate on pre-established routes.

Alas, there is no public transportation on any of the Family Islands; or at airports, as the taxi drivers' union is too powerful. Likewise, few hotels are permitted to operate their own transfer service for guests.

Car

Bahamians are generally cautious and civilized drivers, and main roads are usually in good condition. Those that await their turn are often indented with deep potholes. Believe any Bahamian who warns you that a road is bad.

DRIVER'S LICENSE

To drive in the Bahamas you must have a current license from your home country or state. A visitor can drive on his or her home license for three months.

FUEL

Esso, Shell and Texaco maintain gas stations on most islands. Gas stations are usually open from 8am to about 7pm. Some close on Sunday. In Nassau and Freeport you'll find stations open 24 hours a day. Gasoline costs US$3.50 per US gallon. Credit cards are accepted in major settlements, elsewhere, it's cash only, please!

RENTAL

Several major international car-rental companies have outlets in Nassau and Freeport, along with smaller local firms. In the Family Islands there are some very good local agencies. Ask your hotel for recommendations, or look for display boards at the airport.

Renters must be 21 (some companies rent only to those 25 or older). Collision damage waiver insurance is US$15 a day. Local companies may not offer insurance.

You usually rent for a 24-hour period, with rates starting at US$70 (from around

THE BAHAMAS

US$80 in Nassau and from US$60 for smaller islands).

Golf carts can be rented on the smaller islands and cays for US$40 per day.

ROAD RULES

Always drive on the *left*-hand side. At traffic circles (roundabouts), remember to circle in a clockwise direction, entering to the left. You must give way to traffic already in the circle. It is compulsory to wear a helmet when riding a motorcycle or scooter.

Taxi

There's no shortage of licensed taxis in Nassau and Freeport, where they can be hailed on the streets. Taxis are also the main local transportation in the Family Islands, where they meet all incoming planes.

All taxi operators are licensed. Taxi fares are fixed by the government according to distance: rates are usually for two people. Each additional person is charged a flat rate of US$3. Fixed rates have been established from airports and cruise terminals to specific hotels and major destinations. These rates should be displayed in the taxi. However, you should beware some crafty scams in Nassau and Freeport, where an unscrupulous driver may attempt to charge additional people the same rate as the first and second person.

Turks & Caicos

Donkeys, horses and chickens ramble around in tatty, contented groups on Grand Turk's winding roads. Its narrow, sleepy streets are lined with faded 1800s houses swathed in brilliant scarlet bougainvillea, while leafy trees cast dappled shade over passing bicycles carrying locals, or 'Belongers,' who smile while asking, 'How are you today?'

Days of snorkeling and diving drift by, while quiet evenings are spent sipping spiced rum. In fishermen's bars, expats and 'Belongers' alike engage in noisy debate about development plans for their island. Meanwhile, the ocean's depths, full of flickering colorful life and velvety darkness, quietly envelope the birthing whales, which inspire such awe in their human visitors.

Across these waters, Caicos Islanders welcome guests to share their natural riches; with clusters of intimate and pristine resorts dotted with swaying palm trees. Here, Bahamian and foreign artists ply their wares, and perfect beaches are lined with honey-brown sunbathers and warm glistening shallows. Marinas' small cafés and bars doze in the daytime and awaken at sunset as boats return, with damp passengers talking of curious iguanas and gentle stingrays.

FAST FACTS

- **Area** Over 40 islands together add up to 430 sq miles (1113 sq km) of land
- **Capital** Cockburn Town, Grand Turk
- **Country code** ☎ 649
- **Departure tax** US$35 (normally included in ticket prices)
- **Famous for** Diving with and watching whales; 230-mile-long (370km) coral reef; US astronaut John Glenn landing off Grand Turk from space in 1962
- **Language** English
- **Money** US dollar (US$); US$1 = €0.77 = £0.53
- **Official name** Turks & Caicos Islands
- **People** Belongers and residents
- **Population** 19,960
- **Visa** Not required by North American, UK and most Western European travelers. Other nationalities need to get them in advance; see p119.

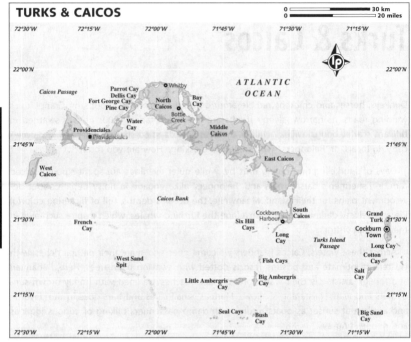

TURKS & CAICOS

(p107)

HIGHLIGHTS

- **Diving** (p107) Take a dive off Grand Turk to visit and embrace the island-divers' two pet groupers.
- **Grace Bay Beach** (p108) Sitting astride an island pony, take a sunset canter along the glorious stretches of this beach.
- **Turtle Cove** (p112) Head to a Provo nightspot for a boisterous night of bingo or exuberant karaoke.
- **North Caicos** (p115) Bicycle around lush North Caicos on a day trip, spotting gangly flamingos and predatory ospreys.
- **Salt Cay** (p107) Go whale-watching or diving with beautiful marine gods: humpback whales.

ITINERARIES

- **Three days** Hire a car and explore Chalk Sound, Blue Hills and Grace Bay on Caicos. Then take a trip to observe Little Water Cay's iguanas and French Cay's stingrays.
- **One week** Add on a visit to North, West or South Caicos for some inspiring outdoor adventures.

- **Two weeks** Add a flight to Grand Turk, for night diving and lounging on Governor's beach, and an excursion to Salt Cay.

CLIMATE & WHEN TO GO

The Turks & Caicos' climate is similar to that of the southern Bahamas, though slightly warmer and drier. Temperatures can average 77°F (25°C) in winter and rise to an average of 90°F (32°C) in summer. The hottest months are August to November, and average humidity is 35%. Average annual rainfall is 21in (53cm) and it's wettest in summer.

The winter season is undoubtedly the most popular to visitors, however as with the Bahamas (see p94), this is when hotel prices soar. Try to aim to go somewhere between mid-April to mid-December in the off-season, where there are still many months of truly grand weather.

HISTORY

Recent discoveries of Indian artifacts on Grand Turk have shown that the islands evolved much the same indigenous culture as did their northern neighbors. Locals even claim that the islands were Christopher Columbus' first landfall in 1492 (see p59).

The island group was a pawn in the power struggles between the French, Spanish and British, and remained virtually uninhabited until 1678, when some Bermudian salt traders cleared the land and created the *salinas* (salt-drying pans) that still exist on several islands.

Fast forward to the 1900s, when the US military built airstrips during WWII and John Glenn splashed down just off Grand Turk in 1962, putting the islands in the international spotlight.

In 1973, the Turks & Caicos became a separate crown colony of Great Britain. More recently, in 1984, Club Med opened its doors on Providenciales (Provo), and the Turks & Caicos started to boom. In the blink of an eye, the islands, which had lacked electricity, acquired satellite TV.

The Turks & Caicos relied upon the exportation of salt, which remained the backbone of the British Crown colony until the 1950s. Today finance, tourism and fishing generate most income, but the islands could not survive without British aid. The tax-free offshore finance industry is a mere minnow compared with that of the Bahamas, and many would be astonished to discover that Grand Turk, the much-hyped financial center, is just a dusty backwater in the sun.

The per capita GDP in 2000 was estimated at US$9600. Illegal drug trafficking, a major problem, has also been a source of significant revenue for a few islanders.

Relations between islanders and British-appointed governors have been strained since 1996, when the incumbent governor's comments suggesting that government and police corruption had turned the islands into a haven for drug trafficking appeared in the *Offshore Finance Annual,* and opponents accused him of harming investment. Growing opposition threatened to spill over into civil unrest. The issue created a resurgence in calls for independence, calls that still continue today.

THE CULTURE

The islands have their own identity, but are as devoutly religious as their northern neighbors. This doesn't stop some from having a tipple on Sunday, when the pubs (strictly speaking) aren't serving.

HOW MUCH?

- **Two-tank dive** US$70
- **Comfortable double room** US$120
- **Day's car hire** US$80
- **Original painting** US$20
- **Mango gelato** US$3.50

LONELY PLANET INDEX

- **Gallon (imperial) of gas** US$3.50
- **Liter of bottled water** US$1.80
- **Bottle of Turks Head beer** US$3
- **Souvenir T-shirt** US$20 to US$30
- **Street snack: chicken and fries** US$6

Turks & Caicos islanders ('Belongers') are descended from the early Bermudian settlers, Loyalist settlers, slave settlers and salt rakers.

Many expats, notably Brits, are employed in the hospitality and finance industries, having escaped the cities and miserable weather of Europe. Others are 'retirement-aged swashbucklers' or those openly avoiding conversations about their origins!

More recently, hundreds of Haitians have fled their impoverished island and landed on the Turks & Caicos Islands, many on their way to Miami's streets of gold. Some residents and Belongers resent the Haitians intrusion into the islands' scarce economic resources.

Nightlife is relatively subdued, except in Provo where a large number of lively bars and restaurants cater to the tourist trade. All the islands have funky bars, where bands play traditional rake 'n' scrape music and the locals (mostly men) engage in dominoes or watch TV.

ARTS

Though slow to develop, the arts scene on the Turks & Caicos Islands has begun to blossom. Traditional music, folklore and sisal weaving evolved during colonial days, and have been maintained to this day.

The local art scene has been dominated by the Haitian community, but other artists are gaining recognition. Much of the work is inspired by the islands' scenery and marine life, with its vibrant Caribbean colors. The shopping section in Providenciales (p114) profiles a few really talented local artists.

ENVIRONMENT
The Land
The islands are predominantly semiarid, notably Salt Cay and much of South Caicos and Grand Turk, which were denuded of vegetation to dissuade rainfall during the heyday of the salt industry. The larger islands of North, Middle and East Caicos are more lush, with creeks, sand flats, lagoons and marshy wetlands. Most of the sandy beaches – some of the finest on the planet – are on the north and west shores, facing the open ocean.

More than 30 protected areas have been set aside to conserve delicate ecosystems and wildlife habitats.

Wildlife
There are almost as many donkeys, wild horses and cattle as humans, though they stay in the wilds. Their forebears once carried 25lb (11.3kg) burlap bags of salt from the ponds to the warehouses and docks. Having earned their rest, they were set free.

Iguanas once inhabited much of the Turks & Caicos until they lost their lives to introduced dogs and cats, and their habitats to development. Now Little Water Cay, Fort George Cay and Ambergris Cays are all protected iguana reserves.

The waters are favored by four species of turtle; hawksbills (an internationally endangered species, although sadly not recognized in this region), green, loggerheads and, occasionally, leatherbacks.

More than 175 species of seabirds and waders have been sighted, of which 78 are migratory land birds. Ospreys are numerous and easily spotted, as are sparrow hawks and barn owls. Flamingos – once numerous throughout the chain – are now limited to West, North and South Caicos, where you may also see Cuban herons.

Frigate birds are more commonly seen here than in the Bahamas, as are pelicans.

A flourishing population of bottle-nosed dolphins lives in these waters. Also, some 7000 North Atlantic humpback whales use the Turks Island Passage and the Mouchoir Banks, south of Grand Turk, as their winter breeding grounds between January and March. Manta rays are commonly seen during the spring plankton blooms off of Grand Turk and West Caicos.

FOOD & DRINK
As in the Bahamas, conch (the chewy meat of a large gastropod), lobster, soft-shell crab and fresh fish (often blackened with Cajun seasoning) are island favorites, along with spicy Jamaican jerk chicken and fresh fruits, such as sapodillas and sugar apples.

However, the food is a lot healthier here than in the Bahamas; there are more fruit and vegetables available (imported from Haiti), and not so many fried dishes. The cooking is more sophisticated, with distinctive French influences, especially apparent in Caicos. More vegetarian choices also appear on menus, although they are still pretty scarce.

More people drink wine here than in the Bahamas, and the local brew is a full-flavored Turks Head beer. There is some delicious rum on the market, such as the black and spicy Gosling, which makes wonderfully potent cocktails.

TURKS ISLANDS

The Turks group comprises Grand Turk and its smaller southern neighbor, Salt Cay, in addition to several tiny cays. The islands lie east of the Caicos Islands, separated from them by the 22-mile-wide (35km) Turks Island Passage.

GRAND TURK
Grand Turk is a charming, offbeat gem with a rare sense of innocence. A brush-covered, bean-shaped dot of an island, it is just 6.5 miles (11km) long and 1.5 miles (2.4km) across at the widest.

Cockburn Town, the main settlement, has been the administrative and political capital of the archipelago for more than 400 years. Today it also claims to be the business and financial center (banks are registered here, but don't have a physical presence), yet it remains as sleepy as a capital can be. Semiwild horses, cattle and donkeys roam the outer streets, while picturesque houses dating from 1800 look out at pristine emerald seas.

The island's middle is dominated by several salinas, from which a peculiar odor sometimes arises. Salt – 'white gold' – was the island's most important export until the industry collapsed in 1962. Pocketed limestone cliffs rise along the north and east shores.

There are nice beaches along all shores; inland, caves once used by Lucayan Indians await discovery.

Grand Turk Cays Land & Sea Park incorporates the tiny Gibb's, Penniston, Long and Martin Alonza Pinzon Cays; important nesting sites for seabirds. A few hundred yards off Grand Turk's leeward shore, 1.5 miles (2.4km) south of Cockburn Town, the shallow seabed opens into a deep blue chasm more than 8000ft (2438m) deep. The diving and fishing here is fabulous. Salt Cay attract whales and eagle rays to its waters, making a spectacular dive a lifetime memory.

Getting There & Around

AIR
For flight information, see p119.

Taxis meet incoming flights; to Cockburn Town costs US$7. There are no buses, but pre-booked rental cars will meet your plane.

BICYCLE
You can rent a bicycle at **Sea Eye Diving** (Duke St) for US$15 per day and from **Pirate's Hideaway Guesthouse** (☎ 946-6909; www.saltcay.tc; Victoria St) on Salt Cay for around US$10 per day.

BOAT
A ferry runs bi-weekly from Grand Turk to Salt Cay (US$12 round-trip). Contact **Salt Cay Charters** (☎ 231-6663; piratequeen3@hotmail .com). Whale-watching boat trips with this bunch cost US$75.

CARS & SCOOTERS
You're hardly likely to need a car in town, but do pay attention anyway to the one-way system along Duke and Front St. You can rent air-con cars from:

Ed-Rico's Rent-a-Car (☎ 946-1744, 946-1042; seacair@tciway.tc; Churchill Bldg, Front St) Will do airport pickup/drop offs.

Tony's Car Rental (☎ 231-1806; Airport Rd) Located at the airport.

Val's Scooter Rentals (☎ 946-1022, 946-1022; Duke St) Near Water's Edge restaurant. Rents out scooters for US$40 per day.

GOLF CARTS
Golf carts can be hired from **Pirate's Hideaway Guesthouse** (☎ 946-6909; www.saltcay.tc; Victoria St) on Salt Cay from around US$35 per day.

TAXI
Several locals, such as Errico from Ed-Rico's (left), operate taxis on Grand Turk. Ask at your hotel or restaurant for recommendations. If you hire a taxi for an island tour, be sure to negotiate the fare beforehand.

Cockburn Town
pop 5525
Cockburn Town belies all notions of a nation's 'capital.' Everything happens on the two main streets, lined with old street lamps and colonial buildings. Some of the latter are salt warehouses built of limestone; others are fine wooden structures, with steep roofs, shuttered windows and shaded doorways. Many of the houses are hemmed in by low stone walls to keep out wild cattle and donkeys. Most people live in more-modern homes in the eastern 'suburbs,' where the land rises to Colonel Murray's Hill.

ORIENTATION
The heart of town is sandwiched between the ocean and the salt pond named Red Salina. Front St runs one way, along the waterfront, then narrows and becomes Duke St three blocks south of the government plaza.

Pond St runs parallel 50yd (46m) to the east, along Red Salina. To the north, Pond St divides: Hospital St runs north to the hospital and Lighthouse Rd runs northeast to the lighthouse at Northeast Point, then divides to follow the waterfront to Governor's Beach and the dock, or southeast to the airport.

INFORMATION
Businesses and government offices close at 3pm on Friday. Some businesses open from 9am to 1pm on Saturday. Public phones can be found at most central places.

Cable & Wireless (☎ 946-2200; cwtci@tciway.tc; Front St) Offers Internet access.

Federal Express (☎ 231-6097)

Grand Turk Hospital (☎ 946-2333; Hospital Rd)

Police (☎ 946-2299; Hospital Rd)

Post office (☎ 946-1334; Front St)

Scotiabank (☎ 946-2507; Front St)

Turks & Caicos Islands Tourist Board (☎ 946-2321; turksandcaicostourism.com; Front St)

AWE-INSPIRING DIVING

Dive Sites: Grand Turk

- **Black Forest** Five types of black coral cling to an undercut festooned with sponges.
- **McDonald's** Everything from groupers to angelfish hang out near this coral arch.
- **Tunnels** Sand chutes slope down to the entrance of twin tunnels that drop to 100ft (30.5m) and emerge in a sponge theme park.

Dive Sites: Caicos Islands

- **Amphitheater** This bowl shaped undercut at 85ft (26m) curves into the Caicos Passage. Whales, sharks and manta rays often pass by.
- **Chimney** Garden eels populate this 10ft-wide (3m) cut in the plate coral.
- **Coral Stairway** A series of coral steps leads to a sand cellar that is Grand Central Station for schooling eagle rays.
- **Shark Hotel** Check in at this 'hotel' to commune with reef and blacktip sharks. The wall has a sponge-encrusted coral chimney that descends 130ft (39.6m).

Dive Sites: French Cay

- **Dax Canyon** The wall starts at 45ft (13.7m) and drops to a shelf at 150ft (45.7m). Large eagle rays are frequent visitors.
- **Rock 'n' Roll** A huge coral mound marks this wall dive, renowned for eagle rays, sharks, moray eels and a rainbow of sponges.

SIGHTS

The Turks & Caicos Island Tourist Board has free Heritage Walk pamphlets.

Front St

Many waterfront government building sites are weathered but retain a faded glory, notably the handsome **General Post Office**. A small plaza contains the Columbus Monument, which claims cheekily and definitively that the explorer landed here on October 12, 1492. Nearby, four large cannons point to sea. The fringing coral reef is protected within **Columbus Landfall National Park**.

The **Philatelic Bureau** displays scores of the beautiful stamps for which the Turks & Caicos are justly famous.

Some important historic buildings further north include little **St Mary's Anglican Church**, **St Thomas Anglican Church**, the pink-faced **Victoria Public Library**, **Oddfellows Lodge** and the battered **Masonic Lodge**.

Turks & Caicos National Museum (☎ 946-2160; www.tcmuseum.org; Front St; admission nonresidents US$5; ⏰ 9am-4pm Mon, Tue, Thu & Fri, 9am-6pm Wed, 9am-1pm Sat) displays eclectic miscellany exhibits of the old salt industry and of life on the coral reef. Its central exhibit is the remains of the oldest authenticated shipwreck in the Americas. A gallery upstairs contains a 3-D underwater display and local wildlife information.

Duke St

South of the heart of downtown, Duke St is lined by stone walls behind which several mansions of the wealthy have been turned into rakish little inns, notably the old Turks Head Inn (sadly now belonging to a film production company) and Salt Raker Inn.

Around Town

A century-old cast-iron **lighthouse** still blinks myopically from Northeast Point. **Corktree** and **Pillory Beaches** are good for bathing.

Lovely pine-shaded **Governor's Beach** lies 1.5 miles (2.4km) south of town, and is a popular picnic and party spot. Unfortunately, plans for cruise-ship stops may informally 'sequester' this part of the island.

Waterloo (1815) is the official Governor's residence. The island's dock is here, and the old US missile-tracking station where astronaut John Glenn was debriefed when he splashed down just off Grand Turk in 1962.

Dirt roads lead south to **White Sands Beach** for snorkelers and east to three prime **bird-**

MARINE GODS

Salt Cay, off of Grand Turk, is one of the best spots in the Caribbean to see humpback whales during the winter months. Scores of leviathans arrive to breed in the warm waters of the Silver and Mouchoir Banks, east and south of Salt Cay. They gather each January, February and March to mate and give birth in these waters. Dive outfits in Cockburn Town and Salt Cay both organize whale-watching and diving trips (see below).

watching spots: Hawkes Pond Salina, Hawkes Nest Salina, and South Creek National Park, which protects the mangroves and wetlands along the island's southeast shore.

Sun-drenched **Salt Cay** provides a picturesque vision of 19th-century life. Donkeys and wild cattle far outnumber human inhabitants, as do iguanas.The cay is a haven for diminishing numbers of green and hawksbill turtles, which come ashore to lay their eggs in the sand. Dive sites include Wanda Lust, known for its plankton-rich waters that attract whales and eagle rays; Kelly's Folly, a rolling coral garden, with hawksbill turtles, morays and parrotfish; and HMS *Endymion*, a never-salvaged, 18th-century British warship bristling with cannons and massive anchors in a coral canyon just 25ft (7.6m) down. See p55 for more on Salt Cay diving.

ACTIVITIES

There are a number of diving outfits (also offering snorkeling trips) in Cockburn and Salt Cay, testament to how many of the locals and visitors make the most of these fabulous coral reefs. Following are popular choices.

Diving & Snorkeling

Oasis Divers (☎ 946-1128; www.oasisdivers.com; Duke St) offers two-tank dives (US$70), popular night dives (US$40) and equipment rentals for reasonable rates. Ask to meet the island's two pet groupers. Packages and special excursions include trips to the wonderful Gibbs Cay, where you can also handfeed stingrays (US$50 plus diving rates).

Sea Eye Diving (☎ 946-1407; www.seaeyediving .com; Duke St) is a small outfit offering a trip to Gibbs Cay (US$50). It has two-tank (US$60) and night dives (US$45).

Salt Cay Divers (☎ 946-6906; www.saltcaydivers.tc) offers two-tank dives for US$80 and many excellent dive/stay packages. January to March the whales are in town, and its seven-night packages include whale-watching and five days' diving from US$1090; excellent value.

Sport Fishing

You're able to charter a boat for fishing from **Dutchie's** (☎ 946-2244; Airport Rd) for US$300 to US$400 per day.

For fishing events, see p117.

FESTIVALS & EVENTS

See p117 for a list of festivals and events on Grand Turk, most of which happen in and around Cockburn Town.

SLEEPING

There are a number of rental houses downtown and around the island that are particularly good for families. The owners of the Manta House have two adjacent self-contained cottages, and Dale at Oasis Divers manages another family house.

Cockburn Town

Manta House (☎ 946-1111; www.grandturk-mantahouse .com; Duke St; s/d US$70/75; ✕ ⊠) This updated guesthouse has rooms in an idyllic, old, wooden single-story home. It has polished wood floors, romantic Caribbean pastels and tasteful décor, and it's just across from a tiny beach in town, and the Sand Bar.

Around Cockburn Town

Bohio Dive Resort & Spa (☎ 946-2135; www.bo hioresort.com; Front St; s/d per 3 nights US$450/600;

AUTHOR'S CHOICE

Island House (☎ 946-1519; www.islandhou se-tci.com; PO Box 36, Grand Turk; d US$90; ℗ ✕ ⊠ ⊠) Book ahead for discounted rates, and to beat the regulars, at this attractive and relaxed Mediterranean-style whitewashed villa set on the crest of a hill. Spacious, spotless suites are comfy but include contemporary kitchens and baths. Rooms have cable TV and balconies with hammocks. Room rates include use of vehicles and free airport transfers. Beaches are a 10-minute drive from this tranquil and friendly place. Great value.

(P ✕ 🔧 🛏) This pristine and attractive beachside resort offers rooms with ocean-view balconies, as well as a top-class restaurant and a dive outfit, with diving packages. Recommended.

Salt Cay

Pirate's Hideaway Guesthouse (☎ 946-6909; www .saltcay.tc; Victoria St, Salt Cay; r US$120; ✕ 🔧) This Hansel-and-Gretel-style B&B abounds with stained glass, Haitian artwork, and murals on a pirate theme. The dark wood floors, nautical-themed baths (including shell-lined tubs) and lively tropical decor add to the character of its comfy rooms. A bar and restaurant, and balconies overlooking the sea, make this a favorite stop for many.

Trade Winds Lodge (☎ 946-6906; www.trade winds.tc; Victoria St, Salt Cay; r US$145; ✕ 🔧) This new beachside property offers weekly packages. Rooms are light, bright and comfortably furnished, and come with kitchens or kitchenettes and screened patios. The lodge also has bicycles, a barbecue and ocean views.

EATING & DRINKING

Courtyard Café (☎ 946-2666; Duke St; mains US$5-15; ☯ breakfast & lunch) This friendly café serves the best breakfast in town. The all-in omelettes are delicious and filling, and the light lunches can be enjoyed in a shady courtyard. Waffles, cinnamon rolls, and bagels are some other breakfast staples on offer.

Water's Edge (☎ 946-1680; Duke St; mains US$6-24; ☯ breakfast, lunch & dinner; 🖥) This informal restaurant-bar has the best spot in town, and makes the most of it. A wooden deck overlooks the beach, and is perfect for a yummy crab salad, Cajun snapper and cocktails.

Sand Bar (☎ 946-1111; Duke St; ☯ noon-1am) This is a small, but vibrant, bar that attracts an eclectic crowd of exgovernors, animated lawyers and passersby to sip killer rum cocktails and consume bar food on the beachside decking.

SHOPPING

Island Creations (☎ 946-1594; Duke St; ☯ 8am-5pm or 6pm) At the south end of Duke St, this small store sells beautiful hand-dyed silk slips, T-shirts and dresses.

X's Place (☎ 946-1299; Duke St; ☯ 9:30am-dark Mon-Sat) This is a trove of Haitian art and antiques, including hand-drawn maps, and carved items.

CAICOS ISLANDS

The Caicos chain is an arc comprising the islands of West Caicos, Providenciales (the main tourist gateway and hot spot), North Caicos, Middle Caicos, East Caicos, and South Caicos, as well as numerous small isles and cays.

PROVIDENCIALES
pop 8850

As recently as 1964, the island of Providenciales (colloquially called 'Provo') did not have a single wheeled vehicle. Provo is now the most developed island of the Turks & Caicos Islands and tourism is booming.

Caicos' iconic beach begins east of Turtle Cove and stretches along the north shore's 5-mile-long (8km) Grace Bay to Leeward Marina, with creamy white sand and extraordinarily aquamarine waters.

A wealth of resort hotels and residential developments are expanding along the north shore at a rate of knots. This is especially so now that seven-story buildings are permitted on the seafront, both saddening and infuriating residents and Belongers.

East of Provo, the north shore and offshore waters are protected within Princess Alexandra National Park. The south shore is a series of connecting lakes and sounds. Away from the beaches, Provo's charm lies in its western rugged hills and ridges and national parks.

Yet Caicos still has a quiet charm that makes the place a pleasure to explore, and the Belongers a delight to chat and joke with. The island's tiny cays and surrounding pockets of sparkling sea are visually and sensually stunning. They can be reached easily by chartered boat or excursion, while miles and miles of coral reefs lie temptingly close to shore. Smith's Reef, offshore from the Turtle Cove Marina, and the beach outside the Coral Gardens Hotel both offer fabulous, easy and highly rewarding snorkeling.

Orientation

The main highway, Leeward Hwy, runs east from downtown along the island's spine, ending near Bird Rock. A coastal highway, Grace Bay Rd, parallels Grace Bay.

A separate coast road runs northwest from downtown to Blue Hills and Wheeland settlements, beyond which it turns into a dirt track to Northwest Point. A fourth road runs south from downtown to Sapodilla Bay.

Information

EMERGENCY
Fire (☎ 946-4444)
Police (☎ 946-4259)

MEDICAL SERVICES
Associated Medical Practices Clinic (☎ 946-4242; Leeward Hwy) Has several private doctors. The clinic has a recompression chamber.
Provo Discount Pharmacy (☎ 946-4844; Central Sq Plaza, Leeward Hwy; ☻ 8am-10pm)

MONEY
First Caribbean (☎ 946-4245; Butterfield Sq, Leeward Hwy)
Scotiabank (☎ 946-4750; Cherokee Rd) Has a 24-hour ATM.
Western Union (☎ 946-5484; Butterfield Sq, Leeward Hwy)

POST
DHL Worldwide Express (☎ 946-4352; Butterfield Sq, Leeward Hwy)
Federal Express (☎ 946-4682; www.fedex.com; Center Complex, Leeward Hwy)
Post office (☎ 946-4676; Old Airport Rd; ☻ 8am-noon & 2-4pm Mon-Thu, 8am-12:30pm & 2-5:30pm Fri) Next to the police station.

TELEPHONE
There are public phone booths at several roadside locations. You dial ☎ 111 to place credit-card calls.
Cable & Wireless (☎ 111; PO Box 78 Leeward Hwy) Make calls here; has telephone information.

TOURIST INFORMATION
Tourist information booth (Arrivals Hall, Providenciales International Airport)
Turks & Caicos Tourism (☎ 946-4970; www.turk sandcaicostourism.com; Stubbs Diamond Plaza, Provo; ☻ 9am-5pm Mon-Fri)

Sights

Pickings for sightseers are quite slim downtown, but history buffs should check out the ruins of **Cheshire Hall** (Leeward Hwy), a plantation house constructed in the 1790s by British Loyalists.

A rugged dirt road (for 4WD vehicles only) leads from the settlement of Wheeland, northwest of downtown, to **Malcolm Roads**,

a superb 2-mile-long (3.2km) beach that's good for snorkeling and is popular with locals on weekends. Following this arduous, windy, hilly, rocky track, you're soon amid cacti, with views over the inland saline lakes.

Another dirt road leads from Crystal Bay Resorts, northwest of Wheeland, to **Northwest Point**. From there, you can walk east to a lighthouse. It's a desperate drive, with deep sand and potholes, and you shouldn't attempt it unless you have much courage and a large 4WD.

Protecting reefs off of Provo's west shore, Northwest Point Marine National Park also encompasses several saline lakes that attract breeding and migrant waterfowl. The largest is **Pigeon Pond**, inland. This part of the park is the Pigeon Pond & Frenchman's Creek Nature Reserve. Other ponds – notably **Northwest Point Pond** and **Frenchman's Creek** – encompass tidal flats and mangrove swamps along the west coast, attracting fish and fowl in large numbers. You'll have to hike here, and come equipped with food and water.

CHALK SOUND NATIONAL PARK
The waters of this 3-mile-long (5km) bay, 2 miles (3.2km) southwest of downtown, define 'turquoise.' The color is uniform: a vast, unrippled, electric-blue carpet eerily and magnificently studded with countless tiny islets.

A slender peninsula separates the sound from the sea. The peninsula is scalloped with beach-lined bays, notably **Sapodilla Bay**. A horribly potholed road runs along the peninsula; although it is accessible, drive carefully! Unfortunately, large vacation homes line both sides of the peninsula from top to toe, which clip the views and hinder some public access from the roads to the water and beaches.

At the far eastern end of the Sapodilla Bay peninsula, a rocky hilltop boasts **carvings** on slabs of rock, dating back to 1844. The slabs are intricately carved with Roman lettering that records the names of sailors apparently shipwrecked here and the dates of their sojourns. The carvings are reached via a rocky trail that begins 200yd (183m) east of the Mariner Hotel; it leads uphill 200yd (183m) to the summit, which offers wonderful views over the island and Chalk Sound.

Caicos Conch Farm (☎ 946-5643/5330; fax 946-5849; tour adult/child US$6/3; ⏰ 9am-4pm Mon-Fri, 9am-2pm Sat), close to the northeastern tip of Provo, claims to be 'the world's only conch farm.' This place is a little creepy, and is basically battery-farming the critters. Nonetheless, it is striving to protect the Caribbean queen conch from extinction by raising the mollusks commercially for export and local use. On a 20-minute tour, you can learn how conchs are grown from eggs to adults.

THE CAYS
French Cay
This tiny cay, about 15 miles (24km) due south of Provo, is an uninhabited wildlife sanctuary protecting over 2000 nesting and migrating species of birds, including frigate birds and ospreys. Stingrays gather to give birth, and nurse sharks are drawn in summer. Supposedly it is an old French pirate lair.

Day trips here include swimming and snorkeling with the 'friendly' sharks in summer, and with gentle stingrays year-round.

Little Water Cay
Northeast of Provo and separated from it by the 400yd-wide (366m) channel, Little Water Cay is a nature reserve within Princess Alexandra National Park and is the home of about 2000 endangered rock iguanas. Please don't feed or touch the iguanas. Also keep to the trails to avoid trampling their burrows and the ecologically sensitive plants. Look out for Curious Iguana, so-named for obvious reasons!

Pine Cay
Two miles (3.2km) northeast of Provo, Pine Cay is an 800-acre (324-hectare) private cay that welcomes visitors by prior arrangement. It has a small cadre of seasonal residents that includes Bill Cosby, Denzel Washington and Jimmy Buffett, who has a passion for bonefishing here.

Fort George Cay
This tiny cay, a stone's throw north of Pine Cay, is a national historic site, with the remains of an 18th-century British fort built to protect the Caicos Islands from attack. Divers and snorkelers can inspect barnacle-encrusted cannons lying on the bottom of

the ocean. The site is protected within Fort George Land & Sea National Park.

Dellis Cay
Next north in the necklace, Dellis is one of the best isles for shelling, thanks to a combination of tidal patterns and current. No shells may be taken away! Leave them for others to admire.

Activities
DIVING & SNORKELING
All the dive operators offer a range of dive and snorkel options, from introductory 'resort courses' to Professional Association of Diving Instructors (PADI) certification (US$350 to US$395).

Most offer free hotel pickup and drop-offs. Dive sites include the other Caicos islands and cays.

Art Pickering's Provo Turtle Divers (☎ 946-4232; www.provoturtledivers.com; Turtle Cove Marina), also with facilities at the Ocean Club Resort, offers two-tank/night dives for US$95/65. Tailored trips to French Cay and West Caicos are popular.

Dive Provo (☎ 946-5040; www.diveprovo.com; Ports of Call plaza, Grace Bay Rd) has two-tank/night dives (US$100/71) at sites around the island, plus photo and video services.

Big Blue (☎ 946-5034; www.bigblue.tc; Leeward Marina) organizes ecoadventure and kayaking tours on North Caicos (US$60), along with its diving trips and courses. A useful refresher course costs US$125. Two-tank dives are US$135 and the diving packages offer good value (four days of two-tank diving, US$485). Turtle Cove Inn (opposite) and Comfort Suites (p112) also have good dive packages.

SPORT FISHING & BONEFISHING
A plethora of boat charters and trips can be arranged from Leeward and Turtle Cove Marinas (see opposite). Try the following:

Catch the Wave Charters (☎ 941-3047; catchthewave@tciway.tc; Leeward Marina) runs a heap of chartered trips, from US$400/800 per half-/full day for three fishing fans, and cruisers from US$500/1050 per half-/full day for up to eight people. Yummy luxury lobster and wine picnics, and barbecues, can be provided.

Captain Barr Gardiner (☎ 946-4874; www.provo.net/bonefish) is a veteran bonefishing guide. Call to arrange a tailored half-/full-day fishing trip.

JOJO: A NATIONAL TREASURE

For more than a decade, a 7ft (2m) bottle-nosed male dolphin called JoJo has cruised the waters off of Provo and North Caicos. When he first appeared, he was shy and limited his human contact to following or playing in the bow waves of boats. He soon turned gregarious and has become an active participant whenever people are in the water. In 1995, JoJo crossed the Turks Island Passage and appeared off of Grand Turk, where he spent a month.

JoJo is now so popular that he has been named a national treasure by the Ministry of Natural Resources. JoJo even has his own warden, who studies his behavior and looks out for him as part of the **JoJo Dolphins Project** (☎ 941-5617; www.marinewildlife.org; PO Box 153, Providenciales, Turks & Caicos).

JoJo, as with any wild dolphin, interprets attempts to touch him as an aggressive act, and will react to defend himself, so please bear that in mind if you're lucky enough to experience his playfulness and companionship for a while.

TURKS & CAICOS

BOAT EXCURSIONS

J & B Tours (☎ 946-5047; www.jbtours.com; Leeward Marina) is a friendly team who runs a heap of great affordable trips to suit all tastes, budgets and ages. Offerings include a half-day trip that takes in a snorkel and visit to some protected iguanas (adult/child US$35/20) to a romantic island getaway (US$225 per couple) or glowworm cruise (adult/child US$60/40). Also available are power-boat charters (from US$675 per person), deep-sea fishing charters (from US$150 per person) and waterskiing (US$60 per person).

Undersea Explorer Semi Submarine (☎ 231-0006; www.caicostours.com; Turtle Cove Marina; adult/child US$40/30) takes you on a cruise to the reef in a boat with a glass-observatory. The observatory is 5ft (1.5m) below the waves, and was developed for Australia's Great Barrier Reef.

OTHER ACTIVITIES

Phillip Outten (☎ 941-3610; phillipoutten@tciway.tc; Venetian Rd, off Leeward Hwy), one of the island's noted artists (see p114) and a really nice chap, offers horseback rides along the beach (US$60 per 1½ hours).

Turtle Parasail (☎ 941-0643; www.captainmarvins parasail.com; Leeward Marina) offers parasailing (US$70) and banana-boat rides (US$25).

Windsurfing Provo (☎ 946-5649/241-1687; windpro@tciway.tc; Ocean Club & Ocean Club West) has windsurfing (US$25 per hour), sailing (US$90 per day) and kayaking (US$15 per hour) on offer.

Most resorts offer tennis.

Festivals & Events

See p117 for a list of festivals and events on Providenciales.

Sleeping

The majority of Provo's accommodation is in condominium complexes or pricy resorts. There are the all-inclusive holiday camps, such as Sandals and Breezes, that can save a dollar or two on food. Several dozen villas are also available for rent along Chalk Sound and the Sapodilla peninsula.

Browse the following websites: www.wherewhenhow.com, www.provo.net and www.tcimall.tc/villas. Also check the hotels' websites listed here for some great discounts.

DOWNTOWN & TURTLE COVE

Airport Inn (☎ 941-3514; fax 941-3281; Airport Plaza; r US$65-75; ✕ ✕) A perfect option if you're in transit between islands – this small inn is at the airport. It has rooms with modern decor, cable TV and phone; some have kitchenettes. It offers special rates for airline crew, and guests enjoy free rides to the beach, plus 15% off of car-rental rates.

Miramar Resort (☎ 946-4240; www.miramarresort.tc; Turtle Cove; d US$120; P ✕ ✕ ✕) Set on a hill above the Turtle Cove Marina, it is a steep walk up and down from Miramar to the area's bars and restaurants. However, the rooms are spacious, attractive and airy, with great views. All rooms come with refrigerators, cable TV and phone and Internet connection. The resort has a pool, gym, tennis court and wine-bar and a fairly gloomy restaurant.

Turtle Cove Inn (☎ 946-4203; www.turtlecovehotel.com; Turtle Cove Marina; d US$85; P ✕ ✕ ✕) Don't pay any extra here for a view of the marina;

it's not really justified. The rooms overlook a small pool and, although this place is a bit tired, it is a good budget option, set in the centre of the Turtle Cove's small bar-and-restaurant strip. There are some excellent dive packages available, too.

GRACE BAY & EAST PROVIDENCIALES

Sibonné Hotel & Beach Club (☎ 946-5547; www .sibonne.com; Grace Bay; r US$175; P ✕ 🕸 🕸) This small, romantic inn sits on the beach, and has comfortable rooms set around a garden that's strewn with hammocks and palm trees. A fabulous restaurant and bar sit adjacent to the freshwater pool and overlook the beach. The renowned Bay Bistro serves a delicately delicious grilled vegetable and brie tart, and desserts involve lots of chocolate wickedness. What else do you need other than elasticized clothes?

   Coral Gardens (☎ 941-3713; www.coralgardens .com; Grace Bay; d US$300; P ✕ 🕸 🖳 🕸) Offers huge, well-lit two-bedroom suites with king-size beds and wrap-around plate-glass windows that open to verandas over a twin-pool complex. The Whitehouse Reef – perfect for great snorkeling – is directly offshore. Because it's tucked out of the main drag of restaurants, you will need transportation.

   Sands (☎ 941-5199; www.thesandsresort.com; Grace Bay; d US$225; P ✕ 🕸 🕸) Stay in the superb modern condos at this quiet beachside resort. Sands is also blessed with the convivial

---

AUTHOR'S CHOICE

Comfort Suites (☎ 946-8888; www.comfort suitestci.com; Grace Bay; r US$150; P ✕ 🕸 🕸) Inland from the beach, this comfortable, friendly and amazingly efficient hotel is a great deal. It's central to Grace Bay's restaurants and bars, and is a shortish walk to the beach. The rooms are cheerful and spacious, and furnished with sofas, refrigerator, coffeemaker, cable TV, in-room safe and ceiling fans. A complimentary breakfast of fattening croissant and *pain au chocolat* (chocolate-filled croissant-like pastry) is served in the courtyard alongside the lively outdoor bar and small swimming pool. Good dive packages should also be checked out.

Hemingway's Bar & Restaurant; the cocktails and mango-and-shrimp salad are delicious.

Eating & Drinking

There are some lovely French influences in the Caicos restaurants, and this doesn't just mean lots of cream and butter sauces. Subtle flavorings and combinations create some imaginative menus that even vegetarians will love.

DOWNTOWN & TURTLE COVE

Banana Boat Bar & Grill (☎ 941-5706; mains US$15-18; 🕙 lunch & dinner) This atmospheric and gaily painted place, adjoining Turtle Cove Marina, serves good grilled dishes, burgers and Bahamian cooking. The nightlife is brilliant: CD night is on Thursday (bring your own along, and preferably not Leonard Cohen or The Wiggles). There's a calypso or reggae band on Friday; karaoke is on Saturday, with renditions sung to much mirth and commentary; and Bingo is on Sunday, with jackpots of up to US$15,000! The latter is a very raucous event that could possibly be the best night in town.

   Tiki Hut (☎ 941-5341; Turtle Cove Inn, mains US$10-25; 🕙 breakfast, lunch & dinner Mon-Sat) Adjoining Turtle Cove Marina, this is a good place for breakfast, but an even better place for Wednesday night's US$10 barbecue; a 13-year tradition that certainly packs out the place. Chicken, ribs or steaks are served with sautéed vegetables and with garlic-mashed potatoes so creamy they would make an Irishman cry. Buckets of beer at US$20 are guzzled by this happy crowd. Don't miss out!

   Baci Ristorante (☎ 941-3044; Harbour Towne Plaza, Turtle Cove; mains US$10-27; 🕙 lunch & dinner Tue-Fri, dinner only Sat & Sun) This cool, classy place has terracotta-tiled floors and wrought-iron furnishings, along with a bougainvillea-shaded patio. It serves some truly grand grub; blackened snapper with lemon sauce, penne with vodka-flavored chicken, and luscious chocolate pâté with crème anglaise and fruit coulis.

GRACE BAY & EAST PROVIDENCIALES

There's a heap of informal eateries at the Ports of Call plaza and along Grace Bay Rd within a five-minute walk of Comfort Suites, all with vegetarian dishes on their menus. The North Shore has some good Bahamian takeouts.

Calico Jack's (☎ 946-5120; upstairs, Ports of Call plaza; mains US$8-20; ☺ 5-10pm Sun-Fri) This lively bar and restaurant is known for its gazpacho (US$5) and yummy great-value pizza. It's the place to be on Friday night, on the outdoor deck carousing with the band and fun-loving residents.

Danny Buoy's Irish Pub and Restaurant (☎ 946-5921; Grace Bay Rd; mains US$9-15; ☺ lunch & dinner) A Celt set up this pub, and did a genuine job on it. Walk in and see the polished wooden bar, draught beers and row of bum-shined bar stools, and you would swear that you're in a misty part of boggy Ireland. That is, apart from the Becks on offer and a menu that would please an English country lord no end; bangers and mash with baked beans, fish-and-chips – oh, simple joys. Live music and quiz nights add to the fun.

Island Scoop Icecreams (☎ 241-4230; Grace Bay Plaza, Grace Bay Rd; ice cream US$3; ☺ 10am-9pm) A couple of very smart cookies are selling this lush and creamy ice cream, and gelato and sorbet, to cafés around the island. Try the wonderful mango gelato; it will coat your taste buds with sensual magic.

Coco Bistro Restaurant (☎ 946-5369; Ports of Call plaza, Grace Bay Rd; mains US$25-30; ☺ lunch & dinner) The combined tropical and rustic style of this indoor/terrace restaurant is obviously French, as is the influence on the menu. Surrounded by abundant Haitian art, choose from fresh indoor dining, or alfresco on a palm-shaded patio, plus creative dishes, such as mussels in curry and hurricane ginger shrimp.

Bambooz Bar & Grill (☎ 946-8146; Salt Mills Plaza, Grace Bay Rd; mains US$9-18; ☺ dinner) *The* hot spot. Thursday night's karaoke brings in the political and religious hoi polloi, as well as some serious crooners. The action starts at around 9pm and on weekends will go until the early hours.

Shopping

A large selection of beachy items, casual clothing and batiks is offered at **Tattooed Parrot** (☎ 946-5829), Marilyn's Crafts and the Night & Day Boutique, all in the Ports of Call plaza.

Getting There & Around

AIR
For flight information to and from the Caicos Islands, see p119.

> **AUTHOR'S CHOICE**
>
> **Grace's Cottage** (☎ 946-8147; www.point grace.com; Point Grace; mains US$26-35; ☺ lunch & dinner) The stage for possibly the finest dining in Caicos is set with an old wood-lined bar, and with intimate tables dressed in crisp white linen that sit in a courtyard among flowering shrubs. The superb dishes are unpretentious and delicious – gorgonzola and broccoli soup, grilled mango with lemon and orange duck, and chocolate soufflé. A romantic and very special meal is enhanced by professional and friendly staff.

There is no bus service from Providenciales International Airport. A taxi from the airport to Grace Bay costs US$16 one way for two people; each extra person costs US$5. Some resorts arrange their own minibus transfers.

BICYCLE
Provo Fun Cycles & Autos (☎ 946-5868; provo funcycles@tciway.tc; Ports of Call plaza) and **Scooter Bob's** (☎ 946-4684; scooter@provo.net; Turtle Cove Marina Plaza) rent out mountain bikes for US$15 per day.

BOAT
A plethora of boat charters and trips can be arranged to the islands and cays from Leeward and Turtle Cove Marinas (see p111).

BUS
Sporadic buses run routes to some of the settlements out of town. Ask at the tourist office for schedules.

CAR & MOTORCYCLE
Mandatory insurance costs US$14 and a one-off government tax is also payable. Most rental companies offer free drop-off and pickup. The local companies are also very good, and may be cheaper than the internationals. A minimum age of 25 years may be required.

Rental agencies **Hertz** (☎ 941-3910; mystique@ tciway.tc), **Avis** (☎ 946-4705; www.avistci.com) and **Budget** (☎ 946-4079) are at the airport. Hertz also has an outlet at Southern Shores Centre and Budget has an outlet at Town Centre Mall, both on Leeward Hwy.

PAINTINGS & CRAFT MEMORIES

Any art fan will love the range of original and affordable pieces of art on sale. Some are sold in local stores and hotel reception areas, starting at around US$15 for an original oil or acrylic painting. Many of these paintings are copies of original Haitian artworks, but still show real talent. Some regional stars:

» **Dwight A Outten** (☎ 941-4545; Art Provo; www.artprovo.com; Ocean Club Plaza) It obviously flows in the blood, for Dwight's flamingos, indigenous birds and island houses are similarly as catching and arguably as good as the paintings of his Rastafarian cousin Phillip Outten.

» **Phillip Outten Gallery** (☎ 941-3610; phillipoutten@tciway.tc; Venetian Rd, Leeward Hwy) Some people consider this genial Rastafarian the leading artist in the Turks & Caicos. His home – gaily painted in Rasta colors – is his gallery, and he always welcomes visitors. His best paintings are of the animals and nature he so obviously relishes.

» **Jean Taylor Gallery** (☎ 231-2708; Grace Bay Plaza, Grace Bay Rd) The gallery opens on demand only, but Taylor's unique vision of Bahamian life and humor can be seen at Art Provo (see later in this box).

» **Anna Bourne** Lives on Provo and paints on silk with French dyes. The North Caicos Art Society in Whitby (North Caicos) sponsors local art, emphasizing silk-screen painting, of which Bourne is perhaps the leading artist in the genre.

Al Vern's Craft Market sits on the side of Turquoise Rd, and is a collection of small huts selling local paintings and crafts. There are some wonderful metal carvings depicting all manner of scenes: underwater mermaids, school buses and cycling Rastafarians. Cut from old car wrecks, painted and varnished, they're truly great.

Bamboo Gallery (☎ 946-4748; www.provo.net/bamboo; Market Place, Leeward Hwy) and **Art Provo** (☎ 941-4545; www.artprovo.com; Ocean Club Plaza) are two fabulous galleries that sell many leading and local artists' vibrant works.

Provo Fun Cycles & Autos (☎ 946-5868; provo funcycles@tciway.tc; Ports of Call plaza), based across the street from Comfort Suites, is friendly and helpful, and rents out good little compact cars and 4WDs from US$45 per day and scooters for US$42. It also rents out bicycles (see p113).

Scooter Bob's (☎ 946-4684; scooter@provo.net; Turtle Cove Marina Plaza) rents out cars and 4WDs from US$60 per day and motorbikes from US$50 per day. It also rents out bicycles (see p113) and snorkeling gear (US$10 per day).

Tropical Auto Rentals (☎ 946-5300; tropical@ tciway.tc; Ocean Club Plaza, Grace Bay) charges from US$65 for compacts and from US$76 for 4WD hire.

TAXI

There are several taxi companies that mainly use minivans. Allow plenty of time, as they often take ages to arrive. You can call VHF channel 06 for the dispatcher, or contact the following companies:

Nell's Taxi Service (☎ 941-3228)
Provo Taxi & Bus Group (☎ 946-5481)

NORTH CAICOS

pop 2075

Little-visited North Caicos appeals to eco-tourists. It gets more rainfall than other islands and hence has more lush vegetation. Traditionally the bread basket of the island chain, in the last century it was also the seat of government for these islands. Farms evolved in colonial times and sloops were built to transport crops to the other islands. Mangoes, oranges, and other fruits and vegetables still thrive beside sea grapes and sugar apples.

There are four tiny settlements; notably Kew, near the island's center, and Bottle Creek, on a breezy coastal bluff 2 miles (3.2km) south of the airport.

North Caicos hosts the **Festarama Festival** each July. This annual regatta includes beach parties and the Miss Festarama Beauty Pageant. In October, the **North Caicos Extravaganza** features a Junkanoo carnival (for details on Junkanoo, see the boxed text in the Bahamas chapter, p72) and Miss Extravaganza beauty contest.

Information

There's a post office in Kew, and Bottle Creek has a small public library. Fax and email service is available in the office of **Papa Grunt's Seafood Restaurant** (☎ 946-7113), adjoining Jo Anne's B&B. The nearest hospital is in Provo (p109). In an emergency, dial ☎ 999 or ☎ 911.

Government clinic Bottle Creek (☎ 946-7194); Kew (☎ 946-7397)

Police Bottle Creek (☎ 946-7116); Kew (☎ 946-7261)

Sights & Activities

The Kew area has several historic ruins, including the interesting **Wades Green Plantation**, granted to a British Loyalist by King George III. The owners struggled to grow sisal and Sea Island cotton until drought, hurricanes and bugs drove them out. The plantation lasted a mere 25 years; the owners abandoned their slaves and left.

Beaches include **Pumpkin Bluff**, **Horsestable** and most importantly, **Whitby Beach**. On any one, yours will be the only Robinson Crusoe footprints. Pumpkin Bluff beach is especially beautiful and the snorkeling is good, with a foundered cargo ship adding to the allure.

Cottage Pond, a 150ft-deep (45.7m) blue hole on the northwest coast, attracts waterfowl such as West Indian whistling ducks, grebes and waders. Bellfield Landing Pond, Pumpkin Bluff Pond and Dick Hill Creek also attract flamingos, as does a large brine lake, **Flamingo Pond**, which floods the center of the island. Here the gangly birds strut around in hot pink. The ponds are protected as individual nature reserves.

A series of small cays off the northeast shore are protected within **East Bay Islands National Park**, and a trio of cays to the northwest form **Three Mary Cays National Park**, another flamingo sanctuary and an osprey nesting site. The **snorkeling** is good at Three Mary Cays and further west at Sandy Point Beach.

Vast bonefish flats extend east of the island. The entire south shore is encompassed by the **Ramsar Site** sanctuary, comprised of a vast series of marsh and intertidal wetlands. It extends to East Caicos, and protects an important breeding site and nursery for waterfowl, lobster, conch and fish.

The creeks are full of schooling bonefish and tarpon.

Sleeping & Eating

The best website displaying the island's accommodation and rentals is www.tcimall.tc. You will also find links to the following options.

Pelican Beach Hotel (☎ 946-7112; www.pelican beach.tc; ✗) The spacious, modestly furnished oceanfront rooms here have wood-paneled walls, tiled floors, and patios with lounge chairs. The private baths are small, but enhanced by hand-painted motifs. There are no telephones or TVs. Breakfasts, sandwich lunches and dinner meals are prepared on request.

There's also a friendly little bar and restaurant, and good local dishes include the freshest of grilled fish and the ubiquitous peas 'n' rice (mains US$12 to US$25).

Ocean Beach Hotel/Condominium (☎ 946-7113; www.turksandcaicos.tc/oceanbeach.com; s/d US$115/130) This nice little place has a homey feel, and all the rooms are on the beachfront with patios. Light rattan furniture adds to the bright atmosphere. An on-site restaurant and bar serves meals on request. Fishing charters are available, and children under 12 stay free.

Jo Anne's Bed & Breakfast (☎ 946-7184; www .turksandcaicos.tc/joannesbnb.com; r US$90; ✗) This is modest accommodation with an adjoining restaurant. The beach is a short walk away. Jo Anne also offers a courtesy van service. Better outfitted and larger villas are available.

Papa Grunt's Seafood Restaurant (☎ 946-7113; mains US$6-8; ✗ breakfast, lunch & dinner) Dinners are by reservation at Jo Anne's no-frills diner (which adjoins the restaurant). Seafood rules, although the fare includes pizza, sandwiches and burgers.

You can buy produce and groceries at KH's Food Store in Whitby and at Al's Grocery in Bottle Creek.

Getting There & Around

AIR

For information on getting to/from the island, see p119.

A taxi from the airport to Whitby costs US$10, one way. Mac of **M&M Tours** (☎ 946-7338) offers island tours for US$30 per hour. You won't need more than three hours to see the entire island.

BICYCLE

You can rent bicycles at Whitby Plaza for (US$20) per day.

BEST OF THE REST

The following islands have some truly terrific displays of natural wealth that would appeal to those seeking extraordinary diving experiences as well as landlubbers who enjoy a good trek or two. Historical ruins and a healthy bird population are simply the icing on the cake.

West Caicos is currently undergoing development, but is renowned for its diving. The **Molasses Reef** harbors the remains of the oldest known shipwreck in the western hemisphere, dating from 1513. The reefs off of the west shore are protected within **West Caicos Marine National Park**. Other prime sites include **Elephant Ear Canyon**, named for the biggest sponges found in the Turks & Caicos, at 95ft (29m). Inland, **Lake Catherine** is a nature reserve that attracts flamingos, ospreys, ducks and waders.

Middle Caicos seems to have been heavily populated in ancient times by Lucayan Indians. There are at least 38 pre-Columbian Lucayan sites on the island, many of which have been excavated by archaeologists. The island boasts miles of beaches, large freshwater lakes and lavish pine forests accessed by 10 miles (16km) of trails along the north coast, created in conjunction with the Turks & Caicos National Trust as part of the Ramsar Site. The historic **Crossing Over Trail** leads from Middle to North Caicos. En route, it passes the ruins of several Loyalist cotton plantations, as well as brine pools favored by cranes and flamingos. The north coast is dramatically scenic, with long sandy beaches and scalloped bays held in the cusps of rugged limestone cliffs. **Conch Bar Caves National Park** protects 15 miles (24km) of underground caverns. Some have lagoons and stalactites and stalagmites. Most have colonies of bats. They were used as sacred sanctuaries by the Lucayan Indians, who left petroglyphs on the walls. The most notable Lucayan site is the **Armstrong Pond Village Historical Site**.

East Caicos is the least visited island. You'll often hear it called 'uninhabited,' although there's an impoverished settlement of Haitians. It's home to small herds of wild cattle and flocks of flamingos flaunting their neon-pink liveries. There are miles of beaches perfect for the adventurous beachcomber.

South Caicos is the smallest Caicos island. First impressions are of an arid wasteland and forlorn, sand-blasted streets roamed by wild horses and donkeys, but a reef and wall run the length of the east coast. You're sure to see plenty of eagle rays, Atlantic rays, blacktip sharks and – the highlight – humpback whales in January and February. Flamingos inhabit the vast salinas on the northeast edge of Cockburn Harbour; about 70 are resident year-round. And the **Annual Commonwealth Regatta** is held on South Caicos each May.

CAR

Car rental costs around US$80 per day. Try the following options:

Gardiners (☎ 946-7141)
Old Nick (☎ 946-7280)

DIRECTORY

Information listed in this directory is specific to the Turks & Caicos Islands. For information pertaining to the entire region, check the book's main Directory (p757).

ACCOMMODATIONS

Refer to the Bahamas Directory (p94) for further information on accommodation.

The **Turks & Caicos Hotel Association** (www.tci mall.tc/tcresorts) has a useful website, while the following agencies arrange villa rentals:

Coldwell Banker (☎ 946-4969; fax 946-8969)
Grace Bay Realty (☎ 941-4105; info@gracebay realty.com)
Prestigious Properties (☎ 946-4379; www .prestigiousproperties.com)
Turks & Caicos Realty (☎ 946-4474; www.tcrealty.com)

ACTIVITIES

The most popular activities are diving and snorkeling, fishing and boating.

In Caicos, a two-tank dive typically costs US$95 to US$100 and a half-day snorkeling trip is around US$65. Fishing can cost

EMERGENCY NUMBERS

Ambulance ☎ 911
Fire ☎ 911
Police ☎ 91

US$400 to US$800 per half-/full day, while windsurfing is US$25 per hour.

A two-tank dive in the Turks typically costs from US$60 to US$80 and snorkeling around US$50 per half-day. Fishing is around US$300 to US$400 per half-/full day.

BOOKS

The Turks & Caicos Islands – Beautiful by Nature by Julia and Phil Davies is a beautiful coffee-table book.

Water and Light by Stephen Harrigan is a splendid memoir by a Texan who 'followed his bliss' and spent several months diving off of Grand Turk.

The Turks & Caicos Islands: Land of Discovery by Amelia Smithers covers the history and idiosyncrasies of these charming islands.

Charles Palmer, a 'Belonger,' as those born on the islands describe themselves, depicts island living and the changes from the early 1950s to the current day in *Living in the Turks & Caicos Islands: From Conch to the Florida Lottery*.

Red Cross Cookbook, published by the Red Cross (as a fundraiser), is sold in the Turks & Caicos. It's a fabulous collection of Caribbean recipes and a bargain at US$10.

CHILDREN

See the Bahamas Directory (p95) for information about traveling with kids.

EMBASSIES & CONSULATES

There are no foreign embassies or consulates in the Turks & Caicos. Contact the relevant officials in Nassau, New Providence.

As a British Crown colony, the Turks & Caicos are represented through British embassies and consulates abroad. There are also British Consulates-General in US cities:

Australia (☎ 02-6270-6666; fax 02-6237-3236; British High Commission, Commonwealth Ave, ACT 2600)

Canada (☎ 514-866-5863; montreal@britainincanada .org; Consulate-General, 1000 De La Gauchetiere St W, Ste 4200, Montreal, Quebec H3B 4W5)

France (☎ 01-44-51-31-00; fax 01-44-51-41-27; British Embassy, 35, rue du Faubourg St Honore, 75383 Paris Cedex 08)

USA San Francisco (☎ 415-617-1300; fax 415-434-2018; British Consulate General, 1 Sansome St, Ste 850, San Francisco, CA 94104); Washington (☎ 202-588-7800; British Embassy, 3100 Massachusetts Ave NW, Washington, DC 20008)

FESTIVALS & EVENTS

Contact **Turks & Caicos Tourism** (☎ 946-4970; www .turksandcaicostourism.com; Stubbs Diamond Plaza, Providenciales) for further details.

South Caicos Regatta (late May) The oldest sea races on the islands receive loud support by merrymaking friends and family on land.

Jags McCartney Relays (May) Grand Turk celebrates this month with events that tax the body and celebrates the islands' culture.

Conch Carnival (June) From night dives and beach bonfires to island music, dancing and kayak races, this four-day funfest on Grand Turk has something for everyone.

Queen's Official Birthday Celebration (June) Features the police marching band playing with jingoistic fervor.

Summerjam (late June) This two-day event on Grand Turk has live bands, beauty contests and general festivities.

Caicos Classic Fishing Tournament (July) This challenge pits man against fish in a popular Provo sporting event.

PRACTICALITIES

▪ **Newspapers & Magazines** There are two newspapers in the Turks & Caicos: the biweekly *Free Press* and the weekly *Turks & Caicos News*.

▪ **Radio & TV** The official Turks & Caicos government radio station is Radio Turks & Caicos (106FM) on Grand Turk. There are several private stations. For contemporary light rock, try 92.5FM; country and western 90.5FM; easy listening 89.3FM; and classical music 89.9FM. WPRT at 88.7FM is a religious and public announcement channel, as is WIV at 96.7FM. Multichannel satellite TV is received from the USA and Canada. The islands have one private TV station.

▪ **Video Systems** VHS is the standard, and tapes can be purchased from photo supply shops.

▪ **Electricity** Hotels operate on 110V (60 cycles), as per the USA and Canada. Plug sockets are two- or three-pin US standard.

▪ **Weights & Measures** The British Imperial and metric systems are both in use. Liquids are generally measured in pints, quarts and gallons, and weight in grams, ounces and pounds.

Provo Summer Festival (July & August) The archipelago's biggest bash is held on Provo and features regattas, float parades, partying and a 'Miss Turks & Caicos Beauty Pageant' that garners noisy input from everyone. These lively events are spread over a week around Emancipation Day.

Grand Turk Game Fishing Tournament (end July/early August) Fish quiver and men quake during this annual event.

Ripsaw Music Festival (August) Rake 'n' Scrape musicians from across the Turks & Caicos gather on Grand Turk to make your toes tap.

Marathon Run (December) The huffers and puffers run with the sleek and oiled across Grand Turk.

Christmas Tree Lighting Ceremony (mid-December) Grand Turk hosts this special event for kids of all ages.

HOLIDAYS

Turks & Caicos national holidays:

New Year's Day January 1
Commonwealth Day March 13
Good Friday Friday before Easter
Easter Monday Monday after Easter
National Heroes' Day May 29
Her Majesty The Queen's Official Birthday June 14 (or nearest weekday)
Emancipation Day August 1
National Youth Day September 26
Columbus Day October 13
International Human Rights Day October 24
Christmas Day December 25
Boxing Day December 26

INTERNET RESOURCES

North Caicos (www.northcaicos.tc) From maps, hotel links and boating charts to where to buy stamps, this site contains much practical information about the island.

Provo.net (www.provo.net) This site concentrates on the tourism aspects of Providenciales and provides some good links to the island's activities.

TCI Online (http://milk.tciway.tc/) A good place to start, with general information about the islands, news and events updated on a weekly basis.

TCIReservations (www.tcireservations.com) A fairly straightforward booking service for many of the mainstream hotels across the islands.

Turks & Caicos Hotel Association (www.tcimall .tc/tcresorts) Information about the association's member hotels with direct links.

Turks & Caicos Islands Gateways (www.tcimall.tc) Hosts businesses involved in the islands' travel and tourism industry as well as community information.

Turks & Caicos Islands Tourist Board (www .turksandcaicostourism.com) The official site of the Turks & Caicos tourism bods and not a bad place to start some research.

MONEY

The Turks & Caicos are unique as a British-dependent territory with the US dollar as its official currency. The treasury also issues a Turks & Caicos crown and quarter. There are no currency restrictions on the amount of money that visitors can bring in.

The country is pricey. Credit cards are readily accepted on Provo and Grand Turk, as are traveler's checks. Elsewhere, you may need to operate on a cash-only basis. Foreign currency can be changed at banks in Provo and Grand Turk, which can also issue credit-card advances and has ATMs. Major credit cards are widely accepted in Caicos and Grand Turk. Credit cards are *not* widely accepted for small transactions in the more remote cays and islands.

International Transfers

If you find yourself in need an emergency cash injection, you can arrange a telegraphic or mail transfer from your account in your home country.

Western Union Grand Turk (☎ 946-2324; Dots Enterprises, Pond St); Providenciales (☎ 941-5484; Town Centre Mall)

Traveler's Checks

Traveler's checks are accepted in Caicos and Grand Turk, but you may be charged a transaction fee of 5%.

TELEPHONE

Phone calls can be made from **Cable & Wireless** (☎ 1800-804-2994), which operates a digital network from its offices in Grand Turk and Provo. Direct dial is standard.

Public phone booths are located throughout the islands. Many booths require phone cards (see opposite).

Hotels charge US$1 per local call, and some also charge for unanswered calls after the receiving phone has rung five times.

Following are some useful telephone numbers:

Local operator (☎ 0)
Directory Assistance (☎ 118)
International Operator Assistance (☎ 115)

Cell (Mobile) Phones

American cell phones can work here, as long as you register with Cable & Wireless 'call roaming' service. Cell phones can be rented from around US$10 per day.

Phone Cards

Phone cards cost US$5, US$10 or US$15, and can be bought from Cable & Wireless outlets, as well as from shops and delis.

You can also bill calls to your Amex, Discover, MasterCard or Visa card by dialing ☎ 1-800-744-7777 on any touchtone phone and giving the operator your card details (there's a one-minute minimum).

Phone Codes

The Turks & Caicos country code is ☎ 649. To call from North America, dial ☎ 1-649 + the local number. From elsewhere, dial your country's international access code + ☎ 649 + the local number. For interisland calls, dial the seven-digit local number. We've included only the seven-digit local number in Turks & Caicos listings in this chapter.

TOURIST INFORMATION
Local Tourist Offices

Cockburn Town (☎ 946-2321; www.turksandcaicos tourism.com; Front St, Cockburn Town, Grand Turk)

Providenciales (☎ 946-4970; www.turksandcaicos tourism.com; Stubbs Diamond Plaza, Providenciales)

Tourist Offices Abroad

Canada (☎ 613-332-6470; rwilson@northcom.net; 29620 Hwy 62N RR#2, Bancroft, Ontario K0L 1C0)

UK (☎ 0181-350-1000; fax 0181-350-1011; 66 Abbey Rd, Bush Hill Park, Enfield, Middlesex EN12RQ)

USA (☎ 800-241-0824; tcitrsm@bellsouth.net; 2715 E Oakland Park Blvd, Ste 101, Ft Lauderdale FL33306)

VISAS

No visas are required for citizens of the US, Canada, UK and Commonwealth countries, Ireland and most Western European countries. Citizens from elsewhere require visas, which can be obtained from British representation abroad (see p117).

TRANSPORTATION

GETTING THERE & AWAY
Entering Turks & Caicos

All visitors need a valid passport; US citizens see the boxed text, p772. Proof of onward transportation is required upon entry.

Air

There are three airports handling international traffic to Grand Turk and Provo, but most international flights arrive at Provo. Other islands have local airstrips.

Providenciales International Airport (PLS; ☎ 941-5670)

Grand Turk International Airport (GDT; ☎ 946-2233)

South Caicos International Airport (XSC; ☎ 946-4255)

Air Turks & Caicos (☎ 941-5481; www.airturksand caicos.com; hub Caicos), the national carrier, has a very good safety record, and flies to Miami, USA, and Nassau, Bahamas.

The following airlines fly to and from Turks & Caicos from within the Bahamas:

Bahamasair (☎ 941-3136; www.bahamasair.com; hub Nassau)

Air Jamaica (☎ 1-800-523-5585; www.airjamaica.com; hub Montego Bay)

GETTING AROUND
Air

Following are airlines flying within the Turks & Caicos:

Air Turks & Caicos (☎ 941-5481; www.airturksand caicos.com; hub Providenciales) Fly from Providenciales to Grand Turk six times daily, North Caicos three times daily, Middle Caicos four times per week, and Salt Cay daily. It also flies from Grand Turk to Salt Cay daily.

Skyking (☎ 941-5464; wwwskyking.tc; hub Providenciales) Flies from Providenciales to South Caicos three times daily, Grand Turk eight times daily and from Grand Turk to South Caicos three times daily.

Bicycle

Cycling is a cheap, convenient, healthy, environmentally sound and above all *fun* way to travel. Bicycles can be rented from many hotels and concessions for around US$20 per day.

Boat

A ferry runs bi-weekly trips from Grand Turk to Salt Cay (US$12, round-trip). Contact **Salt Cay Charters** (☎ 231-6663; piratequeen3@ hotmail.com). Whale-watching boat trips with this company cost US$75.

Bus

Public bus services are limited to a few jitney routes in Provo. Check with the tourist information for regular routes.

Car, Motorcycle & Scooter

Because local transportation is limited, renting a car makes sense if you plan to explore

Provo or Grand Turk. Rentals are around US$80 per day.

Be aware that groups of donkeys, horses, dogs and chickens are likely to stroll at will on and off the roads, so drive slowly, especially around bends!

If you don't rent a car, stick to taxis (expensive) or bicycles for 'scooting' around locally. A government tax of US$15 is levied on car rentals (US$8 on scooter rentals). Mandatory insurance costs US$15.

Driving is on the left-hand side. At roundabouts (traffic circles), remember to circle in a clockwise direction, entering to the left, and give way to traffic already on the roundabout.

Speed limits in the Turks & Caicos are 20mph (around 32km/h) in settlements and 40mph (around 65km/h) on main highways.

Please refer to island destinations for rental companies.

DRIVER'S LICENSE

To rent a car, citizens of the US, Canada, and the UK and Commonwealth countries are required to have a valid driver's license for stays of up to three months. Everyone else requires an International Driving Permit. You must get this permit before you arrive on the Turks & Caicos Islands.

FUEL

Gas stations are plentiful and usually open from 8am to 7pm. Some close on Sunday. Gasoline costs US$3.50 per US gallon. Credit cards are accepted in major settlements. Elsewhere, it's cash only, please!

Taxi

Taxis are available on all the inhabited islands. Most are minivans. They're a good bet for touring, and most taxi drivers double as guides. Be sure to negotiate an agreeable price before setting out.

Cuba

Coconut palms sway in the breeze. The batik-blue water shimmers, and the aroma of freshly grilled snapper wafts down the beach. Suddenly, another cocktail arrives, and the band swings into a number that liquefies hips, distracting you from your snorkel, swim or lunch conundrum. Welcome to Cuba: the picture-perfect idyll.

The driver of a '53 Ford lays on his horn and the *Godfather* theme rings out. A dangerously overflowing bus rumbles past a 'Socialism or Death' billboard while you brush off yet another hustler selling black-market Cohibas. 'Again with the cigars!' you think, watching a guy with a pierced eyebrow and Che tattoo helping an arthritic lady to the bread line. Welcome to Cuba: where contradictions are rife.

Anyone claiming to have Cuba all figured out (and you'll meet many) is either confused or mistaken. Sure, the stereotypes are mostly true – the glorious beaches and erotic nights, slogans on every corner and rum-filled parties until dawn. And the US embargo and other difficulties are daily topics of conversation and consternation. But you can spend a lifetime uncovering the nuances – that's precisely why travelers can't stay away, discovering firsthand what makes this enigmatic island tick.

CUBA

FAST FACTS

- **Area** 42,803 sq miles (110,860 sq km)
- **Capital** City of Havana
- **Country code** ☎ 53
- **Departure tax** CUC$25, cash only
- **Famous for** Cigars, Fidel Castro, salsa
- **Language** Spanish
- **Money** Cuban Convertible Peso (CUC$) and Cuban pesos (CUP; also known as *moneda nacional*, MN). CUC$1 = US$0.90 = €0.77 = UK £0.53 = CUP26
- **Official name** Republic of Cuba
- **People** Cubans
- **Phrases** Qué bolá *(asere)?* (what's up (brother)?); *ciao/ciaocito* (goodbye/bye)
- **Population** 11.2 million
- **Visa** All visitors require a tourist card (CUC$25), which is issued with your plane ticket

CUBA

HOW MUCH?

Room in casa particular CUC$20 to CUC$25

Dinner in casa particular CUC$7

Cross-country bus CUC$51

Concert ticket CUC$10

Internet per hour CUC$6

LONELY PLANET INDEX

Liter of gas CUC$0.80 to CUC$0.95

1.5L bottled water CUC$0.70

Bottle of Bucanero or Cristal CUC$1

Souvenir T-shirt CUC$7

Street snack: pizza CUP7

HIGHLIGHTS

Havana (p127) Experience history, art, architecture, steamy nightlife and an unforgettable street scene in this sensuous city by the sea.

Viñales (p145) Explore some of Cuba's most alluring countryside with rock climbing, horseback riding, caves and a seemingly endless choice of accommodations.

Baracoa (p169) Fall for the charms of Cuba's first city, with intriguing side trips to secluded beaches, waterfalls, caves with freshwater pools, and long miles of hiking trails.

Santiago de Cuba (p162) Immerse yourself in the 'cradle of the revolution,' loaded with history, music and dance, plus scads of interesting nearby sights that can consume an entire vacation.

María la Gorda (p147) With cocktail in hand and hammock gently swinging, chill out at Cuba's very remote, paradisiacal beach, where the scuba diving is tops.

ITINERARIES

One week One week will be gobbled up in and around Havana: the Capitolio, Habana Vieja, museums galore, Plaza de la Revolución, the Malecón, music, dancing and baseball, plus side trips to Playas del Este or Varadero.

Two weeks Have fun with the one-week itinerary above, followed by Viñales, the Che memorial in Santa Clara, en route to Remedios and Cayo Santa María or Trinidad and Playa Ancón.

Three weeks Follow the two-week itinerary, then head east for three days to Santiago de Cuba and then spend another three days exploring around Baracoa.

One month Follow the three-week itinerary, but take the time at explorer pace, with hiking thrown in: Topes de Collantes or Parque Nacional Alejandro de Humboldt.

CLIMATE & WHEN TO GO

There is no bad time to go to Cuba, though July and August are unbelievably hot and room prices jump by 20%. Overbooking can be a problem during Christmas and Easter, which are also peak travel times. Hurricane season (June to November) can dampen spirits and evacuate coastal towns. Festivals happen all year round (see p174).

HISTORY
European Arrivals

Cuba has a history of foreigners meddling, beginning with the invading Arawaks and continuing today with the US embargo and possession of the Guantánamo Naval Base.

When Christopher Columbus neared Cuba on October 27, 1492, he described it as 'the most beautiful land human eyes have ever seen.' Spanish conquistadors, led by Diego Velázquez de Cuéllar, agreed: they came, they saw, they conquered and enslaved – despite resistance by indigenous chiefs Hatuey and Guamá. The inhumane treatment, plus diseases such as smallpox, decimated the native population, and by 1550 only about 5000 survivors remained from a population of around 120,000. The Spanish then turned to enslaving Africans.

By the 1820s, Cuba was the world's largest sugar producer and the US was sweet on it. So important was Cuban sugar, that the US offered – twice – to buy Cuba from Spain. The slave trade continued furiously and by the 1840s there were some 400,000 Africans in Cuba, forever altering the country's makeup.

The Road to Independence

Fed up with the Spanish power structure, landowners plotted rebellion. On October 10, 1868, sugar baron Carlos Manuel de Céspedes launched the uprising at La

CUBA

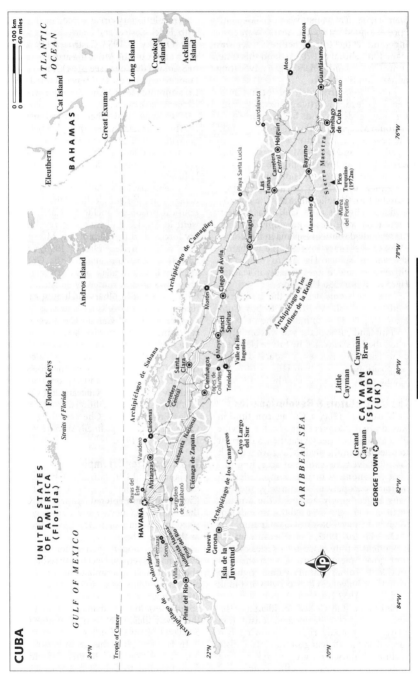

Demajagua. This First War of Independence extended into a Ten Years' War, costing some 200,000 lives before a pact was signed in February 1878. Around this time, some Cuban landowners began advocating annexation by the US.

Enter José Martí. Poet, patriot and independence leader, Martí organized feverishly for independence and, having convinced Antonio Maceo and Máximo Gómez to lead the revolution, landed in eastern Cuba in April 1895: on May 19, Martí was shot and killed. Hero and martyr, his life and legacy have inspired generations of Cubans.

Gómez and Maceo stormed west in a scorched-earth policy that left the country in flames. By this time, Cuba was a mess: thousands were dead, including Antonio Maceo, killed south of Havana in December 1896. On February 15, 1898, the US battleship *Maine,* sent to Havana to 'protect US citizens,' exploded unexpectedly in Havana Harbor, killing 266 US sailors.

After the *Maine* debacle, the US scrambled for control, even trying to buy Cuba again (for US$300 million). The only important land battle of the war was on July 1, when the US Army, led by future US president Theodore Roosevelt, attacked Spanish positions on San Juan Hill (p166). The Spaniards surrendered on July 17, 1898.

The US, Dictators & Revolutionaries

In November 1900, a Cuban constitution was drafted. Connecticut senator Orville Platt attached a rider giving the US the right to intervene militarily in Cuba whenever it saw fit. Given the choice of accepting this Platt Amendment or remaining under US military occupation indefinitely, the Cubans begrudgingly accepted the amendment; in 1903, the US used the amendment to grab the naval base at Guantánamo.

On May 20, 1902, Cuba became an independent republic, led by a series of corrupt governments, starting with the first president, Tomás Estrada Palma, right up to dictator Fulgencio Batista, who first took power in a 1933 coup.

Batista was duly elected president in 1940, when he drafted a democratic constitution guaranteeing many rights. Following two corrupt and inefficient governments, Batista positioned himself for a comeback, and on March 10, 1952, staged another coup.

A revolutionary circle formed in Havana, with Fidel Castro and many others at its core. On July 26, 1953, Castro led 119 rebels in an attack on the Moncada army barracks in Santiago de Cuba (see p164). The assault failed when a patrol 4WD encountered Castro's motorcade, costing the attackers the element of surprise.

Castro and a few others escaped into the nearby mountains, where they planned their guerrilla campaign. Soon after, Castro was captured and stood trial; he received a 15-year sentence on Isla de Pinos (now Isla de la Juventud).

In February 1955, Batista won the presidency in fraudulent elections and freed all political prisoners, including Castro, who went to Mexico and trained a revolutionary force called the 26th of July Movement ('M-26-7'). On December 2, 1956, Castro and 81 companions alighted the *Granma* at Playa Las Coloradas in the Oriente. The group was quickly routed by Batista's army, but Castro and 11 others (including Argentine doctor Ernesto 'Che' Guevara, Fidel's brother Raúl, and Camilo Cienfuegos) escaped into the Sierra Maestra.

In May of the next year, Batista sent 10,000 troops into the mountains to liquidate Castro's 300 guerrillas. By August, the rebels had defeated this advance and captured a great quantity of arms. Che Guevara and Camilo Cienfuegos opened additional fronts in Las Villas Province, with Che capturing Santa Clara. Batista's troops finally surrendered on December 31, 1958.

The Revolution Triumphs

On January 1, 1959, Batista fled, taking with him US$40 million in government funds. Castro's column entered Santiago de Cuba that night and Guevara and Cienfuegos arrived in Havana on January 2. And the rest, as they say, is history.

The revolutionary government immediately enacted rent and electricity reductions, abolished racial discrimination and nationalized all holdings over 400 hectares, infuriating Cuba's largest landholders (mostly US companies). Many Cubans also protested at the new policies: between 1959 and 1970, 500,000 Cubans said *adios.*

In January 1961, the US broke off diplomatic relations and banned US citizens from traveling to Cuba. On April 17, 1961, some 1400 CIA-trained émigrés attacked Cuba, landing at Playa Girón and Playa Larga in the Bahía de Cochinos (Bay of Pigs). The US took a drubbing.

After this defeat the US declared a full trade embargo *(bloqueo)* in June 1961. In April 1962, Khrushchev installed missiles in Cuba, sparking the Cuban Missile Crisis and bringing the world to the brink of nuclear war. Six days later, only after receiving a secret assurance from Kennedy that Cuba would not be invaded, Khrushchev ordered the missiles be dismantled. Cuba was excluded from the deal-making.

Marked by inconsistency and bureaucracy, the Cuban economy languished despite massive injections of Soviet aid. Conversely, educational advances were rapid fire, particularly the 1961 literacy campaign that taught every Cuban to read and write. Meanwhile, Cuba started supporting revolutionary efforts in Latin America and Africa. In November 1966, Guevara launched a guerrilla campaign in Bolivia. Unfortunately, the Cuban model didn't translate well to Bolivia, and US-backed Bolivian troops captured Guevara on October 8, 1967, killing him the following day.

The Wall Falls & the Special Period

When the Eastern bloc collapsed in 1989, US$5 billion in annual trade and credits to Cuba vanished, forcing President Castro to declare a five-year *período especial* (special period) austerity program, technically ongoing. Rationing and rolling blackouts were instituted and food was scarce. Cubans share their survivor stories of this time willingly.

In August 1993, the US dollar was legalized to provide a fast cash injection. Class differences re-emerged as people with dollars gained access to goods and services not available in CUP; touts and prostitutes known as *jineteros/as* (jockeys) reappeared.

When it comes to sore subjects, US immigration policy runs a close second to the embargo. The Cuban Adjustment Act (1966) grants residency to any Cuban arriving on US shores. This has sparked immigration crises, including the Mariel boatlift in 1980 when 125,000 people left and the 1994 *balsero* crisis when some 35,000 people on makeshift rafts struggled across the Florida Straits, many died.

Cold War Redux

George W Bush has rolled back US policy to resemble the worst of the Cold War years: 70% of 'legal' travel – by students, athletes, scientists, etc – to Cuba was eliminated; 14 Cuban diplomats were expelled from the US; and the chief of the US Interests Section in Havana, James Cason, began organizing dissident groups throughout Cuba. More than 70 dissidents connected to Cason were arrested in Cuba in 2003 for 'conspiring with enemies of the state,' and sentenced to varying jail terms. Though some have since been released, the arrests were criticized by Human Rights Watch and former US president Jimmy Carter, who visited Cuba in 2002, the first president to visit since Calvin Coolidge in 1928. In April 2003, Cuba was elected to the UN Human Rights Commission.

In 2004, Cuba withdrew dollars from circulation, and switched over to *peso convertibles* (convertible pesos or CUCs), a nationally produced hard currency. Dollars were – and still are – taxed at 10%, injecting cash into the strapped economy. In April 2005, the economy got another shot of fiscal steroids when all hard currencies began to be taxed by 8%, including US dollars, so that greenbacks are now taxed at 18% in relation to CUCs (ouch!). Major trade deals signed with Venezuela and China provide hope for the future.

In May 2004, the White House released its plan for the transition to democracy in Cuba.

THE CULTURE

In Cuba, money is a consuming topic because hard currency rules: there are places you can go and things you can buy with CUCs but not with CUP. This double economy has reinvigorated the class system that the revolution has worked to neutralize, and the re-emergence of haves and have-nots is among the most ticklish issues confronting Cuba today. The double economy is also one of the most confounding issues facing many travelers; romance is the other. Unfortunately, they're often intertwined as relationships with foreigners are considered a cash cow.

Though housing is free, acute shortages mean even four generations may live under one roof. This cramps love lives and Cubans will tell you it's why the country has one of the world's highest divorce rates.

Most homes don't have a phone or computer, infinitesimally few have Internet access, and disposable income – disposable anything – is an oxymoron. All of these issues has a huge effect on lifestyle and you'll notice are the topic of many conversations as you travel around.

ARTS
Music

Son or salsa: thanks to the tremendous success of bands like Los Van Van and the Buena Vista Social Club phenomenon, most of the world equates Cuban music with one of these forms. Nevertheless the global vernacular heavily influences Cuban music.

Son was originally played by a guitar, tres (a Cuban guitar with three sets of double strings), double bass, bongo and two singers who played the maracas and claves (sticks that tap out the beat). Respected founders of son include Ñico Saquito, Trio Matamoros and Arsenio Rodríguez.

In the 1940s and '50s, son bands grew, playing rumba, chachachá (cha-cha) and mambo. The reigning mambo king was Benny Moré (1919–63), known as 'El Bárbaro del Ritmo' (The Barbarian of Rhythm). You will still hear his voice floating out from bars.

Jazz, considered music of the enemy in the revolution's most dogmatic days, has always seeped into Cuban sounds. Jesus 'Chucho' Valdés' band Irakere, formed in 1973, broke the Cuban music scene wide open with its heavy Afro-Cuban drumming laced with jazz and son.

Hip-hop and rap are taking the younger generation by storm. Groups like Obsession and Anónimo Consejo perform regularly and everyone comes out for the Havana Hip Hop Cuban Rap Festival in August (see p174). For more suggestions, see the boxed text, left.

Thrash metal dominates the rock world; head-bang with energetic groups such as Zeus and Trauma at Patio de María in Havana (p141). Interactivo, X Alfonso and Elmer Ferrer are among the master stylemixers leading the next generation of Cuban musicians.

ENVIRONMENT
The Land

Cuba covers about 42,803 sq miles (110,860 sq km), all told. At 776 miles (1250km) from east to west, the main island is the world's 15th largest.

Cuba's 3570 miles (5746km) of coastline and vibrant coral reef (home to over 900 fish species and 410 sponge and coral species) is a marine wonderland. Though more prone to winter cold fronts, the north shore has the Caribbean standard powdery sands and turquoise sea. The southern coast is more aggressive, bedeviled by diente de perro (jagged rocks that line the shore), but has good fishing and unexplored pockets.

Over millions of years, Cuba's limestone bedrock has been eroded by underground rivers, creating interesting geological features like the 'haystack' hills of Viñales. Cuba has several important mountain ranges providing good hiking opportunities, including the Sierra del Escambray in the center of the country (see p160) and the Sierra Maestra in the Oriente, featuring Pico Turquino (6470ft/1972m), Cuba's highest peak.

Wildlife

Cuba hosts 350 varieties of birds, including the toothpick-sized zunzuncito (bee hummingbird), the world's smallest bird. Cuba also boasts the world's smallest toad, the ranita de Cuba (Cuban tree toad, 0.4in/1cm).

Land mammals have been hunted almost to extinction, except for the indigenous

---

TOP 10 MUSICIANS TO CATCH LIVE

No visit to Cuba is complete without seeing some live music. Keep an eye out for concerts by these musicians.

- Interactivo
- Los Van Van
- Sinfónica Nacional
- Síntesis
- Elmer Ferrer
- Charanga Habanera
- Chucho Valdés
- Anónimo Consejo
- Zeus
- Frank Delgado

jutía (tree rat), an 8.8lb (4kg) edible rodent. Marine fauna is more inspiring: manatees frequent Bahía de Taco and whale sharks swim around María la Gorda (August to November). Leatherback, loggerhead, green and hawksbill turtles also frequent Cuban seas. *Carey* (turtle) is a common menu item in coastal areas; travelers are encouraged to refrain.

There are 90 types of palm, including the *palma real* (royal palm); the national tree, it figures prominently in Cuba's coat of arms and the Cristal beer logo (you'll see plenty of those!). Reforestation programs have been a priority for the Cuban government, having planted over three million trees since 1959.

At present, more than 14% of the country is protected in some way. There are six national parks: Parque Nacional Península de Guanahacabibes and Parque Nacional Viñales, in Pinar del Río; the Gran Parque Natural Montemar (aka Parque Nacional Ciénaga de Zapata) in Matanzas; Parque Nacional Desembarco del Granma in Granma and Gran Parque Nacional Sierra Maestra (straddling Granma and Santiago de Cuba Provinces); and Parque Nacional Alejandro de Humboldt in Guantànamo.

Environmental Issues

Cuba's schizophrenic environmental policy cuts to the heart of the problem: how can a developing nation provide for its people *and* maintain high ecological standards?

One disaster, most agree, was the 1.2 mile–long (2km) stone *pedreplén* (causeway) constructed to link offshore Cayo Sabinal with mainland Camagüey. This massive project involved piling boulders in the sea and laying a road on top, causing irreparable damage to bird and marine life habitats. *Pedreplénes* were also constructed to Cayo Jutías (p145) and Cayo Santa María (p155).

The construction of giant resorts on virgin beaches exacerbates the clash between human activity and environmental protection. Rounding up dolphins to provide tourist entertainment doesn't help. Overfishing, agricultural runoff, industrial pollution and inadequate sewage treatment have contributed to the decay of coral reefs.

Reforestation programs, and river and bay clean-ups provide hope.

FOOD & DRINK

Let's face it, you don't come to Cuba for the food (especially if you're Muslim or have high cholesterol). Cuban meals always feature *congrí* (rice flecked with red or black beans), fried plantains and salad. Pork and fried chicken are the ubiquitous protein. Beef is rare; you may see *ropa vieja,* which is shredded beef livened with peppers and onions. It's akin to a national dish.

Tap water quality is variable and most Cubans live with some stomach amoebas. To be safe, drink bottled water *(agua natural)* or boil it (the local method).

Paladares are privately owned restaurants serving reliable meals in the CUC$7 to CUC$12 range. You'll pay more if you arrive with a *jinetero* (tout). Vegetarians should find decent meals in casas particulares (private homes renting out up to two rooms).

CITY OF HAVANA

pop 2.2 million

Havana (La Habana) is the Caribbean's biggest city, with the entire whorl of politics, culture, education and attitude befitting a great urban center. The city has suffered little damage during the past 200 years, and Habana Vieja, a Unesco World Heritage site, is the finest surviving colonial complex in the Americas. Go beyond the exquisitely restored core, however, and neglect – like pollution – is everywhere. Buildings collapse regularly, residents have to bucket-haul water from street pipes, and garbage overfloweth.

But the people are resourceful, gracious and outgoing, despite it all. Habaneros are hardscrabble, to be sure, but still exuberantly friendly, leaving their indelible mark on any visit.

INFORMATION

Emergency

Ambulance (☎ 7-55-11-85, 7-55-21-85)

Immigration

Inmigración (Map pp134-5; Calle Factor al final & Santa Ana, south of Tulipán, Nuevo Vedado) For visa extensions.

Internet Access

Cibercafé Capitolio (Map pp130-1; ☎ 7-862-0485; Prado & Brasil; per 30min/hr CUC$3/5, ☒ 8am-8pm) Inside main entrance of Capitolio Nacional.

CUBA

HAVANA IN...

Two Days

Fortify yourself with a casa particular breakfast before touring the **Capitolio** (p132) and choosing art or war at the **Museo Nacional de Bellas Artes** (p132) or the **Museo de la Revolución** (p132). A stroll along the **Malecón** (p133) is mandatory, after which Chinatown stir-fries beckon. At night, salsa and swoon at Centro Habana's **Casa de la Música** (p141).

Habana Vieja (opposite) will gobble up day two with gorgeous art and architecture; galleries in **Plaza Vieja**, books in **Plaza de Armas**, and the cathedral in **Plaza de Catedral** (all opposite). At night, it's the **Tropicana** (p142) or **Casa de la Trova** (p141).

Four Days

Follow the two-day itinerary, visiting the **Plaza de la Revolución** (p133) and supping at a **paladar** (p138). On day four, ferry across the bay to tour the **old forts** (p143) and sip sunset cocktails by the sea. Dine divinely at **El Paseo** (p140) in the Hotel NH Parque Central or at **Café del Oriente** (p139) in Plaza de San Francisco.

One Week

Top off the four-day itinerary with a day trip to the turquoise waters of Playas del Este, dancing the night away at **El Chevere** (p141). Spend the next day shaking your booty at a **rumba** in Callejón de Hamel and **shopping** (p142) at the outdoor craft markets. Save your last day for Che, visiting the famous **monument** (p153) in Santa Clara.

Citmatel (Map pp134–5; ☎ 7-831-1321; Calle 15 No 551 btwn Calles C & D; per 1/2/5 hrs CUC$6/10/20; ⏳ 8:30am-5pm Mon-Sat)

Etecsa Habana Vieja (Map pp130-1; ☎ 7-860-4477; Habana 406 cnr Obispo; ⏳ 9am-6pm) Vedado (Map pp134-5; Calle 23 cnr 0, Centro de Prensa Internacional; ⏳ 8am-7pm) There's a little-used ATM at the Habana Vieja branch.

Medical Services

Cira García (☎ 7-204-2811; www.cira.sld.cu; Calle 20 No 4101, cnr Av 41, Playa)

Hospital Nacional Hermanos Ameijeiras (Map pp134-5; ☎ 7-877-6053; fax 7-33-50-36; San Lázaro No 701 at Padre Varela) Enter below the parking lot off Padre Varela (ask for 'CEDA' in Section N).

Tryp Habana Libre (Map pp134-5; ☎ 7-55-45-93; Calle L btwn Calles 23 & 25, Vedado) A good pharmacy.

Money

Banco de Crédito y Comercio Habana Vieja (Map pp130-1; ☎ 7-862-5006; Aguiar No 310 near Obispo; ⏳ 8:30am-1:30pm Mon-Fri); Vedado (Map pp134-5; ☎ 7-870-2684; Calle 23 in Airline Bldg)

Banco Financiero Internacional Centro Habana (Map pp134-5; ☎ 7-873-6496; Plaza Carlos III); Habana Vieja (Map pp130-1; ☎ 7-860-9369; cnr Oficios & Brasil); Vedado (Map pp134-5; ☎ 7-55-44-29; Calle L btwn Calles 23 & 25 in Tryp Habana Libre)

Banco Metropolitano Calle M (Map pp134-5; ☎ 7-55-33-16/17/18; Línea & Calle M); Paseo (Map pp134-5; ☎ 7-830-1962; Línea off Paseo); Vedado (Map pp134-5; ☎ 7-879-2074; Av de la Independencia, in the post office)

Cadeca Habana Vieja (Map pp130-1; Oficios & Lamparilla, facing Plaza de San Francisco; ⏳ 8am-7pm Mon-Sat, 8am-1pm Sun); Habana Vieja (Map pp130-1; Obispo No 257 btwn Aguiar & Cuba; ⏳ 8:30am-10pm) ATMs here; Vedado (Map pp134-5; Calle 23 btwn K & L; ⏳ 7am-2:30pm, 3:30-10pm); Vedado (Map pp134-5; Línea btwn Paseo & Calle A) Cadeca gives cash advances and changes traveler's checks at higher commissions than banks.

Photography

You can download digital photos at the Centro de Prensa Internacional and Av de Italia branches.

Photo Service Centro Habana (Map pp130-1; ☎ 7-863-3195; Av de Italia); Vedado (Map pp134-5; ☎ 7-836-5031; Calles 23 & 0 in Centro de Prensa Internacional; ⏳ 8:30am-8pm); Vedado (Map pp134-5; ☎ 7-55-39-74; Calle 1 & Paseo in Galerías de Paseo; ⏳ 9am-6pm)

Post

DHL (Map pp134-5; ☎ 7-832-2112; Calzada No 818 btwn Calles 2 & 4; ⏳ 8am-5pm Mon-Fri)

Post office Centro Habana (Map pp130-1; Prado at the Gran Teatro); Habana Vieja (Map pp130-1; Oficios No 102, Plaza de San Francisco); Vedado (Map pp134-5; Línea & Paseo; ⏳ 8am-8pm Mon-Sat); Vedado (Map pp134-5; Av de la Independencia, near Plaza de la Revolución;

(⊙ 24hr) The many services at the Vedado branch include photo development and a bank.

Tourist Information

Infotur Airport (☎ 7-266-4094; Terminal 3 Aeropuerto Internacional José Martí; ⊙ 8:30am-5:30pm); Habana Vieja (Map pp130-1; ☎ 7-863-6884; www.infotur.cu; Obispo cnr of San Ignacio; ⊙ 10am-1pm, 2-7pm); Habana Vieja (Map pp130-1; ☎ /fax 7-866-3333; cnr Obispo & Bernaza) Arranges tours, sells maps and phone cards, has transportation schedules.

SIGHTS
Habana Vieja
PLAZA DE CATEDRAL

'Music set in stone' was how novelist Alejo Carpentier eulogized the **Catedral de San Cristóbal de la Habana** (Map pp130-1; San Ignacio & Empedrado; ⊙ 9-11:30am), and its baroque double towers do exude lyrical ambience, especially at night. Elevated to a cathedral in 1788, it's one of the oldest in the Americas.

Be sure to visit the **Centro Wilfredo Lam** (Map pp130 1; ☎ 7 861-2096; San Ignacio No 22 cnr Empedrado; admission CUC$2; ⊙ 10am-5pm Mon-Sat), which displays work by one of Cuba's leading modern painters and hosts shows by local and international artists.

The **Museo de Arte Colonial** (Map pp130-1; ☎ 7-862-6440; San Ignacio No 61; admission CUC$2; ⊙ 9am-7pm), displays colonial furniture and decorative arts in the **Palacio de los Condes de Casa Bayona** (Map pp130–1), the oldest house (1720) on the square.

PLAZA DE ARMAS

The **Palacio de los Capitanes Generales** (Map pp130–1) is one of Cuba's most majestic buildings. Construction began in 1776, and from 1791 to 1902 it was home to Spanish and US power players, after which it became the presidential palace. Since 1968 it has housed the **Museo de la Ciudad** (admission unguided/ guided CUC$3/4; ⊙ 9am-6pm). Highlights include peacocks, a spooky crypt and an eerie Jesus.

Former HQ of the Spanish vice-governor, the **Palacio del Segundo Cabo** (Map pp130-1; ☎ 7-862-4378; O'Reilly No 4; admission CUC$1; ⊙ 9am-6pm Mon-Sat) is another baroque beauty (built in 1772). Today, it has a leafy inner courtyard and the **Sala Galería Raúl Martínez**.

On the northeast side of the Plaza de Armas is the Americas' oldest colonial fortress, the **Castillo de la Real Fuerza** (Map pp130–1), built between 1558 and 1577.

The west tower is crowned by the famous bronze weather vane **La Giraldilla**. The saucy dame probably looks familiar – she's the Havana Club logo.

In 1519, the Villa de San Cristóbal de la Habana was founded on the spot marked by the 1828 **El Templete** (Map pp130-1; admission CUC$1; ⊙ 8:30am-6pm), a neoclassical Doric chapel. The first mass was held below a ceiba tree similar to the one at the entrance (touch it for good luck).

PLAZA DE SAN FRANCISCO

Another of Havana's picturesque plazas, **Plaza de San Francisco** (Map pp130–1) is a seaside beauty distinguished by the domed **Lonja del Comercio** (1909), now Havana's chicest office space. The south side of the square is dominated by the **Iglesia y Monasterio de San Francisco de Asís**. Originally constructed in 1608 and rebuilt between 1719 and 1738, today it's a **concert hall** (⊙ concerts 8pm) hosting classical recitals and a **museum** (☎ 7-862-3467; admission CUC$1; ⊙ 9am-5:30pm), with access to Havana's tallest church tower.

On the water, two blocks south of here, is the **Museo del Ron** (Map pp130-1; ☎ 7-861-8051; Av del Puerto No 262 at Sol; admission CUC$5; ⊙ 9am-5pm Mon-Fri, 10am-4pm Sat & Sun). The interesting bilingual tour explains the entire brewing process, from cane cutting to finished product (you'll get to quaff amber Añejo Reserva in the tasting room). The scale model of the Central La Esperanza is especially cool.

PLAZA VIEJA

One of Havana's most dazzling public spaces, **Plaza Vieja** (Map pp130–1), dating from the 16th century, has several sites not to be missed (including Cuba's only microbrewery!). On the northwest corner is the **Cámara Oscura** (☎ 7-866-4461; admission CUC$1; ⊙ 9am-5:30pm), providing live, 360-degree city views from atop a 115ft-tall (35m) tower. Next door is **Fototeca de Cuba** (☎ 7-862-2530; Mercaderes No 307; admission free; ⊙ 10am-5pm Tue-Sat), a photo gallery with intriguing exhibits.

On the plaza's south side is the oddball **Museo de Naipes** (Map pp130-1; Muralla No 101 cnr of Mercaderes; donations accepted; ⊙ 8:30am-5pm Tue-Sat, 9am-1pm Sun), with 2000 playing cards, including Mussolini, Scooby Doo and U Thant. Next door is **La Casona Centro de Arte** (☎ 7-861-8544; www.artnet.com/la casona.html; Muralla No 107; admission free; ⊙ 8:30am-5:30pm Mon-Sat),

CUBA

HABANA VIEJA & CENTRO HABANA

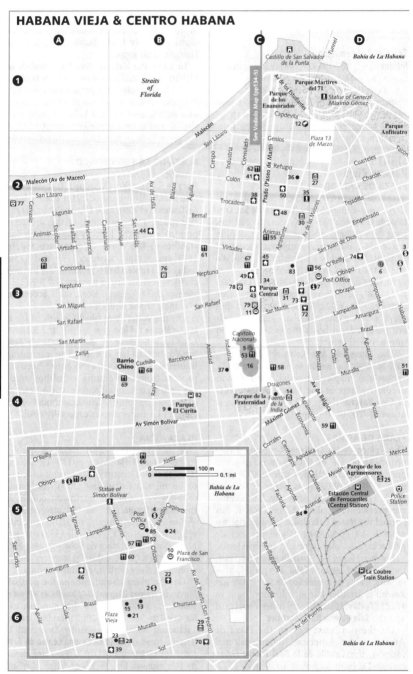

CUBA

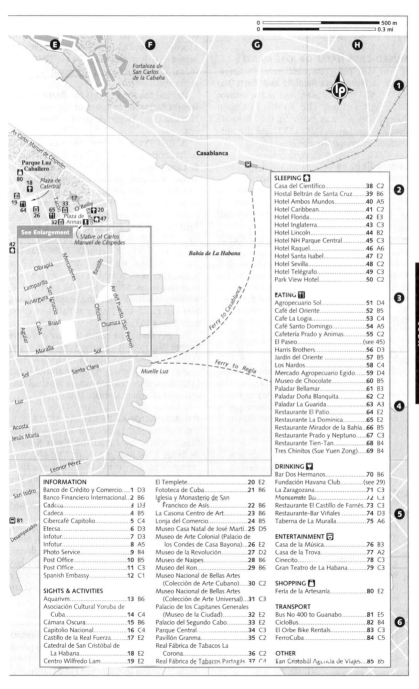

0   500 m
0   0.3 mi

Fortaleza de
San Carlos
de la Cabaña

Casablanca

Av Carlos Manuel de Céspedes

Parque Luz
Caballero
80
18   Plaza de
Catedral
19
26   64   65   33   O'Reilly
  17
  20
  32   Plaza de   47
  Armas

See Enlargement
42   Statue of Carlos
Manuel de Céspedes

Obrapía
Mercaderes
Lamparilla
San Ignacio
Amargura
Baratillo
Oficios
Churruca (San Pedro)
Aguiar
Cuba
Brasil
Muralla
Sol

Bahía de La Habana

Ferry to Casablanca

Ferry to Regla
Muelle Luz

Sol
Santa Clara
Luz
Acosta
Jesús María

Leonor Pérez

San Isidro
81
Desamparados

SLEEPING
Casa del Científico.....................**38** C2
Hostal Beltrán de Santa Cruz.......**39** B6
Hotel Ambos Mundos.................**40** A5
Hotel Caribbean........................**41** C2
Hotel Florida.............................**42** E3
Hotel Inglaterra.........................**43** C3
Hotel Lincoln.............................**44** B2
Hotel NH Parque Central.............**45** C3
Hotel Raquel.............................**46** A6
Hotel Santa Isabel......................**47** E2
Hotel Sevilla..............................**48** C2
Hotel Telégrafo..........................**49** C3
Park View Hotel.........................**50** C2

EATING
Agropecuario Sol.......................**51** D4
Café del Oriente.........................**52** B5
Cafe La Logia.............................**53** C4
Café Santo Domingo...................**54** A5
Cafetería Prado y Animas............**55** C2
El Paseo...............................(see 45)
Harris Brothers..........................**56** D3
Jardín del Oriente **57** B5
Los Nardos...............................**58** C4
Mercado Agropecuario Egido.....**59** D4
Museo de Chocolate...................**60** B5
Paladar Bellamar........................**61** B3
Paladar Doña Blanquita...............**62** C2
Paladar La Guarida.....................**63** A3
Restaurante El Patio....................**64** E2
Restaurante La Dominica.............**65** E2
Restaurante Mirador de la Bahía..**66** B5
Restaurante Prado y Neptuno......**67** C3
Restaurante Tien-Tan..................**68** B4
Tres Chinitos (Sue Yuen Zong).....**69** B4

DRINKING
Bar Dos Hermanos.....................**70** B6
Fundación Havana Club...........(see 29)
La Zaragozana...........................**71** C3
Monserrate Bar..........................**72** C3
Restaurante El Castillo de Farnés..**73** C3
Restaurante-Bar Viñales..............**74** D3
Taberna de La Muralla.................**75** A6

ENTERTAINMENT
Casa de la Música.......................**76** B3
Casa de la Trova.........................**77** A2
Cinecito....................................**78** C3
Gran Teatro de La Habana............**79** C3

SHOPPING
Fería de la Artesanía...................**80** E2

TRANSPORT
Bus No 400 to Guanabo..............**81** E5
CicloBus...................................**82** B4
El Orbe Bike Rentals...................**83** C3
FerroCuba................................**84** C5

OTHER
San Cristóbal Agencia de Viajes...**85** B5

INFORMATION
Banco de Crédito y Comercio.....**1** D3
Banco Financiero Internacional...**2** B6
Cadeca.....................................**3** D3
Cadeca.....................................**4** B5
Cibercafé Capitolio.....................**5** C4
Etecsa......................................**6** D3
Infotur......................................**7** D3
Infotur......................................**8** A5
Photo Service.............................**9** B4
Post Office...............................**10** B5
Post Office...............................**11** C3
Spanish Embassy.......................**12** C1

SIGHTS & ACTIVITIES
Aquarivm.................................**13** B6
Asociación Cultural Yoruba de
   Cuba....................................**14** C4
Cámara Oscura..........................**15** B6
Capitolio Nacional......................**16** C4
Castillo de la Real Fuerza............**17** E2
Catedral de San Cristóbal de
   La Habana.............................**18** E2
Centro Wilfredo Lam...................**19** E2

El Templete...............................**20** E2
Fototeca de Cuba.......................**21** B6
Iglesia y Monasterio de San
   Francisco de Asís....................**22** B6
La Casona Centro de Art.............**23** B6
Lonja del Comercio.....................**24** B5
Museo Casa Natal de José Martí...**25** D5
Museo de Arte Colonial (Palacio de
   los Condes de Casa Bayona).....**26** E2
Museo de la Revolución..............**27** D2
Museo de Naipes.......................**28** B6
Museo del Ron...........................**29** B6
Museo Nacional de Bellas Artes
   (Colección de Arte Cubano).....**30** C2
Museo Nacional de Bellas Artes
   (Colección de Arte Universal)...**31** C3
Palacio de los Capitanes Generales
   (Museo de la Ciudad)..............**32** E2
Palacio del Segundo Cabo...........**33** E2
Parque Central...........................**34** C3
Pavillón Granma.........................**35** C2
Real Fábrica de Tabacos La
   Corona..................................**36** C2
Real Fábrica de Tabacos Partagás..**37** C4

with quality art exhibits in a fantastic colonial palace.

MUSEO-CASA NATAL DE JOSÉ MARTÍ
If you visit only one *casa natal* in Cuba,
make it **Museo-Casa Natal de José Martí** (Map
pp130-1; ☎ 7-861-3778; Leonor Pérez No 314; admission
CUC$1; ☯ 9am-6:30pm). The 'apostle of Cuban
independence' was born in this humble
dwelling on January 28, 1853, and the museum displays all the ephemera.

Centro Habana
CAPITOLIO NACIONAL & AROUND
Washington, DC and Havana have more in
common than you may think – just behold
the **Capitolio Nacional** (Map pp130-1; ☎ 7-863-7861;
admission unguided/guided CUC$3/4; ☯ 9am-7pm),
which is similar to the US Capitol Building, but richer in detail.

Initiated in 1929, the Capitolio took 5000
workers three years, two months and 20 days
to build at a cost of US$17 million. Every-
thing is monumental here, from the huge
bronze doors to the 108,045lb (49-tonne),
56ft (17m) statue of the republic, the third-

CIGAR FACTORY TOURS
Three factories offer identical tours: you
visit the ground floor where the leaves
are unbundled and sorted, moving to the
upper floors to watch the tobacco get
rolled, pressed, banded and boxed. These
are factories, remember, where people toil
for around CUP200 a month, and some
visitors find that the factories smack of a
human zoo. Still, if you have even a passing
interest in tobacco, Cuban work environments or economies of scale, you'll enjoy
one of the CUC$10 tours (in English, French
or Italian) at:

Real Fábrica de Tabacos La Corona
(Map pp130-1; ☎ 7-862-0001; Calle Agramonte
No 106 btwn Colón & Refugio; ☯ tours 9:30am-
3pm Mon-Fri) Built in 1842.

Real Fábrica de Tabacos Partagás
(Map pp130-1; ☎ 7-862-0086; Industria No 520
btwn Barcelona & Dragones; ☯ tours every 15min
9:30-11am & noon-3pm) Built in 1845.

Romeo y Julieta (Map pp134–5; ☎ 7-870-
5195; Padre Varela No 852 at Benjumeda; ☯ tours
10am-3pm Mon-Fri) Far from any tourist sites, you
may get lucky here and have a personalized tour.

largest indoor bronze statue in the world
(only the Buddha in Nava, Japan, and the
Lincoln Memorial in Washington, DC, are
bigger). Below the Capitolio's 203ft-high
(62m) dome, a 24-carat diamond replica is
set in the floor.

Behind the Capitolio is the **Real Fábrica de
Tabacos Partagás**; for tours of this and other
Havana cigar factories, see the boxed text,
left.

Across Prado, beyond the Fuente de la
India sculpture, the **Asociación Cultural Yoruba
de Cuba** (Map pp130-1; ☎ 7-863-5953; www.nnl-cuba
.org/obinibata; Prado No 615; admission adult/student
CUC$10/3; ☯ 9am-5pm) provides a good over-
view of Santería; there are free *tambores*
(drum jams/ceremonies) here on alternate
Fridays at 4:30pm (when museum entry is
free). Consultations are also on offer.

Just north of the Capitolio is the **Gran Teatro de La Habana** (Map pp130-1; ☎ 7-861-3077; Prado
No 458 at San Rafael; guided tours CUC$2; ☯ 9am-6pm),
built between 1907 and 1914. An outrageously beautiful building inside and out,
you can catch the National Ballet of Cuba
here (see p142).

Across from the Gran Teatro is **Parque
Central** (Map pp130-1) and the very first Martí
statue erected in Cuba (1905). The men
laughing and arguing near the statue is the
famous *esquina caliente*, where baseball fanatics debate their favorite teams.

MUSEO NACIONAL DE BELLAS ARTES
This collection is housed in two buildings, collectively called the **Museo Nacional
de Bellas Artes** (Map pp130-1; ☎ 7-861-5777; www
.museonacional.cult.cu; admission CUC$8 for both or CUC$5
individually; ☯ 10am-6pm Tue-Sat, 10am-2pm Sun). The
Colección de Arte Universal (Map pp130-1; Agramonte
& San Rafael) houses a ho-hum permanent collection rich in Grecian urns.

The **Colección de Arte Cubano** (Map pp130-1;
Trocadero btwn Agramonte & Av de las Misiones), however, is world-class. Split into three floors,
all wheelchair-accessible, the museum has
a sculpture garden, café and contemporary
art – look especially for works by Kcho,
Portocarrero and Wilfredo Lam.

MUSEO DE LA REVOLUCIÓN
Since 1976, the glass-encased **Pavillón Granma**
(Map pp130-1) facing the Colección de Arte
Cubano has been home to the 59ft (18m)
'yacht' *Granma* that ushered Fidel Castro and

81 others into world history in 1956. Today, this is one of the revolution's holiest shrines and has the eternal flame to prove it.

The **Museo de la Revolución** (Map pp130-1; ☎ 7-862-4093; Refugio No 1; admission CUC$4, cameras extra; ☉ 10am-5pm) is housed in the former Palacio Presidencial (1913–20), site of the 1957 Batista assassination attempt. Tiffany's of New York decorated the interior. Everything you wanted to know about the Cuban Revolution is here; a pity guided tours (CUC$2) are only in Spanish.

Vedado

Vedado (forest reserve) is a suburban, sedate part of Havana. Beatles fans should visit **Parque Lennon** (Map pp134-5; Calles 15 & 17 btwn Calles 6 & 8) with its hyper-realistic bronze of John lounging on a bench. Every December 8 there are musical vigils here commemorating his life.

Running along the Río Almendares below the bridge on Calle 23, **Parque Almendares** (Map pp134-5) is a wonderful oasis in the heart of chaotic Havana. Benches line the river promenade, plants grow profusely and there are many facilities here, including an antiquated **miniature golf course**, the **Anfiteatro Parque Almendares** (p141) and a **playground**. Take a 20-minute stroll through old growth trees in the **Bosque de la Habana** and you'll feel transported (don't go solo – this isolated spot is considered unsafe by locals).

Although the gigantic **Plaza de la Revolución** (Map pp134-5) has come to symbolize the Cuban Revolution, most of the buildings date from the Batista era. On important occasions, President Castro addresses up to 1.2 million supporters from in front of the star-shaped, 466ft-high (142m) **Memorial José Martí** (☎ 7-59-23-47; admission CUC$5; ☉ 9:30am-5pm Mon-Sat) and 56ft (17m) Martí statue. Join the crowd on May 1 if you want to experience it yourself. There's a thoughtful museum dedicated to José Martí inside the memorial; ride the elevator to the enclosed 423ft-level (129m) viewpoint – the highest structure in Cuba. The **Ministry of the Interior** on the plaza's north side is easily identifiable by its huge 'Che' mural.

Havana has become synonymous with the **Malecón** (Map pp134-5), its 5-mile (8km) seawall that was constructed in 1901. Though you've probably seen many photos of this seaside scene, the pastiche of architectural gems in Havana's unrivaled afternoon light is enchanting.

Two blocks off the Malecón at Calle M is **El Focsa** (Map pp134-5), the monstrous green and yellow architectural wonder (or blunder, depending on your viewpoint) that is Cuba's tallest building.

HAVANA FOR CHILDREN

There is no lack of fun things to do here including visiting the freshwater **Aquarivm** (Map pp130-1; ☎ 7-863-9493; Calle Brasil No 9 btwn Mercaderes & Oficios; admission CUC$1; ☉ 9am-5pm Mon-Sat, 9am-1pm Sun), the fantastic **playground** on the Malecón (at Tacón), replete with rides, and the beach at **Playas del Este** (p144). Culturally, there's **La Colmenita** children's theater at the Teatro Nacional de Cuba (p142), **Cinecito** (Map pp130-1; ☎ 7-863-8051; San Rafael No 68 at Consulado) with kids' movies, and activities at the **Museo Nacional de Bellas Artes** (☉ 3pm Sat, 11am Sun) are all available (see opposite for contact details).

TOURS

As the tour agencies are all government-run, tours are essentially the same, lasting a half-day to a full day, with pickup and drop-off at your hotel. Tours include a four-hour city tour (CUC$15), a 'Hemingway' tour (from CUC$20), a Varadero day trip (from CUC$35, including lunch and open bar) and the Tropicana Nightclub (starting at CUC$65). Other options include tours to Viñales (CUC$44) and a Trinidad–Cienfuegos overnight (CUC$129). The Varadero day trip and city tours always receive high marks. For tours of Habana Vieja, San Cristóbal is highly recommended.

Cubanacán (Map pp134-5; ☎ 7-833-4090; www .cubanacan.cu; Calle 23 No 156 btwn Calles O & P)
Cubatur (Map pp134-5; ☎ 7-833-3142, 7-834-4111; www.cubatur.cu; Calle 23 cnr Calle M)
San Cristóbal Agencia de Viajes (Map pp130-1; ☎ 7-861-9171/2, 7-866-4102; www.viajessancristobal .cu; Calle de los Oficios No 110 bajos btwn Lamparilla & Amargura)

SLEEPING
Budget
CENTRO HABANA
Casa del Científico (Map pp130-1; ☎ 7-862-4511, 7-863-8103; Prado No 212 at Trocadero; s/d with shared bath CUC$26/31, with private bath CUC$45/55; ☒ ▢) This elegant old building with grand stairways,

CUBA

VEDADO

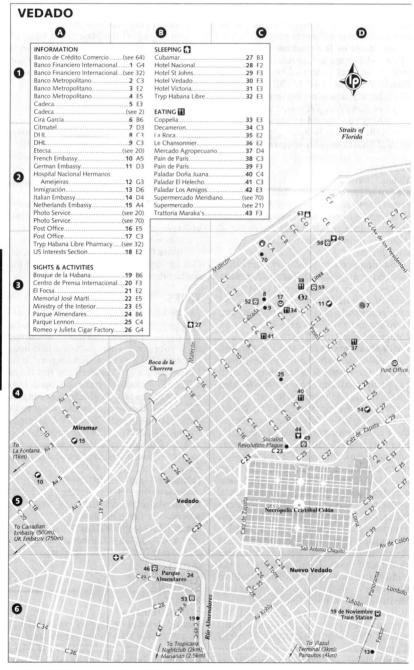

INFORMATION
Banco de Crédito Comercio........(see 64)
Banco Financiero Internacional.......**1** G4
Banco Financiero Internacional..(see 32)
Banco Metropolitano....................**2** C3
Banco Metropolitano....................**3** E2
Banco Metropolitano....................**4** E5
Cadeca..**5** E3
Cadeca.....................................(see 2)
Cira García..................................**6** B6
Citmatel......................................**7** D3
DI IL...**8** C3
DHL..**9** C3
Etecsa.....................................(see 20)
French Embassy.........................**10** A5
German Embassy........................**11** D3
Hospital Nacional Hermanos
    Ameijeiras.............................**12** G3
Inmigración...............................**13** D6
Italian Embassy.........................**14** D4
Netherlands Embassy................**15** A4
Photo Service...........................(see 20)
Photo Service...........................(see 70)
Post Office................................**16** E5
Post Office................................**17** C3
Tryp Habana Libre Pharmacy.....(see 32)
US Interests Section..................**18** E2

SIGHTS & ACTIVITIES
Bosque de la Habana..................**19** B6
Centro de Prensa Internacional...**20** F3
El Focsa....................................**21** E2
Memorial José Martí....................**22** E5
Ministry of the Interior................**23** E5
Parque Almendares....................**24** B6
Parque Lennon...........................**25** C4
Romeo y Julieta Cigar Factory.....**26** G4

SLEEPING
Cubamar....................................**27** B3
Hotel Nacional...........................**28** F2
Hotel St Johns...........................**29** F3
Hotel Vedado............................**30** F3
Hotel Victoria............................**31** E3
Tryp Habana Libre.....................**32** E3

EATING
Coppelia....................................**33** E3
Decameron................................**34** C3
La Roca.....................................**35** E2
Le Chansonnier.........................**36** E2
Mercado Agropecuario...............**37** D4
Pain de París.............................**38** C3
Pain de París.............................**39** F3
Palador Doña Juana...................**40** C4
Palador El Helecho.....................**41** C3
Palador Los Amigos....................**42** E3
Supermercado Meridiano...........(see 70)
Supermercado...........................(see 21)
Trattoria Maraka's......................**43** F3

Straits of Florida

Malecón

Boca de la Chorrera

Miramar

To
La Fontana
(1km)

To Canadian
Embassy (500m);
UK Embassy (750m)

Vedado

Calz de Zapata

Socialist Revolution Plaque

Necrópolis Cristóbal Colón

San Antonio Chiquito

Av de Colón

Post Office

Nuevo Vedado

La Torre

Parque
Almendares

Av Kohly

Tulipán

19 de Noviembre
Train Station

To Tropicana
Nightclub (2km);
Marianao (2.5km)

To Vlazul
Terminal (3km);
Panautos (4km)

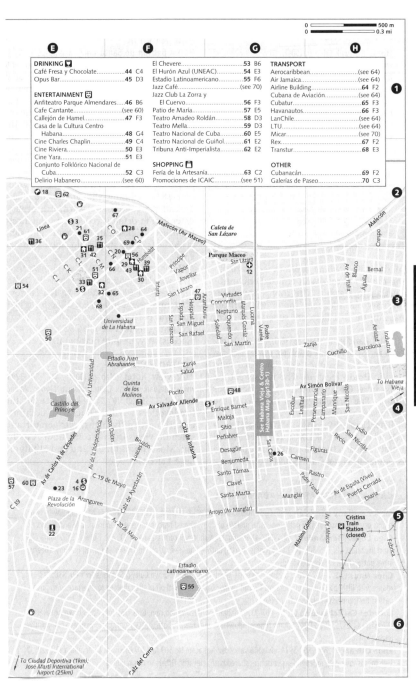

AUTHOR'S CHOICE

Hotel Raquel (Map pp130-1; ☎ 7-860-8280; www.habaguanex.com; Calle Amargura cnr San Ignacio; s/d incl breakfast CUC$115/200; 🔀 🖳) Location, elegance and amenities distinguish this beautifully restored 1905 art deco palace. The marble-pillared lobby with its stained-glass ceiling bespeaks a style of which Havana could use more. In the heart of Habana Vieja, but away from the maddening crowds, the Raquel has only 25 rooms, each outfitted with comfortable cast-iron furnishings, beautiful tile floors and fine linens. Most have balconies and views and all boast deep bathtubs. There's a gym with sauna and massages, and the restaurant is kosher.

---

marble columns and roof terrace overlooking the Prado makes an atmospheric introduction to Havana. The rooms are rather ordinary but adequate; rooms with private bath on the 3rd floor are superior in every way.

Hotel Caribbean (Map pp130-1; ☎ 7-860-8233; Prado No 164 btwn Colón & Refugio; s/d incl breakfast CUC$36/54; 🔀) Another popular place with terrific Prado location. The rooms can be noisy here. Go for something on the upper floors. The price includes the use of the room safe – use it.

Hotel Lincoln (Map pp130-1; ☎ 7-862-8061; Av de Italia; s/d incl breakfast CUC$39/46; 🔀) Deep inside Centro Habana (not for the timid), this place is similar to Hotel Caribbean (above).

Midrange

HABANA VIEJA

Hostal Beltrán de Santa Cruz (Map pp130-1; ☎ 7-860-8330; www.habaguanex.cu; San Ignacio btwn Sol & Muralla; s/d CUC$76/120; 🔀) A restored, 11-room colonial palace, this star is rising fast in the Habaguanex galaxy. Most of the spacious rooms have balconies overlooking the courtyard and all have sumptuous bathrooms with tubs; the location, just steps from Plaza Vieja, is five star.

Hotel Florida (Map pp130-1; ☎ 7-862-4127; www.hotelflorida.cu; Obispo No 252 cnr Cuba; s/d incl breakfast CUC$90/150; 🅿 🔀 🖳) This three-story colonial (1836) building, with arches and pillars around the central courtyard, is a beauty. Attention to detail is reflected in the nicely furnished, high-ceilinged rooms and fantastic beds. This stately old hotel also has an elegant café.

Hotel Ambos Mundos (Map pp130-1; ☎ 7-860-9529; www.hotelambosmundos.cu; Obispo No 153 at Mercaderes; s/d/tr CUC$80/130/186; 🔀 🖳) Famous as Hemingway's hotel (*For Whom the Bell Tolls* was partially written in room 511, still accepting visitors at CUC$2 a pop), this place is tatty, despite new paint.

CENTRO HABANA

Park View Hotel (Map pp130-1; ☎ 7-861-3293; www.hotelparkview.cu; Calle Colón cnr Morro; s/d incl breakfast CUC$50/80; 🅿 🔀) This place off the Prado offers terrific value, with comfortable rooms, spiffy baths, refrigerator and splendid views from the 7th-floor restaurant. Most rooms on the 2nd and 5th floors have balconies.

CASAS PARTICULARES – HABANA VIEJA

Mercy & Vlady (☎ 7-867-2736; Cuba No 505 btwn Brasil & Muralla; r CUC$30; 🔀) A-list colonial with two rooms opening onto interior patio, one with private balcony, shared bath, refrigerator; sunroof, safe and friendly.

Olga López Hernández (☎ 7-867-4561; olgarene@hotmail.com; Cuba No 611, Apt 1 btwn Luz & Santa Clara; r incl breakfast CUC$25-30; 🔀) Two rooms sharing bath – one leads to a living room and small balcony, cheery inner patio. Others in this building.

Chez Nous (☎ 7-862-6287; cheznous@ceniai.inf.cu; Brasil No 115 btwn Cuba & San Ignacio; r CUC$30; 🔀) Big rooms with little balconies, refrigerator, TV and shared bath; the room off of the fabulous roof terrace with private bath is best; professional; French spoken.

Lourdes Cal Echevarría (☎ 7-867-9329; habanalourdes@yahoo.com; Brasil No 361, Apt 1 btwn Aguacate & Villegas; r CUC$25; 🔀) Clean rooms (one windowless) with private bath; passageway patio with rockers; positive female energy.

Elvia Olivares (☎ 7-867-5974; elviaoli@yahoo.es; Aguacate No 509 Apt 402 btwn Sol & Muralla; r CUC$20; 🔀) Two rooms, one with independent entrance, shared bath; elevator. Others in this building.

CHRISTOPHER P BAKER

Pink Sand Beach (p89), Eleuthera, the Bahamas

Capitolio Nacional (p132), City of
Havana, Cuba

MARTIN LLADÓ

DAVE LEWIS

Grace Bay Beach (p108), Turks & Caicos

Catedral de San Cristóbal (p129), City of Havana, Cuba

ALFREDO MAIQUEZ

JERRY ALEXANDER

Blue Lagoon Restaurant (p218), Port Antonio, Jamaica

CHRISTOPHER P BAKER

Inspiration stone, Nine Mile Museum (p222), Jamaica

Captain Keith Tibbetts wreck (p193), Cayman Brac, Cayman Islands

MICHAEL L

CASAS PARTICULARES – CENTRO HABANA

This part of the city can be gritty, but it is close to sights and nightlife. Most independent apartments are here.

Familia Puig (☎ 7-862-2330; www.casapuig.tripod.com; Amistad No 178 altos btwn Neptuno & Concordia; r CUC$25; ✖) Two tranquil and safe rooms in platinum location; friendly and reliable; highly reader-recommended.

Joel y Yadilis (☎ 7-863-0565; Industria No 118 btwn Trocadero & Colón; r CUC$25, 2-bedroom apt CUC$40; ✖) Full apartment has dining room, living room, kitchen and two bedrooms; rent one or both.

Margot y Amalia Urrutia (☎ 7-861-7824; Prado No 20 Apt 7-A; r CUC$25-35) Two rooms (one big, one small) with sea views, gorgeous wraparound porch has El Morro and Capitolio views; English & French spoken. Also rent in Apt 6-A.

Casa de Osmany (☎ 7-863-8733; Consulado No 223 btwn Ánimas & Trocadero; r CUC$35; ✖) Four identical, spotless rooms, each with bath, approach a hostal feel; great location; good for groups.

Niurka o Rey (☎ 7-863-0278; Aguila No 206 bajos btwn Ánimas & Virtudes; r CUC$20; ✖) Independent love nest, TV and refrigerator, but no windows.

María Elisa Navarro (☎ 7-862-4434; San Nicolás No 166 2nd fl btwn Ánimas & Virtudes; r CUC$25; ✖) Two quiet, nicely furnished rooms share bath; stereo.

Norma Pineda Pérez (☎ 7-863-8236; Barcelona No 62 1st fl btwn Aguila & Amistad; r CUC$25) Two rooms share bath; porch and courtyard; good for long term.

María Amparo (☎ 7-863-7437; San Lázaro No 409 btwn Manrique & Campanario; r CUC$20; ✖) One block from Malecón, friendly, safe and quiet.

Hotel Inglaterra (Map pp130-1; ☎ 7-860-8595; www.grancaribe.cu; Prado No 416; s/d/tr CUC$84/120/168; P ✖ 🖳) This historic hotel, built in 1875, is not the prime place to stay that it once was (noisy rooms, reports of theft from rooms, swarming hustlers). The rooftop La Terraza bar has excellent views.

VEDADO

Hotel Victoria (Map pp134-5; ☎ 7-833-3510, 7-833-3625; www.hotelvictoriacuba.com; Calle 19 No 101 & Calle M; s/d/tr incl breakfast CUC$65/90/126; P ✖ 🖳 🍸) This intimate, 31-room hotel off of the main thoroughfare is a good option if you want more personable service than offered by the biggies. Rooms are tight, but well equipped with refrigerator, safe and minibar. Built in the roaring '20s, it has style.

    Hotel Vedado (Map pp134-5; ☎ 7-836-4072; Calle O No 244 btwn Calles 23 & 25; s/d incl breakfast CUC$65/82; ✖ 🖳 🍸) Slightly better value than the St John's, this hotel is more professional, and has a small business center and massage services. Staying at either of these places puts you in the heart of *jinetero* country, but steps from stellar Trattoría Maraka's (p140).

    Hotel St John's (Map pp134-5; ☎ 7-833-3740; Calle O No 216 btwn Calles 23 & 25; s/d incl breakfast CUC$56/80; ✖ 🍸) The rooftop pool is a puddle and the staff unresponsive, but the beds are good, the baths clean and western-facing rooms

have excellent Malecón views. Use the safe-deposit box.

Top End

HABANA VIEJA

Hotel Santa Isabel (Map pp130-1; ☎ 7-860-8201; www.habaguanex.com; Baratillo No 9; s/d incl breakfast CUC$160/200; P ✖ 🖳) This charmer on Plaza de Armas is loaded with architectural details, amenable staff and perks like views, terraces and tubs. Jimmy Carter and Robert Plant stayed here. The suites (from s/d CUC$180/300), with large balconies, are especially nice. Technically five (Cuban) stars, we've received complaints about frayed furnishings and lax housecleaning.

CENTRO HABANA

Hotel NH Parque Central (Map pp130-1; ☎ 7-860-6627; www.nh-hotels.com; Neptuno btwn Agramonte & Prado; s/d incl breakfast CUC$205/270; P ✖ 🖳 🍸) This is central Havana's five-star hotel, with the facilities, location and service to prove it. The 277 warm rooms have king-size beds, and separate shower and soaking tub; most have balconies with Capitolio views. There's a gym, Jacuzzi, massages and a dynamite restaurant, El Paseo.

    Hotel Sevilla (Map pp130-1; ☎ 7-860-8560; fax 7-860-8582; Trocadero No 55 btwn Prado & Agramonte; s/d incl breakfast CUC$144/196; P ✖ 🖳 🍸) This elegant Moorish-esque palace from 1908

CASAS PARTICULARES – VEDADO

Ana Livia Grimany Rojo (☎ 7-830-4311; g&f@ecme.netcons.com.cu; Calle 23 No 1103 btwn Calles 8 & 10; r CUC$25; 💥) Two connecting rooms share kitchen and small terrace; lovely and antique-filled; perfect for family.

Mercedes González (☎ 7-832-5846; mercylupe@hotmail.com; Calle 21 No 360, Apt 2-A btwn Calles G & H; r CUC$30; 💥) Two rooms, with TV and refrigerator; bigger room has terrace access; balcony; gregarious hostess.

José A García (☎ 7-830-9367; josevedado1003@yahoo.es; Calle 23 No 1003 btwn Calles 4 & 6; r incl breakfast CUC$25-30) Gorgeous colonial home with tiled floors, 33ft (10m) ceilings and grand baths; English, French and Italian spoken.

Liset y David (☎ 7-835-2085; Calle 27 No 910 bajos btwn Calles 4 & 6; studio apt CUC$30; 💥) Small, independent studio with kitchen, TV, phone and small patio; discounts for long term.

Silvia Vidal (☎ 7-833-4165; silviavidal602@yahoo.es; Paseo No 602 btwn Calles 25 & 27; r CUC$25-30; P 💥) Unbelievably palatial home with one independent cabaña with kitchen, another connecting to garden; refrigerator; big dogs here.

Luis Alberto Gómez Garcés (☎ 7-832-7811; rociany@yahoo.com; Calle 15 No 305 bajos btwn Calles H & I; studio apt CUC$30; 💥) Independent entrance; full eat-in kitchen; darkish.

Fefita (☎ 7-830-1516; Calle 27 No 912 btwn Calles 4 & 6; r CUC$25; 💥) Incredible colonial home on corner lot with wraparound balcony; discounts for long-term stays.

---

an exudes Old World aura. Clean, safe and recommended, there's a sauna and fitness club, and the Sevilla's swimming pool is open to nonguests (CUC$5). For unforgettable views (but largely forgettable food), check out the 9th-floor restaurant-bar.

Hotel Telégrafo (Map pp130-1; ☎ 7-861-1010, 7-861-4741; www.hoteltelegrafo.cu; Prado No 408 cnr Neptuno; s/d CUC$90/150; P 💥 🖳) This well-located historic hotel (1888) updated to new millennium standards is sharp, but the smallish rooms are coldly modern. The staff, however, is efficient and professional;

AUTHOR'S CHOICE

La Fontana (Map pp134-5; ☎ 7-202-8337, 7-890-4947; www.lafontanahabana.com; Calle 3ra A No 305 cnr 46, Miramar; 🕐 noon-midnight) You will think that you have died and gone to Spain when you dine in the leafy surroundings of this Miramar paladar (a privately owned restaurant), one of Havana's top dining experiences. Kalamata olives, carpaccio and smoked salmon – if you want away from Cuban cooking, this is the place for you. Red snapper ceviche in cilantro (CUC$6), a deliciously smoky trifecta of sausages (CUC$5), grilled octopus with pesto (CUC$8) or rabbit in honey and Dijon reduction (CUC$12) is just the start.

The desserts, such as the mocha mousse (CUC$4), are exquisite. Great wine list too, of course.

---

extras like beeping elevators for the sight-impaired and deep, plush couches on every floor are appreciated.

VEDADO

Hotel Nacional (Map pp134-5; ☎ 7-873-3564; www.hotelnacionaldecuba.com; Calles O & 21; s/d/tr CUC$120/170/210; P 💥 🖳 🖳) An architectural stunner perched over the Malecón, the Nacional is a landmark edifice with 442 surprisingly plain rooms, but you stay here more for the legacy than the creature comforts. The 6th, executive floor has its own reception, fax, meeting rooms and secretarial staff (s/d/tr CUC$150/210/240).

Tryp Habana Libre (Map pp134-5; ☎ 7-55-40-11; Calle L btwn Calles 23 & 25; s/d CUC$140/160; P 💥 💥 🖳 🖳) Havana's biggest hotel has 572 grand, comfortable rooms outfitted with modern furnishings in soothing tones. All rooms have balconies and views. It's popular with European package tourists.

EATING
Paladares
CENTRO HABANA

Paladar La Guarida (Map pp130-1; ☎ 7-264-4940; Concordia No 418 btwn Gervasio & Escobar; 🕐 noon-3pm, 7pm-midnight) This wildly popular paladar does a tasty sea bass in coconut reduction and a novel Indian-inspired lamb. Appetizer fans will be ecstatic here. Housed in a classic Centro Habana palace/tenement, the dining rooms are interestingly eclectic, if cramped. Reservations are essential.

Paladar Doña Blanquita (Map pp130-1; Prado No 158 btwn Colón & Refugio; meals CUC$7-9; ☻ noon-10pm) The balcony here overlooking Prado is a romantic spot for classic Cuban cuisine. The service is friendly, the food reliable and the price right. Enter through the pink, unmarked doorway and go upstairs.

Paladar Bellamar (Map pp130-1; Virtudes No 169 near Amistad; dishes CUC$6-8; ☻ noon-10pm) A good standby, the amiable family here offers classic chicken, pork and fish.

VEDADO

Decameron (Map pp134-5; ☎ 7-832-2444; Línea No 753 btwn Paseo & Calle 2; appetizers CUC$3.50-5.50, mains CUC$5-16; ☻ noon-midnight) Nothing mediocre will pass your lips at this intimate Italian restaurant. Veggie pizza, lasagna, sinful *calabaza* (pumpkin) soup, decadent risotto, filet mignon: it's all good. There's a decent wine list and vegetarian options.

Le Chansonnier (Map pp134-5; ☎ 7-832-1576; Calle J No 257 btwn Calles 13 & 15; appetizers CUC$2.50-5, mains CUC$6-12; ☻ 12:30pm-12:30am) You'll sup in your own elegant dining room in this Vedado mansion-turned-paladar specializing in French flavors. Rabbit in red wine, chicken smothered in mushrooms, and the-meal-in-itself salad are some of the offers in this gay-friendly establishment. Save room for dessert.

Paladar El Helecho (Map pp134-5; ☎ 7-831-3552; Calle 6 No 203 btwn Línea & Calle 11; mains CUC$4.50-7; ☻ noon-11pm Tue-Sun) Tucked along a leafy side street in western Vedado, this little place serves tasty Cuban food. The nice atmosphere is complemented by decent prices and good portions.

Also recommended:

Paladar Doña Juana (Map pp134-5; ☎ 7-832-2699; Calle 19 No 909 btwn Calles 6 & 8; appetizers CUC$2-4.50, mains CUC$4.50-8; ☻ noon-midnight) This unmarked, roof-terrace paladar does reliable pork, chicken and fish standbys; steep stair access.

Paladar Los Amigos (Map pp134-5; ☎ 7-830-0808; Calle M No 253 at Calle 19; mains CUC$6-8; ☻ noon-midnight) A handy location for flavorful Cuban food in plastic-plant ambience.

Restaurants
HABANA VIEJA

Jardín del Oriente (Map pp130-1; ☎ 7-860-6686; Amargura btwn San Ignacio & Mercaderes; meals under CUC$2.50; ☻ 10am-10pm) A lovely garden setting and extraordinary meal deals have brought this

place instant success. Extras like balsamic vinegar and Dijon mustard help.

Restaurante Mirador de la Bahía (Map pp130-1; Obispo No 61, Plaza de Armas; mains CUC$2.50-7; ☻ noon-midnight) Dazzling harbor views and live music distinguish this roof terrace restaurant on the 5th floor above the Museo Nacional de Historia Natural. The food is passable, but there's a full bar. Sunset mojito (a cocktail made from rum, mint, sugar, seltzer and fresh lime juice), anyone?

Restaurante La Dominica (Map pp130-1; ☎ 7-860-2918; O'Reilly No 108 at Mercaderes; pizzas CUC$6.50-9.50, meals CUC$6-18; ☻ noon-midnight) There's good service, a varied menu with heaps of veggie options, plus a CUC$3 lunch special earn points here. The Caesar salad (CUC$9) feeds two and the thin-crust, brick-oven pizza is delicious.

Restaurante El Patio (Map pp130-1; ☎ 7-867-1034/5; elpatio@enet.cu; San Ignacio No 54 at Empedrado; appetizers CUC$8.50-10, mains CUC$9-20; ☻ noon-midnight) Take umbrella drinks on the patio facing the cathedral while whetting your appetite for prosciutto-wrapped asparagus (CUC$9), shellfish in basil sauce (CUC$18) or the praiseworthy filet mignon (CUC$18).

Café del Oriente (Map pp130-1; ☎ 7-860-6686; cafédeloriente@enet.cu; Oficios 112 at Amargura, Plaza de San Francisco; appetizers CUC$5-15, mains CUC$14-30; ☻ noon-11pm) Dine divinely on smoked salmon with caviar (CUC$12), mussels with truffles (CUC$18) or chateaubriand with béarnaise sauce (CUC$20). A glass of port finishes things. Tuxedo-clad waitstaff deal out efficient service with a smile.

CENTRO HABANA

Tres Chinitos (Sue Yuen Tong; Map pp130-1; ☎ 7-863-3388; Dragones No 355 btwn San Nicolás & Manrique; meals CUC$4-8; ☻ noon-midnight) Long lines at this Chinatown favorite aren't for wontons but rather for the pizza, lasagna and beautiful salads. Kill line time dreaming about a CUC$4 pizza with red peppers, mushrooms, black olives and onions.

Restaurante Tien-Tan (Map pp130-1; ☎ 7-861-5478; taoqi@enet.cu; Cuchillo No 17 btwn Zanja & San Nicolás; mains CUC$4-15; ☻ 11am-11pm) Of all the cookie-cutter places on the Cuchillo, this is by far the best. The sizzling beef platter (CUC$10) and sweet and sour pork (CUC$6.50) are highly recommended, as is the wonton soup. The upstairs dining room is better.

CUBA

El Paseo (Map pp130-1; ☎ 7-860-6627; Neptuno btwn Prado & Agramonte, NH Parque Central; appetizers CUC$6-14, mains CUC$13-25; ☼ dinner only) Ay! Were we there right now, we'd be ordering the snails in puff pastry with hazelnuts (CUC$14) or the lobster roasted in coffee sauce (CUC$25). This place maintains the highest international standards and the surroundings match the gourmet menu.

Café Santo Domingo (Map pp130-1; Obispo No 159 btwn San Ignacio & Mercaderes; snacks CUC$3.50 or less; ☼ 24hr) Tucked away upstairs beyond a good bakery is this café hideaway. The sandwiches and pizzas are big and tasty, plus there are eggs and bacon (CUC$1.10) for breakfast.

Cafe La Logia (Map pp130-1; ☎ 7-861-5657; Capitolio; admission CUC$4; ☼ 9am-7pm) With tropical atmosphere to spare, this breezy terrace bar-café provides excellent views of all the Capitolio action. It does a fresh veggie sandwich (CUC$2.50).

Harris Brothers (Map pp130-1; ☎ 7-861-1644; O'Reilly No 526; ☼ 9am-9pm Mon-Sat) One of the best places for groceries, with a large liquor selection, as well as cheeses, olives and other goodies.

Fruits and veggies are sold at *agros* (vegetable markets) including **Agropecuario Sol** (Map pp130-1; Calle Sol btwn Habana & Compostela), and **Mercado Agropecuario Egido** (Map pp130-1; Av de Bélgica btwn Corrales & Apodaca; ☼ 7am-2pm).

Also worth your time and money:

Los Nardos (Map pp130-1; ☎ 7-863-2985; Prado No 563 btwn Brasil & Dragones; appetizers CUC$2-4, mains CUC$4-9; ☼ noon-midnight) Candlelit atmosphere and inventive food like lamb in rosemary sauce; sensational prices and lumberjack-sized portions.

Restaurante Prado y Neptuno (Map pp130-1; ☎ 7-860-9636; Prado cnr Neptuno; appetizers CUC$4-7, mains CUC$4-9; ☼ noon-midnight) Modern Italian place with lots of good, creative salads, pastas and seafood; the *jinetera* (a woman who attaches herself to male foreigners for monetary or material gain) factor dampens the appetite, somewhat.

Cafetería Prado y Ánimas (Map pp130-1; Prado cnr Ánimas; ☼ 8am-10pm) Delicious iced coffee (CUC$1.50).

Museo de Chocolate (Map pp130-1; ☎ 7-866-4431; Mercaderes cnr Amargura; ☼ 10am-5:45pm Tue-Sun) Steaming cups of hot chocolate (CUC$0.55); also housemade chocolates (box of 12/18 CUC$4/5).

VEDADO

Trattoría Maraka's (Map pp134-5; ☎ 7-833-3740; Calle O No 260 btwn Calles 23 & 25; mains under CUC$8;

☼ noon-11:45pm) Real olive oil and mozzarella, and a wood oven mean the pizza (CUC$4 to CUC$6) here is among Havana's best. Try the Greek salad (CUC$7), gooey lasagna or spinach cannelloni. Bug the waitstaff or get lost in the crowd.

La Roca (Map pp134-5; ☎ 7-834-4501; Calle 21 No 102 cnr M; specials CUC$3-4; ☼ 11am-1am) A gentleman in a tuxedo holds open the wooden door and you step into Havana c 1954: the piano man croons *My Way*, sunlight refracts through stained glass and the menu lists voluminous specials for under CUC$4. Who cares that the tablecloths are stained?

Pain de Paris Calle 25 (Map pp134-5; Calle 25 No 164 btwn Infanta & O; ☼ 8am-midnight); Línea (Map pp134-5; Línea btwn Paseo & Calle A; ☼ 24hr) This chain serves reliable cappuccino, croissants (chocolate, ham and cheese etc), napoleons and other pastries.

Coppelia (Map pp134-5; ☎ 7-832-6184; Calles 23 & L; ☼ 11am-10:30pm Tue-Sun) Havana's ice-cream scene is legendary, especially here; enter the *divisa* (dollar) part on Calle 23 or wait in line for the real deal (per scoop CUP2).

Mercado Agropecuario (Map pp134-5; Calle 19 btwn Calles A & B) Havana's 'gourmet' market with fresh herbs and rarer produce; prices reflect the selection.

The supermarket below El Focsa (p133) has good variety, as does **Supermercado Meridiano** (Map pp134-5; ☎ 7-832-1434; Calle 1 & Paseo in Galerías de Paseo).

DRINKING
HABANA VIEJA

Taberna de La Muralla (Map pp130-1; ☎ 7-866-4453; San Ignacio cnr Muralla, Plaza Vieja; ☼ 10am-1am) Cuba's one and only microbrewery has a great corner spot on the plaza, a sizzling grill menu and light and dark house brews (per mug/minikeg CUC$2/6).

Bar Dos Hermanos (Map pp130-1; ☎ 7-861-3514; San Pedro No 304 cnr Sol; ☼ 24hr) A wonderful old wooden dive, the food and live music here are surprisingly good; the salty atmosphere adds to the flavor.

Fundación Havana Club (Map pp130-1; ☎ 7-861-1900; Av del Puerto; ☼ 9am-midnight) For something more upscale, try the Bar Havana Club inside here, serving rum concoctions and live music nightly.

Restaurante-Bar Viñales (Map pp130-1; O'Reilly cnr Compostela) For local atmosphere, you can't beat this big, open place featuring strong cocktails and colorful characters.

CENTRO HABANA

Rather than rubbing sunburned elbows with the tour-bus crowd in El Floridita, head to the nearby **Monserrate Bar** (Map pp130-1; ☎ 7-860-9751; Obrapía No 410) or **La Zaragozana** (Map pp130-1; ☎ 7-867-1040; Av de Bélgica, cnr Obispo; ⊗ noon-midnight), with foot-stomping flamenco from 9pm. Between the two, **Restaurante El Castillo de Farnés** (Map pp130-1; ☎ 7-867-1030; Av de Bélgica No 361 at Obrapía; ⊗ noon-midnight) is a pleasant post-theater place, with sidewalk tables.

VEDADO

Opus Bar (Map pp134-5; Calzada & Calle D above Teatro Amadeo Roldán; ⊗ 3pm-3am) With individual candlelit tables and overstuffed chairs, this is Havana's (good) approximation of a lounge. The wall of windows makes it a great sunset spot.

For a more intellectual scene, check out the basement bar at the **Centro de Prensa Internacional** (Map pp134-5; Calles 23 & O; ⊗ 9am-7pm), where journalists talk shop. Breezy **Café Fresa y Chocolate** (Map pp134-5; Calle 23 cnr 12) is similar, only it's actors and directors instead of writers.

ENTERTAINMENT

Traditional Music

Casa de la Trova (Map pp130-1; ☎ 7-879-3373; San Lázaro No 661 near Parque Maceo; admission free; ⊗ 8-11pm Tue-Sun) Headquarters of Havana's *son* sound, classic Cuban music fans will enjoy the jams that coalesce here regularly.

El Hurón Azul (Map pp134-5; ☎ 7-832-4551; Calles 17 & H; admission CUC$1-5) Uneac is the nerve center of official art and intellectual life in Cuba, and this is its social club. Head here for an Afro-Cuban *peña* (musical performance or get-together) on Wednesday, boleros from 10pm to 2am Saturday, or jazz and *trova* (traditional poetic singing) from 5pm Thursday.

Hotel Nacional (Map pp134-5; admission CUC$25; ⊗ 9pm Sat) Yes, members of the Buena Vista Social Club still gig at this hotel (p138).

Conjunto Folklórico Nacional de Cuba (Map pp134-5; ☎ 7-830-3060; Calle 4 No 103 btwn Calzada & Calle 5; admission CUC$5; ⊗ 3pm Sat) has a steamy Sábado de Rumba – audience participation is encouraged. Another recommended

rumba happens at the wild **Callejón de Hamel** (Callejón de Hamel btwn Aramburu & Hospital; admission by donation; ⊗ 11am).

Jazz

Jazz Club La Zorra y El Cuervo (Map pp134-5; ☎ 7-833-2402; Calles 23 & O, Vedado; admission CUC$5-10; ⊗ 10pm) The freestyle jazz here is a nice change from salsa, especially during International Jazz Fest jams. The Sunday matinee (at 3pm, admission CUC$3) with rock cover band Dimensión Vertical is great fun.

Jazz Café (Map pp134-5; ☎ 7-55-35-56; Calle 1 & Paseo, Galerías de Paseo; drink minimum CUC$10; ⊗ noon-late) This upscale club overlooking the Malecón is perfect for sunset cocktails. At night, the club swings into action with jazz, *timba* (contemporary salsa) and salsa.

Rock, Reggae & Rap

The biggest January 1 free concerts happen in the Tribuna Anti-Imperialista (Los Van Van usually headlines).

Patio de María (Map pp134-5; Calle 37 No 262 btwn Paseo & Calle 2; admission CUP5; ⊗ 10pm-2am) This legendary club near the Teatro Nacional is a great indoor-outdoor venue packed with black-clad, head-banging Habaneros.

Anfiteatro Parque Almendares (Map pp134-5; Calle 23 & Río Almendares; admission CUP2-5) This riverside amphitheater hosts terrific concerts by the likes of Frank Delgado and Interactivo. Regular *peñas* include reggae at 8pm on Friday and rap at 8pm on Saturday.

Salsa

Casa de la Música Centro Habana (Map pp130-1; ☎ 7-878-4727; Av de Italia; matinee CUC$2-4, night CUC$10-20) Miramar (☎ 7-202-3868; Calle 20 No 3308 cnr Av 35; ⊗ 10pm Tue-Sat) Famous bands like NG la Banda and Pupi y Su Son Son play here regularly to a mixed crowd.

Delirio Habanero (Map pp134-5; ☎ 7-873-5713; Paseo & Calle 39; admission CUC$5-15; ⊗ 6pm-late Tue-Sun) This plush lounge upstairs in the Teatro Nacional de Cuba hosts everything from young *trovadores* to salsa stars. The deep couches overlook the Plaza de la Revolución.

Nightclubs

El Chevere (Map pp134-5; ☎ 7-204-4990; Calles 49-A & 28-A in Parque Almendares; admission CUC$10-15; ⊗ 11pm-4am) One of Havana's hottest discos, this place hosts a good mix of locals and tourists.

Cafe Cantante (Map pp134-5; ☎ 7-879-0710; Paseo & Calle 39; admission CUC$5-10; ☿ 9pm-4am Tue-Sat) Beside the Teatro Nacional de Cuba, this is a popular disco with quality live salsa music and dancing. Síntesis lights up the place on Friday nights from 10pm.

Cabarets

Tropicana Nightclub (☎ 7-267-0110; Calle 72 No 4504 at Av 43, Marianao; admission from CUC$65, camera extra; ☿ box office 10am 4pm, show at 10pm) Cuba's most famous nightclub opened in 1939 and is still going strong. Buy your tickets directly from the box office and you can choose your own table (important, as switched tables and botched reservations are common). When bookings are light, bar seats may be available (CUC$25), not sold in advance.

Theater

Gran Teatro de La Habana (Map pp130-1; ☎ 7-861-3077; Prado & San Rafael; admission CUC$10; ☿ box office 9am-6pm Mon-Sat, 9am-3pm Sun) This magnificent theater is closely associated with its most famous resident: the acclaimed Ballet Nacional de Cuba and its founder Alicia Alonso.

Teatro Nacional de Cuba (Map pp134-5; ☎ 7-879-6011; Paseo & Calle 39; per person CUC$10; ☿ box office 9am-5pm & before performances) This modern theater on the Plaza de la Revolución hosts landmark concerts, foreign theater troupes, the La Colmenita children's company and the Ballet Nacional de Cuba.

Teatro Amadeo Roldán (Map pp134-5; ☎ 7-832-4522; Calzada & Calle D; admission CUC$10) This modern, 886-seat theater is the seat of the Orquesta Sinfónica Nacional (performing at 11am on Sunday, in season). Try to catch master Leo Brouwer conducting. Major concerts (eg Egberto Gismonti, Aldo Pérez-Gavilán) also go down here.

Other spaces:

Teatro Mella (Map pp134-5; ☎ 7-833-5651; Línea No 657 btwn Calles A & B; admission CUC$5-10)

Teatro Nacional de Guiñol (Map pp134-5; ☎ 7-832-6262; Calle M btwn Calles 17 & 19; adult/child CUC$3/2; ☿ 3pm Fri, 10:30am & 5pm Sat & Sun) Puppet shows and children's theater.

Cinemas

Havana has a vibrant cinema scene, with some 200 theaters citywide. Movie tickets cost CUP2; most theaters show Cuban movies and mainstream fare flowing from Hollywood.

Cine Yara (Map pp134-5; ☎ 7-832-9430; Calles 23 & L) Havana's most famous cinema also has the best popcorn.

Cine Riviera (Map pp134-5; ☎ 7-830-9564; Calle 23 No 507 near Calle G) Also hosts quality rock and pop concerts on occasion (admission CUC$10).

Cine Charles Chaplin (Map pp134-5; ☎ 7-831-1101; Calle 23 No 1157 btwn Calles 10 & 12) The theater of the Instituto Cubano del Arte e Industria Cinematográfico (ICAIC) has special screenings (premieres, foreign films, festivals etc) and Dolby surround sound.

Sports

Estadio Latinoamericano (Map pp134-5; ☎ 7-870-6526; Zequiera No 312 at Pedro Pérez; admission CUP3; ☿ 8:30pm Mon-Sat, 1:30pm Sun) Baseball games happen at this 58,000-seat stadium in Cerro, just south of Centro Habana, from October to April (and beyond if Havana's Industriales make the play-offs).

SHOPPING

Fería de la Artesanía (Map pp130-1; Tacón btwn Tejadillo & Chacón; ☿ Wed-Sat) Paintings, *guayaberas* (pleated, buttoned men's shirts), woodwork, Che everything, jewelry and more can be haggled over at this open-air handicraft market.

Fundación Havana Club Shop (☿ 9am-9pm) Come to the Fundación Havana Club (p140) for cool Havana Club gear, such as martini glasses (CUC$6) or mojito glasses (CUC$2).

Fería de la Artesanía (Map pp134-5; Malecón btwn Calles D & E; ☿ 10:30am-6pm Mon, Tue & Thu-Sun) This big artisan market distinguishes itself with its huge selection of paintings and historic ephemera – stamps, coins, baseball cards etc.

Promociones de ICAIC (Map pp134-5; ☎ 7-832-9430; Calles 23 & L, in Cine Yara) A fabulous selection of movie posters, T-shirts and classic Cuban films are sold here. Another outlet is inside Café Fresa y Chocolate (p141).

GETTING THERE & AWAY
Air

José Martí International Airport is at Av de la Independencia, 15.5 miles (25km) southwest of Havana. Terminal 1, southeast of the runway, handles domestic Cubana flights. A couple of miles away on Av de la Independencia is the dreaded Terminal 2, which receives direct flights from the US (closed until further notice). Most international flights use Terminal 3, a modern facility, 1.5 miles (2.5km) west of Terminal 2. Aerocaribbean and Aerogaviota use Terminal 5 (aka the Caribbean Terminal). For information on flights to Havana, see p177 and p178.

To book a flight, take a number at **Cubana de Aviación** (Map pp134-5; ☎ 7-834-4949; www.cubana.cu; Airline Bldg, Calle 23 No 64; ☼ 8:30am-4pm Mon-Fri, 8:30am-noon Sat). **Aerocaribbean** (Map pp134-5; ☎ 7-879-7524/25; www.aero-caribbean.com; Airline Bldg, Calle 23 No 64) is located a couple of doors down.

Bus

The **Víazul** (☎ 7-881-1413; www.viazul.cu; Calle 26 & Zoológico, Nuevo Vedado) terminal is inconveniently located 1.9 miles (3km) southwest of Plaza de la Revolución. Infotur (p129) and **Cubatur** (Map pp134-5; Calle 23 cnr M) sell tickets. See the boxed text below for bus services.

The Santiago de Cuba bus stops at Santa Clara (CUC$18).

Taxi

Taxis at the **Víazul** (Calle 26 & Zoológico, Nuevo Vedado) terminal offer fares for up to four people to Varadero (CUC$44), Pinar del Río (CUC$54), Santa Clara (CUC$72) Cienfuegos (CUC$88) and Trinidad (CUC$102).

Train

Trains depart from Havana's **Estación Central de Ferrocarriles** (Map pp130-1; ☎ 7-861-7651, 7-862-1920; Av de Bélgica & Arsenal). Foreigners are supposed to buy hard-currency tickets at **FerroCuba** (Map pp130-1; ☎ 7-862-4971, 7-861-8540; Arsenal near Aponte; ☼ 9am-6pm). See the boxed text, p144, for train services.

GETTING AROUND
To/From the Airport

For all practical purposes, there is no public transportation from the airport to the city center, and taxi drivers work this to their full advantage. A taxi should cost around CUC$15, but you'll be told CUC$25; bargain hard. A taxi between any of the terminals costs CUC$3.

Bicycle & Moped

El Orbe Bike Rentals (Map pp130-1; Av de las Misiones; ☼ 9am-6pm Mon-Sat) rents out beat-up cruisers for CUC$2/12 per hour/day. You have to leave identification as deposit; there's a parts and service store on site.

Rumbos (☎ 7-203-3376; Av 3 btwn Calles 28 & 30, Playa; rental per 1/2/3/24hr CUC$10/13/15/24) The only place to rent mopeds.

Local Transportation

To get from Vedado to Centro Habana, the No 200 bus is the best bet (stops across from Centro de Prensa Internacional) or the P4 (stops across from Coppelia).

Panataxi (☎ 7-55-55-55) has the cheapest official taxis. Fancier taxis can be ordered from **TaxiOK** (☎ 7-204-0000) and **Transgaviota** (☎ 7-267-1626).

Coco taxis are the yellow eggs-on-wheels you will see zipping all over town; the taxis carry three people and cost CUC$0.50 per kilometer.

AROUND HAVANA
Parque Histórico Militar Morro-Cabaña

The sweeping views of Havana from this side of the bay are lovely and a trip to the old forts of the **Parque Histórico Militar Morro-Cabaña** is worthwhile. Beat the heat with a drink at one of the shoreline bars or come at sunset – sensational. If you only visit one of the sites out here, make it La Cabaña.

SERVICES FROM HAVANA'S VÍAZUL BUS TERMINAL

Destination	Cost (one way)	Distance	Duration	Schedule
Cienfuegos	CUC$20	158 miles (254km)	5 hours	8:15am, 1pm
Pinar del Río	CUC$11	101 miles (162km)	2½ hours	9am
Santiago de Cuba	CUC$51	535 miles (861km)	16 hours	9:30am, 3pm, 8pm
Trinidad	CUC$25	208 miles (335km)	6 hours	8:15am, 1pm
Varadero	CUC$10	87 miles (140km)	3 hours	8am, 8:30am, 4pm
Viñales	CUC$12	117 miles (189km)	3¼ hours	9am

SERVICES FROM HAVANA'S ESTACIÓN CENTRAL DE FERROCARRILES

Destination	Cost (one way)	Distance	Schedule
Cienfuegos	CUC$11	158 miles (254km)	7:30am, alternate days
Pinar del Río	CUC$6.50	101 miles (162km)	10:35pm, alternate days
Santa Clara	CUC$10	171 miles (276km)	3:15pm daily
Santiago de Cuba	CUC$50/62	535 miles (861km)	5:05pm, alternate days

The **Castillo de los Tres Santos Reyes Magnos del Morro** (☎ 7-863-7941; admission incl museum entrance CUC$4; ☺ 8am-8pm) was erected between 1589 and 1630 on an abrupt limestone headland to protect the entrance to the harbor. In 1762, the British captured El Morro by attacking from the landward side and digging a tunnel under the walls. In 1845, the first lighthouse in Cuba was added to the castle (admission CUC$2). There is also a **maritime museum**.

The **Fortaleza de San Carlos de la Cabaña** (admission CUC$4; ☺ 9am-6pm) was built between 1763 and 1774 to deny attackers the long ridge overlooking Havana. It's one of the largest colonial fortresses in the Americas, replete with grassy moats, ancient chapel and cobblestone streets. Dictators Gerardo Machado y Morales and Batista used the fortress as a military prison, and Che Guevara established his postrevolution headquarters here. Be sure to visit the creative Havana skyline **mirador** (viewpoint) on the other side of the **Museo de Comandancia del Che** here.

Nightly at 9pm, a cannon is fired on the harbor side of La Cabaña by a squad attired in 19th-century uniforms, a hold-over from Spanish times when these shots signaled that the city gates were closing. The **cañonazo** (admission CUC$6) begins at 8:30pm, followed by a concert by Moncada, a geriatric rock band.

Cyclists can cross the bay from Havana with the specially designed CicloBus leaving from Dragones and Águila on Parque El Curita. A taxi from Habana Vieja should cost around CUC$3.

Playas del Este

Havana's pine-fringed Riviera, Playas del Este, begins at Bacuranao, 11 miles (18km) east of Havana, and continues east through **Santa María del Mar** (the nicest of the beaches here) to Guanabo, 16.7 miles (27km) from the capital. These beaches provide an effortless escape from Havana should you need it, and there are many casas particulares in Guanabo (look for the green triangle).

The beach is lined with **rentals** including windsurfers (per hour CUC$6), catamarans (per hour CUC$12) and beach chairs (per three hours CUC$2). Several simple fish restaurants line the beach.

Bus No 400 to Guanabo leaves hourly from the rotunda at Desamparados near the train station in Habana Vieja. Bus No 405 runs between Guanabacoa and Guanabo.

A taxi from Playas del Este to Havana will cost around CUC$20.

PINAR DEL RÍO PROVINCE

Tobacco leaves and pine trees, sugarcane and bright carpets of rice: come to Pinar del Río Province for some green. With rock climbing, caving, diving and birding sprinkled throughout two Unesco Biosphere Reserves and one World Heritage site, this is Cuba's outdoor adventure hub.

Viñales is famous for its *mogotes* (limestone hills like misshapen marshmallows) and is one of Cuba's most photogenic areas.

To the east is the tobacco-growing region of San Juan y Martínez and the Vuelta Abajo plantations, where the world's finest tobacco thrives in the sandy soil. The majority of export-quality tobacco comes from here. The best time to visit is at harvest time, from January to March.

Moving west, tobacco gives way to the scrubby Parque Nacional Península de Guanahacabibes. This wonderful area boasts remote beaches (with ace scuba diving), bird-watching and hiking.

Recently, Pinar has taken the brunt of Cuba's hurricanes, getting hit back-to-back

by Charley and Category 5 Iván in August
and September, 2004.

Getting There & Away

With few recommendable sights and a
swarm of pesky *jineteros*, the city of Pinar
del Río is useful for transportation, but little else. From the Pinar del Río bus station
(Adela Azcuy between Colón and Coman-
dante Pinares), Víazul leaves for Viñales
daily at 11:30am (CUC$6) and Havana at
2:25pm (CUC$11). Purchase tickets at the
window upstairs from 8am to 7pm.

Here is also where you hire cars for a day
in Viñales (CUC$35 and up or CUC$15
one-way). Private/state taxis to María la
Gorda will cost CUC$35/CUC$50 one-way;
there is no public transportation.

Getting Around

Horse carts (CUP1) on Isabel Rubio near
Adela Azcuy go to the Hospital Provincial
and out onto the Carretera Central.

VIÑALES

Tucked within the Sierra de los Órganos,
16.7 miles (27km) north of Pinar del Río, is
Parque Nacional Viñales, a Unesco World
Heritage site and one of Cuba's most magnificent natural settings. A fertile plain of
several valleys separated by pincushion hills
called *mogotes*, these limestone formations
play host to a healthy rock-climbing scene.
Viñales, founded in 1875, is also the name of
the main valley village (population 14,279).

This is a good area for explorers: rent a
moped or bike and poke through the Valle
Ancón or up to Cayo Jutías; rock climb;
hike deep into the Gran Caverna de Santo
Tomás; or arrange a horse and guide to visit
spots not in any guidebook.

Information

Banco de Crédito y Comercio (☎ 8-79-31-30; Salva-
dor Cisneros No 58; ꙮ 8am-noon & 1:30-3pm Mon-Fri)
Cadeca (☎ 8-79-63-34; Salvador Cisneros & Adela
Azcuy; ꙮ 8:30am-6pm Mon-Sat)
Cubanacán (☎ 8-79-63-93; Salvador Cisneros No 63C;
ꙮ 8:30am-12:30pm & 1:30-9pm; Internet per hr CUC$5)
Etecsa (Ceferino Fernández No 3; Internet per min
CUC$0.10) Make international calls here.
Inmigración (cnr Salvador Cisneros & Ceferino Fernández;
ꙮ 8am-5pm Mon-Fri)
Post office (☎ 8-79-32-12; Ceferino Fernández No 14;
9am-6pm Mon-Sat)

Sights

Two of the coolest sights in town are independently operated affairs. Across from
the Cupet, look for a funky gate hung with
fresh fruit. This is the **Jardín de las Hermanas
Caridad** (Salvador Cisneros No 5; donations accepted;
ꙮ 8am-5pm), a sprawling, nearly 100-year-
old garden. Cascades of orchids bloom beside plastic doll heads, lilies grow in soft
groves and turkeys run amok.

Just past the baseball stadium – look for
the giant T-Rex and teeny Martí – is the
Mundo Prehistórico Museo Parque (Adela Azcuy
Norte No 6; donations accepted; ꙮ 9am-6pm), an outdoor labyrinth of local natural history. Created by Jesús Arencibia, his explanations of
the fossils and endemic plants are peppered
with humor, poetry and lore.

The **Museo Municipal** (☎ 8-79-33-95; Salvador
Cisneros No 115; admission CUC$1; ꙮ 9am-10pm Mon-
Sat, 8am-noon Sun) occupies the former home
of independence heroine Adela Azcuy
(1861–1914). The small, but earnest, collection focuses on the history of Viñales,
replete with reconstructed cave. Hikes set
out from here (see p146).

About 2.5 miles (4km) west of Viñales
is the **Mural de la Prehistoria** (admission CUC$1;
ꙮ 8am-7pm), a 393ft-long (120m) paint-
ing on the side of Mogote Dos Hermanas.
Designed in 1961, it took 15 people five
years to complete. Ponder the psychedelic/
horrific spectacle with a drink at the bar.
Horseback riding is available (per 15 minutes/
one hour CUC$1/5). For phenomenal val-
ley views, hike the **Sendero Al Mural** at the
base of the cliff to the top of the *mogote*;
allow an hour, round-trip.

The spectacular **Gran Caverna de Santo
Tomás** (admission CUC$8; ꙮ 9:30am-3:30pm) is not
to be missed. With over 28.6 miles (46km)
of galleries on eight levels, it's Cuba's largest cave system. Headlamps are provided
for the 0.6 mile (1km), 90-minute guided
tour (in Spanish or English) that takes in
surreal formations including giant stalagmites and stone percussive pipes. The
cavern is at El Moncada, 8.7 miles (14km)
west of the Dos Hermanas turn-off and 0.9
miles (1.5km) off of the road to Minas de
Matahambre.

For an idyllic **beach**, head north to **Cayo
Jutías** (admission incl 1 drink CUC$5). The *pedreplén*
begins 2.5 miles (4km) west of Santa Lucía.
Restaurante Cayo Jutías (ꙮ 9am-5pm) is here. The

CUBA

fastest, prettiest route is via El Moncada and Minas de Matahambre. Two private rooms are available for rent in Santa Lucía or you can camp.

Activities

HIKING

The Museo Municipal (p145) offers five **walking tours** (CUC$5; 9am & 3pm) that make a great introduction to the area. Tours last from two to four hours and are expertly led in French, English, Spanish or Portuguese. Longer hikes can be arranged.

The **Maravillas de Viñales trail** (admission CUC$1, payable at the trailhead) is a 3.1 mile (5km) signposted hike beginning 1.2 miles (2km) before El Moncada, 8 miles (13km) from the Dos Hermanas turn-off. This makes a good three-hour hike with endemic plants and orchids lining the trail; it's not quite a loop and leaves you about 547yd (500m) downhill from the trailhead.

ROCK CLIMBING

Viñales is gaining a reputation as one of the premier rock-climbing spots in the Americas. At last count there were 150 routes at all levels of difficulty, with more opening all the time. October to April is the preferred climbing season. Climbers should check www.cubaclimbing.com for the skinny and bring extra gear to share, as local supplies are ridiculously limited.

Sleeping

Campismo Dos Hermanas (8-79-32-23; s/d CUC$11/15; P) The setting among the *mogotes* can't be beat. The two- and four-bed concrete cabins here are a good place to meet other travelers. There's a restaurant, horseback riding and hiking around the nearby *mogotes*. It fills fast, especially on weekends when Cubans come to party.

Hotel Rancho San Vicente (8-79-62-01; s/d incl breakfast CUC$40/50; P) Nestled in a grove 4.3 miles (7km) north of Viñales village, this hotel will make you go 'ahhhhh.' Skip the 20 older cabins and go straight for the new wooden units (Nos 6 to 43) with lovely natural furnishings, delicious baths and sliding glass doors onto a porch. There are on-site sulfur baths and massage.

La Ermita (8-79-60-71; s/d incl breakfast CUC$54/69; P) With its dazzling hilltop views and cozy furnishings, this is a top pick, 1.2 miles (2km) east of Viñales village. Too bad the walls are so thin. Poolside mojitos are highly recommended. Horseback riding (CUC$5 per hour) is available. This is the only hotel within easy walking distance of town.

Eating & Drinking

El Estanco II (Carretera de Puerto Esperanza; 10am-11pm) This is a decent pizza and beer place on the road half a mile (1km) north of town. A pizza costs CUC$1, a plate of spaghetti twice that.

CASAS PARTICULARES – VIÑALES

Casa El Cafetal – Martha Martínez (8-79-33-14; Adela Azcuy Norte Final; r CUC$15-20; P) Simple, clean room tucked in outstanding locale amid orchards with *mogote* views; gracious hosts.

Ricardo Suárez (8-79-32-69; Salvador Cisneros No 46; r CUC$20;) Spiffy independent room with private terrace, views, two beds.

Villa El Niño (Adela Azcuy Norte No 6; r CUC$20;) New, spotless room across from baseball stadium with *mogote* views from front porch.

Villa Caricia (8-75-33-76, 8-79-60-16; lhdez@princesa.pri.sld.cu; Camilo Cienfuegos No 7A; r CUC$15-20; P) Quiet room with independent entrance and terrace in modern house; friendly hosts; private.

Xiomara Duarte (8-79-32-18; Orlando Nodarse No 50; r CUC$15) Exuberant and flexible hosts compensate for the regular, but comfortable, rooms. Great herb garden.

Villa La Rueda – Orestes & Catalina (8-79-33-69; Salvador Cisneros No 214; r CUC$20; P) Room with independent entrance opens onto patio with views; Villa Cristina at No 206 also recommended.

Villa Cary (8-79-32-37; Salvador Cisneros No 8; r CUC$15-20;) Plain room leads onto patio; nice front porch; reader recommended.

Flora Lozano (8-79-33-19; Salvador Cisneros Interior, Edificio Colonial No 2, Apt 3; r CUC$15) Clean room with refrigerator and shared bath behind Policlínico in Microbrigade building.

Villa Onelio Paez Rodríguez (8-79-33-80, 8-79-33-94; Adela Azcuy No 46; r CUC$15;) Two rooms, one with independent entrance; small patio.

Restaurante Las Magnolias (☎ 8-79-60-62; ⊙ 8am-4pm) The coziest place to eat out here is across from La Cueva del Indio. Sink into the complete lunch (CUC$8) in the attractive patio here.

Next door to Restaurante Las Magnolias is the snack bar **Rincón del Indio** (⊙ 7am-9pm). Other simple places include **Restaurante Las Brisas** (☎ 8-79-33-53; Salvador Cisneros No 96; ⊙ 11am-2pm & 6-9pm), a passable state place where you can fill up for under CUC$4, and **Cafetería Cubanitas** (Adela Azcuy & Rafael Trejo; ⊙ 9:30am-10pm) for sandwiches and snacks.

Viñales' *mercado agropecuario* is 109yd (100m) from town at the west end of Salvador Cisneros toward Dos Hermanas. Get your peso rum and bread here.

Of the many places within spitting distance of Viñales serving *asado* (roast pork), the **restaurant** (☎ 8-79-62-60; ⊙ 11:30am-7pm) at the Mural de la Prehistoria is the tastiest. Roasted and smoked over natural charcoal, the sublime pork melts in your mouth. The CUC$15 complete lunch is huge. A good second choice is **Ranchón y Finca San Vincente** (☎ 8-79-61-10; ⊙ noon-5pm) near the Cueva del Indio exit.

Entertainment

There are two places in town at which to party.

Patio del Decimista (☎ 8-79-60-14; Salvador Cisneros No 102; admission free; ⊙ music from 9pm) Serves live music nightly and cold beers on its patio

El Viñalero (Salvador Cisneros No 105; ⊙ 7:30am-midnight) Across the street from Patio del Decimista, this place also has live music and sidewalk tables.

The Casa de la Cultura, situated on the main square, has a full program of cultural activities.

Getting There & Around

To reach Viñales from the south, you take the nauseatingly curvy road (16.7 miles/27km) from Pinar del Río; from Havana, take the unmarked spur road at km136; Viñales is 16 miles (26km) further on.

BUS

Víazul (Salvador Cisneros No 63A; ⊙ 8am-noon & 1-3pm) is opposite Viñales' main square. The Havana departure via Pinar del Río is at 1:30pm daily (CUC$12).

CAR

The following agencies rent out wheels:
Cubanacán (☎ 8-79-63-93; Salvador Cisneros No 63C; ⊙ 9am-7pm) Has mopeds (per day CUC$23) and bicycles (per day/week CUC$6/20), and transfers to Cayo Levisa (CUC$25) and María la Gorda (one-way CUC$15).

Havanautos (☎ 8-79-63-90) At the Cupet; rents out mopeds.

Micar (☎ 8-79-63-30; Salvador Cisneros)

TAXI

Taxis parked alongside the square will take you to Pinar del Río (CUC$10) or Gran Caverna de Santo Tomás (CUC$16, round-trip).

MARÍA LA GORDA

'Fat Maria' is the name shared by Cuba's most remote mainland beach and its fun hotel/dive center, about 93 miles (150km) southwest of Pinar del Río. Located on the Península de Guanahacabibes (a Unesco Biosphere Reserve), the area is a splendid combination of mangroves, white sands, teal waters and coral rock. In September 2004, Hurricane Iván uprooted trees and clogged reefs with 160mph (257 km/h) winds. Marine biologists estimate it will take up to five years for the coral to recuperate, and the reserve's 172 species of birds are feeling the pain too. Still, María la Gorda is one of Cuba's most idyllic beaches – recommended if you want sand and sea without package tourists.

Estación Ecológica Guanahacabibes (☎ 84-32-77; www.ecovida.pinar.cu/Png/index.htm; ⊙ 7:30am-3:30pm) offers a number of guided tours in Spanish, English or Italian to Cabo de San Antonio (per person CUC$10; five hours). During the 67-mile (108km) round-trip you will have rough *diente de perro* (dog's teeth) rock on one side and brilliant blue sea on the other. Iguanas, *jutías* (an edible tree rat) and birds are highlights. You supply transportation.

Of the two **hiking trails**, Cueva las Perlas (CUC$8, two hours, 1.9 miles/3km) is superior, highlighted by dense forest and Pearl Cave, a multigallery cave system of which 328yd (300m) is accessible. Much of the Del Bosque al Mar 'hike' (CUC$6, 1½ hours, 0.9 miles/1.4km) is on hot tarmac. Its saving grace is the terrific shoreline cenote filled with tropical fish.

There are 30 identified **dive sites** with incredible concentrations of fish, including El

Valle de Coral Negro, a 328ft-long (100m) black-coral wall, and El Salón de María, a 65ft-deep (20m) cave with feather stars and Technicolor corals. The **Puertosol International Dive Center** (☎ 82-77-81-31; per dive CUC$35, plus CUC$7.50 for equipment; ☷ courses 9am & 3pm) at Hotel María la Gorda offers certification and introductory courses and night dives. Snorkelers can ride along for CUC$12.

Four clean, comfortable rooms with private bath are available at the **Radar Meteorológico La Bajada** (☎ 84-32-77; per person CUC$9; ☷). Bring food (plus extra to share) to prepare in the kitchen. Camping is possible on the coastal road between here and Hotel María la Gorda.

Next to the meteorological station is the **Restaurante La Bajada** (☷ 8:30am-10:30pm), with cold beers, fried chicken, pork fillets and loud music.

Hotel María la Gorda (☎ 82-77-81-31, fax 82-77-80-77; s/d incl breakfast CUC$50/68; ☷ ☷), right on a palm-fringed beach, has intimate wooden cabins tucked into the forest 82yd (75m) from the beach (author's choice), or concrete motel-type buildings with refrigerator and porch (some face the parking lot) on the beach. Good (for Cuba) buffet meals cost CUC$11/15 for lunch/dinner. Far from a posh resort, hammocks strung between palm trees and dive talk over rum highballs is what this place is about. The hotel doesn't accept credit cards.

Transtur (☎ 84-75-01-30) at the hotel offers 4WD service with driver to Cabo de San Antonio (CUC$50, four persons max), and transfers to Viñales (CUC$15 per person) and Havana (CUC$120, four persons max).

The marina at Cabo San Antonio provides mooring and services for foreign boats.

CENTRAL CUBA

Long, boring stretches of sugarcane and cows belie the jewels that await travelers in central Cuba. Venture into the provinces of Matanzas, Villa Clara, Cienfuegos or Sancta Spíritus, and you'll discover some of Cuba's most varied and intriguing sights. These include colonial Trinidad, the pristine beaches at Varadero and Cayo Santa María, hiking in Topes de Collantes and important historic monuments including the Che memorial in Santa Clara.

Santa Clara and Sancti Spíritus Provinces played a pivotal role in the triumph of the Cuban Revolution, as these were the fronts where Che Guevara and Camilo Cienfuegos fought – and won – respectively.

Getting There & Away

There are international airports at Varadero and Cienfuegos; see p774 for details of international flights to Cuba.

Víazul (www.viazul.cu) has daily departures from Havana to Varadero; Havana to Trinidad (stopping in Cienfuegos); Varadero to Trinidad (stopping in Santa Clara); Trinidad to Santiago de Cuba; and Havana to Santiago de Cuba stopping in Santa Clara.

Driving or cycling, you have the choice of the Autopista, a multilane highway that makes for fast driving, or the Carretera Central. While the latter is certainly more scenic, the driving can be laborious as you dodge horse carts, goats and tractors.

VARADERO
pop 18,000

At the end of the Vía Blanca, 87 miles (140km) east of Havana, is Varadero, Cuba's Cancún. One foreign tourist in three comes to Cuba specifically to vacation in Varadero and with reason: the sun, sand and aquamarine sea combine with the all-inclusive resorts (where room, food and drink – except top-shelf liquor – activities and entertainment are included in the price) for the perfect tropical getaway. And yet, Varadero lacks intimacy and authenticity, and independent travelers (who are *technically* prevented from renting private rooms) may come away disappointed.

Information

IMMIGRATION
Inmigración (1ra Av & Calle 39; ☷ 9am-noon & 1:30-3:30pm Mon-Fri) Extend visas here; stamps are sold at Banco de Crédito.

INTERNET ACCESS
Most hotels have Internet at CUC$6 per hour.
Etecsa Central Varadero (☎ 45-61-41-38; 1ra Av cnr Calle 30; ☷ 9am-9pm); Plaza América (☎ 45-66-86-65)

MEDICAL SERVICES
Clínica Internacional Servimed (☎ 45-66-77-10; 1ra Av 1 & Calle 60; ☷ 24hr) Medical or dental consultations

(CUC$25); hotel calls (CUC$50). There's a good, 24-hour pharmacy here.

Servimed Farmacia Internacional (Plaza América, Av Las Américas & Calle 61; ☺ 9am-7pm) A well-stocked pharmacy.

MONEY
In Varadero, hotels and meals are payable in euros. Most hotels have currency exchange desks.

Banco de Crédito y Comercio (☎ 45-61-26-16; 1ra Av at Calle 36; ☺ 9am-1:30pm & 3-5pm Mon-Fri) Expect lines.

Banco Financiero Internacional (☎ 45-61-18-69; 1ra Av & Calle 32; ☺ 9am-3pm Mon-Fri, 9am-5pm Sat & Sun); Plaza América (☎ 45-66-82-72; at Av Las Américas & Calle 61; ☺ 9am-noon & 1-6pm Mon-Fri, 9am-6pm Sat & Sun)

Cadeca (☎ 45-66-78-59; Av de la Playa & Calle 41; ☺ 8:30am-6pm Mon-Sat, 8:30am-noon Sun) Western Union here.

PHOTOGRAPHY
Photo Service (☎ 45-66-72-91; Calle 64 No 456 btwn Avs 2da & 3ra; ☺ 9am 10pm) Downloads digital photos.

Photoclub (☎ 45-66-70-15; 1ra Av & Calle 42)

POST
DHL (☎ /fax 45-66-73-30; 1ra Av No 3903 btwn Calles 39 & 40; ☺ 8am-noon & 1:30-5:30pm Mon-Fri)

Post office (☎ 45-61-22-14; Av 1 at Calle 36; ☺ 8am-6pm Mon-Sat)

TRAVEL AGENCIES
Cubanacán (☎ 45-66-70-61; Av Playa & Calle 2)

Cubatur (☎ 45-61-44-05; fax 45-66-70-48; 1ra Av & Calle 33; ☺ 8:30am-6pm)

Havanatur Tour & Travel Av Las Américas (☎ 45-66-77-08; Av Las Américas; ☺ 8am-8pm); Central Varadero (☎ 45-61-43-85/6; Av de la Playa btwn Calles 36 & 37; ☺ 8am-6pm)

Sights
The **Museo Municipal de Varadero** (☎ 45-61-31-89; Calle 57, off 1ra Av; admission CUC$1; ☺ 9am-6pm) displays period furniture and Varadero history in a large, two-story beach mansion erected in 1921.

Parque Josone (1ra Av & Calle 58; admission free; ☺ 9am-midnight) is Varadero's Central Park. The expansive, shady grounds feature an attractive lake with quaint bridges and geese flitting about; rowboat rides are CUC$2 per hour. There are restaurants, plus a public **swimming pool** (admission CUC$2) that's surprisingly uncrowded.

Everything east of the gate on Av Las Américas, beyond Calle 64, once belonged to the US chemical millionaire Irénée Dupont de Nemours, including a three-story mansion called Xanadú (now a B&B; see p150) and a golf course.

Some 1.9 miles (3km) east on Autopista Sur is the 328yd (300m) **Cueva de Ambrosio** (admission CUC$3) which has 47 pre-Columbian drawings. Discovered in 1961, the cave also served as a refuge for escaped slaves and is part of the laughable **Reserva Ecológica Varahicacos** (☺ 9am-4:30pm). There's more earth moving than preserving happening here and ongoing resort construction has left only a scratch of protected land. The best site out here is **Playa Las Calaveras** (admission CUC$3; ☺ 9am-5pm), a shrinking, but beautiful, beach.

Activities
DIVING & SNORKELING
There are over 30 dive sites around Varadero, with a good mix of beginner and more advanced wreck and cave dives. There is only one shore dive, however, and boat dives require an hour in transit (each way). Conditions are often too rough in the winter, when divers are driven to Playa Girón on the south coast (90 minutes).

Varadero has three dive centers, all with similar offers including 26ft (8m) introduction dives at Playa Coral (one/two tanks CUC$40/60), boat dives (one/two tanks CUC$50/70 or four/six tanks CUC$105/150), and cave and night dives (CUC$50). Snorkelers can ride along for CUC$25. All offer American Canadian Underwater Certifications (ACUC) courses.

Acua Diving Center (☎ 45-66-80-64; Av Kawama btwn Calles 2 & 3) Nitrox here.

Barracuda Diving Center (☎ 45-61-34-81; cnr 1ra Av & Calle 59) Multilingual center; dives leave from Aquaworld-Marina Chapelín on Autopista Sur. Fishing trips also leave from here.

Marina Gaviota (☎ 45-66-77-55; dir.marina@delvar.gav.tur.cu) On the eastern tip of the peninsula; diving equipment is in top shape.

SKYDIVING
Skydiving adventures happen at the **Centro Internacional de Paracaidismo** (☎ 45-66-72-56, 45-66-72-60; skygators@cubairsports.itgo.com), based at the old airport just west of Varadero. Tandem jumps (CUC$150, plus CUC$45/50 for

photo/video) leap from 3000m giving you 35 seconds of free fall. The center, opened in 1993, has an impeccable safety record. Jumps are scheduled only in good weather, so go at the first opportunity.

Tours

The most intriguing boat trips are the all-day **catamaran cruises** (per person includes snorkeling gear, open bar & seafood lunch CUC$75) to Cayo Blanco. Terrific coral and tons of fish are highlights at this offshore cay, reached after an hour of sailing. The trip price includes shameless caged-dolphin interaction. Boats leave from **Marina Gaviota** (☎ 45-66-77-55; dir .marina@delvar.gav.tur.cu; ☽ tours 9 & 10am) at the eastern end of the peninsula and **Aquaworld-Marina Chapelín** (☎ 45-66-75-50, 45-66-78-00; www .aquaworldvaradero.com; ☽ tours 9am) on Autopista Sur. The latter also offers a catamaran **sunset cruise** (per person CUC$25; ☽ tours 5pm Mon & Fri).

Sleeping

Varadero is an extremely popular destination, so reservations are a good idea.

The state authorities maintain their tourism monopoly here by prohibiting individuals from renting rooms. In practice, private rooms are available (CUC$20 to CUC$25); you'll be approached at the bus terminal with offers.

BUDGET

Club Herradura (☎ 45-61-37-03; Av de la Playa btwn Calles 35 & 36; s/d incl breakfast CUC$50/67; ☒) This crescent-shaped hotel is right on the beach, providing salty views from the balcony and living room shared between every two units. The beds are squishy and the tiny showers awkward, but the location is tops – there's a nice terrace bar and grill, too.

Apartamentos Mar del Sur (☎ 45-61-22-46; 3ra Av & Calle 30; 1-/2-bedroom apt CUC$60/86; P ☒ ☐ ☒) Affording some independence, the spacious one- and two-bedroom apartments here are nothing fancy, but they are well equipped (kitchen has everything). The hotel itself has many services, making this good value, especially for families or small groups.

The intimate **Hotel Pullman** (☎ 45-66-71-61; fax 45-66-74-95; 1ra Av 1 btwn Calles 49 & 50; s/d incl breakfast CUC$44/56; ☒) has long been a favorite for its fair value and good, nontouristy location. A quiet section of beach is 164yd (150m) away. The affiliated, though less attractive,

Hotel Dos Mares (☎ 45-61-27-02; fax 45-66-74-99; 1ra Av & Calle 53; ☒) has the same prices.

MIDRANGE

Villa Tortuga (☎ 45-61-47-47; Calle 7 btwn Camino del Mar & Av Kawama; all-inclusive s/d CUC$58/90; P ☒ ☐ ☒) This good-value resort in western Varadero is squeezed between the beach and canal, meaning even the cheap rooms have views. There are tons of activities and all the rooms have balconies. The food is not bad.

Hotel Internacional (☎ 45-66-70-38; www.gran caribe.cu; Av Las Américas; s/d incl breakfast CUC$80/114; P ☒ ☐ ☒) Opened in 1950 as the sister hotel to Miami's Fontainebleau, the Internacional is Varadero's most fabulous retro resort. It retains its '50s charm, but rooms are modernish and the facilities extensive, including tennis courts and massages (all right on the beach). Upgrade to a sea-view (extra CUC$5) or all-inclusive level (extra CUC$30).

Villa Los Delfines (☎ 45-66-86-92; fax 45-66-77-27; Av de la Playa & Calle 38; s/d incl breakfast & dinner CUC$75/97; ☒ ☐ ☒) One of Varadero's best-value places, the 100 smart rooms here come packed with extras like minibar and safe. This resort has its own protected beach area and is cozier than Varadero's bigger complexes.

Villa Cuba (☎ 45-66-82-80; 1ra Av & Calle C; all-inclusive s/d/tr CUC$170/280/305; P ☒ ☐ ☒) Interesting architecture, a variety of accommodation and loads of activities make this a good choice. Families should investigate the two- to six-bedroom villas featuring living room, refrigerator, TV and patio. There are four rooms for disabled guests.

Hotel Bella Costa (☎ 45-66-72-10; fax 45-66-71-74; Av Las Américas; all-inclusive s/d/tr CUC$120/180/160; P ☒ ☐ ☒) This Iberostar installation abutting the golf course is a good choice for travelers with children. In addition to the kids' club and pool, accommodation is in individual villas that provide privacy/bonding.

TOP END

Mansión Xanadú (☎ 45-66-84-82, 45-66-77-50; www .varadergolfclub.com; Av Las Américas; s/d incl breakfast & greens fee CUC$160/210; P ☒ ☐) Varadero's most exclusive accommodation is in the Dupont Mansion. The six rooms retain the 1930s furniture (some disastrously repainted) and decor from Dupont's days and have luxurious marble baths and sea-facing balcony.

Hotel Meliá Varadero (☎ 45-66-70-13; www.solmeliacuba.com; all-inclusive s/d CUC$270/320; P ⅗ 🗔 🗟) This stunning resort has a seven-story central atrium dripping with vines that create a natural curtain from the open dome to the lobby. The rooms overlook the golf course or the beach and it's a popular honeymoon spot. You have to walk a bit to reach the beach.

Meliá Paradisus del Oro (☎ 45-66-87-00; www.solmeliacuba.com; s/d all-inclusive CUC$195/390; P ⅗ 🗔 🗟) Toward the eastern end of the peninsula, this classy five-star resort has funky style to spare, with an open layout that integrates the surrounding natural beauty. The beach here is an amazing bend of blue, the rooms are ultraromantic – lots of billowing gauze – and the food is exquisite.

Eating

The atmospheric stretch of Camino del Mar between Calles 9 and 14 is full of quaint surf and turf places.

Mi Casita (☎ 45-61-37-87; Camino del Mar btwn Calles 12 & 13; meals CUC$10-17; ☻ noon-11pm) This one is right on the beach.

Castel Nuovo (☎ 45-66-77-86; 1ra Av at Calle 11; pizzas CUC$2.50-6.50, pasta CUC$2.50-5; ☻ 10am-11pm) This is a solid Italian restaurant; the vegetarian pie (CUC$3.50) is a thing of beauty and the CUC$7 special is one of Varadero's best deals (before 7pm).

Restaurante La Bodegona (☎ 45-61-14-30; Av de la Playa & Calle 36; ☻ noon-10:30pm) Dark wood, leather chairs and a wraparound porch stand out here. Stick to the delicious paella (vegetable/seafood CUC$4.25/7), saving room for flan al ron (rum flan; CUC$2.25). Your after-dinner smoke in the upstairs cigar lounge comes with beach views.

Casa del Queso Cubano (Restaurante La Fondue; ☎ 45-66-77-47; Av Las Américas cnr Calle 62; fondue CUC$7-15; ☻ noon-11pm) Yes, this is the real deal: cheese, beef, chicken, shrimp and chocolate fondues just like mom used to make. One is big enough for two, unless you're famished. The minuscule salad (CUC$2) is a rip-off.

Lai-Lai (☎ 45-66-77-93; 1ra Av & Calle 18; ☻ noon-11pm) This mansion on the beach offers novel Chinese food, including beef in oyster sauce (CUC$6), a sizzling shrimp

platter (CUC$12) and fish in orange sauce (CUC$5). There's a separate kiddie menu.

Restaurante Mansión Xanadú (☎ 45-66-84-82; Av las Américas; appetizers CUC$5-9, mains CUC$14-30; ☻ dinner) For a phenomenal gourmet meal, head to these historic digs, where the distinguished menu features items such as salmon carpaccio with anise (CUC$9), roasted lamb in basil butter (CUC$14) and veal medallions au poivre (CUC$16). Reservations are recommended.

Bim Bom (☎ 45-61-14-50; 1ra Av btwn Calles 24 & 25; ☻ 10am-11pm) Head straight to this place for exotic ice-cream flavors such as tiramisu and hazelnut.

Panadería Doña Neli (☎ 45-61-44-47; 1ra & Calle 43; ☻ 24hr) For yummy, fresh pastries.

There's a grocery store on the ground floor of **Plaza América** (Av las Américas; ☻ 9am-6pm Mon-Sat, 9am-noon Sun), with excellent munchies, plus liquor and wine galore.

Drinking

Bar Benny (Camino del Mar btwn Calles 12 & 13; ☻ noon-midnight) A tribute to the 'Barbarian of Rhythm' Benny Moré, this place has jazz-den energy, with photos of the legendary musician lining the walls and his velvety voice oozing from the sound system. Highly recommended for post-*playa* (beach) cocktails.

Bar Mirador (Av Las Américas; ☻ noon-midnight) On the top floor of the Mansión Xanadú, this bar boasts a beautiful Moorish interior and 360-degree views; there's live music for accompaniment.

Calle 62 (Av las Américas cnr Calle 62; ☻ 24hr, live music 9pm-midnight) A fun, open-air bar with tasty light meals and live music nightly.

Entertainment

CABARETS

Cabaret Cueva del Pirata (☎ 45-66-77-51; Autopista Sur; admission CUC$10 open bar; ☻ 10pm-2am Mon-Sat) About half a mile (1km) east of Hotel Sol Elite Palmeras, this club presents scantily clad dancers in a cabaret show with a buccaneer twist (eye patches, swashbuckling moves etc). Inside a natural cave, this is a popular place attracting a young crowd; once the show's over, the disco begins.

Cabaret Continental (Av Las Américas; admission CUC$25 open bar; ☻ show 10pm Tue-Sun) In the Hotel Internacional, this is an extravagant 2½-hour floor show. After midnight the cabaret becomes a disco (admission CUC$5).

NIGHTCLUBS

Discoteca La Pachanga (☎ 45-66-71-32; Av 1 & Calle 13 in Hotel Acuazul; admission CUC$3; ☉ 11pm-3am) This friendly nightspot is one of Varadero's hottest clubs.

Palacio de la Rumba (Av las Américas final; admission CUC$15; ☉ 11pm-3am) Folks are ecstatic that this place has reopened, as it was universally recognized as Varadero's best disco. It's right on the beach if you want to step out for a moonlit stroll.

Shopping

For one-stop shopping, the big artisan market at Parque de las 8000 Taquillas (1ra Av between Calles 44 and 46) is the place.

ARTex Handicraft Market (1ra Av & Calle 12; ☉ 9am-9pm) This market, conveniently located next to an ARTex store, has an excellent selection of CDs, T-shirts and musical instruments.

Casa del Habano (☎ 45-61-14-30; 1ra Av btwn Calles 31 & 32; ☉ 9am-6pm) Head here for cigars – this place is warmly recommended for its top-quality merchandise and helpful service.

Galería de Arte Varadero (Av 1 btwn Calles 59 & 60; ☉ 9am-7pm) Unique treasures such as antique jewelry and other heirlooms are here.

Taller de Cerámica Artística (☉ 9am-7pm) Located next door to Galería de Arte Varadero, you can buy artistic pottery here – some exquisite, some like art therapy from the psych ward – made on-site.

For US-style consumerism and useful services, head to Plaza América, Varadero's largest shopping complex.

Getting There & Away

AIR

International flights arrive at **Juan Gualberto Gómez** (VRA; ☎ 45-24-70-15), 16 miles (26km) from Varadero. See p774 for details. Airline offices in Varadero:

Aerocaribbean (☎ 45-61-14-70; 1ra Av btwn Calles 54 & 55)

Air France (☎ 45-66-82-85; annavarro@airfrance.fr; 1ra Av cnr Calle 30)

Air Transat (☎ 45-61-27-31; fax 45-61-18-00; Calle 30 & 3ra Av, in Apartamentos Mar del Sur No 215)

Cubana de Aviación Airport (☎ 45-61-30-16); Central Varadero (☎ 45-61-18-23/24/25; 1ra btwn Calles 54 & 55; ☉ 8am-8pm)

BUS

Terminal de Omnibus (Calle 36 & Autopista Sur) has departures with **Víazul** (☎ 45-61-48-86; ☉ 7am-noon & 1-7pm) to Havana at 8am, 4pm and 6pm daily (CUC$10) and Trinidad at 7:30am (CUC$20, six hours, 163 miles/262km), stopping in Santa Clara (CUC$11, 3½ hours, 113 miles/182km).

Alternatively, you can book a Havana transfer at hotel tour desks and travel agencies (CUC$20 to CUC$25 one-way).

CAR

There is a CUC$2 toll each way between Varadero and Havana. Car rental:

Havanautos Airport (☎ 45-25-36-30); Av Kawama (☎ 45-61-37-33; btwn Calles 8 & 9); Hotel Internacional (☎ 45-66-70-38)

Micar (☎ 45-66-73-32; 1ra Av & Calle 20)

Rex Hotel Meliá las Américas (☎ 45-66-77-39); Airport (☎ 45-66-75-39)

Transtur Av 1 & Calle 21 (☎ 45-66-73-32); Airport (☎ 45-25-36-21)

Getting Around

A taxi costs CUC$20 to CUC$25 from the airport to Varadero. Call **Transtur** (☎ 45-61-44-44), **OK Taxi** (☎ 45-61-16-16) or **Transgaviota** (☎ 45-61-97-62). If you're traveling with a bike, note that Transgaviota uses large cars.

A horse and buggy around Varadero costs CUC$5 per person for a 45-minute tour or CUC$10 for a two-hour tour, which is plenty of time to see the sights.

Varadero Beach Tour (all-day ticket CUC$5; ☉ tours hourly 9am-8pm) is a handy bus with 42 well-marked stops linking the resorts and shopping centers. Tickets are sold at hotel tourism desks.

Moped and bicycle rentals are available all over town. Mopeds cost CUC$9/25 by the hour/day, with overnight specials for CUC$25 (5pm to 9am). Bicycles cost CUC$2 per hour or CUC$5/8/10 for three/five/10 hours. Rentals:

Vía rentals (3ra Av cnr Calle 32) Lots of bikes and mopeds.

FM 17 (1ra Av cnr Calle 17) Bike rentals.

SANTA CLARA

pop 210,680

About 172 miles (276km) from Havana, the awesome Che Memorial is here in the provincial capital and history buffs will enjoy the museums, monuments and sites associated with the triumph of the Cuban Revolution. If Santa Clara bores you, don't whine, head north to Remedios – one of Cuba's best detours.

CASAS PARTICULARES – SANTA CLARA

Consuelo Ramos Rodríguez (☎ 422-20-20-64; Independencia No 265, Apt 1 btwn Pedro Estévez & San Isidro; r CUC$20; 🍴) Two big, spotless rooms with refrigerator; English spoken; amiable mother-daughter team.

Teresita Chaviana Arca (☎ 422-20-36-19; General Roloff No 5 btwn Cuba & Colón; r CUC$20; 🍴) Very friendly family has sparkling room with all-tile bath and narrow patio; private.

El Castillito (☎ 422-29-26-71; Céspedes No 65A btwn Maceo & Pedro Estévez; r CUC$20; 🍴) Very central, good value room has refrigerator, TV and terrace.

Hostal Ido (☎ 422-20-50-08; Céspedes No 24 btwn Maceo & Parque Vidal; r CUC$15-20) Airy, independent room with private entrance has small patio.

Villa Lissette (☎ 422-20-74-87; villa_lissette@web.correosdecuba.cu; Lorda No 58 bajos btwn Independencia & Martí; r CUC$15-20; 🍴) Two rooms share bath, both have TV and refrigerator; repeatedly reader recommended.

Familia Pérez (☎ 422-20-05-76; joandyluis@yahoo.com; Independencia No 109 btwn Plácido & Luis Estévez; r CUC$20-25; 🍴) Darkish room in central location; bath has tub; jungle cat rugs will repulse animal lovers.

Information

IMMIGRATION

Inmigración (Av Sandino cnr of Sexta; ⏰ 8am-noon & 1-3pm Mon-Thu) Visa extensions.

INTERNET ACCESS

InfoInternet (Marta Abreu No 55 btwn Máximo Gómez & Villuendas; per mln CUC$0.10; ⏰ 9am-noon & 1-5pm Mon-Sat)

Palmares (Marta Abreu No 10 cnr Villuendas; per hr CUC$5; ⏰ 9am-11:30pm Mon-Fri, 9:30am-10pm Sat & Sun)

MEDICAL SERVICES

Farmacia Campa (Independencia Este & Luis Estévez; ⏰ 8am-8:30pm)

Policlínico Docente José R Leon Acosta (☎ 422-20-22-44; Serafín García Oeste No 167 btwn Alemán & Carretera Central)

MONEY

Banco Financiero Internacional (☎ 422-20-74-50; Cuba No 6 & Rafael Trista)

Bandec (☎ 422-21-81-15; Rafael Tristá & Cuba; ⏰ 8am-2pm Mon-Fri, 8-11am Sat)

Cadeca (☎ 422-20-56-90; Rafael Tristá & Cuba on Parque Vidal; ⏰ 8:30am-6pm Mon-Sat, 8:30am-12:30pm Sun)

PHOTOGRAPHY

Photo Club (☎ 422-20-85-34; Marta Abreu No 10)

POST

DHL (☎ 422-20-89-76; Cuba No 7 btwn Rafael Tristá & Eduardo Machado; ⏰ 8:30am-4pm Mon-Fri, 8am-2pm Sat, 8am-noon Sun)

Post office (☎ 422-20-69-76; Colón No 10; ⏰ 8am-6pm Mon-Sat, 8am-noon Sun)

Sights

The **Monumentos a Ernesto Che Guevara** and **Tren Blindado** are within walking distance of the Parque Vidal if you have good legs; otherwise catch a taxi or horse carriage.

MONUMENTO ERNESTO CHE GUEVARA

This monument, mausoleum and museum **complex** (Av de los Desfiles; admission free; ⏰ 8:30am-9pm Tue-Sun), 1.2 miles (2km) west of Parque Vidal via Rafael Tristá, is in a vast square guarded by a bronze statue of 'El Che.' The statue was erected in 1987 to mark the 20th anniversary of Guevara's murder in Bolivia, and the sublime mausoleum below contains 38 stone-carved niches dedicated to the guerillas killed in that failed revolutionary attempt. In 1997 the remains of 17 of them, including Guevara, were recovered from a secret mass grave in Bolivia and reburied here. Fidel Castro lit the eternal flame on October 17, 1997. The adjacent museum collects the details of Che's life and the Battle of Santa Clara.

MONUMENTO A LA TOMA DEL TREN BLINDADO

This boxcar **museum** (admission CUC$1; ⏰ 8:30am-7pm Mon-Sat, 8:30am-noon Sun), east on Independencia just over the Río Cubanicay, marks the spot where 18 men led by Che Guevara captured a 22-car armored train containing 408 heavily armed Batista troops. Amazingly, this battle on December 29, 1958, only lasted 90 minutes. Some travelers love this place, others leave uninspired.

PARQUE VIDAL & AROUND

The most impressive building in the city is the 1885 **Teatro La Caridad** (Máximo Gómez;

performances CUC$2), in the northwest corner of Parque Vidal, with frescoes by Camilo Zalaya. Opera singer Enrico Caruso performed here. The **Museo de Artes Decorativas** (☎ 422-20-53-68; Parque Vidal No 27; admission CUC$2; ☻ 9am-6pm Mon, Wed & Thu, 1-10pm Fri & Sat, 2-10pm Sun), just east of Teatro La Caridad, is an 18th-century building packed with period furniture and treasures. The inner patio is a treat.

West of the park is the **Museo de la Ciudad** (Independencia & JB Zayas; admission CUC$1; ☻ 8:30am-noon Mon, 8:30am-noon & 1-5pm Tue-Sun), showing the history of Santa Clara; check here for nighttime cultural activities.

Parque Vidal is closed to traffic (cyclists must also dismount and walk their bikes).

Sleeping

Hotel Santa Clara Libre (☎ 422-20-75-48; fax 422-68-63-67; Parque Vidal No 6; s/d incl breakfast CUC$27/36; ☒) That minty-green skyscraper is the 131-room Santa Clara Libre, favored by Cuban honeymooners and low-end tours. Some rooms are comically cramped, but all come with satellite TV, phone and hot-water bath. There are good views from the 11th-floor bar. The hotel facade is bullet-pocked from one of the revolution's final battles.

Eating & Drinking

El Castillo (9 de Abril No 9 btwn Cuba & Villuendas; ☻ noon-11pm) This gem serves quality meals of pork, chicken or liver with *congrí* and salad for CUP35. Take it away or eat at the counter flanked by marble pillars and mosaic tiles.

El Sabor Latino (☎ 422-20-65-39; Esquerra No 157 btwn Julio Jover & Berenguer; meals CUC$10-12; ☻ noon-midnight) The only legal paladar left in town offers complete pork, chicken or fish meals with rice, salad and *tostones* (fried plantain patties) for CUC$10.

Peso ice cream with attitude is at **Coppelia** (Calle Colón cnr Mujica; ☻ 10:30am-midnight Tue-Sun). **Cafeterías Piropo** (Lorda & Independencia; ☻ 10am-10pm) has formidable ice-cream sundaes. There's a small well-stocked **agropecuario** (Cuba No 269 btwn EP Morales & General Roloff) in the center. **Panadería Doña Neli** (Maceo Sur at 9 de Abril; ☻ 7am-6pm) sells bread. **Praga** (Independencia cnr Villuendas; ☻ 8:30am-5pm Mon-Sat, 8:30am-noon Sun) is Santa Clara's largest grocery store.

Entertainment

Club Mejunje (Marta Abreu No 107; ☻ 4pm-1am Tue-Sun) This is a hip bar and performance space set among the ruins of an old building. There are concerts, children's theater and the occasional drag show.

Teatro Laboratorio (Marta Abreu No 111; ☻ performances 8pm) A few doors down from Club Mejunje is Teatro Laboratorio, with cutting-edge theater.

El Bar Club Boulevard (☎ 422-21-62-36; Independencia No 2 btwn Maceo & Pedro Estévez; admission CUC$2; ☻ 10pm-2am Tue-Sun) A fun cocktail lounge with comedy acts and live music.

La Marquesina (☻ 9am-1am) A lively bar attached to the Teatro La Caridad. Love or hate the chanteuse singing to Casio keyboard accompaniment.

Villa Clara ('La Villa,' aka Las Naranjas) are the arch rivals of Havana's Industriales; catch a game at Estadio Sandino, east of the center via Av 9 de Abril.

Shopping

Stroll 'El Bulevar,' Independencia, between Maceo and Zayas for good secondhand clothes and consignment shops.

Fondo Cubano de Bienes Culturales (Luis Estévez Norte No 9 btwn Parque Vidal & Independencia) Sells Cuban handicrafts.

ARTex (☎ 422-21-43-97; Colón No 16 btwn Machado & Rafael Tristá; ☻ 9am-5pm Mon-Sat, 9am-noon Sun) This large place has CDs, souvenirs and some musical instruments.

SERVICES FROM SANTA CLARA NACIONALES BUS STATION

Destination	Cost (one way)	Distance	Duration	Schedule
Havana	CUC$18	171 miles (276km)	4 hours	7:50am, 3:25pm, 8:35pm
Trinidad	CUC$8	55 miles (88km)	3 hours	10:50am
Varadero	CUC$11	113 miles (182km)	3¼ hours	5:10pm
Santiago de Cuba	CUC$33	366 miles (590km)	12 hours	7:30pm, 11:45pm, 1:55am

SERVICES FROM SANTA CLARA TRAIN STATION				
Destination (one way)	Cost	Distance (variable)	Duration	Schedule
Cienfuegos	CUC$2.10	41 miles (67km)	2 hours	7am Mon-Sat
Havana	CUC$10-17	171 miles (276km)	5-6 hours	4:02am, 6:12am, 8:20am daily, 3:50am, 11:55pm alternate days
Santiago de Cuba	CUC$41	366 miles (590k)m	10 hours	10:40pm alternate days

Getting There & Away

Several Canadian tour companies fly to Aeropuerto Abel Santamaría; see p774 for more.

The **Nacionales Bus Station** (☎ 422-20-34-70) is 1.5 miles (2.5km) out on the Carretera Central toward Matanzas, 547yd (500m) north of the Che monument. Tickets for Víazul are sold in the 'Boletines en USD' office on your right as you enter the station. For daily departures see the boxed text, p154.

The **intermunicipal bus station** (Carretera Central), just west of the center via Marta Abreu, has daily buses to Remedios (CUC$1.45, 28 miles/45km).

The **train station** (☎ 422-20-28-95/6) is straight up Luis Estévez from Parque Vidal on the north side of town. The **ticket office** (Luis Estévez Norte No 323) is across the park from the station.

In theory, trains serve the destinations shown in the boxed text above.

Getting Around

Local transportation is mostly by *coche* (horse cart), with an important route along Marta Abreu toward the bus stations and Che monument (CUP1). From the train station to the center, catch the 'Materno' (CUP2).

A bici-taxi tour of outlying sights costs CUC$7 for two people.

Mopeds are rented from **Cubatur** (☎ 422-20-85-34; Marta Abreu No 10; ☺ 9am-8pm) for CUC$17 per day.

Taxis in front of the national bus station and around Parque Vidal charge CUC$7 to Remedios, CUC$45/70 one-way/round-trip to Cayo Santa María and CUC$40 to Havana, or call **Cubataxi** (☎ 422-20-25-80).

REMEDIOS

pop 48,908

Ask Cubans, ask travelers: Remedios – where historic homes line cobblestone streets and relaxing in the park solicits nary a 'pssst' or whistle – is one of Cuba's prettiest towns. The laid-back air of Remedios shatters every December 24 for the **Parrandas**, a night of maniacal fireworks zipping around spectacular floats and glittery-costumed dancers.

Sights & Activities

Dating from the late 18th century, the fine **Parroquia de San Juan Bautista de Remedios** (Camilo Cienfuegos No 20 on Parque Martí; ☺ 9am-11am Mon-Sat) is famous for its gilded altar. The pregnant Inmaculada Concepción (with charming pearl teardrops) is said to be unique in Cuba. If the front doors are closed, go around to the rear.

Visiting the **Museo de las Parrandas Remedianas** (Máximo Gómez No 71; admission CUC$1; ☺ 9am-6pm), two blocks off Parque Martí, is the next best thing to partying here on December 24. There's a photo gallery, scale models of floats and graphic depictions of how the fireworks are made. Another room is jammed with the feathers, headdresses and tassels from the year previous.

You can escape to **Cayo Santa María**, 40 miles (65km) from Remedios, for a day on Central Cuba's most brilliant beach. Come soon, before the best of it is gobbled up by the megaresorts being constructed. The prettiest stretches are alongside Villa las Brujas and at the end of the Meliá resorts' access road. The latter is good for camping. The cay is accessed via the *pedreplén* (CUC$2 toll; no Cubans allowed).

Sleeping & Eating

Hotel Mascotte (☎ 42-39-51-44/45; Parque Martí; s/d CUC$38/44; ☒) Built in 1869, this beautiful colonial is Remedios' only hotel. The nicest of the 10 rooms are Nos 1 and 5; some rooms have balconies. The hotel restaurant, Las Arcadas, serving standard meat and seafood fare, is the only choice in town, aside from a

---

CASAS PARTICULARES – REMEDIOS

Hostal El Patio – Elsa Valdés (☎ 42-39-52-20; José A Peña No 72 btwn Hnos García & A Romero; r CUC$20-25; ✖) Terrific, well-furnished room in back patio; refrigerator; private; good value.

Hostal Las Chinitas (☎ 42-39-53-16, 42-39-57-84; Independencia No 21A btwn Brigadier González & Maceo; r CUC$25; ✖) Bright, spotless room, plus dining & living room; refrigerator; gracious hosts; good meals.

Hostal Casa Cari (José A Peña No 54 btwn Maceo & Brigadier González; r CUC$20; ✖) Big, clean room in nice colonial house opens onto sunny patio.

Hostal Colonial – Maŕia del Portal & Mario Alonso (☎ 42-39-54-03; Brigadier González No 36 btwn Independencia & José A Peña; r CUC$20-25; ✖) Simple, darkish room in home of older couple; reader recommended.

---

few basic cafeterias like **La Fé** (Máximo Gómez No 126), opposite the Parroquia; the curvaceous stone counter is impressive.

Getting There & Away

The bus station is at the entrance to town, near the excellent 28-mile (45km) road to Santa Clara. There is service to Santa Clara (CUC$1.45, one hour, five daily) and Havana (CUC$8, 6½ hours, 7:15pm alternate days).

A taxi from the bus station to town costs CUC$5 if you bargain.

CIENFUEGOS
pop 139,137

The 'pearl of the south,' Cienfuegos is the charming capital city of Cienfuegos Province and has an 'undiscovered' feel. The town is laid out on an orderly grid system. Calle 37 ('Prado') runs 1.9 miles (3km) south to seaside Punta Gorda.

Information
IMMIGRATION
Inmigración (☎ 432-52-10-17; Av 46 No 2901 btwn 29 & 31; ✖ 9am-3pm Mon-Thu)

INTERNET ACCESS
Cybercafé En Mi Cuba (☎ 432-51-18-77; Av 54 No 3518 btwn 35 & 37; per hr CUC$6; ✖ 9am-11pm)
Etecsa (☎ 432-51-52-53; Calle 31 No 5402 btwn Avs 54 & 56; per hr CUC$6; ✖ 8:30am-7:30pm)

MEDICAL SERVICES
Clínica Internacional (☎ 432-55-16-22; fax 432-55-16-23; Calle 37 No 202, Punta Gorda) Dental emergencies handled; 24-hour pharmacy.

MONEY
Banco de Crédito y Comercio (☎ 432-51-57-47; Av 56 at Calle 31)
Banco Financiero Internacional (☎ 432-55-16-57; Av 54 at Calle 29)

Cadeca (☎ 432-55-22-21; Av 56 No 3314 btwn Calles 33 & 35)

PHOTOGRAPHY
One Hour Photo (☎ 432-55-22-98; Calle 37 No 5217 btwn Avs 52 & 54; ✖ 8am-10pm) Lithium batteries and selection of Agfa film.

POST
DHL (☎ 432-51-10-31; Av 54 No 3514 btwn Calles 35 & 37)
Post office Av 56 cnr Calle 35 (☎ 432-51-82-84); Bulevar (Av 54 No 3514 btwn Calles 35 & 37)

Sights

The most interesting sights are clustered around Parque José Martí and 1.9 miles (3km) south in Punta Gorda.

The town turns on **Parque José Martí**, with its compulsory statue of Cuba's apostle rendered in marble and the **Arco de Triunfo** (arch of triumph, unique in Cuba), dedicated to Cuban independence.

Teatro Tomás Terry (☎ 432-51-33-61; www.azurina.cult.cu; Av 56 No 2701 btwn Calle 27 & 29; tours CUC$1, performances CUC$5; ✖ 9am-6pm), on the north side of Parque Martí, was built between 1887 and 1889. This famous 950-seat auditorium opened in 1895 with Verdi's *Aïda*. The seats are carved from Cuban hardwoods (ouch!) and there's an impressive ceiling fresco by Camilo Salaya.

Around the eastern side of the park is the neoclassical, 1869 **Catedral de la Purísima Concepción** (☎ 432-52-52-97; Av 56 No 2902; donations accepted; ✖ 7am-noon), with twin towers and French stained-glass windows.

At the south end of Punta Gorda is the Moorish-style, 1917 **Palacio de Valle** (☎ 432-51-12-26; Calle 37 at Av 2; admission incl drink CUC$1; ✖ 10am-10pm), an outrageous jumble of tiles, turrets and crenellated edges. The interior details are exquisite.

The **Centro Recreativo La Punta** (⊙ 10am-10pm) has a gazebo and bar on the point's southern tip and is a top sunset spot.

Rancho Luna is a pretty bend of beach 11 miles (18km) south of Cienfuegos; it makes a good day trip. There are 32 **scuba diving** sites here with caves, sunken ships, profuse marine life (including whale sharks from August to November) and dazzling coral gardens. **Snorkeling** (per person CUC$16) is also possible; arrangements can be made through Marina Puertosol Cienfuegos or any of the local travel agencies.

The multiple waterfalls, individual bathing pools and gorgeous mountain setting make **El Nicho** (admission CUC$5; ⊙ 8:30am-6:30pm) one of Cuba's most spectacular natural attractions. You can swim, hike and horseback ride (per hour CUC$2) and there's a restaurant. Tucked into the Sierra del Escambray just 90 minutes from Cienfuegos via Cumanayagua, the road to here is rough, but a regular car can handle it.

Activities

The **Marina Puertosol Cienfuegos** (☎ 432-55-12-41, fax 432-55-12-75; Av 8 & Calle 35 Punta Gorda) rents out motorboats (CUC$35 for eight people,

two hours) and leads fishing trips (from CUC$150 for four people, four hours). Snorkeling and scuba diving tours leave daily from Rancho Luna.

Nearby, **Club Cienfuegos** (☎ 432-52-65-10; Calle 35 btwn Avs 10 & 12; ⊙ 10am-1am Sun-Fri, 10am-2am Sat) has a pool and parking-lot-turned-beach in a bayside setting. There's a bar, a restaurant, and amusement park for the children.

Live-aboard charters sail from **Blue Sail Charter** (☎ 432-55-66-19; www.bluesailcaribe.com; charters starting at CUC$1900 per week), which berths six beautiful boats at Club Cienfuegos; English, French, German and Dutch are spoken.

Sleeping

Cubanacán Boutique La Unión (☎ 432-45-10-20, 432-45-16-85; Calle 31 cnr Av 54; s/d incl breakfast CUC$80/90; P ⊠ ⬚ ⬚) Comfortable and classy with multilingual staff, this gem is the standard setter. The 49 antique-furnished rooms are big, the powerful showers hot and the beds luxurious. Rooms have balconies; get a massage or hit the Jacuzzi.

Hostal Palacio Azul (☎ 432-55-58-28/9; Calle 37 No 201 btwn Avs 12 & 14; s/d/tr CUC$32/32/42; ⊠) This restored palace with terrific seaside location

---

CASAS PARTICULARES – CIENFUEGOS

Town Center
Alberto Suárez (☎ 432-55-64-52; Av 60 No 3908 btwn Calles 39 & 41; r CUC$20; ⊠) Two sparkling, well-equipped independent rooms; private roof patio; delicious breakfast.
Casa de Anita (☎ 432-51-94-77; Av 56 No 4314 btwn Calles 43 & 45; r CUC$20; ⊠) Spiffy house near bus and train stations; hospitable.
Elias Álvarez Hernández (☎ 432-52-28-07; elias_cuba@yahoo.es; Calle 57 No 4813 btwn Avs 48 & 50; r CUC$15-20; ⊠) Two independent, clean rooms a bit out of the center; English spoken.
Doña Deysi (☎ 432-51-84-67; Av 5 No 4124 btwn 41 & 43; r CUC$20; ⊠) Two rooms; upper has more air and light.
Dr Claudio & Iliana (☎ 432-51-97-74; Av 54 No 4121 btwn Calles 41 & 43; r CUC$25; ⊠) Two darkish but comfortable rooms with private bath, though one is clear across kitchen.

Punta Gorda
Villa Lagarto Maylin y Tony (☎ 432-51-99-66; villalagarto2004@yahoo.es; Calle 35 No 4B btwn 0 & Litoral; r CUC$35; ⊠ ⬚) Two rooms at water's edge; wraparound balcony with hammocks; sea views and access. Neighbor also rents out.
Hospedaje Ochún – Alejandro López (☎ 432-54-94-49; Calle 35 No 16 btwn 0 y Litoral; r CUC$25; ⊠) Small seaside house with big hospitality; refrigerator; patio.
Villa Mery (☎ 432-51-88-80; bernardocanto@yahoo.es; Av 6 No 3509 btwn Calles 35 & 37; r CUC$25; ⊠) Two rooms with independent entrance onto patio; refrigerator; roof terrace.
Guest House Castaño (☎ 432-52-52-51; Calle 37 No 1824 cnr 20; r CUC$30; ⊠) Two kitschy rooms in house with two patios, roof terrace and full bar.

has seven unique rooms that have soaring ceilings, beautiful tile work and grand baths; value-added upstairs units have views and balconies.

Eating

Vinos Pizza (☎ 432-55-11-21; Calle 31 No 5418 btwn Avs 54 & 56; pizza from CUC$1.50; ☼ noon-3pm & 6pm-midnight) Reliable and tasty soups, pizzas and lasagna (CUC$5) are here. *Familiar* pizzas (starting at CUC$4) feed two.

Paladar El Criollito (☎ 432-52-55-40; Calle 33 No 5603 btwn Avs 56 & 58; ☼ noon-11:30pm) Cienfuegos' only (legal) private restaurant, this friendly spot offers fresh, filling meals with pork, chicken or fish and all the fixings for CUC$7.

Restaurant 1869 (☎ 432-45-16-85; Calle 31 cnr Av 54; appetizers CUC$2.50-8.50, mains CUC$8-15; ☼ breakfast, lunch & dinner) Cienfuegos' finest dining happens at the Boutique La Unión hotel. Appetizers like salmon with asparagus (CUC$8.50) and mains including roast beef stuffed with bacon and carrots (CUC$12) distinguish this place. There's an extensive wine list, separate dessert menu and upscale dinner buffet (CUC$13).

Restaurante La Plaza (Av 34 btwn Calles 37 & 39, Punta Gorda; mains under CUC$2; ☼ noon-3pm & 6:30-10pm) The local pick serves big portions of reliable *comida criolla* in agreeable environs, replete with *son* quartet.

La Lobera (☎ 432-52-65-10; Calle 37 btwn Avs 10 & 12, Punta Gorda; ☼ noon-3pm & 6-9pm) The finer, affordable restaurant at Club Cienfuegos does steak with all the fixings for under CUC$10. The wraparound terrace with sea views makes it.

Café Teatro Terry (Av 56 No 2703 btwn Calles 27 & 29; ☼ 9am-midnight Mon-Sat, 9am-1pm Sun) This café with patio overlooking Parque Martí serves espresso and ice-cream sundaes (CUC$2). Poetry readings and live music at 10pm on Friday and Saturday are a big draw.

Also recommended:

Restaurante Prado (Calle 37 cnr Av 56; mains CUP4-6) Vegetarian peso cafeteria with salads, fruit and rice options.

Coppelia (Calle 37 & Av 52) Peso ice cream for CUP2 a scoop.

Drinking

Bar Terrazas (☎ 432-55-10-20; Av 54 & Calle 31) Upstairs at the Boutique La Unión, this bar is a good central option. Sip a mojito and enjoy fine city views; live music starts up at 10pm.

Billiards Club (☎ 432-52-65-10; Calle 37 btwn Avs 10 & 12; ☼ 10am-1am Sun-Fri, 10am-2am Sat) Shoot a rack at this bar with bay views and big-city vibe at the Club Cienfuegos.

The terrace bar at the Palacio de Valle scores for its architectural details and its ambience.

Entertainment

Jardines de la UNEAC (☎ 432-51-61-17; Calle 25 No 5413 btwn Avs 54 & 56; admission CUC$2) This welcoming outdoor patio venue hosts Afro-Cuban and *trova peñas*.

El Benny (☎ 432-55-11-05; Av 54 No 2907 btwn Calles 29 & 31; admission CUC$3; ☼ 9pm-1am Tue-Fri & Sun, 9pm-2am Sat) This sharp place has quality live music, before turning into a disco with a healthy mix of salsa, pop and *regguetón* (Spanish-speaking dancehall).

Teatro Tomás Terry (☎ 432-51-33-61; www.azurina.cult.cu; Av 56 No 2701 btwn Calle 27 & 29; admission CUC$5; ☼ box office 11am-3pm & 1½hr before curtain) Premier performances happen at this architectural showpiece on the north side of Parque Martí.

Shopping

Most likely whatever you desire can be found on El Bulevar – the pedestrian mall on Ave 54 between Calle 37 and Parque Martí. Otherwise try:

ARTex El Topacio (Av 54 No 3510 btwn Calles 35 & 37) Good CD and book selection.

El Embajador (Av 54 cnr of Calle 33; ☼ 8:30am-6pm Mon-Sat, 10am-6pm Sun) Cigars, coffee and rum; adjoining café in which to enjoy them.

Promociones del ICAIC (Calle 37 No 5001 btwn Avs 50 & 52) Cuban cinema posters, T-shirts, and video cassettes.

Maroya Gallery (☎ 432-55-12-08; Av 54 No 2506 on Parque Martí; ☼ 9am-6pm) Fabulous paintings, folk art and hand-painted clothing.

Getting There & Away

Air Transat has charter flights from Montreal, Toronto and other Canadian cities. See p774 for details of international flights to Cuba.

The **train station** (☎ 432-52-54-95, 432-52-83-30; Av 58 & Calle 49; ☼ ticket window 8am-3:30pm Mon-Fri, 8-11:30am Sat) is across from the bus station. At the time of writing, the only feasible service was to Santa Clara (CUC$2.10, two hours, 4:10am Monday to Saturday).

The **bus station** (☎ 432-51-57-20; Calle 49 btwn Avs 56 & 58) was under construction during research; in the meantime, the train station doubles as the bus station.

Víazul has daily departures to Havana (CUC$20, four hours, 9:40am and 4:40pm) and Trinidad (CUC$6, 1½ hours, 12:25pm & 5:10pm). To reach other destinations from Cienfuegos, connect in Trinidad.

Check the blackboard for local buses to Rancho Luna (CUC$1). Collective taxis here may take you to Santa Clara (CUC$3) or Cumanayagua (CUC$1) en route to El Nicho.

OK Taxi (☎ 432-55-71-00; Calle 31 btwn Avs 54 & 56) or **Cubataxi** (☎ 432-51-91-45; Av 50 No 3508 at Calle 37) go to Santa Clara (CUC$30), Trinidad (CUC$37) and Rancho Luna (CUC$8).

Getting Around
You can rent mopeds at **Rent-A-Moped** (Calle 37 cnr Av 48; per hr/day/week CUC$8/21/120; ☺ 9am-noon & 1-5pm Mon-Fri, 9am-3pm St, 9am-noon Sun). Otherwise jump on a *coche* (CUC$1) along Prado. It's a pleasant way to travel between town and Punta Gorda.

TRINIDAD
pop 52,896
Oozing charm, the fastidiously preserved colonial town of Trinidad and the adjacent Valle de los Ingenios (together a Unesco World Heritage site) are Cuba's most popular destinations. Near to the white sands of Playa Ancón and the lush slopes of Topes de Collantes, Trinidad has an unrivaled ambience. Some towns absorb tourists – and hustlers – well. Trinidad isn't one of them. Stay outside the historic core for a more local scene.

Information
IMMIGRATION
Inmigración (Julio Cueva Díaz off Paseo Agramonte; ☺ 8am-5pm Tue-Thu) South of the train station; visa extension stamps are sold at Banco de Crédito y Comercio.

INTERNET ACCESS
Cafe Internet Las Begonias (Antonio Maceo No 473 at Simón Bolívar; per hr CUC$6; ☺ 9am-11pm) Good place to meet other travelers.
Etecsa (☎ 419-4129; General Lino Pérez No 274; per hr CUC$6; ☺ 8am-7pm) On Parque Céspedes.

MEDICAL SERVICES
Servimed Clínica Internacional Cubanacán (☎ 419-6240; General Lino Pérez No 103 at Anastasio Cárdenas; ☺ 24hr) Consultations before/after 4pm CUC$25/30. On-site pharmacy.

MONEY
Banco de Crédito y Comercio (☎ 419-2405; José Martí No 264)
Banco Financiero Internacional (☎ 419-6107; cnr Camilo Cienfuegos & José Martí; ☺ 8am-3pm Mon-Fri) Cash advances; ridiculously long lines.
Cadeca (☎ 419-6263; Martí No 164 btwn Lino Pérez & Camilo Cienfuegos)

PHOTOGRAPHY
Photo Service (José Martí No 192 btwn Camilo Cienfuegos & General Lino Pérez; ☺ 9am-9pm)

POST
Post office (Antonio Maceo No 418 btwn Colón Zerquera)

TRAVEL AGENCIES
Cubanacán (☎ 419-6142; www.cubanacan.cu; cnr José Martí & Zerquera)
Cubatur (☎ 419-6314; www.cubatur.cu; Calle Maceo cnr Rosario)

Sights & Activities
Near Plaza Mayor is the lush **Museo Histórico Municipal** (Casa Cantero; ☎ 419-4460; Simón Bolívar No 423; admission CUC$2; ☺ 9am-5pm Sat-Thu), where the ill-gotten wealth of slave trader Justo Cantero is well displayed in the stylish, neoclassical rooms. The view from the top of the tower alone is worth the admission price.

Near to the church is the **Museo Romántico** (☎ 419-4363; Echerri No 52; admission CUC$2; ☺ 9am-5pm Tue-Sun) in the Palacio Brunet, built between 1740 and 1808. The mansion-turned-museum collects 19th-century furnishings, china and such. As with most houses, the kitchen and bath are the most interesting rooms.

Housed in the former San Francisco de Asís convent, the photogenic **Museo Nacional de la Lucha Contra Bandidos** (☎ 419-4121; Echerri No 59 at Piro Guinart; admission CUC$1; ☺ 9am-5pm Tue-Sun) is distinguished by its yellow campanile, the only part of the original building remaining. The collection relates to the struggle against counterrevolutionary bands in the Sierra del Escambray (1906–65). Climb the tower for good views.

For a bird's-eye view of Trinidad, walk up Simón Bolívar, between the Iglesia Parroquial and the Museo Romántico, to the ruined 18th-century **Ermita de Nuestra Señora de la Candelaria de la Popa**. From here, it's a 30-minute uphill hike to 590ft-high (180m) **Cerro de la Vigía**, which delivers broad vistas of Trinidad, Playa Ancón and beyond.

CASAS PARTICULARES – TRINIDAD

Hostal Las Mercedes (☎ 419-3107; las_mercedes_2004@yahoo.es; Camilo Cienfuegos No 272 btwn Maceo & Francisco Codania; r CUC$20; P   ✖) Two well-kept rooms in spectacular colonial home open onto lovely courtyard; English spoken.

Aleida Calzada Portieles (☎ 419-4316; Juan Márquez No 20 btwn Jesús Menéndez & José Mendoza; r CUC$20-25; ✖) Spacious room with refrigerator off of private patio faces nice garden; friendly señora.

Bernardo & Sarahi (☎ 419-3543; bernatdad@yahoo.com; Francisco Petersen No 179 btwn Zerquera & M Guerra; r CUC$15-20) Comfortable, quiet room with large bath and tub leads to sunny patio; friendly hosts; excellent meals.

Hostal Digna Aguila Ibargollin (☎ 419-4301; manuelca2@hotmail.com; Frank País No 476 btwn Fidel Claro & Santiago Escobar; r CUC$15-20; P   ✖) Two rooms, one leading to terraced patio; English spoken; droolinducing food aromas.

Orlando Rodríguez Ramos (☎ 419-2110; Antonio Guiteras No 229 btwn Frank País & Miguel Calzada; r CUC$20; ✖) Entire upstairs, large balcony, dining room, refrigerator, privacy.

María C de Zayas Font (☎ 419-3725; mariaelenatrindad@yahoo.com; Camilo Cienfuegos No 126 btwn Frank País & Miguel Calzada; r CUC$15-20; ✖) Two big rooms in colonial house face courtyard; English spoken; mosquito nets on request.

Cabaña's (☎ 419-3910; Gustavo Izquierdo No 103A cnr Simón Bolívar; r CUC$20; ✖) Central, lovely and tranquil upstairs room with private terrace.

Ruben Santander Marin ('Pipo'; ☎ 419-3320; Maceo No 553 btwn Santiago Escobar & Piro Guinart; r CUC$20; P   ✖) Two clean, safe rooms near bus station; upstairs is airier and has refrigerator; big family atmosphere.

Luis Grau Monedero (☎ 419-3253/2165; Zerquera No 270 btwn Maceo & José Martí; r CUC$20; ✖) Two rooms in colonial house share bath; big roof terrace; hilarious art.

Rogelio Ayala (☎ 419-3067; Maceo no 526 btwn Simón Bolívar & Piro Guinart; r CUC$15-20; ✖) Colonial house with back patio; reader recommended.

Playa Ancón, 7.4 miles (12km) south of Trinidad, is an inviting ribbon of white beach lapped by tranquil, blue waters – perfect for a day peddle. There's an excellent reef for **snorkeling** and **scuba diving** 109yd (100m) offshore. The seven-hour **snorkeling tour** (per adult/child incl lunch & open bar CUC$40/30; ◷ 9am) to Cayo Blanco gets rave reviews; black coral and bountiful marine life are highlights. All the Trinidad agencies arrange these trips or go to **Cubanacán Naútica Trinidad** (☎ 419-4754), a few hundred meters north of Hotel Ancón. They also offer **sailboat charters**.

Dozens of crumbling 19th-century *ingenios* (sugar mills) dot **Valle de los Ingenios**. The royal palms, waving cane and rolling hills are timelessly beautiful, especially seen from the saddle (see Tours, right). The valley's main sight is the 1750 **Manaca Iznaga** (admission CUC$1), 10 miles (16km) east of Trinidad, a 144ft-high (44m) tower with exquisite 360-degree views. The tourist train stops here; it's an hour to walk from the local train station at Meyer (see p162).

Topes de Collantes, the rugged 56 mile-long (90km) Sierra del Escambray mountain range some 12 miles (20km) northwest of Trinidad, has some of Cuba's best unguided **hiking**. The **Carpeta Central information office** (☎ 42-54-02-31; ◷ 8am-5pm) sells a topographical map of the area (CUC$2.50), offers camp sites (CUC$10) and guides. The most popular hike is the 1.5-mile (2.5km), 2½-hour round-trip trek to the **Salto del Caburní** (per person CUC$6.50), a 203ft (62m) waterfall cascading into cool swimming holes. It's difficult to get here without a car.

Tours

Cubatur and Cubanacán sell the same excursions, including the popular Valle de los Ingenios sugar train tour (per adult/child CUC$10/5, tours start at 9:30am), horseback riding tours to the Cascada El Cubano (CUC$18 including transportation, park entrance fee, lunch and guide) and day hikes to Topes de Collantes (per adult/child CUC$29/20).

Freelance guides lead horseback riding trips to the Valle de los Ingenios or Cascada El Cubano (per person for three/six hours CUC$7/15), plus CUC$6.50 park entry fee for Cascada El Cubano.

Sleeping

Hotel La Ronda (☎ 419-4011; Martí No 238; s/d incl breakfast CUC$34/48; ✖ ▣) A basic, well-located option right on Parque Céspedes, this restored hotel has 19 rooms arranged around a central courtyard. Quieter rooms are at the back.

Hostal Mesón del Regidor (☎ 419-6572/3; Simón Bolívar No 424 near Ernesto Valdés; s/d/tr incl breakfast CUC$39/48/66) Only a lucky few succeed in booking one of the four tidy rooms in this restored mansion right off of the Plaza Mayor. In addition to the superb location, the attached restaurant and bar are perks.

Eating

Paladar Sol y Son (Simón Bolívar No 283 btwn Frank País & José Martí; meals CUC$6-8; ✖ noon-3pm & 7:30-11pm) The food is good at this popular paladar, so expect a wait. Dining is in a courtyard to the sound of music. English is spoken. Skip the fish.

Paladar Estela (☎ 419-4329; Simón Bolívar No 557, meals CUC$7-8; ✖ 2-11:30pm) Choose the dining room or pretty rear garden to take your meals in this place above the Plaza Mayor. Portions are voluminous and the staff friendly.

Trinidad Colonial (☎ 419-6473; Antonio Maceo No 402 at Colón; meals under CUC$5; ✖ 11:30am-10pm) Good portions of Cuban cuisine are served in the elegant 19th-century Casa Bidegaray. Try the smoked pork.

Mesón del Regidor (☎ 419-6456; Simón Bolívar No 424; ✖ 10am-10pm) Specializing in grilled meats, this is one of the restaurants crowded with lunching tour groups.

Cremería Las Begonias (☎ 419-6404; Antonio Maceo No 473 at Simón Bolívar; ✖ 9am-10pm) Hide out in the back patio with a milkshake, ice cream, or coffee. Another branch of this popular cafeteria is across the street, with burgers, and sandwiches.

Tienda Universo (José Martí; ✖ 9:30am-1pm & 1:30-5pm Mon-Sat, 9:30am-noon Sun) Near Bolívar in the Galería Comercial Universo, this is Trinidad's best grocery store.

The stretch of Martí around Lino Pérez and Camilo Cienfuegos is crowded with peso stalls, selling pizza, *cajitas* (takeout meals that come in small boxes) and snacks.

Entertainment

Casa de la Música (☎ 419-3414; admission free; ✖ 10pm) The wide stairway leading to this club off of the Plaza Mayor is Trinidad's hottest spot. There are always lots of travelers taking in the 10pm show and salsa concerts are held in the rear courtyard (admission CUC$2).

The **Casa de la Trova** (☎ 419-6445; Echerri No 29; admission CUC$1; ✖ 9pm-2am) can be either exhilarating or bogus depending on the package-tourist-to-Cuban ratio. Nearby, the **Palenque de los Congos Reales** (Echerri at J Menéndez; admission free) offers energetic salsa and *son*, heavy on the Afro-Cuban beat.

Las Ruinas del Teatro Brunet (Antonio Maceo No 461 btwn Simón Bolívar & Zerquera; admission CUC$1), hosts an athletic Afro-Cuban show at 10pm from Tuesday to Friday, and a Cuban folklore show from 10pm Saturday in a crumbling colonial patio. Check here for drumming and dance classes.

Shopping

There's an excellent **arts and crafts market** (Jesús Menéndez) in front of the Casa de la Trova. This is souvenir heaven – however, avoid the black coral and turtle-shell items (these animals are endangered and the products are prohibited in many countries).

You can buy locally produced artwork at the **Casa de la Cultura Julio Cueva Díaz** (Zerquera No 406). **Yami Martínez** (☎ 419-3017; www.yami.trinidadphoto.com; Maceo No 413 btwn Zerquera & Colón) creates funky sculptures that you can buy directly from her home studio.

For CDs and musical instruments, it's the **Casa de la Música**, up the stairway beside the Iglesia Parroquial.

Getting There & Away

BUS

The **bus station** (Piro Guinart No 224), accessed via Gustavo Izquierdo, has a left-luggage room. See the boxed text, p162, for services.

CAR

The quickest route to Trinidad from Havana is via Santa Clara and Manicaragua, offering beautiful mountain scenery. The coastal route from Cienfuegos, though slower, is lined with little beaches and fishing villages.

TAXI

For trips to Havana (CUC$25) or Cienfuegos (CUC$37), **Cubataxi** (☎ 419-2214) can be contracted at the bus station.

SERVICES FROM TRINIDAD'S BUS STATION

Destination	Cost (one way)	Distance	Duration	Schedule
Cienfuegos	CUC$6	50 miles (81km)	1½ hours	8am, 3pm
Havana	CUC$25	208 miles (335km)	6 hours	8am, 3pm
Santa Clara	CUC$8	55 miles (88km)	3 hours	2:30pm
Santiago de Cuba	CUC$33	361 miles (581km)	11½ hours	8:15am
Varadero	CUC$20	163 miles (262km)	6 hours	2:30pm

TRAIN

The local train through the Valle de los Ingenios stops at Iznaga and Condado, terminating in Meyer, 12 miles (19km) north of Trinidad (CUC$3, 40 minutes round-trip, 9:30am).

The return train to Trinidad leaves from Meyer at 1:30pm, giving you a few hours to explore the valley; you can also hop on the return train at Condado. This service has gained a reputation as 'the runaway train' for its penchant for derailing. Due to Cuban vagaries, you may pay CUC$10 for this trip.

The Trinidad **terminal** (☎ 419-4223) is a pink house across the tracks on the west side of the station.

Getting Around

You can rent bicycles (per day CUC$3) beside **Cubataxi** (☎ 419-2214) at the bus station.

Transtur (☎ 419-6110; cnr Maceo & Zerquera) at Cubatur rents out mopeds (per day/week CUC$20/126), as does another desk at Las Ruinas del Teatro Brunet (p161).

A coco taxi costs around CUC$4 to Playa Ancón.

EASTERN CUBA

'El Oriente.' Even the name for the eastern part of the country rings exotic. Travelers who make it out this way will experience another side of Cuba – slower paced and more remote, so deeply steeped in history, it sometimes feels like a different time and a separate place.

Getting There & Away

Santiago de Cuba's Aeropuerto Antonio Maceo receives international flights. Domestic flights connect Havana and Holguín, Santiago de Cuba and Baracoa.

Train travel, though slow, is a possibility between the provincial capitals, Havana and Santiago de Cuba.

Getting Around

The northern route between Holguín and Baracoa is a terrible stretch of torn-up road that, although only 130 miles (210km), takes over five hours to drive; the only local transportation up this way is by truck.

SANTIAGO DE CUBA

pop 443,926

Santiago de Cuba ('Santiago') is the island's second-largest city and a strong rival to Havana in literature, music and politics. During the 19th century, French settlers arrived, contributing to the Haitian, African and Spanish mosaic that makes this Cuba's most Caribbean city. Traditional Cuban *son* traces its roots to this area and music fans swoon for Santiago.

Wedged between the sparkling Caribbean Sea and pine-clad slopes of the Sierra Maestra, the scenery here is stunning, especially from Pico Turquino (6470ft/1972m), Cuba's highest peak.

History

Founded in 1514, Santiago de Cuba was the first Cuban capital (1515–1607). After the capital shifted to Havana and Santiago's gold reserves and indigenous labor started giving out, the city lost prominence; despite being the 'cradle of the revolution,' it still nurses an inferior complex.

On July 26, 1953, Fidel Castro and his companions stole away from the Granjita Siboney 12.4 miles (20km) southeast of Santiago and attacked the Moncada Barracks. At his trial here Castro made his famous 'History Will Absolve Me' speech, which became the basic platform of the Cuban Revolution.

Information

EMERGENCY

Police (☎ 106; Corona cnr Sánchez Hechevarría)

IMMIGRATION

Inmigración (Calle 13 near Av General Cebreco, Vista Alegre; ☺ 8am-5pm Mon, Tue, Thu & Fri) Immigration stamps are sold at the Banco de Crédito y Comercio at Felix Peña No 614 on Parque Céspedes.

INTERNET ACCESS

The Hotel Casa Granda (p166) has Internet access for CUC$6 per hour.

Etecsa (Heredia at Félix Peña; per hr CUC$6; ☺ 7:30am-7pm)

MEDICAL SERVICES

Clínica Internacional Cubanacán Servimed (☎ 22-64-25-89; Av Raúl Pujol cnr Calle 8, Vista Alegre; consultations CUC$25; ☺ 24hr) Some English-speaking staff, plus a dentist.

Farmacia Cubanacán (☎ 22-64-25-89; Av Raúl Pujol cnr of Calle 8; ☺ 24hr) Best pharmacy. Another is in the Meliá Santiago de Cuba, open from 8am to 6pm.

Farmacia Las Américas (Av Victoriano Garzón No 422; ☺ 24hr)

Hospital Provincial Saturnino Lora (☎ 22-64-56-51; Av de los Libertadores; ☺ 24hr)

MONEY

Banco de Crédito y Comercio (☎ 22-62-80-06; Felix Peña No 614) ATM on Heredia.

Banco Financiero Internacional (☎ 22-62-20-73; Felix Peña No 565; ☺ 8am-4pm Mon-Fri)

Cadeca (☎ 22-68-61-76; Aguilera No 508; ☺ 8:30am-6pm Mon-Sat, 8:30am-noon Sun) Others are in the Meliá Santiago de Cuba and Hotel Las Américas.

PHOTOGRAPHY

Photo Service José A Saco (General Lacret; ☺ 9am-9pm Mon-Sat, 9am-2pm Sun); Av Garzón (Av Garzón; ☺ 9am-9pm)

POST

Post office (Aguilera No 519)

TRAVEL AGENCIES

Cubatur (☎ 22-62-31-24, 22-62-87-37; agencia stgo@ciges.inf.cu; Av Garzón No 364 btwn Calle 3 & 4; ☺ 8am-8pm)

Rumbos (☎ 22-68-60-33, 22-62-48-23; Gral Lacret at Heredia; ☺ 7:30am-8pm) Organises excursions, mopeds, bus and air tickets. The staff is helpful, with English spoken.

Sights

PARQUE CÉSPEDES & AROUND

Most visits begin on **Parque Céspedes**, where a bronze bust memorializes Carlos Manuel de Céspedes, the man who declared Cuban independence in 1868. Some of Santiago de Cuba's most impressive buildings ring this park, including the 1522 **Casa de Diego Velázquez** (Felix Peña No 602), the oldest house still standing in Cuba. This Andalusian-style showpiece now houses the **Museo de Ambiente Histórico Cubano** (☎ 22-65-26-52; admission CUC$2; ☺ 9am-1pm, 2-5pm Mon-Thu & Sat, 2-5pm Fri, 9am-1pm Sun), with its collection of period furnishings.

You can't miss the five-nave **Catedral de Nuestra Señora de la Asunción**, situated on the south side of the park. Cuba's first cathedral was built here in the 1520s; the present cathedral with its coffered ceiling, dome and graceful archangel was completed in 1922.

Two blocks downhill from the park is the **Balcón de Velázquez** (Bartolomé Masó & Mariano Corona; admission with/without camera CUC$1/free), the site of an old Spanish fort with lovely harbor views. Three long blocks downhill on Bartolomé Masó is the **Fábrica de Tabacos César Escalante** (☎ 22-62-23-66; Av Jesús Menéndez No 703; admission CUC$5; ☺ 9-11am & 1-3pm), a working cigar factory open for visits.

On Heredia, east of the Hotel Casa Granda, is a strip of culturally significant buildings. These include the colorful **Museo del Carnaval** (☎ 22-62-69-55; Heredia No 303; admission CUC$1; ☺ 9am-4pm), displaying the history of Santiago's Carnaval tradition. Drop in for the talented **danza folklórico performance** (admission CUC$1; ☺ 4pm).

Pio Rosado, the alley running alongside the Museo del Carnaval, leads up to the quite fabulous neoclassical building housing the **Museo Municipal Emilio Bacardí Moreau** (☎ 22-62-84-02; admission CUC$2; ☺ 9am-6pm Mon-Sat, 9am-4pm Sun). Founded in 1899 by famous rum distiller and first mayor of Santiago de Cuba, Emilio Bacardí y Moreau (1844–1922), this is one of Cuba's oldest functioning museums and features exhibits relating to the 19th-century independence struggles, plus European and Cuban paintings.

Eight blocks northwest of Parque Céspedes is the important **Museo-Casa Natal de Antonio Maceo** (☎ 22-62-37-50; Los Maceos No 207, admission CUC$1; ☺ 9am-5pm Mon-Sat), where the

CUBA

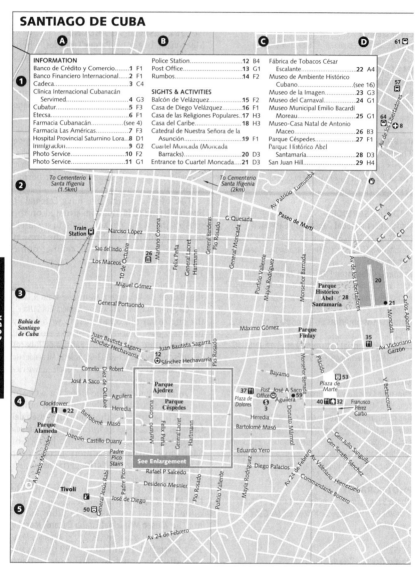

SANTIAGO DE CUBA

INFORMATION
Banco de Crédito y Comercio.......**1** F1
Banco Financiero Internacional.....**2** F1
Cadeca................................**3** C4
Clínica Internacional Cubanacán
Servimed.............................**4** G3
Cubatur................................**5** F3
Etecsa.................................**6** F1
Farmacia Cubanacán..................(see 4)
Farmacia Las Américas................**7** F3
Hospital Provincial Saturnino Lora..**8** D1
Inmigración...........................**9** G2
Photo Service.........................**10** F2
Photo Service.........................**11** G1

Police Station........................**12** B4
Post Office...........................**13** G1
Rumbos................................**14** F2

SIGHTS & ACTIVITIES
Balcón de Velázquez..................**15** F2
Casa de Diego Velázquez.............**16** F1
Casa de las Religiones Populares..**17** H3
Casa del Caribe......................**18** H3
Catedral de Nuestra Señora de la
Asunción............................**19** F1
Cuartel Moncada (Moncada
Barracks)...........................**20** D3
Entrance to Cuartel Moncada....**21** D3

Fábrica de Tabacos César
Escalante...........................**22** A4
Museo de Ambiente Histórico
Cubano.............................(see 16)
Museo de la Imagen..................**23** G3
Museo del Carnaval..................**24** G1
Museo Municipal Emilio Bacardí
Moreau.............................**25** G1
Museo-Casa Natal de Antonio
Maceo..............................**26** B3
Parque Céspedes......................**27** F1
Parque Histórico Abel
Santamaría.........................**28** D3
San Juan Hill.........................**29** H4

independence war general was born on June 14, 1845.

During the 1895 war he was second in command, after Máximo Gómez, and died fighting in western Cuba in 1896. This museum exhibits highlights of Maceo's life, including the tattered flag flown in battle.

CUARTEL MONCADA (MONCADA BARRACKS)

The **Parque Histórico Abel Santamaría** (Gral Portuondo & Av de los Libertadores) is the home to the hospital that was occupied by revolutionary forces on July 26, 1953, during the attack on the adjacent Moncada Barracks.

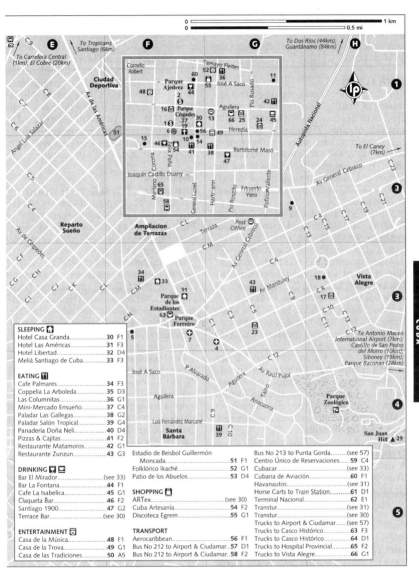

The **Cuartel Moncada** (Moncada Barracks) is where more than 100 revolutionaries led by Fidel Castro attacked Batista's troops on July 26, 1953. At the time, this was Cuba's second-most-important military garrison. The revolutionaries had hoped the assault would spark a general uprising throughout Cuba, but things went awry

and the armed struggle was put on hold for another 3½ years.

A major **museum** (☎ 22-62-01-57; admission CUC$2; ⏰ 9:30am-5:30pm Mon-Sat, 9:30am-12:30pm Sun) can be visited through gate No 3 (on Gral Portuondo near Moncada), where the main attack took place. The outer walls are still bullet-pocked. The museum outlines the history of Cuba, with heavy emphasis on the revolution.

A scale model of Moncada illustrates the 1953 assault.

VISTA ALEGRE

Broad, tree-lined avenues mark the entrance to Santiago de Cuba's old upperclass neighborhood of **Vista Alegre**, on the east side of town. There are some intriguing museums here like the **Museo de la Imagen** (☎ 22-64-22-34; Calle 8 No 106; admission CUC$1; ☺ 9am-5pm Mon-Sat), encapsulating the history of Cuban photography and including fascinating little spy cameras and cool Fidel photos.

Northwest is the **Casa de las Religiones Populares** (Calle 13 No 206; admission with/without guide CUC$2/1; ☺ 9am-6pm Mon-Sat), with a bright collection of all things Santería; visit on a saint's day like December 4 (Santa Barbara) for an all-night drum jam. Around the corner is the **Casa del Caribe** (☎ 22-64-22-85; alarduet@casadelcaribe .cult.cu; Calle 13 No 154; admission free; ☺ 9am-5pm Mon-Fri & concert nights), founded in 1982 to study Caribbean life. Afro-Cuban dance, percussion and culture classes (per hour CUC$10) can be arranged here.

South of here via Av Raúl Pujol is **San Juan Hill** (admission free). On this spot on July 1, 1898, Cuban, US and Spanish troops battled things out. Two weeks later the Spanish surrendered. Some of the original cannons and trenches can still be seen, and there are numerous monuments.

CEMENTERIO SANTA IFIGENIA

A visit to the 1868 **Cementerio Santa Ifigenia** (Av Crombet; admission CUC$1; ☺ 8am-6pm), 1.2 miles (2km) north of the city center, is a stroll through history. Many of the giants of Cuban history are found among the 8000 tombs here, including Cuba's national hero, José Martí (1853–95). The Martí Mausoleum (1951) is flanked by the muses and there's a dramatic changing of the guard every half-hour. Buried here are those who died during the 1953 attack on the Moncada Barracks, and Carlos Manuel de Céspedes (1819–74), the father of Cuban independence.

CASTILLO DE SAN PEDRO DEL MORRO

A Unesco World Heritage site, the **Castillo de San Pedro del Morro** (☎ 22-69-15-69; admission

CUC$4; ☺ 9am-5pm Mon-Fri, 8am-4pm Sat & Sun) perches dramatically on a 197ft-high (60m) promontory, 6.2 miles (10km) southwest of town via Carretera del Morro. Built between 1633 and 1693, El Morro is considered the best-preserved 17th-century Spanish military complex in the Caribbean. Inside the castle is a museum tracing the naval battle here of 1898. The ribbon of coast backed by the Sierra Maestra is a memorable sight.

A taxi from Parque Céspedes with a 30-minute wait costs CUC$10.

Sleeping

Hotel Libertad (☎ 22-62-77-10; Calle Aguilera No 658; s/d CUC$32/38; ☒ ☐) A good location and fair prices make this 18-room hotel right on Plaza de Marte a good choice, though some rooms are windowless – blech. The restaurant is decent value, too.

Hotel Las Américas (☎ 22-64-20-11, 22-68-72-25; Av de las Américas & Av Gral Cebreco; s/d incl breakfast CUC$53/69; P ☒ ☐ ☎) By far the most popular hotel for groups, this place is conveniently located and has lots of facilities (restaurant, 24-hour cafeteria, nightly entertainment, car rental etc). Watch for overcharging in the restaurant.

Hotel Casa Granda (☎ 22-65-30-21/22; www.gran caribe.cu; Heredia No 201; s/d incl breakfast CUC$78/112; ☒ ☐) This elegant 58-room hotel (1914) overlooking Parque Céspedes is the city's most atmospheric. It's a great place at which to stay, if you can get a room – it's that popular. The hotel's 5th-floor Roof Garden Bar has excellent cathedral views. There's nightly music at the Terrace Bar.

Meliá Santiago de Cuba (☎ 22-68-70-70; www .solmeliacuba.com; Av de las Américas & Calle M; s/d CUC$90/115, ste from CUC$145; P ☒ ☒ ☐ ☎) If you want top service and quality, head to this mirrored monster by Cuban architect José A Choy. Rooms are business-traveler comfortable with real bathtubs and city or mountain views.

Eating

Paladar Las Gallegas (Bartolomé Masó No 305; meals CUC$8; ☺ 1-10:45pm) Around the corner from the cathedral, this place packs them in with full meals of pork, chicken or lamb. Try for an intimate table on the plant-filled balcony.

Paladar Salón Tropical (☎ 22-64-11-61; Fernández Marcané No 310, Reparto Santa Barbara; meals CUC$6-8; ☺ 5pm-midnight Mon-Sat, noon-midnight Sun) Go with

CASAS PARTICULARES – SANTIAGO DE CUBA

Casco Histórico
Zoila Mejías & Juan Carlos Macías (☎ 22-62-49-79; Bartolomé Masó No 159 btwn Corona & Padre Pico; r CUC$20; ⊠) Terrific upstairs suite with views, full kitchen and eating area; terrace; gracious hosts.
José y Clara Aurora (☎ 22-65-88-45; shachy@eco.uo.edu.cu; Pio Rosado No 865 btwn Santa Rosa & José de Diego; r CUC$20; ⊠) A spotless room with twin beds in friendly home near Parque Céspedes; good English spoken.
Casona de San Jerónimo (☎ 22-62-07-68; http//:casasantiago.topcities.com; Sanchéz Hechavarría No 571 btwn Mayía Rodríguez & Donato Marmol; r CUC$20-25; ⊠) Two rooms north of Plaza Dolores, with refrigerator, one with independent entrance; reader recommended.
Andrés & Ramona Gámez (☎ 22-62-45-69; Corona No 371 Altos btwn Gral Portuondo & Trinidad; r CUC$15-20; ⊠) Two rooms in bustling/loud house; excellent roof terrace with views; great hot water; friendly.
Nercy & Oscar (☎ /fax 22-65-21-92; Sanchéz Hechavarría No 560 btwn Mayía Rodríguez & Donato Marmol; r CUC$15-20; ⊠) Two rooms, one interior and generic, other with own entrance, TV, refrigerator, plants and patio.
Manrique Nistal Bello (☎ 22-65-19-09; abarreda@abt.ou.edu.cu; José de Diego No 565 btwn Pio Rosado & Porfirio Valiente; r CUC$25; ⊠) Two rooms share bath, refrigerator and eating area in upstairs of house; roof terrace with views; out of center.
Ylia Deas Díaz (☎ 22-65-41-38; Hartmann No 362 near Gral Portuondo; r CUC$20, ⊠) Well-maintained colonial house near center.
Delmis Sánchez (☎ 22-62-33-56; Diego Palacios No 172 btwn Corona & Padre Pico; r CUC$20; ⊠) Spacious room in colonial house; refrigerator; dark interior patio.

Vista Alegre
Marcía Segares Vives (☎ 22-64-42-32; marrero@mediras.scu.sld.cu; Calle 17 No 2 cnr Av General Cebreco; r CUC$20; ⊠) Room with giant bathroom and fully equipped kitchen; patio; busy corner.
Rosa Coutín (☎ 22-64-12-42; Calle 10 No 54 btwn Calles 3 & 5; r CUC$20; P ⊠) Two spiffy rooms with independent entrance and refrigerator; quiet street.
Adela Perdomo Gondin (☎ 22-64-16-21; Calle 10 No 201 cnr Calle 7; r CUC$20; ⊠) Big room with refrigerator and glorious tiled bathroom and tub in colonial house.
Angela Casillo (☎ 22-64-15-51; Calle 8 No 60 Altos btwn Calle 1 & 3; r CUC$20; ⊠) Two big rooms off giant terrace; also rent downstairs.
Pilar Jiméenez de la Cruz (☎ 22-64-29-62; Calle 17 No 1 bajos btwn Calle 4 & Av General Cebreco; r CUC$20; ⊠) Spotless room with refrigerator; no window.
Rafaela Chacón Aguilera (☎ 22-64-16-55; Calle 4 No 407 Altos, cnr Calle 17; r CUC$20; ⊠) Friendly and helpful señora rents out one room.
Niurka Reyes González (☎ 22-64-42-42; Calle 4 No 407 bajos, cnr Calle 17; r CUC$20; ⊠) One room in comfortable colonial house; tremendous front porch.

a fat appetite to this rooftop paladar a few blocks south of the Hotel Las Américas. Try the succulent smoked pork; the *yuca con mojo* (cassava with a sauce made of oil, garlic and bitter orange) is especially delicious here.

Cafe Palmares (Calle M across from Meliá Santiago de Cuba; meals under CUC$3; ⏲ 24hr) A cool, leafy courtyard setting is complemented by many egg, pizza and sandwich options. Fresh juice and espresso make this a good breakfast or postbar choice.

Restaurante Matamoros (☎ 22-62-26-75; west side of Plaza de Dolores; meals CUC$2.50-6; ⏲ 11am-10pm) Meals come with all the fixings here, plus a fabulous *son* trio serenading; try the house specialty of shrimp and chicken

smothered in sauce (CUC$5) or the mighty tasty pork steak (CUC$2.50).

Restaurante Zunzun (Tocororo; ☎ 22-64-15-28; Av Manduley No 159; ⏲ noon-10pm Mon-Sat, noon-3pm Sun) Dine in bygone bourgeois style in this palace-turned-restaurant with inventive offerings like chicken curry (CUC$7), paella (CUC$15) or cheese plate (CUC$6). Expect professional, attentive service.

Other recommendations:
Pizzas & Cajitas (Bartolomé Masó No 260 at Gral Lacret; dishes CUP1-20; ⏲ 7am-11pm)
Coppelia La Arboleda (☎ 22-62-04-35; Av de los Libertadores & Av Victoriano Garzón; ⏲ 10am-11:40pm Tue-Sun) Almost as good as Havana's Coppelia (p140). Line up on Av de los Libertadores by asking for *el último*.

Las Columnitas (Hartmann cnr Tamayo Fleites; meals CUC$3-6; ☻ 8am-2am) Full shrimp (CUC$6) or pork (CUC$3) meals, plus burgers and cold beer in pleasant covered patio.

Mini-Mercado Ensueño (Mayía Rodríguez cnr Aguilera at Plaza de Dolores; ☻ 9am-7pm Mon-Sat, 9am-5pm Sun) Big supermarket.

Panadería Doña Neli (Aguilera & Plácido on Plaza de Marte; ☻ 7:30am-8pm) Cakes and pastries.

Drinking

Cafe La Isabelica (Aguilera & Porfirio Valiente; ☻ 9am-9pm) Strong peso coffee in a smoky cantina-type atmosphere.

Terrace Bar (Heredia No 201; ☻ 10am-1am) Santiago's most popular drinking spot is at the Hotel Casa Granda, with its terrific park views and accomplished minstrels.

Santiago 1900 (☎ 22-62-35-07; Bartolomé Masó No 354; ☻ noon-midnight) Choose from two atmospheric drinking spots in this old Bacardí palace: the back patio buzzing with locals or the quieter balcony bar upstairs. Hard-currency patrons don't wait in line.

Also recommended:

Claqueta Bar (Felix Peña No 654) Live music and hot dancing are hallmarks of this local bar.

Bar La Fontana (Gral Lacret, off José A Saco; ☻ noon-2am) Saloon-cocoon with low stools around individual tables (in CUP).

Bar El Mirador (Av de las Américas & Calle M; ☻ 9pm-2am) Splendid views and classy vibe on the 15th floor of the Meliá (p166).

Entertainment

Casa de la Trova (☎ 22-65-26-89; Heredia No 208; admission CUC$2; ☻ 11am-3pm & 8:30-11pm Tue-Sun) The most famous (and touristy) of all the city's clubs, this is where the nueva *trova* originated. The atmosphere varies from inspiring to canned.

Patio Los Dos Abuelos (☎ 22-62-33-02; Francisco Pérez Carbo No 5; admission CUC$2; ☻ noon-2am Mon-Sat) This club on Plaza de Marte features traditional Cuban music in an energetic mixed local/tourist atmosphere. The schedule is posted.

Casa de las Tradiciones (Rabí No 154; admission CUC$1; ☻ from 8:30pm) This hip spot in the Tivolí district hosts some of Santiago de Cuba's most exciting ensembles and musicians, who take turns improvising. Friday nights are reserved for straight up, classic *trova*. Did you hear that, Nico Saquito fans?

Casa de la Música (☎ 22-65-22-27; Corona btwn José A Saco & Aguilera; admission CUC$5; ☻ 10pm-2:30am) This semiswanky place features live salsa, followed by taped disco. Come ready to shake that thang.

Folklórico Ikaché (Hartmann No 552 cnr Fleites; ☻ 2pm Sat) Afro-Cuban dance performances happen on Saturday in this tumbledown palace headquarters.

Estadio de Béisbol Guillermón Moncada (☎ 22-64-26-40; Av de las Américas; admission CUP1; ☻ 7:30pm Tue-Thu & Sat, 1:30pm Sun) On the northeastern side of town about half a mile (1km) north of Hotel Las Américas; catch a game with some of the country's most rambunctious baseball fans – they're even more so since Santiago won the national championship in 2005.

Shopping

Discoteca Egrem (Saco No 309; ☻ 9am-5pm) This retail outlet of Egrem Studios has a large collection of CDs, with an especially good selection of local musicians. There is also a good CD shop situated in the Casa de la Música.

ARTex (Gral Lacret btwn Aguilera & Heredia) From mouse pads to muumuus, this shop collects any souvenir imaginable.

Cuba Artesanía (Felix Peña No 673 at Bartolomé Masó; ☻ 9am-9pm) Cuban handicrafts and ice-cold drinks go well together here.

Getting There & Away

AIR

Antonio Maceo International Airport (SCU; ☎ 22-69-86-14) is 4.3 miles (7km) south of Santiago de Cuba, off the Carretera del Morro.

For domestic and Caribbean flight information, see p177; for international details, see p774.

Airlines offices include:

Aerocaribbean (☎ 22-68-72-55; www.aero-caribbean.com; Gral Lacret No 701 at Heredia; ☻ 9am-noon & 1-4:30pm Mon-Fri, 9am-noon Sat)

Cubana de Aviación Town Center (☎ 22-65-15-77/78/79; Saco & Gral Lacret; ☻ 8:45-11am & 1-3pm Mon-Fri); Airport (☎ 22-69-10-14)

BUS

Terminal Nacional (National Bus Station; Av de los Libertadores at Calle 9) is 1.9 miles (3km) northeast of Parque Céspedes.

For **Víazul** (☎ 22-62-84-84) services see the boxed text, p169.

JOHN ELK III

Parque de Bombas (p334), Ponce, Puerto Rico

Carnaval (p305), Dominican Republic

ALFREDO MAIQUEZ

PIERCE & NEWMAN

Cycling (p200), Cayman Islands

El Yunque (p328), Puerto Rico

JOHN ELK III

St Thomas Carnival (p370), St Thomas, US Virgin Islands

Bequia (p611), St Vincent
& the Grenadines

Les Salines (p577), Martinique

Coral World (p355), St Thomas, US Virgin Islands

SERVICES FROM SANTIAGO DE CUBA'S NATIONAL BUS STATION

Destination	Cost (one way)	Distance	Duration	Schedule
Baracoa	CUC$15	145 miles (234km)	5 hours	7:30am
Havana	CUC$51	535 miles (861km)	16 hours	9am, 3pm & 8pm
Santa Clara	CUC$33	367 miles (590km)	11½ hours	9am, 3pm & 8pm
Trinidad	CUC$33	361 miles (581km)	11½ hours	7:45pm

TRAIN

The modern **train station** (☎ 22-62-28-36; Av Jesús Menéndez), northwest of the center, has trains to many destinations. The Havana *'especial'* service (first/second class CUC$62/50, 14½ hours, 535 miles/861km, 7:45am alternate days and 6:05pm daily) also stops in Santa Clara (first/second class CUC$41/33, 10 hours, 366 miles/590km).

The easiest way to verify schedules and buy tickets is at **Centro Único de Reservaciones** (☎ 22-65-21-43; Aguilera No 565 bajos; ☻ 8:30am-3:30pm Mon-Fri). For day-of-departure tickets, you have to go to the *'última hora'* window outside the train station; arrive by 8am.

Getting Around

TO/FROM THE AIRPORT

A taxi to the airport costs CUC$5. Taxis congregate in front of the Meliá Santiago de Cuba and around Parque Céspedes, or call **Cubataxi** (☎ 22-65-10-38/39).

Bus Nos 212 and 213 (40 centavos) travel to the airport; No 212 is better for going to the airport, while No 213 is better coming from the airport.

CAR & MOPED

Cubacar Airport (☎ 22-69-41-95); Meliá Santiago de Cuba (☎ 22-68-71-77)

Havanautos Airport (☎ 22-68-61-61); Hotel Las Américas (☎ 22-68-71-60; ☻ 8am-10pm) Hotel Las Américas has mopeds (rent for CUC$27 per day).

Transtur Casco Histórico (☎ 22-68-61-07; below Hotel Casa Granda; ☻ 9am-8pm); Hotel Las Américas (☎ 22-68-72-90)

HORSE CART

To get into town from the train station, catch a southbound horse cart (CUP1) to the clock tower at the north end of Alameda Park, from which Aguilera (to the left) climbs steeply up to Parque Céspedes. Horse carts between the Terminal Nacional bus station (they'll shout *'Alameda'*) and the train station (CUP1)

run along Av Juan Gualberto Gómez and Av Jesús Menéndez, respectively.

TRUCK

Camiones (trucks) run from the city center to the Moncada Barracks and the Hospital Provincial (near the Terminal Nacional); hop on along Corona one block west of Parque Céspedes or on Aguilera. Trucks for Vista Alegre also travel along Aguilera; there's a stop facing the Etecsa building. From the Hotel Las Américas to the *casco histórico* (the city's historic center), trucks stop at the Parque de los Estudiantes rotary.

BARACOA

pop 42,285

A mellow, colonial town on a tropical headland between two bays, Baracoa is one of Cuba's best destinations. Beaches, hiking and a national park are all in the vicinity.

Columbus described El Yunque, the anvil-shaped mountain that shimmers west across the Bahía de Baracoa, in his journal. Today it's a popular day hike. Founded in December 1512 by Diego Velázquez, Baracoa was the first Spanish settlement in Cuba. It served as the capital until 1515, when Velázquez moved to Santiago de Cuba.

Information

Banco de Crédito y Comercio (☎ 21-4-2771; Antonio Maceo No 99; ☻ 8am-2:30pm Mon-Fri)

Cadeca (☎ 21-4-5346; José Martí No 241)

Cubatur (☎ 21-4-5306; cubaturbaracoa@enet.cu; Calle Martí No 181) Tours in English, Italian and German; tickets on Víazul.

Etecsa (Antonio Maceo cnr Rafael Trejo, Parque Central; Internet access per hr CUC$6; ☻ 7am-7pm)

Farmacia Principal Municipal (Antonio Maceo No 132; ☻ 24hr)

Hospital General Docente (☎ 21-4-3014) Found 1.2 miles (2km) along the road to Guantánamo.

Inmigración (Antonio Maceo No 48 at Peraleju; ☻ 8am-noon & 2-4pm Mon-Fri) Visa extensions.

CUBA

Sights & Activities

The most fascinating attraction in Baracoa is the **Museo Arqueológico Cueva del Paraíso** (admission CUC$2; 8am-6pm). It is built into a cave, with a setting that is reason enough to visit. Among the stalactites are spatulas for vomiting, pipes for smoking hallucinogens, and the remains of what may prove to be indigenous rebel Guamá. The expert docents here also lead **cave tours**. To reach the museum, head up the steps from Coroneles Galano.

The 1883 **Catedral de Nuestra Señora de la Asunción** (Antonio Maceo No 152; donations accepted; mass 6pm daily plus 9am Sun), located on Parque Central, houses the Cruz de La Parra; experts agree that this is the last remaining cross out of some two dozen that the Spaniards erected throughout Latin America (the one in Santo Domingo is a copy). Knock on the last door on Calle Maceo to gain access.

Facing the cathedral is a bust of Indian chief **Hatuey**, who was burned at the stake by the Spanish in 1512. A powerful sculpture depicting his fate is housed in the 1802 **Museo Fuerte Matachín** (21-4-2122; Martí at Malecón; admission CUC$1; 8am-noon & 2-6pm) at the southern entrance to town. There are pretty bay views from here and a good overview of local history.

For a pleasing day trip, hike southeast of town, past the stadium and along the beach for about 20 minutes to a bridge crossing the Río Miel. After the bridge, turn left at the fork; after 15 minutes you reach **Playa Blanca** (admission CUC$2), an idyllic picnic spot. Head right at the fork and after about 45 minutes you will come to the blue and yellow **homestead of Raudeli Delgado**. For a donation (per person CUC$3 to CUC$5), Raudeli will lead you on a 30-minute hike into a lush canyon and to the **Cueva del Aguas**, a cave with a freshwater swimming hole.

Summiting 1867ft (569m) **El Yunque** (per person CUC$13) delivers stupendous views. The hike is hot (bring water), but the crystal currents of the Río Duaba and a 23ft (7m) **waterfall** provide relief. Take the road toward Moa for 3.7 miles (6km) and then turn left at the signposted spur. The trailhead is 2.5 miles (4km) further on. Touts in Baracoa will offer to take you 'the back route' (CUC$7 to CUC$10).

For a taste of hidden Cuba, where early morning rainbows arch over the sea and women carry burdens on their heads, take a road trip through the palm-studded valley to **Playa Bariguá**, 10.6 miles (17km) from Baracoa. A further 2.5 miles (4km) along, you come to Boca de Yumurí, where there's a **black sand beach** and **boat trips** (CUC$2) up the jungle-fringed river.

You won't find a prettier beach up here than **Playa Maguana**, an idyllic, white-sand beauty 13.7 miles (22km) northwest of Baracoa.

Grab yourself some shade under a palm and a cold beer from the snack bar and try to figure out how to tweak your itinerary to stay here for a while. Check if one of the four rooms at **Villa Maguana** (s/d incl breakfast CUC$50/65) is available.

CASAS PARTICULARES – BARACOA

Casa Betty (21-4-2567; Ruber López No 33 btwn Céspedes & Ciro Fria; r CUC$20;) Comfortable room with two beds, refrigerator; patio; sublime food.

Fermín Pita Caballero (21-4-5158; Martí No 393; r CUC$20;) Terrific private room off patio abutting the sea; near entrance to town.

Rolando Leyva & Rosa Elvira Calderín (21-4-3634, 21-4-3580; Frank País No 19 btwn Maceo & Martí; r CUC$20;) Two rooms in central house, on quiet side street; back patio.

Andrés Abella (21-4-3298; Maceo No 56 btwn Coliseo & Paralejo; r CUC$15-20) Two rooms off plant-filled, postage-stamp patio; shared bath.

Yolanda Quintero (21-4-2392; Céspedes No 44 btwn Ruber López & Calixto García; r CUC$20;) Homey feel at this classic wooden house with little plot of land out back; reader recommended.

Pedro Soffi & Mariana (21-4-2184; sofi@toa.gtm.sld.cu; Maceo No 27 btwn Castillo Duany & Peraljo; r CUC$20;) Nice folks with one room; great front patio.

Elda Matos Matos (21-4-2684, 21-4-3815; yamnara@try.gtm.jovenclub.cu; Calle Libertad No 42 near Mariana Grajales; r CUC$20;) Big, quiet, airy room off the beaten track.

Sleeping

Hostal La Habanera (☎ 21-4-5273/4; Maceo No 68 cnr Frank País; s/d incl breakfast CUC$39/50; ❄ ⬛) The 10 sharp, comfortable rooms here come with lovely tiled bathrooms (and tubs). Located on the main plaza, this place sells out fast. Room Nos 1, 8, 9 and 10 have floor-to-ceiling doors opening onto balconies overlooking the park.

Hotel El Castillo (☎ 21-4-5223; Loma del Paraíso; s/d CUC$42/58; P ❄ ⬛) This historic castle, once part of the Spanish fort, is a relaxed, friendly place, with only 34 rooms (some dark and dampish). There are good bay and El Yunque views from the pool. It's a 10-minute walk from town up the steps on Frank País or Calixto García.

Eating

The local specialty is *cucurucho* – grated coconut mixed with sugar (small/large cone CUP3/6). Hot chocolate is another Baracoa delicacy.

Bar Restaurante La Colonial (☎ 21-4-5391; Martí No 123; meals CUC$8-9; ❄ noon-midnight) This paladar has an impressive patio dining setup and a varied menu including shrimp, shark, squid and swordfish, plus the usual chicken and pork.

Casa Tropical (☎ 21-4-3437; Martí No 175; meals CUC$7) Good portions of well-prepared food are served efficiently in comfortable surroundings here; try the fish in coconut milk.

Casa del Chocolate (Antonio Maceo No 123; ❄ 8am-9pm) Steaming cups of supersweet hot chocolate (40 centavos) is the house specialty; grab a table with the toothless old dudes.

Cafetería Piropo (Antonio Maceo No 142; light meals CUC$1-3; ❄ 24hr) Flowering terrace, pool table, chicken, burgers and cold drinks make this Baracoa's main hangout. Right across from Parque Central, it's a good spot to connect with people; there are also live music nights.

Restaurante La Habanera (☎ 21-4-5273/4; Maceo No 68; meals CUC$2.50-8.50; ❄ 7am-10pm) Baracoa's most interesting menu features fish specialties like 'la Baracoesa,' with malanga and *mojo*. Located in Hostal La Habanera, the dining room is breezy and there is a full bar too.

La Ferretera (Martí No 206 near Céspedes; ❄ 9am-5:30pm Mon-Sat, 9am-12:30pm Sun) is a large grocery store and **Dulcería La Criolla** (Martí No 178) is a small bread bakery.

Entertainment

Casa de la Trova Victorino Rodríguez (Antonio Maceo No 149A; admission CUC$1; ❄ 9pm) For *trova* and *son*, head to this fun venue next to the cathedral, where talented musicians rely heavily on the *Buena Vista Social Club* set.

El Ranchón (admission CUC$1; ❄ 10pm) Up 146 steep stairs at the western end of Coroneles Galano, El Ranchón has an enchanting hilltop setting with a bird's-eye view. There's sometimes good live music. Otherwise, it's taped disco and salsa.

From October to April, baseball games are held at the Estadio Manuel Fuentes Borges, southeast along the beach from Fuerte Matachín.

Getting There & Away

Planes and buses out of Baracoa are sometimes fully booked, so avoid coming here on a tight schedule without an outbound reservation.

Cubana de Aviación Airport ☎ 21-4-2580); (Calle Martí No 181 (☎ 21-4-2171; ❄ 8am-noon &1-3pm Mon-Sat) flies from Havana to Baracoa (CUC$128, 2½ hours one-way) at 11:30am on Thursday and 9am on Sunday.

The **National Bus Station** (☎ 21-4-3880; Av Los Mártires & José Martí) has daily Víazul departures to Santiago de Cuba (CUC$15, five hours, 145 miles/234km), leaving at 2:15pm.

The **Intermunicipal Bus Station** (Galano & Calixto García) has daily trucks to Moa, passing Parque Nacional Alejandro de Humboldt (CUP5, 1½ hours, 48 miles/78km), with departures from 5am, and Yumurí (CUP1, one hour, 17 miles/28km), with departures at 8am & 3pm.

Getting Around

There's a helpful **Havanautos** (☎ 21-4-5343/4) office at the airport. Mopeds can be rented from the Hotel El Castillo for CUC$14/18/26 per four/eight/24 hours.

A shuttle bus runs from Parque Central to Playa Maguana daily (round-trip CUC$4) at 10am.

A taxi to Boca de Yumurí is CUC$5.

PARQUE NACIONAL ALEJANDRO DE HUMBOLDT

A Unesco World Heritage site 25 miles (40km) northwest of Baracoa, this beautiful national park perched above the Bahía de Taco should serve as a paradigm for

Cuba's protection efforts. The 148,260 acres (60,000 hectares) of preserved land includes pristine forest, 1000 flowering plant species and 145 ferns, making it the Caribbean's most diverse plant habitat. As for fauna, it's the home to the world's smallest frog and the endangered manatee, both of which you can see hiking here.

Hikes are arranged at the **visitors center** (☎ 21-38-14-31; hikes per person CUC$5-10). The three hikes currently offered are the challenging 4.3 mile (7km) Balcón de Iberia loop, with a 23ft (7m) waterfall, El Recrea, a 1.9 mile (3km) bayside stroll and the Bahía de Taco boat tour (with a manatee-friendly motor developed here); December to February is the best time to see these elusive beasts.

You can arrange a tour through Cubatur in Baracoa or get here independently on the Moa-bound truck.

DIRECTORY

This directory is specific to Cuba. For information pertaining to the entire region, check the book's main directory (p757).

ACCOMMODATIONS

Cuba has everything from little beach cabins to luxe five-star resorts. Solo travelers are penalized as far as prices go, paying

75% of the price of a double room. Prices quoted here are for the high season; off-season prices are 10% to 25% cheaper. Pre-arranging accommodation here is difficult; never pay for anything up front. Cubans are not allowed in hotel rooms.

Independent travelers usually stay in casas particulares, private homes offering good value. Accommodation is rented by the room (CUC$15 to CUC$35; bargaining possible); except where noted, rooms have private bath. By law, casas can only rent out two rooms, with a maximum of two people per room (parents with children excepted). Mixed foreign and Cuban couples will not be rented rooms in some casas and in certain towns (eg Viñales) without showing marriage papers.

Arriving at a casa particular with a hustler increases the room price by CUC$5. Meals in casas are usually the best value for money (breakfast CUC$3, dinner CUC$7).

Campismos are concrete cabins, usually with air-con and bath (CUC$10 to CUC$15 per cabin, sleeps four) managed by **Cubamar** (Map pp134-5; ☎ 7-832-1116; www.cubamarviajes.cu; Calle 3 & Malecón). Cubamar also rents out Campertour mobile homes (caravans), which accommodate four adults and two children (CUC$165 per day, plus CUC$400 refundable deposit).

ACTIVITIES
Diving & Snorkeling

As the biggest Caribbean country, with 3570 miles (5746km) of coastline, Cuba is known for all things aquatic, including diving and snorkeling. There are over 30 dive centers throughout Cuba (www.nautica.cu/centros .htm) managed by either Marinas Puertosol, Cubamar or Cubanacán Naútica.

Dives cost CUC$35, while certification courses are CUC$300 to CUC$350 and introductory courses cost CUC$35 to CUC$50. The most popular diving areas covered in this book are María la Gorda (p147) and Playa Rancho Luna (p157). Varadero (p149) has over 30 dive sites, but only one with shore access.

Hiking

Top hikes include the Cuevas las Perlas stroll (p147); summiting flat-topped El Yunque (p170) and exploring Parque Nacional Alejandro de Humboldt (p171).

There are lamentably few independent hikes. Try the Salto del Caburní trail (Topes de Collantes, p160), or the various hikes around Viñales (p146).

Rock Climbing

The Viñales valley (p146) has over 150 routes (at all levels of difficulty, with several 5.14s) in one of Cuba's prettiest settings, and the word is out among the international climbing crowd. Independent travelers will appreciate the free rein that climbers enjoy here; of all Cuba's outdoor adventures, rock climbing is the most DIY by far.

Due to the heat, the climbing season is from October to April. For more information, visit the website of **Cuba Climbing** (www.cubaclimbing.com).

BOOKS

Non-Spanish reading material is ridiculously scarce and expensive, so pack some books if you like to read on the road; Lynette Chiang's travelogue *The Handsomest Man in Cuba* is a worthy companion.

Covering the First War of Independence to the present, *Cuba: A New History*, by Richard Gott, is the latest, broadest history of the island. You can acquaint yourself with Cuba's most revered poet and intellectual in the *José Martí Reader: Writings on the Americas*.

Taking a frank, but reverent look at the revolution is *Cuba: Neither Heaven Nor Hell*, by María López Vigil. For a traveler's point of view on this confounding island, *Enduring Cuba*, by Zoë Bran is highly recommended.

Cuban exile literature is a cottage industry: try works by Christina García, Reinaldo Arenas or Achy Obejas.

CHILDREN

Children are integrated into all parts of Cuban society: at concerts, restaurants, church, political rallies and parties. Travelers with children will find this embracing attitude heaped upon them, too.

One aspect of local culture parents (and children) may find uncomfortable is the physical contact that is so typically Cuban·

strangers ruffle kids' hair, give them kisses or take their hands with regularity.

Shortages of diaper wipes, children's medicine, formula etc, can be a challenge, but Cubans are very resourceful: ask for what you need and someone will help you out.

Children travel for half-price on trains, buses and flights. Most hotels offer room discounts. For ideas on fun kids' stuff in Havana, see p133.

CUSTOMS

For the full scoop on Cuba's complicated customs regulations, see www.aduana.islagrande.cu. Travelers can bring in personal belongings (including photography equipment, binocular, musical instrument, tape recorder, radio, computer, tent and bicycle), but no global positioning systems or 'items attempting against good manners.' Canned, processed and dried foods are no problem. You can export 23 cigars without a receipt.

EMBASSIES & CONSULATES
Cuban Embassies & Consulates

Australia (☎ 02-9698-9797; www.users.bigpond.com /consulcu/consulate.html; PO Box 2382, Sydney, NSW 2012)
Belgium (☎ 02-343-0020; fax 02-344-9691; Robert Jonesstraat 77, 1180 Brussels)
Canada (☎ 613-563-0141; www.embacuba.ca; 338 Main St, Ottawa, Ontario K1S 1E3);
France (☎ 01-45-67-55-35; fax 01-45-66-80-92; 16 rue de Presles, 75015 Paris)
Germany (☎ 030-9161-1811; Stavanger Strasse 20, 10439 Berlin)
Italy (☎ 06-574-2347; fax 06-574-5445; Via Licina No 7, 00153 Rome)
Mexico (☎ 05-280-8039; fax 05-280-0839; Presidente Masarik 554, Colonia Polanco, 11560 Mexico, DF)
Netherlands (☎ 070-360-606 l; www.enmbacuba.nl/; Scheveningseweg 9, 2517 KS, The Hague)
Spain (☎ 91-401-6941; Conde Penalver No 38, 28006 Madrid)
UK (☎ 020-7240-2488; fax 020-7836-2602; 167 High Holburn, London WC1 6PA) Closest embassy to Ireland.
USA Cuban Interests Section (☎ 202-797-8609; fax 202-986-7283; 2630 16th St NW, Washington, DC 20009)

Embassies & Consulates in Cuba

Australia See Canada.
Canada Embassy (☎ 7-204-2516; fax 7-204-2044; Calle 30 No 518 at Av 7, Playa); Consulate (☎ 45-61-20-78; fax 45-66-73-95; Calle 13 No 422, Varadero) Also represents Australia and New Zealand.

France Embassy (Map pp134-5; ☎ 7-201-3121; Calle 14 No 312 btwn Avs 3 & 5, Miramar)
Germany Embassy (Map pp134-5; ☎ 7-833-2569; fax 7-833-1586; Calle 13 No 652, at Calle B, Vedado)
Italy Embassy (Map pp134-5; ☎ 7-204-5615; fax 7-204-5661; Av 5 No 402, Miramar)
Netherlands Embassy (Map pp134-5; ☎ 7-204-2511; fax 7-204-2059; Calle 8 No 307 btwn Avs 3 & 5, Miramar)
New Zealand See Canada.
Spain Embassy (Map pp130-1; ☎ 7-866-8029; fax 7-866-8015, Capdevila No 51 at Agramonte, Centro Habana)
UK Embassy (☎ 7-204-1771; fax 7-204-8104; Calle 34 No 702 at Av 7, Miramar) Also represents New Zealand.
US Interests Section (Map pp134-5; ☎ 7-833-3551, 7-834-4401; Calzada btwn Calles L & M, Vedado)

FESTIVALS & EVENTS

For more information on festivals and events, visit www.afrocubaweb.com/festivals.htm.

Liberation & New Year's Day (January 1) Big street parties countrywide; outdoor concerts in Havana.
Baseball playoffs (late April; location varies) Two weeks of top ball.
Día de los Trabajadores (May 1, May Day) Massive rallies in Plazas de la Revolución countrywide.
Fería Internacional Cubadisco (second week of May; Havana) The Cuban Grammys, with too many stellar concerts from which to choose.
Festival del Caribe, Fiesta del Fuego (first week of July; Santiago de Cuba) Raucous week-long festival celebrating Caribbean dance, music and religion.
Day of the National Rebellion (July 26) In a different province each year, this celebrates the 1953 attack on the Moncada Barracks.
Carnaval, Santiago de Cuba (last week of July) The country's oldest and biggest.
Festival de Rap Cubano Habana Hip Hop (mid-August) Everyone's bustin' rhymes in this wildly successful international event.
Festival Internacional de Ballet (mid-October) Tremendous biennial event packed with performances; 2006 & 2008.
Festival Internacional de Jazz (first week of December) Straight ahead, be-bop, Latin, far out or funkified jazz happens here.
Festival Internacional del Nuevo Cine Latino-americano (first week of December) This prestigious film festival features hundreds of screenings.
Las Parrandas (December 24; Remedios) Extravagant fireworks and floats in one of Cuba's most outrageous festivals.

GAY & LESBIAN TRAVELERS

While Cuba can't be called a queer destination (yet), it's more tolerant than many other Latin American countries and you can hear closet doors being slammed or squeaked open all the time. Although the old 'don't ask, don't tell' lifestyle still exists, the more accepting climate can be largely attributed to the hit movie *Fresa y Chocolate*, which sparked a national dialogue about homosexuality (among men at least, but not so much for lesbians). Antidiscrimination laws also play a role.

As there are no gay bars, Cuban queer culture revolves heavily around cruising and private *fiestas de diez pesos* (private parties charging CUC$2 cover). These mostly gay parties – with a healthy dose of fag hags, bifolks and friends – are moving shindigs held on Friday and Saturday nights (starting at midnight); head to Cine Yara (p142) in Havana and chat up the crowds of partygoers to find out where that night's party is happening. Drag shows – like most Cuban cultural activities – feature talented artists and are another fixture on the queer calendar; ask around.

Violence against gay travelers who take men back to their casa particular is not unheard of, so – as always – cruise at your own risk.

HOLIDAYS

There are only a few holidays that may affect your travel plans, when shops close and local transportation is erratic. These are:
January 1 Triumph of the Revolution; New Year's Day
May 1 International Worker's Day; no inner-city transportation
July 26 Celebrates start of the revolution on July 26, 1953.
October 10 Start of the First War of Independence
December 25 Declared an official holiday after the Pope's 1998 visit.

INTERNET ACCESS

Access to the Internet is provided by Etecsa (per hour CUC$6); you have to show your passport. Laptop connections in hotels and casas particulares are rare. Scanners, printers and other peripherals are typically not available.

MONEY

This is a tricky part of any Cuba trip and the double economy takes some getting used to. Two currencies circulate throughout Cuba – Cuban convertible pesos (CUC) and Cuban pesos (CUP), also called *moneda nacional*

DENOMINATIONS & LINGO

The convertible peso (CUC) comes in multicolored notes of one, three, five, 10, 20, 50 and 100 pesos. Take care, as the bills look extremely similar. Convertible coins come in five, 10, 25 and 50 cents and one- and five-peso denominations. You can tell them from the Cuban peso coins by their subtle octagonal edge.

The Cuban peso (CUP) comes in notes of one, five, 10, 20, 50 and 100 pesos, and coins of one (rare), five and 20 centavos, and one and three pesos.

With their typical linguistic flair, Cubans have lots of money slang and the double economy lingo can be confusing. Take care when negotiating in 'pesos,' a term commonly used for both *moneda nacional* and hard currency convertible pesos.

Convertible pesos (CUC$) Called dollars, *divisa, chavitos*, kooks (for the abbreviation CUC) or simply pesos.
Cuban pesos (CUP) Also called *moneda nacional* (MN) or simply pesos.
Dollars Are gone, but the name endures; prices are almost always quoted in dollars when really they mean convertible pesos.
Kilos Slang for cents.

(MN). Most prices in this chapter are quoted in convertible pesos (CUC$) and nearly everything tourists buy is in this currency (eg accommodations, rental cars, bus tickets, museum admissions and Internet access).

Convertible pesos can only be bought and sold in Cuba with Canadian dollars, euros, British pounds, Swiss francs, Mexican pesos and Japanese yen; these currencies are exchanged at the global exchange rate for the dollar, plus an 8% tax tacked on by the Cuban government. US dollars are also convertible, but with an 18% tax. Convertible pesos are useless outside Cuba; you can reverse-exchange currency at the airport before you pass through immigration. Euros are accepted at nearly all resorts. Do not change money on the street as scams are rampant and there's no benefit to you.

Cuban pesos sell at 26 to 1 against the convertible peso, and while there are many things you can't buy with *moneda nacional,* there's quite a lot you can, including street food, movie tickets and bodega cigars.

ATMs & Credit Cards

Cash is king. Busted machines, finicky phone lines and other Cuban randomness means even the top hotels sometimes experience difficulties processing credit cards. Still, ATMs are becoming more common and they can be handy, when they're working. At banks, cash advances are free; in Cadecas there's a 1% commission. Visa is the most widely accepted credit card.

Due to embargo laws, no credit card issued by a US bank or subsidiary is accepted in Cuba.

Traveler's Checks

While they add security, traveler's checks are a hassle in Cuba. In addition to commissions, cashing them takes time, and smaller hotels don't accept them. They're virtually useless in the provinces. If you insist on carrying them, get Thomas Cook checks.

TELEPHONE
Cell (Mobile) Phones

Cuba's cell phone monopoly is **Cubacel** (www .cubacel.com); you have to buy prepaid cards, plus pay CUC$3 per day. You are charged for both incoming *and* outgoing local calls (from CUC$0.52 to CUC$0.70 per minute). International rates are CUC$2.70 per minute to the US and CUC$5.85 per minute to Europe. Only 900 MHz, unlocked phones work here; you can rent one for CUC$7 per day.

Phone Cards

Etecsa is where you buy phone cards, send and receive faxes, use the Internet and make international calls. Blue public Etecsa phones (most broken) are everywhere. Phone cards (magnetic or chip) are sold in convertible-peso denominations of CUC$5, CUC$10 and CUC$20, and *moneda nacional* denominations of CUP3, CUP5 and CUP7. You can call nationally with either, but you can only call internationally with convertible-peso cards.

CUBA

Phone Codes

To call Cuba from abroad, dial your country's international access code, then Cuba's country code ☎ 53, the city or area code and the local number. To call internationally from a Cuban payphone, dial ☎ 119, the country code, the area code and the number. To the US, you just dial ☎ 119, then 1, the area code and the number.

To place a collect call (reverse charges or *cobro revertido*) through an international operator, dial ☎ 012. This service is not available to all countries. You cannot call collect from public phones.

To call between provinces, dial ☎ 0 + area code + number. To call Havana from any other province, you just dial ☎ 7 + number. Area codes have been included in the phone listings in this chapter.

Phone Rates

Local calls are CUP0.05 per minute, while interprovincial calls cost from 35 centavos to CUP1 per minute.

International calls made with a card cost CUC$2.45 per minute to North America and CUC$5.85 to Europe/Oceania. Operator-assisted calls cost CUC$3.71 and CUC$8.78, respectively.

TIME

Cuba is five hours behind GMT/UTC, the equivalent of Eastern Standard Time in the US and Canada. Cuba normally observes daylight saving time from April to September, during which time it's only four hours behind GMT/UTC. This practice was suspended in 2004, however, and this was still the case at the time of publication.

TOILETS

Cuban sewer systems are not designed to take toilet paper and every bathroom has a small waste basket beside the toilet for this purpose. Aside from in top end hotels and resorts, you should discard your paper in this basket or risk an embarrassing backup.

VISAS & TOURIST CARDS

Visitors initially get four weeks in Cuba with a *tarjeta de turista* (tourist card) issued by their airline or travel agency. Unlicensed US visitors buy their tourist card at the airline desk in the third country through which they're traveling to Cuba (US$25); they are welcomed in the country like any other tourist. You cannot leave Cuba without presenting your tourist card (replacements cost CUC$25).

The 'address in Cuba' line should be filled in with a hotel or legal casa particular, if only to avoid unnecessary questioning.

Business travelers and journalists need visas. Applications should be made through a consulate at least three weeks in advance, preferably longer.

Extensions

Obtaining an extension is easy: go to an immigration office and present your documents and CUC$25 in stamps (obtainable at Bandec or Banco Financiero Internacional). You'll receive an additional four weeks, but can exit and re-enter and start over again. Attend to extensions at least a few business days before your visa is due to expire.

Licenses for US Visitors

Since 1961, the US government has limited the freedom of its citizens to visit Cuba. To travel 'legally' to Cuba, most Americans must obtain written permission (a 'license') from the Treasury Department. This has become increasingly difficult since 2004, when President Bush further restricted travel to Cuba. Licenses are never issued for the purpose of tourism.

For more information, contact the **Licensing Division** (☎ 202-622-2480; www.treas.gov/ofac; Office of Foreign Assets Control, US Department of the Treasury, 2nd fl, Annex Bldg, 1500 Pennsylvania Ave NW, Washington, DC 20220). Travel arrangements for those eligible for a license can be made by specialized US companies such as Marazul (see p774).

Under the Trading with the Enemy Act, goods originating in Cuba are prohibited from being brought into the US. Cuban cigars, rum, coffee etc will be confiscated by US customs. Possession of Cuban goods inside the US or importing them from a third country is also illegal.

US citizens without a license traditionally visit Cuba via Canada, Mexico, the Bahamas, Jamaica or another third country. Since US travel agents and airlines are prohibited from handling arrangements, US citizens use a foreign travel agency or arrange air travel independently.

Immigration officials in Cuba do not stamp US passports, instead stamping the tourist card, which is collected upon departure.

The US government has an 'Interests Section' in Havana, but US visitors are advised to go there only if something goes terribly wrong. Therefore, unofficial US visitors are especially careful not to lose their passports while in Cuba, as this would put them in a very difficult position. 'Unauthorized' US citizens traveling to Cuba can be subject to fines (see the boxed text, below).

TRANSPORTATION

GETTING THERE & AWAY
Entering Cuba

Whether it's your first time or 50th, it's exciting waiting to pass beyond the locked doors of immigration to enter Cuba. The procedure is straightforward as long as you have a passport valid for six months, an onward ticket and your tourist card (see opposite).

Air

Cuba has 11 international airports and over 60 carriers serving the island. See p774 for information on traveling from outside the Caribbean to (and from) Cuba.

Cuba's national airline is **Cubana de Aviación** (www.cubana.cu). Its modern fleet flies major routes and its fares are usually the cheapest. Still, overbooking and delays are nagging problems and it charges stiffly for every kilo above the 20kg allowance.

Jamaica is a major transportation hub to Cuba. Cubana flies from Kingston and Montego Bay to Havana daily, as does Air Jamaica, with numerous convenient connections from the US.

Cubana also flies twice a week to Havana from Guadeloupe/Martinique, Santo Domingo and Puerto Príncipe. The latter two flights stop in Santiago de Cuba first. One flight a week goes from Grand Cayman to Havana with Aerocaribbean and three times a week with Cayman Airways.

From the Bahamas, Cubana flies daily between Nassau and Havana (US$276, round-trip); Bahamasair flies three times a week. US citizens cannot purchase Nassau–Havana tickets online or anywhere in the US.

The following airlines fly to/from Cuba from within the Caribbean:

Aerocaribbean (☎ 7-870-4965, 7-879-7524; www.aero-caribbean.com; hub Havana)

Aerocaribe (☎ 7-204-8667; www.aerocaribe.com; hub Cancún)

Air Jamaica (☎ 7-833-2447; www.airjamaica.com; hub Montego Bay)

Air Transat (☎ 7-204-3802/04; www.airtransat.com; hub Toronto)

Copa Airlines (☎ 7-204-1111; www.copaair.com; hub Panama City)

Cubana de Aviación (☎ 7-834-4949; www.cubana.cu; hub Havana)

Mexicana de Aviación (☎ 7-833-3532; www.mexicana.com.mx; hub Mexico City)

TACA (☎ 7-833-3114; www.taca.com; hub San Salvador)

Sea

Marinas around Cuba accepting foreign vessels include María la Gorda, Marina Hemingway (Havana), Cienfuegos, Varadero, Trinidad and Santiago de Cuba. Harbor anchorage fees are CUC$10 per day

---

TRAVEL BAN PENALTIES

Together with the embargo against Cuba, the US government enforces what is known as a 'travel ban,' preventing its citizens from visiting Cuba. Technically a treasury law prohibiting US citizens from spending money in Cuba, it has largely squelched leisure travel for over 40 years.

The 1996 Helms-Burton Bill imposes fines of up to US$50,000 on US citizens who visit Cuba without government permission. It also allows for confiscation of their property. In addition, under the Trading with the Enemy Act, violators may also face up to US$250,000 in fines and up to 10 years in prison. The authors and publisher of this guide accept no responsibility for repercussions suffered by US citizens who decide to circumvent these restrictions. You are strongly encouraged to visit www.cubacentral.com to inform yourself of the latest legislation on Capitol Hill, and to review the Office of Foreign Assets Control regulations limiting travel (www.treas.gov/ofac).

or 45 centavos per foot for a pier slip with water and electric hookups.

There are no scheduled ferry services to Cuba.

GETTING AROUND
Air
Cubana de Aviación (☎ 7-834-4949; www.cubana.cu) and its regional carrier **Aerocaribbean** (☎ 7-833-3621; www.aero-caribbean.com), fly between Havana and Santiago de Cuba three times daily and Baracoa on Thursday and Sunday (stopping in Santiago de Cuba). One-way tickets are half the price of round-trip.

Bicycle
Cuba is bike country, with bike lanes and with drivers accustomed to sharing the road, countrywide. Spare parts are difficult to find; *Poncheras* fix flat tires and provide air.

Bicycle theft is rampant, except at *parqueos* – bicycle parking lots costing CUP1, located wherever crowds congregate (markets, bus terminals etc). Riding after dark is not recommended. Trains with baggage carriages *(coches de equipaje* or *bagones)* take bikes for CUC$20. These compartments are guarded, but take your panniers with you and check over the bike when you arrive. Víazul buses also take bikes.

Bus
Bus travel is a dependable option with **Víazul** (☎ 7-881-1413, 7-881-5652, 7-881-1108; www.viazul.cu; Calle 26 & Zoológico, Nuevo Vedado), which has punctual, air-con coaches to destinations of interest to travelers. Reservations are advisable during peak travel periods (June to August, Christmas and Easter) and on popular routes (Havana–Trinidad, Trinidad–Santa Clara and Santiago de Cuba–Baracoa). Routes are: Havana–Viñales, Havana–Varadero, Havana–Trinidad, Varadero–Trinidad, Havana–Santiago de Cuba, Trinidad–Santiago de Cuba and Santiago de Cuba–Baracoa. The buses also stop at all provincial capitals.

Car & Moped
Your home license is sufficient to rent and drive a car or moped in Cuba.

FUEL & SPARE PARTS
Cupet and Oro Negro *servicentros* (gas stations) selling hard-currency gas are nearly everywhere. Gas is sold by the liter and is either regular (per liter CUC$0.80) or *especial* (per liter CUC$0.95). Either works equally well.

RENTAL
Renting a car in Cuba is straightforward with your passport, driver's license and refundable CUC$200 deposit (in cash or with non-US credit card). You can rent a car in one city and drop it off in another for a reasonable fee. The cheapest cars start at CUC$45 per day.

Contracts for three days or more come with unlimited kilometers. In Cuba, you pay for the first tank of gas when you rent the car (at CUC$0.95 per liter) and return it empty (no refunds for gas left in the tank). Drivers under 25 pay a CUC$5 fee; additional drivers on the same contract pay a CUC$15 surcharge.

Check over the car carefully before driving off as you'll be responsible for any damage or missing parts. Make sure there is a spare tire of the correct size, a jack and lug wrench. Check that there are seatbelts and that all the doors lock properly. Take the optional CUC$10 per day insurance.

We have received many letters about poor/nonexistent customer service, bogus spare tires, forgotten reservations and other car-rental problems. The more Spanish you speak and the friendlier you are, the more likely problems will be resolved to everyone's satisfaction (tips to the agent may help). Always be ready to go to Plan B.

The following companies have offices nationwide:

Havanautos Airport (☎ 7-649-5197; www.havanautos .cu); Tángana (☎ 7-836-4766; Malecón & Calle 13)

Micar Airport (☎ 7-833-0101; www.micarrenta.cu); Vedado (Map pp134–5; ☎ 7-832-0202; Calle 1 & Paseo in Galerías Paseo) Has the most economical cars.

Rex Airport (☎ 7-642-6074; www.rex-rentacar.com); Vedado (Map pp134–5; ☎ 7-836-7788; Línea & Malecón) Luxury cars and limousines.

Transtur Airport (☎ 7-266-4406; www.transtur.cu); Vedado (Map pp134–5; ☎ 7-55-36-98; Calles 25 & L)

ROAD CONDITIONS
The Autopista and Carretera Central are generally in good repair. While motorized traffic is refreshingly light, bicycles, pedestrians, tractors and livestock can test your driving skills. Driving at night is not recommended due to variable roads, crossing

cows, poor lighting and drunk drivers (an ongoing problem despite a government educational campaign).

Signage, though improving, is still sadly appalling.

ROAD RULES
Cubans drive how they want, where they want. Seatbelts are required and maximum speed limits are technically 50km/hr (around 30 mph) in the city, 90km/hr (around 62 mph) on highways and 100km/hr (around 55mph) on the Autopista.

There are some clever speed traps along the Autopista. Speeding tickets start at CUC$30 and are noted on your car contract (deducted from your deposit when you return the car).

Local Transportation
BICI-TAXI
Bici-taxis are big tricycles with a seat behind the driver. Tourists pay CUC$1; agree on the price beforehand. By law, bici-taxis are not allowed to take tourists (who are expected to take regular taxis) and they're taking a risk by carrying foreigners.

BUS
Very crowded, very steamy, very Cuban – guaguas (local buses) are useful in bigger cities. There is always a line at paradas (bus stops). Shout 'el último?' to determine who is last in line. You 'give' el último when the next person arrives, thereby knowing exactly where you fall in line.

Buses cost from 40 centavos to CUP1. You must always walk as far back in the bus as possible and exit through the rear. Make room to pass by saying 'permiso,' and wear your pack in front.

HORSE CART
Many provincial cities have coches (horse carts) that trot on fixed routes.

TAXI
Car taxis are metered and cost CUC$1 to start, CUC$0.75/km thereafter. Cabbies usually offer foreigners a flat, off-meter rate that works out close to what you'll pay with the meter.

Train
Public railways operated by Ferrocarriles de Cuba serve all the provincial capitals and are a great way to experience Cuba if you have time and patience. Departure information provided in this book is purely theoretical. Getting a ticket in hard currency is usually no problem, though Spanish-speaking travelers frequently travel on trains for the peso price. The most useful routes for travelers are Havana–Santiago de Cuba and Havana–Santa Clara. The bathrooms are foul. Watch your luggage and bring food.

Truck
Camiones (trucks) are a cheap, fast way to travel within or between provinces. Every city has a provincial and municipal bus stop with camion departures.

CUBA

Cayman Islands

With an Americanized sheen buffed by the almighty dollar, the Cayman Islands are distinct from their Caribbean counterparts in substance and style. Here you'll find divers clad in Day-Glo wetsuits, English folk checking the cricket score over a tipple, and in George Town, plenty of cruise-shippers shopping for duty-free Waterford crystal.

For anyone wanting to find out what it *really* means to be Caymanian, it's a simple matter of leaving behind the condos and high-rise hotels and getting to know the easy-going inhabitants of Grand Cayman and its 'sister islands,' Cayman Brac and Little Cayman. There's an infectious, easygoing way of life here that you'll be given to emulate. Scratch below the surface and you'll discover a distinct culture founded only a few centuries ago upon – and inextricably bound with – the sea.

It's the same sea that will color every aspect of your visit in shades of azure, turquoise and indigo. Below these warm, tranquil waters is a world of stingrays, tropical fish and brightly colored corals. Towering underwater walls, shipwrecks and reefs have made the Caymans legendary among divers and snorkelers, and mile upon mile of pristine beaches and predictably glorious sunsets poll well with extreme-relaxation enthusiasts. The beguiling personality of the Cayman Islands will win you over with its own brand of Caribbean flair.

FAST FACTS

- **Area** 100 sq miles (259 sq km)
- **Capital** George Town, Grand Cayman
- **Country code** ☎ 345
- **Departure tax** US$25 (usually included in the price of your air ticket – cruise-ship visitors are exempt)
- **Famous for** Diving, banking and iguanas
- **Language** English
- **Money** Cayman Islands dollar (CI$); US dollars accepted. CI$1 = US$1.25 = €1.01 = £0.69
- **People** Caymanians
- **Population** 40,000
- **Visa** Not required for nationals of the USA, Canada, UK, most Commonwealth countries and some European countries. Available from a British consulate or embassy for £28 (US$51).

HIGHLIGHTS

- **Diving & Snorkeling** (p187) Live the life aquatic in waters celebrated for unparalleled visibility, precipitous walls, healthy reefs and rich marine life.
- **Seven Mile Beach** (p187) Enjoy maximum repose on a beautiful white-sand beach, or saunter up to one of the beachside bars for a frosty mudslide or rum punch.
- **Stingray City** (p187) Take a snorkeling excursion to this famous southern stingray feeding spot, and serve 'em up a meal of chopped squid.
- **Cayman Brac** (p192) and **Little Cayman** (p195) Savor the traditional Caymanian charm and exquisite diving, hiking, biking and bird-watching on these remote, lightly populated islands.
- **Owen Island** (p196) Brush off your Robinson Crusoe fantasies and kayak or swim out to this tiny, idyllic island that's just off the coast of Little Cayman.

HOW MUCH?

- Taxi from Owen Roberts International Airport to George Town US$12.50
- Guided snorkeling trip US$30
- Stingray City dive/snorkel trip US$50/30
- Meal of fresh fish in a touristy restaurant US$25
- Meal of fresh fish in a local restaurant US$12

LONELY PLANET INDEX

- Gallon (imperial) of gas US$3.55
- Liter of bottled water US$2
- Bottle of Stingray Beer US$4
- Souvenir T-shirt US$22
- Street snack: slice of rum cake US$4.50

ITINERARIES

- **Three days** Sun yourself on Seven Mile Beach, visit the Cayman Turtle Farm and snorkel in Stingray City.
- **One week** Add to the three-day itinerary a visit to Hell, hiking at the Botanic Park, and an excursion to Rum Point.
- **Two weeks** Add on Cayman Brac for some nature hikes and deep relaxation on gorgeous secluded beaches.
- **Three weeks** Add on Little Cayman for a little world-class diving, fishing and bird-watching.

CLIMATE & WHEN TO GO

The peak season for tourism is from mid-December to mid-April, when the temperature averages a pleasant 75°F (23.9°C) during the day and 68°F (20°C) during the night, and humidity is at its lowest. During the off-season, temperatures average 83°F (28.3°C). Crowds dissipate, particularly on Cayman Brac and Little Cayman, bringing lodging rates down by as much as 40%. Rainfall is highest from mid-May through to October, with frequent afternoon showers that clear as quickly as they arrive.

HISTORY

For the first century after Christopher Columbus happened upon the Caymans in 1503, the islands were uninhabited by people – which may explain why multitudes of sea turtles were happy to call the place home. The sun-bleached landscape languished in a near-pristine state, undisturbed but for the occasional intrusion of sailors stopping in to swipe some turtles and fill up on fresh water.

No permanent settlers set up house until well after the 1670 acquisition of the islands – and its turtles – by the British Crown, which has held dominion over the three islands ever since. Once settlers started trickling in from Jamaica in the early 18th century, Caymanians quickly established their reputation as world-class seafarers. From the 1780s, Caymanian shipbuilding industry produced schooners and other seacraft used for inter-island trade and turtling.

By 1800, the population numbered less than 1000 – of whom half were slaves. After the Slavery Abolition Act was read at Pedro St James (p191) in 1835, most freed slaves remained, and by 1900 the Caymans' population had quintupled.

Until the mid-20th century, the economy would remain tied to the sea with fishing, turtling and shipbuilding as the main industries. Divers put the Caymans Islands on the international tourist map as early as the 1950s; islanders were understandably protective of

CAYMAN ISLANDS

their little slice of paradise, and were slow to relinquish their isolation. By the next decade, however, Caymanians had begun fashioning the tax structure that's made Grand Cayman an economic powerhouse – and designing an infrastructure that's made it a capital of Caribbean tourism.

In September 2004, Hurricane Ivan gave Grand Cayman a body blow, causing such widespread destruction that tourism was halted and a curfew enforced for several months to prevent looting. Fortunately, Cayman Brac and Little Cayman did not receive a direct hit and damage to the smaller islands was limited.

THE CULTURE

For centuries, the Caymans had been left to simmer undisturbed in their own juices as the rest of the world rushed headlong into modernity. As recently as forty years ago (aside from a few adventurers and fishing nuts) there were few tourists. Electric power was provided solely by noisy generators, and most islanders did without power. What has occurred between then and now constitutes a Caymanian cultural revolution. With the advent of large-scale tourism and big business banking, life on the islands has changed so rapidly that cultural discourse has turned to measuring what's been gained and lost.

Historically, the population is an amalgamation with Jamaican, North American, European and African roots, but contemporary Cayman has become even more multifaceted. For better or worse, a large influx of expatriate workers – representing 78 countries and growing ever greater in number in the aftermath of Hurricane Ivan – has led Caymanians to become a minority in their own country. The upside is that the Cayman Islands has a remarkably rich social fabric that truly celebrates diversity.

At stake, however, is the cultural legacy of this religious, seafaring nation. Borrowing a theme from the islands' traditional folk songs, which regularly feature the laments of sailors longing to return home, many islanders speak with nostalgia of the old ways. In response, the Cayman National Cultural Foundation has been charged with stimulating and promoting local culture; you can get a taste of it yourself at the annual Cayfest cultural festival (p198).

ARTS

While the art scene in the Caymans may fail to scintillate visiting urbanites, it is gathering steam and beginning to garner notice in the world at large. The National Gallery (p187) was opened in 1996 to promote and encourage the embryonic art scene of the islands. An art collective known as Native Son and comprised of homegrown artists Wray Banker, Al Ebanks, Luelan Bodden and Horatio Estaban has exhibited locally and internationally, while late-blooming visionary artist 'Miss Lassie' has become well known abroad in 'outsider art' circles. (Her death in 2003 was cause for spontaneous national mourning.) Unsurprisingly, underwater photography is widely practiced in the Caymans, most notably by Cathy Church, whose Underwater Photo Centre & Gallery provides a focal point. To get the lowdown on cultural events on the islands, visit the Cayman National Cultural Foundation's site at www.artscayman.org.

ENVIRONMENT
The Land

Located approximately 150 miles (241km) south of Cuba and 180 miles (290km) west of Jamaica, the Cayman Islands consist of Grand Cayman and two smaller islands – Cayman Brac and Little Cayman – 75 miles (120km) to the northeast and 5 miles (8km) apart. All three islands are low-lying, flat-topped landmasses, although Cayman Brac does have a 140ft (42.6m) cliff that affords a natural vantage point from which to watch the sun drop into the sea. In fact, the Caymans are the tips of massive submarine mountains that just barely emerge from the awesome Cayman Trench, an area with the deepest water in the Caribbean.

The Waters

Encircling all three of the islands are shallow waters and a reef system harboring one of the world's richest accumulations of marine life. At Bloody Bay Wall, on the north shore of Little Cayman, the seafloor ends abruptly at a depth of only 18ft (5.4m) to 25ft (7.5m), dropping off into a 6000ft (1800m) vertical cliff. Along its sheer face grows an astonishing variety of corals, sponges and sea fans and thousands of mobile creatures going about their daily business as the occasional diver looks on, agog.

Wildlife

The Caymans' dry land is not quite as exciting as its waters, but it still gives nature lovers plenty to do and see. With nearly 200 native winged species, the islands offer outstanding bird-watching. Keep your eyes open and you'll spot parrots, boobies, yellow-bellied sapsuckers, herons and egrets. Reptiles include celebrities such as green sea turtles and blue iguanas, and plenty of common geckos and lizards (the latter sometimes making an appearance in the baths of luxury hotels).

The Caymans aren't lush, but they do support a fair swag of plant life. Mahogany was once abundant but has been mostly logged. Poisonous species include maiden plum (a weed with rash-causing sap), lady's hair or *cowitch* (a vine with fiberglass-like barbs) and the vicious manchineel tree, which produces a skin-blistering sap. Take care not to shelter under a manchineel in the rain! Other indigenous plants are cochineal, used as a shampoo as well as eaten, and pingwing, whose barbed branches were once fashioned into a natural fence.

FOOD & DRINK

Although it is found on fewer menus these days, sea turtle remains the national dish. These days, it's farm-raised and served in soups and stews or as a braised steak.

As in the Bahamas, conch is a popular item on restaurant menus. This large pink mollusk is cooked with onion and spices in a stew; fried up as fritters; or sliced raw and served with a lime marinade. Environmentally concerned diners may want to pass: the Caymanian appetite for conch has resulted in overfishing, even in the protected zones of the islands' reefs.

Jamaican-style 'jerk' seasoning is widely used in Caymanian food, and the roadside sight of a smoking oil drum turned on its side is your cue to pull over and fill up on spicy jerk chicken, pork or shrimp.

Other local favorites include oxtail, cow foot, salt beef with beans and mackerel with green bananas. For dessert, try 'heavy cake,' a dense confection made from starchy ingredients such as grated cassava, cornmeal, yam and liberal quantities of brown sugar.

Wash it all down with a 'jelly ice,' chilled coconut water sucked from the shell, or perhaps a bottle of Stingray Beer, the local brew. Or, if you can handle a thousand extra calories, slurp a mudslide, the creamy cocktail – a potent concoction of Kahlua, Baileys and vodka – that locals claim was invented on Rum Point.

GRAND CAYMAN

pop 37,000

The largest, most visited and most populated of the Cayman Islands, Grand Cayman retains a distinctly British flavor despite its massive influx of American tourists. With nearly 700 banks – most of them hidden – Grand Cayman is the world's fifth-largest financial center. Tourists, however, are mostly interested in the dive outfitters, palm-thatched bars and the beautiful white-sand Seven Mile Beach.

Depending on whether or not cruise ships are in port, the compact, colonial capital of George Town is either buzzing with life or taking a nap. For those with a zeal for shopping, George Town's got the goods, and, better yet, they're sold duty-free. The island's other districts – West Bay, Bodden Town, East End and Northside – each have a distinct character and are worth exploring.

In September 2004, Hurricane Ivan gave Grand Cayman a thrashing it will never forget. The island's tropical landscape was given a buzz cut and hundreds of homes, hotels and businesses suffered irreparable damage. Displaying panache and determination, Grand Caymanians quickly got their tourism infrastructure up and running and it wasn't long before the visitors returned to find the landscape changed but the beaches and diving as glorious as ever.

Information

BOOKSTORES

BookNook (☎ 949-7392; Anchorage Centre, Harbour Dr, George Town) Limited stock of general interest titles, including regional travel guides.

EMERGENCY

Police (RCIP; ☎ 949-4222; Elgin Ave, George Town)

INTERNET ACCESS

Café del Sol Internet Coffee House (☎ 946-2233; cnr West Bay Rd & Lawrence Blvd, Seven Mile Beach; half-/1hr US$3/5; ☑ 7am-7pm Mon-Sat, 8am-7pm Sun) The cheapest access in the most comfortable surroundings.

CAYMAN ISLANDS

MEDICAL SERVICES

Cayman Islands Hospital (☎ 949-8600; Hospital Rd, George Town) Houses a state-of-the-art **recompression chamber** (☎ 555; 🕑 24hr).

MONEY

George Town, it seems, has nearly as many banks as people. Filling your wallet with

the brightly colored currency is optional if you're flush with greenbacks: US currency is accepted everywhere.

POST

Main post office (☎ 949-2474; cnr Edward St & Cardinal Ave, George Town; 🕑 8:30am-3:30pm Mon-Fri, 8:30-11:30am Sat)

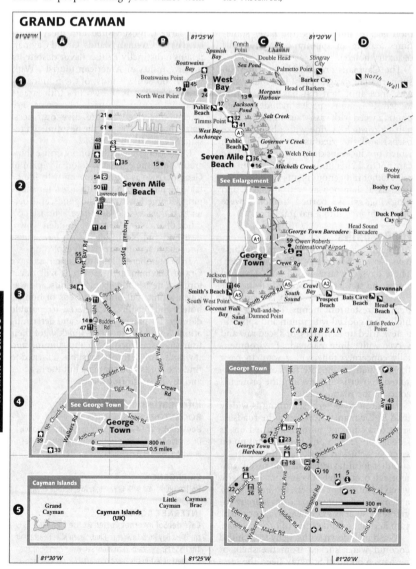

TOURIST INFORMATION

Department of Tourism (☎ 949-0623; www
.caymanislands.ky; the Pavilion, Cricket Sq, Elgin St,
George Town; ◷ 9am-5pm Mon-Fri) The Cayman
Islands' tourism department operates information booths
that are located at the Owen Roberts International Airport
and at the North Terminal cruise-ship dock at George
Town harbor.

Getting There & Around

For information on getting to (and from)
Grand Cayman, see p199.

TO/FROM THE AIRPORT

There's a taxi queue just outside the airport
building. Fares are set by the government,
based on one to three people sharing a ride.

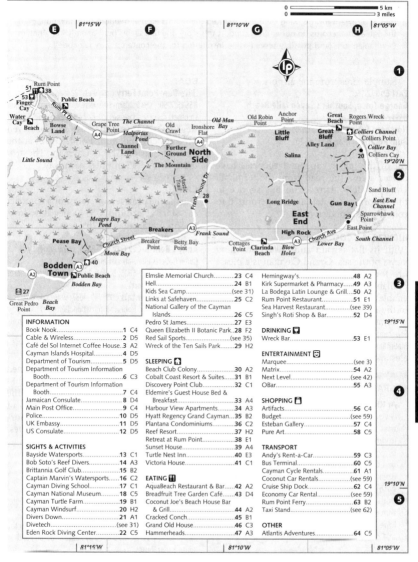

INFORMATION		
Book Nook	**1**	C4
Cable & Wireless	**2**	D5
Café del Sol Internet Coffee House	**3**	A2
Cayman Islands Hospital	**4**	D5
Department of Tourism	**5**	D5
Department of Tourism Information Booth	**6**	C3
Department of Tourism Information Booth	**7**	C4
Jamaican Consulate	**8**	D4
Main Post Office	**9**	C4
Police	**10**	D5
UK Embassy	**11**	D5
US Consulate	**12**	D5

SIGHTS & ACTIVITIES		
Bayside Watersports	**13**	C1
Bob Soto's Reef Divers	**14**	A3
Brittannia Golf Club	**15**	B2
Captain Marvin's Watersports	**16**	C2
Cayman Diving School	**17**	C1
Cayman National Museum	**18**	C5
Cayman Turtle Farm	**19**	B1
Cayman Windsurf	**20**	H2
Divers Down	**21**	A1
Divetech	(see 31)	
Eden Rock Diving Center	**22**	C5

Elmslie Memorial Church	**23**	C4
Hell	**24**	B1
Kids Sea Camp	(see 31)	
Links at Safehaven	**25**	C2
National Gallery of the Cayman Islands	**26**	C5
Pedro St James	**27**	E3
Queen Elizabeth II Botanic Park	**28**	F2
Red Sail Sports	(see 35)	
Wreck of the Ten Sails Park	**29**	H2

SLEEPING 🏠		
Beach Club Colony	**30**	A2
Cobalt Coast Resort & Suites	**31**	A1
Discovery Point Club	**32**	C1
Eldemire's Guest House Bed & Breakfast	**33**	A4
Harbour View Apartments	**34**	A3
Hyatt Regency Grand Cayman	**35**	B2
Plantana Condominiums	**36**	C2
Reef Resort	**37**	H2
Retreat at Rum Point	**38**	E1
Sunset House	**39**	A4
Turtle Nest Inn	**40**	E3
Victoria House	**41**	C1

EATING 🍴		
AquaBeach Restaurant & Bar	**42**	A2
Breadfruit Tree Garden Café	**43**	D4
Coconut Joe's Beach House Bar & Grill	**44**	A2
Cracked Conch	**45**	B1
Grand Old House	**46**	C3
Hammerheads	**47**	A3

Hemingway's	**48**	A2
Kirk Supermarket & Pharmacy	**49**	A3
La Bodega Latin Lounge & Grill	**50**	A2
Rum Point Restaurant	**51**	E1
Sea Harvest Restaurant	(see 39)	
Singh's Roti Shop & Bar	**52**	D4

DRINKING 🍷		
Wreck Bar	**53**	E1

ENTERTAINMENT 🎭		
Marquee	(see 3)	
Matrix	**54**	A2
Next Level	(see 42)	
OBar	**55**	A3

SHOPPING 🛍		
Artifacts	**56**	C4
Budget	(see 59)	
Esteban Gallery	**57**	C4
Pure Art	**58**	C5

TRANSPORT		
Andy's Rent-a-Car	**59**	C3
Bus Terminal	**60**	C5
Cayman Cycle Rentals	**61**	A1
Coconut Car Rentals	(see 59)	
Cruise Ship Dock	**62**	C4
Economy Car Rental	(see 59)	
Rum Point Ferry	**63**	B2
Taxi Stand	(see 62)	

OTHER		
Atlantis Adventures	**64**	C5

THE WRECK OF THE 10 SAILS

Just ask any international sea captain: the coral reefs that encircle the Cayman Islands are beautiful but potentially deadly. This fact was borne out on a fateful night in February, 1794: the *Cordelia*, leading a convoy of merchant ships bound from Jamaica to Britain, ran aground on the reef at East End. In a tragic case of crossed signals, the warning issued from the *Cordelia* to the other ships was misinterpreted as a call to follow more closely, and one by one nine more ships crashed into the reef.

Fortunately for the imperiled sailors, the able mariners living on the island's craggy East End sprang into action, showing great heroism in ensuring that no lives were lost. Popular legend states that as a reward for this, King George III granted the islands eternal freedom from taxation. Even though actual records do not entirely support this story, the tale seems permanently ingrained in Caymanian lore (and possibly served as an inspiration for the contemporary tax code!).

Sample fares from the airport:

East End US$60
George Town, Southern Seven Mile Beach US$12.50
Northern Seven Mile Beach US$25
Rum Point/Cayman Kai US$70

All of the major car-rental agencies have offices across the road from the terminal. Unfortunately, there is no bus service to the airport, and hotels are not permitted to collect guests on arrival.

BICYCLE & SCOOTER

With its flat terrain and always stunning views of the sea, Grand Cayman is a pleasure for cyclists (many hotels make bikes available to guests). Renting a scooter will enable you to easily reach the far reaches of the island.

Cayman Cycle Rentals (☎ 945-4021; Coconut Place Shopping Center, West Bay Rd, Seven Mile Beach; per day mountain bikes/scooters US$15/30) rents both bicycles and scooters.

GRAND CAYMAN FOR CHILDREN

At **Kids Sea Camp** (in the US ☎ 800-934-3483; www.kidseacamp.com; ☼ Jul-Aug), the family that arrives together, dives together. This inventive travel package is designed to bring families closer together, underwater. Organized excursions to a number of great dive and snorkeling sites, combined with access to age-appropriate instruction, make this a good option for families that want to push the active vacation envelope. Kids Sea Camp is hosted by Divetech at Cobalt Coast Resort & Suites (p191)

BOAT

The **Rum Point Ferry** (☎ 949-1234; adult/child return US$15/7.50; ☼ 9:30am-10:30pm winter, 8am-10:30pm summer) carries passengers between the Hyatt Regency dock (on the east side of Seven Mile Beach) and Rum Point (p192) at the far east end of Grand Cayman. The trip takes around 45 minutes each way.

CAR

During the peak season, rates for a compact car start at around US$40 per day; low-season rentals may be 25% less.

Reputable providers:

Andy's Rent-a-Car (☎ 949-8111; www.andys.ky; Owen Roberts International Airport)
Budget (☎ 949-5605; budget@candw.ky; Owen Roberts International Airport)
Coconut Car Rentals (☎ 949-4037; www.coconutcar rentals.com; Owen Roberts International Airport)
Economy Car Rental (☎ 949-1003; www.economycar rental.com.ky; Owen Roberts International Airport)

LOCAL TRANSPORTATION

The public **bus terminal** (☎ 945-5100), located adjacent to the public library on Edward St in downtown George Town, serves as the dispatch point for buses to all districts of Grand Cayman. The system uses color-coded logos on the buses to indicate routes.

The main routes:

West Bay (fare US$1.90; ☼ every 15min 6am-11pm Sun-Thu & 6am-midnight Fri & Sat) Served by Route 1 (yellow) and Route 2 (lime green) buses.
Bodden Town (fare US$1.90; ☼ every 30min 6am-11pm Sun-Thu & 6am-midnight Fri & Sat) Served by Route 3 (blue) buses.
East End (fare US$2.50; ☼ hourly 6am-9pm Sun-Thu & 6am-midnight Fri & Sat) Served by Route 4 (purple) and Route 5 (red) buses.

CAYMAN ISLANDS

Northside (fare US$2.50; ⏰ hourly 6am-9pm Sun-Thu & Sat & 6am-midnight Fri) Served by Route 5 (red) buses.

TAXI

Taxis are readily available at Owen Roberts International Airport, from all resorts and from the taxi stand at the cruise-ship dock in George Town. They offer a fixed rate per vehicle or per person to all points on Grand Cayman. A sign with current rates is posted at the dock.

GEORGE TOWN & SEVEN MILE BEACH

pop 21,000

The cosmopolitan, economic powerhouse of the Caribbean, George Town sends a potent wind of pure capitalism right up Cuba's nether region. Overlooking a grand harbor, the capital city of the Caymans is compact and eminently walkable. Traditional wooden buildings cozy up to modern shopping courts where visitors can acquire anything from authentic doubloons to high-end perfume and jewelry, all at attractive duty-free prices.

Extending north from town is the famous Seven Mile Beach. Nearly its entire length is bursting with condos and bristling with satellite dishes, but the beach is exquisite. You'll see immediately what all the hullabaloo is about. With its gentle stretches of soft white sand, temperate waters and famous sunsets, you've found the archetypal Caribbean beach.

Most of Grand Cayman's hotels, restaurants and shopping complexes line the island's busiest thoroughfare, West Bay Rd, which travels alongside Seven Mile Beach.

Sights

Housed in George Town's oldest building, the **Cayman National Museum** (☎ 949-8368; cnr Harbour Dr & Sheddon Rd, George Town; adult/child US$5/3; ⏰ 9am-5pm Mon-Fri, 10am-4pm Sat) presents a variety of exhibits on the islands' cultural and natural history and an engaging audiovisual presentation.

A short walk north of the museum, on Harbour Dr, is the interesting **Elmslie Memorial Church**, built in 1920 by a shipbuilder-cum-architect named Captain Rayan. With a roof resembling the hull of a schooner, the church looks like it could float away.

At the **National Gallery of the Cayman Islands** (☎ 945-8111; www.nationalgallery.org.ky; ground fl, Harbour Pl, South Church St, George Town; admission free; ⏰ 9am-5pm Mon-Fri, 11am-4pm Sat), the Caymans' fledgling visual art scene is given room to breathe. While most of the exhibitions are imports, there's always some choice local art on display.

Activities

DIVING & SNORKELING

True to its reputation as a world-class diving destination, Grand Cayman has 160 dive sites from which to choose. Some are known to be teeming with marine life, others are noted for reef-encrusted shipwrecks, and many feature dramatic drop-offs into the abyss.

Nearly 50 diving operations rent out and sell equipment, offer certification courses, and provide guided diving and snorkeling excursions.

An official website – www.divecayman .ky – offers complete information on sites and providers.

On your offshore excursion to **Stingray City** you'd better take your waterproof camera, because your friends back home won't believe it. Considered by many bubble-blowers to be the world's best 12ft (3.6m) dive, this stretch of sandy seafloor in Grand Cayman's North Sound is the meeting place for southern stingrays hungry for a meal. As soon as you enter the water, several of the beautiful prehistoric-looking creatures will glide up to you to suck morsels of squid from your tentative fingers. Half- and full-day excursions are offered by nearly every dive operator, including **Divers Down** (☎ 916-3751; www.diversdown.net; Coconut Pl, West Bay Rd, Seven Mile Beach; dive/snorkel trip US$50/30) and **Off the Wall Divers** (☎ 945-7525; www.otwdivers.com; dive/snorkel trip US$45/20).

From **Eden Rock Diving Center** (☎ 949-7243; www.edenrockdive.com; 124 South Church St, George Town; 1-/2-tank dive US$45/55), overlooking the George Town harbor, it's an easy matter to shore dive to the beautiful caves, tunnels and grottoes of two of the Caymans' most celebrated dive sites: Eden Rocks and Devil's Grotto. Guided shore dives begin at US$55.

Red Sail Sports (☎ 945-8745; www.redsailcayman .com; Hyatt Regency Grand Cayman, West Bay Rd, Seven Mile Beach; 1-/2-tank dive US$60/85) is the largest and best-known of the diving providers, offering excursions islandwide.

CAYMAN ISLANDS

Also recommended:

Bob Soto's Reef Divers (☎ 945-4099; bobsotos@ candw.ky; North Church St, George Town; 1-/2-tank dive US$50/85) Located at the Lobster Pot, this diving institution was one of the first.

Cayman Diving School (☎ 949-4729; www.cayman divingschool.com; Greenery Plaza, Seven Mile Beach; resort/open-water certification/divemaster course US$110/425/700) Multilanguage diving instruction.

Divetech (☎ 946-5658; www.divetech.com; Cobalt Coast Resort & Suites, West Bay; 1-/2-tank dive US$45/85) Located near the awesome North Wall.

OTHER WATER SPORTS

Independent paddlers will find rental **kayaks** (s/d US$20/25) at the public beach on Seven Mile Beach. Located on the breezy East End, **Cayman Windsurf** (☎ 947-7492; Morritt's Tortuga Resort, George Town) was put out of business by Hurricane Ivan but plans to offer lessons and rentals from September 2005.

FISHING

The clear, warm waters of the Caymans are teeming with blue marlin, wahoo, tuna and mahimahi. Charter a boat (half-day charters US$375 to US$550, and full-day charters US$650 to US$1200) with an experienced Caymanian captain and hook some real action:

Bayside Watersports (☎ 949-3200; bayside@candw .ky; Batabano Rd, Morgans Harbour) True Caymanian hospitality and fishing expertise.

Captain Marvin's Watersports (☎ 949-3200; www .captainmarvins.com; Waterfront Centre, North Church St, George Town) In business since 1951.

GOLF

Plenty of great sunshine and two world-class courses make the Caymans a prime destination for golf nuts.

Brittannia Golf Club (☎ 949-8020; Hyatt Regency Grand Cayman, West Bay Rd, Seven Mile Beach; greens fee US$50-100), designed by Jack Nicklaus, is reminiscent of legendary Scottish courses with its traditional 'links' layout.

The **Links at Safehaven** (☎ 949-5988; www .safehaven.ky; Safehaven Dr, Seven Mile Beach; greens fee US$100) was temporarily closed at time of research, in the wake of Hurricane Ivan. Under normal conditions, this par 71, 18-hole beauty is a favorite in the Caribbean.

HORSEBACK RIDING

For experienced and novice riders alike, there's something profoundly pleasurable about a thrilling gallop or leisurely trot on an unspoiled beach.

Nikki's Beach Rides (☎ 916-3530, 945-5839; 1½hr excursion US$75) is well regarded for engaging tours led by the amiable Caymanian owner. Small groups of up to six ride along the beach and through scenic inland wetlands.

Honeysuckle Beach Trail Rides (☎ 916-5420; 1½hr excursion US$60) offers a slightly less personalized experience with larger groups, but it's still a quality operation. Private rides are also offered (per person US$85).

Tours

It's possible to visit the underwater world without even mussing up your hair on an **Atlantis Adventures** (☎ 949-7700; www.atlantisadven tures.com; 32 Goring Ave, George Town; ☾ morning, afternoon & evening) submarine expedition. A 90-minute journey (US$450) on a sophisticated research submarine will take you and a friend 1000ft (300m) beneath the surface to explore sheer vertical walls, towering limestone pinnacles and bizarre sea creatures. A different submersible takes larger groups (adult/teen/child US$84/59/42) to a depth of 100ft (30m). Atlantis also offers an interesting three-hour **kayaking tour** (US$72; ☾ Tue-Thu) of Grand Cayman's coastal environment, including secluded shorelines, inlets, bird-nesting areas, sea grass, and mangrove communities.

Sleeping

There are heaps of accommodations on Grand Cayman, including fine hotels, condos and guest houses. Most properties on the island suffered the wrath of Hurricane Ivan; to visitors, this means that some normally peaceful properties may be still undergoing renovation when you arrive.

Lodging on Grand Cayman is not cheap, but the high quality of accommodations and easy access to the splendid Caribbean Sea does much to make amends.

BUDGET

Eldemire's Guest House Bed & Breakfast (☎ 949-6987; www.eldemire.com; Glen Eden Rd, George Town; d US$90-105, 2-/3-bedroom ste $125/200; P 🗙 🐾) The best option for independent budget-minded travelers is this amiable guest house on the South Sound, within walking distance of central George Town. The basic suites have kitchens; room guests enjoy a spacious and well-equipped common kitchen and complimentary continental breakfasts. Rental bikes are available (per day US$10) and snorkeling trips to Stingray City can be arranged at a considerable discount (trips US$15). Take South Church St from downtown and turn left on Glen Eden Rd.

Harbour View Apartments (☎ 949-5681, 949-4168; www.harbourviewapartments.com; West Bay Rd, George Town; regular/deluxe studio US$99/125, apt US$149; P ✗) Independent divers like this budget option for its easy access to good shore-diving. The large apartments and studios are simply furnished and clean, with full-size kitchens. Close proximity to George Town and public transit make this a good option for those without wheels.

MIDRANGE

Beach Club Colony (☎ 949-8100; bchclub@candw.ky; West Bay Rd, Seven Mile Beach; standard/superior/ocean front r US$180/225/300; P ✗ 🖳 🛎) Located 3 miles (4.8km) from George Town, this well-run hotel has tasteful tropical decor and a laid-back ambience. Guest rooms are bright and cheerful, and interconnecting rooms are available on request.

Sunset House (☎ 949-7111; www.sunsethouse.com; 390 South Church St, George Town; courtyard/oceanview/apt US$165/210/300; P ✗ ✗ 🖳 🛎) Billed as 'for divers, by divers,' this well-rated operation offers an impressive array of diving amenities from customized diving boats and specialized guides to a famed under-water photography center. The motel-style rooms are not fancy but are adequate in comfort and cleanliness. A happening watering hole called My Bar and the excellent Sea Harvest Restaurant (p190) round out the offerings.

Discovery Point Club (☎ 945-2243; www.discovery pointclub.com; West Bay Rd, Seven Mile Beach; d US$225, 1-/2-bedroom ste US$395/455; P ✗ ✗ 🖳 🛎) This oceanfront condo hotel is recommended for its cheerfully appointed, spacious apartments with kitchens and brilliant ocean views. The beach is well tended with palm-thatched shelters and excellent snorkeling opportunities.

Victoria House (☎ 945-9626; www.victoriahouse .com; West Bay Rd, Seven Mile Beach; studio US$260, 1-/2-bedroom ste US$385/490, 2-/3-bedroom penthouse ste US$415/495; P ✗) This quiet and relaxing place on the northern end of Seven Mile Beach offers 25 sparkling clean beachfront condos with screened-in porches. The beach and common areas have plenty of ham-mocks and lounge chairs that are perfect for watching one day turn into the next. The beach here is rarely crowded, and the prime snorkeling spot of Cemetery Reef is a short swim away.

TOP END

Plantana Condominiums (☎ 945-4430; www.plantana cayman.com; West Bay Rd, Seven Mile Beach; 1-bedroom garden/oceanview US$315/440, 2-bedroom gardenview US$390-430, 2-bedroom oceanview US$540, 1- or 2-bedroom penthouse US$540-590; P ✗ ✗ 🖳 🛎) This well-run operation stands out among Grand Cay-man's many rental condos for its spacious units and convenient location. The units come fully equipped and are simply fur-nished; screened porches, an oceanside pool and several shady beach *palapas* (thatch-roofed shade structures) sweeten the deal.

Hyatt Regency Grand Cayman (☎ 949-1234, in the US 888-591-1234; www.grandcayman.hyatt.com; West Bay Rd, Seven Mile Beach; island/oceanview US$515/940; P ✗ ✗ 🖳 🛎) The Hyatt's tasteful blend of Caribbean charm with a refined British splendor goes over well with its pampered clientele. Spacious landscaped grounds af-ford privileged beach access, and diving and sightseeing excursions are readily available. The Jack Nicklaus–designed golf course (see Brittania Golf Club, opposite), a de-luxe spa and exquisite and well-appointed beachfront suites nearly justify their respec-tive price tags.

Eating & Drinking

GEORGE TOWN

Breadfruit Tree Garden Café (☎ 945-2124; Eastern Ave; mains US$4-8; lunch & dinner, closed Sun) This unpretentious spot serves local favorites such as curried goat (US$6), oxtail soup (US$6) and roast chicken (US$8).

Singh's Roti Shop & Bar (☎ 946-7684; cnr Doctor Roy's Dr & Shedden Rd; mains US$6-8; lunch & dinner, closed Sun; ✗) For a delicious bargain-priced meal, head to this cheerful hole-in-the-wall spot for some tongue-searing roti (fast food of curry filling, often potatoes and chicken, rolled inside flat bread). The bar, which has drink specials every Friday evening, is a really good place to chat up gregarious locals, homesick Jamaicans and blissed-out divers.

Sea Harvest Restaurant (☎ 949-7111; 390 South Church St, George Town; mains US$16-32; ☺ breakfast, lunch & dinner; ☻) This unpretentious restaurant at Sunset House serves delectable daily seafood specials. Choose between a bright, air-conditioned dining room or a breezy patio at the water's edge. The adjacent watering hole, My Bar, is a popular spot that really gets rocking on Sunday nights.

Hammerheads (Harbour Dr; mains US$10-20; ☺ lunch & dinner) The talented bartenders never have an idle moment at this good-time joint perched over the harbor. The menu favors seafood and contains a few standouts, including a sinful bacon-wrapped shrimp appetizer (US$11).

Grand Old House (☎ 949-9333; South Church St; mains US$22-34; ☺ lunch Mon-Fri, dinner daily; ☻) If nothing but a farm-raised turtle steak will do, head to this Grand Dame of restaurants for some proper colonial hospitality and a wine list that will shock and awe.

SEVEN MILE BEACH

Coconut Joe's Beach House Bar & Grill (☎ 943-5637; West Bay Rd, Seven Mile Beach; dinner mains US$8-21; ☺ breakfast, lunch & dinner; ☻) If your idea of fun was formed on a boozy spring break of yore, then this place is for you. Tiki torches, bar swings and rock and roll add to the lowbrow ambience. Don't deny yourself a chance to try the signature dish: Tortuga Rum barbecue ribs (US$17).

AquaBeach Restaurant & Bar (☎ 946-6398; West Bay Rd, Seven Mile Beach; mains US$10-22; ☺ dinner; ☻) This beachside place is good for a night out. It attracts a young crowd for delicious Mexican and Caribbean cuisine served either outdoors or in private thatched

---

AUTHOR'S CHOICE

Hemingway's (☎ 949-1234; Hyatt Regency Grand Cayman, West Bay Rd, Seven Mile Beach; mains US$28-36; ☺ lunch & dinner; ☒ ☻) This quality restaurant enjoys a reputation for some of the best seafood on the island, and that's really saying something. The menu features creations like sugarcane-skewered tempura lobster and coconut shrimp with mango marmalade. Grab a table with a beach view and settle in for the island's finest Caribbean nouvelle cuisine. Reservations are required.

---

huts or in an underwater-themed dining room. After dinner, head next door to the Next Level (below) nightclub for the sometimes sizzling dance scene.

La Bodega Latin Lounge & Grill (☎ 946-8115; West Shore Center, Seven Mile Beach; lunch mains US$9-12, dinner mains US$24-35; ☺ lunch & dinner; ☻) This popular recent arrival to the cuisine scene serves imaginative fare with names like 'Plantain Crusted Mahi Mahi with Cubano Fufu.' After dinner, live music and latin dancing ensue.

Kirk Supermarket & Pharmacy (☎ 949-7022; cnr North Church St & Eastern Ave, Seven Mile Beach; ☺ closed Sun) This is a well-stocked American-style grocery store near Seven Mile Beach.

Entertainment

Cayman's after-dark scene is flourishing; following Hurricane Ivan, the island's festive mood is palpable.

The legal drinking age is 18. Bars close at 1am Monday through Friday and at midnight on Saturday and Sunday; nightclubs kick out the jams until 3am Monday through Friday and generally have cover charges ranging from US$5 to US$12. Liquor stores generally close at 7pm and on Sunday.

NIGHTCLUBS

OBar (☎ 943-6227; Queens Court Plaza, West Bay Rd, Seven Mile Beach; ☺ 10pm-3am Mon-Fri; Ⓟ ☻) It's all about the dancing at this unpretentious nightclub and lounge.

Matrix (☎ 949-7169; Islander Complex, West Bay Rd, Seven Mile Beach; ☺ 8pm-3am Mon-Fri; Ⓟ ☻) This high-energy dance hall has a massive dance floor and nightly themes. Tip/warning: Wednesday is karaoke night.

Next Level (☎ 946-6398; West Bay Rd, Seven Mile Beach; ☺ 8pm-3am Mon-Fri; Ⓟ ☻) When the DJs are hot – and they usually are – this place has the freshest and funkiest scene on the island.

CINEMAS

Marquee (☎ 949-4011; cnr West Bay Rd & Lawrence Blvd, Seven Mile Beach) This is a two-screen theater showing first-run Hollywood fare.

Shopping

Grand Cayman provides the perfect vacation for travelers who prize a duty-free shopping mall as highly as a secluded beach. At the duty-free malls clustered around the waterfront, savings are significant for consumer goods such as watches, jewelry, sunglasses, designer clothing, cameras, crystal, spirits and cosmetics. You will also encounter a plethora of local treasures, including shell jewelry, thatch work, wood carvings, crocheted items, pepper sauces, tropical fruit jams, honey and Caymanite (Cayman's semiprecious stone) figurines. There is no sales tax in the Cayman Islands.

A worthy few places to check out:

Artifacts (☎ 949-2422; Harbour Dr, Waterfront, George Town; ☺ 10am-5pm Mon-Sat) Take home a few Spanish pieces of eight and doubloons.

Esteban Gallery (☎ 946-2787; Ground fl, AAL Trust Bank Bldg, Waterfront, George Town; ☺ 10am-5pm Mon-Sat) The place for Caymanite sculptures by noted local artist Bracker Horacio Esteban.

Pure Art (☎ 949-9133; South Church St, George Town; ☺ 9am-5pm Mon-Sat) Head here for locally made arts and crafts.

AROUND GRAND CAYMAN

Outside of George Town, Grand Cayman's other districts offer many engaging attractions and a more heartfelt expression of traditional island life. From the craggy coastline of West Bay to the quiet seclusion of the east and north coasts, the rest of the island offers explorers plenty to do, see and ponder.

West Bay

Situated north of George Town is West Bay, home to a large number of native Caymanians and the site of many of the island's oldest seafarers' cottages.

SIGHTS

The **Cayman Turtle Farm** (☎ 949-3893; North West Point Rd; adult/child US$6/3; ☺ 8:30am-5pm), the only one of its kind in the world, raises green sea turtles from hatchlings to behemoths averaging over 300lb (135kg). While protecting wild populations by meeting market demand for turtle products, the farm has, over the years, also released more than 28,000 hatchlings into the waters surrounding the Cayman Islands. Visitors can peer into tanks filled with specimens ranging from babies to massive adults moshing about in their breeding pond. A gift shop sells souvenirs and turtle products (which are illegal to import into many countries, including the USA).

Forget what Dante said about **Hell** (☺ closed Sun) having nine circles. As it turns out, the tiny community is comprised primarily of a post office, a gift shop and an old outcrop of iron shore that someone once called 'hellish.' While sending a postcard home from Hell clearly has a certain appeal, as a tourist attraction this outpost possesses limited charm. The gift shop is home to an attendant who asks 'How the hell are you?' and 'Where the hell are you from?' as he dispenses souvenirs, impervious to eye-rollers.

SLEEPING & EATING

Cobalt Coast Resort & Suites (☎ 946-5656; www .cobaltcoast.com; garden-view/oceanfront r US$200/250, 2-/3-bedroom ste US$295/475; P ⚠ ☐ 🖳) On the northwest shore of Boatswains Bay a few miles north of Seven Mile Beach, this diving resort successfully combines a mellow island vibe with luxurious Caribbean elegance. On site is a decent restaurant and bar, Duppies, a 120ft (36m) dock and the Divetech (p188) dive center.

Cracked Conch (☎ 945-5217; Northwest Point Rd; mains US$12-32; ☺ lunch & dinner; ⚠) This oceanfront restaurant located next to the turtle farm is a veritable institution, having long served up flavorful Caymanian dishes ranging from seafood, turtle and conch to mouthwatering jerk pork, beef and chicken. The bar features daily sunset happy hours and on Sunday there's a Caribbean buffet (US$18).

Bodden Town

pop 5000

Located 10 miles (16km) from George Town is Bodden Town, which served the Cayman Islands as its capital until the mid-19th century. Sadly, this vibrant village bore the brunt of Hurricane Ivan's wrath in September 2004, and many of the old-style cottages that had survived lesser storms finally succumbed to the ravages of the sea.

Even in the midst of the massive reconstruction effort, Bodden Town is worth a visit if only for **Pedro St James** in nearby Savannah. An imposing Caribbean great house dating from 1780, 'Pedro's Castle' has served over the years as everything from jail to courthouse to parliament before making the transition to **museum** (☎ 947-3329; Pedro Rd, Savannah; adult/child US$8/4; ☺ 9am-5pm), quite recently. Touted as the Caymans' 'birthplace of democracy,' it was here in 1831 that

CAYMAN ISLANDS

the decision was made in favor of a public vote for elected representatives. Just as momentously, this is where the Slavery Abolition Act was read in 1835. The grounds showcase native flora, and there's a multimedia presentation evoking 18th century Cayman. To get here, take the coastal road from George Town to Savannah and make a right turn at the Esso Station.

Turtle Nest Inn (☎ 947-8665; www.turtlenestinn .com; r US$129, oceanview apt US$169-199; P ⊠ 🖳 🛋) is an intimate, well-priced small hotel with comfortable apartments overlooking an empty beach. Each apartment includes a queen-size bed and a double pull-out couch; some can be converted into two-bedroom units. Meals are available by arrangement.

East End

Life moves at a slower pace on the East End, the least-developed district on Grand Cayman. It's a prime destination for nature lovers and others who eschew the hubbub of George Town and that rather long beach. The craggy shoreline here overlooks a number of shipwrecks and provides a nice vantage point from which to observe windsurfers in their element. To the east of the village is the **Wreck of the Ten Sails Park**, commemorating the spot where a legendary shipwreck (p186) occurred in 1794.

Queen Elizabeth II Botanic Park (☎ 947-3558; Frank Sound Dr; adult/child US$7.50/5.25; ☯ 9am-5pm) received a body blow from Hurricane Ivan in 2004, but it is still the very best place for nature buffs who want to experience the island's native species. The park is home to orchids (in bloom late May through June), iguanas (elusive) and parrots, as well as other birds.

The nearby **Mastic Trail** meanders through the old-growth forest that once supplied early settlers with timber. The 2-mile-long trail gives hikers the chance to experience a fascinating exploration deep into the old-growth forest of Grand Cayman's wild interior. To get here, rent a care or take the Northside/East End bus from the George Town library (US$2.50). Ask the driver to drop you at the visitors center, and arrange to be picked up.

A remote and extremely personable lodging choice, **Reef Resort** (☎ 947-3100; www .thereef.com.ky; Queens Hwy, Collier Bay; studio/ste/villa US$290/395/595; P ⊠ 🖳 🛋) is a superb isolated getaway. The studios, suites and villas are bright and look out over a stretch of uncrowded beach. There is an Internet café, liquor store and dive shop. Good eats are provided by Castro's Hideaway Bar & Grill, where local legend the Barefoot Man entertains on Tuesday and Thursday night.

Northside

pop 1100

Geographically isolated from the rest of the island, and the last district to be settled, Northside's earliest residents were freed slaves in search of unclaimed land. Today, the district is windswept and uncrowded, providing a direct link to Grand Cayman's past.

At beautiful **Rum Point**, swinging in hammocks and snorkeling are the main activities. A daily ferry service (see p186) discharges visitors from Seven Mile Beach for an afternoon of blissful relaxation.

The **Retreat at Rum Point** (☎ 947-9135; www .theretreat.com.ky; Northside/Rum Point; 1-/2-bedroom condo US$300/395, deluxe/oceanfront condo US$480/595; P ⊠ ⊠ 🖳 🛋) dominates a sweeping expanse of sandy beach and offers for rent privately owned condos with screened porches. Amenities include a tennis court, gym, sauna, racquetball court, and laundry facilities.

Rum Point Restaurant (☎ 947-9412; Northside/ Rum Point; mains US$25-40; ☯ lunch & dinner; ⊠) is a pricey but pleasant place serving delicious seafood and local favorites. Nearby, the **Wreck Bar** (☎ 947-9412; mains US$8-14; ☯ 10am-5pm) is the quintessential laid-back beach bar known islandwide for a sinfully decadent cocktail called the mudslide. Also served is delicious bar food including jerk pork sandwiches and burgers. On Saturday there's live music on the beach.

CAYMAN BRAC

pop 1800

'The Brac' – so called after the Gaelic word for 'bluff' – is the most easterly of the Cayman Islands. With a population of 1600 and at only 14 sq miles (36km), the island is of great interest to ecotourists with its miles of hiking trails, intriguing beaches and an unquantifiable resource called tranquility.

The Brac is dominated by the **Bluff**, a dramatic, wedge-shaped, limestone formation that rises gently from the flatlands of the west end to a height of 140ft (42m), traveling the length of the island before plunging into the sea. The road to the top passes through the **National Trust Parrot Reserve**, a nesting ground for the islands' endangered emerald green native species, and ends at a lighthouse at the blustery Northeast Point.

The island's four main settlements – West End, Stake Bay, Watering Place and Spot Bay – are on the western or northern ends. Resorts and beaches are clustered along the southern tip, including the peaceful expanses of the public beach.

History

Cayman Brac's first settlers were boatbuilders, turtlers and fishers who started arriving from Grand Cayman in 1833. Trading relations were established between the tiny island and Jamaica, Cuba and Central America; exports mainly comprised turtle shell, jute rope, coconut and cows. By 1932, the Brac sustained a population of 1200. That same year a hurricane brought death and much damage to the isolated island, and islanders took shelter in caves as many houses were washed out to sea. Electricity, along with the first wave of tourists, did not make it to Cayman Brac until the 1960s.

Information

INTERNET RESOURCES

Independently run websites provide excellent information on the Brac's offerings:

Brac (www.thebrac.com) In-depth information on lodging and activities.

Nature Cayman (www.naturecayman.com) Tailored for nature nuts.

Sister Islands (www.sisterislands.com) General information about Cayman Brac and Little Cayman.

MEDICAL SERVICES

Faith Hospital (☎ 948-2243; Stake Bay) A recently upgraded modern facility.

MONEY

Cayman National Bank (☎ 948-1551; West End Cross Rd; 9am-5pm Mon-Fri) Has an ATM and currency exchange.

POST

Post office (☎ 948-1422; Stake Bay; 8:30am-5pm Mon-Fri) Internet access is available in the lobby (per half-hour US$4).

TOURIST INFORMATION

Tourist office (☎ 948-1649; www.caymanislands.ky; North Bay Rd; 8:30am-5pm Mon-Fri) Hidden away just east of the airport adjacent to the West End Community Park, this is a good resource for lodging and activities information.

Sights & Activities

The **Cayman Brac Museum** (☎ 948-2622; Stake Bay; admission by donation; 9am-noon & 1-4pm Mon-Sat) is a highly likeable little place with a collection that highlights a time when the island was cut off from the rest of the world.

Hiking is a grand way to see the island. A network of 38 trails link 'Cayman Brac Heritage Sites,' which include beaches, caves, scenic vistas and interesting historic sites. The *Heritage Sites & Trails* brochure is available at the visitors center.

With crystal waters affording superb visibility and 41 permanent dive moorings, Cayman Brac attracts its share of **diving** and **snorkeling** enthusiasts. Of particular interest is the wreck of a 315ft (94.5m) Russian frigate now named the *Captain Keith Tibbetts*. It was purchased from Cuba and intentionally sunk offshore off the northwest of the island in 1996, to serve as a dive attraction.

Two well-run dive providers operate on the western end of the island:

DIVI Tiara (☎ 948-1553; www.diviresorts.com; Stake Bay; 1-/2-tank dive US$33/60, snorkeling trips US$10-20)

Reef Divers (☎ 948-1642; www.bracreef.com; West End; 1-/2-tank dive US$45/75, snorkeling trips US$15-30) Based at the Brac Reef Beach Resort.

The Brac is home to wizened Caymanian **fishing** captains **Edmund Bodden** (☎ 948-0535) and **Lemuel Bodden** (☎ 948-1314), both of whom offer bone, tarpon, reef and deep-sea fishing excursions.

Sleeping & Eating

Accommodations range from casual Caymanian guest houses to resort hotels catering to diving enthusiasts. Lodging prices are cheaper here than elsewhere in the Caymans.

Johanson's Cottage (☎ 948-0277; gjohanson@erols.com; Stake Bay; cottage US$90; P) Cayman Brac has several cottages for rent, but none as pleasant as this one. Superior snorkeling at the doorstep and access to a two-seater kayak and bicycles sweeten the deal.

La Esperenza (☎ 948-0531; North Rd, Spot Bay; 2-/3-bedroom apt US$70/90; mains US$8-16; lunch & dinner; P) This friendly Caymanian-run

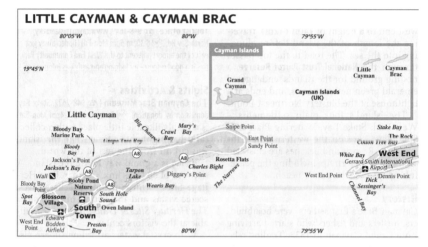

LITTLE CAYMAN & CAYMAN BRAC

operation on the northeast end offers great value on well-equipped apartments, which sleep four to six people. Each comes with a spacious, fully equipped kitchen. Across the street is a restaurant of the same name serving island favorites, and a bar attracting a local crowd. A rental car is available for guests (per day US$30).

Brac Reef Beach Resort (☎ 948-1323; www .bracreef.com; West End; d US$189; P 🞩 🖳 🕱) This relaxed resort is recommended for its 40 bright and cheerful rooms with patios or balconies overlooking a large pool. Also on-site is Reef Divers, offering high-quality excursions. Bicycles and kayaks are available for guests. The on-site restaurant, the Palms, serves delicious local seafood albeit at inflated prices. The poolside Tipsy Turtle Bar is not as cute as its name.

AUTHOR'S CHOICE

Walton's Mango Manor (☎ 948-0518; www .waltonsmangomanor.com; Stake Bay; d incl breakfast US$90-100; P 🞩) Unique on the island, this B&B is set among a lush tropical garden that's ripe with breadfruit and mango. Originally the home of a sea captain, this large Caymanian house is decorated with traditional antiques, including a banister made from the mast of an old sailing schooner. Large home-style breakfasts are served each morning, and guests may use a common refrigerator and microwave.

DIVI Tiara Beach Resort (☎ 948-1553, in the US 800-801-5555; www.diviresorts.com; West End; standard/ deluxe US$110/152; P 🞩 🖳 🕱) Diving is the *raison d'être* at this welcoming, well-run resort on the lovely white-sand beach of the island's southwest corner. Daily dive itineraries are offered to the shipwrecks and reefs, as is dive instruction for skill levels from novice to advanced. Standard rooms feature a patio or balcony, two double beds and private bath; the deluxe rooms are distinguished by ocean views.

Aunt Sha's Kitchen (☎ 948-1581; West End; mains US$8-16; 🕑 breakfast, lunch & dinner) This bright-pink bar and restaurant overlooking the sea is a lively local favorite serving delicious seafood dishes including Cayman-style lobster (US$21).

Captain's Table (☎ 948-1418; West End; mains US$14-32; 🕑 lunch & dinner; 🞩) This, the fanciest of Cayman Brac's restaurants, offers an extensive menu of steaks, seafood and American-style dishes. Meals are served either in the dining room or by the pool.

Getting There & Around

Flights from Grand Cayman to Cayman Brac's **Gerrard Smith International Airport** (☎ 948-1222) are offered daily by Cayman Airways and Island Air. Cayman Airways (see p200 for contact details) operates a weekly nonstop jet service from Miami to Cayman Brac on Saturday.

Unfortunately, there's no public transportation on Cayman Brac, but the negligible

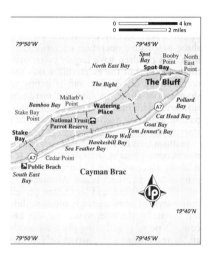

crime rate – and the amiability of the locals – makes hitchhiking safe and easy. The mere sight of a visitor marching down the roadway often results in ride offers by passing motorists. Bicycles may be rented or borrowed from the resorts and are available from many guest houses. Taxis are few; it's a good idea to book in advance for your ride from the airport. Lodging providers will pick you up by prior arrangement. Renting a car is recommended as the best way to sample the island's many interesting beaches and natural and historical sites.

Brac Rent-A-Car (☎ 948-1515; scottaud@candw.ky; Stake Bay)

CB Rent-A-Car (☎ 948-2329; cbrentals@thebrac.com; Gerrard Smith International Airport)

Elo's Taxi (☎ 948-0220)

Hill's Taxi (☎ 948-0540)

LITTLE CAYMAN

pop 115

Predominantly undeveloped and remote, Little Cayman is the smallest and most tranquil of the Cayman Islands. Located 89 miles (143km) northeast of Grand Cayman and 5 miles (8km) west of Cayman Brac, the place has far more iguanas than humans and attracts a special kind of traveler who craves solitude and loves nature. As your twin-prop plane swoops down over the vivid turquoise sea and onto the grass landing strip of the tiny airport, you'll know that

you have arrived at one of the Caribbean's most unspoiled and untrammeled destinations, a place were drivers are reminded that 'Iguanas Have the Right of Way.'

Little Cayman is universally regarded as one of the world's great diving destinations. With a permanent population of just over 100, there are often more divers here than residents.

Information
INTERNET ACCESS
McLaughlin Enterprises (☎ 948-1619; per 15min US$6.25) Found next door Village Square Store, you can get online here (albeit not cheaply).

MEDICAL SERVICES
Little Cayman Clinic (☎ 948-1051; Blossom Ave, Blossom Village; ☷ 9am-1pm Mon, Wed & Fri, 1-5pm Tue & Thu) The clinic is normally staffed by nurses, but a doctor visits on Wednesday afternoon.

MONEY
Cayman National Bank (☎ 948-0051; Guy Banks Rd, Blossom Village; ☷ 9am-2:30pm Mon & Thu) There is no ATM on Little Cayman, and this bank is only open two days each week, so plan accordingly.

POST
Post office (☎ 948-0016; Blossom Village; ☷ 8-11am & 1-3pm Mon-Fri) This tiny post office is located next to the airfield.

TELEPHONE
Public phones can be found at the airport, near the clinic and at the Hungry Iguana restaurant.

Village Square Store (☎ 948-1069; Guy Banks Rd, Blossom Village; ☷ closed Sun) Phone cards can be purchased here.

Sights & Activities
People who love **bird-watching** are deeply gratified by the **Booby Pond Nature Reserve**, home to one of the hemisphere's largest breeding populations of red-footed boobies and a large colony of swooping frigate birds. Overlooking the pond is the **National Trust Visitors Centre** (☷ Mon-Sat), with information on the feathered frolickers and a viewing platform with binoculars. Opposite the pond is the one-room **Little Cayman Museum** (☎ 948-1033; Guy Banks Rd; admission free; ☷ 3-5pm Mon-Fri) containing local artifacts and beach treasures.

What makes Little Cayman a **diving** and **snorkeling** mecca? In a word: walls. Incredible walls. The **Bloody Bay Marine Park** is legendary among divers who come from all over the world for a truly exhilarating experience. Here, near the shore and at a depth of only 18ft (5.4m), the Bloody Bay wall plummets vertically into aquamarine infinity as the divers hovering over the abyss wonder whether they are hallucinating (for more information on diving in this area, see p53).

Little Cayman has 57 dive sites marked with moorings. Snorkelers and shore divers find plenty of satisfaction at many well-known sites.

Recommended diving outfitters:

Conch Club Divers (☎ 948-1026; www.conchclub.com; Guy Banks Rd; 1-/2-tank dive US$45/75)

Pirates Point Resort (☎ 949-1010; Guy Banks Rd; 1-/2-tank dive US$40/73)

Sam McCoy's Diving & Fishing Lodge (☎ 948-0026; www.mccoyslodge.com.ky; North Coast Rd; 1-/2-tank dive US$35/65)

Southern Cross Club (☎ 948-1099; www.southern crossclub.com; Guy Banks Rd; 1-/2-tank dive US$50/80)

Little Cayman's shallow coastal waters and flats offer **fishing** action year-round. In the grassy flats and sandy bottoms are wily bonefish, and tarpon are frequently caught in the small land-locked brackish lake. A short distance offshore beyond the drop-off, anglers find action from blue marlin and other game fish. Sam McCoy's Diving & Fishing Lodge (below) and Southern Cross Club (right) both provide excursions.

Resembling the place where Tom Hanks lost his mind in *Castaway*, tiny **Owen Island** is easy to reach by kayak or by swimming from Southern Cross. The beach here is a tranquil bastion of loveliness that will infuse your best dreams long after departing. Bring a picnic and a special friend.

Sleeping & Eating

Few guests stay only one night, and longer stays receive considerable discounts.

Sam McCoy's Diving & Fishing Lodge (☎ 948-0026; www.mccoyslodge.com.ky; North Coast Rd; nondiving accommodations package s/d/tr US$170/290/375; P X) This unpretentious, family-owned and -operated inn is a friendly place in a stunning location. The rooms are modest but comfortable, and the price includes

three home-cooked meals each day. In days of yore, Sam McCoy established the first shore-based dive operation on Little Cayman. His children have largely taken over the business, but the elder still makes the scene at the on-site bar and is happy to share stories about his days as a merchant seaman and his lifelong preoccupation with fishing. Half-day deep-sea fishing charters start at US$400.

Southern Cross Club (☎ 948-1099; www.southern crossclub.com; Guy Banks Rd; cottage US$240; P X X) A classy place offering 11 bungalows on a private 262yd (240m) beach. All meals are included; breakfast and lunch are served buffet-style in an exceedingly pleasant dining room. In the afternoons, the bar becomes a popular gathering place for locals and island visitors alike, particularly for the Friday evening barbecues.

Paradise Villas (☎ 948-0001; www.paradisevillas .com; Bossom Village; s/d/tr villa US$160/185/200; P X X) This well-run operation near the airstrip offers free-standing, well-equipped cottages arranged on a gorgeous stretch of beach. Each cottage has a sea view, veranda and hammock.

Hungry Iguana (☎ 948-0007; Blossom Village; lunch mains US$5-11, dinner mains US$20-30; X lunch & dinner) Next to Paradise Villas is this pleasant restaurant and bar with its breezy dining room and ocean terrace. The menu includes well-prepared pasta, seafood, meat and poultry, and dinner specials each night keep things interesting.

Village Square Store (☎ 948-1069; Guy Banks Rd, Blossom Village; X closed Sun) Head here for groceries, beer and other basic necessities.

Getting There & Around

Flights from Grand Cayman to Little Cayman's **Edward Bodden Airfield** (☎ 948-0021) are offered daily by Cayman Airways and Island Air. See p200 for more information. At last visit, construction was finally to begin on a long-planned new airport which will eventually replace the tiny airstrip.

Bicycling is the preferred mode of transportation on the island, and nearly every hotel makes them available for guests. If you just simply must burn fossil fuels, **McLaughlin Rentals** (☎ 948-1000; Guy Banks Rd) and **Island Scooter Rentals** (☎ 926-2929; Guy Banks Rd; rental per day US$30) rents cars and scooters, respectively.

CAYMAN ISLANDS

DIRECTORY

Information in this directory is specific to the Cayman Islands. For information pertaining to the entire Caribbean region, see the Directory chapter (p757).

ACCOMMODATIONS

The Caymans offer many comfortable accommodations options. Quite a few resorts cater specifically to divers and include excursions and equipment rentals in their prices. Those on a top-end budget can expect each day to shell out upwards of US$300 per person for accommodations and basic meals, and much more depending on proclivity for duty-free perfume and/or charter boats.

The midrange for lodging is around US$200 and if you hope to travel on a shoestring, you may want to sit down before reading further: the lowest-priced accommodations start at around US$100.

Budget travelers may be able to cut costs by sharing self-catering accommodations and doing more lounging on the beach than diving.

Rates quoted are for walk-ins during the high season (mid-December through mid-April) and do not include the 10% government tax and 10% to 15% service tax. Low-season rates are as much as 40% cheaper.

ACTIVITIES

Unsurprisingly, most recreational activities on these islands have something to do with sea water and sunscreen. Opportunities for water sports abound on all three islands. You'll really be missing out if you come to the Caymans without strapping on a mask and taking a peek underwater.

PRACTICALITIES

- **Newspapers & Magazines** Caymanian Compass, Cayman Net News, Cayman Activity Guide, What's Hot
- **Radio** Radio Cayman – 89.9FM & 105.3FM
- **Video Systems** NTSC
- **Electricity** 110V, 60Hz (US-style)
- **Weights & Measures** Imperial

Diving & Snorkeling

The Cayman's extensive marine-park system and endlessly fascinating dive sites are perfect for all skill levels. With 265 moored sites, and plenty of shore diving and snorkeling possibilities, the only question is where to start. All three islands have fine-tuned dive operations ready to submerse you.

Other Water Sports

The reef-protected shorelines are ideal for sea kayaking, and the breezy east end of Grand Cayman offers bodacious windsurfing.

Please don't go turtling, but fishing is a fine way to pass a day or three; the seas are rife with bonefish, blue marlin, tuna and wahoo. Plenty of guides and charter companies can lead you to the best action, both from shore and in deep waters. Grand Cayman has a small fleet of modern, well-equipped sport fishing boats available, and smaller charter boats and excellent local captains are available in Cayman Brac and Little Cayman.

Land-based Activities

Hiking is a very popular pursuit on Grand Cayman's Mastic Trail (p192) and on Cayman Brac's many well-marked trails (p193).

On Little Cayman, the large mangrove swamp that dominates the southwestern coast is a big draw for bird-watching enthusiasts (p195). Over the three islands, some 200 winged species including boobies, frigate birds, and the endangered Cayman Brac parrot keep bird-watchers blissfully busy.

On Grand Cayman, two excellent golf (p188) courses, including the Caribbean's only Jack Nicklaus–designed course, draw repeat visitors year after year. And if you've ever dreamed of horseback riding (p188) on the beach, your day has come.

BOOKS

The '32 Storm by Heather McLaughlin is a moving selection of stories. They tell of the hurricane that killed 67 people and that flattened almost every building on Cayman Brac and Little Cayman in 1932.

EMERGENCY NUMBERS

Ambulance (☎ 555)
Fire (☎ 911)
Police (☎ 911)

CAYMAN ISLANDS

Founded Upon the Seas by Michael Craton is an engaging, comprehensive history of the Cayman Islands.

The Adventure Guide to the Cayman Islands by Paris Permenter and John Bigley provides a good introduction and plenty of practical information on activities both in and out of the water.

Birds of the Cayman Islands by Patricia Bradley is about as easy to find as a yellow-bellied sapsucker, but it's not a bad reference so it's worth the search.

CHILDREN

Families with children couldn't hope for a better travel destination than the Cayman Islands.

Most hotels have plenty of rooms that sleep four people or more, and many offer babysitting services and activity programs. The gentle sandy beaches provide a relatively safe playground for kids of all ages, and older kids can accompany the adults and enjoy the many water sports activities. Kids of all ages can attend Kids Sea Camp (p186) on Grand Cayman.

EMBASSIES & CONSULATES

Cayman Islands' Embassies & Consulates

There are no Cayman Islands' embassies or consulates in other countries. The Caymans are a British Crown Overseas Territory, so all inquiries should be directed to British embassies, high commissions or consulates:

Australia (British High Commission; ☎ 02-6270-6666; Commonwealth Ave, Yarralumla, Canberra)
Canada (British High Commission; ☎ 613-237-1530; 80 Elgin St, Ottawa K1P 5K7)
Cuba (British Embassy; ☎ 7-204-1771; Calle 34 No 7024/4 entre 7ma Avenida y 17, Miramar)
France (British Embassy; ☎ 01-44-51-31-00; 35 rue du Faubourg St Honoré, 75383 Paris)
Germany (British Consulate-General; ☎ 0211-944-8171; Yorckstrasse 19, 40476 Düsseldorf)
Ireland (British Embassy; ☎ 01-205-3700; 29 Merrion Rd, Ballsbridge, Dublin 4)
Jamaica (British High Commission; ☎ 510-0700; PO Box 575, 28 Trafalgar Rd, Kingston 10)
Netherlands (British Consulate-General; ☎ 020-676-43-43; Koningslaan 44, 1075 AE Amsterdam)
New Zealand (British High Commission; ☎ 04-924-2822; 44 Hill St, Wellington 1)
UK (Foreign & Commonwealth Office; ☎ 020-7008-8438; King Charles Street, London SW1A 2AH)

US Miami (British Consulate; ☎ 305-374-1522; Suite 2800, 1001 Brickell Bay Dr, Miami FL 33131); Washington (British Embassy; ☎ 202-588-7800; 3100 Massachusetts Ave, Washington DC 20008)

Embassies & Consulates in the Cayman Islands

Jamaica (☎ 949-9526; Rankin Plaza, Eastern Ave, PO Box 431, George Town)
UK (☎ 244-2434; Governor's Office, 4th fl, Government Administration Bldg, Elgin Ave, George Town)
US (☎ 945-1511; Unit 7, Grand Harbour Shops, George Town)

FESTIVALS & EVENTS

The following events all take place on Grand Cayman, with the exception of Pirates Week, which is celebrated on all three islands.

Cayfest (☎ 949-5477; www.artscayman.org; mid-April) An annual celebration of Cayman art and culture.
Cayman Islands International Fishing Tournament (☎ 945-3131; www.fishcayman.com; mid-April) This high-stakes fishing tournament is the premier angling event of the western Caribbean.
Batabano (☎ 949-7121; www.caymancarnival.com; early May) The Cayman Islands' Carnival is a colorful parade of costumes, music and dancing.
Pirates Week (☎ 949-5849; www.piratesweek festival.com; late October) A wildly popular family-friendly extravaganza is kicked off with a mock pirate invasion from the sea. For 10 days, music, dances, costumes, games and controlled mayhem fill up the streets. However, just remember to book your transportation and lodgings well in advance.

HOLIDAYS

New Year's Day January 1
National Heroes' Day Fourth Monday in January
Ash Wednesday Late February
Easter (Good Friday to Easter Monday inclusive) March/April
Discovery Day Third Monday in May
Queen's Birthday Second Monday in June
Constitution Day First Monday in July
Remembrance Day Third Monday in November
Christmas Day December 25
Boxing Day December 26

MONEY

The official currency is the Cayman Islands dollar (CI$), permanently fixed at CI$0.80 to US$1. Cayman dollars and US dollars are accepted throughout the islands. The local currency comes in CI$1, 5, 10, 25, 50 and 100 notes.

TELEPHONE
Cell (Mobile) Phones
Cell phones compatible with 800MHz or TDMA networks can roam in the islands. **Cable & Wireless** (☎ 949-7800; Anderson Sq, George Town) offers a pay-as-you-go service, and rents phones at its retail outlet in George Town.

Phone Codes
The Cayman Islands country code is ☎ 345. To call from North America, dial ☎ 1-345 + the local number. From elsewhere, dial your country's international access code followed by ☎ 345 + the local number. We have included only the seven-digit local number in Puerto Rico listings in this chapter.

Phone Cards
Cable & Wireless prepaid calling cards in denominations of CI$5 and CI$10 are available throughout the islands. Rates to the US, UK, Canada and Caribbean destinations (excluding Cuba) average US$0.50 per minute; other destinations will incur a charge of US$1.25 per minute.

Cable & Wireless also has a credit-card call service called 1-800-CALL-USA but it is wildly expensive and should be used only as a last resort.

TOURS
Explore Cayman (☎ 947-4043; www.explore-cayman .com; full-day tours US$89) Offers three excellent ecologically minded tours on Grand Cayman: 'Off the Beaten Track'; 'The Other Beaches'; and 'Mastic Trail & Botanic Park.'

Silver Thatch Tours (☎ 916-0678; silver@hotmail .com; half-day tours US$40-50) Caymanian guide Geddes Hislop offers excellent and informative outings on Grand Cayman. They're geared toward naturalists, and include the Caymans' best bird-watching tour.

VISAS
Visas are not required by nationals of the UK, Canada, USA, most Commonwealth countries and some European countries. However, holders of passports from Australia, France, Germany, Ireland, the Netherlands, Spain and Italy do require visas. Visas are not required by cruise-ship passengers.

Tourist visas are valid for 30 days and can be extended for up to three months, and can be obtained from any British consulate or embassy for a fee of £28 (US$51).

TRANSPORTATION

GETTING THERE & AWAY
Entering the Cayman Islands
All visitors, including US citizens (see the boxed text, p772), are required to have a valid passport and a return ticket. Because the Cayman Islands straddle established drug trafficking routes, officials scrutinize incoming passengers for contraband as a matter of course.

Air
The main passenger airport in the Cayman Islands, **Owen Roberts International Airport** (GCM; ☎ 949-5252), is located 1.5 miles (2.5km) east of George Town on the island of Grand Cayman. Cayman Brac is served by **Gerrard Smith International Airport** (CYB; ☎ 948-1222). On Little Cayman, **Edward Bodden Airfield** (LYB; ☎ 948-0021) flights land on a grass airstrip.

For details of international flights to the Cayman Islands, see p773.

The following airlines provide service within the Caribbean:

Aerocaribbean (in Havana ☎ 53-7-45-3013, in Cayman Islands 945-0871; www.aero-caribbean.com; hub Jose Martí International Airport, Havana)

Air Jamaica (in the Caribbean ☎ 800-523-5585, in Cayman Islands 949-2300; www.airjamaica.com; hub Norman Manley International Airport, Kingston)

Cayman Airways (in the Cayman Islands ☎ 949-2311; www.caymanairways.com; hub Owen Roberts International Airport, George Town)

Sea
Numerous cruise-ship lines drop anchor in George Town Harbour from Monday to Saturday, unloading passengers for a few hours of duty-free shopping, diving and snorkeling, or lounging on nearby Seven Mile Beach.

Most cruises from the US last one to two weeks and include other western Caribbean destinations such as Cozumel and Progreso, Mexico; Key West and Miami, Florida; and Montego Bay and Ocho Rios, Jamaica. See p777 for more information on cruises.

Those entering Cayman waters by private yacht should display the red ensign version of the Cayman flag and report to the port authority in George Town to clear customs and immigration.

CAYMAN ISLANDS

GETTING AROUND

Air

Flights from Grand Cayman to the 'sister islands' Cayman Brac and Little Cayman are offered daily by Cayman Airways and Island Air.

Cayman Airways (☎ 949-2311; www.caymanairways .com) Provides a jet service between Grand Cayman and Cayman Brac (Monday and Thursday to Sunday) and daily turboprop service to both 'sister islands.'

Island Air (☎ 949-5252; www.islandair.ky) Operates four scheduled flights daily between Grand Cayman, Cayman Brac and Little Cayman via 19-passenger turboprop Twin Otter aircraft. Day trips and private charters are available.

Bicycle

Bikes are readily available on all three islands and are often included as part of an accommodations package. Flat terrain, relatively light traffic and near-constant sea access make bicycling a pleasure, particularly on the 'sister islands.'

Boat

The **Rum Point Ferry** (☎ 949-1234; adult/child return US$15/7.50; ☻ 9:30am-10:30pm winter, 8am-10:30pm summer) carries passengers between the Hyatt Regency dock (on the east side of Seven Mile Beach) and Rum Point (at the far east end of Grand Cayman).

Bus

A fleet of beige-and-white minibuses serves all districts of Grand Cayman. The **bus terminal** (☎ 945-5100) is next to the public library on Edward St in downtown George Town and serves as the dispatch point for all eight routes. Fares are from US$1.90 to US$2.50.

There are no bus services available on Cayman Brac and Little Cayman.

Car & Motorcycle

DRIVER'S LICENSE

Visitors must obtain a temporary driver's license (US$7.50) from the police station or car-rental agency; you'll need to show a valid international driver's license or one from your home country.

RENTAL

The simplest way to explore the Caymans is by car. Traffic on the islands is light, making driving a pleasure.

Demand for rentals is high, and the rental fleet took a hit during Hurricane Ivan, so it's a very good idea to book as well in advance as possible.

Many rentals feature right-hand drive, and most rental 4WDs and vans also have left-hand stick shift. A variety of models at competitive rates is available in Grand Cayman. On Cayman Brac, there is a limited number of cars and there are fewer still on Little Cayman.

You must be aged at least 21 to rent a car in the Cayman Islands, and some rental agencies' insurance will not cover renters under 25; check with your rental company in advance.

Scooter and motorcycle rentals are available on all three islands.

ROAD RULES

Driving is on the left-hand side of the road in the Cayman Islands, and the wearing of seat belts is mandatory. Iguanas have right of way.

Jamaica

Jamaica, the alluring green gem of the western Caribbean, is a world unto itself. To many people, Jamaica means reggae and Rastafarianism. Others come to renew their pact with the sun goddess on stunning coral beaches. Pulsing with music and awash in the zesty smells of its singular cuisine, Jamaica is a destination for the senses.

You can choose a villa with your own private beach; laugh your vacation away at a party-hearty resort; or enjoy the camaraderie of backpackers at an economical guesthouse. Some visitors come solely to concentrate on the three Rs: reggae, reefers and rum. Others crave water sports, horseback riding, fishing, golf or any number of more offbeat adventures. You'll find colonial-era estates to explore, along with centuries-old botanical gardens, forts and evocative colonial great houses.

Take to the back roads and hills and, bringing humility with you, you may discover how gracious and hospitable Jamaicans can be. Buy some jerk chicken or 'pepper swimp' from roadside vendors, share time at sea with a local fisherman, learn about herbal remedies from a 'market mammie' or a guide in 'de bush.' Travel with an open mind, and you'll have 'no problem, mon!'

FAST FACTS

- **Area** 4400 sq miles (11,391 sq km)
- **Capital** Kingston
- **Country code** ☎ 876
- **Departure tax** J$1000 (US$20)
- **Famous for** Reggae, Rastas and 'chill'
- **Language(s)** English, patois
- **Money** Jamaican dollars (J$); J$100 = US$1.61 = €1.34 = UK£0.90
- **Official name** Jamaica
- **People** Jamaicans
- **Phrases** No problem, mon. Respect.
- **Population** 2.7 million
- **Visa** Not required by residents of the US, Canada, the UK and Ireland for stays of six months or less. For other nationalities, see p240. Visas cost US$20 to US$50 depending on citizenship.

JAMAICA

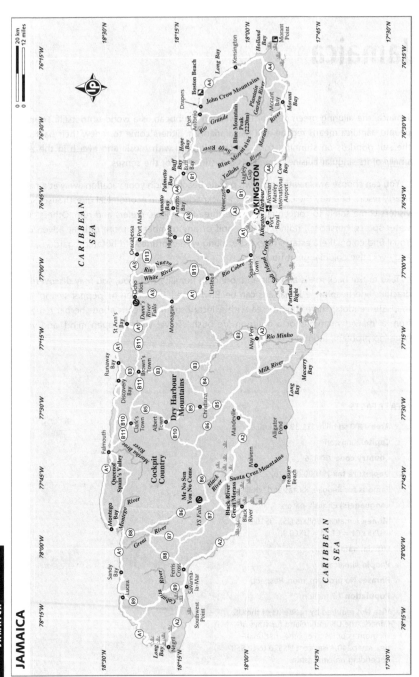

HIGHLIGHTS

- **Negril** (p230) Indulge in some laid-back sunning by day and live reggae by night in the Caribbean's capital of 'chill.'
- **Portland parish** (p215) Enjoy maximum repose on the beaches and delve into the many natural wonders of Jamaica's most beautiful parish.
- **Bob Marley Museum** (p209) Take the pulse of Kingston and look deeper into the life of Jamaica's most revered contemporary hero.
- **Red Stripe Reggae Sumfest** (p224) Dance deep into the morning at Jamaica's world-class midsummer reggae festival.
- **Great Morass** (p235) Travel by boat deep into river country that's teeming with wildlife.

ITINERARIES

- **Three days** Lounge around on the beach in Montego Bay or Negril, catch some live reggae, watch the sun set, hit a local attraction or two, and then do it again.
- **One week** Add on a journey to the mellow, less-touristed town of Treasure Beach.
- **Two weeks** Precede the above itineraries with an energetic visit to Kingston (the heartbeat of Jamaica), followed by a jaunt into the high Blue Mountains.
- **Three weeks** After Kingston and the Blue Mountains, chill out with an herbal tonic on the rootsy beaches of Long Bay or get busy visiting the natural and cultural attractions of Portland parish. Continue with the one week itinerary.

CLIMATE & WHEN TO GO

Jamaica is a year-round destination: winter is usually warm by day and mild to cool by night; summer months are hot. The rainy season extends from May to November, with peaks in May and June and in October and November.

Rain usually falls for short periods (normally in the late afternoon), and it's quite possible to enjoy sunshine for most of your visit during these months. In Portland parish, however, it can rain for days on end.

The high-tourist ('winter') season runs from mid-December to mid-April, when hotel prices are highest. Many hotels charge peak-season rates during Christmas and Easter.

HOW MUCH?

- Taxi from Montego Bay's airport to the 'Hip Strip' US$10
- Guided snorkeling trip US$30
- Rio Grande raft trip US$60
- Meal of fresh fish in a touristy restaurant US$12
- Meal of fresh fish in a local restaurant US$7

LONELY PLANET INDEX

- Gallon of gas US$4.50
- Liter of bottled water US$0.50
- Bottle of Red Stripe beer US$2.50
- Souvenir T-shirt US$10
- Street snack: jerk chicken US$4

HISTORY
Columbus & the Spanish Wave

Jamaica's first tourist was none other than Christopher Columbus, who landed on the island in 1494. At the time, there were perhaps 100,000 peaceful Arawak Native Americans who had settled Jamaica around AD 700. Spanish settlers arrived from 1510, and quickly introduced two things that would profoundly shape the island's future: sugarcane production and slavery. By the end of the 16th century, the Arawak population had been entirely wiped out, worn down by hard labor, ill-treatment and European diseases.

The Brits Dig In

In 1654, an ill-equipped and badly organized English contingent sailed to the Caribbean. After failing to take Hispaniola, the 'wicked army of common cheats, thieves and lewd persons' turned to weakly defended Jamaica. Despite the ongoing efforts of Spanish loyalists and guerilla-style campaigns of freed Spanish slaves (*cimarrones* – 'wild ones' – or Maroons), England took control of the island.

Consequences of Slavery

New slaves kept on arriving, and bloody insurrections occurred with frightening frequency. The last and largest of the slave

JAMAICA

revolts in Jamaica was the 1831 Christmas Rebellion, inspired by 'Daddy' Sam Sharpe, an educated slave and lay preacher who incited passive resistance. The rebellion turned violent, however, as up to 20,000 slaves razed plantations and murdered planters. When the slaves were tricked into laying down arms with a false promise of abolition – and then 400 were hanged and hundreds more whipped – there was a wave of revulsion in England, causing the British parliament to finally abolish slavery in 1834. See the boxed text, p223, for more.

The transition from a slave economy to one based on wage labor caused economic chaos, with most slaves rejecting the starvation wages offered on the estates and choosing to fend for themselves. Desperation over conditions and injustice finally boiled over in the Morant Bay Rebellion.

The Rocky Road to Independence

A banana-led economic recovery was halted by the Great Depression of the 1930s, and then kick-started again by the exigencies of WWII, when the Caribbean islands supplied food and raw materials to Britain. Adult suffrage for all Jamaicans was introduced in 1944, and virtual autonomy from Britain was granted in 1947. Jamaica seceded from the short-lived West Indies Federation in 1962 after a referendum called for the island's full independence.

Post-independence politics have been dominated by the legacy of two cousins: Alexander Bustamante, who formed the first trade union in the Caribbean just prior to WWII and later formed the Jamaican Labor Party (JLP), and Norman Manley, whose People's National Party (PNP) was the first political party on the island when it was convened in 1938. Manley's son, Michael, led the PNP toward democratic socialism in the mid-1970s, causing a capital flight at a time when Jamaica could ill afford it. Bitterly opposed factions engaged in open urban warfare preceding the 1976 election, but the PNP won the election by a wide margin and Manley continued with his socialist agenda.

Coming To Terms

The US government was hostile to the socialist path Jamaica was taking, and when Manley began to develop close ties with Cuba, the CIA purportedly planned to topple the Jamaican government. Businesses pulled out, the economy went into sharp decline and the country lived virtually under siege. Almost 700 people were killed in the lead-up to the 1980 elections, which were won by the JLP's Edward Seaga. Seaga restored Jamaica's economic fortunes somewhat, severed ties with Cuba and courted Ronald Reagan's USA. Relatively peaceful elections in 1989 returned a reinvented 'mainstream realist' Manley to power; he retired in 1992, handing the reins to his deputy, Percival James Patterson, Jamaica's first Black prime minister.

The Present & Future

The year 2004 came to an end with two momentous events: Hurricane Ivan bounced off of Jamaica en route to the Cayman Islands, causing widespread damage, and Seaga announced his retirement after more than three decades of life in politics. As for the future, Prime Minister Patterson, now in his fourth consecutive term in office, has announced his hope that Jamaica will be a republic by the time he leaves office in 2007, confirming the island's gradual movement away from the shadow of its former colonial master.

THE CULTURE

Jamaica has a complicated and challenging culture, with layer upon layer shaped by a tormented past. Jamaicans are also an intriguing contrast. Much of the population comprises the most gracious people you'll ever meet: hardworking, happy-go-lucky, helpful, courteous, genteel and full of humility. If you show them kindness, they will give it back in return. However, charged memories of slavery and racism have continued to bring out the spirit of anarchy latent in an ex-slave society that's divided into rich and poor. Jamaicans struggling hard against poverty are disdainful of talk about a 'tropical paradise.'

There will be times when the traveler will come face to face with the startling realities of life in this volatile society. Some nervous nellies barricade themselves in all-inclusive resorts, but to do so is a shame and wholly unnecessary. Violence rarely intrudes on the foreign visitor; it is mostly restricted to drug wars and impassioned political feuds in the ghettos of Kingston. And harassment by overzealous hustlers (see p237) is usually merely a nuisance, and one the Jamaica Tourist Board has been working hard to address.

Most visitors return home with memories of a warm people who display quick wit and ready smiles. And those who take the time to scratch below the surface may learn something about an island, a country, the world.

Population
The nation's motto – 'Out of Many, One People' – reflects Jamaica's diverse heritage. Tens of thousands of West Africans, plus large numbers of Irish, Germans and Welsh, arrived throughout the colonial period, along with Hispanic and Portuguese Jews and those whom Jamaicans call 'Syrians' (a term for all those of Levantine extraction). Following emancipation in 1834, Chinese and Indians arrived as indentured laborers from Hong Kong and Panama. A second wave of Hong Kong Chinese has settled in recent years, bringing new vitality to retail trade.

Religion
Jamaica claims to have the greatest number of churches per square mile in the world, with virtually every imaginable denomination represented. More than 80% of Jamaicans identify as Christian.

Jamaica also has several quasi-Christian, quasi-animist sects that are generically named Revivalist cults after the post-emancipation Great Revival, during which many Blacks converted to Christianity. The most important Revivalist cult is Pocomania, which mixes European and African religious heritages.

RASTAFARIANISM
Rastafarians, with their uncut, uncombed hair grown into long sun-bleached tangles known as 'dreadlocks' or 'dreads,' are synonymous with the island in the sun. There are perhaps as many as 100,000 Rastafarians in Jamaica. They adhere to an unorganized religion – a faith, not a church – that has no official doctrine or dogmatic hierarchy and is composed of a core of social and spiritual tenets that are open to interpretation. Not all Rastafarians wear dreads, for example,

and others do not smoke ganja (marijuana). All adherents, however, accept that Africa is the Black race's spiritual home to which they are destined to return.

ARTS
Jamaica has evolved a powerful artistic and cultural expression rooted in African traditions, while quintessentially Jamaican styles have evolved across the spectrum of the arts. In addition, Jamaica's crafts industry supports tens of thousands of artisans, who offer a cornucopia of leatherwork, ceramics, shell art, beadwork and basket-weaving.

Literature
Through the years, Jamaican literature has been haunted by the ghosts of slave history and the ambiguities of Jamaica's relationship to Mother England. The classic novels tend to focus on survival in a grim colonial landscape and on escape to Africa, which often proves more grim. Most well-known, perhaps, is Herbert de Lisser's classic *White Witch of Rose Hall*. This plantation-era tale – now an established part of Jamaican lore – tells of Annie Palmer, a wicked mistress of Rose Hall (see p229) who supposedly murdered three husbands and several slave lovers.

Contemporary Jamaican fiction is also filled with sometimes gritty, sometimes poignant stories of perseverance and survival. For instance, *Power Game*, by Michael Thewell, concerns a country boy who comes to Kingston, turns into a 'rude boy' (armed thug), and becomes fatally enmeshed in the savage drug culture. A number of female Jamaican authors have gained notice in recent years with their poignant novels: Christine Craig *(Mint Tea)*, Patricia Powell *(Me Dying Trial)*, Michelle Cliff *(Land of Look Behind)* and Vanessa Spence *(Roads Are Down)*, among others.

Cinema
Jamaica's most powerful films (or, in local parlance, 'flims') have been gritty streetwise dramas depicting the harrowing realities of urban life. Native-born singer Jimmy Cliff rocketed to fame in *The Harder They Come* (1973), in which he starred as a rude boy in Kingston's ghettoes. The brilliant cult movie was produced and directed by Kingstonian Perry Henzell.

Rick Elgood's emotionally engaging 1997 film *Dancehall Queen* found an international audience for its powerful tale of redemption for a struggling, middle-aged street vendor who finds a novel way of escaping the mean streets of Kingston through the erotic intoxication of dancehall music. Jamaica's highest-grossing film of all time is Chris Browne's 2000 crime drama *Third World Cop,* in which old friends straddling both sides of the law must come to terms with each other.

Music

From hotel beach parties in Negril or Montego Bay to the raw 'sound-system' discos of Kingston's working-class suburbs, Jamaica reverberates to the soul-riveting sounds of calypso, soca and, above all, reggae. Music is everywhere. And loud!

Reggae is the heartbeat of Jamaica, though it is actually only one of several distinctly Jamaican sounds, and the nation's musical heritage runs much deeper. Inspired by the country's rich African folk heritage, music spans *mento* (a folk calypso), ska, rock-steady, 'roots' music, and contemporary dancehall and ragga. Kingston is the 'Nashville of the Third World,' with recording studios pumping out as many as 500 new titles each month.

Reggae is synonymous with one man: Robert Nesta Marley. Bob Marley's legacy continues to thrive, as witnessed in the month-long celebration held in Ethiopia in early 2005, marking the 60th anniversary of his birth. There's even talk in Jamaica about elevating Marley to 'National Hero' status, a mantle reserved only for the nation's most pivotal figures.

The term dancehall, although used to mean a sound-system venue, is also used specifically to refer to a kind of Caribbean 'rap' music that focuses on earthly themes dear to the heart of young male Jamaicans, principally 'gal business,' gunplay and ganja. This is hardcore music, named for the loosely defined, outdoor venues at which outlandishly named 'toasters' (rapper DJs) set up mobile discos with enormous speakers, and singers and jive-talking DJs pumped up with braggadocio perform live over instrumental rhythm tracks.

Ragga is the in-vogue, ever-evolving, techno-driven music of the current dance-hall generation – an often angry, in-your-face musical form echoing the restlessness of Jamaican youth. The music reflects a technological rather than aesthetic leap (to the lay-listener, ragga is associated most strongly with egotistical DJs spouting crass lyrics over a usually monotonous yet always fast-paced, compulsive, computerized, two-chord beat).

The sheer creativity and productivity of Jamaican music has had a profound effect around the world. As reggae continues to attract and influence a massive international audience, Jamaica's sound system–based dancehall culture informs contemporary rap, rave and hip-hop cultures.

ENVIRONMENT

Much of the coast is fringed by coral reefs harboring an astonishing array of marine life. Visitors can forsake sandals for hiking boots and follow mountain trails, shower in remote waterfalls, and shoot birds through the lens of a camera. Several areas have been developed as ecotour destinations, most notably the Black River Great Morass, a swampland penetrated by boat.

The Rio Grande Valley is a premier destination for hiking. The Blue Mountains have been opened up in recent years; for a taste of these rugged heights try a climb up Blue Mountain Peak (7402ft; 2221m). Negril's Great Morass is being developed as an eco-attraction protecting fabulous birdlife and wetland ecosystems.

The Land

Most of Jamaica's land mass is rugged and mountainous, reaching 7402ft (2221m) in the Blue Mountains, where the world's most sought-after coffee is grown. Pockets of wild and forbidding jungle terrain give way to swampy wetlands harboring endangered crocodiles and manatees. Parched cactus-covered savannas line the south coast, where traditional fisherfolk draw their pirogues and nets up on otherwise lonesome dark-brown beaches.

With its dramatic, fertile landscape and ever-changing topography, Jamaica is the Caribbean's garden. Fans of flora are enchanted by more than 3000 species of flowering plants. Palm trees are nearly everywhere, including the stately royal palm (a Cuban import), which grows to over 100ft

(30m). Fruit trees include ackee – the staple of Jamaican breakfasts – mango and breadfruit.

Wildlife

The island has more than 255 bird species. Stilt-legged, snowy-white cattle egrets are ubiquitous, as are 'John crows,' or turkey vultures, which are feared in Jamaica and are the subject of several folk songs and proverbs. *Patoo* (a West African word) is the Jamaican name for the owl, which many islanders superstitiously regard as a harbinger of death. Jamaica has two species: the screech owl and the endemic brown owl. There are also four endemic species of flycatchers, a species of woodpecker, and many rare species of doves.

Coral reefs lie along the north shore, where the reef is almost continuous and much of it is within a few hundred yards of shore. Over 700 species of fish zip in and out of the exquisite reefs and swarm through the coral canyons: wrasses, parrotfish, snappers, bonito, kingfish, jewelfish and scores of others. Barracudas, giant groupers, tarpon and nurse sharks are frequently seen. Further out, the cobalt deeps are run by sailfish, marlin and manta rays. Last but not least, three species of endangered marine turtles – the green, hawksbill and loggerhead – lay eggs on Jamaica's beaches.

FOOD & DRINK

Dining in Jamaica ranges from wildly expensive restaurants to humble roadside stands where you can eat simple Jamaican fare for as little as US$1. Most hotels incorporate Jamaican dishes in their menus. Food bought at grocery stores is usually expensive, as many of the canned and packaged goods are imported. Cheap fresh fruits, vegetables and spices sell at markets and roadside stalls islandwide.

Jamaica's homegrown cuisine is a fusion of many ethnic traditions and influences. The Arawaks brought callaloo (a spinach-like green), cassava (a root vegetable), corn, sweet potatoes and several tropical fruits to the island. The Spanish adopted native spices, which were later enhanced by spices brought by slaves from their African homelands. Immigrants from India brought hot and flavorful curries, often served with locally made mango chutney.

Middle Eastern dishes and Chinese influences have also become part of the national menu. And basic roasts and stews followed the flag during three centuries of British rule, as did Yorkshire pudding, meat pies and hot cross buns.

Jamaica's most popular dish is jerk, a term that describes the process of cooking meats smothered in tongue-searing marinade. Jerk is best served hot off the coals wrapped in paper. You normally order by the pound (US$4 worth should fill you up).

Naturally, there's a strong emphasis on seafood. Snapper and parrotfish are two of the more popular species. A favorite is *escoveitched* fish, which is pickled in vinegar then fried and simmered with peppers and onions.

Many meals are accompanied by starchy vegetables – 'breadkinds' – such as plantains and yam, or other bread substitutes such as pancake-shaped cassava bread (or *bammy*) and johnnycakes (delicious fried dumplings, an original Jamaican fast food).

Red Stripe is the beer of Jamaica. Crisp and sweet, it's perfectly light and refreshing. Rum ranges from dark rums to a mind-bogglingly powerful white (clear) rum, the libation of choice for poorer Jamaicans.

KINGSTON

pop 700,000

Dramatically situated between ocean and mountains, Jamaica's lively, teeming, unrepentantly in-your-face capital city rewards travelers who have nerve enough to become familiar with its streets.

Kingston has earned a spotty reputation among would-be visitors for its infamous slums and headline-grabbing social strife. It's true that the city's street culture can be intimidating, but with a little vigilance the savvy traveler can sidestep the squalor to safely experience Kingston's singular sizzle. Those who linger discover the heartbeat of Jamaica and its center of commerce and culture.

There's a well-developed and cosmopolitan cultural scene, compelling historic sites and a vivacious nightlife with everything from jazz and lively theater to reggae concerts. Kingston has a large middle class, and vast acres of well maintained streets lined with modern houses. It is also a city

JAMAICA

divided, with hovels and high-rises side by side. The vast shantytowns that push at the city's margins are for the most part hidden from tourist view, as is the controlled anarchy of the inner-city ghettoes. Not a city for the meek, chaotic and vibrant Kingston reflects the gritty soul of the nation.

HISTORY

Kingston was founded in 1693 by survivors of the devastating earthquake that flattened nearby Port Royal (see p214). Though whacked repeatedly by more earthquakes and hurricanes, the port city prospered throughout the 18th century, becoming one of the most important trading centers in the western hemisphere and an important transshipment point for slaves destined for the Spanish colonies.

In 1872, Kingston supplanted Spanish Town as Jamaica's capital. In spite of an early 20th-century economic boom, the city's slow physical decline seemed assured as sprawling shantytowns put down roots around the old city's perimeter.

In the 1960s, the Urban Development Corporation reclaimed the waterfront. Several historic landmarks, including Victoria Market, were razed to make way for a complex of gleaming new structures, including the Bank of Jamaica and the Jamaica Conference Centre. About the same time, Kingston's nascent music industry was beginning to gather steam, lending international stature and fame to the city. This, in turn, fostered the growth of New Kingston, an uptown area of multistory office blocks, banks, restaurants, shops and hotels.

KINGSTON IN...

Two Days

Visit the **Bob Marley Museum** and the **National Gallery** (opposite), tour **Devon House** (opposite), and take in a meal to remember at **Norma's on the Terrace** (p212) or the **Red Bones Blues Café** (p213).

Four Days

Add on an excursion to **Port Royal** (p214) for a peek into Jamaica's distant past, and head into the Blue Mountains for Sunday brunch at **Strawberry Hill** (p215).

ORIENTATION

The city overlooks the seventh-largest natural harbor in the world, with the waterfront on its southern border. It spreads out in a fan shape from the harbor and rises gently toward the foothills and spur ridges of the Blue Mountains.

The historic area just north of the waterfront forms the city center. Downtown is arranged on a grid system, while New Kingston, or 'uptown,' is defined by several major roads, including the main drag of Knutsford Blvd, Half Way Tree Rd and Hope Rd.

INFORMATION

Bookstores

Bookland (☎ 926-4035; 53 Knutsford Blvd) A good selection on island history, folklore and culture.

Emergency

Police (☎ 922-9321; 79 Duke St)

Internet Access

Most upscale hotels along Knutsford Blvd provide in-room dial-up Internet access and have business centers with Internet service.

Café What's On (☎ 929-4490; Devon House courtyard, Hope Rd; per 15min $1) Adjacent to the historic Devon House, this is a pleasant place to get online.

Laundry

Express Laundromat (☎ 978-4319; 30 Lady Musgrave Rd)

Medical Services

Ambucare Ambulance Service (☎ 978-2327; 202 Mountain View Ave)
Bellevue Hospital (☎ 928-1380; 6-1/2 Windward Rd, Kingston 2)

Money

Uptown, you will find more than a dozen banks located along Knutsford Blvd. Most have foreign-exchange counters as well as 24-hour ATMs.

Scotiabank (☎ 922-1000; cnr Duke & Port Royal Sts) Has its main foreign-exchange center immediately east of the Jamaica Conference Centre.

Post

FedEx (☎ 960-9192; 75 Knutsford Blvd)
Post office Main branch (☎ 922-2120; 13 King St); New Kingston branch (☎ 926-6803; 115 Hope Rd)

Tourist Information

Jamaica Tourist Board (JTB) Airport (☎ 924-8024); Headquarters (☎ 929-9200; fax 929-9375; 64 Knutsford Blvd; ◷ 8:30am-5:30pm Mon-Fri) The headquarters in New Kingston maintains a small research library.

DANGERS & ANNOYANCES

The island averages three murders per day, and 75% of these occur in Kingston. Most of the murders are drug-related or politically inspired and occur in the ghettos, although the level of general violence and crime has escalated frighteningly throughout the city in recent years.

Avoid Kingston entirely during periods of tension, when localized violence can spontaneously erupt. If you're in town when street violence flares up, definitely avoid downtown, and adhere to any curfews that police may impose.

Stick to the main streets – if in doubt, ask your hotel concierge or manager to point out trouble areas. New Kingston is generally safe for walking, as are most main roads. Avoid West Kingston if you can (especially Trench Town, Jones Town, Greenwich Town and Tivoli), particularly west of the Parade, downtown.

Foreigners, especially White tourists, stand out from the crowd. Fortunately, visitors to Kingston are not hassled to anywhere near the degree they are in the north-coast resorts. Still, don't loiter! Constant alertness is called for.

SIGHTS
Downtown

Some visitors – particularly those having just arrived in Jamaica – find the intense urban environment of downtown Kingston a bit daunting. As long as you keep your eyes open and are selective in choosing your friends, a visit to the city's historic center can be enjoyed in relative safety.

For several blocks, the waterfront is paralleled by the breeze-swept, 400yd-long (365m) harborfront **Ocean Blvd**. Nearby, the **National Gallery** (☎ 922-1561; 12 Ocean Blvd; adult/child US$2/1; ◷ 10am-4:30pm Tue-Thu, 10am-4pm Fri, 10am-3pm Sat & Sun) does a smashing job of making its case for Jamaican art with a coherent and moving collection of works by John Dunkley, Edna Manley and other big names in the Jamaican artistic pantheon. Guides are free, but tips are welcome.

At the national mint and treasury is the small but fascinating **Museum of Coins & Notes** (☎ 922-0750; cnr Nethersole Pl & Ocean Blvd; admission free; ◷ 9am-4pm Mon-Fri), displaying Jamaican currency through the centuries.

Half a mile (800m) up King St from the waterfront you reach the **Parade**, the streets surrounding William Grant Park at the bustling heart of the downtown mayhem. Notable buildings include the historic **Kingston Parish Church**, dating from 1699, and the stately **Ward Theatre**.

Uptown

The beautiful **Devon House** (☎ 929-6602; 26 Hope Rd; admission US$5; ◷ 9am-5pm Tue-Sat), built in 1881, is a classic Jamaican 'great house' that will delight antique lovers and history buffs. The shaded lawns attract couples on weekends. The former carriage house and courtyard are home to two of Jamaica's more famous restaurants (see p212). Admission includes a guided tour.

The most-visited site in Kingston is the **Bob Marley Museum** (☎ 927-9152; 56 Hope Rd; adult/student US$10/9; ◷ 9:30am-4pm Mon-Sat). An Ethiopian flag flutters above the gate of the red-brick manse that Marley turned into his Tuff Gong Recording Studios. Dominating the forecourt is a gaily colored statue of the musical legend. Some of the guides are deathly solemn, but the hour-long tour provides fascinating insights into Marley's life. The former recording studio out back is now an exhibition hall and theater, where the tour closes with a fascinating film of his final days. No cameras or tape recorders are permitted.

ACTIVITIES

Built in the 1920s and one of Jamaica's oldest courses, **Constant Spring Golf Club** (☎ 924-1610; 152 Constant Spring Rd) has a par-70 course and boasts a swimming pool and bar, and tennis, squash and badminton courts.

Spartan Health Club (☎ 927-7575; 9 Lady Musgrave Rd; nonmembers US$10) A modern gym.

YMCA (☎ 926-0801; 21 Hope Rd cnr Trafalgar Rd; Kingston 10; pool use US$2)

Putt 'n' Play Mini-Golf Park (☎ 906-4814; 78 Knutsford Blvd; adult/child & senior US$8/4; ◷ 5-11pm Mon-Thu, 5pm-midnight Fri, 11am-midnight Sat & Sun), next to the Liguanea Golf Club, is an 18-hole miniature golf course complete with miniature waterfalls, meandering streams, ponds, sand traps and natural obstacles.

JAMAICA

UPTOWN KINGSTON

INFORMATION
Bookland...........................1 C4
British Embassy..................2 C4
Café What's On...................3 B3
Canadian Embassy..............4 C4
Express Laundromat.............5 D4
FedEx..............................6 C4
German Embassy.................7 B3
Jamaica Tourist Board..........8 C4
Police..............................9 B6
Post Office.......................10 E2
US Embassy......................11 C5

SIGHTS & ACTIVITIES
Bob Marley Museum............12 D2
Devon House.....................13 B3

Putt 'n' Play Mini-Golf Park.......14 B5
Spartan Health Club................15 D5
YMCA................................16 B3

SLEEPING
Altamont Court....................17 C5
Christar Villas......................18 E2
Four Seasons.......................19 B4
Hilton Hotel........................20 C5
Knutsford Court Hotel...........21 B4
Mayfair Hotel......................22 B2
New Chelsea Hotel &
    Amusement Centre.............23 B5
Sandhurst...........................24 D2
Shirley Retreat House.............25 C3
Valerie Dean's Guest House......26 D3

Labels on map:
To Constant Spring Golf Club (2.5km)
Lindsay Cres
Constant Spring Rd
Dunrobin Ave
Gore Tce
Red Hills Rd
W Kings House Rd
W King House Dr
Waterloo Rd
Kingsway Rd
Devon House
Derrymore Rd
Eastwood Park Rd
Constant Spring Rd
Nelson Mandela Park
Molynes Rd
Hope Rd
Half Way Tree
Hagley Park Rd
To Tinson Pen Aerodrome (4km); Port Royal (8km)
Maxfield Ave
Half Way Tree Rd
Cecelio Ave
Ruthven Rd
Chelsea Ave
Grove Rd
New Kingston
Emancipation Park
Knutsford Blvd
Oxford Rd
Beechwood Ave
Norwood Rd
Lyndhurst Rd
Half Way Tree Rd
Retirement Rd
Cross Roads
Rousseau Rd
Slipe Rd
Eureka Rd
Old Hope Rd
Ripon Rd
Haughton Ave
Trafalgar Rd
Holborn Rd
Dumfries Rd
Grenada Cres
Barbados Ave
Dominica Dr
Trinidad Tce
St Lucia Ave
Altamont Cres
Hailing Rd
Belmont Rd
Braemar Ave
Seaview Ave
Montrose Rd
Lady Musgrave Rd
Old Hope Rd
Arthur Wint Dr
Tom Redcam Dr
Jamaica House
Hope Rd
E Kings House Rd
Marley Rd
Liguanea
Hillcrest Ave
King's House Ave
Sandhurst Cres
Paddington Tce
Mason Rd

To Downtown Kingston:
Doreen's Restaurant (1km); Scotiabank (1.5km);
Main Post Office (1.5km); Bus Terminal (3km);
Ward Theatre (3km); The Parade (3km);
National Gallery (3.5km); Museum of Coins & Notes (3.5km);
Bellevue Hospital (4km); Crafts Market (4km);
Port Royal (8km); Norman Manley
International Airport (19.5km)

JAMAICA

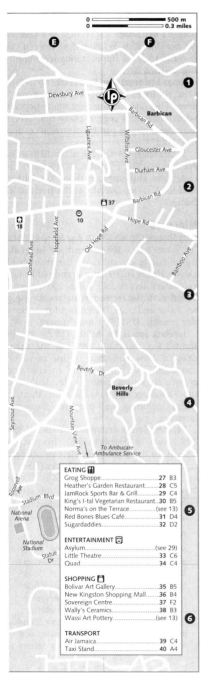

FESTIVALS & EVENTS

Carnival (Easter; www.jamaicacarnival.com) Kingston's week-long Carnival brings costumed revelers into the streets in droves. There's reggae and calypso, of course, but soca is king. Carnival ends with the Road March, when the two camps parade through the streets in carnival costume.

Jamaica Coffee Festival (October; ☎ 922-4200) Jamaica's world famous coffee is something to celebrate at this family-friendly festival.

Fireworks on the Waterfront (December 31; ☎ 922-4200) Ring in the new year on the Kingston waterfront with 100,000 others.

SLEEPING

Most hotels are in uptown and New Kingston. The pickings are virtually nonexistent downtown. Rates are usually the same year-round.

Budget

Valerie Dean's Guest House (☎ 978-4859, 813-0098; www.mikuzi.com; 5 Upper Montrose Rd, Kingston 6; basic/superior r US$30/60, deluxe US$40-50; P 🍴) This exceedingly pleasant place near the Bob Marley Museum has eight bright, comfortable rooms (many with kitchenettes) in a handsome home. All but one basic room have hot water and air-con. The two highest priced options are decked out with art and antiques and are more like small apartments. The lush garden provides a pleasant spot for repose.

New Chelsea Hotel & Amusement Centre (☎ 926-5803; fax 929-4746; 5 Chelsea Ave; r US$40; P 🍴) This is a basic option. Older rooms are dark but modern rooms in an annex are slightly better. All feature air-con, hot water and cable TV. A fifth night is free. It has a pool hall and amusement center, plus a disco and rooftop bar.

Midrange

Mayfair Hotel (☎ 926-1610; mayfair@in-site.com; 4 W Kings House Dr, Kingston 10; r standard/superior US$58/70, s/d ste 88/128; P 🍴 🏊) North of Devon House, the Mayfair offers 32 basic but clean and well-lit rooms with utility furniture and telephone. Standard rooms lack TV. Its best feature is the views toward the Blue Mountains.

Sandhurst (☎ 927-8244; 70 Sandhurst Cres, Kingston 6; s US$40, d US$45-50, d with air-con US$50; P 🍴 🏊) This eccentric favorite in a quiet, residential, Liguanea neighborhood has spotlessly kept pale-blue rooms with black-and-white tile floors, utility furniture and an air of Miami in the 1960s. Some have TV and telephone and private veranda. A dining terrace has views toward the Blue Mountains.

Shirley Retreat House (☎ 927-9208, 946-2678; 7 Maeven Rd, Kingston 10; standard/superior r incl continental breakfast US$60/70; P ✷) A pleasant option operated by the United Church of Jamaica, this unique place offers four simply furnished, well-lit rooms with hardwood floors, pleasant fabrics, fans, and private bath with hot water. Two rooms have small TVs, and one has air-con. Meals are cooked on request.

Altamont Court (☎ 929-5931; altamont@n5.com .jm; 1 Altamont Cres, Kingston 5; studio/ste US$95/120; P ✷ 🖳 🕃) This attractive New Kingston favorite offers lush foliage and 58 modern, clean, one-bedroom studios, well-equipped suites, and facilities including an attractive restaurant, a neophyte business center and a small pool with bar.

Christar Villas (☎ 978-3933; www.christarvillas hotel.com; 99A Hope Rd, Kingston 6; r US$93, studios US$117, 2-bedroom ste US$163-175; P ✷ 🖳 🕃) Here you can choose from modern, pleasantly furnished studio apartments and one- and two-bedroom suites with satellite TVs and full kitchen. Rates include tax. There's a self-service laundry, a restaurant and a gym.

Top End

Four Seasons (☎ 926-8805, 800-526-2422; www.hotel fourseasonsja.com; 18 Ruthven Rd, Kingston 10; standard/ deluxe r US$80/98; P ✖ ✷ 🖳 🕃) A venerable English-style, German-run place, this hotel exudes an aged European ambience with its mahogany wall panels and doors, gilt chandeliers and French curtains. Rooms in the original house, though modest, are spacious, lofty, airy and light. Rooms in the garden units and in the annex offer a more amenable, resort-style feel.

Hilton Hotel (☎ 926-5430, in the UK 0845-7581-595; www.hilton.com; 77 Knutsford Blvd, Kingston 5; r US$130-210, ste US$255-300; P ✖ ✷ 🖳 🕃) This modern hotel is strongly oriented toward the business traveler. The rooms have all the bells and whistles, and there's a fitness center, boutique, tennis courts, business center and the stylish Jonkanoo Lounge for night owls.

EATING & DRINKING

Kingston's cuisine scene doesn't pander to tourists, but like the city itself, it reflects a stimulating mix of cultural influences.

Budget

Doreen's Restaurant (cnr Old Hope Rd & Caledonia Ave; meals US$1.50-9; 🕑 7:30am-10pm) Doreen's is popular with the impecunious seeking filling Jamaica fare.

King's I-tal Vegetarian Restaurant (☎ 929-1921; 41 Half Way Tree Rd; meals US$1-10; 🕑 breakfast, lunch & dinner) This unassuming joint, quite popular with Rastas and reggae celebrities, serves ackee stew, veggie patties, natural juices and even tofu.

Sugardaddies (☎ 925-7267; cnr Hope Rd & Hillcrest Ave; meals US$1.50-9; 🕑 breakfast, lunch & dinner) Inexpensive and unpretentious 'Caribbean soul food' is the specialty at this lively local haunt.

Midrange

Grog Shoppe (☎ 968-2098; 26 Hope Rd; meals US$10-20; 🕑 lunch & dinner Mon-Sat, brunch Sun) In an atmospheric brick edifice on the grounds of Devon House (p209), this grand old Jamaican eatery serves dishes like ackee crepes, baked crab backs, and roast suckling pig with rice and peas. It's known for its Sunday brunch (US$17). Come hungry.

JamRock Sports Bar & Grill (☎ 754-4032; 69 Knutsford Blvd; 🕑 lunch & dinner) On the main drag in New Kingston is this in-vogue restaurant and bar drawing an educated crowd. Its selling point is decidedly not the TVs all around but rather the extensive menu including well-prepared Jamaican favorites.

Heather's Garden Restaurant (☎ 926-2826, 960-7739; 9 Haining Rd; 🕑 lunch & dinner) This place is known for its tasty, moderately priced fare ranging from Jamaican crab backs (US$12) and buffalo chicken wings (US$5) to cottage pie (US$8), charbroiled lamb chops (US$15), kebabs and seafood.

AUTHOR'S CHOICE

Norma's on the Terrace (☎ 968-5488; 26 Hope Rd; mains US$12-36; 🕑 lunch & dinner Mon-Sat) On a candlelit terrace at Devon House (p209), this famous restaurant fuses local flavors with international influences into such dishes as red pea bisque with rum, and – get ready! – jerk smoked pork chops in guava sauce with rum-soaked raisins and fruit flambé. Wrap it all up with a dessert called English trifle.

Top End

Red Bones Blues Café (☎ 978-8262; 21 Braemar Ave; meals US$20-40; 🕑 11am-1am Mon-Fri, 7pm-1am Sat) Red Bones Blues is *the* in-spot in town, and is recommended for its warm and lively ambience and imaginative cuisine. Meals are served on the patio or in a welcoming dining room. Try the peppered garlic shrimp served in an avocado or papaya shell (US$26). In the comfortable bar, there's good conversation, live jazz and blues on Friday nights, and def poetry on the last Wednesday night of the month.

ENTERTAINMENT
Nightclubs

Quad (☎ 754-7823; 20-22 Trinidad Tce) This is a welcome new addition to Kingston's nightlife scene. Quad is actually four clubs with distinct personalities: on the main floor is Christopher's Jazz Club, a tony and tasteful jazz bar where the city's movers and shakers move and shake. In the basement is Taboo, a naughty gentleman's club featuring pole dancers from the Eastern bloc (entrance US$10). On Wednesday, Friday and Saturday, two clubs open on the top floor: Voodoo Lounge, which draws an older, more urbane crowd, and Oxygen, which attracts a 20-something set ready to get sweaty until 4am. The US$10 admission gives you the run of the house, except for Taboo.

Asylum (☎ 929-4386; 69 Knutsford Blvd) Down the street from Quad, this is another happening scene that packs in crowds Tuesday through Sunday. Tuesday is ladies' night with free admission until 11pm; Wednesday is popular for vintage sounds.

Theater

Little Theatre (☎ 926-6129; 4 Tom Redcam Dr) Puts on plays, folk concerts, pantomimes and modern dance throughout the year. The main season is July through August, and a 'mini season' is held each December.

Ward Theatre (☎ 922-0453; North Pde) This is home to the National Dance Theater Company, known for its rich repertory that combines Caribbean, African and Western dance styles.

Sport

Sabina Park (☎ 967-0322; South Camp Rd) *The* place for cricket! The 30,000-seat arena hosted its first test match in 1929 and has been a focal point for the sport ever since. It's currently undergoing a major upgrade in preparation for the 2007 World Cup to be held throughout the Caribbean region. Attending a match – particularly an international test – is an unforgettable cultural experience whether you're a fan or not.

SHOPPING
Crafts Stalls

Crafts Market (Pechon & Port Royal Sts; 🕑 Mon-Sat) In an old iron building on the waterfront, this market has dozens of stalls selling wickerwork, carvings, batiks, straw hats and other crafts. Watch your wallet!

Local Art & Galleries

Bolivar Art Gallery (☎ 926-8799; 1D Grove Rd) Works by Jamaica's leading artists; fine books; antiques and maps.

Wally's Ceramics (☎ 926-4898; 9 Merrick Ave) Quality ceramics.

Wassi Art Pottery (☎ 906-5016; Devon House, 26 Hope Rd) Marvelous vases, planters, plates, bowls etc, each hand-painted and signed by the artist.

Shopping Malls

Several modern malls are concentrated on Constant Spring and Hope Rds. Two of the largest are **Sovereign Centre** (106 Hope Rd) and **New Kingston Shopping Mall** (Dominica Dr).

GETTING THERE & AWAY
Air

Norman Manley International Airport (KIN; ☎ 924-8546; www.manley-airport.com.jm) handles international flights. Domestic flights depart and land at **Tinson Pen Aerodrome** (☎ 924-8452; Marcus Garvey Dr) in west Kingston.

Air Jamaica (☎ 888-359-2475; 4 St Lucia Ave, Kingston 5) has its headquarters uptown. Air Jamaica Express offers daily service to/from Montego Bay and Ocho Rios from both Norman Manley International Airport and Tinson Pen.

TimAir (☎ 952-2516, 979-1114; www.timair.net) is an air-taxi service connecting Kingston with Montego Bay, Negril, Ocho Rios, Port Antonio and Mandeville.

Bus

Buses, coasters and route taxis run between Kingston and every point on the island. They arrive and depart from the bus terminal (Beckford & Pechon Sts), five blocks west of the

Parade. The terminal adjoins Trench Town, and travelers should exercise caution when passing through. For bus services, see the boxed text below.

GETTING AROUND
To/From the Airport

Norman Manley International Airport is located midway along the Palisadoes, about 20 miles (32km) southeast of downtown Kingston. The bus stop is opposite the airport police station. Bus No 98 operates about every 30 minutes between the airport and the west side of the Parade (US$1). Route taxis also operate between the airport and West Parade (US$1.75).

A taxi between the airport and New Kingston will cost about US$25. From Tinson Pen Aerodrome a taxi costs about US$8 to New Kingston, and a bus to the Parade, downtown, is about US$0.25.

Bus

The main downtown terminus for local buses is at North and South Parade and Half Way Tree junction. Kingston's **bus system** (JUTC; ☎ 749-3196; ⏲ 5am-10pm) runs Mercedes-Benz and Volvo buses, including buses for the disabled; fares are US$0.35 to US$0.50.

Taxi

Taxis are numerous in Kingston except when it rains, which is when demand skyrockets. Use licensed cabs only (they have red PPV license plates). Taxis wait outside most major hotels. Taxi companies are listed in the *Yellow Pages*. Fares from New Kingston to downtown are about US$8. There is a taxi stand uptown at the south side of Nelson Mandela Park.

AROUND KINGSTON

Port Royal (population 1200) is a dilapidated, ramshackle place of tropical lassitude, replete with important historical buildings collapsing to dust. Today's funky fishing hamlet was once the pirate capital of the Caribbean. Later, it was the hub of British naval power in the West Indies, but the remains give little hint of the town's former glory.

The English settled the isolated cay in 1656. They called it 'Cagway' or 'The Point' and built Fort Cromwell (which was renamed Fort Charles after the Restoration in 1660). Within two years, General William Brayne was able to report that 'there is the faire beginning of a town upon the poynt of this harbor.' A massive earthquake in 1692 put an end to Port Royal's ascension as survivors crossed the harbor to settle on the firmer ground of what would become Kingston.

The town has many fascinating historic sites, including old **Fort Charles** itself. An excellent map called 'Port Royal: A Walking Tour' is included in *Port Royal* by Clinton V Black, which you can buy in the gift store of Morgan's Harbour Hotel.

Lime Cay, a picture-perfect uninhabited island with white sand and accessible snorkeling, is 15 minutes by boat from Port Royal. Boats run from Morgan's Harbour Hotel, or they can be obtained by asking local fishermen at the pier (US$5). On weekends there are food stalls; at other times bring a picnic.

Morgan's Harbour Hotel (☎ 967-8075; fax 967-8073; s/d from US$130/150; P ⏚ ⏚) is an atmospheric though overpriced hotel within the grounds of the old naval dockyard. It has 63 spacious air-con rooms with terra-cotta tile floors and French doors opening onto balconies.

Sadly, the ferry connecting downtown Kingston to Port Royal is history. Bus No 98 runs from the Parade in downtown Kingston several times daily (US$0.60). A route taxi from the Parade in Kingston costs about US$0.75; a licensed taxi costs

SERVICES FROM KINGSTON BUS TERMINAL

Destination	Cost (one way)	Distance	Duration	Schedule
Ocho Rios	US$4	54 miles (87km)	1½ hours	Four daily
Port Antonio	US$4	61 miles (98km)	1½ hours	Four daily
Montego Bay	US$8	119 miles (191km)	3 hours	Four daily

about US$35 one way. Morgan's Harbour Hotel offers free airport transfers to guests. Otherwise, it's about US$15 for the five-minute taxi ride.

THE BLUE MOUNTAINS

The Blue Mountains rise northeast of Kingston and soar in green pleats to a knife-edged backbone that extends west-northwest and east-southeast for 30 miles (48km). The chain is flanked to the east by the lower John Crow Mountains; to the west are the less distinct Port Royal Mountains. Travelers are drawn by the area's fabulous hiking and scenic beauty.

Sleeping & Eating

Strawberry Hill (☎ 944-8400; www.islandoutpost.com /StrawberryHill; r/ste/villa US$275/475/675; P 🗶 🔀 🔋) This luxury retreat at 3100ft (945m), one hour by car from Kingston, is just north of Irish Town. The 12 Caribbean-style cottages range from studio suites to a four-bedroom, two-story house built into the hillside. Each cottage is a statement in elegance. A sumptuous breakfast is included in the rates, as are transfers. Birding and hiking tours are offered. No children are allowed. Many Kingstonians make the tortuous drive to Strawberry Hill for some of the finest nouvelle Jamaican cuisine on the island (dinner US$18 to US$45). Reservations are advised. Strawberry Hill also hosts a calendar of special events throughout the year, and provides a range of tours into the mountains.

Mount Edge B&B (☎ 944-8151; d per night/week US$50/250, cottage US$30-50) This exceptional budget option perched on the edge of the mountains rising from Newcastle, 1½ hours from Kingston, has three rooms and two simple cottages. The spacious, no-frills lounge has a kitchen and wide glass windows on all sides. Delicious meals are prepared by a Rasta named Ox (breakfast/dinner US$5/8.50), who also will arrange tours into the mountains.

BLUE MOUNTAINS-JOHN CROW NATIONAL PARK

This national park covers the forest reserves of the Blue and John Crow Mountain Ranges. Many stalwart hikers make the journey here to scale **Blue Mountain Peak**, Jamaica's highest mountain at 7402ft (2256m).

The ramshackle village of Hagley Gap is the gateway to Blue Mountain Peak. The road forks in the village, where a horrendously denuded dirt road for Penlyne Castle begins a precipitous ascent. Penlyne Castle is the base for the 7-mile (11km), 3000ft (915m) ascent to the summit. Most hikers stay overnight at one of three simple lodges near Penlyne Castle before tackling the hike in the wee hours. The most popular is **Wildflower Lodge** (☎ 929-5395; r with/without bath US$33/13, cottage US$55), 400yd (366m) east of the ridge crest at Penlyne Castle. Guides (half-/full day US$30/50) can be hired locally at Hagley Gap, Penlyne Castle or from the lodge.

Getting There & Away

From Kingston, simply follow Hope Rd uphill to Papine, a market square and bus station, where Gordon Town Rd leads into the mountains. At the Cooperage, the B1 (Mammee River Rd) forks left steeply uphill for Strawberry Hill and Newcastle. Gordon Town Rd continues straight from the Cooperage and winds east up the Hope River Valley to Gordon Town, then steeply to Mavis Bank and Hagley Gap. It is possible to catch an inexpensive route taxi from Papine.

NORTHERN JAMAICA

The northeast coast is Jamaica's windward corner, where surf rolls ashore into perfect beach-lined coves and waves chew at rocky headlands. Colonial-era edifices are relatively few, though beautiful pocket-size beaches line the shore. You'll also find several unspoiled fishing villages where budget travelers can ease into a laid-back local lifestyle.

Beautiful Portland parish, presided over by the sleepy town of Port Antonio, is the least developed resort area in Jamaica – a fact that endears it to many. Further west, the bustling port of Ocho Rios provides a convenient staging ground for excursions to some of Jamaica's most popular attractions, including the incomparable Dunn's River Falls.

PORT ANTONIO
pop 13,000

Port Antonio is the capital of Portland parish and Jamaica's main banana port. The melancholic town still has the tropical lassitude of a maritime harbor, and there is little of the hustle of Montego Bay or Ocho Rios. Goats snoozing in the shade of verandas sum it all up. Take their cue and chill out for a while, amid some of Jamaica's most stunning scenery.

Information

D-Tech (☎ 993-4184; upstairs, 3 West St; Internet access per 30min US$1.25; ☼ 9am-7pm Mon-Sat)

Jamaica Tourist Board (☎ 993-3051; fax 993-2117; City Centre, Harbour St; ☼ 8:30am-4:30pm Mon-Fri) Operates a poorly stocked office that's barely worth a visit.

Port Antonio Hospital (☎ 993-2646; Nuttall Rd) Above town on Naylor's Hill, south of West Harbour.

Portland Parish Library (☎ 993-2793; 1 Harbour St; Internet access per 30min US$0.80; ☼ 9am-6pm Mon-Fri, 9am-1pm Sat) Near the entrance to the marina.

Post office (☎ 993-2651) On the east side of the town square.

RBTT Bank (☎ 993-9755; 28 Harbour St)

Scotiabank (☎ 993-2523; 3 Harbour St)

www.portantoniojamaica.com This is a good starting point for tourist information.

Sights

Port Antonio's heart is the main square at the junction of West and Harbour Sts. It's centered on a **clock tower** and backed by a handsome red-brick Georgian **courthouse** topped by a cupola. From here walk 50yd (45m) down West St to the junction of William St, where the smaller Port Antonio Sq has a cenotaph honoring Jamaicans who gave their lives in the two world wars.

On the west side of the square is the clamorous and colorful **Musgrave Market**. To the north is the imposing facade of the **Village of St George**, a beautiful three-story complex with an exquisitely frescoed exterior in Dutch style. Fort George St leads to the Titchfield Peninsula, where you'll find several dozen Victorian-style gingerbread houses, including **DeMontevin Lodge** (see opposite), an ornate rust-red mansion. Continue north to the remains of **Fort George** at the tip of the peninsula, dating from 1729. Several George III–era cannons can still be seen mounted in their embrasures in 10ft-thick (3m) walls.

Activities

Lady G'Diver (☎ 715-5957, 844-8711; ladygdiver@cwjamaica.com; 2 Somerstown Rd) is a full-service dive shop at Port Antonio Marina; dive boats leave at 11am and 2pm daily.

Grand Valley Tours (☎ 993-4116; valleytours@cwjamaica.com; upstairs, 12 West St) offers guided hikes in the Rio Grande Valley, plus horseback riding, bird-watching, and other trips of interest to ecotourists.

Eight miles (13km) east of town is the **San San Golf Course & Bird Sanctuary** (☎ 993-7645; 9/18 holes US$50/70; ☼ 8am-5pm), an 18-hole course laid out along valleys surrounded by rainforest. There's a clubhouse, a small pro shop and bistro dining.

Festivals & Events

A Fi Wi Sinting (late February; ☎ 715-3529; www.fiwisinting.com) This festival features traditional music, song, dance and a marketplace.

Portland Jerk Festival (July; ☎ 715-5465) A food festival for folks in love with the hot and spicy.

International Marlin Tournament (October; ☎ 927-0145) Anglers rejoice at this time-honored fishing tournament.

Sleeping

Visitors to Port Antonio and environs enjoy some of the most economical lodging on the island. For a good overview, visit the website of **Port Antonio Guest House Association** (www.go-jam.com).

Jamaica Heights Resort (☎ 993-3305; www.jamaicaheights.net; Spring Bank Rd; d US$75; P ⚐) This splendid hilltop plantation home is set amid lush gardens with incredible views. The six rooms and two studios are tastefully furnished with white wicker and antiques, plus four-poster beds. A spa offers massage and treatments, and there's a beautiful plunge pool plus a nature trail.

Ocean Crest Guest House B&B (☎ 993-4024; 7 Queen St; r US$35-70) This favorite continues to inspire positive mail from readers. Some of the downstairs rooms are dark, but make amends with gleaming tile floors and antique reproduction furnishings. There's a well-equipped communal kitchen. At time of research, four bright rooms (US$70) on the top floor with balconies and views of Port Antonio and its picturesque bay were being unveiled: a welcome addition indeed.

Holiday Home (☎ 993-2425, 993-2882; 12 King St, PO Box 11; s US$30, d US$35-40) This charming home has nine rooms. They're basic and small, and some have shared baths, but the rooms are spick-and-span. Breakfasts are cooked to order.

DeMontevin Lodge (☎ 993-2604; 21 Fort George St, PO Box 85; r US$27-115; ⊠) This venerable Victorian guesthouse boasts a homey ambience and a blend of modern kitsch and antiques reminiscent of granny's parlor. The 13 simple bedrooms (six with private baths) are timeworn, but as clean as a whistle. Behind the lodge is an ancillary building with small budget doubles.

Hotel Mocking Bird Hill (☎ 993-7267; www .hotelmockingbirdhill.com; PO Box 254; garden-view/ superior r US$210/240; P ⊠) This is the place for relaxed, button-down ambience. All rooms are lovingly appointed with well-chosen fabrics and modern art and appliances. Trails lead through the lush hillside gardens…fabulous for birding!

Eating & Drinking

Norma's at the Marina (☎ 993-9510; Ken Wright Pier; meals $11-20; ⦿ lunch & dinner) This can be a forlorn place when a cruise ship is not in port – but some may find the solitude blissfully peaceful. Steaks, chops and fish prepared in the continental style are served at outdoor tables overlooking the impressive marina.

Shadows (☎ 828-2285; 40 W Palm Ave; meals US$6-24; ⦿ lunch & dinner) Serves high-quality Jamaican, American and Chinese cuisine, unintentionally mirroring the local population. The seafood specials are a hit with the locals. In the evenings, the place turns into a nightclub; vintage reggae is featured on Tuesday and Sunday.

Dicky's Sweet Banana Spot (☎ 993-9591; meals from US$15; ⦿ dinner) This offbeat hut on the A4, half a mile (800m) west of town, offers the best bargain in town. 'Dicky' and Joy Butler serve five-course meals, with huge portions. It has only two tables (reservations are essential; you need to order the same morning).

Golden Happiness (☎ 993-4524; cnr Harbour & West Sts; dishes under US$5; ⦿ lunch & dinner) Reasonable-quality Chinese dishes – including a vast menu of chop sueys and sweet-and-sour dishes – are available; you can request half-orders. The ambience is barely detectable.

Roof Club (☎ 993-3817; 11 West St) This is Port Antonio's infamous hang-loose, rough-around-the-edges reggae bar. It's relatively

dead midweek, when entry is free. But on weekends (US$6) it hops, especially on Thursday – 'Ladies Nite.'

Getting There & Around

Ken Jones Aerodrome (☎ 913-3173), 6 miles (9.5km) west of Port Antonio, accepts charter flights.

A **transportation center** (Gideon Ave) extends along the waterfront. Buses, coasters and route taxis leave regularly for Port Maria (where you change for Ocho Rios) and Kingston.

Eastern Rent-a-Car (☎ 993-3624, 993-2562; 16 West St) Car and 4WD rentals.

JUTA (☎ 993-2684) Taxi transfers from Montego Bay (US$230) and Kingston (US$200) airports.

AROUND PORT ANTONIO
Rio Grande Valley

The Rio Grande rushes down from the Blue Mountains through a deeply cut gorge to the sea. The region is popular for **hiking**, but trails are confusing and demanding and should not be attempted without a guide (see opposite).

Rafting is also a big draw. Passengers make the three-hour, 6-mile (9.5km) journey on poled bamboo rafts from Grant's Level or Rafter's Village, just east of Berridale, all the way to St Margaret's Bay. En route, you'll pass through Lovers Lane, a moss-covered narrow stream where you're supposed to kiss and make a wish. Try **Rio Grande Tours Ltd** (☎ 913-5434; Port Antonio; per raft US$60; ⦿ 9am-5pm).

To enter the valley, take Red Hassell Rd south from Port Antonio to Fellowship.

Frenchman's Cove

This small cove, near the town of Drapers 5 miles (8km) east of Port Antonio, boasts one of the prettiest **beaches** (admission US$3.50; ⦿ closed Tue) for miles. A stream winds lazily to a white-sand beach that shelves steeply into the water. Bring insect repellent. There's a snack bar and a secure parking lot. A route taxi from Port Antonio costs US$1.

Drapers San Guest House (☎ 993-7118; Hwy A4, Drapers; d incl breakfast US$48-52) is an agreeable guesthouse above Frenchman's Cove comprising two cottages with five doubles and one single room (two share a bath), all with fans and louvered windows. There's a lovely lounge and communal kitchen. A minimum two-night stay is required; rates include breakfast.

Blue Lagoon

Located 7 miles (11km) east of Port Antonio, the Blue Lagoon is embraced by a deep, natural amphitheater with forest-clad sides. The 180ft-deep (54m) lagoon opens to the sea through a narrow funnel, but is fed by freshwater springs that come in at about 140ft (43m) deep. Access is via **Blue Lagoon Restaurant** (☎ 993-7791, ☒ lunch & dinner), where you can rent snorkeling equipment (US$5) and paddleboats (US$10). You can also take a bamboo raft cruise to Cocktail Beach and Monkey Island (US$15). A route taxi from Port Antonio to the Blue Lagoon costs US$1.

Fairy Hill & Winnifred Beach

Fairy Hill, 8 miles (13km) east of Port Antonio, is a small cliff-top hamlet. A dirt road leads steeply downhill to Winnifred Beach – a great place to hang with 'real' Jamaicans. The turn-off to the beach is opposite the Jamaica Crest Resort. You can catch a route taxi here from Port Antonio (US$1.50).

Mikuzi Vacation Cottages (☎ 978-4859; www .mikuzi.com; Hwy A4, Fairy Hill; garden/1-/2-bedroom cottage US$25/30/75), with privileged access to Winnifred Beach and beautifully landscaped grounds, is an economical place that can't be beat. Two tastefully appointed cottages and a small house are presided over by a warm and attentive caretaker. The cheaper garden cottage lacks a kitchen. Discounts are given for longer stays.

Boston Beach

Boston Beach, 9 miles (14.5km) east of Port Antonio, is a pocket-size beach shelving into jewel-like turquoise waters. High surf rolls into the bay, making this perhaps the best surfing spot in Jamaica; surfboards in various states of decay are available for rent on the beach.

Boston Beach is known for highly spiced jerk chickens and pork sizzling away on smoky barbecue pits along the roadside. Some contend that jerk was invented here. Also on the scene is the Maroon Prophet, a roots bush doctor selling his handmade tonic and blood cleanser, made from roots and bushes according to tradition. Here's to your health!

A route taxi from Port Antonio will cost you US$1.50.

Long Bay

Now that Negril (see p230) has lost its patina of countercultural credibility, free spirits look to Long Bay to assume the mantle of Jamaica's hippest hideaway. Set in a dramatic 1-mile-wide (1.5km) bay, the hamlet appeals to budget travelers and surfers, and has drawn a number of expats who have put down roots and opened guesthouses. Predictably, as Long Bay's reputation for laid-back charm continues to attract notice, developers have noticed too. At the time of research, construction of two high-rise hotels was about to begin.

Casual visitors should know that drugs are rife, and an aggressiveness toward foreign visitors has been sensed on past visits.

SLEEPING & EATING

Yahimba (☎ 402-4101; www.yahimba.com; cabañas US$55) These simple thatch-roofed, African-style cabañas situated on the beach next to Cool Runnings are sublimely copacetic. Each has a private bath, shower and double bed.

Villa Seascape (☎ 913-7762; Hwy A4; d US$50-60; **P**) This well-maintained guesthouse offers two buildings with a total of five modest, nicely furnished rooms with fans. Two rooms share a bath. Breakfast is included; other meals are prepared to order. The sea licks the walls of the veranda.

Cool Runnings Beach Bar & Grill (☎ 387-9305; meals US$5-8; ☒ lunch & dinner) This good-time joint on the beach is a good first stop; the proprietor represents local guesthouses and can help you find accommodations. The food is well prepared and tasty – all is made from scratch, including a wickedly rich mayonnaise. One of the signature dishes is a lovely coconut cream fish (US$8). On Saturday night there's a beach party playing old roots reggae and R&B.

Chill-Out (☎ 913-7171; meals US$4-10; ☒ lunch & dinner) Just down the beach from Cool Runnings is another popular thatched beachfront eatery and bar. Try the steamed fish and vegetables liberally seasoned with allspice (US$9). Sound-system parties are frequently held in the evenings.

GETTING THERE & AWAY
The fare to Long Bay from Port Antonio by route taxi is about US$3.

OCHO RIOS

pop 8200

Ocho Rios, situated 67 miles (108km) east of Montego Bay, is backed by green hills and fronted by the wide, scalloped stretch of Turtle Beach and a reef-sheltered harbor. 'Ochi,' as it is known, is a popular destination with cruise ships, which disgorge 400,000 passengers a year into its compact, charmless streets.

While the town itself is nothing to write home about, engaging nearby attractions, lively nightlife and well-developed infrastructure make Ocho Rios a serviceable base for exploring the island's fascinating northern coast.

Information

Bryan's Bookstores LTD (☎ 795-0705; Shop 12-15, Island Plaza) Has a wide range of titles about Jamaica, including maps.

Cable & Wireless (☎ 974-9906; Shop 13-15, Island Plaza) Offers long-distance calling.

CIBC (☎ 974-2824; 29 Main St) Has foreign exchange facilities and ATM.

Internet Jungle (☎ 974-9906; Shop 13-15, Island Plaza; Internet access per 15min/30min/1hr/all day US$2.50/5/10/20) In the Cable & Wireless office.

Jamaica Tourist Board (☎ 974-7705, 974-3866; fax 974-2586; Shop 3, Ocean Village Shopping Centre, Main St; 8:30am-5pm Mon-Thu, 8:30am-4pm Fri) This office doesn't offer much in the way of literature, but staff will spend time helping you suss out Ochi's transportation, lodging and attractions.

Police station (☎ 974-2533) Off DaCosta Dr, just east of the clock tower.

Post office (Main St; 8am-5pm Mon-Sat) Opposite the Ocho Rios Craft Park.

Scotiabank (☎ 974-2081; Main St) Has foreign exchange facilities and an ATM.

St Ann's Bay Hospital (☎ 972-2272) In St Ann's Bay, about 7 miles (11km) west of Ocho Rios. Your hotel's front desk can arrange a doctor's visit.

Dangers & Annoyances

Ocho Rios' biggest annoyance is the persistent entreaties of hustlers, who are especially thick around the clock tower and DaCosta Dr.

Avoid the area immediately behind the market south of the clock tower. Use caution at night anywhere, but particularly on James St, a poorly lit street with several nightspots and a hangout strip of ill repute.

Sights

To visit Jamaica and not climb **Dunn's River Falls** (☎ 974-5944; www.dunnsriverja.com; adult/child US$10/8; 8:30am-5pm), on the A3, 2 miles (3.2km) west of town, is like touring France without seeing the Eiffel Tower. Join hands in a daisy chain at the bottom and clamber up the tiers of limestone that stairstep 600ft (183m) down to the beach in a series of cascades and pools. The water is refreshingly cool and the falls are shaded by a tall rainforest.

Swimwear is essential. There are changing rooms and lockers (US$5) on the beach, as well as an orchid garden, children's playground, a crafts market, jerk stalls, snack bars and a restaurant. A warning: expect to be given the hard sell here by professional hustlers. Get here before 10am, when the tour buses arrive, or plan your visit for when the cruise ships aren't in town (Saturday to Tuesday).

The main beach is the long crescent of Ocho Rios Bay Beach, locally known as **Turtle Beach** (adult/child US$1/0.50), stretching east from Turtle Towers condominiums. There are changing rooms, water-sport concessionaires, and palms for shade. **Island Village Beach** (admission US$3; 6am-6pm), at the west end of Main St, is a peaceful, smaller beach with a complete range of water sports.

Shaw Park Gardens (☎ 974-2723; Shaw Park Rd; admission US$10; daily) is a tropical fantasia of ferns and bromeliads, palms and exotic shrubs, spread out over 25 acres (10 hectares) and centered on an 18th-century great house. Trails and wooden steps lead past waterfalls that tumble in terraces down the hillside. A viewing platform offers a bird's-eye vantage over Ocho Rios. There's a bar and restaurant. The gardens are signed from opposite the public library on the A3.

Reggae Xplosion (☎ 675-8895; admission US$7; 9am-5pm Mon-Fri, 10am-5pm Sat), at Island Village, is billed as an 'interactive reggae experience' and dedicated to Jamaica's modern musical heritage. The impressive museum is divided into *mento*, ska, reggae, dancehall and other sections, including one commemorating Bob Marley.

Activities

Virtually the entire shoreline east of Ocho Rios to Galina Point is fringed by a reef, and it's great for diving and snorkeling. You can arrange dives and snorkeling at most resorts or at **Watersports Enterprise** (☎ 974-2244; Turtle Beach; 1-/2-/4-tank dive US$45/70/140).

If you're after a round of golf, head to **Sandals Ocho Rios Golf & Country Club** (☎ 975-0119; Bonham Spring Rd; 9/18 holes US$70/100; 🕓 7:30am-5pm), 4 miles (6.5km) southeast of town and signed off of the A3.

See below for activity-based tours.

Tours

Chukka Cove Adventure Tours (☎ 927-2506; www .chukkacove.com; tours US$50-100) offers an invigorating menu of quality excursions including horseback ride 'n' swim, river tubing, 4WD safari, the Zion Bus Line to Nine Mile (see p222) and a unique forest canopy tour.

Hooves (☎ 972-0905; www.hoovesjamaica.com; tours US$55-100) leads several interesting horseback tours, including Heritage Beach Trail, Bush Doctor Mountain Trail and Rainforest River Trail.

Blue Mountain Bicycle Tours (☎ 974-7075; www .bmtoursja.com; adult/child US$/89/65) leads excellent full-day biking tours from Ocho Rios to the Blue Mountains, featuring a hair-raising mountain descent and a dip at a waterfall.

Festivals & Events

Ocho Rios Jazz Festival (June; ☎ 927-3544; www .ochoriosjazz.com) Top names in jazz, under the stars.

Hi Pro High Goal Family Tournament (August; ☎ 952-4370; shane@tobyresorts.com; St Ann Polo Club) Features Jamaica's best polo families in competition.

Sleeping

Ocho Rios and environs offers everything from simple guesthouses to opulent resorts.

BUDGET

Pencianna Guest House (☎ 974-5472; 3 Short Lane; d US$35; P) This downtown option reminded one reader of an Italian pension. The rooms are small yet immaculately kept, with shiny red tile floors and crisp linens. Some have shared baths. The owners prepare Jamaican meals from US$5.

Little Shaw Park Guest House (☎ 974-2177; littleshawpark_2000@yahoo.com; 21 Shaw Park Rd; d US$50, studio apt US$60; P ⛱) This trim place offers rooms amid 1.5 acres (0.6 hectares) of beautifully tended lawns and bougainvillea, with a gazebo and hammocks. There are several

spacious (though dark) cabins with homey decor, and well-lit studio apartments with nicer furnishings and cable TV. Meals are available by request.

MIDRANGE

Ocean Sands Resort (☎ 974-2605; www.caribbean coast.com/nhotels/oceansands; 14 James St; s/d US$45/55; P ⛱ 🅿) This attractive property has an oceanfront setting and its own pocket-size beach, with coral, at your doorstep. A tiny restaurant sits at the end of a wooden wharf. The 35 pleasant rooms have French doors that open onto private balconies. Rates include breakfast.

Fisherman's Point Resort (☎ 974-5317; fisherm anspoint@cwjamaica.com; s/d US$100/160; P ⛱ 🅿) Located near the cruise ship pier, this old favorite has 60 elegant apartments with kitchenettes, bamboo furnishings, satellite TV and private balconies. There's a bar and seafood restaurant; meal plans are available.

Sandcastles Resort (☎ 974-5626, 800-537-8483; sandcastles@cwjamaica.com; 120 Main St; d/tr US$125/135, 1-/2-bedroom ste US$160/200; P ✕ ⛱ 🖥 🅿) This pleasant and popular all-suite resort has studios and one- and two-bedroom suites in various configurations. All have cable TV and modern furnishings. There's a lively sports bar.

Hibiscus Lodge (☎ 974-2676; fax 974-1874; 87 Main St; standard/deluxe r US$126/138; P ✕ ⛱ 🖥 🅿) A well-run hotel perched on a breezy cliff-top setting amid lush grounds, this hotel offers spacious but modestly furnished rooms. There's a small cliff-top pool, an atmospheric bar, plus a fine restaurant.

Seville Manor (☎ 795-2901; fax 974-4054; 84 Main St; d/studio US$46/76; P ⛱) This small charmer tucked away off Main St has 28 rooms with cable TV, modern furnishings and a cozy ambience. It has a restaurant and bar.

TOP END

Royal Plantation Spa & Golf Resort (☎ 974-5601; www.royalplantation.com; s & d US$450-590, ste/villa US$1290/1450, all-inclusive s US$610-1610, d US$770-1930; P ✕ ⛱ 🖥 🅿) Nestled above its own private bay, this graceful resort offers 80 spacious oceanfront suites in six categories, all chock-full of amenities and Edwardian antique reproductions. Lush grounds cascade down to two beaches. Three restaurants, a full-service spa, tennis courts and water sports add to the sparkle.

Eating

As a major resort, Ochi offers a satisfying variety of restaurants from simple but hearty vegetarian fare to haute cuisine. The following restaurants are all within walking distance of downtown.

BUDGET

Bibibips Bar & Grill (☎ 974-7438; 93 Main St; meals US$6-12; ☺ breakfast, lunch & dinner) This breezy oceanfront bar and restaurant overlooks Mahogany Beach and serves chicken wings (US$6), crab, Cajun fries (US$5.50), burgers and the like.

Little Pub Sports Grill (☎ 974-2324; 59 Main St; meals US$5-10; ☺ lunch & dinner) This totally touristy yet enjoyable place serves good American breakfasts. An eclectic lunch and dinner menu is strong on steak and seafood at modest prices.

MIDRANGE

Veggie Kitchen & Health Food (☎ 974-5797; 11 Island Plaza; meals US$2-6; ☺ lunch & dinner) Healthy appetites rejoice! Here you'll get breakfasts such as plantain porridge, lunches such as brown stew with rice and peas; corn and veggie patties; ackee and gluten; and veggie burgers.

Passage to India (☎ 795-3182; 50 Main St; meals US$6-15; ☺ closed Mon) If curry is on the agenda, head here for airy rooftop dining, superb Indian and Indo-Chinese fusion cuisine, and a large vegetarian menu.

Ruins at the Falls (☎ 974-8888; 17 DaCosta Dr; meals US$9-30; ☺ lunch year-round, dinner Dec 15-Apr 15) This Jamaican-Chinese restaurant is set amid tropical gardens with a bridal-veil waterfall and pools. An all-inclusive lunchtime buffet (Monday to Saturday; US$14) includes beverages, live entertainment and garden tour.

Delish Restaurant & Café (☎ 974-6410; 16 Main St; meals US$7-14; ☺ closed Sun) This hip place offers a meld of international cuisines, natural juices and coffee drinks.

TOP END

Toscanini (☎ 975-4785; Harmony Hall; meals US$7-24; ☺ closed Mon) For some of Jamaica's most superlative fare, head to Harmony Hall, about 4 miles (6.5km) east of town on the A3, for this welcoming restaurant and its celebrated daily menu. You'll salivate over dishes like Roquefort salad (US$10) and

shrimp sautéed with garlic and hot pepper flambé with Appleton rum (US$18). Leave room for desserts such as strawberry tart or plum strudel (US$7). Treat yourself!

Drinking

Jimmy Buffett's Margaritaville (☎ 675-8800; Island Village; nightclub admission US$10-20) This ostentatious behemoth offers a boozy good time with its three bars, rooftop whirlpool tub and an endlessly entertaining water slide.

Ruins Pub (☎ 974-9712; 17 DaCosta Dr) This classy joint offers a peaceful environment for enjoying a quiet drink.

Entertainment

Island Village (☎ 974-8353; www.islandjamaica.com; cnr Main St & DaCosta Dr; adults Mon-Fri US$10, Sat & Sun US$5, children & seniors US$5) This contrived 'Jamaican coastal village' has a beach, upscale craft shops, movie theater, cyber center, Jimmy Buffett's Margaritaville (see above), Reggae Xplosion (see p219) and an amphitheater for live performances. The entrance fee includes a guided tour of Reggae Xplosion museum, plus live shows and use of the beach and facilities. Admission is free after 5pm.

Amnesia (☎ 974-2633; 70 Main St; admission US$5) The happening dance club.

Roofe Club (☎ 974-1042; 7 James Ave; admission US$3) The place to get down and dirty with the latest dancehall moves. It can get rough.

Shopping

Shopping is big business in Ocho Rios. There is a wide variety of duty-free shops located on Main St.

Wassi Art (☎ 974-5044; www.wassiart.com; Bougainvillea Dr; artworks US$6-4000; ☺ closed Sun) Here you'll witness scores of rising and established Jamaican masters creating exquisite works of art. To get here, take Milford Rd (A3) and watch for the signs.

Ocho Rios Craft Park (Main St) and **Dunn's River Craft Park** (Dunn's River Falls) have dozens of craft stalls.

Getting There & Away

Boscobel Aerodrome (☎ 975-3101) is 10 miles (16km) east of town No international service lands here. **Air Jamaica Express** (at Boscobel ☎ 726-1344, 888-359-2475) serves Ocho Rios with scheduled flights from Montego Bay, with connecting services.

Buses, coasters and route taxis arrive and depart Ocho Rios from the **transportation center** (Evelyn St); direct services to Montego Bay and Port Antonio operate throughout the day. To take a route taxi to Kingston, take the short ride to Fern Gully bus yard and transfer there. If you're coming from the east, you will be deposited at the taxi stand near One Love Park, up the hill from the harbor.

JUTA (☎ 974-2292) is the main taxi agency catering to tourists. A licensed taxi costs about US$90 per person between Montego Bay and Ocho Rios, and about US$80 between Ocho Rios and Kingston (US$100 to the airport).

Car rental rates are cheaper in Ocho Rios than elsewhere on the island, averaging US$50/300 for the day/week.

Island Car Rentals (☎ 974-2334; www.islandcar rentals.com; Main St)

Salem Car Rentals (☎ 974-0786; www.salemcar rentals.com; 7 Sand Castles Complex)

Getting Around

Ocho Rios has no bus service within town. Coasters and route taxis ply Main St and the coast road (US$1 for short hauls; US$4 to Boscobel Aerodrome).

Government-established licensed taxi fares from downtown include: Dunn's River (US$25), Firefly (US$55), Prospect Plantation (US$22) and Shaw Park Gardens (US$22).

AROUND OCHO RIOS
Nine Mile

Despite its totally out-of-the-way location 40 miles (64.5km) south of Ocho Rios, the village of Nine Mile is firmly on the tourist map for pilgrimages to Bob Marley's birth site and resting place. At the **Nine Mile Museum** (☎ 999-7003; ninemilejamaica.com; admission US$12; ☯ 8am-5:30pm), a Rastafarian guide leads pilgrims to the hut – now festooned with devotional graffiti – where the reggae god spent his early years. Another highlight is 'inspiration stone' (or 'Mt Zion Rock') on which Marley sat and learned to play guitar. Marley's body lies buried along with his guitar in an 8ft-tall (2.4m) oblong marble mausoleum inside a tiny church of traditional Ethiopian design.

Each year on February 6, this is the site of Bob Marley's birthday celebration – fans from around the world make the trek to play and hear music throughout the night.

Getting to Nine Mile is no simple matter. The site is extremely secluded, but all cab drivers know the route (haggle hard for a reasonable fare; US$75 is common). A far easier way to visit is via Chukka Cove's '**Zion Bus Line' tour** (☎ 927-2506; www.chukkacove.com), which departs from Ocho Rios (see p220).

Firefly

About 20 miles (32km) east of Ocho Rios is **Firefly** (☎ 997-7201; Port Maria, St Mary; admission US$10; ☯ closed Sat & Sun), which makes for one of the most interesting excursions in Jamaica. The cottage, set amid wide lawns high atop a hill, was the home of Sir Noel Coward, the English playwright, songwriter, actor and wit. Today the house is a museum, looking just as it did on Sunday, February 28, 1965, the day the Queen Mother visited. Coward lies buried beneath a plain white marble slab on the wide lawns where he entertained so many illustrious stars of stage and screen. Firefly is well signed along three different routes from the A3.

MONTEGO BAY & AROUND

Montego Bay is the second-largest city on the island and Jamaica's most important tourist resort. The region boasts a greater concentration of well-preserved colonial houses than any other, some of which are working plantations that offer guided tours. Several championship golf courses, horse stables and the island's best shopping add to the region's appeal.

MONTEGO BAY

pop 120,000

The thriving port city of Montego Bay (MoBay) is resort Jamaica at its purest and most puerile, where a crowded tourist mishmash of one-way streets full of honking cars and pedestrians almost obscures the scintillating beaches, the golf courses, the historic houses and the mountain-village life going on behind the narrow coastal strip.

Despite MoBay's reputation as a hustlers' city, there are attractions that make it worth being asked 'Hey, Jake! Smoke?' every few steps. Many admirable Georgian stone buildings and timber houses still stand downtown, and there is an excellent variety of arts and crafts. Every kind of water sport is offered, although most of the good beaches are the private domains of resort hotels.

Those seeking a budget holiday with a lively nightlife, and shops and markets packed with bargains, will be right at home, as will those seeking to spend a week idly sunning at an all-inclusive upmarket resort. And for those who want to venture deeper into the mysteries of Jamaica, MoBay's locale on the central northwestern coast makes a serviceable base from which to conduct your explorations.

Information

BOOKSTORES

Sangster's Bookshop (☎ 952-0319; 2 St James St) The largest bookstore in town, albeit only modestly stocked.

EMERGENCY

Fire (☎ 952-2311)

INTERNET ACCESS

Cyber Shores (☎ 971-8907; Gloucester Ave; per 15min/1hr US$2/7.50; 🕓 8am-8:30pm) At Doctor's Cave Beach, has a wireless network that serves the beach.

MEDICAL SERVICES

Cornwall Regional Hospital (☎ 952-5100; Mt Salem Rd) Has a 24-hour emergency room.

MONEY

Exchange bureau (🕓 24hr) In the arrival hall at Sangster International Airport.

FX Trader (☎ 952-3171; 37 Gloucester Ave) At the Pelican (p228); one of a number of money exchange bureaus downtown.

POST

Post office (☎ 979-5137; Gloucester Ave; 🕓 8am-5pm Mon-Fri) This branch office is on the Hip Strip, adjacent to Doctor's Cave Beach Hotel.

TOURIST INFORMATION

Jamaica Tourist Board Airport (☎ 952-3009); Cornwall Beach (🕓 8:30am-4:30pm Mon-Fri, 9am-1pm Sat); Gloucester Ave (☎ 952-4425; fax 952-3587) Opening hours are variable.

Official Visitors Guide (www.montego-bay-jamaica.com) An up-to-date online resource to MoBay and environs.

Dangers & Annoyances

Montego Bay has a reputation for tourist harassment by hustlers. Visitors can expect to be approached in none-too-subtle terms by locals offering their services, and the barrage of young men selling drugs is a wearying constant. Uniformed members of the Montego Bay Resort Patrol police the strip. Downtown is not patrolled, and you need to keep your wits about you.

Sights

The bustling, cobbled **Sam Sharpe Sq** is centered on a small bronze fountain dedicated to Captain J Kerr, a pioneer in the banana trade. The square is named for national hero, the Right Excellent Samuel Sharpe (1801–32), leader of the 1831 Christmas Rebellion (see the boxed text, p224). At the square's northwest corner is the **National Heroes Monument**, an impressive statue of Paul Bogle and Sam Sharpe, Bible in hand, speaking to three admiring listeners cast in bronze. Also on the northwest corner is the **Cage**, a tiny cut-stone and brick building built in 1806 as a lockup.

At the southwest corner is the copper-domed **Civic Centre**, a handsome colonial-style cut-stone building on the site of the ruined colonial courthouse. It contains the **Museum of St James** (☎ 971-9417; admission US$3; 🕓 9:30am-4:30pm Tue-Thu, 9:30am-3:30pm Fri, 10:30am-2:30pm Sat), with relics and other exhibits tracing local history from Taino days to the recent past.

Many of the most interesting buildings in town are clustered along Church St. The highlight is **St James Parish Church** (☎ 952-2775; Church St), regarded as the finest church on the island. Inside, you can view the beautiful interior, which contains a stunning

---

PREACHING RESISTANCE

The week-long Christmas Rebellion that began on Kensington Estate on December 27, 1831, and engulfed much of the Montego Bay region was the most serious slave revolt to rock colonial Jamaica. Its impact and the public outcry over the terrible retribution that followed were catalysts for the British Parliament passing the Abolition Bill in 1834.

The instigator of the revolt was Samuel Sharpe (1801–32), the slave of a Montego Bay solicitor. Sharpe, a deacon of Montego Bay's Burchell Baptist Church, used his forum to encourage passive rebellion.

In 1831, Sharpe counseled fellow slaves to refuse to work during the Christmas holidays. Word of the secret, passive rebellion spread throughout St James and neighboring parishes. The rebellion turned into a violent conflict when the Kensington Estate was set on fire. Soon, plantations and great houses throughout northwest Jamaica were ablaze, and Sharpe's noble plan was usurped by wholesale violence. Fourteen colonialists were murdered before colonial authorities suppressed the revolt. Swift and cruel retribution followed.

More than 1000 slaves were killed. Day after day for six weeks following the revolt's suppression, magistrates of the Montego Bay Courthouse handed down death sentences to scores of slaves, who were hanged two at a time, among them 'Daddy' Sam Sharpe. He was later named a national hero.

---

stained-glass window behind the altar and a number of notable marble monuments.

Activities

Doctor's Cave Beach (☎ 952-2566; adult/child US$5/2.50; ⏰ 8:30am-6pm) is Montego Bay's most excellent beach. There's a food court, Internet café, grill bar, gift shop and water sports, plus changing rooms.

Walter Fletcher Beach, at the south end of Gloucester Ave, is the venue for the **Aquasol Theme Park** (☎ 940-1344; adult/child US$5/3; ⏰ 9am-10pm), with netball, volleyball, tennis courts, water sports, the MoBay 500 go-cart track and Voyage Sports Bar & Grill. It rents out lockers, beach mats, and chairs and umbrellas. Reggae parties are a regularly scheduled attraction.

Montego Bay is world-renowned for **golf**; three championship courses are east of town in Ironshore, and a fourth course, at Tryall, is a 30-minute journey west. See the boxed text, p228.

Nature lovers won't want to miss the **Montego Bay Marine Park** for its coral reefs, rich flora and fauna, and shoreline mangroves. The park extends from the eastern end of Sangster International Airport westward (almost 6 miles; 9.5km) to the Great River, encompassing the mangroves of **Bogue Lagoon**. You can set out with a guide to spot herons, egrets, pelicans and waterfowl, while below, in the tannin-stained waters, juven-

ile barracudas, tarpon, snapper, crabs and lobsters swim and crawl. Authority is vested in the **Montego Bay Marine Park Trust** (MBMPT; ☎ 971-8082; www.montego-bay-jamaica.com/mbmp; Pier 1, off Howard Cooke Dr). MBMPT maintains a meager **Resource Centre** (⏰ 9am-5pm Mon-Fri) with a library on the vital ecosystem.

Here you will also fine first-rate diving and snorkeling with a variety of sites. These range from teeming patch reefs to awe-inspiring walls that begin in as little as 35ft (11m) of water. **Resort Divers** (☎ 953-9699, 940-1183; www.resortdivers.com; Holiday Inn, Rose Hall Rd; 4-/5-dive package US$140/180, 'discover scuba' package US$90; certification US$395) offers dives and certification courses and rents out equipment.

The waters off of Jamaica's north coast offer spectacular **game fishing**. Beyond the north-shore reefs, the ocean floor plummets for thousands of feet. Deep-water game fish use the abyss – known as 'Marlin Alley' – as a migratory freeway. Half- and full-day charters can be booked through hotels, at Pier 1 Marina, or from **Rhapsody Cruises** (☎ 979-0102; Shop 204, Chatwick Plaza).

Rhapsody also offers three-hour **chartered cruises** (US$55; ⏰ 10am-1pm & 3-6pm) with an open bar and a snorkeling stop in the Marine Park. A bus will pick you up at your hotel.

Festivals & Events

Montego Bay's most celebrated annual events are its two high-profile music festivals.

Red Stripe Reggae Sumfest (July; ☎ 953-4573; www
.reggaesumfest.com; weekend/event pass US$76/165) Ja-
maica's premier reggae festival typically includes more than
50 world-class reggae artists. It starts with a beach party
on Walter Fletcher Beach, followed by four theme nights,
including a 'street jam' on Gloucester Ave.

Air Jamaica Jazz & Blues Festival (late January;
☎ 888-359-2475, 800-523-5585; www.airjamaica.com;
single night/event pass US$50/135) Brings internationally
acclaimed acts to Cinnamon Hill near Rose Hall for three
nights of music under the stars.

Sleeping

Montego Bay boasts the largest number of
guest rooms of any resort area in Jamaica.
Most of the Bay's hotels are clustered along
Gloucester Ave; deluxe resorts nestle on
their own beaches east of town at Ironshore
and Mahoe Bay.

BUDGET

Linkage Guest House (☎ 952-4546, 979-0308; 32
Church St; s/d US$18/20, r with private bath US$25) Located downtown far away from the strip is
this backpackers favorite offering 15 rooms
in an old wooden house. They're simple
but clean and have fans, louvered windows,
and hot water in the shared baths. Meals
are served. The owners also offer Maroon
heritage tours (US$50).

Caribic House (☎ 979-6073; fax 979-0322; 69 Gloucester Ave; standard s/d US$45/51, garden view US$49/57,
superior ocean view US$59/69; ☒) This compact,
no-frills option directly opposite Doctor's
Cave Beach is a favorite of budget-minded
Europeans. It has 15 basic rooms with refrigerators and large baths, and one 'superior' room with kitchen, dining room and
three beds.

MIDRANGE

Toby Resorts (☎ 952-4370; www.tobyresorts.com;
cnr Gloucester Ave & Sunset Blvd, PO Box 467; s/d/tr
US$85/98/110; ℗ ☒ ☒) This pleasant resort
offers 72 rooms surrounding a pool and
sundeck with bar. Rooms are nicely furnished with faux-marble floors and pine-
and-rattan furniture, plus phones. Most
have small verandas. Facilities include a
games room and two bars.

Coral Cliff Hotel (☎ 952-4130; www.coralcliff
jamaica.com; 165 Gloucester Ave, PO Box 253; superior s/d/tr
US$110/130/140, d/tr ste US$180/200; ℗ ☒ ☒ ☒)
This 21-room hotel, attached to the Coral
Cliff Gaming Lounge, offers nine centenary

rooms with a yesteryear charm, 10 modern
rooms furbished with appealing tropical
decor, and two suites in elegant plantation
style with spacious balconies. There's an
atmospheric restaurant plus flamboyant
video-slot lounge.

Knightwick House (☎ 952-2988; tapas45@hotmail
.com; Corniche Rd; s US$45, d US$65-70; ℗ ☒) Behind and above Coral Cliff, this delightful
B&B has terra-cotta floors, wrought-iron
railings, abundant artwork and three ap-
pealingly furnished bedrooms that are well
lit and airy. Each has a balcony. Its restaurant, Tapas (see p228), is justly acclaimed.
Rates include full breakfast.

Buccaneer Beach (☎ 952-6489; fax 979-2580; 7
Kent Ave; r standard/ocean view US$79/88; ℗ ☒ ☒)
This small, modest property has a homey
feel. Its 51 air-con rooms have tile floors,
phones, cable TVs and safety boxes, plus
large balconies. The reclusive location at
the end of Kent Ave is a five-minute walk
from Gloucester Ave.

Ramparts Inn (☎ 979-5258; fax 979-5259; 5 Ramparts Close; d US$50; ℗ ☒ ☒) This pleasantly
atmospheric inn on Miranda Hill offers 10
rooms boasting lots of dark timber and natural stone. Its intimate bar and the TV lounge,
which serves as a dining room, are exquisitely old world English. The small pool is a
satisfying place to catch some sunrays.

Doctor's Cave Beach Hotel (☎ 952-4355; www
.doctorscave.com; PO Box 94; s/d standard US$110/115,
superior US$125/130, ste US$145; ℗ ☒ ☒ ☒) The
hotel's labyrinthine corridors lead to well-
appointed rooms and suites decorated in
tropical themes. The lush gardens at the
back are tight up against the cliff face,
where there's a whirlpool. A splendid restaurant opens onto a small swimming pool
and has live entertainment. The Grotto Bar
hosts a lively cocktail party on Tuesday and
Saturday from 6pm to 7pm.

TOP END

Sunset Beach Resort & Spa (☎ 979-8800, 800-
888-1199; www.sunsetbeachjamaica.com; Sunset Dr; d
US$250-310, ste $450; ℗ ☒ ☒ ☒) Located at
the end of the Montego Freeport Peninsula,
this 420-room, twin high-rise, upscale all-
inclusive resort offers five categories of
rooms with ocean or bay view, all with
one king-sized or two double four-poster
mahogany beds. The vast lobby opens to a
massive pool bar.

MONTEGO BAY

JAMAICA

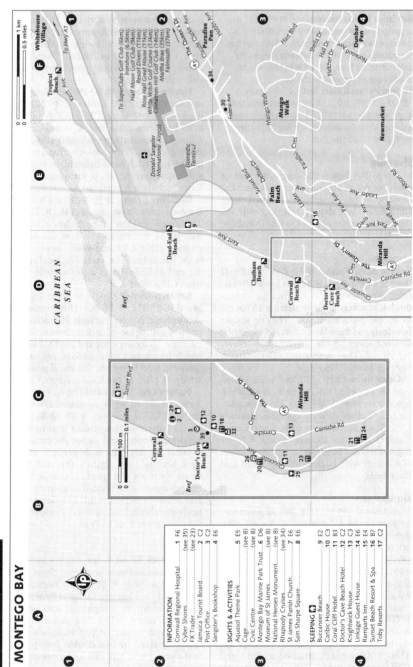

To Whitehouse Village
To Hwy A1

To SuperClubs Golf Club (6km);
Ironshore (6.5km);
Half Moon Golf Club (9km);
Resort Divers (11km);
Rose Hall Great House (11km);
White Witch Golf Course (13km);
Cinnamon Hill Great House (14km);
Cinnamon Hill/Rose Hall (25km);
Martha Brae (37km);
Falmouth (37km)

CARIBBEAN SEA

Reef

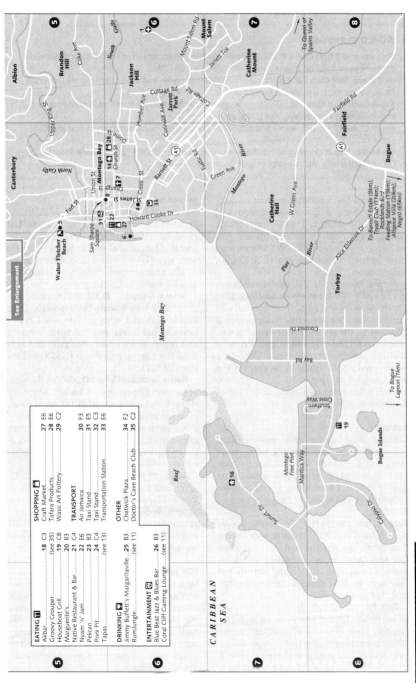

See Enlargement

EATING 🍴
Akbar..................................18 C3
Groovy Grouper..................(see 35)
Houseboat Grill..................19 C8
Marguerite's........................20 B3
Native Restaurant & Bar.......21 C4
Nyam 'n' Jam.....................22 E6
Pelican...............................23 B3
Pork Pit..............................24 C4
Tapas.................................(see 13)

DRINKING 🍸
Jimmy Buffett's Margaritaville..25 B3
Rumjungle..........................26 B3

ENTERTAINMENT 🎭
Blue Beat Jazz & Blues Bar....26 B3
Coral Cliff Gaming Lounge.....(see 11)

SHOPPING 🛍
Craft Market......................27 E6
Tafara Products...................28 E6
Wassi Art Pottery................29 C2

TRANSPORT
Air Jamaica........................30 F3
Taxi Stand.........................31 E5
Taxi Stand.........................32 C3
Transportation Station.........33 E6

OTHER
Chatwick Plaza....................34 F2
Doctor's Cave Beach Club......35 C2

JAMAICA

WORLD CLASS GOLF

Cinnamon Hill Golf Club (☎ 953-2650; www.wyndham-jamaica.com) Six miles (9.5km) east of MoBay, this impressive recent arrival has a course playing from sea level to 900ft (274m).

Half Moon Golf Club (☎ 953-3105; www.jamaicagolfresort.com) About 3 miles (5km) east of Ironshore this classic, spacious course is sculpted from coastal foothills.

SuperClubs Golf Club (☎ 953-2800; www.superclubs.com/activities/golf/sc_golf.asp) Nestled among the verdant hills rising from Ironshore, 700ft (214m) above sea level.

Tryall Club (☎ 956-5681; www.tryallclub.com) A picturesque championship course with a unique layout, just east of Ironshore.

White Witch Golf Course (☎ 953-2800; www.ritzcarlton.com/resorts/rose_hall_jamaica/golf) At the Ritz-Carlton Rose Hall hotel, this truly gorgeous option boasts panoramic views.

The price tag is justified by four restaurants, five bars, a disco, slot casino and nightly entertainment, plus four tennis courts, three pools, a state-of-the-art gym and spa, a high-tech business center, and three beaches with water sports. A Kiddies Club caters to families.

Allspice Villa (☎ 912-3623; www.allspicevilla.com; Rock Pleasant Mt; 1-/2-bedroom ste incl breakfast US$200/375; P 🖳 🖭) Nestled high in the hills 20 minutes from MoBay is this glorious recent addition to the thriving villa rental scene, offering a reclusive romantic getaway with jaw-dropping panoramic views. There is a lovely pool and a spacious Jacuzzi on the veranda, and the breakfast is sumptuous. There's a three-day minimum, and reservations are required.

Eating

Montego Bay has the most cosmopolitan cuisine scene in all of Jamaica, with everything from roadside jerk chicken to nouvelle Jamaican dining. Most restaurants double as bars, encouraging guests to make a night of it.

BUDGET

Nyam 'n' Jam (☎ 952-1922; 17 Harbour St; breakfast US$5, lunch or dinner US$8; 🕑 breakfast, lunch & dinner) This local fave has the real deal Jamaican fare and daily specials including standards like jerk meat, and callaloo and saltfish, but also more esoteric choices like cow mouth, cow foot and oxtail.

Pork Pit (☎ 952-1046; 27 Gloucester Ave; meals US$3-7; 🕑 lunch & dinner) The Pork Pit is world-famous. Here you eat at open-air picnic tables beneath a shade tree. Finger-lickin' jerk chicken and pork costs from US$3 with yams 'festival,' and sweet potatoes extra.

MIDRANGE

Pelican (☎ 952-3171; Gloucester Ave; meals US$6-12; 🕑 breakfast, lunch & dinner; ✗) This is a steadfast good-value favorite with upscale locals. Its menu of Jamaican dishes includes stew peas with rice (US$6) and it also serves sirloin steaks and seafood. Take a sweater. The Sunday buffet is US$12.

Groovy Grouper (☎ 952-3680; meals US$6-14; 🕑 breakfast, lunch & dinner) At Doctor's Cave Beach Club and open till late, the Groovy Grouper has a fabulous beachside location and serves snacks, Jamaican fare, and seafood from *escoveitched* fish (US$8) to lobster (US$21).

Native Restaurant & Bar (☎ 979-2769; 29 Gloucester Ave; meals US$6-18; 🕑 lunch & dinner) Modestly elegant and recommended for good food, pleasant ambience and fair prices. It offers a free hotel shuttle. The menu ranges from salads to classic Jamaican dishes and vegetarian options (US$6 to US$8) to sumptuous seafood feasts (US$8 to US$18).

Akbar (☎ 957-0113; 71 Gloucester Ave; meals US$7-18; 🕑 lunch & dinner) Opposite Doctor's Cave Beach Club, Akbar is recommended for superb Indian cuisine and tremendous atmosphere. It offers a reasonably priced and broad menu that includes tandoori and vegetarian dishes.

TOP END

Tapas (☎ 952-2988; Corniche Rd; meals US$8-22; 🕑 dinner) Located on the veranda of Knightwick House (p225) and behind Coral Cliff Gaming Lounge, this excellent restaurant bills itself as 'where the chefs eat.' The changing creative menu features mouthwatering dishes such as snapper Camembert, lamb tzatziki and smoked marlin soup.

Marguerite's (☎ 952-4777; Gloucester Ave; meals US$8-33; ☼ dinner) Adjoining Margaritaville (see below), this is a great place to watch the sunset over cocktails, followed by dinner on the elegant cliff-top patio. The pricey menu edges toward nouvelle Jamaican, but also includes sirloin steak and a seafood platter (US$33).

Houseboat Grill (☎ 979-8845; houseboat@cwjamaica.com; Southern Cross Blvd; meals US$12-32; ☼ dinner Tue-Sun) Anchored in Bogue Bay at Montego Bay Freeport is one of Jamaica's topnotch restaurants, offering warm ambience and a changing menu of eclectic Caribbean fusion cuisine. You can dine inside, or reclusively out on the sundeck. Reservations are recommended on weekends.

Drinking

Jimmy Buffett's Margaritaville (☎ 952-4777; Gloucester Ave; admission after 10pm US$5) This wildly popular place claims to have 'put the hip into the Hip Strip'…who woulda thunk that anything having to do with Jimmy Buffett could obtain a cachet of cool? Four open-air bars, 15 big-screen TVs, and dance floors on decks overhanging the water offer plenty of diversion.

RumJungle (☎ 952-4130; Gloucester Ave) In the Coral Cliff Gaming Lounge (below) and offering a nightly cabaret, this is MoBay's most atmospheric bar.

Entertainment

Blue Beat Jazz & Blues Bar (☎ 952-4777; Gloucester Ave) Montego Bay's first martini jazz and blues bar offers sophisticated entertainment and Asian-Caribbean fusion cuisine. It's next to Marguerite's restaurant (above).

Coral Cliff Gaming Lounge (☎ 952-4130; Gloucester Ave; ☼ 24hr) This medium-size gamblers haunt has over 100 video-slot machines, big-screen TVs and free drinks, with fashion shows, cabarets and/or live jazz nightly.

Shopping

MoBay's streets spill over with stalls selling wooden carvings, straw items, jewelry, ganja pipes, T-shirts and other touristy items. For the largest selection, head to the downtown **Craft Market** (Harbour St) that extends for three blocks between Barnett and Market Sts.

Tafara Products (☎ 952-3899; 36 Church St) An African/Rastafarian cultural center selling books, arts and crafts, and natural foods.

Wassi Art Pottery (☎ 952-6698; St James Plaza) Magnificent handcrafted pottery.

Getting There & Around

Air Jamaica (☎ 922-4661, in the US 800-523-5585; 9 Queen's Dr) operates scheduled flights between MoBay's Donald Sangster International Airport, Kingston's Norman Manley International Airport and Tinson Pen Aerodrome, and Ocho Rios.

TimAir (☎ 952-2516, 979-1114; www.timair.net) air taxi service connects Montego Bay with Negril, Ocho Rios, Port Antonio, Kingston and Mandeville.

Buses, coasters and route taxis arrive and depart from the **transportation station** (Barnett St), at the south end of St James St.

Montego Bay Metro Line (☎ 952-5500; 19A Union St) links MoBay with suburbs and outlying towns; the fare is US$0.50.

Taxi stands are opposite Doctor's Cave Beach and downtown at the junction of market and Strand Sts, and by the bus terminal. The fare from the airport to Gloucester Ave is US$10.

These rental car companies have offices at Donald Sangster:

Avis (☎ 952-0762)

Budget (☎ 952-3838)

Hertz (☎ 979-0438)

Island Rental Car (☎ 952-5771)

AROUND MONTEGO BAY
Barnett Estate

The sea of sugarcane south of Montego Bay is part of **Barnett Estate** (☎ 952-2382; Granville Main Rd; ☼ 9:30am-5pm), a plantation owned and operated since 1755 by one of Jamaica's preeminent families, the Kerr-Jarretts. On the grounds, the **Bellfield Great House** (☎ 952-2382; prearranged tours US$10; ☼ 10am-5pm), built in 1735, has been restored and is now a showcase of 18th-century colonial living. The estate is on Fairfield Rd, about 800yd (730m) east of Doctor's Hospital. It's poorly signed: take the right turn at the Y-fork marked for Day-O Plantation, then turn right at Granville Police Station.

Rose Hall Great House

This **mansion** (☎ 953-2323; adult/child under 12 US$15/10; ☼ 9am-6pm), with its commanding hilltop position 2 miles (3.2km) east of Ironshore, is the most famous great house in Jamaica. Part of the attraction is the legend of Annie Palmer, the 'White Witch of Rose Hall,' a multiple murderer said to haunt the house. Her bedroom upstairs is

JAMAICA

decorated in crimson silk brocades. The cellars now house an old-English-style pub and a well-stocked gift shop. There's also a snack bar.

To get here, take a charter taxi (US$25), or a route taxi from the Barnett St Transportation Station in Montego Bay (US$1) and walk 1 mile (1.6km) up from the main road. Alternately, you can arrange a tour at any hotel.

Falmouth

Few other towns in Jamaica have retained their original architecture to the same degree as Falmouth, which has a faded Georgian splendor. The city, 23 miles (37km) east of Montego Bay, has been the capital of Trelawny parish since 1790. On weekends, farmers come from miles around to sell their produce, recalling the days when Falmouth was Jamaica's major port for the export of rum, molasses and sugar.

Route taxis leave for Falmouth from the Barnett St Transportation Station in Montego Bay (US$2) several times each day.

Martha Brae

Most visitors come to this small village, 2 miles (3.2km) due south of Falmouth, for the exhilarating 1½-hour **rafting** trip on the Martha Brae River. Long bamboo rafts poled by a skilled guide cruise down the river and stop at 'Tarzan's Corner' for a swing and swim in a calm pool. Trips begin from Rafter's Village, about 1 mile (1.6km) south of Martha Brae. A raft trip costs US$60 per raft (one or two people). Contact **River Raft Ltd** (☎ 952-0889; www.jamaicarafting.com). Remember to tip your raft guide.

Route taxis make the 10-minute ride from Falmouth to Martha Brae during daylight hours on a continuous basis (US$0.75). There are also regular buses.

Rocklands Bird Feeding Station

You don't have to be a bird nerd to love **Rocklands** (☎ 952-2009; admission US$8; ◷ 9am-5pm), where hummingbirds, saffron finches and many other birds come to feed from your hand. You can visit through a hotel-sponsored tour, or by private cab or rental car. The half-mile (800m) road leading to the sanctuary is rough. The turn-off from the B8 is 200yd (182m) south of the signed turn-off for Lethe.

NEGRIL & THE WEST

The highlight of the wild west coast is Negril, Jamaica's capital of cool and casual. Negril nestles at the westernmost tip of Jamaica, providing a grandstand seat for sunsets. It also boasts superb coral reefs that make for excellent scuba diving, and a large swamp area – the Great Morass – that is an ecotour haven.

NEGRIL
pop 3000

Negril, 40 miles (65km) west of Montego Bay, is Jamaica's fastest-growing resort and the vortex around which the island's fun-in-the-sun vacation life whirls. Despite phenomenal growth in recent years, Negril is still more laid-back than anywhere else in Jamaica (it's one of the few places where you can tan the whole booty). You'll probably interact with locals more here than in other resort areas given that woodcarvers hawk their crafts on the beach, makeshift stalls selling health foods and jerk-pork line the roads and mellow greetings are proffered freely by locals. And although magic-mushroom omelettes show up on restaurant menus, you don't need one to consider sunsets over Negril's long beach to be hallucinogenic.

Orientation

Negril is divided in two by the South Negril River, with Long Bay to the north and West End to the south. The apex is Negril Village, which lies immediately south of the river and is centered on a small roundabout – Negril Sq – from which Norman Manley Blvd leads north, West End Rd leads south and Sheffield Rd goes east and becomes the A2, which leads to Savanna-la-Mar, 19 miles (31km) away.

Information

Easy Rock Internet Café (☎ 957-0671; West End Rd; per hr US$5) The most pleasant and personable place to surf the digital wave.

Jamaica Tourist Board/TPDCo (☎ 957-4803, 957-9314; Times Sq Plaza, PO Box 2989, Negril PO; ◷ 9am-5pm Mon-Fri)

Negril Beach Medical Center (☎ 957-4888; fax 957-4347; Norman Manley Blvd; ◷ 9am-5pm, doctors on call 24hr) Has a laboratory that's open Tuesday and Friday.

Police station (☎ 957-4268; Sheffield Rd)
Post office (☎ 957-9654; West End Rd) Between A Fi Wi Plaza and King's Plaza.
Scotiabank (☎ 957-4236) Fifty yards (45.5m) West of Negril Plaza; has foreign exchange service and an ATM.
Top Spot (☎ 957-4542) In Sunshine Village, is well stocked with international publications.

Sights & Activities

The blindingly white, world-famous 7-mile-long (11km) beach of **Long Bay** is Negril's main claim to fame. The beach draws gigolos and hustlers offering everything from sex to aloe massages and, always, 'sensi.' 'Pssst! Bredda, you want ganja? Negril de place to get high, mon!' Tourist police now patrol the beach, but by law all Jamaican beaches must permit public access, so the hustlers are free to roam. Water-sports concessions line the beach. By night, this section is laden with the blast of reggae from disco bars.

Booby Cay is a small and lovely island half a mile (800m) offshore from Rutland Point in Long Bay. The island is named for the seabirds that nest there, but the beautiful coral beach is the main draw. Water-sports concessionaires can arrange boats for about US$25 round-trip.

Three miles (5km) south of Negril Village, the gleaming-white, 66ft-tall (20m) **Negril Lighthouse** (West End Rd; admission free; ☉ 9am-sunset) illuminates the westernmost point of Jamaica. Wilson Johnson, the superintendent, will gladly lead the way up the 103 stairs for a bird's-eye view of the coast.

The waters off of Negril are usually mirror-calm – ideal for all kinds of **water sports**. Numerous concessions along the beach rent out jet skis (about US$40 for 30 minutes), plus sea kayaks, sailboards and Sunfish (about US$15 per hour). They also offer waterskiing (US$25 for 30 minutes) and banana-boat rides (using an inflatable banana-shaped raft towed by a speedboat; US$15).

Negril offers extensive offshore reefs and cliffs with grottoes, with shallow reefs perfect for **scuba diving** and **snorkeling**. Visibility often exceeds 100ft (30m), and seas are dependably calm. Most dives are in 35ft to 75ft (10.5m to 22.5m) of water. Expect to pay about US$5 an hour for masks and fins from concession stands on the beach. Try the **Negril Scuba Centre** (☎ 957-4425; neg .scuba.center@cwjamaica.com; West End Rd; 1-/2-tank dive US$30/55).

Negril's waters are teeming with tuna, blue marlin, wahoo and sailfish and provide excellent action for **sport fishing** enthusiasts. **Stanley's Deep Sea Fishing** (☎ 957-0667; deepseafishing@cwjamaica.com) offers custom fishing trip charters (up to six people for four/eight hours costs US$400/700).

The Negril Hills provide excellent terrain for rip-roaring mountain biking. **Rusty's X-Cellent Adventures** (☎ 957-0155; rustynegril@hotmail .com; tours US$40) offers guided bike tours.

Festivals & Events

Negril Music Festival (mid-March; ☎ 968-9356) A beach bash featuring leading Jamaican and international reggae stars, calypso artists and other musicians.
Spring Break Jamaica Beachfest (mid-April) Negril is thronged for this exercise in Bacchanalian excess.

Sleeping

As with Montego Bay, Negril boasts a stunning array of accommodations. Budget travelers are particularly spoiled for choice with scores of places charging less than US$75 per night and many at half that sum. Many hotels enjoy a beach location, but up on the cliffs of the West End are Negril's most remarkable digs.

LONG BAY

Negril Yoga Centre (☎ 957-4397; www.negrilyoga .com; Norman Manley Blvd; r US$38-70; ⊠ 🎇) The eight rustic yet quite atmospheric rooms and cottages – most with refrigerators and fans – surround an open-air, thatched, wood-floored yoga center set in a garden. Options range from a two-story, Thai-style wooden cabin to an adobe farmer's cottage; all are pleasingly if modestly furnished. The staff make their own yogurt, cheese and sprouts and cook on request. Yoga classes are offered (guests/visitors US$8/10), as is massage (US$60). There's a communal kitchen. This is a good option for women traveling alone and for families with children.

Westport Cottages (☎ 957-4736, 307-5466; Norman Manley Blvd; s/d US$15/20) This offbeat place is popular with the laid-back backpacking crowd (amiable owner Joseph Mathews says it is approved for 'smoke-friendly heartical people'). Joseph has 17 very rustic huts with well-kept outside toilet and cold shower, plus mosquito nets and fans. Newer rooms to the rear are preferred. A well-equipped communal kitchen is available; bicycles

(US$5 per day) and snorkeling equipment are provided.

White Sands (☎ 957-4291; www.whitesandsjamaica.com; standard/deluxe r US$72/101, 1-bedroom apt US$141, villa US$394; ❌ ▣) The best value on the beach is this attractive property where options range from simple yet elegant one-bedroom octagonal units to a four-bedroom, four-bath villa (sleeping eight people) with its own pool. The tiled units sit in a well maintained garden with a pool. The parrot recites dub poetry.

Sea Splash Resort (☎ 957-4041, 800-254-2786; www.seasplash.com; standard/1-/2- bedroom ste US$99/179/199; ℗ ❌ ▣) At this elegant resort on the beach the suites are tastefully appointed, each with large balcony, fully equipped kitchenette, screened-off bedroom and plenty of amenities. There is a handsome beach bar, and guests gain access to the facilities at the nearby Swept Away resort.

Country Country (☎ 957-4273; www.countrynegril.com; standard/deluxe cottages US$155/175; ❌) This color-crazy charmer has that mellow Negril vibe down cold. On offer are 14 air-con wooden cottages with gingerbread trim and fretwork; hot pastels dominate and lend a chic warmth. Some have king-size beds and separate sitting areas.

WEST END

Blue Cave Castle (☎ 957-4845; www.bluecavecastle.com; West End Rd; tower/deluxe/superior/penthouse r US$60/75/75/100; ❌) You've got to love this atmospheric all-stone concoction perched atop the cliff. In addition to the best view of Negril, it has 14 bedrooms, each with ceiling fan, CD player and refrigerator; superior rooms also have air-con and cable TV. Stairs lead down to a sparkling grotto.

Xtabi (☎ 957-0120; www.xtabi-negril.com; West End Rd; economy/standard r US$60/79, cottages US$194) This pleasant option is a good buttoned-down bargain. You can choose economy rooms, standard rooms, simple garden cottages or seafront, clifftop bungalows that are quaint and octagonal. They're pleasingly appointed, if nothing fancy. The bar is lively and the restaurant appealing. It has sunning platforms built into the cliff. Massage is offered.

Tensing Pen (☎ 957-0387; www.tensingpen.com; West End Rd; r winter US$150-475; ❌ ❌) This quite tranquil, reclusive option has 12 thatched

cottages on 2 acres (0.8 hectares); most are 'pillar houses' on the coral cliffs, amid natural gardens. All have exquisite bamboo and hardwood details, though otherwise rooms differ markedly in decor. Massages (US$65) and yoga classes (US$15) are a popular recent arrival, as is an extravagant lodge serving guests exquisite Jamaican fare. Breakfast is included.

Eating & Drinking

Negril has plenty of upscale, elegant restaurants and just as many economical local-flavored joints serving vegetarian food, pasta, seafood and jerk chicken for a song.

LONG BAY

Kuyaba on the Beach (☎ 957-4318; meals US$7-20; ☾ breakfast, lunch & dinner) At the Kuyaba Hotel on the beach, this is a perennial favorite, a thatched, open-air restaurant with heaps of ambience. The lunch menu features burgers (US$7) and gourmet sandwiches, plus superb pepper shrimps (US$10). For dinner, check out a wide range of pasta dishes (US$11 to US$20), a superb lobster bisque, or the Cuban crab and pumpkin cakes with papaya mustard (US$15). Live music is featured.

Tamboo Inn (☎ 957-4282; meals US$7-22; ☾ breakfast, lunch & dinner) Near Kuyaba is this bamboo-and-thatch, two-story restaurant (lit by brass lanterns at night) with a varied menu that includes a breakfast of 'pigs in a blanket' (US$7), pancakes and sausage

(US$6) and a fruit platter with ice cream (US$5). It also has snack foods such as deep-fried lobster niblets, plus sandwiches and pizzas (US$5 to US$22).

WEST END

Hungry Lion (☎ 957-4486; West End Rd; meals US$8-12.50; ☽ dinner) This chic, pleasant restaurant cooks up some of the best Jamaican chow in town. Sure, red snapper slow-cooked in foil is a common dish, but they do something to it here that puts it over the top (US$12.50). The menu features several veggie choices including a toothsome quesadilla (melted cheese and vegetables served in a tortilla) with cucumber ceviche (US$8).

Rockhouse Restaurant & Bar (☎ 957-4373; West End Rd; meals US$5-18; ☽ breakfast, lunch & dinner) At the Rockhouse resort, this is recommended for nouvelle Jamaican treats such as vegetable tempura with lime and ginger, specialty pastas and jambalaya. Lamplit at night, it's a romantic spot. It serves large and hearty breakfasts (average US$5), including muesli and pancakes.

Lighthouse Inn (Busha's Place; ☎ 957-4052; West End Rd; meals US$8-20; ☽ breakfast & dinner) This inn serves splendid appetizers, such as mozzarella with tomatoes, goat cheese and olives. The three-course dinner (US$15) is a real bargain. Meals include an excellent seafood platter, lobster in curry and red snapper stuffed with callaloo. The lively tropical decor is enhanced by candlelight.

Royal Kitchen (☎ 775-0386; West End Rd; meals US$3-7; ☽ lunch & dinner) This happy shack serves up I-tal (all-natural, vegetarian) fare from the heart.

Entertainment

Negril's reggae concerts are legendary, with live performances every night in peak season, when there's sure to be some big talent in town. A handful of venues offer weekly jams, and they have a rotation system so that they all get a piece of the action. Big-name acts usually perform at MXIII in the West End, and at Roots Bamboo on Long Bay. You'll see shows advertised on roadside billboards and hear about them on megaphone-equipped cars.

Jungles (☎ 957-4005; ☽ closed Mon & Tue) A classic nightclub on Long Bay Beach, with a thronged and sweaty dance floor downstairs and a pleasant deck with pool tables.

Getting There & Away

Negril Aerodrome is at Bloody Bay, about 7 miles (11km) north of Negril Village. See p240 for information on domestic charters.

Dozens of coasters and route taxis run between Negril and Montego Bay. The two-hour journey costs about US$6. You may need to change vehicles in Lucea. Be prepared for a hair-raising ride. Minibuses and route taxis also leave for Negril from Donald Sangster International Airport in Montego Bay (the price is negotiable, but expect to pay about US$10).

A licensed taxi between Montego Bay and Negril will cost about US$60.

Getting Around

Negril stretches along more than 10 miles (16km) of shoreline, and it can be a withering walk. Coasters and route taxis cruise Norman Manley Blvd and West End Rd. You can flag them down anywhere. The fare between any two points should never be more than about US$2. Tourist taxis display a red license plate. Fares run about US$3 per 2 miles (3.2km).

Jus Jeep (☎ 957-0094; fax 957-0429; West End Rd)

Vernon's Car Rentals (☎ 957-9724, 957-4354; fax 957-4057) At Fun Holiday Beach Resort and Shop 22, Negril Plaza.

AROUND NEGRIL

The **Great Morass**: with a name like that, how could you possibly resist? This virtually impenetrable 2-mile-wide (3.2km) swamp of mangroves stretches 10 miles (16km) from the South Negril River to Orange Bay. The swamp is the island's second-largest freshwater wetland system and forms a refuge for endangered waterfowl. The easiest way to get a sense of the place is at the **Royal Palm Reserve** (☎ 957-3115; admission US$10; ☽ sunrise-sunset year-round, ☽ visitors center 9am-5pm), where a mile-long (1.6km) boardwalk meanders through the morass, and a 44ft (13.5m) wooden observation tower allows the visitor to have a bird's-eye view of the amazing flora and fauna below.

Caribic Vacations (☎ 957-3309; Norman Manley Blvd, Negril) and other local tour operators run trips to the reserve. To explore the Great Morass outside the Royal Palm Reserve, negotiate with villagers who have boats moored along the South Negril River (just northeast of Negril Village), or with fishermen at Norman Manley Sea Park, at the north end of Bloody Bay. It should cost approximately US$35 for two hours.

SOUTHERN JAMAICA

If you are unimpressed with the promises of an 'all-inclusive' vacation package, Jamaica's southern coast just may be for you. For now, at least, this far-flung region remains free from the excesses of mass tourism. If you live to travel off of the beaten track amid unspoiled scenery, you'll be in heaven.

TREASURE BEACH

Treasure Beach is the generic name given to four coves – Billy's Bay, Frenchman's Bay, Calabash Bay and Great Pedro Bay – with rocky headlands separating lonesome, coral-colored sand beaches. Calabash Bay is backed by the Great Pedro Ponds, which is a good spot for birding.

You'll be hard-pressed to find a more authentically charming and relaxing place in Jamaica. The sense of remoteness, the easy pace and the graciousness of the local farmers and fisherfolk attract travelers seeking an away-from-it-all, cares-to-the-wind lifestyle. Many have settled – much to local pride.

It's said that Scottish sailors were shipwrecked near Treasure Beach in the 19th century, accounting for the preponderance of fair hair, green eyes and reddish skin.

Information

The nearest bank is in Southfield, 10 miles (16km) east of Treasure Beach.

Jake's Place (see right) is an unofficial tourist information source. Here you can book boat rides along the coast and into the Great Morass, plus fishing trips and mountain-bike tours (US$30 to US$35 per person). Also visit www.treasurebeach.net, a good starting point for information.

The post office is on a hillside beside the **police station** (☎ 965-0163), between Calabash Bay and Pedro Cross.

Sleeping & Eating

Shakespeare Cottage (☎ 965-0120; r from US$12) Some 200yd (182m) east of the Treasure Beach Hotel, this place has five rooms with

fans, and private baths with cold water only. You can share use of a kitchen.

Ital Rest (☎ 863-3481, 421-8909; r US$40) An atmospheric out-of-the-way place with two exquisite (if rustic), clean, all-wood thatched cabins with showers, toilets and solar electricity. An upstairs room in the house has a sundeck. Kitchen facilities are shared.

Treasure Beach Hotel (☎ 965-0110; www.treasure beachjamaica.com; superior s/d US$99/110, deluxe d US$144; P ✗ ☞) This rambling property nestled on a hillside overlooking the beach offers 36 rooms including 16 spacious, deluxe oceanfront suites that feature king-size, four-poster beds, cable TVs, tile floors and patios. There are two swimming pools, a whirlpool and a volleyball court; sailing and snorkeling are offered.

Jack Sprat Café (meals US$3-9; ☼ lunch & dinner) On the edge of Jake's property, this is a barefoot and buttoned-down beachside eatery. It's open all day and offers a simple menu of sandwiches, salads, smoked marlin and lobster, plus superb pizzas at night (US$3 to US$8). The jukebox plays pure vintage reggae.

Winsome's Restaurant (meals US$7-20) At Treasure Beach Hotel, this is a pleasant alternative. It serves Jamaican and continental dishes.

Getting There & Around

There is no direct service to Treasure Beach from Montego Bay, Negril or Kingston. Take a coaster or route taxi to Black River

---

AUTHOR'S CHOICE

Jake's Place (☎ 965-3000; www.jakesjamaica .com; r US$95-195, cottages US$195-325; P) Eclectic and endearing are understatements for this rustic, rainbow-colored retreat. Local kids and fishermen wander in and out as if they own the place, adding to Jake's unique charm. There are 13 single rooms (many perched over the sea), four two-bedroom cottages, a three-bedroom villa and a well-appointed house. The decor follows Greek and Muslim motifs, with onion-dome curves, blood-red floors, and walls and rough-hewn doors inset with colored bottles and glass beads. There's also an atmospheric **restaurant** (meals US$8-18). Is it recommended? You bet.

(US$3), then connect to Treasure Beach (US$1.75).

Jake's Place (see the boxed text) arranges transfers from MoBay for US$95 (up to four people), car and motorcycle rental, and transfers by taxi.

BLACK RIVER

Peaceful and picturesque, the town of Black River is a far cry from the heady days of the 18th and 19th centuries, when it prospered from the export of logwood, from which a Prussian-blue dye was extracted. These days, the town's somnolent charms provide a perfect backdrop for weary explorers seeking respite from the physical demands of travel. Most who come are less interested in the town than in exploring the southern half of the **Great Morass**, which extends inland from the mouth of the Black River. The waters, stained by tannins and dark as molasses, are a complex ecosystem and a vital preserve for more than 100 bird species. The morass also forms Jamaica's most significant refuge for crocodiles, about 300 live in the swamps. Locals take to the waters in dugout canoes, tending funnel-shaped shrimp pots made of bamboo in the traditional manner of their West African forebears.

A number of places in Black River offer Great Morass tours. **South Coast Safaris** (☎ 965-2513; fax 962-9272), on the east side of the bridge, offers 1½-hour journeys aboard the *Safari Queen* four times daily; the cost per person is US$20, or US$35 including lunch and a visit to YS Falls (below). The trips leave from the old warehouse on the east bank of the river.

You can also hire a guide to take you up-river in his canoe or boat for about US$15 to US$25, round-trip. Ask near the bridge in town.

Midday tours are best for spotting crocodiles; early and later tours are better for birding. Take a shade hat and mosquito repellent.

YS FALLS

Among Jamaica's most spectacular falls, this series of eight **cascades** (☎ 997-6055; adult/child US$10/6; ⊙ 9:30am-3:30pm Tue-Sun, closed last 2 weeks Oct) fall 120ft (36.5m) and are separated by cool pools that are perfect for swimming. The falls are hemmed in by limestone cliffs and are surrounded by towering forest.

The falls are on the YS Estate, 3.5 miles (5.5km) north of the A2 (the turn-off is 1 mile (1.6km) east of Middle Quarters). The entrance is just north of the junction of the B6 toward Maggotty.

Buses travel via YS Falls from the Shakespeare Plaza in Maggotty. On the A2, buses, coasters and route taxis will drop you at the junction to YS Falls, from where you can walk (it's about 2 miles/3.2km) or catch an Ipswich-bound route taxi.

DIRECTORY

This directory is specific to Jamaica. For information pertaining to the entire region, check p757.

ACCOMMODATIONS

From the cheerful brouhaha of the resort centers to the laid-back, beach-happy towns of the western and southern coasts, Jamaica offers a satisfying range of accommodations for every budget and style. If you're traveling on a shoestring, head to a simple guest-house, where rooms can be had for US$30 to US$60. Midrange hotels – offering relative comfort with basic security, private baths, pools, air-con and satellite TV – are priced up to US$150. Many of these personable

---

PRACTICALITIES

- **Newspapers & Magazines** The *Jamaica Gleaner* newspaper is the high-standard one; its rival is the *Jamaica Observer*. The best domestic magazine is Air Jamaica's *Sky Writings*.

- **Radio & TV** There are 25 radio stations and seven TV channels; most hotels have satellite.

- **Electricity** The voltage used is 110V, 50Hz. Sockets are usually two or three-pin – the US standard.

- **Video Systems** NTSC is the system used in Jamaica.

- **Weights & Measures** Jamaica is transitioning from imperial to metric; distances are measured in kilometers, and gas in liters, but coffee is strictly by the pound.

JAMAICA

EMERGENCY NUMBERS

Ambulance (☎ 011)
Fire (☎ 110)
Police (☎ 119)

---

small hotels have splendid gardens, views of the sea or both. If you've decided to splurge, Jamaica's incomparable luxury hotels rank among the finest in the world.

Rates quoted are for the high season (mid-December to April), unless otherwise noted. At other times rates can be 20% to 60% lower.

ALL-INCLUSIVE RESORTS

For better or worse, Jamaica was the spawning ground for the all-inclusive resort. At chains like **Sandals** (www.sandals.com), **Couples** (www.couples.com) and **SuperClubs** (www.superclubs.com), guests pay a set price and (theoretically) pay nothing more once setting foot inside the resort.

VILLAS

Jamaica boasts hundreds of private houses for rent, from modest cottages to lavish beachfront estates. These arrangements are very cost-effective if you're traveling with family or a group of friends. Many include a cook and maid. Rates start as low as US$400 per week for budget units with minimal facilities. More-upscale villas begin at about US$850 weekly and can run to US$10,000 or more for a sumptuous multibedroom estate.

Holiday Solutions (www.rentjamaica.com) Lists scores of economical short-term accommodations.

Jamaican Association of Villas & Apartments (JAVA; ☎ 974-2508; www.villasinjamaica.com; PO Box 298, Ocho Rios)

ACTIVITIES
Diving & Snorkeling

Jamaica offers fabulous diving and snorkeling, especially along its northern shore and west coast. Underwater treasures range from shallow reefs, caverns and trenches to walls and drop-offs just a few hundred yards offshore. The waters offer exceptional visibility, and water temperatures are above 80°F (26.6°C) year-round.

Diving occurs mostly in and around the Montego Bay and Negril marine parks, in proximity to a wide range of licensed dive operators offering rental equipment and group dives. Many sites remain relatively unexplored and uncrowded. By law, all dives in Jamaican waters must be guided, and dives are restricted to a depth of 100ft (30m).

Dives cost US$50/80 for one-/two-tank dives. A snorkeling excursion, which generally includes equipment and a boat trip, costs US$25 to US$40. 'Resort courses' for beginners (also called 'Discover Scuba') are offered at most major resorts (about US$80), which also offer Professional Association of Diving Instructors (PADI) or National Association of Underwater Instructors (NAUI) certification courses (US$350 to US$375) and advanced courses.

Golf

If golf is your passion, welcome to nirvana. Jamaica has 12 championship courses, more than any other Caribbean island. All courses rent out clubs and have carts. See also the boxed text on p228 for a list of golf clubs in Montego Bay.

Jamaica Golf Association (☎ 925-2325; www.jamaicagolfassociation.com; Constant Spring Golf Club, PO Box 743, Kingston 8)

Sport Fishing

Jamaica's waters are a pelagic playpen for schools of blue and white marlin, dolphin fish, wahoo, tuna and dozens of other species. Deepwater game fish run year-round through the deep Cayman Trench that begins just 2 miles (3.2km) from shore.

Charters can be arranged for around US$400/600 per half-/full day through hotels or directly through operators in Montego Bay, Negril, Ocho Rios and Port Antonio. A charter includes captain, tackle, bait and crew. Most charter boats require a 50% deposit.

For a more 'rootsy' experience, local fishermen will take you out in 'canoes' (narrow longboats with outboards) using hand lines.

Surfing

Although Jamaica is little known as a surfing destination and board rentals on the island can be difficult to come by, the east coast is starting to attract surfers for its respectable waves coming in from the Atlantic. Boston Beach, 9 miles (14.5km) east of Port Antonio, is a well-known spot, as is

Long Bay, 10 miles (16km) further south. The southeast coast, including the Palisadoes Peninsula, also gets good surf.

Surfing Association of Jamaica/Jamnesia Surf Club (☎ 750-0103; www.geocities.com/jamnesiasurfclub; PO Box 167, Kingston 2) provides general information about surfing in Jamaica, and operates a surf camp at Bull Bay, 8 miles (13km) east of Kingston.

Jah Mek Yah (☎ 435-8806, in the US 954-594-9619; www.theliquidaddiction.com/jaspots.html; Morant Bay, St Thomas) is a surf lodge in Jamaica's unspoiled eastern corner offering relaxed, rootsy surf packages.

BOOKS

There's a great number of excellent books in print describing Jamaica's eminently rich cultural, historical and natural landscape.

Music fans are perhaps the most spoiled by choice. *Reggae Explosion,* by Chris Salewicz and Adrian Boot, is a large-format photo-essay book tracing the history of reggae. The definitive and engaging *Catch a Fire: The Life of Bob Marley,* by Timothy White, analyzes the forces that shaped Marley's political and spiritual evolution. *Reggae Bloodlines: In Search of the Music and Culture of Jamaica,* by Stephen Davis and Simon Peter, takes a broader look.

Several memoirs and novels seek to capture the essence of life on the island. Swashbuckling Hollywood hero Errol Flynn, who lived in Jamaica for many years, recalls his colorful experiences in his autobiography *My Wicked, Wicked Ways.* Anthony Winckler was a teacher in Jamaica during an epoch of anti-White sentiment (during the tension-filled late 1970s) – he tells of his experience in the novel *Going Home to Teach.* Russell Banks' *The Book of Jamaica* tells the story of an American expatriate college professor who delves into Jamaica and Rastafarianism with unexpected results. Jean Rhys' *Wide Sargasso Sea* is a sultry tale of post-emancipation Jamaica.

Understanding Jamaican Patois, by Emilie Adams, provides an understanding of English as spoken in Jamaica. Cassidy and RB LePage's *Dictionary of Jamaican English* is the definitive lexicon on patois.

CHILDREN

Some all-inclusive resorts cater specifically to families and have an impressive range of amenities for children. Most hotels also offer free accommodations or reduced rates for children staying in their parents' room. Many hotels provide a babysitter or nanny by advance request. At hotels that aren't family resorts, it's a good idea to prearrange necessities such as cribs, babysitters, cots and baby food.

DANGERS & ANNOYANCES

If you don't like reggae music (you can't escape it!), can't cope with poverty or power outages, and hate being hustled, then Jamaica is definitely not for you. Moreover, if you prize efficient service, this place is liable to drive you nuts. To savor Jamaica properly, to appreciate what makes people passionate about the place, it pays to be idiosyncratic. To rest content here you have to 'get' Jamaica, to take the punches in stride. If you can handle that, and if you like travel with a raw edge, you'll love it.

Many visitors to Jamaica are concerned about crime. Although most violent crime occurs in ghettoes far from tourist centers, many readers continue to report being robbed, mugged or scammed, despite government claims that crime against visitors has dropped.

Drugs – particularly ganja (marijuana) – are readily available in Jamaica, and you're almost certain to be approached by hustlers selling them. Possession and use of drugs in Jamaica is strictly illegal and penalties are severe. Roadblocks and random searches of cars are common. If you *do* buy drugs in Jamaica, don't be foolish enough to take any out of the country. If you get caught in possession, you will *not* be getting on your plane home, however small the amount. A night (or a lengthy sentence) in a crowded-to-bursting Jamaican lock-up is dangerous to your health! At any given time, an average of over 200 foreigners are serving prison sentences in Jamaica for drug offences.

The traveler's biggest problem in Jamaica is the vast army of hustlers who harass visitors, notably in and around major tourist centers. Hustlers walk the streets looking for potential buyers of crafts, jewelry or drugs, or to wash cars, give aloe vera massages or offer any of a thousand varieties of services. If you as much as glance in their direction, they'll attempt to reel you in like a flounder.

EMBASSIES & CONSULATES
Jamaican Embassies & Consulates
Canada High Commission (☎ 613-233-9311; hc@jhc
ottawa.ca; Standard Life Bldg, Suite 402, 275 Slater St,
Ottawa, Ontario KIP 5H9); Consulate General (☎ 416-598-
3008; jcgtoronto@attcanada.net; Suite 402, 214 King St W,
Toronto, Ontario M5H 1KA)
Germany Embassy (☎ 030-859-9450; info@jamador.de;
Schmargendorfer Strasse 32; 12159 Berlin)
UK High Commission (☎ 0207-823-9911; hc@jhcuk.com;
1-2 Prince Consort Rd, London SW7 2BZ)
USA Embassy (☎ 202-452-0660; 1520 New Hampshire
Ave NW, Washington, DC); Consulate General (☎ 212-935-
9000; 2nd fl, 767 3rd Ave, New York, NY 10017); Consulate
General (☎ 305-374-8431; fax 305-577-4970; 842 Ingra-
ham Bldg, 25 SE 2nd Ave, Miami, FL 33131)

Embassies & Consulates in Jamaica
More than 40 countries have official diplomatic representation in Jamaica. Except
for a couple of Montego Bay consulates,
all are located in Kingston. If your country
isn't represented in this list, check 'Embas-
sies & High Commissions' in the yellow
pages of the Greater Kingston telephone
directory.
Australia (☎ 926-3550, 926-3551; 64 Knutsford Blvd,
Kingston 5)
Austria (☎ 929-5259; 2 Ardenne Rd, Kingston 10)
Canada Embassy (☎ 926-1500; 3 West Kings House Rd,
Kingston); Consulate (☎ 952-6198; 29 Gloucester Ave,
Montego Bay)
France (☎ 978-0210; 13 Hillcrest Ave, Kingston 6)
Germany (☎ 926-6728; 10 Waterloo Rd,
Kingston 10)
Italy (☎ 978-1273; 10 Rovan Dr, Kingston 6)
Japan (☎ 929-7534; 1 Kensington Cres, Kingston 5)
Mexico (☎ 926-6891; 36 Trafalgar Rd, Kingston 10)
Netherlands (☎ 926-2026; 53 Knutsford Blvd,
Kingston 5)
Russia (☎ 924-1048; 22 Norbrook Dr, Kingston 8)
Spain (☎ 929-6710; 25 Dominica Dr, Kingston 5)
Sweden (☎ 941-3761; Unit 3, 69 Constant Spring Rd,
Kingston 10)
Switzerland (☎ 978-7857; 22 Trafalgar Rd,
Kingston 10)
UK High Commission (☎ 510-0700, 926-9050;
bhckingston@cwjamaica.com; 28 Trafalgar Rd, Kingston);
Consulate (☎ 912-6859; Montego Bay)
US Embassy (☎ 929-4850, after hrs 926-6440;
kingstonacs@state.gov; Life of Jamaica Bldg, 16 Oxford St,
Kingston); Consulate (☎ 952-0160, 952-5050; uscons
agency.mobay@cwjamaica.com; St James Plaza, 2nd fl,
Gloucester Ave, Montego Bay)
Venezuela (☎ 926-5510; 36 Trafalgar Rd, Kingston 10)

FESTIVALS & EVENTS
Air Jamaica Jazz & Blues Festival (late January;
☎ 888-359-2475, 800-523-5585; www.airjamaica.com;
Montego Bay) Locally and internationally acclaimed artists
perform in an outdoor setting.
A Fi Wi Sinting (late February; ☎ 715-3529; www
.fiwisinting.com; Port Antonio) A festival featuring tradi-
tional music, song, dance and a marketplace.
Trelawny Yam Festival (late March; ☎ 610-0818;
Montego Bay) A food festival celebrating the culture and
heritage of 'yam country.'
Carnival (March to April; www.jamaicacarnival.com;
Kingston) Street parties and soca music all night long.
Spring Break (March to April; Negril & Montego Bay) Get
your groove on and party all night long.
Calabash International Literary Festival (late May;
☎ 922-4200; www.calabashfestival.org; Treasure Beach)
A daring, acclaimed literary festival on the untamed south
coast.
Ocho Rios Jazz Festival (June; ☎ 927-3544; www.ocho
riosjazz.com; Ocho Rios) Top names in jazz, under the stars.
Portland Jerk Festival (July; ☎ 715-5465; Port Antonio) A food festival for folks in love with the hot and spicy.
Red Stripe Reggae Sumfest (July; ☎ 953-4573;
www.reggaesumfest; Montego Bay) The mama of all reggae festivals brings the top acts to the masses.
International Marlin Tournament (October;
☎ 927-0145; Port Antonio) Anglers rejoice at this time-
honored fishing tournament.
Jamaica Coffee Festival (October; ☎ 922-4200;
Kingston) Jamaica's world-famous coffee is something to
celebrate at this family-friendly festival.
Fireworks on the Waterfront (December 31;
☎ 922-4200; Kingston) Ring in the new year on the
Kingston waterfront with 100,000 others.

GAY & LESBIAN TRAVELERS
Jamaica is an adamantly homophobic nation. Homosexual intercourse between men
is illegal, and antigay hysteria is a staple of
musical lyrics. Homosexuality is a subject
that evokes extreme reactions among Jamaicans, and it is difficult to hold a serious
discussion on the topic.

Most Jamaican gays are still in the closet.
Nonetheless, many hoteliers are gay-
tolerant, and you should not be put off from
visiting the island. Just don't expect to be
able to display your sexuality openly without an adverse reaction.

HOLIDAYS
Public holidays:
New Year's Day January 1
Bob Marley Day February 6

Ash Wednesday Six weeks before Easter
Good Friday, Easter Monday March/April
Labour Day May 23
Emancipation Day August 1
Independence Day August 6
National Heroes' Day October 19
Christmas Day December 25
Boxing Day December 26

INTERNET ACCESS

Many upscale hotels provide in-room, dial-up access for laptop computers. Other hotels offer guests email and Internet access through business centers. Most town libraries now have Internet access (per 30 minutes US$1). Most towns also have at least one commercial entity where you can access the Internet.

INTERNET RESOURCES

Everything Jamaican (www.everythingjamaican.com) Noteworthy for its energetic online community.
Jamaica National Heritage Trust (www.jnht.com) A guide to Jamaica's history and heritage.
Jamaica Yellow Pages (www.jamaicayp.com) A handy online presentation of the Jamaican phone directory.
Jamaicans (www.jamaicans.com) An eclectic site seeking to reflect the Jamaican experience.
Visit Jamaica (www.visitjamaica.com) The tourist board's presentation of Jamaica to travelers, with plenty of destination, attractions and lodging information.

LANGUAGE

Officially, English is the spoken language. In reality, Jamaica is a bilingual country, and English is far more widely understood than spoken. The unofficial lingo is patois (pa-twah), a musical dialect with a staccato rhythm and cadence, laced with salty idioms and wonderfully and wittily compressed proverbs.

Patois evolved from Creole English and a twisted alchemy of the mother tongue peppered with African, Portuguese and Spanish terms and, in the last century, Rastafarian slang. Linguists agree that it is more than simplified pidgin English, and it has its own identifiable syntax.

Patois is deepest in rural areas, where many people do not know much standard English. Although it is mostly the lingua franca of the poor, all sectors of Jamaica understand patois, and even polite, educated Jamaicans lapse into patois at unguarded moments.

Most Jamaicans vary the degree of their patois according to whom they're speaking.

MONEY

The unit of currency is the Jamaican dollar, the 'jay,' which uses the same symbol as the US dollar ($). Jamaican currency is issued in bank notes of J$10, J$20, J$50, J$100 and J$200. Coins are issued for 10 cents, 25 cents, J$1 and J$5. The official rate of exchange fluctuates daily, and as of July 2005 it was about J$60 to US$1 and J$75 to €1.

Prices for hotels and valuable items are usually quoted in US dollars, which are widely accepted.

Commercial banks have branches throughout the island. Those in major towns maintain a foreign exchange booth. Traveler's checks are widely accepted in Jamaica, although some hotels, restaurants and exchange bureaus charge a hefty fee for cashing them. Most city bank branches throughout Jamaica now have 24-hour ATMs linked to international networks such as Cirrus or Plus.

TELEPHONE

Jamaica has a fully automated, digital telephone system operated by **Cable & Wireless Jamaica** (☎ 888-225-5295; www.cwjamaica.com), which has offices islandwide where you can make direct calls. Another option is privately run 'call-direct centers,' where an operator places a call on your behalf and you're directed to the appropriate phone booth. You will be charged 'time and charge,' in which the operator will advise you of the cost upon completion of your call.

Major hotels have direct-dial calling; elsewhere you may need to go through the hotel operator, or call from the front desk. Hotels add a 15% government tax, plus a service charge, often at sticker-shock rates.

Cell (Mobile) Phones

You can bring your own cellular phone into Jamaica, but if your phone is locked by a specific carrier, don't bother. Another option is to purchase an inexpensive cellular phone (from US$35) at a **Digicel** (☎ 888-344-4235; www.digiceljamaica.com) or **bMobile** (☎ 888-225-5295; www.cwmobile.com/jamaica) outlet and purchase a prepaid phone card. These are sold in denominations of up to J$1000, and

JAMAICA

you'll find them at many gas stations or stationery shops.

Phone Cards
Public phones require a prepaid phone card, available from Cable & Wireless Jamaica offices, retail stores, hotels, banks, and other outlets displaying the 'Phone Cards on Sale' sign. The card is available in denominations of J$20 to J$500. For international calls, you can also buy WorldTalk calling cards, good for use on any phone, including public call boxes and cellular phones.

Phone Codes
Jamaica's country code is ☎ 876. To call Jamaica from the US, dial ☎ 1-876 + the seven-digit local number. From elsewhere, dial your country's international dialing code, then ☎ 876 and the local number.

For calls within the same parish in Jamaica, just dial the local number. Between parishes, dial ☎ 1 + the local number. We have included only the seven-digit local number in Jamaica listings in this chapter.

VISAS
Nationals of the UK, Ireland, US and Canada don't require a visa for stays of up to six months. Nationals of Austria, Belgium, Denmark, Finland, Germany, Iceland, Israel, Italy, Luxembourg, Mexico, the Netherlands, Norway, Sweden, Switzerland, Turkey and Commonwealth countries (except Sri Lanka and Pakistan) can stay for three months without a visa. Nationals of Argentina, Brazil, Chile, Costa Rica, Ecuador, France, Greece, Japan, Portugal and Spain don't need a visa for stays of up to 30 days.

All other nationals require visas (nationals of most countries can obtain a visa on arrival, provided they are holding valid onward or return tickets and evidence of sufficient funds).

TRANSPORTATION

GETTING THERE & AWAY
Entering Jamaica
All visitors must arrive with a valid passport. As of December 31, 2005, US citizens must show a valid US passport when traveling from the Caribbean in order to re-enter the US (see the boxed text, p772).

Immigration formalities require every person to show a return or ongoing airline ticket when arriving in Jamaica.

Air
Jamaica has international airports in Montego Bay and Kingston. The majority of visitors to Jamaica arrive at Montego Bay's **Donald Sangster International Airport** (MBJ; ☎ 952-5530). In Kingston, **Norman Manley International Airport** (KIN; ☎ 924-8546; www.manley airport.com.jm) is around 11 miles (17.5km) southeast from downtown.

For international travel to/from Jamaica from outside the Caribbean, see p775. The following airlines fly to/from Jamaica from within the Caribbean:

Air Jamaica (☎ 888-359-2475; www.airjamaica.com; hub Kingston)

American Eagle (☎ 800-433-7300; www.aa.com; hub San Juan)

British West Indies Air (BWIA; ☎ 924-8364, 800-538-2942; www.bwee.com; hub Trinidad)

Cayman Airways (☎ 926-1762, 926-7778; www .caymanairways.com; hub Grand Cayman)

LIAT (☎ 888-844-5428; www.liatairline.com; hub Antigua)

Sea
Jamaica is a popular destination on the cruising roster, mainly for passenger liners but also for private yachters.

If all you're after is a one-day taste of Jamaica, then consider arriving by cruise ship. Port visits usually take the form of one-day stopovers at either Ocho Rios or Montego Bay. See p777 for more information on cruises.

Many yachters make the trip to Jamaica from North America. Upon arrival in Jamaica, you *must* clear customs and immigration at Montego Bay, Kingston, Ocho Rios or Port Antonio.

In addition, you'll need to clear customs at *each* port of call.

GETTING AROUND
Air
There are four domestic airports: Tinson Pen in Kingston, Boscobel near Ocho Rios, Negril Aerodrome and Ken Jones Aerodrome at Port Antonio. Montego Bay's Donald Sangster International Airport has a domestic terminal adjacent to the international terminal.

Air Jamaica Express (☎ 922-4661, in the USA 800-523-5585; www.airjamaica.com/express.asp) Operates a scheduled service between Kingston, Montego Bay and Ocho Rios on a daily basis.

TimAir (www.timair.net) Montego Bay (☎ 952-2516, 979-1114); Negril (☎ 957-5374) This air taxi service serves Montego Bay, Negril, Ocho Rios, Port Antonio, Kingston and Mandeville.

Bicycle

Mountain bikes and 'beach cruisers' can be rented at most major resorts (US$10 to US$20 per day). However, road conditions are hazardous, and Jamaican drivers are not very considerate to cyclists. For serious touring, bring your own mountain or multi-purpose bike. You'll need sturdy wheels to handle the potholed roads.

Bus

Traveling by public transportation could be the best – *or worst!* – adventure of your trip to Jamaica. The island's extensive transportation network links virtually every village and comprises several options that range from standard public buses to 'coasters' and 'route taxis.' These depart from and arrive at each town's transportation station, which is usually near the main market. Locals can direct you to the appropriate vehicle, which should have its destination marked above the front window (for buses) or on its side.

COASTERS

'Coasters' – private minibuses – have traditionally been the workhorses of Jamaica's regional public transportation system. All major towns and virtually every village in the country is served.

Licensed minibuses display red license plates with the initials PPV (public passenger vehicle) or have a Jamaican Union of Travelers Association (JUTA) insignia. JUTA buses are exclusively for tourists. They usually depart their point of origin when they're full, often overflowing, with people hanging from the open doors. Guard your luggage carefully against theft.

PUBLIC BUSES

Kingston and Montego Bay have modern municipal bus systems. Throughout the island, bus stops are located at most road intersections along the routes, but you can usually flag down a bus anywhere (except in major cities, where they only pause at designated stops). When you want to get off, shout 'One stop!' The conductor will usually echo your request with, 'Let off!' The following fares apply to public buses: Kingston metropolitan region US$1; Montego Bay licensed area US$0.50; and rural areas US$0.25 flat rate, plus US$0.05 per kilometer.

ROUTE TAXIS

These communal taxis are the most universal mode of public transportation, reaching every part of the country. They operate like coasters (and cost about the same), picking up as many people as they can squeeze in along their specified routes. A 30-minute ride typically costs about US$2; a one-hour ride costs about US$3.

Most are white Toyota Corolla station wagons marked by red license plates. They should have 'Route Taxi' marked on the front door, and they are not to be confused with identical licensed taxis, which charge more.

Car

Exploring by rental car can be a joy. There are some fabulously scenic journeys, and with your own wheels you can get as far off the beaten track as you wish, discovering the magic of Jamaican culture beyond the pale of the touristy areas.

A paved coastal highway circles the entire island (in the southern parishes it runs about 20 miles – 32km – inland). Main roads cross the central mountain chains, north to south, linking all of the main towns. A web of minor roads, country lanes and dirt tracks provides access to more-remote areas.

DRIVER'S LICENSE

To drive in Jamaica, you must have a valid International Driver's License (IDL) or a current license for your home country or state, valid for up to six months. You can obtain an IDL by applying with your current license to any Automobile Association office.

FUEL & SPARE PARTS

Many gas stations close after 7pm or so. In rural areas, stations usually close on Sunday. At time of research, gasoline cost about US$2 per liter. Cash only, please! Credit cards are not accepted.

RENTAL

Several major international car-rental companies operate in Jamaica, along with dozens of local firms. Rates begin at about US$50 per day and can run as high as US$125, depending on the vehicle. Some companies include unlimited mileage, while others set a limit and charge a fee for excess miles driven. Most firms require a deposit of at least US$500, but will accept a credit card imprint. Renters must be 21 years of age (some companies will rent only to those 25 years of age or older).

Avis (www.avis.com) Kingston (☎ 924-8293); Montego Bay (☎ 952-0762)

Budget (www.budget.com) Kingston (☎ 924-8762); Montego Bay (☎ 952-3838); Ocho Rios (☎ 974-1288)

Dollar (www.dollar.com) Montego Bay (☎ 953-9100); Ocho Rios (☎ 974-7000)

Hertz (www.hertz.com) Kingston (☎ 924-8028); Montego Bay (☎ 979-0438)

Island Car Rentals (☎ from the USA 800-892-4581; www.islandcarrentals.com) Kingston (☎ 926-8861, 926-5991); Montego Bay (☎ 952-5771); Ocho Rios (☎ 974-2334) Jamaica's largest and most reputable car-rental company offers five categories of cars ranging from US$49 to US$83 per day.

ROAD CONDITIONS

The main roads are usually in reasonable condition, despite numerous potholes. Many secondary roads – B-roads – are in appalling condition and best tackled with a 4WD vehicle. Most roads are narrow, with frequent bends.

ROAD HAZARDS

Jamaican drivers rank among the world's rudest and most dangerous. Cars race through towns and play hopscotch with one another, overtaking with daredevil folly. Jamaica has the third-highest auto fatality rate in the world, behind Ethiopia and India. Use extreme caution and drive defensively, especially at night when you should be prepared to meet oncoming cars that are either without lights or blinding you with their high-beams. Use your horn liberally, especially when approaching blind corners.

ROAD RULES

Always drive on the left. Remember: 'Keep left, and you'll always be right.' Here's another local saying worth memorizing: 'De left side is de right side; de right side is suicide!'

The speed limit is 30mph (about 50km/h) in towns and 50mph (around 80km/h) on highways. Jamaica has a compulsory seatbelt law.

Taxi

Taxi fares are set by the government according to the distance that is traveled. Fares are expensive, but are cheaper if you share the cost with other passengers. Meters are generally not used. It is possible to negotiate a fare that is less than the stated price; agree on a fare before getting into a taxi. Rates are posted at some hotels. Only use taxis with red license plates having a PPV designation.

Don't be misled by drivers who may want to take you somewhere other than where you want to go. Some drivers receive incentives from establishments for delivering customers.

Haiti

For most outsiders, Haiti typifies a failed state of insurrections, poverty and social malaise. It has always stood out in the media as the dark side of Hispaniola, the island Haiti shares with the more laid-back Dominican Republic. But a look beyond the headlines reveals a kind and deeply spiritual people, who reach back to their African roots more than any other Caribbean nation.

Haiti's difference lies in its history; after independence in 1004 the country was isolated from the full brunt of European colonial influences. Art, influenced by the fascinating Vodou culture, has dominated life ever since.

Although Haiti's lack of infrastructure, grinding poverty and ravaged environment may leave even the most hardened traveler somewhat shell-shocked, it is still a very rewarding place to visit. More than anything, it's the culture that travelers come to see. Visiting Haiti's artists and its galleries, for example, is one of the best ways to get a feel for the place.

You need an open mind and a sense of humor to survive in Haiti. It's no wonder that Graham Greene called his novel about Haiti *The Comedians* – there is always the suspicion that you are playing a part in a surreal comedy when you visit.

FAST FACTS

- **Area** 10,715 sq miles (27,750 sq km)
- **Capital** Port-au-Prince
- **Country code** ☎ 509
- **Departure tax** US$30 plus 10 gourdes by air; travelers departing by land to the Dominican Republic are charged US$10. An additional charge of 10 gourdes (about US$0.40) might be levied.
- **Famous for** Vodou
- **Language** Creole, French
- **Money** Haitian gourdes (HTG); HTG10 = US$0.25 = €0.20 = UK£0.14
- **Official name** Republic of Haiti
- **People** Haitians
- **Phrases in Creole** *Alo* (hello); *merci* (thank you); *au revoir* (goodbye); *se konbyen kob li koute?* (how much is it?)
- **Population** 7 million
- **Visa** US$25 (issued on arrival)

HAITI

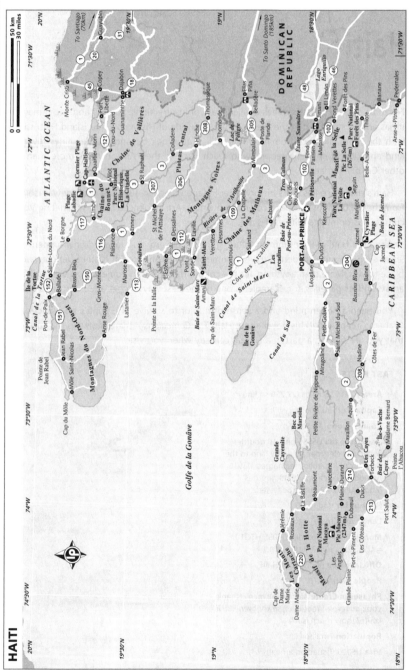

HIGHLIGHTS

- **Port-au-Prince** (p250) A challenging but rewarding city, with rowdy street life, colorful murals, urban Vodou culture and a plethora of handicrafts.
- **Jacmel** (p254) Crumbling grand architecture, a thriving artistic community and Haiti's most spectacular Carnival.
- **Citadelle** (p256) This vast and historic 19th-century fortress provides sweeping views of the northern landscape.
- **Vodou** (p248) A fascinating religion and an intrinsic part of everyday life in Haiti. Vodou festivals occur throughout the year.
- **Parc National Macaya** (p255) One of Haiti's last virgin cloud forests, with beautiful terrain and great hiking trails.

ITINERARIES

- **One week** Stay two days in Port-au-Prince, then two days in Jacmel and finally take a flight north to visit the Citadelle.
- **Two weeks** Follow the itinerary above at a more relaxed pace, and add on Parc National La Visite and some north-coast beaches near Cap-Haïtien.
- **One month** You can see the whole of Haiti in a month, with time for scuba diving, trekking in Parc National Macaya and a horse ride from Jacmel to Bassins Bleu.

CLIMATE & WHEN TO GO

Torrential rains during the hurricane season (September) can cause the already diabolical roads to become engulfed in mud. If you plan to visit during Carnival (usually celebrated in January or February, depending on the position of Ash Wednesday in the Catholic calendar), book well in advance as a good hotel may be hard to find. Otherwise, hotel prices generally don't fluctuate through the year.

HISTORY

The earliest known inhabitants to Hispaniola arrived around 2600 BC in huge dugout canoes, probably from what is now eastern Venezuela. They were called the Tainos, and by the time Christopher Columbus landed on the island in 1492, they numbered some 400,000. However, within 30 years of Columbus' landing, the Tainos were gone, wiped out by disease and abuse.

The demise of the Tainos meant that the Spaniards had to turn to Africa for slaves, the first wave arriving in Hispaniola in 1520. But Spanish control of the island was lackluster, and soon French colonists were moving to the island, mostly the western half. In 1731 the Spanish finally recognized the French colony, known as St-Dominigue, and drew up a border along the lines of two rivers.

Dissension arose in St-Dominigue around the time of the island's division. The mulattos (offspring of White masters and female slaves) demanded equal rights with Whites while the slaves sought freedom. Revolt became commonplace and with Spanish support, slave leaders Jean François, Jean Biassou and François Dominique Toussaint L'Ouverture took on their masters and won, forcing France to abolish slavery.

World's First Black Republic

In May 1803, while Haiti was still under French rule, former slave and rebel leader

HOW MUCH?

- **Taxi from Port-au-Prince to Pétionville** US$8
- **Meal in a touristy restaurant** US$12
- **Snickers bar** US$1
- **Bottle of five-star Haitian rum** US$17
- **Double room in a midrange hotel** US$80

LONELY PLANET INDEX

- **Liter of gas** US$0.70
- **Liter of water** US$2.50
- **Bottle of Prestige beer** US$0.81
- **Souvenir T-shirt** US$10
- **Street snack: sweet cookie** US$0.30

Jean-Jacques Dessalines took the French tricolor flag and, ripping the white out of it, declared he was ripping the White man out of the country. The red and blue were stitched together, the initials RF (République Française) were replaced by *Liberté ou la Mort* (Liberty or Death) and Haiti's flag was born.

Dessalines won a decisive victory against the French at the Battle Vertières, which hastened the surrender of Cap-Haïtien. So, on January 1, 1804, at Gonaïves, Dessalines proclaimed independence for St-Dominigue and restored its Taino name, Haiti, meaning 'mountainous land.'

Emulating Napoleon Bonaparte, Dessalines crowned himself Emperor of Haiti and ratified a new constitution that granted him absolute power. However, his tyrannical approach to the throne inflamed large sections of society to revolt – his death in an ambush at Pont Rouge, on October 17, 1806, marked the first of many violent overthrows that would plague Haiti for the next 200 years.

Dessalines' death sparked a civil war between the Black north, led by Lieutenant Henri Christophe, and the mulatto south, led by General Alexandre Pétion. Fighting continued until Christophe's death in 1820, after which the new southern leader, Jean-Pierre Boyer, brought the entire country under his rule and established a tenuous peace.

During his reign, Boyer took advantage of a revolt against Spanish rule in Santo Domingo by invading and annexing it in 1821. The whole of the island remained under Haitian control until 1849, when the eastern part proclaimed independence as the Dominican Republic.

The next half-century was characterized by continued rivalry between the ruling classes of wealthy mulattos and Blacks. Of the 22 heads of state between 1843 and 1915, only one served his full term in office; the others were assassinated or forced into exile.

US Intervention

By the beginning of the 20th century the US had begun to recognize that Haiti's proximity to the Windward Passage gave the country strategic importance. The stretch of sea between Haiti and Cuba was an important shipping route from the newly opened Panama Canal to the eastern coast of the US.

When Haitian President Vilbrun Guillaume Sam was killed by an angry civilian mob in 1915, the Americans took this as their chance to invade Haiti, in theory aiming to stabilize the country. The occupation furthered the economic interests of the US in Haiti, raising its share in the Haitian market to about 75%. The occupation brought predictable resistance, with fighting from 1918 to 1920, climaxing with a revolt led by Charlemagne Péralute in the north and Benoit Batraville in the Artibonite. The revolt was brutally suppressed, costing the lives of about 2000 Haitians, and is still bitterly remembered by anti-Americans in the country today. The occupation proved costly and the US finally pulled out in 1934.

The Duvaliers & Aristide

Haiti's string of tyrannical rulers reached its zenith in 1956 with the election of François Duvalier, whose support came from the burgeoning Black middle class and the politically isolated rural poor. But he knew where the dangers lay and within months acted swiftly to neutralize his opponents.

Duvalier consolidated his power by creating the notorious Tontons Macoutes. The name refers to a character in a Haitian folk story, Tonton Macoute (Uncle Knapsack), who carries off small children in his bag at night. The Tontons Macoutes were a private militia who could use force with impunity in order to extort cash and crops from a cowed population. In exchange for this privilege, they afforded Duvalier utmost loyalty and protection.

'Papa Doc' died on April 21, 1971 and was succeeded by his son Jean-Claude 'Baby Doc' Duvalier. Periodic bouts of repression continued until major civil unrest forced Baby Doc to flee to France in February 1986.

Control changed hands between junta leaders until finally the Supreme Court ordered elections for December 1990. A young priest named Father Jean-Bertrand Aristide, standing as a surprise last-minute candidate with the slogan *'Lavalas'* (Flood), won a landslide victory.

It is difficult to guess what reforms Aristide and his Lavalas government might have achieved, because after seven months in office, an alliance of rich mulatto families and army generals, worried about their respective business and drug interests, staged a bloody coup.

The Organization of American States (OAS) and the US immediately condemned the coup, calling for economic sanctions. Four years of extreme economic hardship passed before Haitian leader, General Raoul Cédras, finally left for exile in Panama, allowing for a return of President Aristide.

Aristide faced much opposition in the following years, but his party, Fanmi Lavalas, remained popular enough to win elections in May and July 2000.

Haiti Today

The year 2004 marked the 200th anniversary of Haiti's independence. Ironically reflective of its own history, the anniversary year was marred by civil unrest, a bloody uprising, another political vacuum and a traumatic string of natural disasters that claimed thousands of lives.

After failing to implement democratic reforms, the embattled Aristide faced a three-week armed revolt in February 2004. Seizing farmland and whole towns, rebels finally captured Port-au-Prince and forced Aristide into exile; first to the Central African Republic, then Jamaica and finally to South Africa. Aristide maintains that he never vacated his post, but was forced into exile by US agents (a claim the US denies). US-backed Gerard Latortue assumed the prime ministership, but faces ongoing violence by both pro-Aristide supporters and private militia who have reclaimed several towns.

The ongoing political chaos was exacerbated by the enormous devastation wrought by Tropical Storm Jeanne, which killed more than 3000 in September 2004, and left more than 200,000 people homeless. The worst-hit areas were around Gonaïves, where hospitals sat half-buried in mud and doctors were forced to perform amputations without electricity or running water. In the wake of the storms, international food aid was looted by armed gangs.

With a per capita income of US$380, Haiti is the poorest country in the western hemisphere. More than 700 political prisoners languish in jail. Unemployment stands at 80% and literacy is less than 50%. The average lifespan is 52 years. Still, Haitians have proven that progress can be made despite the enormous obstacles, evidenced by the fact that Haiti is one of the few developing nations to reduce its HIV infection rate, bringing the number down from 6% in 2001 to 3% in 2004. Further development will depend on new leadership and the outcome of elections, although any new head of state can expect serious economic, political and social challenges.

THE CULTURE

Haiti is predominantly made up of peasants who live a subsistence lifestyle in rural areas. Traditionally, the men plant and harvest the crops, while the women care for the children, prepare meals and sell surplus crops at the market.

Their small, usually two-room wooden houses have no electricity, and food preparation takes place outside on a charcoal fire. If faced with difficult and arduous work, the men work together on one piece of land in a communal work team called a *kombit*. Neighbors and friends, sometimes called by the sound of a conch-shell trumpet, work for free and are compensated by a feast at the end of the day. In the evenings after eating, the group often relaxes by playing *Krik? Krak!*, an oral game of riddles.

As the growing population's demands on the land have reached breaking point, many peasants have sought a better life in the capital. But the mass exodus from the land has created teeming slums, such as Cité Soleil. Here much of the communal spirit of the countryside is lost in the everyday grind as about 200,000 people occupy 1.9 sq miles (5 sq km) of land, mainly reclaimed sea swamp, in some of the most brutal and demoralizing conditions imaginable.

Another life altogether prevails in the cool hills above Port-au-Prince. The country's elite, the 1% of society that has 44% of the wealth, lives in mansions surrounded by high walls, in and above Pétionville.

Haiti is home to almost eight million people, of whom 79% are rural, living off agriculture. People of African origin make up about 95% of Haiti's population. The other 5% is made up of mulattos, Middle Easterners and people of other races. Members of the mulatto class, which constitutes half of the country's elite and controls most of the economy, are the descendants of African slaves and French plantation owners.

RELIGION

While almost everyone practices Vodou, it is commonly held that 80% of the population is Catholic and 20% Protestant. Due to his distrust of foreign power within the Haitian Catholic Church, François Duvalier created an indigenous episcopacy in the 1960s. The predominantly Bretagne Jesuits and the Holy Ghost Fathers (another group of Catholic priests) were sent into exile and replaced with a more indigenous clergy.

This resultant Catholic hierarchy not only remained silent about the brutal regime, but even included the dictator in their public prayers. However, even though the bishops were Duvalierists, at a grassroots level the Church took its inspiration from the current of liberation theology that flowed across Latin America in the mid-1970s. The Ti Legliz (Little Church) was born and began to flourish. Houses of worship doubled as adult learning centers and political forums for students. With help from the Church-supported Radio Soleil, the Ti Legliz was instrumental in the downfall of Jean-Claude Duvalier.

The Protestant churches in Haiti, with the exception of the Methodists, have been much less political. Many churches from North America, mainstream and otherwise, continue to pour missionaries and money into the country. Their memberships have grown, usually in relationship to the amount of food aid the churches can offer.

ARTS

For its size and population, Haiti has an abundance of artists – they are predominantly painters, but also metalworkers and Vodou flag makers. Much of Haitian art has been classified as 'naïve' or 'primitive,' partly due to its simple style and avoidance of classical perspective.

The major factor contributing to the singular vision of Haiti's artists is their inextricable link with Vodou. Artists serve the *lwa* (Vodou spirits) by painting murals to decorate the walls of temples and making elaborate sequined flags for use in ceremonies.

Hector Hyppolite, now considered Haiti's greatest painter, was a Vodou priest, and his allegiance to the spirit world never faded during his years of success. Some of Hyppolite's paintings can be seen at the Musée d'Art in Port-au-Prince.

VODOU

Vodou is one of the most maligned religions on the planet. Many people imagine it to be a mass of superstitions based on fear and ignorance, lacking any religious traditions. This negative portrayal comes partly from sensational Hollywood movies, but also dates back to the early 19th century when Haitian culture was demonized due to the slave revolt that culminated in the declaration of independence in 1804.

Vodou has its roots in the animist spirit religions of 14th-century West Africa. The slaves, brought from Dahomey (present-day Benin) and the Congo, carried their beliefs with them on the slave ships from Africa. The Vodou that is practiced today is a synthesis of these religions crossed with residual rituals from the Taino Indians.

In order to retain their own beliefs while humoring the missionaries, slaves replaced their sacred objects with icons of the Catholic saints. To this day, Vodou altars display chromolithographs (color pictures) of Catholic saints; the images are the same as those you would see in a church but the meanings are different, with each surrogate Catholic saint signifying a different spirit from the vast pantheon.

There are three denominations in Vodou: Orthodox, Makaya and Kongo. All believe in only one God, called Gran Met (Great Master), and lesser entities called *lwa*, spirits summoned through prayer, song, drumming and dance. The *lwa* possess Vodou initiates, and manifest and identify themselves by singing, dancing, healing the sick and offering advice.

Vodou has played a large part in both the inspiration and organization of the struggle for independence, and many of the early revolutionaries were Vodou priests. But Vodou has also been outlawed at various times; in 1941, under President Elie Lescot, Vodou altars were burned and sacred Mapou trees cut down. The Catholic Church now coexists with and tolerates the practice of Vodou in Haiti.

Musical expression in Haiti reflects both the fusion of cultural influences and, more recently, popular resistance and struggle in Haitian politics. Vodou ceremonies have always been accompanied by music, song and dance. During the ceremony, the *houngan* (priest) salutes and greets the *lwa* from the pantheon. Each *lwa* is announced by its own particular ritual drum beats and songs brought over by the slaves from 16th-century West Africa.

Rara is a Vodou performance ritual held during the weeks before Easter, when temple ceremonies are taken to the streets. *Racines* (roots) music grew out of the Vodou-jazz movement of the late 1970s. Vodou jazz was a fusion of American jazz with Vodou rhythms and melodies. One of the leading proponents of the new musical form was the drummer Aboudja, who sought to rediscover Haiti's African roots (a recurring theme in Haitian art) through music.

In the years since independence, intellectual Haitians have created a strong school of indigenous literature to counter prevailing imperialist concepts of Haiti as a nation of primitive savages. A movement that positively embraced Haiti's unique cultural identity (following the US occupation of 1915–34) is usually referred to as Noirisme. The most important Noirisme writers were Jean Price-Mars and Jacques Roumain, author of *Les gouverneurs de la rosée* (Masters of the Dew), considered to be Haiti's finest work of literature.

Sadly, after the ascendancy of Noirisme in political life, the Duvalier dictatorship effectively torpedoed Haitian intellectual and literary life. Throughout those dark years more books were written by Haitians outside of the country than by those in it, mainly characterized by anti-Duvalier views.

ENVIRONMENT

The Land

Haiti occupies the mountainous western third of Hispaniola, sharing a 241-mile-long (388km) border with the Dominican Republic. About the size of the US state of Maryland, the country is cut by hundreds of rivers and streams, many of which bring torrential flood waters and eroded soil during the hurricane season. Rising above these river valleys are four mountain chains; Haiti's tallest mountain is 8773ft (2674m) Pic La Selle,

located in the southeast of the country. Haiti's largest drainage system, the Artibonite river, extends 248.5 miles (400km) through the center of the country. The river was dammed in its upper reaches in 1956, forming the Lac de Péligre behind Haiti's major hydroelectric facility. Its delta, south of Gonaïves, is a key rice-producing area.

Wildlife

Haiti is rich in birdlife, with 220 species, including the palmchat and the La Selle thrush. The gray-crowned palm tanager is a species unique to Haiti. Water birds include American flamingo and the black-capped petrel, a seabird that nests in the high cliffs of Massif de la Selle and the Massif de la Hotte.

Despite major habitat destruction, some endemic animals remain, including a small population of manatees in the coastal waters. Of the four types of sea turtle here, the largest is the leatherback, which can weigh up to 1326lb (600kg). Reptiles include iguanas and American crocodiles, which can be seen at Étang Saumâtre.

Environmental Issues

Haiti is a popular university case study in environmental degradation and disaster, perhaps equaled only by Madagascar and the more devastated parts of the Amazon rainforest. Unchecked clearing of the land for food production and fuel wood has depleted massive tracts of broadleaf forest. Only a small portion of virgin forest survives, including forests on Pic Macaya (7700ft; 2347m) and Massif de la Selle.

The destruction of the forests for firewood and farmland has caused an untenable amount of soil erosion. An estimated 14,826 acres (6000 hectares) of arable land are lost annually to soil erosion, causing negative growth in the agricultural sector. Erosion has also left urban areas in a precarious position; 3000 people died in the floods of 2004. Meanwhile, the neighboring Dominican Republic and its intact forest cover came out of the same storm system relatively unscathed.

FOOD & DRINK

Most cafés offer a *plat complet,* usually *diri ak pwa* (rice and beans), *bannann peze* (fried plantain), salad and your choice of meat – or more often, whatever is available.

HAITI

The meats offered are *poule* (fried chicken), *tasso* (jerked beef), *griyo* (fried pork), *kabri* (goat) and *lambi* (conch). The dish can be served with *sòs Kreyol* (tomato-based Creole sauce), *ti malice* (onion and herb sauce) or a *sòs vyann* (meat sauce). Seafood is widely available, including lobster and conch, and is very reasonably priced.

Haiti produces wonderful coffee: Rebo and Haitian Blue are two brands that are produced mainly for export. Haiti also grows sugarcane, which is made into rum and *clairin,* a cheap cane spirit. The Haitian rum company is called Barbancourt, and both its three- and five-star varieties are excellent.

PORT-AU-PRINCE

pop 2,000,000

Port-au-Prince sprawls from the docks and waterside slums of the bay up to the sides of the surrounding mountains, where it meets the more affluent town of Pétionville – in reality a suburb of Port-au-Prince. It's a very colorful, animated city, teeming with people and traffic. The center of the city is compact and manageable on foot, and the rowdy street life is enthralling.

INFORMATION

Amex (☎ 223-8671; top fl, Agence Citadelle, 35 Place du Marron Inconnu; ☷ 8am-1pm & 2-4pm Mon-Fri, 8:30am-12:30pm Sat) Exchanges traveler's checks.

Hôpital du Canapé Vert (☎ 245-0205/0281/0984; 83 Rte du Canapé Vert) Has a 24-hour emergency department.

Maison de Tourisme (☎ 222-8659; cnr Rues Capois & Magny; ☷ 8am-4pm Mon-Fri) Good source of information for travelers.

Police (☎ 114, 223-2301)

Red Cross (☎ 118, 245-1171) Offices on Rue des Miracles and Rue Eden.

Semicom (☎ 222-1895; 165 Rue Capois) Internet café located 0.6 miles (1km) south of Champs de Mars; other options are located around Ave John Brown.

Sogebank (Delmas 30) Exchanges US dollars. Another branch is close to Hotel Oloffson.

DANGERS & ANNOYANCES

Street crime is a fact of life in Port-au-Prince, so take sensible precautions. Don't be ostentatious or keep your cash in your back pocket as the pickpockets are skillful.

It is very unwise to walk around after dark, even around touristy areas such as Champs de Mars. Avoid visiting the slum areas, such as Cité Soleil off Rte Nationale 1 and Cité Liberté off Blvd Harry Truman.

SIGHTS

The main area for sightseeing is within and around the **Champs de Mars**, the large park built in 1953 that runs from the Palais National to Rue Capois. Here you'll find a couple of museums and the **Palais National**. The **Place des Héros de l'Independence**, east of the palace, contains the statues of the founders of independent Haiti. The *Statue of the Unknown Slave* depicts a runaway slave blowing a conch-shell trumpet as a call to begin the revolution.

The **Musée du Panthéon National** (Mupanah; National Museum; ☎ 222-8337; Place du Champs de Mars; admission free; ☷ 10am-4pm Mon-Thu, 10am-6pm Fri, 3-5pm Sat & Sun) contains various items of historical interest, including King Christophe's suicidal pistol and the rusting anchor of Columbus' flagship, the *Santa María.*

The **Musée d'Art Haïtien** (Museum of Haitian Art; ☎ 222-2550; Rue Légitime; admission US$0.50; ☷ 10am-4pm Mon-Sat), at the southern edge of Champs de Mars, has a permanent collection of Haiti's finest naïve art. The **Centre d'Art** (58 Ruelle Roy), originally an artists' cooperative, is on a quiet street off Rue Capois several blocks south of Champs de Mars.

The **Ste Trinité Episcopalian Cathedral** (cnr Ave Mgr Guilloux & Rue Pavée) is located just north of Champs de Mars. Its interior is decorated with fantastic biblical murals painted by the country's greatest naïve artists, including Philomé Obin and Wilson Bigaud. Two blocks north of Ste Trinité, the **Notre Dame Catholic cathedral** (cnr Rues Dr Aubry & Bonne Foi) is the city's largest ecclesiastical building.

SLEEPING

Most of the city's hotels are in Pétionville (see p253). Hotels can usually arrange for an airport pickup or drop-off for around US$20.

Wall's Guest House (☎ 249-4317; walls@haitianmail .com; 8 bis Rue Mackandal; shared r per person incl breakfast & dinner US$25) A Canadian couple runs this homey guesthouse. Its cheerful atmosphere attracts numerous young volunteers who work in Haiti.

St Joseph's Home for Boys Guest House (☎ 257-4237; sjfamily@pobox.com; 48 Rue Herne; shared r per person incl breakfast & dinner US$30) A budget option.

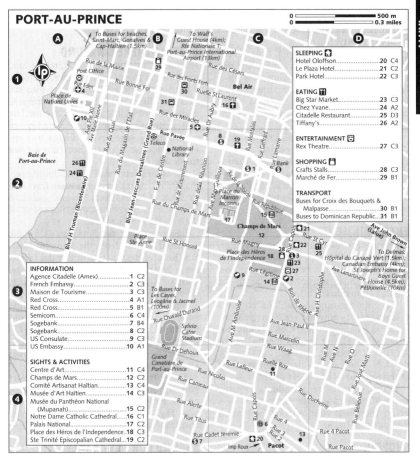

PORT-AU-PRINCE

0 — 500 m
0 — 0.3 miles

SLEEPING 🏠
Hotel Oloffson........................**20** C4
Le Plaza Hotel.......................**21** C2
Park Hotel.............................**22** C3

EATING 🍴
Big Star Market......................**23** C3
Chez Yvane............................**24** A2
Citadelle Restaurant................**25** D3
Tiffany's................................**26** A2

ENTERTAINMENT 🎭
Rex Theatre............................**27** C3

SHOPPING 🛍
Crafts Stalls...........................**28** C3
Marché de Fer.........................**29** B1

TRANSPORT
Buses for Croix des Bouquets &
  Malpasse..............................**30** B1
Buses to Dominican Republic...**31** B1

INFORMATION
Agence Citadelle (Amex)................**1** C2
French Embassy.............................**2** C3
Maison de Tourisme.......................**3** C3
Red Cross....................................**4** A1
Red Cross....................................**5** B1
Semicom......................................**6** C4
Sogebank.....................................**7** B4
Sogebank.....................................**8** C2
US Consulate................................**9** C3
US Embassy................................**10** A1

SIGHTS & ACTIVITIES
Centre d'Art................................**11** C2
Champs de Mars..........................**12** C3
Comité Artisanat Haïtien..............**13** C4
Musée d'Art Haïtien.....................**14** C3
Musée du Panthéon National
  (Mupanah)...............................**15** C2
Notre Dame Catholic Cathedral.....**16** C1
Palais National............................**17** C2
Place des Héros de l'Independence..**18** C3
Ste Trinité Episcopalian Cathedral...**19** C2

From Rte de Delmas, go down Delmas 91, take Rue La Plume (third right) and turn left at the end of the road. St Joe's is the last house on the right.

Hotel Oloffson (☎ 223-4000/4102; 60 Ave H Christophe; r/bungalow/ste per person incl buffet breakfast US$72.90/88.50/115.90, 2nd person additional US$10; 🏊) At the junction of Rue Capois and Ave H Christophe, no trip to Haiti is complete without spending at least one night at this hotel. It was captured in Graham Greene's novel *The Comedians*, part of which was written here.

Park Hotel (☎ 222-4406/8721; fax 221-8721; 23 Champs de Mars; s/d US$48.40/64.40; 🏊 🖥) Slightly cheaper than the Oloffson, this sleepy little town house is set back from the road, near Champs de Mars.

Le Plaza Hotel (☎ 223-9800/8697/9773, 222-0766; hiplaza@acn2.net; 10 Rue Capois; s US$70-90, d US$80-100, plus 10% tax & energy charge per day US$5; 🏊 🖥) Offers the best facilities downtown, with 104 rooms around a tropical garden, as well as a bar, restaurant and swimming pool.

EATING

Most of the hotels in downtown Port-au-Prince have restaurants with Haitian, French and American menus. While dining cheaply in the evening can be a bit of a problem, it's not impossible, and there's always the option of heading up the hill to Pétionville (see p253).

Citadelle Restaurant (1 Rue St Cyr; mains US$1-3.50; 🕐 lunch & dinner) The Citadelle is a friendly,

HAITI

dilapidated eatery serving Haitian delights, which can be eaten inside, on the veranda or in the courtyard.

Chez Yvane (☎ 222-0188/7676; 19 Bicentenaire; dishes US$4; ⏰ 8am-6pm Mon-Sat, 8am-4pm Sun) Also known locally as Chaffeur Gide, this place has the look of an American diner yet the food is exclusively Creole. It has a bright conservatory at the back, overlooking the parking lot and the bay.

Tiffany's (☎ 222-3506/0993; 12 Bicentenaire; dishes US$7-9; ⏰ 11am-6pm Mon-Fri) Cool, dark and spacious, with a delicious Haitian and French menu. Prices are quite reasonable.

Big Star Market (Rue Capois) Next to the Rex Theatre, self-caterers can shop for all kinds of food here.

ENTERTAINMENT

There are no real bars in Port-au-Prince; however, most restaurants serve alcohol and can get quite lively – many also host live music. Most music venues lie up the hill in Pétionville (right).

Government-funded outdoor concerts take place every now and again on the bandstand on Champs de Mars. Live bands also occasionally play at the **Rex Theatre** (☎ 222-1848/1176; 41 Rue Capois), opposite the Champs de Mars. You can buy tickets for concerts at the Big Star Market next door.

If you wish to see a Vodou ceremony you will have to engage the services of a guide. Inquire at your hotel or the Maison de Tourisme (p250).

SHOPPING

Marché de Fer (Iron Market; cnr Blvd Jean-Jacques Dessalines & Rue des Fronts Forts) About four blocks west of the Notre Dame cathedral, this hellish treasure trove is both a food and craft market, selling everything from baskets of dried mushrooms to various Vodou ephemera. A rather stressful shopping experience, it's open daily.

Comité Artisanat Haïtien (29 Rue 3) If it gets too much, try this craftmakers' collective based in Pacot, which has a good selection of colorfully painted miniature metal *taptaps* (converted pickups with bench seats) and basketware. There are crafts stalls next to the Musée d'Art Haïtien.

If you want to buy magnificent sequined Vodou flags, it's more fun to go to the artists themselves. Most of them live in Bel Air, an old quarter just north of the Notre Dame cathedral.

GETTING THERE & AROUND

For more information on international travel to and from Port-au-Prince, see p775.

Caribintair (☎ 246-0737; www.gocelestial.com /caribintair_Schedule.htm) is Haiti's most reliable domestic airline, and the main one used by diplomats and aid workers. At the time of writing there were several flights to Cap-Haïtien and Les Cayes. Check the website for details.

Buses for southwest Haiti, including Jacmel (US$2, three hours), depart from the junction of Rue Oswald Durand and Blvd Jean-Jacques Dessalines, one block west of the Sylvio Cator Stadium.

Buses to Croix des Bouquets (US$0.80, one hour) depart from the statue of Madame Kolo, at the junction of Rue des Fronts Forts and Rue de Centre. For Malpasse, jump on a *taptap* from Croix des Bouquets (about US$1).

Buses to Cap-Haïtien (US$6.50, nine hours), Gonaïves (US$3.50, five hours) and St-Marc (US$2, 3½ hours) depart from the Estation O'Cap beside the Shell gas station, at the confluence of Blvd Jean-Jacques Dessalines and Blvd La Saline.

The Port-au-Prince International Airport is 8 miles (13km) north of the town center. Expect to pay around US$20 for a taxi. The collective taxis, called *publiques*, cost US$0.40 a trip.

AROUND PORT-AU-PRINCE
Pétionville

Pétionville has evolved from a hill resort into a middle- and upper-class suburb of Port-au-Prince. Most of the city's restaurants, nightlife and exclusive shops are up in Pétionville, as are most of its hotels. The streets are cleaner, but the area still retains a shabby, construction-site atmosphere.

There are no obvious tourist sights, but it's worth soaking up the relaxed atmosphere for a couple of days. Place St Pierre, at the top of the hill, has a small flower market and the grassy square is a good place to people-watch.

INFORMATION

Companet Cyber Café (Rue Lamarre; per 30min US$2; ⏰ 9am-7pm Mon-Sat) Centrally located Internet café.

Haitian Association for the Tourism & Hotel Industry (Apt 5, Choucoune Plaza, Rue Lamarre; 8am-4pm Mon-Fri)

Promobank (Rue Faubert & Rue Rigaud; 9am-1pm & 3-5pm Mon-Fri, 9am-1pm Sat) This bank will change traveler's checks.

Voyages Lumière (249-6177, cell 557-0753; www .voyagelumierehaiti.com) Reliable tour operator based in Pétionville. There's no office but they will meet you at your hotel.

SLEEPING & EATING
Most of the large international standard hotels are found in Pétionville, and budget accommodations are limited. Unless stated otherwise, all places listed feature air-con and hot-water baths, and prices include breakfast and taxes.

Doux Sejour Guest House (257-1560; fax 257-6518; 32 Rue Magny; d US$30) This friendly guest-house has airy reception areas and a large balcony terrace overlooking a quiet side street. Ask to see a few rooms, as some are better than others.

Hotel Caraïbe (257-2524; hotelcaraibe@access haiti.com; 13 Rue Leon Nau; s/d US$59/81, d in house US$94;) The good-value and midbudget Caraïbe is an extremely well-run hacienda-style guesthouse, and has a swimming pool and spotless rooms.

Hotel Montana (229-4000; htmontana@aol.com; Rue F Cardozo; s US$98, ste US$118-140, plus 10% tax & per additional person US$10;) Located off Ave Pan Américaine. The reception areas are furnished with wonderful Art Deco walnut furniture, while the 96 guest rooms are a mixture of Art Deco and colonial styles.

Hotel Kinam (257-0462/6525; www.hotelkinam .com; Place St Pierre; s/d US$55/66, s/d ste US$116/138, plus 10% tax & daily energy charge US$5;) A good choice within the heart of Pétionville, it combines character and modern amenities, such as air-con and TV, and it has a swimming pool.

Fior di Latte (256-8474; Choucoune Plaza; mains US$6-11; lunch & dinner Mon-Sat) This is an extremely popular weekend venue serving delicious, authentic Italian-style pizza, pasta and ice cream under a vine-covered canopy. This really is a place where people come to be seen.

La Voile (257-4561; 32 Rue Rigaud; mains US$30-40; dinner only) One of the fanciest places in town, La Voile specializes in seafood, but vegetarians are also well catered for.

GETTING THERE & AROUND
Pétionville is only a half-hour's drive from the center of Port-au-Prince, 15 minutes without traffic.

Tropical Airways (250-1880/27/28; www.tropical-haiti.com; Ave Pan Américaine) conducts regular flights from Port-au-Prince to Cap-Haïtien (US$65/120 one way/round-trip) and Port-de-Paix (US$80/145).

Taptaps and buses run regularly from the junction of Ave Pan Américaine and Rue Lamarre and along Rte de Delmas to Port-au-Prince (5 gourdes). Most *taptaps* for Port-au-Prince leave Pétionville from the junction of Rue Grégoire and Ave Pan Américaine. You can catch a *taptap* to Kenscoff (10 gourdes) from Place St Pierre outside Hotel Kinam.

East of Port-Au-Prince
To get a taste of rural Haiti without straying too far from the capital, head east to **Croix des Bouquets**, best known for its iron workers in the **Noailles district**.

East of Croix des Bouquets, the main road reaches **Étang Saumâtre**, Haiti's largest saltwater lake. The lake supports over 100 species, including flamingos and American crocodiles. If you have time, it's worth making a detour to also visit **Trou Caïman**, an excellent place for spotting waterfowl.

Parc National Forêt des Pins is the largest remaining tract of pine forest in Haiti, covering the far east fringe of the Massif de la Selle, south of Malpasse. There is an official entrance to the forest on the road between Fonds Verettes and Forêt des Pins, where you can find some small cabins that can be rented for the night.

North of Port-Au-Prince – Côte des Arcadins
Rte Nationale 1 is the main highway to Cap-Haïtien via Gonaïves. It skirts the coast, called the Côte des Arcadins, for most of the first 49.5 miles (80km) between Cabaret (the former Duvalierville satirized in Greene's *The Comedians*) and St-Marc. It is here that most of the country's beach resorts are situated. **Wahoo Bay Beach** (556-5646, in Port-au-Prince 298-3410; www.wahoobaybeach.com; Rte Nationale 1; d US$80-100, apt US$130) is an attractive resort with lush gardens and a huge swimming pool.

If you wish to take public transportation, catch a bus or *taptap* in Port-au-Prince

HAITI

from Estation O'Cap beside the Shell gas station, at the confluence of Blvd Jean-Jacques Dessalines and Blvd La Saline.

SOUTHERN HAITI

JACMEL

pop 15,000

Jacmel is about a 74.5-mile (120km) drive southwest of Port-au-Prince, via one of the best roads in the country. A busy coffee port at the turn of the 20th century, it retains much of its late-Victorian grace with wide and sleepy streets lined by elegant town houses. Jacmel has had a longstanding kinship with artists and the arts, and it has now become a refuge for artists from all over Haiti and the world. Much of Jacmel's creativity can be seen in the fantastic papier-mâché masks made for the pre-Lent Mardi Gras festivities.

Information

Associations des Micro-Enterprises Touristiques du Sud'Est (AMETS; 40 Rue d'Orléans; ☑ 8am-4pm Mon-Fri, 8am-2pm Sat) This tourist office can direct you toward the *ateliers* (artist's workshops). It can also arrange car and horse rental, and excursions.
Banque Nationale de Crédit (BNC; Grand Rue; ☑ 8:30am-4pm Mon-Fri, 8:30am-1pm Sat) Exchanges currency.
BizNet (Rue Vaivres; per 30min US$2) An Internet café.

Sights & Activities

Close to the seafront, Rue du Commerce has many fine examples of 19th-century warehouses; at the eastern end of the street are the **customs house**, an old 18th-century **prison** and the **wharf**. There are **merchants' mansions** strewn all over town in varying states of decay, including Manoir Alexandre, a rickety old hotel, and Salubria Gallery (right).

East of Place d'Armes, the town square, is a red-and-green baroque **Marché** built in 1895, which resembles a scaled-down version of the grand iron market in Port-au-Prince. The pretty 19th-century **Cathédrale de St Phillippe et St Jacques** (Rue de l'Eglise) is close to the market.

Sleeping & Eating

While Jacmel is an obvious tourist destination, it doesn't have many places to stay. It can be difficult to find a hotel room during Carnival, when you should book ahead.

Guy's Guest House (☎ 288-3421; http://guysguest house.com/; Ave de la Liberté No 52; r per person incl breakfast from US$13) Next to the Tabernacle Protestant Church, Guy's is central and popular with Peace Corps workers. Rooms are clean and most have shared baths.

Hôtel la Jacmelienne sur Plage (☎ 288-3451/ 3504, 222-4899; hoteljacmelienne@hotmail.com; Rue St-Anne; s/d US$50/60, plus 10% tax & energy charge; ☑) Long considered the place to stay in Jacmel, the Jacmelienne has an enviable beachside position and well-furnished rooms that catch the Baie de Jacmel breeze.

Yaquimo Restaurant & Bar (Ave de la Liberté; dishes US$4-10) If you're looking for a restaurant with live music, try this place by the beach.

Shopping

Salubria Gallery (☎ 288-2390; 26 Rue Seymour Pradel) This eclectic gallery, owned by an American professor Robert Bricston, shows off most of the masters of Haitian art, including Fortuné Gerard, Préfète Duffaut and Lafortune Felix, as well as exotic artifacts from overseas.

Getting There & Around

Jacmel's new bus stand is 2 miles (3.2km) out of town, on the road to Port-au-Prince. Hourly buses for Port-au-Prince (three hours) and Léogâne (1½ hours) cost 40 gourdes (US$1.80), and *taptaps* to Cayes Jacmel (and the nearby beaches) cost 5 gourdes. The drive from Port-au-Prince takes about two hours.

AROUND JACMEL

There are several good **beaches** around Jacmel; the best beach is at **Cyvadier Plage**, 6 miles (10km) east of town. There are beach bungalows here, with hot-water baths, for about US$40 per night.

Around 7.5 miles (12km) inland from Jacmel, reached on horseback or on foot, is **Bassins Bleu**, a spectacular grotto of cascades and cobalt-blue pools.

There are many guides in Jacmel who will, for a fee, take you on the journey by horse, which takes about two hours each way. It is advisable to negotiate the full price before you set off to avoid endless squabbling en route. Consider paying about US$10 per person, but you may have to pay more. A broad hat and sunblock are recommended.

PARC NATIONAL LA VISITE

One of the most spectacular hikes in Haiti is across the western section of Massif de la Selle, from Kenscoff to Seguin. The hike takes six or seven hours. Once you reach Seguin, you can sleep overnight in the cozy **Auberge de la Visite** (☎ 246-0166, 257-1579; r incl all meals US$50), a guesthouse with sweeping views of the sea.

If you don't want to walk all the way, it's also possible to take a 4WD from Kenscoff to the point where the road becomes impassable by vehicle, where you can be met by staff from the Auberge de la Visite with horses (US$20 per horse, book four days in advance).

LES CAYES

pop 46,000

Les Cayes is Haiti's fourth-largest city, although it's still rather sleepy and laid-back. There's not too much in the town itself, but it makes a good stopover on the huge journey to Jérémie or Parc National Macaya, and there are good beaches at the nearby Île-à-Vache.

The best place to stay is at the **Concorde Hotel** (☎ 286-0277; 49 Rue Gabions de Indigenes, PO Box 46; d with breakfast US$32), which is basic but has comfortable rooms with fans. Buses to Port-au-Prince (US$3, six hours) leave when full. For travel to and from Jacmel, take a Port-au-Prince bus and change at Léogâne.

ÎLE-À-VACHE

pop 5000

About 9 miles (15km) off the coast of Les Cayes, the 12.5-mile-long (20km) Île-à-Vache makes a good tropical getaway, complete with colorful rural houses, plantations and unspoiled beaches. Its history is tied closely with that of Captain Morgan, the famous buccaneer who was based here for a while.

An upmarket resort at Caye Coq, **Port Morgan** (☎ 286-1600; www.port-morgan.com; d US$60) has a great view of the bay, with comfortable rooms and good facilities.

Boats leave the Les Cayes wharf hourly (US$1, 30 to 45 minutes) landing at the village of Madame Bernard on the island's northern coast. Alternatively it's possible to charter a fishing sail boat at the wharf for around US$30 for the one- to two-hour trip across the water.

PARC NATIONAL MACAYA & JÉRÉMIE

The mountains in Parc National Macaya contain a number of rough trails that cut through some beautiful terrain. The most challenging trek, taking four days round-trip, is to the top of Pic Macaya.

Within the park, the University of Florida camp at Plaine Durand offers basic facilities, such as toilets, running water and a campsite. Guides at the camp charge US$6 a day per person.

To reach the park, take a *taptap* from Les Cayes as far as Dubreuil and then proceed on foot to the University of Florida project headquarters, a four-hour hike.

If you've come this far, and you have an extra day or two, it's worth carrying on for 28 miles (45km) to the charming seaside town of Jérémie. There are several places to stay here, including the adequate **Auberge Inn** (☎ 284-5174; aubergeinn@netscape.net; 6 Ave Emile Roumer; s/d incl breakfast US$35/45).

Daily *taptaps* travel to Jérémie from Les Cayes (US$5, three hours). The trip from Port-au-Prince takes 12 hours.

NORTHERN HAITI

CAP-HAÏTIEN

pop 100,000

Known as O'Cap to the locals, Cap-Haïtien has a more Latin feel than the rest of Haiti. The streets, laid out in a grid system, owe more to Spanish architecture than French, and are small and narrow, so there is always a shady side to walk on. In comparison to Port-au-Prince, the city has a relaxed and parochial atmosphere, especially in the early evenings when the majority of residents hang out and chat on their balconies.

Information

Banque de l'Union Haïtienne (BUH; Rue 17 A) Change money here, or try Promobank, located in the same building.

Teleco Office (☎ 262-0000/0219; Rue 17; ⊙ 24hr) Between Rue A and the Boulevard, you can place national and international calls here.

Sights

If you follow the Boulevard north until it enters the suburb of Carenage, and then continue north, you'll come across three French fort sites.

The first, **Fort Etienne Magny**, is on your left as you head north; all that remains is a small group of cannons.

The next is **Fort St Joseph**, on the right on the edge of the cliff. If you continue north until the road peters out at Rival Beach, then continue along the sand for 438yd (400m), you'll reach **Fort Picolet**. Although the fort itself is in ruins, some quite large walls and brick staircases are still standing, and you will find an amazing array of cannons.

Sleeping & Eating

Hotel Columbia (Rue 5 K; s/d incl breakfast US$8/10) A small, friendly family-run guesthouse, Columbia has clean and basic rooms on a quiet street.

Hotel Mont Joli (☎ 262-0300, 222-7764; MontJoli@aol.com; Rue B, Carenage; s/d/tr/q US$75/94/105/115; ⌕) Built in many layers on a steep hill north of the old town center this hotel is worth dropping by for a cocktail just to admire the view over the city. Rooms come with TV and private bath.

Café de l'Alliance (☎ 262-4236; Rue 15 D; mains US$4-8; ⏲ breakfast & lunch Mon-Sat) Attached to the Alliance Français library is this smart café serving sandwiches, omelettes and salads.

Getting There & Away

For more information on international and domestic flights to and from Cap-Haïtien, see p259.

The bus station for destinations south along Rte Nationale 1, such as Gonaïves (US$3, four hours), St-Marc (US$5, seven hours) and Port-au-Prince (US$6.50, nine hours), is at the city gates on Rue L. If you're heading to Port-au-Prince, leave early as it's not advisable to arrive in the area of La Saline, where buses terminate, after dark.

BEACHES

The continuation of Rue 21 heads west out of Cap-Haïtien, winding through the hills to the northwest coast of the cape. Here you will discover some of the most beautiful coastal scenery in Haiti, with lush forested hills tumbling into the Atlantic Ocean.

The road hits the north coast of the cape near **Cormier Plage**, a lovely beach and resort, and ends on the western edge of **Plage Labadie**, a small walled-off peninsula.

Taptaps (US$1) going to Cormier Plage and Plage Labadie leave regularly from Rue 21 Q near the gymnasium in Cap-Haïtien.

SANS SOUCI & THE CITADELLE

Henri Christophe's splendid palace, Sans Souci, and the awe-inspiring mountaintop fortress, the Citadelle, can be seen on a day trip from Cap-Haïtien. Sans Souci is on the edge of the small town of Milot, 12.4 miles (20km) south of Cap-Haïtien.

The **Sans Souci palace**, commissioned by Christophe in 1810, was completed in 1813. It was designed to be the equal of Versailles in France, and in its glory days was possibly a serious rival. The palace was ransacked after the fall of Christophe, and finally ruined by an 1842 earthquake.

From Sans Souci, it's a 3-mile-long (5km) walk to the Citadelle, situated in the Parc Nationale Historique La Citadelle. If you have a vehicle, you can drive another 2.2 miles (3.5km) to a parking area at the foot of the Citadelle.

It took Henri Christophe 15 years to build the **Citadelle**, a vast mountaintop fortress, constructed to combat another invasion by the French. The astounding structure was completed in 1820, having employed up to 20,000 people, many of whom died during the arduous task. With 13ft-thick (4m) walls that reach heights of 131ft (40m), the fortress was impenetrable.

Entrance tickets for both sites are sold in the parking lot close to Sans Souci. The official rate for a combined ticket is 35 gourdes (US$1) per person, plus 100 gourdes (US$6) for a guide. If you wish to ascend by horse, the rate is 50 gourdes (US$3) per horse – don't forget you must pay for your guide's horse as well. Having said this, some travelers end up paying upward of US$30 for the whole shebang, so bargain hard.

GONAÏVES

pop 64,000

Gonaïves is a handy place to stay if you want to break your journey between Cap-Haïtien and Port-au-Prince, or if you're visiting for either the Soukri or Souvenance festivals (see p258). Jean-Jacques Dessalines declared Haiti's independence here in 1804, and his wife, Claire Heureuse, is buried in the local cemetery. If you need to stay the night, try the **Family Hotel** (☎ 274-0600; Ave des Dattes; r with fan/air-con US$24/28; 🏴 📺), which is run by a Canadian, English-speaking family.

Express buses and *taptaps* run between Gonaïves and Port-au-Prince's Estation O'Cap (US$3.50, five hours) and Cap-Haïtien (US$3, four hours). Mopeds in Gonaïves operate as fast and cheap taxis, costing 4 gourdes a ride.

DIRECTORY

Information listed in this directory is specific to Haiti. For information pertaining to the entire region, check the book's main Directory (p757).

ACCOMMODATIONS

Cheap accommodations are scarce in Haiti. In some areas it is possible to stay in local homes for around US$10 per person. The budget hotels that do exist are almost

---

> **EMERGENCY NUMBERS**
>
> ▪ **Ambulance** (☎ 118)
> ▪ **Fire** (in Port-au-Prince ☎ 223-1028)
> ▪ **Police** (☎ 114)

---

exclusively aimed at Haitian or Caribbean travelers.

Hotels that are used to accommodating foreigners charge from US$60 per double upward. The accommodations are variable, and you can end up paying the same price for a basic room in a city as for a room in a beachside fort with four-poster beds. There are also international standard hotels charging around US$100 per double, which have plenty of mod cons and constant hot water. However, even these can be a bit run-down.

ACTIVITIES

While not as developed as in other parts of the Caribbean, Haiti still has some great opportunities for snorkeling and scuba diving. At Amani, near St-Marc, divers can descend along a famous wall that is home to what is believed to be the world's largest sea sponge, the Elephant's Ear. Other dive sites include Les Arcadins and Île de la Gonâve and, on the north coast, the beach resort of Cormier Plage.

Haiti also has a few places for walking and climbing. Two national parks, Macaya (p255) and La Visite (p255), have been established to preserve some of Haiti's natural riches, and it is possible to hike in both of these areas.

Amateur ornithologists can delight in Haiti's bird-watching possibilities. The best place for spotting water birds is northwest of Croix des Bouquets at Trou Caïman. High-altitude species, such as the threatened La Selle thrush and the white-winged warbler, can be spotted at Parc National La Visite.

BOOKS

An essential companion for any visitor to Haiti, *Libète: A Haiti Anthology*, edited by Charles Arthur and Michael Dash, covers Haitian history from the Arawak Indians to Aristide. This immensely readable collection of short extracts, many by Haitian authors, is breathtaking in its scope and detail.

> **PRACTICALITIES**
>
> ▪ **Newspapers & Magazines** Major private dailies in Haitian include *Le Matin* and *Le Nouvelliste*. Among the weekly papers, *Haiti Progrés* has a very good English section, while *Libète* is the leading weekly newspaper published in Creole. *Haiti Info* (Haiti Information Bureau, BP 15533, Pétionville, Haiti) is an excellent English-language news and analysis bulletin.
>
> ▪ **Radio & TV** Both the Voice of America and the BBC World Service transmit in Haiti over a short-wave frequency. Local radio stations worth trying include Radio Haiti Inter (106.1 FM) and Metropole (100.1 FM). There are eight TV stations in Port-au-Prince. Most hotels have cable TV, mostly US channels, including CNN.
>
> ▪ **Video Systems** The predominant video format is NTSC.
>
> ▪ **Electricity** Electric power is 115V to 125V (60 cycles). The sockets are designed to accommodate two- and three-pin, flat-pronged plugs (similar to the US and Canada).
>
> ▪ **Weights & Measures** Metric system.

Graham Greene's *The Comedians* is set in Haiti during the reign of Papa Doc. Both an excellent, thoughtful novel and a somber portrayal of life under a dictatorship, the book angered Papa Doc so much that he banned it in Haiti.

DANGERS & ANNOYANCES

Because of ongoing political turmoil and poverty, Haiti has been demonized by the media, and embassies advise against non-essential travel to the country. They also advise those that do travel there to register with their embassy or consulate on arrival.

True, the political situation can be volatile and is unpredictable enough that the risk of getting caught up in a riot is very real, but most trouble occurs in slum areas that are easily avoided. If you stumble upon a demonstration, return to your hotel immediately.

In popular spots, such as the Citadelle, persistent 'guides' who attach themselves to you can ruin the whole trip. Try to discourage them before you set off, as it's very hard to not pay them after they've run up a mountain alongside you.

EMBASSIES & CONSULATES
Haitian Embassies & Consulates

Belgium (☎ 02-649-7381; embhaiti@ip.etecsa.cu; 160 Ave Louise, Brussels 1050) Also covers the UK and Netherlands.
Canada (☎ 613-238-1628; 112 Rue Kent, Ste 1308, Ottawa K1P 5P2)
Dominican Republic (☎ 767-686-5778; amb. haiti@codetel.net.do; 33 Av Juan Sánchez Ramírez, Santo Domingo)
France (☎ 01-47-63-47-78; fax 01-42-27-02-05; 10 Rue Théodule Ribot, BP 275, Cédex 28, 75827 Paris)
Germany (☎ 3088-554-134; fax 3088-554-135; Meinekestr 5, 10719 Berlin) Also covers Denmark.
USA (☎ 202-332-4090; embassy@haiti.org; 2311 Massachusetts Ave NW, Washington, DC 20008)

Embassies & Consulates in Haiti

Embassies and consulates are in either Port-au-Prince or Pétionville.
Canada (☎ 249-9000; www.dfait-maeci.gc.ca/haiti /menu-en.asp; Delmas btwn 75 & 71, Port-au-Prince)
Dominican Republic (☎ 257-0383/1650/1208; fax 257-9215; 121 Ave Pan Américaine, cnr Rte El Rancho, Pétionville)
France (☎ 222-0951/0952, 223-8118; fax 223-9858; 51 Place des Héros de l'Independence; Port-au-Prince)
Germany (☎ 257-8782/7280; germanem@haitelonline .com; 2 Impasse Claudinette, Bois Moquette, Pétionville)

UK (☎ 257-3969; fax 257-4048; Hotel Montana, Rue F Cardoza, Pétionville) Off Ave Pan Américaine.
USA Embassy (☎ 222-0200/0269/1770/0327; http://us embassy.state.gov/posts/ha1/wwwhhome.html; Bicentenaire, Port-au-Prince) Consulate (☎ 223-0989/8853/9324/7011; fax 223-5515; 104 Rue Oswald Durand, Port-au-Prince; ✉ American citizen service 7.30am-2pm Mon, Tue, Wed & Fri, 7.30-11am Thu)

FESTIVALS & EVENTS

There are several saint's days and smaller festivals celebrated throughout the year, particularly during July and August. The celebrations can be equally as energetic as Mardi Gras, but are more manageable in size. Watch out for the following festivals:
Soukri (January 6) Held near Gonaïves.
Carnival Held during the week before Mardi Gras, in Jacmel.
Souvenance (Good Friday) Held near Gonaïves.
Our Lady of the Assumption (October 15) A country-wide festival.

HOLIDAYS

Following are the major public holidays in Haiti.
Independence Day January 1
Mardi Gras January/February (three days before Ash Wednesday)
Good Friday March/April
Assumption Day August 15
Anniversary of Henri Christophe's Death October 8
Anniversary of Jean-Jacques Dessalines' Death October 17
Battle of Vertières Day/Armed Forces Day November 18
Discovery of Haiti Day December 5
Christmas Day December 25

MONEY

The official currency is the gourde, and there are 100 centimes to 1 gourde, though US dollars are widely used. In the past the gourde was fixed to the US dollar at a rate of five gourdes to the dollar. Although this is no longer the rate, the 5-gourde bill is still referred to as 'one Haitian dollar,' the 10-gourde bill as 'two Haitian dollars' and so on.

Credit cards are accepted at car-rental companies, some resorts and major airlines. Exchanging traveler's checks can be problematic: Promobank is the only bank that changes them. Make sure to use US dollar traveler's checks only and bring your purchase receipt, as the bank will ask to see it.

TELEPHONE

Telecommunications in Haiti is atrocious. With phone lines often out of service, many businesses have several phone numbers; if the first doesn't work, try the others. Cell (mobile) phone numbers are more reliable.

Haiti's country code is ☎ 509. We've included only the seven-digit local number in Haiti listings in this chapter. To reach an international operator, dial ☎ 00; for information on international calls, dial ☎ 00-09.

VISAS

Upon entering the Republic of Haiti, visitors from most Western countries must present a passport valid for at least six months. At this time a three-month (90-day) visa is issued for US$25. If you wish to stay in Haiti for longer than 90 days, you must apply for a visitor/resident visa before you travel. The visa lasts five years and costs US$21.20.

If you wish to extend your tourist visa once in Haiti, contact the **Ministry of Foreign Affairs** (☎ 222-1243/8482) in Port-au-Prince.

TRANSPORTATION

GETTING THERE & AWAY
Entering Haiti

It's more difficult to enter Haiti via the airport, compared to the land border with the Dominican Republic. But with a bit of bribe money, it won't be difficult getting through – have a few crisp US dollars on hand as you pass through customs. No particular nationalities are barred from entering Haiti.

Air

Port-au-Prince has the main international airport, officially called **Guy Malary International Airport** (☎ 246-4105), but better known as Port-au-Prince International Airport, especially when booking tickets from abroad. Cap-Haïtien has the country's second-largest airport. For information on international flights to/from Haiti, see p775.

The following airlines fly to and from Haiti from within the Caribbean:

Aerocaribbean (☎ in Port-au-Prince 222-5900, in Cuba 7-879-7524; www.aero-caribbean.com; hub Havana)

Air Caraïbes (☎ 224-1415, 224-1416; www.aircaraibes .com; hub Guadeloupe)

Air Jamaica (☎ in Port-au-Prince 250-0946, in USA 800-523-5585; www.airjamaica.com; hub Montego Bay)

Land

There are three points where you can cross from Haiti into the Dominican Republic and vice versa. One is near Malpasse/Jimaní in the south, on the road that links Port-au-Prince to Santo Domingo. A second crossing point is near Ouanaminthe/Dajabón in the north; the border crossing is on a road that connects Cap-Haïtien and Santiago. The third border crossing is at Belladère/Elías Piña. These crossings close at 6pm.

When you leave Haiti, you must have your passport and the yellow entry card you received upon arrival. Likewise, tourists leaving the Dominican Republic will be asked to produce their passports and tourist cards.

GETTING AROUND
Air

With the atrocious road conditions in Haiti, domestic flights are a popular and quick way of getting from point to point. The flight between Port-au-Prince and Cap-Haïtien is especially useful, as it covers the same distance as a nine-hour bus ride within 30 minutes. A useful service is **Mission Aviation Fellowship** (☎ 510-8086, 250-3992; www.maf.org), which does charter flights around the country. You may be able to tag along on an already booked flight. For regularly scheduled flights, try Caribintair (p252).

Boat

There are quite a few islands and remote areas around Haiti only accessible by ferry or sailboat. Daily routes include Port-au-Prince to Jérémie; Côte des Arcadins to Île de la Gonâve; Ste Louis de Nord and Port-de-Paix to Île de la Gonâve; and Les Cayes to Île-à-Vaches. Smaller speedboats also cover some of these routes.

In some of the more remote coastal regions, fishing boats provide taxi services, charging around the same as *taptaps*. Fix the price before you board, as the owner may try to charge for the whole boat rather than a single ticket. Boats are rarely comfortable and often dangerously overcrowded.

Bus & Taptap

Traveling around by bus or *taptap* is the cheapest way to see Haiti. Fares vary from US$1 to US$7, depending on the destination. There are no timetables; buses leave

HAITI

when filled. Port-au-Prince and Cap-Haïtien have several departure points, depending on the destination, which will be written on the front of the bus. See the relevant sections for details. If you have a choice, a bus is usually faster and more comfortable than a *taptap*.

Car & Motorcycle

Driving in Haiti is dangerous. Most of the roads are terribly rutted, traffic signs are lacking, and if you have an accident, you could encounter problems with angry locals. If you do drive, you will need either a valid International Driving Permit or a current license from your home country.

It is possible to rent a car in Haiti, with fees from US$60 to US$75 a day, plus insurance, for an economy car; 4WDs start at around US$100 per day. Check the agencies at the airport. Hiring a car and driver will set you back US$150 per day.

Taxi

Port-au-Prince and Cap-Haïtien have a brilliant system of collective taxis called *publiques,* which charge 10 gourdes (about US$0.40) per trip. If you get into an empty *publique,* make sure the driver doesn't take the red ribbon off the mirror. This signifies that they are treating you as a private commission. If you want to hire a *publique* and driver for your private use, negotiate the deal before you set off. In smaller towns, taxi services are operated by motorcycle, where you should pay no more than 5 gourdes (about US$0.25) per trip.

Dominican Republic

The Dominican Republic (DR) is justly famous for its beaches – broad bands of white sand bounded by pastel waters and tall coconut trees. But the DR has more to offer than many realize. The north coast is one of the best places in the world for windsurfing and kiteboarding and there's great whale-watching off of the Samaná Peninsula. The DR has the Caribbean's highest peak – Pico Duarte at 10,417ft (3175m) – and whether or not you climb it, the rugged area makes for fun hiking, biking and white-water rafting.

The Dominican Republic is also home to many New World firsts – the first hospital, the first university and the first paved road. It is not a stretch to say that the modern history of the Americas began here.

It is a country of layers, of men playing dominoes on aluminum tables, wood-frame houses painted bubblegum pink, of cockfights and sweet coffee. And nowhere is baseball – by nature a slow game   so imbued by the raucous celebration of its fans.

While there is no shame in spending a week pampering yourself at an all-inclusive resort (the DR is famous for those too!), this is a country of remarkable depth and grace, and it's well worth exploring.

FAST FACTS

- **Area** 18,817 sq miles (48,717 sq km)
- **Capital** Santo Domingo de Guzmán
- **Country code** ☎ 809
- **Departure tax** Air: up to US$20 depending on length of stay. Land: US$20.
- **Famous for** Baseball, cockfighting, merengue, cigars, Columbus landing here first
- **Language** Spanish
- **Money** Dominican Republic pesos (RD$); RD$10 = US$0.35 = €0.30 = UK£0.28
- **Official name** República Dominicana
- **People** Dominicans
- **Phrases** *Siempre a su orden* (you're welcome); *gua-gua* (bus)
- **Population** 9 million
- **Visa** At border or airport US$10

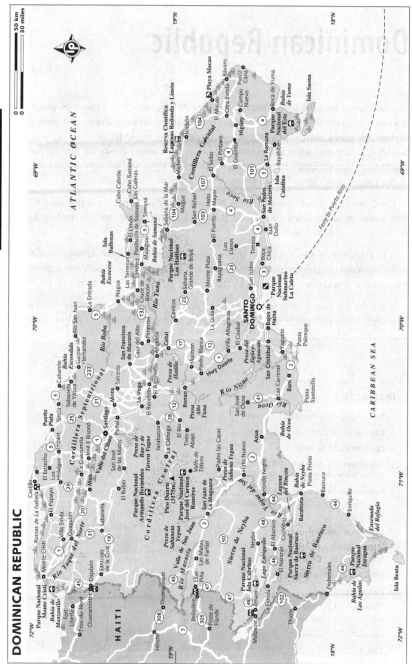

DOMINICAN REPUBLIC

HIGHLIGHTS

- **Carnaval** (p274) Let your hair down during a month of celebrations around the country. They culminate in the capital with an exuberant parade and street party featuring brightly colored costumes and fantastic masks.
- **Baseball** (p277) Join the crowds at Estadio Quisqueya in Santo Domingo for world-class baseball accompanied by dancing in the stands and thousands of shouting and gesticulating fans who live and die on every play.
- **Whale-watching** (p286) From mid-January to mid-March, see humpback whales frolicking, splashing and performing terrific leaps off Samaná.
- **Pico Duarte & Valle de Tétero** (p300) Take in the river-etched Tétero Valley, an excellent side trip on your way up the Caribbean's tallest peak.
- **Playa Rincón** (p289) Kick back and relax on 2 miles (3.2km) of beautiful deserted beach, sandwiched between a thick palm forest and amazing blue waters.

HOW MUCH?

- **Taxi from Las Américas airport to Santo Domingo** US$25 to US$30
- **Three-hour guided tour around Santo Domingo's Zona Colonial** US$20 to US$30
- **Day of diving in Las Terrenas (gear included)** US$25 to US$35
- **Meal of fresh fish in a touristy restaurant** US$8 to US$10
- **Meal of fresh fish in a local restaurant** US$4 to US$6

LONELY PLANET INDEX

- **Gallon (imperial) of gas** US$3.25
- **Liter of bottled water** US$1
- **Bottle of Presidente beer** US$1.25
- **Souvenir T-shirt** US$8
- **Street snack: ham and cheese empanada** US$0.75

ITINERARIES

- **Five days** Spend a day in Santo Domingo before zipping up to Samaná for whale-watching and spend some beach time at Las Galeras.
- **Ten days** First follow the five-day itinerary, spending a couple of days in Santo Domingo. Then head to Jarabacoa and Cabarete for some adventure tours and Los Haitises national park for a tour of ancient cave paintings.
- **Two weeks** Do the ten-day tour, then end your stay with three or four days at an all-inclusive in Bávaro or Punta Cana.

CLIMATE & WHEN TO GO

Except in the central mountains, temperatures don't vary much in the Dominican Republic, averaging a summery 81°F (28°C) to 87°F (31°C) in most places for much of the year. Tropical humidity can make the temperatures feel higher, though sea breezes help mitigate the effect. The rainy season is May to October, though in Samaná and on the north coast it can last until December. August and September constitute hurricane season.

The main foreign tourist seasons are December to February and July to August, and Semana Santa (the week before Easter). Expect higher prices and more crowded beaches at these times – Semana Santa is especially busy. February has great weather and you can enjoy Carnaval and the whales in Samaná. November is good, too – you'll miss the whales but catch baseball season.

HISTORY

First Arrivals

Before Christopher Columbus arrived, the indigenous Tainos ('friendly people') lived on the island now known as Hispaniola. Tainos gave the world sweet potatoes, peanuts, guava, pineapple and tobacco – even the word 'tobacco' is Taino in origin. Yet the Tainos themselves were wiped out by Spanish diseases and slavery. Of the 400,000 Tainos that lived on Hispaniola at the time of European arrival, fewer than 1000 were still alive 30 years later. None exist today.

Independence & Occupation

Two colonies grew on Hispaniola, one Spanish and the other French. Both brought thousands of African slaves to work the land. In 1804, after a 70-year struggle, the French colony gained independence. Haiti, the Taino name for the island, was the first majority-Black republic in the New World.

In 1821, colonists in Santo Domingo declared their independence from Spain. Haiti, which had long aspired to unify the island, promptly invaded its neighbor and occupied it for more than two decades. But Dominicans never accepted Haitian rule, and on February 27, 1844, Juan Pablo Duarte – considered the father of the country – led a bloodless coup and reclaimed Dominican autonomy. The country resubmitted to Spanish rule shortly thereafter, but became independent for good in 1864.

The young country endured one disreputable military leader after the other. In 1916, US President Woodrow Wilson sent the marines to the Dominican Republic, ostensibly to quell a coup attempt, but they ended up occupying the country for eight years. Though deeply imperialistic, this occupation succeeded in stabilizing the DR.

Trujillo's Rise to Power

Rafael Leonidas Trujillo, a former security guard and the eventual chief of the Dominican national police, muscled his way into the presidency in February 1930 and dominated the country until his assassination in 1961. He implemented a brutal system of repression, killing and imprisoning political opponents. Though he was himself partly Black, Trujillo was deeply racist and xenophobic. In October 1937, he ordered the mass extermination of Haitians along the international border. In a matter of days, some 20,000 Haitians were hacked to death with machetes and their bodies dumped into the ocean.

Balaguer's Turn

Joaquín Balaguer was Trujillo's puppet president at the time of Trujillo's assassination. Civil unrest and another US occupation followed Trujillo's death, but Balaguer eventually regained the presidency, to which he clung fiercely for the next 12 years. And like his mentor, Balaguer remained a major political force long after he gave up official control. In 1986, he became president again, despite frail health and blindness. He was as repressive as ever, and his economic policies sent the peso tumbling.

Dominicans whose savings had evaporated protested and were met with violence

from the national police. Many fled to the USA. By the end of 1990, 12% of the Dominican population – 900,000 people – had moved to New York.

Reviled by his own people, Balaguer fixed the 1990 and 1994 elections to stay in power. But by then the military had grown weary of his rule. Balaguer agreed to cut his last term short and hold elections – amazingly enough, he did just that.

A Progressive President

On June 31, 1996, Leonel Fernández, a 42-year-old lawyer who grew up in New York City, was elected president. Fernández shocked his nation by firing the defense minister and forcing two dozen generals into retirement. Dominicans braced for a military reaction, but none came, and Leonel (as he is affectionately called) presided over four years of strong economic growth. He was criticized, however, for failing to alleviate poverty and corruption.

The Bubble Pops

A former tobacco farmer named Hipólito Mejía succeeded Fernández in 2000. Though he'd promised to expand social programs, one of Mejía's first acts as president was to cut spending and increase fuel prices by 30%. The faltering US economy ate into Dominican exports as well as cash remittances and foreign tourism. The Dominican peso began a steep devaluation in October 2002, sinking from RD$17 to the dollar to as low as RD$52 per dollar, before stabilizing at RD$28 to RD$30 per dollar.

Leonel Returns

In May 2004, Leonel Fernández returned to the national stage by soundly defeating Mejía in the presidential elections. In September of that year, the southeast was lashed by Tropical Storm Jeanne. Many of the high-end resorts were closed and rural areas suffered major crop losses. Months later, fallen trees were still unmoved and roads and bridges remained in disrepair. Destruction was much worse in Haiti, however, where more than 1000 people died in flooding and mudslides.

As the US economy regains its footing, Dominicans are feeling the benefits; however, prices remain elevated, especially for utilities and gasoline. Still, spirits are high and were buoyed even more when Domini-can outfielder Vladimir Guerrero of the Anaheim Angels was voted the American League's Most Valuable Player in 2004 – per-haps more amazing was that two of the other three top vote-getters were also Dominican.

THE CULTURE

Most Dominicans are friendly and outgoing, and quick to offer assistance and hospital-ity. Tourists should never hesitate to ask for help finding an address or deciding which local bus to take. That is not to say that Dominicans are pushovers – few shy away from saying what they think, usually loud enough so everyone can hear and join in. Togetherness ranks high in the minds of many Dominicans, who delight in parties, dancing and parades. This being a Carib-bean country, many Dominicans share a gentle and unhurried view of things and an appreciation of small pleasures.

Almost a quarter of Dominicans live in Santo Domingo, which is without ques-tion the country's political, economic and social center. But beyond Santo Domingo, much of the DR has a distinctly small-town feel, with dirt roads, people sitting on front stoops, and burros being led down city streets. There is also an obvious agricultural presence; spotted cows grazing alongside the roads; horses and tractors working the land; and trucks loaded with produce.

The Dominican Republic is a Catholic country, but not to the degree practiced in other Latin American countries; the many churches are well maintained but often empty. It is not surprising, therefore, that there is a fairly free attitude toward premarital and recreational sex. It does not extend to homosexuality, however, which is still fairly taboo. Machismo is also strong here but, like in merengue dancing, many Dominicans experience the roles of men and women as more complementary than confrontational. Indeed, Dominicans – both men and women – are often baffled by the strong negative reaction of foreign women toward men's 'appreciation,' which usually includes passing comments like 'hola, preciosa' (hi, beautiful) and not-so-subtle glances at one's backside.

A less obvious but more powerful force in the DR is race or – more accurately – color, as nearly all Dominicans are a mix of Euro-pean and African descent. As in most coun-tries with colonial pasts, the upper classes are disproportionately white and light-skinned, while the poor and working classes are predominantly dark-skinned. At the same time, they tend to think of themselves as one group rather than many different ones. The same is not true regarding Haitians and Haitian-Dominicans, who are physically much darker than most native Dominicans and are widely viewed as violent or uncouth. Whether racism or national chauvinism, it is the most disturbing feature of an otherwise rich and gracious society.

SPORTS
Baseball

This national pastime is in season from Oc-tober to January. There are six professional teams – Licey and Escojido, both from Santo Domingo, the Águilas from Santiago, the Gigantes from San Francisco, the Estrellas from San Pedro de Macorís, and the Azu-queros from La Romana – and an untold number of formal and semiformal teams around the country. Many Dominican play-ers are stars in the US major leagues, which Dominican fans also follow religiously. The official website for the professional **Domini-can winter league** (www.lidom.com) contains game schedules and news around the league.

Cockfighting

Even more than baseball, cockfighting is the traditional sport of the Dominican Re-public. Almost every town and city in the DR has a *gallera* (cockfighting ring) where specially-bred roosters are pitted against each other in bloody, to-the-death bouts. Gambling on fights is part of the sport, all conducted under a strict honor code. That said, some small-town rings are decidedly seedy and tourists should be alert for trouble. Santo Domingo has numerous cockfight-ing rings; by far the most prestigious – and safe – is the Coliseo Gallístico Alberto Bonetti Burgos (p278), which regularly hosts international competitions.

You can certainly argue that cockfighting amounts to cruelty to animals – after all, the point is for one animal to kill the other for the sake of entertainment. But it is more complicated than that. While detractors concentrate on the fact that the roosters are killed, Dominicans (and others around the world) focus on the clash itself – the roosters' strength, intensity and willingness to fight to the death resonate in a country that has endured so much civil strife and outside manipulation. The most successful birds are revered in much the same way that Secretariat or Seabiscuit are remembered by horse-racing fans. The fighting rooster is also the symbol of a number of political parties and social organizations.

ARTS
Music
Merengue is truly the national music, and from the moment you arrive you'll hear it being played on the bus, at the beach, in the taxi, everywhere, and usually at high volume. Top Dominican merengue groups include Los Hermanos Rosario, Coco Band, Milly y Los Vecinos and, perhaps the biggest name of all, Juan Luis Guerra.

If merengue is the DR's urban sound, *bachata* is definitely its 'country.' This is the music of breaking up and losing out, working hard and playing even harder. Top performers include Raulín Rodríguez, Antony Santos, Luis Vargas and Leo Valdez.

Literature
Most of the popular writing being done by Dominicans today is coming from emigrants and their children living in the US. Among the better known are Julia Álvarez (*How the García Girls Lost their Accents*, 1991, and *In the Time of the Butterflies*, 1995) and Junot Díaz, whose short-story collection *Drown* is written in English and liberally sprinkled with Dominicanisms. Other notable contemporary Dominican writers include José Goudy Pratt, Jeannette Miller and Ivan García Guerra.

ENVIRONMENT
The Land
If a nation's wealth could be measured by its landscape, the Dominican Republic would be the richest country in the Caribbean. Here you can reach the Caribbean's highest point – Pico Duarte at 10,417ft (3175m) – and its lowest – Lago Enriquillo at 130ft (40m) below sea level. Bisecting the country is the mighty Cordillera Central mountain range, which makes up one-third of Hispaniola's landmass. In the lowlands are a series of valleys filled with plantations of

coffee, bananas, cacao, rice, tobacco and many other crops. Almost 1000 miles of coastline includes bountiful coral reefs, multitudes of tiny islands, and sheltered banks where humpback whales gather to breed.

Wildlife
Over 250 species of birds have been found in the Dominican Republic, including numerous endemics, and the country is known for its humpback whales, manatees and other marine mammals. Among a rich variety of reptiles, the most interesting of all has to be the Jaragua lizard, found in 1998, which is the world's smallest terrestrial vertebrate – adults measure only 1in (25mm).

Environmental Issues
The Dominican Republic can easily see, in Haiti, the negative effects of deforestation – lack of trees and ground cover were largely to blame for the severity of flooding and mudslides that killed more than 1000 Haitians during Tropical Storm Jeanne in September 2004. The Dominican Republic has set aside large areas of forest as national parks and scientific reserves, but illegal logging remains a problem.

The large-scale tourist development along the coast is another potential environmental problem. While a few resorts have adopted eco-friendly practices, like limited use of plastic cups and not using bleach in laundry – they are the exception, not the rule. Heavy boat traffic – not to mention the construction of piers suitable for large ships – can damage fragile coral reefs.

FOOD & DRINK
Food
The basis of most meals here are rice and beans that are served separately or mixed together. Bananas and yucca are other popular starches – both are served boiled, though you will also see bananas sliced and fried (*tostones*) or mashed up into a dish called *mangú* (or *mofongo* if it's mixed with pork rind).

As on any island, seafood figures prominently in the national diet. Grouper and snapper are the most common dinner fish and are usually served baked or grilled with a sauce – *al coco* (in coconut sauce) or *a la diabla* (a spicy tomato-based sauce) are favorites. Other seafood dishes include a type of ceviche typically made with octopus and called *pulpo a la vinaigrette*.

Beef, chicken and pork are also part of Dominican cuisine, though the preparations are generally less creative than in other countries. One exception is guinea hen broiled with red wine, a popular dish in the central highlands.

Street food is limited mostly to *empanadas* and *pastelitos* (meat- or cheese-filled pastries) that are sold from carts or bus-station snack shops.

Fruit Drinks

The Dominican Republic makes great fruit drinks. *Batidas* (smoothies) consist of crushed fruit, water, ice and several tablespoons of sugar, and sometimes they also contain a little milk. Popular *batidas* include *batida de piña* (pineapple) and *morir soñando* (literally, 'to die dreaming'), an unlikely combination of milk and orange juice.

Other popular nonalcoholic Dominican drinks include *limonada* (lemonade) and *mabí*, a delicious drink made from the bark of the tropical liana vine.

Alcoholic Drinks

It's tough to beat Dominican *ron* (rum) for quality. Dozens of local brands are available, but the big three are Brugal, Barceló and Bermudez, which all come in *blanco* (clear), *dorado* (golden), and *añejo* (aged) varieties.

There are a handful of locally brewed beers, including Presidente, Quisqueya, Bohemia and Soberante. It's customary for friends to share a Presidente Grande – a 40oz (1.2L) bottle – that's brought to tables in a wood or plastic container and small glass cups.

SANTO DOMINGO

pop 2.2 million

As in many Latin America countries, the Dominican Republic's political, economic and cultural energies are concentrated in its capital. And like its counterparts, Santo Domingo is a city of profound contrasts, where immense wealth and grinding poverty coexist in close quarters. It's a city of Catholics, yet there's no shortage of brothels; there are five-star hotels and frequent power outages; the heat can be oppressive, but the people are optimistic and patient.

Santo Domingo is also a city of firsts: it contains the New World's first hospital, first university, first paved road and first two-story residence, as well as its oldest working church, the oldest monastery and oldest surviving European fortress. In a very real sense, this is where Europe and the Americas first truly mingled. It is the very nexus from which Earth-altering social, political and environmental events would grow.

And beyond all its historic gravity, Santo Domingo – or *la Capital* as Dominicans

---

SANTO DOMINGO IN...

Two Days

Eat breakfast at **Plaza de la Hispanidad** (p272). While your energy's high, visit the **Museo de las Casas Reales** (p271), **Fortaleza Ozama** (p272) and the **cathedral** (p271). Eat lunch at **Parque Colón** (p272) and stroll along Arzobispo Portes and Padre Billini streets – attractive colonial lanes with churches, small parks and pedestrian alleyways. Check out the shops and activity along El Conde. For an evening drink and dinner head to **Mesón D'Barí** (p276) or **La Bodeguita de la Habana Vieja** (p276) in Gazcue.

In the morning, take a taxi to **Faro a Colón** (p272). Return to the **Zona Colonial** for lunch and a visit to the **Amber museum** (p271) or **Larimar museum** (p271). Later, take a cab out to the **Jardín Botánico Nacional** (p273), which is lovely in the late afternoon.

Four Days

Follow the two-day tour. On the third day, visit the Zona Colonial's less-visited sites, like **Monasterio de San Francisco** (p272) and **Mercado Modelo** (p279). Spend the evening among Dominicans at a **baseball game** (p277) or even a **cockfight** (p278). On your last day, browse the shops and galleries in Zona Colonial for gifts to take back home.

DOMINICAN REPUBLIC

CENTRAL SANTO DOMINGO (ZONA COLONIAL)

INFORMATION
Abel Brawn's Internet World.........1 E4
Banco de Reservas........................2 G3
Casa de Teatro.............................3 G5
Centro Cultural Español...............4 G4
Colonial Tour & Travel.................5 G4
Editorial Duarte...........................6 G3
French Embassy............................7 G4
Lavandería Tin.............................8 D5
Librería Pichardo.........................9 E5
Mapas GAAR.............................10 D5
Politur.......................................11 E4
Post Office.................................12 G4
Scotiabank................................13 G3
Tourist Office............................14 G4
Trinidad & Tobago Embassy.......15 G3

SIGHTS & ACTIVITIES
Capilla de Nuestra Señora de los
  Remedios...............................16 G3
Catedral Primada de América......17 G4
Convento de la Orden de los
  Predicadores..........................18 G5
Fortaleza Ozama........................19 H4
Iglesia de la Regina Angelorum...20 F5
Iglesia de Nuestra Señora de las
  Mercedes...............................21 E4

Iglesia de Santa Clara................22 G5
Monasterio de San Francisco......23 F3
Museo Alcázar de Colón............24 G2
Museo de las Casas Reales.........25 G3
Museo del Larimar.....................26 G4
Museo Infantil Trampolín...........27 G4
Museo Mundo de Ambar...........28 F2
Panteón Nacional......................29 G3
Parque Colón.............................30 G4
Parque Duarte...........................31 F5
Plaza de la Hispanidad..............32 G2
Puerta del Conde.......................33 D5
Ruinas del Hospital San Nicolás
  de Barí...................................34 F3

SLEEPING 🏠
Antiguo Hotel Europa................35 G3
El Beaterio Guest House............36 F5
Hotel Conde de Peñalba............37 G4
Hotel Doña Elvira......................38 E5
Hotel Freeman..........................39 G4
Hotel Palacio.............................40 F4
Refugio del Pirata......................41 F3
Sofitel Nicolás de Ovando..........42 G4

EATING 🍴
Coco's Restaurant.....................43 G5

Comedor el Puerto....................44 G5
La Crêperie...............................45 G2
Mesón D'Bari............................46 F4
Restaurant & Bar Palmito
  Gourmet................................47 E6

DRINKING 🍷
Bobo's.....................................48 F4
K-ramba Bar.............................49 G5

ENTERTAINMENT 🎭
Aire Club..................................50 E4

SHOPPING 🛍
Ambar Maldo Gift Shop.............51 G2
Artesanía Elisa..........................52 F5
Atelier Gallery...........................53 F6
Bettey's Galería.........................54 G4
Boutique del Fumador...............55 G4
Encuentro Artesanal.................56 F2
Galería de Arte María del Carmen..57 G4
Mercado Modelo......................58 E3
Museo del Tabaco.....................59 G4
Swiss Mine...............................60 G4

TRANSPORT
Ferries del Caribe......................61 H4

To Caribe Tours Bus Terminal (1km);
Netherlands Embassy (1km);
Centro Olímpico (2.5km);
Estadio Quisqueya (3.5km);
Metro Bus Terminal (4.5km);
Terra Bus (5km);
Parque Zoológico Nacional (5.5km);
Jardín Botánico Nacional (7km)

To Italian Embassy
(100m)

Av Pedro Henríquez Ureña

Palacio
Nacional

Av 30 de Marzo

C Imbert

C 16 de Agosto

Benito González

Hernando de Gorjón

C MI. María Castillo

C Charles Pret

C Uruguay

C Cesar Nicolás Penson

C Luisa O Pellerano

C Julio Verne

Juan Isidro Pérez

To Museo del Hombre
Dominicano/Museo de
Arte Moderno (1km);
Guácara Taína (6.5km);
Aeropuerto Internacional Herrera/
Coliseo Gallístico Alberto
Bonetti Burgos (8km)

Av Bolívar

Parque
Independencia

Altar de
la Patria

Polvorín

33

10

8

Espaillat

Av Bolívar

Enrique Henríquez

To Expreso Santo Domingo
Bávaro Bus Terminal (1.5km);
Haitian Embassy (1.5km);
United States Embassy (1.5km);
Canadian Embassy (2km);
UK Embassy (3km);
Spanish & Japanese
Embassies (4.5km);
Cuban Embassy (7.5km);
Jamaican Embassy (7.5km)

C Santiago

C Dr. Delgado

Leonor de Ovando

Las Carreras

Av Independencia

Cemetery

Canela

Pina

Palo Hincado

Estrelleta

El Número

To San Judas (25m);
Clínica Abreu (100m);
Vivan (125m);
Banco Popular (200m);
Giada Tours & Travel (250m);
Gazcue Hotels (250m);
Car rental agencies (2km);
Malecón (2km);
Hotel Santo Domingo (7km)

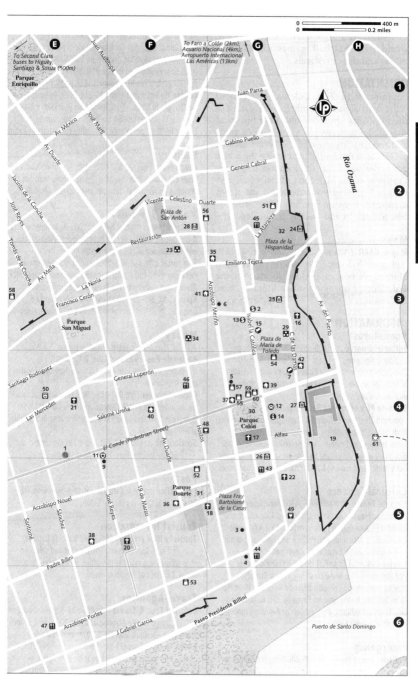

typically call it – is a terrifically fun place to visit, with a huge Carnaval celebration, world-class baseball games and several music and dance festivals.

ORIENTATION

For travelers, the Zona Colonial (Hotel Zone) is the heart of Santo Domingo, where most of the museums, churches and other historical sites are located, as well as hotels, restaurants and services. Just west of the Zona Colonial is Gazcue, a residential area where the hotels are better value but the location less ideal. Further east, the Malecón (officially called Av George Washington) is the broad waterfront avenue where Santo Domingo's high-rise hotels, nightclubs and casinos are located.

Maps

Mapas GAAR (☎ 809-688-8004; www.mapasgaar.com .do; Espaillat; ☾ 8:30am-5:30pm Mon-Fri) This is Santo Domingo's best map store, located on the 3rd floor of an aging office building near El Conde.

INFORMATION
Bookstores

Editorial Duarte (☎ 809-689-4832; cnr Arzobispo Meriño & Mercedes; ☾ 8am-7pm Mon-Fri, 8am-6pm Sat) This dusty shop in the Zona Colonial has a good selection of Spanish-language fiction books, foreign-language dictionaries and maps.

Librería Pichardo (José Reyes at El Conde; ☾ 8am-7pm Mon-Thu, 8am-5:30pm Fri, 8am-1pm Sun) This street-front bookstore has mostly Latin American history plus some antiques and curios – we spotted a seven-language dictionary when we passed by. The owner is a friendly guy, but you may still have to bargain hard to get a good price.

Cultural Centers

Casa de Teatro (☎ 809-689-3430; www.arte-latino .com/casadeteatro; Av Arzobispo Meriño 110; admission varies; ☾ 9am-6pm & 8pm-3am Mon-Sat) A fantastic arts complex with a gallery, theater and open-air bar and performance space. Popular on weekends.

Centro Cultural Español (Spanish Cultural Center; ☎ 809-686-8212; www.ccesd.org; cnr Av Arzobispo Meriño & Arzobispo Portes; admission free; ☾ 10am-9pm Mon-Sat) Run by the Spanish Embassy, this institute regularly hosts art exhibits, film festivals and musical concerts, all with a Spanish bent.

Emergency

Politur (Tourist Police; ☎ 689-6464; cnr El Conde & José Reyes; ☾ 24hr)

Internet Access, Telephone, & Fax

Abel Brawn's Internet World (☎ /fax 809-333-5604; 2nd fl, Plaza Lomba; Internet access per hr US$1.40; ☾ 9am-9pm Mon-Sat, 10am-4pm Sun) Calls to the USA are US$0.30 per minute; to Europe US$0.50 per minute. A fax to the USA costs US$0.50 per page; to Europe $0.75 per page.

Centro de Internet (☎ 809-238-5149; Av Independencia 201; per hr US$1; ☾ 8:30am-9pm Mon-Sat, 8:30am-3pm Sun) Calls to the USA are US$0.17 per minute; to Europe US$0.21 per minute. This office is located in Gazcue.

Laundry

Lavandería Tin (☎ 809-687-3400; Arzobispo Nouel btwn Espaillat & Palo Hincado; ☾ 8am-6pm Mon-Sat) Washing and drying is US$4 per load, up to 14lb (6.4kg).

Medical Services

Clínica Abreu (☎ 809-688-4411; cnr Av Independencia & Burgos; ☾ 24hr) Located near Av Independencia, this is widely regarded as the best hospital in the city.

San Judas (☎ 809-685-8165; cnr Av Independencia & Pichardo; ☾ 24hr) A pharmacy and minimart near Clínica Abreu that delivers to the Zona Colonial and Gazcue.

Vivian (☎ 809-221-2000; cnr Av Independencia & Delgado; ☾ 24hr) Similar to San Judas.

Money

All of the following banks have ATMs.

Banco de Reservas (cnr Isabel la Católica & Las Mercedes; ☾ 8am-5pm Mon-Fri, 9am-1pm Sat) Located in Zona Colonial.

Banco Popular (☎ 809-685-3000; Farmacia Carmina, cnr Av Independencia & Pasteur; ☾ 9am-8pm Mon-Sat, 9am-1pm Sun) This bank's in Gazcue and it's not available after hours.

Scotiabank (cnr Isabel la Católica & Las Mercedes; ☾ 8:30am-4:30pm Mon-Fri) In Zona Colonial.

Post

Post office (Isabel la Católica; ☾ 8am-5pm Mon-Fri, 9am-noon Sat) Facing Parque Colón.

Tourist Information

Tourist office (☎ 809-686-3858; Isabel la Católica 103; ☾ 9am-3pm Mon-Fri) There's a limited selection of brochures and maps at this office, which faces Parque Colón. English and French spoken.

Travel Agencies

Colonial Tour & Travel (☎ 809-688-5285; www.colon ialtours.com.do; Calle Arzobispo Mériño 209; ☾ 8:30am-1pm & 2:30-5:30pm Mon-Fri, 8:30am-noon Sat)

Giada Tours & Travel (☎ 809-686-6994, 264-3704; giada@verizon.net.do; Hostal Duque de Wellington, Av Independencia 304; ☾ 8:30am-6pm Mon-Fri, 9am-2pm Sat)

DANGERS & ANNOYANCES

The Zona Colonial is generally very safe to walk around, day or night, though be alert for pickpockets in crowded areas. On the Malecón be extra cautious if you've been drinking or are leaving a club or casino especially late. Like in any big city, stick to well-lit and well-trafficked areas as much as possible, and be inconspicuous with your cash, jewelry, cameras etc.

SIGHTS & ACTIVITIES

Most of Santo Domingo's historical and interesting sites are in the Zona Colonial, and are easily explored on foot. Sites further afield, like the Faro a Colón and Jardín Botánico, are best reached by taxi.

Zona Colonial

Most of the structures in the colonial district contain walls that were erected in the 16th century, though the years have brought changes, like new facades or added floors. Beyond its many historical sites – the area is listed as a World Heritage site – the Zona Colonial is also a great place to explore and to linger. The west end of Arzobispo Portes is especially attractive, with colonial homes, stone churches and pleasant parks.

MUSEUMS

There are many worthwhile museums in the Zona Colonial. Here are the best of the bunch.

The **Museo de las Casas Reales** (Museum of the Royal Houses; ☎ 809-682-4202; Calle de las Damas; adult/student US$1/0.15; ☺ 9am-5pm Tue-Sun), near Plaza de la Hispanidad, showcases colonial period objects ranging from Taino artifacts to dozens of hand-blown wine bottles and period furnishings. Also on display is an impressive antique weaponry collection acquired by dictator/president Trujillo in 1955.

Once the home of Columbus' son Diego and his wife, Doña María de Toledo, the beautifully restored **Museo Alcázar de Colón** (Museum Citadel of Columbus; ☎ 809-682-4750; Plaza de la Hispanidad; admission US$1.75; ☺ 9am-5pm Tue-Sun) houses many objects said to have belonged to the Columbus family. The building itself – if not the objects inside – is definitely worth a look.

The DR is one of the world's top sources of amber, and the impressive collection at

Museo Mundo de Ambar (☎ 809-682-3309; www .amberworldmuseum.com; Arzobispo Mériño 452; admission US$2; ☺ 9am-6pm Mon-Sat, 9am-1pm Sun) includes excellent examples of both domestic and international amber. Look for samples containing various critters and bugs – there's an entire room dedicated to ants. Signs in Spanish and English explain amber's origin, mining process and common uses.

Museo de Larimar (☎ 809-689-6605; www.larimar museum.com; Isabel la Católica 54; admission free; ☺ 9am-6pm Mon-Sat, 9am-1pm Sun) is on the 2nd floor of a jewelry shop and – despite the location – is quite impressive. It contains a remarkable display of the beautiful blue stone and relates just about everything there is to know about the subject. Signage is in English and Spanish.

CHURCHES

With about a dozen churches in the Zona Colonial, you'll be hard pressed to leave town without bumping into a couple.

Catedral Primada de América (admission free; ☺ 9am-4pm) is the oldest cathedral in operation in the Américas. Diego Columbus set the first stone in 1514, but construction didn't begin in earnest until the arrival of the first bishop in 1521. Numerous architects worked on the cathedral until 1540, which is why its vault is Gothic, its arches are Romanesque and its ornamentation is baroque. The entrance faces Parque Colón.

Built in 1510, **Convento de la Orden de los Predicadores** (Hostos & Padre Billini; admission free; ☺ irregular hrs) was the first convent of the Dominican order in the Americas. It is also the place where Father Bartolomé de las Casas – the famous chronicler of Spanish atrocities committed against indigenous peoples – did most of his writing. Be sure to take a look at the vault of the chapel; it is remarkable for its stone zodiac wheel, which is carved with mythological and astrological representations.

Constructed during the first half of the 16th century, **Iglesia de Nuestra Señora de las Mercedes** (Church of Our Lady of Mercy; cnr Las Mercedes & José Reyes; admission free; ☺ irregular hrs) was reconstructed on numerous occasions following pirate attacks, earthquakes and hurricanes. The church is remarkable for its pulpit, which is sustained by a support in the shape of a serpent demon.

DOMINICAN REPUBLIC

Other notable churches in the Zona Colonial include **Capilla de Nuestra Señora de los Remedios** (cnr Calle de las Damas & Las Mercedes), **Iglesia de Santa Clara** (cnr Padre Billini & Isabel la Católica) and **Iglesia de la Regina Angelorum** (cnr José Reyes & Padre Billini).

HISTORICAL SITES

Beside the cathedral is the historic **Parque Colón**, containing several shade trees and a large statue of Admiral Columbus himself. It is the meeting place for area residents, and it's alive all day long with tourists, townsfolk, hawkers, guides, taxi drivers, shoeshine boys and tourist police.

The **Plaza de la Hispanidad**, in front of the Alcázar de Colón, has been made over many times, most recently during the early 1990s in honor of the 500th anniversary of Columbus' arrival in the New World. The plaza is a large, open area that makes for a lovely stroll on a warm afternoon and it has several outdoor restaurants along its west edge.

The **Fortaleza Ozama** (Ozama Fortress; ☎ 809-686-0222; Calle de las Damas; admission US$0.50; ☉ 9am-6:30pm Mon-Sat, 9am-4pm Sun), at the south end of Calle de las Damas, is the oldest colonial military edifice in the New World. Construction was commenced in 1502 and it served as a military garrison and prison until the 1970s, when it was opened to the public for touring. **Torre del Homenaje** (Tower of Homage) is the main structure, with 6ft-thick (1.8m) walls containing dozens of riflemen's embrasures and offering great rooftop views. Near the door there are several guides, whose knowledge of the fort is generally quite impressive. A 20-minute tour should cost around US$3.50 per person.

Originally constructed in 1747 as a Jesuit church, the **Panteón Nacional** (National Mausoleum; Calle de las Damas; admission free; ☉ 9am-5pm Tue-Sun) was also a tobacco warehouse and a theater before dictator Trujillo restored the building in 1958 as the final resting place of the country's most illustrious persons. The mausoleum is next to Plaza de María de Toledo. Shorts and tank tops are discouraged.

The **Monasterio de San Francisco** (Monastery of St Francis; Hostos; btwn Emiliano Tejera & Restauración), the first monastery in the New World, belonged to the first order of Franciscan friars who arrived to evangelize the island. Dating from 1508, the monastery was set ablaze by Sir Francis Drake in 1586, rebuilt, devastated by

an earthquake in 1673, rebuilt, ruined by another earthquake in 1751 and rebuilt again. From 1881 until the 1930s it was used as an insane asylum – portions of the chains used to secure inmates can still be seen – until a powerful hurricane shut it down for good.

The ruins of the New World's first hospital, **Ruinas del Hospital San Nicolás de Barí** (Hostos), located near Las Mercedes, remain in place as a monument to Governor Nicolás de Ovando, who ordered it built in 1503. So sturdy was the edifice that it survived centuries of attacks by pirates, earthquakes and hurricanes. It remained virtually intact until 1911, when, after being damaged by a hurricane, much of it was ordered to be knocked down so that it wouldn't pose a threat to pedestrians. Today, visitors can still see several of its high walls and Moorish arches. Note that the hospital's floor plan follows the form of a Latin cross.

The **Puerta del Conde** (Gate of the Count; Calle El Conde) owes its name to the Count of Peñalba, Bernardo de Meneses y Bracamonte, who in 1655 led the successful defense of Santo Domingo against an invading force of 13,000 British troops. The gate is the supreme symbol of Dominican patriotism because right beside it, in February 1844, a handful of brave Dominicans executed a bloodless coup against occupying Haitian forces; their actions resulted in the creation of a wholly independent Dominican Republic. It also was atop this gate that the very first Dominican flag was raised. The gate is at the west end of Calle El Conde.

Around Zona Colonial

Santo Domingo has a number of interesting sites outside of the Zona Colonial. For most, it's easiest to get to them by taxi.

Certainly the most intriguing monument in Santo Domingo, both for its contents and history, is the imposing and controversial **Faro a Colón** (Columbus Lighthouse; ☎ 809-592-1492, ext 251; Parque Mirador del Este; admission US$2.25; ☉ 9am-5:15pm Tue-Sun). The Faro's massive cement flanks stretch nearly a block and stand some 10 stories high, forming the shape of a cross. High-powered lights on the roof can project a blinding white cross in the sky, but are rarely turned on because doing so causes blackouts in surrounding neighborhoods. At the intersection of the cross's arms is a guarded tomb that purportedly contains

Columbus' remains. However, Spain and Italy dispute that claim, both saying that *they* have the admiral's bones. Inside the monument a long series of exhibition halls display documents (mostly reproductions) relating to Columbus' voyages and the exploration and conquest of the Americas. A very worthwhile visit.

The lush grounds of the **Jardín Botánico Nacional** (National Botanical Garden; ☎ 809-567-6211; Av República de Colombia; admission US$1.25; ☺ 9am-6pm) span 0.77 sq miles (2 sq km) and include vast areas devoted to aquatic plants, orchids, bromeliads, ferns, endemic plants, palm trees, a Japanese garden and much more. An open-air trolley takes passengers on a pleasant half-hour turn about the park (US$1.25, departures every 30 minutes until 4:30pm) and is especially enjoyable for children.

The **Museo del Hombre Dominicano** (Museum of the Dominican Man; ☎ 809-689-4672; admission US$0.75; ☺ 10am-5pm Tue-Sun) houses an impressive collection of Taino artifacts, including stone axes and intriguing urns. Other displays focus on slavery, the colonial period and Carnaval, with masks and costumes used in celebrations around the country. Unfortunately, the explanations are all in Spanish and the displays are very old-fashioned. English-speaking guides can be requested at the entry – the service is free, but small tips are customary.

The permanent collection at the **Museo de Arte Moderno** (Museum of Modern Art; admission US$0.35; ☺ 10am-6pm Tue-Sun) includes paintings and a few sculptures by the Dominican Republic's best-known modern artists, including Luís Desangles, Adriana Billini, and Martín Santos, but the temporary exhibits on the lower floors tend to be much fresher and more inventive than those upstairs.

SANTO DOMINGO FOR CHILDREN

Santo Domingo is not a bad place for children to visit, but neither is it particularly kid-friendly. The Museo Infantil Trampolín in the Zona Colonial is truly remarkable, but your options after that are just so-so. Perhaps more difficult than the lack of age-appropriate sights is the lack of quiet parks and open green space – **Parque Duarte** (cnr Av Padre Billini & Duarte) is a flagstone plaza with little passing traffic and really the only spot in the Zona Colonial where you can sit on a bench and let the kids romp about.

If you're traveling with children, do not miss the **Museo Infantil Trampolín** (Children's Museum; ☎ 809-685-5551; www.trampolin.org.do; Calle de las Damas; adult/child US$3.50/1.75; ☺ 9am-6pm Tue-Fri, 10am-7pm Sat & Sun). Kids (and adults, if they like) are led through a high-tech, hands-on natural history, biology, science, ecology and social museum all wrapped up into one. The museum includes exhibits dedicated to the formation of earth (complete with earthquake machines and volcano simulations), the human body (featuring skeletons, mammoth eyes and brains, and even a body-parts jungle gym), and the island's ecosystems. Enthusiastic guides lead kids though the exhibits, keeping them captivated with explanations and interesting questions. Truly a place where learning is fun. Most tours are in Spanish, but English-speaking guides are available.

Showing its age, the **Acuario Nacional** (National Aquarium; ☎ 809-766-1709; Av España; admission US$1; ☺ 9:30am-5:30pm Tue-Sun) won't wow many adult travelers, but children are invariably delighted by the main attraction there – an enormous tank with a clear underwater walkway where you can watch turtles, sting rays and huge fish pass around the sides and overhead. There's also a large shark tank and a pool where you can reach down and pet endangered slider turtles, part of a breeding project. Signs are in Spanish only.

The **Parque Zoológico Nacional** (National Zoological Park; ☎ 809-562-3149; Av los Reyes Católicos; admission US$1; ☺ 9am-6pm Tue-Sat), one of the largest in Latin America, has a reasonably impressive collection of animals, from rhinos to chimps, though some of the enclosures are disappointingly cramped. For a nominal fee you can cruise the large grounds by shuttle. The zoo is located in a somewhat seedy neighborhood; a taxi here costs around US$5. Be sure to arrange a return trip with the driver, as you won't find many cabs out here.

TOURS

Interesting and informative **walking tours** of the Zona Colonial are offered on a daily basis by a number of official guides. Tours cover the most important buildings in the zone and can be tailored to your specific interests. Walks typically last 2½ hours and cost between US$20 and US$30. Guides can be found in Parque Colón – typically sitting next to the cathedral or hanging out under

DOMINICAN REPUBLIC

the trees. Guides are dressed in khakis and light blue dress shirts and have licenses with the official state tourism logo on it – ask to see it before you start your tour. Also be sure to agree upon a fee before setting out.

FESTIVALS & EVENTS

Carnaval (February) Celebrated with great fervor throughout the country every Sunday in February, culminating in a huge blowout in Santo Domingo on the last weekend of the month or the first weekend of March. Costumes, especially masks, are central to the celebration – prize-winning groups from around the country compete for the year's top honors here.

Latin Music Festival (June) Held at the Centro Olímpico (Olympic Stadium). This huge three-day event attracts the top names in Latin music – jazz, salsa, merengue and *bachata*. Salsa king Tito Rojas and merengue living-legend Fernando Villalona are among the dozens of featured artists that regularly attend.

Merengue Festival (July & August) The largest festival in the country, a two-week celebration of the DR's favorite music, held every year at the end of July and beginning of August. Most of the activity is on the Malecón, but there are related events across the city.

SLEEPING

Most independent travelers stay in the Zona Colonial, where there are some excellent midrange and top-end options, but surprisingly few budget ones. There's better value in Gazcue, a quiet residential area southwest of Parque Independencia, but you're half a mile (800m) from the heart of the Zona Colonial. High-rise hotels are on the Malecón and are best if you want to be near the nightclubs and casinos.

Zona Colonial

BUDGET

El Refugio del Pirata (☎ 809-687-1572; www.refugio hotel.com; Arzobispo Meriño 356; r US$35; ✹) This place has some good rooms and some awful ones. Recently remodeled rooms are small but have comfortable double beds, modern baths and quaint stenciling on the walls, plus air-con, fan, cable TV and a small mini-refrigerator. Unremodeled rooms aren't worth the price. There is a tiny kitchen for guest use, but it's not cleaned regularly. Call ahead if you will be arriving after 6pm, as otherwise the reception closes early.

Hotel Freeman (☎ 809-689-3961; Isabel la Católica 155; s/d US$25/30; ✹) Just half a block from Parque Colón, this hotel offers basic but clean rooms with two queen-size beds, private hot-water bath, air-con and cable TV. A breezy balcony at the top of the stairs provides a great view over the street.

MIDRANGE

Antiguo Hotel Europa (☎ 809-285-0005; www.anti guohoteleuropa.com; cnr Arzobispo Meriño & Emiliano Tejera; s/d/tw US$63/68/73; P ✹) This hotel, near Plaza de la Hispanidad, has 52 charming rooms all with Spanish tile floors, comfortable beds, and modern amenities. Ask for a room with a balcony. Complimentary continental breakfast is served in a classy rooftop restaurant.

El Beaterío Guest House (☎ 809-687-8657; elbea terio@netscape.net; Av Duarte 8; s/d with breakfast US$55/60, with air-con US$60/70; ✹) Originally a 16th-century nunnery, the Beaterío is now a small guesthouse offering 11 austere rooms. Each has wood-beam ceilings, stone floors and 9ft (2.7m) doors, and all are equipped with modern amenities. The setting is impressive but the rooms are a bit cramped for the price. The elegant reading room, however, is a good place to relax.

Hotel Conde de Peñalba (☎ 809-688-7121; www .condepenalba.com; cnr El Conde & Arzobispo Mériño; s/d with windows US$65/75, without windows US$60/70, tw US$80; ✹ 🖳) This place is right on Parque Colón and rooms here are comfortable and have small baths, good air-con and cable TV. Many boast balconies overlooking the park, which is a major plus. The lack of an elevator may be inconvenient to some.

AUTHOR'S CHOICE

Hotel Doña Elvira (☎ 809-221-7415; www .dona-elvira.com; Padre Billini 209; loft without/ with air-con US$60/65, ste US$110/100; r with air-con US$90-100, without air-con US$80-90; P ✹ 🖳 🖳) Located in a beautifully renovated colonial building, this small hotel offers 13 casually elegant rooms with exposed stone walls, Spanish tile floors and sumptuous linens. Rooms come in various sizes – from a small room with a loft to a spacious suite with an outdoor bathtub. A lush garden with a mosaic-tiled pool, a rooftop solarium and a comfortable reading room round out an already tranquil setting. Full breakfast for two is included in the rate. A gem of a hotel.

TOP END

Sofitel Nicolás de Ovando (☎ 809-685-9955; www
.sofitel.com; Calle de las Damas; s with breakfast US$220-336,
d with breakfast US$238-354; P ⊠ 🖳 🖳) Located
inside the historic Hostal de Ovando – the
home of the first governor of the Americas –
the Sofitel is one of the city's finest hotels.
The beautifully renovated rooms and suites
exude a simple elegance with high, wood-
beamed ceilings, original stone walls, and
handcrafted iron-work furniture. Guests also
enjoy a welcoming pool, a modern fitness
center, a comfortable library and spectacular
views. It's near Plaza de María de Toledo.

Hotel Palacio (☎ 809-682-4730; www.hotel-palacio
.com; Duarte 106; s US$80-90, d US$88-98; P ⊠ ⊠ 🖳)
This German-owned hotel occupies a huge
17th-century mansion (with some recent
additions) featuring original stone walls
and beautiful wood banisters. The 34 large
rooms have thick beds, modern baths fix-
tures, cable TV, minibar and security box.
Some have whirlpool baths and small terraces opening onto leafy interior courtyards. There's a Jacuzzi and small open-air
exercise area on the roof.

Gazcue

BUDGET

Hotel La Danae (☎ 809-238-5609; Calle Danae 18; r
US$28-35; ⊠) Sixteen rooms all with air-con,
fan, cable TV, minirefrigerator and (best
of all) a clean common kitchen for guest
use. The cheaper rooms are in the original
building, and some travelers prefer them
for their high ceilings, which lend a feeling
of extra space. All rooms have just one bed;
the patio in front is nice for reading.

MIDRANGE

Hostal Duque de Wellington (☎ 809-682-4525; www
.hotelduque.com, Av Independencia 304; s US$48-68, d
US$62-78; P ⊠) This is a large hotel with a
friendly, old-fashioned atmosphere. Rooms
here range from standards to suites. All are
attractively decorated and feature air-con,
fan, telephone, cable TV and security box;
2nd-floor rooms have nice, high ceilings.
There is a restaurant and a travel agency on-
site, and other good eating options nearby.

Hostal Alcaldeza (☎ 809-685-0825; Crucero Ah-
rens 2; r US$45-50) Though it doesn't look like
much from the front, this family-run hotel
offers cozy well-appointed rooms all with
comfortable beds, spotless baths and cable

TV. There is no view – the hotel is all on
one floor and boxed in by houses on either
side – but the remodeled rooms have small
patios and get better light.

Malecón

Hotel InterContinental (☎ 809-221-0000; www.inter
continental.com/santodomingo; Av George Washington 218;
r US$190-210; P ⊠ ⊠ 🖳 🖳) With a beauti-
ful lobby and hip bar-lounge area, the Inter-
Continental oozes cool class. Arguably the
finest hotel on the Malecón, rooms here are
impeccably outfitted and guests can make
use of tennis courts, a fine swimming pool,
spa services, even a karaoke bar. There's a
casino and night club on-site.

Meliá Santo Domingo Hotel (☎ 809-221-6666;
www.solmelia.com; Av George Washington 365; s/d
US$100/140; P ⊠ ⊠ 🖳 🖳) Another of the
Malecón's top hotels, the Meliá has an inviting lobby area and bar and a great 2nd-
floor swimming-pool area. The rooms are
comfortable and well-appointed, including
in-room Internet access, though the decor
is a tad dowdy. Ask for a room above the
5th floor for the best views. The hotel also
has tennis courts, a health spa, a casino and
a popular dance club.

EATING

Santo Domingo has a good selection of restaurants in various price ranges. The ones
in the Zona Colonial are usually the most
convenient, but there are some excellent
options in Gazcue as well.

Zona Colonial

Comedor el Puerto (☎ 809-686-1669; cnr Av Arzobispo
Meriño & Av del Puerto; mains US$2.50; ⊙ lunch Mon-Fri)
For classic Creole cooking in an entirely
Dominican setting, head to this family-run
joint. For US$2.50 a plate, you'll have your
choice of three types of meat dishes, two
types of beans, a massive amount of rice,
and a small salad. Great for the food and
even better for the experience.

La Crêperie (☎ 809-221-4734; La Atarazana 11; mains
US$4-12; ⊙ lunch & dinner, closed Tue) One of the
many eateries on Plaza de la Hispanidad, this
is the place to go for crepes. Try an entree
like La Classique (ham and cheese, US$4) for
lunch or La Speciale (Nutella and almonds,
US$6) for dessert. Good salads, too.

Restaurant & Bar Palmito Gourmet (☎ 809-221-
5777, cnr Arzobispo Portes 401 & Santomé; mains US$9-14;

AUTHOR'S CHOICE

Mesón D'Barí (☎ 809-687-4091; cnr Hostos & Salomé Ureña; dishes US$6-12; ☻ lunch & dinner) Occupying a beautifully restored colonial home on a quiet corner in the Zona Colonial, the Mesón D'Barí manages to exude cool confidence and a warm welcome at the same time. A long varnished-wood bar with stools stretches most of the length of one wall, while smartly set tables occupy the rest of the dining area. On the walls hang excellent artwork, most by local artists and most for sale. (In fact, some magazines also list the restaurant as an art gallery.) The *cangrejos guisados* (grilled crab) is the specialty, though the guinea hen in wine sauce (a highland favorite) is excellent, as are the steak and seafood dishes. Popular for the bar as much as the food service, Mesón D'Barí is usually quiet midweek but can get crowded on weekends with upper-crust *capitalinos*. There's live music (jazz, latin, some rock) on many weekend nights, played from a small stage in the back.

☻ lunch & dinner, closed Tue) A relaxed but classy restaurant, the Palmito Gourmet offers top-notch Creole food in an old-world setting. Specialties include *guinea al vino tinto* (hen in red wine sauce) and *mondongo en salsa Criolla* (tripe in a Creole sauce). There's live music on weekends.

Coco's Restaurant (☎ 809-687-9624; Padre Billini 53; mains US$10-30; ☻ lunch & dinner) In this eclectic, chic restaurant, the British chef and co-owner serves up a creative menu that changes on a weekly basis. Meals are based on French and Thai food but you can expect such taste treats as yucca pancakes with sour cream and caviar, and beef and coconut curry with popadom, rice and chutney. As a nod to the motherland, roast beef with Yorkshire pudding is offered on Sunday.

Gazcue

La Bodeguita de la Habana Vieja (☎ 809-476-7626; Av Independencia 302; mains US$7-12; ☻ lunch & dinner Tue-Sun) Cuban dishes are the specialty here, including *tamales Santiagueros,* a variation of the Mexican dish from Santiago de Cuba, and *ropa vieja* (literally 'old clothes'; shredded beef served in a tomato-based salsa). There's live music – mostly mariachi, strangely enough – every night starting at 9pm.

Ananda (☎ 809-682-7153; Casimiro de Moya 7; mains US$3-10; ☻ lunch & dinner Mon-Sat, lunch Sun) Run by the 'International Society of Divine Realization' and doubling as a yoga center, this cafeteria-style restaurant offers excellent and varied vegetarian food – brown rice, roast beans, bananas and eggplant figure prominently.

Hermanos Villar (☎ 809-682-1433; cnr Av Independencia & Pasteur; mains US$2-9; ☻ breakfast, lunch & dinner) A big busy diner with cafeteria-style service in front and a bar and tables in back,

and a sandwich menu several pages long. You have to assert yourself to get any service, but the food is very good.

DRINKING

The Zona Colonial has several fun watering holes, most of which start getting lively around 11pm.

Encuentro Artesanal (☎ 809-687-1135; Arzobispo Meriño 407; mains US$1-3; ☻ 10am-8pm Mon-Sat) Set in a cozy and colorful room at the back of a high-end boutique (p278), the drinks here will purportedly relieve such ailments as anxiety, arthritis and fatigue. They'll even just quench your thirst. Coffee drinks are also served.

Bobo's (☎ 809-689-1183; Hostos 157; ☻ 11am-3pm & 6pm-2am Mon-Sat) An urban-chic lounge with an Asian flair, this is the place to head if you want to dress up, drink a martini and immerse yourself in Dominican yuppyhood.

K-ramba Bar (☎ 809-688-3587; Isabel la Católica 1; ☻ 10am-3am Mon-Sat) This is a small place with indoor and outdoor tables, and drinks are served strong and fast. It's popular with expats and fellow travelers.

ENTERTAINMENT
Nightclubs

Guácara Taína (☎ 809-533-0671; Av Mirador del Sur 655; admission US$10) By far the most unique place to hear live merengue or salsa is in this giant club, located entirely inside a bat cave. It's so big that it can hold more than 2000 people, and in times past it has. Now it's primarily a tourist haunt – a stop of the cruise-ship crowd. The club is difficult to find, but every taxi driver in the city knows where it is. The club is vivacious from midnight till about 5am Thursday through Sunday.

The hotels on the Malecón have Santo Domingo's largest and most popular night clubs: the Jubilee at the **Renaissance Jaragua** (☎ 809-221-2222; Av George Washington 367) is a longtime hot spot, but the clubs at the **Inter-Continental** (☎ 809-221-0000; Av George Washington 218) and **El Napolitano** (☎ 809-687-1131; Av George Washington 101) also draw crowds, especially on weekends. Discos operate from Tuesday through Saturday and open around 9pm, but things don't get hopping until 11pm or later. Admission is US$3 to US$5 when there's a DJ (most nights), US$10 when there's a band. The clubs attract the capital's wealthiest and hippest, and they dress up when they go dancing. Short-sleeved shirts, tennis shoes and jeans are not allowed.

Gay & Lesbian Venues

Unfortunately, Santo Domingo is home to few gay and lesbian businesses. Those that manage to open their doors often close or change names. At the time of research, the following were particularly popular.

Aire Club (☎ 809-689-4163; Calle de las Mercedes 313; ⏰ 7pm-4am Wed-Sun) Considered the hottest club on the gay scene, Aire is a place where people come to see and be seen. Located in a rambling colonial home, this place gets going around 11pm and stays full until the sun rises. Top 40 music rules the dance floor and drag shows are regularly featured. Lesbians and straights are very welcome.

O'Hara's Place (☎ 809-682-8408; Danae 3; ⏰ 6:30pm-midnight) This cool cozy bar in Gazcue has a pool table and just a few tables inside on a welcoming patio that faces the street. Good music and a mellow atmosphere prevail. The manager's name is Scarlet, which may just be a coincidence.

Casinos

There are casinos at most of the large hotels on the Malecón, including the **InterContinental** (☎ 809-221-0000; Av George Washington 218), the **Hotel Santo Domingo** (☎ 809-221-1511; Av Independencia at Av Abraham Lincoln) and **El Napolitano** (☎ 809-687-1131; Av George Washington 101). They generally open at 4pm and close at 4am.

Sports
BASEBALL

Béisbol isn't just big in the Dominican Republic, it's huge. The 48-game Dominican winter league runs from mid-November until early February, and a number of major leaguers from the US play here as well. If you are in Santo Domingo – or anywhere in DR – during baseball season, definitely go to a game.

IN THE STANDS

Steaming BBQ chicken, free-flowing rum, marimba breaks, and bets shouted out at break-neck speed. Watching a baseball game in Santo Domingo's Quisqueya Stadium is more than just a day at the park, it's an event reminiscent of a raging party, an off-track betting office, and the World Series combined. It is one of the best places in the world to watch a baseball game.

As soon as you enter the 16,000-seat stadium, the experience begins. Vendors press through packed stands selling snacks and beer to eager fans. When a customer orders a drink, the vendor takes a bottle of beer and smashes a chunk of ice into a plastic cup. With a flip of the wrist, another bottle is poured into the cup and before you can say thank you, the vendor is moving on, having started your bar tab for the game. He'll return periodically to make sure your cup is full and to give you the latest odds offered by bookies who cruise 'Wall Street' – the uppermost tier of the grandstand.

The bookies are hard to miss; they stand throughout the game, yelling out bets and having bets yelled to them. They'll accept wagers on almost anything – the next inning's score, the following pitch, the direction of the next hit – and they do it in a frenzy, shouting at the top of their lungs, each bookie trying to be heard over the others.

But whether or not they're betting, the most important people in the stands are the fans. Dominicans take baseball very seriously; they discuss innings effusively and know players' stats. They jump up excitedly and embrace the closest stranger when their team makes a good play; they also slump down in their seats when an error is made. And although opposing fans often sling insults at each other, fights rarely break out at Quisqueya. Excitement and fun rule the day.

Estadio Quisqueya (☎ 809-540-5772; cnr Av Tiradentes & San Cristóbal) This stadium is the home field for two of the DR's six professional teams, and games are held Tuesday, Wednesday, Friday and Saturday at 8pm, and Sunday at 5pm. Tickets range from US$1.50 for the bleachers up to US$14 on the baseline. If you're here off-season, check the paper for information on the Liga del Verano (Summer League), which are minor league games held in smaller stadiums around town.

COCKFIGHTING

Coliseo Gallístico Alberto Bonetti Burgos (☎ 809-565-4038; Av Luperón; admission US$7-17.50) This is the country's most prestigious *gallera* (cockfighting ring), with the largest events drawing rooster handlers from as far away as Colombia and Brazil. Matches are held Wednesday and Friday at 6:30pm and Saturday at 3pm; in the high season (December to April) a match could have 30 or 40 fights and last into the wee hours. While it's the most traditional of Dominican pastimes, even more so than baseball, cockfighting is certainly not for everyone. Fights are to the death – some are quick, others are torturous bloody affairs that can last up to 15 minutes (the official limit before a fight is called off). The *gallera* is across from Aeropuerto de Herrera.

SHOPPING

Santo Domingo has a good variety of shopping alternatives; the best and most accessible stores are in the Zona Colonial.

Amber & Larimar

Considered national treasures, amber and larimar are sold widely throughout Santo Domingo. For a sure thing, try one of the following.

Swiss Mine (☎ 809-221-1897; El Conde 101; ☼ 9am-6pm Mon-Fri, 10am-4pm Sat) This shop, on Parque Colón, sells some of the finest-quality amber and larimar around; the design work is also unsurpassed. English, French, Italian and German are spoken.

Ambar Maldo Gift Shop (☎ 809-688-0639; Calle La Ataranza; ☼ 10am-5pm Mon-Sat) With an eclectic selection of amber and larimar jewelry, this makes a great stop if you like to hunt for unique pieces. Prepare to bargain hard – prices have been marked up in anticipation of the ritual.

Art

Santo Domingo's galleries tend to offer more and better Dominican art than Haitian, though you can find good examples of both in the following shops.

Bettye's Galería (☎ 809-688-7649; Plaza de María de Toledo, Isabel la Católica 163; ☼ 9am-6pm closed Tue) With an explosion of outstanding pieces, this is a good place to begin (and even end!) the search for a unique work of art. If you like antiques, a fine selection of jewelry and furnishings can be found here as well.

Atelier Gallery (☎ 809-688-7038; Arzobispo Portes 120; 10am-8pm Mon-Sat) Art sold here is of the type you would expect to see in any fine modern-art museum; traditional work – paintings, sculpture, pottery – is top tier and experimental pieces are the norm. Quite impressive.

Galería de Arte María del Carmen (☎ 809-682-7609; Arzobispo Mériño 207; ☼ 9am-7pm Mon-Sat, 10am-1pm Sun) Specializing in paintings, this gallery has been in business long enough to attract a wide range of talented Dominican artists.

Cigars

If you want to sample some of the finest *tabacos* around, drop by the Boutique del Fumador (☎ 809-685-6425; El Conde 109; 9am-7pm Mon-Sat, 10am-3:30pm Sun) or the Museo del Tabaco (☎ 809-689-7665; El Conde 101; ☼ 9:30am-8pm). Both are located on Parque Colón and are owned by the same tobacco company – Monte Cristi de Tabacos. At either shop you can watch as two workers roll cigars in the shop window – a sampling of the 45 unseen employees who roll away the day in the Boutique del Fumador. Montecristo, Cohiba and Caoba brand cigars are sold at both shops. Prices vary from US$2 to US$6 per cigar and boxes cost up to US$110.

Handicrafts

Encuentro Artesanal (☎ 809-687-1135; Arzobispo Meriño 407; ☼ 10am-8pm Mon-Sat) At this urban-chic shop, you'll find beautiful woodwork, paintings, kitchenware, hip clothing and unique jewelry. Hands down, the best all-around selection of high-end handicrafts in the Zona Colonial.

Artesanía Elisa (☎ 809-682-9653; Arzobispo Nouel 54; ☼ 9am-6pm Mon-Sat) Specializing in traditional faceless dolls, you'll find hundreds of handcrafted porcelain beauties here; all figurines are dressed in late 18th-century

---

FOUR TESTS FOR AMBER

There are some exceptional pieces of amber in the Dominican Republic. To test for authenticity, try one of the following:

- Examine the amber under a fluorescent lamp. If the glow changes, it's amber. If it doesn't, it's plastic. Most legitimate amber dealers have a fluorescent light on hand for this purpose.

- Rub the piece against cotton and bring it close to your hair. If your hair moves, the amber is real. Amber acquires static electricity. Plastic doesn't.

- Place unadorned amber in a glass of salt water. If it floats, it's amber. If it sinks, it's plastic. Remember, though, that this won't work if the piece is in a setting.

- Ask the salesperson to hold a match to the amber. Heated amber gives off a natural resin, plastic a chemical odor. Experts know how long to heat amber before it is damaged.

---

garb and are priced according to the size and detail of each (US$10 to US$550).

Markets

Mercado Modelo (Av Mella btwn Tomás de la Concha & Del Monte y Tejada; ☺ 9am-5pm) This lively trading center just north of the Zona Colonial offers some great buys if you are accomplished in the art of bargaining. Here, you'll find a carnival of woodcarvings, Haitian paintings, amber jewelry, musical instruments, love potions and wicker art. Note that although it's pleasantly bustling during the day, the area becomes somewhat sketchy after sunset.

GETTING THERE & AWAY

Air

Santo Domingo has two airports: the main one, **Aeropuerto Internacional Las Américas** (☎ 809-549-0328, 947-2225) is about 30 minutes east of town, while the smaller Aeropuerto Internacional Herrera is near the west edge of the city. Most international flights come into and depart from Las Américas.

For details on international air travel to and from the Santo Domingo area, see p306 and p774.

Domestic carriers and air-taxi companies in Santo Domingo:

AeroDOMCA (☎ 809-567-1195; Aeropuerto La Herrera)
Caribair (☎ 809-542-6688; Aeropuerto La Herrera)
Take Off (☎ 809-552-1333; www.takeoffweb.com; Aeropuerto La Herrera) Service from Santo Domingo (La Herrera airport) to Punta Cana, and from Punta Cana to Puerto Plata and Samaná (Aeropuerto Arroyo Barril).

Bus

The country's two main bus companies – **Caribe Tours** (☎ 809-221-4422; cnr Avs 27 de Febrero & Leopoldo Navarro) and **Metro** (☎ 809-566-7126; Calle Francisco Prats Ramírez) – have individual depots west of the Zona Colonial. Metro is behind Plaza Central mall, 55yd (50m) east of Av Winston Churchill. Caribe Tours has the most departures, and covers more of the smaller towns than does Metro. Both lines use large, comfortable and fairly modern passenger buses. Be sure to call ahead to confirm the schedule and ticket price, and always arrive at least 30 minutes before the stated departure time.

A number of 2nd-class buses leave from the vicinity of **Parque Enriquillo** (Zona Colonial). A bus stop just west of the park on Calle Caracas services Higüey (US$4.25, 2½ hours, every 20 minutes from 6am to 7pm), Santiago (US$2.80, two hours, take any Sosúa bus), and Sosúa (US$5.65, five hours, nine departures from 6:30am to 3:30pm). All buses make numerous stops en route. Ask about *expreso* buses that are slightly more expensive but have air-con and stop less frequently.

To get to Haiti, **Terra Bus** (☎ 809-531-0383; Plaza Lama, cnr Avs 27 de Febrero & Winston Churchill) offers bus service to Port-au-Prince at 11:30am every day. The trip, in a comfortable, air-conditioned coach, takes about six hours and costs US$39. If possible, reserve at least two days in advance as the bus is frequently full.

Car

Numerous international and domestic car rental companies have offices in Santo Domingo proper and at Las Américas International Airport. Rates average around US$55 per day for a compact car, including taxes and insurance – prices are somewhat lower off-season. For more information on rental requirements, see p307.

DOMINICAN REPUBLIC

Advantage Rent-a-A-Car Av Independencia 506
(☎ 809-685-4000); Airport (☎ 809-549-0536)
American International Av Independencia 1069
(☎ 809-687-0505); Airport (☎ 809-549-0621)
Avis Av Independencia (☎ 809-685-5095; cnr Av Independencia & Socorro Sánchez); Airport (☎ 809-549-0468)
Budget Av John F Kennedy (☎ 809-566-6666; cnr Avs John F Kennedy & Lope de Vega); Airport (☎ 809-549-0351)
Dollar Av Independencia 366 (☎ 809-221-7368); Airport (☎ 809-549-0738)
Europcar(☎ 809-688-2121; Av Independencia 354)
Hertz Av José María Heredia 1 (☎ 809-221-5333); Airport (☎ 809-549-0454)
McAuto Av George Washington (☎ 809-688-6518; cnr Av George Washington & Peynado); Airport (☎ 809-549-0373)
National (☎ 809-549-8303; Airport)
Nelly Av Independencia 654 (☎ 809-687-7997); Airport (☎ 809-549-0505)
Thrifty Airport (☎ 809-549-0717)

GETTING AROUND
To/From the Airport
There are no buses to or from Aeropuerto Internacional Las Américas (the main one) or Aeropuerto Internacional Herrera. From Las Américas, a taxi into town costs US$25 to US$30, with little room for negotiation. The fare from Herrera is more reasonable at US$10 – there's no permanent taxi stand here, but a couple of cabs meet every flight.

Bus
City buses (US$0.25) tend to follow major thoroughfares, including Av Independencia (eastbound) and Av Bolivar (westbound), both of which intersect with Parque Independencia in the Zona Colonial.

Car
Driving can be difficult in Santo Domingo due to traffic and aggressive drivers, especially those of taxis and buses. Many midrange and top-end hotels have parking with 24-hour guards. Otherwise you'll probably have to leave your rental on the street. Do not leave any valuables inside in either case.

Público
More numerous than buses are *públicos* – mostly beat-up minivans and private cars that follow the same main routes but stop anywhere that someone flags them down (US$0.35). Be prepared for a tight squeeze – drivers will cram seven or even eight passengers into an ordinary four-door car.

Taxi
Taxis in Santo Domingo don't have meters, so you should always agree on the price before climbing in. The standard fare is US$4, less within the Zona Colonial. Taxi drivers don't typically cruise the streets, but you can always find one at Parque Colón and Parque Independencia. You can also call a cab; try **Apolo Taxi** (☎ 809-537-7771), **Super Taxi** (☎ 809-536-7014) or **Taxi Express** (☎ 809-537-7777).

THE SOUTHEAST

The Dominican Republic's best beaches are in the southeast, with deep white sand and spectacular turquoise water backed by thick stands of tall coconut trees. (Developers and marketers have dubbed the area Costa de Coco, or Coconut Coast, though it's not a term many Dominicans use.) With such beautiful beaches comes tourist development and nowhere more so than in the Dominican Republic. All-inclusive resorts, close to 100 at last count, dot the coast from just outside Santo Domingo clear around to Playa Macao – some 125 miles (200km), not counting the innumerable inlets, coves and promontories that typify Hispaniola's perimeter. This is the vital heart of tourism in the Dominican Republic, drawing hundreds of thousands of beach-goers every year.

BÁVARO & PUNTA CANA
If the southeast has the best beaches in the DR, then Bávaro and Punta Cana have the best beaches of the southeast. Punta Cana (Grey-Haired Point) is the easternmost tip of the country. And though it's the name many travelers recognize, there are just a few resorts and a beautiful seaside golf course here. Several miles north, Bávaro is significantly more developed, with more than 30 resorts plus the area's best options for independent travelers.

Orientation
Punta Cana is south of the airport and Bávaro is north of it. In Bávaro, a small one-road enclave called El Cortecito has several independent hotels, as well as restaurants, an ATM, Internet access and shops. A short distance west is a collection of three adjoining outdoor malls known collectively at Plaza Bávaro and containing additional shops and services. Continuing past Plaza Bávaro there

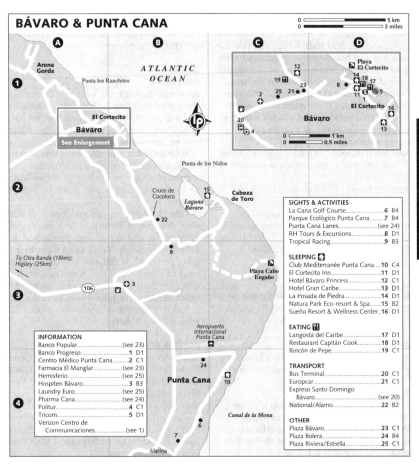

BÁVARO & PUNTA CANA

INFORMATION
Banco Popular	(see 23)
Banco Progreso	1 D1
Centro Médico Punta Cana	2 C1
Farmacia El Manglar	(see 23)
Hemisferio	(see 25)
Hospiten Bávaro	3 B3
Laundry Euro	(see 25)
Pharma Cana	(see 24)
Politur	4 C1
Tricom	5 D1
Verizon Centro de Comunicaciones	(see 1)

SIGHTS & ACTIVITIES
La Cana Golf Course	6 B4
Parque Ecológico Punta Cana	7 B4
Punta Cana Lanes	(see 24)
RH Tours & Excursions	8 D1
Tropical Racing	9 B3

SLEEPING
Club Mediterranée Punta Cana	10 C4
El Cortecito Inn	11 D1
Hotel Bávaro Princess	12 C1
Hotel Gran Caribe	13 D1
La Posada de Piedra	14 D1
Natura Park Eco-resort & Spa	15 B2
Sueño Resort & Wellness Center	16 D1

EATING
Langosta del Caribe	17 D1
Restaurant Capitán Cook	18 D1
Rincón de Pepe	19 C1

TRANSPORT
Bus Terminal	20 C1
Europcar	21 C1
Expreso Santo Domingo Bávaro	(see 20)
National/Alamo	22 B2

OTHER
Plaza Bávaro	23 C1
Plaza Bolera	24 B4
Plaza Riviera/Estrella	25 C1

is another small commercial center, Plaza Riviera/Estrella, before you reach an intersection with a gas station and the main bus terminal and police station. Plaza Bolera, just west of the airport, is nearest Punta Cana and has a police station, restaurants and some services.

Information

EMERGENCY
Politur (Tourist Police; ☎ 809-686-8227) Next to the bus terminal in Bávaro and at Plaza Bolera in Punta Cana.

INTERNET ACCESS
Hemisferio (☎ 809-552-0883; Plaza Riviera/Estrella; per hr US$1.75; ◷ 8am-8pm Mon-Sun) Internet access in an air con office on the 2nd floor.

Punta Cana Lanes (☎ 809-959-4444; Plaza Bolera; per hr US$4.25; ◷ 4pm-midnight Mon-Thu, 4pm-2am Fri, 1pm-2am Sat, 1pm-midnight Sun) Popular bowling alley with an Internet café.

Tricom (El Cortecito; per hr US$3; ◷ 9am-11pm) El Cortecito's only Internet café.

LAUNDRY
Most hotels offer laundry service but it's always costed by the piece, which can make washing your clothes more expensive than the clothes themselves.

Laundry Euro (☎ 809-552-1820; Plaza Riviera/ Estrella; ◷ 8am-8pm Mon-Sat, 8am-5pm Sun) Charges by the load – US$4.50 for up to 16lb (7.3kg) – with same-day service if you drop it off in the morning.

MEDICAL SERVICES

Every all-inclusive hotel has a small on-site clinic and medical staff, which can provide first aid and basic care to guests and non-guests alike. For serious cases, head to one of several good private hospitals in the area.

Centro Médico Punta Cana (☎ 809-552-1506) The name notwithstanding, this is the main private hospital in Bávaro, with a multilingual staff, a 24-hour emergency room and an in-house pharmacy. It's between Plaza Bávaro and the bus terminal.

Farmacia El Manglar (☎ 809-552-1533; Plaza Bávaro; 8am-midnight) Free delivery service to area hotels (until 10pm only).

Hospiten Bávaro (☎ 809-686-1414) Fittingly, this is the best private hospital in Punta Cana, with English-, French- and German-speaking doctors and a 24-hour emergency room. It's between the airport and the turn-off to Bávaro.

Pharma Cana (☎ 809-959-0025; Plaza Bolera; 9am-10pm Mon-Sat, 8am-11pm Sun)

MONEY

Banco Popular (Plaza Bávaro; 9am-4pm Mon-Fri)
Banco Progreso El Cortecito supermarket (9am-9pm Mon-Sat); Plaza Bolera (9am-4pm Mon-Fri)

POST

Most all-inclusive hotels will post letters and postcards for guests, for a small premium.

TELEPHONE

Tricom (El Cortecito; 9am-11pm) Calls to USA are US$0.42 per minute, to Europe US$0.70 per minute.
Verizon Centro de Comunicaciones (El Cortecito supermarket; 9am-5pm) Calls to USA are US$0.35 per minute; to Europe US$0.77 per minute.

TOURIST INFORMATION

There are no official tourist offices in Bávaro or Punta Cana. Your hotel concierge desk can be helpful, but will almost always recommend guided tours over independent activities.

Sights
BEACHES

Although the big resorts can and do restrict the use of their beach chairs and umbrellas to hotel guests, the actual beach is, by law, public and you can walk along the water and set up your towel wherever you like.

El Cortecito has a pretty beach that's open to all, though it can get a bit crowded. It's a good place for parasailing or for walking to even better beaches in front of nearby resorts.

Cabo Engaño is an isolated beach at the southern end of Bávaro, where you'll find great shells and are all but guaranteed to have it to yourself. You'll need a car to get here, preferably a full-size or SUV. On the road to Cabeza de Toro, turn right on the first dirt road past the go-cart track. The beach is just a few miles down, but the road is bad enough that it'll take you a good 20 minutes to get there.

PARQUE ECOLÓGICO PUNTA CANA

About 550yd (500m) south of Punta Cana Resort and Club, the **Parque Ecológico Punta Cana** (☎ 809-959-8483; www.puntacana.com; adult US$10, child US$5; 8am-4pm) offers 1½-hour tours of a portion of the reserve known as Parque Ojos Indígenas (Indigenous Eyes Park), so named for its 11 freshwater lagoons all fed by an underground river that flows into the ocean.

Dozens of bird, plant and insect species are readily visible. Unfortunately, there is no hotel pickup service; a cab here from Bávaro will run upwards of US$30.

AREA CODE SCAM

The Dominican Republic's area code – 809 – is at the heart of a scam that has victimized Americans and Canadians since 1996. Here's how it works: a message is sent via email, voice-mail, or post claiming that the recipient has either won a valuable prize or that a relative is in trouble. To collect the prize or to get information, the person must call an 809 telephone number. Since this only requires a 1 to be placed before it – like a domestic phone call – the caller has no idea that the call is an international one.

Once the victim calls, a series of recorded messages convinces him to stay on the line; for every minute he waits, he's charged US$25. A pricey call, even if it's just five minutes long! How do scammers get away with it? The Dominican government permits companies to use its area code for pay-per-call services, and foreign governments have no way of regulating that.

PARQUE NACIONAL LOS HAITISES

Meaning 'land of the mountains,' this 465-sq-mile (1200-sq-km) park at the southwestern end of the Bahía de Samaná contains scores of lush hills jutting some 100ft to 160ft (30m to 50m) from the water and coastal wetlands. The knolls were formed one to two million years ago, when tectonic drift buckled the thick limestone shelf that had formed underwater.

The area receives a tremendous amount of rain, creating perfect conditions for subtropical humid forest plants such as bamboo, ferns and bromeliads. In fact, Los Haitises contains over 700 species of flora, including four types of mangrove, making it one of the most highly biodiverse regions in the Caribbean.

Los Haitises is also home to 78 species of birds, 13 of which are endemic to the island. Those seen most frequently include the brown pelican, the American frigate bird, the blue heron, the roseate tern and the northern jacana. If you're lucky, you may even spot the rare Hispaniolan parakeet, notable for its light green and red feathers.

The park also contains a series of limestone caves, some of which contain intriguing Taino pictographs. Drawn by Hispaniola's native inhabitants using mangrove shoots, the pictures depict faces, hunting scenes, whales and other animals. Several petroglyphs (images carved into the stone) can also be seen at the entrance of some caves and are thought to represent divine guardians.

Land and boat excursions inside the park leave from Samaná and the small town of Sabana de la Mar, across the bay. Trips typically last half a day and include sailing around land formations and through mangroves, exploring Taino caves, and relaxing on the beach. For details, see p287.

Activities

About 550yd (500m) west of the Punta Cana airport, **Punta Cana Lanes** (☎ 809-959-4444; Plaza Bolera; 🕑 4pm-midnight Mon-Thu, 4pm-2am Fri, 1pm-2am Sat, 1pm-midnight Sun) has 20 bowling lanes (US$8.75 per hour); the rate includes two pairs of shoes (additional pairs US$1 each).

A short distance down the road to Cabeza de Toro, **Tropical Racing** (☎ 809-707-5164; per 20min US$15-58; 🕑 10am-10pm) offers nine-horsepower go-carts with top speeds of 46mph (74km/h) and a winding 1000yd (915m) racetrack on which to drive them. Daytime is good for kids; nighttime is cooler, but also busier and a bit rowdier. The track offers free hotel pickup if you make reservations ahead of time.

La Cana Golf Course (☎ 809-959-2262; www.punta cana.com; Punta Cana Resort & Club; 9/18 holes US$88/144; 🕑 7:30am-6pm) is Punta Cana's top golf course, designed by PB Dye and featuring several par-5s and challenging hill and sand features. The course has stunning ocean views.

Tours

Vendors ply the beach selling basic tours, like snorkeling and glass-bottom boat tours. **RH Tours & Excursions** (☎ 809-552-1425; www.rhtours .com; El Cortecito; 🕑 9am-7pm) offers more-formal excursions, including to Parque Nacional

Los Haitises (US$79), Isla Saona (US$79), and Santo Domingo's Zona Colonial (US$49).

Sleeping

Always book all-inclusive vacations online or through a travel agent, as they can offer discounts of up to 50% off of rack rates. If you find a great deal, check up on the resort by logging onto hotel review sites – two good ones are **TripAdvisor** (www.tripadvisor.com) and **Debbie's Dominican Republic Travel Page** (www .debbiesdominicantravel.com) – bearing in mind that most resorts cater to a particular niche, whether it's families, honeymooners, golfers, or the spring break crowd. The resorts listed below get consistently high marks, and are followed by some nonresort alternatives.

BÁVARO

Natura Park Eco-resort & Spa (☎ 809-221-2626; www.blau-hotels.com; Cabeza de Toro; d per person US$135; P ⚌ 🏊) This resort has won numerous awards for its efforts to reduce its environmental impact, including bleach-free laundry, integrated waste-water systems, even reusable beach cups (instead of the plastic cups so ubiquitous elsewhere). Rooms are simple but comfortable, with unobtrusive decor, low beds, and large glass doors opening onto balconies or terraces. The pool is a bit small, but the beach is quite nice. Small lagoons on the grounds are home to egrets, flamingos and other water birds. The hotel is well marked – in Cabeza de Toro bear left at the radio tower.

Hotel Bávaro Princess (☎ 809-221-2311; www .princesshotelsandresorts.com; Playa Bávaro; d per person US$210; P ☒ ☑) Along a glorious stretch of beach, these 750 all-suite accommodations are set on immaculately tended grounds. Eight restaurants offer a variety of eating choices and themes. Be sure to reserve early for à la carte restaurants to guarantee a spot. Same goes for the chairs on the beach. A water-sports center, four tennis courts, several bars and a discotheque round out this fine hotel.

PUNTA CANA

Club Mediterranée Punta Cana (☎ 809-687-2767; www.clubmed.com; Punta Cana; d per person US$235; P ☒ ☑) Geared toward families and active-minded travelers, Club Med offers snorkeling, kayaking, windsurfing, water-skiing, tennis, water exercises, three kids' activity clubs and even a flying trapeze. Rooms are comfortable, though not luxurious, and are set on lush grounds. Request a room near the reception area as some are located up to a half a mile (800m) away. Highly recommended.

RESORT ALTERNATIVES

The Costa de Coco's 'regular' hotels are located in or around El Cortecito.

La Posada de Piedra (☎ 809-221-0754; www.la posadadepiedra.com; r with shared/private bath US$35/45) This place has three rustic cabañas on the beach and two comfortable rooms with private baths inside the owners' home – the latter share a balcony with fantastic ocean views. An excellent-value place, considering the location.

El Cortecito Inn (☎ 809-552-0639; www.hotel cortecitoinn.com; d/tw with breakfast US$42/60; P ☒ ☑) This hotel, just steps from the beach, offers comfortable though somewhat dated rooms on well-tended grounds, all with balcony. Unfortunately, maintenance is lacking and service is abysmal – check that everything's working in your room before moving in. Nice pool.

Hotel Gran Caribe (☎ 809-552-1039; www.granca ribe.it; Playa Bávaro; s/d with breakfast US$45/62; P ☒)

☑ ☑) This quiet hotel has 36 comfortable rooms surrounding an hourglass-shaped pool. Rooms are small but the attractive decor and rooftop solarium more than make up for it. Guests can use the facilities at a nearby beach club free of charge.

Sueño Resort & Wellness Center (☎ 809-552-1690; Playa Bávaro; s/d without breakfast US$85/140, with breakfast US$85/150, all-inclusive US$100/180; P ☒ ☑ ☑) Designed for maximum relaxation and rejuvenation, rooms here are smallish but lovingly appointed, with pretty wood furniture, thick comfortable beds, and an in-room whirlpool tub. An on-site spa offers pedicures, facials, massages and more.

Eating

With so many all-inclusive resorts, the restaurant selection is somewhat limited.

Restaurant Capitán Cook (☎ 809-552-0645; El Cortecito; mains US$11-18; ☻ lunch & dinner) A long-time favorite serving excellent seafood dishes, prepared in a spotless outdoor kitchen. The complimentary appetizers – breaded crabmeat, hush puppies (deep-fried cornbread) and more – are almost a meal on their own. This place is bustling, especially on Sunday. Ask about the free lunchtime boat service to/from area resorts.

Langosta del Caribe (☎ 809-552-0774; El Cortecito; mains US$11-18; ☻ breakfast, lunch & dinner) This beachside restaurant offers good but pricey lunchtime specials featuring grilled lobster, shrimp kebabs, a seafood platter, dessert, and drinks (US$30 to US$50). Ask about promotions like free transportation and complimentary snorkel trips.

Rincón de Pepe (☎ 809-552-0603; Bávaro shopping center; mains US$8-15; ☻ lunch & dinner Mon-Sat) A classy but low-key restaurant that serves quality Spanish food at sunny outdoor tables or inside an airy, hot-pink dining area. You may even forget you're in a mall.

Getting There & Away

AIR

The Costa de Coco is served by the modern Aeropuerto Internacional Punta Cana, located on the road to Punta Cana about 5.5 miles (9km) east of the turn-off to Bávaro. **American Airlines** (☎ 809-959-2420), **Air France** (☎ 809-959-3002) and **LAN** (☎ 809-959-0144) all have offices at the airport. **Swissport** (☎ 809-959-3014) handles ticketing and other ground services of various carriers that serve Punta Cana airport, including US Airways.

Taxi fares between the airport and area resorts and hotels are surprisingly reasonable, ranging from US$9 to US$30.

BUS

Bávaro's main bus terminal is located a mile (1.6km) inland from El Cortecito.

Expreso Santo Domingo Bávaro (Bávaro ☎ 809-552-0771; Santo Domingo ☎ 809-682-9670; cnr Juan Sánchez Ruiz & Máximo Gómez, Santo Domingo) has direct first-class services between Bávaro and the capital, with a stop in La Romana. Departures times in both directions are at 7am, 10am, 2pm and 4pm (US$3.75, four hours).

To all other destinations, take a local bus to Higüey from Bávaro's main terminal and transfer there (US$2, one hour, every 15 minutes from 6am to 9pm).

Getting Around

Local buses go back and forth on the coastal road between the main bus terminal and Cruce de Cocoloco. They are supposed to pass every 15 to 30 minutes, but can sometimes take up to an hour.

Renting a car for a day or two is a good way to see less-touristed areas along the coast. Rates are high, starting at US$70 per day. Agencies include **Europcar** (☎ 809-686-2861; Plaza Punta Cana; ☷ 8am-6pm), and **National/Alamo** (☎ 809-688-5069; Cruce de Cocoloco; ☷ 8am-6pm Mon-Sat, 8am-5pm Sun).

Otherwise, you can call a **taxi** (☎ 809-552-0617), with trips costing from US$5 to US$30, or catch one in front of any hotel. Motoconchos (motorcycle taxis) are a cheaper option for short distances, but not are recommended for longer trips or at night. Water taxis can be found on El Cortecito beach (US$10 to US$50).

PENÍNSULA DE SAMANÁ

The Samaná Peninsula is a small sliver of land – just 25 miles (40km) long and 9 miles (15km) wide – but a major destination for independent-minded tourists. It offers the deserted beaches and small town atmosphere that many travelers envision when they plan their trip (but that they may find lacking elsewhere in the Dominican Republic). It has excellent hiking and horseback riding; arguably the best diving in the country; and, from mid-January to mid-March, some of the best whale-watching in the world. And it has a broad range of accommodations, from good budget options (finally!) to classy high-end resorts. For photos and more information, check out the sites **SamanaOnline** (www.samanaonline.com) or **Samananet** (www.samananet.com).

Samaná has an intriguing history as well. In the early 1820s, around 5000 Black freemen and former slaves left the US and relocated to Haiti, which at that time occupied the entire island of Hispaniola. (It was part of the same repatriation movement that took former slaves to Liberia, West Africa.) About half of the free men settled in Samaná; today, a community of their descendants still speak a form of English and celebrate a number of traditional Africanesque festivals.

Ironically, Samaná was nearly annexed by the US some 45 years later. Looking to establish a military base in the Caribbean, the Grant administration offered to buy the peninsula for US$2 million or, better yet, to incorporate the Dominican Republic into the US on the same basis as Texas. But after two years of negotiation, the US senate rejected the plan, and the base was eventually built in Guantánamo, Cuba.

SAMANÁ
pop 50,000

Samaná town is a tranquil community with brightly colored houses clinging to the surrounding hillsides and a small business district near the water. Some 30,000 people come here during the two-month whale-watching season; the rest of the year Samaná receives far fewer visitors, and most are headed to or from the coastal towns of Las Terrenas and La Galeras, or taking the ferry across the bay.

Orientation

Just about everything you'll need in Samaná is within 100yd (90m) of the main pier. To make it even easier, the main first-class buses arrive and depart directly across from the pier. The hotels are reachable on foot, but a bit far if you're lugging bags. *Guaguas* (local buses) leave from the municipal market, about half a mile down the road toward Sánchez.

Information

Banco Popular (Av la Marina; 8:15am-4pm Mon-Fri, 9am-1pm Sat)

BanReservas (Calle Santa Barbara; 8am-5pm Mon-Fri, 9am-1pm Sat)

Farmacia Giselle (☎ 809-538-2303; Calle Santa Barbara; 8am-10pm Mon-Sat, 8am-Sun) Near Julio Labandier.

Hospital (Calle San Juan) This is a very basic place near the Palacio de Justicia.

Lavandería Santa Barbara (Calle Santa Barbara; 8:30am-6pm) Same-day laundry service is available (US$1 per pound/500g).

Post office (cnr Calle Santa Barbara & 27 de Febrero; 8:30am-5pm Mon-Fri)

Tourist office (☎ 809-538-2332; Calle Santa Barbara; 8:30am-3pm Mon-Fri) Good for regional maps. Basic English, Italian and French spoken.

Verizon Centro de Comunicaciones (☎ 809-536-2133; Calle Santa Barbara; Internet access per hr US$1.75; 8am-1pm & 2-10pm Mon-Sat, 9am-1pm Sun) This place near Cristóbal Colón offers Internet access and international calls (US$0.32 per minute to the USA; US$0.74 per minute to Europe).

Sights & Activities

CAYO LEVANTADO

About 4.5 miles (7km) southeast of Samaná is Cayo Levantado, a small island with dense vegetation and a beautiful beach. Unfortunately, the island is inundated with tour groups from all-inclusive resorts and scores of vendors hawking jewelry and cheap handicrafts, and much of the charm is lost. Boatmen at the pier will bring you here for US$15 to US$20 each way.

WHALE-WATCHING

Samaná is one of the top places in the world to observe humpback whales. The season begins around January 15 and continues to March 15. See the boxed text, below, for more information.

Victoria Marine (☎ 809-538-2494; www.whalesamana.com; adult/child aged 5-10/child under 5 US$48/28/free; 8:30am-1:30pm & 3-6pm) is Samaná's most-recommended whale-watching outfit, owned and operated by Canadian marine biologist Kim Beddall, who was the first to recognize the scientific and economic importance of Samaná's whales back in 1985. Victoria Marine tours use a large two-deck boat with a capacity for 60 people. Onboard guides offer interesting facts and information in various languages, and sodas and water are provided. Tours leave at 9am and last three to four hours. There is also a 1:30pm trip when demand is high. Some tours include a stop at Cayo Levantado on the return.

If Victoria Marine is booked solid or you just want to comparison shop, **Samaná**

TRAVELING GIANTS

Every winter more than 10,000 humpback whales – virtually the entire North-Atlantic population of the creatures – leave their feeding grounds around Greenland and Iceland and head south to the Caribbean. In mid-January they reach their destination, the waters around the Samaná Peninsula, where they remain for two months to court and breed. Most of the whales swim 2000 to 3000 miles (3200km to 4800km) to get here, though several individuals identified in Samaná were later spotted off the coast of Norway, a trip of some 4500 miles (7200km). This is one of the longest migrations of any mammal.

Before leaving, the whales gorge themselves on invertebrates and fish, consuming up to 1.5 tons a day. It's not without reason – there is no food for the whales in the Caribbean and they depend on the fat they accumulate up north to survive their long journey south. In all, most of the whales go six months without a single meal and lose a fifth of their body weight.

That's not to say they aren't busy. Once in the Dominican Republic, the whales commence their famous antics – slapping their flippers, lifting their tails, leaping partially or entirely out of the water and returning with a tremendous splash. Scientists still don't know why the whales do it – perhaps as a form of communication or to simply break loose barnacles – but males, females and calves all join in.

Adult male humpbacks also sing long complicated songs that are made up of a variety of grunts, chirps and squeals. The music can be heard up to 20 miles (32km) away, and marine biologists believe that this song is used to attract females. Curiously, the whales all sing the same basic song, which evolves over time so that the following year, it will be a new song

Tourist Service (☎ 809-538-2740; Av la Marina 6; sa mana.tour@verizon.net.do; ☉ 8:30am-12:30pm & 2:30-6pm Mon-Fri, 8:30am-12:30pm Sat) and **Moto Marina** (☎ 809-538-2302; Av la Marina; ☉ 8am-6pm) offer similarly priced tours.

CASCADA EL LIMÓN
El Limón is a 165ft (50m) waterfall a short distance from the town of El Limón. Travel agencies in Samaná offer trips here for around US$45, including transportation, horses, guide and lunch. However, it's perfectly easy and much cheaper to do the trip yourself by taking a *gua-gua* to El Limón. See Las Terrenas (p295) for more details.

PARQUE NACIONAL LOS HAITISES
This national park, with its scores of tiny, jungly islands and thick mangrove forests, makes for great exploring by boat. Victoria Marine (opposite) and other tour outfits in town offer trips here for around US$45 per person, including guide and transportation to, and inside, the park. For more information on the park, see the boxed on p283.

Sleeping
Hotel Bahía View (☎ 809-538-2186; d/tw with fan US$15.50/20, tw with balcony US$23.50, tw with air-con US$27; ☒) This place is the best deal in town, though it's a bit removed from the center.

Rooms here are basic and clean, with hot water and a good restaurant downstairs. You probably won't need air-con, but the balcony rooms are worth the extra cost if you appreciate having more light and space.

Hotel Tropical Lodge (☎ 809-538-2840; www .samana-hotel.com; Av La Marina; d/tw with breakfast US$46/70; ☒ ☒) Samaná's nicest hotel is built on a hillside and has great bay views from the swimming pool and breakfast area.

Rooms aren't exactly deluxe, but they're large and perfectly comfortable. The five-minute walk to town can be a slight drag, especially at night, though the on-site restaurant serves reliable meals, including fish, pizza and crepes.

Eating & Drinking
Restaurant Le France (☎ 809-538-2781; Av la Marina; mains US$5-12; ☉ lunch & dinner Tue-Sun) Also known as Chez Tony, the menu at this small, open-air place ranges from Dominican-style chicken and pork to French dishes like beef tartare and homemade pâté. Low-key, friendly service with a few upscale flairs, such as the tartare being created right at your table.

Restaurant Chino (☎ 809-538-2215; Calle San Juan 1; mains US$4.50-12.50; ☉ lunch & dinner) Located on a hill with a fantastic view of the Samaná Bay, this aptly named restaurant serves up

DOMINICAN REPUBLIC

---

altogether. Another way that males attract females is through muscle and intimidation – males are known to bloody their heads as they ram and rake one another to win a female's attention.

After mating, a single calf is born 11 to 12 months later. A newborn humpback whale typically measures 9ft to 13ft (3m to 4m) and weighs up to 2 tons (2000kg). Calves are nursed for nearly a year, drinking milk that's 50% fat and, as a result, gain up to 100lb (45kg) per day – that's close to 4lb (1.8kg) every *hour*. A whale calf doubles its body length in its first year alone.

Whale-watching trips typically depart around 9am and sail for about 45 minutes before arriving in the area known as the sanctuary, a protected area covering more than 7700 sq miles (20,000 sq km).

Once inside the breeding zone, the captain slows the boat and everyone is asked to look for the telltale spout, the spray a whale makes as it exhales near the surface. As soon as a whale is spotted, the captain directs the boat toward it and more often than not, observers are rewarded with breathtaking acrobatics. The larger boats have expert guides on board to explain whale behavior and to answer any questions. Boats are only permitted to stay with a whale or a group of whales for 30 minutes. When that time is up, the boat turns away, the whales continue on their way, and everyone aboard scans the water for another spout. Excursions typically last about three hours and sometimes include a stop on Cayo Levantado, a touristy but beautiful island a short distance from Samaná town. Drinks and light snacks are often provided. For more details, see opposite.

large portions of Chinese favorites – think won ton soup, spring rolls and chop suey. Dishes are tasty if a bit greasy.

Café de Paris (Av La Marina; dishes US$4-10; ☺ breakfast, lunch & dinner) Next to Le France, this eclectic restaurant-bar has decent pizzas, including the house specialty made with chicken, onion, garlic, olives and egg. Crepes are served salty or sweet, and you can order a variety of salads.

You also can get cheap eats at a series of food stands that line Av La Marina near Calle Maria Trinidad Sánchez. Beginning around 6pm, and running until the early hours of the morning, fried chicken is served up with Presidente beers for Dominican and foreign customers alike. If you have trouble finding them, just listen for the *bachata* blasting from the west side of town.

Getting There & Away

AIR

The nearest airport in regular operation is Aeropuerto Internacional El Portillo, just outside of Las Terrenas (p295).

BOAT

Transporte Maritimo (☎ 809-538-2556; Av la Marina) provides a ferry service across the Bahía de Samaná to Sabana de la Mar (US$3.50, one hour, 7am, 9am, 11am and 3pm). From here, you can catch *gua-guas* to various destinations throughout the southeast and to Santo Domingo.

BUS

Facing the pier, **Caribe Tours** (☎ 809-538-2229; Av la Marina) offers a bus service to Santo Domingo six times daily at 7am, 8:30am, 10am, 1pm, 2:30pm and 4pm (US$7.50, 4½ hours). The same bus stops along the way at Sánchez (US$2, 30 minutes), Nagua (US$2.15, one hour) and San Francisco de Macorís (US$3, 1½ hours).

A block west, **Metro** (☎ 809-538-2851; cnr Av la Marina & Rubio y Peñaranda) offers a similar service to Santo Domingo twice a day at 8am and 3:30pm (US$8, 4½ hours). Like it's competitor, it stops at Sánchez (US$2.30, 30 minutes), Nagua (US$2.30, one hour), and San Francisco de Macorís (US$3.50, 1½ hours).

For service to towns nearby, head to the **gua-gua terminal** (Av la Marina) at the *mercado municipal*, near Angel Mesina. From here, trunks and minivans head to Las Galeras

(US$1.75, 45 minutes, every 15 minutes from 6am to 6pm), Limón (US$1.75, 30 minutes, every 15 minutes from 6am to 6pm), and Sánchez (US$1.75, 45 minutes, every 15 minutes from 6am to 4:30pm). You can also hail *gua-guas* on the main drag but you may not get a seat.

Getting Around

Samaná is easily covered on foot, or you can catch a taxi or a motoconcho with a passenger cab. Both can be found near the pier or hailed on the main drag (US$1 to US$3).

CAR

Rental rates for a 4WD (the only vehicle available) are US$70 to US$90 per day, with tax and insurance included. Two convenient agencies are **Joseba Rent-a-Car** (☎ 809-538-2124; Av la Marina; ☺ 8am-noon & 2-5pm Mon-Sat) and **Xamaná Rent Motors** (☎ 809-538-2380; Av la Marina; ☺ 8am-noon & 2-6pm).

LAS GALERAS

Before 1990, there were only two simple hotels in this rapidly changing fishing community 17 miles (28km) northeast of Samaná. Today there are more than a dozen hotel and bungalow options and almost as many restaurants. But the town still retains a peaceful, laid-back quality that – along with some of the DR's best beaches and outdoor activities – make this a favorite stop for many travelers.

Orientation

The road from Samaná winds through lovely, often-forested countryside before reaching the outskirts of Las Galeras. There's one main intersection in town, about 55yd (50m) before the highway dead-ends at the beach, and most hotels, restaurants and services are within walking distance from here.

Information

There is no post office, but Internet Las Galeras sells express stamps.

Clinic (☎ 809-538-0020; ☺ 24hr) The Casa Marina Bay resort has a small clinic that nonguests can use in emergencies. It's 1100yd (1km) east of town. For more serious matters go to Samaná or Las Terrenas.

Farmacia Joven (☎ 809-538-0103; Calle Principal; ☺ 8am-9:30pm Mon-Sat) This pharmacy near the main crossroad has basic meds.

Gift Shop & Internet Habiby (Plaza Lusitania, Calle Principal; Internet access per hr US$3.50; ☻ 8:30am-1pm & 2-8pm Mon-Sat) This place, just steps away from Internet Las Galeras, was setting up shop when we passed through. Prices promised to be significantly cheaper.

Hermanos Cruz Agente de Cambio & Rent-A-Car (☎ 809-341-4574; Calle Principal; ☻ 8am-6pm Mon-Sat, 8am-noon Sun) There is no bank or ATM in Las Galeras but you can exchange cash dollars and euros here.

Internet Las Galeras (Calle Principal; Internet access per hr US$6.25; ☻ 8:30am-8pm Mon-Sat, 9am-12:30pm & 2:30-8pm Sun) This Internet cafe at the main intersection offers reliable – if pricey – Internet connections. It also sells stamps for international destinations (US$1.60) and will post mail left in its drop box.

Verizon Centro de Comunicaciones (Plaza Lusitania, Calle Principal; ☻ 9am-noon & 1-6pm) To call home, this place charges US$0.35 per minute to the USA and US$0.77 per minute to Europe.

Sights
PLAYA RINCÓN
Named one of the top 10 beaches in the Caribbean by *Condé Nast*, Playa Rincón is composed of several long, softly curving beaches stretching almost 2 miles (3.2km), the sand nearly white and the water multihued. A cluster of restaurants serves mostly seafood and rents out beach chairs. Most people arrive by boat taxi – the standard option is to arrive around 9am and leave at 4pm (US$12 to US$15 per person). You can also drive here – the turn-off is 4.5 miles (7km) south of town on the road to Samaná – though the last half-mile (800m) or so is too rough for small or midsize cars.

PLAYITA
Better than the town beach, Playita (Little Beach) is easy to get to on foot or by motoconcho. It's a broad swatch of tannish sand, with mellow surf that's backed by tall palm trees and simple food shacks. On the main road just south of town, look for signs for Hotel La Playita pointing down a dirt road headed west.

PLAYAS MADAMA & FRONTÓN
These two beautiful and isolated beaches are reachable by foot or boat; Madama is a small beach tucked into a narrow bay and framed by high bluffs, and Frontón is a rustic beauty that rivals Playa Rincón. If walking, the trail begins near Karin y Ronald (see p290). In the first half-mile (800m) you'll pass a

German beer garden before reaching the first of two cut-offs to Playa Madama. Whichever cut-off you take, however, it's another 1.25 miles (2km) to the Madama. If you continue on the main trail and pass the second cut-off you'll eventually run into the cut-off to Playa Frontón. From there it's 2.5 winding miles (4km) to the beach itself. You can also take a boat to either of these beaches for around US$17 per person, round-trip.

LA PUERTA DEL FERMAMENTO
Better known as El Punto, this spectacular vista point is a 3 mile (5km) walk from Karin y Ronald (p290).

To get here, simply continue past the turn-offs to Playa Madam and Frontón and keep climbing up, up, up. Budget at least an hour to get to the top.

BOCA DEL DIABLO
'Mouth of the Devil' is an impressive blowhole, where waves rush up a natural channel and blast out of a hole in the rocks. Car or motorcycle is the best way to get here – look for an unmarked dirt road 4.5 miles (7km) south of town and about 110yd (100m) beyond the well-marked turn-off to Playa Rincón. Follow the road east for about 5 miles (8km), then walk the last 110yd (100m) or so.

Activities
DIVING
Cabo Cabrón (Bastard Point) is one of the north coast's best dive sites and is an easy boat ride from Las Galeras. Other popular sites in the area include **Piedra Bonita**, a 55yd (50m) stone tower that's good for spotting jacks, barracudas and sea turtles; **Cathedral**, an enormous underwater cave with an opening to sunlight; and a sunken 180ft (55m) container ship haunted by green morays.

Casa Marina Bay Dive Center (Dive Samaná; ☎ 809-538-2000; Casa Marina Bay Resort; ☻ 7am-6pm) is located at the far end of the Casa Marina Bay Resort beach and is open to nonguests. The shop may close if business is slow, so definitely call ahead before making the trip out here. One-/two-tank dives are US$60/114 including all equipment (US$5 to US$12 less if you have your own). Four-and six-dive packages bring the per-dive rate down to US$48 to US$52, including gear.

HORSEBACK RIDING

The Belgian owners of Karin y Ronald offer horseback riding tours (US$42/54 per half-/full day) that are highly recommended to various spots around Las Galeras, including Boca del Diablo, El Punto lookout, and Playas Madama and Frontón.

MOUNTAIN BIKING

Not to be outdone by their countrymen, the Belgian owners of **La Bella Aventura** (labellaventura@hotmail.com) offer half- and full-day mountain biking tours in the area, for around US$42 per person. Tours can be tailored to the length, difficulty and destination you prefer.

Tours

While you can visit many of the beaches and sights included in tours on your own or by motoconcho, organized tours usually include reliable transportation and a professional and knowledgeable guide.

Aventura Tropical (☎ 809-538-0249; Calle Principal; ☽ 8am-7pm Mon-Sat, 8am-1pm Sun) Offers numerous day trips including whale-watching in Samaná Bay (US$80 per person), land and boat excursions through Parque Nacional Los Haitises (US$70 per person), hikes to the area's isolated beaches (US$20 per person), and village tours that include a cockfight and stops in a typical home and primary school (US$69 per person). Overnight trips can also be arranged, including visits to the waterfalls in Jarabacoa, rafting in Río Yaque del Norte, and climbing Pico Duarte, the highest peak in the Caribbean.

Guariquén (☎ 809-248-5648, 538-0201; guariquen lasgaleras@hotmail.com; ☽ 8am-6pm) An Italian-run development foundation that offers area tours to help support its water, sanitation and other community projects. Tours go the sights listed above, plus an iguana farm and a saltwater lagoon. Guariquén also has a nascent volunteer program – for information on that or any tours, call or stop by Hotel Todo Blanco just east of the main intersection.

Sleeping

BUDGET

Paradiso Bungalows (☎ 809-967-7295; ruby@playa rincon.com; Calle Principal; r US$25) Less than 110yd (100m) from the beach, at the crossroads, Paradiso Bungalows has seven clean cabins with one double bed each and a ceiling fan. All rooms have cold-water baths and screened windows. Porches with rocking chairs make a nice place to laze away an afternoon.

Juan y Lolo Bungalows (☎ 809-538-0208; www.juanylolo.com) For more options in the Para-

diso Bungalows style, and range, try this place, which is 110yd (100m) west of main intersection.

Karin y Ronald (r US$30, bungalow US$54) This place is removed from the center, 1.5 miles (2.5km) east of town, but is ideally located for exploring the less-visited beaches and sights east of Las Galeras. Two cozy rooms and a bungalow are set in a lush garden and have tiled baths, fans and shaded patios. The friendly Belgian owners will personally take you on horseback rides or will draw you a map if you prefer to explore the area on foot. Meal plans are offered although a common kitchen is available.

MIDRANGE

Apart Hotel La Isleta (☎ 809-538-0016; www.la-isleta.com; 1-bedroom apt US$65) Located near the end of the main drag, 165yd (150m) west of Calle Principal, this hotel offers six charming apartments, each with a fully equipped kitchen, a sitting area that can double as a small bedroom and a loft with a queen size bed. All apartments also have porches with enviable views of the ocean. Perfect for a couple looking for some R&R or for a family with young children. Rates drop considerably in the low season and for stays of a week or longer.

La Bella Aventura (labellaventura@hotmail.com; r with breakfast US$42, house US$54) Three small split-level houses (one occupied by the owners) and a comfortable stand-alone room share a large grassy lot where the east-west road bends toward the ocean, 275yd (250m) west of the main intersection. All are constructed of brightly painted cement and have clean private baths (some cold water only), fan, firm beds, sleeper sofas and 24-hour solar/battery power; the houses have small kitchens. All also use rainwater instead of the semisalted groundwater that's used by most other hotels.

TOP END

Villa Serena (☎ 809-538-0000; http://villaserena.com; r with breakfast US$140; P ⚡ ⚡) The most upscale hotel in town is a bit overpriced, though admittedly is quite pretty. Each of the 21 bright spacious rooms is decorated differently, but all have comfortable beds and a sea-facing balcony or terrace. The large oceanfront garden and swimming pool are attractive and well maintained. Use of hotel kayaks and bicycles is included. It's 330yd (300m) east of the main intersection.

Eating

Pizzeria (Calle Principal; mains US$6.50-8.50; breakfast, lunch & dinner, closed Tue) The best thin-crust pizza this side of Santo Domingo can be found in this open-air joint; pizzas come crisp, loaded with toppings, and are big enough for two. Look for the sign of the leaning tower of Pisa toward the entrance of town. Delivery is available.

Chez Denise (809-538-0219; Calle Principal; mains US$4-14; breakfast, lunch & dinner Mon-Sat) Specializing in crepes – salty, sweet, and just down-right good – this restaurant serves excellent French pancakes. Seating is in a pleasant open-air dining room near the crossroads with tables overlooking Calle Principal. Service can be exasperatingly slow but the wait is worth it.

El Kiosko (mains US$5-7; breakfast, lunch & dinner) On the beach at the end of Calle Principal, this thatch-roofed restaurant serves up tasty Dominican dishes at weathered picnic tables.

Patisserie Boulangerie Français (Calle Principal; mains US$1-3.50; breakfast, lunch & dinner Tue-Sun) Down a small footpath off of Calle Principal near the crossroads, a bright yellow clapboard house offers excellent French breads and some tempting pastries. Coffee drinks and continental breakfast combinations are also available.

Entertainment

While the nightlife is pretty mellow in this town, two bars/discotheques – **Chez Manuel** (Calle Principal) and **VIP** (Calle Principal) – are hopping on most weekends by around 9pm. Located about 55yd (50m) apart, you'll be hard pressed to miss either once the *bachata* starts playing. Popular with locals, expats and travelers alike. No cover charge.

Getting There & Around

The only public transportation out of town are *gua-guas* that head to Samaná (US$1.75, 45 minutes, every 15 minutes from 7am to 5pm) from a terminal near the beach. A motoconcho ride around Las Galeras costs around US$0.50 to US$1.

If you can swing it, renting a 4WD is an excellent way to explore the peninsula. **RP Rent-A-Car** (809-538-0249; Calle Principal;

8am-7pm Mon-Sat, 8am-1pm Sun) and **Hermanos Cruz Agente de Cambio & Rent-A-Car** (809-341-4574; Calle Principal; 8am-6pm Mon-Sat, 8am-noon Sun) both rent out 4WD vehicles for US$60 to US$90 per day. While definitely pricey, you'll be glad you have the extra power on the areas' rough roads. **Xamaná Rent Moto** (809-538-0208; 9am-noon & 3-6pm Mon-Fri, 9am-noon Sat & Sun) rents out motorcycles as well (US$25 per day). It's 50yd (50m) west of the intersection.

Mountain bike rentals are also available at **Piccola Italia** (809-325-4018; Calle Principal; 8am-noon & 3-7pm Mon-Sat), a shop near the entrance to town. Most bicycles are 21-speed and in good condition (US$12.50 per day).

LAS TERRENAS

pop 15,000

Although Las Terrenas has grown from a rustic fishing village into a bustling tourist destination it still exudes a small-town quality. The main road is congested with motoconchos and ATVs (all-terrain vehicles), but the sand road along the beach gets quieter the further you walk, with scattered hotels on the inland side and pretty beaches with tan sand, high palm trees and calm aquamarine waters on the other. The nightlife is much livelier here than in Las Galeras or Samaná.

Orientation

The road from Samaná to Las Terrenas makes a sharp left when it hits town and turns into Av Duarte. The main drag in town, Av Duarte has banks, Internet, laundry and other services. Where the highway bends and turns into Av Duarte, a dirt road continues along the beach, eventually hitting a cluster of bars and restaurants known as Pueblo de los Pescadores. The best beaches are beyond that, as well as a number of hotels and restaurants.

Information

BOOKSTORES

Newsstand (Av Duarte; 9am-8pm) This stand at the back of Plaza Taína sells day old *New York Times, Le Monde*, and other international papers for a hefty mark up.

EMERGENCY

Politur (Tourist Police; 809-754-2973; Av Emilio Prud'Homme; 24hr)

INTERNET ACCESS

L'entract.com (Plaza Taína, Av Duarte; per hr US$4.25; ⏰ 9am-1pm & 3:30-7:30pm Mon-Sat)

Verizon (Av Duarte near Plaza Taína; per hr US$1.75; ⏰ 8am-10pm)

LAUNDRY

Lavandería Ami (Av Duarte; ⏰ 8am-6pm Mon-Sat) This laundry next to Plaza Rosada charges US$2.25 per wash, US$3.50 per dry cycle. Detergent and fabric softener are US$0.75 each, and the drop-off service is US$1 extra. There's a same-day service if you drop off early.

MEDICAL SERVICES

Farmacia Rodríguez Rodríguez (☎ 809-240-6084; Av Duarte; ⏰ 8am-8pm Mon-Sat, 8am-6pm Sun)

Hospital Pablo A Paulino (☎ 809-274-6474, ext 24; Calle Matias Mella; ⏰ emergency room 24hr)

MONEY

Banco Popular (Av Duarte; ⏰ 9am-5pm Mon-Fri, 9am-1pm Sat) Across the street from BanReservas, just east of the river. Has a 24-hour ATM.

BanReservas (Av Duarte; ⏰ 9am-6pm Mon-Fri, 9am-1pm Sat) Has a 24-hour ATM.

Fort Knox Money Exchange (El Paseo shopping center, Calle Alberto Camaño; ⏰ 8am-1pm & 4-8pm Mon-Sat, 10am-1pm Sun)

POST

Post office (El Paseo shopping center, Calle Alberto Camaño; ⏰ 9am-1pm & 3-5pm Mon-Fri)

TELEPHONE

Verizon (Av Duarte; ⏰ 8am-10pm) This place near Plaza Taína offers calls to the USA US$0.32 per minute; to Europe US$0.74 per minute.

TOURIST INFORMATION

There is no official tourist office in Las Terrenas, but many hotels offer area maps and provide helpful information.

Sights & Activities

CASCADA EL LIMÓN

A half-hour from Las Terrenas is the small town of El Limón, whose primary attraction is the Cascada El Limón, an impressive 165ft (150m) waterfall with a swimming hole. Just about everyone who visits does so on horseback, and a dozen or more *paradas* (horseback-riding operations) in town and on the highway toward Samaná offer tours. All outfits offer essentially the same thing: a 30- to 60-minute ride up the hill to the waterfalls, 30 to 60 minutes to take a dip and enjoy the scene, and 30 to 60 minutes to return, with lunch at the end. Your guide – who you should tip, by the way – will be walking, not riding, which is the custom.

Spanish-owned **Santí** (☎ 809-452-9352; limon santi@terra.es; ⏰ 8am-7pm), in El Limón, is the most popular of the *paradas* and also the most expensive, charging US$24.50 per person with lunch or US$15.50 without (10% discount if you show this book). The lunch is excellent and the guides and staff (all adults) are better paid than elsewhere. Most other operators charge around US$7/14 without/with lunch; try **Parada la Manzana** (☎ 809-360-9142; ⏰ 8am-4pm), 3 miles (5km) from town near El Limón, or **Parada María y Miguel** (☎ 809-282-7699; ⏰ 7am-5pm), 1.25 miles (2km) from town toward El Limón. A motoconcho to either costs US$1 to US$2.

DIVING & SNORKELING

Las Terrenas has reasonably good diving and snorkeling and at least three shops in town to take you out. Favorite dive spots include a **wreck** in 92ft (28m) of water and **Isla Ballenas**, visible from shore, with a large underwater cave. Most shops also offer special trips to **Cabo Cabrón** near Las Galeras and **Dudu cave** near Río San Juan. Standard one-tank dives average US$40 with equipment, less if you have your own. Four-, 10- and 12-dive packages bring the per-dive costs to around US$26 to US$35 including equipment. Two-tank Cabo Cabrón and Dudu trips cost about US$80 to US$100, including gear, lunch and transportation.

Snorkelers also go to Isla Ballenas, which has good shallow coral flats (US$20 per person, one hour). A popular full-day snorkel trip is to **Playa Jackson**, stopping in two or three locations (US$60 per person including lunch, with a minimum of six people).

Among a handful of dive shops in town, the most conveniently located are **Sea Tribe Diving Center** (⏰ 8:30am-1pm & 3-6:30pm Mon-Sat), which is across from El Paseo shopping center and is open on Sunday in the high season, and **Tropical Diving Center** (☎ 809-240-9619; www.tropical divingcenter.com; Av Italia; ⏰ 8am-4pm).

BEACH RENTALS

Pura Vida (☎ 809-862-0485; ⏰ 10am-5:30pm) is a good place to rent out surfing, kiteboarding and windsurfing gear, with decent prices.

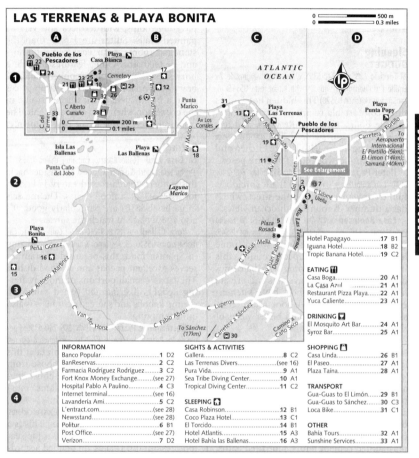

LAS TERRENAS & PLAYA BONITA

It's on the beach across from El Paseo shopping center.

COCKFIGHTING

Two Italian dive instructors have rented and completely renovated Las Terrenas' old **gallera** (cockfighting ring; Av Duarte), just past Plaza Rosada. Fights are held every Sunday from 3pm to 7pm, and average around a dozen match-ups per night. While many *galleras* are rather seedy places, the idea here is to provide a safe, comfortable place for tourists and locals alike to experience this quint-essential Dominican sport/pastime. The fights are certainly not watered-down – they are bloody, to-the-death affairs – and betting is still an integral part of the event.

Volunteers help explain rules, strategy and wagering to cockfight neophytes.

Tours

Bahía Tours (☎ 809-240-6088; www.bahia-tours.com; Av Duarte 237; 🕙 9am-1pm & 3:30-7pm Mon-Fri, 9:30am-1pm & 4:30-6:30pm Sat) is a full-service travel agency that books airline tickets, hotels and car rentals, as well as organizes area tours. Popular day trips include whale-watching in Samaná Bay (US$66 per person), excursions to Parque Nacional Los Haitises (US$60), 4WD tours to El Rincón beach (US$70), and horseback riding to El Limón waterfalls (US$25).

Sunshine Services (☎ 809-240-6164; cnr Calle del Carmen & Calle Libertad; 🕙 9am-1730pm & 4 9pm Mon-Fri, noon-4pm Sat) offer similar (and similarly

DOMINICAN REPUBLIC

priced) excursions as those offered by Bahía Tours.

Sleeping

BUDGET

El Torcido (☎ 809-240-6395; eltorcido.gitta@gmx.de; Av Emilio Prud'Homme; r without/with kitchenette US$15/18, cabaña with kitchen US$20) This hidden hotel offers three comfortable rooms each with gleaming tile floors, bright white walls, and terraces. If you can swing it, the cabaña – a freestanding house with a large kitchen and great porch – is worth the few extra pesos.

Hotel Papagayo (☎ 809-240-6131; fax 809-240-6070; Carr a Portillo; r US$28; P) If El Torcido is full, try this place, just up the street, which has a number of rooms with ocean views.

Casa Robinson (☎ /fax 809-240-6496; Av Emilio Prud'Homme; r US$30, studio US$35, 1-bedroom apt US$45; P) Set within brightly colored wood-frame houses on well-landscaped grounds, this hotel offers 13 cozy rooms with balconies or terraces. All rooms have fans and private hot-water baths, and most have kitchenettes. Those on the 2nd floor afford considerably more privacy and better views of the towering palm trees.

MIDRANGE

Iguana Hotel (☎ 809-240-5525; www.iguana-hotel.com; d/q bungalows with breakfast US$70/100) Down a quiet dirt road at the far end of the beach, the Iguana Hotel's location will be a disadvantage for some but a godsend for others. Eight free-standing bungalows occupy a leafy lawn and garden area; all have red-painted cement floors, blue tiled baths, A-frame ceilings, good fans and pleasant front patios. A large and well-equipped kitchen is available for guest use.

Coco Plaza Hotel (☎ 809-240-6172; jesuscampelo@hotmail.com; Calle Chicago Boss 2; r US$45, studio US$60-80, apt US$85-100; 🖳) Rooms in this four-story, Mediterranean-style hotel vary in size and layout, but all are clean and tastefully decorated. All include breakfast and feature air-con, refrigerator, hot-water baths, fans, cable TV and a safe. Studios and apartments have small modern kitchens. Big discounts are available in the low season.

TOP END

Tropic Banana Hotel (☎ 809-240-6110; www.tropicbanana.com; Calle Alberto Camaño; d/tw US$100/110, ste US$140, inc breakfast; P 🖳 🖳) Facing Playa las Terrenas, the Tropic Banana features simple snug rooms, with terraces and yellow-painted walls. Suites are larger than the standard rooms, with cool cement floors and better baths. Other features include a horseshoe-shaped pool, snooker table, library even a hair salon. High-season prices seem a bit inflated, but it's decent value in the off-season when prices drop by half. The restaurant here is one of the best in town.

Eating

La Casa Azul (Calle Alberto Camaño; mains US$3-12, 🕑 breakfast, lunch & dinner) Once a beachside shack, this modern thatch-roofed eatery is known for its excellent seafood dishes. The mussels in garlic (US$10) are particularly good. It's also a nice place to watch the sunset.

Yuca Caliente (☎ 809-240-6634; Calle Alberto Camaño; mains US$10-23; 🕑 lunch & dinner) Specializing in Spanish food, this oceanside restaurant serves excellent paellas and seafood dishes. The tapas – small portions of mouthwatering delights like *bacalao* (dried salt cod), shrimp kabobs and sautéed octopus – is also quite tempting.

Restaurante Pizza Playa (☎ 809-240-6399; Pueblo de los Pescadores; meals US$2-10; 🕑 lunch & dinner) There are 37 different types of pizza at this cheerful, well-located eatery. Choose from a cheese and tomato pie or the house special with mozzarella, shrimp clams, mussels, calamari and chunks of fish.

Casa Boga (☎ 809-240-6110; Pueblo de los Pescadores; mains US$12-25; 🕑 lunch & dinner Mon-Sat) This is a tiny but highly recommended Basque seafood restaurant. Dishes are divided according to the type of fish – surface, bottom, and a category just for *róbalo*, a delicious whitefish that thrives where freshwater rivers and inlets run into the ocean. The beachfront open-air dining area is easy to miss – look for the sign and menu posted at the entrance of a little passageway between two restaurants.

Drinking

Syroz Bar (☎ 809-866-5577; Calle Alberto Camaño; 🕑 6pm-4am Mon-Sat) A cool jazz bar and lounge that occasionally features live Brazilian music. The seating is outdoors on a pleasant deck overlooking the Caribbean, or indoors in an Asian-themed bar area that is lit mostly by candles. Striking Dominican, Haitian and Thai art adorns the walls.

El Mosquito Art Bar (☎ 809-857-4684; Pueblo de los Pescadores; ☯ 6pm-midnight Sun-Fri, 4pm-midnight Sat) A small, hipster bar with low sofas on its beachside patio instead of tables and chairs. The drink list goes on for pages, including Long Island ice tea, whiskey sour, several martinis and a dozen different whiskeys. Good for tapas, too.

Shopping

There are three **shopping centers** (Av Duarte; ☯ 9am-8pm Mon-Sat, 9am-3pm Sun) bunched together in Las Terrenas: Plaza Taína, Casa Linda and El Paseo.

Each has several high-end boutiques, eateries and a smattering of kitschy shops.

Getting There & Away

AIR

Aeropuerto Internacional El Portillo is a one-strip airport (with no terminal) a few miles east of Las Terrenas. The occasional arrival of a charter flight from Europe gives it its international credentials.

AeroDOMCA (Las Terrenas ☎ 809-240-6571; Santo Domingo ☎ 809-567-1195) operates propeller planes between El Portillo and Santo Domingo (US$65, 30 to 50 minutes, twice daily), stopping first at Aeropuerto Las Américas and then jumping over to Aeropuerto de Herrera. Return flights depart from Herrera airport only (US$55, 30 minutes, twice daily). Tickets and information are available at the office of Bahía Tours (p293).

The air-taxi service costs the same and requires a minimum of just three people. Flights leave whenever the passenger chooses – the most popular destinations are Las Américas airport (US$65 per person), Herrera airport (US$55) and Punta Cana (US$85). Flights can also be arranged to La Romana, Puerto Plata, and El Cibao airport in Santiago.

BUS

Las Terrenas has two *gua-gua* stops at opposite ends of Av Duarte. *Gua-guas* headed to Sánchez (US$1.40, 30 minutes, every 25 minutes from 7am to 6pm) take on passengers at a stop 550yd (500m) south of Calle Luperon.

Those going to El Limón (US$1.75, 20 minutes, every 15 minutes from 7am to 5pm) leave from the corner of Av Duarte and the coastal road.

Getting Around

You can walk to and from most places in La Terrenas, though getting from one end to the other can take a half-hour or more. Taxis charge US$10 each way to Playa Bonita and US$15 to US$20 to El Limón. Motoconchos are cheaper – US$1.75 to Playa Bonita – but are less secure. Both stop in front of El Paseo shopping center and motoconchos are plentiful on Av Duarte and around Pueblo de los Pescadores. A bike can also be handy for getting around town – **Loca Bike** (☎ 809-889-3593; ☯ 8am-noon & 2-6pm) at the west end of Playa Las Terrenas rents out bikes for US$10.50 per day.

PLAYA BONITA

A few miles west of Las Terrenas is Playa Bonita (Pretty Beach), a half-mile-long curve of tan sand, swaying coconut trees and aquamarine surf, backed by a handful of hotels with good but pricey restaurants. While the beach itself isn't spectacular – it's narrow and much of it is strewn with seaweed – Playa Bonita is still an attractive and restful place to spend an afternoon, with fewer people and traffic than at Las Terrenas. The west end of the beach is broader and flatter, and the hotels here do a better job of keeping it clean.

There's a public **Internet terminal** (per hr US$6.25; ☯ 7am-11pm) at Hotel Bahía las Ballenas. **Las Terrenas Divers** (☎ 809-240-6066; ☯ 9:30am-noon & 3-5pm) is at the same hotel, offering dive trips and courses (one tank US$34, 10 tanks US$280, open-water certificate US$345) as well as snorkel trips to Isla Ballenas (US$15, one hour) and Playa Jackson (US$25 to US$30 per person, minimum three people). You can also rent kayaks, boogie boards and surfboards by the hour or the day.

Sleeping & Eating

Hotel Atlantis (☎ 809-240-6111; www.atlantis-beach hotel.com; s US$60, d $70-100; P ☒) This rambling place has 18 charming rooms that unexpectedly appear around bends and at the bottom of staircases, at the top of a mushroom-shaped building and halfway through walkways. Each room is uniquely decorated and – like the setting – comes in surprising sizes and shapes. Many rooms have enviable ocean views and all are just seconds away from a nice stretch of beach.

DOMINICAN REPUBLIC

Air-con costs an extra US$10. A fine French restaurant boasting the chef of former French president François Mitterrand is also on the premises. Breakfast is included in the rate.

Hotel Bahía las Ballenas (☎ 809-240-6066; www
.las-terrenas-hotels.com; d with breakfast US$95-110) All 32 rooms at this well-kept resort are decorated in either Creole, Mexican or south-of-France style. Sounds gimmicky, but it comes off well here, thanks mainly to the outstanding quality of the rooms themselves. Spacious, with high thatched ceilings, all have thick comfortable beds, stylish furnishings, great tile floors and a toilet and shower area that is open at the top for a bit of outdoorsy charm. An open-air restaurant has colorful tables with cushioned chairs, and serves creative Dominican dishes like roast goat or fish in lime and almond sauce. There's a swimming pool and an on-site dive shop.

Getting There & Away

By car, Playa Bonita is reached by a single road that turns off from the Sánchez–Las Terrenas highway. It's possible to walk from Playa Bonita to Playa Las Ballenas in Las Terrenas via a coastal dirt/mud trail that is fairly steep at one section. A taxi ride here is US$10, a motoconcho around US$1.75.

NORTH COAST

Though the north coast's once vibrant resort scene has definitely declined – you could call it the Acapulco of the Dominican Republic – independent and adventure-sport tourism is booming. Windsurfing put the north coast on the map, but it has since become a mecca for kiteboarders, surfers, divers and mountain-bike riders. And not just for experts – there are plenty of schools, independent instructors and tour operators that introduce newcomers to any or all of the sports practiced here.

CABARETE

pop 45,000

This is the center of the north coast's adventure sport activity. One look at the beach will prove as much, with the colorful windsurfing sails brightening the shore and dotting the aquamarine water. The activity is relatively new – a decade ago there were only a handful of hotels here – and the crush of people,

cars and motoconchos can be off-putting at first. But don't let the congestion prevent you from stopping – Cabarete's boisterous nightlife and ideal conditions for windsurfing, kiteboarding and other sports make it well worth your sticking around.

Orientation

Cabarete is built around the main highway, which runs right through the middle of town. Virtually all the hotels, restaurants and shops are on the main drag, making it a jam-packed though easy-to-navigate place.

Information

BOOKSTORES

Bill's Books (☎ 809-753-5800; ☼ 2-5pm Mon, Wed & Fri) A small bookshop in the far east end of town with plenty of beach trash and the occasional good find.

Luis Anselmo Gift Shop (☎ 809-640-3299; ☼ 8:30am-7pm) This shop in the east end of town sells day-old international magazines and newspapers at five times the newsstand rate.

EMERGENCY

Politur (Tourist Police; ☎ 809-571-0713; Carr a Gasper Hernandez; ☼ 24hr) Just east of town.

INTERNET ACCESS

Internet Center (per hr US$3.50; ☼ 9am-9pm Mon-Sat) This place in the west end of town has data ports to connect your laptop.

Kaoba Internet (Hotel Kaoba; per hr US$1.75; ☼ 7am-11pm) In the west end of town.

INTERNET RESOURCES

Active Cabarete (www.activecabarete.com) Info on Cabarete's many outdoors and sports activities.

LAUNDRY

Lavandería Familiar Cabarete (☎ 809-751-4353; ☼ 8am-7pm Mon-Sat) This laundry in the west end of town offers same-day service if clothes are dropped off early (US$0.70 per pound/500g). Delivery is available.

MEDICAL SERVICES

Servi-Med Medical Office (☎ 809-571-0964; ☼ 24hr) This clinic in the center of town has four MDs, one dentist and a chiropractor. English and German spoken.

MONEY

Banco Popular (☼ 9am-5pm Mon-Fri, 9am-1pm Sat) West end of town.

Scotiabank (☼ 8:30am-4:30pm Mon-Fri, 9am-1pm Sat) In the east end of town.

POST
There is no post office in Cabarete but hotels often post guest mail.

TELEPHONE
Centro de Telecomunicaciones (9am-9pm Mon-Sat) On a walkway just east of Villa Taína in the west end of town, this center charges US$0.32 per minute to the US and US$0.74 to Europe.
Tele-Vimenca (8am-10pm Mon-Fri, 10am-5pm Sat) This place offers the same prices as Centro de Telecomunicaciones. It's located near Hotel Laguna Blu in the center of town.

TRAVEL AGENCIES
Ozone Travel (USA ☎ 888-824-6359; www.ozone travel.com) Florida-based travel agency specializing in kiteboarding vacations in Cabarete and around the world.

Sights
Cabarete's beaches are its main attractions, and not just for sun and sand. The beaches are each home to a different water sport, and they are great places to watch beginner and advanced athletes alike.

Playa Cabarete, the main beach in front of town, is the best place for watching windsurfing, although the very best windsurfers are well offshore at the reef line. You can still look for them performing their huge high-speed jumps and even end-over-end backflips.

Bozo Beach is on the western downwind side of Playa Cabarete, and so-named because of all the beginner windsurfers and kiters who don't yet know how to tack up wind and so wash up on Bozo's shore. There are more kiteboarders at Bozo and the surf here is good for boogie boarding. Both Cabarete and Bozo have nice sand and tall palm trees.

Kite Beach is half a mile (800m) west of town and a sight to behold on windy days, when scores of kiters negotiate huge sails and 100ft (30m) lines amid the waves and traffic. On those days, there's no swimming here, as you're liable to get run over.

Playa Encuentro, 2.5 miles (4km) west of town, is the place for surfing (though top windsurfers and kiters sometimes head here to take advantage of the larger waves). The beach itself is okay, but the strong tide and rocky shallows make swimming here difficult.

Activities
WINDSURFING
While kiteboarding has grabbed much of the limelight of late, windsurfing is the sport that put Cabarete on the map and it's still extremely popular. The combination of strong, steady winds, relatively shallow water and a rockless shore create perfect conditions for the sport. Windsurfing generally needs stronger winds than kiteboarding – May through July is the best time, when average wind speeds exceed 15mph (around 24km/h).

The broad bay directly in front of town is used by beginner and expert windsurfers. The calm waters close to shore are ideal for learning to stand up and control the board and sail, while a coral reef about 550yd (500m) from shore creates large swells and breakers that advanced windsurfers use to perform tricks. In general, windsurfing is harder to master than kiteboarding, but the lessons are less expensive and novices tend to suffer fewer faceplants and ego injuries than in kiteboarding. Board and sail rentals average US$20 to US$25 per hour, US$50 to US$55 per day, or US$230 to US$270 per week, plus insurance (usually about US$45 per week.) Private lessons cost around US$40 per hour or US$150 for a four-session course (less for groups). Recommended schools:
Club Nathalie Simon (CNS; ☎ 809-571-0848; www .cabaretewindsurf.com; 9am-6pm) Very professional operation at the west end of main beach offering high quality equipment for differing skill levels. Sea kayaks, boogie boards and Hobie cats also rented.
Fanatic Windsurf Center (☎ 809-571-0861; www .fanatic-cabarete.com) This place at the east end of main beach has somewhat older equipment but notably lower prices. Free intro-to-windsurfing class every Monday, Wednesday and Friday at 10am.

SURFING
Some of the best waves for surfing on the entire island – up to 13ft (4m) – break over reefs 2.5 miles (4km) west of Cabarete at Playa Encuentro. Several outfits here and in town rent out surfboards (US$10 to US$20 per half-day) and offer instruction (three-hour course US$30 to US$40 per person, five-day surf camp US$110 to US$175 per person). You can also rent gear and arrange classes at most kiteboarding and windsurfing schools, which coordinate with the surf

KITEBOARDING

Cabarete is one of the top places in the world to kiteboard, a relatively new sport that entails strapping yourself to a modified surfboard and a huge inflatable wind foil and skimming and soaring across the water.

Kite Beach, 1.25 miles (2km) west of Cabarete, has perfect kiteboarding conditions, but can get very crowded. Bozo Beach, at the west end of the city beach, is also a good spot and has fewer people.

Kiteboarding schools offer multiday courses for those who want to learn – most people need at least six hours of instruction but nine or 12 is recommended. Costs average US$240 to US$275 for six hours, US$350 to US$400 for nine, and US$420 to US$450 for 12. Schools and instructors vary considerably in personality, so spend some time finding one where you feel comfortable. Kiteboarding is a potentially dangerous sport and it is essential that you feel free to ask questions and voice fears or concerns and that you receive patient, ego-free answers in return.

Kite Board Cabarete (☎ 809-856-9853; www.kiteboardcabarete.com) A one-man operation offering specialized training for advanced kiters (per hour US$60, three-day intensive course US$440).

Kitexcite (☎ 809-571-9509; www.kitexcite.com; Extreme Hotel, Kite Beach) Uses radio helmets and optional off-shore sessions – ergo, less waiting and walking time – to maximize instruction.

Laurel Eastman Kiteboarding (☎ 809-571-0564; www.laureleastman.com; Hotel Caracol Beach Club) Friendly, safety-conscious shop located on Bozo Beach and run by one of world's top kiteboarders.

Sleeping

Stay at Kite Beach if you want to be as close to the kiteboarding action as possible. The beach is pretty, but not swimmable when the wind is blowing and scads of kiters are crisscrossing the water and launching from the shore. Each of the following hotels has an on-site (or affiliated) kiteboarding school.

Agualina (☎ 809-571-0805; www.agualina.com; Kite Beach; r US$70, studio US$85, apt US$150; P ⋈ ⊠) Opened in 2004, this may be the most comfortable lodging in Cabarete. Studios and apartments have stylish, well-equipped kitchens and large, modern baths with glass showers and gleaming fixtures.

Kite Beach Hotel (☎ 809-571-0878; www.kitebeachhotel.com; Carr a Sosúa; s/d with breakfast US$52/58; s/d ste US$85/92; 1-bedroom apt US$140-160; P ⋈ ⊡ ⊠) Completely renovated in 2005, this oceanfront hotel boasts well-appointed rooms with gleaming tile floors, good-sized baths, and satellite TV. All suites and apartments have balconies that afford at least partial ocean views.

shops. Two recommended surf schools are **Take Off** (☎ 809-963-7873; www.321takeoff.com; Playa Encuentro) and **No Work Team** (☎ 809-571-0784; Villa Taína Hotel) – ask at Happy Surfpool.

DIVING

Dolphin Dive Center (☎ 809-571-3589; www.dolphindivecenter.com; ⌚ 9am-1pm & 2-6pm Mon-Sat) is a Sosúa-based shop with an office in Cabarete (in the far east of town) where you can arrange fun dives, certification courses and dive safaris. Transportation can be arranged to Sosúa, where the majority of dive sites are located. One-tank dives are US$31/46 with/without your own gear, or US$25/36 per dive with a 10-dive package. Snorkel trips also available (US$15 to US$18, one hour).

Tours

Iguana Mama (☎ 809-571-0908, USA 800-849-4720; www.iguanamama.com; ⌚ 8am-5pm) is one of the most highly-regarded tour operators in the Dominican Republic, and for good reason. Founded by an American and currently owned and operated by a friendly Basque expat, Iguana Mama offers a variety of excursions and activities, from 'canyoning' and 'cascading' (climbing, rappelling, sliding and swimming through a series of waterfalls and land gorges) to more-mellow outings like sailing and horseback riding. The shop, located near the east end of town, specializes in mountain-bike tours, which also range in length and difficulty: the half-day downhill rides though local villages are easy and fun, while more-serious bikers should consider the challenging 12-day cross-country tours. Iguana Mama also operates good three-day Pico Duarte trips.

Festivals & Events
Master of the Ocean (February; ☎ 809-963-7873; www.masteroftheocean.com) Usually held in the last week of February, this event features individual windsurfing, kiteboarding and surfing divisions, but the real test is the namesake category: a triathlon of all three events. The event began in 2002.
International Sand Castle Competition (March; www.castillosdearena.org) For almost two decades, sand sculpture enthusiasts have convened on Cabarete in the first week of March for the chance to display and test their skills. The competition also includes a Kids Day.
Dominican Jazz Festival (October; www.drjazzfestival .com) Held in Puerto Plata, Sosúa and Cabarete at the end of October, this jazz festival attracts top musical talent from around the country and abroad.

Sleeping
BUDGET
Hotel Laguna Blu (☎ 809-571-0802; r US$25, tw without/with kitchenette US$35/53; **P ⚡**) Although not much to look at from the outside, the rooms at Laguna Blu, located in the center of town, 82yd (75m) off the main road, are surprisingly comfortable and clean and include ceiling fans and private hot water baths. Avoid the pool.

Hotel Alegría (☎ 809-571-0455; Callejón 2; r without/with ocean view US$22/30, studio US$45) Hidden down one of Cabarete's few side streets, the cheapest rooms are small and somewhat dim, but clean and perfectly adequate. Ocean-view rooms are larger, with 2nd-floor balconies and good light.

MIDRANGE
Albatros Hotel & Condos (☎ 809-571-0841; h.albatross@verizon.net.do; r without/with kitchenette US$35/60, 1-/2-bedroom apt US$75/100; **P ⚡**) The Albatros, in the west end of town, offers clean and cheerful rooms surrounding a welcoming swimming pool.

Standard rooms have a sitting area, ceiling fan and refrigerator. Studios and apartments come in various sizes; the smallest is a regular-sized room with a kitchenette, the largest is a two-story condo. Ask for a room facing the lagoon, as a street-side generator can be loud.

TOP END
Villa Taína Hotel (☎ 809-571-0722; www.villataina.com; d with breakfast garden-/ocean-view US$75/95, tw US$95/120; **⚡ ⚡ ⚡**) This appealing boutique hotel, also in the west end of town, has 55 tastefully decorated rooms, each with balcony or terrace, air-con, comfortable beds, in-room data ports and modern baths. There is a small clean pool and a nice beach area fringed by palm trees. A 1½-hour windsurfing lesson is included in the rate.

Eating
Cabarete's beach is lined with restaurants, all boasting an open-air dining area facing the water. The view and breeze are terrific, but you pay for it in the meal prices. Some spots are worth the splurge, but in general you'll find much better values off the beach.

BUDGET
Hexenkessel (☎ 809-571-0493; mains US$3.50-11; ⏰ 24hr) Reminiscent of a German beer garden, this place on the east side of town specializes in potato pancakes with ground beef (US$6.50), fried Bavarian bratwurst (US$4), and, if you order a day in advance, whole roasted pork knuckle with sauerkraut (US$20).

Coco Rico (☎ 809-847-1094; mains US$6-12; ⏰ dinner) Great rotisserie chicken, served in huge half- or whole-bird portions with boiled veggies and fries are served here. You'll find it down a walkway toward the public parking lot in the west end of town. Fish and beef dishes are also available. Red-and-white tablecloths and simple wood tables complete an appealing provincial look.

MIDRANGE
Paradise (☎ 809-979-4863; mains US$7-12; ⏰ breakfast, lunch & dinner) Tucked in between a sandwich shop and an uninspired miniature golf course in the west end of town, this open-air eatery offers excellent Italian, French and fusion specialties. The chicken curry pasta (US$8) is superb.

Mirós on the Beach (☎ 809-571-0888; mains US$12-17; ⏰ dinner) High quality Moroccan food (and other select international fare) is served here, in a classy, slightly bohemian setting in the middle of town. Specialties include duck *tagine* (a stew slow-cooked in a round earthenware dish with a conical lid) with couscous and 'Calypso curry' (seafood slow-simmered in coconut milk and curry masala). Great ocean view and live jazz on Saturdays.

Drinking

The drinking and party scene in Cabarete is fun and predictably raucous, with bars open to the wee hours almost every night of the week.

LAX (9am-1am) Everyone starts the night at this mellow bar with drink specials, house music and pizzas until 10:30pm (in case you get hungry).

Around midnight everyone tends to migrate down the beach to **Onno's** (809-571-0461; 9am-5am) or **Bambú** (6pm-6am), adjacent bars with loud music, drink specials and hours of dancing. Somewhere around 4am, people make their way home to rest before the wind picks up in the afternoon. (Pity the surfers – the best waves are at 6am.)

Shopping

Carib Bic Center (809-571-0640; 9am-7pm) This is the best of the smattering of shops catering to water-sports enthusiasts. Here you'll find a good variety of sporting equipment and accessories. It's in the east end of town.

Planet Arte (809-571-3686; 8am-10pm) This shop sells unique, high-quality handicrafts in the center of town, including handmade paper and amber and larimar jewelry.

Getting There & Around

Minibuses to Río San Juan (US$1.75, one hour), Sosúa (US$1, 30 minutes) and Puerto Plata (US$1.75, one hour) trundle through town every 15 to 30 minutes, picking up passengers along the way. **Taxis** (809-571-0767) are good for getting to Kite Beach (US$3) and Playa Encuentro (US$10/18 one way/return) – you can catch these in the middle of town. Motoconchos cover the same ground for less but are much more accident-prone. At the east end of town, **Sandro's Rent A Car** (809-571-9716; 8am-6pm) rents out vehicles starting at US$40 per day.

CENTRAL HIGHLANDS

The backbone of the Dominican Republic is the mighty Cordillera Central mountain range, which runs from the Haitian border nearly to Santo Domingo and accounts for more than 30% of the DR's land mass. The mountains are protected by two huge adjoining national parks that provide excellent hiking opportunities, whether easy

---

CLIMBING PICO DUARTE

At 10,417ft (3175m), Pico Duarte is the highest point in the Caribbean and the crown jewel of the Armando Bermúdez and José del Carmen Ramírez National Parks, which together cover some 580 sq miles (1500 sq km) of rugged mountain terrain. Amazingly, Pico Duarte was not climbed until 1944, as part of a celebration commemorating the 100th anniversary of Dominican independence. During the late 1980s, the government began cutting trails in the parks and erecting cabins, hoping to boost tourism to the country. Nowadays, some 3000 people climb the peak every year.

There are 47 known amphibians in the parks and several mammal species, most notably the wild boar, which was introduced. They reside chiefly in areas that are difficult to access on foot. Much easier to see are the parks' birds, which include the Hispaniolan parrot, the woodpecker, the white-necked crow, and the Dominican Republic's national bird, the palm chat.

Getting to the Top

The most common route up Pico Duarte begins in the town of La Ciénega, 25 miles (40km) from Jarabacoa and at the edge of the park. From here, it's 14 miles (23km) in each direction with about 7500ft (2286m) of vertical ascent, accounting for all of the hills and valleys encountered along the way. Most people make the trip in two or three days, usually rising early on the second day to catch the sunrise from the summit – on a clear day both the Atlantic and Caribbean are visible. If you have time, a rewarding side trip is to Valle de Tétero, a broad valley with sparkling mountain rivers and Taino petroglyphs.

strolls to area waterfalls or the three-day assault on the Caribbean's highest mountain, Pico Duarte. The town of Jarabacoa is not the biggest city in the interior – that would be Santiago – but its proximity to the mountains make it the region's main tourist destination.

JARABACOA

pop 27,500

At 2630ft (800m) above sea level, Jarabacoa is sometimes described as 'Switzerland in the tropics.' While that is no small exaggeration, the mountain setting and cool crisp climate here can be a welcome change from the muggy lowlands and coastal areas. Many wealthy Dominicans maintain weekend homes in and around town and this is also a favorite getaway for *capitalinos* of all walks of life.

Beyond its pleasant climate, Jarabacoa has the country's best outdoor options, including impressive waterfalls, white-water rafting, horseback riding and mountain bike riding.

Also popular is 'canyoning,' an adventure sport that entails sliding, jumping, and rappelling down a narrow river gorge. And Jarabacoa is the most logical staging area for an ascent of Pico Duarte.

Orientation

Av Independencia and Calle María N Galán, one block over, are Jarabacoa's main north–south streets – Parque Central is at one end of Av Independencia and the Caribe Tours bus terminal at the other. The city's major east–west street is Calle del Carmen, which borders Parque Central and is the road you take from Jarabacoa to get to Rancho Baiguate.

Information

A&G Servicios Multiples (☎ 809-574-4044; Av Independencia 43; 8am-10pm) Calls to the USA US$0.32 per minute; to Europe US$0.74 per minute.

Banco León (cnr Duarte & Mario N Galán; 8:30am-4/5pm Mon-Fri, 9am-1pm Sat) Has a 24-hour ATM.

Centro de Copiado y Papelería (☎ 809-574-2902; cnr Duarte & Av Independencia; Internet access per hr US$1; 8am-noon & 2-8pm Mon-Fri, 8am-7pm Sat)

Clínica Dr Terrero (☎ 809-574-4597; Av Independencia 40; 24hr)

Farmacia Miguelito (☎ 809-574-2755; Mario N Galán 70; 7:30am-9:30pm Mon-Sat, 7:30am-4pm Sun) Free delivery.

Net Café (1st fl, Plaza Ramírez, Parque Central; Internet access per hr US$.70; 9am-1am)

Policía Turística (Tourist Police; ☎ 809-754-3216; cnr José Duran & Mario N Galán; 24hr) Behind the Caribe Tours terminal.

Practicalities

The easiest and most assured way of climbing Pico Duarte is with an organized trip. All three of the tour operators listed on p302 can arrange trips and this is the way most people go.

That said, it's not difficult to organize a trip yourself, especially if you speak some Spanish. Make your way to La Ciénega, where you can hire a local guide (US$20 per day), who will insist you hire a pack mule (US$10 per day). Purists scoff, but, for most, hiring a mule or two is a practical and remarkably cheap way to bring all the equipment, provisions and water you need without worrying about weight – they even carry your personal gear. The mule is useful if someone gets hurt – the main reason the guides want them along – and some people even ride them up instead of hiking. Discuss with the guide how long you have and any side trips you'd like – Valle de Tétero, for example – and together you can plan your trip. Guides typically bring along tools like a hatchet for cutting firewood, but it's worth double-checking. You are expected to bring food for yourself and your guide – basic provisions usually suffice.

You can also hire independent guides in Jarabacoa – expect to pay around US$275 per person (minimum two) for a two-night, three-day trip that includes transportation to/from Jarabacoa, food, all equipment, pack mules and guide services. The best way to locate one is to ask at your hotel for a recommendation.

The park has several cabins, outfitted with bunks, which hikers are free to use. However, a serious rat problem makes staying in them somewhat unnerving. If possible, bring your own tent or ask your guide or tour operator about renting one. The cabins have simple camp kitchens and rather unappealing latrines.

Entrance to the park is US$3, payable in La Ciénega.

DOMINICAN REPUBLIC

Post office (⊗ 8am-noon & 2-4pm Mon-Fri) At the north end of Av Independencia.

Progreso (Calle Luis F Gomez Uribe; ⊗ 8:30am-4/5pm Mon-Fri, 9am-1pm Sat) Near Av Independencia, with a 24-hour ATM.

Tourist office (☎ 809-574-7287; 2nd fl, Plaza Ramírez; ⊗ 9am-1pm & 2-6pm Mon-Fri) Basic info and a few maps. Spanish only.

Sights & Activities

You can easily visit Jarabacoa's waterfalls independently, but most other activities are only available with organized excursions.

WATERFALLS

There are three waterfalls in the vicinity of Jarabacoa that can be visited in a day.

Salto de Jimenoa Uno is definitely the prettiest, a 195ft (60m) waterfall that pours from a gaping hole in an otherwise solid rock cliff. (A lake feeds the waterfall via a subsurface drain.) There's a nice swimming hole, but the water is icy cold.

Salto de Jimenoa Dos is a 130ft (40m) cascade with an appealing bathing pool. The waterfall is 550yd (500m) from the parking lot and reached by a series of narrow suspension bridges and leafy trails.

Salto de Baiguate is also in a lush canyon but isn't nearly as impressive as the others, nor is the pool as inviting. It's also a bit harder to get to because of the poor road conditions.

Any of the motoconcho drivers around town can take you to one, two or all three of the falls for around US$12 to $17 per person. Hiring a taxi or pickup costs around US$50 to US$75, a good option if you're in a group or not keen on motoconchos. No matter how you go, be sure to clarify with your driver how long you'll stay at each place – some try to rush you through. If you're driving, Salto de Jimenoa Uno is 4.5 miles (7km) past the gas station on the road toward Constanza; for Salto de Jimenoa Dos, look for a well-signed turn-off 2.5 miles (4km) north of town. Salto de Baiguate is difficult to get to without a guide.

WHITE-WATER RAFTING

The **Río Yaque del Norte** is the longest river in the country and the only place where you can go white-water rafting. It's no Zambezi, of course, but has enough rolls and holes to keep things interesting. The water is frigid – you'll wear a wetsuit under your life jacket – but, overall, this is a fun way to spend a day.

CANYONING

Canyoning here involves hiking down into a deep canyon just below Salto de Jimenoa Uno, leaping 50ft (15m) from the top of an enormous boulder into the chilly Río Jimenoa, swimming down part of the river, then rappelling twice down rocky cliff faces to solid-rock landings. There are two levels – one for beginners and another for more-experienced climbers. Tours are offered by Rancho Baiguate and Rancho Jarabacoa.

Tours

Jarabacoa has two main tour operators, whose main clientele are Dominican groups from the capital and foreign guests of all-inclusive resorts near Puerto Plata, to the north. However, independent travelers are always free to join any of the trips, usually by just calling the day before. Canyoning and longer hiking trips (including Pico Duarte) should be arranged several days in advance.

Rancho Baiguate (☎ 809-574-6890; www.rancho baiguate.com.do; Carretera a Constanza) and **Rancho Jarabacoa** (☎ 809-248-7909; ranchojarabacoa@hot mail.com; Carretera a Salto de Jimenoa Dos) offer all of the activities described in this section at similar prices: 1½-hour tours of one or two waterfalls on horseback (without/with lunch US$10/16 per person), 4WD (without/with lunch US$16 per person), ATV (s/d US$30/40) or mountain bike (US$8 per person). Canyoning trips last 3½ hours and cost US$56. Pico Duarte trips can be three, four or five days, and vary in price depending on the number of people in the group. For two people, expect to pay US$310/437/540 for a three-/four-/five-day outing. With five people, the rates fall to US$210/270/340. Note that a three-night tour may include two nights in a hotel.

Iguana Mama (☎ 809-571-0908, USA 800-849-4720; www.iguanamama.com; ⊗ 8am-5pm) is a highly recommended tour operator based in Cabarete in the east end of town. It offers tours around Jarabacoa, including mountain biking and climbing Pico Duarte. Trips usually leave from Cabarete, but you can also pick up the tour in Jarabacoa. See p298 for details.

Sleeping

The first listing here is in the center; the others are outside of town.

Hotel Brisas de Yaque (☎ 809-574-4490; cnr Luperón & Prof Pelegrina Herrera; r US$25; ❄) The best option in town offers cozy rooms with exposed brick walls, wood trim and nice balconies. Be sure to ask for one facing west – the view of the surrounding mountains is excellent.

Rancho Baiguate (☎ 809-574-6890; www.rancho baiguate.com.do; Carretera a Constanza; full-board d per person US$64, s US$74; P ❄) Rancho Baiguate has boxy but comfortable rooms with private hot-water bath, screened windows, ceiling fan, heater and shiny enamel paint to dress up the cinder-block construction. With plenty of open space, this is a good place to stay if you have kids and/or plan on joining some of the many tours offered here. It's 3 miles (5km) from town.

Hotel Gran Jimenoa (☎ 809-574-6304; Av La Confluencia; www.granjimenoa.com; d/tw with breakfast US$47/67; P ❄ ❄) Several miles from town, this is Jarabacoa's best hotel and good value if it's in your price range. All 28 large rooms have air-con, comfortable beds, tile floors and a terrace looking onto the hotel's attractive swimming pool – numbers 206 and 306 are the best. Be sure to check out the restaurant, perched right on the bank of the roaring Jimenoa river.

Eating

Deli Café de la Montaña (☎ 809-574-7799; cnr Calle del Carmén & Mario N Galán; mains US$2.25-5; ❄ lunch & dinner Tue-Sun) Great for vegetarians but good for anyone looking for a light meal, this eatery offers excellent sandwiches and wraps, hearty salads and good pita pizzas.

Restaurante El Rancho (☎ 809-574-4557; Av Independencia 1; mains US$4-10; ❄ breakfast, lunch & dinner) On the northern edge of town, El Rancho offers a varied menu of chicken and beef dishes, crepes, and seafood. The walls of this semidressy, open-sided restaurant are graced with handsome local paintings, although the motoconcho traffic outside detracts somewhat from the setting.

D'Lo Ultimo (☎ 809-574-7591; Av Independencia; mains US$3.50-10.50; ❄ breakfast, lunch & dinner, closed Thu) This modest Dominican eatery near Sánchez offers reliable and tasty meals. Be sure to ask about the daily special; you can often get a salad, a meat-based entrée with a side of rice and a dessert for US$5 to US$6.

Getting There & Away

Caribe Tours (☎ 809-574-4796; Calle José Duran) offers the only bus service to and from Jarabacoa. Departures to Santo Domingo (US$5.25, 2½ hours, 7:30am, 10am, 1:30pm and 4:30pm) also service La Vega (US$1.75, 30 minutes). It's near Av Independencia.

Next door, a **gua-gua terminal** (cnr Av Independencia & José Duran) provides frequent service to La Vega (US$1.40, 45 minutes, every 10 to 30 minutes from 5:30am to 6:30pm). If you prefer to hire a cab to La Vega, the ride costs around US$14.

Getting Around

The town of Jarabacoa is easily managed on foot but to get to outlying hotels and sights you can flag down a motoconcho during the day. During the evening, or if you prefer a bit more comfort, call **Jaraba Taxi** (☎ 809-574-6464) or just catch a cab at the corner of José Duran and Av Independencia.

Car rental rates average US$40 to US$45 per day at both of these agencies, less if you rent for a week or more:

Chachi Rent A Car (☎ 809-574-2533; Carretera a Salto Jimenoa km 1.5; ❄ 8am-noon & 2-6pm Mon-Sat)

Francis Rent A Car (☎ 809-574-2981; Carretera a Salto Jimenoa km 2; ❄ 8am-noon & 2-6pm Mon-Fri, 8am-7pm Sat, 8am-5pm Sun)

DIRECTORY

ACCOMMODATIONS

Lodging in the Dominican Republic is more expensive than many travelers expect. A reliable room with private bath averages US$20 to US$30 per night in most areas. Hotels at this level typically offer hot water and 24-hour electricity, and occasionally cable TV and air-con. Midrange hotels average US$35 to US$75 per night and typically include all the above, and sometimes breakfast or off-street parking. High-end hotels are US$100 or more and have all the amenities you'd expect.

The Dominican Republic is famous for its affordable, all-inclusive resorts. Once you factor in eating expenses, most all-inclusive

> **EMERGENCY NUMBERS**
>
> **Ambulance, Fire & Police** (☎ 911)

DOMINICAN REPUBLIC

DOMINICAN REPUBLIC

resorts qualify as midrange. Definitely check the Internet or a travel agency for specials.

ACTIVITIES

WINDSURFING & KITEBOARDING

The DR is one of the top places in the world for windsurfing and kiteboarding. The wind blows hardest in Cabarete, a town on the north coast given over almost wholly to the two sports. Cabarete has numerous schools for those interested in either. See the boxed text, p298, for detailed information on kiteboarding.

DIVING & SNORKELING

On the southern coast, warm Caribbean waters and abundant tropical fish make for fun, easy dives. On the north coast, the Atlantic waters are cooler and less transparent but the terrain includes more canyons, swim-throughs, caverns and rock outcrops.

HIKING

The highland town of Jarabacoa is the jumping-off point for ascents of the Caribbean's tallest peak, Pico Duarte at 10,417ft (3175m). Hiking through the Valle de Tétero, a beautiful valley with rivers and indigenous petroglyphs, makes a rewarding side trip.

MOUNTAIN BIKING

Several tour operators – like Iguana Mama in Cabarete (p298) – offer highly recommended mountain-bike tours ranging from half-day downhill rides to 12-day cross-country excursions.

WHALE-WATCHING

From mid-January to mid-March, thousands of humpback whales congregate in and around the Bay of Samaná, making it one best whale-watching spots in the world.

BOOKS

Lonely Planet's *Dominican Republic* has much more information on traveling in the DR. Baseball fans should pick up *Sugarball: The American Game, the Dominican Dream,* by Alan M Klein, and *The Tropic of Baseball,* by Rob Ruck.

For more on the DR's music, try *Bachata: A Social History of Dominican Popular Music,* by Deborah Pacini Hernandez, and *Merengue: Dominican Music and Dominican Identity,* by Paul Austerlitz. *Why the Cocks Fight,* by Michele Wucker, examines Dominican-Haitian relations through the metaphor of cockfighting, popular in both countries.

CHILDREN

All-inclusive resorts can be a convenient and affordable way for families to travel, as they do away with decisions on when and where to eat, what to do, and where to stay. For independent-minded families, the DR has plenty of family-friendly beaches and outdoor activities.

There are few kid-specific parks or attractions, however.

DANGERS & ANNOYANCES

Some guests at all-inclusive resorts report having items stolen from their rooms. As in any hotel, don't leave money or valuables in plain view.

Use the room safe (if one is available) or lock items in an inside pocket of your suitcase.

EMBASSIES & CONSULATES
Dominican Republic Embassies & Consulates

For the contact information of all Dominican embassies and consulates, check out the website of the **Secretaría de Estado de Relaciones Exteriores** (www.serex.gov.do). When it's functioning, it's a good resource.

Australia (☎ 02-9363-5891; 343a Edgecliffe Rd, Sydney, NSW 2027)

Canada (☎ 613-569-9893; www.drembassy.org; 130 Albert St, Suite 418, Ottawa, Ontario KIP 5G4)

France (☎ 01-53-53-95-95; www.amba-dominicaine-paris.com; 45 Rue de Courcelles, Paris 75008)

Germany (☎ 228-364-956; embajada_dominicana@hotmail.com; Burgstrasse 87, 53177 Bonn)

Haiti (☎ 257-9215; fax 509-257-0568; 121 Av Panamericaine, Pétionville, Puerto Principe)

Italy (☎ 06-320-0441; embajadadominicanait@yahoo.it; Via Pisanelli No 1, Int 4; Rome 00196)

Jamaica (☎ 755-4154; domemb@cwjamaica.com; 32 Earls Court, Kingston 8, Kingston)

Japan (☎ 03-499-6020; fax 03-499-2627; Rm 904, Kowa 38 Bldg, 4-12-24 Nishi-Azabu Minato-Ku 106-0031, Tokyo)

Netherlands (☎ 02-647-1062; Terschellingerstraat 6, 1181 HK, Amsterdam)

Spain (☎ 94-427-6388; consul@repdom.euskalnet.net; José Ma Escuza 20-6A, 48013 Bilbao)

UK (☎ 0207-727-6285; http://dominicanrepublic.embassyhomepage.com; 139 Inverness Terrace, Bayswater, W2-6JF, London)

USA (☎ 202-332-6280; embassy@us.serex.gov.do; 1715 22nd St NW, Washington, DC 20008)

Embassies & Consulates in the DR

Canada (☎ 809-685-1136; Av Eugenio de Marchena 39, Santo Domingo)

Cuba (☎ 809-537-2113; Calle FP Ramírez 809, Santo Domingo)

France (☎ 809-687-5270; Calle de las Damas 42, Santo Domingo) Between Luperón & El Conde.

Haiti (☎ 809-686-5778; cnr Calle Juan Sánchez Ramírez 33 & Av Máximo Gómez, Santo Domingo)

Italy (☎ 809-682-0830; Calle Rodríguez Objío 4, Santo Domingo)

Jamaica (☎ 809-482-7770; Av Enriquillo 61, Colonia Los Cacicazgos, Santo Domingo)

Japan (☎ 809-567-3365; 8th fl, Torre BHD office Bldg, cnr Calle Luís Thomen & Av Winston Churchill, Santo Domingo)

Netherlands (☎ 809-565-5240; Max Henríquez Ureña 50, Santo Domingo)

Spain (☎ 809-535-6500; 4th fl, Torre BHD office bldg, cnr Calle Luís Thomen & Av Jiménez Moya, Santo Domingo)

Trinidad & Tobago (☎ 809-688-1645; Isabel La Católica 171, Santo Domingo)

UK (☎ 809-472-7111; cnr Avs 27 de Febrero 233 & Av Tiradentes, Santo Domingo)

USA (☎ 809-221-2171; cnr Avs César Nicolás Penson & Máximo Gómez, Santo Domingo)

FESTIVALS & EVENTS

If there's any generalization to be made about Dominicans, it is that they take holidays and celebrations very seriously.

Carnaval (February) Celebrated with great fervor throughout the country every Sunday in February, culminating in a huge blowout in Santo Domingo the last weekend of the month or the first weekend of March. Masks and costumes figure prominently in every town's celebration – Santiago even hosts an international Carnaval mask competition.

Independence Day (February 27) On this day in 1844, the Dominican Republic gained independence from Haiti, which had occupied the DR shortly after the latter declared independence from Spain. The day is marked by street celebrations and military parades.

Semana Santa 'Holy Week,' in March, is the biggest travel holiday in the country and much of Latin America. Everyone heads to the water – expect crowded beaches, innumerable temporary food stands, and music day and night.

Santo Domingo Merengue Festival Santo Domingo hosts the country's largest and most raucous merengue festival. For two weeks at the end of July and beginning of August, the world's top merengue bands play for the world's best merengue dancers.

HOLIDAYS

New Year's Day January 1
Epiphany/Three Kings Day January 6
Our Lady of Altagracia January 21
Duarte Day January 26
Independence Day, Carnaval February 27
Holy Thursday, Holy Friday, Easter Sunday March/April
Pan-American Day April 14
Labor Day May 1
Foundation of Sociedad la Trinitaria July 16
Restoration Day August 16
Our Lady of Mercedes September 24
Columbus Day October 12
UN Day October 24
All Saints' Day November 1
Christmas Day December 25

MONEY

The Dominican monetary unit is the peso, indicated by the symbol RD$. There are one- and five-peso coins, while paper money comes in denominations of 10, 20, 50, 100, 500 and 1000 pesos.

DOMINICAN REPUBLIC

ATMs

Banco Popular, Banco Progreso, Banco de Reservas, Banco León, and Scotiabank all have ATMs that accept most foreign debit cards.

Black Market

Moneychangers will approach you in a number of tourist centers, but you get equally favorable rates and a much securer transaction at an ATM, bank or exchange office.

Credit Cards

Visa and MasterCard are accepted widely, especially in areas frequented by tourists. Some businesses add a surcharge for credit card purchases (typically 16%).

Taxes & Tipping

There are two taxes on food and drink sales: a 12% to 16% value-added tax and a 10% service tax, but it is customary to leave an additional 10% tip. It is also common to tip tour guides, bellhops (US$1 to US$2 per bag) and hotel housecleaners (US$1 to US$2 per day).

TELEPHONE & FAX

Call centers are the easiest way to make international phone calls. Or buy a Verizon 'Comunicard,' available at many hotels and minimarts, and follow the Spanish/English instructions printed on the back. You must dial the area code (☎ 809) for all calls within the DR, even local ones. The area code has been included in all local listings in this chapter. To call the USA or Canada, simply dial 1, then the area code and number.

VISAS

Tourist cards, available upon arrival for US$10, are issued to foreign visitors from Australia, Austria, Belgium, Brazil, Canada, France, Germany, Greece, Ireland, Italy, Mexico, Netherlands, Spain, Sweden, Switzerland, the UK and the USA.

TRANSPORTATION

GETTING THERE & AWAY
Entering the Dominican Republic

All foreign visitors must have a valid passport to enter the Dominican Republic (US travelers see the boxed text, p772). A tourist card is purchased on arrival – see left. For more information on traveling from outside the Caribbean to (and from) the Dominican Republic, see the main Transportation chapter (p770).

At airports, neither immigration nor customs officials pay much attention to tourists carrying an ordinary amount of luggage. Border officials may be more scrutinizing.

Air

The Dominican Republic has seven international airports:

Aeropuerto Internacional Cibao (STI; ☎ 809-581-8072) Serves Santiago and the interior.

Aeropuerto Internacional El Portillo Airstrip near Las Terrenas that gets busiest during whale-watching season.

Aeropuerto Internacional Gregorio Luperón (POP; ☎ 809-586-1992) Serves Playa Dorada and Puerto Plata.

Aeropuerto Internacional La Romana (LRM; ☎ 809-689-1548) Near La Romana.

Aeropuerto Internacional Las Américas (SDQ; ☎ 809-549-0081) Outside Santo Domingo and is the country's main international airport.

Aeropuerto Internacional María Montez (BRX; ☎ 809-524-4144) Near Barahona.

Aeropuerto Internacional Punta Cana (PUJ; ☎ 809-959-2473) Serves Bávaro and Punta Cana.

Carriers that service other countries in the Caribbean:

Air Antilles Express (☎ 809-648-648; www.airantilles.com; hub Guadeloupe)

Air Caraïbes (☎ in the US 877-772-1005; www.aircaraibes.com; hub Guadeloupe)

Air Jamaica (☎ 809-872-0080; www.airjamaica.com; hub Kingston)

LIAT (☎ 888-844-5428; www.liatairline.com; hub Antigua)

Land
BORDER CROSSINGS

There are three main border crossings between the Dominican Republic and Haiti: Jimaní/Malpasse in the south on the road between Port-au-Prince and Santo Domingo; in the north at Dajabón/Ouanaminthe between Cap-Haïtien and Santiago; and further south at Belladère/Elías Piña. Borders open 8am to 6pm but it is always a good idea to arrive early.

When leaving the Dominican Republic, travelers will be asked to produce their passports and tourist cards. From Haiti, you must have your passport and the yellow entry card you received upon arrival.

BUS

Terra Bus (☎ 809-531-0383; Plaza Lama, cnr Avs 27 de Febrero & Winston Churchill, Santo Domingo) offers an air-con service from Santo Domingo to Port-au-Prince, Haiti.

Sea

Ferries del Caribe (Santo Domingo ☎ 809-688-4400; Santiago ☎ 809-724-8771; Mayagüez, Puerto Rico ☎ 787-832-4400; San Juan, Puerto Rico ☎ 787-725-2643) offers the DR's only international ferry service, connecting Santo Domingo and Mayagüez, Puerto Rico. The ferry departs Santo Domingo on Sunday, Tuesday and Thursday at 8pm and returns from Mayagüez on Monday, Wednesday and Friday at 8pm. The trip takes 12 hours and costs around US$124/165 one way/return in an airplane-style seat, or around US$220 per person for two people in a private room with an exterior window.

GETTING AROUND

Air

The main domestic carriers and air taxi companies:

AeroDOMCA (☎ 809-567-1195; www.aerodomca.com; Aeropuerto Internacional Herrera) The main domestic carrier, with regular and charter service to and between all the DR's airports, including Las Américas airport, Las Terrenas and Punta Cana.

Caribair (☎ 809-542-6688; www.caribair.com.do; Aeropuerto Internacional Herrera) Domestic service to all DR airports except Las Terrenas, plus select cities elsewhere in the Caribbean.

Take Off (☎ 809-552-1333; www.takeoffweb.com; Aeropuerto La Herrera) Service from Santo Domingo (La Herrera airport) to Punta Cana, and from Punta Cana to Puerto Plata and Samaná (Aeropuerto Arroyo Barril).

Bicycle

The DR's under-maintained highways are not well suited for cycling, though mountain biking on back roads can be rewarding. There are a number of recommended tours available from Jarabacoa (p302) and Cabarete (p298).

Bus

There are two classes of bus service in the DR: first class is in comfortable air-con buses, often with TVs and a movie. Fares are low – the most expensive first-class ticket is less than US$10. Reservations aren't usually necessary.

FIRST CLASS SERVICE

Caribe Tours (☎ 809-221-4422; cnr Avs 27 de Febrero & Leopoldo Navarro, Santo Domingo) The most extensive bus line, with services everywhere but the southeast.

Expreso Santo Domingo Bávaro (☎ 809-682-9670; cnr Juan Sánchez Ruiz & Máximo Gómez, Santo Domingo) Connects Santo Domingo and Bávaro with a stop in La Romana.

Metro (☎ 809-566-7126; Calle Francisco Prats Ramírez, Santo Domingo) Serves nine cities, mostly along the Santo Domingo–Puerto Plata corridor. The office is behind the Plaza Central mall, 55yd (50m) east of Av Winston Churchill.

GUA-GUAS

Gua-guas vary in size, from minivans to midsize buses with room for around 30 passengers. They don't have toilet facilities, and only occasionally have air-con. Unlike regular buses, *gua-guas* stop all along the route to pick up and drop off passengers. Wherever long-distance buses don't go, you can be sure a *gua-gua* does. *Gua-guas* rarely have signs, so ask a local if you're unsure which one to take. Most pass every 15 to 30 minutes and cost US$1 to US$2. Simply wave to be picked up.

Car & Motorcycle

RENTAL

Renting a car is a great way to see the country without wasting time waiting for buses. Prices range from US$40 to US$100 per day. Motorcycles can also be rented, but only experienced drivers should do so because of poor road conditions. If you bust a tire – the most common car trouble here – a *gomera* is a tire repair and retail shop.

You must have a valid driver's license and be at least 25 years old to rent a car. You will be required to show a major credit card or leave your passport as a deposit. Be sure to ask about the 'deductible' (the amount you pay out-of-pocket before insurance kicks in) and whether the insurance covers damage to your tires or windows.

See p279 for a list of car-rental agencies in Santo Domingo.

ROAD HAZARDS

In large cities, especially Santo Domingo, the sheer number of cars, trucks, buses and motorcycles makes for hectic driving. On highways, especially the secondary ones, roads may be unpaved for long sections and often have large potholes.

DOMINICAN REPUBLIC

ROAD RULES

Road rules in the Dominican Republic are the same as most countries in the Americas, and the lights and signs are the same shape and color you find in the USA or Canada. Seatbelts are required at all times. Street lights are often ignored in small towns – watch what other drivers are doing.

Local Transportation

BUS

Large cities like Santo Domingo have public bus systems that operate as they do in most places around the world. However, *públicos* (see right) pass much more frequently.

MOTOCONCHOS

Motoconchos are motorcycle taxis, and are usually cheaper and easier to find than ordinary taxis. Motoconcho drivers often gather at large intersections or cruise around looking for passengers. In some smaller towns, they are the only form of public transportation, so most travelers use them at least once or twice. However, a shocking number of people, including tourists, have been hurt or killed in motoconcho accidents.

A few 'dos and don'ts' for safe riding: don't take a motoconcho in the rain or for long distances, especially if it means getting on the highway; don't share the motoconcho with another passenger; do be careful not to burn your leg on the muffler,

especially when getting on or off; be sure your feet are well placed and your grip on the handholds is firm before setting off; and don't be afraid to ask the driver to slow down *(Más despacio, por favor!)* – if he doesn't respond, ask to be let off *(Déjame aquí, por favor.)*. As with ordinary taxis, agree on a price beforehand.

PÚBLICOS

These are banged-up cars, minivans or small pickup trucks that pick up passengers along set routes, usually main boulevards. *Públicos* (also called *conchos* or *carros*) don't have signs but the drivers will hold their hands out the window to solicit potential fares. They are also identifiable by the crush of people inside them – up to seven in a midsize car! To flag one down simply hold out your hand – the fare is US$0.30. If there is no one else in the car, be sure to tell the driver you want *servicio público* (public service) to avoid paying private taxi rates.

TAXIS

Dominican taxis rarely cruise around looking for passengers – instead they wait at designated *sitios* (stops) at hotels, bus terminals, tourist areas, and public parks. You also can phone a taxi service (or ask your hotel receptionist to call for you). Taxis do not have meters – agree on a price beforehand.

Puerto Rico

First you feel the heat: searing and tropical, pressing in on your clothes. Then the sounds start to penetrate: *bomba* and *plena* and salsa and…are those West African rhythms? You can be sure of it. And how about that language? A hybrid of Caribbean Spanish and US slang, peppered with long-ago words from Yoruba and Taino cultures, two diverse peoples that mixed intimately when slavery forced them into the sugar fields and gold mines of Latin America. Can't believe your eyes and ears? You're not dreaming – you're in Puerto Rico.

It's hard to fathom that all of this vibrant energy and history is contained on one tiny island that's small enough to traverse (twice!) in a day. Consider Puerto Rico's myriad options: the beach and casinos of Isla Verde, art and culture in Old San Juan, the world's largest radio telescope, and underground caves. There's hiking in protected reserves, kayaking in luminescent bays, and world-class diving and snorkeling on Vieques, Culebra and along the western coast. And Ponce is known for magnificent colonial celebrations.

You'll also quickly see why Puerto Rico is known as America's 51st state: strip malls, chain stores and fast-food restaurants as well as drug stores, highways and efficient national park systems abound. But if you can take the infrastructure for what it is and look through it to the island's great natural beauty – a blend of tangled dark jungle, flat dry plains, steeply curving mountains dropping down to azure seas – you're in for a fabulous time.

PUERTO RICO

FAST FACTS

- **Area** 3500 sq miles (9060 sq km)
- **Capital** San Juan
- **Country code** ☎ 787
- **Departure tax** It costs US$14.10 to leave the island; normally included in the price of your ticket
- **Famous for** Rum and baseball
- **Languages** Spanish and English
- **Money** US dollars; US$1 = €0.82 = UK£0.55
- **Official name** Puerto Rico
- **People** Puerto Ricans
- **Phrases** *Qué pasa?* What's happening? *Esta todo hablado.* It's all understood.
- **Population** 4 million
- **Visa** Unnecessary for most countries (see p340)

PUERTO RICO

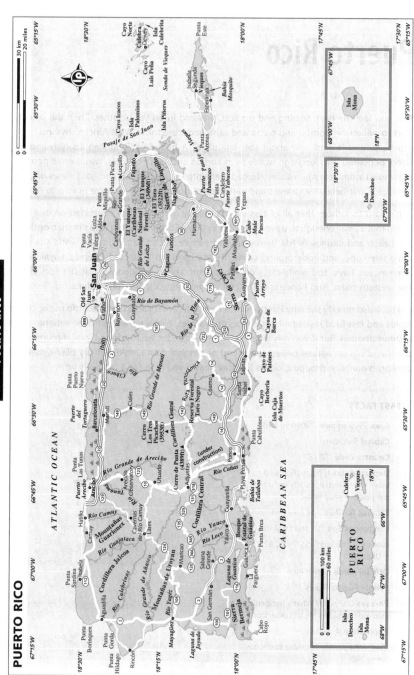

HIGHLIGHTS

- **San Juan** (p314) Explore sexy, sassy and sinfully fun San Juan, with beaches, nightlife and a historic old town that shines any time of year.
- **Culebra** (p331) and **Vieques** (p329) Relax on blow-your-mind beaches, and snorkel and dive in some remote, undiscovered locations.
- **El Yunque** (p328) Spend a day (or even two) in the only tropical rainforest in the US commonwealth, enjoying the deep greens and cool showers that characterize this ecosystem.
- **Ponce** (p333) Catch an open-air music festival in the beautiful main square of Puerto Rico's most colonial city.
- **Arecibo Observatory** (p328) Get behind this giant radio telescope, where extraterrestrial communication looks like a distinct possibility.

ITINERARIES

- **Three Days** Laze on San Juan beaches – Ocean Park, Condado, Isla Verde. Old San Juan museums, galleries and monuments are worth a day, and bar hop on Calle Fortaleza at night. Take a trip to the rum factory in Bayamón and then bronze on the beach again.
- **One Week** Pick up on day three above, rent a car and get to El Yunque for a day of hiking and river swimming. Check out

Playa Luquillo then head to the Camuy caves and the Arecibo Observatory before returning to San Juan.

- **Two Weeks** Reverse the order of the last two days above, going first to Arecibo and then moving toward El Yunque. Take the ferry to Vieques and spend a night or two on the island and then head over to Culebra. Check out Playa Flamenco, spending at least one night there. After a mid-morning ferry ride back, drive to Ponce and use that as a base to check out Guánica forest, then move up the coast to La Parguera and Rincón.

CLIMATE & WHEN TO GO

It's a rare day indeed when temperatures fall below 60°F (16°C) in Puerto Rico. Generally it's 80°F (27°C) and sunny. Dry season is December to March, but the months you really want to keep an eye on are those between June and November, aka Hurricane Season. August, September and October are the most vulnerable months. October tends to be very rainy and road wash-outs occur frequently. Rains sometimes extend well into November.

HISTORY

Indigenous peoples are thought to have arrived – via a raft from Florida – around the 1st century AD, quickly followed by groups from the Lesser Antilles. The Tainos created a sophisticated trading system on the island they named Borinquen, and became the reigning culture, although they were terminally fighting off Carib invaders.

All that changed forever in 1508, when Juan Ponce de León came back for a second and closer look at the island he had glimpsed from one of Christopher Columbus' ships. Driven by a desire for gold, Spanish Conquistadores enslaved, murdered, starved and raped natives with impunity. Virtually wiped out by war, smallpox and whooping cough, a few remaining Tainos took to the mountains. Soon Dutch and French traders became frequent visitors, dropping off human cargo from West Africa. By 1530, West African slaves – including members of the Mandingo and Yoruba tribes – numbered about half the population of 3000 in Puerto Rico.

And so it went for several generations. The Spanish-American War of 1898 finally pried Puerto Rico out from under the yoke

PUERTO RICO

of the Spanish Empire, but it established the small island as a commonwealth of the United States – Borinquen was liberated from Spain, but not quite free.

Operation Bootstrap poured money into the island and set up highways, post offices, supermarkets and a few military posts. Puerto Ricans have accepted the US economic and military presence on their island, with varying degrees of anger, indifference and satisfaction, for more than 100 years now – but the strong *independentista* movement that wanted to cut all ties with the US in the 1950s has mostly receded into the background. The biggest question for Puerto Ricans – a passionately political people who muster at least a 90% voter turnout on election days – is whether to keep the 'status quo' or become, officially, America's 51st state.

In the November 2004 gubernatorial elections, which were hotly contested for months and involved several hand recounts, the 'status quo' candidate eventually won. Until 2008, at least, Puerto Rico will remain a commonwealth – but beyond that, it's anybody's guess.

THE CULTURE

As a predominantly Catholic country (albeit widely mixed with African and indigenous practices), Puerto Ricans treasure family values and family pursuits and often have three or more generations living in the same home. But they don't interpret 'family-friendly' as being closed-minded. They are fiercely and justifiably proud of their mixed European, African and indigenous ancestry – in a country where skin tones range from the darkest coal to freckled white (sometimes even in the same family), it's no mean feat to have created a culture where all are welcome.

Gay and lesbian visitors to the island will notice the welcoming atmosphere – there are a few conservative groups who in the past raised a ruckus when a cruise-ship company touted San Juan as a 'gay' destination, but they were quickly shushed by the progressive majority who were embarrassed by the ugly display of discrimination.

Population

Long a pastoral oasis, Puerto Rico has become one of the most densely populated places on earth during the second half of the 20th century. Currently more than four million people live on the island. These statistics can be deceptive, however, because the bulk of the island's population has migrated to a handful of urban areas. At least 1.6 million people live in metropolitan San Juan, while the cities of Caguas, Ponce, Mayagüez, Aguadilla and Arecibo account for another million citizens. Beyond the *tapones* (traffic jams) that result from the cities' endless arrays of traffic lights and narrow streets, Puerto Rico remains a place of windy peaks, quiet cane fields and empty beaches.

ENVIRONMENT
The Land

At 100 miles long and 35 miles wide (161km x 56km), Puerto Rico is clearly the little sister of the Greater Antilles (Cuba, Jamaica and Hispaniola). With its four principal satellite islands and a host of cays hugging its shores, Puerto Rico claims approximately 3500 sq miles (9060 sq km) of land, making the commonwealth slightly larger than the Mediterranean island of Corsica or the second-smallest state in the USA, Delaware.

Puerto Rico has more than a dozen well-developed and protected wilderness areas, most of which are considered *reservas forestales* (forest reserves) or *bosques estatales* (state forests). The best known is the 43-sq-mile (111-sq-km) Caribbean National Forest, generally referred to as El Yunque, which dominates the cloudy yet sun-splashed peaks at the east end of the island. Bosque Estatal de Guánica, on the southwest coast, is home to a tropical dry forest ecosystem.

National forest campground and reservation information can be obtained by calling ☎ 800-280-2267. General information about federal lands is also available from the Fish & Wildlife Service at the **Federal Information Center** (☎ 800-688-9889).

Wildlife

Endangered giant sea turtles, such as the hawksbill, green and leatherback, nest on Puerto Rican beaches, particularly on the island of Culebra. Puerto Rico's vast coral reefs are the nurseries and feeding grounds for hundreds of species of tropical fish. It offers some of the best places in the world for divers to come face-to-face with large barracudas, manta rays, octopus, moray eels and nurse sharks.

El Yunque is home to more than 60 species of bird, including the greenish-blue, red-fronted Puerto Rican parrot, which is on the edge of extinction. The coastal dry forest of Guánica features more than 130 bird species, largely songbirds.

Snakes are everywhere, but remember that none of them are poisonous, including the Puerto Rican boa, which grows to more than 7ft (2.1m).

Keep your eyes peeled for small-boned Paso Fino horses, brought to the island by the Spanish conquistadors. In many places, but particularly in Vieques, they roam freely across the roads in untamed herds.

Environmental Issues
Puerto Rico has long suffered from a number of serious environmental problems, including population growth and rapid urbanization, deforestation, erosion of soil, water pollution and mangrove destruction.

To combat the mounting destruction of the island's environment, citizens in many municipalities have formed local environmental action groups. Contact one of these organizations listed if you see or hear of a problem or – even better – want to collaborate with professionals and volunteers to help save the island:

Caribbean Environmental Information (☎ 751-0239)
Conservation Trust of Puerto Rico (☎ 722-5834)
Natural History Society of Puerto Rico (☎ 726-5488; www.naturalhistorypr.org)

Puerto Rican Association of Water Resources (☎ 977-5870)
Puerto Rican Conservation Foundation (☎ 763-9875)

FOOD & DRINK
With the plethora of fast-food restaurants and sudden influx of exotic fusion dishes in restaurants, getting hold of authentic Puerto Rican food – *comida criolla* or *cocina criolla* – can be quite a challenge! Similar in many ways to Central and Latin American cuisine, *comida criolla* features a lot of deep-fried salty snacks, inventive combinations of yucca, plantains (green bananas) and fragrantly spiced rice dishes. For an island, Puerto Rico's surprisingly light on fish dishes, but chicken and beef are present at just about every meal.

That said, there are a growing number of vegetarian restaurants in Puerto Rico, particularly in Old San Juan and San Juan, but even regular restaurants often carry vegetarian dishes nowadays. When a restaurant specifically does vegetarian/vegan food it's noted here, but chefs in many restaurants are often willing to prepare vegetarian dishes upon request. Vegans want to be careful, as butter or meat renderings often find their way into beans and rice.

Usually eaten between about 7am and 9am, typical Puerto Rican breakfasts are light and simple. Lunch is available between 11:30am and 2pm. Puerto Ricans usually go cheap on this event, flocking to fast-food

---

SAN JUAN IN...

Two Days
Find a hotel with casino and beachfront access – bronze up and then hit the gaming tables. Give the next day to the monuments, forts and galleries of **Old San Juan** (p315). Dine along **Calle Fortaleza** (p324).

Four Days
Expand your time in **Old San Juan** (p315) and throw in a visit to the **Bacardi Rum Factory** (p328). Rent a car and head to **El Yunque** (p328) for a day. Finally, shop 'til you drop in **Condado** (p326) and squeeze in one last beach run, or dine in one of the beautiful restaurants in **Gran Hotel El Convento** (p321).

One Week
Head into the 'burbs for Santurce's **Museo de Arte de Puerto Rico** (p320) and the **Museo de Oller** (p320) in Bayamón. Turn to water sports for a break: snorkel, scuba or sail off **Isla Verde** (p320) or **Condado** (p320).

outlets for burgers and the like, or gathering around street vendors selling a variety of fried finger foods.

Dinners, served between about 6pm and 10pm, are more expensive, and a legion of prosperous islanders have developed a tradition of going out to restaurants – especially on Thursday, Friday and Saturday – as a prelude to a long 'night on the town.'

A list of highly acclaimed gourmet restaurants is published in *Qué Pasa,* the Puerto Rico Tourism Company's (PRTC) bimonthly magazine.

SAN JUAN

pop 442,447 (1.6 million including suburbs)

In Puerto Rico you must accept that all roads lead to San Juan, and not just because it's home to more than one-third of all islanders. This is where the island's heartbeat is – a place of great economic opportunity; beautiful, gleaming buildings; a university; multiple art galleries; museums; and a sophisticated nightlife that doesn't get revved up until well after midnight.

And why would you want to skip San Juan, anyway? It's not just the glamorous high-rise hotels and sleek condos along the beaches of Condado, Isla Verde and Ocean Park that you'd miss, but also the working-class charm of Santurce, the raucous student energy of Río Piedras, and the turbulent pace of downtown Hato Rey.

Then there's the crown jewel, the magnificent walled city that the world has come to know as Old San Juan (Viejo San Juan). This working, breathing community, rife with cobblestone streets, pastel-colored town houses, Romanesque arches, wrought-iron balconies, intimate courtyards and striking vistas has the look and feel of a Spanish colonial city. Chock-full of restaurants, clubs, bars, shops and museums, Old San Juan offers the traveler more entertainment per square foot than New York City – at a pace that is definitely laid-back and totally Latin.

Alternative lifestyles are warmly welcomed in San Juan, and in places – most notably Condado – the city is as openly gay-friendly as Miami Beach. Some inns and B&Bs are set aside solely for gay and lesbian patrons, but generally speaking, if

your money is good, you'll be considered a valued customer anywhere.

At first glimpse some people are taken aback by the vast number of fast-food restaurants and outlet malls that overrun most parts of San Juan – you just have to close your eyes to that aspect of the city and look for what's unique underneath the overlay of modern life.

ORIENTATION

Starting at the westernmost tip of the city and working backward toward the Aeropuerto Internacional de Luis Muñoz Marín (LMM), you've got Old San Juan, the tourist center and most visually appealing part of town.

Next comes Condado, flashy and full of big buildings and hotels along Av Ashford, and then Miramar and Santurce, a little south of the beach and mostly filled with working-class families. Ocean Park is a private community (with gates) lying along the water between Condado and Isla Verde; its main street is Av McLeary. The final stop in the city is Isla Verde (although technically it is in Carolinas, a suburb of San Juan). Av Isla Verde is a long stretch of hotels and casinos along a narrow but pretty white beach; the only drawback is the proximity of the airport. Large jets thunder overhead every 20 minutes or so for most of the day.

INFORMATION
Bookstores
Bell, Book & Candle (Map pp318-19; ☎ 728-5000; 102 Av José de Diego, Condado) Pulls in the vacation crowd and offers a wide range of English titles.

Bookshop (Map pp316-17; ☎ 724-1815; 201 Calle Cruz near Plaza de Armas, Old San Juan) A great place to familiarize yourself with the latest Puerto Rican authors, in English translation or original Spanish.

Bookworm (Map pp318-19; ☎ 722-3344; 1129 Ave Ashford) Gay literature in Spanish and English as well as mainstream picks. Very helpful and friendly staff.

Emergency
In *any* kind of emergency, just call ☎ 911. Beware: you may find that the telephone directory and tourist publications list nonfunctioning local numbers for emergency services.

Fire (☎ 722-1120)
Hurricane Warnings (☎ 253-4586)

Isla Verde Police (☎ 449-9320)
Medical (☎ 754-2222, 343-2550)
Rape Crisis Hotline (☎ 877-641-2004)
Río Piedras Police (☎ 765-6439)
Tourist Zone Police (☎ 911 or 726-7020, English spoken, 24hr)

Internet Access
Cybernet Café Condado (Map pp318-19; ☎ 724-4033; 1128 Av Ashford; per hr US$5-6; 🕙 10am-10pm); Isla Verde (☎ 791-3138; 5575 Av Isla Verde; per hr US$5-6; 🕙 10am-10pm)
Diner's Internet (Map pp316-17; ☎ 724-6276; 311 Calle Tetuan, Old San Juan; 🕙 10am-10pm)

Laundry
Rates run about US$1.50 to US$2 per wash and US$0.50 per 10 minutes to dry.
Condado Cleaners (Map pp318-19; ☎ 721-9254; 63 Calle Condado; 🕙 7am-8pm Mon-Fri, 8am-5pm Sat) Promises a fast turn around, and delivers too.
La Lavandería (Map pp316-17; ☎ 717-8585; 201 Calle Sol, Old San Juan; 🕙 7am-9pm Mon-Thu, 7am-8pm Fri-Sun) Has to be the Laundromat with the best view in town.

Medical Services
Ashford Memorial Community Hospital (Map pp318-19; ☎ 721-2160; 1451 Av Ashford, Condado) Probably the best-equipped and most convenient hospital for travelers.
Walgreens Old San Juan (Map pp316-17; ☎ 722-6690; cnr Calles Cruz & San Francisco); Condado (Map pp318-19; ☎ 725-1510; 1130 Av Ashford) You will find US drugstore chains like Walgreens all over the city. The Condado branch is open 24 hours.

Money
Banco Popular LMM airport (☎ 791-0326; Terminal C); Old San Juan (Map pp316-17; ☎ 725-2635; cnr Calles Tetuán & San Justo) Near the cruise-ship piers and Paseo de la Princesa; Condado (Map pp318-19; Av Ashford); Isla Verde (Av Isla Verde).

Post
Main post office (☎ 767-2890; 585 Av Roosevelt, Hato Rey; 🕙 7:30am-4:30pm Mon-Fri, 8:30am-noon Sat) General delivery mail comes here.
Old San Juan post office (Map pp316-17; ☎ 723-1281; 153 Calle Fortaleza; 🕙 7:30am-4:30pm Mon-Fri, 8:30am-noon Sat) Convenient for travelers.

Tourist Information
Departamento de Recursos Naturales y Ambientales (DRNA; Department of Natural Resources; Map pp318-19; ☎ 724-8774; www.drna.gobierno.pr in Spanish; Av Muñoz Rivera, Pda 3½, Puerta de Tierra)

For information on camping, including reservations and permits, contact this department or visit its office.
Puerto Rico Tourism Company (PRTC; ☎ 800-223-6530, 721-2400; www.prtourism.com); LMM airport (☎ 791-1014; 🕙 9am-5:30pm) Old San Juan (Map pp316-17; ☎ 722-1709; La Casita, Calle Comercio & Plaza de la Darsena near Pier 1) Distributes information in English and Spanish. At the LMM airport, you can stop at the information counter between Terminals B and C or visit the PRTC's desk on the lower (arrivals) areas of Terminals B and C.

DANGERS & ANNOYANCES
Under no circumstances should you walk into La Perla, the picturesque yet poverty-stricken enclave outside the north wall of Old San Juan. Avoid the neighboring cemetery at night as well. Some travelers have been mugged during daylight hours along the eastern end of Calle Norzogaray by drug addicts who hang out in the alleys and park near here. Puerta de Tierra is also a no-no once the sun sets. Avoid Calle Loíza in Santurce, and the Plaza del Mercado in Río Piedras at night.

SIGHTS
Old San Juan
LA CASITA
Looking just like a pink gatehouse, La Casita (Little House; Map pp316–17) greets visitors near the cruise-ship docks in 'lower' Old San Juan, in the outskirts of the walled city that rises on the hill to the north. Stop here for the weekend craft market. Also look for the food vendors selling fruit, icy *piraguas* (snow cones) and other treats.

EL ARSENAL
On the point of land called La Puntilla is a low, gray fortress with a Roman proscenium entrance. This is **El Arsenal** (Map pp316-17; ☎ 724-1877, 724-5949; admission free; 🕙 8:30am-4pm Mon-Fri), a former Spanish naval station that was the last place to house Spanish military forces after the US victory in the Spanish-American War. Today, the Arsenal is home to the fine- and decorative-arts divisions of the **Instituto de Cultura Puertorriqueña** (☎ 724-0700; www.icp .gobierno.pr), and hosts periodic exhibitions in three galleries.

LA PRINCESA
Further along the paseo, poised against the outside wall of the city, is La Princesa (Map

PUERTO RICO

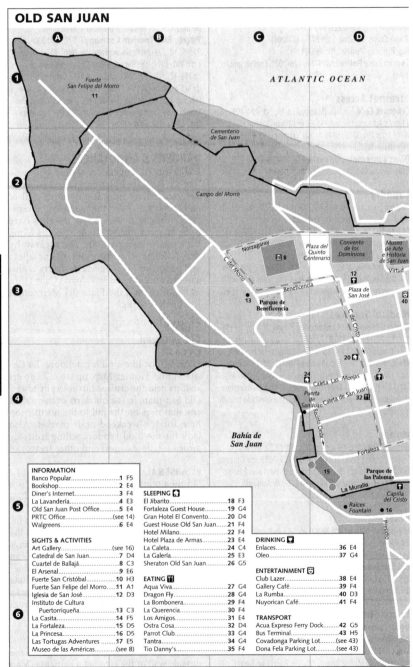

OLD SAN JUAN

A   B   C   D

ATLANTIC OCEAN

Fuerte San Felipe del Morro **11**

Cementerio de San Juan

Campo del Morro

Norzagaray

Plaza del Quinto Centenario

Plaza de los Dominicos

Convento de los Dominicos

Museo de Arte e Historia de San Juan

Virtud

8

12

Beneficencia

13   Parque de Beneficencia

Plaza de San José

C del Morro

C del Cristo

40

20

24   Caleta Las Monias

7

Puerta de San Juan

Caleta de San Juan

32

Recinto Oeste

Bahía de San Juan

15

Fortaleza

Parque de las Palomas

La Muralla

Raíces Fountain

16

Capilla del Cristo

Presidio

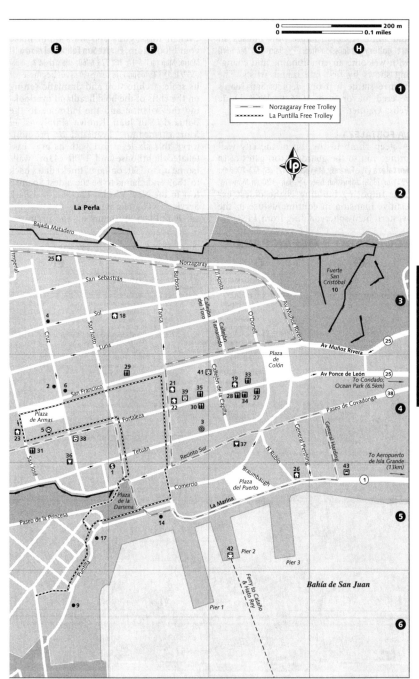

PUERTO RICO

pp316–17). Once a harsh jail, the long, gray-and-white stone structure now houses an **art gallery** (admission free; 9am-4pm Mon-Fri) with welcome air-conditioning and changing shows by first-rate island artists. The bronze statue in front depicts San Juan's revered mayor from 1946 to 1968, Doña Felisa Gautier.

LA FORTALEZA

A steep climb to the top of the city wall brings you to the guarded iron gates of **La Fortaleza** (The Fortress; Map pp316-17; 721-7000 ext 2211 or 2358; admission free; 9am-3:30pm Mon-Fri). This imposing building is the oldest executive mansion in continuous use in the western hemisphere, dating from 1533.

FUERTE SAN FELIPE DEL MORRO

Even if forts, guns and wars don't make your blood hum, **Fuerte San Felipe del Morro** (El Morro; Map pp316-17; 729-6960; adult/child & senior US$2/1; 9am-5pm) is impressive because of its scale, architecture and dramatic setting on the cliffs of the bold headland overlooking the Atlantic and the entrance to the Bahía de San Juan. Known simply as 'El Morro' (meaning headland or promontory), this six-level fort with its gray castellated lighthouse and 140ft (43m) walls (some up to 15ft, or 4.6m, thick) dates back to 1539 and claims to be the oldest Spanish fort in the New World. The National Park Service (NPS) maintains this fort and the small military museum on the premises.

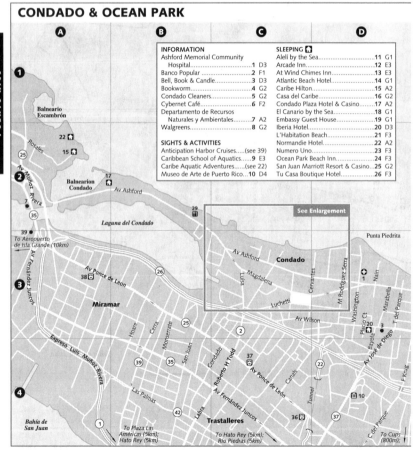

CONDADO & OCEAN PARK

PUERTO RICO

INFORMATION			SLEEPING		
Ashford Memorial Community			Aleli by the Sea	11	G1
Hospital	1	D3	Arcade Inn	12	E3
Banco Popular	2	F1	At Wind Chimes Inn	13	E3
Bell, Book & Candle	3	D3	Atlantic Beach Hotel	14	G1
Bookworm	4	G2	Caribe Hilton	15	A2
Condado Cleaners	5	G2	Casa del Caribe	16	G2
Cybernet Café	6	F2	Condado Plaza Hotel & Casino	17	A2
Departamento de Recursos			El Canario by the Sea	18	G1
Naturales y Ambientales	7	A2	Embassy Guest House	19	G1
Walgreens	8	G2	Iberia Hotel	20	D3
			L'Habitation Beach	21	F3
SIGHTS & ACTIVITIES			Normandie Hotel	22	A2
Anticipation Harbor Cruises	(see 39)		Numero Uno	23	F3
Caribbean School of Aquatics	9	E3	Ocean Park Beach Inn	24	F3
Caribe Aquatic Adventures	(see 22)		San Juan Marriott Resort & Casino	25	G2
Museo de Arte de Puerto Rico	10	D4	Tu Casa Boutique Hotel	26	F3

Displays and videos in Spanish and English document the construction of the fort over almost 200 years, as well as El Morro's role in rebuffing the various attacks on the island by the British and the Dutch.

CUARTEL DE BALLAJÁ

On the 2nd floor of these barracks you will find the **Museo de las Américas** (Museum of the Americas; Map pp316-17; ☎ 724-5052; admission free; ⓨ 10am-4pm Tue-Fri, 11am-5pm Sat & Sun). As it expands, the museum plans to give an overview of cultural development in the New World. Current exhibits include artifacts excavated in Old San Juan, an impressive *santos* (saints) collection and displays of other traditional crafts. Hours for both the barracks and the museum are the

same. Tours in Spanish or English are available with advance reservations.

IGLESIA DE SAN JOSÉ

Facing the plaza is the **Iglesia de San José** (Map pp316-17; ☎ 725-7501; admission free; ⓨ 7am-3pm Mon-Wed & Fri, 8am-1pm Sat, 8am-12:15pm Sun), the second-oldest church in the Americas. Established in 1523 by Dominicans, this church with its vaulted Gothic ceilings still bears the coat of arms of Juan Ponce de León (his family worshiped here), a striking carving of the Crucifixion and ornate processional floats. For 350 years, the remains of Ponce de León rested in a crypt here before being moved to the city's cathedral down the hill.

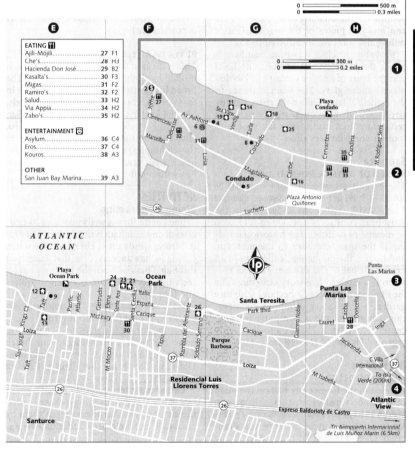

FUERTE SAN CRISTÓBAL

Along Calle Norzagaray, the street veers away from the ocean and the city's wall butts up against **Fuerte San Cristóbal** (Map pp316-17; ☎ 729-6960; adult/child & senior US$2/1; ☼ 9am-5pm), the old city's other major fortification. In its prime, San Cristóbal covered 27 acres (11 hectares) with a maze of six interconnected forts protecting a central core with 150ft (46m) walls, moats, booby-trapped bridges and tunnels. The fort was constructed to defend Old San Juan against land attacks from the east via Puerta de Tierra.

CATEDRAL DE SAN JUAN

Every Spanish colonial city must have its cathedral, and the **Catedral de San Juan** (Map pp316-17; ☎ 722-0861; admission free; ☼ 8am-4pm), next to the Gran Hotel El Convento, fills that need admirably. The building dates back to 1521 and includes pieces of the original Gothic ceiling and staircase constructed in 1529.

Probably the chief reason to visit here is to see the marble tomb of Ponce de León and the body of religious martyr St Pio displayed under glass. The main entrance to the cathedral faces Calle del Cristo, a shady street of posh boutiques, trendy bars and restaurants that capture the fancy of both tourists and islanders alike.

Santurce

MUSEO DE ARTE DE PUERTO RICO

The biggest **art museum** (MAPR; Map pp318-19; ☎ 977-6277; 299 De Diego Avenue, Santurce; adult/child & senior US$5/3; ☼ 10am-5pm Tue-Sun; **P**) in the Caribbean consists of 130,000 sq ft (12,080 sq meters) of facilities. The historical building is the main entrance to the museum, and houses the permanent collection in 18 exhibition halls. The east wing of the museum is a modern five-story structure. The facility boasts a 5-acre (2-hectare) sculpture garden, a three-story atrium, a conservation laboratory and a computer-learning center (ActivArte). There's also the highly regarded **Pikayo** (☎ 721-6194) restaurant.

Río Piedras

MUSEO DE OLLER

Located in the former city hall on the plaza of Bayamón's historic district, this **museum of art & history** (☎ 785-6010; admission free; ☼ 9am-4pm Tue-Sat) pays tribute to native son Francisco Oller (1833–1917), considered the

first Latin-American Impressionist. Most of Oller's great works are displayed elsewhere, but the restored neoclassical museum building is worth a peek if you are in the area. The collection includes some Oller portraits, Taino artifacts and sculptures by Tomas Batista, another local artist.

Beaches

PLAYA CONDADO

Rounding a point of coral at the east end of the Condado beach, you'll see the beach of **Playa Ocean Park** (Map pp318–19) sprawling in front of you – flat, broad, sugary and uncrowded. There are a number of low-key beach concessions here and some popular guest houses. Many of the city's leisure class come here to walk, jog, swim, play paddle ball or read the morning paper. The broader strand in front of the Atlantic Beach Hotel is popular with gays.

PLAYA ISLA VERDE

This is the best beach in San Juan, although it often has light seaweed in the water. The broad beach stretches for well over a mile in front of the condo towers and chic hotels, like the Water Club and Wyndham El San Juan. This is the Copacabana of Puerto Rico, alive with tourists, beach bunnies, *playeros* (beach hippies) and water-sports/umbrella/ beach-chair vendors. All of the hotels sport beachfront pubs and restaurants.

ACTIVITIES

Diving & Snorkeling

While Puerto Rico is well known for its first-class diving, San Juan is not the best place for it. Strong winds often churn up the water. Condado has an easy dive that takes you through a pass between the inner and outer reefs into coral caverns, overhangs, grottos and tunnels.

Eco-Action Tours (☎ 791-7509; ecoactiontours@yahoo.com) can do just about any tour imaginable, but for far less than you'll pay if you book the same trip through your hotel. Snorkeling and kayaking trips range from US$40 to US$69, and for a trip to Culebra it's US$89.

Caribe Aquatic Adventures (Map pp318-19; ☎ 724-1882, 281-8858) keeps changing its base around the city, but you can always reach them by phone. In spite of their wanderlust, the operators here are reliable and have 20 years of experience with this environment. One-/two-tank dives cost about US$55/85.

Snorkelers and divers in need of gear should check out **Mundo Submarino** (☎ 791-5764; Laguna Gardens Shopping Center, Isla Verde).

Kayaking

Las Tortugas Adventures (Map pp316-17; ☎ 725-5169; www.kayak-pr.com; 4 Calle la Puntilla) will give you a good workout and some thrills as you circle the island that is home to Old San Juan and Puerta de Tierra. Owner Gary also has two- and four-hour tours of the Laguna Piñones, as well as trips off the south coast and the east coast.

Sailing

To rent a small sailboat or powerboat, contact the **Caribbean School of Aquatics** (Map pp318-19; ☎ 728-6606; 1 Calle Taft, suite 10F, Condado).

For a cruise around Bahía de San Juan, call **Anticipation Harbor Cruises** (Map pp318-19; ☎ 725-3500; San Juan Bay Marina; adult/child US$12/6). Its one-hour evening party cruise with free munchies, open wine and soda bar, live music and dancing is good value.

TOURS

Walking-tour vendors in San Juan seem to come and go with the frequency of twitchy squirrels on a high-tension wire. One outfit that stands the test of time is María Alexandra Pla's **Colonial Adventures** (☎ 793-2992, 888-774-9919). She offers themed walking tours of Old San Juan with bilingual guides. Offerings include historic, antique/art, shopping and mystery walks. Tours cost US$16 to US$22. Debbie Ramos at **Legends of Puerto Rico** (☎ 531-9060) also operates popular tours like the night-time 'Walk Among the Dead.'

SLEEPING
Old San Juan
BUDGET

La Caleta (Map pp316-17; ☎ 725-5347; www.thecaleta .com; 11 Caleta Las Monjas; apt per week from US$350, shorter stays negotiable; 🔊) Set on a quiet street, this three-story apartment building has some balconies that catch the trade winds, and overlook La Fortaleza and the Plazuela de la Rogativa at the entrance to Bahía de San Juan. The small rooms are a bit bare – concrete floors and no decorations – but all have phones and kitchenettes. The sunny penthouse suite is the prettiest option.

Guest House Old San Juan (Map pp316-17; ☎ 722-5436; 205 Calle Tanca; r with fan or air-con US$40; 🔊) The cheapest rooms are minuscule and a bit dingy and the shared baths slightly unappealing. Larger rooms are slightly more attractive. But it's probably the most affordable place in Old San Juan and it's on a beautiful street.

El Jibarito (Map pp316-17; ☎ 725-8375; 280 Calle Sol; r US$60) You won't go hungry because this small guesthouse is right over a restaurant of the same name. If you don't mind feeling like you are sleeping in someone else's house, then this is a good and clean budget option.

Fortaleza Guest House (Map pp316-17; ☎ 721-7112; 361 Calle Fortaleza; r without bath per night/week from $65/125) Spanish-only at this guesthouse! Tiny rooms in homey settings are quite a bargain at weekly prices. Not much privacy and you'll see some ants, but overall it's a safe and fun place to stay.

MIDRANGE

La Galería (Map pp316-17; ☎ 722-1808; www.thegallery inn.com; 204-206 Calle Norzagaray; r with breakfast US$145-350; 🅿 🔊) This is a series of connecting town houses overlooking the ocean from a perch near the city's northern wall. Jan D'Sopo and her husband, Manuco Gandía,

---

AUTHOR'S CHOICE

Gran Hotel El Convento (Map pp316-17; ☎ 723-9020; www.elconvento.com; 100 Calle del Cristo; r US$165-400; 🅿 🔊 🖥 🔊) The front door says it all – solid wood, built in the 1600s, and still guarding the entrance to El Convento, which literally was a convent once for wealthy women from Spain widowed in the New World. El Convento sits in a beautiful section of the old town and absolutely is worth a visit, whether you stay overnight or not. Anyone is welcome to check out the restful atrium inside and drink or eat at any of the very upbeat bars and restaurants. To go upstairs, just call on the white courtesy phone in the lobby. The mother-superior suite is utterly breathtaking – not so opulent as elegant, and steeped in a very unique kind of Old World charm. No matter what room you stay in, however, a night at El Convento is a very special experience.

have decorated this 18th-century compound with a vast collection of their own art. Gorgeous rooms and an even better patio view.

Hotel Milano (Map pp316-17; ☎ 729-9050; www .hotelmilanopr.com; 307 Calle Fortaleza; r with continental breakfast US$95-155; 🕸) A renovated 19th-century building, located on one of the busiest streets in the heart of Old San Juan, the Milano is right on Calle Fortaleza, just steps from the hottest restaurants in Old San Juan. Rooms are bland but clean and comfortable, rather like a chain hotel but with slightly more personality.

Hotel Plaza de Armas (Map pp316-17; ☎ 722-9191; www.ihphoteles.com; r US$90-175; 🕸) In the heart of Old San Juan this modern and new hotel offers little to attract the eye inside, but does offer every possible convenience in terms of location. Rooms are a bit stuffy.

TOP END

Sheraton Old San Juan (Map pp316-17; ☎ 721-5100; 101 Calle La Marina; r US$225-575; 🅿 🕸 🛋) Facing the cruise-ship docks, this nine-story, convention-style hotel that used to be a Wyndham offers 240 rooms with all the amenities for the luxury-minded, including a major casino. While comfortable, it is a chain hotel. Bland decor and atmosphere come with the territory.

Condado & Ocean Park

BUDGET

Embassy Guest House (Map pp318-19; ☎ 800-468-0615; 1126 Calle Sea View; r US$65-90; 🅿 🕸 🛋) A favorite budget spot among gay travelers – although others like it too – the Embassy encourages guests to have fun in its Jacuzzi with bar. The rooms show their age a bit but since the oceanfront location is sublime, it's hardly worth fussing about.

Arcade Inn (Map pp318-19; ☎ 728-0668; 8 Calle Taft; r US$75-80; 🕸) Families like the beach cottage vibe of this almost, but not quite, waterfront B&B. The rooms are bright and inviting and there's plenty of shared space for wee ones to run about. Kitchen available.

Aleli by the Sea (Map pp318-19; ☎ 725-7313; 1125 Calle Sea View; r US$65-110; 🅿 🕸) In the heart of Condado this inn has nine units with private baths, as well as shared living room, kitchen and seaside sundeck. If you can pony up for the higher-priced rooms the stay will be much more enjoyable – the less expensive ones are a bit depressing and sterile.

Casa del Caribe (Map pp318-19; ☎ 722-7139; 57 Calle Caribe; r US$75-165; 🕸) A bit run-down and shabby in places, this B&B isn't a bad option if you just want to sit on the beach and relax. In the off-season, when the prices are sure to be low, this is an even better deal. Dogs welcome.

MIDRANGE

Atlantic Beach Hotel (Map pp318-19; ☎ 721-6900; www.atlanticbeachhotel.net; 1 Calle Vendig; r US$105-155; 🕸) The Atlantic Beach has been the soul of San Juan's gay community for decades. This place has a knowledgeable and funny staff, and 37 spacious plain rooms right on the broadest part of Condado beach. Also has an on-site restaurant and a popular terrace bar.

At Wind Chimes Inn (Map pp318-19; ☎ 800-946-3244; www.atwindchimesinn.com; 53 Calle Taft; r US$85-115; 🅿 🕸 🛋 🛋) Prices will fall in off-season, making this even more of a bargain. At Wind Chimes is modeled along the lines of a Spanish villa and feels quite homey, with passably pretty rooms and a nice pool with Jacuzzi.

Iberia Hotel (Map pp318-19; ☎ 723-0200; 1464 Av Wilson; r US$95-115; 🕸) Another gay-friendly option, this Spanish-looking small hotel with 30 units is in an exclusive residential neighborhood of Condado. You get all the amenities plus a terrace, solarium and restaurant. This place offers a lot of style and attention to detail for the price.

Numero Uno (Map pp318-19; ☎ 726-5010; 1 Calle Sta Ana; r US$115-215; 🅿 🕸 🛋) Just east of Condado beach in Ocean Park, there is a lot of charm in this distinctive whitewashed beach house surrounded by coconut palms. Owned by a former New Yorker who's spruced everything up nicely, Numero Uno lives up to its name.

Ocean Park Beach Inn (Map pp318-19; ☎ 728-7418; 3 Calle Elena; r US$90-165; 🅿 🕸) Catering to gay men and women, the inn features 10 rooms with private entrances, refrigerators, baths and ocean/garden views just one block from the beach.

L'Habitation Beach (Map pp318-19; ☎ 727-2499; www.habitationbeach.com; 1957 Calle Italia; r US$90-120; 🕸) A very popular guesthouse often frequented by gay couples, L'Habitation welcomes everybody with equal enthusiasm. Rooms are big, clean and decorated in a very homespun style. The private beach is quite nice, and there's an on-site bar.

El Canario By the Sea (Map pp318-19; ☎ 533-2649; www.canariohotels.com; 4 Calle Condado; r US$100-115; 🅇) There are three Canario inns around Condado – agents here at the 'By the Sea' can assist you in reserving at any one of the properties. Each of the small hotels has 25 to 40 units with cable TV, phone and continental breakfast. You get a quiet, clean, well-lighted place.

Tu Casa Boutique Hotel (Map pp318-19; ☎ 727-5100; 2071 Calle Cacique; P 🅇 🅇) A very pretty boutique hotel just two blocks from the beach, Tu Casa also rents bicycles to zip around on. Rooms are beautifully coordinated and the romantic suite is a real knockout.

TOP END

Condado Plaza Hotel & Casino (Map pp318-19; ☎ 727-721-1000; www.condadoplaza.com; 999 Av Ashford; r US$300-1350; 🅇) The hotel steals the show with a fitness center, spa, bi-level suites, seven restaurants, live entertainment and great salsa. It even has its own private beach facing Fuerte San Gerónimo across the inlet.

Caribe Hilton (Map pp318-19; ☎ 721-0303; www .caribehilton.com; Calle Rosales; r US$260-450; P 🅇 🅇 🅇) Situated on Calle Rosales off Av Muñoz Rivera in Puerta de Tierra, this is a good bet if you want luxury near Old San Juan, as well as access to a beach and tennis courts. With 672 newly renovated rooms and nine restaurants, this place is really an all-inclusive resort.

Normandie Hotel (Map pp318-19; ☎ 729-2929; www.normandiepr.com; Av Muñoz Rivera; r US$200-325; 🅇 🅇 🅇). Next door to the Caribe Hilton, more affordable and smaller with 189 units, this hotel is an art-deco masterpiece. It echoes with the ghosts of the jet set who used to scandalize the island 50 years ago by cavorting nude in the pool. For a large hotel, this place has soul.

San Juan Marriott Resort & Casino (Map pp318-19; ☎ 722-7000; www.marriotthotels.com; 1309 Av Ashford; r US$265-525; P 🅇 🅇) Rising from the ashes of the burned-out Dupont Plaza in 1995, this Marriott has turned into a pretty beachfront property, with two pools and 525 units.

Isla Verde
BUDGET

Mango Inn (☎ 726-4230; 20 Calle Uno; www.themango inn.com; US$70-105; P 🅇 🅇) It's all good but the location – the Mango just happens to be on the wrong side of the highway. But if you

don't mind a hop over to the beach, then the Mango is perfect for a budget traveler. The pool is small but cute, and fresh flowers adorn the rooms.

Casa Mathiesen (☎ 726-8662; 14 Calle Uno Este; r US$70-89; P 🅇 🅇) A pedestrian bridge over the expressway connects you to the beach and restaurant. Rooms come with kitchenette but are tiny. If you can live with that, however, this is a good deal. The owners also run **Green Island Inn** (☎ 800-677-8860; 36 Calle Uno Este; r US$58-78; 🅇 🅇) down the street, within a mile of the airport. Both a restaurant and a pool are on site.

Casa de Playa (☎ 800-916-2272, fax 727-1334; 86 Av Isla Verde; r US$90-160; 🅇) This is a former private beach villa set amid an explosion of palms. There are now 20 units here with all the mod cons. The beach bar has a loyal following.

MIDRANGE

La Playa Hotel (☎ 791-1115; www.hotellaplaya.com; 6 Calle Amapola; r US$95-135; 🅇 🅇) Amid the schlock highway art, fast-food joints, car-rental agencies and condo towers of Isla Verde, this place is an oasis on the beach. You get a room with all the comforts in a beachfront property. There is also a popular, moderately priced restaurant-bar on the premises.

Empress Oceanfront (☎ 800-678-0757; 2 Calle Amapola; r US$140-200; 🅇 🅇) For a dramatic location, this hotel can't be beaten. It commands a small peninsula at the water's edge of Calle Amapola. The pool and restaurant are part of a deck that stands on pilings stretching out over the ocean.

Courtyard Inn (☎ 791-0404; www.marriott.com; 7012 Boca de Cangrejos; r US$150-300; P 🅇 🅇 🅇) This is one of the island's best deals. Right on the beach (sunshades, chairs and towels available) with two beautiful pools, an open-air bar and a more formal restaurant inside, it's also got a casino that's small but fun – a good choice for beginners, since croupiers don't mind explaining the rules.

TOP END

Water Club (☎ 728-3666; www.waterclub.com; 2 Calle Tartak; r US$289-995; P 🅇 🅇 🅇) San Juan's most high-profile luxury boutique beach hotel has 11 floors, 84 spacious rooms and ocean views from every guest's quarters. The lobby decor includes waterfalls behind glass, theatrical lighting and filmy white draperies. The 11th floor (rooftop) has a sundeck and a wet bar with futons, sofas and a fireplace. Individual attention is the watchword with the staff.

Ritz Carlton Hotel & Casino (☎ 800-241-3333;www.ritzcarlton.com; 6961 Hwy 187; r US$325-2500; P 🞉 🖳 🖳) A huge, square monolith with festive lights strung all year round, the Ritz keeps a tight grip on its front door – nonguests aren't exactly welcomed (that's why it's the favorite celebrity hangout). Rooms are, as you would expect, swanky, swell and sumptuous.

Wyndham El San Juan Hotel & Casino (☎ 800-468-2818; www.wyndham.com; 6063 Av Isla Verde; r US$395-450; P 🞉 🖳 🖳) El San Juan still has it, even after 40 years. The hotel's advertising claims nightlife here is reminiscent of 1950s Havana, and this is no lie. Bring your tux and platinum card.

EATING
Old San Juan
Parrot Club (Map pp316-17; ☎ 725-7370; 363 Calle Fortaleza; dishes US$18-32; 🕑 lunch & dinner) Vibrating with splashy orange, blue and yellow decor, the Parrot Club features sounds of live jazz and the tastes of '*nuevo Latino*' cuisine. The fact that the menu is written in 'Spanglish' hints at the fusion cookery that goes into recipes like crabcakes *caribeños* (Caribbean version of crabcakes).

Dragon Fly (Map pp316-17; ☎ 977-3886; 364 Calle Fortaleza; dishes US$10-25, 🕑 dinner) This is hip eatery number two on Calle Fortaleza, and it's right across the street from the Parrot Club (same owner). Dragon Fly looks like an intimate little Penang bordello with its flaming red walls and fabrics and it draws a sexy-looking crowd to the bar. Latin/Asian fusion cuisine is very light and appealing.

AUTHOR'S CHOICE

La Querencia (Map pp316-17; ☎ 723-0357; 320 Calle Fortaleza; dishes US$16-26, 🕑 dinner) A beautifully restored old town-house full of color – try drinks in the red bar up front and dinner in the warm, candle-lit green room in back. It's a good place to take children who like interesting food; the menu rotates but does steaks, paella, lots of seafood and Puerto Rican classics like *mofongo* (fried balls of mashed plaintain) and *lechon asado* (roast suckling pig).

Aquaviva (Map pp316-17; ☎ 722-0665; 364 Calle Fortaleza; dishes US$30-40; 🕑 dinner only) And Aquaviva makes three, all owned by the same person. The white decor with lamps shaped like *aguavivas* (jellyfish) is, naturally, quite aquatic looking and the fresh seafood bar impossible to resist.

Los Amigos (Map pp316-17; 253 Calle San Jose; sandwiches US$2-4; 🕑 until 5pm) Don't let the completely unprepossessing exterior fool you – this is the best place around for a traditional, inexpensive Puerto Rican breakfast or lunch.

La Bombonera (Map pp316-17; ☎ 722-0658; 259 Calle San Francisco; mains US$5-10) Sanjuaneros claim the baked goods here cannot be matched, and they relish the endless free refills of *café con leche* (coffee with milk).

Tio Danny's (Map pp316-17; ☎ 723-0322; 313 Calle Fortaleza; dishes US$8-22; 🕑 lunch & dinner) To get a real Old San Juan vibe, step into Danny's and sit at the bar. Big, steaming plates of *arroz con pollo* (rice with chicken) and plantains come out of the kitchen with reassuring regularity. Mexican food served in the al fresco area out back.

Ostra Cosa (Map pp316-17; ☎ 722-2672; 154 Calle Cristo; dishes US$15-30) Touting itself as an 'aphrodisiac restaurant' with creative menu offerings like royal smashed potato with octopus (US$15), Ostra Cosa's lush garden does make you feel like you've stepped into a secret earthly paradise. Perfect for couples.

Tantra (Map pp316-17; ☎ 977-8141; 356 Calle Fortaleza; dishes US$13-27; 🕑 lunch & dinner) The bar prides itself on innovative drinks (try the Black Martini) and the kitchen prides itself on innovative dishes (try anything). Indo-Latin cuisine and it's darn good.

Condado & Ocean Park
Don't let the prevalence of second-rate hotel restaurants, tourist traps and fast-food chains deter you – there's good eating to be found along this stretch of beach.

Ajili-Mójili (Map pp318-19; ☎ 725-9195; 1052 Av Ashford; dishes US$14-23; 🕑 lunch & dinner) The menu is high-end *comida criolla* – island-style pork loin with *mofongo* (fried balls of mashed plaintain), for example – and the atmosphere heady and romantic. Candles, sweeping views, lots of attention from the staff – come prepared to be pampered, and dress up rather than down.

Ramiro's (Map pp318-19; ☎ 721-9049; 1106 Av Magdalena; dishes US$25-37; 🕑 lunch & dinner) It's a good idea to make reservations for Ramiro's, which some would say has replaced Ajili-Mójili as the city's 'best' restaurant. Dishes like lamb with spiced root vegetables and guava sauce, and crabmeat and avocado salad certainly make a good argument on for Ramiro's.

Zabo's (Map pp318-19; ☎ 725-9494; 14 Calle Candida; dishes US$12-30; ☽ lunch & dinner) Very creative dishes like mango and curry rice and rosemary pork chops with garlic merlot sauce make Zabo's a hit with the foodie crowd in town, and the breezy colonial-style building makes you feel like you've stepped miles away from the crowded city street.

Che's (Map pp318-19; ☎ 726-7202; 35 Calle Caoba; dishes US$12-24; ☽ lunch & dinner) Almost all of the Sanjuaneros and expats say Che's has the best Argentinean food around; once you taste the *churrasco* or *parrillada* (boiled or grilled, marinated steak), or even the veal chops, you won't disagree.

Migas (Map pp318-19; ☎ 721-5991; 1400 Calle Magdalena; dishes US$15-35; ☽ lunch & dinner) The latest trendy boutique restaurant to open up on Magdalena, Migas is high on the list of bar-hopping Sanjuaneros. Some come for drinks and others for the food – miso-glazed salmon, classic French steak frites, spicy duck with orange glaze – and others hang out just to enjoy the sleek elegance and fashionable buzz.

Hacienda Don José (Map pp318-19; ☎ 722-5880; 1025 Av Ashford; dishes US$5-12; ☽ breakfast, lunch & dinner) A bit touristy, yes, but also right on the beach and serving plentiful dishes at comparatively low prices. Breakfast will set you back less than US$5. Drinks are also very affordable and you can take your meal on the beachfront patio. Not bad.

Salud (Map pp318-19; ☎ 722-0911; 1350 Av Ashford; dishes US$5-15; ☽ breakfast & lunch) Veggie eaters will find a pleasant surprise here. Both a health food store and café, this narrow little place serves up a spicy stew of roots and vegetables for US$5 and you can stock up on veggie protein if you are heading out of town.

Via Appia (Map pp318-19; ☎ 725-8711; Av Ashford; pizza US$7-14) Right next door to Salud, you'll find the Condado area's favorite pizza restaurant, with its shady streetside tables.

Kasalta's (Map pp318-19; ☎ 727-7340; 1966 Calle McLeary; dishes US$4-10; ☽ 6am-10pm) This is a Cuban bakery on Ocean Park's main drag that opens early for those who have watched the sun rise through the open doorway of a bar or club. Inside this old-style cafeteria with display cases filled with treats, you can order up a *cubano* (grilled sandwich with chicken, ham, cheese, lettuce and tomato), grilled ham and cheese, steak sandwich, omelette or one of a dozen sweet confections to eat with your steaming mug of *café con leche*.

Isla Verde

Ferrari Gourmet (☎ 982-3115; 51 Ave Isla Verde; dishes US$6-14; ☽ lunch & dinner) Try to picture an elegant pizza joint and you'll get a feeling for Ferrari Gourmet – simple pizzas and snacks, but oh so tastefully done. Wine by the glass, too.

Casa Dante (☎ 726-7310; 39 Av Isla Verde; dishes US$14-22; ☽ lunch & dinner) Casa Dante is a family-run restaurant that serves more variations of *mofongo* than one would think humanly feasible. All are delicious, and you can stick to fajitas or enchiladas or a basic steak if that's what you prefer.

Shogun (☎ 268-4622; dishes US$5-14; ☽ lunch & dinner) Lots of Japanese restaurants line the Isla Verde strip. This is one of the most popular, serving standard fare like tuna, maki and California rolls, or specialty rolls that you can put together yourself or pick from the á la carte menu.

DRINKING & ENTERTAINMENT

Traditional bars tend to open in the mid-to-late afternoon to catch the post-siesta or after-work happy-hour crowd. Dance clubs and live-music venues tend to open between 9pm and 10pm, but only start to get busy after 11pm. Monday to Thursday most places will close by midnight or 1am. On weekends, it's late, late hours – at least until 3am or 4am and often later if the crowd is big.

Dance Clubs

Club Lazer (Map pp316-17; ☎ 721-4479; 251 Calle Cruz) A long-time favorite in Old San Juan, Lazer draws all the young kids on shore leave from their jobs on the cruise ships, their passengers and Sanjuaneros who are too young, gay or 'alternative' for mainstream clubs. This mix makes the scene at Lazer arguably more wild, crazy and cosmopolitan because these people come from all over the globe and will never see each other again…unless they want to. The music ranges from house, electronica, *regguetón* (Spanish-speaking dancehall) to rap and hip-hop.

Asylum (Map pp318-19; ☎ 723-3416; 1420 Av Ponce de León) A lot of night owls – both straight and gay – end their Sunday morning dance-athons at Asylum. The crowd is mostly 18 to 23, except on gay nights when it's older.

Latin & Live Music Venues

La Rumba (Map pp316-17; ☎ 725-4407; 152 Calle San Sebastián) This is what you came to Puerto Rico for – a club so packed with people of all races and ages that it matters not if you are an expert twirler or a rank neophyte who can't even spell syncopation. It won't get busy until after 11pm, when the live bands start warming up, but soon enough the trickle of people through the door will turn into a torrent and you'll be caught up in a warm tropical crush of movement. Expect *bomba* (inspired by African rhythms and characterized by call-and-response dialogues), *plena* (African rhythms beat out with traditional percussion instruments), salsa, samba and, of course, rumba music.

Nuyorican Café (Map pp316-17; ☎ 977-1276; 312 Calle San Francisco) This café arrived on the scene in 2001 and quickly became the hottest live jazz venue (nightly) in the city. The entrance is on the alley, Callejón de la Capilla, between Calles San Francisco and Fortaleza. Some nights also include poetry reading. Step into the little bar in the alley for a beer, lots of locals and pleasant conversation.

Gallery Café (Map pp316-17; ☎ 725-8676; 305 Calle Fortaleza) This café in the old city features jazz on Wednesday night, and funk, hip-hop, Latin jazz and techno Thursday to Saturday. Happy hour specials run till 9pm on Friday. You get a well-dressed local yuppie gang here.

Oleo (Map pp316-17; ☎ 977-1083; 305 Calle Recinto Sur) Loud house music in an art-filled space that's been lovingly decked out in vibrant, flashy colors.

Wet & Liquid (☎ 728-3666) Inside the Water Club (see p323), this bar is where well-heeled guests mingle with well-heeled drinkers on the make. Fashionable and full of fashion-istas, this is where you are mostly likely to bump into a model (male or female).

Enlaces (Map pp316-17; ☎ 977-0754; 255 Calle Cruz) In Old San Juan, this hip-hop lounge plays some heavy beats and attracts a late-teen, early 20-something crowd.

Gay & Lesbian Venues

Eros (Map pp318-19; ☎ 722-1131; 1257 Av Ponce de León) If you want a place with a Latin feel, where the disc jockey mixes some of the heavier New York house sounds with Latin rock and salsa, try here. Eros is next to the Teatro Metro in the Santurce/Miramar district. The scene starts at about 10pm and cranks till 4am on weekends. While basically a gay venue, this hot dance scene on Saturday nights draws free spirits from all quarters of the gay, lesbian, bi and straight world. The place to take a walk on the wild side.

Kouros (Map pp318-19; ☎ 977-0771; 1515 Av Ponce de León) Open only on the weekends, Kouros is probably the most glamorous disco in town and it caters to a gay male and fe-male crowd particularly (although certainly anyone is welcome). If you want to put on something slinky and get hot and sweaty under a strobe light, check out Kouros.

Cups (☎ 268-3570; 1708 Calle San Mateo) Bars catering exclusively to women are hard to come by in San Juan, but this one in San-turce is a laid-back women's scene popular with couples and cruisers.

You can start to get the lay of the land by stopping in at the Atlantic Beach Hotel (p322). The terrace bar at this hotel packs in a huge crowd for its Sunday T-dance with drag revues and male strippers on most weekends. Weeknights draws a steady crowd as well.

Every Sunday night at Asylum (left) is gay night.

SHOPPING

There are several beautiful boutiques and clothing stores lining Av Ashford in Con-dado. For arts and crafts, the shopping is in Old San Juan. Calles San Francisco and Fortaleza are the two main arteries in and out of the old city, and both are packed cheek by jowl with shops. Running perpendicular at the west end of the town, Calle del Cristo is home to many of the old city's most chic establishments.

Visitors should note that many of the craft vendors in Old San Juan are actually selling imports from South America, so do not proceed with the illusion that you are buying the unique produce of Puerto Rican artisans. Gathered around Plaza de Armas you'll find many recognizable brand names.

GETTING THERE & AWAY

Air

International flights arrive at and depart from San Juan's Aeropuerto Internacional de Luis Muñoz Marín (LMM), about 8 miles (12.8km) east of the old city center. See p341 and p776 for details of flights.

Private aircraft, charter services and the bulk of the commuter flights serving the islands of Culebra and Vieques arrive at and depart from San Juan's original airport at Isla Grande, on the Bahía de San Juan in the city's Miramar district. See p341 for details.

Público

There is no islandwide bus system. *Públicos* (taxis) form the backbone of public transportation in Puerto Rico and can provide an inexpensive link between San Juan and other points on the island, including Ponce (US$8) and Mayagüez (US$12). *Públicos* are generally shared taxis in the form of minivans that pick up passengers along pre-determined routes.

In San Juan the major *público* centers include the LMM airport, two large *público* stations in Río Piedras (Centro de Públicos Oeste and Centro de Públicos Este) and – to a lesser extent – the Plaza de Colón in Old San Juan.

GETTING AROUND

To/From the Airport

The bus is the cheapest option. Look for the 'Parada' sign outside the arrivals concourse at LMM. The B40 bus will get you from the airport to Isla Verde or Río Piedras. From there you can take other buses to Old San Juan or Condado.

There are also airport shuttle vans or limousine kiosks on the arrivals concourse. There is a good chance that you can join up with other travelers headed along your way. Once the van fills, you'll pay around US$7 to Isla Verde, US$9 to Condado and US$12 to Old San Juan.

Getting to LMM airport from hotels in the San Juan area is easy. Staff at virtually all of the midrange and top-end hotels will arrange for a taxi or airport shuttle van to pick you up in front of your lodging at your request. Depending on how many people share the cost of the ride, you can expect to pay between US$4 and US$20.

If you go it alone, there are fixed prices between the airport and Isla Verde (US$8), Condado (US$12) and Puerta de Tierra/ Old San Juan (US$16).

Bus

The **Autoridad Metropolitana de Autobuses** (AMA; Metropolitan Bus Authority & Metrobus; ☎ 767-7979) has a main bus terminal in Old San Juan near the cruise-ship piers. These are the routes taken most often by travelers (bus numbers are followed by associated route descriptions):

B40 LMM Airport, Isla Verde, Piñones and Río Piedras.
M1 & M9 Old San Juan, Río Piedras via various routes.
B21 Old San Juan, Condado, Stop 18 (Santurce), Plaza Las Américas.
A5 Old San Juan, Stop 18, Isla Verde.
C10 Hato Rey, Stop 18, Condado, Isla Grande.

Beware! The A5 bus that goes from Isla Verde to Old San Juan runs through the dangerous housing project of Loísa. In fact, if you want to go to Condado from Isla Verde you must get off near here at Stop 18 in Santurce; the surrounding area is rife with violent crime.

Car

Traffic, parking, the maze of thoroughfares and the danger of being carjacked make having and using a rental car in the city a challenge. Old San Juan has the city's two safest and most accessible parking facilities: Covadonga parking lot on Calle Recinto Sur just as you enter town, and next to that Dona Fela, which is slightly cheaper. For access to El Morro or the nightlife of Calle San Sabastián, check out the underground lot (beneath Parque Beneficencia off Calle Norzagaray) at the upper end of town. Parking costs US$2.50 for the first hour, and 75¢ for additional hours.

Ferry

A commuter ferry service called the **Acua Expreso** (Map pp316-17; ☎ 788-1155; 6am-9pm every 30 min; US$1) connects the east and west sides of Bahía de San Juan, Old San Juan and Cataño. In Old San Juan the ferry dock is at Pier 2, near the Sheraton Old San Juan.

Taxi

Cab drivers are supposed to turn on the meter for trips around town but that rarely happens. Insist on it, or establish a price from the start. Meters, when or if they do go on, charge US$2 initially and US$1.50 per mile or part thereof. You'll also pay US$1 per piece of luggage. There's a US$5 reservation charge; add a US$1 surcharge after 10pm.

Taxis line up at the south end of Calle Fortaleza in Old San Juan; in other places they can be scarce. Don't make yourself a mugging target by standing on a deserted street waiting for one to pass by – call from the nearest hotel. Try **Metro Taxi Cabs** (☎ 725-2870) or **Rochdale Radio Taxi** (☎ 721-1900); they usually come when you call.

Train
The Tren Urbano started a test service in December 2004. To learn its current status, check with the PRTC (p315).

AROUND SAN JUAN
Bacardi Rum Factory
Called the 'Cathedral of Rum' because of its six-story pink distillation tower, the **Bacardi plant** (☎ 788-8400; Hwy 888, Bayamón; admission free; ☼ 8:30am-4:30pm Mon-Sat) covers 127 acres (51 hectares) and stands out like a petroleum refinery across from Old San Juan, near the entrance to the bay. The world's largest and most famous rum-producing family started their business in Cuba more than a century ago, but they began moving their operation to this site in 1936. Today the distiller produces some 100,000 gallons of rum per day and ships 21 million cases per year worldwide.

Arecibo Observatory
Getting up to the Arecibo observatory and the world's largest **radio telescope** (☎ 878-2612; www.naic.edu; adult/child & senior US$4/2; ☼ noon-4pm Wed-Fri, 9am-4pm Sat, Sun & most holidays) is almost as exciting as the site itself. From Hwy 129, follow the roller-coaster ride through *mogotes* (tall hills) on narrow, two-lane roads – Hwy 635 and then Hwy 625 – that lead to the observatory.

The size and complexity of the space-age, 20-acre (8-hectare) 'dish,' set in a sinkhole between a cluster of hills, is simply mind-boggling. The actual receiving and transmitting instruments – which do rotate – are suspended by cables 50 stories above the dish and weigh more than 600 tons (609,630kg). And, yes, there is an ongoing Search for

Extraterrestrial Intelligence (SETI) program here like the one Jodie Foster obsesses over in the movie *Contact*, some of which was filmed here.

Parque de las Cavernas del Río Camuy
This **park** (☎ 898-3100; adult/child/senior US$10/7/5; ☼ 8am-3:45pm Wed-Sun & holidays) is home to one of the largest cave systems in the world and is definitely worth a stop (but call ahead if it's been raining – too much water causes closures).

Trolleybus trips and ample walking among stalagmites and stalactites make this a fun trip for the whole family. If you come early enough you can do the caves in the morning and the observatory in the afternoon. They are a 30-minute drive apart.

EASTERN PUERTO RICO

The proximity of San Juan's dense urban atmosphere to the lush green rainforest-covered hills of El Yunque is almost too good to be true – in just under 30 minutes you can be standing alongside a crystal-clear river listening to coquí frogs make their distinctive sounds.

And there's more: a few minutes beyond the magnificence of El Yunque is Playa Luquillo, where you can loll under the sun on white sands while rain clouds bump up against the mountain peaks behind you. For those who really want to get off the beaten track, you can take a quick ferry or plane ride to the untrammeled Spanish Virgin Islands, otherwise known as Culebra and Vieques.

LUQUILLO & AROUND
El Yunque
Covering some 28,000 acres (11,332 hectares) of land in the Luquillo mountains, this verdant, tropical rainforest is impressively healthy and bountiful, and some of the island's old trees still remain (1000 years and growing!). The views of the valleys, Atlantic, Caribbean and eastern islands are inspiring; the temperatures are cool; the hiking is heart-pounding; and the streams and waterfalls are rejuvenating. The first place of note that most people stop at is **El Portal Visitor's Center** (☎ 888-1880; www .southernregion.fs.fed.us/caribbean; Hwy 191, adult/child

& seniors US$3/$1.50, under 5 free 🕑 9am-5pm, closed Christmas Day). Built in 1996, El Portal is the key for visitors who want to understand more about El Yunque and tropical rainforests. Driving from San Juan, follow Hwy 3 to Hwy 191, watching for a large sign announcing 'El Yunque Portal' on the right side of the road. Then keep going uphill.

Playa Luquillo

This **balneario** (public beach; admission free, parking US$2; 🕑 8:30am-5:30pm) has been criticized in recent years for getting too crowded and a bit unkempt. But if you come on a quiet winter weekday, then you'll likely still be entranced by the broad white sweep of sand and gentle warm waves. It also has a wheelchair-accessible area and is great for children. Follow Hwy 3. You'll know you've arrived when you see the numerous food stalls lined up along the highway.

Sleeping & Eating

Río Grande Plantation Eco Resort (☎ 887-2779; www.riograndeplantation.com; Hwy 956, Río Grande; r US$100-175, villas US$150-300; P 🕹 🔊) The grounds at this former sugar plantation and mill are immense and picturesque, with a rushing river and birds flying every which way. Rooms are large, with big baths, cable TV and minirefrigerators. Great for kids.

Trinidad Guest House (☎ 889-2710; 6A Ocean Drive; d with bath US$87; 🔊) Fronted by big palm trees in a pretty, outdoor courtyard, this guesthouse is on Playa Luquillo. There are 10 rooms, six with private baths (small, but pretty), and rates include a breakfast of delicious bread and fresh fruit.

Brass Cactus (☎ 889-5735; Hwy 193; meals US$8-25) Not at all a prickly place, the Brass Cactus serves hearty American pub fare with the odd traditional dish thrown in. Children will find lots to eat (burgers, fries, chicken fingers).

Lolita's (☎ 889-5770; Hwy 3; mains US$6-11; 🕑 noon-10pm Tue-Sun) This eatery is 3 miles (4.8km) east of town on the south side of Hwy 3. A soft taco costs US$1.75, and many dinners run under US$8. Imported Mexican mariachis provide the music.

Getting There & Away

Públicos run from San Juan ($4) to and from the Luquillo plaza. Aside from that, you'll need your own wheels.

VIEQUES

pop 10,000

Also know as La Isla Nena (Little Girl Island), Vieques is the larger and better known of the Spanish Virgin Islands, in part because it made headlines in 2002 when residents succeeded in ousting the US Navy. Having tired of the navy's military training exercises that dropped live ordnance around parts of the island, Viequenses staged sit-ins, protests and all sorts of civil disobedience until the navy pulled out.

Now residents are struggling to keep afloat economically while not giving over their beloved island to developers (including the Puerto Rican government), who are vying for chunks of land with disquieting intensity.

For now, at least, the beaches are still heartbreakingly pristine and the long-term residents – expats and locals alike – stubbornly refuse to give up their laid-back island lifestyle.

There are two small settlements on the island: Isabella Segunda (Isabella II), where the ferry from Fajardo docks, and Esperanza, which is a 20-minute drive across the island.

Information

Unless otherwise noted, all of these addresses are in Isabella Segunda.

MONEY

It's a good idea to carry cash on the island (but watch out for petty thieves) because there's only one ATM and lots of places don't take plastic.

Banco Popular (☎ 741-2071; Calle Muñoz Rivera; 🕑 8am-3pm Mon-Fri) The only game in town, or on the island, for finances. The ATM does sometimes run dry, especially on Sunday nights.

POST

Post office (☎ 741-3891; Calle Muñoz Rivera 97; 🕑 8:30am-4:30pm Mon-Fri, 8am-noon Sat) Across from the Banco Popular, this is the island's only post office. It will take general delivery letters.

TOURIST OFFICES

Puerto Rico Tourism Company (PRTC; ☎ 741-0800; www.gotopuertorico.com; Calle Carlos LeBrun 449; 🕑 8am-5pm) Friendly and helpful staff are on hand to give out maps, brochures and lots of other literature on island life.

Sights

ORCHID, RED, GARCIA, SECRET & BLUE BEACHES

All these south-shore beaches, which used to be on navy land, can be reached by entering the Garcia Gate on Hwy 997.

Red Beach usually has a few cabanas up to shade bathers from the sun. Garcia Beach and Secret Beach are the next coves along the road. Blue Beach, at the east end of the Camp Garcia road, is long, open and occasionally has rough surf. Orchid Beach, at the eastern tip of the US Fish & Wildlife Reserve, is often deserted, with wide, deep blue waters (not good for children).

SOMBÉ

This long, half-moon-shaped bay, also known as Sun Bay, is less than a half mile east of Esperanza. It's the island's *balneario* (public beach), with all the facilities you have come to expect in Puerto Rico. It's sheltered and popular with families, campers and wild horses.

Activities

Vieques has some great sites for snorkeling and diving (see the boxed text, p339).

The island's dive shop shut down recently, but **Chipper** (☎ 741-3224) will take small groups out upon demand. He's got all the necessary equipment and knows the best spots for beginner, intermediate and expert divers.

Martineau Bay Resort (☎ 741-4100) has a dive master on hand who will do tours for non-guests, equipment provided.

Sleeping

ESPERANZA

Bananas (☎ 741-8700; www.bananasguesthouse.com; r US$45-70; 🖳) If you want to be at the heart of Esperanza's action (not quite an oxymoron), head here. The accommodations are basic and the front rooms are noisy, but it's a fair price for a room. The very best part is the great atmosphere – funky, relaxed and everything a Caribbean hideaway should be.

Trade Winds (☎ 741-8666; www.enchanted-isle.com/tradewinds; r US$55-75; 🖳) Harry and Janet Washburn run this popular guesthouse and inn with 10 rooms, including three terrace rooms that have a harbor view and catch the breeze. The biggest delight is probably the fabulous

open-air deck where meals are served – it offers splendiferous views of the ocean.

Acacia Apartments (☎ 741-1856; acaciaapts@aol.com; 236 Calle Acacia; r US$75-105) Four airy apartments in a three-story, tower-like building, which offers spectacular views of mountains and sea from its 2nd- and 3rd-floor decks, as well as its rooftop patio (St Croix is visible on clear days). Free washing machine. The managers also have spacious, airy apartments (US$750 to US$950) at their mountaintop house **A Breeze** in the barrio of Destino.

Ted's Guesthouse (☎ 741-2225; www.vieques-island.com/rentals/ted; Calle Hucar 3; r US$80-125) Three apartments in Ted's house, all impeccably clean and delightfully appointed – you'd think you were in a big name resort. Secure parking facilities and great views from the rooftops.

ISABELLA SEGUNDA

Bravo Beach Hotel (☎ 741-1128; www.bravobeachhotel.com; North Shore Rd, 1 above the lighthouse, Bravos de Boston; r US$125-225, villa US$425) Bravo's boutique building makes each room look like a tiny jewel box – pretty colors, high-tech gadgetry (including wi-fi) and egg-shaped lamps are the norm. The on-site restaurant – Chef Michael's FoodWorks – serves some delectable treats.

Casa La Lanchita (☎ 800-774-4717; www.viequeslalanchita.com; North Shore Rd 374, Bravos de Boston; r US$80-150) This place is a really great option for families – there's a lap and a kiddie pool. Although it looks like a guesthouse, it's actually comprised of separate apartments, and each unit comes with a kitchenette.

Ocean View (☎ 741-3696; 751 Calle Plinio Peterson; r US$75-100) This place feels a bit like an institution, but you can walk to several of the town's best bars and the staff are friendly. Rooms are clean – some have lovely ocean views – but not all that pretty.

Casa de Amistad (☎ 741-3758; www.casadeamistad.com; 27 Calle Benitez Castano; r without/with bath US$45/$55; 🖳) A really fun and comfortable place to crash in downtown Isabella Segunda, Casa de Amistad has seven rooms, plus you get use of the rooftop deck and little pool.

Eating

ESPERANZA

La Sirena (☎ 741-4462; Calle Flamboyan; US$16-30; 🕑 lunch & dinner) Franco-British owners churn out creative food like crabcakes, mussels in white-wine sauce, lobster in coconut-flavored rum and Puerto Rican *mofongo* stuffed with either pork, shrimp or chicken; and steaks.

Bananas and **Trade Winds** both have popular restaurants on-site.

ISABELLA SEGUNDA

Trópico (☎ 741-4000; Rte 200; dishes US$8-20; ☻ dinner) The menu here rotates daily – there is a grill night, fish night, paella night and so on. Many of the dishes are served with vegetables grown right on the 6-acre (2.4-hectare) plot inhabited by the restaurant, and the owners are happy to make vegetarian dishes.

El Patio Bar & Restaurant (☎ 741-6381; Calle Antonio Mellado; dishes US$2-15; ☻ breakfast, lunch, dinner) Rub elbows with the locals at El Patio, a laid-back place with outdoor tables and succulent, savory *comida criolla*.

Taverna Español (☎ 741-1175; Calle Carlos Lebrun cnr Benitez Castaño; mains US$8-16; ☻ lunch & dinner) The tavern has been around for a long time and the wear and tear is starting to show, but this is where Viequenses come to get their seafood fix.

Wai Nam (☎ 741-0622; Calle Plinio Petersen; US$4-12; ☻ lunch & dinner) Under the Ocean View hotel is Vieques' only Chinese restaurant. The entrees are rather formulaic and bland, but the price is right and you can sit and stare out across the mountains and ocean.

Getting There & Around

On the island there's little access to public transportation. You have to rent a car or scooter, or take a taxi. Taxis can be found at the ferry dock.

AIR

Vieques Air Link (☎ 888-901-9247, San Juan Vieques 741-8331, Fajardo-Vieques 741-3266) is a major carrier here, flying to Culebra and Fajardo on demand and San Juan daily. It also flies to St Croix, USVI. **Isla Nena Air Service** (☎ 863-4447, 741-1577; www.islanena.8m.com) flies on demand to Culebra, Fajardo and San Juan, and **Air Sunshine** (☎ 888-879-8900, 741-7900; www.airsunshine.com) flies to St Thomas, St Croix and Tortola as well as San Juan.

CAR & SCOOTER RENTAL

Extreme Scooters (☎ 435-9345; per 24hr US$40-50, US$60 deposit required) The biggest game in town is just

uphill from the ferry, and they are responsible. Call ahead and they'll deliver to you.

Island Car Rentals (☎ 741-1666)
Maritza's Car Rental (☎ 741-0078)
Martineau Car Rental (☎ 787-0087)
Steve's Car Rental (☎ 741-8135)

FERRY

Call the **Puerto Rican Port Authority** (☎ 863-0705, 800-981-2005; ☻ 8-11am & 1-3pm Mon-Fri) for vehicle reservations (required) or call the Vieques office (☎ 741-4761; ☻ 8-11am & 1-3pm Mon-Fri) at the ferry dock in Isabella Segunda. For ferry schedules see p341.

CULEBRA

pop 2500

Closer to St Thomas than to Puerto Rico, Culebra has long been an expat favorite and you'll find that most of the shop and hotel owners in Dewey – the only town – are Americans. But there's plenty of lively back-and-forth between locals and those who adopted the island at a later age, and overall Dewey gives off a homey, happily integrated feel. And it sure is fun!

It's hard to top Culebra for family vacations, with plenty of beaches where the wave size seems built for small-fry, and the resplendent nature beats anything they've ever seen on the telly.

For information about the magnificent diving and snorkeling on the island, check in at the dive shop across from the ferry dock. See also the Diving & Snorkeling chapter (p55).

Information

MONEY

Banco Popular (☎ 742-3572; Calle Márquez; ☻ 8:30am-2:30pm Mon & Wed-Fri)

POST

Post office (☎ 742-3862; Calle Márquez; ☻ 8:30am-4:30pm Mon-Fri, 8:30am-noon Sat) Right in the center of town.

TOURIST INFORMATION

Tourist office (☎ 742-3116, ext 441; Calle William Font; ☻ 8:30am-3:30pm Mon-Fri) Very basic information can be found in this yellow building near the health clinic. There are also good websites to turn to: everybody agrees that Bruce Goble of La Loma gift shop runs the island's best website (www.culebra-island.com), and there's also www.culebra.org and www.islaculebra.com.

Sights

PLAYA FLAMENCO
There's a reason this beach is deemed one of the Caribbean's best – it's simply gorgeous. This is the only public beach on the island with toilet and shower facilities and kiosks that sell food. Camping is allowed in the seaside grove of trees.

PLAYA ZONI
Head to the extreme eastern end of the island and you'll eventually run out of road at this beach. It is long and straight, with beautiful Caribbean islands popping up in the distance, but it's an isolated place, so use the buddy system when swimming.

PLAYA CARLOS ROSARIO
If you follow a path west from the parking lot at Playa Flamenco, a 12- to 15-minute hike over the hill will bring you to a small, nameless beach. Keep going, crossing the narrow peninsula and down to the sandy basin and shade trees. You can snorkel on either side of the barrier reef here by swimming through the boat channel – look for the white plastic bottle marker – at the right side of the beach. But be *very* careful: water taxis and local powerboats cruise the area, and in 1998 a long-time Culebra resident and diver was struck and killed by a boat.

For really spectacular snorkeling, work your way along the cliffs on the point south of the beach, or head about 0.25 miles north to a place called The Wall, which has 40ft (12m) drop-offs and rich colors. Carlos Rosario took a lot of shelling before the navy moved to Vieques; you may see ordnance in the water. It could be live; don't mess!

Activities
Culebra features some of Puerto Rico's most amazing dive spots (see the boxed text, p339). You can rent snorkel gear for about US$10 to US$12 a day from **Culebra Dive Shop** (☎ 742-0566) and from **Culebra Divers** (☎ 742-0803). Half-day (US$25) and full-day (US$50) boat and snorkeling trips are also offered, along with dive instruction and trips. One-tank dives cost around US$60; two-tank trips run at about US$90.

Glass Bottom Boat (☎ 501-0011) will take you wherever you want to go around the island, as well it offers a variety of trips to neighboring cays.

Sleeping & Eating
Mamacita's (☎ 742-0090; www.mamacitaspr.com; r US$85-100; ☒) Pretty pinks and bright blues abound at this Caribbean-style hotel-restaurant-bar. Rooms are simple but attractive and some overlook the canal. A long-time favorite of locals and expats.

Bahia Marina (☎ 742-3112, toll free ☎ 1-866-CULEBRA; www.culebraplanners.com; US$95-135; ☐) Built like mini-condos, each unit has a bedroom, two baths and a kitchen/living area with satellite TV and high-speed Internet. There's a full-service bar and restaurant on the premises; great for families and large parties, it's also wheelchair accessible.

Costa Bonita (☎ 742-4000; www.costabonitaresort .com; Punta Carenero; US$175-US$300; ☐ ☒ ☐ ☒) Locals bitterly opposed this new resort but Costa Bonita succeeded in opening in 2004 – it's comparatively eco-friendly, however, and beautiful to boot. Great amenities, including docks for sailboats, speedboat and plane service from St Thomas, St Croix, San Juan and other Caribbean locations.

Club Seabourne (☎ 742-3169; www.clubseabourne .com; r/villas US$165/549; ☒) Club Seabourne ranks near the top of the island's luxury accommodations list. It lies 1.5 miles (2.4km) south of the drawbridge on the Punta del Soldado road and has one of the best restaurants on the island.

Posada La Hamaca (☎ 742-3516; www.posada .com; r US$70-90) An attractive building with Spanish architecture right on the canal, La Hamaca pales a bit in comparison to Mamacita's next door, but overall is a good deal. Rooms are simple, some with kitchenettes, and most have private baths.

Hotel Kokomo (☎ 742-0683; r US$45-85; ☒) Impossible to miss, Hotel Kokomo is the bright yellow hotel directly across from the ferry dock. New management has given this old building a new lease of life; rooms are still basic, but now they are clean and cheery enough. The cheapest have shared baths.

Dinghy Dock (☎ 742-0581; mains US$7-18) Almost as popular as Mamacita's, the Dinghy Dock is across the bridge on the left. Great seafood and strong drinks.

Tamarindo Bar & Grill (☎ 742-0345; Tamarindo Estates; mains US$14-22; ☒ Thu-Sun dinner) This bar and grill is at the boutique resort on a dirt road that takes you to a small beach called Playa Tamarindo. You can sit on the terrace or take a candlelit table right on the beach.

Getting There & Away

AIR

Culebra gets excellent air service from San Juan and Fajardo on the commuter carriers that also serve Vieques; see p341 for details. **Isla Nena Air Service** (☎ 863-4447, 863-4449; www .islanena.8m.com) can be chartered for flights to St Thomas and **Air St Thomas** (☎ 791-4898; www.airstthomas.com) does charter flights to St Croix, St Thomas and many other Caribbean islands, with stopovers at Vieques or Culebra on demand.

FERRY

If you need to confirm the schedule, call the **Fajardo Puerto Rican Port Authority office** (☎ 863-0705, car reservations ☎ 800-981-2005; ☒ 8-11am & 1-3pm Mon-Fri; Culebra office ☎ 742-3161; ferry dock, Dewey; ☒ 8-11am & 1-3pm Mon-Fri). For ferry schedules, see p341.

Getting Around

CAR/SCOOTER

With more than 200 guestrooms and several dozen vacation villas for rent, Culebra's cars are in high demand. Reservations are essential in high season.

Carlos Jeep (☎ 742-3514, 613-7049)
Coral Reef (☎ 742-0055)
Dick's (☎ 742-0062)
Jerry's Jeeps (☎ 742-0587)
Thrifty Car Rental/JM Scooter Rentals (☎ 742-0521)
Willy's (☎ 742-3537)

TAXI

Público vans run between the ferry dock and Playa Flamenco for US$2. Some local entrepreneurs double as taxi drivers.

Willy's (☎ 742-3537, 396-0076) generally meets every ferry and also arrives on your door when booked. If he's busy and you're stuck for a ride, try **Romero** (☎ 378-0250) or **Kiko's Transportation** (☎ 742-2678).

SOUTH & WEST COASTS

A stunning change of scenery awaits you along the southern coast – particularly west of the main city, Ponce. The central mountains tumble down to denuded plains that once were full of sparse bushes – everything was cleared away to make room for sugar plantations in the 1800s. Now there's little to catch the eye – outside of the colonial

charms of Ponce – until you arrive at Bosque Estatal de Guánica, a fabulous 'dry forest' that brings to mind the deserts of southern Arizona. Unbelievably, it's little more than an hour's drive from El Yunque's fecund greenery.

PONCE

pop 194,636

The historic center of this otherwise modern city is full of great charm and quaint architecture. Unfortunately, you must battle an outer layer of congested traffic and annoying stop lights to reach it.

Once that's over though, and you arrive at the city's heart, you'll find the serene beauty of the Plaza Las Delicias, a sun-dappled and fountain-filled colonial-era square. Aside from one unfortunate transgression (a string of fast-food joints on the corner) it's a very authentic and tranquil cityscape with a wonderful sense of place.

Ponce also has a waterfront pavilion, boardwalk and beach south of the city at a site called Paseo Tablado La Guancha, often simply called 'La Guancha.' There are dozens of attractive restaurants and cafés here, live salsa music on weekends and one of the liveliest weekend scenes for families and youth on the island.

Information

Candy & Magazine Store (Calle Isabel 72; ☒ 7am-6pm Mon-Fri, 8am-6pm Sat, 8am-1pm Sun) Small shop with one computer, but easily found downtown. Many hotels have Internet service for guests.
Ponce Tourism Office (Parque de Bombas; ☎ 284-3338; www.ponceweb.org; Plaza Las Delicias; ☒ 9am-5:30pm) Can't miss the big red structure in the middle of the park, and inside are friendly, English-speaking staff, ready with brochures, answers and suggestions.

Sights & Activities

PLAZA LAS DELICIAS

This is the quintessential Spanish-colonial plaza, and it lives up to its name that translates as 'Plaza of Delights.' In the daytime the square is filled with window shoppers, children intent on their own games and groups of elderly men quietly playing dominoes under shady trees. A string of pretty cafés and eateries circle the park (ignore the fast-food restaurants that blight one corner). But it's at its best at night, when violet and pink lights dance in the waters

PUERTO RICO

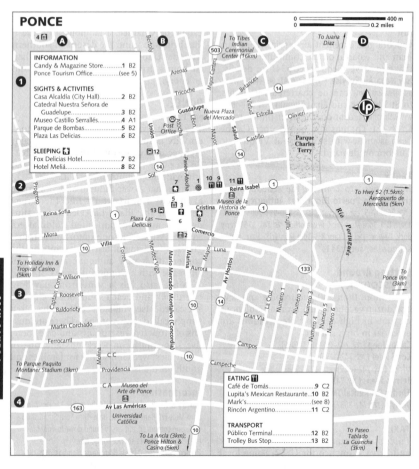

PONCE

INFORMATION
Candy & Magazine Store..........1 B2
Ponce Tourism Office..............(see 5)

SIGHTS & ACTIVITIES
Casa Alcaldía (City Hall).............2 B2
Catedral Nuestra Señora de
Guadalupe............................3 B2
Museo Castillo Serrallés............4 A1
Parque de Bombas....................5 B2
Plaza Las Delicias......................6 B2

SLEEPING
Fox Delicias Hotel.....................7 B2
Hotel Meliá.................................8 B2

EATING
Café de Tomás.............................9 C2
Lupita's Mexican Restaurante..10 B2
Mark's.......................................(see 8)
Rincón Argentino.....................11 C2

TRANSPORT
Público Terminal.......................12 B2
Trolley Bus Stop.......................13 B2

of the **Fuente de Leones** (Fountain of Lions), a monument rescued from the 1939 World's Fair in New York. In the shadows, statues of island legends like Luis Muñoz Marín and famous *danza* composer Juan Morel Campos fix their eyes on eternity.

Painted a soothing blue and white, and with twin bell towers that blaze silver in the midday sun, the **Catedral Nuestra Señora de Guadalupe** (☎ 842-0134; admission free; ☻ 6am-1pm Mon-Fri; 6am-noon & 3-8pm Sat & Sun) is actually a newcomer to this site in the center of Plaza Las Delicias. Built in 1931, it stands in the place where colonists erected their first chapel in the 1660s, which (along with subsequent structures) succumbed to earthquakes and fires.

PARQUE DE BOMBAS

An Arabian-styled, red-and-black-striped building, **Parque de Bombas** (☎ 284-3338; admission free; ☻ 9:30am-5pm) stands back-to-back in the plaza with the cathedral and is the most photographed building in all of Puerto Rico.

Built as part of an agricultural exhibit that came to the city in 1882, the building later became the home of the city's volunteer firemen and functioned as a firehouse until 1990.

Now it has been restored as a museum to highlight the numerous fires that have plagued the city over the last century and the firefighters who struggled to contain the conflagrations.

MUSEO CASTILLO SERRALLÉS
If you are curious about the lifestyles of Puerto Rico's rich and famous, duck into the **Museo Castillo Serrallés** (Serrallés Castle Museum; ☎ 259-1770; 17 El Vigía; adult/senior/child US$3/2/1.50; ☻ 9:30am-5.30pm Tue-Sun). The Moorish-style castle's red-tile roof, turrets and verandas date to the 1930s, when the baron of the island's Don Q rum empire decided to build a monument to his wealth.

PASEO TABLADO LA GUANCHA
Ponce built this great half-mile (0.8km) boardwalk in the mid-1990s to overlook the town's yacht harbor and *club náutico*. Today there is a seaside concert pavilion with dozens of bars and restaurants, often great live salsa, an obligatory observation tower and a well-maintained public beach.

Sleeping
Fox Delicias Hotel (☎ 290-5050; www.foxdeliciashotel .com; 6963 Calle Isabel; r US$85-250; P ⓧ ⌨ ⌱) A glam and modern hotel, the Fox Delicias is a great favorite among sophisticated San-juaneros who like the fresh, bright colors, and three very sleek cocktail lounges spread throughout the hotel.

Hotel Meliá (☎ 842-0260, 800-44-UTELL; home.coqui .net/melia; 2 Calle Cristina; r US$85-120; P ⓧ ⌨ ⌱) Just east of the plaza, this historic hotel has 80 rooms on four floors. The carpet and walls may look a bit worn in some places (it is a century-old hotel), but beds are big and baths fully modernized.

Ponce Inn (☎ 841-1000; r US$85-95; ⓧ ⌨ ⌱ P) Situated on Hwy 1 on your way to the airport, this former Days Inn is a good place for a family. There's an on-site restaurant, laundry and a Jacuzzi, as well as Internet hook-up in each room.

Holiday Inn & Tropical Casino (☎ 844-1200; www .sixcontinentshotels.com; 3315 Ponce By Pass; r US$110-160; P ⓧ ⌨ ⌱) Holiday Inn sits on a hill west of town on Hwy 2. Attractions include a small casino and a pastoral setting with a good view of the mountains and the distant Caribbean. Pretty rooms, if a bit bland.

Ponce Hilton & Casino (☎ 259-7676; www.hilton .com; 1150 Av Caribe; r US$210-280; P ⓧ ⌨ ⌱) This 153-room Hilton is off Hwy 14, the road to the La Guancha boardwalk on the Caribbean, and offers the most deluxe accommodations in town.

Eating
Mark's at the Meliá (☎ 842-0260; Hotel Meliá, Calle Cristina; dinner mains US$14-26; ☻ dinner) One of Ponce's favorite spots for haute cuisine lies inside the Hotel Meliá (left). Mark's has been written up in every major foodie magazine on the island and is renowned for *comida criolla* dishes presented with French flair.

Lupita's Mexican Restaurante (☎ 848-8808; 60 Calle Isabel; dinner mains US$9-15; ☻ lunch & dinner) Big neon signs in the window attract an upbeat, local crowd full of fun. The food is plentiful, homemade and heavy on beans and rice. Burritos cover the plate entirely and fajitas arrive sizzling hot.

Café de Tomás (☎ 840-1965; Cnr Calles Isabel & Mayor; mains US$4-20; ☻ lunch & dinner) Also called Tompy's, Café de Tomás serves vegetarian dishes and salads, as well as all kinds of sandwiches. Many full meals cost less than US$7.

Rincón Argentino (☎ 284-1762; Calle Salud; mains US$10-22; ☻ dinner) The inside courtyard, dripping with soft lights and heavy palm fronds, has got to be one of the most romantic places in town. The mains are mostly steak and chicken dishes, with a few seafood and pasta creations. Live piano music on weekends. Good wine list.

La Ancla (☎ 840-2450; 9 Av Hostas Final; dishes US$13-27; ☻ dinner) Near the Ponce port, this restaurant has paella for two and a huge Sunday brunch that will leave you groaning at the table.

Getting There & Around
Four miles (6.4km) east of the town center off Hwy 1 on Hwy 5506 is the Aeropuerto de Mercedita (Mercedita Airport). **Cape Air** (☎ 848-2020) has five flights a day departing for San Juan.

The *público* terminal is on Calle Unión just a couple of blocks north of the plaza. You can get vans from here to all of the major towns on the south coast and the central mountains. There are also plenty of long-haul vans headed to Río Piedras in San Juan (about US$10) and Mayagüez (about US$8).

CAR
Avis (☎ 842-6184)
Dollar (☎ 843-6940)
Hertz (☎ 842-7377)

PUERTO RICO

TAXI
Cooperativa de Taxis (☎ 848-8248).
Ponce Taxi (☎ 642-3370)

TROLLEY
Ponce has free trolley buses and a fake train that runs on the roads. Check with the tourism office for schedules.

BOSQUE ESTATAL DE GUÁNICA

When you visit the Bosque Estatal de Guánica (Guánica State Forest, also known as Guánica Biosphere Reserve), make sure you stop by the **ranger station** (☎ 821-5706; admission free; ⌚ 9am-5pm) to pick up some maps before exploring this marvelous park. You can take a half-hour hike to a beach through three different kinds of forests, tramping the coast until you find a secluded cove for sunning, before hiking back to your car by a different trail. And all of this takes place in an area where birds, bullfrogs, the pale blue Caribbean and the sunshine make music together.

Since scientists estimate that only 1% of the earth's dry forest remains, the 9500-acre (3845-hectare) Bosque Estatal de Guánica is a rare sanctuary indeed. The forest's uneven rainfall and drainage patterns have created an unusual variety of habitats for more than 700 varieties of plants (48 in danger of extinction), which attract a large number of birds.

Some studies claim that at least 40 of the 111 species of birds found in Puerto Rico turn up in Guánica. Everyone agrees that Guánica is a preferred habitat for nine of the island's 14 endemic species, which include the Puerto Rican woodpecker, the Puerto Rican emerald hummingbird, the Puerto Rican lizard cuckoo and the Puerto Rican nightjar, which is one of the island's highly endangered species. With 36 miles (58km) of trails and over 10 miles (16km) of undeveloped Caribbean coastline, Guánica is a first-rate attraction to nature lovers.

To get here, follow Hwy 116 south toward Guánica from Hwy 2. Turn left (east) onto Hwy 334 and follow this road as it winds up a steep hill through an outlying barrio of Guánica. Eventually, the road penetrates the forest, and after cresting the hills it ends at the ranger station, a picnic area and scenic overlook of the forest and the Caribbean to the south. The southern extent of the eastern

section of the forest – including Bahía de la Ballena (Whale Bay) and the ferry to Gilligan's Island – is also accessible by Hwy 333, to the south of Guánica.

LA PARGUERA

A salty, sleepy fishing town by day, La Parguera is a favorite nightlife hangout for vacationing Puerto Ricans at night. The people who fall in love with this village have discovered that once you launch into this watery world on a kayak, sailboard, small outboard or dive boat, La Parguera becomes a maze of mangrove canals, bays and islands. Five miles (8km) offshore you can find some of the best diving in Puerto Rico at the 'Wall' (see the boxed text, p339).

Once you pass through the depressing towns on the approach, you'll see signs heralding freshly painted guesthouses, *paradores* and restaurants. Dive and windsurfing shops dot the short main street; boat docks jut south into watery canals lined with mangroves. Several vacation condo developments spread across the upland fields beneath a tall steep hill.

Activities

Paradise Scuba Center (☎ 899-7611; paradisescubapuertorico@hotmail.com; Rte 304) will take you offshore to Cayo Enrique or Cayo Laurel on a four-hour snorkeling excursion (US$45) that includes drinks and snacks. For US$65, you can take a sunset snorkeling trip that includes swimming after dark in Bahía Fosforescente. Many scuba fanatics use this dive service to dive at places like the Wall and Trench Alley to see big morays, barracuda and sea turtles. A two-tank dive at the Wall is US$85; a night dive is US$60. You can rent snorkeling gear for US$15 a day.

Parguera Divers (☎ 899-4171; www.pargueradivers.com; near Parador Posada Porlamar) does regular trips to the Wall, two-tank dives (US$80) and one-tank dives (US$45) offered, plus US$15 for equipment rental. Open-water certification courses available too.

Sleeping

Parador Posada Porlamar (☎ 899-4015; posada@caribe.net; Hwy 304; r US$65-110) A number of charter boats work out of the Posada's private dock and it's a great hangout for divers and fishers. There's a good restaurant on site, and children are welcome.

Parador Villa Parguera (☎ 899-7777; www.elshop .com; Hwy 304; r US$80-90) On the main street across from the church, this two-story hotel with 63 units comes closest to luxury accommodation in town with its waterfront dock, private balconies, harbor views, landscaped seaside grounds and large swimming pool. There is also a gourmet restaurant and nightclub.

Andino's Chalet and Guesthouse (☎ 899-0000; 133 Calle 8; r from US$45, apt US$125) About two blocks east of the center of town, you are some distance from the water here, but you do get a breezy terrace and private bath in contemporary facilities.

Eating

La Casita (☎ 899-1681; Rte 304; mains US$10-22; ☺ lunch & dinner Tue-Thu) A happy-go-lucky family establishment that is a big hit with the locals. Lots of seafood dishes and big lobster plates for under US$25.

La Parguera Steakhouse (☎ 899-3400; Hwy 304; mains US$15-19) Just up the road from La Casita, this steakhouse is a good bet for *churrasco* (US$14).

Guajataco (☎ 808-0303; Rte 304) A snazzy little open-air Mexican joint on your left as you go downhill into town, Guajataco's serves snack-sized *empanadillas* and tacos.

Getting There & Around

Públicos come and go irregularly from a stop near the small waterfront park and boat piers in the center of the village. Service is basically local to nearby towns such as Lajas (US$1), where you can move on to bigger and better van-stands in bigger and better municipalities.

The fastest drive here is Hwy 2 via Hwy 116 from Guánica. Follow the signs for the last couple of miles on Hwy 304.

RINCÓN
pop 15,000

What's not to love about Rincón? There's great surfing, diving and whale-watching opportunities around Isla Desecheo, a small island 13 miles (21km) offshore, not to mention a wonderfully laid-back barefoot ambience, no traffic, eclectic *paradores* and tempting bakeries, all set in an area full of green mountains and cow pastures pushing up against the Caribbean.

The opportunities for first-rate snorkeling, diving and surfing are endless and there are a good number of very dependable and skilled operators in Rincón who are as interested in protecting natural resources as they are in making a buck. This is a combination not always seen in ecotourism-dependent locations. Once Rincón works its surfer magic on your heart, it's very hard to leave.

Activities
DIVING & SNORKELING

Greg Carson's **Taíno Divers** (☎ 823-6429) is at the little marina west of the center of town, near the Black Eagle restaurant. The shop rents out snorkeling gear for about US$15 a day and also offers diving adventures off Desecheo, sunset cruises, whale-watching, kayaking and more. Two-tank dives are about US$95. Snorkelers head for Steps beach in calm conditions. Steps lies off Hwy 413, just north of town.

ALL THAT GLITTERS IS NOT GOLD

Puerto Rico is blessed with three bioluminescent bays filled with tiny organisms that give off an eerie glow to warn away predators. Bringing tourists through these bays at night is big business, but there's a problem: pollution. Engine oils kill the organisms, and so does bug spray with DEET (don't use it).

To avoid damaging these endangered bays, only book tours with operators who use kayaks or electric motors. **Golden Heron Kayaks** (☎ 615-1625; www.golden-heron.com; US$50-95) on Vieques has the best bay of the three.

Yokahú Kayaks (☎ 604-7375, 863-5374) covers the Fajardo bay, which is the second-best option.

Sadly, in La Parguera, home to the third bay, most tour operators only use motorized engines. The bioluminescence has been greatly reduced as a consequence. If you're offered a ride, check that it will be in a boat that's safe for the environment. If not, turn the operator down, and make sure to tell them why you are saying no.

SURFING

Hot Wavz Surf Shop (☎ 823-3942) is on the lighthouse road and can hook you up with whatever you need, or rent you a surfboard to fit conditions for US$20 to US$25; boogie boards run about US$15.

Sleeping & Eating

Lazy Parrot Inn (☎ 823-5654; www.lazyparrot.com; Hwy 413; r US$85-135; ⓟ ✕ ⓦ) This pretty inn sits on the ridge above the north-facing beaches, next to the bakery/deli (parking across the street on the hill). Harmonious grounds, with a bar overlooking a Jacuzzi and pool, and an on-site restaurant that serves delicious seafood.

Casa Verde Guesthouse (☎ 605-5351; www.find -paradise.com; Hwy 413, Beach Rd; apt US$60; ⓟ ✕) A surfer-friendly guesthouse with super-modern accommodations – one-, two- and three-bedroom choices are available.

Sandy Beach Inn (☎ 823-1146; r US$60-90, apt US$115) Luli and 'surf dog' Lenny Intreglia have been running 'SBI' for over 15 years, and they get lots of repeat guests, both surfers and landlubbers. The three-story hillside operation offers terrific views from the popular rooftop bar and restaurant.

Amirage Apartments (☎ 823-6454; www.procean front.com; Rte 429, ste US$125; ⓟ ✕ ⓛ ⓦ) Besides the private balcony in your room, you'll have access to a Jacuzzi in a shady courtyard, free snorkel and kayak equipment and your own private kitchen (with dishwasher!)

Rincón of the Seas (☎ 823-6189; www.rinconofthe seas.com; Hwy 115; r US$180-495) A very glamorous option right on the beach, this big hotel has fabulously decorated art-deco suites. Staff are more than willing to hook you up with snorkeling and scuba diving trips.

Rock Bottom Bar & Grill (☎ 605-5351; Hwy 413, Beach Rd) An upbeat and popular place right next to Casa Verde Guesthouse, Rock Bottom has good food and even better late-night music and fun.

Getting There & Around

Rincón doesn't have an airport, but there are two in the area: Mayagüez and Aguadilla.

The *público* stand is situated just off the town plaza on Calle Nueva. Expect to pay about US$4 if you are headed north to Aguadilla or US$1.50 to go south to Mayagüez (you can access San Juan from either of these cities).

The easiest way to approach the town is via the valley roads of Hwy 402 and Hwy 115, both of which intersect Hwy 2 south of the Rincón peninsula.

You will pay US$20 or more for a taxi from either the Aguadilla or Mayagüez airport, and you definitely need a car to move around to the various attractions in Rincón. There are rental-car sites at both the Mayagüez or Aguadilla airports.

DIRECTORY

ACCOMMODATIONS

There are no youth hostels in Puerto Rico, and very few dorm room–style accommodations near local universities. Most options are guesthouses (like B&Bs), inns, hotels and *paradores* (midrange to high-end hotels that get regular surprise visits from the tourism board). Vacation rentals are a good idea for long-term guests or big groups. Most hotels rates are for a room, where you specify what type of bed you want (double versus twin). If you have more than two to a room you'll be charged more, but solo travelers are mostly not given any price break.

ACTIVITIES

Puerto Rico's tropical climate and variety of land/seascapes make the island a mecca for outdoor activities.

The semiprotected waters off the east end of Puerto Rico, which include the islands of Culebra and Vieques, provide the setting for racing and cruising aboard sailboats. You can count on the trade winds blowing 12 to 25 knots out of the east almost every day. A number of marinas meet sailors' needs in the Fajardo area. The largest is the **Puerto del Rey Marina** (☎ 860-1000), with 750 slips and room for vessels up to 200ft (79m) long.

Among both tourists and islanders, the most popular hiking area in Puerto Rico is the national rainforest at El Yunque (p328). All the commonwealth's *reservas forestales* offer good hikes, as does the dry forest in Guánica (p336).

EMERGENCY NUMBERS

Ambulance, fire & police (☎ 911)

PRACTICALITIES

- **Newspapers & Magazines** *San Juan Star* (www.sanjuanstar.com) is a bilingual daily newspaper and *Puerto Rico Breeze* is a biweekly paper on gay nightlife in San Juan. *Que Pasa!* is a bimonthly magazine published by the PR Tourism Office.

- **Radio & TV** US TV is broadcast across the island. The English-language radio station is WOSO San Juan, at 1030AM. Elsewhere, radio is mostly in Spanish.

- **Video Systems** Puerto Rico uses VHS for videos.

- **Electricity** Puerto Rico has the 110 volt AC system used in the USA.

- **Weights & Measures** Puerto Rico follows the US system with two exceptions: all distances you see on road signs are in kilometers and gas is pumped in liters.

Since the 1968 world surfing championships at Rincón, surfers the world over have known that Puerto Rico ranks with a few sites in Mexico and Costa Rica as some of the biggest and best winter surfing in all of the Americas. If you stay close to San Juan, you will find the surfers' scene at the beaches eastward from Isla Verde. But for the big stuff, you need to make a pilgrimage west to Rincón and Isabela, which host numerous important competitions each year.

Puerto Rico played host to the Ray Ban Windsurfing World Cup in 1989, and the sport has been booming here ever since. Hotdoggers head for the surfing beaches at Isla Verde or, better yet, the rough northwest coast.

BOOKS

Stories from Puerto Rico/Historias de Puerto Rico (Passport Books 1999) contains island folk tales in English and Spanish; very good reading and lots of information.

Puerto Rico Mio: Four Decades of Change (Smithsonian Institute Press, 1990) by Jack Delano. This acclaimed book offers insightful and moving glimpses into Borinquen life by a photographer who has been shooting Puerto Rico since 1941.

CHILDREN

Puerto Ricans love children – it doesn't matter who they belong to – and even more, they love family. So traveling with youngsters is rarely a hassle. There are some hotels that won't take children under a certain age but it's very rare. Several museums and hotels offer child rates or discounts – don't be afraid to ask. If renting a car, make sure that the rental agency has a car seat for you and if taking a taxi any long distance, bring one with you. Children should carry some form of ID in case of an emergency.

DISABLED TRAVELERS

Puerto Rico is surprisingly compliant with the *American Disabilities Act*. Most modern hotels have at least one room set up for special needs clients. All the ferries to Culebra and Vieques are wheelchair-accessible and Playa Luquillo has a wheelchair-accessible stretch of sand.

EMBASSIES & CONSULATES

Puerto Rico is represented by US diplomatic offices abroad; see p370 for a list of some offices.

EMBASSIES & CONSULATES IN PUERTO RICO

The following official buildings are located in San Juan.

Austria (☎ 766-0799; Plaza Las Américas, Río Piedras)
Canada (☎ 790-2210; 107 Calle Cereipo Alturas, Guaynabo)
Netherlands (☎ 759-9400; Mercantil Plaza, Hato Rey)
Mexico (☎ 764-0258; Bankers Finance, Hato Rey)
Spain (☎ 758-6090; Mercantil Plaza, Hato Rey)
UK (☎ 727-1065; 1509 Calle Lopez Landron, Santurce)
Venezuela (☎ 766-4255; Merantil Plaza, Hato Rey)

UNDER THE SEA

Great dives for every ability level:
Vieques Anchor Reef and Patti's Reef (novice), Blue Reef (intermediate)
Culebra Cayo Ratón and Whale Rock (intermediate), Sail Rock (multi-level)
Fajardo Cayo Lobos, Spurs, Palomenitos (novice and intermediate)
La Parguera The Wall (expert) is said to be the *ne plus ultra* of diving sites
Rincón Desecheo Island (all levels) is on par with the Red Sea and Great Barrier Reef

FESTIVALS & EVENTS

Carnaval, Ponce (February) Laid-back Ponce gets pretty wild during this week, in the six days preceding the beginning of Catholic Lent, with *vejigante* masks (colorful paper maché masks depicting often-scary characters from African and European mythology) and costumes overflowing in the streets

Coffee Harvest Festival, Maricao (mid-February) A celebration of Maricao's principal product, with lots of caffeine-fueled dancing.

Cinco Días con Nuestro Tierra (second week in March) Held in Mayagüez, this is one of the island's agricultural/industrial fairs, featuring local produce.

Festival de Mavi, Juana Diaz (April) Mavi, or *mabi* in Spanish, is a fermented drink invented by Tainos that uses local bark as its primary ingredient. This festival is as much about honoring Taino heritage as it is about drinking mavi.

Fiesta Nacional de la Danza, Ponce (mid-May) This is a perfect opportunity to learn about the old-fashioned *danzas* that were practiced during colonial times.

Festival Casals, San Juan Internationally renowned, the Casals festival brings musicians from around the world to remember Pablo Casals, who lived most of his adult life in Puerto Rico.

Fiesta de San Juan Bautista Day, San Juan (June 24) A big, national party that ends with walking backwards into the ocean for a midnight dip.

Fiesta de Santiago Apostal, Loíza Aldea (end of July) The place to come for an African-influenced party. This is a fiesta worthy of Bahía in Brazil – parades, fabulous drum ensembles, *vejigante* masks and costumes revive saints, such as Santiago, who according to the traditions of Santería are incarnations of West African gods.

Hatillo Masks Festival, Hatillo (December 28) The island's third major festival of masks. Features masked devils prowling the streets as incarnations of the agents of King Herod, who sent his soldiers into the streets of Judea to find and kill the Christ child. Kids think it is great fun to run and hide from the maskers.

HOLIDAYS

New Year's Day January 1
Three Kings Day (Feast of the Epiphany) January 6
Eugenio María de Hostos' Birthday January 10; honors the island educator, writer and patriot.
Martin Luther King Jr Day 3rd Monday in January
Presidents' Day 3rd Monday in February
Emancipation Day March 22; island slaves were freed on this date in 1873
Palm Sunday Sunday before Easter
Good Friday Friday before Easter
Easter Sunday in late March/April
Jose de Diego Day April 18
Memorial Day last Monday in May

Independence Day/Fourth of July July 4
Luis Muñoz Rivera's Birthday July 18; honors the island patriot and political leader
Constitution Day July 25
Jose Celso Barbosa's Birthday July 27
Labor Day first Monday in September
Columbus Day 2nd Monday in October
Veterans' Day November 11
Thanksgiving Day fourth Thursday in November
Christmas Day December 25

MONEY

Puerto Rico uses US currency. ATMs are called ATHs in Puerto Rico (for *a todos horas* – at all hours) and are common in most shopping areas and even in many small-town banks.

TELEPHONE

The Puerto Rican area code is ☎ 787. To call from North America, dial ☎ 1-787 + the seven-digit local number. From elsewhere, dial your country's international access code followed by ☎ 787 + the local number. To call within Puerto Rico, just dial the local number. We have included only the seven-digit local number for Puerto Rico listings in this chapter.

VISAS

US residents don't need visas to enter Puerto Rico; however if they are planning to work or study they should check on the latest regulations with their embassy. Canadians don't need visas for stays of up to 180 days, as long as they aren't working or studying during that period. Citizens of most European countries, Australia and New Zealand can waive visas through the Visa Waiver program. All non-US and Canadian travelers planning to stay for longer than 90 days need a visa: contact the closest US embassy and be prepared to pay US$100.

TRANSPORTATION

GETTING THERE & AWAY
Entering Puerto Rico

US nationals need proof of citizenship (such as a driver's licence with photo ID) to enter Puerto Rico, but should be aware that if they're traveling to another country in the Caribbean (other than the US Virgin Islands, which, like Puerto Rico, is a US territory), they must have a valid passport in order to re-enter the US (see the boxed text, p772). Visitors from other countries must have a valid passport to enter Puerto Rico.

Air

Aeropuerto Internacional de Luis Muñoz Marín
(SJU; ☎ 749-5050) – commonly shortened to LMM – in San Juan, is a major Caribbean hub. Chances are that you will be arriving and departing from the airport in San Juan, but Aguadilla's **Aeropuerto Rafael Hernández** (BQN; ☎ 891-2286), at the former Base Ramey on the island's northwest tip, has some scheduled international flights. Ponce and Mayagüez each has a small airport for domestic flights. San Juan's original airport at Isla Grande, on the Bahía de San Juan in the Miramar district, services private aircraft and the bulk of the commuter flights to the Puerto Rican islands of Culebra and Vieques.

For information on international flights to Puerto Rico, see p776. The following airlines fly to/from Puerto Rico from within the Caribbean:

Air Flamenco (☎ 724-1105; www.airflamenco.net; hub Culebra)
Air Jamaica (☎ 800-523-5585; www.airjamaica.com; hub Kingston)
Air St Thomas (☎ 800-522-3084; www.airstthomas .com; hub St Thomas)
Air Sunshine (☎ 888-879-8900; www.airsunshine.com; hub San Juan)
American Eagle (☎ 800-433-7300; www.aa.com; hub Chicago, USA)
Cape Air (☎ 800-352-0714; www.flycapeair.com; hub San Juan)
Caribbean Sun (☎ 866-864-6272; www.flycsa.com; hub San Juan)
COPA (☎ 722-6969; www.copaair.com; hub San Juan)
Isla Nena Air Service (☎ 741-6362; www .islanena.8m.com; hub Fajardo)
LIAT (☎ 800-468-0482; www.liatairline.com; hub St Kitts)
Vieques Air Link (☎ 888-901-9247; www.vieques -island.com/val; hub San Juan)
Seaborne Airlines (☎ 888-359-8687; www.sea borneairlines.com; hub St Thomas)

Sea
CRUISE SHIP
San Juan is the second-largest port for cruise ships in the western hemisphere (after Miami). More than 24 vessels call San Juan their home port or departure port, and every year new cruise ships either originate sailings from San Juan or make San Juan a port of call. The ships dock at the piers along Calle La Marina, which are just a short walk from the cobblestone streets of Old San Juan.

FERRY
Transportation Services Virgin Islands (☎ 863-0582; www.caribecay.com) runs a high-speed passenger ferry from Fajardo to St Thomas, US Virgin Islands.

For a true seafaring adventure, consider the ocean-going ferry between Mayagüez and Santo Domingo, Dominican Republic (see p307 for details).

GETTING AROUND
Air
Perhaps because Puerto Rico is a relatively small island, or perhaps because it has such a 'car culture,' the commonwealth's domestic air transportation system is rather basic. The bulk of Puerto Rico's domestic air traffic links San Juan to the offshore islands of Culebra and Vieques. Fares to Vieques are one way/round-trip $45/90; fares to Culebra are about $50/90. You can also fly between San Juan, Ponce, Aguadilla and Mayagüez.
Air Flamenco (☎ 724-6464; www.airflamenco.net) Flies from San Juan to Culebra and Vieques.
American Eagle (☎ 800-433-7300; www.aa.com; hub Chicago, USA) Flies from San Juan to Mayagüez and Aguadilla.
Cape Air (☎ 800-352-0714; www.flycapeair.com; hub San Juan) Flies from San Juan to Aguadilla, Mayagüez, Ponce and Vieques.
Isla Nena Air Service (☎ 742-0972; www .islanena.8m.com; hub Fajardo) Flies from San Juan and Fajardo to Culebra and Vieques.
M&N Aviation (☎ 722-5980) Offers sightseeing trips and charter flights to destinations around Puerto Rico.
Vieques Air Link (San Juan–Vieques ☎ 888-901-9247, San Juan–Culebra ☎ 722-3736; www.viequesisland .com/val) Flies from San Juan to Culebra and Vieques.

Boat
The **Puerto Rican Port Authority Office** (☎ 800-981-2005, 863-0705) handles the solid and safe ferry service from Fajardo to Vieques and Culebra. Reservations are required to take a car on a transport ferry (a bit of a hassle). Passenger ferries run more frequently. Roundtrip is US$4. Schedules:

Fajardo–Culebra Passenger Ferry (9:30am & 3pm Mon-Fri, 9am, 2:30pm & 6:30pm Sat & Sun) Schedule varies on holidays.
Fajardo–Culebra Cargo Ferry (3:30am, 4pm & 6pm Mon-Fri, also 10am Wed & Fri)
Fajardo–Vieques Passenger Ferry (9:30am, 1pm & 4:30pm Mon-Fri, 9am, 3pm & 6pm Sat & Sun & holidays)
Fajardo–Vieques Cargo Ferry (4am & 1:30pm & 6pm Mon-Fri)

A ferry runs from Vieques to Culebra, leaving from Isabella Segunda at 6am Monday to Friday. A ferry sometimes runs from Culebra to Vieques at 5pm Monday to Friday, but check in advance.

Bus

Públicos – large vans that pick up and drop off passengers with great frequency and little haste – run between a few of the major cities, but it's a very slow (although cheap) way to travel. You'd better have a lot of time if you choose this method of transportation.

Car

A car is definitely the easiest way to get around the island and costs about $45 to US$65 per day, depending on availability. Several good highways now link San Juan to just about every other major point with a drive of less than two hours. Scooters are available for rent on Culebra and Vieques (about US$40 per day) – they are not safe to ride on any major roads.

If you rent a car, take all the insurance options, unless you already have good coverage on your credit card. Be aware that if you rent a car and then take it on the ferry to Vieques or Culebra (not an easy feat to get a reservation, by the way) the rental agency will not cover any damage. In fact, they will tell you it's against their policy to take the cars to the islands. Nobody will stop you if you take the chance, but if you have an accident, no tow truck's coming to get you. You'll be liable for the whole auto.

DRIVING LICENSE
A valid driver's license issued from your country of residence is all that's needed to rent a car.

FUEL & SPARE PARTS
Garages and gas stations are few and far between in Puerto Rico. It's a good idea to carry extra fuel in the trunk if you are doing heavy driving. Be aware that gas is sold in liters on the island.

ROAD RULES
Basically, there are none. Watch your back, don't tailgate, and ignore the general craziness of local drivers. Drive on the right-hand side of the road. On major highways, using a turn signal to indicate a lane change seems to amuse drivers – if you give them advance warning of where you're going, it just makes it easier for them to cut you off.

US Virgin Islands

When Christopher Columbus named this archipelago 'the Virgins,' he saw pristine islands with protected bays, verdant hillsides bursting with tropical flora and shoals of fat fish living on the offshore reefs. Even today, visitors hold their breath for a moment upon first glimpsing these emerald isles. The island of St John boasts 9500 acres (3845 hectares) of parkland with unblemished forests and sublime beaches, plus the town of Cruz Bay, where hippies and Rasta men intermingle with snowbirds (North Americans who come to the Virgin Islands for the warm winters) and archeologists. St Croix, the 'big stepsister' whose location 40 miles (64km) south makes her geographically and psychologically isolated, features fertile land where Danish colonialism flourished.

Most people arrive on St Thomas, however, where the pressures of time, growth and economics have shot an arrow into the island's heart. Almost 60,000 people live on this island, just 12 miles (19km) long. Duty- and tax-free shopping bring mass tourism and dizzying cruise-ship traffic to the port town of Charlotte Amalie. Islanders now realize that they need to protect their island, but only time will tell whether the need for preservation outweighs the lure of the almighty dollar. Regardless, beyond the busy shopping districts, the island's spectacular beaches beckon and the rhythms of reggae or calypso swirl through the air.

FAST FACTS

- **Area** 136 sq miles (352 sq km)
- **Capital** Charlotte Amalie, St Thomas
- **Country code** ☎ 340
- **Departure tax** None
- **Famous for** Duty-free shopping in St Thomas, Cruzan rum
- **Language** English
- **Money** US dollar; US$1 = €0.82, = UK£0.55
- **People** US Virgin Islanders
- **Phrases** Night bring day, mon (Out of the gloom comes brightness); Wind at your back, mon (a parting comment that means, literally, 'I hope the wind stays at your back,' ie I hope you have an easy day).
- **Population** 110,026
- **Visa** Unnecessary for most countries (see p371)

US VIRGIN ISLANDS

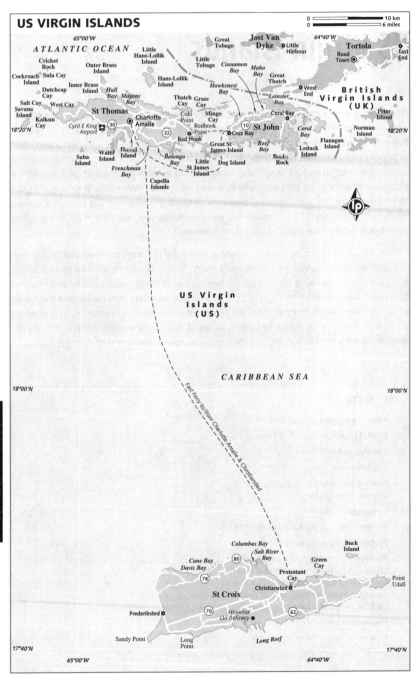

HIGHLIGHTS

- **Buck Island** (p366) Take a catamaran trip around this marine sanctuary.
- **Coral World** (p355) Get close and personal with sharks, barracudas and manta rays.
- **Getting wet** (p360 and p364) Grab a snorkel and submerge yourself in the crystal-clear waters of St John's protected bays or scuba dive along the coral-encrusted wall at St Croix's Cane Bay.
- **Charlotte Amalie** (p355) Shop your tax-free, duty-free heart out while touring St Thomas' historic main town.
- **Off the beaten track** (p358) Encounter wild pigs, donkeys and goats while hiking along one of 22 trails in St John's Virgin Islands National Park.

ITINERARIES

- **One Week** Spend a couple of days shopping and eating in Charlotte Amalie, then head over to St John for a few days of hiking and snorkeling.
- **Two Weeks** Do it all: after a couple of days in Charlotte Amalie, stay at one of St Thomas' north-coast resorts for a week. Dive to your heart's content on St Croix, then ferry over to St John for another week.

CLIMATE & WHEN TO GO

The weather is reliably balmy with daily highs ranging between 77°F (25°C) in winter and 82°F (28°C) in summer. Easterly trade winds keep the humidity lower than on most other Caribbean islands. Rain usually comes in brief tropical showers. The wettest months are July to October, making the winter months the most reliable for good weather. Those willing to risk a little rain will find much better hotel deals in the off and shoulder seasons (spring and fall).

HISTORY
Early History

Archeologists date the Virgin Islands' habitation back to about 2000 BC, when Pre-Ceramic Siboneys, possibly nomads from North America, moved southward to the Virgin Islands. They were followed by Taino Indians, who were later wiped out by Caribs – master mariners and ruthless warriors – who wiped out Taino settlements.

On Christopher Columbus' second trip to the Caribbean in 1493, he christened

---

HOW MUCH?

- Taxi from St Thomas' airport to Charlotte Amalie US$6
- Bottle of Cruzan rum US$7
- Snorkel gear rental US$7-10/day
- Passenger ferry from St Thomas to St John US$7 (one way)
- Seaplane flight from St Thomas to St Croix US$92 (round-trip)

LONELY PLANET INDEX

- Gallon (imperial) of gas US$2.48
- Liter of bottled water US$2
- Bottle of Carib beer US$4
- Souvenir T-shirt US$10
- Street snack: fresh fruit smoothie US$5

---

these isles Santa Ursula y Las Once Mil Vírgenes in honor of a 4th-century princess and her 11,000 maidens.

The islands remained under Spanish control until the English defeated the Spanish Armada in 1588. England, France and Holland were quick to issue 'letters of marque,' which allowed 'privateers' the rights to claim territory and protect those claims.

One king's privateer became every other king's pirate. Blackbeard (Edward Teach) operated in the Virgin Islands before 1720, with a collection of other rascals including Henry Morgan, and Calico Jack Rackham with Anne Bonny and Mary Read, his female partners in plunder.

The Danes and English bickered over the islands steadily, while building vast sugar and tobacco plantations. The English held colonies on islands east of St John, while the Danes held St Thomas to the west. St John remained disputed territory. Finally, in 1717 the Danes sent a small but determined band of soldiers to St John and drove the British out. The Narrows between St John and Tortola in the British Virgin Islands (BVI) became the border that has divided the eastern (Danish, now US) Virgins from the British Virgins for more than 250 years.

US VIRGIN ISLANDS

Slavery & Liberation

The West Indies grew rich producing sugar and cotton for Europe. In pursuit of profits, the Danish West India and Guinea Company declared St Thomas a free port in 1724, and purchased St Croix from the French in 1733. By the end of the century, the number of African slaves exceeded 40,000.

Harsh living conditions and oppressive laws drove slaves to revolt. Meanwhile, sugar production in Europe and American tariffs on foreign sugar cut into the islands' profits. The deteriorating economy put everyone in a foul mood. Something had to give and it finally did in 1848, when Blacks on St Croix forced the legal end to slavery.

Blacks remained in economic bondage. Life in the islands was dismal. Average wages for field workers were less than 15¢ a day. A series of labor revolts left the plantation infrastructure in ruins.

Meanwhile, the US, realizing the strategic value of the islands, negotiated with Denmark to buy the Danish-controlled Virgins. The deal was almost done in 1867, but the US Congress rejected the idea of paying US$7.5 million (more than it had paid for Alaska).

As WWI began in Europe, the US grew concerned that German armies might invade Denmark and claim the Danish West Indies. Finally, the US paid the Danes US$25 million in gold, making the purchase of St Thomas, St Croix, St John and their satellites the most expensive US government land purchase, at US$290 per acre.

In 1917, the US Navy took control of the islands, bringing draconian rule, racism and gangs of misbehaving sailors. The US tried to enforce Prohibition here, a hilarious concept for an economy tied to the production, sale and distribution of rum. In 1931, President Herbert Hoover traveled to the Virgins, stayed for less than six hours and made a speech in which he declared, 'It was unfortunate that we ever acquired these islands.'

In 1934, however, President Franklin Delano Roosevelt visited and saw the potential that Hoover had missed. Soon, the US instituted programs to eradicate disease, drain swamps, build roads, improve education and create tourism infrastructure.

In 1936, the US Congress passed the Organic Act, which guaranteed US citizenship to all citizens in the US Virgin Islands (USVI). When Cuba's doors closed to American tourists in 1959, the Virgin Islands welcomed the rush of sun-seekers. Cruise ships made St Thomas their featured stop, and yachties discovered the superb sailing.

The islands have endured more than their share of political corruption scandals – nepotism, cronyism and bribery have long been a way of life. The past four decades have brought unprecedented growth in tourism, and with it a mushrooming population and associated crime.

THE CULTURE
The National Psyche

The USVI are an unincorporated territory of the USA, and the islands participate in the US democracy by sending an elected, nonvoting representative to the US House of Representatives. All citizens of the USVI are US citizens, but they cannot vote in presidential elections. While most islanders enjoy the benefits of 'being American,' they are heartily happy to not deal with the politics and often frenzied pace of American life.

Though the USVI wear a veneer of mainstream American culture, with conveniences like shopping malls and fast food, West African culture is a strong presence. On these islands, everyone has arrived trailing a culture from somewhere else and there is a real respect for differences.

Population

Since 1970, the USVI's population has quadrupled, although current growth appears to have plateaued. Economic opportunities draw immigrants from other parts of the West Indies, along with 'continentals' (US mainlanders), who come to escape the politics and busyness of American life, or retire in the sun.

Blacks outnumber Whites by more than four to one. The descendants of former slaves, Blacks now dominate the political and professional arenas on the islands.

ARTS
Music

The USVI have a rich musical heritage, with influences of colonists from England, Ireland, Spain, France, Denmark and Holland.

Reggae and calypso tunes blast from vehicles and emanate from shops, restaurants and beach bars. *Quelbe* and *fungi* (*foon*-ghee, also an island food made of cornmeal and fish) are two types of folk music. *Quelbe* is a blend of jigs, quadrilles, military fife and African drum music, with *cariso* lyrics (often biting satire) from slave field songs. *Fungi* uses homemade percussion like washboards, ribbed gourds and conch shells to accompany a singer. The best time to experience island music is during the 'jump up' parades and competitions associated with major festivals like Carnival on St Thomas and St John, or at St Croix's Cruzan Christmas Fiesta (see p370).

Architecture

Charlotte Amalie and Christiansted showcase traditional West Indian architecture, a loose adaptation of late-18th-century English-Georgian (neoclassical) style. Construction used a mix of ship-ballast brick, 'rubble' (a blend of coral, molasses and straw) and wood.

Literature

The University of the Virgin Islands sponsors the journal *The Caribbean Writer,* which offers a compendium of poems and short fiction by major Caribbean writers.

Painting

The most celebrated painter to come from the USVI is Camille Pissarro. Born in St Thomas in 1830 as Jacob Pizarro, the son of Spanish Jews, young Jacob grew up on Main St in Charlotte Amalie. Eventually, he became an accomplished painter, moved to Paris and changed his name. Pieces of the painter's work are on display at the Camille Pissarro Gallery (p355) and at Government House (p351), both in Charlotte Amalie.

ENVIRONMENT
The Land

The USVI archipelago consists of about 50 islands, 1100 miles (1770km) southeast of Miami and 40 miles (64km) east of Puerto Rico. They are the northernmost islands in the Lesser Antilles chain and, along with the BVI, form an irregular string of islands stretching west to east. The one exception to this string is the USVI's largest island, St Croix, which lies about 40 miles (64km) south.

St Thomas is the second-largest island. St John is east of St Thomas, the last of the USVI before the chain becomes the BVI.

As with almost all of the islands ringing the Caribbean Basin, the USVI owe their existence to a series of volcanic events that built up layers of lava and igneous rock, creating islands with three geographical zones: the coastal plain, the coastal dry forests and the central mountains. Except for St Croix, the coastal plain is a narrow fringe, with a ridge of high mountains dominating their interiors.

The mountain slopes are dense subtropical forests. All of the timber is second or third growth; the islands were stripped for sugar, cotton and tobacco plantations in the colonial era. There are no rivers and very few freshwater streams. Coral reefs of all varieties thrive in the shallow waters near the seashores. The shores host a few pockets of mangrove swamps, including Salt River Bay on St Croix.

Wildlife

Very few of the land mammals that make their home in the Virgin Islands are natives; most mammal species have been accidentally or intentionally introduced to the island over the centuries. Virtually every island has a feral population of goats and burros, and some islands have wild pigs, white-tailed deer, cattle, horses, cats and dogs. Other prevalent land mammals include mongooses and bats.

The islands are home to a few species of snake (none of which are poisonous), including the Virgin Island tree boa.

More than 200 bird species – including the official bird, the bananaquit – inhabit the islands. One of the joys of winter beachcombing is watching the aerial acrobatics of brown pelicans as they hunt for fish.

Environmental Issues

The USVI have long suffered from serious environmental problems, including deforestation, soil erosion, mangrove destruction and a lack of freshwater. During the 18th century, logging operations denuded many of the islands to make room for plantations, subsequently eroding untold acres of topsoil. The demise of the agricultural economy in the late 19th century allowed the islands to reforest, and in recent years the island governments have set aside forest land and began work on a series of forest conservation projects.

US VIRGIN ISLANDS

But population growth and rapid urbanization continue to pose the greatest threats. If not for the desalination plants (which make freshwater out of seawater) the islands couldn't support even a quarter of their population, let alone visitors. When a hurricane strikes, power and diesel facilities shut down. Islanders with enough foresight and money keep rainwater cisterns for such emergencies, but folks without suffer.

While islanders still have a long way to go toward undoing generations of environmental damage and preserving their natural resources, the past decade has seen an increase in the level of awareness, resources and action dedicated to conservation efforts.

The following agencies are working toward environmental preservation:

Bureau of Environmental Enforcement
(☎ 774-3320)
Friends of the Virgin Islands National Park
(☎ 779-4940)
National Marine Fisheries Law Enforcement Division (☎ 774-5226)

FOOD & DRINK
Food
Soup and stew are staples in West Indian cooking. Many soups use ground provisions (roots) and fruits to add texture, taste and vitamins. *Dasheen* (taro root) tastes like potato. Its green leaves are a primary ingredient in the islands' famous callaloo soup (see the boxed text, right).

Pate (*paw*-tay) is the islands' most popular finger food. It is a fried pastry of cassava (yucca) or plantain dough stuffed with spiced goat, pork, chicken, conch, lobster or fish. Another popular dish is roti, flatbread envelopes stuffed with curried meat, fish or poultry. Island cooks often serve *fungi*, which is made from cornmeal, with fish and gravy.

Meat dishes are primarily curried or barbecued with tangy spices. *Daube* meat is pot roast spiced with vinegar and native seasonings. *Souse* is another spicy one-pot dish made from boiled pigs' feet with a sauce of limes and hot pepper.

Fish and shellfish are common, and cooks will bake, grill, stew or boil whatever is the daily catch. Conch (pronounced 'conk') is often fried into crispy fritters. Be aware that overfishing of conch has meant it is heading for the endangered species list.

THE SECRET OF CALLALOO

Thick green callaloo soup is legendary among West Indian cooks, who protect their own secret ingredients. Here is a recipe gathered during conversations with several St Thomas matriarchs:

- one small salted turkey
- 1½lb (680g) of red snapper
- meat of two crabs
- 3lb (1.36kg) of spinach or dasheen leaves
- 12 okra
- one large onion
- one clove of garlic
- one sprig each of thyme and parsley
- several pieces of hot pepper
- one stalk of celery
- two tablespoons of vinegar

Boil turkey meat in three quarts of water until tender. Boil fish, remove bones and add to the stock. Add crabmeat. Add vegetables and spices after they have been put through a grinder. Boil rapidly for 30 minutes. Serve with *fungi*.

Vegetarianism is uncommon on the islands, but many restaurants offer veggie options.

Drinks
While tap water is usually safe, you're better off with bottled water, especially if you have a sensitive stomach. 'Bush tea' is made from the aromatic leaves of indigenous plants.

Foxy's Lager and Blackbeard's Ale are two local (and delicious) microbrews and St Cruzan rum is served everywhere. Although only loosely enforced, you have to be 18 to legally consume booze.

ST THOMAS

pop 51,653
Beloved darling of the cruise-ship industry and bustling capital of the USVI, St Thomas has a bit of an identity crisis. Few ports rival the scenic drama of Charlotte Amalie

(a-*mall*-ya), the Caribbean's busiest shopping district. But every day, thousands of passengers flood the 30-sq-mile (78-sq-km) island like a ship displacing water. The island's reputation for being mobbed with tourists in the throes of a shopping frenzy turns some travelers away. Some locals say that inept political leaders and greedy entrepreneurs have sold out their land to multinational conglomerates, the US' car culture, fast-food chains and consumerism. Others argue that controlled tourism only adds to the island's natural charm.

The good news is that St Thomians have looked up from counting their money to take stock. Island media run daily news and editorial coverage of citizens speaking up against government corruption, crime and lack of foresight. Preservation groups are fighting to stop development on the remaining untouched beaches.

Orientation

The capital of the USVI and the main town is Charlotte Amalie, on the south shore of St Thomas, just 2 miles (3.2km) east of the airport. The bulk of St Thomas' resorts and attractions lie along the beaches of the East End, within a mile or two of Red Hook, home to the East End's business district and ferry terminal. The northwest coast has a string of spectacular bays, including world-renowned Magens Bay.

Information

The following places are located outside Charlotte Amalie. See also Information in the Charlotte Amalie section (p351).

Greatful Deli & Coffee Shop (☎ 775-5160; 6500 Red Hook Plaza; per 15min US$2; ☼ 7am-6pm Mon-Sat, 8am-3pm Sun) Four terminals in this groovy café have Internet access.

Hemingway's Book Shop (☎ 775-2272; Red Hook Plaza; ☼ 9am-5pm Mon-Sat, to 4pm Sun) Sells both new and used books.

Roy Schneider Community Hospital (☎ 776-8311; 48 Sugar Estate Rd at Rte 313; ☼ 24hr) On the east side of Charlotte Amalie, this full-service hospital has an emergency room, recompression chamber and doctors in all major disciplines.

St Thomas Visitors Bureau (☎ 774-8784; Tolbod Gade, Charlotte Amalie; ☼ 9am-5pm Mon-Sat) This hyper-air-conditioned office has brochures, maps and a rest room. There's a satellite visitors center serving cruise ships at the Havensight dock.

Getting There & Around

See p371 for details on how to get to and from St Thomas.

TO/FROM THE AIRPORT

If you are in a hurry, a taxi is your best bet. The fare for one passenger going between Charlotte Amalie and the airport is US$6; it's US$13 to/from Red Hook. Cabs are readily available at the airport.

BUS

The territorial **Division of Transportation** (Vitran; ☎ 774-5678) operates air-conditioned buses over the length of the island. Fares are US$1. Look for the Vitran bus stop signs on Rtes 30 and 38.

CAR

St Thomas has a handful of car-rental agencies, some of which have outlets at the airport and resort hotels. A lot of rental agencies pitch Jeeps to tourists, but be aware that Jeeps lack a lockable trunk. Some agencies prohibit you from taking their cars to St John, and they claim they know you've been there if they see St John's distinct yellow dust on the car.

Avis (☎ 800-331-1084; www.avis.com)
Budget (☎ 776-5774, 800-626-4516; www.budgetstt .com)
Dependable Car Rentals (☎ 800-522-3076; www .dependablecar.com)
Discount Car Rentals (☎ 776-4878; www.discount car.vi)
Hertz (☎ 800-654-3131; www.hertz.com)

TAXI

Territorial law requires that taxi drivers carry a government-set rate sheet, and prices are listed in the readily available free tourist guide *St Thomas/St John This Week*.

Many taxis are vans that carry up to 12 passengers. These service multiple destinations and may stop to pick up passengers along the way, so their rates are usually charged on a per-person basis. Following are current per-person rates for some of the island's most popular destinations from Charlotte Amalie.

Destination	Cost
Frenchtown	US$3
Havensight	US$5
Magens Bay	US$8.50
Red Hook	US$10

US VIRGIN ISLANDS

CHARLOTTE AMALIE
pop 12,000

With more than 1000 cruise-ship visits a year, Charlotte Amalie is the most popular cruise-ship and duty-free destination in the Caribbean. Yet this town is much more than a shopping mall. From the harbor's edge, the town buildings, whitewashed with red-hipped roofs, spread across the narrow coastal plain and blossom over a cluster of pointed hills.

Orientation

Located midisland on the south shore of St Thomas, Charlotte Amalie stretches about 1.5 miles (2.4km) around St Thomas Harbor from the Havensight district on the east side (where the cruise ships dock) to Frenchtown on the west.

Spanning the area between Waterfront Dr and Dronningens Gade (Main St), a score of alleys lined with colonial warehouse buildings house upscale shops and urban malls. Street signs are labeled with original Danish names. North St, for example, is Norre Gade (*gaa*-da, which is 'street' in Danish). Main St and Back St have signs in English as well as Danish and are generally called by their English names.

MAPS

Free maps of St Thomas, available at the tourist offices and at the airport, usually have enlarged insets of Charlotte Amalie.

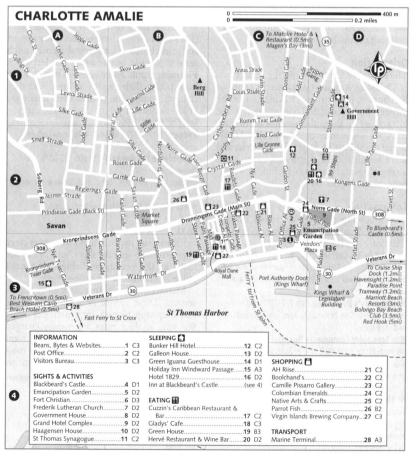

CHARLOTTE AMALIE

INFORMATION		SLEEPING		
Beans, Bytes & Websites...........1 C3		Bunker Hill Hotel......................12 C2		
Post Office..............................2 C2		Galleon House.........................13 D2		
Visitors Bureau........................3 C3		Green Iguana Guesthouse..........14 D1	SHOPPING	
		Holiday Inn Windward Passage...15 A3	AH Riise...................................21 C2
SIGHTS & ACTIVITIES		Hotel 1829..............................16 D2	Boolchand's.............................22 C2
Blackbeard's Castle....................4 D1		Inn at Blackbeard's Castle........(see 4)	Camille Pissarro Gallery............23 C2
Emancipation Garden..................5 D2			Colombian Emeralds.................24 C2
Fort Christian...........................6 D3		EATING	Native Arts & Crafts..................25 C2
Frederik Lutheran Church............7 D2		Cuzzin's Caribbean Restaurant &	Parrot Fish...............................26 B2
Government House.....................8 D2		Bar......................................17 C2	Virgin Islands Brewing Company...27 C3
Grand Hotel Complex..................9 D2		Gladys' Cafe............................18 C3	
Haagensen House.....................10 D2		Green House............................19 B3	TRANSPORT
St Thomas Synagogue...............11 C2		Hervé Restaurant & Wine Bar.....20 D2	Marine Terminal.......................28 A3

US VIRGIN ISLANDS

Information

You'll find Chase Manhattan, Citibank, First Bank, Scotiabank and Banco Popular in Charlotte Amalie. For tourist information, see p349.

AT&T Calling Center (☎ 777-9201) In Havensight next to the tram station, has more than 15 phone booths plus fax and copying services for travelers.

Beans, Bytes & Websites (☎ 776-7265; 5600 Royal Dane Mall; per min US$0.15; ⊗ 7am-6pm Mon-Sat, 7am-1pm Sun) The best place to reconnect with your electronic mailbox, with more than a dozen terminals, plus wireless Internet. The attached café (p354) has good coffee and munchies.

Dockside Bookshop (☎ 774-4937; Havensight Mall; ⊗ 9am-5pm Mon-Sat, 11am-3pm Sun) Excellent bookstore, with plenty of regional titles.

Main post office (☎ 774-3750; zip code 00804) On the west side of Emancipation Garden. There are several satellite post offices, including one just west of the Marine Terminal, and one in the Havensight Mall. Most post offices are open 7:30am to 4:30pm Monday to Friday and 7:30am to noon Saturday.

Dangers & Annoyances

A pirates' den almost from its inception, Charlotte Amalie has some big-city problems including drugs, poverty, prostitution and street crime. Savvy travelers who take reasonable precautions should have no problems. Avoid the Savan section of town, a red-light district to the west where the island's underworld takes its deepest hold. Savan is the area surrounding Main St west of Market Sq and north of the Holiday Inn Windward Passage hotel.

Sights

EMANCIPATION GARDEN & AROUND

Emancipation Garden is the heart of Charlotte Amalie and is the spot where town officials read the emancipation proclamation after slaves were freed on St Croix in 1848. Carnival celebrations and concerts take place here, but mostly folks kick back under shade trees with a cold drink from the Vendors' Plaza, where sellers hawk sarongs, batik dresses, souvenir T-shirts and Prada knock-offs.

Red-brick **Fort Christian** (☎ 776-4566; donation US$1; ⊗ 8:30am-4:30pm) is just east of Emancipation Garden and is the oldest colonial building in the Virgin Islands, dating back to 1666. Over the years, the fort has functioned as a bastion, jail, governor's residence

and a Lutheran church. The museum inside has exhibits on Virgin Islands history.

The 1839 **Grand Hotel Complex**, composed of four neoclassic/Tuscan-designed buildings on the north side of Emancipation Sq, houses popular shops and restaurants. Across the street on Norre Gade (North St), the **Frederik Lutheran Church** is one of Charlotte Amalie's architectural gems.

During the 19th century, the church had segregated congregations – one West Indian, the other Danish. The church is open on Saturday and you can attend services on Sunday.

GOVERNMENT HILL

Government House (☎ 774-0001; 21-22 Kongens Gade; admission free; ⊗ 9am-noon & 1-5pm Mon-Fri), with three stories and a hipped roof, is one of St Thomas' most famous buildings. The grand white mansion was built between 1865 and 1867. Restored in 1994, it currently houses the offices of the territorial governor. You can walk around the first two floors, you'll see paintings by noted local artists, including island-born Camille Pissarro.

Blackbeard's Castle (☎ 776-1234; ⊗ 8am-6pm) watches over the town from the top of Government Hill. In the 18th century, this five-story masonry watchtower was allegedly the lookout post of pirate Edward Teach, alias Blackbeard, who found St Thomas a useful haven from which to ambush unsuspecting merchant ships.

The Inn at Blackbeard's Castle surrounds the turret (see p353). It's worth the climb up Government Hill (come in the cool of the morning), and the entry fee includes use of the inn's three pools. You can tour the site on your own (US$10) or join a one-hour **historic walking tour** (US$20; ⊗ departs 9:30am), which tours the castle and other historic sites.

Halfway down Government Hill from Blackbeard's Castle, a steep set of stairs leads through a canopy of trees back to the commercial district. These are the so-called **99 Steps**, which were constructed using ship-ballast brick in the mid-18th century. There are actually 103 steps, but no matter. Midway along the steps is the **Haagensen House** (☎ 774-9605; adult/child US$6/3; ⊗ 9am-4pm), a restored 1830s town house holding a small museum that splendidly evokes Danish colonial life.

ST THOMAS SYNAGOGUE

The second-oldest Hebrew temple in the western hemisphere (the oldest is on the island of Curaçao), **St Thomas Synagogue** (☎ 774-4312; www.onepaper.com/synagogue; admission free; ⏰ 9:30am-4pm Mon-Fri) is a National Historic Landmark. The current building dates from 1833, but Jews have worshipped here since 1796, from Sephardic Jews from Denmark to today's 600-person Reform congregation. The temple floor is made of sand to symbolize the flight of the Israelites out of Egypt and across the desert.

The synagogue's **Weibel Museum** has exhibits depicting 300 years of Jewish history in the West Indies.

FRENCHTOWN

Occupying a peninsula on the western side of St Thomas Harbor, a community of many brightly painted frame houses was populated by the island's 'Frenchies,' Huguenots who immigrated to St Thomas during the mid-19th century from St Barth. Nowadays, the quiet neighborhood has some good restaurants that overlook the harbor (see p354).

To get here from town, take a taxi (per person US$3), or walk west past the Marine Terminal, where the seaplanes take off, and turn left just past the post office. The walk takes about 25 minutes.

HAVENSIGHT

A hundred years ago, the wharfs and surrounding area on the east side of St Thomas Harbor (known today as Havensight) was a bustling steamship wharf and coaling

station. Today, as many as six cruise ships tie up to the **West India Company Cruise Ship Dock** (still others moor in the harbor). When passengers disembark, they find **Havensight Mall**, a massive compound of buildings that houses dozens of shops and restaurants. Taxis travel to and from Havensight regularly (US$5 per person).

PARADISE POINT TRAMWAY

Built in 1994, this **aerial tramway** (☎ 774-9809; www.stthomasskyride.com; adult/child US$16/8; ⏰ 9am-5pm, to 9pm Tue-Thu in winter) scales 700ft (213m) up Flag Hill to the scenic outlook on Paradise Point. From a base station across the street from the Havensight Mall, you take the seven-minute ride up in modern gondolas. At the top, there is a restaurant, bar, gallery of shops, tropical bird show and a short nature trail.

Sleeping

Rack rates at St Thomas' hotels look steep, but because many visitors sleep on cruise ships, there is a lot of competition to fill their rooms, so you can usually pick up significant last-minute discounts. The rates listed here are for high season (December 15 to April 30); rates are about 20% lower in the off season.

CHARLOTTE AMALIE
Budget

Galleon House (☎ 774-6972, 800-524-2052; www.galleonhouse.com; r US$70-140; 🅿 🖵) A good budget option, this 12-room property spreads along the west side of Government Hill, behind the Hervé restaurant in the heart

---

NORTH COAST BEACHES

Hull Bay Lying to the west around Tropaco Point from Magens Bay, Hull Bay is the island's most popular surfing beach and usually a gem of solitude when Magens Bay is overrun. This strand lies at the base of a steep valley and has excellent shade along its entire length. When the surf is up, youth from all over the island abandon jobs and school to catch a wave.

Little Magens Bay This stunning stretch of sand is the only nude beach on the island. But beware: the beach is on private property, and it has a reputation for rampant theft. Take the dirt road that leads off Magens Rd to the right just before the entrance to Magens Bay. Follow the dirt road for 200yd until you see rocks and a cliff to your left and a trail that leads down an embankment to the beach.

Magens Bay The mile of sand that fringes heart-shaped Magens Bay 3 miles (5km) north of Charlotte Amalie makes almost every travel publication's list of beautiful beaches. The seas here are calm, the bay broad and the vista of the surrounding green hills dramatic. Magens Bay has picnic tables and changing facilities, many food vendors and a water-sports operation. The beach is open 6am to 6pm. Admission is US$1 per car and US$1 per person. A taxi from Charlotte Amalie will cost US$8.50 per person.

US VIRGIN ISLANDS

of the town's historic district. With good vistas of town and harbor, this place offers a sense of being in the middle of things, yet above it all. Rooms are small and darkish, but clean, and eight have patios. You also get a full complimentary breakfast, and an attractive veranda, pool and deck look out on the red roofs of the historic district.

Bunker Hill Hotel (☎ 774-8056; www.bunkerhill hotel.com; 7A Commandant Gade; d/ste US$79/98; ⊠ ⊠ ⊠) A modern, spotless, three-story 16-room inn built around a sunny pool deck and courtyard. Each room has a refrigerator, big bathroom and some have patios. Some of the inner rooms are dark, so ask for one with lots of light. Full breakfasts are complimentary.

Midrange & Top End

Mafolie Hotel (☎ 774-2790, 800-225-7035; www.ma folie.com; 7091 Estate Mafolie; s/d/ste US$97/107/145; ⊠ ⊠ ⊠) On Mafolie Hill, 850ft (259m) above town, the Mafolie offers a dramatic vista, the feel of a Danish colonial villa and a popular alfresco restaurant (p354). The hotel's 22 rooms have private bath and simple, pleasant decor.

Green Iguana Guesthouse (☎ 776-7654; www .thegreeniguana.com; 37B Blackbeard's Hill; r US$120-150; ⊠ ⊠ ⊠) Beside the Inn at Blackbeard's Castle, this homey place surrounds a lush garden and overlooks St Thomas Harbor. There are several room configurations, but the nine spacious rooms have private baths, microwaves, refrigeratorss and bright, welcoming decor. Guests have access to the pool at Blackbeard's Castle.

Inn at Blackbeard's Castle (☎ 776-1234, 800-344-5771; www.blackbeardscastle.com; d US$115-195; ⊠ ⊠ ⊠) At the top of the 99 Steps, the inn surrounds the pirate's watchtower on the hilltop above Charlotte Amalie. All 12 rooms feature period West Indian furnishings, refrigerator and private balcony. There are three pools, including one right at the base of the historic tower. The previous owners ran an excellent restaurant/bar here; when they sold the property, the restaurant closed down. St Thomas residents are still mourning the loss. The hotel organizes free shuttles for guests going to nearby restaurants.

Hotel 1829 (☎ 776-1829, 800-524-2002; www .hotel1829.com; r US$105, r with view US$180-220; ⊠ ⊠ ⊠) Located next to the Hervé restaurant, this inn, completed in 1829, blends the atmosphere of a Victorian gentlemen's club

and a colonial villa. Exposed rubble walls, beamed ceilings and period West Indian furnishings characterize the property. There is a free continental breakfast and a small pool for guests. No children under 12 are allowed.

Holiday Inn Windward Passage (☎ 774-5200, 800-524-5389; www.holidayinn.st-thomas.com; r US$195-300; ⊠ ⊠ ⊠ ⊠) For decades, this four-story, block-long hotel on Waterfront Dr has been the town's centerpiece. With 151 rooms, it has the feel of a business hotel, and even at its busiest, the pool in the central courtyard seems tranquil. From the hotel, it's an easy walk along the waterfront to the restaurants and shopping in the historic district.

Bluebeard's Castle (☎ 774-1600, 800-225-3522; www.equivest.com; Bluebird's Hill; r from US$250; ⊠ ⊠ ⊠ ⊠) With its sprawling white-stucco facade, this castle-hotel on the eastern edge of Charlotte Amalie looks a lot like the fortress it once was. Fifty years ago it was the island's premier resort, and while it can no longer compete with the Ritz-Carlton and Marriott resorts for chic, Bluebeard's still offers first-class rooms, pools, restaurants and service.

AROUND CHARLOTTE AMALIE

Best Western Carib Beach Hotel (☎ 774-2525, 800-792-2742; www.caribbeachresort.com; 70-C Lindbergh Bay; r US$100-170; ⊠ ⊠ ⊠ ⊠) One of the best values for a beachfront stay in the Caribbean, this on-the-beach hotel just a 0.25-mile (400m) from the airport and 2.5 miles (4km) from downtown has 60 oceanfront rooms. You will also find a pool, restaurant and a popular pool bar.

Marriott's Frenchman's Reef Beach Resort (☎ 776-8500, 800-524-2000; www.marriottfrenchman-sreef.com; 5 Estate Bakkeroe; r from US$250) Just 3 miles (5km) east of Charlotte Amalie's center on Flamboyant Pt, this eight-story megaresort has 500 rooms, three pools, five restaurants and eight bars. You'll find Jacuzzis, four lit tennis courts, diving instruction and sailing trips offered here. Call ahead to find out about promotions; it often offers excellent rates.

Marriott's Morning Star Beach Resort (r US$450-750) Virtually next door to the Frenchman's Reef resort (and same contact details), this exclusive and quieter spot spreads out along the beach. It has 96 rooms in several cross-shaped villas tucked among shady palms.

Bolongo Bay Beach Club (☎ 775-1800, 800-524-4746; www.bolongobay.com; 7150 Bolongo Bay; s/d from US$185/195; P ✖ ✖ ✖) Nestled along 1000ft (305m) of crescent beach, family-owned Bolongo has a fun, casual resort ambience. All 75 rooms and 20 villas have ocean views, private patios and 1st-class amenities. On the waterfront is a complete array of water sports, and there are tennis courts, a fitness center and a 53ft (16m) catamaran for day sails and diving trips. You can also do the all-inclusive plan (s/d US$300/400).

Eating

CHARLOTTE AMALIE

Beans, Bytes & Websites (☎ 777-7089; 5600 Royal Dane Mall; coffee & bagel US$3.50; ✖) This chic little cyberbistro has yummy coffee, bagels and croissants. The best place to surf the Web.

Cuzzin's Caribbean Restaurant & Bar (☎ 777-4711; 7 Back St; sandwiches US$8, dinner meals US$10-19; ✖ lunch & dinner) Everybody's favorite stop for West Indian cuisine, where the scent of onions, peppers and curry will draw you from half a block away. You can go light with the spicy calypso chicken wings (US$4) or get into something more serious like the fresh curried conch (US$18).

Green House (☎ 774-7998; cnr Store Tvaer Gade & Waterfront Dr; burgers US$8, dinner meals US$10-16; ✖ from 11am) Raised a half-story above the surrounding sidewalks, this cavernous, open-air restaurant overlooks the harbor. The cuisine is predictable American pub fare, but the menu is extensive, with burgers, pizzas and seafood. After 10pm, the Green House becomes a rocking party scene.

Mafolie Restaurant (☎ 774-2790; 7091 Estate Mafolie; meals US$14-24; ✖ dinner only) Sitting high above the bay at the Mafolie Hotel, the

---

AUTHOR'S CHOICE

Gladys' Cafe (☎ 774-6604; Royal Dane Mall; meals US$7-14; ✖ 7am-4:30pm Mon-Sat, 8am-2:30pm Sun; ✖) With the stereo blaring beside her, Gladys belts out Tina Turner tunes while serving some of the best West Indian cuisine around. There is no view here, but the bistro setting, friendly staff and delicious food make up for it. This is a great place to come for a full breakfast or a bowl of callaloo soup. Buy a bottle of Gladys' famous hot sauce for US$5.

---

dining patio here offers incredible alfresco dining. Cool breezes, candle light and striking vistas complement the Caribbean-and-Creole infused seafood, such as fresh red snapper, crab and lobster. An extensive wine list offers choices in all budgets and the friendly staff can help you pick the perfect meal.

Hervé Restaurant & Wine Bar (☎ 777-9703; Government Hill; meals US$25-55; ✖ lunch Mon-Fri, dinner daily; ✖ ✖) Specializing in Swiss-French cuisine and five-star service, Hervé has an elegant atmosphere with indoor and terrace seating, both with views of the downtown rooftops and harbor. Background jazz plays while the breeze swooshes in from the bay. A good menu choice is the surf-n-turf (US$50), or try the well-prepared veal roulade or seafood dishes. You'll need reservations on weekends.

Iggie's (☎ 775-1800; Bolongo Bay Beach Club; meals US$7-12; ✖ lunch & dinner) In a large open-air pavilion overlooking a broad beach, this casual place is lots of fun. A sand volleyball court sits beside the restaurant, which serves great sandwiches, burgers and seafood entrees, plus a kids' menu. Things kick up at night, when the place grooves to a festive bar atmosphere.

FRENCHTOWN

Several restaurants huddle around the parking lot in Frenchtown.

Frenchtown Deli (☎ 776-7211) This is a popular takeout stop for breakfast and lunch with a view of Hassel Island and the harbor. You can get a bagel with cream cheese and a cup of coffee here for under US$3.50. A thick turkey sandwich for lunch cost you about US$7.

Hook, Line & Sinker (☎ 776-9708; 2 Honduras; ✖ lunch & dinner Mon-Sat, brunch Sun; P) This open-air mom-and-pop operation on the water welcomes all people like old friends. Locals love the Sunday brunch (US$14). The menu has a good mix of sandwiches, salads, pastas and seafood entrees, such as the almond-crusted yellowtail.

Epernay Wine Bar & Bistro (☎ 774-5348; mains US$12-22; ✖ dinner only Mon-Sat; P ✖) Next to the Frenchtown Deli, this is a great place to meet fellow hipsters while hanging out at the bistro's bar, or settle at a shadowy table. Delicious starters like steamed mussels (US$9) complement mains such as sesame-crusted tuna (US$21). Beware, this small place is usually smoky.

Shopping

As a duty-free, tax-free port, St Thomas is a shopper's paradise. You can find bargains on everything from jewelry and electronics, to perfume and booze. US citizens can leave with up to US$1200 worth of purchases without paying the customs agent.

Business hours in most of the island stores are 9am to 5pm Monday to Saturday; stores open on Sunday if cruise ships are in town.

You'll find hundreds of shops around Main St, Back St and the colonial warehouses in Charlotte Amalie, and at Havensight Mall compound adjacent to the cruiseship dock. Vendors' Plaza, in front of Fort Christian, boasts an eclectic mix of crafts, costume jewelry and souvenir T-shirts. Be sure to stop by the following stores:

AH Riise (☎ 776-2303; 37 Main St) Sells everything from Rolex watches to liquor.

Boolchand's (☎ 776-0794; 31 Main St) One of the Caribbean's largest camera retailers.

Camille Pissarro Gallery (☎ 774-4621; 14 Main St) Sells a dwindling collection of reproductions of Pissarro's famous island scenes; it also sells work by other island artists.

Colombian Emeralds (☎ 774-3400; Grand Hotel Complex & Havensight Mall) Has a reputation throughout the Caribbean for offering good value on high-quality gems.

Native Arts & Crafts (☎ 777-1153; Tolbod Gade) Next to the visitors center, this is the place to buy gifts made by St Thomian craftspeople.

Parrot Fish (☎ 776-4514; cnr Store Tvaer Gade & Back St) Sells authentic, hard-to-find recordings (not bootlegs) of calypso, reggae and steel-band music.

Virgin Island Brewing Company (☎ 714-1683; 1C Royal Dane Mall) Serves free samples and good prices on Blackbeard Ale and Foxy's Lager.

RED HOOK & EAST END

The East End has the bulk of the island's major resorts and a good collection of restaurants. Red Hook is the only town to speak of on this end, though it's small, built around the Red Hook Ferry Dock and a busy marina. The American Yacht Harbor complex has good shops and restaurants, as does the Red Hook Plaza across the street.

For details of useful facilities, see Information on p349.

Sights & Activities

CORAL WORLD

This 4.5-acre (1.8-hectare) **marine park** (☎ 775-1555; www.coralworldvi.com; 6450 Estate Smith Bay; adult/child US$18/9; ☯ 9am-5pm), at Coki Point, is the most popular tourist attraction on St Thomas. The 80,000-gallon Caribbean Reef Tank accurately depicts the marine life on offshore coral reefs. The Undersea Observatory gives visitors a 360-degree view of life 15ft (4.5m) under water. Topside, you can visit a shark tank, turtle pool, stingray pool, touch pool and a mangrove lagoon. Iguanas run wild, and you can follow them along short nature trails. Staff hold scheduled feedings and give talks about biology, reef ecology and habitat conservation.

The site has restaurants and gift shops, along with changing rooms if you want to visit nearby Coki Beach. You can find discount coupons to Coral World in some of the free tourist guides.

EAST END BEACHES

Coki Bay, right at the entrance to Coral World, is a protected cove with excellent snorkeling, but beware – the beach can get very crowded.

A west-facing beach in front of the eponymous resort, **Secret Harbour** could hardly be more tranquil. It is protected from breezes as well as waves, and the water remains shallow a long way offshore. The resort has a watersports operation, and this is one of the best places to learn to windsurf.

To reach **Vessup Beach**, a long, broad strand overlooking St John and the BVI, follow a dirt road around the south side of the harbor at Red Hook until you reach Vessup Bay Marina. Serious windsurfers love this spot.

The **Sapphire Beach Resort** just off Rte 38 is perhaps the most welcoming of all the island's resorts to transient beach visitors. The Sapphire Beach volleyball games here can get spirited, as can the party scene on Sunday afternoon, when the resort brings in live bands.

SAILING

During the last 25 years, the bulk of the Virgin Islands' bareboat yacht charters have migrated to the BVI, but St Thomas still has a few charter operations. Expect to pay US$55 a person for a four-hour trip and about US$100 for a full-day adventure. The trips generally include a catered lunch, free drinks and snorkel gear. Trips depart from the Sapphire Beach Marina and from American Yacht Harbor in Red Hook, where you

US VIRGIN ISLANDS

can also rent powerboats for about US$200 per day, or organize fishing trips.

DIVING & SNORKELING

St Thomas features several premier dive sites, and most island resort hotels have a dive service on the property. Most dive centers charge about US$55 for a one-tank dive, or US$85 for two. They also rent snorkeling gear for about US$10. Recommended dive shops are:

Chris Sawyer Diving Center (☎ 775-7320; www .sawyerdive.vi; retail center at American Yacht Harbor) Mostly boat dives out of the Wyndham Sugar Bay Resort, also night dives and trips to BVI's wreck RMS *Rhone*.

Coki Beach Dive Club (☎ 775-4220; www.cokidive .com) Just steps away from Coki Beach, offer shore and night dives, plus Professional Association of Diving Instructors (PADI) courses.

Dive In! (☎ 777-9029; www.diveinusvi.com; Sapphire Beach Resort) Mostly boat dives, PADI certification courses.

KAYAKING

Virgin Islands Ecotours (☎ 779-2155; Rte 32 at Holmberg's Marina) offers a 2½-hour guided kayak tour and snorkeling expedition. The trip takes you through a mangrove lagoon to a coral rubble beach for snorkeling. Rates run about US$50.

Sleeping

Prices listed are based on high-season occupancy unless otherwise noted.

Pavilions and Pools (☎ 775-6110; 6400 Estate Smith Bay; d US$250-275; P ⊠ ⊠ ⊠) The very cool thing about this small hotel is that each of the 25 suites has its own pool – yeah, you read that right! Suites have full kitchens, and separate bedrooms with sliding doors that open to your own pool. You can spend days here and never put on a stitch of clothing. When you're ready to put on a bikini, the friendly staff will shuttle you to nearby Sapphire Beach. The on-site restaurant serves grilled fish nightly (US$20 to US$35).

Point Pleasant Resort (☎ 775-7200, 800-524-2300; www.pointpleasantresort.com; 6600 Estate Smith Bay; d from US$255; P ⊠ ⊠ ⊠) On a steep hill overlooking Water Bay, this family-run property opened in the 1970s and was the first truly ecosensitive resort on St Thomas. The place still has lots of charm. It has 128 spacious suites in multi-unit cottages tucked into the hillside forest. Each unit has a full kitchen, separate bedroom and

large porch. The resort also has walking trails, three pools set at different levels and a beach. One of the island's best restaurants, the Agavé Terrace, is perched on the resort's hillside.

Sapphire Beach Resort & Marina (☎ 775-6100, 800-524-2090; www.sapphirebeachresort.com; 6720 Estate Smith Bay; d from US$325; P ⊠ ⊠ ⊠) Beautiful Sapphire Beach is more than 0.5 miles (0.8km) long and the resort is an attractive option for families. Rooms are studio-style suites with all the amenities; there are about 170 separate guest quarters in a collection of large multistory buildings facing the beach and the resort's marina.

Wyndham Sugar Bay Resort (☎ 777-7100, 800-996-3426; www.wyndhamsugarbayresort.com; 6500 Estate Smith Bay; d from US$350; P ⊠ ⊠ ⊠) On grounds decorated with tropical flowers and perched above a sheltered beach, this giant hotel is the island's only truly all-inclusive resort. There are 300 rooms, three interconnecting pools, a fitness center, tennis courts, water sports and a kids' program.

Eating & Drinking

Greatful Deli & Coffee Shop (☎ 775-5160; 6500 Red Hook Plaza; sandwiches US$7; ☻ 7am-6pm Mon-Sat, 8am-3pm Sun; P ⊠) Oh, you gotta love this place. The male waitstaff are bearded, tattooed pirate-looking guys who are full of cheer and like to call customers 'amigo.' The place is redolent with the scent of 10 varieties of fresh-roasted coffee and grilled veggies, and the click of fingers on computer keyboards (see p349). You can do breakfast for under US$5, and there are plenty of veggie options.

Señor Pizza (☎ 775-3030; slice US$2, large pie US$18; ☻ lunch & dinner) Right next door to Red Hook Plaza, this place serves the island's best pizza. It can get busy with takeout orders in the evening, when vacationers in East End villas decide they don't feel like cooking.

Duffy's Love Shack (☎ 779-2080; 650 Red Hook Plaza; meals US$8-12; ☻ lunch & dinner; P) This pub is just a frame shack in the middle of a paved parking lot, but it's a legendary stopping place for travelers visiting the East End. Duffy's creates its own atmosphere with high-volume rock and crowds in shorts and tank tops. The food is classic pub fare. The big attractions here are people-watching and the killer cocktails.

Molly Malone's (☎ 775-1270; American Yacht Harbor; meals US$6-20; ✆ breakfast, lunch & dinner; 🦶) A re-creation of a friendly Irish pub, Molly's has a huge menu, and lots of (indoor and outdoor) seating. It's a great place to watch sports on overhead TVs, or cool off with a brew at the bar.

You'll find two great restaurants at the Point Pleasant Resort, including the highly respected **Agavé Terrace & Bar** (☎ 775-4142; mains US$30-50; ✆ dinner only), whose deck hangs out in thin air over a steep slope, giving diners a breathtaking view of St John and the BVI. It serves excellent seafood. Also here is **Fungi's on the Beach** (☎ 775-4142; full meals from US$12.50; ✆ from 11am), a fun place to try delicious local cuisine.

ST JOHN

pop 4300
Just 3 miles (5km) from St Thomas, St John seems a world away. Mellow and rugged, simple and laid-back, St John is all about relaxing in nature's bounty.

Where St Thomas is loaded with homes and businesses, St John is largely wilderness: almost three-quarters of the island falls within the borders of the Virgin Islands National Park. While commuters cause traffic jams on St Thomas, feral donkeys stop traffic on the byways of St John. And while almost every beach on St Thomas has a luxury resort, many beaches on St John don't even have a parking lot.

Orientation
At 9 miles (14.5km) long and 5 miles (8km) wide, St John rises above the surrounding sea like a peaked green cap. All but the extreme east and west ends of the island lie within the borders of the national park and will remain forever wild. Cruz Bay at the West End is St John's port of entry, with constant ferry traffic and most of the island's shops, restaurants and pubs.

The settlement of Coral Bay at the East End is the sleepy domain of folks who want to feel like they're living on a frontier. Centerline Rd (Rte 10) scales the island's heights and proceeds east–west along the mountain ridges to connect St John's two communities. The North Shore Rd (Rte 20) snakes along the north coast and connects

the most popular beaches, bays and campgrounds. The wildest and least accessible areas of St John lie along the south shore and the extreme east end of the island.

Information
Connections (in Cruz Bay ☎ 776-6922, in Coral Bay 779-4994; www.connectionsstjohn.com; per 30min US$5; ✆ 8:30am-5:30pm Mon-Sat) Internet access. The Cruz Bay office is on the corner of Prince and King Sts. The Coral Bay office is in the small complex of shops surrounding Skinny Legs restaurant.

Myrah Keating Smith Community Health Center (☎ 693-8900; ✆ 8am-8pm Mon-Fri) About 2 miles (3.2km) east of Cruz Bay on Centerline Rd, this is the place to come for routine medical attention.

Post office (☎ 779-4227) In Cruz Bay, directly across the street from the passenger ferry dock.

St John Visitors Center (☎ 776-6450; ✆ 9am-5pm Mon-Sat) A small building next to the post office, across the street from the BVI ferry dock in Cruz Bay.

US Customs & Immigration (☎ 776-6741; ✆ 8am-noon & 1-5pm) In a building adjoining the wharf for ferries serving the BVI. If you arrive on one of these ferries or on a yacht from the BVI, you must clear customs and immigration here before proceeding into town.

Getting There & Away
Passenger ferries between Charlotte Amalie and Cruz Bay run about every two hours and cost US$7 one way. Ferries run almost every hour between Red Hook and Cruz Bay, costing US$3 one way. Car ferries from Red Hook to Cruz Bay run hourly and cost US$22/35 one way/round-trip. For more information, see p373.

Ferries also travel to Jost Van Dyke and Tortola in the BVI (see p372).

Getting Around
BUS
Vitran (☎ 774-5678; fare US$1) operates air-conditioned buses over the length of the island via Centerline Rd. Buses leave Cruz Bay in front of the ferry terminal at 6am and 7am, then every hour at 25 minutes after the hour until 9:25pm.

CAR
St John has a handful of car-rental agencies. All have outlets within walking distance of the ferry terminal.

Rates generally run from US$45 per day. Vendors rent Jeeps and SUVs to handle the rugged terrain. Rental agencies:

US VIRGIN ISLANDS

C & C Jeep Rentals & Taxi Service (☎ 693-8169)
Delbert Hill Car Rental (☎ 776-6637)
O'Connor Car Rental (☎ 776-6343)
St John Car Rental (☎ 776-6103)

TAXI
Territorial law sets the taxi rates on St John. Grab a cab at the waterfront in Cruz Bay or call the **St John Taxi Association** (☎ 774-3130) for a pickup.

TOURS
The street and parking lot in front of the ferry dock in Cruz Bay swarm with cabs offering island tours. A two-hour circuit of the island costs about US$45 for one or two passengers. You pay US$18 per person when three or more take the tour.

CRUZ BAY
Thirty years ago Cruz Bay was a dusty customs port where almost nothing moved in the midday sun. Today, St John's only town grooves with many shops and restaurants, all within walking distance of the ferry terminals. The laid-back scene makes it a fun place to hang out. Don't be surprised if you catch the sweet scent of burning herb floating through the air. You'll mix with hippies and sea captains, snowbirds (North Americans who come to the Caribbean for its warm winter) and reggae worshippers. At some point during the town's evolution, folks began calling it 'Love City.' The nickname came as an attempt to sum up the New Age aura of freedom, independence and upscale chic that now permeates the whole island.

Virgin Islands National Park
In the early 1950s, the US millionaire Laurence Rockefeller discovered and fell in love with the nearly abandoned St John and began purchasing large tracts of land. He built the Caneel Bay resort and donated more than 5000 acres (2023 hectares) to the US government. The land became an official national park in 1956, and over the years the government has added another 4000 acres (1619 hectares), plus 5650 underwater acres (2286 hectares). More than a million visitors a year stop at the park, making it the most popular single attraction in all of the Virgin Islands.

The **National Park Service** (NPS; ☎ 776-6201) runs a visitors center on the dock across from the Mongoose Junction shopping arcade. It's an essential first stop for all travelers interested in exploring the miles of shoreline, pristine reefs and 22 hiking trails (see the boxed text, below).

More than 30 species of tropical birds nest in the park, including the bananaquit, hummingbirds and smooth-billed ani. Green iguanas and geckoes, hawksbill turtles and an assortment of feral animals roam the land. Largely regenerated after 18th-century logging, the island flora is a mix of introduced species and native plants.

Activities
DIVING & SNORKELING
St John has some spectacular dive sites, all of which are accessed by boat, including wreck dives on the *General Rogers* and RMS

US VIRGIN ISLANDS

HIKING ON ST JOHN

With more than 9500 acres (3845 hectares) of national park and 22 maintained trails, St John is paradise for tropical hikers. The National Park Visitors Center has excellent maps, and any reasonably fit hiker can safely hit the trails without a local guide. Nevertheless, joining a hiking tour led by a professional can be well worth the cost for the natural and human history you'll learn from your leader. Get a list of guides from the visitors center.

The National Park Service sponsors a number of hikes, including birding expeditions and shore hikes, but its best-known offering is the **Reef Bay Hike** (☎ 776-6201 ext 238; US$20; for reservations ⊙ 9:30am-3pm Mon & Thu). This begins at the Reef Bay trailhead, 4.75 miles (7.6km) from Cruz Bay on Centerline Rd. The hike is a 3-mile (5km) downhill trek through tropical forests, leading past petroglyphs and plantation ruins to a swimming beach at Reef Bay, where a boat runs you back to Cruz Bay.

Park trails include a number of old plantation roads that lead through wet forests and dry forests to ruins, archeological sites, mountain peaks and hidden shores. Trails have identifying signs at the trailheads. A brochure called *Trail Guide for Safe Hiking* gives descriptions of each route.

Rhone. A two-tank trip including gear costs US$85 (about US$140 to the *Rhone*). The following shops also offer dive certification, snorkeling trips and boat trips to the BVI.

Cruise Bay Watersports (☎ 776-6234; www.divest john.com; Palm Plaza, behind Lumber Yard)

Low Key Watersports (☎ 693-8999; www.dive lowkey.com; Wharfside Village)

BOATING

The following are in Wharfside Village.

Arawak Expeditions (☎ 693-8312; www.arawakexp .com) Offers guided sea kayak tours (including lunch US$90; from 10am to 6pm daily). It also offers mountain biking tours (half/full day US$50/90).

Noah's Little Arks (☎ 693-9030) Operates out of Low Key Watersports and rents 12ft (3.6m) inflatable dinghies with 15hp engines (half/full day US$75/130).

Ocean Runner Powerboat Rentals (☎ 693-8809) Rents larger speedboats for US$265 to US$365, plus gas.

Festivals & Events

The one big event on the island is **St John's Carnival**, which begins around July 1 and climaxes on July 4 or 5. The event aims to celebrate Emancipation Day (July 3) and the US Independence Day (July 4).

Sleeping

St John's accommodations appeal to two groups: one is upper-middle-class vacationers, the other adventure travelers keen on camping and ecotourism. Low-cost, no-frills guesthouses, once staple accommodations on the island, are disappearing fast in the face of gentrification. Prices listed below are winter high-season rates.

Inn at Tamarind Court (☎ 776-6378, 800-221-1637; www.tamarindcourt.com; d/q US$148/240; ☒ ☒) There are no water views or private decks here, but the shady courtyard with its casual bar and restaurant make for a good place to kick back with other guests, hoist a jar and exchange local knowledge. Most of the 20 rooms are small and simply furnished. An economy room has a shared bath (US$75).

Serendip Condos (☎ 776-6646, 888-800-6445; www .serendipstjohn.com; studio/1-bedroom unit US$131/195; ℗ ☒ ☒) Located on the hill above Cruz Bay, this place offers a lot for a moderate price, although it's a 0.75-mile (1.2km) hike along Rte 104 to town. There are 10 studios and one-bedroom units in three-story buildings. Each unit has a private balcony and full kitchen.

Lavender Hills Estates (☎ 779-6969, 800-348-8444; www.lavenderhill.net; 1-/2-bedroom ste US$195/295; ℗ ☒ ☒ ☐ ☒) Above Gallows Point a short walk south of the business district, this multistory purple building has 12 spacious suites with tile floors, rattan furnishings and private porches. Guests enjoy the convenience of the pool and laundry.

Gallows Point Resort (☎ 776-6434, 800-323-7229; www.gallowspointresort.com; d US$295-495; ℗ ☒ ☒ ☐ ☒) On the promontory overlooking the harbor on the south side of Cruz Bay, Gallows Point has 14 private villas amid lushly landscaped grounds. Each suite has private terraces and decks, a living room, full kitchen, one or two bedrooms and large bath. There's a small beach with excellent snorkeling just offshore. Many of the condo units have vaulted ceilings; all have a collection of French doors that open onto water views. Furnishings are wicker creations with vibrant floral patterns. When you consider that you can cook meals in your villa, the price doesn't seem so high. Swanky ZoZo's restaurant on the property has great views for a sunset dinner.

Westin Resort (☎ 693-8000, 800-808-5020; www .westinresortstjohn.com; d from US$370; ℗ ☒ ☒ ☐ ☒) For the utmost in luxury, the Westin has all the hallmarks of a contemporary five-star resort. Two hilly miles (3.2km) south of Cruz Bay on Rte 104, the resort has a 0.25-acre (0.1-hectare) pool, a palm-shaded beach fronting Great Cruz Bay, a fitness center, spa, lit tennis courts and four restaurants. The hotel has 282 rooms, plus 90 condo units on the hill across the road.

Caneel Bay (☎ 776-6111, 888-767-3966; www .caneelbay.com; d from US$450; ℗ ☒ ☒ ☐ ☒)

US VIRGIN ISLANDS

Built in 1955 around the ruins of an old sugar plantation just 2 miles (3.2km) north of Cruz Bay, Caneel Bay offers old-school elegance on 170 acres (69 hectares) of national park land. Seven beaches, landscaped rolling hills, miles of hiking trails, 11 tennis courts and five restaurants – we're just getting started. Luxurious accommodations in 166 guestrooms and cottages feature plantation-style furnishings from Indonesia and loads of privacy. Service is top of the line. Rates drop dramatically in the off and shoulder seasons.

Eating & Drinking

Starfish Market (☎ 779-4949; Southside Rd; ☺ 8:30am-6pm) A full-service supermarket, with good produce, a deli, and wide selection of beer and wine.

Chilly Billy's Lumberyard Café (☎ 693-8708; 13-38 Enighed Gade; breakfast US$7-9; ☺ 8am-2pm; ☒) Islanders swear by the omelettes, breakfast burritos and strawberry pancakes at this breakfast joint upstairs in the yellow Lumberyard building up the hill from the car-ferry dock.

Panini Beach (☎ 693-9119; Wharfside Village; meals US$8-20; ☺ lunch & dinner; ☒) Enjoy lunchtime panini sandwiches or northern Italian pasta and pizza at this trattoria, with indoor and outdoor harborside dining.

Woody's Seafood Saloon (☎ 779-4625; meals US$8-14; ☺ lunch & dinner; ☒) St John's daily party starts here at 3pm, when the price on domestic US beers drops to US$1. By 4pm, the crowd in this tiny place has spilled over onto the sidewalk. Bartenders pass beers out a streetside window. While lots of folks show up at this cramped bar to drink with fellow tanned bodies, a traveler can actu-

---

AUTHOR'S CHOICE

Rhumb Lines (☎ 776-0303; Meada's Plaza; ☺ closed Tue) Tucked in a lush courtyard in Meada's Plaza, this little restaurant has incredible food and even better prices. Enjoy superb salads, sandwiches and fresh, healthy tropical cuisine served by happy, friendly hippies. At night, try selections from the 'pu pu' menu (US$3 to US$6 each), a mix of tapas-like treats. Indoor and outdoor seating under thatched umbrellas.

---

ally get some reasonable pub food, such as grilled fish.

Duffy's Love Shack (☎ 776-6065; King St; meals US$8-15; ☺ lunch & dinner) A step child of the original on St Thomas, this Duffy's, while still a party venue, has a mellower scene and a nice upstairs eating area for reasonably priced bar food.

Morgan's Mango (☎ 693-8141; meals US$13-28; ☺ lunch & dinner) Just across from the car-ferry landing, this is a good mid-priced restaurant with imaginative Caribbean recipes. The terrace of this hillside restaurant offers a view of the harbor while you dine on items such as Haitian voodoo snapper or Cuban citrus chicken. The owners often bring in live acoustic acts, making it a good choice for a fun or romantic night out.

Stone Terrace Restaurant (☎ 693-9370; meals from US$25; ☺ dinner only Tue-Sun) Family-owned and -operated on the southern edge of the village, it's all about candle light, linen and great wine at this open-air bistro. The menu here includes black peppercorn-encrusted tuna, seared duck and rack of lamb.

NORTH ISLAND

Most of the national park's major attractions are accessed by the North Shore and Centerline Rds. A rental car is the easiest way to access the area, but taxis will also drop you at beaches for a nominal fee.

Sights & Activities

ANNABERG SUGAR MILL RUINS

Part of the national park, these ruins at Leinster Bay on the north side of the island are the most intact sugar plantation ruins in the Virgin Islands. A 30-minute, self-directed walking tour (US$4) leads you through the slave quarters, village, windmill, rum still and dungeon.

The schooner drawings on the dungeon wall may date back more than 100 years. Park experts offer **demonstrations** (☺ 10am-2pm Tue-Fri) in traditional island baking, gardening, weaving and crafting.

BEACHES

Most beaches have rest rooms and changing facilities, and most are excellent for snorkeling. You can rent snorkeling gear at dive shops in Cruz Bay (p358), or at Trunk and Cinnamon Bays. The NPS publishes an oft-photocopied but useful brochure called

---

WILD KINGDOM

Whether you are camping, hiking or driving on St John, it will not be long before you have a close encounter with one or more of the island's troublesome population of feral animals. According to rough estimates from the National Park Service, 500 goats, 400 donkeys, 200 pigs and hundreds of cats are the descendants of animals abandoned in the island jungle. White-tailed deer and mongooses are two other exotic species that now have successful breeding colonies.

Park rangers are most concerned with the goats and pigs, whose foraging wipes out under-brush and leaves hillsides prone to erosion. Many of the animals have grown adept at raiding garbage cans and food supplies in the camping areas, and the donkeys meandering on island roads pose a serious hazard to drivers.

Do not tempt these animals by offering them food or leaving food or garbage where they can get at it. And do not approach them for petting or taking a snapshot. They may look harmless, but they are all capable of aggression.

Where's the Best Snorkeling? which you can pick up at the NPS visitors center.

Caneel Bay
This is the main beach in front of the dining terrace at the Caneel Bay resort. The resort has seven beaches, but this is the one it permits visitors to use. It's a lovely beach, with fair snorkeling off the east point. You must sign in as a visitor at the guardhouse when you enter the resort property.

Hawksnest Bay
The bay here is dazzling to behold, a deep circular indentation between hills with a broken ring of sand on the fringe. Some scenes from the film *Christopher Columbus: The Discovery* were shot here.

Oppenheimer's Beach
On the eastern edge of Hawksnest Bay, the beach and house here are not part of the national park; they belonged to Dr Robert Oppenheimer, one of the inventors of the atomic bomb. His daughter left the land to the children of St John.

Jumbie Bay
Jumbie is the common word for ghost in the Creole dialect, and this beach east of Oppenheimer's has a plethora of ghost stories. Look for the parking lot on the North Shore Rd that holds only three cars. From here, take the wooden stairs down to the beach.

Trunk Bay
This long, gently arching beach is the most popular strand on the island and charges a

US$4 fee. The beach has lifeguards, changing facilities, toilets, picnic facilities, snorkel rental, a snack bar and taxi stand. No question, the beach is scenic, but it often gets packed. Everyone wants to try the underwater snorkeling trail.

Cinnamon Bay
The next bay east of Trunk Bay, this exposed sweeping cove is home to the Cinnamon Bay Campground (below). The beach has amenities including showers, toilets, a restaurant and grocery store. You can rent sailboards and sea kayaks here.

Leinster Bay
This bay adjoins the grounds of the ruined Annaberg Plantation at the northeast end of the island. Park in the lot at the plantation and follow a dirt road/trail around Leinster Bay. The best snorkeling is on the offshore fringing reef of Watermelon Cay.

Sleeping
Anyone uninterested in staying at the big resorts will love the two ecoresort options on the north island.

Cinnamon Bay Campground (☎ 776-6330, 800-539-9998; www.cinnamonbay.com; camp site/4-person tent US$27/58, 4-person cottages US$70-90) About 6 miles (9.6km) east of Cruz Bay on the North Shore Rd (Rte 20), this campground/ecoresort sits along a mile-long crescent beach at the base of forested hills. It's really a campers' village with a general store, snack bar and a restaurant, but with thick vegetation giving plenty of privacy. There are three accommodations options.

US VIRGIN ISLANDS

You can use your own tent; stay in a 10ft x 14ft (3m x 4.2m) tent that sits on a solid wood platform and comes equipped with four cots, a lantern, ice chest, and cooking capabilities; or stay in a cottage – a 15ft x 15ft (4.5m x 4.5m) concrete shelter with two screened sides, electric lights, cooking capabilities and ceiling fan. You can get a beachfront, water-view or forest location. Everyone uses the public toilet facilities and cold-water showers.

Maho Bay Camps (☎ 776-6240, 800-392-9004; www.maho.org; d US$110) About 8 miles (13km) east of Cruz Bay on North Shore Rd (Rte 20), is Stanley Selengut's award-winning ecosensitive tent resort.

This resort has grown into a complex with 114 units. Each of the 16ft x 16ft (5m x 5m) tents, complete with kitchen, sits on a platform on a steep, forested hillside, with decks overlooking the offshore islands. The tents are so far off the ground, and the surrounding vegetation is so thick, it's like living in a tree house. The resort's 'green' philosophy includes water conservation: community toilets are low-flush units, and showers have pull-chains for brief dousing.

High above the tent camps **Harmony Studios** (US$195-220) has condos with a private bath, kitchen and deck, with solar-generated electricity, rainwater-collection and roof wind scoops for cooling.

CORAL BAY

Two hundred years ago, Coral Bay was the largest settlement on St John. Known originally as 'Crawl' Bay, presumably because there were pens or 'crawls' for sea turtles here, this settlement owes its early good fortune to the largest and best-protected harbor in the Virgin Islands.

Today, Coral Bay's village center has dwindled to a school and a handful of shops, restaurants and pubs clustered around the base of a hill dominated by the **Emmaus Moravian Church**, built by Moravian missionaries in 1733. Rte 107 leads to **Salt Pond Bay** and the island's most remote beaches and coastal wilderness.

Horseback Riding

Carolina Corral (☎ 693-5778; 13 Carolina Rd; rides US$55) offers two-hour beach, trail and sunset rides on horses and donkeys.

Sleeping & Eating

Concordia Eco-tents (☎ 693-5855, 800-392-9004; Estate Concordia; d US$135-200) Maho Bay's Stanley Selengut has built nine 'tent-cottages' on stilts, strung together by boardwalks on the steep hillside. Each shelter has a living area, camp kitchen, bedroom and private bath complete with a composting toilet and solar-heated shower. It's very quiet and remote, so you'll want a rental car.

Vie's Snack Shack (☎ 963-5033; meals US$6-10; ⏰ 10am-5pm Tue-Sat) Vie Mahabir opened this plywood-sided restaurant next to her house in 1979, just after the government paved the road. She wanted to make a living while raising her 10 children. In the process, she built a reputation as a treasured island storyteller and chef. Come for the garlic chicken with johnnycakes.

Skinny Legs (☎ 779-4982; meals US$8-12; ⏰ lunch & dinner) You'll find salty sailors, bikini-clad transients and East End snowbirds at this open-air grill just past the fire station. Overlooking a small boatyard, it's not about the view, but the jovial clientele and lively bar scene. Try a tasty cheeseburger, or grilled *mahimahi* (white-meat fish) sandwich.

ST CROIX

pop 60,000

'We don't have mass anything,' explained a Cruzan woman, overlooking the beach as the sun dipped behind disappearing rain clouds. 'It's like anti corporate, and you know it as soon as you get here.' Hallelujah.

Thanks to its geographic isolation, 40 miles (64km) south of the other Virgins, St Croix's vibe is distinctly relaxed. The island's fertile coastal plain earned it the nickname 'Garden of the Antilles' for its natural affinity for growing sugarcane. The sugar plantations are long gone, but remnants of the colonial days are visible throughout the island, including the historic districts of Christiansted and Frederiksted, the island's two main towns.

More than half of the islands residents are the descendants of former slaves; about 30% are second- or third-generation immigrants from Puerto Rico; quite a few are young, White Americans who come to run the island's restaurants, inns and sports operations.

Economically, the island turns to industry as well as tourism. The Hovensa Oil refinery on the south shore is the fifth largest in the world. Most of the oil comes from Venezuela, is refined here and exported, along with sulfur and other by-products.The refinery employs up to 6000 people, helping to raise the standard of living on the island. The overall feeling on St Croix is that it's a real place, a small-town cosmopolitan haven mostly free of commercialism.

Getting There & Around

Henry E Rohlsen Airport is on the southwest side of St Croix and handles flights from the US, many connecting via San Juan, Puerto Rico or St Thomas; see p371.

Seaborne Airlines (☎ 773-6442, 888-359-8687; www.seaborneairlines.com; one way/round-trip US$66/93; 25min) flies seaplanes between St Thomas and St Croix, and the fast ferry, the 600-passenger **Salacia** (☎ 719-0099; www.virginislands fastferry.com; round-trip US$70; 75min) sails between the two islands.

Taxis are unmetered so it's best to settle your fare in advance. The set rate per person to Christiansted from the airport is US$13. **Vitran** (☎ 778-0898; fare US$1) buses travel along Centerline Rd between Christiansted and Frederiksted.

St Croix has several car rental agencies, and cars cost about US$45 per day. Many rental companies will pick you up at the airport or seaplane dock. Local companies include:

Budget (☎ 778-9636)
Centerline Car Rentals (☎ 778-0450, 888-288-8755)
Gold Mine Car Rental (☎ 773-0299)
Olympic (☎ 773-2208)

CHRISTIANSTED
Orientation

Kings Wharf is the commercial landing where, for more than 250 years, ships landed with slaves and set off with sugar or molasses.

Today it's lined with restaurants, shops and bars. The historic district stretches southwest of here along a grid of narrow one-way streets.

The main arteries through town are King St (eastbound) and Company St (westbound). Gallows Bay is a shopping district across the harbor to the east.

Information

Governor Juan F Luis Hospital (☎ 776-6311) Next to the Sunny Isle Shopping Center on Centerline Rd, 2 miles (3.2km) west of Christiansted.
Post office (☎ 773-3586; cnr Company St & Market Sq; 7:30am-4:30pm Mon-Fri, 8:30am-noon Sat)
St Croix Visitors Center (☎ 773-0495, 800-372-8784; www.st-croix.com; 53 Company St; 8am-5pm Mon-Fri) A small visitors center that serves the cruise ships in Frederiksted.
Strand Street Station Internet Cafe (☎ 719-6245; 1102 Strand St; per 30min US$5; 9am-7pm Mon-Sat, 10am-2pm Sun) Has several computers, sells phone cards and stamps.

Sights & Activities
CHRISTIANSTED NATIONAL HISTORIC SITE

In the yellow buildings on the town's east side, this **historic site** (☎ 773-1460; 2100 Church St; admission US$3; 8am-5pm Mon-Fri, 9am-5pm Sat & Sun) includes **Fort Christiansvaern** (Christian's Defenses), an impressive four-point citadel and the best-preserved Danish fort in the West Indies. Built between 1738 and 1749 out of Danish bricks (brought over as ships' ballast), the fort protected citizens from the onslaught of pirates, hurricanes and slave revolts, but its guns were never fired in an armed conflict. After 1878, the fort served as a prison and courthouse for the island. Visitors touring the fort will find cannons in place on the ramparts, plus a magazine, soldiers quarters furnished in period decor, prison cells and a kitchen, as well as a small military museum.

Other buildings on or near the site include the **Old Danish Scale House**, where the Danish weighed hogsheads of sugar for export. The **Custom's House**, recognizable by its sweeping 16-step stairway, served as the Danes' customs house for more than a century. Nearby, three-story neoclassical **Danish West India and Guinea Company Warehouse** served as company headquarters; slaves were auctioned in its central courtyard. Next door, the 1753 **Steeple Building** served as Church of Lord God of the Sabaoth, the island's first house of worship.

Half a block away between King and Company Sts, the U-shaped **Government House** evolved into one of the most elaborate governor's residences in all of the Lesser Antilles. Visitors can enter via the sweeping staircase on King St and explore the huge 2nd-floor reception hall.

US VIRGIN ISLANDS

PROTESTANT CAY

This small triangular cay, located less than 200yd (180m) from Kings Wharf (a five-minute ferry ride, round-trip US$3), is the site of a small resort. The resort's beach bar-restaurant and wide, sandy beach are open to the public. No other West Indies port has such a perfect little oasis so close at hand.

Festivals & Events

St Croix Agricultural Festival (mid-February) This festival has three days worth of food, music, crafts and livestock at the fairgrounds on Centerline Rd.

St Patrick's Day (March 17) Cruzans go all out with a parade in Christiansted.

St Croix Half-Ironman Triathlon (early May; ☎ 773-4470) Participants bid for the qualification of Ironman.

Danish West Indies Emancipation Day (July 3) Cruzans celebrate with a holiday from work, beach parties, family gatherings and plenty of fireworks over the Christiansted harbor.

Cruzan Christmas Fiesta (December 17 to January 7) This event puts a West Indies spin on the Christmas holiday. Most of the events happen in and around Christiansted.

Sleeping

Pink Fancy (☎ 773-6448, 800-524-2045; www.pink fancy.com; 27 Prince St; d US$95-150; Ⓟ ✕ ✕ ▣) In a historic 1780 Danish town house, this B&B has 13 rooms in four buildings, a pool and a bar where your hosts serve compli-

mentary drinks each evening. All rooms include a kitchenette.

Danish Manor Hotel (☎ 773-1377, 800-524-2069; www.danishmanor.com; 2 Company St; d US$110-135; ✕ ✕ ▣) This pink hotel, built around a courtyard in the heart of the restaurant district, is excellent value. There are 34 smallish but clean and comfortable rooms, some with kitchenettes and distant sea views.

Hotel Caravelle (☎ 773-0687, 800-524-0410; www.hotelcaravelle.com; 44A Queen Cross St; d US$135-165; Ⓟ ✕ ✕ ▣) Located on the waterfront, this property has 43 spacious rooms, plus a pool with sundeck overlooking the harbor.

King Christian Hotel (☎ 773-6330, 800-524-2012; www.kingchristian.com; 59 Kings Wharf; d standard/ superior US$100/135; Ⓟ ✕ ✕ ▣) You can't miss this three-story, sand-colored building that looks like a Danish warehouse (which it was 200 years ago) right next to the National Park Service sites. Many dive operations and tour boats have offices on the 1st floor. The 39 rooms include refrigerators and safes as well as the usual amenities. There is a small pool, but most guests take the ferry to the beach at Protestant Cay.

Hotel on the Cay (☎ 773-2035, 800-524-2035; www.hotelonthecay.com; d from US$175; ✕ ✕ ▣) A truly cool place to stay, 7-acre (2.8-hectare) Protestant Cay sits in the harbor a stone's throw from the Christiansted boardwalk, just a three-minute ferry ride away. The

---

DIVING ST CROIX

If you are a scuba enthusiast worth your sea salt, you cannot miss the north shore dives at Cane Bay Drop-Off, North Star Wall and Salt River Canyon, or the Butler Bay wreck dives. Frederiksted Pier is an exceptional dive, especially at night.

One of the best things about diving at St Croix is that while almost all the dive operators offer boat dives, many of the most exciting dives, such as Cane Bay, involve beach entries with short swims to the reef. On the deep side of the reef (just 100yd to 200 yd offshore), there is a wall that drops off at a 60-degree slope to a depth of more than 12,000ft (3658m). All the operators hit all the dive sites and charge about US$50 for one-tank dives, about US$80 for two tanks (both including equipment).

Cane Bay Dive Shop (☎ 773-9913, 800-338-3843; www.canebayscuba.com) This is a professional, friendly five-star PADI facility, across the highway from the beach and the Cane Bay Drop-Off, and with shops in both Christiansted and Frederiksted.

St Croix Ultimate Bluewater Adventures (☎ 773-5994, 887-567-1367; www.stcroixscuba.com; 14 Caravelle Arcade) Another ultra-professional shop in the Caravelle Arcade.

Other reputable shops include **Anchor Dive Center** (☎ 800-532-3483; www.anchordivestcroix.com) and **Dive Experience** (☎ 800-235-9047; www.divexp.com).

55 rooms come with private balconies and kitchenettes. The broad, white-sand beach has plenty of water-sports vendors and it's a great place to visit whether you stay at the hotel or not.

Eating

Morning Glory Coffee & Tea (☎ 773-6620; US$7-12; ☻ no dinner, closed Sun; Ⓟ ☒) In the Gallows Bay Market just east of downtown, this bright deli caters to vacationers and businessfolk coming into town from the East End. Breakfast is the big attraction here, with granola, croissants and eggs. Also delicious sandwiches.

Turtles (☎ 772-3936; 55 Company St; ☻ 8am-4pm Mon-Fri) Come to this central deli in a courtyard off Company St for smooth coffee breakfasts and big homemade sandwiches.

Luncheria (☎ 773-4247; 6 Company St; burritos US$8; ☻ lunch & dinner) This fun Mexican cantina will satiate your desire for delicious margs and burritos, whether you eat here or take out. The setting is a nice shaded courtyard with café tables.

Kim's Restaurant (☎ 773-3373; 45 King St; meals US$9-12; ☒) Come here for dynamite West Indian cooking and friendly conversation with cook and manager 'Big Kim.' The ambience is simple with peach-and-white tablecloths and a courtyard. Try the curried chicken, served with rice and salad.

Fort Christian Brew Pub (☎ 713-9820; Kings Wharf at King's Alley; lunch US$8-12, dinner US$16-21; ☻ lunch & dinner; ☒) Right on the boardwalk overlooking Protestant Cay, this is a great spot to sample drafts of the Virgin Island's homebrew, Foxy's Lager. The New Orleans menu features jambalaya and spicy shrimp *étouffée* (a delicious, tomato-based stew).

Mix Lounge (☎ 733-5762; meals US$8-22; ☻ 8am-11pm; ☒) Opened in 2004, this groovy martini bar-slash-sports bar at the west end of the boardwalk has an extensive menu offering a mix of seafood, salads and tapas-style snacks. Sunday brunch (US$25) features caviar, oysters and mimosas, accompanied by live music.

Kendrick's (☎ 773-9199; cnr King & Company Sts; meals US$18-40; ☻ dinner only Tue-Sat; ☒ ☒) Chef David Kendrick's award-winning restaurant has long set the standard for Cruzan gourmands. You can sit inside the colonial cottage or eat in the courtyard.

> **AUTHOR'S CHOICE**
>
> **Tutto Bene** (☎ 773-5229; 2006 Eastern Suburb; meals US$17-30; ☻ dinner only; Ⓟ ☒ ☒)
> Elegant yet casual, friendly and sophisticated, this fantastic Italian restaurant 0.5 miles (0.8km) east of Christiansted oozes greatness. The friendly, informative staff know the menu and each other well (in fact, they take an annual sailing trip together to the BVI each year), which makes the service relaxed and extremely efficient. The menu offers generous portions of fresh fish, chicken and meat entrees and creative pasta dishes. The nightly specials will rock your world. There's no view and only a couple of tables outside, but here the atmosphere and food is perhaps better than an ocean view.

AROUND CHRISTIANSTED

The area west of Christiansted has two very distinct sides to its topography and character. First, there are the wild mountains and beaches of the so-called rainforest area along the north shore. This is the site of some of the island's most dramatic scenery, spectacular diving and popular resorts. South of the mountains is the broad coastal plain that once hosted sugar plantations. Today, the area is largely a modern commercial and residential zone where most of St Croix's population lives.

Along the north shore, about 4 miles (6.4km) west of Christiansted on Rte 80, the **Salt River National Historic Park** is the only documented site where Christopher Columbus landed on US soil. In 1993, almost 700 acres (283 hectares) surrounding the Salt River estuary became an ecological reserve. The best way to see the bay is by kayak with **Caribbean Adventure Tours** (☎ 778-1522; www.stcroix kayak.com; 2½-hr-tour US$45) at the Salt River Marina on the west side of the bay.

Beach seekers hit palm-fringed **Hibiscus Beach**, less than 2 miles (3.2km) west of Christiansted off Rte 75. There are two hotels with a beachside restaurant and bars here, and good snorkeling.

A long, thin strand along Rte 80 about 9 miles (14.5km) west of Christiansted, **Cane Bay** marks the border between some of the best reef dives on the island and the steep hills of the rainforest. This beach stretch is a favorite as there are several small hotels, restaurants, bars and the Cane Bay Dive Shop (see the boxed text, p364).

Sleeping & Eating

Several small inns and guesthouses dot this area. Check out www.smallinnsstcroix.com for other suggestions.

Hibiscus Beach Hotel (☎ 773-0121, 800-442-0121; www.1hibiscus.com; 4131 La Grande Princesse; s/d from US$170/180; P ✗ ✗ ✗) The 38 rooms here spread through a collection of beachfront, colonial-style villas amid a coconut grove. Each room comes with a private patio or balcony. There is a popular beachfront bar and restaurant here too, with a view across the water to Christiansted.

Cane Bay Reef Club (☎ 778-2966, 800-253-8534; www.canebay.com; 114 North Shore Rd; r US$150; P ✗ ✗) This is a great value because each of the nine rooms is like its own little villa overlooking the beach. The decor is dated but all suites include kitchens and private patios virtually hanging over the sea. There is a pool and a seaside sundeck. The water-side bar is a popular place.

Waves at Cane Bay (☎ 778-1805, 800-545-0603; www.canebaystcroix.com; North Shore Rd; partial/full kitchen US$140/155) At the east end of Cane Bay, this small, kid-friendly hotel reflects the laid-back personalities of owners Suzanne and Kevin Ryan. You can snorkel or dive right off the rocks out front or lounge in the saltwater pool. The excellent restaurant here serves dinner.

Carambola Beach Resort (☎ 778-3800; www .carambolabeach.com; garden-/ocean-view r US$180/210; P ✗ ✗ ✗ ✗) The former Rockefeller resort is west of Cane Bay, and it's simply gorgeous. Guests stay in one of the red-roofed villas on the mountainside overlooking Davis Bay. There are 150 suite-sized rooms with all the trimmings, plus three restaurants, a world-class golf course, an on-site dive operator and tennis courts.

Drinking

After a day of diving at Cane Bay, climb out of the ocean and head to the **No Name Beach Bar** (across from the beach) or **Off the Wall** (at the east end), both open-air pubs with burgers, nachos and quesadillas, plus a happy crowd of drinkers.

EAST END
Buck Island Reef National Monument

With about 30,000 visitors a year, Buck Island is probably the most visited single attraction on St Croix. This small island (176 acres or 71 hectares, 1 mile or 1.6km long by 0.5 miles or 0.8km wide) lies 1.5 miles (2.4km) off the northeast coast of St Croix and sits at the center of an 880-acre (356-hectare) marine sanctuary. The sea gardens and marked underwater trail create first-rate snorkeling and shallow diving. Protected beaches have facilities and cooking grills you can fuel with driftwood. A hiking trail circles the west end and leads to an impressive observation point.

Another reason to visit Buck Island is simply the trip itself. Most visitors travel here aboard tour boats from Christiansted, 5 miles (8km) to the west.

Point Udall

Point Udall is the easternmost geographic point in the US territory. As you face into a 25-knot trade wind, the vista from the promontory high above the surf-strewn beaches is enough to make you hear symphonies. Others simply like the challenge of hiking the steep trails down the hillside to the isolated beaches on the south side of the point.

BUCK ISLAND TOURS

Several tour operators carry passengers to Buck Island. Most boats leave from Kings Wharf. Expect to pay US$50/75 (half/full day) per person, including snorkeling gear. The following are some of the most popular tour operators.

Big Beard Adventures (☎ 773-4482; www.bigbeards.com) Trips aboard catamaran sailboats, leaving from the Pan Am Pavilion.

Milemark Watersports (☎ 773-2628; www.milemarkwatersports.com) Offers half- and full-day trips aboard a large dive boat or catamaran, leaving from Kings Wharf.

Teroro II (☎ 773-3161) A trimaran sailboat whose captain will entertain you completely; trips leave from Green Cay Marina, east of Christiansted.

Sleeping

Buccaneer (☎ 773-2100, 800-255-3881; www.the buccaneer.com; 5007 Estate Shoys; r from US$295; ☒ ☒ ☒ ☒ ☒) Just 2 miles (3.2km) east of Christiansted, this historic resort continues to set the standard in Caribbean luxury. Owned and operated by the Armstrong family since 1947, the resort, though it has 138 rooms spread out on 340 luscious tropical acres (138 hectares), has an intimate, homey atmosphere.

Several room configurations tuck into separate buildings and cottages surrounding the main three-story hotel that overlooks a cove and beach. Each room has its own patio, refrigerator and full amenities. Active guests will appreciate the golf course, eight-court tennis center, water-sports shack and health spa. There are four restaurants, including The Terrace, with wonderful sunset views (meals US$25 to US$40). Don't be surprised if you see celebrities sharing one of the three beaches, or sipping a rum punch at the bar.

Divi Carina Bay Beach Resort (☎ 773-9700, 877-773-9700; www.divicarina.com; 25 Estate Turner Hole, Grapetree Bay; r from US$145) Many locals come to this splashy resort to visit the 10,000-sq-ft (929-sq-meter) **casino** (☎ 773-1529) and visitors come to stay at the 120 oceanfront rooms or 20 one-bedroom villas. Modern amenities abound. Guests can choose from two restaurants, two pools, a 1000ft (305m) beach, tennis courts or the island's only casino.

FREDERIKSTED

Once Frederiksted was the island's major commercial port, but today most goods arrive on the island at the oil refinery's artificial harbor on the island's south side.

Except when cruise ship arrivals dominate the Frederiksted Pier, the town looks the part of a classic Caribbean outpost. It seems an almost motionless village of colonial buildings lying beside a painted turquoise sea. The town's population is only slightly higher than it was two centuries ago. Although Cruzans generally stick to Christiansted for urban accoutrements, and most cruise ship passengers stay here for only a few hours, Frederiksted has some beautiful Victorian colonial architecture.

Notable sites include the Old Customs House and Fort Frederick, where a small museum opens up for visiting cruise-ship passengers. **Fort Frederik Beach** is the public strand just north of the fort. When the prevailing trade winds are blowing, this beach remains as sheltered as a millpond; you can swim off the beach for some excellent snorkeling around the pier.

Sleeping

With its out-of-the-mainstream, laissez-faire ambience, Frederiksted is the center for gay life on St Croix. All of the hotels listed here are gay-friendly.

Frederiksted (☎ 772-0500, 800-595-9519; www.frederikstedhotel.com; 442 Strand St; poolside/oceanside dUS$100/110; ☒ ☒ ☒ ☒) This 40-room downtown hotel calls itself 'a modern inn with old island charm.' Four floors are built around a courtyard and small pool, and many rooms have patios overlooking the pier. Rooms have tiled floors and standard hotel-style furnishings and a refrigerator. A bar and restaurant are on the premises.

Sand Castle on the Beach (☎ 772-1205, 800-524-2018; www.sandcastleonthebeach.com; 127 Estate Smithfield; d/q from US$130/250; ☒ ☒ ☒ ☒) Right on the beach about a mile (1.6km) south of Frederiksted, this four-building establishment with 19 rooms is one of the few gay and lesbian–oriented hotels in the USVI. Recently renovated rooms come with kitchenettes; most have sea views. In addition to swimming off the long beach, you can also sun or take a dip in the freshwater pool. There is also a video library and gas grills for cookouts, or you can have lunch or dinner at the oceanside restaurant aptly named the Beach Side Café.

Eating

Turtles (☎ 772-3676; 37 Strand St; sandwiches US$8; ⏰ 8:30am-3pm Mon-Sat) Like its sister in Christiansted, this deli makes killer sandwiches on homemade bread. Good coffee too.

Changes in L'Attitude (☎ 772-3090; meals US$8-18) Travelers and islanders alike gather at this beach bar just north of Frederiksted at Rainbow Beach. With Tex-Mex cuisine and a Jimmy Buffet vibe, this is a good place eat some fresh fish after a day at the beach (there are free beach chairs, changing rooms and showers here too).

Blue Moon (☎ 772-2222; 17 Strand St; meals US$15-35; ⏰ lunch Tue-Fri, dinner Tue-Sat, brunch Sun; ☒ ☒) Caribbean, vegetarian and Cajun cuisine are served up in this restored colonial warehouse, considered one of the best restaurants on the island. There's live jazz Friday and Saturday nights, and at Sunday brunch.

Le St Tropez (☎ 772-3000; 227 King St; ✆ dinner only; ✕ ✕) As authentic as it gets, this French bistro overflows with the spirit and sophistication of the Mediterranean. There are only 15 tables in this intimate courtyard-terrace restaurant that drips with the sound of Louis Armstrong and the scents of *coq au vin*. Call early for reservations.

AROUND FREDERIKSTED

Most of St Croix's rain falls over the mountains at the northwest corner of the island, producing a thick, damp forest of tall mahogany, silk cotton and white cedar. Only about 40 inches of rain fall here per year, which means the **Caledonia Rainforest** is not a true 'rainforest,' but no matter. This place looks the part, with clouds, dripping trees and earthy aromas.

Tucked into a steep hillside at the heart of the rainforest on Mahogany Rd, about 15 minutes' drive from Frederiksted, is the unusual outdoor woodworking and sculpture studio called **St Croix Leap** (☎ 772-0421; Rte 76 Brooks Hill; ✆ 8:30am-5pm Mon-Fri, 10am-4pm Sat). Here, master sculptor 'Cheech' leads a band of apprentice woodworkers in transforming chunks of fallen mahogany.

Paul & Jill's Equestrian Stables (☎ 772-2880; www.paulandjills.com), 1.5 miles (2.4km) north of Frederiksted on Rte 63, offers trail rides

---

PARTY PIGGIES

The wildest place to eat on the West End is the **Montpellier Domino Club** (☎ 772-9914), off Rte 76 in the rainforest. The club is set in a series of open-air pavilions beneath the dripping vegetation, and the cuisine is modern West Indian with fried chicken and fish offerings (around US$10).

Weekend afternoons and evenings pack in the customers with live entertainment such as calypso bands. But the big attraction here is the famous beer-swilling swine: tourists line up to pay US$1 to watch pigs gnaw open cans of nonalcoholic brewskis and swill the contents. These porkers used to drink the real thing until offspring were born suffering the symptoms of alcohol withdrawal. Oink.

---

that lead through hidden plantation ruins and the rainforest to hilltop vistas.

Estate Whim Plantation Museum

Just a few miles outside Frederiksted on Centerline Rd lies St Croix's most striking evocation of its colonial sugarcane history. Only a few of the original 150 acres (61 hectares) of Whim Plantation survive as the **museum** (☎ 772-0598; adult/child US$6/1; ✆ 10am-4pm Mon-Sat), but the grounds thoroughly evoke the days when 'King Cane' ruled the island. Guided tours leave every 30 minutes.

Cruzan Rum Distillery

If you are curious about how the Nelthropp family, one of the last of the Virgin Island distillers, makes their popular product in handcrafted oak barrels, stop by for a tour of the **distillery** (☎ 692-2280; www.cruzanrum.com; 3 Estate Diamond; adult/child US$4/1; ✆ 9am-4pm Mon-Fri). The tour takes about 20 minutes, after which you get to sip some of the good stuff. The factory is about 2 miles (3.2km) east of Whim Plantation.

St George Village Botanical Garden

Continuing east on Centerline Rd, you'll get to these **gardens** (☎ 692-2874; adult/child US$5/1; ✆ 9am-5pm). This 16-acre (6.5-hectare) park built over a colonial sugar plantation does for the flora and fauna what Whim Plantation does for the grandeur of plantation days.

DIRECTORY

ACCOMMODATIONS

Staying in the USVI can be downright expensive. However, hotels are at the mercy of the tourism traffic so if you travel in the off or shoulder seasons, or even if things are slow in the peak months, rates can drop as much as 40%. It's always a good idea to call ahead to check out deals. You'll be charged an 8% hotel tax, plus a 10% service charge.

If you're planning on staying a while, you might want to look into renting a condo or villa. Newspapers usually have print and online listings (check www.virginislanddaily news.com). The following are respected property managers with rentals in desirable locations:

Calypso Realty (☎ 774-1620)
Paradise Properties (☎ 779-1540, 800-524-2038)
McLaughlin Anderson Villas (☎ 774-2790, 800-537-6246)
Viva! VI Vacations & Villas (☎ 779-4250)

ACTIVITIES

The tropical climate and variety of land and seascapes make the islands a mecca for outdoor activities including playing and swimming in the surf.

Sailing is excellent in the calm bays, and several charter companies offer trips, rentals and lessons.

Diving & Snorkeling

Both diving and snorkeling here are superb, with warm water temperatures and incredible visibility. St Thomas and St John feature nearshore fringing reefs that sit atop the shallow Virgin Bank.

St Croix sits atop its own narrow bank and divers can explore sheer walls and slopes absolutely encrusted with colorful corals. Snorkelers can step in the water almost anywhere and find plenty of tropical fish, sea turtles, even nurse sharks. Dive operators run day trips out of the major ports and resort hotels.

Fishing

The USVI host several deep-sea fishing tournaments. Marlin is a spring/summer fish, sailfish and wahoo run in fall, and dorado show up in winter. Charters run out of American Yacht Harbor in Red Hook.

Hiking

The most popular hiking area is the 9500-acre (3845-hectare) Virgin Islands National Park on St John, with about 23 miles (37km) of hiking trails (see the boxed text, p358).

Sailing

Some of the world's best sailing is in the USVI. Several companies rent boats, offer day sails and charters (see the boxed text, p398). If you want to learn to sail, **Annapolis Sailing School** (☎ 800-638-9192) in Christiansted on St Croix books three-and five-day learn-to-sail vacations.

The following companies offer charters from St Thomas:
Caribbean Sailing Charters (☎ 800-824-1331; American Yacht Harbor)
CYOA Yacht Charters (☎ 777-9690, 800-944-2962; Frenchtown Marina)
Island Yacht Charters (☎ 775-6666, 800-524-2019; American Yacht Harbor)

For an up-to-date list of charters check the **Sail magazine website** (www.sailmag.com). To find crewed yachts in the USVI contact the **Virgin Islands Charterboat League** (☎ 774-3944, 800-524-2061).

Surfing & Windsurfing

In general, winter is the best surfing season, when swells roll in from the northeast and set up some point breaks of 6ft (1.8m) and higher at places like Hull Bay on St Thomas. Bring your own board; it is hard to find rental equipment in the islands.

BOOKS

If you like the lilt of West Indian dialogue, check out Bob Shacochis' *Easy in the Islands*, a collection of short stories that won an American Book Award.

Mariners will want *The Cruising Guide to the Virgin Islands*, by Nancy and Simon Scott, and *Street's Cruising Guide to the*

US VIRGIN ISLANDS

Eastern Caribbean. Birders should check out *A Guide to the Birds of Puerto Rico & the Virgin Islands*, by Herbert Rafaela. *Common Trees of Puerto Rico and the Virgin Islands*, by EL Little and FH Wadsworth, has everything you ever wanted to know about manchineel and mango trees.

The Virgin Islands: America's Caribbean Outpost, by James Bough and Roy Macridis, investigates the US' role in the Virgin Islands. Isidor Paiewonsky's *Eyewitness Accounts of Slavery in the Danish West Indies* is an important historical book. Many islanders consider local author Harold Willocks' thick tome *The Umbilical Cord* the best portrait of their islands past and present.

If you've got a restless 10 to 14 year old, they'll get hooked on *My Name is Not Angelica* by Scott O'Dell, an incredible historical novel set in 1733 St Thomas.

Caribbean Cooking, by Judy Bastry, and *Virgin Islands Native Recipes*, by Mildred Anduze, unfold the mysteries of Creole cuisine.

CHILDREN

Very much a family-oriented destination, the USVI are a great place to bring kids. Many resorts have children's programs and babysitting services.

Many hotels offer deals for children, and restaurants often have special menus or discounts.

Caribbean Nanny Care (☎ 473-7500; www.caribbeannannycare.com) offers babysitting services by trained, professional nannies. They will come to your hotel or take the kids off your hands for US$40 per hour (minimum four hours). It also rents out gear like car seats, strollers and baby monitors.

DANGERS & ANNOYANCES

St Thomas and St Croix both have reputations for crime, mostly robbery and petty theft. If you lock up your belongings and avoid walking alone at night, you should be fine.

EMBASSIES & CONSULATES
US Virgin Islands Embassies & Consulates

US diplomatic offices representing the USVI abroad and providing visa services include the following:

Australia Melbourne (☎ 03-9526-5900; 553 St Kilda Rd, Victoria); Sydney (☎ 02-9373-9200; Level 59 MLC Centre, 19-29 Martin Pl, NSW 2000)
Canada (☎ 613-238-5535; 100 Wellington St, Ottawa, Ontario K1P 5T1)
France (☎ 01-43-12-22-22; 2 av Gabriel, 75382 Paris)
Germany (☎ 030-8305-0; Neustädtische Kirchstr, 4-5 10117 Berlin)
Ireland (☎ 01-668-8777; 42 Elgin Rd, Ballsbridge, Dublin)
Netherlands (☎ 020-575 5309; Museumplein 19, 1071 DJ Amsterdam)
New Zealand (☎ 04-462 6000; 29 Fitzherbert Tce, Thorndon, Wellington)
UK (☎ 0207-499-9000; 24 Grosvenor Sq, London W1A 1AE)

Embassies & Consulates in the US Virgin Islands

With the exception of those listed below, there are no foreign embassies or consulates.

Denmark (☎ 776-0656; www.dkconsulateusvi.com; Scandinavian Center, Havensight Mall, Bldg 3; Charlotte Amalie; St Thomas)
Sweden (☎ 774-6845; 1340 Taarneberg; Charlotte Amalie, St Thomas)

FESTIVALS & EVENTS

St Croix Agricultural Festival (mid-February) This three-day event features island crafters, food stalls, bands and more.
International Rolex Cup Regatta (early April; ☎ 775-6320) World-class racing boats and crews gather at St Thomas for this regatta three-day event.
St Thomas Carnival (April; ☎ 774-8774) Stemming from West African masquerading traditions, the St Thomas carnival is the second-largest carnival in the Caribbean after the one at Port-of-Spain, Trinidad.
St John Carnival (early July; ☎ 776-6450) A smaller version of the St Thomas Carnival.
Cruzan Christmas Fiesta (December 17-January 7; ☎ 773-0495) Puts a West Indies spin on the holidays; most of the decorations and events focus on Christiansted.

GAY & LESBIAN TRAVELERS

Gays and lesbians have been some of the islands' most prominent entrepreneurs and politicians for decades. Sadly, however, the climate of 'don't ask, don't tell' still permeates. Of the three islands, St Croix is the most 'gay-friendly.'

HOLIDAYS

US public holidays are celebrated along with local holidays in the USVI. Banks, schools and government offices (including post offices) are closed, and transportation, museums and other services are on shorter schedules.

New Year's Day January 1
Three Kings Day (Feast of the Epiphany) January 6
Martin Luther King Jr's Birthday Third Monday in January
Presidents' Day Third Monday in February
Holy Thursday & Good Friday Before Easter
Easter & Easter Monday Late March or early April
Memorial Day Last Monday in May
Emancipation Day July 3. Island slaves were freed on this date in 1873.
Independence Day (aka Fourth of July) July 4
Supplication Day In July (date varies)
Labor Day First Monday in September
Columbus Day Second Monday in October
Liberty Day November 1
Veterans' Day November 11
Thanksgiving Day Fourth Thursday in November
Christmas Day & Boxing Day December 25 & 26

INTERNET RESOURCES
www.stthomasthisweek.com Online version of the ubiquitous weekly magazine.
www.usvi.net Comprehensive information on everything from hotels and restaurants to island arts and activities.
www.usviguide.com Specific information on each of the three main islands, with helpful transportation information.
www.usvitourism.vi Official site for the USVI Department of Tourism.

MONEY
The US dollar is used throughout the USVI. You'll find Chase Manhattan, Citibank, First Bank, Scotiabank and Banco Popular on the main islands. Although hours may vary slightly, most banks are open 9am to 3pm Monday to Thursday, 9am to 5pm Friday.

TELEPHONE
Pay phones are readily available. Local calls cost US$0.25, but you're better off using a phone card, readily available at shops and kiosks. The country code is ☎ 340, but you just dial the seven-digit local number in the islands. To call from North America, dial ☎ 1-340 + the local number. From elsewhere, dial your country's international dialing code + ☎ 340 + the local number. We've included only the seven-digit local number in USVI listings in this chapter.

Most cell (mobile) phones that work in the US will work on the islands as well, often with no extra fee. It's best to contact your provider before you leave to find out what type of service you can expect (and how much it will cost).

TOURIST INFORMATION
The **US Virgin Islands Department of Tourism** (www.usvitourism.vi) has locations on the three main islands. See the Information section under each of the islands for details.

VISAS
Under the US State Department's Visa Waiver Program, visitors from most Western countries do not need a visa to enter the USVI if they are staying less than 90 days. If you are staying longer, or if your home country does not qualify under the Visa Waiver Program (check www.state.gov), you'll need to obtain a B-2 visa (US$100), which you can get at any US embassy.

TRANSPORTATION

GETTING THERE & AWAY
Entering the US Virgin Islands
US nationals need proof of citizenship (such as a driver's licence with photo ID) to enter the USVI, but should be aware that if they're traveling to another country in the Caribbean (other than Puerto Rico, which, like the USVI, is a US territory), they must have a valid passport in order to re-enter the US (see the boxed text, p772). Visitors from other countries must have a valid passport to enter the USVI.

Air
Airports on both St Thomas and St Croix handle international air traffic, but the bulk of international flights arrive and depart from St Thomas, coming through Puerto Rico.

Cyril E King Airport (STT; ☎ 774-5100; www.viport .com/aviation.html) A modern facility less than 2 miles (3.2km) west of Charlotte Amalie.
Henry E Rohlsen Airport (STX; ☎ 778-0589; www .viport.com/aviation.html) Located on the southwest side of St Croix .

See p777 for information on getting to USVI from outside the Caribbean. The following

See p777 for information on getting to USVI

US VIRGIN ISLANDS

airlines fly to/from USVI from within the Caribbean:

Air St Thomas (☎ 776-2700; www.airstthomas.com; hub St Thomas)

Air Sunshine (☎ 888-879-8900; www.airsunshine.com; hub San Juan)

American Eagle (☎ 868-669-4661; www.aa.com; hub Houston)

Cape Air (☎ 800-352-0714; www.flycapeair.com; hub San Juan)

Clair Aero (☎ 784-495-2271; www.clairaero.com; hub Tortola)

Liat (☎ 774-2313; www.liatairline.com; hub Antigua)

Seaborne Airlines (☎ 888-359-9687; www.seaborne airlines.com; hub St Thomas)

Sea
CRUISE SHIP
St Thomas is the most popular cruise ship destination in the Caribbean, with more than 1000 arrivals each year. For the most part, these ships dock at the West India Company dock in Havensight on the eastern edge of St Thomas Harbor.

Cruise Line International Association (CLIA; ☎ 212-921-0549; www.cruising.org) is a New York–based company that provides information on cruising and individual lines. See also p777 for more information.

FERRY
US Virgin Islands to British Virgin Islands
There are excellent ferry connections linking St Thomas and St John with the BVI's Tortola, Virgin Gorda and Jost Van Dyke. You must have a valid passport to travel between USVI and BVI.

Several ferries offer service from the Marine Terminal in Charlotte Amalie to Road Town (Tortola), often via West End (Tortola). All have several daily departures and similar costs (round-trip US$40, 1½ hours). Try **Smith's Ferry Services** (☎ 775-7292), **Native Son** (☎ 774-8685) or **Road Town Fast Ferry** (☎ 777-2800).

Speedy's (☎ 284-495-5240) has sailings (one way/round-trip $35/60, two hours including stop at customs on Tortola) on Tuesday, Thursday and Saturday between Charlotte Amalie and Virgin Gorda, via Road Town (Tortola).

Inter-Island Ferry Services (☎ 776-6597) and the **Nubian Princess** (☎ 775-4700) both offer three daily sailings between Cruz Bay and

Tortola's West End (round-trip US$35, 30 minutes). Inter-Island Ferry Services also has two sailings daily between Red Hook and Jost Van Dyke (BVI), via St John (round-trip US$40, 45 minutes).

US Virgin Islands to Puerto Rico
Passengers can take the high-speed passenger ferry **Caribe Cay** (☎ 787-863-0582; www.caribe cay.com; two hours; $55 one way) to Fajardo, Puerto Rico. This Fajardo-based company departs St Thomas every Saturday at 4:30pm from Charlotte Amalie's waterfront, at the foot of Raadet's Gade. You need to purchase tickets on the Friday before, so call ahead to make arrangements with a representative. Return trips to St Thomas depart Fajardo Saturdays at 8am.

GETTING AROUND
Air
A soaring floatplane is the best way to get back and forth between St Thomas and St Croix. **Seaborne Airlines** (☎ 773 6442, 888-359-8687; www.seaborneairlines.com) runs many trips each day from the Marine Terminal in Charlotte Amalie, or the seaplane dock in Christiansted (one way/round-trip US$66/93; 25 minutes). There's a baggage restriction of just 30lb (16kg; US$0.50 per extra pound); if you have a lot of luggage, you might want to take the fast ferry (p363) or a regular flight. Seaborne also flies to San Juan and Culebra, Puerto Rico.

Cape Air (☎ 800-352-0714; www.flycapeair.com; hub San Juan) also flies between St Thomas and St Croix.

Bus
Vitran (☎ 774-5678) operates air-conditioned buses over the length of St Thomas, St John and St Croix. Fares are US$1 and buses run daily between 5:30am and 9:30pm.

Car
Driving is the most convenient way to get around individual islands, but be prepared for unique driving conditions. First, driving is on the left-hand side of the road, and the steering column is on the left also. You'll see signs reminding you to 'keep your shoulder to the shoulder' and 'stay left!' Island roads are narrow, steep and twisting; stray cows, goats and chickens constantly wander onto the roads.

Drivers don't always heed the rules of the road here, often stopping dead in the middle of the road to talk to friends.

A common gesture is the flap: when drivers are about to do something (stop, turn etc), they extend their arm out the window and waggle their hand up and down like a flapping bird.

RENTAL

Many of the major international car rental companies operate in the Virgin Islands, along with plenty of local firms. Most rental companies require that you to be at least 21, have a major credit card and a valid driver's license. Rental companies have desks at the St Thomas and St Croix airports.

High-season rates begin at about US$45 per day and can run as high as US$100, but you'll get a better price for a weekly rental. See the island entries in this chapter for car-rental agencies.

Ferry

The islands have frequent and inexpensive ferry services. The full ferry schedules are printed in the free *St Thomas/St John This Week* magazine, which you can pick up anywhere.

ST THOMAS TO ST JOHN

A ferry departs Red Hook for Cruz Bay (one way US$3, 20 minutes) at 6:30am, 7:30am, then hourly from 8am to midnight daily. It departs Cruz Bay hourly from 6am to 11pm daily.

The ferry service between Charlotte Amalie and Cruz Bay (one way US$7, 45 minutes) departs Charlotte Amalie at 9am, 11am, 3pm, 4pm and 5:30pm daily, and Cruz Bay at 7:15am, 9:15am, 11:15am, 1:15pm, 2:15pm and 3:45pm daily. In Charlotte Amalie, catch the ferry at the waterfront, at the foot of Raadet's Gade.

Boyson, Inc (☎ 776-6294) and **Republic Barge** (☎ 997-4000) both run car ferries between Red Hook and Cruz Bay (round-trip US$35; 20 minutes), which means there are sailings almost every hour. The first sail is at 6am, the last one at 7pm.

ST THOMAS TO ST CROIX

The 600-passenger **Salacia** (☎ 719-0099; www .virginislandsfastferry.com), otherwise known as the 'fast ferry,' travels between St Thomas and St Croix during high season (late November to May) only (round-trip US$70, 75 minutes). From St Thomas it departs from the Marine Terminal in Charlotte Amalie, and the Gallow's Bay Terminal in Christiansted on St Croix.

Taxi

Territorial law requires that taxi drivers carry a government-set rate sheet, and those rates are published in the free *St Thomas/St John This Week* or *St Croix This Week*.

Many taxis are open-air pickup trucks with bench seats and awnings, able to carry up to 12 passengers. To hail one, stand by the side of the road and wave when a cab approaches.

US VIRGIN ISLANDS

British Virgin Islands

Looking for neon lights, casinos and high-rise buildings? Well, you've come to the wrong place. A wonderful mix of uninhabited cays, mountainous islands and hundreds of welcoming anchorages, the British Virgin Islands (BVI) are a sailor's fantasy, a diver's bliss and a traveler's hip-hip-hooray.

Forget shopping and pretentious resorts. The BVI's blend of West Indian culture, young professional Britons, salty mariners and feisty millionaires keeps the islands energized. Everyone, it seems, is happy to be here. And why not? More than 60 islands flank the Sir Francis Drake Channel – that's a lot of beach and a lot of surf to play in. Tortola, the largest island and primo provisioning stop, grooves to a funky beat; Virgin Gorda offers secluded resorts and submerged boulders; Jost Van Dyke is the playful island, where it's just impossible to take anything too seriously, while Anegada, a coral atoll only 28ft (8.5m) above sea level, is home to prehistoric iguanas, rare birds and pristine beaches.

This British overseas territory, part of the British West Indies, is a treat. Whether you're a seasoned sailor or a landlocked terrestrial, you'll be changed by the BVI, where it's all about getting wet, sucking lobster tails and sipping sunshine.

FAST FACTS

- **Area** 59 sq miles (153 sq km)
- **Capital** Road Town, Tortola
- **Country code** ☎ 284
- **Departure tax** US$5 by sea (cruise ship passengers pay US$7); US$15 by air (plus US$5 security tax)
- **Famous for** Sailing ecstasy, the Baths, incredible diving
- **Language** English
- **Money** US dollar; US$1 = €0.82 = UK£0.55
- **People** British Virgin Islanders
- **Phrases** Oi, y'alright, mon?
- **Population** 21,000
- **Visa** Not necessary for tourists

HIGHLIGHTS

- **The Baths** (p391) Snorkel amid giant rocks, where the sea fills the grottoes between boulders on Virgin Gorda.
- **Charter boat** (p398) Sail through the islands on a charter boat – it may be more affordable than you realize.
- **Foxy's Tamarind Bar** (p394) Swill a pint of Foxy's Lager at this legendary bar on Jost Van Dyke.
- **RMS Rhone** (p389) Scuba dive on this famous shipwreck off Salt Island.
- **Off-the-beaten track** (p395) Make your way over to Anegada for a few days of pristine exploration.

ITINERARIES

- **Three Days** Stay in one of Tortola's resorts and be sure to book a day's sailing trip to one of the out islands.
- **One week** Spend a day or two in Tortola's Cane Garden Bay, then ferry to Virgin Gorda for a couple more. Plan a three-day sailing trip or learn to scuba dive.
- **Two weeks** Follow the one-week itinerary and utilize the ferries by adding a trip to Jost Van Dyke.

CLIMATE & WHEN TO GO

Reliably balmy with gentle trade winds, the BVI's temperature averages 77°F (25°C) in the winter and 82°F (28°C) in summer. Though the islands average less than 50 inches of rain each year, count on brief tropical showers between July and October. Hurricane season hits its peak from July to September.

Most visitors come between December and February, but November, April and May are good times too, as hotel prices are lower and the cruise ships are not yet in full swing.

HISTORY

On Christopher Columbus' second trip to the Caribbean, Carib Indians led him to an archipelago of pristine islands that he dubbed Santa Ursula y Las Once Mil Vírgenes (St Ursula and the 11,000 Virgins), in honor of a 4th-century princess raped and murdered, along with 11,000 maidens, in Cologne by marauding Huns.

The earliest Spanish charts of the islands identify Tortola (Turtledove) and Virgin Gorda (Fat Virgin). After sailing past the

---

HOW MUCH?

- **Taxi from Tortola's airport to Road Town** US$18
- **Two-tank scuba dive trip** US$80
- **Round-trip ferry from Tortola to Virgin Gorda** US$20
- **Half-day sailing trip** US$60
- **Fresh fish at a restaurant** US$20

LONELY PLANET INDEX

- **Liter of gas** US$2.60
- **Liter of bottled water** US$2
- **Bottle of Carib beer** US$2
- **Souvenir T-shirt** US$20
- **Street snack: roti** US$10

Virgins, Columbus traveled west to Puerto Rico and Jamaica.

By 1595, the famous English privateers Sir Francis Drake and Jack Hawkins were using the Virgin Islands as a staging ground for attacks on Spanish shipping. In the wake of Drake and Hawkins came French corsairs and Dutch freebooters. All knew that the Virgin Islands had some of the most secure and unattended harbors in the West Indies. Places like Sopers Hole at the West End of Tortola and the Bight at Norman Island are legendary pirates' dens.

While the Danes settled on what is now the US Virgin Islands (USVI), the English had a firm hold on today's BVI. The middle island of St John remained disputed territory until 1717, when the Danish side claimed it for good. The Narrows between St John and Tortola has divided the eastern Virgins (BVI) from the western Virgins (USVI) for more than 250 years.

Following WWII, British citizens in the islands clamored for more independence. In 1949 BVI citizens demonstrated for a representative government and got a so-called presidential legislature the next year. During the 1960s Britain's administrative mechanisms for its Caribbean colonies kept changing shape and, by 1967, the BVI had become an independent colony with its own political parties, a Legislative Council and an elected Chief Minister.

BRITISH VIRGIN ISLANDS

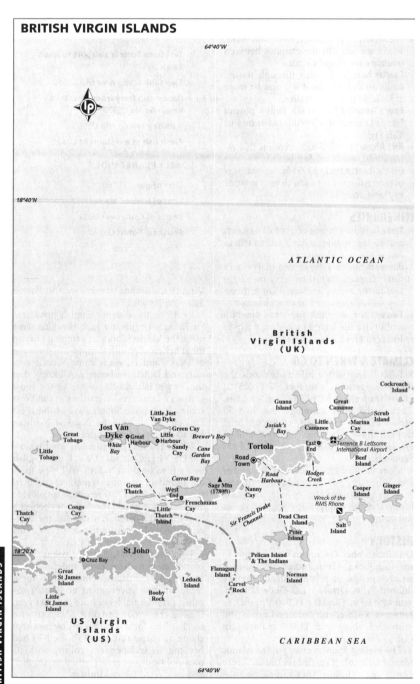

In 1967, Britain's Queen Elizabeth II made the first of many royal visits to the BVI, casting a glow of celebrity on the islands that they enjoy to this day. In the past four decades the islands have seen unprecedented growth in the tourism and sailing industries.

THE CULTURE

The BVI have one of the most stable economies in the Caribbean, with tourism generating about 45% of all income.

In the mid-1980s the government began offering offshore registration to companies wishing to incorporate in the islands, and incorporation fees now generate substantial revenues, with about 500,000 companies currently on the register. The population of sailors, locals and seasonal workers has been infused with British accountants, trust lawyers and investment brokers who came to Tortola to handle international business interests, be it leaping through taxation loopholes or waxing creative on the plethora of offshore accounts. The result is a nice mix of professional people, who soon loosen up with the heat and relaxed attitude, West Indians working the tourist trade or raising livestock, and adventurers whose biochemistry is intricately tied to the seas.

ENVIRONMENT
The Land

Like other islands fringing the Caribbean, the BVI owe their existence to a series of volcanic eruptions that built up layers of lava and igneous rock, creating islands with three geographical zones: the coastal plain, coastal dry forests and the steep central mountains that dominate the island interiors. The one exception is easternmost Anegada, which is a flat coral island. Sage Mountain on Tortola is the highest point in the islands at 1780ft (542m). Except where houses perch precariously on impossibly steep slopes, the mountains are dense subtropical forests. All of the timber is second- or third-growth; the islands were stripped for sugar, cotton and tobacco plantations in the colonial era. The Virgins have no rivers and very few freshwater streams.

Thousands of tropical plant varieties grow in the BVI, and a short drive can transport a nature lover between entirely different ecosystems. Mangrove swamps,

BRITISH VIRGIN ISLANDS

coconut groves and sea-grape trees dominate the coast, while mountain peaks support wet forest with mahogany, lignum vitae, palmetto and more than 30 varieties of wild orchid.

Islanders also grow and collect hundreds of different roots and herbs as ingredients for 'bush medicine.' Psychoactive mushrooms grow wild (and are consumed) on the islands, particularly on Tortola (see the boxed text, below).

Wildlife

Few land mammals are natives; most were accidentally or intentionally introduced. Virtually every island has a feral population of goats and burros, and some islands have wild pigs, horses, cats and dogs.

More than 200 species of bird inhabit the island, adding bright colors and a symphony of sound to the tropical environment. A few snake species (none of which are poisonous) slither around, along with a host of small and not-so-small lizards, including the 6ft-long (1.8m) rock iguanas of Anegada and the common green iguana found throughout the islands. Anoles and gecko lizards are ubiquitous. Numerous species of toad and frog populate the islands, including the piping frog and the giant toad, which secretes poisonous white venom from its eyes.

Environmental Issues

Rapid urbanization, deforestation, soil erosion, mangrove destruction and a lack of freshwater keep environmentalists wringing their hands with worry. On Tortola, almost all of the flat land has been developed, and houses hang on mountain slopes like Christmas ornaments. High population growth and density have kept sewage treatment plants in a constant scramble to prevent the islands soiling themselves.

As with the islands' other environmental problems, mangrove destruction was at its worst decades ago with the rush for development. Some bays now lined with marinas, hotels and businesses, such as the harbor at Road Town, were mangrove estuaries just 50 years ago. Environmentalists began fighting to preserve the remaining mangroves in the 1980s, and the late 1990s brought some victories in this arena.

Desalination plants make freshwater out of seawater and without them the islands would seriously lack water. When a storm strikes, islands lose power and diesel facilities shut down, forcing islanders to use rainwater cisterns.

Environmental concerns have resulted in the formation of the **BVI National Parks Trust** (☎ 494-3904; www.bvinationalparkstrust.org), which protects 15 parks and six islands, including the Dogs and Fallen Jerusalem, which are excellent dive sites. The entire southwest coast of Virgin Gorda is a collection of national parks that includes the giant boulder formations at the Baths.

FOOD & DRINK

Soup and stew are staples. Generally, cast-iron pots are used for 'boilin' down' soups or stews, such as *pepperpot* – which combines oxtail, chicken, beef, pork and calf's foot with a hot pepper and *cassareep* (from

---

MAGIC MUSHROOMS

Psychoactive mushrooms *(psilocybin)* grow wild on Tortola. If you're into partying, someone will eventually tempt you with 'shrooms' or shroom tea. Shrooms are legal to possess and consume in the BVI, but illegal to sell.

There are dozens of species, but the primary distinguishing feature of most *psilocybin* mushrooms is that they bruise blue when handled.

Depending on how much you consume, mushrooms generally take 30 to 60 minutes (up to two hours) to 'kick in.' The effects of ingestion resemble a short LSD trip, producing significant physical, visual and perceptual changes. The 'trip' can last up to six hours, but for many people, there is an additional period of time when it is difficult to fall asleep and reality is skewed.

Depending on the strength and size of the dose, Tortola's shrooms can give you anything from a mild high to a wall-melting, toilet-hugging bad trip. Note: mixing shrooms with alcohol is asking for trouble.

cassava). *Tannia* (a root vegetable) soup is another traditional offering, as is *calabeza* (pumpkin) soup. Another popular dish is *roti* (*root*-ee), which are flatbread envelopes stuffed with curried meat, fish or poultry, often served with a tangy mango chutney.

Fungi (*foon*-ghee) is made from cornmeal and is usually served with fish and gravy. *Daube* meat is a pot roast seasoned with vinegar, onion and native spices. *Souse* is another spicy one-pot dish made from boiled pig's feet with a sauce of lime and hot pepper. Most dishes arrive with johnnycakes (fried bread).

The BVI are home to the popular cocktail called the Painkiller, a yummy mix of rum, orange juice, pineapple juice and a touch of coconut cream.

TORTOLA

Viewed from offshore Tortola oozes a sense of enchantment, with sharp mountain peaks glowing purple in the mist, covered with frangipani, ginger and bursting bougainvillea. Despite being used by many travelers simply as a jump-off point, Tortola is actually a big diamond in the rough, offering a lot to people willing to take the time to penetrate its busy facade.

The island is both the governmental and commercial center of the BVI, as well as the air and ferry hub. About 80% of the BVI's 21,000 citizens live and work here. On the south shore, Road Town is a thickly settled mix of commercial development, industrial sites, marinas, hotels and West Indian homes.

Many travelers head to the north shore, where guesthouses and mountain villas mingle with beachside resorts. As singer Jimmy Buffett insinuates in his anthem to Cane Garden Bay, anyone who misses the beaches and nightlife on the north shore of Tortola has missed a land of peace and plenty.

In Spanish, Tortola means 'turtledove.' Today, most of the namesake doves are gone, but you can still hear them on neighboring Guana Island, where their distinctive cooing fills the air.

Orientation

At 21 sq miles (54 sq km) in area, Tortola lies less than 2 miles (3.2km) east of St John in the USVI, across a windswept and current-ripped channel called the Narrows. This long, thin, high island stretches 14 miles (22.5km) from west to east but is rarely more than 2 miles (3.2km) wide. The altitude of Tortola's mountain spine creates steep slopes that come almost to the water's edge on the island's north and south shores. A fringe of scalloped bays ring the island; the deepest of which is the harbor for the BVI's largest town and capital, Road Town.

Getting There & Around

Terrence B Lettsome Airport (EIS; ☎ 494-3701) is on Beef Island, connected to Tortola by a toll bridge on the east end of the island. Most international flights from North America and Europe connect through a hub (see p400).

There are two ports of entry for ferries; one is at the main ferry terminal in Road Town, the other is at West End, on the west end of the island. Ferries travel to Virgin Gorda from Road Town only. You can take ferries from either Road Town or West End to Charlotte Amalie on St Thomas; ferries to St John (USVI) or Jost Van Dyke depart from West End (see p401).

Public transportation is almost nonexistent and people either rent cars or make use of the efficient taxis. Although everything looks close on the map, the ruggedness of Tortola's topography makes for slow travel.

CAR

There are several good local car-rental agencies on the island. All drivers must purchase a Visitor's Temporary Driver's License (US$10), available at the car-rental agency. Hold onto this in case you end up renting a car on another island.

High-season rates begin at about US$45 per day, and can run as high as US$80, but you'll get a better price for a weekly rental. **Hertz** Road Town (☎ 494-6228); airport (☎ 495-6600) **International Car Rentals** (☎ 494-4715; Road Town) **Jerry's Car Rental** (☎ 495-4111, 800-430-7648; West End) A good option if you're coming in on a West End ferry. Jerry will pick you up at the dock.

TAXI

Taxis are convenient and essential if you're not renting a car. Several are the open-air variety, with bench seats and awnings, able to carry 12 passengers. The fare from Road

Town to the West End, Cane Garden Bay and the airport is the same (US$18). From West End to the airport it's US$36. See p401 for reputable taxi companies.

ROAD TOWN

Road Town looks, smells and sounds like the boomtown it is. This small town is the bustling administration stop for anyone traveling through the BVI. From here, you can take ferries to the outlying islands, including Virgin Gorda and the USVI.

The capital takes its name from the island's principal harbor, Road Bay, which has served as a 'roadstead' (staging area) for fleets of ships for centuries. By day, the town's roads clog with traffic that stirs up dust and shakes your spine with the winding of transmission gears. Even the harbor seems on the verge of chaos with the comings and goings of scores of charter yachts, ferries and occasional cruise ships. It's both exciting and a little overwhelming.

Most of the town's pubs and restaurants are along Waterfront Dr. Despite the name, little of this road actually skirts the sea, and the town (perhaps because of hurricanes) largely turns its back to the harbor.

Main St, Road Town's primary shopping venue, is a nice retreat for anyone seeking shade and quiet. This narrow street winds along the western edge of town and has a collection of wooden and stone buildings dating back about 200 years.

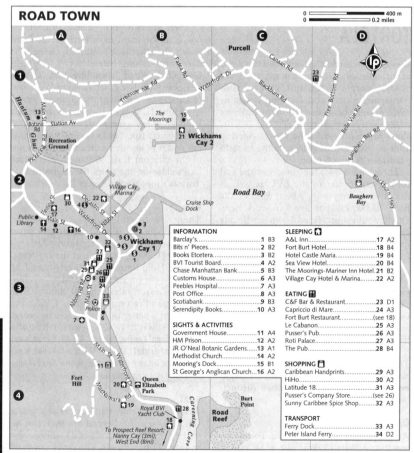

ROAD TOWN

0 — 400 m
0 — 0.2 miles

Purcell

Pasea Rd
Canaan Rd
Waterfront Dr
Blackburn Rd
Treasure Isle Rd
Free Bottom Rd
Belle Vue Rd
Baughers Bay Rd
Blackburn Hwy

The Moorings
Wickhams Cay 2

Huntums Ghut
Botanic Rd
Station Av
Recreation Ground
Pickering Rd

Village Cay Marina
Road Bay
Baughers Bay

Ferris St
DeCastro St
Nibbs St
Waterfront Dr
Cruise Ship Dock

Public Library
Main St

Wickhams Cay 1

Abbott Rd
Main St
Police

Main St
Waterfront Dr

Fort Hill
MacNamara Rd
Queen Elizabeth Park
Royal BVI Yacht Club
Careening Cove
Burt Point
Road Reef

To Prospect Reef Resort; Nanny Cay (3mi); West End (8mi)

Information

BOOKSTORES

Books Etcetera (☎ 494-6611; Wickhams Cay 1; ☯ 9am-5pm Mon-Sat)

Serendipity Books (☎ 494-5865; Main St; ☯ 9:30am-5:30pm Mon-Sat)

INTERNET ACCESS

Bits 'n' Pieces (☎ 494-5957; Wickhams Cay 1; US$3 per 15min; ☯ 8am-5pm Mon-Fri, 9am-noon Sat) Just down from Books Etcetera, in the office of Caribbean Yacht Management, this place has four terminals and a printer.

MEDICAL SERVICES

Peebles Hospital (☎ 494-3467; Main St) At the south end of Main St, this hospital has 40 beds and complete emergency services.

MONEY

Branches of Barclay's, Scotiabank and Chase Manhattan bank are all found on Wickhams Cay 1 in Road Town. All these banks have ATMs.

POST

Post office (☎ 494-7423; Main St; ☯ 8am-4pm Mon-Fri, 9am-1:30pm Sat) The main PO is at the south end of Main Street. There are small regional offices at Cane Garden Bay, Carrot Bay, East End and West End.

TOURIST INFORMATION

BVI Tourist Board (☎ 494-3864, 800-835-8530; www.bvitouristboard.com; Akara Bldg, Wickhams Cay 1; ☯ 9am-5pm Mon-Fri) Facing the Village Cay Hotel and the cruise ship dock (look for the banner) the main office provides the free BVI map, which is sufficient for navigating roads.

Tourist office (☎ 494-7260; ☯ 9am-5pm) This small office is at the ferry terminal.

Dangers & Annoyances

Road Town has little street crime, but areas can become suddenly desolate after dark. Long Bush Rd, in the northwest corner of town, has a number of rowdy West Indian bars and clubs. Don't walk alone there at night.

Sights

The **JR O'Neal Botanic Gardens** (☎ 494-4997; cnr Botanic Rd & Main St; admission US$3; ☯ 8am-dusk) is a four-acre (1.6 hectare) national park and a pleasant refuge from Road Town's traffic, noise and heat. Benches are set amid indigenous and exotic tropical plants and there is

also an orchid house, a lily pond, a small rain forest and a cactus grove. The herb garden is rife with traditional bush medicine plants.

In the heart of Main St, the stark, white rubble walls of the **HM Prison** date back to the 18th century. The fortress is still a working jail, and you can hear muffled voices and radio music from the cells at night. East of the prison, **St George's Anglican Church** (☎ 494-3894) is another survivor of the 18th century. Inside is a copy of the 1834 Emancipation Proclamation that freed Britain's slaves in the West Indies. To the west of the prison, the 1924 **Methodist Church** (☎ 495-9619) is a fine example of a classic West Indian timber-framed construction.

Standing at the extreme south end of Main St, and looking like an imperial symbol, whitewashed 1880 **Government House** (admission US$3; ☯ 9am-2pm Mon-Sat) was once the British Governor's residence. Today it's a small museum with period furniture and historic artifacts.

Activities

In the minds of many sailing enthusiasts, the BVI are the charter-boat capital of the world, with companies offering hundreds of sailboats for rent, or crewed boats for hire (for details, see the boxed text, p398).

The following are well-known day-sail operators, who run trips to Virgin Gorda, Jost Van Dyke, Anegada or Norman Island. Generally rates start at about US$60 per person for a half-day (four hours) and US$85 for a full day (eight hours).

Patouche II (☎ 248-494-6300; www.patouche.com; HR Penn Marina) Found next to the pub, *Patouche II* is a 48ft (14.5m) catamaran, or powerboat. Snorkeling gear and instruction is included.

White Squall II (☎ 494-2564; www.whitesquall2.com; Village Cay Marina, A Dock) Sail on this traditional 80ft (24m) schooner.

Other places with boats and equipment rentals:

Last Stop Sports (☎ 494-0564; www.laststopsports .com; Wickhams Cay II, Mooring's Dock) Offers great rates on kayak rentals (US$30/35 a single/double) and windsurfing equipment (minimum five-day rental starting at US$120). It also rents bikes and dive gear.

M&M Powerboat Rentals (☎ 495-9993; www .powerboatrentalbvi.com; Village Cay Marina, B Dock) M&M rents 15ft (4.5m) and 22ft (6.6m) outboards for US$125 and US$250 a day.

The marinas at nearby Prospect Reef Resort (p384) and Nanny Cay (p384) offer a full range of charters and water sports.

Several good dive operators are based on Tortola, in and around Road Town. See p397 for information.

Festivals & Events

Tortola plays host to an almost endless list of yacht races, including the **Annual Spring Regatta & Sailing Festival** (☎ 494-3286; www.bvi springregatta.org). One of the Caribbean's biggest parties, the regatta began with friendly competition between local sailors in 1972.

The event has continued to gain momentum and today it features six fun-filled days of small- and large-craft races that take place throughout the BVI around early April. The races provide a time-honored excuse to spend evenings swilling beer, sipping rum, listening to live music and partying with sailors and crew from around the world.

Land-based celebrations are hard to come by with the exception of the **BVI Emancipation Festival** (☎ 494-3134), which occurs over two weeks at the end of July and beginning of August. During this time, Tortola rocks from the West End to the East End, celebrating its African-Caribbean heritage.

Sleeping

BUDGET

Sea View Hotel (☎ 494-2483; seaviewhotel@surfbvi .com; cnr Waterfront Dr & MacNamara Rd; r US$60-145; P ✖ ✖ ✖) At the west end of town, this clean oasis run by Ishma Christopher has about 20 small rooms as well as efficiency apartments. Some rooms have a porch with a garden or sea view. There is a small pool, a deck, a bar and breakfast service. You must sample or buy some of Ishma's homemade hot-pepper sauce, which she bottles in recycled rum containers.

A&L Inn (☎ 494-6343; 3 Fleming St; r US$75; ✖) Anyone looking for a cheap place to stay will do well at this 2nd-floor hotel just off Main St. The 14 rooms have private baths, two double beds and small refrigerators; some have balconies. Basic to the core, but clean and close to the Road Town action.

MIDRANGE & TOP-END

Fort Burt Hotel (☎ 494-2587; www.bviguide.com/fort burt; d standard/ste US$120/200; P ✖ ✖ ✖ ✖) The hotel rises on the ruins of a 300-year-old Dutch fort that once guarded the harbor from a steep hillside above Waterfront Dr. The 12 rooms have all amenities; most have sweeping sea views and some suites even have private pools. There is a gourmet restaurant on site (opposite).

Moorings-Mariner Inn Hotel (☎ 494-2332, 800-535-7289; www.bvimarinerinn.com; Wickhams Cay 2; d/ste US$170/230; P ✖ ✖ ✖ ✖) Adjacent to the Moorings, one of the BVI's biggest yacht-charter companies, the Mariner Inn has 40 luxurious rooms with balconies (ask for one overlooking the harbor). There's a jumbo pool, restaurant and bar. Even if

---

GET WET!

When there's great diving everywhere, it's hard to come up with a 'best of,' but here's a highly subjective attempt (in no particular order):

Top Five Dive Sites

- **Wreck of the RMS Rhone** (see p389 and p55) This famous 310ft (94m) shipwreck sits in just 30ft to 90ft (9m to 27m) of water off Salt Island, making it an accessible wreck dive for all levels.

- **Blond Rock** A pinnacle between Dead Chest and Salt Islands, this coral ledge has many caves, crevices and deep holes.

- **Alice's Wonderland** This spot off Ginger Island has some of the best deepwater coral formations in the BVI.

- **The Indians** Just off Norman Island, three cone-shaped rock formations rise from 36ft (10.8m) underwater to 30ft (9m) above water.

- **Angel Reef** Off Norman Island, this site is a crossroads for species from different habitats, with shallow canyons rising to the surface.

Top Five Snorkeling Sites

- **Brewers Bay** Tortola
- **Loblolly Bay** Anegada
- **The Baths** Virgin Gorda
- **Dry Rocks East** Cooper Island
- **The Caves** Norman Island

AUTHOR'S CHOICE

Village Cay Hotel & Marina (☎ 494-2771; www.villagecay.com; Wickhams Cay 1; r from US$150; P ⊠ ⊠ ⊠) This marina is the heart of Road Town, with a restaurant and hotel overlooking the yacht slips in Road Bay. The hotel has 19 rooms and two condos. The rooms, with refrigerators, have all the first-class amenities of a resort at a fraction of the price. The hotel's pierside restaurant is a popular place for yacht charterers to 'chill' before or after going to sea. The hotel has laundry service for guests.

---

you're not a yachtie, you should come by for a cocktail.

Hotel Castle Maria (☎ 494-2553; hotelcastle maria@surfbvi.com; MacNamara Rd; r US$85-140; P ⊠ ⊠ ⊠) At the south end of Main St, near Queen Elizabeth Park and just up from Waterfront Dr, is this 30-room property with the look of an art-deco mansion. The secluded pool, restaurant and bar are gay-friendly.

Eating & Drinking

Tortolians love to eat out, and Road Town has plenty of restaurants for every wallet. Most restaurants get creative with the sea's bounty, adding a wonderful mix of flavors to grilled fish and lobster. After the dinner hour many restaurants become popular drinking establishments.

Capriccio di Mare (☎ 494-5369; Waterfront Dr; meals US$7-14; ⊗ breakfast, lunch & dinner Mon-Sat) Set on the porch of a classic West Indian house across from the ferry dock, this Italian café draws both locals and travelers. Breakfast includes fresh pastries and cappuccino. Lunch and dinner feature salads, pasta dishes and pizza.

Roti Palace (☎ 494-4196; Abbott Hill Rd; rotis US$8-15; ⊗ lunch & dinner) On a side street that leads up the hill off Main St near the Sunny Caribbee Spice Shop, this cramped little restaurant has some of the best roti on the island.

Pusser's Pub (☎ 494-3897; Waterfront Dr; meals US$8-14; ⊗ lunch & dinner; ⊠) This landmark English-style pub is popular for pizza, burgers and sandwiches in its lively, heavily air-conditioned atmosphere.

Pub (☎ 494-2608; meals US$8-22; ⊗ breakfast, lunch & dinner Mon-Sat, dinner only Sun) On the waterfront

near Fort Burt Hotel is this Road Town institution. You can dine on the deck at the harbor's edge on steaks, ribs, lobster and fresh fish. Lots of folks show up at night to sip cold beers.

Fort Burt Restaurant (☎ 494-2587; meals US$8-25; ⊗ breakfast, lunch & dinner) With a delightful view of the harbor, this upscale restaurant in the Fort Burt Hotel (opposite) serves dishes created by students of the nearby New England Culinary Institute. It's a great place to come for romantic dinners.

C&F Bar & Restaurant (☎ 494-4941; meals US$12-20; ⊗ dinner Mon-Sat) For totally authentic West Indian cuisine, come to this neighborhood joint in Purcell Estate, east of Road Town. It's worth the trouble it takes to find (take a cab your first trip – about US$6 from the ferry dock). Tortolians show up in droves to consume barbecue seafood and curry dishes from chef Clarence Emmanuel.

Shopping

Road Town doesn't create a mass shopping frenzy like many other port towns; however, it is capable of providing you with a shopping fix. Craft hawkers come out in droves around Wickhams Cay 1 when there are cruise ships in port, but the good shops are on Main St. Note that no buildings have addresses, but everything is easy to find. Storekeepers stay open 9am to 5pm weekdays and 9am to 1pm Saturday.

Caribbean Handprints (☎ 494-3717) Sells locally designed silk-screened fabric by the yard.

HiHo (☎ 494-7694; www.go-hiho.com) Sells BVI-brand clothing inspired by the windsurfing competition Hook-in-Hold-on, held annually since 1979.

AUTHOR'S CHOICE

Le Cabanon (☎ 494-8660; Waterfront Dr; panini sandwiches US$10, dinner mains from US$12; ⊗ lunch & dinner) This delectable tropical French bistro, created by Parisian Christophe Boisgirard, is a treat whether you come at lunch, for a panini sandwich, or for seafood dinners flavored with French West Indian flair. The open-air terrace, carved from a classic West Indian house, becomes a lively and friendly scene at night. The chef flies in all of his provisions from the French island of St Martin.

Latitude 18 (☎ 494-7807; www.latitude18.com) Stocks good-quality souvenir T-shirts and sunglasses.

Pusser's Company Store (☎ 494-2467; www.pussers.com; Waterfront Dr) Reachable by footpath from Sunny Caribbee, this shop sells nautical clothing and accessories. You can also buy bottles of Pusser's Rum here (the blend served on Her Majesty's Royal Navy ships for 300 years).

Sunny Caribbee Spice Shop (☎ 494-2178; www.sunnycaribbee.com) A favorite for its colorful array of island-made spices like 'mango fire.'

AROUND ROAD TOWN

Just west of Road Town the road hugs the shoreline past a couple of historic sites and big resorts. The ruined walls and foundations of the **William Thornton Estate** plantation great house lie unpreserved and unguarded just west of Nanny Cay. Thornton went on to design the US Capitol Building in Washington, DC.

Halfway between Road Town and West End, the **Dungeon** is a ruined fort built in 1794 by the Royal Engineers. It was dubbed the Dungeon because its underground cell holds remnants of what might be prisoners' graffiti.

Closer to the West End, **Fort Recovery** is the BVI's oldest intact structure. Villas now surround the fort (see right).

Sleeping & Eating

Prospect Reef Resort (☎ 494-3311, 800-356-8937; www.prospectreef.com; r US$160-480; P ☒ ☒ ☒) Just beyond Fort Burt, on the western border of Road Town, sits Tortola's largest resort. The 137 rooms come in several configurations, from garden studios (US$160) to two-bedroom villas (US$480). There are all the amenities you'd expect from a 44-acre (17.5-hectare) seaside resort…except a beach. The resort compensates by running a regular glass-bottom ferry to Peter Island, 3 miles (5km) offshore. Guests also have the use of an Olympic lap pool and the specially constructed tide pools. Tennis, diving instruction, fishing and yacht charters are at your doorstep.

Nanny Cay Resort & Marina (☎ 494-2521, 800-742-4276; www.nannycay.com; s/d standard US$115/160, ste US$200/245; P ☒ ☒ ☒) Nanny Cay, 2 miles (3.2km) west of Road Town, describes itself as 'an island unto itself,' and the description

fits. This 42-room resort has two pools, two restaurants, a tennis court, marina, windsurfing school, dive shop, mountain bike center, boutiques and a minimarket – in short, it's a self-contained pleasure dome on a 25-acre (10-hectare) islet. Rooms have kitchenettes, private balconies and wooden cathedral ceilings.

Villas of Fort Recovery Estate (☎ 495-4354, 800-367-8475; www.fortrecovery.com; villas US$260-795; P ☒ ☒ ☒) Surrounding the fort ruins, these villas are all about luxury and privacy. One- and four-bedroom villas spread out on a private beach in the shadow of the old fort's Martello tower. There is also a pool in a garden setting. Everything is top drawer, with expansive views of St John and Norman Islands.

Callaloo (☎ 494-2347; meals US$22-45; ☽ lunch & dinner) Based on the Prospect Reef Resort, overlooking the lagoon, Callaloo specializes in Caribbean gourmet cuisine.

WEST END

The small settlement of West End has the main ferry terminal for vessels going to and from the USVI (see p400). Frenchman's Cay is the small island attached to the West End. **Sopers Hole** (www.sopershole.com), the former site of a 16th-century pirate's den, is a major anchorage, with a marina and shopping wharf, which has some great restaurants and bars. Anyone needing transportation from here can call **West End Taxi Association** (☎ 495-4934).

Sleeping & Eating

Jolly Roger Inn (☎ 495-4559; www.jollyrogerbvi.com; r with private/shared bath US$70/86; ☽ 8am-late) On the north side of Sopers Hole, next to the ferry dock, this popular restaurant and bar has a great waterfront location and the chefs serve up delicious grilled fish and pizzas. Locals and travelers flock to the Caribbean barbecue on Friday and Saturday nights. Above the restaurant are five budget rooms, three with shared bath.

Pusser's Landing (☎ 495-4554; Sopers Hole; meals US$8-18; ☽ lunch & dinner) Set on the waterfront, this fun pub offers outdoor harborside seating and Margaritaville ambience. There are nightly all-you-can-eat specials, but the best deal is the daily happy hour from 5pm to 7pm, when chicken wings go for US$0.25 each.

CANE GARDEN BAY AREA

On the north shore, Cane Garden Bay is a turquoise cove ringed by a semicircle of steep hills. Only a few miles from Road Town as the crow flies, the winding, steep roads travel over the mountains, making it about a 25-minute drive. With a beautiful 1-mile (1.6km) sandy beach and plenty of bars and restaurants overlooking the water, the area is the island's most popular beach and party zone, with accommodations for every budget. South of Cane Garden Bay are a series of picturesque bays.

Rid yourself of visions of a sprawling resort area, however; the sheer mountains dominate the landscape, so everything hugs the water along a small strip of road. Speckled amid the holiday zone are small West Indian settlements; you're living among locals, which is a great way to get immersed in the culture.

Sights & Activities

You can't miss the funky **North Shore Shell Museum** (☎ 495-4714; Carrot Bay; admission free), which also serves great meals in its restaurant (see p387). Just off the North Coast Rd at the west end of Cane Garden Bay, the **Callwood Rum Distillery** (tour US$1; ☯ 8:30am-6pm Mon-Sat) is the oldest continuously operated distillery in the Eastern Caribbean. The Callwood family has been producing Arundel rum here for generations, using copper vats and wooden aging casks. A small store sells the delicious local liquor.

BEACHES

Brewers Bay, a palm-fringed bay on the north shore east of Cane Garden Bay, has excellent snorkeling and a tranquil scene – possibly because getting here involves an expensive cab ride and brake-smoking ride down steep switchbacks. There are a couple of beach bars and a campground here.

Cane Garden Bay could be on the postcard that drew you to the BVI in the first place. The gently sloping crescent of sand stretches for almost 1 mile (1.6km) with a backdrop of steep green hills. It's a popular yacht anchorage and there's plenty of water-sports vendors and beachside bars. When cruise ships arriving in Road Town bus passengers over for the day, the scene can get crowded in a hurry.

Apple Bay, southwest of Cane Garden, is the 'surfing beach,' especially in late December

to February when the consistent swells roll in. On many maps, Apple Bay includes Cappoons Bay, home of the infamous Bomba's Surfside Shack (see the boxed text, p386).

Long Bay is an attractive 1-mile (1.6km) stretch of white-sand beach that spreads west of Apple Bay. **Smuggler's Cove**, at the island's southwestern tip, has good snorkeling.

SAGE MOUNTAIN NATIONAL PARK

At 1780ft (543m), Sage Mountain is the Virgin Islands' highest peak. This 92-acre (37-hectare) park is laid out with seven trails. Pick up a trail map at the attractive **Mountain View restaurant** (☎ 495-9536; admission free; ☯ dawn to dusk), which sits at the trailhead (excellent sunsets).

The park is not a rainforest in the true sense, because it receives less than 100in (254cm) of rain a year, but the lush area possesses many rainforest characteristics. Hikers should keep an eye open for the 20ft (6m) fern trees and other flora that have not changed since the days of the dinosaurs. You'll also see spectacular vistas of both the USVI and BVI.

Shadow, a friendly West Indian man, offers **horseback riding** (☎ 494-2262; US$50 per person) from Shadow's Ranch.

Sleeping

BUDGET

Brewers Bay Campground (☎ 494-3463; camp site/ prepared tent US$15/40) Tortola's only commercial campground is just 2 miles (3.2km) north of Road Town and around the bend from Cane Garden Bay. Nevertheless, it's difficult to reach over treacherous mountain roads. Public transportation is virtually

---

AUTHOR'S CHOICE

Lighthouse Villas (☎ 494-5482; travel-watch .com/lighthouse; Cane Garden Bay; d/q US$220/375; Ⓟ ☒ ☒) These six immaculate villas, in a white three-story building just behind the Old Works Inn, are incredible value. Each villa has a kitchen and sitting area, plus French doors opening onto balconies spitting distance from the bay. Owner Malcia Rymer goes out of her way to welcome guests and encourages them to take advantage of the common Jacuzzi and barbecue grill.

nonexistent so you need a car or to take a cab. The sites sit under sea-grape trees and tall palms right on the beach. You can bring a tent or use the prepared sites, which include two cots, linens and everything you need to cook. There's a beach bar for beer and other sustenance.

MIDRANGE

Rhymer's Beach Hotel (☎ 495-4820; Cane Garden Bay; d US$95; P ⅏) On the beach and right in the center of the action, Rhymer's is probably the oldest of the area's inns. The big pink concrete building with its restaurant and laundry shows serious signs of hard use, but the price and energy of the place make up for it. Rooms are mostly studios with kitchenette and patios.

Ole Works Inn (☎ 495-4838; www.quitorymer.com; Cane Garden Bay; d with hill/beach view US$95/130; ⅏ ⅏) Across the street from Quito's Gazebo, this bright yellow hotel can't be beat for ambience. Reggae master Quito Rymer has created this inn of 18 small rooms within the walls of a 320-year-old rum factory.

Heritage Villas (☎ 494-5842; www.heritagevillas bvi.com; Windy Hill; 1-/2-bedroom apt US$165/250; P ⅏ ⅏ ⅏) High on Windy Hill between Cane Garden Bay and Carrot Bay, this place has nine spacious apartments that seem to hang out in thin air. There's a pool, sundeck and restaurant. You will need a car to get around from here and there's a two-night minimum stay.

TOP END

Sugar Mill Hotel (☎ 495-4355; www.sugarmillhotel.com; Apple Bay; d/q US$295/340; P ⅏ ⅏ ⅏) In a league of its own for ambience, intimacy and customer service, this boutique hotel rises from the ruins of the Appleby Plantation that gave Apple Bay its name. The centerpiece of the property is the gourmet restaurant (opposite). Guests stay in the 16 studios and suites that hide on the steep hillside among mahogany trees, bougainvillea and palms. There is a pool up on the hill and a small beach across the road.

Sebastian's Seaside Villa (☎ 495-4212; www.sebas tiansvillas.com; Little Apple Bay; r US$200-375, P ⅏ ⅏ ⅏) Well known for its friendly staff and its lovely beachside accommodations, all 26 rooms have teak furnishings, a sea view, balcony and a refrigerator or kitchen. There's a good beachside restaurant here as well (see opposite).

Long Bay Beach Resort & Villas (☎ 495-4252, 800-729-9599; www.longbay.com; r from US$295; P ⅏ ⅏ ⅏) This 52-acre (21-hectare) resort has more than 70 rooms, plus additional private homes and rental villas planted among the vegetation on the southwestern tip of the island. With several pools, tennis courts, jogging trails, restaurants and bars, this place can keep you entertained for a week.

Eating & Drinking

Many restaurants in this area turn into bars at night, offering live music, dancing or just solid bar time. In the winter high-season most restaurants serve breakfast, lunch and dinner.

Rhymer's (meals US$15-25) The beach bar at this hotel (left) caters to the crews from yachts who are sick of cooking on board.

BOOZE, BRAS & THE BOMBA SHACK

The best-known pub on Tortola is **Bomba's Surfside Shack** (☎ 495-4148; Cappoons Bay), literally a shack built from nailed-together beach refuse, with signs that challenge 'sexy' females to get naked. Apparently this has somehow worked, as the bar's decor consists of ceilings strung with bras and panties.

Bomba's is famous for its monthly full-moon parties, which feature an outdoor barbecue, live reggae, plenty of dancing and drinking. Bomba serves free psychoactive mushroom tea (see the boxed text, p378) and up to five hundred people show up for these bacchanals. While plenty of people (especially males) come away saying they have never been to a better party, a lot of women look back on their experience at the Bomba Shack with horror and regret at the poor choices they made under the influence of mushrooms and rum punch.

Many women refuse to patronize the bar, claiming the scene degrades women and takes advantage of unsophisticated teenage girls, who seem drawn to the place like fish to bait… while the sharks circle in the shadows.

AUTHOR'S CHOICE

Quito's Gazebo (☎ 495-9934; Cane Garden Bay; meals US$8-25; ☺ lunch & dinner) This beachside bar takes its name from its owner and reggae master, Quito Rymer, whose band has toured with Ziggy Marley. You can dance up a storm to Quito's reggae rhythms, and hundreds pack the restaurant on weekends to do just that. Rotis and fresh salads make for popular light luncheons. At night grilled items such as snapper fill the menu.

Rhymer's serves a great breakfast (about US$6) and the dinner menu includes fish and ribs. The bar draws beachgoers seeking refreshment.

Myett's Garden & Grille (☎ 495-9648; Cane Garden Bay; meals US$8-25; ☺ breakfast, lunch & dinner) Just down the beach, Myett's draws a lot of people from charter boats and has a lush tropical setting. The food can be hit-and-miss, but you can get good seafood. Live bands play Friday through Monday nights.

Paradise Club (☎ 495-4606; Cane Garden Bay; meals US$14-25; ☺ lunch & dinner) Also known as the Big Banana, this is one of the larger, busier and louder restaurant/bars. You can get dishes like coconut shrimp, barbecue chicken and ribs. At night there's often live reggae.

North Shore Shell Museum (☎ 495-4714; Carrot Bay; meals US$7-18; ☺ breakfast, lunch & dinner) This zany mix of fascinating museum and eatery, owned by Egberth Donovan, specializes in delicious big breakfasts and grilled fish dinners. The staff often lead the patrons in making *fungi* music (ie music made by scratch bands) blowing and banging on conch shells. Dinner reservations are a good idea.

Palm's Delight (☎ 495-4863; Carrot Bay; meals under US$12; ☺ lunch & dinner) Located right on the water's edge, this family-style West Indian restaurant serves up great cheap eats and local ambience. Friday nights provide a lively scene, with families eating on the patio and a bar crowd watching cricket or baseball on the TV.

Sugar Mill Hotel (☎ 495-4355; www.sugarmill hotel.com; Apple Bay; meals US$15-30; ☺ breakfast, lunch & dinner) Owners Jeff and Jinx Morgan, contributing writers for *Bon Appetite* mag-

azine, oversee the menu, cooking and presentation of meals in the restored boiling house of the plantation's rum distillery (see opposite). Reservations are a must.

Sebastian's on the Beach (meals US$8-20; ☺ breakfast, lunch & dinner) At Sebastian's Seaside Villa (opposite), this is a favorite and offers beachfront dining.

EAST ISLAND

Tortola's eastern end is a mix of steep mountains, remote bays and thickly settled West Indian communities. Beef Island, the large isle off the eastern end of Tortola, is home to the BVI's only major airport. A few resorts and guesthouses, marinas, quiet beaches and an exceptional collection of restaurants beckon travelers here, but a car is essential to explore the area.

Beaches

Josiahs Bay is a dramatic windswept strand with a surfable point break in winter, and a small beach bar surrounded by acres of empty space. Several charming and inexpensive guesthouses lie inland on the valley slopes.

Lambert Bay is east of Josiahs and home to Lambert Beach Resort (p388) and a wide, palm-fringed beach.

Trellis Bay, a broad semicircular beach east of the airport on Beef Island, is a crowded yachting anchorage with a small island (and restaurant) in the center of the bay. Trellis Bay is also the landing for Virgin Gorda's North Sound express ferry and home to a water-sports operator, a sculptor's studio, a general store and funky guesthouse.

Sleeping

Serendipity House (☎ 499-1999; www.serhouse.com; Josiahs Hill; r from US$110; ⓟ ☒ ☒ ☒) For some tropical seclusion about half a mile (800m) from Josiahs Bay, this is one of the best values on Tortola, with special deals for longer stays. Canadians Carol and Bill Campbell welcome travelers with the invitation to 'spend a vacation, not a fortune.' There are four units, ranging from an apartment to a two-bedroom villa, all with full kitchens.

Tamarind Club Hotel (☎ 495-2477; www.tamarind club.com; r US$110-160; ⓟ ☒ ☒ ☒) Just 100yd (91m) down the hill from Serendipity House, these red-roofed West Indian–style villas surround a central garden and pool. Each room has a private bath and veranda.

Beef Island Guest House (☎ 495-2303; d US$110; ℗ ✗) Located on Trellis Bay next to De Loose Mongoose restaurant, this place is just a five-minute walk to the airport and therefore an excellent choice for anyone with a late arrival or early departure. It's also convenient to the North Sound ferry to Virgin Gorda. Set on a thin beach among a grove of low coconut palms, the one-story guesthouse looks more like a contemporary West Indian home than an inn, but the four guest rooms have unexpected character. All rooms come with fans.

Lambert Beach Resort (☎ 495-2877; www.lambert beachresort.com; d US$160-365) On a long, white strand, near the northeast corner of the island, this remote resort is good for families or anyone who wants to arrive and stay put. Unless you have a car, coming and going won't be easy. A meal plan is available (US$70 per person) for the resort's excellent restaurant. Most of the 38 units are large, one-bedroom suites in four-unit villas. The pool has a swim-up bar, waterfalls and a huge children's pool.

Pusser's Marina Cay Resort (☎ 494-2174; www .pussers.com; s/d US$154/198, d villa US$295) Lying just east of Beef Island, 8-acre (3-hectare) Marina Cay is home to this secluded hotel (four rooms, two villas), with an excellent open-air restaurant and bar, a dive shop and water-sports rentals. A free ferry runs from Trellis Bay on Beef Island.

Eating

De Loose Mongoose (meals US$7-15; ✆ closed Mon) Next to the Beef Island Guest House (left), this is a good place to have breakfast, eat lunch or watch the sunset over dinner. Try the conch fritters, arguably the best in the BVI.

Last Resort (☎ 495-2520; Trellis Bay; meals US$12-25; ✆ dinner) On an islet in Trellis Bay, this restaurant features a changing dinner menu featuring fish, meat and pasta dishes. The big attraction is owner Tony Snell's cabaret

---

OUT ISLANDS

The BVI 'out islands' (a Creole expression for remote or undeveloped cays) are a wonderful mix of uninhabited wildlife sanctuaries, luxurious holiday-homes for the rich and famous, and provisioning stops for sailors. Some you can access by ferry, but most require you to come by charter or private boat.

Guana Island

One mile (1.6km) off Tortola's northeast tip, this 850-acre (340-hectare) undeveloped island is the seventh-largest island in the BVI. Guana takes its name from a rock formation called the 'Iguana Head' that juts out from a cliff at the northwest corner of the island.

In the mid-1930s, Beth and Louis Bigelow bought the island and invited intellectuals to 'rusticate' on their island. Dr Henry Jarecki and his wife, Gloria, bought the island in 1975. Both ardent conservationists, the Jareckis saw the opportunity to establish Guana as a private nature preserve. **Guana Island Club** (☎ 494-2354, 800-544-8262; www.guana.com; villas US$850-1500) accommodates only 30 guests, who enjoy a total tropical retreat. You can rent the entire island for US$11,500 a day.

Norman Island

Since 1843, writers have alleged that treasure is buried on Norman Island, supposedly the prototype for Robert Louis Stevenson's book *Treasure Island*. It fits the bill: Norman is the largest uninhabited island in the BVI.

Two fantastic beach bars lure boaters. The **William Thornton** ('Willie T'; ☎ 494-0183) is a schooner converted into a restaurant-bar and moored in the bight. On the beach, **Billy Bones** (☎ 494-4770) is an open-air pavilion. Both have good food and the owners often bring in live West Indian bands or just crank Bob Marley and Jimmy Buffett over high-voltage sound systems.

Weekends are always a huge party scene and, as one local puts it, 'Everyone just gets f---ing mental.'

act following dinner. Sailors get here by boat, but landlubbers can call the free ferry service from the resort's hotline telephone at the Trellis Bay ferry dock.

Secret Garden (☎ 495-1834; Josiahs Bay Plantation; meals US$7-21; ☽ dinner) One of the most delightful places to eat on Tortola. Outdoor tables are set amid the distilling buildings of the old plantation (now an art gallery and boutique). Owner Kim Peters Millman offers an exceptionally imaginative menu that ranges from grilled swordfish Creole to coconut chicken or Bajan flying-fish pie. Reservations required.

Fat Hog Bob's (☎ 495-1010; Maya Cove; meals US$7-30; ☽ 7am-late) With a 100ft (30m) porch at the seaside, this fun-times rib house offers a huge and surprisingly creative menu, featuring things like babyback ribs marinated in Guinness and crab-stuffed steak.

Brandywine Bay (☎ 495-2301; meals US$25-35; ☽ dinner Mon-Sat) One mile (1.6km) east of Road Town, overlooking Sir Francis Drake Channel, this oceanside treat is the signature restaurant of chef David Pugliese. Here you can eat Tuscan-infused seafood, beef and game, served on a breeze-cooled terrace.

VIRGIN GORDA

The 'Fat Virgin's' variety of landscapes is a visual feast kissed with adventure. Beachcombers spend hours walking along the sand-rimmed bays, contemplating seashells and the mystery of tides. Mariners tuck into the protected bays or sail to friendly island outposts. Hikers summit Virgin Gorda Peak, relishing the cool breeze, bromeliads and vistas of the entire archipelago. Snorkelers get sunburned backs through spending hours half-submerged, mesmerized by the underwater life.

This is Virgin Gorda who, until the 1960s, sat quietly day-dreaming. She'd been a supply stop for marauding buccaneers; raised plantations full of sugarcane, ginger, indigo and cattle; and, over the centuries, had as

Peter Island

This lofty L-shaped island, about 4 miles (6.5km) south of Tortola, is the fifth-largest of the BVI and home to the luxurious, all-inclusive **Peter Island Resort** (☎ 800-346-4451; www.peterisland .com). In the late '60s, Norwegian millionaire Peter Smedwig fell in love with Peter Island and built a resort, which he operated until his death in the late 1970s.

The resort recently underwent a multimillion-dollar renovation. Anyone with reservations can come to the island's Tradewinds restaurant. You get here by the Peter Island ferry from Tortola.

Salt Island

This T-shaped island is a forlorn place. The salt making (which gave the island its name) still goes on here, but the RMS *Rhone* is the big attraction. The *Rhone* crashed against the rocks off Salt Island's southwest coast during a hurricane in 1867. Now a national park, the steamer's remains are extensive, making it one of the Caribbean's best wreck dives (see also p55).

Cooper Island

Lying about 4 miles (6.5km) south of Tortola, Cooper Island is a moderately hilly cay and is virtually undeveloped except for the **Cooper Island Beach Club** (☎ 494-3721; www.cooper-island .com), whose restaurant makes it a popular anchorage for cruising yachts.

The Dogs

This clutch of six islands lies halfway between Tortola and Virgin Gorda. Protected by the BVI National Parks Trust, the Dogs are sanctuaries for birds and marine animals (the diving here is excellent).

Necker Island

This private island belongs to Richard Branson, famous adventurer and scion of Virgin Atlantic Airways and Virgin Records. About 1 mile (1.6km) north of Virgin Gorda, Necker is one of the world's most luxurious retreats.

BRITISH VIRGIN ISLANDS

much as 10,000 tons extracted from her copper mine. Then she'd seen the collapse of the plantations and the closing of the mine, and she'd been abandoned until her population declined to about 600 souls.

In the early 1960s, Laurence Rockefeller constructed a resort at Little Dix Bay and the Fat Virgin re-emerged, ready to share her bounty.

The resort brought jobs, roads and utilities. Yachts and more exclusive resorts followed. Soon, the giant granite rock formations of Virgin Gorda's Baths became the BVI's biggest tourist attraction. Now the Fat Virgin giggles with the tickle of tourist's feet and still there is hardly any crime on the island and no rampant commercialism.

Orientation

Virgin Gorda lies 8 miles (13km) east of Tortola. Its elongated serpent shape makes it a particularly easy place to navigate. The main highway, North Sound Rd, runs along the spine.

The prominent Virgin Gorda Peak, 1359ft (414m) high, dominates the northern half of the island. The southern half is a rolling plain called 'the Valley.' The island's main settlement, Spanish Town, lies on the western shore of the Valley; the airport is 1 mile (1.6km) to the east.

Festivals & Events

The island goes crazy on the four days preceding Lent for the **Virgin Gorda Easter Festival** (☎ 495-5181). Spanish Town around Yacht Harbour fills with *mocko jumbies* (costumed stilt walkers representing spirits of the dead), scratch bands, calypsonians, a food fair and parades.

Getting There & Away

AIR

Air Sunshine flies to Virgin Gorda from San Juan, St Thomas and St Croix. Air St Thomas services Virgin Gorda from Charlotte Amalie in the USVI. For details see p400.

SEA

There is a regularly scheduled ferry service between Spanish Town and Road Town, Tortola, and a service between Virgin Gorda's North Sound and Trellis Bay on Tortola. For details see p401.

Getting Around

TO/FROM THE AIRPORT

Virgin Gorda Airport (☎ 495-5621) is on the east side of the Valley. You can count on taxis waiting at the airport when flights are arriving. Expect to pay about US$9 for a ride into Spanish Town; US$18 will get you to the northwest resorts. You will pay about US$20 to get to Gun Creek.

CAR

Virgin Gorda has several car-rental companies, which will pick you up from the ferry and drop you off almost anywhere on the island. You'll pay US$50 to US$80 per day.
L&S Jeep (☎ 495-5297)
Mahogany Car Rentals (☎ 495-5469)
Speedy's Car Rental (☎ 495-5240)

TAXI

Cab rates on Virgin Gorda are some of the highest in the Caribbean. The rate from the northwest beach resorts or Gun Creek to Spanish Town is US$20 for a 3-mile (5km) trip. **Potter Gafford Taxi Service** (☎ 495-5329) and **Mahogany Run Taxi Service** (☎ 495-5469) are the major services on the island.

SPANISH TOWN & THE VALLEY

More of a settlement than a town, the commercial center of Virgin Gorda probably gets its name from a (severe) corruption of the English word 'penniston,' a blue woolen fabric long used for making slave clothing on the island, rather than from any Spanish connections. Islanders referred to their settlement as Penniston well into the 1850s.

The harbor dredged here in the 1960s is home to today's Yacht Harbour mall, the heart of Spanish Town. Overall, Spanish Town is a sleepy place, but the mix of islanders, yachties and land travelers creates a festive vibe.

Information

BVI Tourist Board (☎ 495-5181; Yacht Harbour Mall; ⏰ 9am-5pm Mon-Sat, 10am-2pm Sun) There's a bank here.
Chandlery Ship Store (Yacht Harbour Mall; Internet access per 15min US$5; ⏰ 7am-5pm Mon-Fri, 8am-noon Sat & Sun) Has a couple of computer terminals where you can check your email.
Nurse Iris O'Neal Clinic (☎ 495-5337; ⏰ 9am-4:30pm) On the ridge road in the Valley near the airport. Call ahead.
Stevens Laundromat (☎ 495-5596; Yacht Harbour Mall; ⏰ 8am-noon & 4-8pm)

Sights & Activities

THE BATHS

This collection of **giant boulders** (admission US$3) jumbled at the seaside, near the southwest corner of the island, marks a national park and the BVI's most popular tourist attraction. The rocks form a series of grottoes that flood with seawater.

While the Baths are a site to stir the imagination, the place is generally overrun with tourists. By 10am each morning a fleet of visiting yachts has moored off the coast and tourists have been shuttled in from resorts and cruise ships. Come at sunrise or sunset if you want to wonder at the Baths in private.

Neighboring the Baths, **Spring Bay** is similar. You will find white sand, clear water and good snorkeling off the boulder enclosure called the 'Crawl.' Spring Bay is less crowded than the Baths, but if you really want to get away from people, head south of the Baths on one of the two trails that lead to **Devil's Bay**, a 20-acre (8-hectare) national park at the very southern tip of the island.

COPPER MINE NATIONAL PARK

Near Virgin Gorda's southwest tip, these impressive ruins (which include a chimney, boiler house, cistern and mine-shaft house) are now a national park and protected area. Cornish miners worked the mine between 1838 and 1867. The rugged hillside and coastline on this part of the island make an excellent place for a picnic.

BEACHES

Beachcombers can wander for hours along Virgin Gorda's 14 beaches. The best beaches are **Trunk Bay**, **Little Dix Bay** and – the best – **Savannah Bay**, which features more than 1 mile (1.6km) of white sand. No other beach provides such opportunities for long, solitary walks. Sunsets here can be fabulous.

SAILING

At Yacht Harbour, the 44ft (13m) schooner **Spirit of Anegada** (☎ 496-6825; www.spiritofanegada .com) carries passengers on full- and half-day sailing adventures. Rates are US$55 for a half-day, US$85 for a full day, and US$35 for the sunset sail. The 50ft (15m) sloop **Double 'D'** (☎ 495-6150; www.doubledbvi.com) offers half day sails for US$45 and full days for US$85. Both companies supply lunch and

beverages. **Euphoric Cruises** (☎ 495-5542) rents 18ft to 24ft (5.5m to 7.3m) speedboats for around US$250 a day.

DIVING

Dive BVI (☎ 495-5513, 800-848-7078; www.divebvi.com), at Yacht Harbour and Leverick Bay, has four fast boats that take you diving at any of the BVI sites.

Sleeping

People typically come to Virgin Gorda either for the day or for a resort beach vacation. Most of the latter group head toward resorts reachable from the North Sound Rd.

Ocean View Hotel (☎ 495-5230; r US$90; P ⚙) This guesthouse, across the street from Yacht Harbour, has 12 units above the Wheel House restaurant in a concrete-block building with a spacious 2nd-floor veranda. Rooms are basic but clean and brightly decorated, and the grounds are meticulously maintained.

Bayview Vacation Apartments (☎ 495-5329; www.bayviewbvi.com; d & q US$110-145; P ⚙) These apartments, behind Chez Bamboo restaurant, can be a good deal if you are traveling with three or four people. Each apartment has two bedrooms, a full kitchen, dining facilities and an airy living room. There is a roof deck for sunbathing.

Fischer's Cove Beach Hotel (☎ 495-5252; www .fischerscove.com; d r/cottage US$115/200; P) This beachside hotel, near the southwest end of the island, has a small collection of neat triangular-shaped cottages and a main hotel building with 12 dated studio apartments. The cottages have full kitchens, but no phones, TVs or air-con (the hotel units do). The popular open-air restaurant here overlooks the beach.

Little Dix Bay (☎ 495-5555, 800-928-3000; www .rosewoodhotels.com; villas from US$625; P ⚙ ⚙ ⚙) This major splurge was built by Laurence Rockefeller in the 1960s, and it looks every bit as polished and serene as it did 40 years ago. There are 98 rooms here, in villas poised in a coconut grove along a half-mile (800m) crescent of sugar-sand beach. The lush grounds are redolent with well-tended flowers, and the thatched conical roofs of the public buildings give the resort the feel of a South Seas resort. Rooms are spacious and furnished with elegant fabrics and wicker furniture fit for the Sultan of Brunei.

Eating & Drinking

Wheel House (breakfast, lunch & dinner) At the Ocean View Hotel (p391), this is a breakfast stop for locals. You can get West Indian meals here.

Mad Dog (495-5830; meals US$7-12; breakfast, lunch & dinner) An airy pavilion set among the rocks where the road ends at the Baths. There is often a gathering of local expats and tourists here for piña coladas and sandwiches.

Thelma's Hideout (495-5646; meals US$10-20; breakfast, lunch & dinner) Find this West Indian hangout on the side road leading to Little Dix Bay resort. Seating is in an open-air courtyard, and there is a stage where a band plays during high season. Thelma will serve you breakfast, but most travelers come here for the conch stew (US$12 lunch, US$18 dinner). Make dinner reservations here by 3pm.

Bath & Turtle (495-5239; Yacht Harbour Mall; breakfast, lunch & dinner) On a patio in a courtyard surrounded by the mall, this place is open for breakfast, lunch and dinner. Try the pizza (US$16), the fiesta quesadilla (US$8) or the seared ahi tuna salad (US$15). At night it's a fun pub scene.

Mine Shaft Café (495-5260; meals US$10-20; 10am-late) In a pavilion overlooking the Atlantic on Copper Mine Rd at the southeast end of the island. Patrons come for the burgers, wraps, happy hours and views. Owner Elton Sprauve throws a monthly full-moon party, complete with live music under the stars, warm breezes, cheap rum punch and grilled meats.

Rock Café (495-5482; meals US$16-32; from 4pm;   ) Nestled among the boulders at the traffic circle south of Spanish Town, this place has indoor and outdoor dining, plus a popular terrace bar. The cuisine is mostly Italian, with pastas and fresh fish. Wednesday to Sunday nights the terrace bounces to hip-hop.

Chez Bamboo (495-5752; meals US$30-50; from 3pm) Just north of Yacht Harbour, this bistro (in a converted West Indian home and yard) couldn't be in a better setting, amid candlelight and tropical plants. The chefs specialize in French Creole Caribbean cuisine. Jazz, blues or calypso fills the air on weekend evenings. Our only problem with the place is that it is just drastically overpriced. Still, you may want to make reservations, as this restaurant is popular with the yachties.

Buck's Food Market (495-5423; 7am-7pm) In the Yacht Harbour Mall.

NORTH & EAST ISLAND

The northeast end of Virgin Gorda features the spectacular scenery of North Sound and steep mountain slopes rising up to 1359ft (414m) **Virgin Gorda Peak**, in the protected **Gorda Peak National Park**. Two well-marked trails lead to the summit off the North Sound Rd.

The strand of gently curving beach and vivid blue water at the Mango Bay Resort is called **Mahoe Bay**. **Mountain Trunk Bay**, **Nail Bay** and **Long Bay** lie north of Mahoe Bay and run nearly undisturbed for about 1 mile (1.6km).

At **Gun Point**, a free ferry leaves every 30 minutes to take visitors and staff to the Bitter End and Saba Rock resorts.

Sleeping & Eating

Virgin Gorda Villa Rentals (www.virgingordabvi.com) At the Leverick Bay Resort (below), rents more than two dozen villas in the area.

Bitter End Yacht Club & Resort (494-2745, 800-872-2392; www.beyc.com; d incl meals US$600-790;   ) Just about the coolest place you'll ever go, this all-inclusive resort at the east end of North Sound is in a class of its own. It started as a beach bar and a collection of five cottages in the 1960s. Now it has 95 hillside villas, multiple restaurant/bars and docks that have everything from outboards to cruising yachts, plus a sailing school (see the boxed text, p398). This is a great place for an active couple or families. Some of the villas have air-con; others are open to the trade winds. All accommodations have first-class amenities but no TVs. Rates include three meals a day and unlimited use of the resort's fleet of boats. The resort runs a free water taxi to/from Gun Creek, departing Gun Creek every hour on the half-hour from 7:30am to 10:30pm. Return boats leave on the hour.

Mango Bay Resort (495-5672, 877-626-4622; www.mangobayresort.com; villas from US$275;   ) Overlooking Mahoe Bay, this is a compound of 12 Italian-style villas, from one-bedroom duplexes to four bedroom cottages, all nestled beside the beach.

Leverick Bay Resort (495-7421, 800-848-7081; www.leverickbay.com; hotel r US$119-149;   ) Near the settlement of Gun Creek, this resort functions as hotel, villa-broker and marina. The 14 rooms in the hotel, each with a private balcony, are great value. The hotel has a beach, laundry, tennis court, dive shop, spa, market and Internet café on the property. The popular restaurant, the **Light House** (☎ 495-7369; meals US$8-25; �YY breakfast, lunch & dinner), overlooks the marina and serves up a vast menu including fresh salads, sandwiches, seafood and steak dinners.

Saba Rock Resort (☎ 495-9966; www.sabarock.com; r US$150-250) On the tiny island just off the Bitter End Yacht Club in North Sound, Saba Rock is a boutique resort with eight rooms, a restaurant, two bars and a gift shop. A free shuttle ferries guests from the Bitter End.

Clubhouse Steak & Seafood Grille (buffet US$40; �YY breakfast, lunch & dinner) This is the most popular restaurant at the Bitter End resort. You can get an à la carte menu here, but most people order the buffet: it's monumental in both variety and substance. Make reservations early. To get here you catch the free ferry from Gun Creek; you don't need to be a guest to come over.

Giorgio's Table (Mango Bay Resort; ☎ 495-5684; lunch mains US$12-18, dinner mains US$22-35; �YY lunch & dinner) Serves fine Italian dishes, including Mediterranean fish and beef filet, in a pavilion built on the rocks at the tip of a peninsula.

JOST VAN DYKE

For the last 400 years, Jost (pronounced yoast) has been an oasis for seafarers and adventurers. This small island, less than 5 miles (8km) northwest of Tortola, has developed a reputation that exceeds its mere 4 sq miles (10 sq km). Jost and its satellite cays comprise a retreat of mountains, beaches and coves where only the tide's ebb and flow measures time.

A Dutch pirate (the island's namesake) used the island as a base in the 17th century. In the 18th century Jost became a homestead for Quakers escaping religious tyranny England. Quaker surnames, such as Lettsome and Callwood, survive among the 200 islanders, mostly descendents of freed Quaker slaves.

Electricity only arrived in 1991. Since the late 1960s, calypsonian and philosopher Foxy Callwood (see the boxed text, p394) has wooed mariners clearing customs to indulge in the island's charms.

A few guesthouses, bars and restaurants cater to visitors. So far, the green hills of this island remain undisturbed by development, but if you talk to Foxy, he'll tell you 'da times dey are a changin'.' Just a few years ago, Jost only had two telephones; now its businesses have websites, and tourists can rent Jeeps to buzz about the island. There are no banks on Jost.

Orientation

Ferries to Jost Van Dyke land at the pier in Great Harbour, the island's main settlement. The main road runs along the south shore. If you follow it over the hill to the west for about 1 mile (1.6km), you reach White Bay. Go east for about 2 miles (3.2km) to reach Little Harbour. Further northeast is Diamond Cay National Park and some secluded snorkeling sites.

Festivals & Events

Foxy's Woodenboat Regatta (☎ 495-9258) is held on the US Memorial Day weekend (in May). Since 1974 the annual regatta has drawn in classic wooden yachts for four days of light racing and heavy partying.

Getting There & Away

The easiest way to get to Jost is by ferry from West End on Tortola (see p401). You can also take a ferry from Red Hook which stops to pick up and drop off at Cruz Bay (see p372).

Getting Around

You can catch **Greg Brat's water taxi** (☎ 495-9401) or travel by land with **Ceto's Taxi Service** (☎ 499-6585). You can rent a vehicle from **Paradise Jeep Rental** (☎ 495-9477) in Great Harbour.

GREAT HARBOUR

Jost's main settlement sits between the beach and the foot of the mountains. Kick off your shoes, then hit the restaurants and bars.

Information

The **customs office** (☎ 494-3450; �YY 8:30am-3:30pm Mon-Fri, 9am-12:30pm Sat), on the Great Harbour waterfront, stocks brochures about Jost (businesses, restaurants, hotels etc) and is the de facto tourism office. There's a police station next door.

Sleeping & Eating

Since most of Jost's businesses cater to crews from visiting yachts, almost all of the restaurants and bars stand-by on VHF radio channel 16 to take reservations and announce nightly events.

Rudy's Mariner's Rendezvous (☎ 495-9282; r US$125, meals US$15-30) Rudy George runs this bar, restaurant and convenience store rolled into one. The oceanside restaurant serves delicious seafood. Five basic rooms overlook the harbor, but guests are at the mercy of the lively downstairs bar.

Sea Crest Inn (☎ 495-9024; seacrestinn@hotmail .com; apt US$130; ✂ ✂) On the waterfront, just east of Foxy's, the gracious Ivy Chinnery Moses has four large studio apartments, each with a kitchenette and balcony.

Christine's Bakery (☎ 495-9281; meals US$5-10; ☽ breakfast & lunch) This place is the kind of out-island bakery you dream about. Christine has the settlement filled with the scent of banana bread, coconut and coffee by 8am. This is the place to come for breakfast and lunch. Christine also rents out a couple of rooms above the bakery.

Foxy's Tamarind Bar (☎ 495-9258; meals US$8-30; ☽ lunch & dinner) Foxy's little beach bar put Jost on the map. Local bands play several nights a week in season and draw a mix of islanders and party animals off the boats. The light fare is a mix of rotis (US$12) and burgers (about US$8), plus some good veggie choices. Expect to pay over US$25 for most dinner meals, and make reservations by 5pm. If you want to hear Foxy sing his highly improvisational calypso, he does a set or two Monday to Saturday at 10am and 6pm.

Ali Baba's (☎ 495-9280; lunch mains US$7-15, dinner mains US$20-35; ☽ breakfast, lunch & dinner) Near Rudy's, it has a lazy, down-island atmosphere on its open-air patio. Patrons come for fresh fish and the Monday night pig roast (US$25).

Club Paradise (☎ 495-9267; meals US$8-25; ☽ lunch & dinner) Recognizable by its bright pink paint, it serves delightful West Indian cuisine. Come barefoot and sip a cool brew or dance in the sand – it's all good. The pig gets roasted here on Wednesdays.

WHITE BAY

Jost's most attractive strand of beach hugs a barrier reef that shelters the bay from swells and waves, which makes for good swimming and anchoring. White Bay has a popular camping area, a couple of entertaining beach bars and a small hotel and restaurant.

Sleeping & Eating

Sandcastle Hotel (☎ 495-9888; www.sandcastle-bvi .com; d US$225-270) This beachside gem at the west end of the bay offers four cottages and two rooms set within 70ft (21m) of the shore. There are no phones or TVs in any of the guest rooms. In the hotel, the infamous Soggy Dollar Bar (SDB) takes its name from the sailors swimming ashore to spend wet bills. One of the Caribbean's best beach bars, the SDB is the birthplace

---

ONE FOXY FELLA

Foxy (born 'Philiciano') Callwood started life as one of seven children on Jost Van Dyke in 1938. Since then, this barefoot man with the dreadlocks, chocolate skin and guitar has become famous. The keys to Foxy's celebrity are his irreverent, deep and infectious laughter, the persistent twinkle in his eye and the ability to offer up a melody or piece of philosophy to make each person he meets feel worthy.

'I always happy,' he says, as he wanders around Foxy's Tamarind Bar in a T-shirt and ragged jeans. 'I am so happy my cup is full and running over.'

The public first met Foxy in 1968, when his mother set up a booth on the beach for a festival at Jost and proclaimed it 'Mama's Booth & Foxy's Bar.' Soon word spread among sailors and they've been coming ever since.

Today, Foxy has a boutique selling Foxy memorabilia, a huge two-story restaurant addition tucked behind his open-air bar, and his own private-label rum. Then there is Foxy's Lager, brewed and bottled in St Croix. He authorized the use of his name on the product under an agreement stating, according to him, 'Dat if I think it tastes like s, h, i..., dey takin' my name off of dere.' Every day, Foxy executes the taste test, and so far he claims the lager is ambrosia.

of the Painkiller, the BVI's delicious-yet-lethal cocktail. The restaurant offers a four-course gourmet candlelit dinner for US$32 per person. Ruben Chinnery sings calypso on most Sunday afternoons, when lots of yachts stop by for lunch.

White Bay Villas (☎ 410-571-6692; www.jostvandyke .com; villa per week from US$600) Rents out six private beachfront villas for weekly stays.

White Bay Campground (☎ 495-9312; bare sites US$25, tents US$45) A mix of bare sites and platform tents sit under the shade trees on the fringe of the beach here. This campground is one of the most popular stops for backpackers in the Virgin Islands. On the grounds, Ivan's Local Flavor Bar & Restaurant draws crowds for the cookouts and cold beer.

LITTLE HARBOUR

The east side of Little Harbour has a thin, steep strand of white sand perfect for sunbathing and swimming in water totally protected from wind and waves.

Sleeping & Eating

Sandy Ground Estates (☎ 494-3391; www.sandy ground.com; d per week US$1950, extra person per week US$300) Seven private villas have full kitchens, tiled floors, beautiful furnishings and terraces overlooking Little Harbour.

Sidney's Peace and Love (☎ 495-9271; meals US$8-25; ☿ lunch & dinner) Right on the water, Sidney's serves up West Indian specialties, along with burgers and barbecue. The Monday night pig roast (US$20) is popular. Live reggae bands play here most nights. Saturday night rocks with charter yacht crews. T-shirts left behind by visiting revelers decorate the rafters. A popular T-shirt for sale here proclaims 'Time flies when you ain't doin' shit.'

Abe's by the Sea (☎ 495-9329; meals US$10-30; ☿ breakfast, lunch & dinner) On the east side of the harbor, Abe's specializes in West Indian fish dishes. There's often live *fungi* music at night.

ANEGADA

Sometimes referred to as the 'Mysterious Virgin' or 'Ghost Cay' because of its remote location and killer reef, Anegada takes its name from the Spanish word for 'drowned' or 'flooded.' But whatever you call the east-

ernmost Virgin Island, it's the place to come to for shipwrecks, sharks, lonesome beaches and creatures that go bump in the night.

Lying about 20 miles (32km) to the northeast of Tortola, and 12 miles (19.5km) from Virgin Gorda, Anegada is a coral atoll stretching about 12 miles (19.5km) from west to east and, at most, 3 miles (5km) from north to south. The island is so low – 28ft (8.5m) above sea level at its highest – that mariners often cannot see it to get their bearings until they are trapped in a maze of coral reef. Since the early days of colonization, Anegada's Horseshoe Reef has snared more than 300 ships. Some of these wrecks are legendary, such as that of the HMS *Astrea,* a 32-gun British frigate, and the *Paramatta,* an English steamship.

About 170 people live on Anegada. Some are the descendants of the pirates and wreckers; a few are descendants of Portuguese immigrants. Many families survive on lobster and conch fishing.

History

During the 1960s, a real-estate developer named Kenneth Bates worked a sweetheart deal with the government that allowed him to build a marina and hotel complex. He succeeded in constructing an airport and part of a hotel before islanders drove him off. What Bates could not accomplish, however, the late Lowell Wheatley did, building the low-key Anegada Reef Hotel in the 1970s.

Visitors returned with stories of a wild island, with salt ponds rife with wading birds, wild orchids, blooming cacti and epiphytes. They talked about giant rock iguanas and a booming population of wild goats and cows. Divers claimed they'd never seen so many sharks and pelagics. The government responded by declaring much of the island a wilderness sanctuary, fostering the reintroduction of flamingos to the salt ponds and building a nursery to protect young rock iguanas.

Growing outside interest has led islanders to develop a small clutch of restaurants, beach bars and guesthouses. Still, Anegada is a *very* remote adventure.

Orientation

Shaped like a long sliver of mango stretched west to east, Anegada constitutes about 15 sq miles (39 sq km) of extremely flat land. The island's horizon holds few visual landmarks except for odd clumps of casuarina and coconut trees. Anegada's main road starts at the airport in the center of the island and swings by the Settlement, a picture of dead cars (you can get them on the island, but you can't get them off), hurricane-damaged structures, laundry drying in the breeze and folks feeding goats and chickens. From the Settlement, the road heads west to the yacht anchorage at Setting Point and a number of nice beaches.

Information

The best source of local knowledge on the island is probably Romalia Smith, who staffs the desk at the airport when a flight is due in or out. Lawrence and Lorraine Wheatley, the proprietors of the Anegada Reef Hotel, are also good sources of information. There are no banks on Anegada.

Anegada has some fierce mosquitoes. 'Gallon Nippers' can appear in swarms thick enough to kill wild goats; be prepared with strong repellent.

Sights & Activities

The large salt pond at the west end of the island is home to a flock of flamingos, which were successfully reintroduced to the BVI from 1987. The BVI National Parks Trust designated **Flamingo Pond** and its surrounding wetlands as a bird sanctuary; you can also see egrets, terns and ospreys nesting and feeding in the area.

Tiny **Pomato Point Museum** (☎ 495-9466; admission free; ✆ dinner), attached to the Pomato Point Restaurant, has an interesting mix of archeological sea relics collected by islander Wilfred Creque.

At least two-thirds of Anegada's shoreline is pristine beach, and the clear waters offer unbelievable snorkeling on the offshore reef. Especially notable beaches with shelters and beach bars are **Loblolly Bay** on the northeast shore, about 2 miles (3.2km) from the Settlement, and **Cow Wreck Bay**, which stretches along the northwest end of the island.

Anyone interested in **bonefishing**, **kayaking** or **bicycling** can arrange trips through the Anegada Reef Hotel.

Sleeping & Eating

Anegada Reef Hotel (☎ 495-8002; www.anegadareef .com; garden s/d US$180/250, ocean s/d US$215/275) The heart of the island, this seaside hotel has the feel of a classic out-island fishing camp. Islander Lowell Wheatley and his English wife, Sue, ran this place for years. When Lowell passed away in 2002, his son Lawrence took over and continues to welcome guests. The hotel's 16 rooms and two-bedroom villas overlook the island's yacht anchorage; the fishing dock, restaurant and beach bar constitute the social epicenter of the island. Hotel rates include three meals at the hotel's restaurant (meals US$10 to US$25). A lot of folks cruising in yachts show up in the anchorage off the dock and join the beach party at the open-air bar, while the fish and lobster sizzle on the grill.

Neptune's Treasure (☎ 495-9439; r US$75-105) On the beach near Setting Point, this place is a restaurant, guesthouse and marina rolled into one. There are about six simple guest rooms with private bath. Most people come for the restaurant (meals US$15 to US$22), which stands at the center of a compound built by the Soares family, originally Portuguese fisherfolk from the Azores. The menu here is similar to most of the island's waterfront restaurants, but it offers an enclosed air-conditioned dining room.

Mac's Place Camping (☎ 495-8020; bare sites US$15, 8ft x 10ft tents US$40) At Loblolly Bay, this is without question the premier camping experience on Anegada. The setting is in a shady grove of sea-grape trees just above the beach line, where the landscape opens to the cooling trade winds.

Big Bamboo (☎ 495-2019; meals US$10-25; ✆ lunch & dinner) Aubrey Levons' popular beach restaurant-bar is at the west end of Loblolly Bay. Tony's Taxi and jitneys from the Anegada Reef Hotel make an almost constant cycle between the airport, the yacht anchorage and the Big Bamboo. The restaurant specializes in island recipes for lobster, fish and chicken.

Cow Wreck Beach Bar & Grill (☎ 495-9461; meals US$10-25; ✆ lunch & dinner) In a beachside pavilion on Lower Cow Wreck Beach, this beach bar features lobster, conch and shellfish cooked on the outdoor grill.

Dotsy's Bakery & Sandwich Shop (☎ 495-9667; meals US$7-10; ✆ breakfast, lunch & dinner) This bakery in the Settlement attracts locals to the fresh-baked breads, breakfasts, fish-and-chips, burgers and pizzas.

Getting There & Away

You can only get to Anegada by flying from Tortola or St Thomas, or by boat charter. There is no ferry service. Captain Auguste George Airport lies 1 mile (1.6km) northwest of the Settlement. **Clair Aero** (☎ 495-2271; www.clairaero.com) has scheduled flights departing Tortola at 8am and 5pm on Monday, Wednesday, Friday and Sunday; the flights return from Anegada at 8:20am and 5:20pm (US$66 round-trip).

Getting Around

If you're renting a car, expect to pay about US$75 for a pickup-jitney that carries 10 people at the Anegada Reef Hotel. You will pay around US$50 per day for a Suzuki Samurai at **DW Jeep Rentals** (☎ 495-9677) in the Settlement.

Tony's Taxi (☎ 495-8037) waits for inbound flights, and Tony will give you a three-hour tour of the whole island for about US$50. Shuttles run to the beaches from the Anegada Reef Hotel.

DIRECTORY

ACCOMMODATIONS

One of the best things about the BVI is the range of available accommodations, especially on Tortola, where you can find moderately priced guesthouses as well as swanky resorts. The **BVI Tourist Board** (☎ 494-3134, 800-835-8530; www.bvitouristboard.com) puts out an excellent illustrated booklet called *Intimate Inns, Hotels & Villas* with descriptions of more than 50 rental properties in the BVI.

On every hotel bill, you'll see an added 7% government tax and often a service charge, usually 10% to 15% more.

ACTIVITIES
Diving & Snorkeling

The BVI are volcanic outcrops of a vast underwater plateau that stretches for more

EMERGENCY NUMBERS

- **Police, fire and ambulance** (☎ 999)
- **Tourist information** (☎ 494-3134)
- **Virgin Islands Search & Rescue** (VISAR; ☎ 767, VHF 16)

PRACTICALITIES

- **Newspapers & Magazines** There are three weekly newspapers: *Island Sun*, *BVI Beacon* and *Standpoint*. The free *Limin' Times* lists weekly entertainment.

- **Radio & TV** There are seven radio stations, including ZWAVE (97.3FM, reggae) and ZVCR (106.9FM, Caribbean). Puerto Rico's WOSO, at 1030AM, has international news and weather/storm coverage in case of a hurricane. For BVI TV news, check Channel 5, the local-access channel.

- **Electricity** 110 volts-plugs have two (flat) or three (two flat, one round) pins.

- **Weights & Measures** Imperial.

than 70 miles (113km) where the Caribbean meets the Atlantic. The islands form a protective ring around Sir Francis Drake Channel. The sheltered paradise of secluded coves, calm shores and crystal-clear water provides outstanding underwater visibility, healthy coral and a wide variety of dive and snorkeling sites. Conservation is a big deal here, and there are lots of permanent mooring buoys. Safe, professional dive operators are plentiful and all go to the good spots, including the wreck of the RMS *Rhone*.

In general, expect to pay about US$60 for a one-tank dive, US$85 for two tanks. Most dive operators run trips to the same sites.

We recommend the following dive operators for their professionalism, friendliness and safety.

Dive BVI (☎ 495-5513, 800-848-7078; www.divebvi .com) Offices at Marina Cay, Tortola, and Yacht's Harbour and Leverick Bay, Virgin Gorda.

Dive Tortola (☎ 494-9200; www.divetortola.com; Prospect Reef Marina)

Sail Caribbean (☎ 495-1675; www.sailcaribbean divers.com; Hodges Creek Marina)

Underwater Safaris (☎ 494-3235; Mooring's Dock, Road Town)

Sailing

The BVI's calm waters and protected bays offer some of the best sailing opportunities in the Caribbean. You'll find plenty of opportunity to rent bareboat charters, hire a crewed yacht or sailboat, or take the plunge and learn to sail. See the boxed text, below, for more information.

Surfing & Windsurfing

The BVI offer ideal conditions for beginner and seasoned windsurfers. The water is warm and safe, the winds average a gentle 10 to 15 knots.

On Tortola, **Surf & Sail** (☎ 494-0123; www.go -hiho.com) in Nanny Cay is the biggest windsurfing operator on the islands, with lessons from US$45. In spring, it sponsors the annual Hook-in-Hold-on (Hi-Ho) windsurfing competition. **Last Stop Sports** (☎ 494-1843; The Moorings, Wickhams Cay 2) also offers board rentals and instruction.

Tortola's north coast serves surfers reliable, zippy swells from November to March, especially at the points off Apple Bay, Cane Garden Bay and Josiah's Bay. Last Stop Sports also rents out surfboards for about US$20 per day.

BOOKS

Birders should check out *A Guide to the Birds of Puerto Rico & the Virgin Islands*, by Herbert Rafaela. *Common Trees of Puerto Rico and the Virgin Islands*, by EL Little and FH Wadsworth, has everything you ever wanted to know about manchineel and mango trees. *Sugar Mill Caribbean Cookbook: Casual & Elegant Recipes Inspired by the Islands*, by Jinx and Jefferson Morgan, owners of Tortola's Sugar Mill Hotel and highly acclaimed restaurant (see p386) is filled with delicious recipes. *The Cruising Guide to the Virgin Islands*, by Nancy Scott, is the essential guide for any sailor, accompanied by *Virgin Anchorages*, by Simon and Nancy Scott.

CHILDREN

The BVI are an excellent destination for children. Many of the bigger resorts cater to families and offer special programs for children, including baby-sitting services. Because this is such a big yachting and sailing destination you'll see a lot of families around the marinas. The islands are safe and relatively crime free.

DANGERS & ANNOYANCES

The BVI have very little street crime. Nevertheless, the usual rules of cautious conduct for travelers apply here. Drivers should be careful of wandering cattle. If you drive at

---

YACHT CHARTER BASICS

A felicitous combination of geography and geology positions the BVI as sailing's magic kingdom. You've got a year-round balmy climate, steady trade winds, little to worry about in the way of tides or currents, a protected thoroughfare in the 35 mile-long (56km) Sir Francis Drake Channel, and hundreds of anchorages, each within sight of one another. These factors make the BVI one of the easiest places to sail, which explains why more than a third of all visitors come to do just that.

If you want to sail, there are three basic options: a sailing school; a bareboat charter (bare of crew but fully equipped), with or without a skipper; or a more luxurious crewed charter, complete with captain, cook and crew.

A typical week-long itinerary involves a sampling of the islands, while partially circumnavigating Tortola. The attraction of a sailing vacation is you can sail or stay put as long as you want, look for quiet anchorages or head for the party spots, and add on diving, hiking or shopping trips at will.

The cost of chartering a boat depends on the vessel's size and age and the time of year. It is a misconception that sailing is too expensive; once you do a little research you might be pleasantly surprised.

Choosing a Company

Charter companies depend on their reputations. Ask for references and spend some time talking with the company's representatives. If you're not satisfied, call another company.

For an up-to-date list of services, prices and equipment check the **Sail magazine website** (www.sailmag.com). People looking for a crewed-yacht vacation of the British Virgin Islands can contact the **BVI Charter Yacht Society** (☎ 494-6017, 800-233-8958; www.bvicrewedyachts.com).

night on the island roads, sooner or later you will have a brake-screeching close encounter with a cow. Mosquitoes and sand fleas are an unfortunate part of life; you'll want good bug spray with you.

EMBASSIES & CONSULATES
British Virgin Islands Embassies & Consulates

There are no foreign embassies or consulates in the BVI. British diplomatic offices representing the BVI abroad include the following.

Australia (☎ 02-9254-7521; Level 16, the Gateway, 1 Macquarie Pl, Sydney, NSW 2000)
Canada (☎ 416-593-1290; Suite 2800, 777 Bay St, College Park, Toronto, Ontario M5G 2G2)
France (☎ 01-44-51-31-00; 35 rue de Faubourg, St Honoré, 75008 Paris)
Germany Bonn (☎ 022-891-670; Freidriech-Ebert Allee 77, 53111); Berlin (☎ 030-201-840; Unter den Linden 17/34, 10117)
Ireland (☎ 01-205-3822; 29 Merrion Rd, Ballsbridge, Dublin)
Netherlands (☎ 070-427-04-27; Lange Voorhout 10, 2514 ED, The Hague)
USA (☎ 212-745-0444; 27th fl, 885 2nd Ave, New York, NY 10017)

FESTIVALS & EVENTS
Numerous sailing regattas happen throughout the year.

Below is a list of some of the island events that have cultural as well as entertainment value.

Virgin Gorda Easter Festival (Mid-February; ☎ 495-5181) Held over the four days preceding the Christian Lent period; see p390.
Annual Spring Regatta (Mid-April; ☎ 494-3286; www.bvispringregatta.org) The yachties sail from Road Town; see p382.
Foxy's Woodenboat Regatta (May; ☎ 495-9258) Held on the US Memorial Day; see p393.
HI-HO Races (Late June; ☎ 494-7963) Windsurfers converge on the BVI for the Hook-In-Hold-On races; see opposite.
BVI Emancipation Festival (End of July/beginning of August; ☎ 494-7963) This festival occurs over three weeks; see p382.

GAY & LESBIAN TRAVELERS
While a fair number of islanders and travelers in the BVI are gay, West Indian taboos on the lifestyle are crumbling exceedingly slowly.

You are not likely to meet many 'out' gays or lesbians, nor are you likely to see

Charters
Catamaran Company (☎ 800-262-0308; www.catamaranco.com)
Horizon Yacht Charters (☎ 494-8787, 877-494-8787; www.horizonyachtcharters.com)
Moorings (☎ 494-2331, 800-535-7289; www.moorings.com)
Sunsail Yacht Charters (☎ 495-4740, 800-327-2276; www.sunsail.com)
Tortola Marine Management (☎ 494-2751, 800-633-0155; www.sailtmm.com)

Crewed Boats
Crewed boats are booked by brokers that know the boats and their crews. The following is a list of reputable brokers:
Catamaran Company (☎ 800-262-0308; www.catamaranco.com)
Ed Hamilton & Co (☎ 800-621-7855; www.ed-hamilton.com)
Sailing Vacations (☎ 800-922-4880; www.sailingvacations.com)
Sunsail Sailing Vacations (☎ 800-327-2276; www.sunsail.com)
Virgin Island Sailing Ltd (☎ 800-382-9666; www.visailing.com)
Windjammer Barefoot Cruises (☎ 800-327-2601; www.windjammer.com)

Sailing Schools
Bitter End Sailing School (☎ 494-2745; www.beyc.com) The Bitter End Yacht Club (p392) on Virgin Gorda offers beginner to advanced courses.
Offshore Sailing School (☎ 800-221-4326; www.offshore-sailing.com) At the Prospect Reef Resort (p384) on Tortola, has learn-to-cruise courses.

public displays of affection among gay couples.

HOLIDAYS

New Year's Day January 1
Commonwealth Day second Monday in March
Good Friday Friday before Easter (in March or April)
Easter Monday April
Whit Monday May or June (date varies)
Sovereign's Birthday June (date varies)
Territory Day July 1
BVI Festival Days First Monday to first Wednesday in August
St Ursula's Day October 21
Birthday of Heir to the Throne November 14
Christmas Day December 25
Boxing Day December 26

MONEY

The US dollar is used throughout the BVI. You'll find branches of Banco Popular, First Bank Virgin Islands, First Caribbean Bank, HSBC, Scotiabank and VP Bank on Tortola. Although hours vary slightly, most banks are open 9am to 3pm Monday through Thursday, and 9am to 5pm Friday.

TELEPHONE

Pay phones are readily available in the BVI and are best accessed with a phone card, available at many shops. The BVI country code is ☎ 284, but you only need to dial the seven-digit local number when you're on the islands. To call from North America, dial ☎ 1-284 and the local number. From elsewhere, dial your country's international access code + ☎ 284 + the local number. We have included only the seven-digit local number in BVI listings in this chapter.

TOURIST INFORMATION

The ultrahelpful **BVI Tourist Board** (www.bvi touristboard.com) Tortola (☎ 494-3134); Virgin Gorda (☎ 495-5181) also has some overseas offices:
Germany (☎ 49-210-428-6671; Schwarzbachstr 32, D-40822 Mettmann bei, Dusseldorf)
UK (☎ 44-207-355-9585; 15 Upper Grosvenor St, London W1K 7PJ)
USA (☎ 212-696-0400; 1270 Broadway, Suite 705, New York, NY 10001)

WORK

Everyone except Belongers (naturalized citizens) is required to have a work permit to work in the BVI.

TRANSPORTATION

GETTING THERE & AWAY
Entering the British Virgin Islands

All you need is a valid passport and a return ticket to enter the BVI (US citizens see the boxed text, p772). If you are staying for a few months customs officials might ask to see proof of funds. There are **customs houses** (☎ 494-3864; www.bvi.gov.vg) at the ferry docks in Road Town and West End on Tortola.

Air

Terrence B Lettsome Airport (EIS; ☎ 494-3701) is a modern facility on Beef Island, which is connected to Tortola by a toll bridge. There are no international flights to BVI.

Airlines flying to/from BVI from within the Caribbean:
Air St Thomas (☎ 340-776-2700; www.airstthomas .com; hub St Thomas)
Air Sunshine (☎ 495-8900, 888-879-8900; www.air sunshine.com; hub San Juan)
American Eagle (☎ 495-2559, 868-669-4661; www.aa .com; hub San Juan)
Cape Air (☎ 495-2100, 800-352-0714; www.flycapeair .com; hub San Juan)
LIAT (☎ 340-774-2313; www.liatairline.com; hub Antigua)
Seaborne Airlines (☎ 888-359-8687; www.sea borneairlines.com; hub St Thomas)

Sea
CRUISE SHIP

Cruise ships call at Road Town's harbor on Tortola. Because it's so small, the town can feel easily overwhelmed with the arrival of just one cruise ship. Passengers tend to flock via taxis to Cane Garden Bay beach, or they hop on the ferry to Virgin Gorda for a look at the Baths.

Cruise Line International Association (CLIA; ☎ 212-921-0549; www.cruising.org) is a New York–based company that provides information on cruising and individual lines.

FERRY

Excellent ferries connect Tortola's Road Town and West End with St Thomas, USVI, and West End with St John, USVI. You must have a valid passport to travel between the BVI and USVI.

There are two sailings daily between Jost Van Dyke and Red Hook with **Inter-Island**

Ferry Services (☎ 495-4166), via St John (US$40 round-trip, 45 minutes).

Alternate departure times are made with **Smith's Ferry Services** (☎ 495-4495) and **Native Son** (☎ 495-4617), traveling from Road Town to downtown Charlotte Amalie on St Thomas, first stopping at West End (US$40 round-trip, 1½ hours). **Road Town Fast Ferry** (☎ 494-4454) makes the trip in just under an hour.

There are two daily sailings between Virgin Gorda and Charlotte Amalie, via Road Town (one way/round-trip US$35/60; two hours) with **Speedy's** (☎ 495-5240).

There are three sailings a day each with **Inter-Island Ferry Services** (☎ 495-4166) and **Nubian Princess** (☎ 495-4999), traveling between West End and Cruz Bay, St John (US$35 round-trip, 30 minutes).

GETTING AROUND
Air
Clair Aero (☎ 495-2271; www.clairaero.com; hub Tortola) flies between Tortola and Anegada and between Tortola and Virgin Gorda four times per week. It operates charter flights to most Caribbean destinations too.

Boat
The islands have a frequent and inexpensive ferry service that's easy to navigate, despite convoluted schedules. The full schedules are printed in most of the tourism guides, including the **BVI Welcome Guide** (www.bviwelcome.com), but following are the essentials.

BEEF ISLAND TO NORTH SOUND
North Sound Express (☎ 495-2138) runs ferries from Trellis Bay on Beef Island (near the airport) to the north end of Virgin Gorda, stopping at the Valley, Bitter End and Leverick Bay (US$17 one way, 15 minutes). Reservations are required.

ROAD TOWN TO SPANISH TOWN
Speedy's (☎ 495-5240) and **Smith's Ferry Service** (☎ 495-4495) run trips between Road Town on Tortola and Spanish Town on Virgin

Gorda almost half-hourly (US$20 round-trip, 45 minutes).

WEST END TO JOST VAN DYKE
New Horizon Ferry Service (☎ 495-9278) has five sailings a day between West End and Jost Van Dyke; the last sailing departs West End at 6pm and Jost at 5pm (US$20 round-trip, 20 minutes).

Car
Driving is undoubtedly the most convenient way to get around individual islands, but be prepared for some crazy conditions. Steep, winding roads are often the same width as your car. Chickens and dogs dart in and out of the roadway and, oh, did we mention the goats? Driving is on the left-hand side.

Drivers often stop dead in the middle of the road. Watch for the flap: when drivers are about to do something (stop, turn etc), they flap their arm out the window. Be careful not to lose your keys; there are no locksmiths on the islands.

RENTAL
There are several good local car-rental agencies on the islands. All drivers must purchase a Visitor's Temporary Driver's License (US$10), which you can purchase from the car-rental agency.

High-season rates begin at about US$45 per day and can run as high as US$80, but you'll get a better price for a weekly rental. See the individual islands for car-rental agencies.

Taxi
Taxis are convenient and essential if you're not renting a car. Several are the open-air variety, with bench seats and awnings, able to carry up to 12 passengers.

Beef Island Taxi Association (☎ 495-1982)
BVI Taxi Association (☎ 494-3942)
Waterfront Taxi Stand (☎ 494-3456)
West End Taxi Association (☎ 495-4934)

Anguilla

Bleached white-sand beaches, over 80 restaurants from beachfront seafood shacks to French haute cuisine, the largest range of budget to superluxe hotels just about anywhere in the Caribbean, warm and friendly people…it's tough to find a reason not to go to Anguilla.

Some think the cost is prohibitive, but the benefits are worth it to many. There is not a single chain restaurant on the island, nor are there any of the crowds or casinos that blight Anguilla's less-expensive next-door neighbor, St Martin. Quickly becoming known as a gourmand's destination, Anguilla also boasts some of the best beaches in the Caribbean: long strands of semisecluded miniparadise, with baby-soft sand and swaying palm-tree backdrops. Still others find Anguilla inviting because of its residents. Friendliness isn't an option, it's a way of life. Not waving at someone as you pass by is considered rude.

An informal law most people have abided by here is to not build anything higher than a coconut tree. This ensures tourism is always kept in balance, and Anguillians can keep the unhurried way of life they guard so zealously. Everyone on the island is keeping their fingers crossed that two new golf courses and an airport expansion won't affect the sleepy pace too much, but for now, Anguilla is truly, as they say, 'Tranquility wrapped in blue.'

FAST FACTS

- **Area** 35 sq miles (91 sq km)
- **Capital** The Valley
- **Country code** ☎ 264
- **Departure tax** US$20 airport, US$3 ferry
- **Famous for** Bankie Banx
- **Language** English
- **Money** Eastern Caribbean dollar (EC$); EC$1 = US$0.37 = €0.31 = UK£0.21
- **People** Anguillians
- **Phrases** Limin' (hanging out, preferably on a beach or with a rum punch)
- **Population** 11,561
- **Visa** Not necessary for most nationalities; see p411.

HIGHLIGHTS

- **Shoal Bay East** (p408) Witness in person the poster on your travel agent's wall at the best of Anguilla's many perfect Caribbean beaches.
- **Dune Preserve** (p408) Hanging out at Bankie Banx's *irie*-infused bar/restaurant, especially when reggae legend Bankie himself takes the stage.
- **Staying in Style** (p409) Rent out a villa with a half-dozen of your closest friends for a week.
- **Diving & Snorkeling** (p410 and p410) Explore coral reefs, sunken ships, underwater cliffs or an 18th-century Spanish galleon.
- **Palm Grove** (p408) Spend a few leisurely hours eating fresher-than-fresh lobster and johnnycakes at this beachside shack, aka Nat's Place.

ITINERARIES

- **Three Days** Depending on your budget, stay at Casa Nadine Guest House, the Anguilla Great House or the Malliouhana, while relaxing during the day on the beach, and spending your nights eating your weight in seafood at Tasty's or Hibernia.
- **One Week** Stay at a villa, alternating lounging on the beach with day-tripping to places like Scilly Cay for a lunch with a difference or diving at Prickly Pear Cays, and devoting your nights to chilling at the Dune Preserve, Pump House or Johnno's.

CLIMATE & WHEN TO GO

The average annual temperature is 80°F (27°C), with the hottest weather occurring during the hurricane season from June to November. The average annual rainfall is 35in (89cm). The lightest rainfall is generally from February to April and the heaviest from August to November. High-season rates start around mid-December and go until April. Many hotels shut down for the entire month of September. The best time to go is the end of October to early December, as everything has reopened, the weather is mild and the prices are low. Unless you own a private jet, don't even think about going during Christmas or New Year's: costs can easily double and even triple low-season rates.

HOW MUCH?

- **Taxi from the ferry terminal to The Valley** US$12
- **Day trip of full-day snorkeling and lunch to Prickly Pear** US$80
- **Diving** US$50 for one tank, US$80 for two tanks
- **Fresh fish in touristy restaurant** US$30
- **Fresh fish in local restaurant** US$20

LONELY PLANET INDEX

- **Liter of gas** US$1.12
- **Liter of bottled water** US$2
- **Bottle of Carib beer** US$2
- **Souvenir T-shirt** US$20
- **Street snack: johnnycake** US$1

HISTORY

Anguilla was first settled by American Indians from South America over 3500 years ago. Known as Arawak Indians for the language they spoke, they named the island 'Malliouhana': arrow-shaped sea serpent. Arawak Indians settled the island for millennia, evidenced by many cave sites with petroglyphs and artifacts still visible today and studied by archeologists. Sadly, the two main sites – Big Spring and the Fountain – have been closed to the public recently, but could reopen sometime in 2006 or 2007.

Columbus sailed by in 1493, but didn't land on the island. Britain sent a colony in 1650 to take advantage of soil that was hospitable to growing corn and tobacco. However, it wasn't hospitable to much else, and the plantation colonies that bloomed on nearby Caribbean islands, like St Kitts and Nevis, never defined Anguilla.

Because large-scale plantations didn't take off on Anguilla, smaller-scale industries, such as sailing, fishing and private farming, began to crop up on the island. In 1834 Britain abolished slavery in its colonies, and many Anguillian ex-slaves were able to take up positions as farmers, sailors and fishermen.

Soon after Anguilla formed a federation with St Kitts and Nevis, disliked by most of

ANGUILLA

ANGUILLA

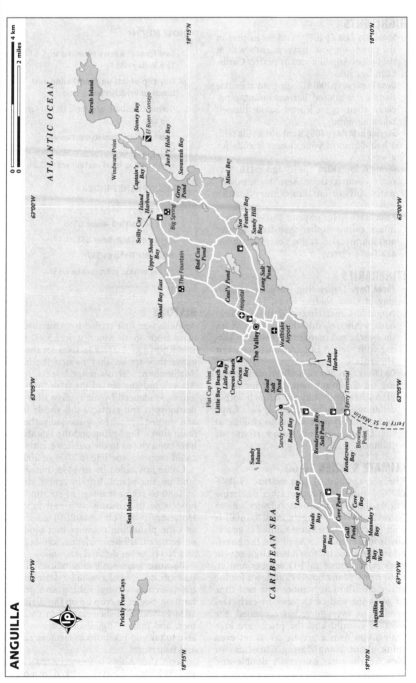

ATLANTIC OCEAN

Scrub Island

Stoney Bay
El Buen Consejo

Windware Point

Jack's Hole Bay

Captain's
Bay

Savannah Bay

Mimi Bay

Scilly Cay
Island
Harbour

Grey
Pond

Sea
Feather Bay

Sandy Hill
Bay

Big Spring

Upper Shoal
Bay

The Fountain

Bad Cox
Pond

Coal's Pond

Long Salt
Pond

Shoal Bay East

Hospital

The Valley

Wallblake
Airport

Flat Cap Point

Little Bay Beach
Little Bay
Crocus Beach
Crocus
Bay

Road
Salt
Pond

Little
Harbour

Sandy Ground

Road Bay

Rendezvous Bay
Salt Pond

Ferry Terminal

Blowing
Point

Sandy
Island

Ferry to St Martin

Seal Island

Long Bay

Rendezvous
Bay

Cove
Bay

Meads
Bay

Cove Pond

Barnes
Bay

Gull
Pond

Maunday's
Bay

Shoal
Bay
West

Prickly Pear Cays

CARIBBEAN SEA

Anguillita
Island

0   2 miles
0   4 km

63°10'W   63°05'W   63°00'W

18°15'N   18°10'N

the ex-slave population. Anguilla was allowed only one freeholder representative to the House of Assembly on St Kitts and was largely ignored, eventually culminating in the Anguilla Revolution in 1967. Anguilla Day marks May 30, 1967, the day Anguillians forced the Royal St Kitts Police off the island for good.

As a result of its revolt with St Kitts, Anguilla remains a British overseas territory. Under the Anguilla constitution, which came into effect in 1982, Britain is represented by a British governor appointed by the queen. The governor presides over an appointed Executive Council and an elected Anguilla House of Assembly.

Financial offshore services now rival tourism as Anguilla's largest moneymaker.

THE CULTURE

One the most welcoming on the planet, Anguillian culture is a blend of West Indian, British and African influences. Naturally, boating is hugely popular, and you'll still see many a race day. Anguillians guard their way of life zealously, and take pride in maintaining the balance between tourist development and the preservation of a thriving local society.

Community and family life is extremely important on Anguilla. Many people call each other 'cousin' or 'uncle,' and they stress a culture of openness and tolerance. Tourists who share these ideals will feel right at home. The standard of living has greatly improved since fishing was the economy's mainstay (up until the 1950s), and now almost three-quarters of the island is employed in tourism or commerce.

ARTS

Anguilla has a small arts and crafts scene, but isn't known for a long history in the arts. There are currently about two-dozen resident artists on the island. A brochure for a self-guided tour is available from the tourist office (p411).

ENVIRONMENT

Anguilla lies 5 miles (8km) north of St Martin, a dry and mostly scrubby island shaped like an eel (its namesake). Almost two dozen white-sand beaches have fostered countless imaginations to linger over whether one could subsist on a diet of coconuts to take an early retirement here.

BANKIE BANX

The most popular musician from Anguilla is reggae musician-cum-businessman Bankie Banx. Although he hasn't gained much popularity outside the Eastern Caribbean, his cameo in the movie *Cool Runnings* brought him international attention. After Hurricane Luis devastated Anguilla in 1995, Bankie recorded *Mighty Wind* to raise money for the victims on Anguilla. He now owns and lives at Dune Preserve (p408), where he runs his multi-level beachfront bar/restaurant/hang-out joint made from driftwood, old boats and a lot of *irie* (well being).

The most commonplace creatures on the island are the many roaming goats and sheep. Hint: if you see a slightly fuzzier-looking goat with its tail down, not up, it's actually a Caribbean sheep.

Like many Caribbean islands, Anguilla desalinates much of its water. Be mindful of letting the water run needlessly.

FOOD & DRINK

Anguilla has a reputation of being an incredibly expensive destination, and restaurant prices are one reason for this. Almost everything sold on Anguilla has been shipped in, driving up prices. Fortunately, many hotel and villa rooms come with fully equipped kitchens, so consider cooking some meals at home to keep costs down.

Lobster (common spiny lobster) and crayfish (spotted spiny lobster) are two locally caught Anguillian specialties. Crayfish, while smaller than lobsters, are reasonably sized creatures that have sweet, moist meat, and are commonly served three to an order.

Tap water usually comes from rooftop cisterns and thus should be boiled before drinking if there's no sign next to the faucet. Bottled water is readily available in grocery stores.

THE VALLEY

pop 1200

The Valley is Anguilla's only real town. The post office (p411) and banks (p411) are located here, and tourists can shop for groceries, as well as check out the handful of shops and sights.

Sights

WALLBLAKE HOUSE

The Valley's most interesting building is the **Wallblake House** (☎ 497-2944), which was built in 1787 and is one of the oldest structures on the island. Tours are held from 10am to 2pm Monday, Wednesday and Friday.

Make sure to also view the interior of the adjacent **church**, which has a unique design incorporating a decorative stone front, open-air side walls and a ceiling shaped like the hull of a ship.

Sleeping & Eating

Casa Nadine Guest House (☎ 497-2358; s/d incl tax & service US$20) As the cheapest accommodations option in the Leeward Islands, you can't fault the less-than-spotless surroundings. Eleven barebones rooms are a 10-minute walk from town (five minutes' walk from Crocus Bay). Rooms have warm showers, surprisingly comfortable mattresses, a kitchen (ask for pots and utensils from the proprietor) and doorless baths, ensuring you'll get to know your traveling companion perhaps a little too well.

Roy's Place (☎ 497-2470; www.roysplaceanguilla .com; Crocus Bay; r US$150, lunch US$7-14, mains US$14-38; ⌣ lunch & dinner; P ✂ ⌨) An English pub on a Caribbean beach with a pet parrot. This is the place to try Anguilla's famous local lobster while enjoying the breezy beachfront patio. Two pounds of lobster costs US$38 (big enough to split), or try a lighter pasta dish. Patrons can use the free high-speed Internet service next to the bar or trade a book at the lending library. Beer is half-price during Friday happy hour (5pm to 7pm) and there is a traditional English lunch on Sunday. Several guest rooms are available.

Roti House (☎ 497-5030; 30 George Hill; roti US$9-15; ⌣ lunch & dinner) Serving goat, chicken, shrimp or vegetable traditional Caribbean roti at a brightly painted roadside shack. Plan to relax for a while along with roaming chickens at one of the four plastic patio tables, as service is as unhurried as the island. Once in a while it serves conch roti, but you have to ask, as it's not on the menu.

IGA Fairplay Food Center (☎ 497-3877; Cosley Rd; ⌣ 8am-9pm Mon-Sat, 8am-noon Sun) Offers a large selection of American and European

food, perfect for cooking in your villa or hotel-room kitchen. Accepts both EC and US dollars.

Produce Market (cnr Wallblake & Landsome) For fresh bananas, vegetables and other local fare.

CENTRAL & WEST ANGUILLA

Heading west from The Valley you'll find some of the best restaurants in Anguilla. Keep an eye out, as many of them are unassumingly placed here and there along the main road, or far down a seemingly impassable dirt road. You'll also find **Sandy Ground** on Road Bay, the closest thing Anguilla has to a travelers' haunt. The crescent-shaped beach is fronted by a few restaurants, bars and small hotels, but stays surprisingly free of crowds, even in high season. Across the road is a large salt pond that was commercially harvested until the 1970s, when it became economically unfeasible.

The pearly white sand at **Rendezvous Bay** beckons one to stroll its full 1.5-mile (2.5km) length. **Shoal Bay West** isn't as stunning as its eastern namesake, but it's got fabulous snorkeling and a few nearby dive sites. **Meads Bay** boasts some of the fancier hotels, but it's still relatively free of attitude. There are annual **boat races** from its beach on the first Thursday in August.

On the way to Sandy Ground, check out **Pyrat Rums** (☎ 497-5003; Road Bay; ⌣ 10am-4pm), where you can sample locally made rum or call ahead for a complimentary factory tour.

Sleeping

BUDGET

Syd-An's Apartments & Villas (☎ 497-3180; www .inns.ai/sydans; Sandy Ground; r with fan from US$90, villa US$115; ✂ ⌨) On Sandy Ground's main strip, across from the beach, Syd-An's has 10 pleasant apartments with separate bedrooms, full kitchens and cable TV situated around a convivial courtyard. Rooms with air-con cost a tad more.

Sea View Guest House (☎ 497-2427; http://inns.ai /seaview; Sandy Ground; 1-/2-bedroom apt US$60/110; P) Across from the beach, both apartments are outfitted for a longer stay with full kitchens and maid service every other day. You'll be downstairs from a local Anguillian family who can help you arrange diving and sightseeing adventures.

La Palma (☎ 497-3260; http://inns.ai/lapalma; Sandy Ground; 1-3 bedroom apt from US$65; P) Directly on the beach, La Palma's two- and three-bedroom apartments have kitchens, cable TV and ceiling fans. They can arrange baby-sitting.

MIDRANGE

Anguilla Great House (☎ 497-6061, in USA 800-583-9247; www.anguillagreathouse.com; Rendezvous Bay; cottage US$220-280; P 🍽 🖭) This most-Caribbean-feeling hotel features West Indies cottages decorated with island touches, private porches and colorful murals. Kayak (US$15 per hour) and Sunfish sailboat (US$35 per hour) rentals are available. A great place for kids.

Rendezvous Bay Hotel and Villas (☎ 497-6549, in the US 800-274-4893; www.rendezvousbay.com; Rendezvous Bay; r US$130-325, villas for 6-8 people US$825-1075; P 🍽 🖭) The most kickback place on the island is famous resident Jeremiah Gumb's former hotel, near the ferry terminal on a beach practically all its own. A great place to meet new friends over cocktails at the bar. Offers tennis, sailing, kayaking, room service, a restaurant and a car-rental agency. Some rooms have full kitchens.

Body & Soul (☎ 497-8363, cell 235-8399; www .anguilla.de in German; Sandy Ground; apt 2/4/6 people US$115/125/140; P 🖭) Your biggest decision while staying at this peaceful retreat: should I take a nap on the beach 10ft (3m) away, or should I just stop at the hammock on my patio? Recently painted and refurbished, this cheery apartment has a full kitchen and three bedrooms. The English-speaking German owner also runs a fitness and massage studio, where visitors can pay per class, as well as a cybercafé next door.

Carimar Beach Club (☎ 497-6881, in USA 800-235-8667; www.carimar.com; Meads Bay; 1-/2-bedroom apt from US$340/455; 🍽) Each bougainvillea-draped Spanish-style apartment is equipped with a full kitchen, living and dining rooms, and a balcony or patio. Ask about off-season diving or honeymoon packages.

TOP END

Malliouhana (☎ 497-6111, in USA 800-835-0796; www .malliouhana.com; Meads Bay; r from US$620; P 🍽 🖭 🖭) On a low cliff at the east end of Meads Bay is one of the island's most fashionable luxury hotels. The rooms are gracefully appointed with Italian tile floors, marble baths, rattan furnishings, original artwork and large patios. Just strolling through the 25 acres (10 hectares) of Mediterranean-style architecture and gardens will instill instant relaxation, and that's before you stroll to one of three adjacent beaches or get a massage at the top-notch spa.

Eating

This is prime territory for impromptu weekend barbecues. If you're lucky, you'll end up on the road east of Malliouhana on a weekend when B&Ds, a mobile barbecue, decides to open; and don't forget to top off your ribs with the bread pudding with rum sauce.

Picante (☎ 498-1616; appetizers US$7-9, mains US$10-16; 🍽 dinner only, closed Tue) A Caribbean taqueria? Why not. This unassuming roadside restaurant on the far west of the island's Albert Hughes Rd is popular with the locals. A Californian couple runs the open-air tin-roofed casual Mexican space that seats about 30 on wood benches. Be careful to keep some room after the delicious home-baked tortillas for enchiladas and fish tacos. A small bar serves margaritas.

Smokey's (☎ 497-6582; Cove Bay; lunch from US$8, dinner from US$10; 🍽 lunch & dinner) Occupying a great spot right on the beach and open until the last person stumbles home, Smokey's offers a menu of local creations and typical American fare. Pizza and burgers are available for lunch, and dishes like curried goat are the mainstay of the dinner menu. Cove Bay is just next to Rendezvous Bay, within easy walking distance.

AUTHOR'S CHOICE

Tasty's (☎ 497-2737; South Hill Rd; breakfast US$5-11, mains US$12-25; 🍽 breakfast & lunch, closed Thu; P) A tad less expensive than the other island favorites, Tasty's offers creatively fused dishes, such as grilled tuna steak with orange Creole sauce or coconut-crusted fish fillet with spicy banana rum sauce. The bright teal and purple walls are covered with shells and tropical murals. South Hill Rd heads west from The Valley.

Ripples (☎ 497-3380; Sandy Ground; mains US$12-25; ⏰ lunch & dinner) The hip and happening spot for locals and travelers alike in Sandy Ground. Serves staples like burgers and salads, but also Caribbean fusion dishes like Cajun fish with pineapple and lime salsa. It's open till midnight.

Entertainment

Dune Preserve (☎ 772-0637; www.dunepreserve.com; ⏰ most of the time) Imagine if a reggae star was given a huge pile of driftwood and old boats, and got to build his very own fort on the beach. The result would be this, one of the grooviest places on the planet. Hometown hero Bankie Banx (see the boxed text, p405) has lived, played and limed here for two-dozen years. Live music takes the stage on Wednesday, Friday and Saturday (plus Tuesday and Sunday during high season) and, if you're lucky, you'll hear Bankie jam himself. Food and drinks are also served. Try the Dune Shine: fresh ginger, pineapple juice, white rum and bitters. Take the road past the Cuisinart resort (a dirt road) and take the first left turn down a seemingly impossible rocky road. This is also the home of the Moonsplash festival (p410).

Johnno's Beach Bar (☎ 497-2728; Sandy Ground; meals US$5.50-12; ⏰ noon-midnight, closed Mon) No shirt and no shoes will still get you service at this happening beach shack. Johnno's offers casual fare and tropical drinks to a blend of locals and travelers. Happy hour is from 5pm to 7pm, and there's live jazz Friday night.

Pumphouse (☎ 497-5154; Sandy Ground; ⏰ noon-3pm & 5pm-2am Wed-Sat) At the north end of Sandy Ground, this former saltworks plant is now one of Anguilla's chillest hotspots. Serving burgers, steaks and a Caribbean international fusion menu, such as Asian-glazed tuna burger for US$19. Order a range of inventive drinks from the 2004 Caribbean Bartender of the Year. Happy hour is from 5pm to 6pm. Live calypso and reggae play several nights a week.

EAST ANGUILLA

Close your eyes and imagine the quintessential Caribbean stretch of white-sand beach. You've just pictured **Shoal Bay East**, a 2-mile-long (3km) beach with pristine sand, thoughtfully placed reefs ideal for snorkeling, glassy turquoise water and a remarkable lack of tourist development.

Island Harbour is a working fishing village, not a resort area, and its beach is lined with brightly colored fishing boats rather than chaise lounges. Travelers staying here enjoy less of a resort feel and more long conversations with locals.

There are another half-dozen beautiful semisecluded beaches, with **Captain's Bay** and **Junk Hole's Bay** the best among them.

Sleeping

Allamanda Beach Club (☎ 497-5217; www.allamanda .ai; Shoal Bay East; apt US$100-165; P ❄ ♨) Just a two-minute walk from the beach, this fabulously priced three-story place isn't fancy, but spacious apartments offer a small separate kitchen, living room, balcony, TV and ceiling fans. Try to get a 3rd-floor room for the view. It's home to Gwen's Reggae Grill, as well as Zara's Restaurant, where you can munch on its famous 'rasta pasta' while listening to the singing chef.

Harbor Lights (☎ 497-4435, in USA 800-759-9870; www.harborlightsanguilla.com; Rose Hill Rd, Island Harbour; incl service charge d US$80, studio US$110-130; P) This sweet family-run place right on the ocean at the east side of town has the area's best-value accommodations. There are four pleasant ocean-view studios, all with full kitchens, and baths with solar-heated showers. There's a common barbecue area, and you can snorkel just a few feet from the deck; diving and other water sports can be arranged.

Shoal Bay Villas (☎ 497-2051; www.sbvillas.ai; Shoal Beach East; studio from US$270, 1-bedroom apt from US$295, 2-bedroom apt US$445, extra person per night US$40; P ♨) A splendid beachfront location, this place has 15 large, comfortable units with tropical decor. All have ceiling fans, a kitchen, and a patio or balcony. Some rooms literally step onto the sandy stretch of perfection that will be your front yard. Baby-sitting available.

Eating

Palm Grove (☎ 497-4224; Junk's Hole Bay; lobster US$25, lobster salad US$15; ⏰ lunch) Just maneuvering down this rocky dirt road will work up a hunger for the fresher-than-fresh lobster at what is quite possibly the only beachfront shack ever featured in *Bon Appétit* magazine. Put your order in with chef/owner Nat for lobster (there are other things on the menu, but why bother?) and his delectable johnnycakes – a doughy flour and cornmeal pastry, like an airy, not-too-sweet donut – and head down to the beach for the hour (or two) wait.

Uncle Ernie's (☎ 497-2542; meals from US$6, fruit coladas US$5; ☺ breakfast, lunch & dinner) At this popular local beach bar west of Shoal Bay Villas, you can get barbecued chicken, ribs or a cheeseburger and wash it down with a US$2 Heineken or an Ernie's special rum punch. There are also more expensive fish, crayfish and lobster offerings. On Sunday afternoon there's live music to be heard.

Smitty's (☎ 497-4300; Island Harbour; meals US$12-25) The proprietor Smitty, as he's known to his friends (and they are many), runs this casual beachside bar and restaurant offering fresh lobster and barbecue chicken and ribs as if it was a barbecue in his backyard. Try the lobster and crayfish combo for US$30.

Hibernia (☎ 497-4290; appetizers US$10-15, mains US$27-39; ☺ lunch & dinner Tue-Sun in winter, dinner Tue-Sat in summer) In the Harbour View residential area, 0.75 miles (1.2km) east of Island Harbour, this is one of the island's top restaurants. Featuring Caribbean nouvelle cuisine with Asian hints, main courses range from chicken to creative seafood dishes, such as lobster tail with Lao rice and papaya with ginger lime sauce (US$39). There's veranda dining and a hillside setting with a spectacular sea view. Pass the gas station heading east and follow the Hibernia signs up the hill and to the left.

Scilly Cay (☎ 497-5123; mains US$25-40; ☺ noon-4pm, bar 11am-5pm, closed Mon & Sep-Oct & in rough weather) Off the coast of Island Harbour, this is a different lunchtime experience. Wave at the island and they'll send a boat over to the Island Harbour pier (behind Smitty's) to pick you up. Sunday afternoon packs in locals and tourists alike for the reggae band, and there's live music on Wednesday and Friday. Reputedly serves the best rum punch on the island.

DIRECTORY

ACCOMMODATIONS

Anguilla has a reputation as an expensive destination because…well, it is. Rooms average about US$300 during winter, but prices drop dramatically in summer. There are several economical options, including the Casa Nadine Guest House (p406), which has rooms for US$20 a night. Many hotel rooms and almost all villas have fully equipped kitchens, so you can do your own cooking and reduce your costs.

High-season rates usually run December 15 to April 15, but it's around Christmas and New Year's when prices rise astronomically. Most hotels charge significantly less in the off season.

Hotels charge a 10% government tax and 10% service charge.

VILLAS
One of Anguilla's many charms is its plethora of villas, available for every taste and budget. It can cost from about US$1000 per week for a studio during summer to US$35,000 per night for a seven-bedroom mansion at Christmas.

To make arrangements you can either contact a booking agent, such as **Island Dream Properties** (☎ 498-3200; www.islanddreamproperties .com), or make plans yourself by checking the website http://villas.ai. Part of the ever-helpful www.news.ai website run by resident Bob Green, this website lists each villa and its direct reservation information.

For true service, **Charanell's Personal Concierge Services** (☎ 478-7866; www.cpcsanguilla.com; weekly per couple/family or group US$275/550) works as a personal hotel concierge to ensure all your needs on the island are met. This lifelong resident of Anguilla also serves as a wedding coordinator and offers baby-sitting services.

Note: roosters don't pay heed to quiet-hour signs posted at hotels or villas, no matter the level of luxury. Bring earplugs.

PRACTICALITIES

■ **Newspapers & Magazines** The weekly Anguillian newspaper comes out on Friday.

■ **Radio & TV** Radio Anguilla is at 1505AM and 95.5FM. Cable TV is available with local programming on Channel 3.

■ **Electricity** The current used is 110V (60 cycles).

■ **Weights & Measures** Imperial system.

ACTIVITIES

Beaches & Swimming

The pure white-sand beaches are high on most Anguillian visitors' list as a must-see, must-relax destination. The most prized beaches are Shoal Bay East and Rendezvous Bay. To get to the secluded beach at Little Bay, hire a fisherman from Crocus Bay (as The Valley's main beach, it's no slouch itself) to ferry you over for US$10 per boat.

Diving

Although it doesn't hold the allure of nearby dive havens, such as St Eustatius or Saba, Anguilla has clear water and good reef formations. In addition, since the mid-1980s a number of ships have been deliberately sunk to create new dive sites, bringing Anguilla's total to almost two-dozen diverse sites.

Offshore islands popular for diving include Prickly Pear Cays, which has caverns, ledges, barracudas and nurse sharks; several wrecks, including the 1772 natural sinking of the Spanish galleon *El Buen Consejo*, 109yd (100m) off Stoney Bay; and Sandy Island, which has soft corals and sea fans.

DIVE SHOPS

Anguillian Divers (☎ 497-4750; www.anguilliandivers.com; Meads Bay) caters to novices and experts alike, offering single dives (US$60 for a daily dive) as well as many courses, such as Professional Association of Diving Instructors (PADI) certification, advanced open water, resort and dive master. Packages are available for US$245 to US$310.

A local with years of experience as a PADI dive master, Doug from **Special 'D' Diving & Charters** (☎ 235-8438; www.dougcarty.com; Sandy Ground) can practically call each fish, shark and turtle by name. And they'll come. Doug is an extremely popular divemaster; reserve ahead. A one-tank dive costs US$80, two tanks US$85.

Horseback Riding

El Rancho del Blues (☎ 497-6164; Blowing Point; 1-/2-hr ride US$35/50) offers trail and beach rides.

Snorkeling & Sailing

Among the offshore islands, one of the most popular destinations is Prickly Pear Cays, which has excellent snorkeling conditions. Tour boats leave Sandy Ground for Prickly Pear at around 10am, returning around 4pm; the cost averages US$80, including lunch, drinks and snorkeling gear. Try **Chocolat** (☎ 497-3394) or if there's no answer check at Ripples restaurant (p408) in Sandy Ground, Doug Carty from **Special 'D' Diving & Charters** (☎ 235-8438; www.dougcarty.com; Sandy Ground) or **Gotcha** (☎ 497-2956) for snorkeling, fishing or just cruising. Shoal Bay East, Sandy Island and Little Bay are other popular snorkeling spots.

> **EMERGENCY NUMBERS**
>
> **Police, Fire, Ambulance** (☎ 911)

FESTIVALS & EVENTS

Moonsplash (www.dunepreserve.com) The hippest of Anguilla's festivals, Bankie Banx invites all his old reggae friends to the Dune Preserve (p408), anytime from late February to early April, for some late-night jamming. Guests have included Third World, the Wailers, and Toots and the Maytals.

Anguilla Summer Festival (July/August; www.festival.ai) Anguilla's carnival is its main festival, which starts on the weekend preceding August Monday and continues until the following weekend. Events include boat races, costumed parades, a beauty pageant, calypso competitions, music and dancing.

Tranquility Jazz Festival (early November; www.anguillajazz.org) This jazz festival attracts big names and local acts, who play to an international audience of jazz aficionados in various hotels and other locations.

HOLIDAYS

Anguilla has the following public holidays:

New Year's Day January 1
Good Friday Late March/early April
Easter Monday Late March/early April
Whit Monday Eighth Monday after Easter
Anguilla Day May 30
Queen's Birthday June 11
August Monday (Emancipation Day) First Monday in August
August Thursday First Thursday in August
Constitution Day August 6
Separation Day December 19
Christmas Day December 25
Boxing Day December 26

INTERNET ACCESS

Public Library (☎ 497-2441; The Valley; per 30min EC$5; 🕑 9am-5pm Mon-Fri, 9am-noon Sat)

INTERNET RESOURCES

www.anguilla-vacation.com The official tourism website for Anguilla is easy to navigate and lists all accommodations by type and price.

www.news.ai A thoroughly researched website written by a local, but can be lacking in updates.

MEDICAL SERVICES

The island's 36-bed **Princess Alexandra Hospital** (☎ 497-2551) is in The Valley.

MONEY

There are four international banks on Anguilla in The Valley, all with ATMs dispensing US and EC dollars.

Scotiabank is next door to IGA Fairplay Food Center, and the other three are centrally located in town.

A 15% service charge is added to most restaurant bills and no further tipping is necessary.

POST

Anguilla's only **post office** (☎ 497-2528; ☷ 8am-4:45pm Mon-Fri) is in The Valley. To mail a postcard or half-ounce letter (14g) costs EC$1.50 to North, South and Central America, and EC$1.90 to Europe.

TELEPHONE

Anguilla's area code is ☎ 264 and is followed by a seven-digit local number. If you are calling locally, just dial the local number. To call from North America, dial ☎ 1-264 + the local number. From elsewhere, dial your country's international dialing code + 264 + the seven-digit local number. We have included only the seven-digit local number in Anguilla listings in this chapter.

TOURIST INFORMATION

Local Tourist Offices

Anguilla Tourist Board (☎ 497-2759, in USA 800-553-4939; www.anguilla-vacation.com; Coronation Ave, The Valley)

Tourist Offices Abroad

Canada (☎ 416-944-8105; xybermedia@aol.com; 116C Hazelton Ave, Toronto, ON M5R 2E4)

Germany (☎ 6257-96-29-20; rmorozow@t-online. de; c/o Sergat Deutschland, IMM Guldenen Wingert 8-C, D-64342 Seeheim)

UK (☎ 0208-871-0012; anguilla@tiscali.co.uk; 7A Crealock St, London SW18 2BS)

USA (☎ 914-287-2400; mwturnstyle@aol.com; 246 Central Ave, White Plains, NY 10606)

VISA

Citizens of many CIS, African and South American countries need to obtain a visa.

TRANSPORTATION

GETTING THERE & AWAY

Entering Anguilla

It's best to travel with a valid passport, and from December 31, 2005, all US citizens will need a valid passport to re-enter the US from any Caribbean country (see the boxed text, p772).

Air

Anguilla's **Wallblake Airport** (AXA; ☎ 497-2514) has recently been expanded to make way for larger American Airlines jet airplanes. Two new golf courses are expected to attract more tourism.

The following airlines fly to and from Anguilla from within the Caribbean:

American Eagle (☎ 497-3131; www.aa.com; hub St Martin)

Caribbean Star (☎ 497-2680; www.flycaribbeanstar .com; hub Antigua)

LIAT (☎ 497-5002; www.liatairline.com; hub Antigua)

Transanguilla (☎ 497-8690; www.transanguilla.com; hub Anguilla)

Winair (☎ 497-2748; www.fly-winair.com; hub St Martin)

Sea

FERRY

Ferries make the 25-minute run from Marigot Bay in St Martin to Blowing Point in Anguilla an average of once every half-hour from 8am to 6:15pm. From Anguilla to St Martin the ferries run from 7:30am to 7pm. As ferry companies change frequently, call the **dispatch center** (☎ 497-6070). The ferry terminal is 4 miles (6km) southwest of The Valley in the small village of Blowing Point.

The one-way fare per person is US$12 (US$15 on the last boat of the day). The fare for the passage is paid onboard the boat.

YACHT

The main ports of entry are at Sandy Ground in Road Bay or Blowing Point. The **immigration and customs office** (☎ 497-2451; ☷ 8:30am-noon & 1-4pm Sun-Fri, 1-4pm Sat) can be contacted on VHF channel 16.

ANGUILLA

GETTING AROUND

There is no public transportation on Anguilla and distances can be vast. Visitors will either need to rent a car or rely on pricy taxi drivers. Day-trippers will get a better taxi deal if they negotiate a tour price for several hours (see right).

Car & Motorcycle

DRIVER'S LICENSE

Visitors must buy a temporary Anguillian driver's license for US$20, which is issued on the spot by the car-rental companies. Make sure each person driving has a valid license, as hefty fines will be imposed on the spot.

RENTAL

Compact air-conditioned cars rent for about US$40 a day (usually US$5 cheaper in summer), with free unlimited mileage in winter.

The agency **Wendell Connor Car Rental** (☎ 497-6894, cell 235-6894; wendellconnor@caribcable .com) will pick you up for no cost. Both **Triple K Car Rental** (☎ 497-2934; hertztriplek@anguilla.net; Airport Rd) and **Island Car Rentals** (☎ 497-2723; islandcar@anguillanet.com; Airport Rd) are a quick taxi ride from the airport.

ROAD RULES & CONDITIONS

In Anguilla, you drive on the left-hand side of the road. Steering wheels can be either on the left or right.

Most roads are potholed if they're paved and full of rocks if they're dirt, making driving an adventure.

The island has six gas stations, all well marked on the tourist maps and our own Anguilla map (p404). Most close on Sunday.

Taxi

From the airport, a taxi will cost US$6 into The Valley, US$12 to Rendezvous Bay and US$22 to Shoal Bay West. From the ferry, it's US$12 to The Valley, US$14 to Sandy Ground and US$20 to Shoal Bay West. Rates are for one to two people, with an additional person paying US$4, after 6pm an extra US$2.

To book a taxi at the airport call ☎ 497-5054, and at the ferry ☎ 497-6089.

Tours

Taxi drivers provide two-hour tours of the island for US$40 for one or two people, US$5 for each additional person.

St Martin/Sint Maarten

St Martin/Sint Maarten is an island of contrasts. It is the world's smallest land mass shared by two countries: France and the Netherlands Antilles. Nicknamed the 'Friendly Island,' its white-sand beaches, gourmet French restaurants, good hiking and nightlife can make this the perfect destination. Many who come here appreciate its duty-free shopping, nonstop casinos, cruise ships and all-inclusive resorts, but for others, this makes St Martin not the relaxing Caribbean vacation they had in mind. There are most definitely places to get away, but cruise ships stopping by kick the whole island into high gear.

Although the Dutch side has lost most of its Dutch influence, the French side maintains its 'Europe in the Caribbean' feel. Casinos are only allowed on the Dutch side.

Part of the reason St Martin is so popular is that it is easy to get to, inexpensive and offers a little of everything for everybody, from secluded bays to pulsating nightclubs. It's a main transportation hub for the surrounding islands as the international Juliana Airport accepts jet airplanes.

FAST FACTS

- **Area** 37 sq miles (96 sq km)
- **Capital** St Martin: Marigot; Sint Maarten: Philipsburg
- **Country codes** St Martin (☎ 590); Sint Maarten (☎ 599)
- **Departure tax** Air: US$6 in Netherlands Antilles, US$25 elsewhere; ferry: US$2
- **Famous for** Beaches, duty-free shopping, casinos, theme restaurants, cruise port
- **Languages** French in St Martin; Dutch in Sint Maarten; English, Creole, Papamientu and Spanish on both sides
- **Money** St Martin: euro (€); Sint Maarten: Netherlands Antillean guilder (NAf); US dollar (US$) on both sides. US$1 = €0.83 = UK£0.55 = NAf1.77
- **Official names** St Martin/Sint Maarten
- **Population** St Martin: 35,000; Sint Maarten: 34,000
- **Visa** Not necessary for visitors from North America or the EU

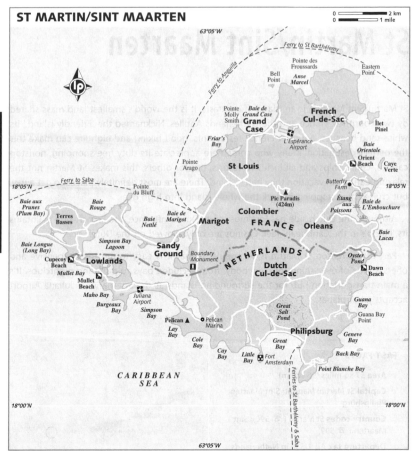

ST MARTIN/SINT MAARTEN

HIGHLIGHTS

- **Grand Case** (p419) Enjoy seafood, French fare or johnnycakes and patties every night while staying in this charming French Caribbean seaside village.
- **Orient Beach** (p420) Stroll the long stretch of white sand, which beckons all tastes with beachfront bars, water sports, chaise lounges and an au naturel section.
- **Pic Paradis** (p419) Climb to the top of St Martin's highest point for an unbeatable view.
- **Nightlife** (p424) Dance until dawn at the *très* chic club Bliss, or try your luck at the nearby blackjack tables.
- **Sunset Beach Bar** (p424) Drink a death-defying piña colada at sunset at this bar

near Juliana Airport, making sure to duck when the planes come through.

ITINERARIES

- **Two Days** Stay at the Caravanserai Beach Resort in Maho Bay and party 'til dawn at Bliss, spending the days on Maho Bay Beach.
- **One Week** After a couple of days in Maho Bay, head to Grand Case and dine in some of the many fine French restaurants. Fill your days with trips to the Butterfly Farm, Pic Paradis, and Dawn, Orient and Cupecoy Beaches.
- **Two Weeks** Follow the one-week itinerary and then head to Marigot to splurge at the duty-free French shops and, now

that you've worked up the courage, drop your swimsuit at Orient Beach for an all-over tan.

CLIMATE & WHEN TO GO

St Martin averages an annual temperature of a perfect 79°F (26°C). July through October sees heat, humidity and, often, hurricanes; many establishments close entirely in September. The best times to visit St Martin are November to early December and May to June.

HISTORY

For a thousand years, St Martin was sparsely populated by Arawak and later the more fierce Carib Indians. They named the island Sualouiga after the brackish salt ponds that made it difficult to settle.

Columbus sailed past on November 11, 1493, which happened to be the feast of St Martin of Tours and thus, the island's namesake. The Dutch, however, were the first to take advantage of the land, a nice stopping-off point between Holland and their new colonies in Brazil and New Amsterdam (modern-day New York City). After a few abortive attempts by the Spanish to regain the island, now found to be brimming with lucrative salt deposits, the French and Dutch ended up fighting for control of it.

As the legend has it, the Dutch and the French decided to partition St Martin from a march originating in Oyster Pond. The French walked northward, the Dutch south. While the French quenched their thirst with wine, the Dutch brought along dodgy gin. Halfway through, the Dutchmen stopped to sleep off the ill effects, creating a much larger French partition.

St Martin became a plantation island much like many of its neighbors. The end of slavery brought an end to the plantation boom, and by 1930 the population stood at just 2000 hearty souls. Ironically, it was WWII that brought tourism to St Martin. In 1943, the US Navy built large runways on the island to use as a base in the Caribbean. The French capitalized by using the runways to fly in tourists, by the 1950s bringing the population of St Martin up to about 70,000 and making tourism the number one industry on both sides of the island.

Sint Maarten was a part of the Netherlands Antilles until 2005, when the five islands (Saba, Curaçao, Bonaire, St Eustatius and Dutch Sint Maarten) met on the Jesurun Referendum to decide the fate of the Netherlands Antilles. Sint Maarten, along with fellow populous island Curaçao, voted overwhelmingly to become an independent country within the Kingdom of the Netherlands.

THE CULTURE

The island culture has its roots largely in African, French and Dutch influences, though scores of more recent immigrants – including many from the Dominican Republic and Haiti – have added their own elements to this multicultural society. The standard of living for these new immigrants is pretty rough, as many are in the country illegally and there is not enough work available.

St Martin has adapted to tourism more than any other nearby island. No more than 20% of the people living on St Martin were born there. The two cultures, Dutch and French, have had to share the smallest land area of any two countries and, as such, have developed a tolerant attitude that allows gays and lesbians and those with alternative lifestyles to feel quite comfortable. Residents coexist with the constant hum of low-lying debauchery that accompanies the dozens of gentlemen's clubs, casinos and thriving discos. Some ignore it, some join in, but most simply accept that their beautiful island home plays host to one long adult spring break.

Topless sunbathing is customary on both sides of the island and nude sunbathing is sanctioned at Orient Beach, where there is a naturist resort (p421).

ENVIRONMENT

The west side of the island is more water than land, dominated by the expansive Simpson Bay Lagoon, which is one of the largest landlocked bodies of water in the Caribbean and has moorings for a large array of boats. The interior is hilly, with the highest point, Pic Paradis, rising 1391ft (424m) from the center of French St Martin.

Herons, egrets, stilts, pelicans and laughing gulls are among the plentiful shorebirds in the island's brackish ponds. Frigate birds can be spotted along the coast, and hummingbirds and bananaquits in gardens. Lizards also are abundant.

Most island water comes from desalinization plants and is costly. Be careful not to take overly long showers, or to let the tap run.

FOOD & DRINK

Food here can be excellent, not too expensive and a brilliant blend of European and Caribbean influences. Although the numbers of theme restaurants and fast-food joints can be overwhelming, especially on the Dutch side, the French side offers a plethora of traditional seafood *lolos* (barbecue stands) and the gourmet capital of the Caribbean, Grand Case (p419).

Note that some restaurants include a 15% service charge in their prices and at others you are expected to tip an equivalent amount.

French wine and Caribbean rum are not in short supply. All over the island you'll find guavaberry stores selling a black-face bottle of the island's signature liqueur.

Although the island sports several desalinization plants, many people still use cisterns. Although the rooftop-caught cistern water is generally safe to drink, bottled water is inexpensive and plentiful.

FRENCH ST MARTIN

MARIGOT

pop 12,500

As the capital of French St Martin, Marigot offers a distinctly European flavor to the island with plenty of good shopping and restaurants, and several sights.

Orientation

Marigot has two commercial centers: the harborfront, with its public market, souvenir stalls and ferry terminal to Anguilla and St Barth; and Port La Royale Marina, a quaint area with higher-end boutiques and more restaurants. The area around Rue du Général de Gaulle connects the two, offering a spectrum of shops and restaurants. The tourist office produces an excellent map of the island.

Information

Bibliothèque Municipale (☎ 87-85-87; Rue du Palais Justice; per 15/30min €1.50/3; ☼ 2-7pm Mon & Tue, 9am-7pm Wed, 11am-7pm Thu & Fri, 9am-1pm Sat)
Change Point (☼ 7:30am-7pm Mon-Sat) Near the marina.
Hospital of St-Martin (☎ 52-25-25)
Inter Change (Rue du Général de Gaulle; ☼ 8am-6:30pm Mon-Sat)
Post office (☎ 51-07-60; 25 Rue de La Liberté; ☼ 7am-5:30pm Mon-Fri, 7:30am-noon Sat) There are card phones outside the post office. Phone cards are sold in the various souvenir shops around town.
Tourist office (☎ 87-57-21; www.st-martin.org; Port de Marigot; ☼ 8:30am-1pm & 2:30-5:30pm Mon-Fri, 8am-noon Sat) Southwest of the marina. There's an information booth on Rue de la République near the ferry terminal.

Sights

Fort Louis was constructed in 1767 by order of French King Louis XVI to protect Marigot from marauding British and Dutch pirates. It's been abandoned for centuries and contains only remnants from bygone eras, but the view alone is worth the 15-minute hike up (past the old hospital) to the ruins.

The **St Martin Archaeological Museum** (☎ 29-22-84; ☼ 9am-4pm Mon-Fri, 9am-1pm Sat) covers everything from the Arawak period to island fashion in the 1930s, and features period photography, historical displays and artifacts from the pre-Colombian period.

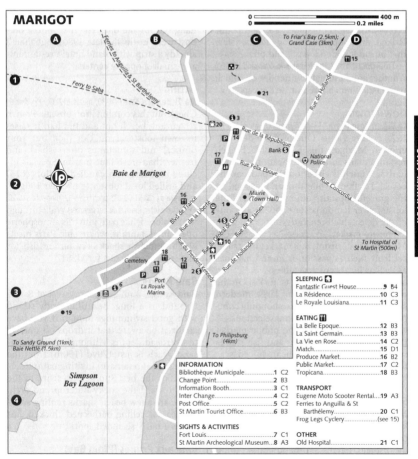

MARIGOT

SLEEPING 🏠
Fantastic Guest House...............**9** B4
La Résidence............................**10** C3
Le Royale Louisiana.................**11** C3

EATING 🍴
La Belle Epoque......................**12** B3
La Saint Germain....................**13** B3
La Vie en Rose.......................**14** C2
Match...................................**15** D1
Produce Market......................**16** B2
Public Market.........................**17** C2
Tropicana..............................**18** B3

TRANSPORT
Eugene Moto Scooter Rental....**19** A3
Ferries to Anguilla & St
   Barthélemy.........................**20** C1
Frog Legs Cyclery...................(see 15)

OTHER
Old Hospital...........................**21** C1

INFORMATION
Bibliothèque Municipale.............**1** C2
Change Point............................**2** B3
Information Booth......................**3** C1
Inter Change............................**4** C2
Post Office...............................**5** C2
St Martin Tourist Office..............**6** B3

SIGHTS & ACTIVITIES
Fort Louis................................**7** C1
St Martin Archeological Museum...**8** A3

Sleeping

Fantastic Guest House (☎ 87-71-09; www.fantastic
guesthouse.com; Rue Low Town; s/d/tr US$50/70/80; ✖)
One of the best deals during the winter, this
19-room family-run charmer has kitchenettes in double and triple rooms, and is just
south of the marina.

Le Royale Louisiana (☎ 87-86-51; centrhotel
.sxm@wanadoo.fr; Rue du Général de Gaulle; s/d incl
breakfast from €45/60; ✖ ✖) This central
hotel has been recently renovated with
more comfortable furnishings, and is one
of the better deals in Marigot. Rooms in
the front can be noisy, but all offer TVs,
phones and refrigerators.

La Résidence (☎ 87-70-37; Rue du Général de Gaulle;
s/d incl breakfast €84/104; ✖) This 21-room hotel

has large, adequate rooms with TV, air-con,
room safes, balconies and minibars.

Eating

MARINA

Port La Royale Marina has a waterfront
lined with restaurants offering everything
from pizza and burgers to seafood and
nouvelle cuisine. There's fierce competition, with some of the island's lowest menu
prices and lots of chalkboard specials. The
best bet is to just wander around and see
what catches your fancy.

La Saint Germain (☎ 87-92-87; crepes around
US$10; ✖ breakfast, lunch & dinner) Head here for
a good selection of crepes. It has a pleasant
spot on the marina.

La Belle Epoque (☎ 87-87-70; breakfast around US$10, lunch around US$14) Harborside La Belle Epoque is large and popular, serving standard fare that includes seafood, pasta and pizza.

Tropicana (☎ 87-79-07; dinner for 2 around US$100) Another good intimate dinner option, which has classic French fare but isn't cheap.

DOWNTOWN

La Vie en Rose (☎ 87-54-42; fish/meat/seafood US$15/ 16/20; ☺ lunch & dinner) One of the oldest eateries in Marigot, this fashionable French restaurant sits in a prime location near the harbor. Lunch is either on the patio or the casual 1st floor while dinner is served in the graceful upstairs dining room. Try the lobster over lemon pasta (US$32) and one of the delectable French desserts.

Produce market (☺ sunrise-2pm Wed-Sat) On Marigot's waterfront, this market has tropical fruit such as passion fruit and bananas as well as local root vegetables.

Match (☺ 9am-8pm Mon-Sat, to 1pm Sun) On the north side of Marigot is this large, modern supermarket at the back of a shopping complex with good deli and wine selections.

There's a complex at the public market that has a dozen bars, *lolos* and fish stands selling sandwiches, Caribbean-spiced seafood with plantains and burgers for around US$7 to US$12.

Shopping
Marigot has the best boutique and knickknack shopping on the island. Be sure to cruise the harborfront's public market for local spices, pareus and handicrafts. Along Rue du Général de Gaulle down to the marina is a bevy of European shops, both famous names and small boutiques.

Getting There & Away
To head around the island on the private minivan bus system, head up to Rue de Holande and wave down the one with the sign you want. From Marigot, you can get to Grand Case and Philipsburg.

ST MARTIN BEACHES
Simpson Bay & Baie Nettlé
Sandy Ground is the long, narrow, curving strip of land that extends west from Marigot, with Baie Nettlé (Nettle Bay) on one side of the road and Simpson Bay Lagoon on the other. Sandy Ground itself is nothing special,

but Baie Nettlé is a lovely beach at which to hang out for the day. The first tourist outpost went up in the late 1980s, but there's already a strip with bland hotels, restaurants and small shopping centers.

EATING
Ma Ti Beach (☎ 87-01-30; meals €12-17; ☺ dinner) Check out this combination upscale French restaurant, beach hut and tiki bar. It raises its own lobster (you can pick out your dinner) and sometimes offers shark and fresher-than-fresh blue marlin. Specials include beefskirt with candied shallots (€15) and grilled local lobster (€4.90 per 100g).

Layla's (☎ 51-00-93; lunch US$8-12, dinner US$16-20; ☺ lunch winter, lunch & dinner summer) Walk through the rainforest-like path into this atmospheric open-air restaurant, where chic Paris meets beach-bum fish shack. Try tartare fish for US$16 or duck breast for US$17.

Baie Rouge
Baie Rouge, 2 miles (3.2km) west of Sandy Ground, is a long, beautiful sandy strand with good swimming, though if you have children be aware that it drops off quickly to overhead depths. Although this golden-sand beach is just 170yd (150m) from the main road it retains an inviting natural setting. For the best snorkeling, swim to the right toward the rocky outcrop and arch. There are a few beach shacks renting snorkel gear or selling barbecued chicken, but this is a fairly secluded spot.

Baie aux Prunes (Plum Bay)
The remote and unspoiled Baie aux Prunes is a gently curving bay with polished shell-like grains of golden sand. The beach is popular for swimming and sunbathing, and it's backed by a little grove of white cedar trees with pink blossoms that attract hummingbirds.

The bay can be reached by turning right 0.8 miles (1.3km) south of Baie Rouge and immediately taking the signposted left fork. After 1.25 miles (2km) you will come to a junction; veer right and continue for another 330yd (300m), where there's a parking area and a short walkway to the beach.

Baie Longue (Long Bay)
Long Beach, at Baie Longue, embraces two splendid miles of seemingly endless white

sand. The only commercial development along the shoreline is the La Samanna hotel, down at the very southern tip. The beach is very big and well off the beaten path – a great place for long strolls and quiet sunsets.

You can get to Long Beach by continuing south from Baie aux Prunes or by taking the La Samanna turn-off from the main road and continuing past the hotel for 870yd (800m).

Friar's Bay

Friar's Bay, 1.25 miles (2km) north of Marigot's center, is a pretty cove with a broad sandy beach. This popular local swimming spot is just beyond the residential neighborhood of St Louis, and the road leading in is signposted. There are a number of beach huts selling burgers, beer and grilled chicken.

COLOMBIER

For St Martin's version of a country drive, take the road that leads 1.25 (2km) inland to the hamlet of Colombier between Marigot and Grand Case. This short, pleasant side trip offers a glimpse of a rural lifestyle that has long disappeared elsewhere on the island. The scenery along the way is bucolic, with stone fences, big mango trees, an old coconut-palm plantation and hillside pastures with grazing cattle.

The road to Colombier begins 380yd (350m) north of the turn-off to Friar's Bay.

PIC PARADIS (PARADISE PEAK)

The 1391ft (424m) Pic Paradis, the highest point on the island, offers fine vistas and good hiking opportunities. The peak is topped with a communications tower and is accessible by a rough maintenance road that doubles as a hiking trail. You can drive as far as the last house and then walk the final 0.8 miles (1km) to the top.

The mountain gets more rain than the rest of the island, and the woods are thick with vine-covered trees and colorful forest birds. Ten minutes up, just before the tower, a sign to the left points the way to the best viewpoint. Take this trail for about 82yd (75m), then veer to the right where the path branches and you'll come to a cliff with a broad view of the island's east side. You can see Orient Salt Pond and the expansive Étang aux Poissons to the east, the village

of Orleans at your feet and Philipsburg to the south.

For those who want to do more serious hiking, a network of trails leads from the Pic Paradis area to Baie Orientale (Orient Bay), Orleans and the Dutch side of the island.

The road to Pic Paradis is 545yd (500m) north of the road to Colombier. Take the road inland for 1.25 miles (2km), turn left at the fork (signed 'Sentier des Crêtes NE, Pic Paradis') and continue 550yd (500m) further to the last house, where there's space to pull over and park.

GRAND CASE

The small beachside town of Grand Case has been dubbed 'Gourmet Capital of the Caribbean.' The beachfront road is lined with an appealing range of places to eat, from local *lolos* to top-notch French restaurants. While dining is the premier attraction, there's also a decent beach and several comfortable accommodations.

Sleeping

Chez Martine (☎ 87-51-59; www.chezmartine.com; 140 Blvd de Grand Case; r incl breakfast US$85, ste $170; P ✖ ☐) Has six air-conditioned rooms with private baths at the side of its restaurant, which has decent fish meals at a good price. There's a shared kitchen and a patio to relax on after a tough day at the beach.

Grand Case Beach Club (☎ 87-51-87, in the US ☎ 800-447-7462; www.grandcasebeachclub.com; studios/1-bedroom units US$250/305; P ✖ ✖ ☐ ☎) On the quiet northeast end of the beach, this gently sprawling place has 73 pleasant condo-like units with full kitchen and balcony. A great place to bring children, as those aged 12 and under stay free in all rooms other than the studios. Plus, there's

---

AUTHOR'S CHOICE

Hotel L'Esplanade (☎ 87-06-55, 866-596-8365; www.lesplanade.com; s/d studio US$230/280, loft US$270/320, ste US$330/380; P ✖ ☐ ☎) Relaxation at its best. This romantic impeccably run hillside hotel is a beach pathway removed from the hustle and bustle. With just 24 sumptuously homey lofts and suites, each with fully equipped kitchen and private terrace, as well as a pool and swim up bar, it'll be tough to leave.

an on-site pool, recreation room and tennis courts. Rates include Continental breakfast at the well-regarded restaurant.

Grand Case Beach Motel (☎ 87-87-75; 6 Blvd de Grand Case; s/d €80/95; ℗ ✸) An older, slightly run-down motel, but with some of the least expensive rooms in Grand Case, and it's directly on a quiet corner of the beach. The 12 rooms aren't in the best of shape, but they're clean and it's quiet. Air-con rooms cost a bit more.

Eating

Each evening, a ritual of sorts takes place on Grand Case's beachfront road, with restaurants placing their menus and chalkboard specials out front and would-be diners strolling along the strip until they find a place that strikes their fancy.

BUDGET

Sunset Creole Cuisine (☎ 29-02-52; Rue des Ecoles; meals €7-11; ⏲ breakfast, lunch & dinner Mon-Sat, breakfast & lunch Sun) A Haitian–Dominican Republican family owns this hidden treasure. By venturing off the main road, you'll discover the best johnnycakes on St Martin – stuffed in the Haitian style with black-eyed peas – as well as calamari sandwiches (€9) or shark steak (€8). Make sure you try a coconut ginger cookie on the way out.

Lolos (meals under US$10) Every day and evening, the barbecues start luring the tourists with their delectable smells. Located along the main pier in the heart of town, a dozen *lolos* sell johnnycakes, rice and peas, chicken legs, spareribs and potato salad, all sold à la carte. Tables are set up for guests to enjoy an outdoor meal.

MIDRANGE & TOP END

L'Hibiscus (☎ 29-17-91; meals €15-26; ⏲ dinner) If you've come to Grand Case for fine dining, L'Hibiscus should be on your agenda. It combines classical French cuisine with tasty Creole spices. For €17, you could get yourself a plate of hot fresh foie gras and passion fruit seeds with hibiscus petals, fried banana plantains and coriander. You're not going to get that anywhere else.

L'Amandier (☎ 87-24-33; ⏲ breakfast, lunch & dinner) A virtual restaurant city, this all-in-one location has a restaurant, bar, beach, swimming pool, art gallery and shop, and offers massages and facials. Be careful to

leave before you melt from total and utter relaxation. Snacks include baguette sandwiches for €10 and main dinner meals come in the likes of beef filet with olive mashed potatoes in rum sauce (€26).

Le Tastevin (☎ 87-55-45; 86 Blvd de Grand Case; appetizers/mains around US$13/21; ⏲ lunch & dinner) Serves excellent high-end French cuisine with a specialty in seafood. Meals include grilled kingfish with olive tapenade and glazed sweet peppers (US$21) with the classic foie gras appetizer (US$18).

Getting There & Away

Grand Case is on the route for the local minivans that regularly circle the island's main road.

FRENCH CUL-DE-SAC

French Cul-de-Sac is a small but spread-out seaside community just north of Orient Bay. While there's no beach of note, local fishers run boats back and forth all day to the white sands of nearby Îlet Pinel.

Îlet Pinel

The most visited of the area's offshore islands, Pinel is just 0.6 miles (1km) from French Cul-de-Sac. Totally undeveloped, it's the domain of day-trippers, who are deposited on the islet's calm west-facing beach, where there's good swimming, a water-sports hut (snorkel gear US$10) and a couple of **lolos** (barbecued chicken meals around US$10).

The island is under the auspices of the national forest system, and two minutes' walk south of the swimming beach is a little roped-off area set aside for snorkelers. For the best coral and fish, head for the single white buoy in the center.

It's easy to get to Pinel – simply go to the dock at the road's end in French Cul-de-Sac, where you can catch a small boat. The five-minute ride costs US$6 round-trip and runs 9am to 4:30pm or 5pm.

ORIENT BEACH

Although this most perfect of beaches has become somewhat of a tourist settlement, it still retains a breezy Caribbean atmosphere. Snorkel-friendly reefs protect 3.5 miles (5.5km) of inviting white-sand beach. Restaurants, bars, water sports and an au naturel resort and beach all call Orient Beach home.

Sights & Activities

Adults and children alike will walk away feeling like veritable butterfly-ologists after a visit to the **Butterfly Farm** (☎ 87-31-21; www .thebutterflyfarm.com; adult/child US$12/6, admission valid for repeat visits; ⏰ 9am-3pm), on a turn-off from the N7 in Quartier d'Orleans. Peer into cocooning chrysalises as butterflies flit above, adding to the magical wonderland feel. Guided tours cover biology, conservation and fun facts. Come early to see the butterflies at their most active.

Sleeping

Club Orient Naturist Resort (☎ 87-33-85; www.club orient.com; 1 Baie Orientale; studios US$137.50-256.25, mini ste deluxe US$162.50-312.50, waterfront beach chalets US$212.50-450, s less €25, children free; P ⏰ 🍴) Come home with no tan lines from this naturist (nudist) resort. Lining its own white-sand beach, Club Orient offers a range of activities, all done au naturel – fine dining, water sports, sunbathing and sailing cruises. Six different levels of accommodations all feature fully equipped kitchens in semidetached cottages. And there's a completely stocked general store and car rental agency available.

La Plantation (☎ 29-58-00; www.la-plantation .com; C5 Parc de La Baie Orientale; studios s US$150-200, d US$185-280, ste from US$265; ⏰ closed Sep & part of Oct; P ⏰ 🍴) Charming suites and villas are brightly decorated to ensure Caribbean glee at all times. Dine poolside or on your oceanfront terrace. These spacious suites and studios can be combined to host large groups or families.

Eating

Near the parking lot at the southern end of the beach you'll find a couple of stalls selling cheap hot dogs and burgers, as well as **Pedro's** (barbecued chicken/fish US$9/12; ⏰ 9am-5pm), a popular beachside bar. One popular stand is Kontiki, but there are a handful of other beach bars nearby offering a similar menu.

OYSTER POND

The Dutch–French border slices straight across Oyster Pond, a largely rural area with a number of small condominiums and other vacation rentals. A marina and most of the accommodations fall on the French side, while the area's finest beach, Dawn Beach, is on the Dutch side (see p424).

Oyster Pond is not a pond, but rather a protected bay whose shape resembles an oyster. For a good vantage of Oyster Pond, take the short path leading up the cactus-studded hill on the northeast side of the bay.

Sleeping

Columbus Hotel (☎ 87-42-52; columbus@wanadoo.fr; s/d incl Continental breakfast from US$100/157) Just a few minutes' walk from the marina, this a newer-style complex has condo-type units. Each has a separate bedroom, TV, phone, kitchenette and a terrace or balcony.

Captain Oliver's (☎ 87-40-26; www.captainolivers .com; s/d incl buffet breakfast from US$140/185; P 🍴) This mini-city at the marina is perhaps the only hotel in the world where you can be in two different countries at once. On the border in St Martin but above Sint Maarten water, the hotel has a sushi bar, minizoo, scuba center, several bars and a fun restaurant (below). Rooms are fairly soulless but equipped with balconies, minibars and spacious furnishings.

Eating

Dinghy Dock Bar (meals from US$5) This snack bar with picnic tables on the marina dock serves up sandwiches, chili dogs and full meals, and has Foster's on tap for some strange reason. Happy hour is 5pm to 7pm. Next door is a small convenience store with groceries, alcohol and sundries.

Captain Oliver's (breakfast buffet US$10, lunch US$13-15, dinner around US$30; ⏰ breakfast, lunch & dinner) An open-air restaurant at the marina dock, this has a breakfast buffet, burgers with fries and seafood and meat dishes at lunch and dinner. Saturday night is lobster-buffet night, with all you can eat for US$33.

DUTCH SINT MAARTEN

PHILIPSBURG

pop 18,000

Philipsburg, Dutch Sint Maarten's principal town, is centered on a long, narrow stretch of land that separates Great Salt Pond from Great Bay. There are some older buildings mixed among the new, but overall the town is far more commercial than quaint. Most of the action is along Frontstreet, the bayfront road, which is lined with boutiques, jewelry shops, restaurants, casinos and duty-free shops selling everything from Danish porcelain to Japanese cameras and electronics.

Orientation

A giant parking lot sits in front of the government building for ample parking. Four streets run east to west, and numerous narrow lanes (called *steegjes*) connect them north to south. Frontstreet has one-way traffic that moves in an easterly direction, and Backstreet has one-way traffic heading west. The north side of Philipsburg is sometimes referred to as Pondfill, as much of this area is reclaimed land.

Information

Banks are plentiful along Frontstreet, including Barclays Bank, and most dish out US dollars or Antillean guilders.

Hospital (☎ 543-1111) East of Philipsburg, in the Cay Hill area.

Post office (⏱ 7:30am-5pm Mon-Thu, to 4:30pm Fri) At the west end of E Camille Richardson St.

Public library (☎ 542-2970; Vogessteeg; Internet access per 30min US$4; ⏱ 9am-12:30pm Tue, Wed & Fri, 4-6:30pm Mon, Wed & Fri, until 9pm Tue & Thu, 10am-1pm Sat)

Sint Maarten Tourist Bureau (☎ 542-2337; www .st-maarten.com; 33 WG Buncamper Rd; ⏱ 8am-5pm Mon-Fri)

Sights

SINT MAARTEN MUSEUM

This little but growing **museum** (☎ 542-4917; Frontstreet 7; admission US$1; ⏱ 10am-4pm Mon-Fri, 10am-2pm Sat) has displays on island history, including Arawak pottery shards, plantation-era artifacts, period photos and a few items from HMS *Proselyte,* the frigate that sank off Fort Amsterdam in 1801. The little shop downstairs sells an assortment of Caribbean arts and crafts.

SINT MAARTEN PARK

'Park' is a misnomer, as this **zoo** (☎ 543-2020; adult/child US$5/2; ⏱ 9am-5pm winter, 10am-6pm summer), across from Great Bay Salt Pond, has several dozen species of mammals and reptiles. Although it's small in scale, it's a fantastic place to bring children to see primates at play, interact with friendly animals in the petting zoo, and marvel at tarantulas and lizards.

MARINA AREA

Great Bay Marina and adjoining Bobby's Marina, on the southeast side of Philipsburg, have a couple of restaurants, a small grocery store, car rental agencies, a dive shop and several stores with marine supplies. For information on crews wanted, boats for sale etc, check the bulletin board next to the Island Water World marine store (which also sells charts).

Sleeping

Seaview Beach Hotel (☎ 542-2323; www.seaview beachhotel.com; Frontstreet; depending on view s US$79-99, d US$99-130, tr US$135-150, q US$145-160; P ✷) Good prices, friendly service and a beachfront location make this a good bet all round. Rooms aren't particularly inviting, but they're comfortable, come with refrigerators and cable TV, and half have balconies facing the ocean. Casino on the 1st floor.

Pasanggrahan (☎ 542-3588, in the US ☎ 800-223-9815; www.pasanhotel.com; 19 Frontstreet; r US$148-178; P ✷) This beachside hotel offers complimentary beach paraphernalia, a social happy hour with snacks, plenty of water sports and even live music every so often. The restaurant and lobby are in a former governor's residence, but most rooms are in less-distinguished side buildings. The standard rooms are simple and small, with a shared seaside balcony. The deluxe rooms are larger and fancier, with private balconies and views of the Great Bay.

Holland House Beach Hotel (☎ 542-2572, in the US ☎ 800-223-9815; www.hollandhousehotel.com; s & d US$140-295; P ✷) Has a central beachfront location in the heart of Philipsburg and 54 spacious rooms. Overall, they're Philipsburg's nicest, featuring hardwood floors, balconies, cable TV, phones and in most cases a kitchenette. Top-floor suites have the best views.

Joshua Rose Guest House (☎ 542-4317; in the US ☎ 800-223-9815; Backstreet 7; standard s/d/tr/q US$55/80/90/130; ✷) Nothing fancy but central, with private baths, TV and refrigerator in each room.

Eating & Drinking

BUDGET

Barefoot Terrace (☎ 542-0360; Wathey Sq; breakfast from US$6, specials US$6-10; ⏱ breakfast & lunch) With an attractive view on the waterfront, this eatery has alfresco dining with breakfast ome-

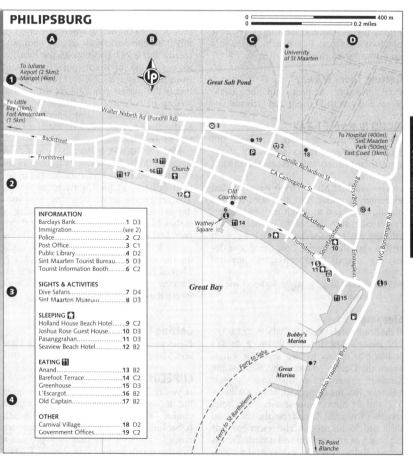

PHILIPSBURG

INFORMATION
Barclays Bank.............................**1** D3
Immigration...........................(see 2)
Police.......................................**2** C2
Post Office...............................**3** C1
Public Library..........................**4** D2
Sint Maarten Tourist Bureau......**5** D3
Tourist Information Booth.........**6** C2

SIGHTS & ACTIVITIES
Dive Safaris...............................**7** D4
Sint Maarten Museum................**8** D3

SLEEPING 🏠
Holland House Beach Hotel.......**9** C2
Joshua Rose Guest House........**10** D3
Pasanggrahan.........................**11** D3
Seaview Beach Hotel...............**12** B2

EATING 🍴
Anand....................................**13** B2
Barefoot Terrace....................**14** C2
Greenhouse............................**15** D3
L'Escargot.............................**16** B2
Old Captain...........................**17** B2

OTHER
Carnival Village......................**18** D2
Government Offices...............**19** C2

---

lettes and lunchtime sandwiches or burgers. Creole specials and a full menu of local dishes, like goat stew, at reasonable prices.

Anand (☎ 542-5706; Hotelsteeg 5; dishes from US$6; 🕙 lunch Mon-Sat, dinner nightly) For a diet change, try this popular little place serving good, cheap East Indian fare. Serves a range of vegetable, chicken, goat and beef dishes.

MIDRANGE & TOP END

Greenhouse (☎ 542-2941; lunch US$10-18, dinner US$15-28) At the north end of the marina, this is a lively spot that pulls in the punters during its happy hour from 4:30pm to 7pm, which has two-for-one drinks as well as half-price snacks. At lunch there are burgers, sandwiches, barbecued ribs and

chicken; while at dinner, meat and seafood dishes are served.

L'Escargot (☎ 542-2483; lunch around US$10, dinner around US$18) A French restaurant in a colorful, gingerbread, 19th-century Creole house, L'Escargot has light lunches such as seafood crepes or quiche with salad. Dinner features various *escargot* (snail) appetizers and main courses such as crisp duck in a choice of guavaberry or pineapple and banana sauce, an island favorite. Friday night is the hugely successful 'La Cage aux Folles' dinner and cabaret. Book in advance.

Old Captain (☎ 542-6988; dishes US$8-30) Recommended Old Captain serves excellent Indonesian, Japanese and Chinese cuisine, including Peking duck, within a beachfront setting. Come for sushi and karaoke on Friday nights. Outdoor seating is available overlooking Great Bay Beach. There is a good vegetarian menu as well.

Getting There & Away
Public buses can be picked up along Backstreet and run to Marigot and Orleans.

MAHO & MULLET BAY
These areas are where the Caribbean and Las Vegas meet. Fancy-schmancy shopping, theme restaurants, resorts and casinos dominate.

The beach at Maho Bay is beautiful and extremely popular, but the faint-hearted should take heed to watch for sandstorms. It's situated at the end of the Juliana Airport runway, and perhaps the world's lone beach with a sign that reads: 'Low flying and departing aircraft blast can cause physical injury.'

Planes do not fly at night so hotel rooms stay relatively quiet.

Sleeping
Maho Beach Hotel (☎ 545-2115, in the US ☎ 800-223-0757; www.mahobeach.com; r from US$190; P ✕ ☒) It has 600 rooms in two separate wings. From the Ocean Terrace wing, wave at the airplane passengers as they pass by your balcony. Rooms come with king-size beds, TV and 24-hour room service. The hotel has its own guest Laundromats, car rental desk and doctor on call. The resort grounds include a casino, several restaurants, fitness center, indoor parking garage and a 1000-seat Vegas-style showroom.

Caravanserai Beach Resort (☎ 545-4000, in the US ☎ 877-796-1002; www.caravanseraibeachresort .com; s & d from US$210, tr from US$245, q from US$300; P ✕ ☒) A small city in itself, this resort is either loved or hated by guests but one thing's certain: those looking for peace and quiet best go elsewhere. It has an inane amount of amenities – tropically decorated rooms with private balcony or patio, cable TV and VCR; four pools, tennis complex, boardwalk, its own beach, a casino, several eating options, tour desk and the hippest night spot on the island, Bliss (right).

Eating & Drinking
Sunset Beach Bar (☎ 545-3998; 2 Beacon Hill Rd; burgers & sandwiches US$6-8, frozen cocktails & virgin drinks

US$6; ✆ 10am-10pm or 11pm) Probably the only restaurant in the world where you feel you might have to duck while sipping your piña colada, lest a 747 bop you on the head on its way to the Juliana Airport. Equidistant from the runway's edge and Maho Beach, this is the perfect place to get drinks that belong in coconuts and listen to almost constant live music. Hint: check in early at the airport, then hitch or catch a US$6 taxi to the bar.

Bliss (☎ 545-3996; breakfast US$10, lunch/dinner around US$13/24; ✆ practically 24hr) This is an all-encompassing experience for those not faint of heart, at the Caravanserai Resort. The restaurant serves breakfast and Sunday brunch with main meals consisting of dishes like duck confit baguette and dorado filet with coconut carrot sauce. House music kicks up at about 11pm each night on the open-air dance floor: Tuesday is Martini Night, Thursday to Saturday is DJ dancing to an international groove. Don't worry if all that dancing makes you get the munchies: the grill is open until 4am.

Getting There & Away
Buses run to Mullet Bay from Grand Case and Marigot.

CUPECOY BEACH
If you're looking for a beach that's quiet but not totally secluded, Cupecoy is a good choice. This pleasant white-sand beach is backed by low sandstone cliffs that are eroded in such a way that they provide a run of small semiprivate coves. There's beach parking down an unmarked drive at the north side of the Ocean Club in Cupecoy.

DAWN BEACH
Dawn Beach, on the east coast near the French-Dutch border, is a lovely white-sand beach with clear turquoise waters. Swimming and snorkeling are good when the seas are calm. Although it's a bit silted, snorkelers can expect to find waving sea fans, soft corals and small tropical fish.

To get to Dawn Beach from French St Martin, follow the road around the south side of Oyster Pond (see p421). There's parking, a shower and snorkel-gear rentals near Mr Busby's, at the north end of the beach.

DIRECTORY

ACCOMMODATIONS

Almost all of the Dutch-side accommodations are between Philipsburg and Mullet Bay, with the majority of rooms in large resorts. A good cluster of reasonable hotels and resorts can be found on the French side at Grand Case and Baie Nettlé, but most resorts are widely dispersed. Accordingly, the places on the French side tend to be more personal and friendly. The most basic rooms run at least US$60, but most resorts and hotels range in the US$125 to US$300 category. Prices drop significantly in the summer.

ACTIVITIES

Beaches & Swimming

The island has beautiful white-sand beaches that range from crowded resort strands to long, secluded sweeps. Most of the best and least-developed beaches are on the French side of the island.

The nudist Orient Beach is understandably crowded, even the clothing-optional section. Long Beach is great for seclusion, while Baie Rouge, Dawn Beach and the islets off the northeast coast are good places for both snorkeling and swimming. All beaches are technically open to the public, although several resorts try to fake people out with privacy signage.

PRACTICALITIES

■ **Newspapers & Magazines** French side: *Saint-Martin's Week, Fax Info, Pelican;* Dutch side: *The Daily Herald, Today* (both in English); *Discover Saint Martin/ Sint Maarten, Sint Maarten Events* and *Ti Gourmet.*

■ **Radio & TV** For island music try Radio Calypso 102.1 or Radio 101.5 for reggae and dance music. Radio Transat is at 106.1FM. SXM-TV6 broadcasts from Phillipsburg in English.

■ **Electricity** 220V, 60 cycles on the French side; 110V, 60 cycles on the Dutch side.

■ **Weights & Measures** Metric.

EMERGENCY NUMBERS

Ambulance St Martin (☎ 29-29-34); Sint Maarten (☎ 130)
Fire & Sea Rescue St Martin (☎ 18); Sint Maarten (☎ 120)
Police St Martin (☎ 17); Sint Maarten (☎ 111)

Diving & Snorkeling

The most popular diving is found at Proselyte Reef, a few miles south of Philipsburg, where in 1802 the British frigate HMS *Proselyte* sank in 50ft (15m) of water.

In addition to the remains of the frigate, there are 10 dive sites in that popular area, including fascinating coral reefs with caverns.

DIVE SHOPS

The following dive shops are full-service facilities and prices are competitive. On average, single dives cost around US$45, while multidive packages lower the price to around US$40 per dive. Night dives are around US$60.

Most of the shops operate open-water certification courses for around US$350 and accept referred students for US$55 or so per dive.

Some of these shops offer half-day Discover Scuba resort courses for beginners, including a little beach dive, for US$45 to US$60.

Aquamania Watersports (☎ 544-2640; fax 544-2476; Pelican Marina, Simpson Bay, Sint Maarten)
Blue Ocean Dive Center (☎ 87-89-73; Royal Food Store center, Baie Nettlé, St Martin)
Dive Safaris Philipsburg (☎ 542-9001; Bobby's Marina, Sint Maarten); Simpson Bay (☎ 545-3213; La Palapa Marina, Sint Maarten)
Octoplus Dive Center (☎ 87-20-62; Grand Case, St Martin)
Scuba Fun Caraibes (☎ 87-36-13; Marina, Anse Marcel, St Martin)
Sea Dolphin Dive Center (☎ 87-60-72; fax 87-60-73; Le Flamboyant Hotel, Baie Nettlé, St Martin)
Sea Horse Diving (☎ /fax 87-84-15; Mercure Hotel, Baie Nettlé, St Martin)

There's decent snorkeling at a number of places, including Baie Rouge, Dawn Beach and the islands of Caye Verte (Green Cay) and Îlet Pinel off the northeast coast.

Scoobidoo (☎ 87-20-28; www.scoobidoo.com; St Martin) has sailing trips that go to Prickly Pear (p410) in Anguilla and St Barth (p430) for around US$80 per person. It also offers sunset cruises and snorkeling trips (US$35 per person).

Golf
The island's golf course, the 18-hole **Mullet Bay Golf** (☎ 545-2801; Sint Maarten), has greens fees of US$109, cart included.

Hiking
The island's most popular hike is up to Pic Paradis, St Martin's highest point. Not only will this hike reward you with great views, but Pic Paradis also serves as a takeoff point for a few longer hikes that reach down to the coast. For details, see p419.

For those who don't want to trek off on their own, guided hikes are offered by **St Martin Action Nature** (☎ 87-97-87), an organization that helps keep the island trails clear, and **Sint Maarten's Heritage Foundation** (☎ 542-4917), which is affiliated with the Sint Maarten Museum in Philipsburg (see p422).

Horseback Riding
Horseback riding is available from **Bayside Riding Club** (St Martin ☎ 87-36-64, Sint Maarten ☎ 547-6822), near Orient Beach and the **OK Corral** (☎ 87-40-72), at Baie Lucas, St Martin. The cost for a one-hour beach ride is typically US$40, a two-hour ride is between US$45 and US$60.

Windsurfing
At Orient Beach, the **Windsurfing Club** (☎ 29-41-57) rents boards from US$20 an hour, US$50 a day and US$220 a week and also teaches courses. The shop also rents surfboards and boogie boards for US$12 to US$15 per half-day.

SCAMS

As one Lonely Planet author discovered personally, crime in St Martin is rampant. Thefts are as common as sunburns. Rental cars have bright orange spots painted on their tires, making them an instant target. *Never* leave valuables in your car. Even if you're just dashing out for…ahem…five minutes.

Other Water Activities
Sint Maarten 12 Metre Challenge (☎ 542-0045; www.12metre.com), at Bobby's Marina in Philipsburg, has three-hour excursions on America's Cup racing yachts, which are large, fast and sleek. Its fleet includes *Stars & Stripes*, the very yacht Dennis Conner used in the 1987 challenge for the America's Cup in Australia. The trips cost US$70 per person.

Sunfish sailboats can be rented at some resort-area beaches as well as at sailing-cruise concessions; deep-sea fishing and yacht charters can be arranged through the marinas. When the swell picks up, Mullet Bay and Orient Bay can be good for boogie boarding.

CHILDREN
St Martin is an especially good place to bring children. Many hotels offer discounts or free stays for children staying with their parents, and activities like the Butterfly Farm (p421) and Sint Maarten Park (p422) offer interactive fun for little ones.

DANGERS & ANNOYANCES
Crime, especially theft but also an increasing number of violent or personal crimes, is growing on the island. Be especially careful of your car and yourself in seemingly secluded destinations such as a deserted beach or at Pic Paradis. Check your rental car doors. Many have had not one, but both locks jimmied open at some point in their lives.

EMBASSIES & CONSULATES
St Martin is represented in your home country by the embassy or consulate of France. Sint Maarten is represented by embassies and consulates of the Netherlands, and by the small number of consulates on Curaçao (see p754).

FESTIVALS & EVENTS
Carnival On the French side, celebrations are held during the traditional five-day Mardi Gras period that ends on Ash Wednesday. It features the selection of a Carnival Queen, costume parades, dancing and music. On the Dutch side, which has the larger Carnival, activities usually begin the second week after Easter and last for two weeks, with steel-band competitions, jump-ups, calypso concerts, beauty contests and costume parades. Events are centered at Carnival Village on the north side of Philipsburg.
Heineken Regatta (early March) This annual event features competitions for racing yachts, large sailboats and small multihulls.

HOLIDAYS

New Year's Day January 1
Good Friday Late March/early April
Easter Sunday/Monday Late March/early April
Queen's Day April 30; Dutch side
Labor Day May 1
Government Holiday The day after the last Carnival parade, about a month after Easter; Dutch side
Ascension Thursday 40th day after Easter
Pentecost Monday Eighth Monday after Easter; French side
Bastille Day July 14; French side
Assumption Day August 15; French side
Sint Maarten Day November 11
Christmas Day December 25
Boxing Day December 26; Dutch side

MONEY

On the French side, restaurants and hotels are split between posting prices in euros or US dollars, while on the Dutch side they're virtually always posted in US dollars.

ATMs blanket the island and transaction fees will cost substantially less than using the exchange bureaus.

SHOPPING

St Martin is the Eastern Caribbean's prime duty-free shopping location. Philipsburg's Frontstreet is the island's most commercial strip and has the largest selection of camera and electronics shops. In both Philipsburg and Marigot, shoppers will find chic boutiques, jewelers and perfume stores carrying top-name European products. In Marigot there's a concentration of shops at the north side of Port La Royale Marina and along the adjacent Rue du Général de Gaulle (see also p418).

Duty-free alcohol is a bargain. You can buy bottles of rum at shops around the island for around US$5.

TELEPHONE

St Martin's area code is 590 and Sint Maarten's is 599. Calls between the two sides are treated as international calls. To call the Dutch side from the French side, dial 00-599 + the seven-digit number. To dial the French side from the Dutch side, dial 00-590-590 + the six-digit number (that's the area code dialed twice).

To dial within the French telephone system, dial 0590 + the six-digit number. To dial within the Dutch telephone system, dial 0599 + the seven-digit number. We have included only the six- and seven-digit local numbers in the listings in this chapter.

TOURIST INFORMATION

See the Information sections under Marigot and Philipsburg for local tourist offices.

Tourist Offices Abroad

ST MARTIN
France (01-53-29-99-99; www.st-martin.org; 30 rue St-Marc, 75002 Paris)
USA (877-956-1234; www.st-martin.org; 675 3rd Ave, Ste 1807, New York, NY 10017)

SINT MAARTEN
Canada (416-622-4300; fax 416-622-3431; 703 Evans Ave, Ste 106, Toronto, M9C 5E9)
USA (877-956-1234; www.st-maarten.com; 675 3rd Ave, Ste 1807, New York, NY 10017)

VISA

Visas are not necessary for North Americans, EU nationals and Australians. Some former Soviet states and many African nationals will need visas.

TRANSPORTATION

GETTING THERE & AWAY

Entering the Island

Citizens of the EU need an official identity card or valid passport. Citizens of most other foreign countries need both a valid passport and a visa for France if entering the island on the French side. From December 31, 2005, US citizens need a valid passport to re-enter the US from the Caribbean (see the boxed text, p772).

A round-trip or onward ticket is officially required of US, Canadians and all non-EU citizens to St Martin, regardless of whether entry is made on the French or Dutch side.

People arriving by yacht can clear immigration at the **office** (542-2222) based in Philipsburg, Sint Maarten.

Air

There are two airports on the island: **L'Espérance Airport** (87-53-03; Grand Case, St Martin) and **Juliana Airport** (SXM; 545-2060; www.pjiae.com; Sint Maarten). All international flights arrive at Juliana Airport (for details see p776) and it is a major hub for carriers such as Winair, which flies on to Anguilla, St Barth, Saba, St Eustatius, Montserrat and other nearby islands. Prop planes head from L'Espérance to St Barth, Guadeloupe and Martinique.

Note that Juliana can be tediously slow and inefficient and getting there three hours before your flight isn't a bad idea. Your best bet is come early and hungry, check in and, if you end up with plenty of time, hitch or catch a US$6 taxi to the Sunset Beach Bar (p424) for a most unique version of airplane food. Buses to Philipsburg and Marigot run from just in front of the airport.

The following airlines fly to/from St Martin/Sint Maarten from within the Caribbean:

Air Antilles Express (in St Martin ☎ 87-35-03; www .airantilles.com; hub Guadeloupe)

Air Caraïbes (☎ 877-772-1005; www.aircaraibes.com; hub Guadeloupe) Flies between Guadeloupe, Martinique, St Barth, St Maarten, Dominica, Dominican Republic and Haiti.

American Eagle (☎ 800-433-7300; www.aa.com; hub San Juan)

BWIA (☎ 800-538-2942; www.bwee.com; hub Port of Spain, Trinidad)

Caribbean Star (☎ 800-744-7827 within Caribbean; www.flycaribbeanstar.com; hub Antigua)

Caribbean Sun (☎ 866-864-6272; www.flycsa.com; hub San Juan)

LIAT (in Sint Maarten ☎ 545-2403; www.liatairline.com; hub Antigua)

Transanguilla (in Anguilla ☎ 264-497-2680; www .transanguilla.com; hub Anguilla)

Winair (in Sint Maarten ☎ 545-2568; www.fly-winair .com; hub Sint Maarten)

Sea
CRUISE SHIP
No less than 12 major companies land in Philipsburg and Marigot. Day-trippers head to duty-free shopping in the main towns or to beach excursions. Sometimes up to four ships a day are in port. For information on cruise ships, see p777.

FERRY
Ferries depart from Marigot, Oyster Pond and Simpson Bay for Anguilla, St Barth and Saba. Ferry companies disappear frequently, so call the **main ferry line** (☎ 87-53-03) in St Martin for the most up-to-date information.

Anguilla
Ferries make the 25-minute journey from Marigot Bay in St Martin to Blowing Point in Anguilla an average of once every 30 minutes from 8am to 6:15pm (from 7:30am to 7pm from Anguilla to St Martin).

The one-way fare is US$12 (US$15 on the last boat of the day). The fare for the passage is paid onboard the boat.

St Barth
The ferry service between St Martin/Sint Maarten and St Barth is choppy: the seas are famous for being rough and the ferries don't run that often.

The main company is **Voyager** (in Marigot, St Martin ☎ 87-10-68, in Philipsburg, Sint Maarten ☎ 542-4096), which has two modern highspeed boats. One leaves from Marigot at 9am and 6:15pm for the 1½-hour journey; it departs from Gustavia at 7:15am and 4:30pm. The fare is one way/same-day round-trip/round-trip US$52/62/72). On Sunday morning and Wednesday, the ferry leaves from Captain Oliver's Marina in Oyster Pond.

The **Edge** (in Sint Maarten ☎ 544-2640), a highspeed catamaran operated by Aqua Mania, takes 45 minutes from Pelican Marina on Simpson Bay. Ferries leave Sint Maarten at 9am and Gustavia at 4pm daily. Check in 15 minutes in advance. Fares are US$44/59/79 for a one-way/same-day round-trip/round-trip.

Saba
The **Edge** (in Sint Maarten ☎ 544-2640) leaves Pelican Marina in Simpson Bay at 9am Wednesday to Sunday (Wednesday, Friday and Sunday August to October), arriving about 10:30am. The departure time is 3:30pm arriving at Pelican Marina at 5pm. Fares are adult/child round-trip US$60/30, one way US$40/20.

YACHT
Yachts can clear immigration at Philipsburg and Marigot. There are marinas at Philipsburg, Marigot, Simpson Bay Lagoon, Oyster Pond and Anse Marcel.

GETTING AROUND
Bicycle
Frog Legs Cyclery (☎ 87-05-11), next to the Match supermarket in Marigot, St Martin,

rents out mountain bikes from US$15 a day and organizes island cycling tours for US$20.

Bus

Buses are plentiful, cheap and simple to use. Large public buses run between Marigot, Philipsburg and Grand Case and, more commonly, private minivans. Each charges from US$1 to US$3, depending on distance. Bus service also runs less often to Mullet Bay, Simpson Bay and Orleans.

In the capitals you have to stand at bus stops, which are found along Backstreet in Philipsburg and on Rue de Hollande in Marigot. In rural areas you can flag down buses anywhere along the route.

Car & Motorcycle

RENTAL

Car rental agencies are abundant on St Martin. During low season, there's no need to book ahead, as you can simply arrive at Juliana Airport and bargain among the 10 or so booths for a price as low as US$25.

High-season rates can run as high as US$45.

The following companies have offices at Juliana Airport, Sint Maarten:

Avis (☎ 545-2316)
Budget (☎ 545-4030)
Dollar (☎ 545-3061)
Hertz (☎ 545-4440)
Paradise Island (☎ 545-2361)
Sunshine (☎ 545-2685)

Eugene Moto Scooter Rental (☎ 87-13-97; eugene moto@wanadoo.fr), located next to the museum in Marigot, St Martin, has the following daily rates, including helmet and lock: €22 for a 450cc (for 14 and up), €27 for a 100cc (license required, can fit two) and €37 for a regular motorcycle.

Scooters don't last long in St Martin and you'll lose your deposit if yours is stolen. Use caution.

ROAD RULES

Driving is on the right side of the road on both sides of the island, and your home driver's license is valid. Road signs and most car odometers are in kilometers.

The amount of traffic in Marigot and Philipsburg can shock visitors expecting a peaceful island getaway. Traffic jams occur regularly, most notably around Juliana Airport at peak times.

Hitchhiking

Although many islanders hitchhike around the island, safety precautions apply, especially for tourists, as petty theft and violent crime have been on the rise.

Taxi

The government-regulated fares should be posted in each taxi. Rates increase in the evening or if there are more than three passengers.

Taxi rates from Philipsburg: US$8 to St Maarten Park, US$12 to Marigot and US$22 to Pic Paradise. From Juliana Airport: US$6 to Maho, US$12 to Marigot and US$20 to Grand Case.

To hail a taxi, call ☎ 147 anytime day or night. Taxi tours of the island last 1½ to three hours and cost US$15 to US$35 per person.

ST MARTIN/ SINT MAARTEN

St Barthélemy

St Barthélemy (St Barth) brings to many minds a jet-setting hot spot for the rich and famous, the sort of place where one could go only by private plane or with at least one Oscar nomination.

And for some people, it is that. But St Barth is also much more. A long-forgotten backwater territory of France, it was all but ignored until St Barth and tourism butted heads, for better or worse. You may hear locals lament about the good ol' days when everyone knew each other and handwoven straw lantana hats were more common than Gucci bags.

Outside of the Christmas season, St Barth can feel more like Bondi Beach, Australia, than St Tropez. Put together six or eight people and renting a villa can be downright affordable. Beaches number in the dozens, many secluded enough to have to yourself.

Many who come to St Barth return year after year, giving the island the feel of an adult summer camp. Restaurateurs take the time to get to know each customer. The island's phone book tends to repeat itself, as a handful of names account for half the natives: Gréaux, Magras, Laplace, Ledee, Brin. St Barth is pricey, but remember, you're paying for a Caribbean stay refreshingly free of casinos, golf clubs and megaresorts.

FAST FACTS

- **Area** 8 sq miles (21 sq km)
- **Capital** Gustavia
- **Country code** ☎ 590
- **Departure tax** €4.50
- **Famous for** Playground of the rich and famous, secluded pristine beaches, French dining and shopping
- **Language** French
- **Money** Euro (€); €1 = US$1.20 = UK£0.69
- **Population** 8000
- **Visa** Not necessary for most nationalities; see p440

HIGHLIGHTS

- **Gustavia** (p434) Feel like you're in a French village as you wander through this gorgeous town.
- **Dining** (p433) Try a different gourmet, seafood or French restaurant every day and night of the week.
- **Anse de Columbier** (p438) Relax on this secluded pure-white beach, which you just might have to yourself during the off-season.
- **Villas** (p438) Spend a week in style, staying with a special someone or half a dozen of your closest friends.
- **Retail therapy** (p440) Shop the quaint boutiques and trendy national chains.

ITINERARIES

- **Two days** Stay at the Hotel Le Village St Jean, spending at least one day at Gouverneur Beach and one sunset on Shell Beach at Do Brazil.
- **Two weeks** Rent a villa overlooking the ocean, adding beach days at Anse de Grand Saline and Anse de Columbier, and striking up conversations with warm-hearted locals at restaurants like Maya's and Restaurant des 3 Forces. Take a snorkeling trip to Île Fourchue and dive for a day or two in the well-protected St Barth Natural Marine Reserve.

CLIMATE & WHEN TO GO

St Barth has two seasons: the *caréme,* the dry season; and the *hivernage,* the hurricane season from July to November, when heavier rains are expected.

During Christmas the rates skyrocket from pricey to outrageously ridiculous, so depending on your budget, this may be a time to avoid.

HISTORY

St Barth never had a big Arawak or Carib Indian presence, due to its inhospitable landscape and lack of freshwater. When Christopher Columbus sighted the island

---

HOW MUCH?

- Taxi from the airport to Gustavia €9
- Half-day snorkeling trip €65
- Two-tank dive €90
- Meal of fresh fish in a touristy restaurant €22
- Meal of fresh fish in a local restaurant €12

LONELY PLANET INDEX

- Liter of gas €1.15
- Liter of bottled water €1
- Bottle of Carib beer €2
- Souvenir T-shirt €18
- Street snack: pain au chocolat €1.50

---

on his second voyage in 1493, he named it after his older brother Bartholomeo.

The first Europeans who attempted to settle the island in 1648 were French colonists, who were soon slaughtered by marauding Carib Indians. Norman Huguenots gave it another try about 25 years later and prospered not due to farming (which was near impossible) or fishing, but by setting up a way station for French pirates plundering Spanish galleons (see the boxed text, p437). You can still hear traces of the old Norman dialect in towns such as Flamands and Corossol.

In 1784 French King Louis XVI gave St Barth to his friend Swedish King Gustaf III, in exchange for trading rights in Göteburg. Many Swedish reminders – such as the name Gustavia, St Barth's continuing duty-free status, and several buildings and forts – are still evident.

Sweden sold St Barth back to France in 1878 after declining trade, disease and a destructive fire made it not worth their while. Until tourism swept through with a vengeance almost a century later, St Barth was not much more than a quaint French backwater.

Throughout the 19th and early 20th centuries, life continued to be tough for residents. Without the typical lush Caribbean vegetation, farming was difficult. Many former slaves emigrated to surrounding

---

THE NAME GAME

Officially named St Barthélemy, its common name can be spelled half a dozen ways – St Barth, St-Barth, St Barth's, St Barts etc – but in all cases, the 'h' is silent.

ST BARTHÉLEMY

ST BARTHÉLEMY (ST BARTH)

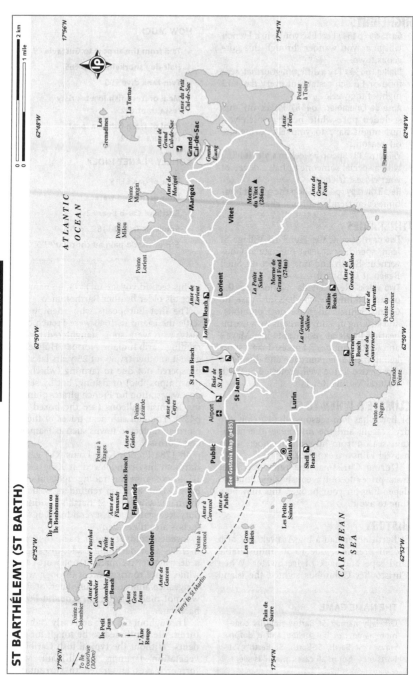

islands to find work, leaving St Barth one of the only islands without a substantial African population.

In the 1950s the tiny airport slowly started bringing in tourists on small planes and private jets. The scrubby island suddenly found new natural resources: beaches, sunsets, quiet. Quick-thinking islanders created laws limiting mass tourism to guard their hard-earned lifestyle. This means you still won't see casinos, high-rise hotels or fast-food chains, but you will pay for the atmosphere.

As tourism income grew on St Barth, the formerly neglectful France started to take notice. On December 7, 2003, the natives of St Barth voted overwhelmingly (90%) to grant themselves more fiscal and political independence from France and Guadeloupe. Following an affirmative vote in the French legislature in late 2005 or early 2006, St Barth becomes an Overseas Collectivity of its own, losing Guadeloupe as its political middleman and gaining a municipal council rather than a single island-wide mayor. Locals hope this will ensure the retention of more of the island's self-generated taxes, as well as allow St Barth to create many of its own regulations and structures. Visitors won't feel any of these changes directly, besides a few more smiles on residents' faces.

THE CULTURE

Most residents of St Barth fall into one of three categories: descendants of hard-working families from Normandy who have called St Barth home for over 300 years; mainlanders setting up expensive shops and restaurants; or foreigners looking for a more relaxed lifestyle. As tourism blossomed over the last 40 years, the first group of residents largely traded in their fishing careers for tourism-related jobs.

The island's culture is relatively laid-back. Islanders are unguarded, spontaneous and sturdy people. Many natives haven't seen their house key for years, nor do they care whether Sylvester Stallone is at the next table. Gays and lesbians will find a welcoming tolerance from most locals.

Although this is a beach resort island, it's also quite French, and wearing bathing suits in town or businesses is considered inappropriate.

ARTS

For hundreds of years, St Barth's residents were too busy toiling in near-impossible conditions to create much art. Today many resident artists sell work in studios scattered around the island, and the St Barth Film Festival (p440) is the only one of its kind to showcase Caribbean talent.

ENVIRONMENT

St Barth's total land area is a mere 8 sq miles (21 sq km), although its elongated shape and hilly terrain make it seem larger. The island lies 15.5 miles (25km) southeast of St Martin.

St Barth has numerous dry and rocky offshore islets. The largest, Île Fourchue, is a half-sunken volcanic crater whose large bay is a popular yacht anchorage, and a destination for divers and snorkelers.

St Barth's arid climate sustains dryland flora, such as cacti and bougainvillea. Local reptiles include lizards, iguanas and harmless grass snakes. From April to August, sea turtles lay eggs along the beaches on the northwest side of the island. The numerous islets off St Barth support seabird colonies, including those of frigate birds.

In recent years St Barth has taken environmental concerns very seriously and has committed to sustainable methods. The island utilizes a color-coded recycling system. Be sure to comply by tossing glass in green containers and plastic in blue containers.

In 2001 St Barth pioneered the first trash incinerator of its kind in the Caribbean. The incinerator is able to simultaneously burn trash, create energy and produce drinkable water, all with less pollution than older incinerators. It comes with a higher price tag, but islanders feel the result is worth it.

FOOD & DRINK

St Barth is a food-lover's dream. It's filled with restaurants for every taste and budget: French haute cuisine, bistro crêperies, Asian fusion and seafood of all sorts. While there aren't many native St Barth dishes, this is perhaps the only place on the planet where you might have a *pain au chocolat* (chocolate-filled croissant-like pastry) for breakfast, Creole-spiced escargot for lunch and curried lobster for dinner.

As you can imagine, wine is plentiful and mostly French. As there are no freshwater

ST BARTHÉLEMY

sources on the island, tap water is desalinized or from cisterns. It is potable but many (even locals) prefer to drink bottled water.

GUSTAVIA

pop 5000
It was only in the 1950s that St Barth became the tourist destination we know today. Gustavia was a sleepy fishing village with a few houses surrounding what has become the island's main harbor. The island's capital is still small and quaint, and everything can be done on foot.

INFORMATION
There are several banks in Gustavia, such as Banque Nationale de Paris and Change Caraibes on Rue du Général de Gaulle, and **Banque des Antilles Française** (29-68-30), all with ATMs.

Public toilets are available behind the tourist office, and include showers for boaters.

Bruyn Hospital (☎ 27-60-35; Rue Jean-Bart) A small hospital, ¼ mile (400m) north of Gustavia.

Centre Alizés (☎ 29-89-89; Rue de la République; per 15min/1hr €3/8) High-speed Internet access. Also rents cell phones for €10 a day or €80 a week.

Doctor (☎ 27-76-03) For after-hours medical attention.

Funny Face Bookstore (☎ 29-60-14) In the Carré d'Or building; stocks English-language books.

Municipal Police (☎ 27-66-66)

Office Municipal du Tourisme (☎ 27-87-27; Quai Général de Gaulle) Will help with accommodations, restaurant recommendations, island tours and activities. Has map for self-guided Gustavia walking tour.

Pharmacie St Barth (☎ 27-61-82; Rue de la République; ☻ 8am-7:30pm Mon-Fri, 8am-1pm & 3:30-7pm Sat & holidays)

Post office (☎ 27-63-63; cnr Rue Jeanne d'Arc & Rue Samuel Fahlberg; ☻ closed afternoons Wed & Sat)

SIGHTS & ACTIVITIES
Fort Gustave
The site of old Fort Gustave has a couple of cannons and a mildly bottle-shaped lighthouse, but most people come here for the fine view of Gustavia and the harbor. An interpretive plaque points out local sights and landmarks. Across the harbor to the south is **Fort Oscar**, which is still used as a military installation, and from where you can see the islands of St Kitts and St Eustatius on a clear day.

TOP FIVE SUNSET-WATCHING SPOTS

No doubt about it, the sunsets here are just prettier than anywhere else. Here are the top five places to watch a sunset:

▪ The beach in Corossol (p438).
▪ The lighthouse at Fort Gustave (left).
▪ Gouverneur Beach (p438).
▪ Anse de Grande Saline (p438).
▪ From a sunset cruise with Splash or Marine Service (p439).

Musée Municipal
At this **museum** (☎ 29-71-55; admission €2; ☻ 2:30-6pm Mon, 9am-12:30pm & 2:30-6pm Tue-Fri, 9am-1pm Sat) you can take a look at historical St Barth, from the Indian settlements to the Swedish occupation, with old photos and traditional clothing.

SLEEPING
Most top-end accommodation is outside of Gustavia.

Sunset Hotel (☎ 27-77-21; www.st-barths.com /sunset-hotel; Rue de la République; s €60-124, d €69-135, tr €96-147; ℙ ✗) The most central hotel in Gustavia, it's also clean, unpretentious and family run. Ten rooms all have phones, TVs and refrigerators. The pricier ones have a stunning view of the harbor and sunset, but get a bit of street noise. Rates also depend on the season. Book ahead.

La Presqu'ile (☎ 27-64-60; s/d €34/51; ℙ ✗) Not only a freakishly good deal for St Barth, but this hotel is also fairly comfortable and central. Rooms are small but clean, and the wrap-around patio offers a beautiful spot to have breakfast and admire the Gustavia harbor, just in front of the hotel.

EATING
Budget
Le Repaire (☎ 27-72-48; Rue de la République) A casual meeting spot in the heart of Gustavia, this Creole open-air restaurant serves eggs and croissants in the morning, and sandwiches and lighter meals all day and evening.

La Crêperie (☎ 27-84-07; Rue du Roi Oscar II; crepes €3-16, panini around €7, ice cream €2.50) Try the Tartiflette, with *reblochon* cheese, potatoes and bacon (€10), or the sweet Bounty with coconut ice cream, nutella and whipped cream.

GUSTAVIA

| 0 | 200 m |
| 0 | 0.1 miles |

To St Jean; Airport

INFORMATION
Banque des Antilles Francaises...1 B3
Banque Nationale de Paris........2 C2
Bruyn Hospital............................3 B4
Centre Alizés.............................4 B2
Change Caraïbes........................5 B2
Funny Face Bookstore..........(see 32)
Municipal Police.......................6 B2
Office Municipal du Tourisme...7 B2
Pharmacie St Barth...................8 B1
Post Office................................9 B3
Public Toilet.........................(see 7)

SIGHTS & ACTIVITIES
Fort Gustave..........................10 B1
Fort Oscar............................11 A2
Marine Service.......................12 B3
Musée Municipal....................13 A2
Océan Must Marina...............14 B2
Totem Surf............................15 C3

SLEEPING
La Presqu'île........................16 B2
Pipiri Palace.........................17 C3
Sunset Hotel........................18 B2

EATING
Eddy's...................................19 C3
Fish Market..........................20 B2
La Repaire............................21 B2
Le Crêperie..........................22 C2
Le Select..............................23 C2
Produce Market....................24 C2
Wall House...........................25 B2

DRINKING
Ti Zouk K'fe.........................26 B3

TRANSPORT
Budget Car Rental...............27 C2
Chez Beranger Car &
  Scooter Rental..................28 C3
Ferry Terminal.....................29 B2
Port Office..........................30 B2
Taxi Stand...........................31 B2

OTHER
Carré d'Or...........................32 B2
St Barth Properties..............33 C3
Sibarth...............................34 C3

ST BARTHÉLEMY

Le Select (☎ 27-86-87; cnr Rue de la France & Rue du Général de Gaulle; salads €5, kebabs €9, burgers €5; 10:50am-2:40pm & 5:30-9:30pm Mon-Sat) Eating a cheeseburger here might make you feel like you're in paradise. Er, at least it did to Jimmy Buffett, who wrote 'Cheeseburger in Paradise' here and was once part owner. At the heart of Gustavia, it's a casual place where one can chill out for a few hours with a cold beer.

Fish Market (Rue de la République) If you've got your own kitchen, come here to pick up still-wriggling supplies. Local fishermen bring in the catches of the day – marlin, wahoo, dorado, tuna, langosta.

Produce Market (Rue du Roi Oscar II) This tiny market sells local fruits and vegetables.

Midrange & Top End

Eddy's (☎ 27-54-17) Look for the teeny doorway practically hidden along a stone wall across from Le Sapotillier. This fusion restaurant blends Creole, Caribbean, Cajun and French influences in a tropical setting for a sensory delight. Try the fish carpaccio (€10) or steamed fish with vanilla sauce (€19).

Wall House (☎ 27-71-83; mains €21, dinner prix fixe €25; closed lunch Sun) Located along the waterfront near the museum, with plenty of outdoor seating. The view here of the harbor is as good as the view of the exquisitely presented dishes. The meals combine a Creole influence with traditional French cuisine, resulting in a blend of ingredients such as duck breast with sweet onion marmalade or

AUTHOR'S CHOICE

Hotel Le Village St Jean (☎ 27-61-39; www
.villagestjeanhotel.com; r €190, cottage & ste €230-
420, 2-bedroom cottage €570; **P** 🔁 🖳 🔧)
Comfort, elegance, charm, great-priced Italian restaurant: this is practically a perfect
home away from home. Family patriarch
André Charneau built the Village himself
in 1968, and it has been lovingly family run
since 1969. Rooms vary from basic hotel
rooms to deluxe cottages with kitchenettes
and patios (the two-bedroom cottage has
its own pool), ensuring good value on any
budget. There are substantial summer discounts. It's a five-minute walk uphill from
the beach. There's a pool with a view and
a Jacuzzi, and an **Internet café** (per 30min
€6; 🕑 7:30am-11pm).

scallop carpaccio. The prix fixe (fixed-price
menu) is a steal.

Pipiri Palace (☎ 27-53-20; cnr Rue du Général de
Gaulle & Rue de la Guadeloupe; appetizers €9-14, mains €17-
32) This fun, tin-roofed restaurant is filled
with rattan chairs and beachy decor. It's a
great place for ribs, lobster or bouillabaisse.

ENTERTAINMENT

Ti Zouk K'fe (☎ 27-90-60; cocktails €4-8, panini €5-12;
🕑 11am-late) Across from the diving out-
fit Marine Service, heading toward Wall
House, is this eclectic bar and restaurant.
It serves casual sandwiches during the day
and there's often music at night.

AROUND GUSTAVIA

Check out pretty **Shell Beach**, where tennis great Yannick Noah co-owns **Do Brazil**
(☎ 29-06-66; lunch €11-18, dinner €18-32), a casually
trendy sandwich bar fronting the beach.
The dinner menu is Brazilian, featuring
exotic tastes like *moqueca* – shrimp, lobster
and fish marinated in coconut milk (€32).
Drinks, snacks and ice cream are available
during the day.

On the road to Corossol is **Public**, a village
centered on a small beach (popular with locals) and the desalinization plant. Here you'll
find **Maya's** (☎ 27-75-73; 🕑 dinner, closed Sun), one
of those places the regulars return to time
and time again for Randy and Maya's personal service. Simultaneously upscale and
unpretentious, and expensive, the waterfront

restaurant has a changing menu that can include tropical salads, fish dishes and Maya's
world-famous coconut tart.

ST JEAN

Many hotels and restaurants line the main
stretch of road in this tourist-heavy village,
making parking difficult. Once you're off
the road, the beach is delightful, the hotels
comfortable and the dining eclectic – ranging from delis to tragically hip, techno-in-
fused attitude factories.

Sleeping

Emeraude Plage (☎ 27-64-78; www.emeraudeplage
.com; Rue de St Jean; r €295-840; **P** 🔁 🖳) A gaggle
of cottages, bungalows and studios set in a
tropical park directly on the St Jean beach.
Tiled rooms all come with a large bedroom
with a private terrace, fully equipped kitchen,
cable TV and continental breakfast. Proximity to the water results in higher prices, but
being able to practically dive from Bungalow D or the villa into the ocean might be
worth it.

Eden Rock (☎ 29-79-89; www.edenrockhotel.com;
cottage €615, classic/premium ste €1095/1750; **P** 🔁 🔧)
St Barth's first hotel, this was recently completely refurbished to even more glory
than the original. The hotel stretches out
and over a rocky promontory down to the
white-coral St Jean beach below. Each suite
and cottage is luxuriously appointed with
fine antiques, swashbuckling colors and an
unbeatable view. Fabulous three- and five-
day discounts over summer.

Eating

La Terrazza (☎ 27-61-39; www.villagestjeanhotel.com;
Hotel Le Village St Jean; appetizers €10-19, mains €18-27;
🕑 closed Wed) The family who run Hotel Le
Village St Jean (left) also run this brightly
charming Northern Italian trattoria and
bar. Specialties include comfort fare such
as baked cannelloni filled with spinach,
squash and *talleggio* cheese. Impossibly, the
view is almost as good as the food.

Kiki-é Mo (☎ 27-90-65; Rue de St Jean; light meals
& pizza €6-14) In the heart of St Jean, this full-
service deli has delectable pizza with top-
pings like grilled vegetables, *talleggio* cheese
and prawns, as well as pasta, sandwiches and
desserts. It also caters for villa rentals.

Match (☎ 27-68-16; ☼ 8am-1pm & 3-8pm Mon-Sat, 9am-1pm & 3-7pm Sun) In the complex across from the airport you'll find this supermarket, a must for all villa renters. Packed with tropical fruit, and European and American food, it's also the best place to pick up reasonable French wines.

EASTERN ST BARTH

GRAND CUL-DE-SAC

Grand Cul-de-Sac has a sandy beach and a reef-protected bay with good conditions for water sports. The area attracts an active crowd, including lots of windsurfers. The beach is along a narrow strip of land that separates the bay from a large salt pond (sand fleas can be a nuisance). Fronting the bay are a couple of hotels and restaurants, along with a windsurfing and water-sports center.

Sleeping & Eating

St Barths Beach Hotel (☎ 27-60-70; www.saintbarthbeachhotel.com; s/d/tr €190/275/330, villa €260-585; P) Thirty-six modern but not particularly attractive rooms are nestled against the beach in a protected bay, with all the amenities one could possibly want. Eight deluxe villas set further back from the beach come with fully equipped kitchen and rental car for each stay. There's also a full gym available to guests.

Hostellerie & Restaurant des 3 Forces (☎ 27-61-25; www.3forces.net; Vitet; s/d US$190/240; P ✖) Called a 'Holistic New Age Inn' by owner and local character Hubert Delamotte, a dead ringer for Salvador Dali and the island's resident astrologer, the 12 rooms, each

---

MONTBARS THE EXTERMINATOR

In addition to having quite possibly the coolest name in history, Mr The Exterminator was a French-born pirate, and not a very nice one at that. He was present when his uncle was killed in a battle with Spanish Conquistadors and he spent the rest of his life exacting revenge (and borrowing a bit of plunder). Legend has it that Montbars buried treasure somewhere between Anse du Gouverneur and Anse de Grande Saline, which has never been found. If you've been looking for a reason to borrow Grandpa's metal detector...

---

with ocean views, are named after a zodiac sign. The restaurant's chef, Jean-Paul Aureille, serves a Provençal menu that changes monthly and includes dishes like pesto frog legs (€24), herbed chicken (€17) and San Trôpez pie, a brioche with a light orange-flower cream sauce (€12). There's a great, inexpensive wine list. It's located up the hill in Vitet, above Grand Cul-de-Sac.

LORIENT

Lorient, the site of St Barth's first French settlement (1648), is a small village fronted by a nice white-sand beach. When it's calm, snorkelers take to the water, but when the waves are happening, this is one of the island's best surfing spots.

Sleeping & Eating

Chateau Gréaux (☎ 73-06-53; elgreaux@wanadoo.fr; studio US$100; P) Staying with this charming couple, a St Barth local and his American wife, feels like you're visiting long-lost family. His family has been on the island for centuries and she runs the St Barth Film Festival (p440), so they're both treasure troves of information. The spacious and impeccably tidy studio up in the hills shares a courtyard and a pool with the main house, but has a private entrance, a patio overlooking the sunset, and its own kitchen and bath.

Le Manoir de Marie (☎ 27-79-27; www.lemanoirstbarth.com; Rte de Salines; r €130-650; P) Although overpriced for the level of service and comfort, this hotel is one of the more unusual places in all of the Caribbean. Meandering paths lead to rustic Norman cottages built in the architectural style of 18th-century France. Cottages range from basic to quite grand, with kitchenettes and private tropical gardens.

Bassin Laurent Villa (☎ 27-66-64; www.st-barths.com/bassin-laurent; cottage per week incl continental breakfast US$3300, 2-person maximum; P) High in the hills overlooking Lorient, with a view of practically the entire world, these two cottages offer an isolated colonial-style retreat. The hospitable English-speaking owners run St Barths Online (p440) and know literally every single detail about the island, and will organize car rental or pickup, dinner reservations etc for you. Ethernet connected.

Le Wok (☎ 27-52-52; Rte de Saline á Lorient; mains around €14; ☼ 6-9pm Tue-Sun) Mixing Caribbean elements and local seafood with French flair, this Asian restaurant is hidden in the hills, attracting mostly locals. It has a charming outdoor patio, and takeaway is available.

GOUVERNEUR BEACH

This is a gorgeous, sandy beach lining a U-shaped bay that's embraced by high cliffs at both ends. It's one of the broadest and most secluded spots in the region, and it makes a splendid spot for sunbathing and picnics.

ANSE DE GRANDE SALINE

A long, lovely beach, broad and secluded, Anse de Grande Saline is named after the large salt pond that backs it. Stilts and other waterbirds flock to the pond, but watch for biting gnats. It's considered one of the best beaches on St Barth by residents. Return visitors make the trek yearly. Bodysurfing is also good here.

WESTERN ST BARTH

COROSSOL

This is one of the last remaining traditional villages on St Barth, and the villagers still speak in an old Norman dialect. The brown-sand beach is lined with blue and orange fishing boats and stacks of lobster traps. Women still weave the leaves of the lantana palm into straw hats, baskets and place mats, which they line up on the walls in front of their homes to attract buyers.

This is where you'll find **Le Musée International du Coquillage** (☎ 27-62-97; admission €3; ⏰ 9am-12:30pm & 3-5pm Tue-Sat), with over 9000 seashells on display. Owner Ingénu Magras started the museum half a century ago, years after he and his father collected seashells from their fishing traps when he was in his teens.

FLAMANDS

A small village on the northwestern side of the island, Flamands retains a pleasantly rural character. The village stretches along a curving bay whose long, broad, white-sand beach and clear waters are very popular with beachgoers. There's easy beach access with streetside parking at the westernmost end of Anse de Flamands.

ANSE DE COLUMBIER

Anse de Columbier is a beautiful, secluded, white-sand beach that's fronted by turquoise

waters and backed by undulating hills. It's reached by boat or via a scenic 20-minute walk that begins at the end of the road in La Petite Anse, just beyond Flamands. The sandy bottom at the beach is ideal for swimming, and there's fairly good snorkeling at the north side. Many snorkeling trips come here; for snorkeling information see opposite.

DIRECTORY

ACCOMMODATIONS

Accommodations on St Barth are all small scale. The island has about 40 hotels, with a combined capacity of only 700 rooms. A recent law forbids hotels to build more than 12 rooms, as St Barth guards its reputation for intimacy. Most places list prices in euros. Most hotels include the tax and service charge in their quoted rates, although a few places add 5% to 10% to the bill.

Every hotel and villa discounts substantially during the off-season.

Villas

In addition to hotels, St Barth has numerous villas for rent. Weekly rates range from about US$1000 per week to over US$100,000 per week, with a staff, several bedrooms and possibly even a gold or fur sink...

The biggest accommodations agency is **Sibarth** (☎ 29-88-90; www.wimcovillas.com; Rue de Centenaire, Gustavia). Also worth checking is **St Barth Properties** (☎ 29-75-05, in USA ☎ 800-421-3396; www.stbarth.com; Rue Samuel Fahlberg, Gustavia).

PRACTICALITIES

- **Newspapers & Magazines** Newspapers include the *Weekly,* published in English on Friday from November to April, and *Today*. Tourist magazines include *St-Barth Magazine, Discover Saint Barthélemy, Tropical St Barth* and *Ti Gourmet*.

- **Radio** Radio Transat 100.3FM.

- **Electricity** The current used is 220V (50/60 cycles). Many hotels offer American-style shaver adapters.

- **Weights & Measures** The metric system and 24-hour clock are used here.

EMERGENCY NUMBERS

Fire (☎ 18)
Police, ambulance (☎ 16)

ACTIVITIES
Beaches & Swimming
St Barth, with its numerous bays and coves, boasts nearly two-dozen beaches. Those looking for 'in-town' beaches will find that St Jean, Flamands, Lorient and Shell Beach all have beautiful, sandy strands. The most famous secluded beaches, Colombier, Saline and Gouverneur, are as close to the picture-perfect Caribbean beach as possible, with long white expanses of sand and gently lapping warm waves. Especially in summer, these beaches can be practically empty.

Diving
If you dive on your own, you must pay a fee and register with the **St Barth Natural Marine Reserve** (☎ 27-88-18). Check at the town hall or any dive outfitters and they will send you through the proper channels. The most popular diving spots are off the islets surrounding St Barth, which are rich in marine life and coral. Almost all of the dive sites and surrounding islands are managed by the Marine Reserve. Try the following options:

Aquati'Barth (☎ 0690-41-97-49; www.aquatibarth .com) Also offers snorkeling.
Marine Service (☎ 27-70-34; http://st-barths.com /marine.service; Quai du Yacht Club, Gustavia; tank dive €55, 10-dive package €480) A full-service center offering snorkeling, diving, half- and full-day private and public sailing charters, and deep-sea fishing.
Splash (☎ 0690-56-90-24; www.splash.gp)

Fishing
Both **Marine Service** (☎ 27-70-34) and **Ocean Must Marina** (☎ 27-62-25) in Gustavia offer shore and deep-sea fishing, where catching tuna, wahoo or blue marlin is common. Renting a 21ft (6.4m) skippered motorboat for deep-sea fishing starts at about €386 for the day for four to seven people.

Horseback Riding
Ranch des Flamands (☎ 39-87-01; Merlette) offers 1½-hour excursions for beginning and experienced riders. Rides depart most days at 3:30pm and cost about €35 per person.

Sailing & Snorkeling
Half-day trips cost about €65 per person, full-day trips €100 and sunset cruises €55. They usually include a meal or buffet, plus drinks and all snorkeling gear.

Carib Waterplay (☎ 27-71-22; caribwaterplay@ wanadoo.fr) Located in St Jean and Corossol.
Coté Mer (☎ 0690-45-06-00; www.cote-mer.com) Half- and full-day snorkeling, plus sunset cruises. Includes open bar, champagne and cold buffet.
Marine Service (☎ 27-70-34; http://st-barths.com /marine.service; Quai du Yacht Club, Gustavia) Offers a half-day snorkel sail aboard the catamaran.
Océan Must Marina (☎ 27-62-25; Gustavia) Offers sailing and snorkeling cruises.
Splash (☎ 0690-56-90-24; www.splash.gp) Runs full-day snorkel and sail trips with gourmet buffet to Île Fourchue.

Surfing
The main surfing spots are at Lorient, Anse des Cayes and Anse Toiny. None of these beaches have surf rentals, so you need to go to St Jean or Gustavia.

Daily prices run €15 for a short board, €20 for a long board and €10 for a boogie board. Discounts can be arranged for longer rentals.

Hookipa Surf Shop (☎ 27-71-31; St Jean)
Totem Surf (☎ 27-83-72; Gustavia)

Windsurfing
Grand Cul-de-Sac, the main windsurfing center, has a large protected bay that's ideal for beginners, and some nice wave action beyond the reef for advanced windsurfers. Both places listed also rent kayaks.

Carib Waterplay (☎ 27-71-22; caribwaterplay@ wanadoo.fr) Located in St Jean and Corossol; offers windsurfing lessons, as well as kayaking, surfing and snorkeling trips.
Wind Wave Power (☎ 27-82-57) Located at St Barths Beach Hotel in Grand Cul-de-Sac; gives 1½-hour windsurfing lessons (about €60).

BUSINESS HOURS
Most businesses close at lunchtime between about noon and 2pm, and many places shut on Wednesday afternoons.

DANGERS & ANNOYANCES
St Barth has a very low crime rate. Besides keeping an eye on valuables left on the beach, no advanced safety precautions are necessary.

ST BARTHÉLEMY

FESTIVALS & EVENTS

A number of festivals are celebrated on St Barth throughout the year.

St Barth Music Festival (mid-January) Features two weeks of jazz, chamber music and dance performances.

Carnival Held for five days before Lent. Includes a pageant, costumes and street dancing, ending with the burning of a King Carnival figure at Shell Beach. Many businesses close during Carnival.

Festival of St Barth (August 24) The feast day of the island's patron saint is celebrated with fireworks, a public ball, boat races and other competitions.

St Barth Film Festival (late April; ☎ 29-74-70; www .stbarthff.org) The only festival of its kind to showcase Caribbean talent in fiction and documentary films.

HOLIDAYS

St Barth has the following public holidays:

New Year's Day January 1
Easter Sunday Late March/early April
Easter Monday Late March/early April
Labor Day May 1
Ascension Thursday Fortieth day after Easter
Pentecost Monday Seventh Monday after Easter
Bastille Day July 14
Assumption Day August 15
All Saints Day November 1
All Souls Day November 2
Armistice Day November 11
Christmas Day December 25

INTERNET ACCESS

An Internet café is available at Hotel Le Village St Jean (see p436).

INTERNET RESOURCES

Known as St Barths Online, **www.st-barths .com** is the go-to place for anything you'd ever want to know about the island. It has links to accommodations and restaurants.

MONEY

The currency used in St Barth is the euro, though US dollars are widely accepted.

SHOPPING

St Barth is a duty-free port and features the most exclusive labels in the world: Dior, Bulgari, Rolex etc. But there is also a thriving industry of small, locally owned boutiques and a local label, Made in Saint-Barth.

TELEPHONE

The telephone system has been a bit confusing since a changeover in 1996. To call St Barth from abroad, dial your country's international access code plus St Barth's area code *twice*, ie ☎ 590-590 + the local six-digit number.

To call from within the French phone system, add '0' in front of the (single) area code, ie ☎ 0590 + the local number. We have included only the six-digit local number for St Barth listings in this chapter.

To dial a cell (mobile) phone, call ☎ 0690 + the number.

Public telephones take all major credit cards and prices are listed.

VISAS

Citizens from the US, UK, Canada, Australia, Japan and New Zealand don't need visas. Citizens of many CIS, African and South American countries require visas from a French consulate valid for admission to the Overseas French Department of Guadeloupe.

TRANSPORTATION

GETTING THERE & AWAY

Entering St Barth

Residents of EU countries need only a national identity card to enter St Barth. Passports are needed for all other nationalities (US citizens see the boxed text, p772).

Air

Located near the village of St Jean, St Barth's only airport, **Aéroport de St-Barthélemy** (SBH; ☎ 27-65-41), has the second-shortest runway in the world (the shortest is on Saba). Because of this, only small planes can land on St Barth, ensuring mass tourism is not to be seen.

The following airlines fly to and from St Barth:

Air Antilles Express (☎ 0890-648-648; www.air antilles.com; hub Guadeloupe)
Air Caraïbes (in French West Indies ☎ 0590-27-61-90; www.aircaraibes.com; hub Guadeloupe)
St Barth Commuter (☎ 27-54-54; www.stbarth commuter.com; hub St Barth)
Winair (☎ 27-61-01; www.fly-winair.com; hub St Martin)

Sea

FERRY

The ferry service between St Barth and St Martin is choppy in a couple of ways: the seas are famous for being rough and the ferries don't run that often.

The main company is **Voyager** (☎ in Marigot, St Martin 0590-87-10-68, in Philipsburg, Sint Maarten 599-542-4096), which has two modern high-speed boats. One leaves Marigot, St Martin, at 9am and 6:15pm for the 1½-hour journey; it departs Gustavia at 7:15am and 4:30pm.

On Sunday and Wednesday, the boat leaves from Captain Oliver's Marina in Oyster Pond, St Martin. Fares are US$52 one way, US$62 for a same-day round-trip and US$72 for a round-trip; payment can also be made in euros.

Also available is the high-speed catamaran, the **Edge** (in Sint Maarten ☎ 599-544-2640), which makes the 45-minute trip to Gustavia daily from Pelican Marina on Simpson Bay, Sint Maarten, at 9am and returns at 4pm. Check in 15 minutes in advance. A one-way trip costs US$44, a same-day round-trip US$59, and a round-trip US$79.

YACHT

Those arriving by yacht can clear immigration at the **port office** (☎ 27-66-97), on the east side of Gustavia Harbor.

GETTING AROUND

There is no bus system on St Barth. Taxis are pricey, so consider renting a car.

Car & Motorcycle

RENTAL

About 10 international and local car-rental companies have booths outside St Barth's airport. Cars can also be rented from most hotels and car-rental agencies in Gustavia (although the cars are kept near the airport). Prices range from US$35 a day in the off-season to US$50 a day in high season. Try the following options:

Alamo (☎ 29-60-12) Located at the airport.

Budget (☎ 27-66-30) Located at the airport and in Gustavia.

Chez Beranger Car & Scooter Rental (☎ 27-89-00) Located in Gustavia.

Ets Dufau (☎ 27-54-83) Located in the shopping complex directly across the street from the airport; rents scooters and motorcycles. Also has an office in Public.

Island Car Rental (☎ 27-70-01) Located at the airport.

ROAD RULES

Driving is on the right-hand side. A driver's license from your home country is valid in St Barth. The speed limit is 45km/h, unless otherwise posted.

Hitchhiking

Hitching is easy and comparatively safe in St Barth, although substantially more difficult the closer one gets to the far corners of the island.

Taxi

Taxi prices go from pricey to outrageous. Rates increase by 50% between 6:30pm and 6:30am, and on Sunday and holidays.

From Gustavia to the airport costs €9, to Vitet €17 and to Petit Cul-de-Sac €20. From the airport it costs €9 to St Jean and €11 to Lorient.

To book a taxi in Gustavia, call ☎ 27-66-31; at the airport, call ☎ 27-75-81.

Tours

Day-trippers can hire a taxi to explore St Barth, either at the driver's discretion or using one of three tourist itineraries, which take 45 minutes, one hour or 1½ hours and cost €39/46/61, respectively. Or you can ask your driver to drop you at a beach and hitch or taxi back.

ST BARTHÉLEMY

Saba

Teeny-tiny Saba (*say*-bah) is like no place on earth. Its volcanic peak rises majestically and vertically straight out of the Caribbean Sea like the tip of an iceberg. You won't find the beaches, casinos, resorts, shopping and nightlife of most other Caribbean islands, but you will find ecolodges, hiking trails and pristinely maintained dive sites rivaled by few. Practically every step you will take on Saba will either be up or down a hill.

Until the 1930s Sabans used trails to get around the island, as it was assumed impossible to build a road. An islander by the name of Joseph Lambert Hassell thought otherwise, and took an engineering correspondence course. In 1943 the Sabans built what is still known as 'the Road.'

Three dive companies and many tour operators offer dives to deep-sea wrecks and pinnacles, sea turtles and coral-reef formations. You'll need a full two weeks just to explore the 12 main hiking trails on the island. What's more, Saba has a surprising number of fantastic restaurants and comfortable accommodations to suit any taste. And, with only 1600 residents, you'll know enough of the friendly locals to feel like family within just a few days.

FAST FACTS

- **Area** 5 sq miles (13 sq km)
- **Capital** The Bottom
- **Country code** ☎ 599
- **Departure tax** US$5 within the Netherlands Antilles, US$20 elsewhere
- **Famous for** Striking volcanic scenery, hiking and diving
- **Languages** Officially Dutch (used in government); English is spoken in schools, homes and everywhere else
- **Money** Netherlands Antillean guilder (NAf); US dollars accepted most places. US$1 = €0.82 = UK£0.55 = NAf1.77
- **People** Sabans
- **Population** 1600
- **Visas** Not necessary for most residents of North America, the EU and Australia

HIGHLIGHTS

- **Diving** (p448) Explore pinnacles and swim among nurse sharks in pristine protected waters.
- **Mt Scenery** (p449) Hike along any one of 12 well-marked trails.
- **Ecolodges** (p446) and **cottages** (p446) Get natural and enjoy a sweat lodge or solar-heated outdoor shower, making sure to try the homemade 'Saba Spice' rum as a nightcap.
- **Runway** (p450) Fly in and out from the world's smallest airport landing.
- **Sea & Learn** (p450) Visit throughout the month of October for this festival, when events are held around the tiny island celebrating its biodiversity.

ITINERARIES

- **Two Days** Get in a morning or afternoon dive on the first day with any of the three dive outfitters. Dine at Ecolodge Rendez Vous (make sure to try the homemade Saba Spice rum) in the evening. Hike up to Mt Scenery the following day, aiming to reach the peak between 11am and noon. Relax with a yoga class at Vitality before a quiet stroll around the Sandy Cruz Trail.
- **One Week** Sign up with Dive Saba to stay at an ecolodge, homey inn or fancy hotel. In between your 10 dives to see nurse sharks, pinnacles and sea turtles, hike the North Coast Trail, stop at Brigadoon for Saturday sushi or fresh fish any night, and catch Monday-night steel-pan music or Friday's outdoor movie at Tropics Cafe.

CLIMATE & WHEN TO GO

Saba's temperature averages 27°C (80°F) in July but in winter can dip down to 17°C (63°F) during the evening. With stately Mt Scenery known as a cloud forest, the island gets substantially more rain – 40in (1000mm) – and cloud cover than the rest of the Caribbean. Saba is the rare island in this region where a visit during July to September is actually pleasant, if there's not a hurricane. The dry season is December to July. Trade winds keep the island cool, especially at night, and blankets are a necessity even on some summer nights.

HISTORY

Saba was intermittently inhabited by Siboney, Arawak and Carib Indians before

---

HOW MUCH?

- **Taxi from the airport to El Momo Cottages** US$15
- **Two-tank dive per day** US$80
- **Meal of fresh fish in a touristy restaurant** US$21
- **Meal of fresh fish in a local restaurant** US$12
- **Saba Marine Park fee per dive** US$3

LONELY PLANET INDEX

- **Liter of gas** US$0.90
- **Liter of bottled water** US$1.50
- **Bottle of Carib beer** US$2
- **Souvenir T-shirt** US$18
- **Street snack: cheese pastechis** US$1.50

Columbus sailed past the island on his second voyage to the New World. Although English pirates and French adventurers briefly inhabited the island, it wasn't until 1640 that the Dutch set up a permanent settlement, the remains of which are still scattered around the island.

Saba changed hands a dozen times or so over the next 200 years, resulting in mostly Irish and English settlers, but Dutch ownership. Life on Saba for these pioneers was difficult at best. Many of the men made their living from the sea, leaving so many women on the island that it became known as 'The Island of Women.'

Because the steep topography of the island precluded large-scale plantations, colonial-era slavery was quite limited on Saba. Those colonists who did own slaves generally had only a few and often worked side by side with them in the fields, resulting in a more integrated society than on larger Dutch islands.

The close-knit community beat seemingly impossible conditions and thrived in this little outpost. Tourism found Saba when an airport was built in 1959. It wasn't until 1970 that Saba got uninterrupted electricity.

Saba was a part of the Netherlands Antilles until 2005, when the five islands (Saba, Curaçao, Bonaire, St Eustatius and Dutch Sint Maarten) met on the Jesurun Referendum to decide the fate of the Netherlands Antilles. Saba, along with Bonaire, voted overwhelmingly to become administered directly by the Netherlands.

THE CULTURE

Saba was founded by mostly British, Irish, Dutch and Scandinavian settlers as well as African slaves, and most long-time residents descend from these families. The largest Dutch influence now is the young diveshop and hotel employees who come over on work visas from the Netherlands.

Visiting Saba feels more like visiting an 18th-century Celtic village than a Caribbean island. One of the charming things

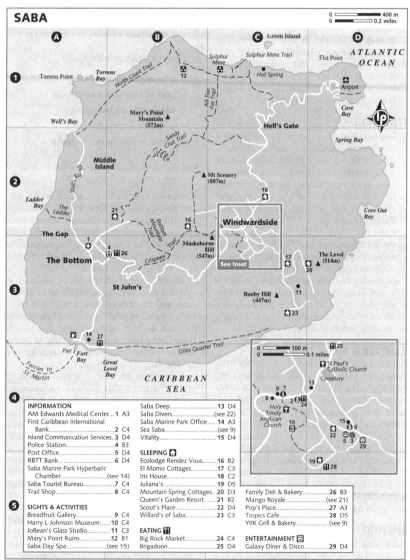

SABA

0 — 400 m
0 — 0.2 miles

ATLANTIC OCEAN

Torrens Point
Torrens Bay
North Coast Trail
Sulphur Mine
Sulphur Mine Trail
Green Island
Flat Point
Hot Spring
Airport
Cove Bay

Well's Bay
Mary's Point Mountain (572m)
All Too Far Trail
Hell's Gate
Spring Bay

Sandy Cruz Trail
Middle Island
Mt Scenery (887m)
18

Ladder Bay
The Ladder
Well's Bay
21
Bottom Mountain Trail
16
Windwardside
Core Gut Bay

The Gap
1
4 26
Crispeen Trail
Maskehorne Hill (547m)
See Inset
17
20
The Level (514m)

The Bottom
St John's
Booby Hill (447m)
11
23

Pier
Fort Bay
14 27
Great Level Bay
Giles Quarter Trail

Ferries to St Martin

CARIBBEAN SEA

Inset map:
0 — 100 m
0 — 0.1 miles
25
St Paul's Catholic Church
Cemetery
13
9 7
8
2
24
Holy Trinity Anglican Church
10
15
22
6
5
29
19
28

INFORMATION
AM Edwards Medical Center...**1** A3
First Caribbean International Bank.................................**2** C4
Island Communication Services..**3** D4
Police Station............................**4** B3
Post Office..................................**5** D4
RBTT Bank.................................**6** D4
Saba Marine Park Hyperbaric Chamber.........................(see 14)
Saba Tourist Bureau..................**7** C4
Trail Shop.................................**8** C4

SIGHTS & ACTIVITIES
Breadfruit Gallery.....................**9** C4
Harry L Johnson Museum.......**10** C4
JoBean's Glass Studio.............**11** C3
Mary's Point Ruins..................**12** B1
Saba Day Spa.......................(see 15)

Saba Deep.............................**13** D4
Saba Divers.........................(see 22)
Saba Marine Park Office........**14** A3
Sea Saba.............................(see 9)
Vitality..................................**15** D4

SLEEPING
Ecolodge Rendez Vous.........**16** B2
El Momo Cottages..................**17** C3
Iris House............................**18** C2
Juliana's.............................**19** D5
Mountain Spring Cottages....**20** D3
Queen's Garden Resort.........**21** B2
Scout's Place.......................**22** D4
Willard's of Saba..................**23** C3

EATING
Big Rock Market...................**24** C4
Brigadoon..........................**25** D4

Family Deli & Bakery..............**26** B3
Mango Royale....................(see 21)
Pop's Place..........................**27** A3
Tropics Cafe........................**28** D5
YIIK Grill & Bakery...............(see 9)

ENTERTAINMENT
Galaxy Diner & Disco...........**29** D4

about Saba is its matching white houses, all decorated with red roofs and green-trimmed doors and shutters. Locals drive leisurely along streets, honking their horns to greet neighbors and friends.

Sabans enjoy a relatively high standard of living. The island is extremely tolerant of differences, starting hundreds of years ago when slave and master had to work side by side to allow the island to thrive. Now gay dive and tour companies are welcomed and even courted by the island. Most Sabans attend one of six churches on the island: three Roman Catholic, two Anglican and one Seventh Day Adventist.

ARTS

Saba has a small handicraft scene and locals produce and sell beautiful items such as hand-blown glass, Saban lace and island paintings. In Windwardside check the Breadfruit Gallery (p446) or even take a glass-blowing class at JoBean Designs Art Glass Studio (p446).

Saba's most famous craft is lace-making. Brought to Saba by a woman sent to live in a Venezuelan convent in the 1870s, the activity took off. By 1928 this women's skill was bringing in a much-needed US$15,000 a year for the tiny island. You can still find Saban lace in many island shops, including the Breadfruit Gallery (p446).

ENVIRONMENT

Five completely separate temperate zones exist on Saba. Starting with steep cliffs that seem to shoot out of the ocean, the land progresses to grassy meadows, slopes with little vegetation, and up to hilltops, rainforests and finally the cloud forest covering the top of Mt Scenery (2877ft; 877m).

For a place as small as Saba, there is an enormous amount of mammal, fish, bird and plant life surrounding the island, both native and introduced. Rare wild orchids peek out along the Road or in the rainforest, and oleander and hibiscus flowers are practically endemic. The elephant ear plant has shade-bearing leaves as big as…well, elephant ears.

For hundreds of years Sabans have been using plants and flowers for healing. Keep on the lookout for a guide to medicinal plants written by the local newspaper reporter and pharmacologists from the American medical university in the Bottom, tentatively titled *Bush Medicines of Saba.*

Bird-watchers will enjoy spotting the plethora of avian life overhead as much as they'll enjoy saying their names: sooty terns, brown boobies, brown noddies, banana quits and pearly eyed thrashers are a handful of the 60 species of birds that call Saba home. Keep an eye out at higher elevations for humming-birds and at lower elevations for red-tailed hawks. Saba has its own unique reptile – the skittish little brown Anoles lizard – seen scurrying around everywhere.

But perhaps the best thing about Saban wildlife is the obvious lack of certain wild-life: mosquitoes are, by and large, absent.

Sabans are extremely environmentally aware, as they're just one step above a bio-sphere project. Water comes from rainwater gathered from rooftop cisterns, a small de-salinization plant or imported bottles. Be as mindful as possible by taking short showers and not running the water longer than absolutely necessary.

Hikers are requested to pay a US$3 hiking fee during a stay. (All trails are on privately owned land; stay on the well-marked trails.) Divers pay a US$3 fee for each dive to support the Saba Marine Park. Additional donations are always welcome.

FOOD & DRINK

For an island that imports almost all its food, Saba has a dizzying array of restaurant choices, from tiny bakery shacks to upscale hotel restaurants. Be sure to try one of the many homemade rums, often flavored with locally grown banana, mango, vanilla or 'Saba Spice.' Many establishments – such as El Momo Cottages and Ecolodge Rendez Vous – make and sell their own blends.

WINDWARDSIDE

Although the Bottom is the capital of Saba, Windwardside is where most of the tourist infrastructure is located.

INFORMATION

First Caribbean International Bank (☎ 416-2216; 🕒 8:30am-3:30pm Mon-Fri)

Island Communication Services (☎ 216-4881; per 30min US$5; 🕒 10am-7pm Mon-Fri, 10am-5pm Sat) High-speed Internet access.

Post office (🕒 8am-noon & 1-5pm Mon-Fri, 8am-noon Sat)

RBTT Bank (☎ 416-2454; ⊗ 8:30am-3:30pm Mon-Fri)
Trail Shop (☎ 416-2630; ⊗ 8:30am-12:30pm &
1:30-3:30pm Tue-Fri, 10am-2pm Sat & Sun) Stocks a large
selection of maps, books and souvenirs. It's a nonprofit
organization set up by the Saba Conservation Foundation.

SIGHTS

The **Harry L Johnson Museum** (admission US$2;
⊗ 10am-noon & 2-4pm Mon-Fri) is in a gardenlike
setting surrounded by wildflowers, including black-eyed susans – the official island
flower. The collection is housed in a 160-
year-old Saban home in the typical style,
whitewashed with green-shuttered windows. On display are Arawak Indian artifacts and memorabilia from Victorian times
on Saba.

JoBean Designs Art Glass Studio (☎ 416-2490;
www.jobeanglass.com; Booby Hill) offers half-day
classes in the intricacies of glassblowing for
old hands and newbies alike. JoBean also
creates many beautiful pieces of her own
for sale; one piece is even owned by Queen
Beatrix of the Netherlands.

The **Breadfruit Gallery** (☎ 416-2509) show-
cases the best of Saban talent, from painting
to lace.

ACTIVITIES

If you're feeling the need to wind down and
stretch, **Vitality** (☎ 416-2751; yoga per 1/6 classes
US$10/55) offers yoga and Pilates classes daily,
as well as natural foods, juices and light
vegetarian meals.

After a long day of diving or hiking (see
p448), relax with a massage, body scrub or
foot treatment at the **Saba Day Spa** (☎ 416-3488;
www.sabadayspa.com; massage with facial US$105). The
owner worked for years with the Ritz Carlton on St Thomas.

MARY'S POINT RUINS

A generation ago Saba was even more
isolated than it is now. One village, Mary's
Point, was a 45-minute walk from even the
next village. In 1934 the Dutch government decided to move every single villager
and house to an area behind Windwardside known as the Promised Land, thus less-
ening the isolation of being so far from any
other signs of civilization. You can see the
ruins of Mary's Point while hiking on the
Sandy Cruz Trail.

SLEEPING
Budget

El Momo Cottages (☎ 416-2265; www.elmomo.com;
s/d cottage with shared bath US$40/55, with private bath
US$55/65, with private bath & kitchen US$80/90; ⊠ ⚲)
Those looking for peace, nature and a balance
of silence and camaraderie will find ecocot-
tage heaven here. Stone paths meander past
oleander bushes and sunbathing iguanas to
reach private cottages, all with beckoning
hammocks. Solar-heated outdoor showers
hand built by the owners ensure a clear, private view of the ocean while you suds up.
The home-baked bread, banana marmalade,
and yogurt and muesli for breakfast can't be
beat…except for maybe sitting around with
new friends sipping homemade mango rum
on the restaurant patio at night.

Midrange

Ecolodge Rendez Vous (☎ 416-3348; www.ecolodge
-saba.com; Crispeen Trail; 4-person cottage without/with
kitchenette US$85/95; ⚲) If staying at the inter-
section of six hiking trails at a place powered
by solar panels sounds better than having
a TV and phone in your room, this might
be for you. Twelve rustic but comfortable
cottages allow guests to feel connected to
nature, and each comes with delightful paintings by local artist Heleen Cornet. Guests
and visitors can use the hot tub and sweat
lodge. It also offers dive packages. Even if
you don't stay here, be sure to visit its restaurant (opposite).

Scout's Place (☎ 416-2740; www.sabadivers.com;
s US$66-94, d US$83-117, extra bed s/d US$35/38) Built
in the traditional gingerbread white-and-
green-trim Saban style, this lively 14-room
hotel is owned by the same German couple
who run Saba Divers (p449). Three categories of rooms start with refrigerator, cable
TV and ceiling fan, while the spacious private cottages have grand four-poster Caribbean beds and balconies with ocean views.
It also offers a range of diving packages, so
check its website for the latest deals. Children's programs are available. The casual
restaurant serves lighter meals and fish for
lunch and dinner, and has a fun atmosphere and porch seating. There's karaoke
in the bar on Friday nights.

Juliana's (☎ 416-2269; www.julianas-hotel.com; s/d
US$110/125; ℗ ⚐ ⚲) In partnership with Sea
Saba (p449), Juliana's will be appreciated by
the diver and nondiver alike. Comfortable

rooms and gracious cottages are all housed in the classic Saban gingerbread-cottage style, with colorful and airy decor. Each comes with a TV/DVD, ceiling fan and terrace. Cottages have kitchenettes. Wi-fi Internet access and digital camera card reader also are available, as are dive-package rates.

Mountain Spring Villas (☎ 416-2265; www.elmomo.com; the Level; villa per day US$100-150, per week US$650-900; P ❄ ☒) Two recently built three-bedroom houses can each accommodate four to six people, next door to each other. On offer are vaulted ceilings, cable TV, fully equipped kitchen and use of the pool at El Momo Cottages, a five-minute walk away. You could swear you could see the entire Caribbean Sea from the front porch.

Top End

Willard's of Saba (☎ 416-2498, 800-504-9861; www.willardsofsaba.com; Booby Hill; s US$300-600, d US$400-700; P ☒) The highest hotel in the Kingdom of the Netherlands, Saba's most upscale hotel offers guests a hot tub, large heated lap pool, tennis court, fitness center and upmarket restaurant. Seven spacious, well-appointed rooms have top-of-the-universe views. Skip the fitness center and just use the built-in stairstepper – your walk up to your room.

Iris House (☎ 416-2246, in the UK 0732-779-258, in the US & Canada 800-883-7222; www.irishousesaba.com; r per week for 2 people US$980, each additional person up to 6 US$175; ☒) Relax at this recently refurbished cottage's pool while peering out at the expansive Caribbean Sea; stroll less than three minutes to most restaurants and sights in Windwardside; or hang out in front of a DVD on a rainy day. Let Jeff know ahead of time and he'll have the refrigerator stocked for you. Prices include tax and a round-trip to the airport or ferry via taxi.

EATING

Brigadoon (☎ 416-2380; ❂ dinner, closed Tue) Saba certainly offers some fantastic restaurants, and this is one of the best. Specials have included coriander-encrusted tuna sashimi and lobster, and sushi is served on Saturday from 6:30pm to 7:30pm. If you're staying around Windwardside, Trish, the ebullient owner and chef extraordinaire, will drive you home if you ask nicely.

Rainforest Restaurant (☎ 416-3348; www.ecolodge-saba.com; Ecolodge Rendez Vous, Crispeen Trail) The red-curry coconut shrimp is famous. Juice

or ice cream made from the local soursop fruit is a rare treat, tasting somewhere between mango, banana and coconut. The restaurant is usually open for breakfast, lunch and dinner, but will shut early if there are no customers. It's best to call ahead.

Tropics Cafe (☎ 416-2469; juices & cocktails US$4-8, breakfast US$3-10, mains US$7.50-17.95; ❂ breakfast, lunch & dinner) As if the filling omelettes and delectable fish sandwiches weren't enough, the side wall opens to a view of the Caribbean Sea. Monday night is Barbecue Surf or Turf, with live steel-pan music, and Friday features an outdoor movie on a 12ft x 18ft (3.6m x 5.5m) screen made by sailmakers on St Martin. Fish is brought in fresh daily by local fishermen. It's the only restaurant on Saba open all day every day.

YIIK Grill & Bakery (☎ 416-2539; lunch & dinner US$4-13) Above Sea Saba and with a fantastic view of the Caribbean Sea, this popular and casual restaurant offers great value. There's a large selection of salads, sandwiches and burgers at lunch, and international cuisine, including pasta dishes and fresh fish, is the order of the day for dinner.

Big Rock Market (☎ 416-2280; ❂ 8am-noon & 2-6pm) Saba's largest grocery store, with an impressive selection of international food and wine.

ENTERTAINMENT

Galaxy Diner & Disco (☎ 416-3878; ❂ 11am-9pm Mon-Thu, 11am-2am Fri & Sat) Nothing fancy for meals – sandwiches, pasta, burgers – but this is the most consistent nightlife spot on the island. DJs spin here once in a while; ask the locals what's on.

AROUND SABA

THE BOTTOM

The Bottom is where you'll find the administrative and governmental buildings. It's not used very often, but the police station is located here. In the front yard is a bell that was rung on the hour every hour until the 1990s.

Saba Medical College is an accredited university offering the first 2½ years of medical education on par with the curriculum offered at US or Canadian medical schools. It administers the hyperbaric chamber (p448) at Fort Bay.

Medical attention can be sought at **AM Edwards Medical Center** (☎ 416-3239).

Sleeping & Eating

Queen's Garden Resort (☎ 416-3494, in the US 800-599-9407; www.queensaba.com; deluxe/superior/royal ste US$350/395/495) A 12-unit luxury resort in a verdant setting half a mile (800m) east of town. Gorgeous views accompany fully equipped rooms with cable TV, a phone, four-poster beds, a kitchen and a separate living room. In addition, one- and two-bedroom units have verandas with their own Jacuzzis. It also has a fitness center, a tennis court and a restaurant, the Mango Royale (below). Rates include breakfast for two. Get creative: they say they can make anything you request.

Family Deli & Bakery (☎ 416-3858; ⏰ 8am-9pm Mon-Sat, 11am-4pm Sun) Serves breakfast, lunch and dinner, and light meals all day, including cheese *pastechis* (deep-fried turnovers). Follow the smell of freshly baked bread.

Mango Royale (☎ 416-3494; www.queensaba .com; Queen's Garden Resort) Mango Royale has a romantic setting and is the trendiest restaurant in Saba. Recently under new management, it planned to offer a different menu each night, from grilled lobster to Italian cuisine.

FORT BAY

Fort Bay is the main port for Saba. If you're diving or arriving by ferry, you will most likely make your way through this tiny enclave. Saba's only gas station is located here.

The **Saba Marine Park office** (⏰ 8am-noon & 1-5pm Mon-Fri, 8am-noon Sat) has a few brochures to give away, and sells marine-park-logo T-shirts and books on diving. The region's only hyperbaric facility, **Saba Marine Park Hyperbaric Chamber** (☎ 416-3288; ⏰ 24hr), is also in Fort Bay, on the right side of the Road as you enter the Bottom from Windwardside.

Although Pop doesn't own it anymore, **Pop's Place** (☎ 416-3327), just along the waterfront, is still a welcoming stop after a dive or hike for a burger or one of the famous lobster sandwiches.

LADDER BAY

Before Fort Bay became Saba's official port, everything – from a Steinway piano to Queen Beatrix – was hauled up to the Bottom via the **Ladder**, a vertical staircase of over 800 steps. The area is now a moder-

ately difficult trail that heads past an abandoned customs house and affords hikers beautiful views.

WELL'S BAY

Saba's only beach is a recent addition after a large storm in 1999, and it's part-time at that. The slight chocolate-sand **beach** only appears at Well's Bay sometime between April and June and disappears again around October/November, but you'll still find many local families and tourists enjoying a dip during the summer The walk down is steep (read: Saban) and it's often deserted, so it's best to arrange a taxi to collect you beforehand. Fifteen minutes' swim to the northeast end of the bay is **Torrens Point**, a gathering spot for tropical fish (and snorkelers in the know).

DIRECTORY

ACCOMMODATIONS

Because Saba is so remote, accommodations aren't nearly as expensive as on other islands. The delightful El Momo Cottages (p446) is one of the cheapest options and the top hotels rarely charge over US$300 per night. Villas are equally as affordable.

The Saba Tourist Bureau (p450) offers help with booking accommodations. Hotels often add a 5% government room tax and 10% service charge.

ACTIVITIES

Diving & Snorkeling

Although it seems hardly possible when you first approach Saba by air or ferry, this volcanic island might be even more scenic below the ocean's surface than above it. Divers, mostly, but also adventurous snorkelers, can find a bit of everything at 26 varied dive sites: steep wall dives just offshore, varied marine life from sharks to sting rays and turtles, and several wreck dives.

But perhaps the most well known of Saba's underwater treasures are the many pinnacles. These marine mountain peaks rise dramati-

SABA

cally out of the ocean's floor, encrusted with coral and sponges, and visited by all varieties of marine life.

The Saba Marine Park has protected the area since 1987. It's the only self-supporting marine park in the world, maintained by a US$3 fee charged for each and every dive, a small price to pay for the pristine conditions. There is a hyperbaric chamber on Saba (opposite), staffed by trained volunteers from the medical university and Saba Marine Park. There is no individual diving on Saba; all divers must register with the Marine Park and go through a dive operator.

For snorkelers, Well's Bay (opposite) and the adjacent Torrens Point are popular spots, and there's even a marked underwater trail. Ladder Bay is also popular, but it's a good 30-minute hike down to the shore from the road and double that back up.

DIVE SHOPS

All three diving outfits have good reputations for safety. Each offers several types of packages, as well as individual dives.

Saba Deep (☎ 416-3347; www.sabadeep.com; Windwardside) Boats leave from Fort Bay.

Saba Divers (☎ 416-2741; www.sabadivers.com; Windwardside) Based at Scout's Place.

Sea Saba (☎ 416-2246; www.seasaba.com; Windwardside)

DIVE TOURS

Dive Saba (☎ in the US & Canada 800-883-7222; www.divesaba.com) offers fantastic deals on airfares, dive packages and hotels in Saba. It's based in the US, but can arrange trips for anyone. Prices start at about US$700 to US$800 for a seven-night, 10-dive package at one

of Windwardside's hotels – Juliana's, El Momo Cottages or Ecolodge Rendez Vous – and go up to US$2800 for a seven-night, eight-dive package staying at the stunning Willard's of Saba (p447).

Hiking

Saba is a hiker's paradise. Many of the trails have been around for centuries and were used by the earliest settlers as the main paths from village to village. Dress in layers, wear sturdy walking shoes and bring water. Some might appreciate a walking stick. Stay on the trails as they traverse private land.

The island's premier hike is to the top of Mt Scenery, a three-part climb that ends at the highest point in all of the Kingdom of the Netherlands. The third and final part of the trail starts behind the Trail Shop in Windwardside and goes straight up and up. The final slog to the top goes up many steps to arrive on top of the cloud forest. The best time to head out is about 9am or 10am to reach the peak at the least cloudy part of the day, around noon, for a view that will make the pain in your calves well worth it.

Other trails include the Sulphur Mine Track, a moderately strenuous hike past hot springs and into an abandoned mine (explore at your own risk), and the relatively easy Sandy Cruz Trail, which leads past the deserted old village of Mary's Point (p446).

Before setting out on a hike, head to the Trail Shop (p446) for endless information on Saba's hiking trails.

It's not illegal to hike on Saba without hiring 'Crocodile James' Johnson, but it might as well be. This knife- and combat fatigue-clad softie is a fifth-generation Saban who knows the island better than anyone. He is the official trail ranger for Saba and has created and/or maintained all 12 trails, but is also knowledgeable about history, botany and wildlife. Contact Johnson through the Trail Shop or on his cell phone (☎ 095-800-195).

The only trail you shouldn't attempt without a guide is the North Coast Trail. All other trails are accessible to experienced hikers.

DANGERS & ANNOYANCES

It's hard to imagine a safer place on the planet. Saba is virtually crime-free, as quick getaways are pretty tough on an island that just built its second road. The island's only snake is nonpoisonous, and there are very few mosquitoes and therefore no malaria.

EMBASSIES & CONSULATES

There are no embassies on Saba. See p754 for locations of consulates in Curaçao.

FESTIVALS & EVENTS

Saba Summer Festival (late July) The island's Carnival is a week-long event including jump ups, a Carnival Queen contest, a calypso-king competition, a costumed parade around the Bottom and a grand-finale fireworks display.

Sea & Learn (October; www.seaandlearn.org) The entire island becomes a learning center for naturalists, scientists and laypeople, who share the richness of Saban flora and fauna, from helping out on a shark research project to learning how to use tropical plants to make medicinal teas.

Saba Days (first week of December) Features sporting events, steel bands, dance competitions, donkey races and barbecues.

GAY & LESBIAN TRAVELERS

Although it's a complete coincidence that Saba's nickname is the 'Unspoiled Queen,' Saba is one of the most gay-friendly spots in all of the Caribbean. It doesn't have the nightlife of St Barth, but this is the spot for gays and lesbians looking for a relaxed outdoor vacation of diving and hiking where they can be openly accepted.

HOLIDAYS

New Year's Day January 1
Good Friday Friday before Easter
Easter Sunday Late March/early April
Easter Monday Late March/early April
Queen's Day April 30
Labor Day May 1
Ascension Thursday Fortieth day after Easter
Christmas Day December 25
Boxing Day December 26

MONEY

The official currency on Saba is the Netherlands Antillean guilder, though US dollars are accepted almost everywhere, and many prices are listed in US dollars at hotels and restaurants.

There is no ATM on the island; however, the First Caribbean International Bank in Windwardside will give you a cash advance (in guilders or dollars) from your ATM card.

POST

There are no addresses or postal codes on Saba. Simply address correspondence to: Ms Johnson, Saba, Dutch West Indies.

TELEPHONE

Saba's country code is ☎ 599 and is followed by a seven-digit local number. If you are calling locally, just dial the seven-digit number. To call the island overseas, dial your country's international access code followed by ☎ 599 + the local number. We have included only the seven-digit local number in Saba listings in this chapter.

TOURIST INFORMATION

On Saba, information can be found at **Saba Tourist Bureau** (☎ 416-2231; www.sabatourism.com; Windwardside; ◷ 8am-5pm Mon-Fri).

Overseas, there's a **tourist office** (☎ 3170-351-28-11; Badhuisweg 173-175; 2587 JP, the Hague) in the Netherlands.

TRANSPORTATION

GETTING THERE & AWAY
Entering Saba

Valid passports are required by all visitors; US citizens – see the boxed text, p772.

Air

Landing at Saba's **Juancho E Yrausquin Airport** (SAB; ☎ 416-2255; Flat Point) is the second-most thrilling activity undertaken on Saba. The first is taking off. The runway doesn't end with a comfy grassy meadow or even a fence, but at a sheer dropoff cliff. Don't worry, though: your pilot must pass a test every month to be able to fly into Saba.

Currently the only airline flying into Saba is **Winair** (☎ 416-2255; www.fly-winair.com; hub St Martin). It has five 15-minute flights a day to/from St Martin, as well as a daily flight to/from St Eustatius.

Sea

Operated by Aqua Mania on Sint Maarten, the **Edge** (☎ in Sint Maarten 599-545-2640; adult/child one way US$40/20, round-trip US$60/30) leaves Pelican Marina in Simpson Bay at 9am on Wednesday to Sunday (Wednesday, Friday and Sunday from August to October), arriving in Saba at about 10:30am. It departs Saba at 3:30pm, arriving at Pelican Marina at 5pm.

GETTING AROUND

There is no bus service on Saba. Most travelers hitchhike, walk along the many trails or use taxis.

Car & Motorcycle

You don't have to be insane to rent a car on Saba, but it would certainly help. Life-long residents won't even attempt some driveways (Willard's hotel is especially notorious). The only two roads are narrow, steep and windy with tight corners, and driving is difficult in just about every way. The island's sole **gas station** (8am-3pm Mon-Sat) is in Fort Bay near the Marine Park.

RENTAL

OK, don't say we didn't warn you. **Caja's Car Rental** (416-2388; takijah77@hotmail.com; the Bottom) rents cars for about US$50 a day.

ROAD RULES

Driving is on the right-hand side of the road. A driver's license from your home country is valid in Saba.

Hitching

Hitching is so common and necessary that it's illegal *not* to pick up a hitchhiker.

Safety cautions do apply, but this is the most common method for tourists to get around.

Taxi

There is no central taxi dispatch number on Saba. Ask your hotel or restaurant to arrange one for you, or try the following taxi drivers on their cell phones:

Eddie (552-1005)
Garvis (552-3418)
Manny (552-8871)

St Eustatius

Those who come to St Eustatius – commonly known as Statia – aren't looking for the typical Caribbean vacation. They are most likely divers, hikers or colonial history buffs, and they might enjoy being relaxed to the brink of boredom.

Statia's license plate reads 'The Historic Gem,' and that history's been a tough one. Statia feels like the little island that could. The selection of restaurants, accommodations and nightlife is slim, but the physical beauty of the island – on the ground and below the sea – is what draws most visitors. Two dozen dive sites showcase Statia's incredible underwater treasures: colonial trading ship wrecks; deliberately sunk newer wrecks with accompanying maps to preplan a diving expedition; coral reefs; and marine life as varied as barracuda, tropical fish and nurse sharks.

Landing in Statia is a bit like stepping back into a niche of the Caribbean from the 1950s. There is only one town on the island, Oranjestad, with lots of wide open spaces to enjoy expansive views, solitude, wandering cows and goats, and secluded beaches. An oil-holding facility – Statia Terminals – gives the island an industrial feel with a constant stream of oil tankers.

FAST FACTS

- **Area** 12 sq miles (31 sq km)
- **Capital** Oranjestad
- **Country code** ☎ 599
- **Departure tax** US$5.65 within Netherlands Antilles, US$12 elsewhere
- **Famous for** Diving, colonial history, not being famous
- **Languages** Dutch officially, English spoken by everyone
- **Money** Netherlands Antillean guilder (NAf); US dollars accepted everywhere. US$1 = €0.82 = UK£0.55 = NAf1.77
- **Official name** Sint Eustatius
- **People** Statians
- **Phrases** *I pas by dei yesterday.* I passed by there yesterday
- **Population** 2800
- **Visa** None needed for citizens of North America and most European countries

HIGHLIGHTS

- **Diving** (p459) Explore the deep with sharks, octopuses, barracuda and centuries-old relics.
- **The Quill** (p459) Hike to the island's highest point at Mazinga and admire the scenery around this dormant volcano.
- **Fort Oranje** (p455) Amble through Statia's colonial buildings and historic fort.
- **Sint Eustatius Museum** (p455) Visit this excellent museum and see what it was like to live in 18th-century colonial Statia.
- **Little Round Hill House** (p458) Step back in time a few decades and get as far off the Caribbean beaten path as possible at these isolated accommodations in northern Statia.

ITINERARIES

- **Two Days** Stay in Lower Town, Oranjestad and dive Hangover Reef, Doobie's Crack and the Charlie Brown wreck.
- **One Week** While diving every other day, spend one day hiking the Quill, another at the Botanical Gardens and Fort de Windt, and a final day at the Sint Eustatius Museum, Fort Oranje and the synagogue ruins.
- **Two Weeks** After seeing the island's sights, contact Stenapa and inquire about volunteering at the Miriam C Schmidt Botanical Gardens or tagging sea turtles at Zeelandia Beach.

CLIMATE & WHEN TO GO

In January the average daily high temperature is 85°F (29°C), while the low averages 72°F (22°C). In July the average daily high is 90°F (32°C) and the average low hovers around 76°F (24°C).

The annual rainfall in Statia averages 45in (114.5cm) and is fairly evenly dispersed throughout the year. Relative humidity is in the low 70s from March to December and in the mid-70s in January and February.

Statia's relative lack of tourism means that prices stay the same most of the year. As a result, it's a good place to come December through April when nearby islands double their prices.

HISTORY

Statia has been the Caribbean whipping boy for centuries. Carib Indians had a settlement on Statia at the time Columbus came

---

HOW MUCH?

- **Taxi from the airport to Lower Town** per person US$5
- **Two-tank dive** US$80
- **Fresh fish in touristy restaurant** US$17
- **Fresh fish in local restaurant** US$9
- **Admission to the Sint Eustatius Museum** US$2

LONELY PLANET INDEX

- **Liter of gas** US$0.96
- **Liter of bottled water** US$1.50
- **Bottle of Carib** US$2
- **Souvenir T-shirt** US$16
- **Street snack: johnnycake** US$2

---

across the island, in 1493. The French arrived next, but it was the Dutch who established the first permanent settlement in 1636. Statia subsequently changed hands 22 times among the squabbling Dutch, French and British.

Statia was the only link between Europe and the New World for much of the 17th century. As the English and French levied duty after duty on their islands, the Dutch made Statia a duty-free island. Subsequently, thousands of ships used Oranjestad as their main stopping point between Europe and the colonies in America, bringing arms and gunpowder to the rebellious colonists, among other things. At its heyday, Statia was home to no less than 20,000 full-time residents, both European colonialists and African slaves.

It was on November 16, 1776, when Statia's most infamous moment happened. An American ship sailing into the harbor fired a 13-gun salute, indicating American independence. Statia responded with an 11-gun salute, cementing itself as the first foreign nation to recognize the new United States of America.

Britain was none too pleased. A British navy admiral launched an attack on Statia in 1781, destroying many warehouses and starting a downhill spiral that produced massive emigration and the demise of Statia's former glory as 'The Golden Rock.'

ST EUSTATIUS

ST EUSTATIUS (STATIA)

0 — 2 km
0 — 1 mile

Boven Bay

Doobie's Crack

Boven (294m)

Venus Bay

Jenkins Bay

ATLANTIC OCEAN

Zeelandia Bay

Little Mtn (200m)

Zeelandia

Concordia Bay

Tumble-Down-Dick Bay

Great Bay

Signal Hill (234m)

Franklin Delano Roosevelt Airport

Concordia

Compagnie Bay

Interlopers Point

Golden Rock

See Oranjestad Map (p456)

Oranjestad

Corre Corre Bay

Oranjestad Bay

The Quill

Gallows Bay

Mazinga (600m)

Miriam C Schmidt Botanical Gardens

CARIBBEAN SEA

White Wall

Charlie Brown Wreck

Hangover Reef

Kay Bay

Fort de Windt

Buccaneers Bay

Back-off Bay

Statia had been a municipality of the Netherlands Antilles, along with Bonaire, Curaçao, Saba and Sint Maarten since 1954. On Statia Day, November 16, 2004, the island adopted a new flag, but in 2005 voted to remain part of the Netherlands Antilles. However, all four other members voted to disband the island nation group, effectually leaving Statia the sole member of the Netherlands Antilles.

THE CULTURE

Most islanders are descendants of African slaves brought over to work on the warehouses in Lower Town and the long-vanished plantations. The culture is a mix of African and Dutch heritages with many expats.

ENVIRONMENT

The Quill (whose name is derived from the Dutch word *kwil,* meaning pit or hole) looms above the southern half of the island. This dormant volcano, which reaches 1968ft (600m) at Mazinga, the highest point on the rim, is responsible for the high, conical appearance Statia has when viewed from neighboring islands.

Cliffs drop straight to the sea along much of the shoreline, resulting in precious few beaches. At the north side of Statia there are a few low mountains, while the island's central plain contains the airport and Oranjestad.

Most of the island is dry with scrubby vegetation, although oleander, bougainvillea, hibiscus and flamboyant flowers add a

ST EUSTATIUS

splash of color here and there. The greatest variety of flora is inside the Quill, which collects enough cloud cover for its central crater to harbor a rainforest with ferns, elephant ears, bromeliads, bananas and tall trees. The island also has 18 varieties of orchids, all but three of which are found within the Quill.

There are 25 resident species of birds on Statia, including white-tailed tropic birds that nest on the cliffs along the beach north of Lower Town, in Oranjestad. There are also harmless racer snakes, iguanas, lizards and tree frogs. Most other animal life is limited to goats, chickens, cows and donkeys.

FOOD & DRINK

Statia isn't known for its cuisine. Roadside barbecue joints pop up, usually on weekends, and are certainly worth an adventurer's try. Better than it sounds, the popular dish 'goat water' is actually more of a goat stew, and can be found at roadside stands and in locals' restaurants.

ORANJESTAD

pop 2200
INFORMATION

The two main banks are First Caribbean National Bank and Windward Islands Bank (WIB). The only ATM is in the building across from WIB.

Computers & More (☎ 318-2596; ccclop@aol.com; per 30min NAf4; ☿ 10am-5pm Mon-Fri, by appointment Sat)

Post office (☎ 318-2207; Cattageweg; ☿ 7:30am-4pm Mon-Fri)

Public library (Internet access per hr US$5; ☿ noon-5pm Mon, 8am-5pm Tue-Fri)

Queen Beatrix Medical Centre (☎ 318-2371)

SIGHTS & ACTIVITIES
Fort Oranje

Right in the center of town, **Fort Oranje** (admission free; ☿ 24hr) is one of the last remaining bastions of Statia's historic past, an intact fort complete with cannons, triple bastions and a cobblestone courtyard. The first rampart here was erected by the French in 1629, but most of the fort was built after the Dutch took the island from the French in 1636. They added to the fort a number of times over the years.

The courtyard has a couple of memorials, including a plaque presented by US Presi-

dent Franklin Roosevelt to commemorate the fort's fateful 1776 salute of the American war vessel *Andrew Doria*. At the time, the British on neighboring Antigua didn't take too kindly to Statia being the first foreign power to officially recognize the new American nation. The British navy later sailed for Oranjestad and, led by Admiral George Rodney, mercilessly bombed it to high heaven, and then took possession of the island and all its wealth.

Sint Eustatius Museum

Chockfull o' history, this **museum** (☎ 318-2288; adult/child US$2/1; ☿ 9am-5pm Mon-Fri, until noon Sat) gives meaning to the Statian tag line and license plate insignia, 'The Historic Gem.' Set up as an upper class colonial-era house, the museum also houses a pre-Columbian collection of artifacts and information on slavery, nautical history and colonial relics. The shady grounds are a wonderful place for a picnic or just to sit and enjoy for a spell.

Government Guesthouse

The Government Guesthouse is the handsome 18th-century stone-and-wood building opposite First Caribbean National Bank. It was thoroughly renovated in 1992 with funding from the EU and is now the government headquarters, with the offices of the lieutenant governor and commissioners on the ground floor and the courtroom on the upper floor.

The building, which once served as the Dutch naval commander's quarters, derived its name from this time, in the 1920s, as a guesthouse.

Synagogue Ruins

Those with a particular interest in Jewish history or old buildings can explore the roofless and slowly decaying yellow-brick walls of the Honen Dalim (Kind to the Poor), an abandoned synagogue dating from 1739. It's 30m down the alleyway opposite the south side of the library. The synagogue is the second oldest in the western hemisphere.

Statia's rising influence as a trade center was accompanied by a large influx of Jewish merchants beginning in the early 1700s. After the 1781 invasion, British troops stole much of the wealth from the Jewish merchants and deported the men.

ST EUSTATIUS

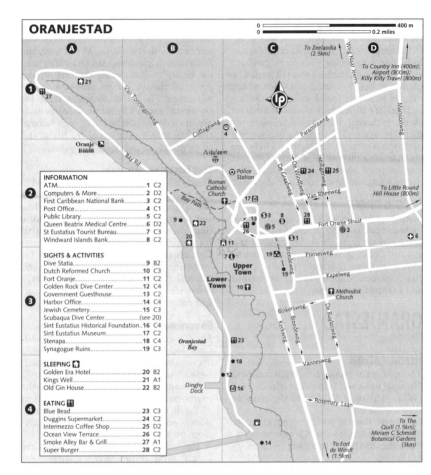

ORANJESTAD

INFORMATION
ATM	1	C2
Computers & More	2	D2
First Caribbean National Bank	3	C2
Post Office	4	C1
Public Library	5	C2
Queen Beatrix Medical Centre	6	D2
St Eustatius Tourist Bureau	7	C3
Windward Islands Bank	8	C2

SIGHTS & ACTIVITIES
Dive Statia	9	B2
Dutch Reformed Church	10	C3
Fort Oranje	11	C2
Golden Rock Dive Center	12	C4
Government Guesthouse	13	C2
Harbor Office	14	C4
Jewish Cemetery	15	C3
Scubaqua Dive Center	(see 20)	
Sint Eustatius Historical Foundation	16	C4
Sint Eustatius Museum	17	C2
Stenapa	18	C4
Synagogue Ruins	19	C3

SLEEPING
Golden Era Hotel	20	B2
Kings Well	21	A1
Old Gin House	22	B2

EATING
Blue Bead	23	C3
Duggins Supermarket	24	D2
Intermezzo Coffee Shop	25	D2
Ocean View Terrace	26	C2
Smoke Alley Bar & Grill	27	A1
Super Burger	28	C2

About 545yd (500m) east of the synagogue ruins is a **Jewish cemetery** with gravestones dating from 1742 to 1843. It was here that clever Jews tried to avoid British plundering. Troops noticed an extremely large number of funerals for such a small community, and upon opening a casket, found valuables instead of bodies.

Dutch Reformed Church
The thick 23.5in (60cm) stone walls of the old Dutch Reformed Church, built in 1755, remain perfectly intact, but the roof collapsed during a 1792 hurricane and the building has been open to the heavens ever since. The grounds are resting place to many of the island's most prominent citizens.

Stenapa
The Sint Eustatius National Parks Foundation is known as **Stenapa** (☎ 318-2884; www.statiapark.org; Lower Town; ☺ 7am-5pm Mon-Thu, 7am-4pm Fri, 9am-noon Sat & Sun) and collectively manages the Statia Marine Park as well as the aboveground national park and the Miriam C Schmidt Botanical Gardens (p458). This nongovernment organization was started in 1998 to protect Statia's ample natural resources. The office has information about diving and hiking, as well as everything about Statian flora and fauna.

Sint Eustatius Historical Foundation
The small historical foundation museum **gift shop** (☎ 318-2856; ☺ 9am-noon Mon-Sat) along

Lower Town sells books and local artwork and crafts. Proceeds support the museum and historical research on Statia.

Diving

Despite Statia's light tourism, there are three dive shops, all in Oranjestad, offering competitive rates. One-tank dives average US$45, two-tank dives US$80. Night dives, certification courses and multidive packages are also available. For information on diving and snorkeling in Statia, see p459.

Dive Statia (☎ 318-2435, in the US 866-614-3419; www.divestatia.com)

Golden Rock Dive Center (☎ /fax 318-2964, in the US ☎ 800-311-6658; www.goldenrockdive.com)

Scubaqua Dive Center (☎ /fax 318-2160; www .scubaqua.com) Swiss- and French-run.

SLEEPING

Kings Well (☎ /fax 318-2538; www.turq.com/kingswell; Van Tonningenweg; s US$75-95, d US$90-140; P ⊠) Has the most character of any accommodations on the island, that is if one doesn't mind bounding Great Danes and squawking pet macaws. The villalike rooms feel like old English cottages; the ocean-view rooms far surpass the garden view, but all contain cozy furnishings, refrigerators and ceiling fans. A fish pond wards off mosquitoes and the plush gardens are almost always in bloom.

Old Gin House (☎ 318-2319; www.oldginhouse.com; s US$125-250, d US$135-275, incl breakfast; P ⊠ ⊠) A bit past its prime, this refurbished 17th-century ginning station (when the dark seeds were removed from cotton plants) came under new management recently. It's hired a French chef and has plans to restore to its former glory. Rooms are comfortably outfitted with king-size beds and satellite TV. The priciest rooms face the ocean, but rooms in the main house are a bit stale. The casual restaurant fronts Oranje Beach and has romantic candles and a view of the sunset; a more upscale restaurant is planned for the historic main house.

Country Inn (☎ /fax 318-2484; countryinn@statiatour ism.com; s/d US$40/55, breakfast extra US$5; ⊠) Walking distance from the airport, Statia's lowest-priced accommodations aren't fancy, but they're clean and quiet. Iris Pompier, the dedicated proprietor, will even cook you one of her fabulous lunches or dinners on request. About a 20-minute walk or quick hitch from town. Credit cards aren't accepted.

> **REEF BALLS**
>
> Statia is in the process of building a sandy beach at Oranjestad. Environmentally-friendly, concrete 'reef balls' anchored in the sea floor in 6.5ft to 13ft (2m to 4m) depths will create a breakwater that allows sand to accumulate, creating an artificial submerged reef, reducing wave energy. Or, in nonscientific terms, no waves, more beach.

Golden Era Hotel (☎ 318-2345, in the US 800-223-9815, in Canada 800-344-0023; goldenera@goldenrock.net; s US$70-120, d US$88-120; P ⊠ ⊟ ⊠) This Swiss-owned hotel commands a central location with several rooms and a terraced restaurant literally on the ocean, and four more rooms with decent ocean views. Rooms can be drab and bedding could use some updating, but the grounds are covered with yellowbells and oleander, and the pool bar practically forces guests to lounge on a beach chair with a mystery novel and a piña colada.

EATING
Budget

Intermezzo Coffee Shop (☎ 318-2520; Heilligerweg; ⓧ breakfast & lunch, closed Sat) The only place to get decent coffee on the island, Intermezzo also serves sandwiches and smoothies. The convivial outdoor seating makes for an excellent place to find conversation, international magazines and enjoy the weather.

Super Burger (☎ 318-2412; snacks up to US$6; ⓧ breakfast, lunch & dinner) The burgers, as super as they are, aren't nearly as good as the famous milkshakes. A good spot to try john-nycakes (corn-flour griddle cakes).

Duggins Supermarket (☎ 318-2150; De Windtweg; ⓧ 8am-8pm Mon-Fri, 6am-9pm Sat, 9am-1pm Sun) As the main supermarket on this duty-free island, Duggins is inexpensive, packed with popular European and American items, and filled with Kittitians who save money by paying for a boat ticket on Sundays and loading up with barrels full of products.

Midrange

Smoke Alley Bar & Grill (☎ 318-2002; Lower Town; nachos US$10, sandwiches US$4.50-9.50; ⓧ lunch & dinner Mon-Sat, DJ & dancing late Fri & Sat) A recent change in ownership will hopefully put the spark

ST EUSTATIUS

back into this former hotspot. Commanding an enviable location directly over the ocean on the turn into Lower Town, this open-air restaurant-cum-nightclub has group bench seating; pulsing music at night; an eclectic crowd of medical students, locals and foreigners; and mediocre food.

Ocean View Terrace (☎ 318-2934; breakfast around US$7, lunch/dinner $11/16; ⊙ closed Sun) In the courtyard next to the Government Guesthouse, this place has a quiet open-air setting, with eggs and omelettes for breakfast and well-priced fish for lunch and dinner.

Blue Bead (☎ 318-2873; breakfast US$5.50-9, lunch US$10, dinner US$17-20; ⊙ breakfast, lunch & dinner) A bar and restaurant at Oranjestad Bay, this offers pleasant water-view dining and reasonable prices. Breakfast is omelettes and freshly baked French bread. Lunch and dinner offer fish, humongous pizzas and fish. Popular in the evening as a local hang-out.

Golden Era (sandwiches & snacks US$4-12, dinner around US$16; ⊙ lunch & dinner) The restaurant of the Golden Era Hotel (p457) boasts a dining room literally *on* the Caribbean ocean, but the outdoor poolside seating is just as lovely. Light lunches, fresh fish and lobster for dinner, and a healthy wine list ensure a relaxing meal after a day of vigorous activity.

AROUND ST EUSTATIUS

FORT DE WINDT

The road south from Oranjestad ends abruptly at Fort de Windt, where a couple of rusty cannons sit atop a cliff-side stone wall. While there's not much else to this small 18th-century fort, you'll be rewarded with a fine view of St Kitts to the southeast. The most interesting geological feature in the area is the white cliffs to the east of Fort de Windt, a landmark readily visible from neighboring islands.

To get there, take the road that runs past the old Dutch Reformed Church and follow it south, through a dry terrain of cacti and stray goats, to its end 2 miles (3km) away.

ZEELANDIA

Zeelandia, about 2 miles (3.2km) northeast of Oranjestad, takes its name from Statia's first Dutch settlers, who were from Zeeland province in the Netherlands.

The dark-sand beach at Zeelandia Bay collects its fair share of flotsam and is not an ideal good beach for swimming; the Atlantic side of the island is turbulent, and there are dangerous currents and undertows. It is a reasonable strolling beach, however, and you can find private niches by walking south along the beach toward the cliffs.

For those who are up for a longer walk, a track from the main road leads north to the partially secluded Venus Bay. There's no beach, but it makes for a nice hike, taking about 45 minutes one way.

MIRIAM C SCHMIDT BOTANICAL GARDENS

The semiwild **Miriam C Schmidt Botanical Gardens** (☎ 318-2884) grow under the watchful eye of the Quill. Volunteers and Stenapa staff have been busy preparing them to show residents and visitors alike the rich biodiversity of Statia. So far, there's a greenhouse, a little office and a wide range of unmarked native plants. Take Rosemary Laan towards the Quill and follow the dirt road that points to the Botanical Gardens. Take care, as it can be rough riding.

LITTLE ROUND HILL HOUSE

Six degrees from anything resembling a rat race, **Little Round Hill House** (☎ 318-2350; junestatia@hotmail.com; Little Round Hill; per person per night/week US$25/140, 3-night minimum; P), a 2-acre (0.8-hectare) property, is for self-sufficient travelers looking for the ultimate in solitude. A virtual compound of relaxation amid a tropical jungle setting, three stand-alone buildings house a full kitchen, living room, outdoor heated shower, and bedrooms that sleep up to four people (and one live-in cat). Pick your breakfast from the garden's fruit trees.

DIRECTORY

ACCOMMODATIONS

Most accommodations are along the waterfront in Lower Town, Oranjestad, or scattered between the town and the airport. There are only four hotels and one guesthouse in all of Statia, so booking ahead is highly advised. Prices range from US$40 to US$150.

The government tax on hotels is 7%. Restaurants charge 15% service fee in lieu of gratuities.

Camping is technically allowed on Statia, although the tourist office has never had a request in its history. If you're willing to pioneer through the bureaucracy, Zeelandia might be the best location to bunker down.

ACTIVITIES
Beaches & Swimming
No one visits Statia for its beaches, which can't compare with those of other islands in the Caribbean and are few in number. Plans are under way to turn Oranje Beach into a bona fide Caribbean beach, with white sand and a walking path (see the boxed text, p457). Volcanic Zeelandia Beach, on the east coast, has rough surf and undertows, butts up against the island's landfill, and is not recommended for swimming; nonetheless, it rates as Statia's second beach.

Diving & Snorkeling
Reef dives, seahorses, colonial trading shipwrecks, giant octopuses, stingrays, barracudas, coral, lobster, tropical fish… the list could go on forever. Statia's diving is regarded as among the best in the Caribbean.

Part of what keeps it this way is the US$6 per day or US$15 per year pass fee paid to Stenapa (p456) to help this foundation maintain the pristine conditions of the Marine Park. Please take only photos and leave all historic objects and marine life alone (fines have been levied at the airport on divers found to have stashed a blue bead or two).

Statia has recently sunk several ships for some of the best wreck diving in the world. The *Charlie Brown* was sunk in 2003 and a map of its cavernous hull and quarters now hangs on the Stenapa wall so divers can plan their route beforehand. Several colonial-era wrecks congregate around Lower Town but the ships have eroded significantly.

Hangover Reef, at the southwest side of the island, is a popular reef dive with a wide variety of sponges, corals and sea fans. It also has many ledges and crevices harbor-

ing lobsters, sea turtles and numerous species of fish.

For a deep dive, Doobie's Crack, a large cleft in a reef at the northwest side of the island, has black-tip sharks and schools of large fish.

See the Diving & Snorkeling chapter (p56) for more on Statia diving.

Snorkeling tours of some of the shallower reefs are available from the dive shops for around US$25. See p457 for details of Statia's dive shops.

Hiking
The tourist office has a free hiking brochure with descriptions of 12 trails, and it can provide information on current trail conditions. Most of the trails are signposted, and some of them are marked with orange ribbons.

The most popular hike is to the Quill, Statia's extinct volcano. The Quill, and its surrounding slopes, was designated a national park in May 1998. The trail leading up the mountain begins at the end of Rosemary Laan in Oranjestad and it takes about 50 minutes to reach the edge of the crater. From there you can continue in either direction along the rim. The trail to the right (southeast) takes about 45 minutes and ends atop the 1968ft (600m) Mazinga, Statia's highest point. The shorter Panorama Track to the left offers great views and takes only about 15 minutes. A third option is the track leading down into the crater, where there's a thick rainforest of tall trees, some with huge buttressed trunks. This steep track, which takes about 30 minutes each way, can be very slippery, so sturdy shoes are essential.

Guided tours about native flora and fauna can be organized through **Stenapa** (☎ 318-2884; www.statiapark.org; Lower Town, Oranjestad), which

ST EUSTATIUS

oversees the national park, or through the tourist office (see below).

EMBASSIES & CONSULATES

There are no embassies on Statia. See p754 for locations of consulates in Curaçao.

FESTIVALS & EVENTS

Statia Carnival (Late July) With 10 days of revelry, this is the island's biggest festival, culminating on a Monday. Music, jump-ups (including early-morning pajama ones), competitions and local food are the highlights.

Statia Day (November 16) Fort Oranje is the site of ceremonies held on Statia Day, which commemorates the date in 1776 when Statia became the first foreign land to salute the US flag. On this date in 2004, Statia adopted a new flag.

HOLIDAYS

New Year's Day January 1
Good Friday Friday before Easter
Easter Sunday/Monday late March/early April
Queen's Birthday April 30
Labor Day May 1
Emancipation Day July 1
Ascension Thursday 40th day after Easter
Antillean Day October 21
Statia Day November 16
Christmas Day December 25
Boxing Day December 26

MONEY

The official currency on Statia is the Netherlands Antillean guilder, though US dollars are accepted almost everywhere.

TELEPHONE

Statia's country code is ☎ 599. If you are calling locally, just dial the seven-digit number. To call the island overseas, dial your country's international access code followed by ☎ 599 + the local number. We have included only the seven-digit local number in Statia listings in this chapter.

TOURIST INFORMATION

The **St Eustatius Tourist Bureau** (☎ 318-2433; www .statiatourism.com; Fort Oranje) has free island maps that show the roads and hiking trails.

Abroad, there's a **tourist office** (Antillen Huis; ☎ 070-306-6111; fax 070-306-6110; Badhuisweg 173-175, 2597 JP 'S-Gravenhage) in the Netherlands.

VISAS

Citizens of North America and most European countries don't need a visa to visit Statia. Other nationalities should check with the Dutch representation in their home country.

VOLUNTEERING

Statia has some amazing opportunities for educational volunteer trips. **Stenapa** (☎ 318-2884; www.statiapark.org; Lower Town, Oranjestad) connects long- and short-term volunteers with opportunities in tagging sea turtles on Zeelandia Beach, maintaining the Miriam C Schmidt Botanical Gardens, staffing the office, cataloguing Statian flora etc. Contact Stenapa for more information.

TRANSPORTATION

GETTING THERE & AWAY
Entering St Eustatius

Visitors need a passport and onward or return ticket; this includes US citizens – see the boxed text on p772.

Air

Franklin Delano Roosevelt Airport (EUX; ☎ 316-2887) is Statia's only airport. It's tiny and currently only accommodates **Winair** (☎ 318-2303; www.fly-winair.com; hub St Martin) puddle jumpers from St Martin.

Sea

There is currently no regular ferry service to Statia. Save for a few dive boats and the odd small ship, no cruise ships alight here.

YACHT

Yachts need to radio the Marine Park at VHF channel 16 or 17 as there are many protected spots around the island and there is only anchorage for about 10 yachts at a time.

GETTING AROUND

Statia has no buses, so renting a car is useful if you want to explore the island properly, which could be done in a day. If you're staying in Oranjestad, you probably won't need a car for most of your stay, but expect to do some serious walking, as the town is spread out.

Car & Motorcycle

Driving is on the right side of the road. Road conditions are spotty outside of Oranjestad and the road to the Miriam C Schmidt

Botanical Gardens can be impassable after rain. Watch out for roaming goats, cows and chickens all over the island, even in Oranjestad.

RENTAL

ARC Car Rental (☎ 318-2595; www.arcagency.com)
Brown's Car Rental (☎ 318-2266) Offers weekend deals.
Rainbow Car Rental (☎ 318-2811/3055; raintour@goldenrock.net; booth at airport) Rents out cars for US$35, plus US$5 for CWD insurance. Weekly discounts.
Sheriff Scooter Rentals (☎ 0523-3544; per day US$20) Ask for Carlos or check at the Old Gin House (p457).

Hitchhiking

The usual safety precautions apply, but hitchhiking on Statia is relatively easy and safe.

Taxi

The island's handful of taxis congregates at the airport after arriving flights.

If you have trouble finding a taxi or would like to book a tour, try friendly **Blondell Berkel** (☎ 523-5341) or **Rosie Lopes** (☎ 318-2811). An island tour costs US$40 for up to five people. All taxi fares run under US$5 per person.

ST EUSTATIUS

St Kitts & Nevis

The island nation of St Christopher (known as St Kitts) & Nevis constitutes a low-key destination. Both are relaxed tropical isles with all the requirements for paradise, though it takes a bit of adventure to see the culture through the resorts. White-sand beaches with palm trees swaying in the soft trade winds: check. Brightly painted festive bars serving drinks that ought to be served in coconuts, or at least with paper umbrellas: check. Friendly locals who have redefined the nature of time into the most agreeable concept of 'island time': check.

Some will find the islands' relaxed nature ideal, while others might get restless after a few days. St Kitts, the much larger of the two, offers more resorts and nightlife, but also has retained much more of the Caribbean personality. A rarity in the Eastern Caribbean, the public transportation system is outstanding on St Kitts, and not bad on Nevis. Nevis is the kinder, gentler island, but a Four Seasons hotel has affected the slow pace tremendously.

A constantly running ferry connects the two, allowing visitors on one island to day-trip to the other. History buffs will appreciate both islands. A bit of cash will afford you a stay at one of the many grand plantations-turned-gracious inns.

FAST FACTS

- **Area** St Kitts: 68 sq miles (176 sq km); Nevis: 36 sq miles (93 sq km)
- **Capital** St Kitts: Basseterre; Nevis: Charlestown
- **Country code** ☎ 869
- **Departure tax** St Kitts: adults US$22, children under 12 US$5; Nevis: US$20.50
- **Famous for** Beaches, historic plantation inns
- **Language** English with a Creole or Patois accent
- **Money** Eastern Caribbean dollar (EC$); EC$1 = US$0.37 = €0.31 = UK£0.21
- **Official name** Federation of St Kitts & Nevis
- **People** Kittitians; Nevisians
- **Phrases** *Menono* (I don't know); *get dat do* (get that done)
- **Population** 46,000 (35,000 on St Kitts; 11,000 on Nevis)
- **Visa** Not required for most nationalities

HIGHLIGHTS

- **Brimstone Fortress** (p469) Explore the only Unesco World Heritage site in the Leeward Islands.
- **Rawlins Plantation** (p470) Upgrade to a plantation inn for the vacation of a lifetime, or just dine here or at any of the other half-dozen or so sumptuous stately plantation inns on the islands.
- **Sunshine's** (p474) Beware the sting of the Killer Bee (the drink, not the insect) on Pinney's Beach in Nevis.
- **Frigate Bay Beach** (p468) and **Pinney's Beach** (p474) Relax on any one of dozens of beaches, including these two on St Kitts and Nevis, respectively.
- **Turtle Beach Bar & Grill** (p471) Commune with wild monkeys, white sand, rum and a pet pig, but be sure to stop by on a day when the cruise ships aren't in.

ITINERARIES

- **Two Days** Spend your first day at Frigate Bay Beach, heading to Sprat Net's for a lively lobster dinner that night. On your second day, catch a ferry over to Nevis for a monkey-spotting hike and end the day watching the sun set over your Caribbean dinner.
- **One Week** Stay at Turtle Beach, day-trip by ferry to Nevis. Spend a day wandering through Brimstone Hill Fortress and take the St Kitts Scenic Railway the last morning before your afternoon flight out.
- **Two Weeks** After leaving the splendor of the beach, head to the ultimate relaxation of Montpelier Plantation Inn on Nevis. Mix beach-going days with a horseback riding excursion and a visit to the sumptuous botanical gardens. Watch at least three sunsets from Banana's Bistro.

CLIMATE & WHEN TO GO

Winter days average a temperature of 81°F (27°C) while summers shoot up to a still respectable 86°F (30°C).

Annual rainfall averages 55in (140cm) and is fairly consistent throughout the year. The driest months are February to June and the hurricane (and rainy) season is July to November.

High season rates start from around mid-December and go to mid-April. The best time to visit, price- and weather-wise, is November and early December.

HOW MUCH?

- **Taxi from airport to Charlestown** US$15
- **Full-day sailing trip, including snorkel and lunch** around US$70
- **Two-tank dive** US$90
- **Meal of fresh fish in touristy restaurant** US$24
- **Meal of fresh fish in local restaurant** US$14

LONELY PLANET INDEX

- **Liter of petrol** US$1.04
- **Liter of bottled water** US$2
- **Bottle of Carib** US$1.50
- **Souvenir T-shirt** US$20
- **Street snack: johnnycake and sausage** US$2

HISTORY

The island known today as St Kitts was called Liamuiga (Fertile Island) by its Amerindian inhabitants. When Columbus sighted the island on his second voyage to the New World, in 1493, he named it St Christopher after his patron saint, later shortened to 'St Kitts.'

Columbus used the Spanish word for 'snow,' *nieves,* to name Nevis, presumably because the clouds shrouding its mountain reminded him of a snowcapped peak. Native Caribs knew the island as Oualie (Land of Beautiful Waters).

St Kitts and Nevis are the oldest British colonies in the Caribbean. Sir Thomas Warner founded a colony way back in 1623, only to be joined soon after by the French, a move the British only tolerated long enough to massacre the native Caribs. In one year, 2000 Caribs were slaughtered, causing blood to run for days at the site now known as Bloody Point.

After a century and a half of Franco-British battles, the 1783 Treaty of Paris brought the island firmly under British control. During this era, sugar plantations thrived on St Kitts.

Nevis had a similar colonial history. In 1628, Warner sent a party of about 100 colonists to establish a British settlement on

ST KITTS & NEVIS

the west coast of the island. Although the original settlement, near Cotton Ground, fell to an earthquake in 1680, Nevis eventually developed one of the most affluent plantation societies in the Eastern Caribbean. As on St Kitts, most of the island's wealth was built upon the labor of African slaves who toiled in the island's sugarcane fields.

By the late 18th century, Nevis, buoyed by the attraction of its thermal baths, had become a major retreat for Britain's rich and famous.

In 1816 the British linked St Kitts and Nevis with Anguilla and the Virgin Islands as a single colony. In 1958 these islands became part of the West Indies Federation, a grand but ultimately unsuccessful attempt

to combine all of Britain's Caribbean colonies as a united political entity. When the federation dissolved in 1962, the British opted to lump St Kitts, Nevis and Anguilla together as a new state. Anguilla, fearful of domination by larger St Kitts, revolted against the occupying Royal St Kitts Police Force in 1967 and returned to Britain as an overseas territory.

In 1983, St Kitts and Nevis became a single nation within the British Commonwealth, with the stipulation that wary Nevis could secede at any time. A period of corruption on St Kitts and pro-independence on Nevis in the 1990s almost brought an end to the federation, and one suspects it might not be long before the two divide for good.

St Kitts and Nevis is one of the 54 members of the Commonwealth and still retains a Governor-General, appointed by the ruling monarch of Britain. The buck actually stops at the prime minister, who is the leader of the ruling political party. Nevis has internal home rule and a separate legislature, as well as an island administration that mirrors that of the federation on a smaller scale.

THE CULTURE

Although the population is predominantly (90%) of African descent, culturally the islands draw upon a mix of European, African and West Indian traditions. Architecture is mainly British in style and cricket is the national sport.

St Kitts, more than Nevis, still feels like a place where people live and work, rather than just a tourist spot. Walk through a residential area on St Kitts on any given night and most residents will be out in the streets, listening to reggae or calypso blaring out of homes and chatting with friends.

St Kitts and Nevis have an interesting mixture of leniency and propriety. You can get fined for using foul language in public, but you can drink while driving (note that doesn't mean you can drive drunk!), so keep an eye out on the road at night. Swimwear should be restricted to the beach and pool areas of resorts.

ENVIRONMENT

Both islands boast grassy coastal areas and plenty of wide beaches, topped off by mountainous rainforest interiors filled with ferns and tall trees. Flowers surround the islands and plumeria, hibiscus and chains-of-love are common along roadsides and in garden landscaping. St Kitts' shape resembles a large chicken drumstick, and the uninhabited southeast peninsula is covered with sparse, desert like cacti and yucca.

The most popular wildlife on the islands is the skittish vervet monkey. Imported by French settlers from Africa, these monkeys can now be seen fairly regularly all over both islands. Even more ubiquitous is the mongoose, imported by plantation owners to curb rats from munching on their sugarcane (luckily for the nocturnal rats, mongooses hunt during the day, and rarely the twain did meet). Both islands provide plenty of avian life for bird-watchers.

FOOD & DRINK

Reasonably priced local fresh fish and other seafood are plentiful on the islands and are generally the best bet. Beef and many other items are imported and tend to be expensive, particularly on Nevis. In Basseterre and Charlestown there are a few good, inexpensive local restaurants, while the plantation inns on both islands offer some fine upscale opportunities for romantic dining.

Tap water is safe to drink everywhere. Cane Spirit Rothschild, more commonly known as CSR, is a clear sugarcane spirit distilled on St Kitts. CSR is often served on the rocks with Ting, a popular grapefruit soft drink. Ting, Ginseng Up and Carib beer are bottled on St Kitts.

ST KITTS

St Kitts offers more variety than its sleepy nation-mate, Nevis. Along with the requisite palm tree–lined white-sand beaches and stately plantation inns come several pulsating casinos, the region's only Unesco site, beach bars and a scenic train ride. St Kitts offers just about any type of Caribbean vacation, whether it be bunking in locally owned inns or spending a week in an international all-inclusive. Kittitians are friendly and welcoming and you'll make quick friends if you use the local minivan public transit systems, especially if you enjoy listening to blasting reggae at breakneck speeds.

BASSETERRE

pop 12,604

Not the most attractive Caribbean capital, Basseterre garners at least a stop for most St Kitts visitors. Restaurants, shops, bars and museums line its crowded streets.

Information

Banks congregate around the Circus, and include First Caribbean International, Royal Bank of Canada and Scotiabank.

Cable & Wireless (Fort St; ☺ 8am-5pm Mon-Fri, to noon Sat) You can make international phone calls and send faxes and telegrams. Dial ☎ 355 to make credit-card calls.

JNF General (☎ 465-2551) The main hospital on St Kitts is at the west end of Cayon St.

Philatelic Bureau (Pelican Mall, Bay Rd) Colorful commemorative stamps are sold here, next door to the post office.

Post office (☎ 465-2521; Bay Rd; ☯ 8am-4pm Mon & Tue, 8am-3:30pm Wed-Fri) Next to Pelican Mall. Postcards to the US/Europe cost EC$0.80/1.20.

St Kitts Tourism Authority (☎ 465-4040; www.stkitts -tourism.com; Pelican Mall, Bay Rd) Sells tickets for the St Kitts Scenic Railway (see the boxed text, p470) and offers information on activities, accommodations and weddings.

Sunsurf Internet Café (☎ 466-5925; sunsurfcafé@caribsurf.com; Cellar, TDC Mall; ☯ 8am-8pm Mon-Sat, 2-7pm Sun)

Sights

The St Christopher Heritage Society is in the process of establishing a substantial **national museum** in the waterfront Treasury Building. It seems to be a long process, mainly due to hurricane damage to the building and the time expended sorting through the museum collection.

The displays will focus on the cultural and historical heritage of the islands. Check with the museum (if it's open) or the tourist office for opening times and admission prices.

Carib Breweries (☎ 465-2309), which brews the wonderful Carib beer, usually offers visitors an informal tour by appointment 10am to 2pm weekdays. The brewery is along the south side of the circle-island road just west of the hospital. There's no fee, but a tip to the tour guide is the norm.

Warner Park Stadium (☎ 466-2007; office ☯ 8.30am-4.30pm Mon-Fri, stadium closed until mid-2006) is in the middle of a massive refurbishment aimed at bringing the park up to international cricket standards, as it aims to host the Cricket World Cup in March, 2007. A few cricket matches will be held leading up to the big event.

Sleeping

BUDGET

Seaview Guest House (☎ 466-5298; seaview@caribsurf .com; Bay Rd; s/d from US$57/69; ☒) Conveniently located opposite the harbor-front and a stone's throw from the ferry terminal, Seaview has 10 rooms that are simple and clean, with private baths. A spotless kitchen is shared by guests.

Trinity Inn Apartments (☎ 465-3226; trinity@carib surf.com; apt US$70; ☒) Four miles (6.5km) west of Basseterre, at Palmetto Point. Housed in a small apartment building on the coastal road are 10 one-bedroom units with kitchens. There's also a pool.

MIDRANGE & TOP END

Ocean Terrace Inn (☎ 465-2754, in the US 800-524-0512, in the UK 0181-350-1000; www.oceanterraceinn .com; Fortlands; r $195-460, extra person aged over 12 per night US$40; ☒ ☒ ☒ ☒) This gently sprawling hotel drapes across a hill five minutes' walk from downtown. Frequented by business and tour groups, OTI (as it's known) boasts three pools set amid lush vegetation and flowering allamanda bushes. Rooms are corporate-looking but comfortable. Amenities include balconies in all rooms, kitchenettes in suites, daily shuttle to Turtle Beach, in-hotel spa, two restaurants featuring Caribbean dishes and seafood, plus full concierge to arrange any sport imaginable. In case Caribbean piracy makes an ugly comeback, head to the three 18th-century cannons gracing the rooftops.

Palms Hotel (☎ 465-0800; www.palmshotel.com; the Circus; ste US$95-180, extra person US$25; ☒) At the heart of Basseterre, this business hotel isn't anything particularly fancy, but the location can't be beat. Simple spacious rooms are comfortably but plainly furnished. Ask about winter discounts.

Eating & Drinking

Redi-Fried (Bay Rd; meals EC$10.50; ☯ until midnight) Next to the cinema, this hole-in-the-wall offers good ol' greasy fried chicken and fries for next-to-nothing prices.

Bambu's (☎ 466-5280; Bank St; breakfast US$6.95-9.25, meals US$5.75-9.65, coladas & daiquiris US$3-6) This popular café near the Circus has an arty decor and Basseterre's best coffee. It serves pizzas, burgers and all sorts of rum-infused drinks in a loud and colorful setting. Happy hour, from 5pm to 7pm Friday, serves up two-for-one Caribs and US$5 special drinks.

Ballahoo Restaurant (☎ 465-4197; breakfasts EC$20, lunch from EC$10-22, dinner EC$35-70; ☯ Mon-Sat) This popular restaurant has a cheery 2nd-floor balcony overlooking the Circus. Full breakfasts include Creole saltfish or pancakes with bacon. At lunch there are rotis, burgers and sandwiches, plus a meal of the day. Dinner offerings include vegetarian stuffed peppers, chicken kebabs, parrotfish fillet and lobster. A tasty treat is the tangy fresh-squeezed ginger beer.

Fisherman's Wharf (☎ 465-2754; meals US$18.50-28.50; ☯ dinner nightly) A good-value, fun place to eat with dining at picnic tables on a waterfront dock below Ocean Terrace Inn.

BASSETERRE

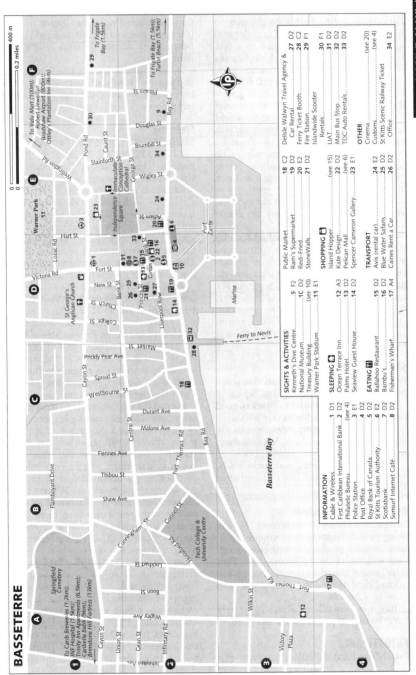

0   400 m
0   0.2 miles

INFORMATION

Cable & Wireless................................	1 D1
First Caribbean International Bank........	2 D2
Philatelic Bureau..............................	(see 4)
Police Station..................................	3 E1
Post Office......................................	4 D2
Royal Bank of Canada.......................	5 D2
St Kitts Tourism Authority..................	6 E2
Scotiabank......................................	7 D2
Sunsurf Internet Café.......................	8 D2

SIGHTS & ACTIVITIES

Kenneth's Dive Centre......................	9 F2
National Museum..............................	1C D2
Treasury Building..............................	(see 10)
Warner Park Stadium........................	11 E1

SLEEPING

Ocean Terrace Inn............................	12 A3
Palms Hotel.....................................	13 D2
Seaview Guest House.........................	14 D2

EATING

Ballahoo Restaurant..........................	15 D2
Bambu's...	16 D2
Fisherman's Wharf............................	17 A4
Public Market..................................	18 C2
Ram's Supermarket...........................	19 D2
Redi-Fried.......................................	20 E2
StoneWalls......................................	21 D2

SHOPPING

Island Hopper.................................	(see 15)
Kate Design....................................	22 D2
Pelican Mall....................................	(see 6)
Spencer Cameron Gallery..................	23 E1

TRANSPORT

Avis (rental car)...............................	24 E2
Blue Water Safaris............................	25 D2
Caines Rent a Car.............................	26 D2
Delisle Walwyn Travel Agency &	
Car Rental....................................	27 D2
Ferry Ticket Booth............................	28 C2
Fire Station.....................................	29 F1
Islandwide Scooter	
Rentals.......................................	30 F1
LIAT..	31 D2
Main Bus Stop.................................	32 D2
TDC Auto Rentals............................	33 D2

OTHER

Cinema..	(see 20)
Customs...	(see 4)
St Kitts Scenic Railway Ticket	
Office...	34 E2

Dinners, including freshly caught snapper fillet and lobster, are cooked to order over an open grill and accompanied by a self-service side buffet. Try the jerk chicken and wings in a tamarind barbecue sauce. Yum.

StoneWalls (☎ 465-5248; Princes St; dinner averages EC$50; ☾ dinner Mon-Sat) StoneWalls is easy to spot – just look for the stone walls! *Newsweek* listed it as one of the top bars in the world, which is saying something. This trendy pub, run by a Canadian-English couple, has a pleasant courtyard setting and offers Creole, Cajun and Caribbean cuisine. Stone-Walls also plays some great reggae and jazz, and is a pleasant place to meet chatty expats and locals alike. It's not the cheapest bar around, though. Reservations for dinner are suggested.

The green-walled, tin-roofed **public market** (Bay Rd) is the best place to pick up fruits and vegetables. There are a couple of grocery stores between the public market and the post office, including Ram's Supermarket, but the best food selection hands down is at the new **Valu Mart** (Wellington St), an American-style supermarket 0.3 miles (500m) north-east of the Cayon St traffic circle on the way to the airport.

Shopping

Pelican Mall (Bay Rd) There are duty-free shops here selling jewelry, watches and liquor.

Island Hopper (cnr Bank & Fort Sts) Stocks a good selection of Caribelle batiks (see p470).

Spencer Cameron Gallery (Independence Sq) On the north side of the square, has island artwork and prints at reasonable prices.

Kate Design (Bank St) Features attractive watercolors, prints, cards and silks by island artist Kate Spencer.

Getting There & Around

Basseterre is easily covered on foot. If you're using public transportation around the island, look for privately owned green mini-vans with an 'H' on the license plate. They usually leave from the main bus stop on Bay Rd and head around the circle-island road at no set schedule.

Buy your ferry tickets to Nevis at the ferry ticket booth just past the main bus stop.

FRIGATE BAY

Frigate Bay, located 3 miles (5km) southeast of Basseterre, is an isthmus with the calm Caribbean-side Frigate Bay Beach on one (the west) side and the condo-lined Frigate Beach North skirting the more treacherous Atlantic side.

Buses generally don't run to Frigate Bay, so if you don't have your own rental car you'll have to plan on doing some hefty walking or rely on taxis.

Sleeping

Angelus Resort (☎ 466-6224; www.angelusstkitts .com; r US$109-350, ste US$250-350, P ⊠ ⊡) It bills itself as 'The Angelus: A Caribbean Life-styles Resort' and can feel a bit cold, but the price, which plummets in the off season, is right. One of the only Leeward Island accommodations with in-room washer/dryer, studios also come with kitchenettes, VCRs and private balconies from which to admire the ocean, the mountains or a golf course. There's a Sunday beach barbecue and on-site spa. Check the website for rotating specials.

Timothy Beach Resort (☎ 465-8597, in the US & Canada 800-288-7991; www.timothybeachresort.com; r for 1-6 people US$120-345; P ⊠ ⊡) This extremely well-priced condo-style resort has a good beachside location on the east side of Frigate Bay Beach. Room price goes up depending on how good the view is, the number of people sharing the room, the number of kitchen amenities and how hot it is (ask about cheaper rates in summer).

Marriott (☎ 466-1200; http://marriott.com/property /propertypage/SKBRB; 858 Frigate Bay Rd; r from US$164; P ⊠ ⊠ ⊡) For a megaresort, this is not a bad choice at all, especially for those traveling with kids. For the little time you're in your room, you'll have a balcony overlooking the ocean (almost all rooms), massaging showerhead and 24-hour room service. Outside, if the beachfront location isn't enough, you'll also have three pools (one adults-only), a golf course, restaurants, activities desk, children's center and a huge full-service spa.

SeaLofts (☎ 465-1075; www.sealofts.com; units US$192-310; P ⊠ ⊡) The two-bedroom town house–style units each have a living room with sofa bed, wicker and rattan furnishings, dining area, full kitchen, large balcony, cable TV and a washing machine and dryer. It's on the beach, and there are two tennis courts and a pool. There's no housekeeping service and thus no service charge.

Eating & Drinking

Mr X's Shiggidy Shack (☎ 663-3983; burgers/lobster US$12/22) In addition to possessing the coolest name in restaurant history, this beachside restaurant/bar/snorkel- and beach chair–monger serves up tasty food and solid drinks. Mr X grills fresh lobster, shrimp and fish in his indoor restaurant, or you can have a burger beachside. Thursday night there's a bonfire and Saturday night has live music.

Monkey Bar (☎ 465-8050; bar menu US$12-24) Right on Frigate Bay Beach, this bar offers the regular St Kitts fare – chicken, fish-and-chips, lobster – but in a hut directly on the sand and serving drinks with names like Turkey on Speed, Screamin' Banshee and Magnetic Monkey.

PJ's Pizza Bar & Restaurant (☎ 465-8373; pizza from EC$19; ☯ dinner) Run by two Canadian women, this is a popular place with both eat-in and take-out service. PJ's also has sandwiches, salads, chili and lasagna and sometimes sells loaves of freshly baked whole-wheat and French bread. Happy hour is 6pm to 7pm, with the last Thursday of every month a tequila happy hour.

Dolce Cabana (☎ 465-1569; the Anchorage; salad/pasta/pizza US$7/13/10; ☯ closed Tue) Classic Italian fare is served with island flair in this popular party spot. Weekend nights have a special theme after dinner ends: Thursday and Sunday karaoke from 9pm to 1am, Friday is dance club, and Saturday changes from a live band to salsa.

Near PJ's Pizza Bar is a minimart, **Ram's** (☯ 9am-6pm Mon-Sat).

NORTHWEST COAST

Visitors will want to travel around the northwest coast of St Kitts by rental car, bus (green minivans) or take the St Kitts Scenic Railway (see the boxed text, p470). On the way you'll find **Bloody Point**, 4 miles (6.5km) west of Basseterre, the site where more than 2000 native Caribs were massacred by joint British and French forces in 1626. Legend has it the place received its name because so much blood was spilled – it ran for three days straight.

After Bloody Point the road swings down to the seaside village of **Old Road Town**, the landing site of the first British settlers in 1623. Amerindians left an earlier mark in the form of petroglyphs, and the 17th-century sugar estate has been turned into Caribelle Batik (p470).

As you continue from Brimstone Hill Fortress (below), you'll pass through lowlands of cane while circling **Mt Liamuiga**, the 3792ft (1137m) volcano that dominates the island's interior.

At the south end of Sadlers, you'll spot an old stone church down in the cane fields; shortly beyond that a sign points to **Black Rocks**. A short drive down that side road ends at coastal cliffs and a view of some seaside lava rock formations. The cliffs are only a five-minute walk from the circle-island road.

Brimstone Hill Fortress National Park

Grandiose **Brimstone Hill Fortress** (☎ 465-2609; foreign visitors adult/child US$8/4; ☯ 9:30am-5:30pm) offers a personal glimpse into the violent and tumultuous past of the former Caribbean colonies. The rambling 18th-century compound, which in its day was nicknamed the 'Gibraltar of the West Indies,' is one of the largest forts in the Caribbean. As a major British garrison, Brimstone Hill played a key role in battles with the French, who seized the fort in 1782 but returned it the next year under the terms of the Treaty of Paris. The treaty ushered in a more peaceful era, and by the 1850s the fort was abandoned.

After a fire swept through Basseterre in 1867, some of the fort structures were partially dismantled and the stones used to rebuild the capital. In the 1960s major restoration was undertaken, and much of the fortress has been returned to its earlier grandeur. Queen Elizabeth II inaugurated the fort as a national park during her visit to St Kitts in October 1985.

The main hilltop compound, the **Citadel**, is lined with 24 cannons and provides excellent views of St Eustatius and Sandy Point Town. Inside the Citadel's old barrack rooms are museum displays on colonial history that feature cannonballs, swords and other period odds and ends. There's also a small collection of Amerindian adzes, a few pottery fragments and a rubbing of the Carib petroglyphs in Old Road Town. Another room contains a display on the American Revolution and the West Indian role in that revolt.

Also worthwhile is the short stroll above the cookhouse to the top of Monkey Hill, which provides excellent coastal views. A small theater next to the gift shop plays a brief video on the fort's history; a nearby canteen sells drinks and sandwiches.

Brimstone Hill, upon which the fortress stands, is an 800ft (240m) volcanic cone named for the odoriferous sulfur vents you will undoubtedly detect as you drive past the hill along the coastal road.

GETTING THERE & AWAY

Buses from Basseterre to Sandy Point Town can drop you off at the signposted road leading up to the fortress, from where it's a half mile (800m) uphill walk on a narrow, winding road. If you're driving up, be sure to beep your horn as you approach blind curves.

Caribelle Batik

The drive to this outstanding **historic manor and shop** (☎ 465-6253; 🕑 8:30am-4pm Mon-Fri) is a history lesson in itself. Just past the nursery school on Wingfield Rd are several large black stones with petroglyphs. Beyond those you'll come across the ruins of a mill. The shop itself is at Romney Manor, site of a 17th-century plantation at Old Road Town. Watch a batik demonstration or purchase high-quality batik clothing, including shirts, pareus and skirts, from the store.

Sleeping

Rawlins Plantation (☎ 465-6221; www.rawlins plantation.com; s/d US$370/480; 🕑 often closes Aug & Sep; P 🖳 🖭) This former sugar estate fits sublimely into its new incarnation as the most gracious of St Kitts' plantation inns, including creating a romantic honeymoon suite out of a stone windmill. Other accommodations are in comfortable cottages with wooden floors, four-poster beds and separate sitting rooms or verandas. Those looking for peace and quiet will appreciate the calm-inducing lack of TV, air-conditioning and telephone, as well as the art studio and drapery of tropical fruit and greenery. The rates for the 10 rooms include breakfast, afternoon tea and dinner. The plantation is toward Mt Liamuiga, 1 mile (1.6km) up a signposted cane road that begins half a mile (800m) east of St Paul's.

Golden Lemon (☎ 465-7260; www.goldenlemon .com; s/d incl breakfast in winter from US$220/325, villas from US$325; P 🖭) If you like the idea of staying at a historic property but want to be at the beach, this fits both bills. Each room in the 17th-century manor house is decorated differently, one in deep russet, the next in candied yellow, all with antique touches like rattan rocking chairs and vaulted plank ceilings. Modern villas circle the beachfront, and a plunge pool graces each one. There are fabulous summer and fall honeymoon packages, but keep in mind that the romantic Great House is more historic than it is soundproof.

Ottley's Plantation Inn (☎ 465-7234, in the US 800-772-3039; www.ottleys.com; r incl breakfast from US$290, cottage US$480; P 🔀 🖭) Pretend you're a 19th-century sugar plantation baron or baroness as you play croquet on the lawn at this grandest of inns. Each room is furnished individually in tasteful colonial decor. Cottages come with a private plunge pool (and sometimes a lounging resident cat). The Mango Orchard Spa (also open to nonguests) faces a forested ravine, making this perhaps the only place in the world where one can watch monkeys frolic during a pedicure. Specials for stays over five nights.

Eating

Rawlins Plantation (lunch buffet/dinner EC$65/120; 🕑 lunch, 1 seating for dinner 8pm) With its splendid

---

ST KITTS SCENIC RAILWAY

If you can get past the cheesiness of the onboard 'St Kitts Railway choir' and the only train to have its own theme song, the double-decker **St Kitts Scenic Railway** (☎ 465-7263; www.st kittsscenicrailway.com; Bay Rd, Basseterre; adult/child US$89/44.50) can be a delightful way to see the entire island, especially for the whole family. Tickets are available at hotels, the tourist office and the station; trains usually run at 9:30am and 1pm or 1:30pm.

The narrow-gauge tracks, built between 1912 and 1926 to haul sugarcane from plantations to Basseterre, are still used for sugarcane production. The track passes by Brimstone Hill Fortress, sugar plantations and beautiful vistas of rainforest, beaches and neighboring islands. A three-minute walk from the airport, this three-hour journey is a good bet for those with afternoon flights, as bags can be stowed, or to see the island from the bottom deck on a rainy day. It even has fabulously clean toilets!

view across cane fields to St Eustatius, this plantation inn (see opposite) is the choice place to have lunch on a circle-island tour. The West Indian lunch buffet, served daily on the patio, includes numerous dishes, such as chicken and breadfruit curry, beef brochettes, flying-fish fritters and fresh-fruit sorbet. Dinner, a set four-course meal, is available by reservation only.

Golden Lemon (lunch EC$30-45, dinner around EC$120) Lunch offerings at this manor house (see opposite) include salads, sandwiches and fish-and-chips. Dinner, by reservation only, changes daily but commonly includes a seafood main dish complete with appetizer, soup and dessert.

Royal Palm Restaurant (breakfast/lunch/dinner US$14/17/68) At Ottley's Plantation Inn (opposite), this restaurant has alfresco dining within the partial stone walls of a former sugar warehouse. Try the Palm's famous banana pancakes for breakfast (US$9.95) or come on Sunday for the champagne brunch. The lunch menu features simple sandwiches and salads, as well as local gourmet items such as coconut-crusted chicken and plantains. At dinner a four-course meal is offered.

Sprat Net Bar & Grill (☎ 465-6314; Old Road Bay; lobster dinner EC$52, with ribs EC$62, with chicken EC$62; ⊗ closed Mon & Tue) A trip to St Kitts wouldn't be complete without a visit to this institution. About 20 extended picnic tables are packed all night with tourists, expats and locals, all enjoying the sunset, camaraderie, drinks and food that's as simple as it is good. Lobster comes with not much more than corn on the cob and a big cup of melted butter to ensure it melts in your mouth. The restaurant is tucked along Old Road Bay, and the parking can be difficult.

SOUTHEAST PENINSULA

St Kitts' southeast peninsula is a scrubby wild plain filled with expansive, white-sand beaches, grassy hills, barren salt ponds and the occasional meandering cow. A decade-old road now allows non-nautical day-trippers to venture around this starkly contrasting part of St Kitts, but much of the land remains free of development. Come here for the best chance of green vervet monkey spotting.

Many dirt paths off the main road lead to beaches and hikes. As you're coming over the hill from Frigate Bay, take the first right

at the post for Shipwreck Bar & Grill, which will lead you to **South Friar's Beach**, a calm bay with a refreshingly uncluttered beach. Stop in for a Carib at Business' Shack, where you can lime away an afternoon with a few drinks, a pile of beach chairs, or chatting with Business himself. Up ahead, a dirt track off to the left leads to **Sand Bank Bay**, a quiet, sheltered beach; taking the later left fork leads to **Cockleshell Bay**, a gray-sand beach with a stunning view of Nevis. This road will eventually lead to **Turtle Beach**, the only development on the Southeast Peninsula, and most visitors' reason for heading here.

It's best to get to this part of the island by car. The Ocean Terrace Inn (p466) in Basseterre runs a shuttle here on non–cruise ship days.

Sleeping & Eating

Turtle Beach Bar & Grill (☎ 465-9086; www.turtlebeach 1.com; apt US$150, weekly US$900, 2nd bedroom per night US$50; ⓟ ⊗) As the only edifice of substance on the peninsula, this all-encompassing bar, hotel, apartment and water-sports mecca at Turtle Beach is second to none. There are two superb apartments available for rent up the hill from the restaurant, each with a full kitchen, large living room and huge deck with great views of Nevis and the bay. The restaurant's conch ceviche and lobster sandwich are worth the trip alone (meals US$7 to US$19). Spend hours enjoying the beach-hangout feel, free kayaks or photo opportunities of food-stealing monkeys. If 400 cruise passengers don't sound like your ideal dining companions, call ahead to see if a ship has booked the restaurant.

NEVIS

Nevis is smaller and more laid-back than its former federation-mate, and some prefer it to St Kitts. Sugar plantations, white sandy beaches and a top-notch botanical garden create a good amount of low-key sightseeing, and a range of horseback riding and windsurfing options keep the body active. A paved road circles the island, and car rentals are inexpensive, making it easy to explore Nevis on a day trip. The island has a forested interior rising to scenic Nevis Peak, which is often cloaked in clouds. The coastal lowlands, where the larger villages are located,

---

GET HITCHED IN PARADISE

Want to get married on a white sandy beach or on a plantation overlooking the ocean? Nevis specializes in cozy weddings and romantic honeymoons, and most upper-end hotels offer special packages. Brides and grooms will need to adhere to a few regulations, but the tourist office (below) or hotel of choice will work with future Mr and Mrs to arrange wedding co-ordinators, marriage officers and locations.

---

are much drier and support bougainvillea, hibiscus and other flowering bushes that attract numerous hummingbirds.

CHARLESTOWN

pop 1700

The ferry from St Kitts docks next to the center of Nevis' capital, where all of the government and business structures coexist with tourist facilities and sweet gingerbread Victorians.

The greater Charlestown area can be readily explored on foot – the museums and the Bath House are within walking distance. Just a 15-minute jaunt north of the center will put you on a lovely stretch of Pinney's Beach that's lined with coconut trees and invites long strolls.

Information

You will find banks north of the tourist office on Main St, including Barclays and Scotiabank.

Alexandra Hospital (☎ 469-5473; Government Rd)

Downtown Cybercafé (☎ 469-1981; Main St; Internet per 15min US$5, long-distance calls to US or Europe per min EC$1.65; ☼ 8am-6pm Mon-Sat) Check your email or call abroad, accompanied by a sandwich or drink. It's across from the museum.

Nevis Tourist Office (☎ 469-7550, in the US 866-55-NEVIS; www.nevisisland.com; ☼ 8am-4pm Mon-Fri, 9am-1pm Sat) A two-minute walk east of the pier. It's packed with staff and helpful brochures to help sort out just about any question.

Philatelic Bureau (☼ 8am-4pm Mon-Fri) Commemorative stamps are sold here, near the public market.

Post office (☎ 469-5521; Main St; ☼ 8am-3:30pm)

Sights & Activities

Occupying a Georgian-style building at the site where American statesman Alexander Hamilton was born in 1757, is the pleasant little **Museum of Nevis History** (☎ 469-5786; Main St; admission US$2, combined with Horatio Nelson Museum US$3; ☼ 8am-4pm Mon-Fri, 9am-noon Sat). In addition to portraits of Hamilton, this museum has period photos with interpretive captions and other bits and pieces of Nevis culture and history. Shady grounds offer a lovely picnic or rest spot.

A couple of minutes' walk up Government Rd from the town center is a small and largely forgotten **Jewish cemetery**, which consists of a grassy field of horizontal gravestones. The oldest stone dates from 1684, and quite a few others date from the early 18th century, when an estimated 25% of the nonslave population on Nevis was Jewish. In addition, it's now believed that the site of the original synagogue, which may be the oldest in the Caribbean, has been identified. An excavation is currently being undertaken about 75yd (68m) south of the cemetery; to get there, take the dirt path that begins opposite the cemetery's southwest corner and follow it to the **ruins** just beyond the government offices.

The **Horatio Nelson Museum** (☎ 469-0408; Building Hill Rd; adult/child US$2/1; ☼ 9am-4pm Mon-Fri, 10am-1pm Sat), about 100yd (91m) east of the old Bath House, contains memorabilia relating to Lord Nelson, who stopped off on this island in the 1780s, where he met and married Fanny Nisbett, the nièce of the island's governor. This former private collection consists largely of mugs and dishes painted with Nelson's image, ceramic statues of the admiral and a few everyday items once used by him.

The **Bath House** was the first hotel built in the Caribbean, in 1778. Now being turned into government offices, its mineral-laden springs below brought spa-goers here in colonial days. The springhouse is now closed, but you can join the locals and bathe in the stream that runs below the Bath House. Women will want to take caution going alone or at night.

Sleeping

Daniel's Deck (☎ 469-5265; s/d US$38/58) Not the cleanest place on the island, but it's cheap, central and most rooms have kitchenettes. All have fans and private baths. The owner, Roosevelt Daniel, can also arrange short-term apartment rentals. To avoid street noise, ask for room 1, 3, 4, 6 or 7.

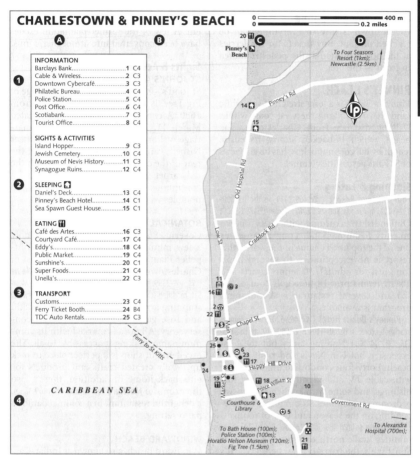

CHARLESTOWN & PINNEY'S BEACH

INFORMATION		
Barclays Bank	1	C4
Cable & Wireless	2	C3
Downtown Cybercafé	3	C3
Philatelic Bureau	4	C4
Police Station	5	C4
Post Office	6	C4
Scotiabank	7	C3
Tourist Office	8	C4

SIGHTS & ACTIVITIES		
Island Hopper	9	C3
Jewish Cemetery	10	C4
Museum of Nevis History	11	C3
Synagogue Ruins	12	C4

SLEEPING		
Daniel's Deck	13	C4
Pinney's Beach Hotel	14	C1
Sea Spawn Guest House	15	C1

EATING		
Café des Artes	16	C3
Courtyard Café	17	C4
Eddy's	18	C4
Public Market	19	C4
Sunshine's	20	C1
Super Foods	21	C4
Unella's	22	C3

TRANSPORT		
Customs	23	C4
Ferry Ticket Booth	24	B4
TDC Auto Rentals	25	C3

Sea Spawn Guest House (☎ 469-5239; seaspawn@ yahoo.com; r US$40-60, discount for longer stays; P 💻) Rooms here are simple, clean and less than 0.6 miles (1km) from both the town and Pinney's Beach. The dedicated owners are upgrading many rooms and adding high-speed Internet. Upstairs rooms have aircon, downstairs rooms come with ceiling fans. There are shared kitchen facilities, and a refrigerator in each room.

Eating

Courtyard Café (breakfast & lunch around EC$12; ⊙ Mon-Sat) Serves local fare in a quiet garden courtyard shaded by banana trees, including breakfast pancakes and lunchtime sandwiches and burgers.

Eddy's (☎ 469-5958; dishes EC$12-25) The food is equally as fun as the atmosphere here. Run by a Canadian–West Indian couple, Eddy's has a pleasant 2nd-floor veranda dining area that overlooks Main St. There's homemade soup and bread, salads and burgers, and chicken stir-fry. Wednesday night is party night, from around 7:30pm till the last person leaves.

Unella's (☎ 469-5574; dishes EC$41-60) A 2nd-floor open-air restaurant, it has good views of St Kitts and a fine selection of seafood dishes, such as fish of the day, snapper and lobster.

The best place to go for produce is the **public market** (⊙ 7am-4:30pm Mon-Sat). **Super Foods** (⊙ 8am-8pm Mon-Sat), at the south side of Main St, is the island's biggest supermarket.

Getting There & Around

Charlestown is tiny so everything can be reached on foot. Buy tickets for the ferries at the booth located at the pedestrian area in front of the pier.

PINNEY'S BEACH

Pinney's Beach is a long stretch of soft white sand that runs along the west coast within walking distance from Charlestown. The beach, which is backed almost its entire length by tall coconut palms, has lovely views of St Kitts across the channel.

Sleeping & Eating

Four Seasons Resort (☎ 469-1111, in the US 800-332-3442, in Canada 800-268-6282; r from US$895-5800) Outlandishly luxurious with every known amenity to humankind. Long regarded as one of the top hotel chains in the world, this resort is no exception, with several pools (one just for adults), 10 tennis courts and a staff tennis pro, 18-hole golf course, full spa and several restaurants. A children's program is available.

Pinney's Beach Hotel (☎ 469-5207; www.pinneys beachhotel.com; s US$50-110, d US$80-170, tr US$105-215; P ☒ ☒) Nothing fancy but the least expensive hotel in Nevis and right on the beach. Forty-four condo-like units all come with cable TV and slightly depressing furnishings, and some with kitchenettes or two bedrooms for families. Room prices vary depending on the season and type of room.

Sunshine's (☎ 469-5817; meals EC$14-20) Ten minutes' walk north on Pinney's Beach is Sunshine's, the party-central beach bar. It's stumbling distance to the ocean and a fun place to hang out (the photos on the walls are comment enough), and many expats and locals do just that. The food – a selection of fish, chicken and lobster dishes – is quite good, but is overshadowed by the legendary drink served here: the Killer Bee. It's a secret concoction of the bar owner, Sunshine, tasting like a nice fruit punch but with a kick like a very large mule.

SOUTH NEVIS

The circle-island road crosses the southern part of Nevis between cloud-shrouded Nevis Peak and Saddle Hill, passing through the districts of Fig Tree and Gingerland. This area was the center of Nevis' sugar industry in colonial days, and there are many

crumbling sugar-mill stacks to evoke that era. A few of the former plantation estates have been converted into atmospheric inns.

Sights & Activities

ST JOHN'S ANGLICAN CHURCH

St John's, on the main road in the village of Fig Tree, is a stone church that dates from 1680. A copy of the church register, dated March 11, 1787, which records the marriage of Lord Horatio Nelson and Frances Nisbett, can be found in a glass case at the rear of the church. If you peek beneath the red carpet in the center aisle you'll find a continuous row of tombstones of island notables who died in the 1700s.

BOTANICAL GARDENS OF NEVIS

Covering 8 acres (3.2 hectares) of land only a few minutes' drive southwest of Montpelier Plantation Inn and just southeast of Charlestown, the **Botanical Gardens of Nevis** (☎ 469-3399; adult/child US$9/4; ☒ 9am-4:30pm Mon-Sat, modified schedule Apr-Oct) displays a rare and stunning array of tropical greenery, orchid and rose gardens, and a rain-forest conservatory. All flora is marked with its common name, making it accessible to all. The excellent gift shop is a perfect place to pick up locally created crafts and products for gifts back home. In addition, there's also the exquisite **Martha's Tea House** (☎ 469-3860), a delightful restaurant in a colonial bamboo patio setting.

WINDWARD BEACH

Windward Beach, also known as Indian Castle Beach, is the only easily accessible beach on the southern part of the island. Backed by beach morning glory and low scrubby trees, it has fine gray sand and fairly active surf. Unless it's a weekend, the odds are good that, with the exception of a few rummaging goats, you'll have the beach to yourself.

To get there, turn south at the Gingerland Post Office in Market Shop and follow the signs.

HORSE RACING

On the way to Windward Beach is the **horse-racing track**, for a Nevisian pastime that takes place on various holidays during the year. The jockeys train throughout most of the year. Whether you're lucky enough to arrive during a race holiday (contact the tourist office in Charlestown for dates) or you just happen upon a training session at this makeshift track, the view of Windward Beach in the background is stunning.

NEVISIAN HERITAGE VILLAGE

Nevisian Heritage Village (☎ 469-5521; Stoney Grove; adult/child EC$8/2.50; ☺ 9am-3:30pm Mon-Sat) is a collection of cottages that gives visitors a view of the social evolution of Nevisian history dating back to Carib times. Homes and shops are outfitted with period antiques and artisan displays. Not to be missed during Culturama (see p478) when residents engage in the old traditions.

Sleeping

Montpelier Plantation Inn (☎ 469-3462; www.mont peliernevis.com; r incl breakfast & afternoon tea US$400-696; P ☒) This 17th-century inn has hosted Horatio Nelson's wedding in 1787 and Princess Diana, but still somehow manages to create a balance between regal and casual. The recently built cottages don't have the romance from the outside, but all 17 rooms are exquisitely decorated with sleep-til-noon beds and every amenity, including DVD players, black-out drapes and luxurious toiletries. Spa services are available. Daily activities include playing beach cricket with the plantation dogs and falling asleep with one of the many library books in the outdoor reading gazebo.

    Golden Rock Plantation Inn (☎ 469-3346; www .golden-rock.com; s/d/tr US$195/210/290, Sugar Mill d US$275; P ☐ ☒) Enjoy the golden glow from the towering Nevis Peak as you sip your afternoon tea on the bougainvillea-covered grounds. The owner's great-great-great-great-grandfather built the lava-stone sugar plantation by hand in the 1810s. Spend an enchanted vacation in a cottage once used as a mill for grinding sugarcane, now a two-level stone suite with a bamboo staircase and four-poster bed. There's a spring-fed pool, tennis court, nature trails and a complimentary beach and town shuttle. Specializes in weddings and honeymoons.

    Hermitage (☎ 469-3477, in the US 800-682-4025; www.hermitagenevis.com; Gingerland; cottage incl breakfast US$325-450, Manor House villa US$790; P ☒) The main plantation house, which is 260 years old and furnished with antiques, serves as a parlor and evening gathering spot. The cottages are pleasantly rustic, with canopied beds, hardwood floors, sitting rooms, ceiling fans, minirefrigerators and lattice-shuttered windows. There's a pool, tennis court and horse treks, but a hammock on each cottage porch beckons.

Eating

Hermitage (lunch around US$25, dinner prix fixe US$50) The restaurant in this plantation house (see left) has pleasant open-air dining. The dinner menu offers a choice of a prix fixe (fixed-price) meal with dishes such as yellowfin carpaccio with ginger, sesame and soy, and pasta with lime cream and caviar. Lunch is a more simple affair, with sandwiches, rotis and salads.

    Montpelier Plantation Inn (lunch/dinner US$14/54) This inn (see left) has a casual terrace where lunch is served and includes sandwiches, chef salads and simple pastas. Dinner is a deluxe prix fixe meal of local dishes and spices.

    Golden Rock Plantation Inn (☎ 469-3346; ☺ lunch & dinner) Has outdoor dining at this inn (see left;) on a cobblestone patio. At lunch, lobster salad (US$20.50) is a specialty, and there are sandwiches from US$6.50. Dinner features a changing four-course meal and requires advance reservations.

OUALIE BEACH

Oualie Beach is a long, laid-back strip of gray sand fronted by waters that are shallow and generally calm. The Oualie Beach Resort has a dive and water-sports shop.

Sleeping & Eating

Oualie Beach Resort (☎ 469-9735; www.oualiebeach .com; d US$245-295, s 10% less; P ☒ ☒) The family who runs Oualie Beach has been on Nevis

---

for 350 years. Classic Caribbean ginger-bread, as the room price goes up, so do the amenities. Starting with at least a queen four-poster mahogany bed and ocean-view patio, deluxe rooms and studios also have kitchenettes, king beds and VCRs. Can be combined for family suites.

Hurricane Cove Bungalows (☎ 469-9462; hcove@caribsurf.com; 1-/2-bedroom cottage from US$200/300; **P** **⊠**) Has a cliff-top location at the north end of Oualie Beach. Accommodations are in pleasantly rustic wooden cottages, each with a kitchen, porch and ceiling fan. In winter a minimum one-week stay is required; at other times, a minimum three-night stay is mandatory.

DIRECTORY

ACCOMMODATIONS

Hotels on St Kitts & Nevis add a 7% government tax, a 2% island enhancement tax, and normally a 10% service charge onto room rates.

There are several resorts on each island, but most accommodations are still small-scale hotels, grand plantation inns, inexpensive guesthouses or condominiums. Hotels on Nevis start around US$200, with the exception of several guesthouses and Pinney's Beach Hotel.

PRACTICALITIES

■ **Newspapers & Magazines** There are three local newspapers: the weekly *Democrat* and *Observer* and the bi-weekly *Labour Spokesman*. The annual *St Kitts & Nevis Visitor* is a good source of general tourist information and can be picked up free at tourist offices and hotels.

■ **Radio** For local radio try FM 90.3, 96.0 or 98.9 for reggae, soca, calypso or island music.

■ **Electricity** Most electric current is 220V, 60 cycles; many hotels supply electricity at 110V.

■ **Weights & Measures** Imperial. Speed-limit signs are in miles, as are rental-car odometers.

EMERGENCIES

Ambulance & Police (☎ 911)

Camping is technically allowed, but neither island is set up with facilities. Contact the tourist board to inquire.

ACTIVITIES
Beaches & Swimming

The islands' beaches have a hard time competing with the white stretches found on Anguilla and Antigua, but there are reasonable strands on St Kitts and a couple of attractive options on Nevis.

St Kitts' best beaches are on the south end of the island at Frigate Bay, Friar's Bay and in the sheltered bays of the southeast peninsula. Beaches along the main body of the island are thin strands of black and gray sands.

On Nevis, Pinney's Beach, which runs north from Charlestown, has a Robinson Crusoe look and feel. It's long and lovely, backed by coconut palms.

There's also a pleasant little beach at Oualie Bay.

Diving & Snorkeling
ST KITTS

St Kitts has healthy, expansive reefs and varied marine life that includes rays, barracuda, garden eels, nurse sharks, sea turtles, sea fans, giant barrel sponges and black coral.

One popular dive spot is Sandy Point Bay, below Brimstone Hill, with an array of corals, sponges and reef fish as well as some coral-encrusted anchors from the colonial era. Among a handful of wreck dives is the 148ft (44.5m) freighter *River Taw,* which sank in 50ft (15m) of water in 1985 and now harbors soft corals and reef fish.

Pro-Divers (☎ 869-466-DIVE; prodiver@caribsurf .com), at Turtle Beach, offers single-tank dives for US$60, two-tank dives for US$90, night dives for US$70, a three-day Professional Association of Diving Instructors (PADI) certification course for US$350 and a half-day snorkeling trip for US$35.

Two other dive operations that offer similar services and rates:

Frigate Bay Divers (☎ 466-8413; Frigate Beach)
Kenneth's Dive Centre (☎ 465-2670, in the US 732-787-8130; Bay Rd) On the east side of Basseterre.

White House Bay, on the southeast peninsula of St Kitts, is a favorite place for snorkeling.

All of the dive companies rent snorkel gear for around US$10 a day, as does **Mr X's Watersports** (☎ 465-4995) at Frigate Bay Beach, which also offers a snorkeling tour for US$20 to US$25.

NEVIS

Nevis' diving scene is a low-key affair, with an emphasis on untouched coral reefs that are seldom visited by divers.

Two popular diving sites are Monkey Shoals, a densely covered reef close to Oualie Beach, and Devil's Caves, on the western side of the island, with coral grottoes and underwater lava tubes in 40ft (12m) of water.

Scuba Safaris (☎ 469-9518; scubanevis@caribsurf .com), at Oualie Beach, offers single-tank dives for US$45, two-tank dives for US$80, night dives for US$70 and also a half-day snorkeling trip for US$35.

Hiking

Both St Kitts and Nevis have an abundance of untouched native vegetation, a good selection of easy and tough treks, and great views from the mountainous interiors. Tracks on St Kitts and Nevis are not well defined, but there are moves to improve the tracks, and it's advisable to do any major trekking with a guide.

Greg's Safaris (☎ 869-465-412; g-safari@caribsurf .com) has a half-day hike into the rainforest of St Kitts for US$40. The guide moves at a comfortable pace suitable for all ages, identifies flora and fauna, and stops to sample fruits along the way. Greg's also offers a full-day tour of Mt Liamuiga volcano for US$80, including lunch.

For a more local feel, try **Glenn Wing** (☎ 466-8830), a one-man hiking guide. A hike through the rainforest up to the Mt Liamuiga crater costs US$35.

On Nevis, **Top to Bottom** (☎ 469-9080; walk nevis@caribsurf.com) offers a choice of well over a dozen hikes, ranging from walks to estate ruins, monkey-spotting hikes in the jungle and the more strenuous hikes to the top of Nevis Peak. Each outing costs US$20, except for the mud-sliding and leg-aching treks to Nevis Peak, which cost from US$30 to US$40.

Horseback Riding

Nevis' horseback rides have a much better reputation than St Kitts.

Rides start at around US$30 for one hour.

Head out to the beach, up to the mountain or both with **Hermitage Plantation Inn** (☎ 469-3477), which also offers carriage rides, or **Nevis Equestrian Centre** (☎ 469-8118; Cotton Ground).

Mountain Biking

Mountain-bike rentals are available on Nevis for US$20 a day from **Winston Crooke** (☎ 469-9682), at Oualie Beach Resort (p475).

Windsurfing

Oualie Bay, at the northwest side of Nevis, catches the trade winds and offers a sandy launch in shallow waters that's good for beginners. There are also opportunities for wave jumping and other advanced techniques.

Windsurfing Nevis (☎ 469-9682), at Oualie Beach, rents out boards for US$20/35 for one/two hours, US$65 a day, and offers beginner lessons for US$50.

Other Water Sports

Mr X's Watersports (☎ 465-4995), on Frigate Bay Beach, rents Sunfish and Hobie Cat sailboats for US$20 to US$30 an hour, offers water skiing for US$15 a circuit, and provides a shuttle to South Friar's Bay for US$5 round-trip. Unlimited snorkeling, sailing, windsurfing, kayaking, and boogie boarding for one day is available for US$60, or four days for US$150.

For kayaking on Nevis, check with **Windsurfing Nevis** (☎ 469-9682) at Oualie Beach.

DANGERS & ANNOYANCES

Common sense should prevail while walking around Basseterre at night.

There has been a spate of strong-arm robberies, especially against the women of Ross University, the veterinary medical school on St Kitts. Be especially careful driving at night.

EMBASSIES & CONSULATES

UK (☎ 0207-937-9522; 10 Kensington Court, 2nd fl, London W85DL)

USA (☎ 202-606-2636, 3216 New Mexico Ave NW, Washington, DC 20016)

FESTIVALS & EVENTS

St Kitts Music Festival (last week in June) This four-day festival brings together top-name calypso, soca, reggae, salsa, jazz and gospel performers from throughout the Caribbean.

Culturama (late July to early August) Nevis has been celebrating this week-long event for over 30 years. It features music, crafts, and beauty and talent pageants, culminating with a parade on Culturama Tuesday.

Carnival (December 24 to January 3) The biggest yearly event on St Kitts, with 10 days of calypso competitions, costumed street dances and steel-band music. Many businesses are closed during this period.

HOLIDAYS

Public holidays on St Kitts & Nevis include the following:

New Year's Day January 1
Good Friday Late March/early April
Easter Monday Late March/early April
Labour Day First Monday in May
Whit Monday Eighth Monday after Easter
Queen's Birthday Second Saturday in June
August Monday First Monday in August
Independence Day September 19
Christmas Day December 25
Boxing Day December 26

MAPS

On St Kitts, the tourist office's *Road Map & Guide* will suffice for most visitors. On Nevis, the *Journey Map* covers practically every crevice on the island and has a detailed road map of both the island and Charlestown. Both maps are available at most hotels, the tourist offices and many shops.

MONEY

The official currency is the Eastern Caribbean dollar, and although US dollars are accepted almost everywhere, ATMs don't carry them on either island. Instead, most large banks will allow you to receive dollars from an inside teller for a US$5 fee.

Hotels and restaurants add a 7% tax and usually a 10% service charge as well. When a restaurant doesn't add a service charge, a 10% tip is appropriate.

POST

When mailing a letter to the islands, follow the addressee's name with the town and then 'St Kitts, West Indies' or 'Nevis, West Indies.'

TELEPHONE

Local numbers have seven digits; St Kitts numbers start with ☎ 465 or ☎ 466 and Nevis numbers with ☎ 469. To make a local call, dial all seven digits. When calling the islands from overseas, dial your country's international access code + the country code ☎ 869 + the local number. We have included only the seven-digit local number in St Kitts & Nevis listings in this chapter.

For directory assistance, phone ☎ 411.

TOURIST INFORMATION
Local Tourist Offices

Nevis Tourist Office (☎ 469-7550, in the US 866-55-NEVIS; www.nevisisland.com; Charlestown; ☷ 8am-4pm Mon-Fri, 9am-1pm Sat)
St Kitts Tourism Authority (☎ 465-4040; www.stkitts-tourism.com; Pelican Mall, Bay Rd, Basseterre)

Tourist Offices Abroad

Canada (☎ 416-368-6707; fax 416-368-3934; 365 Bay St, St 806, Toronto, Ontario M5H 2V1)
Germany (☎ 0603-173-76-30; fax 06031-72 50 81; Leonhardstrasse 22, D-61169 Friedberg)
UK (☎ 0207-376-0881; fax 020-7937 3611; 10 Kensington Court, London W8 5DL)
USA (☎ 212-535-1234, 800-582-6208; fax 212-734-6511; 414 East 75th St, New York, NY 10021)

TOURS

Blue Water Safaris (☎ 466-4933; Princes St, Basseterre, St Kitts) Full-day catamaran cruises for US$65, with snorkeling, lunch on Pinney's Beach, and an open bar thrown in. Sunset and moonlight cruises are US$40 per person, and half-day fishing trips for a maximum of six persons cost US$350.

Kantours (☎ 465-2098; St Kitts) A somewhat mass-market outfit offering half-day circle-island tours for around US$60, as well as deep-sea fishing and catamaran cruises.

Leeward Island Charters (☎ 465-7474; St Kitts) This class act offers a full day of snorkeling and lunch on the *Spirit of St Kitts* catamaran for US$71.50/35.75 for adults/children, as well as sunset cruises for US$45 with complimentary appetizers.

TRANSPORTATION

GETTING THERE & AWAY
Entering St Kitts & Nevis

Visitors from most countries need only a passport to enter St Kitts or Nevis (US citizens see the boxed text, p772), as well as a round-trip or onward ticket.

Air

St Kitts' newly expanded international airport, **Robert Llewellyn Bradshaw Airport** (SKM; ☎ 465-8121), located on the northern outskirts of Basseterre, takes a few large jets.

Nevis International Airport (NEV; ☎ 469-9040), in Newcastle, is a small operation with Winair, LIAT, Nevis Express, Carib Aviation, an ATM and a couple of charter desks.

For information on traveling from outside the Caribbean to/from St Kitts and Nevis, see p776. Most travel to the area is via other Caribbean islands with the following airlines:

American Eagle (☎ 800-433-7300; www.aa.com; hub San Juan, Puerto Rico)

British West Indies Airways (BWIA; ☎ 465-6163; www.bwee.com; hub Trinidad)

Carib Aviation (☎ on St Kitts 465-3055, on Nevis 469-9295; www.candoo.com/carib; hub Antigua)

Caribbean Star (☎ 469-5426; www.flycaribbeanstar .com; hub Antigua)

Caribbean Sun (☎ 465-5929; www.flycsa.com; hub San Juan, Puerto Rico)

LIAT (☎ on St Kitts 465-2286, on Nevis 469-9333; www.liatairline.com; hub Antigua)

Winair (☎ 465-2186; www.fly-winair.com; hub St Martin)

Sea

CRUISE SHIP

Numerous cruise ships visit St Kitts; they dock at Basseterre's deep-water harbor. It can be a good idea to email the tourist office when you know your travel dates to get the cruise schedule, as certain places such as Turtle Beach or the St Kitts Scenic Railway are virtually inaccessible or shut entirely to noncruise passengers.

YACHT

The two ports of entry are Basseterre and Charlestown. On both islands, customs is near the ferry dock and is open 8am to noon and 1pm to 4pm Monday to Friday. Yachters will need cruising permits to visit other anchorages and a special pass to go between the two islands.

GETTING AROUND

Boat

As there is currently no air service between the islands, the ferry is your only choice, besides hiring a fisherman. Ferries range from simple barge-like boats to air-conditioned indoor comfort. Companies change hands often, but the general timetable remains the same. To check the ferry schedule from either island, dial ☎ 466-4636.

Ferries generally run from 7am to 5pm with concentrations around 7:30am, 1pm and 3:30pm to 5pm. There are often later ferries on Friday and Saturday nights and no midday ferry on Sunday. They leave from the marina area on Bay Rd in Basseterre and two blocks from the tourist office in Charlestown. Rates range from US$8 to US$22 round-trip.

Thomas Martin (☎ 664-8142) is a friendly Rasta fisherman in Dieppe Bay by the Golden Lemon in St Kitts who runs boat charters to St Barth, Nevis and Statia for travelers with a sense of adventure who don't mind getting a little wet. Price is negotiable but a one-way trip on his trusty speedboat to Statia costs about US$25.

Bus

On St Kitts, the buses are privately owned minivans and are hard to miss. They're usually careening around corners at breakneck speeds, blasting out hip-hop and reggae beats, and with reassuring names such as 'The Terminator' or 'Love Bus' splattered across the wind-shield. In Basseterre, most leave from the bus stop on Bay Rd. Fares range from EC$2 to EC$5.

Bus service is fairly sporadic and there's no schedule, although buses are generally most plentiful in the early morning and late afternoon. The last bus is usually between 10pm and midnight. To avoid competition with tourist taxis, buses do not normally run to Frigate Bay (or points southeast).

On Nevis, buses run south and east from Memorial Sq in Charlestown and head to the north from Walwyn Sq. Fare ranges from EC$1 to EC$4.

Buses on both islands can resemble minivan taxis, so check the front plate to be sure. An 'H' means private bus and a 'T' means taxi (an 'R' is a rental car and a 'P' or 'PA' is a resident's car).

Car & Motorcycle

DRIVER'S LICENSE

Foreign visitors must purchase a visitor driver's license, which costs EC$50 (or US$20) and is valid for 90 days. The easiest place to get them is at the **police station** (Pond Rd) on the east side of Basseterre, which is open 24 hours and has a separate window designated for issuing visitor licenses. If you're flying into St Kitts and renting a car, the rental agency will usually pick you up at the airport and then stop at the police station on the way to its office.

During weekday business hours, driver's licenses can also be obtained at the Inland Revenue Office, above the post office on Bay Rd in Basseterre.

In Nevis, visitor driver's licenses can be obtained at the Charlestown, Gingerland or Newcastle police stations for EC$62.50.

RENTAL
Nevis
Most places charge US$10 a day more for a CDW.

Parry's Car Rental (☎ 469-5917) in Charlestown is a friendly, locally owned operation. If you're arriving by ferry, call Parry in advance and he'll meet you at the harbor (give him a few minutes). When returning the car, you simply park it near the dock with the keys in the ignition. Rates begin around US$30.

Nevis Car Rental (☎ 469-9837; Newcastle).

TDC Auto Rentals (☎ 469-5690; tdcrentals@caribsurf .com; Bay Rd, Charlestown) Rates are US$30 for a small car. Ask about rental exchange on both islands (minimum three-day rental).

St Kitts
There are numerous car rental agencies on St Kitts. Rates begin at about US$30/180 per day/week with unlimited mileage for a small car such as a Nissan March or Suzuki Swift. In addition, optional collision damage waivers (CDW) cost about US$10 a day plus 5% government levy. With some companies you're still responsible for the first few hundred dollars worth of damage, while with others the CDW waives all liability.

Avis (☎ 465-6507, in the US 800-228-0668; Bay Rd, Basseterre)

Caines Rent a Car (☎ 465-2366; Princes St, Basseterre)

Delisle Walwyn Car Rental (☎ 465-8449; Liverpool Row, Basseterre)

TDC Auto Rentals (☎ 465-2991; West Independence Sq, Basseterre) Both TDC and Avis provide free airport or hotel pick-up. Ask about rental exchange on both islands.

The cheapest scooter rental company is **Islandwide Scooter Rentals** (☎ 466-7841; midasscooter@ caribsurf.com; Pond Rd; ⏰ 9am-5pm Mon-Fri, 9am-2pm Sat). Rental costs are US$27 to US$30 per day, US$162 to US$180 per week.

ROAD RULES
Drive on the left side of the road, often around goats, cows and pedestrians. Speed limits are posted in miles per hour, and are generally between 20mph (30km/h) and 40mph (60km/h). Gas costs about EC$6 per gallon.

Basseterre has quite a few one-way streets, some of which are not clearly marked. Keep an eye out for road signs, and when in doubt, simply follow the rest of the traffic.

On Nevis, gas stations are marked on the *Journey Map* (see p478).

Taxi
Taxis meet scheduled flights. On St Kitts, a taxi from the airport costs EC$18 to Basseterre, EC$29 to Frigate Bay, and EC$47 to St Paul's.

From the Circus (the main taxi stand in Basseterre), it costs EC$10 to anywhere within town, EC$20 to Frigate Bay and EC$85 to Brimstone Hill round-trip. Rates are 25% higher between 11pm and 6am. There's an EC$3 charge for each 15 minutes of waiting. To call a taxi, dial ☎ 465-4253.

Nevis taxi rates include the following: airport to Charlestown and Pinney's Beach hotels US$15, to Montpelier Plantation Inn US$25; from Charlestown to Four Seasons US$8, to Banana's Bistro US$12, and to Golden Rock Hotel US$16. Service between 10pm to 6am adds 50% extra. For taxis call ☎ 469-1483 or ☎ 469-5631 in Charlestown and ☎ 469-9790 in Newcastle.

Taxi island tours on both islands cost around US$60. Those shorter on time rather than cash can take a half-island tour for US$44.

Antigua & Barbuda

If it's sandy beaches with almost unbelievably turquoise water, sun and relaxation you're after, Antigua and Barbuda won't fail to deliver. Although at roughly 11 miles (18km) wide Antigua is a small island, plenty of water-based activities, an abundance of colonial-era historic sites, and some excellent hotels and restaurants mean you'll have plenty to keep you happy on a short vacation.

Old stone windmills from long-abandoned sugar plantations are so plentiful that they are the island's main landmarks. The renovated colonial-era naval base of Nelson's Dockyard attracts yachters from around the world, and the scattered ruins of an extensive hilltop fortress are found at neighboring Shirley Heights.

Antigua's hotels are spread out along its sandy beaches; compared with other bays, Dickenson Bay and neighboring Runaway Bay are crowded with places to stay, but remote resorts can be found scattered around the island.

Barbuda, 25 miles (40km) to the north, is the other half of this dual-island nation. It's a quiet, single-village island sheltering less than 2% of the nation's population. Barbuda gets very few visitors; mainly bird-watchers who come to see its frigate-bird colony, and a few yachters who enjoy its clear waters and remote beaches.

FAST FACTS

- **Area** Antigua: 108 sq miles (280 sq km); Barbuda: 62 sq miles (160 sq km)
- **Capital** Antigua: St John's; Barbuda: Codrington
- **Country code** ☎ 268
- **Departure tax** Antigua: US$20; Barbuda: none
- **Famous for** Antigua: cricket; Barbuda: frigate bird
- **Language** Antigua & Barbuda: English
- **Money** Antigua & Barbuda: Eastern Caribbean dollar (EC$); EC$1 = US$0.37 = €0.31 = UK£0.21
- **People** Antiguans, Barbudans
- **Phrases** No big ting
- **Population** Antigua: 72,000; Barbuda: 1250
- **Visa** Not required for US, EU or Commonwealth visitors

HIGHLIGHTS

- **Half Moon Bay** (p496) Kick back on one of the islands' quietest beaches, where the sand is white and the water turquoise.
- **Nelson's Dockyard** (p492) Explore colonial-era sights, including this 18th-century British naval base.
- **Codrington Lagoon** (p500) Tour the Caribbean's largest rookery, which is home to thousands of frigate birds.
- **Harmony Hall** (p496) Indulge in a leisurely Sunday lunch at this charming Nonsuch Bay inn.
- **St John's** (p486) Soak up some true West Indian character on the colorful streets of town.

ITINERARIES

- **Three or four days** Spend a day wandering St John's, taking in the museum and market before heading south across Fig Tree Dr to Falmouth Harbour and Nelson's Dockyard. Spend the next day or two roaming the rugged east coast, Devil's Bridge, and the fabulous beaches at Half Moon and Nonsuch Bays, not forgetting to stop for a fantastic lunch at Harmony Hall.
- **One week** Heading southwest from the airport, cool down with a swim or snorkel at Darkwood or Johnson's Beaches before stopping overnight at English Harbour and taking in Nelson's Dockyard. Continue counterclockwise around the east coast, via Betty's Hope (inland), up to Dickenson Bay (on the northwest coast) to soak up some rays and underwater sights with a few day's diving. Then make a two-day trip to Barbuda for some incredible bird-watching and relaxing on isolated beaches.

CLIMATE & WHEN TO GO

In January and February, the coolest months, the daily high temperature averages 81°F (27°C), while the nightly low temperature averages 72°F (22°C). In July and August, the hottest months, the high averages 86°F (30°C) and the low 77°F (25°C).

Antigua is relatively dry, averaging about 45in (115cm) of rain annually. The wettest months are September to November, when measurable precipitation occurs, on average, eight days each month. February to April is the driest period, with an average of three rainy days each month.

HISTORY

The first permanent residents in the area are thought to have been migrating Arawaks who established agricultural communities on Antigua & Barbuda about 2000 years ago. Around AD 1200 the Arawaks were forced out by invading Caribs, who used the islands as bases for their forays in the region, but apparently didn't settle them.

Columbus sighted Antigua in 1493 and named it after a church in Seville, Spain. In 1632 the British colonized Antigua, establishing a settlement at Parham, on the east side of the island. The settlers started planting indigo and tobacco, but a glut in the supply for those crops soon drove down prices.

In 1674 Sir Christopher Codrington arrived on Antigua and established the first sugar plantation, Betty's Hope. By the end of the century, a plantation economy had developed, slaves were imported, and the central valleys were deforested and planted in cane. To feed the slaves, Codrington leased the island of Barbuda from the British Crown and planted it with food crops.

As Antigua prospered, the British built numerous fortifications around the island, turning it into one of their most secure bases in the Caribbean. The military couldn't secure the economy, however, and in the early 1800s the sugar market began to bottom out. With the abolition of slavery in 1834, the plantations went into a steady decline. Unlike on some other Caribbean islands, the land was not turned over to former slaves when the plantations went under, but was instead consolidated under the ownership of a few landowners. Consequently, the lot of most people only worsened. Many former slaves moved off the plantations and into shantytowns, while others crowded onto properties held by the church.

A military-related construction boom during WWII, and the development of a tourist industry during the postwar period, helped spur economic growth (although the shantytowns that remain along the outskirts of St John's are ample evidence that not everyone has benefited).

In 1967, after more than 300 years of colonial rule, Antigua achieved a measure of self-government as an Associated State of the UK. On November 1, 1981, it achieved full independence.

Vere Cornwall Bird became the nation's first prime minister, and despite leading a government marred by political scandals, he held that position through four consecutive terms. He stepped down in 1994 to be succeeded by his son Lester.

Another son, Vere Bird Jr, received international attention in 1991 as the subject of a judicial inquiry. The inquiry investigated his involvement in smuggling Israeli weapons to the Medellín drug cartel. His signature on documents, required by Israeli authorities to prove that the weapons were bound for a legitimate buyer, allowed the cargo to be shipped to a nonexistent officer of the Antigua Defence Force. After eight hours in port, the weapons were transferred to a Colombian boat and shipped to the Medellín cartel without interference by customs. As a consequence of the inquiry, Vere Bird Jr was pressured into resigning his cabinet post, but was allowed to keep his parliamentary position. Another son of VC Bird, Ivor, was convicted of cocaine smuggling in 1995.

Throughout the five-term family stronghold on government, controversy continued to surround the Birds. In 1997, Prime Minister Lester Bird announced that a group of ecologically sensitive nearshore islands (including Guiana Island, which had been proposed for national-park status) were being turned over to Malaysian developers to build a 1000-room hotel, an 18-hole golf course and a world-class casino. This was met with widespread protest from environmentalists. In 1999, VC Bird died, aged 89.

Finally, in March 2004, the Bird's tainted golden reign of the 'aviary' (as Antigua had become known) came to a grinding halt with opposition United Progressive Party leader Baldwin Spencer being elected to the helm.

THE CULTURE
The National Psyche

Away from the resorts, Antigua retains its traditional West Indian character, albeit with a strong British stamp. It's manifested in the gingerbread architecture found around the capital, the popularity of steel-band (steelpan), calypso and reggae music, and in festivities, such as Carnival. English traditions also play an important role, as is evident in the national sport of cricket.

Many Barbudans originally come from or have spent time living on their sister island, Antigua, and favor the quieter pace of life on the more isolated Barbuda. In fact, many Barbudans working in tourism are happy with the trickle of tourists that the remote island attracts, and have been reluctant to promote the island as a honeymoon destination or court the kind of development Antigua has seen.

Dress is casual, and simple cotton clothing is suitable attire for most occasions. In a few of the most upscale resort restaurants, jackets and ties are required of men. To avoid offense, restrict swimwear to the beach.

SEND DEM COME

As is the case on other islands in the Caribbean, bus drivers on Antigua try to make their vehicles as distinctive as possible by giving them colorful names. Some of the buses, with names like 'Man Standing By' and 'Send Dem Come,' are making an obvious pitch to riders; others, such as 'Could Be Dangerous' or 'Don't Tes' Me,' sound anything but reassuring. Although there's an element of jest to it all, choosing a bus by the name may prove to be a good way of avoiding some of the more reckless drivers.

Population

Approximately 90% of the 72,000 people who live on Antigua are of African descent. There are also small minority populations of British, Portuguese and Lebanese ancestry. The population of Barbuda is approximately 1250, with most of African descent.

SPORTS

One of the best things Britain did for the West Indies was introduce the local populace to cricket. It soon became the national passion of Antigua and is played everywhere – on beaches, in backyards or anywhere there's some flat, open ground. National and international games are played at the Antigua Recreation Ground in St John's, and although the West Indies team has fallen from the dizzying heights of the 1970s and early '80s, the game is followed religiously, and the atmosphere at a match is electric and enthralling.

Viv Richards (King Viv or the 'Master-Blaster,' as he was known in his heyday), who hails from Antigua, is one of the most famous cricketers of the modern game. Known for his aggressive style of batting, he became captain of the West Indies team, and captained 27 wins in 50 tests between 1980 and 1991. He now acts as a coach, and it's not uncommon to see him strolling around the streets of St John's.

A new 20,000-seat cricket stadium, the Sir Vivian Richards Stadium, 4 miles east of St John's, is scheduled to be built in time for the 2007 Cricket World Cup, which is being held throughout the Caribbean.

Soccer and basketball are increasing in popularity, and national and club soccer games – also played at the Antigua Recreation Ground – can produce much the same atmosphere as cricket.

RELIGION

Nearly half of all Antiguans are members of the Anglican Church. Other religious denominations include Roman Catholic, Moravian, Methodist, Seventh Day Adventist, Lutheran and Jehovah's Witness.

ARTS

Reggae and zouk (the latter means 'party,' and is a rhythmic music that originated in Martinique and Guadeloupe in the 1980s), are both popular on the island. You'll also hear calypso, a style of singing rooted in slave culture that was developed as a means of communication when slaves weren't allowed to speak, and soca, a rhythmic, more soulful style of calypso. By far the most popular musical style on Antigua is Steel pan (steel drum), the melodic percussion music that comes from tapping oil drums topped with specially made tin pans. Originally from Trinidad, the form has been adapted in Antigua, and has become an integral part of the annual Carnival and Christmas festivities.

ENVIRONMENT
The Land

Antigua's land area is 108 sq miles (280 sq km). The island is vaguely rounded in shape, averaging about 11 miles (18km) across. The deeply indented coastline is cut by numerous coves and bays, many lined with white-sand beaches. The southwest corner is volcanic in origin and quite hilly, rising to 1319ft (402m) at Boggy Peak, the island's highest point. The rest of the island, which is predominantly of limestone and coral formation, is given to a more gently undulating terrain of open plains and scrubland.

The island of Barbuda, 25 miles (40km) north of Antigua, has a land area of 62 sq miles (160 sq km). A low-lying coral island, Barbuda boasts a highest point merely 145ft (44.2m) above sea level. The west side of Barbuda encompasses the expansive Codrington Lagoon, which is bound by a long, undeveloped barrier beach.

The country's boundaries also include Redonda, an uninhabited rocky islet less than 1 sq mile (2.6 sq km) in size that lies 25 miles (40km) southwest of Antigua.

Wildlife

As a consequence of colonial-era deforestation, most of Antigua's vegetation is dryland scrub. The island's marshes and salt ponds attract a fair number of stilts, egrets, ducks and pelicans, while hummingbirds are found in garden settings.

Guiana Island, off the northeast coast, has one of Antigua's largest remaining tracts of forest. It's the sole habitat for the tropical mockingbird, and supports the largest colony of nesting seabirds on Antigua. These include tropic birds, roseate terns, brown noddies and endangered whistling ducks. Unfortunately, the government has targeted

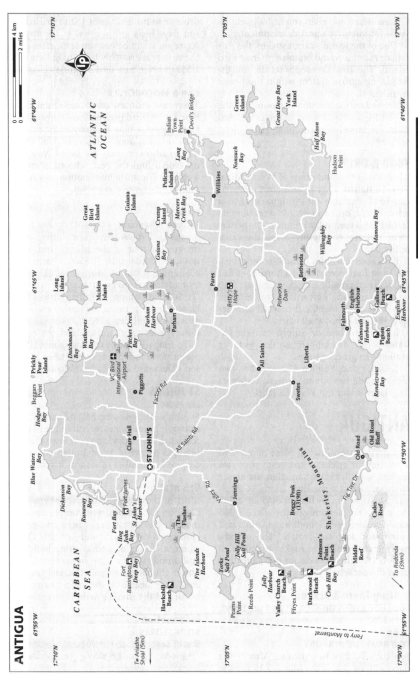

ANTIGUA

ATLANTIC OCEAN

CARIBBEAN SEA

ANTIGUA & BARBUDA

Guiana Island and eight smaller adjacent islands for intensive resort development.

One of the world's rarest snakes, the Antiguan racer, is found on nearby Great Bird Island. The area also supports the fourth-largest mangrove system within the Lesser Antilles.

Barbuda's Codrington Lagoon has the largest frigate-bird colony in the Lesser Antilles. For more information on frigate birds, see p499.

FOOD & DRINK

There's a fairly good range of West Indian, French, Italian, English and North American food available on Antigua and, to a lesser extent, on Barbuda. Most restaurants feature fresh seafood, with one of the better-value options commonly being the catch of the day.

For a good, cheap local snack, order a roti – the West Indian version of a burrito – filled with curried potatoes, chicken or beef. Also try one of the locally grown black pineapples, which are quite sweet, rather small and, despite the name, not at all black.

It's best to boil or otherwise treat tap water before drinking it. Bottled water is available in grocery stores.

Cavalier and English Harbour are two locally made rums, and Antigua brews its own lager under the Wadadli label.

ANTIGUA

Red phoneboxes, English place-names and a passion for cricket – the vestiges of two centuries of British occupation are never far from sight on the little island of Antigua. Most visitors are here, though, to enjoy the corporeal pleasures of the island's 365 sandy beaches, good food, water sports and year-round tropical climate. The island's easily manageable size makes it simple to explore its sights on a day or two's breather from the deckchair.

Getting There & Around

For information on air, bus and sea travel, see p503.

TO/FROM THE AIRPORT

Antigua's VC Bird International Airport is at the northeast side of the island, a 15-minute

drive or so from either St John's or Dickenson Bay. Taxis are plentiful at the airport. Agree on a fare before you start; rates from the airport are roughly US$7 to St John's, or US$21 to Nelson's Yard or Shirley Heights.

CAR & MOTORCYCLE

There are a dozen or so car-rental firms based at VC Bird International Airport. The local agencies may be marginally cheaper than international companies, but check how roadworthy cars are before you sign up. You'll find the best rates on agencies' websites. For more information on car and motorcycle rentals, see p504.

TOURS

Antigua Adventures (☎ 727-3261; www.antigua adventures.com; PO Box 1669, St John's) offers every imaginable tour of the island, from half-island helicopter rides (US$80, 15 minutes), 45-minute tours of Montserrat (US$200) and historical hikes of English Harbour (US$60) to fishing or sailing trips (from US$60 per day, including lunch) and ecotours (half-/full day $US50/90) or gourmet tours (prices vary) of the island.

Touring Antigua by taxi costs about US$70 per car for a half-day tour that takes in Nelson's Dockyard and Shirley Heights.

ST JOHN'S

pop 36,000

St John's, Antigua's capital and commercial center, is home to nearly half of the island's residents. It's a busy little port town that has retained plenty of West Indian character, despite the number of visitors it sees.

Orientation

Most of the town's tourist activity is centered on two harborfront complexes – the modern Heritage Quay, where cruise-ship passengers disembark, and Redcliffe Quay, where a cluster of period stone buildings and wooden huts have been restored to house gift shops, art galleries and restaurants. Popeshead St is the main route to the north and the island's main resort area.

Information
BOOKSTORES

Best of Books (☎ 562-3198; PO Box 433, Redcliffe St; ☺ 9am-6pm Mon-Sat) International titles, newspapers and a children's book section.

ST JOHN'S

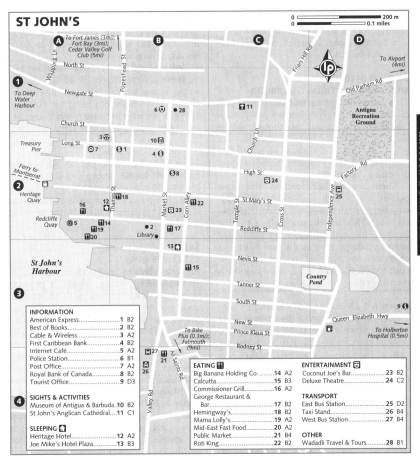

INFORMATION
American Express......................1 B2
Best of Books............................2 B2
Cable & Wireless......................3 A2
First Caribbean Bank...............4 B2
Internet Café.............................5 A2
Police Station............................6 B1
Post Office.................................7 A2
Royal Bank of Canada.............8 B2
Tourist Office.............................9 D3

SIGHTS & ACTIVITIES
Museum of Antigua & Barbuda..10 B2
St John's Anglican Cathedral....11 C1

SLEEPING
Heritage Hotel..........................12 A2
Joe Mike's Hotel Plaza.............13 B3

EATING
Big Banana Holding Co.........14 A2
Calcutta..................................15 B3
Commissioner Grill................16 A2
George Restaurant &
  Bar......................................17 B2
Hemingway's.........................18 B2
Mama Lolly's.........................19 A2
Mid-East Fast Food...............20 A2
Public Market........................21 B4
Roti King...............................22 B2

ENTERTAINMENT
Coconut Joe's Bar..................23 B2
Deluxe Theatre......................24 C2

TRANSPORT
East Bus Station....................25 D2
Taxi Stand.............................26 B4
West Bus Station....................27 B4

OTHER
Wadadli Travel & Tours..........28 B1

EMERGENCY
Police (Newgate St) This is the main police station in town. The police headquarters (☎ 462-0125; American Rd) is located on the eastern outskirts of St John's.

INTERNET ACCESS
Internet Café (☎ 462-1040; Redcliffe St; per hr EC$20; ☷ 8:30am-5:30pm Mon-Fri) FedEx agent, Internet access and computer store.

MEDICAL SERVICES
Holberton Hospital (☎ 462-0251; Hospital Rd) Located just off Queen Elizabeth Hwy.

MONEY
Amex (Long St; ☷ 8:30am-4pm Mon-Thu, 8:30am-5pm Fri)

First Caribbean Bank (Market St; ☷ 8am-2pm Mon-Thu, 8am-noon & 2-4pm Fri)
Royal Bank of Canada (High St; ☷ 8am-2pm Mon-Thu, 8am-noon & 2-4pm Fri)

POST
Post office (Long St; ☷ 8:15am-noon & 1-4pm Mon-Thu, 8:15am-noon & 1-5pm Fri)

TELEPHONE
There is a row of pay phones along Long St, opposite St John's Anglican Cathedral (see p522).
Cable & Wireless (Thames St; ☷ 8am-5pm Mon-Fri, 9am-noon Sat) Card phones as well as a 24-hour phone-card dispenser can be found outside the building.

ANTIGUA & BARBUDA

TOURIST INFORMATION
Tourist office (☎ 462-0480; www.antigua-barbuda
.com; Ministry of Tourism, Queen Elizabeth Hwy; ☒ 8am-
4:30pm Mon-Thu, 8am-3pm Fri)

Sights & Activities
MUSEUM OF ANTIGUA & BARBUDA
This community-run **museum** (☎ 462-1469;
cnr Market & Long Sts; ☒ 8:30am-4pm Mon-Fri, 10am-
2pm Sat) occupies the old courthouse, a stone
building that dates from 1750. It has an
eclectic collection of displays on island history, but everything looks as though it could
do with a dusting.

There is a touchable section with stone
pestles and conch-shell tools, a reconstructed Arawak house, and modest displays
on natural history, the colonial era and the
struggle for emancipation. Probably the
most popular exhibit is the well-worn bat
of former West Indies' cricket team captain, Vivian Richard. An EC$5 donation is
encouraged.

ST JOHN'S ANGLICAN CATHEDRAL
This twin-spired **cathedral** (btwn Newgate & Long
Sts) is the town's dominant landmark. The
original church dated back to 1681, but the
current baroque-style stone structure was
constructed in 1847, after a devastating
earthquake.

The cathedral interior is unusual in that
it's completely encased in pitch pine, creating a church-within-a-church effect that
was intended to buffer the structure from
damage by natural disasters. The interior
can be viewed when the caretaker is around,
which is usually until 5pm.

FORT JAMES
Fort James, a small stronghold at the north
side of St John's Harbour, was first built
in 1675, but most of the present structure
dates from 1739. It still has a few of its
original 36 cannons, a powder magazine
and a fair portion of its walls intact.

Fort Bay, which stretches north from the
fort, is the closest beach to St John's and is
thus popular with islanders.

Festivals & Events
Antigua's renowned 10-day Carnival hits
the streets of St John's from the end of July
to early August; for more information,
see p502.

Sleeping
It's slim pickings for accommodations in
St John's, but most visitors tend to favor
seaside resorts anyway.

Heritage Hotel (☎ 462-1247; heritagehotel@candw
.ag; Thames St; s/d/ste US$85/95/130; ☒ ☒) A good-
value business hotel in a downtown location. The 18-bedroom wing on Heritage
Quay is under renovation, while the 31-
bedroom main block has large, modern,
tiled rooms with floral furnishings, refrig-
eration and dataports.

Joe Mike's Hotel Plaza (☎ 462-1142; joemikes@
candw.ag; PO Box 136, cnr Corn Alley & Nevis St; s/d
US$50/60; ☒) An older central hotel. Rooms
here are a bit drab, but make an easy, central crash pad after a night in the adjacent
minicasino.

Eating
REDCLIFFE QUAY
Big Banana Holding Co (Redcliffe St; pizza EC$22-50;
☒ 8:30am-midnight Mon-Sat) This is a popular
warehouse-style pizzeria, with shady outdoor seating, and serving decent pizza by
the slice or plate.

Commissioner Grill (Redcliffe St; dinner mains EC$40-
85; ☒ 9am-10:30pm Mon-Sat, 6-11pm Sun) An upmarket Creole restaurant with a good reputation.
Features specials like *foungee* (cornmeal)
with fried plantain and codfish, but there's
also steak and chips for homebirds.

Mama Lolly's (Redcliffe St; dishes EC$10-15;
☒ 8:30am-4:30pm Mon-Sat) Try a hearty red-bean
stew or delicious banana-berry smoothie in
this excellent little veggie café with outdoor
seating.

Mid-East Fast Food (Redcliffe St; mains EC$8-18;
☒ 10am-4pm Mon-Sat) Munch on hot falafel,
sharwarma (chicken with pickles) or hummus in pitta while seated at picnic tables
in the shade.

AROUND TOWN
Roti King (St Mary's St; roti EC$12; ☒ 8:30am-midnight,
closed Sun) Join the locals at this takeout
shack for some of the biggest and best roti
in Antigua.

Hemingway's (St Mary's St; dinner EC$30-80;
☒ 8:30am-midnight Mon-Sat) Dig into great burgers and steaks at this popular place, housed
in an attractive 19th-century West Indian
building.

George Restaurant & Bar (☎ 562-4866; Redcliffe
St; dinner mains EC$35-85; ☒ 10am-10pm Mon-Sat) At

Cow Wreck Beach Bar & Grill (p396), Anegada, British Virgin Islands

JOHN NEUBAUER

RMS *Rhone* (p389), Salt Island,
British Virgin Islands

GREG JOHNSTON

Local art, St John's (p486), Antigua &
Barbuda

LEE FOSTER

GREG GAWLOWSKI

Terre-de-Haut (p524), Guadeloupe

MICHAEL LAWRENCE

Nesting leatherback turtle (p702), Trinidad & Tobago

Brimstone Hill Fortress National Park (p469), St Kitts & Nevis

RICHARD CUMMINS

this swanky new 1st-floor veranda restaurant with tropical hardwood furnishings and plants, George serves munchies like jerk chicken and hummus by day and Antiguan specials, such as coconut shrimp, by night.

Calcutta (Corn Alley St; meals EC$7-12; ☺ 8am-5pm Mon-Sat) If you don't mind the bright lighting and plastic tablecloths, tuck into great West Indian curries, roti and local seafood dishes at this new café.

Public Market (Market St; ☺ 6am-6pm Mon-Sat) At the south end of Market St opposite the bus station, this is the best place for fresh fruits and vegetables.

Drinking & Entertainment

Coconut Joe's Bar (Market St) Close to town, the atmosphere here is lively, helped along by the constant loud music that can be heard from its 1st-floor balcony.

Deluxe Theatre (☎ 462-2188; High St) screens box office regulars on weekend nights.

Big Banana Holding Co (opposite) has live music on Thursday nights.

There are several casinos near St John's, including one at Heritage Quay and another at Joe Mike's Hotel Plaza (opposite).

Shopping

Heritage and Redcliffe Quays are lined with souvenir, jewelry and perfume stores aimed at visitors.

You can buy 'duty-free' liquor at Heritage Quay or the airport departure lounge, with Johnnie Walker Red Label selling for around US$18 and Antiguan rum for US$8 (rum can also be bought in local shops around the island for about the same price).

RUNAWAY BAY

With its attractive white-sand beach, calm waters and handful of small, reasonably priced hotels, Runaway Bay is the nearest resort to St John's. Note, however, that the north end of the beach has lost virtually all of its sand since Hurricane Luis, and the process of regeneration has been slow. But from Barrymore Beach Club south there is still a gorgeous sandy strand, and precious few beachgoers to share it with. It's just a short five- to 10-minute walk to the livelier Dickenson Bay. A large **salt pond** stretches along the inland side of Runaway Bay, and in the evening, egrets come to roost at the pond's southern end.

Sleeping & Eating

Barrymore Beach Club (☎ 462-4101; barrymorep@candw.ag; PO Box 1774; r US$115, apt kitchenette US$180-300) A friendly Scottish-run beachfront hotel, with rooms set in landscaped gardens. One- or two-bedroom apartments have pitched roofs, rattan furniture and spacious living areas.

Sunset Cove Resort (☎ 462-3762; fax 462-2684; PO Box 1262; studio/apt from US$100/175; ❄ ☒) Offers studio and one-bedroom apartments, set in landscaped gardens around a pool and close to Runaway beach. Top-floor units have high ceilings, but all have good kitchens, comfy rattan furniture and handy extras, like VCR and phones. Cats nightclub is attached.

Julian's (☎ 726-3233; dinner mains EC$42-78; ☺ closed Mon) On the beach side of Barrymore Beach Club, British chef Julian serves an inventive mix of Creole and international dishes, like blackened snapper with squash or Japanese fish fusion, in classy surroundings.

Millers by the Sea (☎ 462-9414; mains EC$40-60) Right on the beach at Fort James, Millers is a popular seafood spot. It has barbecue specials on Thursday, and nightly live music that ranges from jazz to calypso, as well as a happy hour from 5pm to 7pm.

DICKENSON BAY

Dickenson Bay, Antigua's main moderate-range resort area, is fronted by a long, lovely white-sand beach with turquoise waters and good swimming conditions.

All of Dickenson Bay's action is centered on the beach, which features water-sports' booths, open-air restaurants, and half a dozen hotels and condominiums. It's more touristy than Runaway Bay and can get a little crowded at times. Still, it's a fun scene, with reggae music, vendors selling T-shirts and jewelry, and women braiding hair.

Sleeping & Eating

Antigua Village (☎ 462-2930; www.antiguavillage.com; PO Box 649; studio from US$175; ❄ ☒) A well-maintained beachside condominium complex with 100 units spread around landscaped grounds. They're individually owned so the decor varies, but most are spacious with large balconies, fully equipped kitchens and a shelf of beach reads thrown in.

Siboney Beach Resort (☎ 462-0806; www.siboneybeachclub.com; PO Box 222; apt US$170-310; ❄ ▣ ☒) Popular with honeymooners, Siboney's is a beachside apartment complex set in thick shady vegetation. Apartments are hardly luxurious, but cozy with king-size beds, kitchenettes, louvered balcony or patio doors, and the ubiquitous rattan furnishings.

Dickenson Bay Cottages (☎ 462-4940; www.dickensonbaycottages.com; 1-/2-bed apt US$160/305; 🖳 🖳) A small, secluded complex of nicely furnished cottages set around a pool. Colorful bedrooms are on a mezzanine level overlooking the living and dining area. It's family friendly and a five-minute walk from the beach.

Coconut Grove (☎ 462-1538; dinner EC$50-90) Situated on the beach at Siboney Beach Resort, this popular Creole restaurant serves English breakfasts and sandwiches for lunch. At dinner, dishes range from catch of the day to lobster.

Pari's Pizza (☎ 462-1501; mains EC$24-70; 🕑 11:30am-11:30pm, closed Mon) Almost opposite Dickenson Bay Cottages on the inland road, eat in here or take out decent pizza, steaks and juicy ribs.

Grocery Store (🕑 9am-7pm) A very small store at Antigua Village.

NORTH SHORE

The northern part of the island between Dickenson Bay and the airport has the island's most well-to-do residential areas, a golf course, and a few exclusive villa developments and small upscale resorts.

Sleeping & Eating

Sunsail Club Colonna (☎ 462-6263; www.sunsail.com; PO Box 591; r/apt/villa from US$140/170/190; 🖳 🖳) An attractive Italianate complex with 114 comfortable rooms, apartments and villas on a sandy beach. Expect plenty of action, with tennis, aerobics, sailing and kids' club events happening from morning to night.

Le Bistro (☎ 462-3881; mains EC$80-120; 🕑 dinner, closed Mon) This well-regarded, upmarket French restaurant, inland from Hodges Bay, is considered by some to be Antigua's finest. Dine on confit of duck or lobster bisque in intimate surroundings. Reservations are recommended.

DEEP BAY

West of St John's, Deep Bay is a pleasant little bay with a sandy beach and protected waters. The Royal Antiguan Hotel sits above the beach, and there's a fair amount of

resort activity, but it's a good-sized strand and a nice swimming spot.

The coral-encrusted wreck of the **Andes** lies in the middle of Deep Bay with its mast poking up above the water. Approximately 100 years have passed since this bark caught fire and went down, complete with a load of pitch from Trinidad. The waters are shallow enough around the wreck to be snorkeled, but divers tend to bypass it because ooze still kicks up pretty easily from the bottom.

The remains of **Fort Barrington**, which once protected the southern entrance of St John's Harbour, are atop the promontory that juts out at the northern end of the bay. Although the fort was originally constructed in the mid-17th century, most of the present fortifications date to 1779. To hike up to the fort, simply begin walking north along the beach at Deep Bay; the trail takes about 10 minutes.

A salt pond separates Deep Bay from smaller Hog John Bay, where there's another sandy beach and a couple of hotels.

Located right at the end of the peninsula, the well-established **Hawksbill Beach Resort** (☎ 462-0301; www.hawksbill.com; PO Box 108; s/d all inclusive from US$240/350; 🖳 🖳), situated on 37 acres, offers more than 100 rooms, cottages or apartments, and tends to attract more mature guests. Rooms are airy, some with pitched ceilings and traditional decor, but the best bits are the complimentary water sports, tennis and four beaches, including Antigua's one and only nudist beach.

The resort has a couple of restaurants, one specializing in pasta and seafood.

JOLLY HARBOUR

Jolly Harbour is a marina and dockside condominium village on Antigua's west coast. Marina facilities include a pharmacy, supermarket, dive shop, boat rentals and charters, and a handful of restaurants.

There is a pleasant – albeit busy – white-sand beach south of the marina at Club Antigua and a quieter beach fronting Jolly Harbour.

Sleeping & Eating

Cocobay Resort (☎ 562-2400; www.cocobayresort.com; all-inclusive per person US$170-200; 🅿 🖳 🖳 🖳) This small development on the south side of

Jolly Harbour, popular with young British hipsters, is the area's chicest choice. Stylish Creole garden cottages in pale Mediterranean colors have terracotta-tiled floors and earthy dark-wood furnishings. The picture-postcard infinity pool is only steps away from the lovely Valley Church Beach. Of its two restaurants, one serves informal snacks and has West Indian barbecues on Sunday, while the other fancier option, **Sheer** (mains EC$40-100; ⏲ dinner, closed Mon), serves fineries, such as seared duck breast or lamb shank with langoustines.

Al Porto (☎ 462-7695; meals EC$25-50; ⏲ lunch & dinner) This is the most popular of the marina restaurants. It has harborfront dining, with good pizza and pasta dishes, and pricier meat dishes.

The marina's Epicurean market sells sandwiches, liquor and groceries.

JOLLY HARBOUR TO JOHNSON'S POINT BEACH

Heading south on the coastal road you'll pass one of Antigua's best beaches, **Darkwood Beach**, a wide swath of white sand and turquoise water that makes a great swimming and snorkeling spot. There are some changing rooms, a few deck chairs, and a little beachside hut that serves tasty club sandwiches or barbecued fish during the day.

Johnson's Point Beach, at the southwest corner of the island, is a fine stretch of white sand. And it probably has the best views of rumbling Montserrat to boot. Midway between St John's and English Harbour, Johnson's Point may suit people who want to avoid the more touristed parts of the island without being totally secluded. It's not quite as out of the way as it seems, as buses go by about every half-hour (except on Sunday) on the way to St John's.

FIG TREE DRIVE

After Johnson's Point Beach, the road passes pineapple patches, tall century plants, and pastures with grazing cattle and donkeys. High hills lie on the inland side of the road, topped by the 1319ft (402m) **Boggy Peak**, the island's highest point.

Old Road, a village with both a fair amount of poverty and the luxury Curtain Bluff Hotel, marks the start of Fig Tree Dr. From here, the terrain gets lusher as the road winds up through the hills. The narrow road is lined with bananas (called 'figs' in Antigua), coconut palms and big old mango trees. It's not jungle or rainforest, but it is refreshingly green, and makes a pleasant and rewarding rural drive. The road isn't great, and a 4WD is preferable to a car. A couple of snack bars sell fresh fruit and juices along the way.

Fig Tree Dr ends at the village of Swetes. On the way to Falmouth Harbour you pass through the village of Liberta and by the **St Barnabas Anglican Chapel**, an attractive greenstone-and-brick church built in 1842.

FALMOUTH HARBOUR

The large, protected, horseshoe-shaped bay of Falmouth Harbour has two main centers of activity: the north side of the harbor, where the small village of Falmouth is located, and the more visitor-oriented east side of the harbor, which has most of the restaurants. The east side is within easy walking distance of Nelson's Dockyard.

Sights

On the main road in Falmouth's center is **St Paul's Anglican Church**, Antigua's first church. As one of the island's oldest buildings, dating to 1676, the church once doubled as Antigua's courthouse. You can get a sense of its history by poking around the overgrown churchyard, which has some interesting and quite readable colonial-era gravestones. Charles Pitt, the brother of the English prime minister William Pitt, was buried here in 1780.

Sleeping & Eating

Catamaran Hotel & Marina (☎ 460-1036; www.catamaran-antigua.com; s/d from US$100/115; ✿ ▢) On a little beach at the north side of Falmouth Harbour, this pleasant 16-room hotel is one of the area's better-value accommodation options. The deluxe rooms on the 2nd floor have bathtubs and four-poster queen-size beds, and there are four ground-level units with kitchenettes. It also has its own 30-berth marina.

The following restaurants are all within a few minutes of each other at the east side of Falmouth Harbour. Note that some close during summer when business slacks off.

Le Cap Horn (☎ 460-1194; pizza EC$28-36, mains EC$30-70; ⏲ dinner, closed Sun) This place has two sides: a pizzeria and a French restaurant.

The pizzeria makes brick-oven pizza, from regular tomato and cheese to a seafood version, as well as pasta dishes and a meal of the day (in the pizza price range). The French restaurant offers specials like red snapper in basil sauce and Creole lobster.

Abracadabra (☎ 460-1732; mains EC$30-60; dinner, closed Sun) Popular with young revelers and yachties, this welcoming garden restaurant in a 17th-century building serves fresh pasta and seafood. If you still have energy, stay for the open-air disco after 11pm.

Jackee's Kwik Stop (meals EC$10-25; 8am-4pm Mon-Sat) On the main road, Jackee is renowned for her sandwiches, roti and omelettes made with TLC.

In the marina-harborside complex, on the road leading to Pigeon Beach, is a small supermarket and liquor store.

ENGLISH HARBOUR

English Harbour has the richest collection of historic sites on the island; collectively, they are the centerpiece of the Antigua & Barbuda National Parks system.

Foremost is Nelson's Dockyard, an 18th-century British naval base named for English captain Lord Horatio Nelson, who spent the early years of his career here. Today, it's still attracting sailors as the island's most popular yacht haven.

There are also two hilltop forts flanking the entrance to the harbor, and a couple of little museums. You could easily spend the better part of a day roaming around the sites. Bus routes from St John's end right at Nelson's Dockyard, but you'd need a car to explore the Shirley Heights area on the opposite side of the harbor.

English Harbour is separated from Falmouth Harbour by a slender neck of land that at its narrowest is just a few hundred yards wide.

Information

Bank of Antigua (9am-1pm Mon-Thu, 9am-noon & 2-4pm Fri, 9am-noon Sat) Just 100ft (30.5m) past the entrance to Nelson's Dockyard.

Customs office (8am-4pm; Nelson's Dockyard) On the ground level of the old Officer's Quarters building on the south side of the marina.

Lord Jim's (8am-5pm; Nelson's Dockyard) South of the customs office; sells nautical charts and cruising guides.

Post office (9am-3pm Mon-Fri) At the entrance of Nelson's Dockyard.

The harbor also has **public showers** (6am-6pm) and a **laundry** (per load US$10; 8am-6pm).

Sights

NELSON'S DOCKYARD

This historic **dockyard** (www.nationalparksantigua .com; adult/child under 12 EC$13/free; 9am-5pm) is Antigua's most popular tourist sight, as well as the island's main port of entry for yachts. It can feel a bit like a movie set, walking among the palm-flanked Georgian buildings with hordes of day-trippers, but nevertheless it's an interesting place to visit. The dockyard, which dates from 1745, was abandoned in 1889 following a decline in Antigua's economic and strategic importance to the British Crown.

Restoration work began in the 1950s, and this former royal naval base now has a new life closely paralleling its old one – that of an active dockyard. And it's the only working Georgian marina in the western hemisphere. The handsome old brick-and-stone buildings have been converted into yachting and tourist-related facilities. Many duplicate the buildings' original uses. The bakery, for instance, was originally the officers' kitchen and still has the old stone hearth, while some of the hotel rooms that now house travelers were once used as quarters for sailors whose ships were being careened.

The dockyard is English Harbour's main center of activity, with a small market selling T-shirts and souvenirs; a handful of restaurants; two inns; a dive shop; an art center that sells local artwork and inexpensive prints; and numerous boating facilities – all occupying old naval buildings. Take time to stop at the interpretive plaques that explain the history of the various buildings.

Upon entering, pick up the free map that shows the dockyard sights and businesses. A water taxi from the dockyard across the harbor to Galleon Beach costs US$8, round-trip.

The dockyard's small **museum** (admission free) occupies a former officers' house and features an assorted collection of nautical memorabilia, including clay pipes, rusty swords, muskets, cannonballs and one of Lord Nelson's telescopes. Models of a mid-19th-century schooner and naval brig round off the display. The museum's small gift shop sells books, maps and souvenirs.

FORT BERKLEY

A pleasant 10-minute stroll starting behind the Copper & Lumber Store Hotel leads to the site of this small fort, which overlooks the western entrance of English Harbour. Dating from 1704, it served as the harbor's first line of defense. You'll find intact walls, a powder magazine, a small guardhouse and a solitary cannon, the last of 25 cannons that once lined the fortress walls. There's also a fine harbor view at the top.

SHIRLEY HEIGHTS

With its scattered 18th-century fort ruins and wonderful hilltop views, Shirley Heights is a fun place to explore. A bit over a mile (1.6km) up Shirley Heights Rd you'll reach the **Dow's Hill Interpretation Centre** (admission EC$13, free with Nelson's Dockyard ticket; ☼ 9am-5pm), which features a viewpoint, and an audiovisual presentation on island history and culture.

For the best views and main concentration of ruins, continue past the museum; the road will fork after about 0.5 miles (0.8km). The left fork leads shortly to **Blockhouse Hill**, where you'll find remains of the Officers' Quarters dating to 1787 and a clear view of sheltered Mamora Bay to the east.

The right fork leads to **Fort Shirley**, which has more ruins, including one that has been turned into a casual restaurant and bar. There's a sweeping view of English Harbour from the rear of the restaurant, while from the top of Signal Hill (487ft; 148m), just a minute's walk from the parking lot, you can see Montserrat 28 miles (45km) to the southwest and Guadeloupe 40 miles (64km) to the south. It's a perfect spot to watch the sun go down.

Sleeping

Inn at English Harbour (☎ 460-1014; www.theinn .ag; PO Box 187; s/d from US$231/308; P ✕ ⬜ ⬛) With great views of the bay and, for those who are interested, Eric Clapton's house, this small beach resort on the southeast side of English Harbour looks like a cozy English lodge. Its 34 bright and airy rooms and suites have big balconies and baths, and are furnished with solid teak beds and natural linen spreads. Swim in the infinity pool or play tennis, or enjoy nonmotorized water sports in the bay.

Admiral's Inn (☎ 460-1027; PO Box 713; r US$155-280) Built as a warehouse in 1788, the Inn has 14 rooms above the restaurant in the original brick building and five rooms in a separate modern annex. Rooms vary in size and decor, and some are quite small. Room No 6 is larger and a good choice in the moderate category, while No 3, a quiet corner room with a fine harbor view, is recommended in the superior category; both have hand-hewn open beams. Complimentary transportation is provided to nearby beaches.

Copper & Lumber Store Hotel (☎ 460-1058; www .copperlumberantigua.com; r US$200-350) This beautiful recently restored hotel was built in the 1780s to store the copper and lumber needed for ship repairs. It now has 14 studios and suites, all with kitchens and ceiling fans, and some with antique furnishings. The Georgian suite is so laden with historic character that you could almost imagine Lord Nelson stepping into the scene.

Eating

Admiral's Inn (dinner mains EC$60-90; ☼ breakfast, lunch & dinner) The changing chalkboard menu usually features salads, burgers and curried conch (the chewy meat of a large gastropod) at lunch, with more-elaborate dishes for dinner. There's atmospheric indoor dining as well as outdoor harborfront tables.

Mainbrace Pub (meals US$10-18; ☼ 7:30am-midnight) In the Copper & Lumber Store Hotel (above), this welcoming airy pub serves steaks, sandwiches and British favorites, like shepherd's pie, and sausage and chips.

Dockyard Bakery (☼ 7:30am-4pm Mon-Fri, 7:30am-2pm Sat) Located behind the museum at Nelson's Dockyard, this bakery has sandwiches, breads, meat patties, guava Danishes, carrot cake and other tempting pastries at reasonable prices. You can also order takeout coffee and sip it under the 300-year-old sandbox tree that fronts the bakery.

Shirley Heights Lookout (☎ 460-1785; mains EC$25-50) In a vintage 1791 guardhouse at Fort Shirley, this place has a fantastic view of English Harbour. It serves snack lunches and local dishes at dinner, and is best known for its Sunday barbecues, which are accompanied by steel-band music from 4pm to 7pm and reggae from 7pm to 10pm, with lots of dancing toward the end of the evening. It's so popular that it feels like half the island is attending. There's no admission fee and drinks are reasonably priced. It's one of the island's nicest scenes.

MONTSERRAT   *Alex Leviton*

There was a time when traveling to the island of Montserrat combined two activities that had not been envisioned in tandem very often:

- Caribbean vacation
- Death wish

You don't need a death wish to visit Montserrat anymore, just an ash mask. Budding scientists with an interest in the wrath of nature will enjoy a visit, as will those just looking for some peace and quiet in beautiful surroundings that mirror both the Caribbean and Ireland.

Montserrat had spent several decades as a tight-knit community, priding itself on its image as an unspoiled Caribbean island with no pretensions. And then on July 18, 1995, the Soufrière Hills Volcano (3180ft; 969.3m) decided to give the island a big how-do-you-do, ending 400 years of volcanic dormancy.

The capital and only significant town, Plymouth, was covered in ash and subsequently abandoned, and has remained a ghost town. The 11,000 residents resettled around the island or emigrated abroad, and tourists all but disappeared. Excited vulcanologists swarmed the island declaring a Safe Zone, a Daylight Entry Zone and an Exclusion Zone (the area nearest the volcano).

Still, farmers continued to use this land, and on June 25, 1997, the volcano erupted again, requiring 50 helicopter airlifts and causing 19 deaths. Two months later, a superheated pyroclastic flow (one of the volcanic activities that makes vulcanologists so giddy) wiped out the remainder of Plymouth, and its historically significant architecture and character were lost forever.

The last eruption before this book went to press was in July 2003. Visitors can sometimes watch glowing volcanic rocks tumble down the mountainside at night. The volcano still lets off steam every so often, but life has regained some normalcy for Montserratians, and some off-limit zones have begun to welcome back residents. Tourism in the one-third of the island left in the 'Safe Zone' is low-key, but very welcome.

The friendly people of Montserrat are mostly of African descent, with strong Irish roots. You can still hear an Irish lilt to the accent. St Patrick's Day is a national holiday and Montserrat is known as 'the emerald isle of the Caribbean.'

FAST FACTS

- **Area** 39 sq miles (101 sq km) and expanding
- **Capital** Plymouth (abandoned after volcano)
- **Country code** ☎ 664
- **Departure tax** US$16
- **Famous for** Being the green isle of the Caribbean; massive volcanic eruption in 1995
- **Money** Eastern Caribbean dollar; EC$1 = US$0.37 = €0.31 = UK£0.21
- **Official language** English
- **People** Montserratians
- **Population** 11,000 pre-eruption; now approximately 4000
- **Visa** Not required for nationals of North America and most European countries

Climate

Montserrat's climate is tropical, with a heavier rainfall (averages 60in – 152cm – per year) during the hurricane season of July to November. Although the volcano hasn't erupted since 1997, visitors would be wise to carry an ash mask with them at all times and to keep the radio set to ZJB (91.9FM) for announcements. The climate ranges from 77°F (25°C) in winter to 86°F (30°C) in summer.

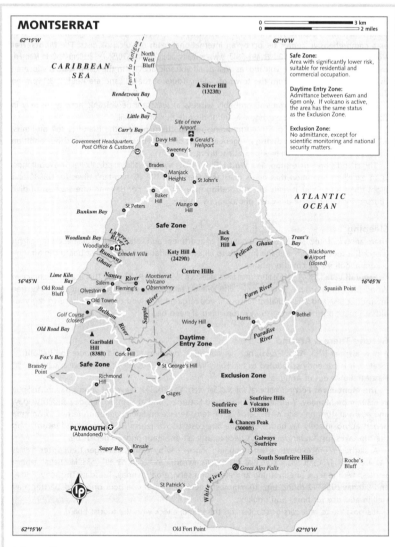

MONTSERRAT

0 _____ 3 km
0 _____ 2 miles

62°15'W 62°10'W

CARIBBEAN SEA

North West Bluff

▲ Silver Hill (1323ft)

Safe Zone:
Area with significantly lower risk, suitable for residential and commercial occupation.

Daytime Entry Zone:
Admittance between 6am and 6pm only. If volcano is active, the area has the same status as the Exclusion Zone.

Exclusion Zone:
No admittance, except for scientific monitoring and national security matters.

Rendezvous Bay

Little Bay

Site of new Airport

Carr's Bay

Government Headquarters, Post Office & Customs

Davy Hill ● Gerald's Heliport
Sweeney's

Brades
Manjack Heights ● St John's

Baker Hill
Mango Hill

Bunkum Bay St Peters

Safe Zone

Jack Boy Hill ▲

Trant's Bay

Woodlands Bay
Woodlands *Lawyers River*
Erindell Villa
Runaway Ghaut

Katy Hill ▲ (2429ft)

Pelican Ghaut

Blackburne ● Airport (closed)

ATLANTIC OCEAN

Lime Kiln Bay *Nantes River*
Montserrat Volcano Observatory

Centre Hills

Old Road Bluff
Salem ● Fleming's ●
Olveston ●
Old Towne

Farm River

Spanish Point

Golf Course (closed)
Belham River
Sappit River

Windy Hill ●
Harris ●

● Bethel

Old Road Bay

Garibaldi Hill (838ft) ▲
Cork Hill

Paradise River

Daytime Entry Zone

Fox's Bay

Safe Zone

Bransby Point
Richmond Hill

St George's Hill

Exclusion Zone

● Gages

Soufrière Hills
Soufrière Hills ▲ Volcano (3180ft)

PLYMOUTH ✪ (Abandoned)

▲ Chances Peak (3000ft)

Galways Soufrière

Sugar Bay Kinsale

South Soufrière Hills

Roche's Bluff

White River ● Great Alps Falls

St Patrick's

62°15'W Old Fort Point 62°10'W

16°45'N 16°45'N

Information

The **Montserrat Tourist Board** (☎ 491-2230; www.visitmontserrat.com) is now located in Olveston. Most hotels on the island were lost in one of the eruptions. There are two hotels left, but a half-dozen cozy B&Bs have picked up a stream of adventurous travelers. The tourist board can assist with accommodation. The current government headquarters is located in Brades, where you can also find the **customs office** (☎ 491-3816) and **post office** (☎ 491-2457).

Caribbean Connections (☎ in the US or Canada 888-255-6889; www.islandhoppingexperts.com) is an excellent resource for travel arrangements and information about Montserrat and other Caribbean destinations.

Sights & Activities

Soufrière Hills Volcano isn't accessible, but there are several good vantage points, as well as a comprehensive center set up by an international team of vulcanologists. The **Montserrat Volcano Observatory** (MVO; ☎ 491-5647; www.mvo.ms; adult/child EC$10/5; ⏱ 8:30am-4:30pm Mon-Fri) monitors the action of the volcano, as well as all volcanic activity in the Caribbean. It's located in Fleming's, up the hill from the town of Salem. Tours of the volcano are held at 3:15pm on Tuesday and Thursday.

Any visitors to Montserrat will probably witness at least a little volcanic activity, usually in the form of a small hybrid earthquake, sulfur dioxide flux or rockfall.

Although much of the ocean surrounding the southern part of the island is still off-limits, what is left of Montserrat's **diving** is legendary. Best of all, it's been left in near-pristine condition because the volcano virtually wiped out tourism.

The island's only dive shop, **Sea Wolf** (☎ 491-6859; www.seawolfdivingschool.com), in Woodlands, is an excellent operation that offers one-tank dives from US$40, two-tank dives for US$80 and night dives for US$60. It rents out **snorkeling** gear for US$10 per day and offers a host of dive courses, including an underwater photography course.

Sleeping

There are two hotels, six B&Bs and a handful of apartment and villa rentals available on the island (check the tourist board website for links to all accommodations). The tourist board can arrange accommodations by email or phone.

Erindell Villa (☎ 491-3655; http://mni.ms/erindell; s/d US$55/65; [P] [💻] [🐕]) This is a good choice in Woodlands. Comfortable rooms come with ceil-ing fans, borrowed snorkeling gear, snacks, free Internet access and a few dialect lessons if you're game. And you don't even have to dig your old ash mask out of storage – they're provided, if need be.

Getting There & Around

A new **airport** (MNI; ☎ 491-2533), not yet named, is opening at Gerald's, where the heliport is located. It is currently scheduled to take only **Winair** (☎ 877-255-6889; www.fly-winair.com; hub Sint Maarten) flights out of Antigua.

The **Montserrat Ferry** (Montserrat Aviation Services; ☎ 491-2533) leaves St John's Bay in Antigua at 6:30am on Monday, Wednesday, Friday and Saturday, and at 9am on Tuesday and Thursday, and again at 4pm on each of these days (no ferry service on Sunday). Return ferries to Antigua depart approximately 1½ hours later. The fare costs US$75 return (US$52 weekend return), and the trip takes just under one hour. Check in at least one hour prior to departure.

A slightly more expensive but beguiling journey is by eight-passenger **helicopter** Antigua (☎ 268-462-3147; Carib Aviation, VC Bird International Airport); Montserrat (☎ 491-2533; Montserrat Aviation Services), with at least one morning and afternoon service on Monday, Tuesday, Thursday, Friday and Sunday (US$112 round-trip, 20 minutes); check in at least one hour prior to departure. Call well in advance for times and bookings.

It's possible to rent cars or scooters on the island; check with the tourist board.

HALF MOON & NONSUCH BAYS

Half Moon Bay, on the southeastern side of the island, is an undeveloped crescent-shaped bay with a beautiful white-sand beach and turquoise waters.

Just north of Half Moon Bay at Nonsuch Bay lies a little slice of Tuscany in the Caribbean: **Harmony Hall** (☎ 460-4120; www .harmonyhall.com; PO Box 1558; r US$165; [🐕]). This delightful six-roomed inn is the perfect place to get away from it all. Set on atmospheric grounds around a converted sugar mill, individually designed rooms have king-sized beds, patios, local art on the walls and Mediterranean tiled baths. Italian food enthusiasts will be in for a treat with lobster ravioli or roast snapper in wine served in the candlelit open-air **restaurant** (mains EC$30-80; ⏱ lunch, dinner Fri & Sat). Harmony Hall also has a fine collection of quality arts and crafts, with changing exhibitions of work by local and regional artists, and a dinghy dock for yachters.

LONG BAY

On the east side of Antigua, Long Bay has clear blue waters and a gorgeous white-sand beach that's reef-protected and good for snorkeling. Two exclusive resorts lie at the ends of the beach, one housing a dive shop. Other than a few private homes and a couple of beach bars, there's little else in the neighborhood. Unless you're looking for total seclusion or don't mind paying hefty taxi fares, you'll need a car if you make a base in this area.

Devil's Bridge

A modest coastal sea arch, Devil's Bridge is at Indian Town Point, an area thought to be the site of an early Arawak settlement. To get here, turn east onto the paved road a third of a mile (0.5km) before the Long Bay Hotel turn-off. After a mile the road ends at a roundabout; from here the arch is a minute's walk to the east. Be careful when you're walking near the arch as the Atlantic breakers that have cut the arch out of these limestone cliffs occasionally sweep over the top.

Long Bay Hotel (☎ 463-2005; www.longbayhotel .com; PO Box 442; r with breakfast & dinner from US$345) On the east end of Long Bay, this upscale, family-run hotel has Creole-style rooms with wicker furnishings and sea views; some have pitched ceilings. Tennis, water sports and diving are available, and the open-air restaurant offers candlelit dining with a lovely ocean view.

BETTY'S HOPE

Just southeast of the village of Pares, **Betty's Hope** (🕙 9am-4pm Tue-Sat) was the island's first sugar plantation, built by Christopher Codrington in 1674 and named in honor of his daughter Betty. Ruins of two old stone windmills, a still house (distillery) and a few other stone structures remain on the site, which is now under the jurisdiction of the Museum of Antigua & Barbuda. Through a combined local and international effort, one of the mills has been painstakingly restored and returned to working condition. The mill is operated only on special occasions, but the windmill sails remain up year-round, with the exception of the hurricane season.

The site's old stable has been converted into a visitors center, and focuses on Antigua's sugar era and the estate's history. A donation of US$2 is appreciated. The road into Betty's Hope is signposted.

BARBUDA

Barbuda, 25 miles (40km) north of Antigua, remains one of the Eastern Caribbean's least-visited places. Other than its frigate-bird colony and its beautiful beaches, most of which are best accessed by private boat, there's not much to attract tourists to this low, scrubby island.

The only village, Codrington, is home to most residents and is the site of the island's airport. Barbuda has three small, exclusive resorts on its southern coast, although these clublike places are so removed from the rest of the island that they have their own landing strip and haven't done much to upset Barbuda's isolation.

Interestingly, most of the 1250 islanders share half a dozen surnames and can trace their lineage to a small group of slaves brought to Barbuda by Sir Codrington, who leased the island in 1685 from the British Crown. The slaves raised livestock and grew food crops, turning Barbuda into a breadbasket to feed laborers working Antigua's sugar plantations. The Codrington family managed to keep their lease, which was negotiated at an annual rental payment of 'one fattened sheep,' for nearly two centuries. Their legacy remains well beyond the town's name – from the communal land-use policies that still govern Barbuda to the introduced goats, sheep and feral donkeys that range freely (to the detriment of the island flora).

Besides having the Caribbean's largest colony of frigate birds, Barbuda hosts tropical mockingbirds, warblers, pelicans, ibis, oystercatchers, herons and numerous kinds of ducks. The island also has wild boar and white-tailed deer, both of which are legally hunted.

Getting There & Around
AIR

Unless you charter a plane or helicopter, your only option for getting to Barbuda by air is with **Carib Aviation** (☎ 462-3147; www .candoo.com/carib), which has 20-minute flights

ANTIGUA & BARBUDA

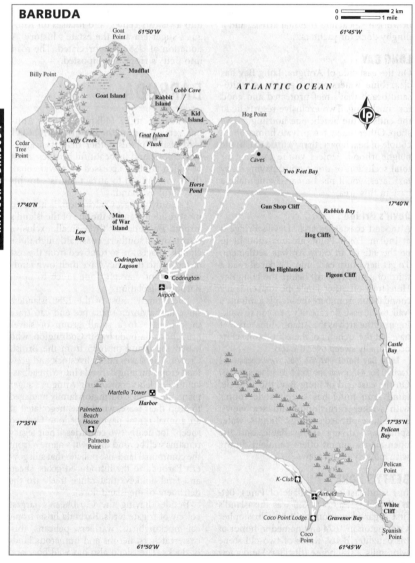

BARBUDA

from Antigua to Barbuda at 7:45am and 5pm daily; flights return from Barbuda to Antigua at 8:15am and 5:30pm. The fare is US$70 round-trip.

BOAT

Barbuda's reefs, which extend several miles from shore, are thought to have claimed

a good 200 ships since colonial times – a rather impressive number, considering that Barbuda has never been a major port.

Some reefs remain poorly charted, and the challenge of navigating through them is one reason Barbuda remains well off the beaten path. If you're sailing to the island, bring everything you'll need in advance, because there are no yachting facilities on Barbuda.

There's no scheduled passenger-boat service to Barbuda, but if you want to try your luck hitching with a private yacht, check around at the marinas on Antigua or take a day tour (below).

CAR & MOTORCYCLE
Barbuda has no public transportation. Distances are too great and the dusty dirt roads too hot to make walking a practical means of exploring. There isn't an established taxi service, but you might be able to arrange to hire someone to drive you around – inquire at your guesthouse or try **Byron Askie** (☎ 460-0164), who also rents out a car for US$50 per day.

Several other locals rent out vehicles. A good place to start is with **Hilroy Thomas** (☎ 460-0015) or **JS Walker** (☎ 460-0619); you should be able to arrange 4WD rental for about US$55 a day. **George 'Prophet' Burton** (☎ 460-0103) has a 14-seater minibus and **Eric Burton** (☎ 460-0465) has a 32-seater bus for hire; both men will act as driver and tour guide, if needed.

TOURS
Barbuda has a reputation for tours that fail to materialize, drivers that don't show up at the airport or some other missing link. Confirm all reservations.

Some Antiguan travel agents, such as **Wadadli Travel & Tours** (☎ 462-2227; Market St), offer day trips to Barbuda that include a visit to the rookery and caves, lobster lunch and time on one of the lovely beaches. They usually need a minimum of four people, and cost US$1200 per person without airfare. **Antigua Adventures** (☎ 727-3261; www.antiguaadventures.com; PO Box 1669, St John's) runs day trips on a powerboat to Barbuda that include a visit to the bird sanctuary, snorkeling and lunch (US$150).

Barbuda Bike Tours (☎ 773-9599; www.barbuda biketours.com) organizes cycle tours of the island, as well as bike rentals from January to May (mountain-bike rental per half-/full day US$20/30).

Alternatively, you can make your own way to Barbuda and pick up a local taxi driver or guide from there. Helpful local artist and café owner **Claire Frank** (☎ 460-0434; 9am-5pm) can arrange tours, with advance notice.

FRIGATE BIRDS
Frigate birds skim the water's surface for fish, but because their feathers lack the water-resistant oils common to other seabirds, they cannot dive into water. Also known as the man-of-war bird, the frigate bird has evolved into an aerial pirate that supplements its own fishing efforts by harassing other seabirds until they release their catch, which the frigate bird then swoops up in midflight.

While awkward on the ground, the frigate bird, with its distinctive forked tail and 6ft (1.8m) wingspan, is mesmerizingly graceful in flight. It has the lightest weight-to-wingspan ratio of any bird and can soar at great heights for hours on end – making it possible for the bird to feed along the coast of distant islands and return home to roost at sunset without having landed anywhere other than its nesting site.

CODRINGTON
The town of Codrington – a modest, low-key place – is on the inland side of Codrington Lagoon, a hefty 3.5 miles (5.6km) north of the nearest beach.

The town begins at the airport – simply walk to the north from there and you'll be in the center of it.

Codrington is home to Barbuda's post office, its bank and its police station, as well as a government house that dates from 1743. However, this is not a town set up for visitors: there are few signs, and only one of its eateries keeps regular hours.

Sleeping & Eating
Nedds Guest House (☎ 460-0059; s/d US$35/60) Located above a grocery store at the head of the airport. Run by MacArthur Nedd, it has four rooms with fans and private bath, and a communal kitchen. McArthur also runs a taxi service.

Palm Tree Guest House (☎ 460-0517; r US$80-120) Next to the bakery in town, this place has eight doubles with private bath, fan and satellite TV. Its restaurant (7:30am–10pm) opens in season, and serves everything from inexpensive breakfast fare and sandwiches to a full lobster meal for about EC$40.

A couple of snack shops are in the village center.

CODRINGTON LAGOON

The expansive, brackish estuary of Codrington Lagoon, which runs along Barbuda's west coast, is an intriguing destination for bird-watchers. Thousands of frigate birds nest in the lagoon's scrubby mangroves – with as many as a dozen birds roosting on a single bush. Because of the density, the birds' nesting sites are all abuzz with squawking.

The most popular time to visit the rookery is during the mating season, from October to February. Male frigate birds put on a colorful display, ballooning up their bright red throat pouches as part of the elaborate courtship rituals. While the males line up in the bushes, arch their heads back and puff out their pouches with an air of machismo, the females take to the sky. When one spots a suitor that impresses her, she'll land and initiate a mating ritual. After mating, a nest is built from twigs that the male gathers. The female lays a single egg that both birds take turns incubating. It takes about seven weeks for the chick to hatch, and nearly six months for it to learn to fly and finally leave the nest.

The nesting site is in the upper lagoon area known as Man of War Island and can be reached only by boat. There are a couple of outboards that can take visitors out to the rookery, but arrangements generally need to be made a day in advance. If you're staying on Barbuda you can arrange it through your guesthouse – the cost is about US$50 per boat for up to four people, and the trip lasts about 75 minutes. For those visiting Barbuda for the day, there are day tours that include the rookery (see p499).

WEST & SOUTH COASTS

The west coast of Barbuda is lined with magnificent white-sand **beaches** and azure waters. From Palmetto Point northward there's a beautiful pinkish strand that extends 11 miles (18km), most of it lining the narrow barrier of land separating Codrington Lagoon from the ocean. Because of its isolation, however, the beach remains largely the domain of one hotel and a few lone boaters. More-accessible beaches are found along the coast south of the harbor, with one of the finest sweeps along the stretch between the two resorts.

The **harbor** has a customs office and a sand-loading operation – Barbuda's sands also glisten on some of Antigua's beaches!

To the northwest of the harbor is the 56ft-high (17m) **Martello Tower**, a former lookout station that from a distance looks like an old sugar mill. About 0.5 miles (0.8km) north of Coco Point is a nice white-sand strand with nearshore coral formations that provide good snorkeling.

The pristine waters of **Gravenor Bay**, between Coco and Spanish Points, are a favored yacht anchorage with reef formations and excellent snorkeling. Near the center of the bay is an old, deteriorating pier, while the ruins of a small **tower** lie about 0.5 miles (0.8km) away to the east.

Archaeologists believe that the uninhabited peninsula leading to **Spanish Point** was once the site of a major Arawak settlement. A dirt track connects both ends of the bay, and another leads northward from the east side of the salt pond.

Sleeping

Beach House (☎ 460-0442; www.caribbeanclubs.net/the beachhouse; ste from US$615; ✱ ▢ ▢) At Palmetto Point, this spectacular property has 21 airy suites that open right onto the pink-sand beach. Their white modernist interiors offer every imaginable amenity. The significant price includes airport transfers and massage on arrival.

K-Club and Coco Point Lodge are two very exclusive resorts at the southern end of Barbuda. Both are incredibly expensive, quite separated from the rest of the island and a bit of a hike to reach.

CAVES

For those who feel like taking a look down under, there are some caves about 5 miles (8km) northeast of Codrington, though if it's been raining recently mud holes may well make it impossible to visit them. **Dark Cave** is an expansive underground cavern with pools of deep water, while another cave near Two Feet Bay contains the faded drawings of Arawaks.

DIRECTORY

ACCOMMODATIONS

Other than a couple of budget guesthouses in St John's and a handful scattered around the island, Antigua is mainly home to resort-type complexes, many of them offering

---

PRACTICALITIES

- **Newspapers & Magazines** Get up on local news with the pro-government *Antigua Sun* or the opposition-leaning *Daily Observer*.

- **Radio** Catch hourly news and weather on Gem radio, at 93.9FM.

- **Video Systems** NTSC is the standard video system.

- **Electricity** The current used mostly is 220V, but some places use 110V, 60 cycles; check first.

- **Weights & Measures** The imperial system is used here.

---

all-inclusive packages. There are a few good-value, moderate-range places around the island, with prices from about US$70 for a double in summer and closer to US$100 in winter. Still, most of Antigua's accommodations easily charge double these prices.

If you plan on traveling in late summer, keep in mind that many of Antigua's hotels close for September, and some extend that a few weeks in either direction.

In addition to the rates given throughout this chapter, an 8.5% government tax and a 10% service charge are added to all accommodations bills. See the main Directory (p757) for budget, midrange and top-end accommodations prices in this book.

ACTIVITIES
Beaches & Swimming
Antigua's tourist office boasts that the island has 365 beaches, 'one for each day of the year.' While the count may be suspect, the island certainly doesn't lack lovely strands. Most of Antigua's beaches have white or light golden sands with turquoise water – many are protected by coral reefs and all are officially public. You can find nice sandy stretches all around the island, and, generally, wherever there's a resort, there's a beach. Prime beaches on the west coast include the adjacent Dickenson and Runaway beaches, Deep Bay and Hawksbill Beach to the west of St John's, and the less populated Darkwood Beach and Johnson's Point Beach to the south. On the east coast, Half Moon Bay and Long Bay are top contenders. Those

visitors based in the English Harbour area can make their way to Galleon Beach and the clear waters of secluded Pigeon Beach. The far ends of some public beaches, including the north side of Dickenson, are favored by topless bathers, and nude bathing is practiced along a section of Hawksbill Beach.

Diving
Antigua has some excellent diving, with coral canyons, wall drops and sea caves hosting a range of marine creatures, including turtles, sharks, barracuda and colorful reef fish. Popular diving sites include the 2-mile-long (3.2km) Cades Reef, whose clear, calm waters have an abundance of fish, and numerous soft and hard corals, and Ariadne Shoal, which offers reefs teeming with large fish, lobsters and nurse sharks. A fun spot for both divers and snorkelers is *Jettias*, a 310ft (94.5m) steamer that sank in 1917, and that now provides a habitat for reef fish and coral. The deepest end of the wreck is in about 30ft (9m) of water, while the shallowest part comes up almost to the surface.

DIVE SHOPS
The going rate is about US$55 for a one-tank dive, US$75 for a two-tank dive and US$65 for a night dive. Nondivers who want to view the underwater world but don't want to overly commit can opt for a half-day resort course that culminates with a reef dive (around US$90). Rates include the rental of tanks and weights, but you'll have to pay an extra US$15 to US$20 for a regulator, BCD (buoyancy compensating device), snorkel, mask and fins. Most places give a discount for payment by cash or traveler's check.

Dive shops in Antigua:

Deep Bay Divers (☎ 463-8000; www.deepbaydivers .com; PO Box 2150, Heritage Quay, St John's)

Dive Antigua (☎ 462-3483; www.diveantigua.com; PO Box 251, Rex Halcyon Cove, Dickenson Bay)

Dockyard Divers (☎ 460-1178; www.dockyard-divers .com; PO Box 184, Nelson's Dockyard)

Jolly Dive (☎ 462-8305; PO Box 744, Jolly Harbour)

Octopus Divers (☎ 460-6286; www.octopusdivers.com; PO Box 2105, Falmouth Harbour)

EMERGENCY NUMBERS

Ambulance (☎ 462-0251)
Police (☎ 462-0125)

Golf

Both **Cedar Valley Golf Club** (☎ 462-0161), a 10-minute drive north of St John's, and **Jolly Harbour Golf Course** (☎ 480-6950), at Jolly Harbour, have an 18-hole course with cart and club rentals.

Hiking

The historical society, which operates the Museum of Antigua & Barbuda (p488), sponsors a culturally or environmentally oriented hike once a month. Walks average about 90 minutes and typically visit old estates or interesting landscapes. The walks are free, but donations are welcome. Call the **museum** (☎ 462-1469) for information on upcoming hikes.

Other Water Activities

Both **Tony's Water Sports** (☎ 462-6326) and **Sea Sports** (☎ 462-3355), at Dickenson Bay, offer a range of boating activities, such as waterskiing (US$35), parasailing (US$55) and jetskiing (US$40). Tony will take groups of up to four people deep-sea fishing (per half-day US$380) or snorkeling (per day US$20).

BOOKS

Antigua's best-known writer is Jamaica Kincaid, who has authored a number of novels and essays including *A Small Place* (1988), which gives a scathing account of the negative effects of tourism on Antigua. Other internationally recognized works by Kincaid include the novel *Annie John,* which recounts growing up in Antigua, and *At the Bottom of the River,* a collection of short stories.

Harvard lecturer Robert Coram penned an incendiary investigation, *Caribbean Time Bomb* (1993), into corruption on Antigua and VC Bird's involvement with the US government.

EMBASSIES & CONSULATES

Antiguan & Barbudan Embassies & Consulates

UK (☎ 020-7486-7073; 15 Thayer St, London W1M5LD)
USA (☎ 202-362-5211; 3216 New Mexico Ave NW, Washington, DC 20016)

Consulates in Antigua & Barbuda

Germany (☎ 462-3174; PO Box 1259, St John's)
UK (☎ 462-0008/9; Price Waterhouse Centre, 11 Old Parham Rd, St John's)

FESTIVALS & EVENTS

Antigua Sailing Week (April) A major, week-long yachting event that begins on the last Sunday in April. It's the largest regatta in the Caribbean and generally attracts about 150 boats from a few dozen countries. In addition to a series of five boat races, there are rum parties and a formal ball, with most activities taking place at Nelson's Dockyard and Falmouth Harbour, where the majority of boats are anchored.
Caribana Festival (May) This is Barbuda's own Carnival, but it's by no means the grand affair of Antigua's Carnival.
Carnival (July & August) Antigua's big annual festival is held from the end of July and culminates in a parade on the first Tuesday in August. Calypso music, steel bands, masqueraders, floats and jump-ups (nighttime street parties) are all part of the celebrations.

HOLIDAYS

Public holidays in Antigua & Barbuda:
New Year's Day January 1
Good Friday late March/early April
Easter Monday late March/early April
Labour Day first Monday in May
Whit Monday eighth Monday after Easter
Queen's Birthday second Saturday in June
Carnival Monday & Tuesday first Monday and Tuesday in August
Antigua & Barbuda Independence Day November 1
Christmas Day December 25
Boxing Day December 26

MONEY

The currency of Antigua & Barbuda is the Eastern Caribbean dollar (EC$), and the official exchange rate is EC$2.72 to US$1.

US dollars are widely accepted. However, unless rates are posted in US dollars, as is the norm with accommodations, it usually works out better to use EC dollars.

MasterCard, Visa and Amex are widely accepted. Credit-card charges are made in US dollars, so businesses that quote prices in EC dollars must convert the bill to a US dollar total. Whenever you intend to pay by credit card it's a good idea to ask about the exchange rate first, as some places use varying exchange rates, potentially overcharging by as much as 8%.

A 10% service charge is added to most restaurant bills, in which case no further tipping is necessary.

TELEPHONE

Almost all pay phones have been converted to the Caribbean Phone Card system. Cards can be bought in areas near the phones and from the Cable & Wireless offices in St John's or English Harbour. They're priced from EC$10 to EC$60, depending on the number of time units they have.

Avoid credit-card phones, as they charge a steep US$2 per minute locally, US$4 to other Caribbean islands or the US, and up to US$8 elsewhere.

Antigua & Barbuda's area code is ☎ 268. To call from North America, dial ☎ 1-268, followed by the seven-digit local number. From elsewhere, dial your country's international access code + ☎ 286 + the local phone number. We've included only the seven-digit local number in Antigua & Barbuda listings in this chapter.

For directory assistance, dial ☎ 411.

VISAS

Visas are not required by most nationalities for stays of less than six months.

TRANSPORTATION

GETTING THERE & AWAY

For details on travel between Antigua and Montserrat, see the boxed text, p530.

Entering Antigua & Barbuda

All visitors need a valid passport (US citizens see the boxed text, p772) and a round-trip or onward ticket, though immigration officials seem to be more interested in where you plan to stay. On arrival, you'll be given an immigration form to complete.

Air

VC Bird International Airport (ANU; ☎ 462-0358) is about 5 miles (8km) from St John's center. There's a tourist information booth, an ATM that accepts Visa, MasterCard, Cirrus and Plus cards, a **bureau de change** (⊙ 8am-9pm Mon-Fri) and a dozen car-rental companies. Nearby is a post office.

For information on traveling from outside the Caribbean to (and from) Antigua and Barbuda, see p772.

You can get a direct or connecting flight from Antigua to any destination in LIAT's or Caribbean Star's network. If you plan to island-hop, it's worth investigating the multi-stop packages on their websites. For information on helicopters to Montserrat, see p496.

The following airlines fly to and from Antigua & Barbuda from within the Caribbean islands:

Air Jamaica (☎ 800-523-5585; www.airjamaica.com; hub Montego Bay, Jamaica)

American Eagle (☎ 800-433-7300; www.aa.com; hub San Juan)

British West Indies Air (BWIA; ☎ 800-538-2942; www.bwee.com; hub Port of Spain, Trinidad)

Carib Aviation (☎ 462-3147; www.candoo.com/carib; hub Antigua) Charters flights to Barbuda.

Caribbean Star (☎ 480-2501; www.flycaribbeanstar .com; hub Antigua)

Caribbean Sun (☎ 866-864-6272; www.flycsa.com; hub San Juan)

LIAT (☎ 462-0700; www.liatairline.com; hub Antigua)

Sea

CRUISE SHIP

Antigua is a port of call for numerous cruise ships. The island's cruise-ship terminal, at Heritage Quay in St John's Harbour, has a duty-free shopping center and a casino. Heritage Quay is within easy walking distance of St John's main sights: the museum, cathedral and historic Redcliffe Quay. Cruise ships also anchor near Falmouth Harbor and taxi their passengers into the harbor for the day. See p777 for more on cruises.

YACHT

A favorite place to clear customs is at Nelson's Dockyard in English Harbour. Other ports of entry are Falmouth Harbour, Jolly Harbour, St John's Harbour, and Crabbs Marina in Parham Harbour. If you're going on to Barbuda, ask for a cruising permit, which will allow you to visit that island without further formalities.

Antigua has many protected harbors and bays, and fine anchorages are found all around the island. Full-service marinas are at English Harbour, Falmouth Harbour, Jolly Harbour and Parham Harbour.

Boaters can make reservations at many restaurants around Falmouth Harbour and English Harbour via VHF channel 68.

Yacht charters can be arranged through **Sun Yacht Charters** (☎ 460-2615) at Nelson's Dockyard.

GETTING AROUND

Bicycle

Paradise Boat Sales (☎ 460 7125) at Jolly Harbour rents out mountain bikes for US$15

ANTIGUA & BARBUDA

for single-day rentals and US$12 per day if you rent for a minimum of two days.

Bike Plus (☎ 462-2453; PO Box 2771, Comache St, St John's), on the road to Falmouth, rents out bikes for US$10 per day.

Barbuda Bike Tours (☎ 773-9599; www.barbuda biketours.com; mountain-bike rental per half-/full day US$20/30) rents out bikes from January to May.

Bus

Antigua's buses are privately owned and are predominantly minivans, although there are a few midsize buses. Fares cost EC$1.50 to EC$4.50. Buses from St John's to Falmouth and English Harbour are plentiful, cost around EC$3 and take about 30 minutes. They start early and generally run until about 7pm. Rush hour is particularly bustling, with lots of buses between 4pm and 5pm. There are very few buses on Sunday.

The main bus station (West Bus Station) in St John's is opposite the public market. All destinations are allocated a number, and each bus displays a number that indicates where it's heading. Notices are posted about with destination numbers. Buses line up in a row and don't actually leave until they're full. So just find the bus you need, hop on, and hope it fills up and leaves before you melt.

Buses to the east side of the island leave from the East Bus Station, near the corner of Independence Ave and High St, and go to Piggots and Willikies. The numbering system doesn't apply here, so you'll need to ask around to find your bus.

There's no bus service to the airport, Dickenson Bay or other resort areas on the northern part of the island.

Public transportation on Barbuda is extremely limited; see p499.

Car & Motorcycle
DRIVER'S LICENSE

When you arrive, you'll need to buy a local driving permit, available from car-rental agencies. It costs US$20 and is valid for three months.

RENTAL

There are more than a dozen car-rental agencies on Antigua, most with representatives at the airport. All of the agencies in the following list rent out cars for around US$50 a day, but can drop as low as US$40 in summer, when things are slow. Discounts are usually offered for longer rentals. Many of the companies also offer 4WDs for the same rates, or for US$5 to US$10 more.

All but the newest rental cars are generally quite beat, mostly because of the poor road conditions. Your best bet (though by no means a sure thing) for getting a roadworthy car is to book with one of the international agencies. Most car-rental agencies will deliver cars to your hotel free of charge.

Rental companies·
Avis (☎ 462-2840; www.avis.com)
Dollar (☎ 462-0362; www.dollar.com)
Hertz (☎ 462-4114; www.hertz.com)
Oakland Rent-A-Car (☎ 462-3021; www.carib-hotels.cmo/antigua/oakland)
Thrifty Rent-A-Car (☎ 462-9532; www.thrifty.com)

At Jolly Harbour, **Paradise Boat Sales** (☎ 460-7125) rents out 50cc scooters for US$35 and 150cc motorcycles for US$40. Rates are 20% less for multiple-day rentals.

See p499 for information on car rental in Barbuda.

ROAD CONDITIONS

Antigua's roads have improved over the last few years, but many are still in bad shape. Roads in the west, north and south are quite good, but to the east of the island they are in need of some repair. Fig Tree Dr is more an off-road rally course, with potholes and gravel to contend with. If you plan to get off the beaten track, it's best to hire a 4WD.

Be aware of goats darting across the road and of narrow roads in built-up areas, which can be crowded with children after school finishes.

Finding your way around Antigua can prove difficult at times. The island is randomly dotted with green road signs pointing you in the right direction, but they peter out the further away you get from the main centers. Private signs pointing the way to restaurants, hotels and a few other tourist spots are far more frequent. Beyond that, the best landmarks are old stone windmills, which are shown on the Ordnance Survey map of Antigua – a very handy item to have if you intend to do extensive exploring.

ROAD RULES

Driving is on the left-hand side. Many rental cars have steering wheels on the left, which can be disorienting. The speed limit is generally 20mph (32km) in villages and 40mph (64km) in rural areas. Numerous gas stations are scattered around the island, including one just outside the airport terminal. Gas sells for around EC$9 per gallon.

Taxi

Taxis are identifiable by number plates beginning with 'H.' Fares are regulated by the government, but be sure to confirm the fare with the driver before riding away. Fares from the airport are US$8 to St John's, US$6 to Runaway or Dickenson Bays, US$16 to Jolly Harbour and US$24 to English Harbour. Fares are for up to four persons; a fifth person costs an additional 25%.

In St John's there's a taxi stand opposite the public market, and taxi drivers also hang around Heritage Quay. Most hotels have taxis assigned to them; if you don't find one, ask at reception.

There is no established taxi service on Barbuda, but you may be able to hire someone to drive you around. See p499 for more information.

Guadeloupe

The island archipelago of Guadeloupe is like a busy chunk of rural France transported to the tropics. As one of the most urbanized of the region's islands, you'll need to scratch beneath the French polish to get a grip on its Creole core. With more Citroëns on the road than in a Jean-Luc Godard movie, and with *boulangeries* (bakeries) and the blare of europop on every street corner, you may feel closer to Paris than Puerto Rico. But head away from the resorts, and you'll find that the buzz of insects in the banana groves, the friendliness of the *paysans* (countryfolk) and the whiff of coconut rum will put you firmly back on Caribbean time.

Guadeloupe's shape inevitably invites comparison to a butterfly, with its two wing-shaped islands. Grande-Terre with its gently rolling hills, vibrant resorts and the bulk of the island's beaches will keep action-seekers happy, while Basse-Terre's rugged mountains wrapped in a dense rainforest of tall trees and lush ferns appeal to those in search of a more natural experience. Much of the interior of Basse-Terre is a national park, where you can hike to the Eastern Caribbean's highest waterfalls and climb the island's highest peak, La Soufrière, a smoldering volcano.

Guadeloupe's surrounding offshore islands make for enjoyable excursions. The most visited, Terre-de-Haut, is a delightful place with a quaint central village and harbor. The other populated islands – Terre-de-Bas, Marie-Galante and La Désirade – offer a glimpse of rural French West Indies that has changed little in recent times.

FAST FACTS

- **Area** 554 sq miles (1434 sq km)
- **Capital** Basse-Terre
- **Country code** ☎ 590
- **Departure tax** none
- **Famous for** Its butterfly shape
- **Languages** French, Creole
- **Money** Euro (€); €1 = US$1.20 = UK£0.69
- **Official name** La Guadeloupe
- **People** Guadeloupean
- **Phrases** *Est-ce que vous voudriez un ti-punch?* (Would you like a ti-punch?)
- **Population** 440,000
- **Visa** None required for residents of the US, Canada or the EU

HIGHLIGHTS

- **Porte d'Enfer** (p519) Picnic and loll around at the lagoon at the 'Gate of Hell.'
- **Parc National de la Guadeloupe** (p519) Explore this extensive park, with its verdant rainforest, magnificent waterfalls and a steaming volcano.
- **Terre-de-Haut** (p524) Take a break on this charming island and check out its grand French fort.
- **Marie-Galante** (p529) Get acquainted with the timeless rural character of this sleepy isle.
- **Le Moule** (p518) Take in the bustle of provincial life.

ITINERARIES

- **Three days** Spend a morning roaming Pointe-à-Pitre before heading west, stopping at Cascade aux Ecrevisses or hiking to La Soufrière, then on to the west coast. Dive at the Réserve Cousteau, then wander east to Grande-Terre, following a clockwise route that takes in the Porte d'Enfer, Le Moule and some well-earned R&R at the beach in Ste-Anne.
- **One week** Follow the plan for three days, then catch a boat to Terre-de-Haut, and cycle to the fort, followed by a day or two exploring Marie-Galante. Head back to the mainland for a hike at Pointe des Chateaux before a satisfying meal in St-François.

CLIMATE & WHEN TO GO

Pointe-à-Pitre's average daily high temperature in January is 83°F (28°C) while the low average is 67°F (19°C).

In July, the average daily high temperature is 88°F (31°C) while the low average is 74°F (23°C).

The annual rainfall in Pointe-à-Pitre is 71in (180cm). February to April is the driest period, when measurable rain falls an average of seven days a month and the average humidity is around 77%. The wettest months are July to November, when rain falls about 14 days a month and the average humidity reaches 85%.

Because of its height, the Basse-Terre side is both cooler and rainier than Grande-Terre. Its highest point, La Soufrière, averages 390in (990cm) of rain per year. The trade winds, called *alizés,* often temper the climate.

HOW MUCH?

- **Taxi from the airport to Point-à-Pitre center** €15
- **One-hour diving trip** €35
- **Comfortable hotel double room** €80
- **Museum ticket** €3.50
- **Local fish meal** €10

LONELY PLANET INDEX

- **Liter of gas** €1.50
- **Liter of bottled water** €2
- **Glass of ti-punch** €3
- **Souvenir T-shirt** €8
- **Street snack:** caramelized nuts €2

HISTORY

When sighted by Columbus on November 14, 1493, Guadeloupe was inhabited by Carib Indians, who called it Karukera (Island of Beautiful Waters). The Spanish made two attempts to settle Guadeloupe in the early 1500s but were repelled both times by fierce Carib resistance, and finally in 1604 they abandoned their claim to the island.

Three decades later, French colonists sponsored by the Compagnie des Îles d'Amérique, an association of French entrepreneurs, set sail to establish the first European settlement on Guadeloupe. On June 28, 1635, the party, led by Charles Liénard de l'Olive and Jean Duplessis d'Ossonville, landed on the southeastern shore of Basse-Terre and claimed Guadeloupe for France. They drove the Caribs off the island, planted crops and within a decade had built the first sugar mill. By the time France officially annexed the island in 1674, a slavery-based plantation system had been well established.

The English invaded Guadeloupe several times and occupied it from 1759 to 1763. During this time, they developed Pointe-à-Pitre into a major harbor, opened profitable English and North American markets to Guadeloupean sugar and allowed the planters to import cheap American lumber and food. Many French colonists actually grew wealthier under the British occupation, and the economy expanded rapidly. In 1763, British occupation ended with the signing

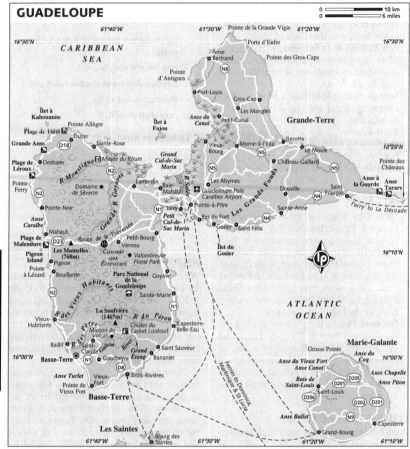

of the Treaty of Paris, which relinquished French claims in Canada in exchange for the return of Guadeloupe.

Amid the chaos of the French Revolution, the British invaded Guadeloupe again in 1794. In response, the French sent a contingent of soldiers led by Victor Hugues, a Black nationalist. Hugues freed and armed Guadeloupean slaves. On the day the British withdrew from Guadeloupe, Hugues went on a rampage and killed 300 royalists, many of them plantation owners. It marked the start of a reign of terror. In all, Hugues was responsible for the deaths of more than 1000 colonists, and as a consequence of his attacks on US ships, the USA declared war on France.

In 1802, Napoleon Bonaparte, anxious to get the situation under control, sent General Antoine Richepance to Guadeloupe. Richepance put down the uprising, restored the pre-revolutionary government and reinstituted slavery.

Guadeloupe was the most prosperous island in the French West Indies, and the British continued to covet it, invading and occupying the island for most of the period between 1810 and 1816. The Treaty of Vienna restored the island to France, which has maintained sovereignty over it continuously since 1816.

Slavery was abolished in 1848, following a campaign led by French politician Victor Schoelcher. In the years that followed, planters brought laborers from Pondicherry, a French colony in India, to work in the cane fields. Since 1871, Guadeloupe has had representation in the French parliament, and since 1946 it has been an overseas department of France.

Guadeloupe's economy is heavily dependent upon subsidies from the French government and upon its economic ties with mainland France, which absorbs the majority of Guadeloupe's exports and provides 75% of its imports. Agriculture remains a cornerstone of the economy. The leading export crop is bananas, the bulk of which grow along the southern flanks of La Soufrière.

THE CULTURE

Guadeloupean culture draws from a pool of French, African, East Indian and West Indian influences.

The mix is visible in the architecture, which ranges from French colonial buildings to Hindu temples; in the food, which merges influences from all the cultures into a unique Creole cuisine; and in the widely spoken local Creole language.

Guadeloupe is one place where you're apt to see women wearing traditional Creole dress, especially at festivals and cultural events. The typical costume consists of a full, brightly colored skirt (commonly a madras-type plaid of oranges and yellows), with a matching headdress, a white lace-trimmed blouse and petticoat, and a scarf draped over the shoulder.

WHAT'S IN A NAME?

At first glance, the names given to the twin islands that make up Guadeloupe proper are perplexing. The eastern island, which is smaller and flatter, is named Grande-Terre, which means 'big land,' while the larger, more mountainous western island is named Basse-Terre, meaning 'flat land.'

The names were not meant to describe the terrain, however, but the winds that blow over them. The trade winds, which come from the northeast, blow *grande* (big) over the flat plains of Grande-Terre but are stopped by the mountains to the west, ending up *basse* (flat) on Basse-Terre.

Population

The population of Guadeloupe (Basse-Terre and Grande-Terre) is about 420,000, with more than half the population aged under twenty. In addition, about 3000 people live on Les Saintes, 1600 on La Désirade and 13,000 on Marie-Galante.

About three-quarters of the population is of mixed ethnicity, a combination of African, European and East Indian descent. There's also a sizable population of White islanders who trace their ancestry to the early French settlers, as well as a number of more recently arrived French from the mainland.

RELIGION

The predominant religion is Roman Catholicism. There are also Methodist, Seventh Day Adventist, Jehovah's Witness and Evangelical denominations, and a sizable Hindu community.

ARTS

Guadeloupe's most renowned native son is St John Perse, the pseudonym of Alexis Léger, who was born in Guadeloupe in 1887. Perse won the Nobel Prize for literature in 1960 for the evocative imagery of his poetry. One of his many noted works is *Anabase* (1925), which was translated into English by TS Eliot.

The leading contemporary novelist in the French West Indies is Guadeloupe native Maryse Condé. Two of her best-selling novels have been translated into English. The epic *Tree of Life* centers on the life of a Guadeloupean family, their roots and the identity of Guadeloupean society itself. *Crossing the Mangrove* (1995) is an enjoyable yarn that gently reveals nuances of rural Guadeloupean relationships as it unravels the life, and untimely death, of a controversial villager.

ENVIRONMENT
The Land

Guadeloupe proper is comprised of two very different twin islands divided by a narrow mangrove channel called the Rivière Salée. The islands are volcanic in origin. Grande-Terre, the eastern island and flatter of the two, has a limestone cover, the result of being submerged during earlier geologic periods. Basse-Terre, the larger, western island, is rugged, lush and mountainous. Guadeloupe's highest point is La Soufrière, a 4812ft (1467m) active volcano.

Of the nearby offshore islands, Les Saintes (5.5 sq miles/14 sq km) is high and rugged, Marie-Galante (61 sq miles/158 sq km) is round and flat and La Désirade (8.5 sq miles/22 sq km) is somewhere in the middle with hills that rise up to an elevation of 895 ft (273m).

Wildlife

Guadeloupe's diverse vegetation ranges from mangrove swamps to mountainous rainforest. Basse-Terre has an abundance of tropical hardwood trees, including lofty *gommiers* (gums) and large buttressed *chataigniers* (chestnut trees), and thick fern forests punctuated with flowering heliconia and ginger plants.

Birds found on Guadeloupe include various members of the heron family, pelicans, hummingbirds and the endangered Guadeloupe wren. A common sighting is the bright yellow-bellied bananaquit, a small nectar-feeding bird that's a frequent visitor at open-air restaurants, where it raids unattended sugar bowls.

You'll probably see drawings of raccoons on park brochures and in Guadeloupean advertising; it is the official symbol of Parc National de la Guadeloupe and its main habitat is in the forests of Basse-Terre.

Guadeloupe has mongooses aplenty, introduced long ago in a futile attempt to control rats in the sugar-cane fields. Agoutis (short-haired, short-eared rabbitlike rodents that look a bit like guinea pigs) are found on La Désirade. There are iguanas on Les Saintes and La Désirade.

FOOD & DRINK
Food

Island cuisine is made up of a well-matched mix of both Creole and French cultures. Locals will equally enjoy a *pain au chocolat* (chocolate-filled croissant-like pastry) and *café crème* (espresso with steamed milk or cream) at 11am, followed by chicken *colombo* (curry) and ti-punch at lunchtime. Guadeloupe is the second-largest consumer of fish per head worldwide so expect it on menus in many delicious guises. *Ouassous* (crayfish), *chatrou* (octopus) and more traditional fish such as *vivanneau* (red

snapper) are generally served simply grilled, or marinated in aromatic Creole spices such as nutmeg, ginger, vanilla and fenugreek. *Lambi* (conch – the chewy meat of a large gastropod)is also prevalent, although overfishing has meant that conch is heading for the endangered species list.

Some typical Guadeloupean dishes include *accras* (a fried mixture of okra, black-eyed peas, pepper and salt), *crabes farci* (spicy stuffed land crabs), *colombo cabri* (curried goat), rice and beans, and breadfruit gratin. Another popular Creole dish is *blaff*, a seafood preparation poached in a spicy broth.

Markets are full of colorful exotic fruits and vegetables; small, sweet bananas and huge avocados, *christophenes* (a common Caribbean vegetable shaped like a large pear), mangoes, pineapples and *maracudjas* (passion fruits).

Drink

Tap water is safe to drink. There are lots of excellent local rums, and some distilleries have tasting rooms. Homemade flavored rums (that have fruit added) are also popular; in bars and restaurants you'll commonly see these in large glass jars behind the counter. A common restaurant drink (and the locals' beverage of choice) is ti-punch, where you're brought white rum, cane sugar and a fresh lime to mix to your own proportions. Locally brewed Corsaire beer goes well with Creole food and lazy days on the beach.

Excellent French wines are served at nicer restaurants, and can also be picked up (for very reasonable prices) at the supermarkets in the larger towns.

POINTE-À-PITRE

pop 21,000
HISTORY

In 1654, a merchant named Peter, a Dutch Jew who settled in Guadeloupe after being exiled from Brazil, began a fish market on an undeveloped harborside jut of land. The area became known as Peter's Point and eventually grew into the settlement of Pointe-à-Pitre, located in the southwest of Grande-Terre.

Guadeloupe's largest municipality, Pointe-à-Pitre is a conglomerate of old and new and is largely commercial in appearance. There

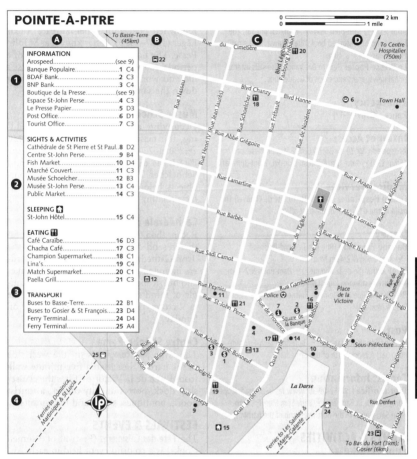

POINTE-À-PITRE

0   2 km
0   1 mile

INFORMATION	
Arospeed	(see 9)
Banque Populaire	**1** C4
BDAF Bank	**2** C3
BNP Bank	**3** C4
Boutique de la Presse	(see 9)
Espace St-John Perse	**4** C3
Le Presse Papier	**5** D3
Post Office	**6** D1
Tourist Office	**7** C3

SIGHTS & ACTIVITIES	
Cathédrale de St Pierre et St Paul	**8** D2
Centre St-John Perse	**9** B4
Fish Market	**10** D4
Marché Couvert	**11** C3
Musée Schoelcher	**12** B3
Musée St-John Perse	**13** C4
Public Market	**14** C3

SLEEPING	
St-John Hôtel	**15** C4

EATING	
Café Caraïbe	**16** D3
Chacha Café	**17** C3
Champion Supermarket	**18** C1
Lina's	**19** C4
Match Supermarket	**20** C1
Paella Grill	**21** C3

TRANSPORT	
Buses to Basse-Terre	**22** B1
Buses to Gosier & St François	**23** D4
Ferry Terminal	**24** D4
Ferry Terminal	**25** A4

GUADELOUPE

---

are a couple of small museums, but other than that the most interesting sight is the bustling harborside market.

ORIENTATION

From the outskirts, Pointe-à-Pitre looks pretty uninviting – a concrete jungle of high-rises and sprawling traffic. Venture into the center, though, and you'll find a much more attractive old town with peeling colonial architecture and palm-fringed streets.

The town hub is Place de la Victoire, an open space punctuated with tall royal palms that extends north a few blocks from the inner harbor. There are sidewalk cafés opposite its west side, a line of big old mango trees

to the north and some older buildings along with the *sous-préfecture* (sub-prefecture) office at the park's east side.

While it's not a major tourist destination, all visitors can expect to at least pass through Pointe-à-Pitre, as it is the main port for ferries to Guadeloupe's outer islands and it also shelters the central bus terminal.

Central Pointe-à-Pitre is quite compact, and nothing is more than a five- or 10-minute stroll from Place de la Victoire.

INFORMATION
Bookstores
Boutique de la Presse (Centre St-John Perse) Sells Institut Géographique National maps of Guadeloupe.

Espace St-John Perse (☎ 82-93-26; 11 Rue de Nozières; ☾ 8am-6pm Mon-Fri, 8am-1:30pm Sat) The largest and best-stocked bookstore in town has a small English-language section.

Le Presse Papier Next to Délifrance, also sells international newspapers and maps of Guadeloupe.

Emergency
Police (☎ 89-77-17)

Internet Access
Arospeed (☎ 83-81-36; 50 Centre St-John Perse; per 15min €3; ☾ 9am-1pm & 2-6pm Mon-Fri, 10am-3pm Sat)

Medical Services
Centre Hospitalier (☎ 89-10-10; Rte de Chauvel) The main hospital is north of the post office.

Money
Banque Populaire (Rue Achille René-Boisneuf; ☾ 8am-noon & 2-4pm Mon-Fri)
BDAF bank (Sq de la Banque; ☾ 8am-noon & 2-4pm Mon-Fri) Next to the tourist office.
BNP bank (Rue Achille René-Boisneuf; ☾ 8am-noon & 2-4pm Mon-Fri)

Post
Post office (Blvd Hanne; ☾ 8am-6pm Mon-Fri, 8am-noon Sat) A block north of the cathedral.

Tourist Information
Tourist office (☎ 82-09-30; www.lesilesdeguadeloupe .com; 5 Sq de la Banque; ☾ 8am-5pm Mon-Fri, 8am-noon Sat) Opposite the northwest end of the harbor.

SIGHTS & ACTIVITIES
Public Markets
There's a fun, colorful **open-air market** (☾ 5am-2pm Mon-Sat) running along La Darse, the inner harbor. Women wearing madras-cloth turbans sell island fruit, vegetables, flowers, pungent spices, handicrafts and clothing, while a few fishing boats docked at the edge of the harbor sell fresh fish. The **Marché Couvert** (cnr Rues Peynier & Schoelcher), another large public market, is just a few blocks to the west and has a good collection of handicrafts and spices. To get here from the waterfront, take the pedestrian Rue St-John Perse.

Musée St-John Perse
This **municipal museum** (9 Rue de Nozières; admission €2.50; ☾ 9am-5pm Mon-Fri, 8:30am-12:30pm Sat) occupies an attractive 19th-century colonial building with ornate wrought-iron

balconies. The museum is dedicated to the renowned poet and Nobel laureate Alexis Léger (1887–1975), better known as St John Perse. The house offers both a glimpse of a period Creole home and displays on Perse's life and work. Perse grew up a bit further down the same street, at No 54.

Musée Schoelcher
Occupying an interesting period building, this **museum** (24 Rue Peynier; admission €1.50; ☾ 8:30am-12:30pm Mon-Sat, 2-5:30pm Mon & Tue, 2-6pm Thu & Fri) is dedicated to abolitionist Victor Schoelcher. The main exhibits are personal objects belonging to Schoelcher, and artifacts relating to slavery.

Cathédrale de St Pierre et St Paul
Rather than the traditional arches, this weathered sand-colored church, nicknamed the 'Iron Cathedral,' is supported by iron girders intended to brace it against earthquakes and hurricanes. The church, which is a couple of minutes' walk northwest of Place de la Victoire, is worth a look, particularly on Sunday.

Centre St-John Perse
The large **port complex** is on the west side of the harbor, less than a five-minute walk from Place de la Victoire. It has the cruise-ship dock, port authority offices, a tourist booth, boutiques, shops and restaurants.

FESTIVALS & EVENTS
The **Fête des Cuisinières** (Festival of Women Cooks) is a colorful event held in early August. Women in Creole dress, carrying baskets of traditional foods, parade through the streets to the cathedral, where they are blessed by the bishop. It is followed by a banquet and dancing.

SLEEPING & EATING
Pointe-à-Pitre has few places to stay and even fewer reasons to spend the night. Shops close early, and the streets are almost empty after dark. If you're looking for island culture or a cozy beachside getaway, you may as well keep moving.

St-John Hôtel (☎ 82-51-57; www.saint-john-perse .com; s/d incl breakfast €85/100; ☒) In the Centre St-John Perse, this two-star member of the Anchorage chain is centrally located and extremely convenient if you're catching an early morning boat. It has 44 compact but otherwise comfortable rooms with small, shared balconies overlooking the harbor.

Chacha Café (☎ 89-61-94; cnr Rues St-John Perse & Quai Layrle; mains €4-12; ☽ 10am-9pm Mon-Fri, 10am-5pm Sat) A small, friendly local bar with a big selection of salads, omelettes and hot specials such as honeyed chicken.

Paella Grill (☎ 82-12-34; cnr Rues Frébault & St-John Perse; mains €7-10; ☽ 7am-4pm Mon-Sat) This scruffy colonial-style café with outdoor seats in the old town is great for people-watching. Try the fish *fricassée* or pork stew. There's a notice board inside that details local services.

Lina's (☎ 24-62-45; cnr Rues Frébault & Delgrés; snacks €3-7; ☽ 7:30am-6pm Mon-Fri, 8:30am-2pm Sat) A trendy café that does good coffee and smoked salmon with avocado- or pesto chicken–type sandwiches on a range of breads.

Café Caraïbe (Place de la Victoire; snacks €4-8) On the west side of the square, this little place has outdoor tables and a French café feel, with salads and crepes as well as French wine and draft beer.

There's a **Match supermarket** (Rue Frébault) north of town; the food stalls outside are a great place to get street food like gratin of *christophene*, and *accras*. The well-stocked **Champion supermarket** (Blvd Chanzy) is one of the few places open Sunday and holidays (until 12:30pm only).

SHOPPING
The harborfront market in Pointe-à-Pitre is a good place to buy island handicrafts, including straw dolls, straw hats and primitive African-style wood carvings. It's also a good spot to pick up locally grown coffee and a wide array of fragrant spices.

One of the most popular island souvenirs is *bois bandé*, the allegedly aphrodisiac bark of a local tree, usually sold soaked in rum. The nice ladies at the market will gladly explain its dosage and effects.

GETTING THERE & AROUND
Air
For information on air travel to and from the region, see p535.

TO/FROM THE AIRPORT
Taxis are easy to find at the airport; it costs about €15 into Pointe-à-Pitre center or you could rent a car on arrival. There's no bus shuttle to town from the airport.

Boat
For information on ferry travel to and from the region, see p535.

Bus
Buses to Gosier, Ste-Anne and St-François leave from Rue Dubouchage at the east side of the harbor. Buses to places in Basse-Terre leave from the northwest side of town near Bergevin Stadium, a 10-minute walk from the center along Blvd Chanzy.

Car & Motorcycle
On weekdays, traffic in the center is congested and parking can be tight. There are parking meters (€1 per hour) along the east side of Place de la Victoire and on many of the side streets throughout the city. Information on car rental is covered on p536.

GRANDE-TERRE

The southern coast of Grande-Terre, with its reef-protected waters, is Guadeloupe's main resort area. The eastern side of the island is largely open Atlantic, with crashing surf and a decidedly rural character. In the interior there's a mix of rolling hills and flat plains, the latter still largely given over to sugarcane.

Turn to above and p536 for information on transportation to Grande-Terre destinations.

BAS DU FORT
Bas du Fort, on the southern outskirts of Pointe-à-Pitre, has Guadeloupe's largest marina, a university and some new condo and hotel developments. The main hotel area is 1.25 miles (2km) by road south of the marina. Bas du Fort takes its name from its location at the *bas* (base) of Fort Fleur-d'Épée.

Aquarium de la Guadeloupe
This small harborside **aquarium** (☎ 90-92-38; adult/child €6/2.50; ☽ 9am-7pm) has 60 species of tropical fish such as the huge suede-skinned sharksuckers, moray and plenty of live coral as well as turtles and sharks. Displays are a little hard to read but it still makes a good hour's distraction. To get here, turn off the N4 east of the roundabout and follow the signs for the marina, not Bas du Fort.

Fort Fleur-d'Épée

This small 18th-century hilltop garrison offers views of Gosier and the island of Marie-Galante. Much of the coral block walls and a few of the buildings stand intact, and there are rusting cannons and flowering flamboyant trees on the grounds. To get here, turn off the N4 at the 'Bas du Fort' sign and head south for about 0.6 miles (1km); an inconspicuous sign on the left marks the side road that leads 872yd (800m) up to the fort.

GOSIER

Guadeloupe's most popular tourist resort is Gosier, 5 miles (8km) southeast of Pointe-à-Pitre. It's really two towns, neatly divided: a cluster of high-rise hotels full of French families on one side and a growing Caribbean village next door.

On the west side of Gosier is a tourist strip with a run of resort hotels, a casino, car rental agents and restaurants. The beach forms a series of scalloped sandy coves, with a hotel backing each cove. The water is generally calm, and all kinds of water sports are vigorously practiced.

Gosier's village center, about a 15-minute walk away, feels a little run-down and lacks the fine beaches found in the main hotel area, but it is more local in character. On the west side of the village center you'll find a park planted with flamboyant, white cedar and tropical almond trees. There's also a small but swimmable beach and a good view across the water to Îlet du Gosier.

Many of Guadeloupe's most popular nightspots, attracting a young and fashionable French crowd until early morning, are clustered together on the outskirts of Gosier on the road to Pointe-à-Pitre.

Information

La Gazette (Ave Général de Gaulle) Sells the Institut Géographique National (IGN) map of Guadeloupe and international newspapers.

Post office (8am-5pm Mon-Tue, Thu & Fri, 8am-noon Wed & Sat) In the Gosier village center.

Sights

Just 654yd (600m) off Gosier village is lovely **Îlet du Gosier**, a little undeveloped island surrounded by calm turquoise waters. This relaxed place has an old lighthouse and attractive white-sand beaches, making it popular with swimmers, sunbathers and families

out for a picnic. A small restaurant serves cold drinks throughout the day and simple fish dishes in the afternoon.

There's decent snorkeling on the northwest side of the island; if you go out about 66ft (20m) from the dilapidated green shed, you'll come to a sunken boat hull harboring big-eyed fish, and a bit beyond you'll find a few coral heads.

Motorboats shuttle beachgoers between Gosier and the island, departing from the little dock at the end of Rue Félix Éboué.

Activities

Beach huts in front of the resort hotels rent out snorkeling gear for €10 a day, windsurfing equipment, Sunfish sailboats and larger Hobie Cat boats. Also available are fun boards, pedal boats and other water-activities gear.

Sleeping

BUDGET

La Formule Économique (84-54-91; fax 84-29-42; 112/120 Lot Gisors, 97190 Gosier; d/studio from €40/50;) Offering *hotellerie à la carte*, it calculates rates based on the amenities you select. There's a terrace bar and a downstairs restaurant. You'll see signs in town directing you to the hotel, about 218yd (200m) up a side road that passes the Jehovah's Witness temple.

Les Flamboyants (84-14-11; fax 84-53-56; Chemin des Phares et Blaises, 97190 Gosier; s/d incl breakfast from €37/45;) On a quiet hilltop location about 0.6 miles (1km) east of the village and a five-minute walk from the nearest bus stop, this cozy hostelry has a view of Îlet du Gosier, a small pool and friendly staff. The 18 compact rooms are suitably simple, with comfortable beds and private baths.

Hotel Pergola Plage (84-44-44; 97190 Gosier; s/d €45/50) Found in town, it has pleasant rooms overlooking a small beach near the center of town. The bar-restaurant down the hill is a popular local watering hole.

MIDRANGE

Canella Beach Residence (90-44-00; www.canella beach.com; Pointe de la Verdure, BP 73, 97190 Gosier; r from €81;) With 146 units in two three-story buildings, studios have rattan furniture, a queen or two twin beds, a little sitting area with sofa bed, TV, phone, a balcony and a kitchenette. Some studios on the ground level are wheelchair-accessible. There are also suites and duplex apartments. Rates include use of the pool, tennis courts, paddleboats and canoes.

Callinago Hotel & Village (☎ 84-25-25; reservations@callinago.com; BP 1, 97190 Gosier; s/d €82/96; ⌗ ⌙) This place has two separate wings: the 'hotel,' with 40 rooms, and the 'village,' with 93 studios. The village units have kitchenettes, while the hotel units have no cooking facilities but include breakfast in the rate.

TOP END

The following are modern beachside resorts with standard top-notch amenities, including swimming pools, activity centers, restaurants and well-appointed rooms with balconies.

La Créole Beach Hôtel (☎ 90-46-46; fax 90-46-66; BP 19, 97190 Gosier; r from €160; ⌗ ⌙) A snazzy 218-room complex, set in exotic gardens, right on the beach. Contemporary rooms have two double beds and French colonial–style furnishings. There are a number of water sports available.

Hôtel Arawak (☎ 84-24-24; fax 84-38-45; BP 396, 97162 Pointe-à-Pitre; r from €150; ⌗ ⌙) An eight-story hotel with 200 rooms, and a tennis and fitness center. Cookie-cutter rooms have tiled floors and inoffensive '80s-style furnishings, some with ocean view.

Auberge de la Vieille Tour (☎ 84-23-23; fax 84-33-43; Montauban, 97190 Gosier; r from €165; ⌙) The lobby of this 180-room inn incorporates an 18th-century windmill, but most of the rooms are in more ordinary buildings. Breakfast is good here and there's tennis on-site.

Eating

Le Lotus d'Or (☎ 84-35-73; 38 Ave Général de Gaulle; mains €9-17; ☽ lunch & dinner) On a hill with great ocean views, this restaurant has Guadeloupe's best Vietnamese cuisine. You can get a full meal of spring rolls or salad, main course, dessert and coffee.

Restaurant de l'Auberge (dinner mains €18-30; ☽ lunch & dinner) The Auberge de la Vieille Tour (see above) has Gosier's most upmarket fine-dining restaurant, serving traditional French and Creole cuisine. Everything's à la carte.

Lollapalooza Café (Ave de Montauban) Crack open some grilled lobster (the house specialty) or feast on a sizzling fajita in this cavernous Cuban-themed café.

The center of Gosier has a number of inexpensive eating options. There are two bakeries right opposite each other at the main intersection. One of them, Brioche Passion, has a few sidewalk tables where you can have coffee and croissants, good inexpensive sandwiches and crepes. For mouthwatering French pastries, cakes and fruit tarts, the bakery across the street is in a class by itself.

In the main beach hotel area, the Créole Village shopping center has half a dozen places at which to eat. Down the hill toward the beach, you'll find an Ecomax supermarket, and there's a daytime produce stand next to the post office.

Drinking & Entertainment

Gosier is easily the most hopping nightlife spot on the island. Most of the fancy hotels have live music and poolside barbecues on a regular basis. The local casino, on the road into town, is a small yet high-stakes joint without any real character; proper dress is *exigée* (mandatory).

Café Cubana (122 Ave de Montauban) Features waitstaff in full Ché Guevara garb mixing up an assembly line of mojitos (a rum cocktail with mint, sugar, seltzer and lime) – something you'd probably best avoid if braving the on-site tango lessons.

La Cheyenne (122 Ave de Montauban; ☽ Fri & Sat) If bachelor or beach-themed nights are your thing, you'll enjoy this massive disco, with big screens and thumping beats.

The outskirts of Gosier, north on the D119 toward Pointe-à-Pitre, host a string of late-night restaurants, bars and discos, a long walk or a quick taxi ride from the hotels.

STE-ANNE

The village of Ste-Anne has a pleasant French West Indian character and is one of the nicest resorts along this stretch of coast. There's a seaside promenade along the west side of town and a lively market and fine white-sand beach stretching along the east side. The beach, which offers good swimming and is shaded by sea-grape trees, is particularly popular with islanders.

Another white-sand beach, **Caravelle Beach**, stretches along the east side of the Caravelle Peninsula, about 1.25 miles (2km) west of the town center. Its main tenant is Club Med, but the entire beach is public; though of course Club Med won't let you play with its toys unless you're staying there. The unmarked road to Caravelle Beach is off N4, opposite Motel l'Accra Ste-Anne.

Sleeping

TOWN CENTRE

Auberge le Grand Large (☎ 85-48-28; www.aubergele grandlarge.com; Chemin de la Plage, 97180 Ste-Anne; r from €73; 🌀 🖳) Opposite Ste-Anne Beach on the corner of the beach access road, these are 15 suitably casual, brightly colored bungalows with tiled floors and phones. You can take breakfast in the shady garden.

Au Verger de Ste-Anne (☎ 88-27-56; www.guade loupe-hebergement.com; 5 Lot Marguerite, 97180; 2-person cottage per week €450; 🌀 🖳) Right in the village, this charming small group of pastel-colored wooden chalets with garden decks and fully equipped kitchens is a good option. The owners can arrange car hire or pick you up from the airport, for a fee.

Le Rotabas (☎ 88-25-60; www.lerotabas.com; BP 30, 97180 Ste-Anne; s/d incl breakfast from €97/104; 🌀 🖳) A friendly, laid-back place with a prime location at Caravelle Beach. It has 44 unpretentious bungalows and rooms, most with refrigerator and radio. There's a pool, and the ocean is just a stone's throw away.

AROUND TOWN

Eden Palm (☎ 88-48-48; www.edenpalm.com; Le Heleux, 97180 Ste-Anne; s/d from €197/230; 🌀 🖳 🖳) This is a classy new four-star hotel built around an old windmill, 3 miles (5km) east of Ste-Anne. With 40 luxury bungalows with contemporary fittings and terraces, there's a *hammas* (Moroccan sauna) for stressed parents, and an imaginative kids' club for busy offspring, with activities like crab fishing and tree planting thrown in.

La Toubana (☎ 88-25-78; http://www.im-caraibes .com/leader-hotels/; BP 63, 97180 Ste-Anne; s/d incl breakfast €97/114; 🌀 🖳) About 1.25 miles (2km) west of central Ste-Anne, on a quiet coastal cliff overlooking the Caravelle Peninsula, there are 33 simple but comfortable garden bungalows here. Baths could do with a spruce up but the setting and ocean view more than make up for that.

Le Club Méditerrannée (☎ 88-21-00; www.club med.com; r incl meals & water sports from €115) A secluded 324-room all-inclusive hotel and bungalow residence on the Caravelle Peninsula, 1.25 miles (2km) west of central Ste-Anne. It has an attractive white-sand beach,

its own dock and all the standard Club Med amenities. You may have to book a week in the high season.

Eating

Opposite Ste-Anne Beach is a row of simple open-air restaurants with tables in the sand and barbecue grills at the side.

Le Coquillage (meals €7-12) This recommended place has meal specials that include crab *farci, blaff, lambi fricassée* and crayfish; it doubles as a dance club at night, with a zouk soiree on Wednesday.

L'Americano (pizza €7-15; 🕑 6:30am-2am) Next to the market, this big friendly restaurant-bar shows football on large screens and serves great pizzas or breakfast pancakes.

Kouleur Kreole (salads €6-8, grills €11-19; 🕑 closed Mon) A popular spot that serves big tasty seafood grills or a variety of fresh salads; it also has a live band on Friday evenings.

Le Kon Tiki (mains €5-11) A 'feet in the water' restaurant that never seems to close and is a good pit-stop for sandwiches, pancakes or ice creams.

At Caravelle Beach, near La Rotabas, there are snack shops selling crepes, hot dogs, sandwiches and other simple eats and there are also a couple of beachside spots offering plate meals from around €8. La Rotabas (left) has a restaurant serving more substantial Creole food at moderate prices.

The restaurant at La Toubana (left) has meals from €18. It has a gorgeous ocean view and specializes in lobster.

ST-FRANÇOIS

St-François is a town with two distinct identities. The west side of town is a sleepy provincial backwater that's quite spread out, while the east side has boomed into Guadeloupe's second-largest tourist area and feels a lot like a small city in south Florida. The center of the action is the deep U-shaped harbor, which is lined with a handful of restaurants, hotels, car-rental offices, boutiques and marina facilities. Just north of the marina there's a golf course.

A small beach fronts Le Méridien hotel, and an undistinguished strand runs along the south side of the town center, but the best beaches in the area are just a 10-minute drive east of town in the direction of Pointe des Châteaux.

St-François is a major jumping-off point for trips to Guadeloupe's smaller islands. The dock for boats to La Désirade, Marie-Galante and Les Saintes is at the south side of the marina, as is free parking.

Information

Arobas Café (per 15min/hr €1.90/6.50; ☺ 7am-2am Mon-Sat, 4pm-2am Sun) At the marina.

Banque Populaire (☺ 7:45am-noon & 2-4:45pm Mon-Fri, 7:45am-12:30pm Sat) Has an exchange office on the north side of the marina.

BNP bank (☺ 8am-noon & 2-4pm) Next to the post office, it has an ATM.

Post office (☺ 8am-noon Mon-Sat & 2-4pm Mon, Tue, Thu & Fri) A block west of the harbor. Phone cards can be purchased at the Match supermarket (below).

Tourist office (☎ 88-48-74; Ave de l'Europe, 97118 St-François; ☺ 8am-noon Mon-Sat & 2-5pm most weekdays, to 12:30pm Wed)

Sleeping

Hotel Kayé La (☎ 88-10-10; hotelkayela@wanadoo.fr; BP 204, 97118 St-François; s/d incl breakfast from €70/78; ⊠) At the marina, this hotel has 75 pleasant contemporary rooms with waterfront balconies. Request an upper-floor room for a water view.

Hotel Residence Pradel (☎ 88-49-85; hotelres.pra del@wanadoo.fr; studio/bungalow per night €54/92; ⊠ ⊡) Overlooking the golf course, this low-key *résidence* has two bungalows and 18 fully equipped studios with phone and TV. There's wheelchair-accessible accommodations and a sauna on site.

Le Kali (☎ 88-40-10; Place du Marché, 97118 St-François; s/d without bath incl breakfast €40/55) In the center of town opposite the market is this laid-back, old-time restaurant with upstairs accommodations. It has a handful of simple rooms, each with a bed and sink and some with air-conditioning.

Le Méridien La Cocoteraie (☎ 88-79-81; cocoteraie@ wanadoo.fr; BP 37, 97118 St-François; r from €230; ⊠ ⊡) A five-story hotel with a little white-sand beach. The 49 suites have all the conveniences you'd expect for the price, though lack imagination, somewhat. There's tennis and golf available.

Eating

TOWN CENTER

Le Kali (meals €8-15) Also a restaurant, Le Kali (see above) offers multicourse dinners including fish, pepper steak and lobster priced by weight.

Jerco Chez Nise (Rue Paul-Tilby; meals €9-18; ☺ lunch Tue-Sun, dinner Tue-Sat) This tiny, recommendable local favorite is a no-frills neighborhood restaurant. What it may lack in atmosphere with its strip lighting and tiled floor it more than makes up for with its delicious Creole cooking.

Quai 17 (mains €8-20; ☺ lunch & dinner) At the end of the row, it's a lively spot that serves pizza, fish and a good selection of salads to people from visiting yachts.

Le Resto des Artistes (mains €7-16; ☺ lunch & dinner Tue-Sun) This touristy spot on the north side of the marina, near the car rental booths, serves surprisingly good Italian favorites such as spaghetti with clams or a range of pizzas, and has a great outdoor waterfront setting.

On the southwest corner of the marina, there's a line of inexpensive harborside eateries that sell pastries, sandwiches, ice cream and grilled foods.

South of the market, there's a local **boulangerie** (Rue de la République) with good croissants and breads. At the northwest side of the marina, there's a large **Match supermarket** (☺ 8:30am-8pm Mon-Sat, 8:30am-1pm Sun); and the **fruit & vegetable market** (Place du Marché) runs every day except Monday.

AROUND TOWN

Some of the best eateries in town are to be found on the road to Pointe des Châteaux.

Iguane Café (☎ 88-61-37; Rte de la Pointe des Châteaux; mains €17-29; ☺ dinner Wed-Mon, lunch Sun) A colorful, exotic dining room full of local artwork, sculpture and huge plants, where the food is the real star. Savor fine modern French cuisine such as rum-soaked lamb or goat's cheese roast in thyme.

Le Ranch Dinette (Rte de la Pointe des Châteaux; mains €3-5; ☺ dinner & lunch Sun) Feast under tiki lights in this funky open-plan diner with Tintin comic-laminated tables, sofas, and bookshelves bulging with French spy thrillers. Borrowing from the tapas concept, you pick from a range of fantastic dishes such as caramelized fish, tuna tartare or roast squash, washed down with decent French plonk.

Also on this strip, Le Colombo is renowned for it lobster.

POINTE DES CHÂTEAUX

Just a 10-minute drive from St-François is windswept **Pointe des Châteaux**, the easternmost point of Grande-Terre. This intriguing

GUADELOUPE

coastal area has white-sand beaches, limestone cliffs and fine views of the jagged nearshore islets and the island of La Désirade.

From the end of the road you can make a couple of short hikes, though the walk to the cross on the hilltop is currently closed. The beach at the end of the point has rough surf and a steep shoreline, but there are more-protected white-sand beaches further to the northwest.

Anse Tarare is a popular nudist beach situated in a sheltered cove 1.25 miles (2km) west of the road's end. The dirt road north of the main road is marked by a sign reading 'Plage Tarare.'

A few minutes' drive to the west, a side road (follow the 'Chez Honoré' signs) leads about 0.6 miles (1km) north to **Anse à la Gourde**, a gorgeous sweep of white coral sands. The waters are good for swimming and snorkeling, but be careful of nearshore coral shelves.

La Paillotte (meals €4-13) is a popular beach shack at the end of the road at Pointe des Châteaux – it sells sandwiches and fresh tropical juices as well as a variety of Creole meals ranging from chicken to lobster.

LE MOULE

The town of Le Moule served as an early French capital of Guadeloupe, and was an important Native American settlement in precolonial times. Consequently, major archeological excavations have taken place in the area, and Guadeloupe's archeological museum is on the outskirts of town.

It's an authentic provincial town with a bustling main street, fish market, cinema, a few art galleries and a scenic harbor. The world surf championships have taken place here and as a base, it may make a good alternative to the crowded resorts of the southern coast. The wide town square has a few historic buildings, including the town hall and a neoclassical Catholic church. Along the river are some discernible waterfront ruins from an old customs building and a fortress dating back to the original French settlement.

There's also a lovely tranquil beach with reef-protected waters and plenty of shade at L'Autre Bord, about 0.6 miles (1km) east of town, while Baie du Moule, on the west side of town, is popular with kayakers and surfers and has its own surf school.

Information

Tourist office (☎ 23-89-03; www.ot-lemoule.com; 32 Rue Duchassaing, 97160 Le Moule; ☯ 8:30am-noon & 2-5pm Mon-Fri, 8:30am-noon Sat)

Sights

The modern **Edgar Clerc Archeological Museum** (adult/child under 12 €2.50/1.50; ☯ 9am-5pm Tue-Sun Sep-Mar, 10am-6pm Tue-Sun Apr-Aug), on a coastal cliff in the Rosette area, has Native American petroglyphs, pottery shards, tools made of shells and stone and an exhibition on local excavations. The museum is about 0.6 miles (1km) north on La Rosette road (D123), on the western outskirts of Le Moule.

Sleeping & Eating

The tourist office can provide a list of vacation rentals, including *gîtes* (small familyrun facilities) and apartments in the area.

Cottage Hotel (☎ 23-78-38; www.cottage-residence .net; Rte de la Plage des Alizés; cottage per night/week €61/330; ☒) A small garden complex with 24 duplex cottages beside a secluded sandy beach. There's a kitchenette downstairs and the cozy sitting rooms also have two sofa beds as well as a double bedroom upstairs.

Afrique Etoile (☎ 23-84-23; 18 Rue Albert Premier; mains €15; ☯ lunch & dinner Tue-Sat, lunch Sun) Tucked away on a laneway off the main drag, this authentic West African restaurant serves delicacies such as Malien couscous (lemon smoked chicken) and *tiep dieu* (Senegalese fish and rice) as well as many vegetarian options.

Stardust Café (6 Rue Achille René-Boisneuf; mains €8; ☯ breakfast, lunch & dinner) On the northeastern corner of the square, this little local cafébar serves hot specials like bouillabaisse or chicken curry as well as sandwiches (€2) and great fresh juices. Sit outside and watch local kids play basketball on the square.

Entertainment

Biz'art Café (☎ 0690-57-13-14) You can't fail to spot the graffiti-covered Citroën 2CV on the main road between Le Moule and St-Francois that marks the entrance to this funky bar and club. Popular with locals, there's live music on Friday and Saturday nights in the downstairs Cuban bar and a salsa and latino club afterwards.

NORTHERN GRANDE-TERRE

The northern half of Grande-Terre is a rural area of grazing cattle, cane fields and abandoned roadside sugar mills. The main sights are the beach at Anse Maurice, east of Gros Cap, and Porte d'Enfer and Pointe de la Grande Vigie, about a 40-minute drive north of Le Moule. The road can be a bit narrow, but it's in good condition and paved all the way.

From Le Moule, drive up past the archeological museum in Rosette, then turn right on the D120 and follow that road north. As you get closer to Porte d'Enfer the route will be signposted.

Anse Maurice

East of Gros Cap, off the D120, the beach at Anse Maurice is scenic, clean and nearly empty. The trade winds keep things cool, but watch out for sunburn.

To get here, take the road across from the post office in Gros Cap, and take a right turn after the water tower. Keep going straight until you get to a parking lot. There's a bar-restaurant open every day.

Porte d'Enfer

Despite its name, Porte d'Enfer (Gate of Hell) is a lovely sheltered cove surrounded by cliffs and backed by a small beach. Inside the cove the water is shallow, but deep enough for swimming, while the entire coastline outside of the cove is tumultuous, with pounding surf and strong currents. There are picnic tables and sea cotton trees near the beach – it would make a pretty spot to break for a picnic lunch.

As you continue north there's a viewpoint about 0.6 miles (1km) beyond Porte d'Enfer that looks back at the beach and the area's craggy coastal cliffs.

About 0.6 miles (1km) further along, look to the east and you'll see a series of seven coastal points, the second of which has a blowhole.

Pointe de la Grande Vigie

The island's northernmost point, Pointe de la Grande Vigie offers scenic views from its high sea cliffs. On a clear day you can see Antigua to the north and Montserrat to the northwest, both about 46.5 miles (75km) away. There's a good view of Grande-Terre's east side from the parking lot, and you can take a short walk out to the furthest point for a view of the west side of the island.

South to Morne-à-l'Eau

South of Port-Louis the road passes inland through a couple of agricultural towns. The coast, however, is largely mangrove swamp.

The main tourist attraction in Morne-à-l'Eau, the largest town in central Grande-Terre, is its **cemetery**, at the intersection of the N5 and N6. Guadeloupe's most elaborate burial ground, it looks like a miniature city, terraced with raised vaults and tombs, many decorated in checkered black and white tiles. Locals are getting a little fed up with tour buses full of strangers gawking and taking photos of their relatives' resting places; a little courtesy and discretion is strongly advised.

Grands Fonds

The central part of Grande-Terre, known as the Grands Fonds (Great Valleys), is an undulating landscape of mounded hills and deeply creviced valleys. It's a pretty rural area that's given over to small farms and lush green pastures and crossed by narrow winding roads.

The northern section of Grands Fonds is home to the Blancs Matignons, descendants of White colonists who settled these hills at the beginning of the 19th century and who have maintained strict isolation ever since.

Grands Fonds is a fun place to drive – expect to get lost in the crisscross of roads; however, as long as you head in a southerly direction, you'll eventually come out at the coast.

To get into the heart of Grands Fonds, simply take the N5 east 0.6 miles (1km) from Morne-à-l'Eau and then turn south on the D109.

BASSE-TERRE

Shortly after entering the island of Basse-Terre from Pointe-à-Pitre, you have a choice of three main routes: north along the coast, south along the coast, or across the interior along the Route de la Traversée, through the national park.

For information on buses through the area, see p536.

ROUTE DE LA TRAVERSÉE

The road that heads across the center of the island, the Route de la Traversée (D23),

GUADELOUPE

slices through the Parc National de la Guade-loupe, the 42,731-acre (17,300-hectare) forest reserve that occupies the interior of Basse-Terre. It's a lovely mountain drive that passes fern-covered hillsides, thick bamboo stands and enormous mahogany and gum trees. Other rainforest vegetation en route includes orchids, heliconia and ginger.

The road begins off the N1 about 15 minutes west of Pointe-à-Pitre and is well signposted. There are a few switchbacks, but driving is not tricky if you don't rush, and it's a good two-lane road all the way. Although the road could easily be driven in an hour, give yourself double that to stop and enjoy the scenery – more if you want to do any hiking or to break for lunch.

Don't miss the **Cascade aux Ecrevisses**, an idyllic little jungle waterfall that drops into a broad pool. From the parking area the waterfall is just a three-minute walk on a well-beaten but lushly green trail. The road-side pull-off is clearly marked on the D23, 1.25 miles (2km) after you enter the park's eastern boundary. Try to go early; busloads of tourists arrive in the late afternoon.

At **Maison de la Forêt**, 1.25 miles (2km) further west, there's a staffed roadside **exhibit center** (☼ 9:30am-4:30pm) with a few simple displays on the forest (in French only). A map board and the beginning of an enjoy-able 20-minute **loop trail** are at the back of the center. The trail crosses a swing bridge over the Bas-David river and then proceeds through a verdant jungle of *gommier* trees, tall ferns and squawking tropical birds.

Continuing west, if the weather's clear you'll find a view of Pointe-à-Pitre from the rear of Gîte de Mamelles (see right).

Before winding down to the coast, there's a very modest zoo, the **Parc des Mamelles** (adult/child €11.50/7.50) on the north side of the road. It features caged raccoons, birds and a few other creatures along a pleasant jungle walk; the admission fee includes a drink at the snack bar. On the same side of the road, a few minutes before the zoo, a signposted road leads up to **Morne à Louis**, which offers a nice hilltop view on a clear day.

Sleeping & Eating

Auberge de la Distillerie (☎ 94-25-91; fax 94-27-68; Sommet Rte de Versailles, 97170 Petit-Bourg; s/d incl break-fast from €55/69; ✖ ☐) On the north side of the D23 about 3.7 miles (6km) west of the

N1, it's an unpretentious and inviting 15-room hostelry. Rooms have TV, a phone, a small refrigerator and a patio strung with a hammock. There's a pool and lots of flower-ing plants on the grounds. It's a 15-minute drive from Pointe-à-Pitre and just a few minutes east of the national park.

For those who want to grab something to eat on the way into the national park, the hotel has a small bakery with crispy ba-guettes and croissants. It also has a Creole **restaurant** (dinner mains €8-14).

A popular lunch break for people touring the island is Gîte de Mamelles, which has a hilltop location on the N11, a five-minute drive west of Maison de la Forêt. The res-taurant takes its name from the smooth double-mounded hills to the south.

NORTHERN BASSE-TERRE

The northern half of Basse-Terre offers in-teresting contrasts. High hills and moun-tains rise above the west coast, providing a lush green setting for the handful of small villages along the shoreline. Although much of the west coast is rocky, there are a couple of attractive swimming beaches, the most popular of which is Grande Anse.

Once you reach the northern tip of the island the terrain becomes gentler and the vegetation dry and scrubby. Continuing down the east coast, the countryside gradu-ally gives over to sugarcane and the towns become larger and more suburban as you approach Pointe-à-Pitre.

Deshaies

A gorgeous harborside village surrounded by green hills and dotted with waterside restaur-ants, Deshaies could probably be dubbed the gourmet capital of Basse-Terre. It has a sheltered bay and is a popular stop with yachters; there's a customs office at the southern end of town. The local sea-faring traditions have carried on into the tourist trade, with several dive shops and deep-sea fishing boats operating from the pier.

Grande Anse, a mere 1.25 miles (2km) north of Deshaies, is a beautiful beach with no de-velopment in sight. There are scenic hills at both ends of the beach and mounds of glistening sand along the shore. While it's arguably the finest beach in Basse-Terre, it's usually not crowded (with the exception of weekends).

Boiling Lake (p552), Dominica

Cathedral of the Immaculate Conception
(p587), Castries, St Lucia

Gustavia (p434), St Barthélemy

Grand Anse (p662), Grenada

Natural Bridge (p736), Aruba

Colorful signage,
Barbados (p625)

Woman blending old and new,
Barbados (p627)

Willemstad (p745), Curaçao

A more secluded spot, **Plage de Tillet** is a lovely beach on a quiet cove; look for the roadside pull-off along the N2, 0.6 miles (1km) northeast of the Fort Royal Touring Club.

Park along the edge of the pavement and continue on foot along the main path heading downhill to the north; you'll reach the beach in a couple of minutes.

SLEEPING

There are a handful of *gîtes* on the road that leads inland from Grande Anse toward Caféière.

Habitation Grande-Anse (☎ 28-45-36; www .grande-anse.com; Plage de la Grande Anse, 97126 Deshaies; per week incl car hire €900; ❄ ⚍) You won't beat the location of this three-star complex of charming Creole-style studios and apartments, right next to the gorgeous Grande Anse beach. Bedrooms have satellite TVs, king-size beds and louvered doors onto terraces overlooking the sea.

Les Terrasses de la Baie (☎ 28-57-17; Pointe de la Batterie, 97126 Deshaies; per week €590; ❄) Here are five colorful, cozy bungalows, complete with hammocks, decks and kitchenettes, set in lush tropical gardens, 872yd (800m) from the village. There's a wonderful openair Creole restaurant here too, with live music at weekends.

Au Ti Sucrier (☎ 28-91-29; 97126, Pointe Ferry; studio/apt per night €92/127; ❄ ⚍) A stone's throw from Plage de Léroux at Pointe Ferry, just south of Deshaies, this place has 14 rustic studios with outdoor kitchens, based around the pool.

EATING & DRINKING

You'll find some of the best food around in the village and its hinterland.

Le Coin de Pécheurs (☎ 28-47-75; mains €13-34; ❄ lunch & dinner) An excellent little restaurant with vaguely nautical decor and a seaside terrace, at the northern entrance to the village, that serves Creole starters of *christophene farcie* (stuffed vegetable) and entrecôtes or grilled fish for mains.

L'Amer (☎ 28-50-43; mains €16-18; ❄ dinner daily, lunch Sun) Almost next door to Le Coin de Pécheurs, this chic, upmarket restaurant with stylish blue and white decked interior and terrace is renowned for its salads and seafood such as delicious king prawns, flambéed in aged rum.

L'Amandine Sarl (☎ 28-45-98; mains €4-6; ❄ lunch) A patisserie-bar-café in the village that's good for a quick sandwich, snack or hot daily special.

Le Mouillage Chez Racine (mains €5-14; ❄ breakfast, lunch & dinner Wed-Mon) Eat in or take away Creole snacks such as *boudin* (black pudding), *accras* or codballs. There's also a children's menu.

La Note Bleue (mains €18) At the south end of town, La Note Bleue has a huge bar that's popular with visiting yachties, and a French restaurant with indoor and outdoor seating.

In the parking area fronting the Grande Anse beach you'll find a couple of food stalls selling inexpensive crepes and sandwiches. **Le Karacoli** (☎ 28-41-17; mains €16-23; ❄ lunch) is an upmarket Creole restaurant with a garden setting right on the Grande Anse beach. It's worth bearing the rather abrupt service for the excellent seafood.

Ste-Rose

In days past, Ste-Rose was a major agricultural town. While sugar production has declined on Guadeloupe and a number of mills have closed, sugarcane is still an important crop in this area. There are vast undulating fields of cane and a couple of rum-related tourist sights on the outskirts of town.

MUSÉE DU RHUM

Dedicated to the history of sugar and rum production (and also with an inexplicable but fascinating collection of giant insects from around the world), this **rum museum** (☎ 28-70-04; adult/child incl small tasting €5/2.50; ❄ 9am-5pm Mon-Sat) is at the site of the former Reimonenq Distillery, about 545yd (500m) inland from the N2 in the village of Bellevue, just southeast of Ste-Rose. Exhibits include an old distillery, cane-extraction gears and a vapor machine dating from 1707.

DOMAINE DE SÉVERIN

A fun place to stop is **Domaine de Séverin** (❄ 8am-12:30pm & 2-5pm Mon-Fri, 8am-12:30pm Sat), a working mill and distillery that doesn't charge an entrance fee and has exhibits in English explaining the distillation process. Visitors are free to walk out back (or take a little train) and get a close-up look at the distillery works, the antique waterwheel and cane crushers and the foaming vats of rum.

GUADELOUPE

In the tasting room are samples of the final products, including a nice, light, citron-flavored rum.

Domaine de Séverin is near the village of Cadet, which is off the N2 midway between Ste-Rose and Lamentin. The turn-off from the N2, as well as the five-minute drive up to the site, is well signposted.

SOUTH TO CAPESTERRE-BELLE-EAU

The N1, the road that runs along the east coast of Basse-Terre, is for the most part pleasantly rural, a mix of sugarcane fields, cattle pastures, banana plantations and small towns.

Valombreuse Floral Parc (adult/child €5/2.50; ☻ 9am-6pm), nestled in the hills west of Petit-Bourg, is a pleasant 34.6-acre (14-hectare) botanical garden. Trails wind through thick growths of flowering heliconia and ginger, and there are lots of orchids, anthuriums and other tropical plants. The road leading off the N1 to the park, 3 miles (5km) inland, is well signposted.

In the center of the village of **Ste-Marie**, a bust of Columbus and two huge anchors comprise a modest roadside monument honoring the explorer who landed on this shore in 1493. If you're up for a dip, try the brown-sand beach, **Plage de Roseau**, on the south side of town.

The road is lined with flamboyant trees on the north side of **Capesterre-Belle-Eau**, a good-sized town that has a supermarket, some local eateries and a gas station.

On the south side of Capesterre-Belle-Eau is the **Allée Dumanoir**, a stretch of the N1 that's bordered on both sides by majestic century-old royal palms.

CHUTES DU CARBET

Unless it's overcast, the drive up to the Chutes du Carbet lookout will reward you with a view of two magnificent waterfalls plunging down a sheer mountain face.

Starting from St Sauveur on the N1, the road runs 5.3 miles (8.5km) inland, making for a beautiful 15-minute drive up through a lush green rainforest. It's a good hard-surfaced road all the way, although it's a bit narrow and twisting. Nearly 2 miles (3km) before the end of the road is a marked stop at the trailhead to **Grand Étang**, a placid lake circled by a loop trail. It's just a five-minute walk from the roadside parking area down

to the edge of the lake, and it takes about an hour more to stroll the lake's perimeter. (Due to the danger of bilharzia infection, this is not a place for a swim.)

The road ends at the **Chutes du Carbet lookout**. You can see the two highest waterfalls from the upper parking lot, where a signboard marks the trailhead to the base of the falls. The well-trodden walk to the second-highest waterfall (361ft; 110m) takes 30 minutes; it's about a two-hour hike to the highest waterfall (377ft; 115m). It's also possible to hike from the lookout to the summit of La Soufrière (see opposite), a hardy three-hour walk with some wonderfully varied scenery.

There are picnic facilities at the lookout, along with a few food stalls selling plate lunches of simple barbecue fare. This is a very popular spot for outings and can get quite crowded on weekends and holidays.

A nice stop on the way back is the flower nursery **Les Jardins de St-Éloi**, where there's a short path through a garden of ginger, heliconia and anthuriums. It's at the side of the road about 1 mile (1.6km) south of Grand Étang; there's no admission charge.

TROIS-RIVIÈRES

Most often visited as a jumping-off point to Les Saintes, Trois-Rivières has a sleepy town center of old, leaning buildings with delicate gingerbread trims and rusting tin roofs. The town is surrounded by lush vegetation and has fine views of Les Saintes, just 6.2 miles (10km) offshore to the south.

Signs at the west side of the town center point the way from the N1 to the dock, 0.6 miles (1km) away, where the ferry leaves for Terre-de-Haut. La Roche Gravée restaurant, a few minutes' walk from the dock, provides parking for ferry passengers.

There's a black-sand beach that's good for swimming at Grande Anse, several miles west of Trois-Rivières.

Parc Archéologique des Roches Gravées

If you're killing time in Trois-Rivières, don't miss the **archaeological park** (admission €1.50; ☻ 9am-5pm), featuring rocks carved with petroglyphs of human, animal and abstract forms. Some of the rocks were found on the site; others were brought from around Basse-Terre. The visitors center at the entrance has informative displays and pamphlets on island history.

GUADELOUPE

Almost as interesting as the petroglyphs, the trail through the park requires some scrambling through boulder fields, around tree trunks and through a garden of native plants. It's nicest in the afternoon, when shadows play through the trees and lizards scatter away from your footsteps.

The park is on the road to the ferry dock, 218yd (200m) north of the waterfront.

LA SOUFRIÈRE

From Trois-Rivières there are a couple of ways to get to La Soufrière, the active 4812ft (1467m) volcano that looms above the southern half of the island.

If you have extra time, you could take the D6 coastal road through Vieux-Fort, a town known for its eyelet embroidery, and then turn north to La Soufrière when you reach Basse-Terre.

However, the most direct route to La Soufrière is to follow the D7 northwest from Trois-Rivières, turn west on the N1 for a few miles and then follow the signs north to St-Claude. This is a nice jungle drive into the mountains; you'll cross some small streams and pass banana plantations before reaching the village of St-Claude, just south of the national-park boundaries. There's no food available in the park, but St-Claude has a few local restaurants and small grocers.

From St-Claude, signs point to La Soufrière, 3.7 miles (6km) to the northeast on the D11. The steep road up into the park has a few beep-as-you-go hairpin turns, and it narrows in places to almost one lane, but it's a good solid road all the way. If it's fogged in, proceed slowly, as visibility can drop to just a few meters.

The closed **Maison du Volcan** is the trailhead for a couple of hour-long walks, including one to Chute de Galleon, a scenic 131ft (40m) waterfall on the Galion river.

There are a couple of viewpoints and picnic areas as the road continues up the mountain for the 15-minute drive to **La Savane à Mulet**, a parking area at an elevation of 3746ft (1142m). From here, there's a clear view straight up La Soufrière (when it's not covered in clouds or mist), and you can see and smell vapors coming from nearby fumaroles.

For an adventurous 1½-hour hike to La Soufrière's sulfurous, moonscape-like sum-mit, a well-beaten trail starts at the end of the parking lot. It travels along a gravel bed and continues steeply up the mountain through a cover of low shrubs and thick ferns. In addition to a close-up view of the steaming volcano, the hike offers some fine vistas of the island. It's also possible to make a four-hour trek from La Savane à Mulet to the Chutes du Carbet lookout (opposite).

The road continues further east another 1.1 miles (1.75km), taking in a lookout and views of sulfur vents before it dead-ends at a relay station.

BASSE-TERRE

pop 14,000

The rather grim administrative capital of Guadeloupe, Basse-Terre is somewhat active on weekdays during work hours, but almost deserted after dark and on weekends, with most shops and restaurants closed. As an old colonial port town, it has a local character that escapes many of the modern resort towns of Grande Terre.

Orientation

The south side of town, along Blvd Gouverneur Général Félix Eboué, has a couple of rather imposing government buildings, including the Palais de Justice and the sprawling Conseil Général, the latter flanked by fountains.

At the north side of town, opposite the commercial dock, is the old town square. It's bordered by the aging Hôtel de Ville (Town Hall), the tourist office, customs and some older two- and three-story buildings that are, overall, more run-down than quaint.

The bus station is on the shoreline at the western end of Blvd Gouverneur Général Félix Eboué. Opposite the north end of the station is the public market.

Information

There's a pharmacy on the square, a Crédit Agricole and a central parking area.
Hospital Ste-Hyacithe (☎ 80-54-54)

Sights

There's an unadorned **cathedral** near the river, about five minutes' walk south of the square. **Fort Louis Delgrès**, which dates from 1643, is at the south side of town, as is the Rivière Sens Marina.

Sleeping & Eating

Relais d'Orléans (☎ 81-13-68; Rue de Lardenoy; r from €25; ﹩) Across from the prefecture, this place has friendly management and small, clean rooms with private bath, and a simple restaurant with authentic Creole food at very affordable prices.

Le Moulin Blanc (cnr Rues Marie Claire & Docteur Cabre; mains €4-8; ﹩ lunch) In the town center, this is a jumping local lunch spot with counter seats, fresh-fruit juices and grilled-meat sandwiches.

La Taverne Royale (Blvd Gouverneur Général Félix Eboué; pizza €5-9; ﹩ lunch Mon-Fri, dinner Mon-Sat) At night, the French crowd files into this funky, over–air-conditioned stone hideout with whole-wheat pizzas and wine by the carafe.

Opposite the bus station is a handful of cheap, if somewhat scruffy, snack shops serving sandwiches. In the evenings, food wagons set up shop on the town's central park, selling sandwiches, crepes and other quickies.

MALENDURE BEACH & PIGEON ISLAND

The road up the west coast from Basse-Terre (N2) follows the shoreline, passing fishing villages, small towns and a few black-sand beaches. The landscape gets drier as you continue north into the lee of the mountains. There's not much of interest for visitors until **Plage de Malendure** (Malendure Beach), a rather popular dark-sand beach that's the departure point for snorkeling and diving tours to nearby Îlet Pigeon (Pigeon Island).

Activities

Jacques Cousteau brought Pigeon Island to international attention a couple of decades ago by declaring it to be one of the world's top dive sites. The waters surrounding the island are now protected as the **Réserve Cousteau**, an underwater park.

There is a tourist information booth and the following dive shops on Malendure Beach:

Archipel Plongée (☎ 98-93-93; www.archipel-plongee.fr; 97132 Pigeon) Runs Fédération Française d'Études et de Sports Sous-Marins (FFESM) and Professional Association of Diving Instructors (PADI) programs.

Centre National de Plongée (☎ 98-16-23; www.cip-guadeloupe.com; Bouillante)

Chez Guy et Christian (☎ 98-82-43; www.plaisir-plongee-caraibes.com; 97132 Pigeon) Offers night dives in addition to day outings.

Antilles Vision (☎ 98-70-34; tours ﹩ 10:30am, noon, 2:30pm & 4:30pm) has a glass-bottom boat tour from Malendure Beach. It takes 80 minutes, including a 40-minute swim, with snorkels for those who wish.

It's a 2.5 mile (4km) drive from Malendure Beach to the beginning of Route de la Traversée (D23) for the **scenic drive** (45 minutes) back to Pointe-à-Pitre (see p519).

Sleeping

In the center of the village of Pigeon, just south of Malendure Beach, there are several private room-for-rent and *gîte* signs.

La Domaine de Malendure (☎ 98-92-12; http://www.im-caraibes.com/leader-hotels/; Malendure, 97125 Bouillante; r incl breakfast from €109; ﹩ ﹩) This three-star 50-room property, close to the beach, is a great place to unwind. Duplex rooms have bright bedrooms on a mezzanine level with sea-view terraces. Explore the Réserve Cousteau with the on-site dive school or just quaff rum cocktails at the pool's swim-up bar.

Le Rocher de Malendure (☎ 98-70-84; www.rocher-de-malendure.gp; Malendure, 97125 Bouillante; studio per night/week €61/380) On a scenic cliff side setting just south of Malendure Beach, you can rent a simple tiled bungalow with kitchenette. The decor is nothing special but the views are worth waking up for. Figure €30 extra for half-board.

Eating

There are huts on Malendure Beach selling cheap sandwiches and snacks, and a couple of simple open-air beachside restaurants with more substantial meals.

For something more upmarket, most people head south to the village of Pigeon. The restaurant at Le Rocher de Malendure (above) is run by two brothers, one of whom trained at the celebrated Bocuse school in France. It has a seaside setting and good French/Creole food specializing in fresh-caught marlin and tuna for around €14.

TERRE-DE-HAUT

Lying 6.2 miles (10km) off Guadeloupe is Terre-de-Haut, the largest of the eight small islands that make up Les Saintes. Since the island was too hilly and dry for sugar plantations, slavery never took hold here.

Consequently, the older islanders still trace their roots to the early seafaring Norman and Breton colonists. The younger generation is a more mixed group, sporting a look best described as 'Rasta pirate.'

Terre-de-Haut is quaint and unhurried, quite French in nature and almost Mediterranean in appearance. Although it's a tiny package, it's got a lot to offer, including a strikingly beautiful landscape of volcanic hills and deep bays. The island has fine protected beaches with good swimming and windsurfing, a fort with a botanical garden, good restaurants and a reasonably priced range of places stay at which to stay. In all, it's one of the most appealing little islands in the Eastern Caribbean, though it can get overrun with tourists on weekends and in the height of the high season.

Although tourism is growing, many islanders still rely on fishing as a mainstay. You can often find the fishers mending their nets along the waterfront and see their colorful locally made boats, called *saintoises,* lined along the shore.

Terre-de-Haut is only 3.1 miles (5km) long and about half as wide. If you don't mind uphill walks you can get around on foot, although many people opt to rent motorbikes. Ferries to Guadeloupe and Terre-de-Bas dock right in the center of Bourg des Saintes, the island's only village. The airstrip is to the east, a 10-minute walk from the village center.

Getting There & Away

AIR

Air Caraïbes (☎ 82-47-00; www.aircaraibes.com) flies to Terre-de-Haut from Pointe-à-Pitre three or four times daily, returning 130 minutes later. The fare is roughly €135 return but check the company's website for special offers.

SEA

L'Express des Îles (☎ 91-69-58; www.express-des-iles .com) leaves for Terre-de-Haut from the east side of the Pointe-à-Pitre harbor at 8am on Tuesday and Thursday, returning from Terre-de-Haut at 4pm. The crossing takes 45 minutes (one-way/round-trip €21/30, two-island pass €45). There's also a seasonal boat service from the **St-François marina** (☎ 88-48-63) from mid-December to mid-May and mid-July to the end of August. The crossing takes 80 minutes, as the boat stops at Marie-Galante en route. Ring to

check schedules as they change frequently and the website may not be up to date.

Brudey Frères (☎ 90-04-48; www.brudey-freres.fr) leaves Pointe-à-Pitre at 8am for Terre-de-Haut, departing Terre-de-Haut at 3:45pm (one-way/round-trip €19/34). In the high season, there's also a Monday and Friday boat from St-François. There's also a sailing from Trois-Rivières to Terre-de-Haut at 9am and 4:30pm with return journeys at 5:45am or 3:45pm (one-way/round-trip €12/18).

There are a few smaller operators that depart from St-François and Ste-Anne. **Iguana** (☎ 22-26-31) leaves St-François from the marina (just behind Hotel Kayé La) at 8am and from the pier in Ste-Anne at 7:30am (round-trip €31). Check at Ste-Anne's marina and the American Bar, on the waterfront at the eastern end of the market, for timetables and to buy tickets.

Getting Around

With advance reservations, most hotels will pick up guests free of charge from the airport or pier.

MOTORCYCLE

Motorbikes are a great way to tour the island. Although roads are narrow, there are only a few dozen cars (and no car rentals) on Terre-de-Haut, so you won't encounter much traffic. With a motorbike you can zip up to the top of Le Chameau and Fort Napoléon, get out to the beaches and explore the island pretty thoroughly in a day. The motorbikes are capable of carrying two people, but because the roads are so windy, it's not advisable to carry a passenger (unless you're an accomplished driver).

There are lots of rental locations on the main road leading south from the pier, but the ones that set up dockside seem as good as any. Try **Localizé** (☎ 99-51-99) or **Archipel Rent Services** (☎ 99-52-63) if you want to book in advance. If you arrive on a busy day it's wise to grab a bike as soon as possible, as they sometimes sell out. Most charge €20 to €25 for day visitors and require a €200 deposit or an imprint of a major credit card. Motorbikes come with gas but not damage insurance, so if you get in an accident or spill the bike, the repairs will be charged to your credit card.

Motorbike riding is prohibited in the center of Bourg des Saintes and helmets are obligatory. You'll see people ignoring

GUADELOUPE

TERRE-DE-HAUT & TERRE-DE-BAS

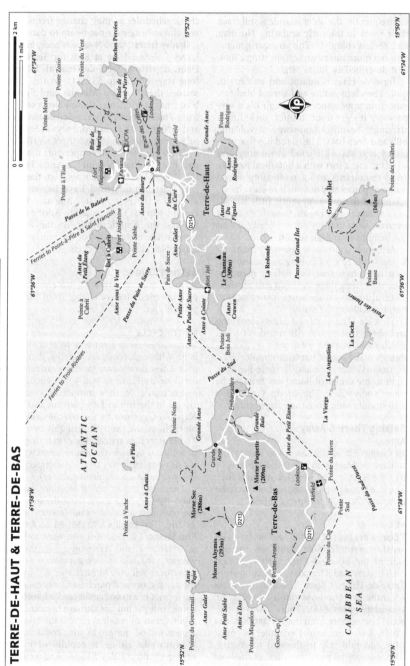

the law, but if you're not wearing a helmet and you run into police, you can expect to be stopped.

TOURS

Air-conditioned minivans provide two-hour tours of the island for around €10 per person, if there are enough people. Look for vans parked along the street between the pier and the town hall right after the ferry arrives.

BOURG DES SAINTES

Home to most of the island's residents, Bourg des Saintes is a picturesque village with a decidedly Norman accent. Its narrow streets are lined with whitewashed, red-roofed houses with shuttered windows and yards of flowering hibiscus.

At the end of the pier is a small courtyard with a gilded column commemorating the French Revolution; it's a bustling place at ferry times, quiet at others. Turn right and in a minute you'll be at the central town square, flanked by the *mairie* (town hall) and an old stone church.

It's a fun town in which to kick around. There are small restaurants, ice cream shops, scooter rentals, art galleries and gift shops clustered along the main road, which is pedestrian-only during the day. Most shops close around 1pm; some reopen in the evening, but in the off season many places stay closed.

A small underwater earthquake just off Les Saintes in late 2004 caused some damage to buildings in the town – you may notice cracks – and the church is consequently undergoing reconstruction.

Information

There are card phones at the pier.

Crédit Agricole (9am-2:30pm Tue, Thu & Fri) The island's sole bank. There's an ATM on Rue de la Grande Anse, next to the tourist office.

Post office On the main road a few minutes' walk south of the town hall.

Tourist office (☎ 99-58-60; www.terredehaut-les saintes.com; 39 Rue de la Grande Anse; 8am-noon & 1:30-4:30pm Mon-Sat, 8am-2pm Sun)

Sleeping

TOWN CENTER

There are room-for-rent signs around the island, but keep in mind that if you're traveling

> **AUTHOR'S CHOICE**
>
> **Auberge Les Petits Saints** (☎ 99-50-99; La Savane; r €100-120;) The charming guesthouse of artist Didier and chef Jean-Paul in the balmy hills just west of the village is a true gem. This former mayor's residence, a homey but luxurious country villa with 12 rooms, is decorated with objets d'art, well-chosen antiques and plenty of TLC. The decked swimming pool has fabulous views over the bay; there's also a studio (€100) and apartment (€130) for rent in the grounds.

during the high season the competition for rooms can be overwhelming, so it's wise to book ahead.

Hotel Coco Playa (☎ 92-40-00; www.cocoplaya .com; Fond de Curé, 97137 Les Saintes; s/d from €91/93;) Choose from 10 marine-, romantic- or Asian-themed rooms and suites, all with seaside terrace and satellite TV in this airy, modern hotel on the edge of the village

La Saintoise (☎ 99-52-50; 97137 Les Saintes; r €58;) A 1960s 10-room hotel on the square opposite the town hall; though not high on amenities – its rooms have private shower and phone – the owners are friendly.

AROUND TOWN

Résidence Iguann'la (☎ 99-57-69; Rte de Grande Anse, 97137 Les Saintes; apt per night/week €81/422;) Between town and the airport, this place has four cozy units with homey furnishings, within walking distance of Grande Anse and the town. All have TV, a kitchen and terrace.

Kanaoa (☎ 99-51-36; www.kanaoa.com; 97137 Les Saintes; r incl breakfast from €60;) Adjacent to Village Creole, this two-star property, five minutes' walk from the village, has 19 simple seaside rooms and bungalows on a little beach.

Eating

There are lots of casual restaurants around town that cater to day-trippers and offer a meal of the day in the €7 to €10 range.

La Saladerie (☎ 99-53-43; Anse Mirre; mains €8-14; closed Tue) A popular spot with nice atmosphere for a good variety of salads and specials of the day; it's a few minutes' walk north of the pier on the main road.

GUADELOUPE

Le Génois (☎ 99-55-45; Mouillage; mains €15-22; ☺ lunch & dinner) A yachtie hangout just north of the ferry dock, with big tables, soft lighting in the evenings and nice ocean views.

Pastarasta (☎ 99-57-40; La Savane; mains €10-16; ☺ lunch & dinner) Another lively late-night favorite, serving fresh fish dishes, depending on the day's catch.

Le Mambo (mains €7-12; ☺ to 10pm if there's a crowd) In the center of town, this cheap 'n' cheerful place has pizzas and Creole specialties like *boudin, fricassée* and fish *blaff*. It's a popular dinner spot.

There's an unpretentious 'feet in the water' restaurant at Kanaoa (p527) that serves reasonable grills and seafood, with lovely views.

Auberge Les Petits Saints (mains €20-30; ☺ dinner Tue-Sun) The open-air terraced restaurant at this hotel (p527) specializes in fresh fish and seafood finely teamed with fresh local produce.

FORT NAPOLÉON

Fans of Patrick O'Brian's novels should head straight for **Fort Napoléon** (admission €3; ☺ 9am-12:30pm), built in the mid-19th century but never used in battle, and now dedicated to a museum of naval history. There's a fine hilltop view of Bourg des Saintes, and you can look across the channel to Fort Josephine, a small fortification on Îlet à Cabrit. On a clear day you can also see Marie-Galante and La Désirade.

The grounds surrounding the fort are planted in cactus gardens, home to some sizable iguanas that are completely unfazed by humans. The fort's barracks contain a museum focusing on maritime history, including local fishing methods and the historic naval battles between the French and British. You can walk through on your own or join an informative 30-minute guided tour conducted in French. Fort Napoléon is 1 mile (1.6km) north of the center of Bourg des Saintes; simply turn left as you come off the pier and follow the road uphill.

BAIE DU MARIGOT

Baie du Marigot is a pleasant little bay with a calm protected beach about 0.6 miles (1km) north of Bourg des Saintes. Even though it's just a 15-minute walk from town, there's very little development in the area and the beach doesn't get crowded. It's fairly close to Fort Napoléon, so you could combine a visit to the two; after visiting the fort, turn left at the bottom of the winding fort road and bear left again a few minutes later as you near the bay.

Sleeping

UCPA (☎ 99-54-94; fax 99-55-28; Baie du Marigot, 97137 Les Saintes) Has 60 rooms in freestanding duplex and quadriplex buildings. It sits alone above Baie du Marigot with its own jetty and a fine sea view. Geared for windsurfers, UCPA offers week-long packages that include accommodations, meals, lessons and unlimited use of sailboards and Hobie Cat catamarans.

BAIE DE PONT PIERRE

The horseshoe-shaped Baie de Pont Pierre is a lovely reef-protected beach with light brown sand and a splendid setting. The bay is backed by sea-grape trees and flanked on both sides by high cliffs, while an offshore islet at its mouth gives the illusion of closing the bay off as a complete circle. It's a very gentle place, with a nice mix of tourists and locals; there are even tame goats that mosey onto the beach and lie down next to sunbathers. The beach is an easy 1-mile (1.6km) walk northeast of Bourg des Saintes.

EAST-COAST BEACHES

The long, sandy **Grande Anse**, immediately east of the airport runway, has rough seas and water conditions, and swimming is not allowed. The north side of this windy beach is backed by clay cliffs.

South of Grande Anse and about 1.25 miles (2km) from town is **Anse Rodrigue**, a nice beach on a protected cove that usually has good swimming conditions.

SOUTHWEST BEACHES

Southwest of Bourg des Saintes 1.25 miles (2km) is **Anse à Cointe**, a good beach for combining swimming and snorkeling. The snorkeling is best on the north side. There is also good snorkeling and a sandy beach at **Pain de Sucre** (Sugarloaf), the basalt peninsula that's about 763yd (700m) to the north.

Anse Crawen, 545yd (500m) south of Bois Joli, is a secluded, clothing-optional beach just a couple of minutes' walk down a dirt path that starts where the coastal road ends. It's a perfect spot for **nude snorkeling**; bring plenty of water and sunscreen.

Bois Joli (☎ 99-50-38; fax 99-55-05; Anse à Cointe, 97137 Les Saintes; s/d from €70/75; ⌗ ⌗) Fronting a golden-sand beach, this three-star hotel looks like something out of Disneyland with its pink ginger-trim bungalows with wooden porches and hump-backed bridge over a glistening pool. Its 31 rooms have tiled floors and Creole-style white furniture. The restaurant has a fine sea view and is a great spot for a romantic meal, with steak and seafood dishes priced around €18.

LE CHAMEAU

A winding cement road leads to the summit of Le Chameau, which at 1014ft (309m) is the island's highest point. There are picture-perfect views of Bourg des Saintes and Îlet à Cabrit on the way up and sweeping views of the other Les Saintes islands, Marie-Galante, Basse-Terre and Dominica from the top of the hill. The summit is capped by an old stone sentry tower that has deteriorated but still has metal steps leading to the top, where there's an unobstructed view as far as the eye can see.

To get to Le Chameau, turn south from the Bourg des Saintes pier and continue 0.6 miles (1km) on the coastal road. At Restaurant Plongée turn inland on the D214; 545yd (500m) later, turn left on the cement road and follow it up 1.1 miles (1.75km) to where it ends at the tower.

From town it's a moderately difficult hour-long walk to the top. A more fun alternative is to ride a motorbike, which takes five minutes.

TERRE-DE-BAS

Lying just 0.6 miles (1km) to the west of Terre-de-Haut, Terre-de-Bas is the only other inhabited island in Les Saintes. A bit less craggy than Terre-de-Haut, Terre-de-Bas once had small sugar and coffee plantations and is populated largely by the descendants of African slaves. It's a quiet rural island, and tourism has yet to take root, but there is a regular ferry service between the islands, making it possible for visitors to poke around on a day excursion.

The main village, Petites-Anses, is on the west coast. It has hilly streets lined with trim houses, a small fishing harbor and a quaint church with a graveyard of tombs decorated with conch shells and plastic flowers. Grande Anse, diagonally across the island on the east coast, is a small village with a little 17th-century church and a nice beach.

One-lane roads link the island's two villages; one of the roads cuts across the center of the island, passing between the two highest peaks – Morne Abymes and Morne Paquette – and the other goes along the south coast. If you enjoy long country walks, it's possible to make a loop walk between the two villages (about 5.6-miles – 9km – round-trip) by going out on one road and returning on the other. Otherwise, there's sometimes an inexpensive *jitney* (private minibus) that runs between the villages.

Petite-Anses has a good bakery and pastry shop, and both villages have a couple of reasonably priced local restaurants.

Getting There & Away

The boat *L'Inter* shuttles between Terre-de-Haut and Terre-de-Bas (€6 round-trip) five times a day between 8am and 4pm.

MARIE-GALANTE

Marie-Galante, 15.5 miles (25km) southeast of Guadeloupe proper, is the largest of Guadeloupe's outer islands. Compared with the archipelago's other islands, Marie-Galante is relatively flat, its dual limestone plateaus rising only 492ft (150m). It is roughly round in shape with a total land area of 61 sq miles (158 sq km).

The island is rural in character; it's pretty much sugarcane and cows, totally untouched by mass tourism. It offers visitors lovely, uncrowded beaches and some pleasant country scenery.

Very few English-speaking tourists come this way, and few islanders speak any English at all.

Marie-Galante has a population of about 13,000, half of whom live in Grand-Bourg, on the southwest coast. Most of the rest are evenly divided between its two smaller towns – St-Louis and Capesterre.

In the early 1800s, the island of Marie-Galante boasted nearly 100 sugar mills, and the countryside is still dotted with their scattered ruins. Today, sugar production is concentrated at one mill, while cane is distilled into rum at three distilleries. Most of the cane is still cut by hand and hauled from the fields using oxcarts.

The **distilleries** are among the island's main 'sights.' The Distillerie Poisson, midway between St Louis and Grand-Bourg, bottles the island's best-known rum under the Père Labat label. Distillerie Bielle, between Grand-Bourg and Capesterre, offers tours of its age-old distillery operation. Both places have tasting rooms and sell rum.

Getting There & Away

AIR
Air Caraïbes (☎ 82-47-00; www.aircaraibes.com) has a couple of flights daily to Marie-Galante from Pointe-à-Pitre (20 minutes) for €135, round-trip. The airport is midway between Grand-Bourg and Capesterre, about 3.1 miles (5km) from either.

BOAT
The interisland crossing to Marie-Galante can be a bit rough, so if you're not used to bouncy seas it's best to travel on a light stomach and sit on deck.

There are two boat companies that make the run to Marie-Galante.

L'Express des Îles (☎ 91-11-05) leaves from the east side of the Pointe-à-Pitre harbor at 8am, 12:30pm and 5pm Monday to Saturday and 8am, 8am, 5pm and 7pm Sunday (one-way/round-trip €21/36). The 12:30pm boat goes via St-Louis, but all other sailings are to Grand-Bourg only.

In winter, L'Express des Îles has a boat service to St-Louis from the **St-François marina** (☎ 88-48-63).

Brudey Frères (☎ 90-04-48) sails to Grand-Bourg, leaving Pointe-à-Pitre at 7:45am, 12:15pm (via St-Louis) and 5:30pm Monday to Saturday and 7:45am, 4:45pm and (occasionally) 7:15pm on Sunday (one-way/round-trip €19/33).

Getting Around

BUS
During the day, except for Sunday, inexpensive minibuses make regular runs between the three villages.

BICYCLE
Bicycles can also be rented from the **Bureau Touristique de Marie-Galante** (☎ 97-77-48; 51 Rue du Presbytère, Grand-Bourg). Roads are generally flat, well paved and free of cars, making Marie-Galante an excellent destination for bike touring.

The downside is the condition of most rental bikes, which are more suited for pedaling around town than for distance riding. Rental costs about €10. You can also hire bikes from Auto Moto Location and Magaloc (see below).

CAR & MOTORCYCLE
Cars, motorbikes and bicycles can be rented from **Auto Moto Location** (☎ 97-19-42), in St-Louis, opposite the police station. **Magaloc** (☎ 97-01-70) rents out all kinds of vehicles and bikes and will deliver almost anywhere on the island.

Cars generally start at €30 to €35 per day and motorbikes at €20.

GRAND-BOURG
Grand-Bourg is the commercial and administrative center of the island. The town was leveled by fire in 1901, and its architecture is a mix of early-20th-century buildings and more recent, drab concrete structures.

The ferry dock is at the center of town. The post office, customs office and town hall are all within a few blocks of the waterfront. There's a pharmacy and a couple of banks with ATMs on the square in front of the church.

The **tourist office** (☎ 97-56-51) can provide you with information on local rental houses, *gîtes* and guesthouses.

Château Murat, about 1.25 miles (2km) from Grand-Bourg on the north side of the road to Capesterre, is an 18th-century sugar estate that's undergone extensive restorations. The grounds are open to the public all the time, and there's a visitors center that is open sporadically.

Sleeping & Eating
Philippe Bavarday (☎ 97-83-94; fax 97-81-90; 97112 Grand-Bourg; d per night/week €30/200; ❉) A member of the Gîtes de France Guadeloupe network, this place has an attractive home with four rooms. It's near the coast, a few miles east of town in the section of Les Basses, between the airport and the center of Grand-Bourg.

Auberge de l'Arbre à Pain (☎ 97-73-69; Rue Docteur Etzol, 97112 Grand-Bourg; s/d €30/45) If you want to be in the center of town, try this auberge a few minutes' walk from the dock. Its seven small, straightforward rooms have private baths. There's a small Creole restaurant on-site.

Le Vert de Terre (☎ 97-80-68; Pointe des Basses; mains €4-10; ☺ 7-11pm) Near the beach is this friendly little music bar that serves hot snacks and *plats du jour* (daily specials). Instruments are there for you to join in the music (if you can, or must) or you can just play backgammon or dominoes.

Opposite the dock you'll find a handful of local cafés and restaurants, most specializing in seafood. There's a bakery and a supermarket about two blocks inland.

Entertainment
The heart of Grand-Bourg's action, such as it is, is on your left as you walk off the ferry dock. It's here that you'll find La Galante des Îles, a loud and smoky bar with cheap snacks. The real draw here is off-track betting – legal gambling on televised horse races from France. You'll need a solid command of French to play the ponies.

ST-LOUIS
pop 4000
This fishing village is the island's main anchorage for yachters as well as a secondary port for ferries from Guadeloupe. There's a little market at the end of the dock, and a couple of restaurants and the post office are just east of that.

Although there are beaches along the outskirts of St-Louis, some of the island's most beautiful strands lie a few miles to the north. The golden sands of Plage de Moustique, Anse Canot and Anse du Vieux-Fort unfold one after the other once you round the point that marks the north end of Baie de St-Louis.

Sleeping & Eating
Hotel Cohoba (☎ 97-50-50; http://www.im-caraibes.com/leader-hotels/; Folle Anse Cocoyer; r from €140; ☒ ☒) Just south of town, at the lovely beach Folle Anse, this three-star property has 100 Creole-style bungalows in landscaped gardens. It's a good spot to practice your water sports.

Village de Ménard (☎ 97-07-40; www.village demenard.com; Section Vieux Fort; bungalows from €60;

☒ ☒) A small complex of 10 comfy bungalows on a cliff overlooking the bay.

Le Refuge (☎ /fax 97-02-95; Section St-Charles, 97134 St-Louis; r €40; ☒) A good *gîte* about 1.25 miles (2km) southeast of central St-Louis. It offers doubles and an optional good multi-course dinner of traditional island fare.

L'Assiette des Îles (☎ 97-10-93; cnr Rues F Eboué & République; mains €12-18; ☺ lunch & dinner, closed Sun) In the town center is this typical small family restaurant that specializes in tasty local fish and seafood dishes.

CAPESTERRE
pop 4100
Capesterre, on the southeast coast, is a seaside town backed by hills. You can explore sea cliffs and hiking trails to the north of the village.

On the south side of town is a beautiful beach, Plage de la Feuillère; a second attractive beach, Petite Anse, is about 0.6 miles (1km) to the southwest.

Sleeping & Eating
Hôtel Hajo (☎ 97-32-76; 97140 Capesterre; r from €45) With an unusual Mediterranean decor and six ocean-view rooms, it's about 1.25 miles (2km) southwest of Capesterre on a rocky strand of Plage Ferriere. There's a reasonably priced French/Creole restaurant on site.

Le Soleil Levant (☎ 97-31-55; d from €40) In the center of town, this place has a peaceful setting with a view of the bay, as well as a downstairs bar-restaurant where locals gather to play dominoes. Larger and more-expensive apartments are also available.

LA DÉSIRADE

About 6.2 miles (10km) off the eastern tip of Grande-Terre, La Désirade is the archipelago's least-developed and least-visited island. Looking somewhat like an overturned boat when viewed from Guadeloupe, La Désirade is 6.8 miles (11km) long and 1.25 miles (2km) wide, with a central plateau that rises 895ft (273m) at its highest point, Grand Montagne.

The terrain is desertlike, with coconut and sea-grape trees along the coast and scrub and cactus on the hillsides. It's too dry and arid for extensive agriculture and though some people raise sheep, most of La Désirade's 1700 inhabitants make their living from fishing and boat building.

The uninhabited north side of the island has a rocky coastline with rough open seas, while the south side has sandy beaches and reef-protected waters.

La Désirade's harbor and airport are on the southwest side of the island in **Beausejour**, the main village. The island's town hall, post office and library are also in Beausejour. There are smaller settlements at **Le Souffleur** and **Baie Mahault**. La Désirade's main road runs along the south coast, joining the villages.

In 1725, Guadeloupe established a leper colony on La Désirade, and for more than two centuries victims of the dreaded disease were forced to make a one-way trip to the island. The **leprosarium**, which was run by the Catholic Sisters of Charity, closed in the mid-1950s. Its remains, a chapel and a cemetery, are just to the east of Baie Mahault.

Sleeping & Eating

L'Oasis du Désert (☎ 20-02-12; r from €28) This hotel-restaurant is a small hostelry in the Desert Saline quarter of Beausejour.

There are also a few rooms in private homes around town for about €25; help with bookings is available from **Location 2000** (☎ 20-03-74).

Two restaurants on the Petite Rivière beach, east of Baie Mahault, are worth the trip. Try the grilled fish or homemade coconut ice cream at the beachfront restaurant **Chez Nounoune** (☎ 20-03-59; menu €16; ☽ lunch Thu-Tue). Slightly more expensive is **Restaurant de la Plage** (☎ 20-01-89) for Creole fare.

Beausejour and Baie Mahault both have a handful of moderately priced seafood restaurants and cheaper snack bars.

Getting There & Away

AIR

Air Caraïbes (☎ 82-47-00; www.aircaraibes.com) flies to La Désirade from Pointe-à-Pitre (20 minutes) daily for €132 round-trip.

BOAT

Sotramade (☎ 20-05-03) leaves from the St-François marina at 8am and 4:45pm daily, with an extra departure at 2pm on Sunday (round-trip €22, 45 minutes).

Getting Around

Bicycle and scooter rentals are available at the ferry dock for €10 to €20 a day. The coastal road is a lot more hilly than it appears from the boat, making bicycling a sweaty workout. Most locals and visitors prefer the scooters.

DIRECTORY

ACCOMMODATIONS

See p757 for details on how accommodations' price ranges are categorized in this book.

Camping

The only established campground on Guadeloupe is **Camping Traversée** (☎ 98-21-23), which has a pleasant seaside setting south of Pointe-Noire on the northwest side of Basse-Terre.

Gîtes

Some of the best-value places to stay are not hotels but small family-run facilities known as *gîtes*. **Gîtes de France Guadeloupe** (☎ 82-09-30; BP 759, 97171 Pointe-à-Pitre) is an association of homeowners who rent out private rooms and apartments. Most of the *gîtes* are quite comfortable; all are rated on a scale of one to three by the association – the higher the number, the higher the standard. The *gîtes* are spread around Guadeloupe, with the largest collection in the Gosier, Ste-Anne and St-François areas. Generally, they're booked by the week, and arrangements can be made in advance through the association. Although rates vary, on average you can find a nice place for around €200 a week for two people. A full list of *gîtes* can be obtained from the association or at the tourist office.

Hotels

There are nearly 8000 hotel rooms in Guadeloupe, most in small to mid-size hotels. The bulk of the accommodations are along the south coast of Grande-Terre, between

---

EMERGENCY NUMBERS

Ambulance (☎ 18, 87-65-43)
Fire (☎ 18)
Police (☎ 17)

GUADELOUPE

Pointe-à-Pitre and St-François. Rooms on the outlying islands of Les Saintes, Marie-Galante and La Désirade are limited.

By Caribbean standards, rates are reasonable and as in France, taxes and service charges are included in the quoted rate; many hotels also include breakfast.

ACTIVITIES
Beaches & Swimming
White-sand beaches fringe Gosier, Ste-Anne and St-François. At the north side of the peninsula leading to Pointe des Châteaux lie two remote beaches: Anse à la Gourde, a gorgeous sweep of white coral sands, and Anse Tarare, the adjacent nudist beach. While most of Grande-Terre's east coast has rough surf, there is a swimmable beach at Le Moule and a little protected cove at Porte d'Enfer. On the west side of Grande-Terre, Port-Louis is the most popular swimming spot, especially on weekends.

The beaches along Basse-Terre's rugged northwest coast are wilder and less crowded, with long, empty stretches of golden sands and views of Montserrat smoldering in the distance. There are also a handful of black-sand beaches along Basse-Terre's southern shore.

Diving
Guadeloupe's top diving site is the Réserve Cousteau, at Pigeon Island off the west coast of Basse-Terre. Spearfishing has long been banned in this underwater reserve, and consequently the waters surrounding

Pigeon Island, which is just 0.6 miles (1km) offshore, are teeming with colorful tropical fish, sponges, sea fans and corals.

There are numerous dive shops in Guadeloupe; see especially the Réserve Cousteau area (p524). Single-dive rates average €35, with discounts on multiple-dive packages.

Golf
The only golf course on Guadeloupe is the 18-hole, par 71, **Golf de St François** (☎ 88-41-87), designed by Robert Trent Jones, in St-François.

Hiking
Guadeloupe has wonderful trails that take in waterfalls, primordial rainforest and botanical gardens. A number of them are simple 10- to 30-minute walks that can be enjoyed as part of a tour around the island.

Serious hikers will find many longer, more rigorous trails in the national park. The most popular are those leading to the volcanic summit of La Soufrière, the island's highest point, and to the base of Chutes du Carbet, the Eastern Caribbean's highest waterfalls. Both make for scenic half-day treks. Keep in mind that this is serious rainforest hiking, so be prepared for wet conditions and wear good hiking shoes.

Horseback Riding
Domaine de Belle Plaine (☎ 0690-58-01-09; www.cheval-guadeloupe.com; Conocor La Boucan, Ste-Rose) has traditional or Western-style riding trails on the beach and interior, from €25.

Snorkeling
Guadeloupe's most popular snorkeling spot is Pigeon Island. **Nautilus** (☎ 98-89-08) offers glass-bottom boat trips from Malendure Beach that include about 20 minutes of snorkeling time.

On Grande-Terre, there's reasonable snorkeling off Îlet du Gosier, which can be reached by boat from Gosier. Snorkeling equipment can be rented at many beachside tourist resorts.

Surfing
Le Moule, Port-Louis and Anse Bertrand commonly have good surfing conditions from around October to May. In summer, Ste-Anne, St-François and Petit Havre can have good wave action.

GUADELOUPE

Windsurfing

Windsurfing is quite popular on Guadeloupe. Much of the activity is near the resorts on the south side of Grande-Terre and on Terre-de-Haut. Windsurfing gear can be rented from beach huts for about €10 an hour.

Union des Centres de Plein Air (UCPA; ☎ 88-64-80; 97118 St-François) has week-long windsurfing/hotel packages in both St-François and Terre-de-Haut.

BOOKS

There are many books in French about Guadeloupe and its flora and fauna, but books in English are harder to find. In Pointe-à-Pitre, try Espace St-John Perse or Boutique de la Presse (see p511).

DANGERS & ANNOYANCES

Bilharzia (schistosomiasis) is found throughout Grande-Terre and in much of Basse-Terre, including Grand Étang lake. The main method of prevention is to avoid swimming or wading in fresh water.

EMBASSIES & CONSULATES

Guadeloupe is represented in your home country by the embassy or consulate of France. See also p763 for details on how the system of embassies and consulates works.

FESTIVALS & EVENTS

Carnival Celebrations are held during the traditional week-long Mardi Gras period that ends on Ash Wednesday. They feature costume parades, dancing, music and other festivities.

Tour Cycliste de la Guadeloupe (early August) A ten-day international cycling race.

HOLIDAYS

Public holidays in Guadeloupe:
New Year's Day January 1
Easter Sunday Late March/early April
Easter Monday Late March/early April
Labor Day May 1
Victory Day May 8
Ascension Thursday 40th day after Easter
Pentecost Monday Eighth Monday after Easter
Slavery Abolition Day May 27
Bastille Day July 14
Schoelcher Day July 21
Assumption Day August 15
All Saints Day November 1
Armistice Day November 11
Christmas Day December 25

MAPS

The best map of Guadeloupe is the No 510 (1:100,000) map published by the Institut Géographique National (IGN), which is sold at bookstores around the island for €7.50. Although the paper quality is inferior, you can get the same detailed IGN map in a glossy version, free of charge, from island car rental agencies.

MONEY

The euro is the island currency. Hotels, larger restaurants and car rental agencies accept Visa (Carte Bleue), American Express and MasterCard (Eurocard).

Avoid changing money at hotel lobbies, where the rates are worse than at exchange offices or banks. Currency exchange offices, called bureaux de change, are scattered along the waterfront of Pointe-à-Pitre, and ATMs (called ABMs, *distributeurs des billets* or *distributeurs automatiques*) will usually give good rates.

TELEPHONE
Cell (Mobile) Phones

Before leaving home, check with your home cell phone service provider to see if they have a roaming agreement with one of the networks in Guadeloupe – if it does, ask how much calls will cost; one network may be cheaper than others.

Many hotels will rent out cell phones on a daily or weekly basis, whereby you prepay call credit, much like a phone card. Ask at the nearest tourist office or your hotel.

Phone Cards

Public phones in Guadeloupe accept French *télécartes* (phone cards), not coins. The cards cost €5, €10 or €15, depending on the calling time, and are sold at post offices and at shops marked *télécarte en vente ici*. For directory assistance, dial ☎ 12.

Phone Codes

The country code for the French West Indies is ☎ 590, as is the area code for Guadeloupe. Thus, to call from abroad dial your country's international access code plus ☎ 590-590 + the local six-digit number.

To call from within the French phone system, omit the country code and add a '0': ☎ 0590 + the local number. We have included only the six-digit local number for the

Guadeloupe listings in this chapter. To dial a cell phone, call ☎ 0690 + the number.

TOURS

Emeraude Guadeloupe (☎ 81-98-28) organizes 'green tourism' sightseeing outings. These trips offer an emphasis on nature and hiking.

VISAS

US and Canadian citizens can stay for up to 90 days without a visa by showing a valid passport (US citizens see the boxed text, p772). EU citizens need an official identity card, passport or valid French *carte de séjour* (visitor card). Citizens of most other countries, including Australia, need a valid passport and a visa from a French consulate valid for admission to the Overseas French Department of Guadeloupe.

TRANSPORTATION

GETTING THERE & AWAY

Entering Guadeloupe

You'll be required to fill out a simple immigration slip on arrival, outlining details of your stay and the purpose of your visit. All visitors officially require a return or onward ticket.

Air

Guadeloupe Pole Caraïbes Airport (☎ 21-14-72) is north of Pointe-à-Pitre, 3.7 miles (6km) from the city center on N5. The terminal has a tourist information booth, car rental booths, a couple of restaurants, a pharmacy and gift shops. The two Tabac Presse newsstands sell phone cards and the IGN map of Guadeloupe. There are car rentals and a taxi stand for transportation, but no airport bus.

During banking hours you can exchange money and traveler's checks at the Crédit Agricole bank in the arrival lounge. You can also exchange US and other major foreign currency bills using the 24-hour currency-exchange ATM next to the bank. Another ATM that accepts credit and bank cards can be found on the upper level next to the self-service restaurant.

For information on major international carriers servicing the region, see p775. The following airlines serve Guadeloupe from within the Caribbean:

Air Antilles Express (☎ 21-14-47; www.airantilles .com; hub Pointe-à-Pitre)
Air Caraïbes (☎ 82-47-00; www.aircaraibes.com; hub Pointe-à-Pitre)
LIAT (☎ 82-13-93; www.liatairline.com; hub Pointe-à-Pitre)

Sea

CRUISE SHIP

Cruise ships dock right in the city at Centre St-John Perse, Pointe-à-Pitre's port complex, which has shops, restaurants and a hotel.

FERRY

There are two companies providing regular boat service between Guadeloupe and Martinique; the larger of the two also has service to Dominica and St Lucia. For information on services between Guadeloupe and its outlying islands, see the relevant sections in this chapter.

Brudey Frères (☎ 90-04-48; www.brudey-freres.fr) has a 350-passenger catamaran with a daily service between Pointe-à-Pitre and Fort-de-France (€57/87 one-way/round-trip). In season, there's an extra boat on Monday, Wednesday, Friday and Saturday.

It also has a daily (except Friday) service between Guadeloupe and Dominica for €55/80 one-way/round-trip and a once- or twice-a-week service to St Lucia (one-way/round-trip €80/115).

Brudey offers discounts for youths and elders. Schedules change, so ring to check current timetables.

L'Express des Îles (harbor office ☎ 91-69-68, admin office 83-72-27; www.express-des-iles.com) operates modern 300-seat catamarans between Guadeloupe, Martinique and Dominica. The boats have both air-conditioned and open-air decks and a snack bar.

Southbound boats leave Pointe-à-Pitre for Dominica at 8am on Monday, Wednesday and Saturday and also at noon on Friday and 2pm Sunday (one-way €60, 1¾ hours). They return from Dominica to Guadeloupe at 11am Saturday, 4pm Monday and Wednesday, 5pm Friday and 5:30pm Sunday.

There's also a three-hour boat to Fort-de-France, Martinique, from Pointe-à-Pitre, leaving at 8am on Tuesday and Friday.

Once a week in the off season, and two or three days a week in the summer and winter peak seasons, there's also a boat between Guadeloupe and Castries, St Lucia.

GUADELOUPE

Departure days and times for these services change frequently and often bear no relation to the printed schedule. The only way to be sure is to call L'Express des Îles or check with a local travel agent.

Buying two one-way tickets with stopovers can make island-hopping in the region very affordable. There are discounts of 50% for children aged two to 11, and 10% for passengers aged under 26, or aged 60 and older.

YACHT
Guadeloupe has three marinas. **Marina de Bas du Fort** (☎ 90-84-85), between Pointe-à-Pitre and Gosier, has 700 berths, 55 of which are available for visiting boats. It can handle craft up to 128ft (39m) in length and has full facilities including fuel, water, electricity, sanitation, ice, chandlery and a maintenance area.

Marina de St-François (☎ 88-47-28), in the center of St-François, has about 250 moorings, as well as fuel, water, ice and electricity.

Marina de Rivière-Sens (☎ 90-00-01), on the southern outskirts of the town of Basse-Terre, has 220 moorings, fuel, water and ice.

Customs and immigration offices are located in Pointe-à-Pitre, Basse-Terre and Deshaies.

The yacht charter companies **Moorings** (☎ 90-81-81), **Stardust Marine** (☎ 90-92-02) and **Star Voyage** (☎ 90-86-26) are based at Marina de Bas du Fort.

GETTING AROUND
Air
Air Caraïbes (☎ 82-47-00; www.aircaraibes.com; hub Pointe-à-Pitre) has daily flights between Pointe-à-Pitre and Marie-Galante, La Désirade and Terre-de-Haut. See those island sections for details.

Bicycle
Dom Location (☎ 88-84-81; Rue St-Aude Ferly, St-François) and CFM (opposite) has mountain bikes for €15 a day.

Boat
Ferries to Les Saintes leave from Pointe-à-Pitre, St-François and Trois-Rivières. Ferries to Marie-Galante leave from Pointe-à-Pitre and St-François. Ferries to La Désirade leave from St-François.

Schedule and fare information is given under the individual island sections in this chapter.

Bus
Guadeloupe has a good public bus system that operates from about 5:30am to 6:30pm, with fairly frequent service on main routes. On Saturday afternoon service is much lighter, and there are almost no buses on Sunday.

Many bus routes start and end in Pointe-à-Pitre – see p513 for details. Schedules are a bit loose and buses generally don't depart Pointe-à-Pitre until they're near capacity. Jump seats fold down and block the aisle as the bus fills, so try to get a seat near the front if you're not going far. Destinations are written on the buses. Bus stops have blue signs picturing a bus; in less developed areas you can wave buses down along their routes.

COSTS
The bus from Pointe-à-Pitre to Gosier costs €1.30 (pay the driver) and takes about 15 minutes. If you're going to the Bas du Fort marina, you can take this bus and get off just past the university. Other fares from Pointe-à-Pitre are €1.90 to Ste-Anne, €2.40 to St-François, €2.80 to Pointe-Noire (via Route de la Traversée) and €3.70 to Basse-Terre.

Car & Motorcycle
DRIVER'S LICENSE
You'll need a European or International Driving Permit to drive on the island.

RENTAL
Several car-rental companies have offices at the airport and in major resort areas. Some agents will let you rent a car near your hotel and drop it off free of charge at the airport, which can save a hefty taxi fare.

Companies generally drop their rates the longer you keep the car, with the weekly rate working out to be about 15% cheaper, overall, than the daily rate. Nearly all companies use an unlimited-kilometers rate.

Rates for small cars are advertised from around €35 per day, although the rates offered on a walk-in basis can vary greatly with the season. It's a competitive market, and when business is slow it's generally possible to find something for as low as €25. At the height of the season you may not find anything available for less than €45, and sometimes all categories of automobiles are sold out completely. Certainly, if you're traveling in winter it's not a bad idea at all to book in advance and you'll generally find the best rates on the web.

Car-rental companies:

Avis (☎ 21-13-54; www.avis.com)
Bespo Loc (☎ 82-01-61; www.bespoloc.com)
Budget (☎ 82-95-58; www.budget.com)
Europcar (☎ 21-13-52; www.europcar.com)
Hertz (☎ 93-89-45; www.hertz.com)
Thrifty (☎ 91-42-17; www.thrifty.com)

CFM Gosier (☎ 84-41-81; D119); St-François (☎ 88-51-00; Le Méridien) rents out scooters for €30 a day and also has bigger bikes.

ROAD CONDITIONS

Roads are excellent by Caribbean standards and almost invariably hard-surfaced, although secondary and mountain roads are often narrow.

Around Pointe-à-Pitre there are multi-lane highways, with traffic zipping along at 110km/h (around 68mph). Outside the Pointe-à-Pitre area, most highways have a single lane in each direction and an 80km/h (around 50mph) speed limit.

ROAD RULES

In Guadeloupe, drive on the right. Traffic regulations and road signs are of European standards. Exits and intersections are clearly marked, and speed limits are posted.

Hitchhiking

Hitchhiking is fairly common on Guadeloupe, particularly when the bus drivers decide to go on strike. The proper stance is to hold out an open palm at a slightly downward angle. All the usual safety precautions apply.

Taxi

Taxis are plentiful but expensive. There are taxi stands at the airport, in Pointe-à-Pitre and in Basse-Terre. The larger hotels commonly have taxis assigned to them, with the drivers waiting in the lobby.

Fares are 40% higher from 9pm to 7am nightly, as well as all day on Sunday and holidays. You can call for a taxi by dialing ☎ 82-00-00 or ☎ 83-99-99 in the Pointe-à-Pitre area, ☎ 81-79-70 in Basse-Terre.

GUADELOUPE

Dominica

Dominica is justifiably dubbed the 'Nature Island of the Caribbean.' With lush, green peaks of over 4000ft (1200m), the last surviving Carib population in the Caribbean and the absence of any major tourist development, you could easily think you had stumbled across virgin soil. Well, almost. You will come across hikers, divers and botanists enjoying the Edenlike scenery above and below the water, but the lack of direct flights means you won't see many package vacationers.

Arriving by air or by sea, you'll first notice Dominica's rugged jungly peaks cloaked in mist, and its dark craggy shoreline. Venture inland on lush rainforest trails past waterfalls, bubbling hot springs and volcanic sites and you'll discover an island pulsating with life. You'll feel you've stumbled onto the set of *Jurassic Park*, with an almost deafening cacophony of insects, frogs and parrots; jungle plants on growth overdrive; and damp aromatic smells emanating from this atmospheric terrain. The dynamic landscape continues under water, with many fantastic diving spots still relatively untouched.

What Dominica lacks in sandy beaches and all-inclusive resorts it more than makes up for in unspoiled rainforest, unique diving spots, vibrant live music and pride in a barely diluted Carib culture.

FAST FACTS

- **Area** 290 sq miles (750 sq km)
- **Capital** Roseau
- **Country code** ☎ 767
- **Departure tax** EC$50 (US$18) for over 12s
- **Famous for** Nature
- **Languages** English, Creole, patois
- **Money** Eastern Caribbean dollar (EC$); EC$1 = US$0.37 = €0.31 = UK£0.21
- **Official name** Commonwealth of Dominica
- **People** Dominicans
- **Phrases** *Bon swé* (Creole); goodnight. *sa ka fete?* how are you?
- **Population** 74,000
- **Visa** Required for residents of former Eastern Bloc countries

HIGHLIGHTS

- **Morne Trois Pitons National Park** (p551) Inhale breathtaking mountain and atmospheric rainforest scenery in this Unesco World Heritage site.
- **Hiking** (p554) Step out on Dominica, from a leisurely walk to Emerald Pool (p550) to an unforgettable trek to Boiling Lake (p552).
- **Diving** (p554) Take the plunge and head for top-notch, little-frequented dive sites.
- **Northern Coast** (p549) Cross the wonderful northern country from Portsmouth along the rugged coast to Pagua Bay.
- **Cabrits National Park** (p548) Explore the park and take in fine views from the ruins of Fort Shirley.

ITINERARIES

- **One day** Start early and drive up the west coast from Roseau to Portsmouth. Explore Cabrits National Park and then travel down the east coast through the Carib Territory, stopping at the Emerald Pool for a dip on your way back across the island.
- **Three days** Basing yourself in the suburb of Castle Comfort, just south of Roseau, you could begin with a day's roam around Roseau and a few days' diving and whale-watching around the southwest coast. Then make your way across the island's interior, taking in Trafalgar Falls, the Emerald Pool and a hike to Boiling Lake. Continue up the northeast coast, stopping in the Carib Territory. Then head around the north of the island and travel back down the west coast through Portsmouth.

CLIMATE & WHEN TO GO

A year-round tropical climate tempered by northeastern trade winds makes Dominica an ideal Caribbean destination for those who prefer a more moderate climate. Temperatures average between 75°F (24°C) and 86°F (30°C) year-round, with cooler temperatures in the mountains. Most visitors come to Dominica between February and June, the island's driest months when humidity is at a manageable average of 65%. April is the driest month with about 10 days of rainfall in Roseau, as opposed to the wettest month, August, when rainfall more than doubles. The rainy season lasts

---

HOW MUCH?

- Taxi from Canefield Airport to Roseau center US$7
- Single-tank dive US$50
- Comfortable hotel double US$80
- Main course in a midrange restaurant US$10
- Average entry to site EC$5

LONELY PLANET INDEX

- Gallon (imperial) of gas EC$9
- Liter of bottled water EC$1.30
- Kubuli beer EC$4.50
- Souvenir T-shirt EC$25
- Street snack: cod ball EC$1

---

from July to late October, almost coinciding with the Caribbean's hurricane season (June to November).

HISTORY

The Caribs, who settled here in the 14th century, called the island Waitikubuli, which means 'tall is her body.' Christopher Columbus, with less poetic flair, named the island after the day of the week on which he spotted it – a Sunday ('Doménica' in Italian) – which fell on November 3, 1493.

Daunted by fierce resistance from the Caribs and discouraged by the absence of gold, the Spanish took little interest in Dominica. France laid claim to the island in 1635 and a few years later sent a contingent of missionaries, who were driven off by the unwelcoming Caribs. In 1660, the French and English signed a neutrality treaty in which they agreed to allow the island to remain in possession of the Caribs. Nevertheless, by the end of the 17th century, French settlers from the neighboring French West Indies began to establish coffee plantations on Dominica. In the 1720s France sent a governor and took formal possession of the island.

For the remainder of the 18th century, Dominica was caught up in the French and British skirmishes that marked the era, with the island changing hands between the two powers several times. In 1805, the French burned much of Roseau to the ground and

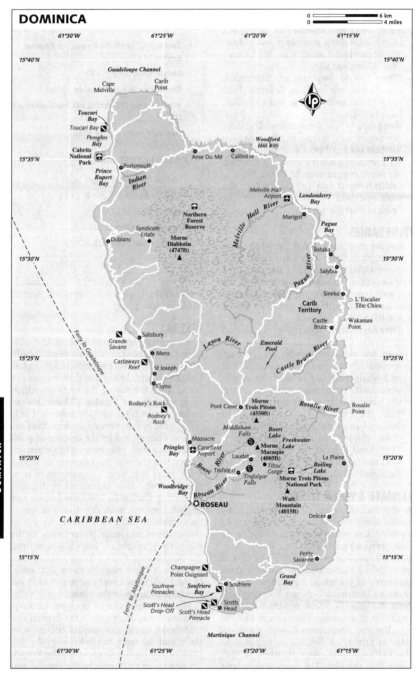

DOMINICA

0 —————— 6 km
0 —————— 4 miles

Guadeloupe Channel

Cape Melville

Carib Point

Toucari Bay
Toucari Bay

Douglas Bay

Cabrits National Park

Portsmouth

Prince Rupert Bay

Indian River

Woodford Hill Bay

Anse Du Mé

Calibishie

Melville Hall River

Melville Hall Airport

Londonderry Bay

Marigot

Pagua Bay

Northern Forest Reserve

Syndicate Estate

Dublanc

Morne Diablotin (4747ft)

Pagua River

Bataka

Salybia

Sineku

L'Escalier Tête Chien

Carib Territory

Castle Bruce

Wakaman Point

Grande Savane

Salisbury

Layou River

Mero

Emerald Pool

Castle Bruce River

Castaways Reef

St Joseph

Layou

Rodney's Rock

Rodney's Rock

Pont Casse

Morne Trois Pitons (4550ft)

Rosalie River

Rosalie Point

Massacre

Pringles Bay

Canefield Airport

Middleham Falls

Boeri Lake

Freshwater Lake

Boeri River

Laudat

Morne Macaque (4005ft)

Titou Gorge

Boiling Lake

La Plaine

Trafalgar

Roseau River

Trafalgar Falls

Morne Trois Pitons National Park

Woodbridge Bay

Roseau River

ROSEAU

Watt Mountain (4015ft)

CARIBBEAN SEA

Delices

Petite Savanne

Champagne Point Guignard

Soufriere Pinnacles

Soufriere

Grand Bay

Soufriere Bay

Scott's Head Drop-Off

Scotts Head

Scott's Head Pinnacle

Ferry to Guadeloupe

Ferry to Martinique

Martinique Channel

DOMINICA

since then the island remained firmly in the possession of the British, who established sugar plantations on Dominica's more accessible slopes.

In 1967, Dominica gained autonomy in internal affairs as a West Indies Associated State, and on November 3, 1978 (the 485th anniversary of Columbus' 'discovery'), Dominica became an independent republic within the Commonwealth.

The initial year of independence was a turbulent one. In June 1979, the island's first prime minister, Patrick John, was forced to resign after a series of corrupt schemes surfaced, including one clandestine land deal to transfer 15% of the island to US developers. In August 1979, Hurricane David, packing winds of 150mph, struck the island with devastating force. Forty-two people were killed and 75% of the islanders' homes were destroyed or severely damaged.

In July 1980, Dame Eugenia Charles was elected prime minister, the first woman in the Caribbean to hold the office. Within a year of her inauguration she survived two unsuccessful coups and in October 1983, as chairperson of the Organization of East Caribbean States, endorsed the US invasion of Grenada.

Dominica's more-recent political history has also been turbulent. After the sudden death of popular Prime Minister Roosevelt Douglas ('Rosie') in 2000, after only eight months in office, his successor – the radical Pierre Charles – also died on the job, four years later. In 2004 the then 31-year-old Roosevelt Skerrit stepped into the breach. A popular choice with young people, Skerrit comes from a Rastafarian farming family in the north of the island. His political longevity remains to be measured.

THE CULTURE
The National Psyche
Dominica draws on a mix of cultures: French place names feature as often as English; African language, foods and customs mingle with European traditions as part of the island's Creole culture; and the Caribs still carve dugouts (canoes), build houses on stilts and weave distinctive basketwork. Rastafarian and Black pride influences are also common.

With an almost 80% Roman Catholic population, conservative traditional values are

PEAKS & VALLEYS
It's said that when Christopher Columbus returned to Spain after his second voyage to the New World, King Ferdinand and Queen Isabella asked him to describe the island of Dominica. Columbus responded by crumpling up a piece of paper and tossing it, with all its sharp edges and folds, onto the table. That, he said, was Dominica.

However, Lonely Planet's *Mexico* guide says Hernán Cortés did the same thing for Mexico. Perhaps this was a habit of conquistadors?

strong. Family holds an important place in Dominican society, so much so that a government poster warning Dominicans of the dangers of transporting illegal drugs lists separation from family (followed by imprisonment and loss of life) as the number one deterrent to the crime.

Population
Dominica's population is approximately 74,000; about a third lives in and around Roseau. While the majority of islanders are of African descent, about 3000 native Caribs also reside on Dominica, most of them on a 3700-acre (1480-hectare) reservation on the eastern side of the island. Dominica has been noted for its number of centenarians; despite being one of the poorer countries in the Western world, it has one of the highest longevity rates. All that fresh air, perhaps?

ARTS
Dominica's most celebrated author, Jean Rhys, was born in Roseau in 1890. Although she moved to England at age 16 and made only one brief return visit to Dominica, much of her work draws upon her childhood experiences in the West Indies. Rhys touches lightly upon her life in Dominica in *Voyage in the Dark* (1934) and in her autobiography, *Smile Please* (1979). Her most famous work, *Wide Sargasso Sea,* a novel set mostly in Jamaica and an unmentioned Dominica, was made into a film in 1993.

ENVIRONMENT
The Land
Dominica is 29 miles (47km) long and 16 miles (26km) wide, and has a total land mass

of 290 sq miles (750 sq km). It has the highest mountains in the Eastern Caribbean; the loftiest peak, Morne Diablotin, is 4747ft (1424m) high. The mountains, which act as a magnet for rain, serve as a water source for the alleged 365 rivers that run down the lush green mountain valleys. En route to the coast, many of the rivers cascade over steep cliff faces, giving the island an abundance of waterfalls.

Wildlife

More than 160 bird species have been sighted on Dominica, giving it some of the most diverse birdlife in the Eastern Caribbean. Of these, 59 species nest on the island, including two endemic and endangered parrot species.

The Sisserou parrot *(Amazona imperialis)*, also called the imperial parrot, is Dominica's national bird. It is about 20in (51cm) long when fully grown, the largest of all Amazon parrots. It has a dark purple breast and belly and a green back.

The Jaco parrot *(Amazona arausiaca)* is somewhat smaller and greener overall, with bright splashes of varied colors. It is also called the red-necked parrot, for the fluff of red feathers commonly found at the throat.

The island has large crapaud *(Leptodactylus fallax)* frogs, small tree frogs, many lizards, 13 bat species, 55 butterfly species, boa constrictors that grow nearly 10ft (3m) in length and four other types of snakes (none poisonous).

The most abundant tree on the island is the *gommier,* a huge gum tree that's tradionally been used to make dugouts.

Environmental Issues

Extended cruise-ship facilities in Roseau and Prince Rupert Bay have resulted in a fivefold increase in cruise-ship arrivals. Liners with a capacity for holding 3000 people dock here to refill water supplies and dump waste, which worries many environmentalists. Tourism on Dominica is otherwise still small-scale.

Despite objections by international environmental groups, Dominica allows whaling to take place in its waters.

FOOD & DRINK

Dominica's national dish is the mountain chicken, which is not a chicken at all but the legs of a giant frog called the crapaud, which is endemic to Dominica and Montserrat. Found at higher elevations, it's a protected species and can only be caught between autumn and February.

Crapaud meat is white and tastes like chicken.

Creole food is prevalent on restaurant menus. Be sure to try callaloo soup – callaloo tastes a bit like spinach. Although no two recipes for the soup are identical, on Dominica it's invariably a flavorful, creamy concoction.

Roadside stands and small-town restaurants typically serve fried chicken, fish-and-chips and tasty bakes along with cold drinks.

The island produces numerous fresh fruits, including bananas, coconuts, papayas, guavas, pineapples and mangoes, the latter so plentiful they commonly drop along the roadside.

Rivers flowing down from the mountains provide Dominica with an abundant supply of freshwater. Though tap water is generally safe, most visitors stick with bottled water.

Dominica brews its own beer under the Kubuli label; you'll see red-and-white signs all over the island with Kubuli's concise slogan – 'The Beer We Drink.'

ROSEAU

Roseau *(rose-*oh) is a colorful West Indian capital, its streets lined with old stone-and-wood buildings. Some buildings are strikingly picturesque, with jalousied windows, gingerbread trim and overhanging balconies, while others are little more than weathered shells leaning precariously out over sidewalks. For the most part, walking Roseau's quieter backstreets feels like stepping back 100 years.

ORIENTATION

Roseau is laid out in an easy to navigate grid system with many of the tourist facilities clustered around the ferry dock. The tourist office and Old Market are close by.

INFORMATION

Internet Access

You can access the Internet at the Cornerhouse café (p545).

Dominica Cable & Wireless (Hanover St; ☉ 8am-7pm Mon-Fri) For phone card, fax and email services.

First Caribbean Bank (Old St)

Lin's Laundry (10 Castle St; load EC$12; ☉ 8am-6pm Mon-Fri, 8:30am-3:30pm Sat)

New Charles Pharmacy (☎ 448-3198; cnr Old & Cork Sts)

Post office (Dame Eugenia Charles Blvd; ☉ 8am-3pm Mon-Wed & Fri, 8am-noon Thu & Sat)

Princess Margaret Hospital (☎ 448-2231) Found in the Goodwill area on the north side of Roseau, off Federation Dr.

Royal Bank of Canada (Dame Eugenia Charles Blvd) Near the Old Market, this bank has an ATM that accepts credit cards and Cirrus and Plus bank cards.

Tourist office (☎ 448-2045; www.dominica.dm; PO Box 293, Roseau; ☉ 8am-5pm Mon, 8am-4pm Tue-Fri) Found on the west side of the Old Market.

SIGHTS & ACTIVITIES
Old Market
The cobblestone plaza and small covered arcade of the Old Market is the site of a former slave market.

Today, the area is used by vendors selling T-shirts, straw hats, baskets and other handicrafts, and it is busiest on Saturday morning.

Dominica Museum
Found on the 2nd floor of the tourist-office building, this worthwhile **museum** (admission EC$2; ☉ 9am-4pm Mon-Fri, 9am-noon Sat) offers an insightful glimpse into the culture and history of the Dominican people.

You'll find Native American artifacts, including stone axes and other tools, *adornos* (Arawak clay figurines) and a *gommier* dugout. Informative displays delve into Carib lifestyles, Creole culture and the slave trade. There's also a collection of French and English colonial coins used on Dominica in the 18th and 19th centuries.

Public Market
Along the riverfront at the northwest end of Dame Eugenia Charles Blvd, you'll find the **public market** (☉ sunrise-4pm Mon-Sat), with fresh fruit, vegetables, herbs and spices – the blowing of a conch shell means there's fresh fish for sale.

Churches
Roseau's **Roman Catholic Cathedral**, on Virgin Lane above the Methodist Church, is an old

stone edifice with an expansive interior. The windows are of typical Gothic shape, but only the upper parts are stained glass; the lower sections are wooden shutters that open to catch cross-breezes.

While the church is not a must-see, it's nicely maintained and worth a peek if you're in the area.

The **Anglican Church**, opposite Peebles Park, is a gray stone-block church that was left with only its shell standing in 1979 after Hurricane David ripped off the original roof. The roof has since been replaced with tin.

Library & Around
The **public library** (Victoria St) was built in 1905 with funding from US philanthropist Andrew Carnegie. It has an old veranda with a sea view, and a grand streetside cannonball tree that blooms in late spring.

Government House, the white mansion with the expansive lawn, and the **Assembly Building** are within about 110yd (100m) of the library.

Botanical Gardens
The 40-acre (16-hectare) **botanical gardens** (admission free), which date from 1890, are on the northeast side of town below Morne Bruce hill. They're a relaxing place to take a stroll. There are big banyan trees, flowering tropical shrubs and an **aviary** housing Jaco and Sisserou parrots, the two parrot species found in Dominica's rainforests (see opposite).

Brochures describing the island's parks and trails are sold at the forestry office.

Nearby, you'll find a **monument** (of sorts) to Hurricane David – a school bus crushed under the weight of a huge African baobab tree that fell during the 1979 hurricane.

FESTIVALS & EVENTS
Roseau is packed solid for **Carnival**, and for the week of **Independence Day**; make hotel reservations in advance or you'll find yourself sleeping well out of town. For more information see p555.

World Creole Music Festival Music continues through the night at this music festival, usually held on the last weekend of October at Roseau's Festival City. Big-name acts from the Caribbean rock on with African *soukous* (dance music), Louisiana zydeco and a wide variety of local bands and dance groups.

DOMINICA

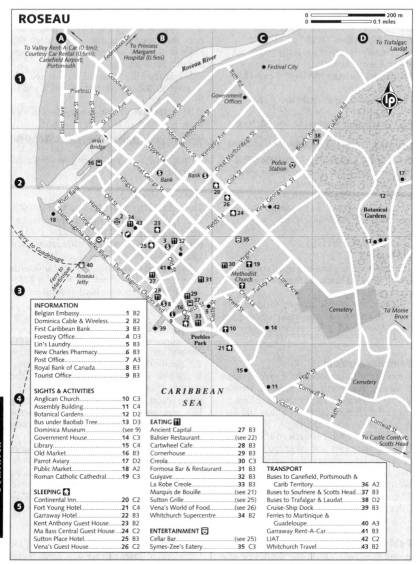

ROSEAU

INFORMATION	
Belgian Embassy	**1** B2
Dominica Cable & Wireless	**2** B2
First Caribbean Bank	**3** B3
Forestry Office	**4** D3
Lin's Laundry	**5** B3
New Charles Pharmacy	**6** B3
Post Office	**7** A3
Royal Bank of Canada	**8** B3
Tourist Office	**9** B3

SIGHTS & ACTIVITIES	
Anglican Church	**10** C3
Assembly Building	**11** C4
Botanical Gardens	**12** D2
Bus under Baobab Tree	**13** D3
Dominica Museum	(see 9)
Government House	**14** C3
Library	**15** C4
Old Market	**16** B3
Parrot Aviary	**17** D2
Public Market	**18** A2
Roman Catholic Cathedral	**19** C3

SLEEPING	
Continental Inn	**20** C2
Fort Young Hotel	**21** C4
Garraway Hotel	**22** B3
Kent Anthony Guest House	**23** B2
Ma Bass Central Guest House	**24** C2
Sutton Place Hotel	**25** B3
Vena's Guest House	**26** C2

EATING	
Ancient Capital	**27** B3
Balisier Restaurant	(see 22)
Cartwheel Cafe	**28** B3
Cornerhouse	**29** B3
Creola	**30** C3
Formosa Bar & Restaurant	**31** B3
Guiyave	**32** B3
La Robe Creole	**33** B3
Marquis de Bouille	(see 21)
Sutton Grille	(see 25)
Vena's World of Food	(see 26)
Whitchurch Supercentre	**34** B2

ENTERTAINMENT	
Cellar Bar	(see 25)
Symes-Zee's Eatery	**35** C3

TRANSPORT	
Buses to Canefield, Portsmouth &	
Carib Territory	**36** A2
Buses to Soufriere & Scotts Head	**37** B3
Buses to Trafalgar & Laudat	**38** D2
Cruise-Ship Dock	**39** B3
Ferries to Martinique &	
Guadeloupe	**40** A3
Garraway Rent-A-Car	**41** B3
LIAT	**42** C2
Whitchurch Travel	**43** B2

SLEEPING
Town Center
BUDGET

Ma Bass Central Guest House (☎ 448-2999; 44 Fields Lane; s/d with fan US$35/45, with fan & bath US$45/50) This is Roseau's best guesthouse. Its friendly owner, Theresa Emanuel (better known as Ma Bass), keeps the place spotlessly clean

and goes out of her way to make guests feel at home. This centrally located three-story building rises above its neighbors and has a balcony with a good view of the town.

Kent Anthony Guest House (☎ 447-2730; 3 Great Marlborough St; s/d US$25/30) These homely 1st-floor accommodations may not be the Ritz but you won't beat it for friendliness or location. The helpful Kent also organizes taxi tours.

Continental Inn (☎ 448-2214; fax 448-7022; 37 Independence St; s/d with bath from US$60/70; 🟦) With 22 simple and compact rooms, this place ranks as one of the more comfortable of Roseau's budget accommodations. Some rooms have just beds and a fan, while others also sport TV and air-con. Credit cards are accepted. There's also a small, inexpensive restaurant.

Vena's Guest House (☎ 448-3286; 48 Cork St; s/d with bath from US$35/45) Occupying the site of author Jean Rhys' birthplace, Vena's sees plenty of return visitors, but the rooms aren't much. There's a popular restaurant attached.

MIDRANGE

Fort Young Hotel (☎ 448-5000; www.fortyounghotel.com; PO Box 519, Victoria St; r US$90-115, ocean-front r US$115-210; 🅿 🟦 🖳 🖳) A few minutes south of the town center, this luxury 74-room hotel incorporates the walls of the 18th-century Fort Young, which once guarded the eastern flank of the capital. The newer oceanfront rooms are the best with stylish furnishings and sofas, big baths and hardwood decks. There are wheelchair-accessible rooms and a spa for chill-seekers.

Sutton Place Hotel (☎ 449-8700; fax 448-3045; PO Box 2333, 25 Old St; r incl continental breakfast from US$95; 🟦) Roseau's answer to a boutique-style hotel – rooms are comfortable but less imaginatively decorated than the stylish lounge area with its leather easy chairs, canvassed art and – that rarity in these parts – subtle lighting.

Garraway Hotel (☎ 449-8800; www.garrawayhotel.com; 1 Dame Eugenia Charles Blvd; r/ste from US$90/130; 🟦 🖳) This modern, business-style hotel at the east end of the bayfront is the nearest you'll find to a midrange chain hotel. Decor uninspiring but pleasant, and the staff is friendly and helpful.

Castle Comfort

If you don't fancy staying in town, there are several decent options on the rocky shore-line of the Castle Comfort area, about 1 mile (1.6km) south of Roseau.

Anchorage Hotel (☎ 448-2638; www.anchoragehotel.dm; PO Box 34; s/d US$66/85; 🟦 🖳) This lively little hotel and dive school overlooks the bay. However, the skeleton of a giant sperm whale beside the pool may not entice novice divers to the water. Rooms are simple but very comfortable with TVs and balconies.

Evergreen Hotel (☎ 448-3288; fax 448-6800; PO Box 309; r from US$95, lodge US$125; 🟦 🖳) A 16-room hotel in a balmy garden setting. Rooms are on three floors and are compact for the price, with pastel bedspreads and some with ocean views. There's also a little detached lodge with sea-view patio.

Castle Comfort Lodge (☎ 448-2188; www.castlecomfortdivelodge.com; PO Box 2253; 4-/7-night package US$670/1050; 🟦) Catering mostly to US visitors, you can stay in this cozy waterfront hotel as part of a dive package that includes meals, two-tank dives, airport transfers and, at an additional cost, whale-watching.

Sea World Guesthouse (☎ 448-5068; r US$50) A little closer to Roseau, this guesthouse has seven simple rooms in a bright yellow building. It's an attractive, clean place with a cozy restaurant facing the rocky beach.

EATING

Budget & Midrange

Cornerhouse (☎ 449-9000; 6 King George V St; ⏰ breakfast & lunch Mon-Fri) This chilled-out, 1st-floor café and book exchange is a great place to hang out. You can munch delicious homemade chili or interesting veggie wraps, and there's also Internet access.

Cartwheel Cafe (Dame Eugenia Charles Blvd; snacks EC$12-15; ⏰ breakfast & lunch Mon-Sat) This laidback little eatery is in a historic waterfront building with thick stone walls. The menu includes standard breakfast items and lunchtime sandwiches.

Creola (☎ 440-2870; 5 Cross Lane; mains EC$25-65; ⏰ breakfast & lunch Mon-Fri & Sat, dinner Wed & Fri) This classy new Creole restaurant in an intimate whitewashed dining room uses almost all local produce in its innovative daily menu. Try the saltfish and green banana pancakes to kickstart your day and (preferably later) one of the five local sorrel, plantain or guava wines.

Ancient Capital (☎ 448-6628; 8 Cork St; mains EC$15-45; ⏰ lunch & dinner Mon-Sat, dinner Sun) Try an eclectic menu of delicious crispy salted chicken, pork in orange or spaghetti marinara by night, or snacks and freshly pressed juices by day.

Guiyave (15 Cork St; lunch buffet EC$33; ⏰ breakfast & lunch Mon-Sat) This eatery has dining on a little 2nd-floor balcony. There are daily specials as well as a buffet of spare ribs, codfish soup and salad.

Formosa Bar & Restaurant (☎ 440-3021; King George V St; mains EC$15-35; ☻ lunch & dinner Mon-Sat, dinner Sun) You can take out, or eat in the tidy air-con room here, tucking into decent Chinese staples such as king prawns with plum sauce or a range of vegetarian dishes.

Vena's World of Food (sandwiches from EC$5, mains EC$25; ☻ lunch & dinner) This open-air courtyard restaurant is connected to Vena's Guest House (p545), and is a popular spot for an after-work drink. Rabbit or goat meals are available at lunch and dinner.

There are a few grocery stores around town; the largest is the **Whitchurch Supercentre** (Old St; ☻ 8am-7pm Mon-Thu, 8am-8pm Fri & Sat), which has a deli with cooked chicken, sliced meats and bakery products. The public market (p543) is the place to get fruit and vegetables.

Top End

Sutton Grille (mains EC$50-120; ☻ breakfast, lunch & dinner) At the Sutton Place Hotel (p545), this outdoor courtyard restaurant has a medieval atmosphere with its thick stone walls and wrought-iron gates. Fancy sandwiches or a buffet lunch are available by day with a more elaborate fish and steak menu later on.

La Robe Creole (3 Victoria St; mains US$15-28; ☻ breakfast, lunch & dinner) A cool and cozy stone-walled pub and long-established family restaurant serving top-notch Creole dishes and seafood all day. The bar has an extensive wine selection and there's a good take-out snack bar downstairs.

Marquis de Bouille (mains US$15-30; ☻ breakfast, lunch & dinner) Although this restaurant (at the Fort Young Hotel, p545) incorporates the stone wall of the fort, it's a bit too hall-like to make for an intimate dining experience. Go for a power breakfast or buffet lunch with mountains of choice. It's also one of the only places on the island where you'll want to dress up for dinner.

Balisier Restaurant (Dame Eugenia Charles Blvd; mains US$22-30; ☻ breakfast, lunch & dinner) Located on the 2nd floor of the Garraway Hotel (p545), Balisier has a great view of Scotts Head. Creole specials like Colombo chicken and goat curry feature, or there's a buffet selection on Wednesday and Friday.

The restaurant at the Anchorage Hotel (p545) has what appears to be just another

hotel menu of local fish and meat dishes but food is surprisingly good, simply cooked and well presented. They must have the biggest breakfast menu in town with over 10 mouth-watering fresh pancake varieties to choose from.

ENTERTAINMENT

Most entertainment is largely limited to a sunset drink at one of the hotel bars.

Fort Young Hotel (p545) has a happy hour from 6pm to 8pm and live steel-pan music a bit later.

On Wednesday there's live music at the Cellar Bar of Sutton Place Hotel (p545) and on Thursday **Symes-Zee's Eatery** (38 King George V St; ☻ 9pm-3am) has a live jazz jam session with talented local musicians.

GETTING THERE & AROUND
Air

There are no international flights into and out of Dominica; see p556 for more information.

Most interisland flights arrive at **Canefield Airport** (DCF; ☎ 449-1990; metoffice@cwdom .dm), just outside Roseau.

TO/FROM THE AIRPORT

Avis is the only car-rental agency at Canefield Airport, but other agencies will provide customers with free airport pickup. Taxis are readily available (five- to 10-minute journey EC$20), but if you're traveling light you could also walk out to the road and catch a bus into town (EC$2, 20 minutes).

Boat

For information on the ferry services between Roseau and Guadeloupe and Martinique (and on to St Lucia) see p556.

Bus

The bus service is operated by private minivans, recognizable by number plates that begin with the letter 'H.' You can hail a passing van from the street. There isn't a bus station, but buses heading southward (including to Castle Comfort, EC$1.50) tend to congregate at the Old Market, while those going north stop at West Bridge.

Car & Motorcycle

For information on car-rental agencies in Roseau, see p557.

DOMINICA

Taxi

You can pick up a taxi on the street or call **Dominica Taxi Association** (☎ 449-8553/235-8648).

AROUND ROSEAU

Morne Bruce is a rather exclusive hillside suburb that's southeast of Roseau. It has a couple of places to stay, but most people who venture up this way do so for the panoramic hilltop view of Roseau and its surrounds.

One way to get to the viewpoint is to drive up and park below the president's office. You can also hike to this point from the botanical gardens; the half-mile (800m) trail begins just east of the parrot aviary.

Sleeping

Itassi Cottages (☎ 448-7247; fax 448-3045; PO Box 1333; 1-2 person cottage US$60) With a view of Roseau and Scotts Head, this is five minutes' drive from town. The cottages are simply furnished in pastel colors and have cooking facilities, phone and TV. The manager prefers to rent out the cottages on a weekly basis (US$380 for one or two people), but accepts daily rentals when they're not full.

Reigate Hall Hotel (☎ 448-4031; reigate@cwdom .dm; s/d/ste US$65/75/105; 🅿 🖳 🔲) In the Reigate area on a hill above Morne Bruce, this former manor house has the character of a small mountain inn and a superb view of Roseau 1 mile (1.6km) below. The 17 rooms are rather simply appointed, but they are modern and have private balconies. There's a small pool, a sauna and a tennis court. The Reigate Hall Hotel is at the very end of a rather tortuous one-lane road.

AROUND DOMINICA

LAYOU RIVER AREA

The Layou River, Dominica's longest river, empties into the sea just south of Layou, at the center of the west coast. The river basin is a peaceful rural area, with bamboo leaning over the riverbanks and banana and coconut trees at the side of the road. When it's not running strong, the river is a popular place for freshwater swimming.

Sleeping & Eating

Sunset Bay Club (☎ 446-6522; www.sunsetbayclub .com; s/d from US$86/127; 🔲) About 1 mile (1.6km)

BROTHERLY LOVE

Philip Warner, son of a 17th-century St Kitts governor, was responsible for a ruthless massacre of Carib Indians on Dominica in 1674. He was also responsible for the murder of 'Indian' Warner, his half-brother.

Indian Warner, who had the same father as Philip but whose mother was a Dominican Carib, left his English upbringing on St Kitts to return to Dominica, where he became a Carib chief. Philip, leading a contingent of British troops intent on seeking vengeance for Carib raids on St Kitts, tricked his half-brother into meeting him on the west coast of Dominica in the village now known as Massacre. Philip then ambushed Indian Warner, along with his entire tribe.

---

north of Salisbury, this snazzy Belgian-run hotel and Professional Association of Diving Instructors (PADI) dive center has a garden setting on a small, clean stretch of beach. There are 12 rooms, a small pool, a sauna and lovely open-air **restaurant** (mains EC$30-50; 🕑 lunch & dinner).

Castaways Beach Hotel (☎ 449-6244; fax 449-6246; PO Box 5; s/d US$80/100) An inviting place on a long, attractive gray-sand beach that's fronted by calm waters. There are 26 rooms in two wings – those in the south wing have one double bed, while those in the north wing have two single beds and are a bit bigger. All are pleasant enough and have ceiling fans, a shower, a phone and oceanfront balconies. There's a dive operation on-site, a small dock, tennis court and the **Four Seasons** (mains EC$22-60; 🕑 lunch & dinner) restaurant, which serves Creole and European fare.

Getting There & Away

There is a bus service from Roseau to Salisbury (EC$5.20, 30 minutes).

NORTHERN FOREST RESERVE

The Northern Forest Reserve is an extensive area that encompasses 22,000 acres (8800 hectares) of land in the interior of the island, including 4747ft (1424m) Morne Diablotin, the island's highest peak. The main habitat of Dominica's two endangered parrot species is in the eastern section of the reserve.

DOMINICA

To get to the reserve, turn east on the signposted road that begins just north of the village of Dublanc and continue to Syndicate Estate, about 4.5 miles (7.25km) inland. There you'll find an easy mile-long loop trail (Syndicate Trail) to a parrot observatory platform, as well as the start of the trail leading up Morne Diablotin, a rugged hike that's best done with a guide – contact the tourist office in Roseau (p543). The best times to see the parrots are in the early morning and late afternoon, when the birds are most active; local guides say the parrots like to hang out where oranges grow.

PORTSMOUTH

Dominica's second-largest town sits on the banks of Prince Rupert Bay. Columbus entered the bay during his fourth voyage to the New World in 1504, and three decades later the Spanish established a supply station here for their galleons.

Cabrits National Park, on the north side of town, and Indian River, to the south, are the area's noteworthy attractions. Other than two rusty shipwrecks in the bay, the town center doesn't have any sights. By day it's a rather sleepy, ramshackle place, but after dark it shows its seedier side – expect some drunken harassment. Ross University just south of town attracts a lot of American medical students, which adds a cosmopolitan flavor to the local demographic.

Douglas Bay, 2 miles (3km) north of Portsmouth, also has a black-sand beach and decent snorkeling. A good paved road leads to Douglas Bay, but the area remains a bit of a backwater that's well off the tourist track.

Information

National Commercial Bank of Dominica (☎ 445-5430) This bank is south of the small parking lot from where you can pick up the bus to Roseau.

Police (Bay Rd)

Sights & Activities
INDIAN RIVER

Just south of town you can expect to be met by a handful of rowers ready and willing to take you on a boat ride up the Indian River. The boats wind up the shady river through tall swamp bloodwood trees, whose buttressed trunks rise out of the shallows, their roots stretching out laterally along the riverbanks. It can be a fascinating outing,

taking you into an otherwise inaccessible habitat and offering a close-up view of the creatures that live at the water's edge.

Though almost everyone you meet in Portsmouth will offer to be your guide, you'll get a lot more from the trip if you go with one of the boaters who work with the Park Service. The rowers, who set up shop along the coastal road at the river mouth, charge EC$35 per person for a tour that takes about 1½ hours, usually with a stop for drinks at the jungle-hut bar.

CABRITS NATIONAL PARK

Cabrits National Park, on a scenic peninsula 1.25 miles (2km) north of Portsmouth, is best known as the site of the impressive 18th-century British garrison, Fort Shirley. In addition to the peninsula, the park encompasses the surrounding coastal area, as well as the island's largest swamp. The Cabrits Peninsula, formed by two extinct volcanoes, separates Prince Rupert Bay from Douglas Bay. The coral reefs and waters of the latter are also part of the park.

The British began construction on the main elements of Fort Shirley in 1774 but three years later the French captured the island and continued construction. Between the vying powers, the garrison was built, but France's effort proved to be counterproductive, as Dominica was returned to the British under the 1783 Treaty of Paris and the fort was subsequently used to repel French attacks.

Fort Shirley had more than 50 major structures, including seven gun batteries, quarters for as many as 600 officers and soldiers, numerous storehouses and a hospital. Following the cessation of hostilities between the British and French, the fort gradually slipped into disrepair, and in 1854 it was abandoned.

Cabrits is a fun place to explore. Some of the fort's stone ruins have been cleared and partially reconstructed, while others remain half-hidden in the jungle. The powder magazine to the right of the fort entrance has been turned into a small museum with restoration exhibits and a display of artifacts unearthed during that work.

The fort is home to scores of hermit crabs, harmless snakes and ground lizards (*Ameiva fuscata*) that scurry about the ruins and along the hiking trails that lead up to the two volcanic peaks. The trail up the 560ft (168m) West Cabrit begins at the back side of Fort Shirley, and the hike takes about 30 minutes. Most of the walk passes through a wooded area, but there's a panoramic view at the top.

Sleeping

Portsmouth Beach Hotel (☎ 445-5142; www.avirtu aldominica.com/pbh.htm; PO Box 34; s/d US$50/60; 🛋) This hotel is situated on a lovely black-sand beach about 0.5 miles (800m) south of town. You'll find 170 rooms with kitchenettes here, although most are rented out to foreign students who attend the nearby Ross University medical school. The rooms are straightforward with tiled floors, showers, phones, ceiling fans and screened louvered windows. There is a pool and a restaurant too.

Picard Beach Cottage Resort (☎ 445-5131; www .avirtualdominica.com/picard.htm; cottages US$100-120) Next to Portsmouth Beach Hotel and sharing the same management, Picard has eight pleasantly rustic wooden cottages with big oceanfront porches. Each has a separate bedroom, a small kitchenette and a dining/living room with two single beds.

Eating

Sister Sea Lodge (☎ 445-5211; sangow@cwdom.dm; Picard Estate; mains EC$35-65) The fish bar at this lodge (see the boxed text, right) serves fantastic, simple barbecued fish, octopus and lobster straight off the boat in a great beachside setting.

Le Flambeau (mains EC$25-40) Located at the Portsmouth Beach Hotel (above), this breezy alfresco restaurant is on the beach. Simple breakfast items cost EC$10, and sandwiches and burgers are about the same price. There are also vegetarian plates and moderately priced fish and meat dinners.

Miss Bali (Lizard Trail Rd; mains EC$20-45; 🕑 lunch & dinner) An authentic North Indian restaurant, patronized mostly by medical students from nearby Ross University. It serves real fish curry, lamb *biryani* and plenty of vegetarian choices.

Indian River Cuisine (☎ 445-5352; Michael Douglas Rd; mains EC$32-65; 🕑 lunch & dinner) A lively, no-frills sports bar-cum-restaurant where you can catch a Premier League match over chicken and chips, or red snapper with rice and ground provisions (root vegetables).

AUTHOR'S CHOICE

Sister Sea Lodge (☎ 445-5211; sangow@cw dom.dm; Picard Estate; s/d US$45/65) A little treasure at the end of leafy Lizard's Trail, Sister Sea Lodge comprises a small group of cottages set in beautifully scented rose and ylang ylang gardens. Run by the congenial German Harta Sango, the large open-plan cottages are reminiscent of the 1970s with large art canvasses, high beamed ceilings, stone-floored baths and macramé hammocks. The lodge's laid-back open-air bar and restaurant (left), on a secluded pebble beach, are Portsmouth's hippest.

Getting There & Away

The bus service to Portsmouth (EC$8, one hour) leaves from the southeast side of the Roseau River near the public market.

PORTSMOUTH TO PAGUA BAY

The route that cuts across the northern neck of the island from Portsmouth to the east coast is a stunning drive through mountainous jungle. The road is winding and narrow, the terrain is all hills and valleys, and the landscape is lush with tropical greenery. Once you reach the coast there are some breathtaking ocean vistas, a couple of one-lane bridges, and plantations with seemingly endless rows of coconut palms.

Calibishie

The first sizable village you will reach on the east coast, Calibishie, is an attractive fishing village with a handful of friendly bars and restaurants, a craft store and a car-rental agency.

There are some good picnic beaches in the area. **Hell's Gate Beach**, half a mile (800m) west of town, looks out onto two striking rock columns, which protrude from the sea – the columns are collectively known as Devil's Rock. However, this beach is unsuitable for swimming. Further east, there are brown-sand beaches at **Woodford Hill Bay** (a good turtle-watching spot) and **Londonderry Bay**, near Melville Hall Airport. Both bays have rivers emptying into them where women gather to wash clothes; at Londonderry the airport fence doubles as the clothesline.

Calibishie makes a good pit stop for lunch or an overnight stay, particularly if you're catching a morning flight from nearby Melville Hall Airport.

SLEEPING & EATING

Calibishie Lodges (☎ 445-8537; www.calibishie-lodges.com; apt US$70-90; ⊠ 🖳 🖳) This small, relaxed residence, run by a young Belgian couple, has six lovely apartments that sleep up to four people. The apartments have good-sized living areas, bright and modern furnishings, and come with balconies. The excellent attached **Bamboo Restaurant** (mains EC$30-65; ⊙ breakfast, lunch & dinner) offers an inventive Creole menu, including dishes such as coconut crayfish and lobster with banana cake. There's a good selection of wine and beers, and you can also imbibe fresh punches.

Warrow's Seaside Lounge (mains EC$20-35; ⊙ lunch & dinner) Found on Calibishie's main drag, this great Creole bar and restaurant has a seaside terrace and serves tasty local fish and chicken dishes.

CARIB TERRITORY

The 3700-acre (1480-hectare) Carib Territory, which begins around the village of Bataka and continues south for 7.5 miles (12km), is home to most of Dominica's 3000 Carib Indians. It's a predominantly rural area with cultivated bananas, breadfruit trees and wild heliconia growing along the roadside. Many of the houses are traditional wooden structures on log stilts, but there are also simple cement homes and, in the poorer areas, shanties made of corrugated tin and tar paper.

The main east-coast road runs right through the Carib Territory. Along the road are several stands where you can stop and buy intricately woven Carib baskets and handicrafts.

Salybia, the main settlement, has a couple of noteworthy buildings. One is the carbet, an oval-shaped community center designed in the traditional Carib style with a high-pitched ribbed roof; in pre-Columbian times, these buildings served as collective living quarters. The Catholic church in Salybia, which also has a sharply pitched roof, is decorated with colorful paintings of Carib life and has a unique altar made from a dugout.

At Sineku, a sign points oceanward to **L'Escalier Tête Chien**, a stairway-like lava outcrop that seems to climb out of the turbulent ocean. This unique, natural formation was thought by the Caribs to be the embodiment of a boa constrictor and it is significant in Carib legends.

After leaving the Carib Territory, the road offers occasional glimpses of the rugged coastline.

There's an intersection 0.5 miles (800m) south of Castle Bruce; take the road marked 'Pont Casse' to continue to the Emerald Pool and the village of Canefield. This road takes you through a scenic mountain valley with a luxuriant fern forest and lots of rushing rivers.

The classy, colonial-style **Beau Rive Hotel** (☎ 445-8992; www.beaurive.com; PO Box 2424; s/d US$85/120; 🖳 🖳), set in tropical gardens overlooking Wakaman Point, lies 1 mile (1.6km) or so north of Castle Bruce. It is run by a Briton and has six elegantly furnished rooms.

Beau Rive also serves a set meat-free dinner (US$20) or a dinner of fish or chicken, all to the tinkle of the grand piano.

Getting There & Away

Buses heading to Canefield (EC$2) and the Carib Territory (EC$9.50) leave from the southeast side of the Roseau River near the public market.

EMERALD POOL

Emerald Pool, which takes its name from its lush green setting, is at the base of a gentle 40ft (12m) waterfall. The pool, deep enough for a little dip, is reached via a 0.3-mile (500m) walk through a rainforest of massive ferns and tall trees.

The path is well defined and easy to follow, although it can get a bit slippery in places. Emerald Pool is generally a serenely quiet area except on cruise-ship days, when one packed minivan after another pulls up to the site.

The pool is on the road that runs between Canefield and Castle Bruce; it's an enjoyable winding drive with thick jungle vegetation, mountain views and lots of beep-as-you-go hairpin turns.

It's about a 30-minute drive from Canefield; the trailhead is marked with a roadside forestry sign.

TRAFALGAR FALLS

On the eastern edge of Morne Trois Pitons National Park, Trafalgar Falls are spectacular and easily accessible. The 0.4-mile (600m) walk to the falls begins at Papillote Wilderness Retreat (see below), about 1 mile (1.6km) east of the village of Trafalgar.

Start the walk at the bottom of the inn's driveway, where you'll find a cement track leading east. Follow the track until you reach a little snack bar; take the footpath that leads downhill from there and in a couple of minutes you'll reach a viewing platform with a clear view of the falls in a verdant jungle setting.

There are two separate waterfalls. Water from the upper falls crosses the Titou Gorge before plunging down the sheer 200ft (60m) rock face that fronts the viewing platform. At the base of the waterfall are hot sulfur springs – there are a couple of basins in which bathers can sit (look for the yellow streaks on the rocks).

The lower falls flow from the Trois Pitons River, which originates in the Boiling Lake area. This waterfall, which is gentler and broader than the upper falls, has a pool at its base that's deep enough and wide enough for an invigorating swim.

Young men hang out at the start of the trail and tout their services as guides. Getting to the viewing platform is straightforward and doesn't require a guide, so if you plan to go only that far, save yourself the 'tip' (roughly EC$20), as the guides call their negotiable fee.

Going beyond the platform is trickier, as getting to the base of the falls requires crossing a river. Depending on how surefooted you are, a guide could be helpful in climbing down the boulders to the lower pool and even more so in clambering over to the hot springs. Guide or not, be very careful with your footing, as the rocks get moss-covered and can be as slippery as ice. This is a serious river, and during rainy spells it may be too high to cross. Flash floods are also a potential danger, as heavy rains in the upper slopes can bring a sudden torrent – if you're in the river and the waters start to rise, get out immediately.

Sleeping & Eating

Papillote Wilderness Retreat (☎ 448-2287; www .papillote.dm; PO Box 2287; s/d US$95/110, with breakfast & dinner per person extra US$35, cottage US$125) This is a delightful little inn nestled in the mountains above Trafalgar village. American owner and naturalist Anne Baptiste has planted the grounds with nearly 100 types of tropical flowers and trees. The rustic inn has eight simple units with private baths, wooden plank floors and patchwork bed quilts made at the local women's co-op. There's also a two-bedroom, two-bath cottage near a waterfall. Bring a bathing suit and relax in the inn's hot-springs pool.

Papillote has good food, with lunchtime salads and hot Creole dishes. Dinner, a full meal (residents EC$35, nonresidents EC$50), is by reservation.

D'Auchamps Cottages (☎ 448-3346; www.avirtual dominica.com/dauchamps/; PO Box 1889; cottages US$50) On the road to Trafalgar Falls and set on a 9-acre (3.6-hectare) estate amid a botanical garden, there are two simple cottages here, each with a kitchen, veranda and bath. The seventh night is free on weekly stays.

Getting There & Away

To get to Trafalgar from Roseau, take King George V St north from the town center. After crossing the Roseau River, continue up the Roseau Valley road for 2.3 miles (3.7km), at which point the road forks; take the right branch. From here it's a 10-minute drive along a narrow potholed road to Papillote, 2 miles (3.2km) away.

Buses go from Roseau to the village of Trafalgar (EC$2.75, 30 to 40 minutes), from where it's about half a mile (800m) to Papillote. Taxis from Canefield Airport to Papillote cost EC$50.

MORNE TROIS PITONS NATIONAL PARK

This national park, in the southern half of the island, encompasses 17,000 acres (6880 hectares) of Dominica's mountainous volcanic interior.

Most of the park is primordial rainforest, varying from jungles thick with tall, pillar-like *gommier* trees to the stunted cloud-forest cover on the upper slopes of Morne Trois Pitons (4550ft/1386m), Dominica's second-highest mountain. The park has many of the island's top wilderness sites, including Boiling Lake, Boeri Lake, Freshwater Lake and Middleham Falls. Hikes to all four start at Laudat (elevation 1970ft/

600m), a small hamlet with fine mountain views.

Emerald Pool, at the northernmost tip of the park, is described on p550.

Sights & Activities

MIDDLEHAM FALLS

The trail to Middleham Falls, one of Dominica's highest waterfalls, takes you on an interesting rainforest walk. More than 60 species of trees, including the tall buttressed chataignier, form a leafy canopy that inhibits undergrowth and keeps the forest floor relatively clear. The treetops provide a habitat for light-seeking flora, including climbing vines, bromeliads and various air plants. The forest is also home to numerous bird species and a tiny species of tree frog.

There are usually guides available at the trailhead who charge about EC$60 to take you to the falls, and the hike takes about 1¼ hours each way. If you don't use a guide, carry a compass and be careful not to stray off the main trail, because it's easy to lose your bearings in the surrounding wilderness.

BOILING LAKE

Dominica's pre-eminent trek is the rugged day-long hike to Boiling Lake, the world's second-largest actively boiling lake (the largest is in New Zealand). Geologists believe the 207ft-wide (62m) lake is a flooded fumarole – a crack in the earth that allows hot gases to vent from the molten lava below. The eerie-looking lake sits inside a deep basin, its grayish waters veiled in steam, its center emitting bubbly burps.

En route to the lake, the hike passes through the aptly named Valley of Desolation, a former rainforest destroyed by a volcanic eruption in 1880. Today, it's an active fumarole area with a barren-looking landscape of crusted lava, steaming sulfur vents and scattered hot springs. The hike follows narrow ridges, snakes up and down mountains and runs along hot streams. Wear sturdy walking shoes and expect to get wet and muddy.

The strenuous 6-mile (9.6km) hike to the lake begins at Titou Gorge, and requires a guide.

OTHER TRAILS

The walk to **Freshwater Lake**, Dominica's largest lake, is a straightforward hike that skirts the southern flank of Morne Macaque. As the 2.5-mile (4km) trail up to the lake is along a well-established 4WD track, this hike doesn't require a guide. It's a relatively gradual walk and takes about 2½ hours round-trip.

Hikers can continue another 1.25 miles (2km) from Freshwater Lake to **Boeri Lake**, a scenic 45-minute walk that passes mountain streams and hot and cold springs. The 130ft-deep (39m) Boeri Lake occupies a volcanic crater that's nestled between two of the park's highest mountains. En route are ferns, heliconia and various epiphytes, as well as the mossy trees of the elfin woodlands that surround the lake.

For a short walk and a dip there's the trail from Laudat to **Titou Gorge**, where a deep pool is warmed by a hot spring. Just above the pool, the gorge narrows, and when the water's calm it's possible to swim upriver to a small cascading waterfall. If you see any brown water being kicked up, then there's a dangerous current and you should stay out of the pool. To get to the trail, turn at the pay phone in Laudat and follow the short road to the utility station. The 0.5-mile (800m) trail follows a narrow canal that feeds water to the hydroelectric plant.

Serious hikers could also hire a guide to tackle **Morne Trois Pitons**, the park's tallest peak, but it's a rough trail that cuts through patches of sharp saw grass and requires scrambling over steep rocks. The trail begins at Pont Casse, at the north side of the park, and takes about five hours round-trip.

Sleeping & Eating

Roxy's Mountain Lodge (☎ /fax 448-4845; PO Box 265; s from US$50, d with kitchenette from US$80) Based in Laudat, Roxy's makes a great base if you're planning to do a lot of hiking. This friendly, family-run place has 17 rooms and an engaging, communal atmosphere. There's a TV room, a small bar and a restaurant with good-value lunchtime sandwiches and dinner meals. Valerie Rock, who runs the guesthouse with her brother, can arrange reliable trail guides and is an excellent source of information about the island.

Getting There & Away

To get to Laudat, take King George V St north from Roseau. After crossing the Roseau River, continue up the Roseau Valley for 2.3 miles (3.7km), at which point the road forks; take the left fork, marked 'Laudat.' The road is narrow and a bit potholed, but it's passable. The trail to Middleham Falls begins on the left 2.5 miles (4km) up; the trail to Freshwater and Boeri Lakes begins opposite the shrine, half a mile (800m) further.

There's regular but limited bus service. Buses to Laudat (EC$4.75, 40 minutes) leave from the Roseau police station every other hour from 6:30am; buses return to Roseau from Laudat about 45 minutes later. Taxis from Roseau to Laudat cost EC$80.

SOUTH OF ROSEAU

The coastal road south of Roseau is a delightful 30-minute drive that takes you through a couple of attractive little seaside villages and ends at Scotts Head. Most of the road skirts the water's edge, although there's a roller-coaster section just before Soufriere that winds up the mountain and gives a bird's-eye coastal view before dropping back down.

Soufriere (population 950) has a picturesque old stone church on the north side of the village. There are steaming sulfur springs in the hills above town, including one about 1 mile (1.6km) inland on the road that leads east from the village center.

Scotts Head (population 800), on the southernmost tip of Dominica's west coast, is a picturesque fishing village and a fun place in which to kick around. It has a gem of a setting along the gently curving shoreline of Soufriere Bay, which is the rim of a sunken volcanic crater. Mountains form a scenic inland backdrop. At the southern tip of the bay is a promontory, also called Scotts Head, which is connected to the village by a narrow, rocky neck of land. It's a short, easy walk to the top of the promontory, where there's a fine coastal view.

The center of village activity in Scotts Head is the waterfront, where brightly painted fishing shacks line the shore, and colorful fishing boats are hauled up onto the sand. It's a lively, welcoming scene, with frequent beach barbecues and dancing in the local bars. The bay offers good swimming and snorkeling, as well as some of the island's best diving.

Sea Kayaking (☎ 448-1665), in the village, offers just that for US$10 per hour and also rents out snorkeling sets (per day US$12).

There is a bus service from the Old Market in Roseau to Soufriere and Scotts Head (EC$3.50, 30 minutes).

DIRECTORY

ACCOMMODATIONS

Dominica has only about 750 rooms available for visitors, mainly in small, locally run hotels and guesthouses along the west side of the island. There are also two mountain lodges (Papillote and Roxy's) just west of Morne Trois Pitons National Park – these are delightful places to stay for those who want to be on the edge of the rainforest. Budget accommodations are comprised largely of guesthouses.

Dominica has a 5% room tax, and the more expensive hotels also add a 10% service charge to bills. See p757 for details on how accommodations price ranges are categorized in this book.

ACTIVITIES

In response to the growing numbers of cruise-ship passengers, the government of Dominica has instituted user fees for all foreign visitors entering ecotourist sites. These include national parks and other protected areas.

The cost is US$2 per site, US$5 for a day pass or US$10 for a weekly pass, and the proceeds go to conservation efforts and maintenance of the park system. Passes are sold by car-rental agencies, tour operators,

---

PRACTICALITIES

- **Newspapers** The *Chronicle* and the *Tropical Star* are Dominica's weekly papers.

- **Radio** Government-owned DBS radio station broadcasts on 88.1FM and 595AM.

- **Video Systems** NTSC is used on the island.

- **Electricity** Seventy per cent of the island's electricity is hydro-generated, with power of 220/240V, 50 cycles.

- **Weights & Measures** Dominica uses the imperial system.

DOMINICA

---

cruise-ship personnel and the forestry department, as well as at all of the major sites, including Indian River, Cabrits National Park, Emerald Pool and Boiling Lake.

Beaches & Swimming

While Dominica doesn't have the sort of gorgeous strands that make it onto brochure covers, it's not without beaches. On the calmer and more popular west coast, they're predominantly black-sand beaches, with the best of the lot in the Portsmouth area.

The east coast has largely open seas with high surf and turbulent water conditions. There are a few pockets of golden sands just south of Calibishie that are sometimes calm enough for swimming and snorkeling, and there are a couple of roadside brown-sand beaches a bit further south.

Diving & Snorkeling

Dominica has superb diving. The island's rugged scenery continues under the water, where it forms sheer drop-offs, volcanic arches, pinnacles and caves.

Many of Dominica's top dive sites are in the Soufriere Bay area. Scotts Head Drop-Off is a shallow coral ledge that drops off abruptly more than 150ft (46m), revealing a wall of huge tube sponges and soft corals. Just west of Scotts Head is the Pinnacle, which starts a few feet below the surface and drops down to a series of walls, arches and caves that are rife with stingrays, snappers, barracudas and parrotfish.

Calmer waters more suitable for snorkelers and amateur divers can be found at another undersea mound, the Soufriere Pinnacle, which rises 160ft (49m) from the floor of the bay to within 5ft (1.5m) of the surface and offers a wide range of corals and fish. Also popular for snorkelers and beginners is Champagne, a subaquatic hot spring off Pointe Guignard, where crystal bubbles rise from underwater vents.

The north side of the island still has lots of unexplored territory. Popular sites north of Roseau include Castaways Reef, Grande Savane, Rodney's Rock, Toucari Bay and the wrecks of a barge and tugboat off Canefield.

For more information on diving in Dominica, see p54.

Note that by law, all dives (shore and boat) in Dominica must be accompanied by a government-registered, licensed divemaster.

DIVE SHOPS

Anchorage Dive Center (☎ 448-2638/2639; www.anchoragehotel.dm; PO Box 34) At Anchorage Hotel in Castle Comfort (p545), just south of Roseau.

Dive Dominica (☎ 448-2188; www.divedominica.com; PO Box 63) At Castle Comfort Lodge (p545); it's the island's oldest dive shop.

East Carib Dive (☎ /fax 449-6575; http://eastcaribdive.free.fr; PO Box 375) Near Salisbury, it's run by a divemaster from Germany.

Nature Island Dive (☎ 449-8181; www.natureislanddive.com) Based in Soufriere, just minutes from many of the island's best dive spots.

The going rate is about US$50 for a one-tank dive or a night dive and US$70 for a two-tank dive. Anchorage offers beginners a resort course with an ocean dive for US$95. A number of the shops offer full PADI certification courses for around US$400.

In addition, Dive Dominica, Nature Island Dive and Anchorage have one-week packages that include accommodations and multiple dives.

All the dive shops offer snorkeling tours or will take snorkelers out with divers. If you're tagging along with divers, make sure they're doing a shallow dive – staring down at a wreck 50ft (15m) under water isn't terribly interesting from the surface.

Hiking

Dominica has some excellent hiking. Short walks lead to Emerald Pool and Trafalgar Falls, two of the island's most visited sights. Cabrits National Park has a couple of short hikes. In the Northern Forest Reserve, there's an easy hike through a parrot reserve and a rugged trail to the top of the island's highest mountain. The Morne Trois Pitons National Park offers serious treks into the wilderness, ranging from jaunts through verdant jungles to an all-day trek across a steaming volcanic valley that ends at a boiling lake.

The short hikes to the more popular destinations can generally be done on your

DOMINICA

own, but most wilderness treks require a guide who's familiar with the route.

Dominica's Forestry Division publishes brochures on many of the trails; each can be purchased for EC$1 or so at the forestry office in Roseau's Botanical Gardens (p543).

Individual hikes are described in relevant sections throughout this chapter.

Kayaking

Nature Island Dive (☎ 449-8181; www.natureisland dive.com), in Soufriere, rents out sea kayaks for US$15 per hour. You can paddle around Soufriere Bay, or take an excursion up the coastline where there are snorkeling sites that can't be reached by land.

Kayak rentals are also available just north of Portsmouth, where you can check out Cabrits National Park and Douglas Bay, with excellent snorkeling spots.

Mountain Biking

Nature Island Dive (☎ 449-8181; www.natureisland dive.com), in Soufriere, rents out mountain bikes and leads guided biking trips. You can explore old estate trails and the nearby sulfur springs; staff can recommend longer outings for serious bikers.

Whale-Watching

Whales and dolphins roam the deep waters off Dominica's sheltered west coast. Sperm whales, which grow to a length of 70ft (21m) and have a blunt, square snout, are the whales most commonly sighted; the main season is October to March. Other resident toothed whales are the orca, pygmy sperm whale, pygmy killer whale, false killer whale and pilot whale. In winter, migrating humpback whales are occasionally spotted as well.

Anchorage Dive Center and Dive Dominica (opposite) run whale-watching boat tours from around 2pm to sunset a few times a week (US$50).

BOOKS

Wild Majesty: Encounters with Caribs from Columbus to the Present Day, by Peter Hulme and Neil L Whitehead, is a lively anthropological account of the life and culture of native West Indian Caribs. *In Search of Eden: Essays on Dominican History,* by Irving W Andre and Gabriel J Christian, provides a good introduction to Dominica's natural history.

EMBASSIES & CONSULATES
Dominican Embassies & Consulates
UK (☎ 0207-370-5194; 1 Collingham Gardens, South Kensington, London SW5 0HW)
USA (☎ 202-332-6280; 820 2nd Ave, Suite 900, New York, NY 10017)

Embassies & Consulates in Dominica
Belgium (☎ 448-3012; Hanover St 20, Roseau)
China (☎ 449-1385; PO Box 56, Roseau)
UK (☎ 448-7655; c/o Courts Dominica Ltd, PO Box 2269, Castle Comfort, Roseau)

FESTIVALS & EVENTS
Carnival Dominica's official celebrations are held on the two days prior to Ash Wednesday, but there are pre-Carnival events running from January. These include weekly competitions and parades: in the two weeks prior to Lent there are calypso competitions, a Carnival Queen contest, jump-ups and a costume parade.
Independence Day The week leading up to Independence Day (November 3), or Creole Day, is packed with events. The vibrant celebration of local heritage includes parades, school kids in traditional outfits and special Creole menus. Live music is performed in restaurants, banks and grocery stores as well as on sidewalks all around Roseau.

HOLIDAYS
Public holidays on Dominica:
New Year's Day January 1
Carnival Monday & Tuesday Two days preceding Ash Wednesday.
Good Friday Late March/early April
Easter Monday Late March/early April
May Day May 1
Whit Monday Eighth Monday after Easter
August Monday First Monday in August
Independence Day/Creole Day November 3
Community Service Day November 4
Christmas Day December 25
Boxing Day December 26

MONEY
Dominica uses the Eastern Caribbean dollar (EC$). At the time of writing, the bank exchange rate for US$1 was EC$2.68 for traveler's checks, EC$2.67 for cash. US dollars are widely accepted by shops, restaurants and taxi drivers, usually at an exchange rate of EC$2.60 or EC$2.65.

Most hotels, car-rental agencies, dive shops, tour operators and top-end restaurants accept MasterCard, Visa and American Express credit cards.

DOMINICA

POST

The main post office is in Roseau; there are small post offices in larger villages. All post-office (PO) boxes listed in this chapter are in Roseau; therefore, box numbers should be followed by 'Roseau, Commonwealth of Dominica, West Indies.' When there's no PO box, the address should include the recipient's town. The use of the word 'Commonwealth' on mail is important to prevent mail being sent to the Dominican Republic by mistake.

TELEPHONE

Dominica's country code is ☎ 767. To call from North America, dial ☎ 1-767 + the seven-digit local number. Elsewhere, dial your country's international access code, + ☎ 767 + the local number. Within Dominica you just need to dial the local number. We've included only the seven-digit local number in Dominica listings in this chapter.

For directory information dial ☎ 118; for international calls, dial ☎ 0.

Dominica has coin and (more commonly) card phones. Buy phone cards at telecommunications offices, the Roseau library and the Canefield Airport gift shop.

VISAS

Only citizens of former Eastern Bloc countries require visas.

TRANSPORTATION

GETTING THERE & AWAY
Entering Dominica

Most visitors to Dominica must have a valid passport; US citizens see the boxed text, p772. French nationals may visit for up to two weeks with an official Carte d'Indentité. A round-trip or onward ticket is – in principle – required of all visitors to the island.

Air

There are no direct flights available from Europe or the US into Dominica, so overseas visitors must first get to a gateway island. There are direct flights to Dominica from Antigua, Barbados, Guadeloupe, Martinique, Puerto Rico, St Lucia and St Martin.

Dominica has two airports: **Canefield Airport** (DCF; ☎ 449-1990), just outside Roseau, and **Melville Hall Airport** (DOM; ☎ 445-7101;

melvillehallairport@yahoo.com), on the secluded northeast side of the island.

On LIAT's printed schedule, the letters C and M after the departure time indicate which airport is being used. There's a **tourist information booth** (6:15-11:30am & 2:15-6pm) at both airports, as well as a handful of car-rental firms.

The following airlines fly into and out of Dominica from within the Caribbean:
Air Caraïbes (☎ 448-2181; www.aircaraibes.com; c/o Whitchurch Travel, Old St, Roseau; hub Guadeloupe)
Air Guadeloupe (☎ 448-2181; c/o Whitchurch Travel, Old St, Roseau; hub Guadeloupe)
American Eagle (☎ 448-0628; www.aa.com; hub Dominican Republic)
Caribbean Star (☎ 448-2181; www.flycaribbeanstar.com; c/o Whitchurch Travel, Old St, Roseau; hub Antigua)
LIAT (☎ 448-2421; www.liatairline.com; King George V St, Roseau; hub Antigua)

Sea

L'Express des Îles (☎ 448-2181; www.express-des-iles.com; c/o Whitchurch Travel, Roseau) connects Dominica with both Pointe-à-Pitre in Guadeloupe (€60/85 one way/return, 1¾ hours, once daily Monday, Wednesday, Friday, Saturday and Sunday) and Fort-de-France in Martinique (€60/85 one way/return, 1½ hours, once daily Monday, Wednesday, Friday, Saturday and Sunday) on modern catamarans. Both services do return trips on the same days. There's also a service to Castries in St Lucia on Friday and Sunday (four hours), returning on Saturday and Sunday.

These schedules change frequently; it's important to confirm departure times a couple of days in advance to avoid getting stranded on the island.

There are discounts of 50% for children aged two to 11 and 10% for passengers under 26 or older than 60.

Caribbean Ferries (☎ 448-2181; www.caribbean-ferries.com; c/o Whitchurch Travel, Roseau) also runs a once-per-day return service between Dominica and St Lucia (Monday, Wednesday and Friday), Martinique (Monday, Wednesday, Friday and Sunday) and Guadeloupe (Monday, Friday and Sunday).

All are seasonal, only going in the winter months.

Brudey Frères (in Guadeloupe 590-590-90-04-48; www.brudey-freres.fr) has a daily (except Friday) service between Dominica and Guadeloupe for €55/80 one way/round-trip.

GETTING AROUND
To/From the Airport
From Melville Hall Airport, there are plenty of car-rental companies and there's also a taxi phone service if you can't find a taxi. The fare is about EC$50 to Roseau or EC$40 to Portsmouth. For details on getting to/from Canefield Airport, see p546.

Bus
Buses, which are usually minivans, run regularly along the coastal routes between Roseau and Scotts Head, and Roseau and Portsmouth, although the further north you go past Canefield the less frequent they become. Generally, they run from 6am to 6pm or a little later Monday to Friday, and until 2pm on Saturday. There aren't any services on Sunday.

Car & Motorcycle
DRIVER'S LICENSE
A local driver's license (US$12) is required, which can be picked up from immigration at either airport or at car-rental agencies any day of the week. Visiting drivers must be between the ages of 25 and 65 and have a valid driver's license and at least two years' driving experience.

RENTAL
Avis (☎ 448-2481) is the only car-rental company right at Canefield Airport. Daily rates begin at US$48.

Budget (☎ 449-2080), in the village of Canefield, has a courtesy phone at the airport, provides free pickup and has relatively attractive rates, beginning at US$40.

There are many other car-rental agencies on the island. Those in Roseau include **Courtesy Car Rental** (☎ 448-7763; Goodwill Rd) and **Garraway Rent-A-Car** (☎ 448-2891). Also try **Valley Rent-A-Car** (☎ In Roseau 448-3233, In Portsmouth 445-5252).

Note that although most car rentals include unlimited mileage, a few local companies cap the number of free miles before a surcharge is added, so be sure to inquire in advance.

In addition to rental fees, most companies charge US$10 to US$15 a day for an optional collision damage waiver (CDW), though even with the CDW you may still be responsible for the first US$800 or so in damages.

ROAD CONDITIONS
Dominica is a visitor-friendly island. Road signs mark most towns and villages, and major intersections are clearly signposted.

Primary roads are usually narrow but in good shape – most are well paved and pothole-free. Secondary roads vary; some of the interior mountain roads are steep, narrow and in bad repair. Be careful of deep rain gutters that run along the side of many roads – a slip into one could easily bring any car to a grinding halt.

ROAD RULES
Dominicans drive on the left-hand side of the road. There are gas stations in larger towns around the island, including Canefield, Portsmouth and Marigot. The speed limit in Roseau and other towns is 20mph (32km/h).

DOMINICA

Martinique

Francophiles will feel right at home on Martinique. Except for the palm trees to remind you that you're somewhere sunnier, the island could be easily mistaken for a provincial region of France. In fact, you'll be hard-pressed to hear English spoken – 80% of the island's visitors hail from France and all locals speak French or Creole. That said, however, Martinique is also home to a fascinating and dynamic Caribbean society, with a distinct culture and a long history of resistance to French authority.

Martinique is volcanic in origin, topped by the 4582ft (1397m) active volcano, Mont Pelée. Pelée last erupted in 1902, gaining an infamous place in history by wiping out the capital city of St-Pierre. Today, the ruins of St-Pierre are Martinique's foremost tourist sight.

Today's capital, Fort-de-France (in many ways similar to Marseilles), is a busy city, the largest the French West Indies. Most of the island's other large towns are modern and suburban, linked to the capital by multilane highways and fast-moving traffic. Nevertheless, nearly a third of Martinique is forested and it's often referred to as the 'Isle of Flowers.' Other parts of the island are given over to pineapples, bananas and sugarcane fields. You can still find sleepy fishing villages, remote beaches and lots of hiking trails into the mountains. Just be sure to brush up on your French before hitting this Gallic outpost.

FAST FACTS

- **Area** 417 sq miles (1080 sq km)
- **Capital** Fort-de-France
- **Country code** ☎ 596
- **Departure tax** None
- **Famous for** Flowers, including hibiscus, frangipani and bougainvillea
- **Languages** French, Creole
- **Money** Euro (€) €1 = US$1.20 = UK£0.69
- **Official name** La Martinique
- **People** Martiniquans
- **Phrases** *La plage est en quelle direction?* Which way to the beach? *Combien ce coute le ti-punch s'il vous plait?* How much is the ti-punch please?
- **Population** 415,000
- **Visa** Most non-EU and non-US citizens need a visa

HIGHLIGHTS

- **St-Pierre** (p569) Explore the town's eerie ruins.
- **Les Salines** (p577) Tune out in a tree hammock, with vast stretches of beach and blue sea in front of you.
- **Route de la Trace** (p570) Cruise across the lush mountainous interior on this scenic rainforest drive.
- **Grand Anse** (p574) Kick back in this sleepy fishing village.
- **Presqu'île de Caravelle** (p573) Ramble the charming fishing village of Tartane on this rugged Atlantic peninsula.

ITINERARIES

- **Three Days** Heading north from a morning's ramble in Fort-de-France, enjoy the scenery of Route de la Trace en route to the Leyritz Plantation. Make a quick detour to Grande Rivière for a good windswept meal. On day two, amble back down the west coast, taking in the fascinating St-Pierre and a night's dive of its offshore wrecks. Finish your break with a bout of sunbathing and water sports at Grand Anse or Anse d'Arlet.
- **One Week** Continuing with the first itinerary, take the coast road south past Diamant and on down to Ste-Anne. Snorkel off the lovely beach at Les Salines. The next day, scoot up the east coast to the Presqu'île de Caravelle (Caravelle Peninsula) and the pretty village of Tartane. Round it all off with a visit to the L'Habitation Fond St-Jacques plantation and the rum museum.

CLIMATE & WHEN TO GO

Martinique enjoys a year-round tropical climate though its busiest tourist period is during the dry season, from December to May, when temperatures average about 85°F (26°C). The rainy season begins in June and continues until the end of November, with heavy showers most days (September is the rainiest month). Martinique's average humidity is high, ranging from 80% in March and April to 87% in October and November. The mountainous northern interior is both cooler and rainier than the coast.

HISTORY

When Christopher Columbus sighted Martinique, it was inhabited by Carib Indians who

---

HOW MUCH?

- Taxi fare from the airport to Fort-de-France center €20
- One-hour diving trip €40
- Comfortable hotel double €80
- Cinema ticket €6
- Meal of fresh fish €10

LONELY PLANET INDEX

- Liter of gas €1.20
- Liter of bottled water €1.50
- Glass of Lorraine beer €3.50
- Souvenir T-shirt €15
- Street snack: crepe €2

---

called the island Madinina, which means 'Island of Flowers.' Three decades passed before the first party of French settlers, who were led by Pierre Belain d'Esnambuc, landed on the northwest side of the island. There they built a small fort and established a settlement that would become the capital city, St-Pierre. The next year, on October 31, 1636, King Louis XIII signed a decree authorizing the use of African slaves in the French West Indies.

The settlers quickly went about colonizing the land with the help of slave labor and by 1640 had extended their grip south to Fort-de-France, where they constructed a fort on the rise above the harbor. As forests were cleared to make room for sugar plantations, conflicts with the native Caribs escalated into warfare, and in 1660 those Caribs who had survived the fighting were finally forced off the island.

The British also took a keen interest in Martinique, invading and holding the island for most of the period from 1794 to 1815. The island prospered under British occupation; the planters simply sold their sugar in British markets rather than French markets. Perhaps more importantly, the occupation allowed Martinique to avoid the turmoil and bloodshed of the French Revolution. By the time the British returned the island to France in 1815, the Napoleonic Wars had ended and the French empire was again entering a period of stability.

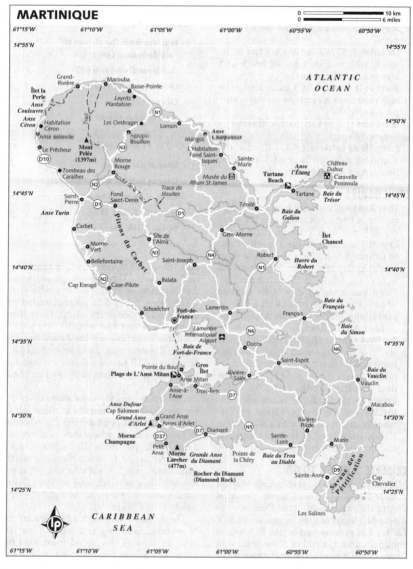

MARTINIQUE

Not long after the French administration was re-established on Martinique, the golden era of sugarcane began to wane, as glutted markets and the introduction of sugar beets on mainland France eroded prices. With their wealth diminished, the aristocratic plantation owners lost much of their political influence, and the abolitionist movement, led by Victor Schoelcher, gained momentum.

It was Schoelcher, the French cabinet minister responsible for overseas possessions, who convinced the provisional government to sign the 1848 Emancipation Proclamation, which brought an end to slavery in the French West Indies. Widely

---

THE EMPRESS JOSEPHINE

Martinique's most famous colonial daughter was the Empress Josephine. Born in Trois-Îlets in June 1763 and baptized Marie Joseph Rose Tascher de la Pagerie, the child, it's rumored, was pronounced by a soothsayer to be a future queen.

After a relatively short-lived marriage to a wealthy army officer, Alexandre de Beauharnais, Josephine began a passionate love affair with a largely unknown military officer named Napoleon Bonaparte. At the age of 33, and six years his senior, Josephine married Napoleon. In 1804, Napoleon was proclaimed Emperor of France and Josephine was crowned empress.

Although she had two children by her first marriage, Josephine was unable to bear Napoleon an heir and in 1809 Napoleon acrimoniously divorced her.

Curiously, Josephine's daughter from her first marriage, Hortense de Beauharnais, married Napoleon's brother and gave birth to a son, Louis, who would take the French throne as Napoleon III in 1852.

---

reviled by the White aristocracy of the time, Schoelcher is now regarded as one of Martinique's heroes.

On May 8, 1902, in the most devastating natural disaster in Caribbean history, the Mont Pelée volcano erupted violently, destroying the city of St-Pierre and claiming the lives of its 30,000 inhabitants. Shortly thereafter, the capital was moved permanently to Fort-de-France. St-Pierre, which had been regarded as the most cultured city in the French West Indies, was eventually rebuilt, but it has never been more than a shadow of its former self.

In 1946, Martinique became an Overseas Department of France, with a status similar to those of metropolitan departments. In 1974 it was further assimilated into the political fold as a Department of France.

THE CULTURE

Martinique's society combines French traditions with Caribbean Creole culture. Politeness is highly valued on Martinique, so brush up on your manners.

Always be respectful, and take your cue from the islanders. Unlike other Caribbean cultures, a laid-back attitude to dress, communication and behavior is frowned upon.

Many of the hotel restaurants enforce a dress code; look for signs that read *tenue correcte est exigée* (correct dress expected). Elsewhere, dress is casual but generally stylish. Topless bathing is common on the island, particularly at resort beaches, but save beachwear for the beach only. In general, always address people with the less familiar *'vous'* rather than *'tu.'*

Population

Martinique's population is about 415,000, and more than a quarter of this live in the Fort-de-France area. The majority of residents are of mixed ethnic origin. The earliest settlers were from Normandy, Brittany, Paris and other parts of France; shortly afterward, African slaves were brought to the island. Later, smaller numbers of immigrants came from India, Syria and Lebanon. These days, Martinique is home to thousands of immigrants – some of them here illegally, from poorer Caribbean islands such as Dominica, St Lucia and Haiti.

ARTS
Literature

The Black Pride movement known as *négritude* emerged as a philosophical and literary movement in the 1930s largely through the writings of Martinique native Aimé Césaire, a poet who was eventually elected mayor of Fort-de-France. The movement advanced Black social and cultural values and reestablished bonds with African traditions, which had been suppressed by French colonialism.

Music

The beguine, an Afro-French dance music with a bolero rhythm, originated in Martinique in the 1930s. A more contemporary French West Indies creation, zouk, draws on the beguine and other French-Caribbean folk forms. Retaining the electronic influences of its '80s origins, with its Carnival-like rhythm and hot dance beat, zouk has become as popular in Europe as it is in the French Caribbean. The Martiniquan zouk band Kassav' has made several top-selling

MARTINIQUE

recordings, including the English-language album *Shades of Black*.

ENVIRONMENT
The Land
At 417 sq miles (1080 sq km), Martinique is the second-largest island in the French West Indies. Roughly 40 miles (65km) long and 12.5 miles (20km) wide, it has a terrain punctuated by hills, plateaus and mountains.

The highest point is the 4582ft (1397m) Mont Pelée, an active volcano at the northern end of the island. The center of the island is dominated by the Pitons du Carbet, a scenic mountain range reaching 3959ft (1207m).

Martinique's irregular coastline is cut by deep bays and coves, while the mountainous rainforest in the interior feeds numerous rivers.

Wildlife
Martinique has lots of colorful flowering plants, with vegetation types varying with altitude and rainfall. Rainforests cover the slopes of the mountains in the northern interior, which are luxuriant with tree ferns, bamboo groves, climbing vines and hardwood trees like mahogany, rosewood, locust and *gommier*.

The drier southern part of the island has brushy savanna vegetation such as cacti, frangipani trees, balsam, logwood and acacia shrubs. Common landscape plantings include splashy bougainvillea, the ubiquitous red hibiscus and yellow-flowered allamanda trees.

Martinique has Anolis lizards, manicous (opossums), mongooses and venomous fer-de-lance snakes. The mongoose, which was introduced from India in the late 19th century, preys on eggs and has been responsible for the demise of many bird species. Some native birds, such as parrots, are no longer found on the island at all, while others have significantly declined in numbers. Endangered birds include the Martinique trembler, white-breasted trembler and white-breasted thrasher.

FOOD & DRINK
Most restaurants serve either Creole or French food with an emphasis on local seafood. Red snapper, conch, crayfish and lobster are popular. The best value at many restaurants is the fixed-price menu, which is sometimes labeled *menu touristique* – a three- or four-course meal that usually runs from €10 to €18, depending on the main course. Remember that this is France, so bring a good book or someone to talk to; it can take a couple of hours for all the courses to be served.

For more moderately priced meals there are a number of Italian restaurants and pizzerias on the island. Bakeries are good budget places to grab a quick meal, because most of them make sandwiches to go and some have a few café tables out front.

The island of Martinique grows much of its own produce, including some very sweet pineapples.

Water is safe to drink from the tap. In restaurants, if you ask for water you'll usually be served bottled water.

The legal drinking age is 18. Lorraine is the tasty local beer, but island rums are far more popular. Martinique's de rigueur *apéritif* is ti-punch, a mixture of white rum, sugarcane juice and a squeeze of lemon. It's a feisty little drink that could fuel you up for the day. Also popular is *planteur* punch, a mix of rum and fruit juice.

FORT-DE-FRANCE

pop 100,000

Fort-de-France, the island capital, is the largest and most cosmopolitan city in the French West Indies. Its harborfront setting with the Pitons du Carbet rising up beyond is a view best appreciated when approaching the city by ferry.

The narrow, busy streets opposite La Savane (the harborfront central park) are lined with a mixture of ordinary offices, bargain-basement shops and crumbling early-20th-century buildings with wrought-iron balconies that wouldn't look out of place in New Orleans.

Give yourself a few hours to wander around and take in the handful of historic sites and museums the city has to offer; most visitors tend to leave the capital by evening when its near-empty streets begin to reveal their seedier side.

ORIENTATION
La Savane, the city park, lines the eastern end of the harbor. Northwest of here you'll

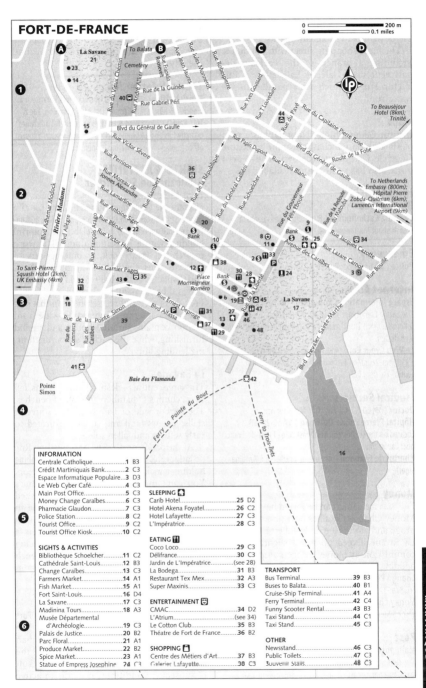

FORT-DE-FRANCE

0 ——— 200 m
0 ——— 0.1 miles

MARTINIQUE

spot the spire of Cathèdral St-Louis, one of the city's most visible landmarks.

The main shopping street with boutiques, including a branch of the Parisian department store Galeries Lafayettes, is Rue Victor Hugo, which runs parallel to the waterfront.

Maps

Institut Géographique National has a map of Martinique, which is sold at the bookstore Centrale Catholique (below). The tourist office also has some maps available.

INFORMATION

Bookstores

Centrale Catholique (57 Rue Blénac) Sells books in French about Martinique, and maps.

Emergency

Police (☎ 63-51-51; Rue Victor Sévere)

Internet Access

Espace Informatique Populaire (☎ 56-19-86; 9 Rue Lazare Carnot; per 15min €2; 8:30am-12:30pm & 5-8pm Mon-Fri) This IT center also offers hourly courses in web design.

Le Web Cyber Café (4 Rue Blénac; per 15min €2; 11am-2am Mon-Fri, 6pm-2am Sat) A smoky but central 1st-floor bar.

Medical Services

Doctor (☎ 60-60-44) For after-hours service.
Hôpital Pierre Zobda Quitman (☎ 55-20-00) Located on the D13 on the northeast side of Fort-de-France near Lamentin.
Pharmacie Glaudon (cnr Rues de la Liberté & Antoine Siger)

Money

Full-service banks can be found next door to Money Change Caraïbes on Rue Ernest Deproge and along Rue de la Liberté, opposite La Savane. Expect to pay a slightly higher commission at moneychangers due to later opening hours.

Change Point (Rue Victor Hugo; 8am-5:30pm Mon-Fri, 8am-12:30pm Sat)
Money Change Caraïbes (4 Rue Ernest Deproge; 7:30am-6pm Mon-Fri, 8am-12:30pm Sat)

Post

Main post office (cnr Rues Antoine Siger & de la Liberté; 7am-6pm Mon-Fri, 7am-noon Sat) Head here to send faxes, buy phone cards and pick up poste restante mail.

Telephone

Public card phones can be found at La Savane, opposite the post office and around the city.

Tourist Information

Tourist office (☎ 60-27-73; www.ot-fortdefrance.fr in French; 76 Rue Lazare Carnot; 8am-5pm Mon, Tue & Thu, 8am-12:30pm Wed & Fri) Has some useful brochures on activities and accommodations. In peak season a tourist office kiosk on Rue Lamartine is open too.

SIGHTS & ACTIVITIES

Bibliothèque Schoelcher

Fort-de-France's most visible landmark, the **Bibliothèque Schoelcher** (Schoelcher Library; Rue de la Liberté; 1-5:30pm Mon, 8:30am-5:30pm Tue-Thu, 8:30am-5pm Fri & 8:30am-noon Sat), is an elaborate, colorful building with a Byzantine dome. The work of architect Henri Pick, a contemporary of Gustave Eiffel, the library was built in Paris and displayed at the 1889 World Exposition. It was then dismantled, shipped in pieces to Fort-de-France and reassembled on this site. The ornate interior is interesting – the front section contains antique books and period furnishing, while the back is still a functioning lending library.

La Savane

This large central park sports grassy lawns, tall trees, clumps of bamboo and lots of benches. The harbor side of La Savane has souvenir stalls, a newsstand and statues dedicated to early settlers and fallen soldiers.

At the park's north side, near bustling Rue de la Liberté, is a **statue of the Empress Josephine** holding a locket with a portrait of Napoleon. You can't miss it – years ago, the statue's head was lopped off and red paint splashed over it. No real efforts have been made to repair the damage. Evidently, the empress is not highly regarded by islanders, who believe she was directly responsible for convincing Napoleon to continue slavery in the French West Indies so that her family plantation in Trois-Îlets would not suffer.

Fort St-Louis

Opposite the south side of La Savane is **Fort St-Louis** (tours €4; tours hourly 10am-3pm). The original fort, built in the Marshal Vauban style, dates from 1640, although most of the extensive fort that stands today is the result of subsequent additions. It is still an active military base and can be visited only as part of a 45-minute tour in French, escorted by a guide and sailor.

Cathèdral St-Louis

With its neo-Byzantine style and 187ft-high (57m) steeple, the **Cathèdral St-Louis** (Rue Schoel-cher) is one of the city's most distinguished landmarks. Built in 1895 by Henri Pick, a block northwest of La Savane, the church fronts a small square and is picturesquely framed by two royal palms. The spacious, elaborate interior is well worth a look.

Musée Départemental d'Archéologie

For displays of Native American artifacts, including stone tools, ritual objects and pottery, head to the **archeological museum** (9 Rue de la Liberté; adult/child under 12 €3/1.50; 1-5pm Mon, 8am-5pm Tue-Fri, 9am-noon Sat). Most engaging are the 100 or so clay *adornos*, the decorative figurines that Arawaks used to adorn vases and bowls. There are also illustrations of the Caribs and a diorama of thatched huts. The presentation is simple and a bit dry, and you can walk through it all in about 20 minutes, but it's still worth the visit. Most signs are in French only.

Palais de Justice

The Palais de Justice, a neoclassical court-house built in 1906, is two blocks northeast of the cathedral and can only be viewed from the outside. The design resembles a French railroad station, as the plaque out front points out. The square fronting the courthouse has a statue of French abolition-ist Victor Schoelcher.

Parc Floral & Public Markets

If you're already in the area, the **Parc Floral**, a public park at the north side of the city, is worth a stroll.

Fort-de-France's early-18th-century, Henri Pick–designed **spice market**, with its colorful stalls piled high with herbs, spices and local flowers, is worth a visit, even if only to grab a few snaps of the local stallholders, many in traditional costume, plying their wares.

A **farmers market** runs along the west side of Parc Floral and spills over into the street along the Rivière Madame. In addition to island-grown fruits and vegetables, the mar-ket sells drinking coconuts and cut flowers. The **fish market** is a block to the south, while

a second and larger public **produce market** is on the north side of Rue Isambert. The markets run from 5am to sundown but get there before noon for best pickings; the busiest day is Saturday and they're closed Sunday.

Outdoor Activities

Madinina Tours (70-65-25; 111-113 Rue Ernest Deproge) organizes local boat and canoe excursions and **Funny Scooter Rental** (63-33-05; 80 Rue Ernest Deproge) rents out mountain bikes – ask for a VTT (*velo tout terrain*; all-terrain bike).

TOURS

Azimuth Tours (60-16-59; 9-11am Sat) runs walking tours of the historic city, beginning in various locations. Ring for details.

FESTIVALS & EVENTS

Guitar Festival (www.cmac.asso.fr in French) A biennial festival held on even-numbered years.

Mardi Gras Carnival A spirited carnival during the five-day period leading up to Ash Wednesday. Much of the activity centers on La Savane, where the streets spill over with revelers, rum-fueled partying, costume parades, music and dancing.

Semi-marathon (November; www.sport-up.fr/semifort defrance in French) A 13.6-mile (22km) marathon around the city.

Martinique Jazz Festival (December) This biennial, week-long festival is held on odd-numbered years.

SLEEPING

While there are quite a few sleeping options in the city, quality can vary. We recommend the following options.

City Center

BUDGET

Carib Hotel (60-19-85; caribhotel@wanadoo.fr; 9 Rue de la Redoute du Matouba; s & d €48;) A great budget choice with a French feel. It has comfortable rooms with bath and telephone, and there's a cozy downstairs bar.

L'Impératrice (63-06-82; fax 72-66-30; 15 Rue de la Liberté, 97200 Fort-de-France; s/d from €50/61;) It looks as though nothing has changed in this little city hotel in a century and judging by the dog-eared furniture and faded wallpaper, it probably hasn't. What it lacks in sheen it more than makes up for in charm and loca-tion, right next to La Savane. Rooms have private baths and phones.

MARTINIQUE

Hotel Lafayette (☎ 73-80-50; www.lelafayettehotel
.com; 5 Rue de la Liberté, 97200 Fort-de-France; s/d from
€50/70; ❄) Rooms here are simple and
clean with rustic furniture and 1970s eider-
downs.

MIDRANGE

Hotel Akena Foyatel (☎ 72-46-46; hotel-akena-foy
atel@wanadoo.fr; 68 Ave des Caraïbes; s/d incl breakfast
€89/92; ❄) The fanciest in-town option, this
place is part of a worldwide chain of French
business hotels. Rooms are immaculately
clean, with all mod cons. Breakfast is taken
on the bright, plant-filled 1st floor.

Around Fort-de-France

Squash Hotel (☎ 72-80-80; fax 63-00-74; 3 Blvd de la
Marne, 97200 Fort-de-France; s/d incl breakfast €113/124;
❄ ⬛) Just west of town, this newly reno-
vated, large business hotel has well-appointed
rooms with shiny '80s-style furnishings, tiled
floors and balconies. A fitness center and
three squash courts should keep the energetic happy.

Le Beausèjour Hotel (☎ 75-53-57; www.lebeause
jour-hotel.com in French; 44 La Jambette, 97200 Fort-de-
France; s/d €61/77; ❄) Located about 10 minutes' drive east of the center of town, this
charming villa in exotic gardens has its own
restaurant and 12 rooms with TVs and private baths.

EATING & DRINKING

There are a number of cafés and restaurants
opposite La Savane on Rue de la Liberté.

Budget

If you want to eat cheaply, you can easily
find takeout food and freshly baked bread
for a picnic in the park. Bakeries selling
pastries and inexpensive sandwiches are
scattered throughout the city. In the evenings, food vans selling crepes, barbecued
chicken and other cheap local food park
along the Blvd Chevalier Ste-Marthe at the
southeast side of La Savane.

Délifrance (Rue de la Liberté; sandwiches from €2.50;
❄ breakfast & lunch) This French chain serves
standard but tasty enough filled baguettes
for palates tired of *accras* (a fried mixture
of okra, black-eyed peas, pepper and salt)
and *boudin* (black pudding).

Super Maxinis (cnr Rues de la Liberté & Perrinon;
mains €4-9; ❄ breakfast & lunch) A cheerful café
for decent daytime snacks, sandwiches and

salads. It's thronged with local workers at
lunchtime.

Jardin de l'Impératrice (☎ 63-06-82; 15 Rue de la
Liberté; mains €4-10; ❄ breakfast, lunch & dinner) This
balmy, colonial '50s-style café, at the hotel
of the same name, is a great place to grab
a coffee or snack (available all day) and to
spend an afternoon people-watching over
your newspaper.

Midrange

La Bodega (☎ 60-48-48; 28 Rue Ernest Deproge; mains
€9-15) Try some *accras* with pasta in this dark,
cozy spot that specializes in Creole and Italian food.

Coco Loco (☎ 63-63-77; Rue Ernest Deproge; mains
€10-30; ❄ closed Sun) Disconcertingly located
on a traffic island between two busy roads,
this place looks like a British chain pub but
its conch curries, meat kebabs and salads
seem to be a winner with tourists.

Restaurant Tex Mex (☎ 60-60-21; 108 Rue Ernest Deproge; mains €10-20) Munch on steaming
fajitas and enchiladas washed down with
a Sol beer in this cozy Mexican joint. Most
nights you'll be serenaded by a live mari-
achi band.

ENTERTAINMENT

Fort-de France's nocturnal action may be
considered tame by some standards – in
fact, young revelers head to the city's outlying resorts for action at weekends. However, there are a handful of piano-bars that
offer live zouk, jazz and French music; you
can pick up fliers at the tourist office or in
hotel foyers, or check out the listings site
www.martiniquescoop.com (in French).

Cinemas

Centre Martiniquais d'Action Culturelle (CMAC;
☎ 70-79-39; www.cmac.asso.fr in French; 6 Rue Jacques
Cazotte, 97200 Fort-de-France; adult/child €7/5) This
arts center runs an interesting program of
indie films and documentaries as part of its
cultural festivals.

Theatre

Théâtre de Fort de France (☎ 59-43-29; Rue Victor
Sévere; adult/child €15/9) Offers a program of traditional drama, dance and mime for adults
and children.

CMAC (☎ 70-79-39; www.cmac.asso.fr in French)
Throughout the year this center hosts the-
atrical shows by Martiniquans and various

touring theater companies in its state-of-the-art auditoriums.

Live Music

L'Atrium (☎ 70-79-39; www.atrium.mq in French; 6 Rue Jacques Cazotte) Based at the CMAC, this relatively new cultural center hosts an impressive range of classical, jazz, opera and world music concerts in its year-round program.

Coco Loco (☎ 63-63-77; Rue Ernest Deproge; ❧ closed Sun) This busy restaurant-bar (see opposite) has live local music at weekends and serves up a heady mix of international cocktails to tourists and expats.

Le Cotton Club (☎ cell 0696-28-60-83; 13 Rue Garnier Pages; ❧ 11:30am-2am) This live music bar has – unusually – live jazz by day during lunch, as well as *spectacles* (proper shows) at night.

SHOPPING

The busy streets of downtown Fort-de-France are crammed with cheap shops selling all manner of trinkets, clothing, jewelry and perfumes.

The main boutique area is along Rue Victor Hugo, particularly from Rue de la République to Rue de la Liberté. Shops in the town center open from 9am to 1pm and from 3pm to 6pm Monday to Friday and from 9am to 1pm on Saturday.

Department Stores

Galeries Lafayette (Rue Schoelcher) This department store, near the cathedral, has a little of everything. Foreigners who pay with traveler's checks or a credit card get 20% off the posted price at this store (and at many of the other upmarket shops).

Local Art

Local handicrafts such as wicker baskets; dolls in madras costumes; wooden carvings; and T-shirts are sold by vendors at the northwest corner of La Savane and at craft shops around the island. There's an artisan market at **Centre des Métiers d'Art** (Rue Ernest Deproge) that has regional handicrafts for sale.

GETTING THERE & AWAY

Air

For information on flights to Lamentin airport, located southeast of Fort-de-France, see p580.

Boat

There are a couple of regular *vedettes* (ferries) between main resort areas and Fort-de-France that provide a nice alternative to dealing with heavy bus and car traffic – they also allow you to avoid the hassles of city parking and are quicker to boot. In Fort-de-France, the ferries dock at the quay fronting La Savane. Schedules are posted at the docks; the ferries leave promptly and occasionally even a few minutes early.

FORT-DE-FRANCE TO POINTE DU BOUT

Somatours Vedettes (☎ 73-05-53) runs a ferry between Fort-de-France and the Pointe du Bout marina. It's quite a pleasant way to cross and takes only 20 minutes. The boat runs daily from 6:45am to 7pm, every 15 minutes Monday to Friday, and every half-hour on Saturday and Sunday, and costs €3/6 one way/round-trip.

FORT-DE-FRANCE TO TROIS-ÎLETS

Matinik Cruise Line (☎ 68-39-19, 68-42-13) runs a ferry about every 75 minutes between Fort-de-France and the town dock in the village of Trois-Îlets. The first boat departs from Trois-Îlets at 6:10am and the last boat returns from Fort-de-France at 5:45pm. The journey takes 15 minutes and costs €4/7 one way/return. There are no boats on Sunday.

Bus

Fort-de-France's busy main bus, or *taxi collectif,* service terminal is at Pointe Simon, on the west side of the harbor. Buses to St-Pierre leave frequently Monday to Saturday, but less frequently on Sunday (€3.20, 45 minutes). Other bus fares from Fort-de-France are to Trois-Îlets (€2.40), Diamant (€5.70), Ste-Anne (€9.80) and Grand-Rivière (€5.70). You can pick up buses to the gardens of Balata, and Morne Rouge, alongside the cemetery south of the Parc Floral; they leave about every 30 minutes during the day, Monday to Saturday.

Car & Motorcycle

There are numerous car-rental agencies at the airport and in town. You'll find the best rates on their websites, and local firms are generally cheaper than international agencies.

An unlimited mileage rate is generally preferable to a lower rate that adds a charge

MARTINIQUE

per kilometer, particularly if you plan on touring the island.

You must be at least 21 years of age to rent a car, and some companies add an extra surcharge for drivers under the age of 25.

Car-rental companies at the airport:

Avis (☎ 42-11-00; www.avis.com)

Budget (☎ 42-04-04; www.budget-antilles.com)

Carib Rentacar (☎ 42-16-15; www.rentacar-caraibes
.com/martinique/index.asp)

Europcar (☎ 73-33-13; www.europcar.mq in French)

Hertz (☎ 51-01-01; www.hertz.com)

Funny Scooter Rental (☎ 63-33-05; 80 Rue Ernest De-proge) rents out scooters for €25 per day or €175 per week, including insurance.

GETTING AROUND
To/From the Airport

The airport is just a 10-minute drive from Fort-de-France. However, be warned – the traffic can move at a frustrating snail's pace during peak times (from 7am to 10am and 4pm to 7pm), so leave yourself around a couple of hours if catching a flight. Taxis are readily available at the airport (about €20 to Fort-de-France). If you need to refuel a rental car, head for one of the 24-hour gas stations on the N5 near the airport.

Because of the taxi union, there's no direct bus service from the airport. However, on the return it's possible, if not terribly practical, to take a Ducos-bound bus from Pointe Simon in Fort-de-France and ask to be dropped off on the highway outside the airport.

Bus

Local buses (or *taxis collectifs*) are minivans marked 'TC' and can be flagged at bus stops around the city.

Car & Motorcycle

Parking in the city is not a problem on weekends and holidays, but is quite a challenge on weekdays. There's a parking lot along the north side of La Savane that's entered at the intersection of Ave des Caraïbes and Rue de la Liberté; it costs €1.50 per hour. Streetside parking is free in the evenings, on Sunday and on holidays.

Taxi

There are plenty of taxis in the city, and there are taxi stands on the western side of La Savane and on Rue de Pavé. Fares are metered (from La Savane to the spice market costs about €10).

NORTHERN MARTINIQUE

Several roads head north from Fort-de-France. The most interesting sightseeing routes are the coastal road (N2) to St-Pierre and the Route de la Trace (N3), which crosses the lush mountainous interior before ending in Morne Rouge. The two routes can be combined to make a fine loop drive; the highlights can be seen in a half-day or the trip could be stretched into a leisurely full-day outing.

FORT-DE-FRANCE TO ST-PIERRE

The N2 north to St-Pierre passes along dry, scrubby terrain and goes through a line of small towns – a merging of modern suburbia and old fishing villages. If you were to drive without stopping, it would take about 45 minutes to reach St-Pierre from Fort-de-France.

It's worth swinging off the highway at **Case-Pilote** to take a peek at the old village center. Turn west off the N2 at the Total gas station and you'll immediately come to a quaint stone church, one of Martinique's oldest. Just 80yd (75m) south is a charming town square with a water fountain, a historic town hall, a tourist office and a moderately priced café. In Case-Pilote, and in the next village, **Bellefontaine**, you can find brightly painted wooden fishing boats called *gom-miers* (named after the trees from which they're constructed) lined up along the shore. At Bellefontaine, look inland at the hillside to spot one of Martinique's more unusual buildings, a blue-and-white house designed in the shape of a boat.

The pretty town of **Carbet**, where Columbus briefly came ashore in 1502, fronts a long sandy beach and has a few tourist amenities, including a bunch of restaurants and a scenic garden.

Anse Turin, a long gray-sand beach that attracts a crowd on weekends, is along the highway 0.9 miles (1.5km) north of Carbet. Opposite the beach is the **Musée Paul Gauguin** (admission €3.50; ☺ 9am-5:30pm), marked by a few inconspicuous signs. This interesting museum contains Gauguin memorabilia, letters from the artist to his wife and reproductions of Gauguin's paintings – including *Bord de Mer I* and *L'Anse Turin – Avec les Raisiniers,* which were both painted on the nearby beach during Gauguin's five-month stay on Martinique in 1887. There's also a collection of works by local artists, more or less in the style of Gauguin, and a basement full of extremely creepy mannequins in period costumes.

Just north of the Gauguin museum is the driveway up to **Le Jardin des Papillons** (☎ 78-33-39; adult/child €4.60/2.30; ⊗ 9am-noon), where the scattered stone ruins of one of the island's earliest plantations have been enhanced with gardens and a butterfly farm. There's a restaurant on-site and a small music museum called **Jardin Musical** (⊗ 1:30-4:30pm), where children can play on larger-than-life musical instruments in an old church.

ST-PIERRE

St-Pierre is on the coast 4.3 miles (7km) south of Mont Pelée, the still-active volcano that destroyed the town in just 10 minutes at the beginning of the 20th century. It's a fascinating, atmospheric town in which to wander around. There are numerous blackened ruins throughout St-Pierre, some of which are little more than foundations, while others are partially intact. Many of the surviving stone walls have been incorporated into the town's reconstruction. Even 'newer' buildings have a period character, with shuttered doors and wrought-iron balconies.

The center of town is long and narrow, with two parallel one-way streets running its length. All of the major sights have signs in French and English, and you can explore the area thoroughly in a few hours.

These days St-Pierre has 6000 residents, which is just one-fifth of the pre-eruption population. The central gathering spot is the waterfront town park, next to the market. A beach of soft black sand fronts the town and extends to the south.

Sights

MUSÉE VULCANOLOGIQUE

This small but very interesting **museum** (Rue Victor Hugo; admission €3.50; ⊗ 9am-5pm), founded in 1932 by American vulcanologist Franck Perret, gives a glimpse of the devastating 1902 eruption of Mont Pelée. On display are items plucked from the rubble, including petrified rice, a box of nails melted into a sculpturelike mass, glass cups fused together by heat and the cathedral tower's cast-iron bell squashed like a saucer. There are also historic photos of the town before and immediately after the eruption. The displays are in English and French.

There's free parking adjacent to the museum, which occupies the site of an old hillside gun battery. From the old stone walls along the parking lot you can get a good perspective of the harbor and city, and you can look down upon a line of ruins on the street below.

RUINS

St-Pierre's most impressive ruins are those of the old 18th-century **theater**, just 109yd (100m) north of the museum. While most of the theater was destroyed, enough remains to give a sense of the former grandeur of this building, which once seated 800 and hosted theater troupes from mainland France. A double set of stairs still leads up to the partial walls of the lower story.

On the northeast side of the theater you can go into the tiny, thick-walled **jail cell** that housed Cyparis, the town's sole survivor (for more on Cyparis' amazing good fortune, see the boxed text, p570).

Another area rich in ruins is the **Quartier du Figuier**, along Rue Bouillé, directly below the vulcanology museum. Two sets of steps, one just north of the theater and the other just south of the museum, connect Rue Victor Hugo with the bayfront Rue Bouillé.

Sleeping & Eating

Residence Surcouf (☎ 78-32-73; www.residencesur couf.com in French; 97250 St-Pierre; studio per week from €245; ⊠) In the foothills of Mont Pelée, 0.9 miles (1.5km) from St-Pierre, this group of fully equipped studio or two-bedroom garden bungalows is simply decorated with bright furnishings.

Habitation Josephine (☎ 78-34-28; dinner menu €10-17) This courtyard restaurant opposite the waterfront park is a friendly family-run operation serving excellent Creole food, including a complete *menu du jour* (menu of the day; €15) and a *menu pecheur* (fisherman's special).

There is an 8 à Huit grocery store in the center of town; a bakery, the Patisserie

---

THE ERUPTION OF MONT PELÉE

At the end of the 19th century, St-Pierre – then the capital of Martinique – was a flourishing port city. It was so cosmopolitan that it was dubbed the 'Little Paris of the West Indies.' Mont Pelée, the island's highest mountain, provided a scenic backdrop to the city.

In the spring of 1902, sulfurous steam vents on Mont Pelée began emitting gases, and a crater lake started to fill with boiling water. Authorities dismissed it all as the normal cycle of the volcano, which had experienced harmless periods of activity in the past.

But on April 25 the volcano spewed a shower of ash onto St-Pierre. Some anxious residents sent their children to stay with relatives on other parts of the island. The governor of Martinique, hoping to allay fears, brought his family to St-Pierre.

At 8am on Sunday, May 8, 1902, Mont Pelée exploded into a glowing burst of superheated gas and burning ash, with a force 40 times stronger than the later nuclear blast over Hiroshima. Between the suffocating gases and the fiery inferno, St-Pierre was laid to waste within minutes.

Of the city's 30,000 inhabitants, the sole survivor, a prisoner named Cyparis, escaped with only minor burns – ironically, he owed his life to having been locked in a tomblike solitary-confinement cell at the local jail. Following the commutation of his prison sentence by the new governor, Cyparis joined the PT Barnum circus where he toured as a sideshow act.

Pelée continued to smolder for months, but by 1904 people began to resettle the town, building among the crumbled ruins.

Pomme Cannelle, south of the cathedral; a wood-fired pizza place, **Pizzaria Marina** (☎ 78-12-01; 🍴 breakfast, lunch & dinner), south of the museum; and another pizzeria, **La Paillote** (☎ 78-29-58; 🍴 breakfast, lunch & dinner), on the waterfront.

ST-PIERRE TO ANSE CÉRON

From St-Pierre, the N2 turns inland but the D10 continues north for 8 miles (13km) along the coast and makes a scenic side drive, ending in 20 minutes at a remote beach. The shoreline is rocky for much of the way and the landscape is lush, with roadside clumps of bamboo.

The limestone cliffs 2.5 miles (4km) north of St-Pierre, called **Tombeau des Caraïbes**, are said to be the place where the last Caribs jumped to their deaths rather than succumb to capture by the French.

The road goes through the town of **Le Prêcheur**, where green and orange fishing boats dot the shoreline, and **Anse Belleville**, a village so narrow that there's only room for a single row of houses between the cliffs and the sea.

A third of a mile (500m) before the end of the road, you will find the interesting **Habitation Céron** (☎ 52-94-53; adult/child aged 5-12 €6/2.30; 🕤 9:30am-5pm, restaurant noon-2:30pm), a former sugar plantation with the working areas and furnace still intact. There's also **horse trekking** (adult/child per 40min €20/6) or **quad-biking**

(per 1½hr €39) around the beautiful grounds of the estate, and a Creole restaurant housed in the former slave quarters. The road ends at **Anse Céron**, a gorgeous black-sand beach in a wild, junglelike setting. Anse Céron is backed by coconut palms and faces Îlet la Perle, a rounded offshore rock that's a popular dive site. Despite the remote location, the beach has a shower, toilets, picnic tables and a snack shop.

A very steep one-lane route continues for 1 mile (1.6km) beyond the beach. This is the start of a six-hour, 12.4-mile (20km) hike to Grand-Rivière (for details on taking this as a guided hike, see p578).

ROUTE DE LA TRACE

The Route de la Trace (N3) winds up into the mountains north from Fort-de-France. It's a beautiful drive through a lush rainforest of tall tree ferns, anthurium-covered hillsides and thick clumps of roadside bamboo. The road passes along the eastern flanks of the pointed volcanic mountain peaks of the Pitons du Carbet. Several well-marked hiking trails lead from the Route de la Trace into the rainforest and up to the peaks.

The road follows a route cut by the Jesuits in the 17th century; islanders like to say that the Jesuits' fondness for rum accounts for the twisting nature of the road.

Less than a 10-minute drive north of Fort-de-France you'll reach the **Sacré-Coeur de**

Balata, a scaled-down replica of the Sacré-Coeur Basilica in Paris. This domed church, in the Roman-Byzantine style, has a stunning hilltop setting – the Pitons du Carbet rise up as a backdrop and there's a view across Fort-de-France to Pointe du Bout below.

The **Jardin de Balata** (☎ 64-48-73; adult/child €6.20/2.30; ☺ 9am-5pm), on the west side of the road 10 minutes' drive north of the Balata church, is a mature botanical garden in a rain-forest setting. Walkways wind past tropical trees and flowers including native begonias, orchids, heliconia, anthuriums and bromeliads. Many of the plants are numbered; you can pick up a free handout that lists 200 of the specimens with their Latin and common French names. This attractive garden takes about 30 to 45 minutes to stroll through and is a great place to photograph flowers and hummingbirds.

After the garden, the N3 winds up into the mountains and reaches an elevation of 1968ft (600m) before dropping back down to **Site de l'Alma**, where a river runs through a lush green gorge. There are riverside picnic tables, trinket sellers and a couple of short trails into the rainforest.

Some 2.5 miles (4km) later, the N3 is intersected by the D1, a winding scenic drive that leads west for about 9 miles (14km), via Fond St-Denis to St-Pierre. Just beyond this intersection, the N3 heads through a cobblestone tunnel, and about half a mile (800m) beyond that, on the east side of the road, is the signposted trailhead for **Trace des Jésu-ites**. This popular hike is 3 miles (5km) long and takes about three hours one way. It winds up and down through a variety of terrain, ranging in elevation from 1016ft (310m) at the Lorrain River crossing to 2197ft (670m) at its termination on the D1.

Continuing north on the N3, the Route de la Trace passes banana plantations and flower nurseries before reaching a T-junction at **Morne Rouge**, which was partially destroyed by an eruption from Mont Pelée in August 1902, several months after the eruption that wiped out St-Pierre. At 1476ft (450m), it has the highest elevation of any town on Martinique, and it enjoys some nice mountain scenery.

About 1.2 miles (2km) north of the T-junction, a road (D39) signposted to Aileron leads 1.8 miles (3km) up the slopes of Mont Pelée, from where there's a rugged trail (four hours round-trip) up to the volcano's summit.

LES OMBRAGES
This **botanical garden** (☎ 53-31-90; adult/child €5/2.50; ☺ 8am-5pm) is at the site of a former rum distillery. A trail passes by stands of bamboo, tall trees with buttressed roots, torch gingers and the ruins of the old mill. It's a nice lush jungle walk.

Tour guides lead 45-minute walks, in French only. Les Ombrages is 270yd (250m) east of the N3, northeast of the town of Ajoupa-Bouillon.

BASSE-POINTE & AROUND
As the N3 nears the Atlantic it meets the N1, which runs along the coast both north and south. The northern segment of the road edges the eastern slopes of Mont Pelée and passes through banana and pineapple plantations before reaching the uninspiring coastal town of Basse-Pointe, birthplace of *négritude* poet Aimé Césaire.

Leyritz Plantation
Dating from the early 18th century, **Leyritz Plantation** (☎ 78-53-92; reservation@plantationleyritz .com; adult/child €2.50/1.25; ☺ 9am-5pm) is a former sugar plantation that now houses a hotel and snazzy restaurant.

The grounds are in a pleasant parklike setting of palm, grapefruit and guava trees, and you can't help but notice the gigantic rubber tree, *cacouichouc*, near the pond. You can stroll around the grounds at your leisure and explore some of the old buildings, though information on slavery and the history of this plantation is sadly sparse. Most intriguing is the former plantation house, a weathered two-story building with period furnishings.

Inside the gift shop near the entrance to the plantation is a minuscule 'museum' that's essentially a small collection of Victorian-style dolls made of dried plants and fibers.

If you're not eating at the plantation you must pay to explore the grounds and visit the museum. The plantation is on the D21, 1.2 miles (2km) southeast of Basse-Pointe.

There are 67 **guest rooms** (☎ 78-53-92; reservation@plantationleyritz.com; 97218 Basse-Pointe; s/d €69/87; ☒ ☒ spread across Leyritz Plantation's grounds, many in the old plantation quarters. Rooms vary, but most are comfortable (though a little short on atmosphere). Some of the nicer ones are in the renovated stone cottages that once served as dwellings for married slaves. It's a popular place with retirees from mainland France, but its secluded country setting may prove too remote for first-time visitors intent on exploring the entire island.

The Leyritz Plantation **Restaurant Le Ruisseau** (lunch mains €10, 3-course lunch €24; ⏱ lunch & dinner) and bar, within the old stone walls of the refinery, are in a funky setting. However, the Creole menu of *accras, colombo* (a spicy, East Indian–influenced dish that resembles curry) and *fricassée* are geared mainly for the tourist palate.

GRAND-RIVIÈRE

From Basse-Pointe, there's an enjoyable 20-minute drive to Grand-Rivière along a winding, but good, paved road. En route you will go through the coastal village of Macouba (where there is a rum distillery), pass two trails leading up the northern flank of Mont Pelée, cross a couple of one-lane bridges and finally wind down into the town.

Grand-Rivière is an unspoiled fishing village scenically tucked beneath coastal cliffs at the northern tip of Martinique. Mont Pelée forms a rugged backdrop to the south, while there's a fine view of neighboring Dominica to the north.

The road dead-ends at the sea where there's a fish market and rows of bright fishing boats lined up on a little black-sand beach. The waters on the west side of town are sometimes good for surfing. The *syndicat d'initiative*, in the town center, has local tourist information and organizes guided hikes in the region.

While there's no road around the tip of the island, there is a 12.4 mile (20km) hiking trail leading to Anse Couleuvre, on the northwest coast. The trailhead begins on the road opposite the quaint two-story *mairie* (town hall), just up from the beach. For more information, see p578.

Sleeping & Eating
Chanteur Vacances (☎ 55-73-73; mains €9-20; ⏱ breakfast, lunch & dinner) A friendly sea-view restaurant in a quiet spot. It serves simple

but excellent Creole cuisine, including the house specialty – that rarity – good-value lobster.

Chez Tante Arlette (☎ 55-75-75; r €30, mains €12-19; restaurant ⏱ noon-9pm; ⏱) About 55yd (50m) from the *syndicat d'initiative*, this Creole restaurant is renowned for its seafood. At the time of writing, four simple rooms were under renovation on the floor above.

Yva Chez Vava (☎ 55-72-72; meals €12-30; ⏱ lunch) On the outskirts of town near the river, people travel far and wide for large helpings of seafood and Antillaise specials here, so it's best to book ahead. Service can be a tad slow.

BASSE-POINTE TO LAMENTIN

The highway (N1) from Basse-Pointe to Lamentin runs along relatively tame terrain and is not one of the island's most interesting drives, although there are a few worthwhile sights. The communities along the way are largely modern towns that become increasingly more suburban as you continue south.

Some 1.2 miles (2km) north of Ste-Marie, lies **L'Habitation Fond St-Jacques** (☎ 69-10-12; ⏱ 9am-5pm), the site of an old Dominican monastery and sugar plantation dating from 1660. One of the early plantation managers, Father Jean-Baptiste Labat, created a type of boiler (the *père labat*) that modernized the distilling of rum. During the French Revolution, the plantation was confiscated by the state and was recently developed as a cultural center by local government. The chapel and most of the living quarters are still intact and there are many ruins on the grounds, including those of the mill, distillery basins, boiling house and sugar factory. The site is 160yd (150m) inland from the N1.

The **Museé du Rhum St James** (☎ 69-30-02; admission free, guided tour €3; ⏱ 9am-5pm Mon-Fri, 9am-1pm Sat & Sun), at the site of St-James Plantation's working distillery, is a fun place to stop. The plantation is on the D24, 220yd (200m) west of the N1, on the northern outskirts of Ste-Marie. There are both indoor and outside displays of old sugar-making equipment, including steam engines, rum stills and cane-crushing gears. There's also a tasting room where you can sample different rums, and if you don't get too heady you could go out back to check out the sugar mill and distillery.

The road continues on south through cane fields and passes the Presqu'île de Caravelle.

Presqu'île de Caravelle

A tour of the peninsula is well worth it for its wild landscape and authentic fishing villages. A gently twisting road leads through lush scenery with spectacular views down through the sugarcane fields to Baie du Galion. On the north side of the peninsula are a couple of nice protected beaches – the long, sandy **Tartane** and, one of the island's nicest, the gently shelving, palm-fringed beach of **Anse l'Étang**.

Tartane, the larger of the two beaches, has lots of fishing shacks, a fish market and colorful *gommier* boats; both places have plenty of beachside restaurants selling everything from crepes and ice cream to pizza and Creole food on the road along the pretty seafront. There's also an ATM and gas station in Tartane. Out at the tip of the peninsula are the deteriorated ruins of Château Dubuc, a 17th-century estate. The master of the estate gained notoriety by using a lantern to lure ships into wrecking off the coast, and then gathering the loot. The site has trails and a small **museum** (admission €2.30).

SLEEPING & EATING

Hotel Restaurant Caravelle (☎ 58-07-32; http:// perso.wanadoo.fr/hotelcaravelle; Route du Château Dubuc; s/d €52/80; ⚡) On the eastern outskirts of Tartane, this is a small, friendly hotel, with steps leading down to the fabulous Anse l'Étang. Recently renovated in charming Creole-African style, the cozy entrance features art and sculpture, and there is a hibiscus-covered, decked terrace with glorious views to the Atlantic. The simple, but comfortable, studios all have colorful furnishings and well-equipped kitchenettes. This is a real gem.

La Table de Mamy Nounou (lunch mains €5-13, dinner menu €22; ⚡ lunch & dinner) The Caravelle's fabulous restaurant features excellent seafood, grills and mouthwatering desserts.

Chez Titine (☎ 58-27-28; mains €6-15; ⚡ lunch & dinner) A family-run business for half a century, Chez Titine is a popular local place with a terrace that serves fresh salads, steaks and fish straight off the boat. You'll find it on the seafront.

SOUTHERN MARTINIQUE

Martinique's south has many of the island's best beaches and most of its hotels. The largest concentration of places to stay is in the greater Trois-Îlets area, which encompasses the overdeveloped uber-resort of Pointe du Bout and the smaller, rather more authentic villages of Grand Anse and Anse d'Arlet. Other major resort areas are Diamant and Ste-Anne.

The interior of the island's southern half is largely a mix of agricultural land and residential areas. Lamentin, the site of the international airport, is Martinique's second-largest city but – like other interior towns – has little of interest to tourists.

TROIS-ÎLETS

This small working town has a central square that's bordered by a little market, a quaint town hall and the church where Empress Josephine was baptized in 1763. Despite its proximity to the island's busiest resort area, the town has (surprisingly) avoided developers' attention so far, though its charm has been tarnished by a constant flow of traffic through its main street.

Pointe du Bout (which uses Trois-Îlets as its postal address) is a few miles west of the town center, as are the island's golf course, the birthplace of Josephine and a small botanical park.

The area's other chief attraction, a sugar museum, is east of central Trois-Îlets.

Musée de la Pagerie

This former sugar estate was the birthplace of the Empress Josephine. A picturesque stone building, formerly the family kitchen, has been turned into a **museum** (☎ 68-33-06; adult/child €5/2; ⚡ 9am-5:30pm Tue-Sun) containing Josephine's childhood bed and other memorabilia. Multilingual interpreters relate anecdotal tidbits about Josephine's life, such as the doctoring of the marriage certificate to make Josephine, six years Napoleon's elder, appear to be the same age as her spouse.

A couple of other buildings on the museum grounds contain such items as the Bonaparte family chart, old sugarcane equipment and love letters to Josephine from Napoleon.

MARTINIQUE

The road leading up to the museum, just over half a mile (800m) inland from the Trois-Îlets, begins opposite the golf-course entrance. You can poke around in the ruins of the old mill opposite the museum for free.

Maison de la Canne

This tastefully restored and worthwhile **sugarcane museum** (☎ 68-32-04; adult/child aged 5-12 €3/0.75; ⊗ 8:30am-5:30pm Tue-Sun) occupies the site of an old sugar refinery and distillery. Artifacts include an old locomotive once used to carry cane from the fields to the distillery, and some antique cane crushers. However, these are less interesting than the period photos and items such as the *Code Noir* (Black Code) outlining appropriate conduct between slaves and Whites. Panels describing the influence of the sugarcane industry on local culture and art also speak volumes about a social history that spanned three centuries. Displays are in French and English. The museum is on the D7, 0.9 miles (1.5km) east of Trois-Îlets' center.

POINTE DU BOUT

Pointe du Bout, Martinique's most developed resort at the southern end of the Baie de Fort-de-France, resembles a miniature Las Vegas with its neon-lit streetscape and fake facades. It's home to Martinique's most-frequented yachting marina and three of its largest resort hotels – expect to pay top euro for a night's bed and board anywhere within spitting distance of the water. The point is a Y-shaped peninsula, with the hotels fringing the coast and the marina in the middle. All roads intersect south of the marina, and traffic can get congested.

There's a public beach – Plage de l'Anse Mitan – which runs along the western side of the neck of the peninsula between Pointe du Bout and Anse Mitan.

Information

Ferries to and from Fort-de-France leave from the west side of Pointe du Bout's marina, where a money-changing office, a laundry, the port bureau and marine supply shops are all clustered together.

The marina also has a newsstand, souvenir shops, boutiques and a Crédit Agricole.

Thrifty, Budget and Avis car-rental agencies have offices near the peninsula's main intersection.

Sleeping

Hotel de la Pagerie (☎ 66-05-30; fax 66-00-99; 97229 Trois-Îlets; s/d €125/140; ⊠ ☲) Tucked between a busy intersection and the inner harbor, this 98-bedroom hotel has straightforward rooms with floral decor – some rooms have kitchenettes. Facilities are somewhat limited, otherwise.

Novotel Carayou (☎ 66-04-04; www.novotel.com; 97229 Trois-Îlets; s/d incl breakfast €235/290; ⊠ ☲) The 200-room family-friendly Carayou sits on the peninsula that forms the northeast side of the marina. The rooms are modern but on the small side, with faux rustic furnishings. A water-sports center, three restaurants, a large pool and tennis courts keep punters happy.

Sofitel Bakoua Martinique (☎ 66-02-02; www .accor-hotels.com; 97229 Trois-Îlets; r from €320, with ocean view €480; ⊠ ☲) Under new management, the area's most exclusive resort caters mostly for well-heeled French vacationers. The 138 rooms and suites are comfortably furnished (the best 40 are on the beach) and guests have access to one of the area's best beaches and the hotel's water toys.

Eating

Délifrance (⊗ 6:30am-7:30pm) Good croissants, pastries, filled baguettes and coffees are the staples at this café, which has outside tables.

Boule de Neige (crepes €4-9, salads €6-16; ⊗ breakfast, lunch & dinner) Next door to Délifrance is this simple café, famous for its homemade ice cream and crepes. Try the Asian salad or the sinful Josephine crepe.

Chez Fanny (mains €10-18; ⊗ breakfast, lunch & dinner) Found on the neck of the peninsula, this is one of the cheaper restaurants in the area. The changing chalkboard menu includes half a dozen daily specials, such as steamed snapper or chicken *fricassée*. Food is served from steamer trays, cafeteria style.

Restaurant La Marine (dinner mains €7-19; ⊗ breakfast, lunch & dinner) An open-air pizzeria and bar fronting the marina. It draws lots of yachters who want to sit back and have a few beers while keeping an eye on their boats.

GRAND ANSE

The idyllic little fishing village of Grand Anse is located on Grand Anse d'Arlet Bay. It's set around a softly sloping beach that's lined with brightly painted fishing boats and a string of restaurants. It's a more peaceful option than the busier resorts further north.

Anse Dufour, a lovely secluded beach that's spectacularly situated at the end of a steep windy trail off the D7, 1.8 miles (3km) north of Grand Anse, is perfect for family swimming. Good snorkeling can be found along the south end of the bay just off Morne Champagne, the volcanic peninsula that separates Grand Anse from Anse d'Arlet; you can hire gear from the dive school **Plongeé Passion** (☎ 68-71-78). A trail at the south end of the beach leads up to the top of Morne Champagne.

Sleeping & Eating
Ti Plage (☎ 29-59-89; mains €9-13; ☒ lunch Tue-Sun) Next door to Localizé, this tastefully decorated little beachside restaurant with decked veranda is famous for its couscous royale special on Friday night. Otherwise, expect delicious smoked fish salad, duck confit or vegetarian galettes.

Ti Sable (☎ 68-62-44; mains €11-19; ☒ lunch & dinner, closed Sep) This popular restaurant is like a big beach hut with fairy lights. It features great local fish dishes like *blanquette de dorade* (sea bream casserole), barbecued meats and exotic salads. It also serves decent kids' menus and mean cocktails, with live music at weekends.

ANSE D'ARLET
Anse d'Arlet is a typical pretty fishing village south of Grand Anse which, unlike many coastal towns, makes the most of its gorgeous beachfront. There's an interest-

---

AUTHOR'S CHOICE

Localizé (☎ 68-64-78; www.localize.fr; Alleé des Raisiniers, 97217 Anse d'Arlet; studios 2/4 people per week €406/833) This small group of charming Creole studios, set in an exotic garden right on a beautiful beach, is undoubtedly the best place to stay in the area. Stylishly decorated with teak furniture, natural linen bedspreads, hammocks on decks and kitchenettes with washing machines, you need only take 10 paces from bed for your prebreakfast dip. Ask for nightly rates when it's less busy or check out the owner's other local hip villa rentals at www.anses-d -arlet.com.

---

ing 18th-century Roman Catholic church in its center, a cinema and a handful of laid-back beach huts selling snacks at the northern end of the village. Some excellent snorkeling can be had around an offshore rock that juts out of the sea.

Sleeping & Eating
Résidence Madinakay (☎ 68-70-76; 3 Alleé des Arlesiens; r €58; ☒) The only accommodations right in the village. These simple, colorful studios all have kitchenettes and balconies.

L'Amerloc (☎ 68-62-79; mains €13-25; ☒ dinner Tue-Sun) In a cozy detached house on the edge of town, there's a simple choice of top-notch dishes like tuna with piquant green salsa or steak with Roquefort. The atmosphere is intimate and relaxed with candlelit tables and rich decor.

DIAMANT
You may be fooled into thinking that Diamant, a small seaside town facing the offshore islet of Rocher du Diamant (Diamond Rock), is a resort. A number of hotels on the outskirts list Diamant as their address, but the center of Diamant is no more than one street and is far more local than touristy in character.

A long and narrow gray-sand beach extends nearly 1.2 miles (2km) along the west side of Diamant; however, there are strong currents in patches, so get advice from your hotel on safe places to bathe.

Sleeping & Eating
Le Patio de l'Anse Bleue (☎ 76-28-83; patio-anse-bl eue@wanadoo.fr; r from €65) This lovely guesthouse, run by a French couple, just over half a mile (800m) west of town, only has three rooms but each is individually decorated with hand-painted furniture. Rooms all face onto a large open-air inner courtyard and Jacuzzi.

Diamant les Bains (☎ 76-40-14; diamantlesbains @martinique-hotels.com; 97223 Diamant; s/d from €70/94; ☒ ☒) A small in-town hotel with an attractive West Indian character. The rooms are slightly outdated and are in the main building or in simple bungalows around the landscaped pool. Two bungalows have wheelchair access and the best bets are the larger ones close to the beach.

Diamond Rock (☎ 76-42-42; resa@diamond rock .com; Pointe de la Chéry, 97223 Diamant; s/d €200/250;

DIAMOND ROCK

The 577ft-high (176m-high) Rocher du Diamant (Diamond Rock) is a volcanic islet 1.8 miles (3km) off the southwestern tip of Martinique. It was once home to 120 British sailors who, for 17 months in 1804–05, used it to harass French vessels trying to navigate the passage.

Having registered the rock as a fighting ship, the unsinkable HMS *Diamond Rock*, the British royal navy was finally outwitted when French Admiral Villaret de Joyeuse allegedly cut loose a skiff loaded with rum in the direction of Diamond Rock, and as the isolated British sailors chugged down the hooch, the French forces retook the island.

🔣 🔣) Formerly the Novotel, this all-inclusive (meals and standard drinks) hotel at the eastern end of the Diamant peninsula has 180 large rooms with somewhat tired pastel and wicker furnishings. However, it's in a gorgeous secluded setting, with extensive gardens, its own breezy beach and good water-sports facilities, including a dive school and offshore fishing.

Planete Diamant (☎ 76-49-82; mains €5-12; 🕙 11am-2am, closed Wed) This small local bar at the western end of the village serves snacks, salads and – best of all – cocktails until the small hours.

Le Ti Pain (☎ 76-40-49; mains €6-20; 🕙 lunch & dinner) Opposite the school, this cozy pizzeria with beach terrace serves hearty pasta staples such as carbonara and *spaghetti al pescadore* (seafood pasta) as well as crispy pizzas.

STE-ANNE

The southernmost village on Martinique, Ste-Anne has an attractive seaside setting with its painted wooden houses and numerous trinket shops. Its most popular swimming beach is the long, lovely strand that stretches along the peninsula to Club Med, just over half a mile (800m) north of the town center. Despite the number of visitors that flock to the town on weekends and during the winter season, Ste-Anne remains a casual, low-key place.

There are also abundant near-shore reef formations that make for good snorkeling.

Sleeping

La Dunette (☎ 76-73-90; www.ladunette.com in French; 97227 Ste-Anne; r incl breakfast from €70; 🔣) In town, this quiet, friendly hotel has 18 fairly spacious rooms, some with sea-view balconies. There's a terraced restaurant overlooking a small beach that fronts the hotel.

Domaine de l'Anse Caritan (☎ 76-74-12; www.anse-caritan.com; Rte des Caraibes; s/d from €112/122; 🔣 🔣) This modern, family-friendly hotel, at the end of a wooded lane just over half a mile (800m) south of the village center, has 96 contemporary rooms with kitchenettes. Rooms are a bit soulless but there's a sandy beach complete with inflatable aquatic playground, canoeing and dive center, so it's unlikely you'll be hanging out in the rooms.

Eating

Poi et Virginie (☎ 76-73-54; mains €12-24; 🕙 lunch & dinner Thu-Mon, dinner Wed, closed Tue) Fresh fish in inventive sauces, grilled lobster and Mexican specials feature at this restaurant that's popular with locals. Sit on the waterside terrace and watch the floodlit fish: it's the nearest you'll get to snorkeling without getting wet.

Les Tameriniers (☎ 76-75-62; 30 Rue Abbé Saffache; mains €10-22; 🕙 lunch & dinner) The most upmarket eatery in town. Try the Creole menu (€40), a three-course feast, including lobster grilled in aged rum.

AUTHOR'S CHOICE

Manoir de Beauregard (☎ 25-08-49; Chemin des Salines; s/d from €100/120; 🕙 closed Sep; 🔣 🔣) This 18th-century manor and grounds, opened as a hotel in the late '60s, still retains the atmosphere of its glory days as a plantation. Walking into the lobby, with its high-beamed ceilings, Louis XV mahogany furniture, marble floors and grand piano is like stepping into an opulent *fin-de-siècle* family home. Rooms in the old house are surprisingly unfussy and have antique sleigh beds and massive bathrooms; 15 airy bungalows on the grounds are tastefully furnished in a similar style. You can dine by moonlight in the excellent restaurant on the veranda. Plans are afoot to open a costume museum on site. The manor is on the main road from Ste-Anne to Les Salines beach.

In the town center, there's a popular snack bar called Jamai'sc on the square that serves grilled meat and fish or **La P'tite Faim** (Rue Abbé Saffachem), which serves good takeout sandwiches and salads.

LES SALINES

Found at the undeveloped southern tip of the island, Les Salines is widely regarded as Martinique's finest beach. The gorgeous long stretch of golden sand attracts hundreds of visitors, scantily clad French tourists and local families alike, on weekends and holidays, but it's big enough to accommodate everyone without feeling crowded. There's plenty of shade and parking on the beach's edge among the hammock-filled trees.

You'll find Les Salines about 3 miles (5km) south of Ste-Anne at the end of the D9. There are showers and food vans near the center of the beach, and about 545yd (500m) further south you'll find snack shops selling reasonably priced sandwiches, burgers and chicken. Camping is allowed on the west side of the beach at weekends and during school holidays.

Les Salines gets its name from Étang des Salines, the large salt pond that backs it. Beware of poisonous manchineel trees (most marked with red paint – see p579 for more information on these trees) on the beach, particularly at the southeast end. There's some good snorkeling at the west end of the beach.

DIRECTORY

ACCOMMODATIONS

Martinique has around about 120 hotels and a dozen or so midsize resorts that have 100 or more rooms. Most of the island's other hotels range from 12 to 40 rooms. By Caribbean standards, nightly rates are moderate, with budget-end hotels averaging about €50, midrange €80 and upper-end about €200.

PRACTICALITIES

■ **Newspapers** The daily *France-Antilles* newspaper centers on news from the French West Indies.

■ **Radio & TV** Tune into Radio France Outre-Mer (RFO) at 92MHz and 94.5MHz on FM or catch up on local TV on networks RFO 1 and RFO 2.

■ **Video Systems** The Secam video system is used on the island.

■ **Electricity** Voltage is 220V, 50 cycles, and plugs have two round prongs.

■ **Weights & Measures** Martinique uses the metric system for weights and measures, and the 24-hour clock.

Taxes and service charges are included in the quoted rates. See p757 for details on how accommodations price ranges are categorized in this book.

Camping

Established campgrounds with facilities are virtually nonexistent on the island. Camping is allowed along the beach at Les Salines and in a few other areas on weekends and during school holidays.

Private Rooms & Apartments

Gîtes de France (☎ 73-74-74, in Paris 01-49-70-75-75; www.gites-de-france.fr; BP 1122, 97209 Fort-de-France) offers rooms and apartments in private homes, with weekly rates beginning at around €150 for two people.

ACTIVITIES
Beaches & Swimming

The beaches on the southern half of the island have white or tan sands, while those on the northern half have gray or black sands. Many of Martinique's nicest beaches are scattered along the southwest coast from Grand Anse to Les Salines. Popular east-coast beaches include those at Cap Chevalier and Macabou to the south and the Presqu'île de Caravelle beaches of Anse l'Étang and Tartane. However, beaches along the northeast side of the island can have very dangerous water conditions and have been the site of a number of visitor drownings.

Diving

St-Pierre has some of the island's top dive sites, with wrecks, coral reefs and plenty of marine life. More than a dozen ships that were anchored in the harbor when the 1902 volcanic eruption hit now lie on the sea bed.

Cap Enragé, northeast of Case-Pilote, has underwater caves harboring lots of sea life. Grand Anse, with its calm waters and good coral, is a popular diving spot for beginners. Rocher du Diamant also has interesting cave formations but trickier water conditions. Îlet la Perle, a rock off the northwest coast, is a good place to see groupers, eels and lobsters when water conditions aren't too rough.

DIVE SHOPS

Expect to pay around €40 for a single dive. Dive shops on Martinique:

Paradis Plongeé (☎ 34-56-10; www.paradisplongee .com) Based in Diamant.

Plongeé Caritan (☎ 76-81-31; www.anse-caritan .com) Located in Ste-Anne.

UCPA (☎ 78-21-03; www.ucpa.com/plongee) This St-Pierre company specializes in wreck dives.

Hiking

Martinique has many hiking trails. From Route de la Trace, a number of signposted trails lead into the rainforest and up and around the Pitons du Carbet. Also popular is the hike to the ruins of Château Dubuc on the Presqu'île de Caravelle.

There are strenuous trails leading up both the northern and southern flanks of Mont Pelée. The shortest and steepest is up the southern flank, beginning in Morne Rouge, and takes about four hours round-trip. The hike up the northern flank is 5 miles (8km) long and takes about 4½ hours one way; two trails begin just east of Grand-Rivière and converge halfway up the mountain.

A bit less strenuous but still moderately difficult is the 12.4-mile (20km) hike around the undeveloped northern tip of the island between Grand-Rivière and Anse Couleuvre. An easy way to do this trail is to join one of the guided hikes organized by the **syndicat d'initiative** (☎ 55-72-74) in Grand-Rivière, which conducts outings. Hikers leave from Grand-Rivière's town hall, arriving in Anse Couleuvre about five hours later and then return to Grand-Rivière by boat.

Other *syndicats d'initiative* organize hikes in other parts of the island, and the **Parc Naturel Regional** (☎ 64-42-59) leads guided hikes several times a week.

Horseback Riding

A number of stables offer horseback riding. The cost of guided outings varies with the destination and length, but is generally around €20 to €40. Stables include:

Black Horse (☎ 68-37-80) In Trois Îlets.

Mer et Nature (☎ 29-04-00) In Trois-Îlets.

Ranch Jack (☎ 68-37-69) Near Anse d'Arlet.

Snorkeling

You'll find that snorkeling is good around Grand Anse and Ste-Anne, and along the coast from St-Pierre to Anse Céron. Most larger hotels rent out snorkeling gear and many provide it free to their guests. Some of the dive shops offer snorkeling trips, while others let snorkelers tag along with divers.

BOOKS

Texaco, a novel by Patrick Chamoiseau that won the prestigious Prix Goncourt, tells the story of the growth and modernization of Fort-de-France through the eyes of some of its poorer inhabitants, and also recounts the riotous heyday and sudden destruction of St-Pierre.

Lafcadio Hearn (1850–1904) visited the island at the end of the 19th century, in the post-slavery period. His travelogue, *Two Years in the French West Indies,* is an evocative account of rural life on the island at that time.

CHILDREN

Children will be well catered for on vacation in Martinique. Most restaurants allow kids to dine as long as they are accompanied by an adult. Practically all hotels will provide cots, and some hotels provide babysitting services. European brands of baby formula, foods and diapers can be bought at pharmacies.

DANGERS & ANNOYANCES

The fer-de-lance, an aggressive pit viper, can be found on Martinique, particularly in overgrown and brushy fields. The snake's bite is highly toxic and sometimes fatal; it's essential for victims to get an antivenin injection as soon as possible. Hikers should be

MARTINIQUE

alert for the snakes and stick to established trails.

There is a risk of bilharzia (schistosomiasis) infection throughout the island; the main precaution is to avoid wading or swimming in freshwater.

Beware of manchineel trees on some beaches, particularly on the south coast, as rainwater dripping off them can cause skin rashes and blistering. They're usually marked with a band of red paint.

After dark, the center of Fort-de-France, particularly around La Savane, is a not a safe place to walk alone; robbery is the main concern.

EMBASSIES & CONSULATES
Martiniquan Embassies & Consulates
Martinique is represented in your home country by the embassy or consulate of France. See p763 for an explanation of the way the system of embassies and consulates works.

Consulates in Martinique
Germany (☎ 50-38-39; Acajou, 97232 Le Lamentin)
Netherlands (☎ 73-31-61; 44/46 Ave Maurice Bishop, 97200 Fort-de-France)
UK (☎ 61-56-30; Route du Phare, 97200 Fort-de-France)

FESTIVALS & EVENTS
Mardi Gras Carnival Martinique has a spirited Carnival during the five-day period leading up to Ash Wednesday, though most of the action centers on Fort-de-France.
St-Pierre Commemorates the May 8, 1902, eruption of Mont Pelée with live jazz and a candlelight procession from the cathedral. On a smaller scale, every village in Martinique has festivities to celebrate its patron saint's day.
Tour de la Martinique (Mid-July) Week-long bicycle race.
Tour des Yoles Rondes (Early August) Week-long race of traditional sailboats.
All Saints Day (Toussaint; November 2) On this day, the graves of the dead are whitewashed and decorated with fresh flowers; in the evening there are church ceremonies and lovely candlelight processions to the cemeteries.

HOLIDAYS
New Year's Day January 1
Good Friday Late March/early April
Easter Sunday Late March/early April
Easter Monday Late March/early April
Ascension Thursday 40th day after Easter
Pentecost Monday Eighth Monday after Easter
Labor Day May 1

Victory Day May 8
Slavery Abolition Day May 22
Bastille Day July 14
Schoelcher Day July 21
Assumption Day August 15
All Saints Day November 1
Fête des Morts November 2
Armistice Day November 11
Christmas Day December 25

INTERNET RESOURCES
www.martinique.org General information on the island, provided by the Martinique Promotion Bureau.
www.martiniquescoop.com (in French) Entertainment and nightlife information.
www.martinique-pages.com Accommodations, sports and cultural listings.

LANGUAGE
French is the official language, but islanders commonly speak Creole when chatting among themselves. English is spoken at larger hotels but is understood rather sporadically elsewhere, so if you don't have a fair command of French, a dictionary and phrasebook will prove quite useful.

MONEY
The euro has been the island's currency since 2001. Hotels, larger restaurants and car-rental agencies accept Visa (Carte Bleue) and MasterCard (Eurocard). Most shops and restaurants in Fort-de-France and other tourist areas accept US dollars, but at criminally poor exchange rates.

POST
There are post offices in all major towns. You can also buy postage stamps at some *tabacs* (tobacco shops), hotels and souvenir shops.

Mailing addresses given in this chapter should be followed by 'Martinique, French West Indies.'

TELEPHONE
For more information on phone cards and making long-distance calls, see p767.

Cell (Mobile) Phones
To see whether you can use your phone on the island's networks (GSM 1800/1900), check with your cell service provider before you leave to see if it has a roaming agreement with any of the French service operators (F-Orange or Bougytel).

Phone Cards

Public phones in Martinique accept French *télécartes* (phone cards), not coins. The cards cost €5, €10 or €15, depending on the amount of calling time on them, and are sold at post offices and at shops with signs that say '*télécarte en vente ici.*'

Phone Codes

Local numbers have six digits, and a three-digit area code (☎ 596). We have included only the six-digit number for Martinique listings in this chapter.

When calling Martinique from outside the island, dial your country's international access code, followed by the ☎ 596 area code *twice* in front of the six digits. When calling from within the French West Indies, dial ☎ 0596 + the local six-digit number.

For directory assistance, dial ☎ 12.

VISAS

US and Canadian citizens can stay up to three months without a visa by showing a valid passport (US citizens see the boxed text, p772). Citizens of the EU need an official identity card, valid passport or French *carte de séjour* (visitor permit).

Citizens of most other countries, including Australia, need a valid passport and a visa from a French consulate valid for admission to the Overseas French Department of Martinique.

TRANSPORTATION

GETTING THERE & AWAY
Entering Martinique

A round-trip or onward ticket is officially required of visitors. This may be checked at customs upon arrival or, if you're coming from within the Caribbean, before you depart for Martinique.

Air

Lamentin International Airport has an **information line** (☎ 0836-68-43-14). For further information on travel to Martinique from outside the Caribbean, see p775.

The following airlines fly to/from Martinique from within the Caribbean:

Air Antilles Express (☎ 42-16-71; www.airantilles .com in French; hub Guadeloupe)

Air Caraïbes (☎ 820-83-58-35; www.aircaraibes.com; hub Guadeloupe)

LIAT (☎ 42-16-02; www.liatairline.com in French; hub Antigua)

Sea
CRUISE SHIP

Cruise ships land at Pointe Simon in Fort-de-France, at the western side of the harbor and within easy walking distance of the city center and main sights. The arrival facilities have phones, rest rooms, a taxi stand and a tourist information booth that opens on cruise-ship days. See p777 for more on cruises.

FERRY

L'Express des Îles (☎ 63-12-11) operates modern catamaran ferries that travel daily between Martinique, Guadeloupe, Dominica and St Lucia.

The smaller **Brudey Frères** (☎ 70-08-50) offers express catamarans between Martinique and Guadeloupe. For detailed information on both of these boats, see p535).

YACHT

The main port of entry is in Fort-de-France but yachts may also clear at St-Pierre or Marin.

Yachting is very popular in Martinique and there are numerous yacht charter companies operating on the island. **Moorings** (☎ 74-75-39), **Stardust** (☎ 74-98-17) and **Sunsail** (☎ 74-77-61) are based at the marina in Marin. **Star Voyage** (☎ 66-00-72) is based at the Pointe du Bout marina.

GETTING AROUND
Bicycle

It's possible to tour most of the island by bike, but cyclists would need nerves of steel on main traffic-clogged roads, where some locals tend to drive rally-style, overtaking on bends at high speed.

Several companies rent out mountain bikes (VTTs), including **BDD** (☎ 66-01-04) in Trois-Îlets or **Sud Loisirs** (☎ 76-81-82) in Ste-Anne.

Boat

There are countless catamaran tours and boat charters operating around the island. For the latest information, check with the tourist office or at your hotel.

MARTINIQUE

Bus

Although there are some larger public buses, most buses are minivans, marked 'TC' (for *taxis collectifs*) on top. Destinations are marked on the vans, sometimes on the side doors and sometimes on a small sign stuck in the front window.

Bus stops are marked *arrêt autobus* or have signs showing a picture of a bus. See p567 for examples of bus fares from Fort-de-France.

Car & Motorcycle

For information on car and motorcycle rental, see p567.

DRIVER'S LICENSE

Your home driver's license is all that you will need to legally drive on Martinique's roads.

ROAD CONDITIONS

Roads are excellent by Caribbean standards, and there are multilane freeways (and rush-hour traffic) in the Fort-de-France area.

ROAD RULES

In Martinique, drive on the right side of the road. Traffic regulations and road signs are the same as those in Europe, speed limits are posted, and exits and intersections are clearly marked.

Taxi

The taxi fare from the airport is approximately €20 to Fort-de-France, €50 to Ste-Anne and €25 to Pointe du Bout or Anse Mitan. A 40% surcharge is added onto all fares between 8pm and 6am and also all day on Sunday and holidays. To book a cab, call **24-hour taxi** (☎ 63-63-62, 63-10-10).

MARTINIQUE

St Lucia

It's little wonder that St Lucia has become one of the most popular honeymoon destinations worldwide. This romantic idyll offers plenty of opportunities for relaxation, with its secluded coves and white sandy beaches, great water sports and plethora of fancy resorts equipped to cater to your every whim.

St Lucia's lush mountainous interior also affords the opportunity to explore atmospheric rainforest terrain and wildlife that includes tall hardwood trees, climbing vines, tree ferns and the indigenous Jacquot parrot, St Lucia's national emblem. But its most dramatic scenery is in the south, where the twin peaks of the Pitons rise sharply from the Soufrière shoreline to form one of the Eastern Caribbean's most distinctive landmarks.

South of lively Castries and the well-trodden tourist trail of Rodney Bay and Gros Islet, you'll find a charming rural island among the sprawling banana plantations and untamed jungle that is dotted with authentic fishing villages and typical West Indian towns where life has changed little in half a century.

FAST FACTS

- **Area** 238 sq miles (616 sq km)
- **Capital** Castries
- **Country code** ☎ 758
- **Departure tax** EC$54
- **Famous for** Jacquot parrot
- **Language** English, Creole
- **Money** Eastern Caribbean dollar (EC$); EC$1 = US$0.37 = €0.31 = UK£0.21
- **People** St Lucians
- **Phrases** *Mwe vié o bwé s'u plé* (Creole patois). I want a drink please.
- **Population** 160,000
- **Visa** None required for citizens of the US, or EU or Commonwealth countries.

HIGHLIGHTS

- **Castries** (p586) Stroll around downtown, from its grand cathedral to colorful rum shops.
- **Pigeon Island** (p592) Explore around fort ruins, and hike, snorkel and rest on a white-sand beach.
- **Soufrière** (p593) Take in this picturesque area, for its fine scenery, great diving, waterfalls and steaming sulfur vents.
- **Jump-ups** (p591 and p593) Participate in the colorful Friday-night jump-ups at Gros Islet and Anse La Raye.
- **Balenbouche Estate** (p595) Explore the old mill and spend the night.

ITINERARIES

- **One Week** Beginning in Castries, head southeast to explore one of the island's nature reserves or to watch turtles on Grande Anse. Make your way back to lively Soufrière and visit the 'drive-in volcano,' then hike Gros Piton before kicking back with some sun and scuba in the northern resorts around Rodney Bay or Gros Islet.
- **Ten Days** Basing yourself in Soufrière, spend a couple of days hiking the interior rainforest trails and visiting Morne Coubaril Estate before diving the reef around nearby Anse Chastanet. After a ramble through the streets of Castries, head up north to the windswept headland of Cap Estate, and explore the military fort remains and walking trails of Pigeon Island National Park. If you still have energy, go horseback riding on the beach at Cas-en-Bas, before flaking out with a sunset dip.

CLIMATE & WHEN TO GO

The most popular (and most expensive) time of year to visit St Lucia is during its driest period from December to March, when the official hurricane season is over (June to end of October). In January the average daily high temperature in Castries is 81°F (27°C), while the nightly low temperature is 68°F (20°C). In July the average daily high is 85°F (29°C), while the nightly low is 72°F (22°C).

Humidity ranges from 76% in February to 83% in November.

HISTORY

Archeological finds on the island indicate that St Lucia was settled by Arawak Indi-

---

HOW MUCH?

- Taxi fare from the airport to Castries center EC$20
- One-hour diving trip EC$105
- Comfortable hotel double room US$80
- Short bus ride EC$3
- Daily beach bed rental EC$20

LONELY PLANET INDEX

- Gallon of gas EC$8
- Liter of bottled water EC$3
- Bottle of Piton beer EC$5
- Souvenir T-shirt EC$20
- Street snack: corn on the cob EC$1

---

ans between 1000 BC and 500 BC. Around AD 800 migrating Caribs conquered the Arawaks and established permanent settlements on the island.

St Lucia was outside the routes taken by Columbus during his four visits to the New World and was probably first sighted by Spanish explorers during the early 1500s. Caribs successfully fended off two British attempts at colonization in the 1600s only to be faced with French claims to the island a century down the road, when they established the island's first lasting European settlement, Soufrière, in 1746 and went about developing plantations. St Lucia's colonial history was marred by warfare, however, as the British still maintained their claim to the island.

In 1778 the British successfully invaded St Lucia, and established naval bases at Gros Islet and Pigeon Island, which they used as staging grounds for attacks on the French islands to the north. For the next few decades St Lucia seesawed between the British and the French. In 1814 the Treaty of Paris finally ceded the island to the British, ending 150 years of conflict during which St Lucia changed flags 14 times.

Culturally, the British were slow in replacing French customs, and it wasn't until 1842 that English nudged out French as St Lucia's official language. Other customs linger, and to this day the majority of people

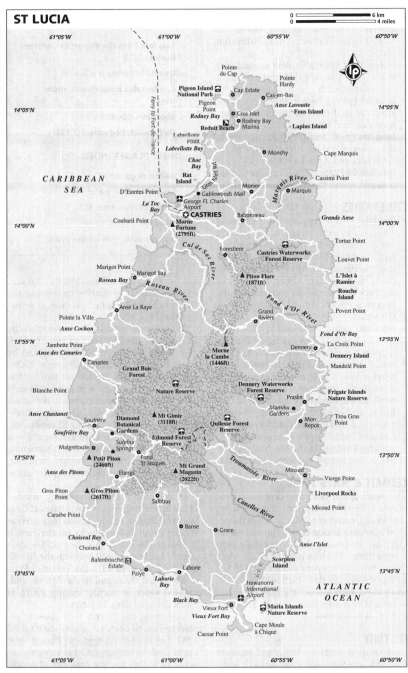

ST LUCIA

0   6 km
0   4 miles

61°05'W   61°00'W   60°55'W   60°50'W

Pointe
du Cap

Pointe
Hardy

**Pigeon Island
National Park**   Cap Estate   Cas-en-Bas

Pigeon
Point   *Anse Lavoutte*

14°05'N   *Rodney Bay*   Gros Islet   *Fous Island*   14°05'N
     Reduit Beach   Rodney Bay
Marina   **Lapins Island**

Labrellotte
Point

Labrellotte Bay   Monchy   Cape Marquis

*Choc
Bay*

**Rat
Island**   Monier   Marquis   Cassimi Point

**CARIBBEAN
SEA**   D'Estrées Point   Gablewoods Mall   *Marquis*   Marquis

*La Toc
Bay*   George FL Charles
Airport

Coubaril Point   **CASTRIES**   Babonneau   *Grande Anse*

14°00'N   **Morne
Fortune
(2795ft)**   14°00'N

Cul de Sac River   Forestiere   Tortue Point

**Castries Waterworks
Forest Reserve**   Louvet Point

Marigot Point   Marigot Bay   **Piton Flore
(1871ft)**   **L'Islet à
Ramier**

Roseau Bay   *Roseau River*   **Rouche
Island**

Anse La Raye   *Fond d'Or River*

Pointe la Ville   Grand
Rivière   Povert Point

Anse Cochon

13°55'N   Jambette Point   *Fond d'Or Bay*   13°55'N
Anse des Canaries   La Croix Point

Canaries   **Morne
la Cambe
(1446ft)**   Dennery   **Dennery Island**

**Grand Bois
Forest**   Mandelé Point

Blanche Point   **Nature Reserve**   **Dennery Waterworks
Forest Reserve**   **Frigate Islands
Nature Reserve**

Anse Chastanet   Praslin

Soufrière   **Diamond
Botanical
Gardens**   *Mamiku
Gardens*   Trou Gras
Point

Soufrière Bay   ▲ **Mt Gimie
(3118ft)**   **Quilesse Forest
Reserve**   Mon
Repos

Malgretoute   *Sulphur
Springs*   **Edmond Forest
Reserve**

13°50'N   ▲ **Petit Piton
(2460ft)**   Fond
St Jacques   ▲ **Mt Grand
Magazin
(2022ft)**   Micoud   13°50'N

Anse des Pitons   Etangs   *Troumassée River*   Vierge Point

Gros Piton
Point   ▲ **Gros Piton
(2617ft)**   **Liverpool Rocks**

Caraibe Point   Saltibus   *Canelles River*   Micoud Point

Banse   Grace

Anse l'Islet

Choiseul Bay

Choiseul   *Balenbouche
Estate*   Laborie   **Scorpion
Island**

13°45'N   Paiye   *Laborie
Bay*   *Hewanorra
International
Airport*   **ATLANTIC
OCEAN**   13°45'N

Black Bay   Vieux Fort   **Maria Islands
Nature Reserve**

Vieux Fort Bay   Cape Moule
à Chique

Caesar Point

61°05'W   61°00'W   60°55'W   60°50'W

Ferry to Fort-de-France

speak a French-based patois among themselves, attend Catholic services and live in villages with French names.

St Lucia gained internal autonomy in 1967 and then achieved full independence, as a member of the Commonwealth, on February 22, 1979.

THE CULTURE
The National Psyche

St Lucians are generally laid-back, friendly people influenced by a mix of their English, French, African and Caribbean origins. For instance, if you walk into the Catholic cathedral in Castries, you'll find a building of French design, an interior richly painted in bright African-inspired colors, portraits of a Black Madonna and child, and church services delivered in English. About 85% of St Lucians are Roman Catholics.

A predominantly African heritage can be seen in the strong family ties that St Lucians hold and the survival of many traditional customs and superstitions. Obeah (voodoo) is still held in equal measures of respect and fear in places like Anse La Raye.

The local Snakeman is visited by islanders for his medicinal powers; one such muscular remedy he uses involves massaging the thick fat of the boa constrictor on aching limbs.

Population

The population is about 160,000, one-third of whom live in Castries. Approximately 85% of all islanders are of pure African ancestry. Another 10% are a mixture of African, British, French and East Indian ancestry, while about 4% are of pure East Indian or European descent.

Multiculturalism

The island's strong Rastafarian movement has become increasingly more politicized in recent years, especially among the marginalized youth, where reports of discrimination and police mistreatment have become rife. A high birthrate to teenage mothers, relatively high unemployment due to the dwindling banana industry and a burgeoning drug trade have also fuelled malaise. Having said that, visitors to the island are more likely to come across a less militant type of Rasta on roadsides, toting a spliff rather than a baton, calmly watching life go by.

ARTS

Derek Walcott, the renowned Caribbean poet and playwright and winner of the 1992 Nobel Prize for literature, is a native of St Lucia. Influenced by Russia's Pushkin and Tolstoy, his work is also affected by his formative years on the island. Walcott, who teaches at Boston University, still maintains his connections with the island. His brother Roderick Walcott is a renowned playwright.

St Lucian novelist Garth St Omer writes fictional stories of village life that warn of colonial and religious oppression.

ENVIRONMENT
The Land

St Lucia is teardrop-shaped, roughly 27 miles (43.5km) in length and 14 miles (22.5km) in width, with a land area of 238 sq miles (616 sq km). The isle's interior is largely mountainous, reaching its highest point at the 3118ft (950m) Mt Gimie in the southwest. Deep valleys, many of which are planted with bananas and coconuts, reach down from the mountains.

The Soufrière area has the island's best-known geological features: the twin volcanic cones of the Pitons, which rise up some 2500ft (762m) from the shoreline, and the hot, bubbling Sulphur Springs, just inland from the town. Despite this little show of geological activity, there hasn't been a volcanic eruption on St Lucia since 1766.

Wildlife

St Lucia's vegetation ranges from dry and scrubby areas of cacti and hibiscus to lush jungly valleys with wild orchids, bromeliads, heliconia and lianas.

Under the British colonial administration, much of St Lucia's rainforest was targeted for timber harvesting. In many ways the independent St Lucian government has proved a far more effective environmental force, and while only about 10% of the island remains covered in rainforest, most of that has now been set aside as nature reserve. The largest indigenous trees in the rainforest are the *gommier,* a towering gum tree, and the *chatagnier,* a huge buttress-trunked tree.

Island fauna includes St Lucia parrots (see the boxed text, p586), St Lucian orioles,

ST LUCIA PARROT

The rainforest is home to the St Lucia parrot *(Amazona versicolor)*, locally called the Jacquot, the island's colorful endemic parrot. Despite the Jacquot's status as the national bird and its appearance on everything from T-shirts to St Lucian passports, it has teetered on the brink of extinction, and occasionally made it onto island dinner tables in times past.

However, a successful effort to educate islanders on the plight of the parrot and new environmental laws seem to be working to save it. Fines for shooting or capturing parrots have been increased a hundredfold, while much of the parrots' habitat has been set aside for protection. So far the protection measures have been a success; the 2000 parrot census found 800 birds, up from less than 100 in the mid-1970s. Most of the parrots nest in the Edmond and Quilesse Forest Reserves, east of Soufrière.

purple-throated Carib hummingbirds, bats, lizards, iguana, tree frogs, introduced mongooses, rabbitlike agouti and several snake species, including the venomous fer-de-lance and the boa constrictor.

FOOD & DRINK
Standard Western fare predominates at most hotels. In contrast, local restaurants generally feature West Indian and Creole dishes, featuring fresh seafood.

Street food is excellent, especially in the morning when it's hot and fresh. Roadside stands around the island serve up treats, like stuffed bakes, fried chicken and fish-and-chips.

Water is generally safe to drink from the tap. The island's local beer, Piton, is a tasty light lager brewed in Vieux Fort, perfect for a day on the beach.

CASTRIES

A stroll through the throbbing streets of Castries is like a sensory explosion of color, sound and smell. From the local stallholders haggling over the price of dasheen (taro) in the bustling market or the weathered faces hanging out on tin-roofed porches, to the smell of fresh rotis drifting from food stalls or the blare of calypso from passing pickup trucks, Castries provides a visceral experience that rings of real St Lucian life.

HISTORY
The city, which was founded by the French in the 18th century, was ravaged by fire three times between 1785 and 1812, and again in 1948. Consequently, most of the city's historic buildings have been lost.

An area that survived the last fire was Derek Walcott Sq, a quiet, central square surrounded by a handful of 19th-century wooden buildings that have gingerbread-trim balconies, an attractive Victorian-style library and the imposing Cathedral of the Immaculate Conception. Opposite the cathedral at the east side of the square is a lofty *saman* (monkey pod) tree that's estimated to be 400 years old.

The small city remains a friendly laid-back place with plenty of West Indian character.

ORIENTATION
Castries, the island's commercial center and capital, is a bustling port city set on a large natural harbor. The liveliest part of the city is just southeast of the port, at Jeremie and Peynier Sts, the site of the colorful Castries Market.

INFORMATION
Bookstores
Book Salon (cnr Laborie & Jeremie Sts) Sells books about the Caribbean.

Cultural Centers
Folk Research Centre (☎ 453-1477; Mt Pleasant) Documents the island's folk history, language and dance.

Emergency
Fire, Medical & Police (☎ 999)
Police Headquarters (☎ 452-3854/5; Bridge St)

Internet Access
ClickCom (☎ 452-4444; 1st fl, La Place Carenage, Jeremie St; per 15min EC$2.50; ☼ 8:30am-4pm Mon-Fri, 8:30am-1pm Sat) Broadband Internet access, fax and phone service.

Medical Services

Victoria Hospital (☎ 452-2421; Hospital Rd) For medical emergencies.

Williams Pharmacy (☎ 452-2797; Bridge St)

Money

Both of the following banks have ATMs that accept Cirrus cards.

Bank of Nova Scotia (☎ 456-2100; William Peter Blvd)

Royal Bank of Canada (☎ 456-9200; William Peter Blvd)

Post

General Post Office (GPO; Bridge St; ✆ 8:15am-4pm Mon-Fri)

Telephone & Fax

There are plenty of card phones located around the city.

Cable & Wireless (Bridge St; ✆ 7:30am-6:30pm Mon-Fri, 8am-12:30pm Sat) For faxes and reduced-rate phone calls.

ClickCom (☎ 452-4444; 1st fl, La Place Carenage, Jeremie St; ✆ 8:30am-4pm Mon-Fri, 8:30am-1pm Sat)

Tourist Information

Tourist office (☎ 452-4094; www.stlucia.org; La Place Carenage, Jeremie St; ✆ 8am-12:30pm & 1:30-4pm Mon-Fri, 9am-12:30pm Sat)

SIGHTS & ACTIVITIES

Cathedral of the Immaculate Conception

The city's Catholic **cathedral** (Laborie St), built in 1897, is a grand stone structure that has a splendidly painted interior of trompe l'oeil columns and colorfully detailed biblical scenes. The island's patron saint, St Lucia, is portrayed directly above the altar. The church richly incorporates both Caribbean and African influences, including images of a Black Madonna and child, and the liberal use of bright red, green and yellow tones.

Morne Fortune

Sitting atop the 2795ft (852m) Morne Fortune, about 3 miles (4.8km) south of Castries center, is **Fort Charlotte**, whose construction began under the French and was continued by the British. Because of its strategic hilltop vantage overlooking Castries, the fort was a source of fierce fighting between the French and British in colonial times. The fort buildings have been renovated and given a new life as the Sir Arthur Lewis Community College.

At the rear of the college, a small **obelisk** monument commemorates the 27th Inniskilling Regiment's retaking of the hill from French forces in 1796. Near the monument you'll also find a couple of cannons and a fairly good view of the coast north to Pigeon Point.

If you just want a good view of the city, there's no need to venture as far as the college. The **scenic lookout** opposite Government House, about half a mile (800m) south of Castries, has a fine view of the port and capital, and also gives a glimpse of the attractive crown-topped Victorian mansion that serves as the residence of the governor-general.

TOURS

Solar Tours & Travel (☎ 452-5898; www.solartoursandtravel.com; 20 Bridge St) offers a variety of specialized gourmet, shopping, Creole and historical tours of Castries and the island.

FESTIVALS & EVENTS

St Lucia Jazz Festival (May; www.sluciajazz.org) Big-name music over four days.

Carnival (July; ☎ 452-1859; www.stluciacarnival.com) Castries' streets buzz with music, costume parade and calypso during this festival.

Creole Heritage Month (October; ☎ 452-2279) A series of events promoting Creole arts and culture organized by the Folk Research Center.

SLEEPING

With a range of resorts so close to the city, accommodations in Castries itself are thin on the ground.

Seaview Apartel (☎ 452-4359; PO Box 527; s/d EC$189/216; ✖) More 'runway view' than 'sea view,' this modern residence is a five-minute bus ride from downtown on the east side of the airport runway. Most of its 10 no-frills units have kitchens, balconies and simple furnishings. Rates include daily maid service.

Bon Appetit (☎ 452-2757; PO Box 884; s/d incl tax & breakfast US$45/55) At the south side of town near the top of Morne Fortune, this place has a lovely ocean view with Martinique on the horizon. Run by Italian couple Renato and Cheryl Venturi, who operate a small on site restaurant, there are five immaculate, simply furnished rooms with fans.

Green Parrot (☎ 452-3399; fax 453 2272; PO Box 648; s/d year-round US$60/75; ✖ ✿) On Morne

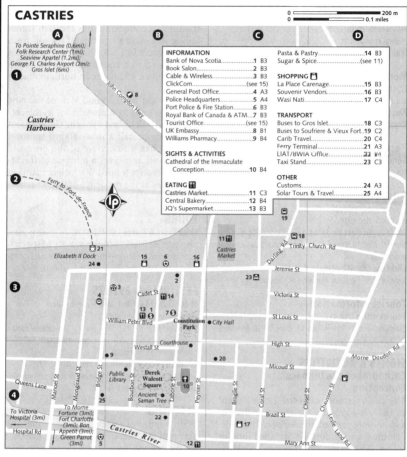

CASTRIES

0 — 200 m
0 — 0.1 miles

INFORMATION

Bank of Nova Scotia	1 B3
Book Salon	2 B3
Cable & Wireless	3 B3
ClickCom	(see 15)
General Post Office	4 A3
Police Headquarters	5 A4
Port Police & Fire Station	6 B3
Royal Bank of Canada & ATM	7 B3
Tourist Office	(see 15)
UK Embassy	8 B1
Williams Pharmacy	9 B4

SIGHTS & ACTIVITIES

Cathedral of the Immaculate Conception	10 B4

EATING

Castries Market	11 C3
Central Bakery	12 B4
JQ's Supermarket	13 B3

Pasta & Pastry	14 B3
Sugar & Spice	(see 11)

SHOPPING

La Place Carenage	15 B3
Souvenir Vendors	16 B3
Wasi Nati	17 C4

TRANSPORT

Buses to Gros Islet	18 C3
Buses to Soufriere & Vieux Fort	19 C2
Carib Travel	20 C4
Ferry Terminal	21 A3
LIAT/BWIA Office	22 B4
Taxi Stand	23 C3

OTHER

Customs	24 A3
Solar Tours & Travel	25 A4

Fortune, which is 3 miles (5km) from town, this place has great views of the harbor. Its 54 comfy rooms with tiled floors and balconies are simply decked out in furniture reminiscent of a few decades gone by. There's a bar, pool room and restaurant.

EATING

Sugar & Spice (☎ 384-7263; Castries Market; mains EC$8-12; ☺ breakfast & lunch Mon-Sat) Located at the northern end of the Castries market, locals swarm to this simple café at lunchtime to order the hearty daily specials, such as red snapper in Creole sauce and lamb stew, which are served with a mountain of carbs in the form of macaroni, rice, dasheen and yam.

Green Parrot Restaurant (☎ 452-3399; lunch EC$10-25, dinner EC$90) The chef at the Green Parrot worked at London's Claridges Hotel, so you can expect some European- and Caribbean-influenced fine dining by night here. A less formal lunch is geared toward local business clientele, while dinner is a more expensive affair, with a four-course meal selected from a full menu. Be sure to snare one of the window tables to enjoy the restaurant's fine hilltop view of Castries and the northwest coast.

Pasta & Pastry (☎ 452-7196; Cadet St; mains EC$13-15; ☺ breakfast & lunch Mon-Sat) This little Italian restaurant attracts local workers for its decent pasta and staples, such as the chicken cacciatore.

Bon Appetit (☎ 452-2757; mains EC$40-90; ✕ lunch Mon-Fri, dinner daily) On Morne Fortune, this is an intimate little restaurant with home-cooked food and a wonderful view. Main dishes include fish and freshwater crayfish, the house specialty. As there are only five tables, reservations are recommended.

JQ's Supermarket (William Peter Blvd; ✕ 8am-5pm Mon-Fri, 8am-4pm Sat) A large, well-stocked grocery store.

Central Bakery (Peynier St) The place for fresh-baked bread and inexpensive coconut pies.

There's a row of bars, restaurants and bakeries along Mary Ann St, perfect for grabbing a sandwich and a beer, and chatting with locals. For good, cheap rotis and local dishes, try the food stalls at the south side of Castries Market. You can get drinking coconuts for EC$1 at the market and at the Darling Rd bus stands. If you're preparing the perfect picnic, you could pick up some fruit at the market.

SHOPPING

On Jeremie St, on the west side of the market, you'll find vendors selling T-shirts, dolls, wood carvings, and other handicrafts and souvenirs.

Both Pointe Seraphine, on the north side of the harbor, and **La Place Carenage** (Jeremie St) have a **duty-free shopping complex** (✕ 9am-5pm Mon-Fri, 9am-2pm Sat) catering to cruise-ship passengers, with about 25 shops selling jewelry, watches, liquor, crystal, china and other imported goods. There are also a couple of clothing shops, including Bagshaws, which sells island-made silk-screened clothing. The business hours fluctuate a bit with the season, and it's open Sunday if cruise ships are in port.

Wasi Nati (☎ 453-1089; Brogile St; ✕ 8am-5pm Mon-Fri) A health-food store that sells whole-foods, diabetic products, vitamins and curious tonics in bottles, irresistibly titled Gas or Bowel, as well as brightly colored 'male-performance' tablets.

GETTING THERE & AROUND
Air
AIRPORTS & AIRLINES
Inter-Caribbean flights generally land at George FL Charles Airport, at Castries, very close to downtown. It has a tourist-information booth, car-rental agencies and a small money-exchange facility.

The main airlines serving St Lucia have offices in Castries. **LIAT** (Derek Walcott Sq; ✕ 8am-4pm Mon-Fri, 8am-noon Sat) also takes bookings for British West Indies Air (BWIA). For more information see p633.

GETTING TO/FROM THE AIRPORT
Taxis are plentiful at George FL Charles Airport. Agree on a fare before you depart; rates from the airport are roughly EC$20 to Derek Walcott Sq in central Castries; EC$40 to Reduit Beach; EC$50 to Rodney Bay Marina; and EC$80 to Marigot Bay.

There are no direct buses; the nearest bus stop is about 1 mile (1.6km) away, at the northern end of the airport runway.

Boat
See p633 for information on boat travel.

Bus
Buses are operated by private owners in minivans. Wait at bus stops or flag one down. In Castries, buses going south to Soufrière and Vieux Fort or north to Gros Islet can be found east of the market on Darling Rd.

Car & Motorcycle
For information on car rental, see p600.

Taxi
You can hail a taxi on the street, ask your hotel to book one for you, or dial ☎ 452-1599. Always agree on a fare before you depart.

NORTHERN ST LUCIA

NORTH OF CASTRIES
Gros Islet Rd runs up the coast connecting northern Castries to Rodney Bay. This area is wall-to-wall with beachside resort hotels, as well as some moderately priced guesthouses. Most of the guesthouses are on the inland side of the road but within walking distance of the beach.

Gablewoods Mall, just south of the Halcyon, has a supermarket, bank, pharmacy, bookstore and Internet access.

Sleeping
The following accommodations are on Gros Islet Rd, 2 miles (3km) north of George FL Charles Airport. They all have restaurants

too. For snacks, head to one of the many outlets at Gablewoods Mall.

Villa Beach Cottages (☎ 450-2884; info@villabeach cottages.com; PO Box 129, Castries; cottages US$115-145, children under 12 free; 🔀 🖳) Set in a tropical garden overlooking the water at Choc Bay, 14 bright, newly renovated cottages and villas decorated in Creole style come complete with four-poster beds, hammocks and barbecues. Nobel Cottage is where Derek Walcott spent many a summer and features his watercolor paintings.

Apartment Espoir (☎ 452-8134; PO Box 269, Castries; studios/d US$60/75) Tucked away at the secluded Labrellotte Bay, the 11 simple studios and one- or two-bedroom apartments with balcony are only a stone's throw from a sandy beach.

Windjammer Landing (☎ 456-9000; www.wind jammer-landing.com; PO Box 1504, Castries; s/d from US$115/230, r with plunge pool from $195; 🔀 🖳) On a quiet beach at Labrellotte Bay, this sprawling villa-style complex has contemporary units, with rattan furniture, terracotta–tiled floors and kitchens. There are two tennis courts, water sports and a free kids' club. Splash out on a three-bed villa if you must, with private chef.

Sandals Halcyon (☎ 452-3081; www.sandals.co.uk; PO Box 399, Castries; 7 nights per person from US$2600; 🔀 🖳 🖳) A 327-room all-inclusive resort and spa on a nice sandy beach and lush gardens, 2 miles (3km) north of the airport at Choc Bay. Rates include meals, water sports and other activities.

RODNEY BAY

Rodney Bay is a large protected bay that encompasses the resort area of Reduit Beach and the village of Gros Islet. An artificial channel cuts between Reduit Beach and Gros Islet, opening to a large lagoon that's the the site of Rodney Bay Marina, the island's largest yachting port.

Rodney Bay Marina is a modern facility with a couple of banks, a car-rental agency, dive shops, a launderette, a bookstore, a travel agency, marine supply shops, a grocery store and some good eating spots – many of which are run by expats. It's a bustling yachters' scene and a good place to make contact with sailors if you're looking to hitch a ride or find a crew job.

In contrast, **Reduit Beach**, southwest of the marina, is a fully fledged tourist resort, with a fine sandy beach, clear blue waters, and a plethora of restaurants and hotels (and crowds). It's a 30-minute round-trip walk by road between the marina and the beach, and a small ferry crosses the lagoon between the two areas several times a day.

Sleeping

Tuxedo Villas (☎ 452-8553; mondesird@candw.lc; PO Box GM508; ste from US$90; 🔀 🖳) This cluster of 10 suites, a short walk from the beach, wouldn't look amiss in Las Vegas with its OTT pink exterior and white garden furniture around the pool. Comfy suites are fully equipped with kitchens and busily patterned living areas.

Coco Kreole (☎ 452-0712; www.cocokreole.com; PO Box GM605, Rodney Bay; r from US$85; 🔀 🖳) A five-minute walk from Reduit Beach, this small new hotel has a funky interior, with huge canvasses of Caribbean artwork on rich-colored walls, low-key Moroccan lamps and exotic velvet cushions at the bar. Rooms are a little less interesting, but are nonetheless well serviced and comfortable. An additional 120 rooms are planned.

St Lucian Byrex Resort (☎ 452-8351; www.rex resorts.com; PO Box 512, Castries; r from US$300; 🔀 🖳) Fronting onto Reduit Beach, this resort is made up of two 'hotels'; the all-inclusive Papillion or the pay-as-you-go Rex. Rooms will appeal to 1980s aficionados, with chrome and pastel furnishings a-go-go. It's a fun place, buzzing with on-site activities and young people.

Royal St Lucian (☎ 452-9999; www.rexcaribbean .com; PO Box 977, Castries; s/d from US$500/610; 🔀 🖳) This may have been the jewel of the Caribbean in its day, but now the lovely, plant-filled airy foyer and gardens are probably its best features. While rooms are fitted with every modern convenience, they're on the small side, with slightly tired-looking furnishings and fittings.

Eating
RESTAURANTS

Great House (☎ 450-0450; Cap Estate; mains EC$60-150; 🕑 dinner) In a former plantation house just off the main Cap Estate road, after the turn-off to Gros Islet, savor French-inspired fine dining, like scallops in champagne *beurre blanc* or grilled lobster, at this chic restaurant.

Buzz Seafood & Grill (☎ 458-0450; mains EC$45-80; 🕑 dinner Tue-Sun, brunch Sun, closed Mon) This popular

new terraced restaurant has an eclectic menu
of Moroccan spiced lamb, shrimp tempura
and delicious homemade desserts, or there's
traditional British pub fare at the bar.

Charthouse (☎ 452-8115; mains EC$50-105; 🕑 din-
ner Mon-Sat) With its appealing waterfront setting, this carnivores den is renowned for its
sizzling steaks and baby back ribs; it also
has a seafood menu and pizza for kids.

Razmataz (mains EC$36-59; 🕑 dinner Fri-Wed) You
can't miss this large hut on sticks, covered
in fairy lights and colored lanterns, on the
main strip. Its cozy atmosphere and top-
notch Indian fare attract hordes of (mostly
British) visitors.

CAFÉS & QUICK EATS
Triangle (meals EC$8-12; 🕑 breakfast, lunch & dinner)
You could have your Christmas lunch here if
you wanted – it never closes – but you probably wouldn't. It may not be gourmet dining
but this covered shack is a great place to try
real West Indian hot snacks, such as cod
balls and rotis (it's open until 2am).

Lime (☎ 452-7061; restaurant mains EC$35-45; buf-
fet EC$15-22; 🕑 lunch & dinner) Ignore the slightly
down-at-heel appearance and piped music
of this bar (open to 1am) and feast on a buffet menu of grilled kingfish, dasheen pie and
green banana salad. The restaurant has more
elaborate seafood and chicken specials.

There are a couple of small stores selling groceries and spirits, and a well-stocked
grocery store at the Rodney Bay Mall.

Entertainment
Late Lime (☎ 452-7061; 🕑 11pm-1am) Above the
Lime (above), this has music and dancing on
Wednesday, Friday and Saturday nights.

Triangle Pub (☎ 452-0334) Across the street
from Late Lime, locals come here to belt out
Whitney classics at its karaoke nights on
Monday, Tuesday and Saturday. It also has
a good comedy night on Friday.

Spinnakers (☎ 452-8491) Right on Reduit
Beach, Spinnakers has calypso and other
music several nights a week.

In the early evening, don't be surprised if
you're served two drinks for each one you
order: many local bars and restaurants are
in competition to see who can put on the
longest and most generous happy hour.

GROS ISLET
Although only up the road, Gros Islet, a small
fishing village of simple wooden houses with
rusting tin roofs and a shore dotted with
painted wooden boats, is a million miles
from the monied development of Rodney
Bay. If you hear a conch shell being blown,
it's the signal that fishing boats have arrived
with a catch to sell.

Although the town doesn't have any sights
per se, there's a small market near the shore
where you can often find fishermen and
women mending nets. The bars along the
beach are the habitual hang-outs of the local
Rastafarian community. Gros Islet is also famous for its spirited Friday-night jump-up,
where islanders and visitors alike grub up on
grilled chicken, swill rum punch and dance
in the streets as best they can.

From Gros Islet, walk a couple of minutes north along the shore and you'll come
to an expansive stretch of white-sand beach
that curves around to Pigeon Island.

The Cricket World Cup in 2007 will see
an influx of visitors to Gros Islet, home of
the Beausejour Stadium. The stadium is
being upgraded to double its current capacity (about 14,000) in time for this major
Caribbean sporting event.

Most buses making the coastal drive north
from Castries terminate in the center of Gros
Islet.

Sleeping
Conch Shell Inn (☎ 450-9318; Marie Therese St; s/d from
US$35/45; 🔀 🖳) There are 10 neat, brightly
painted rooms, all with fan, private bath
and TV in this new guesthouse on the main
street. There's a sea view from the back,
communal kitchen and owner Joan rents
cell phones for EC$10 per day.

Bay Mini Guesthouse (☎ 450-8956; s/d US$33/44; ❷) Further north, you can't miss the intensely orange building overlooking the beach. Its four rooms with bath are rustically furnished, some with kitchenettes.

Henry's La Panache Guesthouse (☎ 450-0765; fax 450-0453; Cas-en-Bas Rd; s/d US$35/45) A relaxed and friendly place in a garden setting about a five-minute walk east of the highway. The rooms are pretty basic, some with home-made bunks, but have refrigerators, fans and private baths. There's a cozy outdoor lounge area with books and games.

Capri (☎ 450-0009; PO Box RB2552, Cap Estate; r US$69-89; ❷ ❷) Expect a warm welcome in this former embassy residence, a few minutes' walk from a sandy beach. Its nine individually furnished rooms, some with four-poster beds, can double up as your own personal massage/tai chi/yoga den during the day. Nice touches, like an honesty bar and access to Le Sport's neighboring spa facilities, add to the experience.

Eating & Drinking

Wall (mains EC$5-15) Visit this greasy spoon in the center of town for carb hits, like burgers and hot snacks.

Mannee's Bakery (Marine St; ☽ 6am-9pm) Sells fresh bread, rolls and pizza slices.

Coretta's Place (Bay St; ☽ breakfast, lunch & dinner) Right on the water, Coretta serves a menu of fresh fish and seafood, straight from the boat to the barbecue, on informal colored outdoor tables.

Village Gate (Dauphin St) Friday night's jump-up action seems to center on this tiny corner bar run by the friendly Junior and his crew.

PIGEON ISLAND NATIONAL PARK

Pigeon Island has a spicy history dating back to the 1550s, when St Lucia's first French settler, Jambe de Bois (Wooden Leg), used the island as a base for raiding passing Spanish ships. Two centuries later British admiral George Rodney fortified Pigeon Island, using it to monitor the French fleet on Martinique. Rodney's fleet set sail from Pigeon Island in 1782 for his most decisive military engagement, the Battle of the Saintes.

With the end of hostilities between the two European rivals, the fort slipped into disuse in the 19th century, although the USA established a small signal station here during WWII.

In the 1970s a sandy causeway was constructed between Gros Islet and Pigeon Island, turning the island into a peninsula, and in 1979 Pigeon 'Island' was established as a national park.

It's a fun place to explore, with walking paths winding around the scattered remains of **Fort Rodney**, whose partially intact stone buildings create a certain ghost-town effect. The grounds are well endowed with lofty trees, including a few big banyans, and fine coastal views.

As soon as you go through the entrance gate, you will see the remains of an 1824 kitchen and officers' mess. While there's people who make a beeline from here to the main fortress at Fort Rodney Hill on the outer point, a walk which takes about 15 minutes, it's enjoyable just to mosey through the ruins and gradually work your way in that direction. A good route is to continue northwest from the officers' mess past the soldiers' barracks (1782) and then loop down toward the bay, where you can pick up the main path.

At the top of Fort Rodney Hill, you'll find a small but well-preserved fortress, a few rusting cannons and a spectacular view. You can see south across Rodney Bay to the gumdrop-shaped hills dotting the coast, and north past Pointe du Cap to Martinique. For more views, continue north past the stone foundations of the ridge battery to the top of the 359ft (109m) **Signal Peak**, about a 20-minute walk.

Admission to **Pigeon Island** (admission EC$10; ☽ 9am-5pm, center closed Sun), administered by the St Lucia National Trust, includes entry to an interpretation center with multimedia historic displays. There's a pub and restaurant selling sandwiches at moderate prices.

Most of the coastline around Pigeon Island is rocky, though there's a nice little sandy beach just east of the jetty.

It's about a 20-minute walk along the causeway from Gros Islet to Pigeon Point.

SOUTHERN ST LUCIA

The main road in the southern part of the island makes a loop that can be done as a full-day trip.

The road to Soufrière is a scenic drive, winding in and out of lush jungle valleys and up into the mountains. It goes through banana plantations, passes the fishing villages of Anse La Raye and Canaries, and offers fine coastal and mountain vistas, including some lovely views of the Pitons as you approach Soufrière.

MARIGOT BAY

Marigot Bay is a lovely sheltered bay that is backed by green hillsides and sports a little palm-fringed beach. The inner harbor is so long and deep that an entire British fleet is said to have once escaped French warships by ducking inside and covering their masts with coconut fronds. The bay was the setting for the 1967 musical *Doctor Dolittle*, starring Rex Harrison.

Doctor Dolittle would hardly recognize the place today, with its string of hotels and beach bars, but it's still a tranquil spot, perfect for wasting the day in a beach chair.

Marigot Bay is a popular anchorage for yachters. Its marina has a customs office and a small market, and sells water, ice and fuel. The **Moorings** (☎ 451-4357) bases its bareboat charters here and runs the marina facilities.

A little pontoon boat shuttles back and forth on request (EC$5 round-trip), connecting the two sides of the inner harbor.

Sleeping & Eating

Marigot Beach Club (☎ 451-4974; www.marigot diveresort.com; PO Box 101, Castries; villas from US$165; 🄼 🄻 🄾) Located on the north side of the bay, this top-notch property and dive center has lovely suites with plush furnishings, good kitchens and living areas. Welcome extras include stereos, coffeemakers and private cell phones. Great location and value.

Dolittle's Restaurant & Beach Bar (Marigot Beach Club; mains EC$40-65; 🕑 lunch & dinner) At a pleasant waterside spot, Dolittle's has lunchtime sandwiches, and barbecued meats, pasta and fish specials by night.

JJ's Cottages Restaurant & Bar (☎ 451-4076; cottages EC$177, mains US$10-24; 🕑 lunch & dinner; 🄼 🄾) JJ's has 10 spacious chalet-style wooden cottages, with big comfy beds and refrigerators. The big barnlike eatery attached is popular with day-trippers for its local cuisine. Try Lucian snapper, octopus *labowi* (garlic curry) or fish *toufee* (coconut curry).

ANSE LA RAYE

South of Marigot Bay, the winding coast road continues to Anse La Raye, a sleepy fishing village that's become the island's Friday-night hot spot. 'Seafood Friday' has eclipsed Gros Islet's jump-up as the place to be on Friday for street food (everything from bakes for EC$1 to grilled lobster for EC$40), loud music and dancing (both in the street, and in at least two nightclubs and numerous bars).

The crowd is mostly local, and the party goes on all night.

During the rest of the week Anse La Raye is a typical island town, with colorful houses and an attractive beach, though swimming is discouraged because of strong currents.

SOUFRIÈRE

Founded by the French in 1746 and named after the nearby sulfur springs, the town of Soufrière has a lovely bay setting. The coastal Pitons provide a scenic backdrop to the south, and the island's highest peaks rise above the rainforest just a few miles inland.

Something of a rough diamond, Soufrière remains the spiritual heart of St Lucia. Unlike the polished resorts at the north of the island, Soufrière has a charm that comes from its ramshackle old weathered buildings, some still adorned with delicate gingerbread trim, and the genuine friendliness of its people.

The main sights – the Sulphur Springs, Morne Coubaril Estate and Diamond Botanical Gardens – are on the outskirts of town and can be visited in a couple of hours. Avoid the plethora of local 'guides' in town, who'll do their best to latch onto you.

Although most visitors are day-trippers on one of the many boat or land tours that include Soufrière, much of what the town has to offer, including its relaxed provincial character, is best appreciated by those who actually stay. Some of St Lucia's best accommodations are in this area.

Information

Soufrière Tourist Office (☎ 459-7419; 🕑 8am-4pm Mon-Fri, 8am-noon Sat) On the waterfront.

Sights & Activities

ANSE CHASTANET

Soufrière's picturesque scenery is equally impressive below the surface of the water.

Anse Chastanet, a lovely sheltered bay just over 1 mile (1.6km) north of Soufrière, has some of the finest nearshore snorkeling and diving on St Lucia. It also makes a fine choice if you're simply up for a swim.

At the beach is a hotel, a dive shop that rents out snorkeling equipment, a bar, and a restaurant that serves both simple snacks and full meals. Anse Chastanet is about a 35-minute walk from Soufrière along the hilly coastal road that skirts the north side of Soufrière Bay. If you're not up for a walk, you can easily arrange a water taxi from the village (EC$60 round-trip).

SULPHUR SPRINGS
With a barren and somewhat moonscapish terrain, these **springs** (admission EC$15; ⊙ 9am-5pm) are pocked with pools of boiling mud and steaming vents. The vents release great quantities of sulfuric gases, which are responsible for the yellow mineral deposits blanketing the area. The putrid smell, resembling rotten eggs, is hydrogen sulfide.

Visitors used to walk up close to the vents and peer directly into the mud ponds until a local guide leading a group of German tourists stepped through the soft earth and plunged waist-deep into the boiling mud. He lived to tell the story, but everything is now viewed from the safety of overlooks.

Despite the fact that this area is promoted as a 'drive-in volcano,' those expecting to peer down into a volcanic crater will be disappointed. The crater walls eroded away eons ago, and now the volcanic activity is along the side of a hill.

It's compulsory to have a guide walk through with you; although the price of the guide is theoretically included in the entrance fee, a tip will be expected.

To get there from Soufrière, go south on the potholed Vieux Fort road, which winds uphill as it leaves town. About a five-minute drive out of Soufrière, take the downhill fork to the left at the Sulphur Springs sign, from where it's half a mile (800m) further to the park entrance.

MORNE COUBARIL ESTATE
This **estate** (☎ 459-7340; adult/child EC$18/9; ⊙ 10am-6pm Mon-Fri, by arrangement Sat & Sun), on the Vieux Fort road about half a mile (800m) north of Sulphur Springs, is an interesting working cocoa and coconut plantation with tradi-

tional buildings, and the ruins of a water and sugar mill. You can also horse trek on the estate or learn about indigenous plant life, with varieties of Liberian coffee, snake plants and water lettuces marked in the gardens.

DIAMOND BOTANICAL GARDENS
The Diamond Estate's **botanical gardens, waterfall and mineral baths** (adult/child under 12 EC$15/7.50; ⊙ 10am-5pm Mon-Sat, 10am-3pm Sun & holidays) are all at the same site.

Paths wind through the gardens, which are planted with tropical flowers and trees, including numerous heliconia and ginger specimens. At the back of the gardens a small waterfall drops down a rock face that is stained a rich orange from the warm mineral waters. The waterfall featured briefly in the movie *Superman II* as the site from where Superman plucked an orchid for Lois Lane.

The mineral baths date from 1784, when they were built atop hot springs so that the troops of King Louis XVI of France could take advantage of their therapeutic effects. The baths were largely destroyed during the French Revolution, but in recent times a few have been restored and are open to visitors.

The Diamond Estate is 1 mile (1.6km) east of the Soufrière town center, via Sir Arthur Lewis St, and the way is signposted. The Old Mill restaurant serves buffet lunches there.

MALGRETOUT
A 20-minute walk along the dirt coastal road south of Soufrière leads to a quiet, undeveloped beach, which is great for snorkeling, and to the mineral **Pitons Waterfall** (admission EC$5) at Malgretout. Not only does this most unfrequented waterfall have a beautiful Eden-like setting, but visitors are allowed to shower in its warm volcanic waters – a situation that is not allowed at the more touristed waterfall at Diamond Botanical Gardens. To get to the falls, travel along the coastal dirt road until you reach a fork that leads on the right to the pensioners' home and secluded **Malgretout beach**, and then continue left up the steep road uphill for about 200yd (180m) – a sign marks the way.

Sleeping
BUDGET & MIDRANGE
Hummingbird Beach Resort (☎ 459-7232; www.istlucia.co.uk; PO Box 280, Soufrière; s/d from US$60/65; ✂ 🖥 🕭) On the north side of the harbor,

AUTHOR'S CHOICE

Stonefield Estate (☎ 459-7037; www.stone fieldvillas.com; PO Box 228, Soufrière; 1- to 3-bedroom villas US$190-600; ✎ 🖳 ☎) This laid-back, family-run property on a former estate is the island's ultimate in understated cool. The 11 hip villas feature sumptuous living areas in natural whitewashed stone and wood, stylishly simple rustic furniture, garden showers, and huge decks (some with private plunge pools) with double hammocks and glorious views over Petit Piton.

this friendly, relaxed hotel is a great place to meet fellow travelers. Its 10 spacious rooms with comfy Creole furnishings (some with four-poster beds) are dotted around the poolside garden, a stone's throw from the beach.

Still Beach Resort (☎ 459-7261; www.thestillresort .com; r from US$65; ✎) A few steps up the hill from the Hummingbird, this newly renovated resort has large, colorfully decked out, though somewhat charmless, rooms and apartments at very reasonable prices.

Camilla's Guesthouse (☎ 459-5379; 7 Bridge St; s/d US$40/60) Seek out the formidable Mrs Camilla at her restaurant on Bridge St if you fancy a homey room with shiny bedspreads in one of her communal guesthouses around town. They're packed with St Lucians on weekends.

TOP END

Mago Estate (☎ 459-5880; www.magohotel.com; PO Box 247, Soufrière; r US$200-500; ✎ 🖳 ☎) Get back to (albeit luxurious) nature in this unique small hotel with cavelike rooms, surrounded by trailing vegetation, set into the mountain rock. Rooms are on the small side, with tasteful ethnic-chic furnishings. Check out the fabulous elevated Julius Caesar suite with a huge open wall looking down over Soufrière and the bay.

Eating

BUDGET

There are a handful of local restaurants offering good food at reasonable prices near the central square that borders Church, Sir Arthur Lewis and Bridge Sts.

Archie's Creole Pot (☎ 459-7760; 9 Bridge St; mains EC$9-15; ✎ breakfast, lunch & dinner) Enjoy great

homemade meat or veggie rotis with all the carb-rich trimmings – dasheen, plantain and sweet potato. It's open till 2am.

Eroline's Foods (Church St) Located in the center of town, this is the local supermarket.

MIDRANGE & TOP END

Hummingbird (mains EC$40-120) Savor delicious, beautifully presented Caribbean and European dishes that feature fresh fish and seafood. Excellent sandwiches and salads are available throughout the day.

Camilla's Guesthouse (☎ 459-5379; 7 Bridge St; mains EC$20-50; ✎ breakfast, lunch & dinner) Take your pick between the flouncy upstairs gourmet Creole restaurant with local specialties, such as goat stew and callaloo (root vegetable) soup, or the less formal café-cum-snack bar downstairs (open until 2am).

Jalousie Hilton (☎ 456-8000; lunch mains EC$25-50) Don't let heavy security at the gate put you off your club sandwich or chicken satay in the spectacular surroundings of this beachside restaurant at the base of the Pitons. Loll around on the (public) beach for the afternoon to get your full money's worth.

Entertainment

Most of the organized nightlife centers around the hotel bars, though you're more likely to sniff out any action in one of the few bars in town.

Sidetrack Café (☎ 461-6656; Darnley Alexander St; ✎ 9am-4am) Kick back over a game of cards and rum punch with locals downstairs, or shake your booty to the big calypso DJ sounds upstairs on the large street-side veranda.

Ladera Resort (☎ 459-7323; PO Box 225, Soufrière) Located on the Vieux Fort road out of town, the bar at this exclusive resort, with its stunning views over the Pitons, is the most dramatic spot for a sunset cocktail.

CHOISEUL

Choiseul, a little village south of Soufrière, has an active handicraft industry, and its roadside arts-and-crafts center is a good place to pick up locally made dolls, baskets, pottery and wood carvings.

Located between Choiseul and Paiye is **Balenbouche Estate** (☎ 455-1244; www.balenbouche .com; r US$45-75), the tranquil 18th-century estate home of the congenial Uta Lawaetz and her daughters. You can stay in the lovingly restored house furnished with simple, beautiful antiques, or in one of three hippyish garden cottages with mosaic-tiled baths. You really feel that you have stepped back in time here; complete the experience with a stroll round the grounds and truly atmospheric jungle-covered mill ruins.

THE SOUTH & EAST COASTS

The road up the east coast from Vieux Fort is relatively straight and uneventful, passing through a few local villages and numerous banana plantations before turning inland at the town of Dennery and making a scenic, winding cut across the mountainous rainforest to Castries. **Grande Anse**, 6 miles (10km) north of Dennery, is renowned for its nesting leatherback turtles. **Desbarra Turtle Watch Group** (☎ 284-2812), a local community group, organizes tours in season (March to August).

Maria Islands Nature Reserve (☎ 454-5014; ☼ 9am-5pm Mon-Fri), east of Vieux Fort, is the only habitat of the *kouwes* snake, one of the world's rarest grass snakes, and the Maria Islands ground lizard. Because it's a sanctuary for terns, noddies and other seabirds, this two-island reserve is only accessible outside the summer nesting season.

Mamiku Gardens (☎ 455-3729; www.mamiku.com; ☼ 9am-5pm) is a fascinating historic garden, between Praslin and Mon Repos, that has been left delightfully unmanicured. Wander among orchids, rock pools and aromatic plants, or visit the medicinal herb garden.

DIRECTORY

ACCOMMODATIONS

Most hotels display rates in US dollars, though they will equally accept payment in EC dollars. St Lucia has a number of good-value, moderately priced guesthouses, with the lion's share in the Rodney Bay area. The all-inclusive resorts phenomenon has made a big impact on St Lucia in recent years, with many hotels in the Rodney Bay area only offering this kind of deal.

The island's main resort area, at nearby Reduit Beach, has reasonably priced mid-range hotels, as do other places scattered around the island. Some of the more unique hotels can be found further south, around Soufrière.

See p757 for a guide to budget, midrange and top-end accommodations price ranges in this book.

ACTIVITIES

Beaches & Swimming

All of St Lucia's beaches are public. On the touristed northwest side of the island there's a fine white-sand beach along the causeway linking Gros Islet and Pigeon Point, and another at Reduit Beach, the resort strip south of Rodney Bay. There are also nice golden strands at Choc Bay, which stretches north from the Sandals Halcyon resort.

Along the southwest coast are numerous coves and bays, many accessible by boat only, that offer good swimming and snorkeling.

The east side of the island is less protected, with rougher water conditions, some off-limits to swimmers.

Diving & Snorkeling

St Lucia's rugged mountain terrain continues beneath the sea as underwater mounts, caves and drop-offs. Most of the diving takes place on the western side of the island, with some of the top sites in the south-central area where the best reefs remain.

Anse Chastanet, near Soufrière, has been designated a marine park. It boasts spectacular nearshore reefs, with a wide variety of corals, sponges and reef fish; it's excellent for both diving and snorkeling.

A popular dive just a bit further south is Keyhole Pinnacles, consisting of coral-encrusted underwater mounts that rise to within a few feet of the surface. For more information, see p56.

There are a couple of wreck dives, including *Lesleen,* a 165ft (50.3m) freighter that was deliberately sunk in 1986 to create an artificial reef. It now sits upright in 65ft (20m) of water near Anse Cochon, another popular dive area. Anse Cochon is also a favored snorkeling stop on day sails to Soufrière.

In addition, there's good snorkeling and diving beneath both Petit Piton and Gros Piton, the coastal mountains that loom to the south of Soufrière. In the main resort

---

EMERGENCY NUMBERS

Ambulance & Fire (☎ 911)
Police (☎ 999)

area north of Castries, Pigeon Island offers fair snorkeling.

DIVE SHOPS

There are a number of dive shops on St Lucia. Expect to pay US$35 to US$45 for a single dive.

Buddies Scuba (☎ 450-8406; www.buddiesscuba.com; PO Box 565, Castries) A Professional Association of Diving Instructors (PADI) facility, based at the Rodney Bay Marina in Castries, with dives to Anse Chastanet and Anse Cochon.

Dive Fair Helen (☎ 451-7716; www.divefairhelen.com) This well-run center offers a variety of courses and packages, and operates out of Vigie Marina and Marigot Bay.

Dolphin Divers (☎ 452-9485; PO Box 1538, Castries) Located at Rodney Bay Marina.

Frog's Diving (☎ 450-8831; www.frogsdiving.com; PO Box 3049, Castries) Located at Rodney Bay.

Scuba St Lucia (☎ 459-7000; www.scubastlucia.com; Anse Chastanet Hotel, PO Box 7000, Soufrière) A long-established PADI facility, it offers one-tank dives, an introductory scuba course, open-water certification courses and referral courses. Boat transportation from Castries is available.

Golf

The **St Lucia Golf & Country Club** (☎ 450-8523), on the northern tip of the island, has an 18-hole par 71 course and offers lessons (per half-hour around EC$105).

Hiking

There are three main trails into the mountainous interior on public lands that are administered by the **Department of Forest & Lands** (☎ 450-2231).

The Barre de L'isle Trail is a good choice if you're on a budget, as you can get to the trailhead from Castries for EC$5 by hopping on a Vieux Fort bus (about 30 minutes). This lush rainforest hike, which is in the center of the island along the ridge that divides the eastern and western halves of St Lucia, leads to the top of the 1446ft (441m) Morne la Cambe. It provides some fine views along the way, and takes about three hours round-trip. The trailhead, which begins at the south side of the highway, is clearly marked; on weekdays Department of Forest & Lands personnel wait at the trailhead to collect the park fee and are available as guides.

As trailhead access for the other two forest-reserve hikes is inland from major roads and bus routes, these hikes are usually undertaken as part of an organized tour. The Des Cartiers Rainforest Trail at the Quilesse Forest Reserve begins 6 miles (9.5km) inland from Micoud and passes through the habitat of the rare St Lucia parrot. The Edmond Forest Reserve Trail begins about 7 miles (11.3km) east of Soufrière, crosses a rainforest of tall trees interlaced with orchids and bromeliads, and offers fine views of St Lucia's highest peak, the 3118ft (950m) Mt Gimie.

While the latter two forest-reserve hikes take only a few hours to walk, the travel time to either trailhead is about 90 minutes one way from Castries, so the hikes are full-day outings. The Department of Forest & Lands and the island's main tour agencies arrange outings several days a week.

A hike up either of the Pitons peaks takes about four hours round-trip, and shouldn't be done without an experienced local guide from the Soufrière tourist office (p593).

Horseback Riding

Trim's National Riding (☎ 450-8273; PO Box 1159, Castries) offers a one-hour ride along the beach in Cas-en-Bas (US$40) and a two-hour ride that also includes crossing the interior to Gros Islet (US$50).

Mourne Coubaril (☎ 459-7340) offers a horseback trail through the working plantation estate for US$50 for about 90 minutes.

Tennis & Squash

Most of the larger hotels have tennis courts. The **St Lucia Yacht Club** (☎ 452-8350), at Reduit Beach, has squash courts open to visitors for a fee (per half-hour US$25).

Windsurfing

A number of the large beachfront hotels, including the Royal St Lucian (p590), at

Reduit Beach, and the Windjammer Landing (p590), between Castries and Gros Islet, rent out windsurfing equipment.

The Vieux Fort area, at the southern tip of the island, gets strong winds and rough seas, making it a favorite with experienced windsurfers looking for a challenge.

BOOKS

Collected Poems, 1948–1984 is a good introduction to St Lucian Nobel prize-winning poet Derek Walcott's work, much of which is influenced by island life and culture.

BUSINESS HOURS

Government and business hours are generally 8:30am to 12:30pm and 1:30pm to 4:30pm Monday to Friday. Many stores are also open 8am to noon Saturday. Bank hours are usually 8:30am to 3pm Monday to Thursday, closing at 5pm on Friday. A few bank branches, particularly in resort areas, are also open on Saturday morning.

DANGERS & ANNOYANCES

Bilharzia (schistosomiasis) is endemic to St Lucia; the general precaution is to avoid wading or swimming in freshwater. Hikers should keep in mind that the poisonous fer-de-lance favors brushy undergrowth, so stick to well-trodden trails.

EMBASSIES & CONSULATES
St Lucian Embassies & Consulates
Germany (☎ 6172-302-324; Postfach 2304, 61293 Bad Homburg)
UK (☎ 0207-937-9522; 10 Kensington Ct, London W85DL)
USA (☎ 202-364-6792; 3216 New Mexico Ave NW, Washington, DC 20016)

Consulates in St Lucia
Germany (☎ 450-8050; Care Service Bldg, Massade Industrial Estate, Gros Islet)
UK (☎ 452-2484/5; NIS Waterfront Bldg, 2nd fl, PO Box 227, Castries)

FESTIVALS & EVENTS
Atlantic Rally for Cruisers (ARC; December) One of the largest transatlantic yacht races, starting in the Canary Islands and ending at Rodney Bay Marina, St Lucia's largest yacht port. About 200 boats cross the finish line.

HOLIDAYS
New Year's Day January 1
New Year's Holiday January 2
Independence Day February 22
Good Friday Late March/early April
Easter Monday Late March/early April
Labour Day May 1
Whit Monday Eighth Monday after Easter
Corpus Christi Ninth Thursday after Easter
Emancipation Day August 3
Thanksgiving Day October 5
National Day December 13
Christmas Day December 25
Boxing Day December 26

Note that when some holidays fall on Sunday, they are celebrated on the following Monday.

MAPS
The best map is the 1:50,000 Ordnance Survey map of St Lucia, which is difficult to find on the island. Less-detailed road maps are available at the local tourist offices.

MONEY
The Eastern Caribbean dollar (EC$) is the island currency. Traveler's checks in US dollars are the most convenient, but checks in Canadian dollars and British pounds can also be changed without difficulty.

Most banks will cash traveler's checks in US, Canadian and British currencies free of charge for transactions of EC$500 or more, and with a nominal charge for lesser amounts.

You can get cash advances using Visa or MasterCard, or make withdrawals from your account using a Cirrus or Plus bank card, from ATMs at the Royal Bank of Canada branches in Castries and Rodney Bay.

Visa, MasterCard and Amex are the most widely accepted credit cards, and can be used for car rentals and at most midrange and top-end restaurants and hotels.

An 8% tax and 10% service charge are added to the bill at all but the cheapest hotels and restaurants; there's no need for additional tipping.

TELEPHONE
There are both card and coin phones around the island. Phone cards are sold at tourist-office booths, Cable & Wireless offices and many stores.

You can send international faxes and make phone calls in Castries from **Cable & Wireless** (Bridge St; ⏰ 7:30am-6:30pm Mon-Fri, 8am-12:30pm Sat) and **ClickCom** (☎ 452-4444; 1st fl, La Place Carenage; ✉ 8:30am-4pm Mon-Fri, 8:30am-1pm Sat).

For local calls, dial the seven-digit number. When calling from North America, add the area code ☎ 1-758. From elsewhere, dial your country's international access code, followed by ☎ 758 and the local number. We have included only the seven-digit local number for St Lucia listings in this chapter.

For more information on phone cards and making long-distance calls, see p767.

TOURS

The **St Lucia National Trust** (☎ 452-5005; natrust@isis .org.lc) can arrange tours to the island's coastal nature reserves: the Maria Island Nature Reserve, off the southeast coast, and the Frigate Islands Nature Reserve, off the east coast; both are popular with bird-watchers.

VISAS

For all foreign visitors, stays of over 28 days generally require a visa.

TRANSPORTATION

GETTING THERE & AWAY
Entering St Lucia

Most visitors must show a valid passport; US citizens see the boxed text, p772. French citizens can enter with a national identity card. Visitors to the island are required to fill in an immigration form on arrival detailing the length, purpose and location of their stay, plus any customs declarations they may have. An onward or round-trip ticket or proof of sufficient funds is officially required.

Air

St Lucia has two airports: **Hewanorra International Airport** (UVF; ☎ 454-6355), in Vieux Fort at the remote southern tip of the island, and **George FL Charles Airport** (SLU; ☎ 452-1156), in Castries near the main tourist area.

Scheduled international jet flights land at Hewanorra, which has a longer runway, while flights from within the Caribbean and charters generally land at the more central George FL Charles Airport.

Both airports have tourist-information booths, taxi stands, card and coin phones, and booths for international and local car-rental agencies. The tourist-information booths book rooms, sell phone cards and

will exchange US cash into EC dollars at slightly disadvantaged rates.

Offices for the main airlines serving St Lucia are in central Castries. For information on flights to St Lucia to/from outside the Caribbean, see p776.

The following airlines fly to/from St Lucia from within the Caribbean:

Air Jamaica (☎ 453-6611; www.airjamaica.com; hub Jamaica)

BWIA (☎ 452-3778; www.bwee.com; hub Trinidad)

Caribbean Star (☎ 453-2927; www.flycaribbeanstar .com; hub Antigua)

LIAT (☎ 452-3056, after hours 452-2348; www.liatair line.com; hub Antigua)

Sea
CRUISE SHIP

Cruise ships dock in Castries. There are a number of berths, some on the east side of the harbor near the town center and others at Pointe Seraphine on the north side of the harbor, where there's a duty-free shopping complex.

FERRY

The ferry service **L'Express des Îles** (www.ex press-des-iles.com) operates a daily 80-minute express catamaran between Castries and Fort-de-France on Martinique. It also has a service on Saturday and Sunday to Guadeloupe (six hours) and Dominica (four hours). Departure days and times change frequently; check in advance with any local travel agent. On St Lucia, tickets can be purchased from **Carib Travel** (☎ 452-2151; PO Box 102, Micoud St).

There is a crossing between St Lucia and Guadeloupe run by **Brudey Frères** (☎ 590-590-90-04-48; www.brudey-freres.fr), in Point-à-Pitre, Guadeloupe, once or twice a week (one way/ return €80/115). Tickets can be purchased from local travel agencies.

For more information on these boats, see p535.

YACHT

Customs and immigration can be cleared at Rodney Bay, Castries, Marigot Bay or Vieux Fort. Most yachties pull in at Rodney Bay, where there's a full-service marina and a couple of marked customs slips opposite the customs office.

It's easy to clear at Marigot Bay, where you can anchor in the inner harbor and dinghy over to the customs office. Castries is a more congested scene, and yachts entering the harbor are required to go directly to the customs dock. If there's no room, you should head for the anchorage spot east of the customs buoy. At Vieux Fort, you can anchor off the big ship dock, where customs is located.

Popular anchorages include Reduit Beach, the area southeast of Pigeon Island, Rodney Bay Marina, Marigot Bay, Anse Chastanet, Anse Cochon and Soufrière Bay.

Yacht charters are available from **Sunsail** (☎ 452-8648) and **DSL Yachting** (☎ 452-8531), both at Rodney Bay Marina, and from the **Moorings** (☎ 451-4357), at Marigot Bay. For addresses and booking information, see p782.

GETTING AROUND
Bus
Bus service is via privately owned minivans. They're a cheap way to get around, and the means by which most islanders get to town, school and work. Buses are frequent on main routes (such as Castries to Gros Islet) and generally run until 10pm (later on Friday); however, there is no scheduled timetable. Very few buses run on Sunday.

If there's no bus stop nearby, you can wave buses down en route as long as there's space for the bus to pull over. Pay the fare directly to the driver.

If you're trying to circle the island by bus, note that afternoon service between Soufrière and Castries is unreliable, so it's best to travel in a counterclockwise direction, catching a morning bus from Castries to Soufrière and returning via Vieux Fort (up the east coast) in the afternoon.

If you're traveling in the southwest of the island, be aware that southbound buses are often completely full, and it's sometimes more convenient to backtrack north to Castries, where you can be sure of getting a seat.

Sample fares from Castries to Gros Islet (Route 1A) or Marigot Bay (Route 3C) are EC$3, to Vieux Fort (Route 2H) EC$8 and to Soufrière (Route 3D) EC$9. Route numbers are displayed on the buses.

Car & Motorcycle
DRIVER'S LICENSE
Drivers on St Lucia must hold an International Driving Permit or purchase a local driving permit (EC$54), which is valid for three months.

RENTAL
Avis, Hertz and National, as well as smaller (and generally cheaper) local firms, operate out of both Hewanorra and George FL Charles airports, nearly all offering unlimited mileage.

The cheapest cars, that are without air-conditioning, rent for about US$45 a day; you'll find the best rates on the Internet.

Car-rental companies offer optional collision damage waiver (CDW) for about US$16 a day, which covers theft and collision damages to the car, but the renter is still responsible for the first US$500 to US$800 in damages. If the CDW is not taken, the renter is usually responsible for the first US$1500 to US$2500 in damages.

If you're planning an extensive tour of the island, it's advisable to hire a 4WD, as many of the roads are steep and smaller ones can become little more than potholed mudslides after a bout of rain.

On the main road between Castries and Rodney Bay, **Wayne's Motorcycle Center** (☎ 452-2059) rents 500cc Honda motorcycles for US$30 a day, helmet included.

ROAD CONDITIONS
Roads vary greatly around the island, with some sections being newly surfaced and others deeply potholed. Make sure you have a workable jack and spare tire available. Many of the interior and southern roads are also very winding and narrow. Gas stations are distributed around the island.

ROAD RULES
On St Lucia, drive on the left-hand side. Speed limits are generally 15mph (24km/h) in towns and 30mph (48km/h) on major roads.

St Vincent & the Grenadines

'A Yachtsman's Paradise,' 'The Jewels of Caribbean,' 'A Piece of Eden' – all of the clichés and tourism slogans ring true in St Vincent & the Grenadines (SVG), a nation of 32 impossibly gorgeous cays and islands. Although traditionally the territory of smugglers, pirates, wealthy yachters, reclusive royalty and rehabbing rock stars, this lost corner of the world is increasingly accessible to travelers.

St Vincent, the northernmost island, is the nation's commercial and political hub, accounting for 90% of both the land area and the population. However, the true attractions are the smaller islands that reach like stepping-stones from St Vincent down to Grenada. Surrounded by coral reefs and clear blue waters, they are some of the region's best spots for diving, snorkeling and boating. In particular, the uninhabited Tobago Cays are perhaps the most striking (and most sought after) destination in the Caribbean.

While all of the Grenadine islands are lightly populated and generally undeveloped, exclusive Mustique, Palm Island and Petit St Vincent are worlds apart from funky, somewhat ramshackle Union Island and St Vincent. That is not to say that one type of island is better than the other – each has its own charm and appeal.

FAST FACTS

- **Area** 150 sq miles (389 sq km)
- **Capital** Kingstown
- **Country code** ☎ 784
- **Departure tax** EC$40
- **Famous for** Deserted islands, yachting, pirates
- **Languages** English, French patois (increasingly rare)
- **Money** Eastern Caribbean dollar (EC$); EC$1 = US$0.37 = €0.31 = UK£0.21
- **People** Vincentians (formal); Vincys (colloquial)
- **Phrases** Check it? (Do you follow me?)
- **Population** 118,000
- **Visa** No visa required

HIGHLIGHTS

- **Tobago Cays** (p619) Marvel at the pristine beaches and reefs of these uninhabited islets.
- **La Soufrière** (p610) Hike St Vincent's picturesque volcano to its crater lake.
- **Bequia** (p611) Visit the most dynamic of the Grenadines, which offers diving, dining, nightlife and beaches, without feeling too overdeveloped.
- **Mustique** (p615) Party with Mick Jagger and David Bowie, or simply laze about at this exclusive getaway.
- **Sunset from the Sea** (p611) Charter a sailboat for some unforgettable views of the sunset over the Grenadines and the shimmering Caribbean.

ITINERARIES

- **Three days** Hike St Vincent's La Soufrière volcano, then move on to the beaches of Bequia or Mustique. For a more relaxing three days, just head straight to the beaches.
- **One week** After Mustique and/or Bequia, explore the Tobago Cays from either Mayreau or Palm Island.
- **Two weeks** Island hop by boat from St Vincent down to Union Island. Fly back up to St Vincent to maximize overall beach time.

CLIMATE & WHEN TO GO

The climate varies between the islands, as the Grenadines to the south are slightly drier and marginally warmer than St Vincent. In St Vincent the dry season runs approximately from January to May. In July, the wettest month, rainfall averages 26 days, while in April, the driest month, it averages only six days. In January the average daily high temperature is 85°F (29°C), while the nightly low average is 72°F (22°C). In July the average daily high is 86°F (30°C), while the nightly low averages 76°F (24°C).

The high season (winter) runs from December to April/May. The wetter months can still be nice, and they keep the islands lush and green.

HISTORY

St Vincent is not as remote as it appears and has actually been inhabited for some 7000 years. Originally it was sparsely populated by the hunter-gatherer Siboney Indi-

HOW MUCH?

The following costs are based on St Vincent prices. Costs are considerably higher on some of the more exclusive and smaller islands.

- Taxi from Kingstown to airport EC$20
- Day trip around St Vincent US$100
- Day of diving off St Vincent US$70
- Meal of fresh fish in a touristy restaurant EC$60
- Meal of fresh fish in a local restaurant EC$20

LONELY PLANET INDEX

- Gallon (imperial) of gas EC$8
- Liter of bottled water EC$3
- Bottle of Hairoun beer EC$4
- Souvenir T-shirt EC$20
- Street snack: boneless chicken roti EC$8

ans. Around two thousand years ago they were replaced by the Arawak Indians, who moved up from present-day Venezuela. The raiding Caribs eventually took over from the Arawaks, but held some of the islands for as little as 100 years before the arrival of the heavily armed Spanish. Fierce Carib resistance kept the Europeans out of St Vincent long after most other Caribbean islands had fallen to the colonists. This was in part because many Caribs from other islands fled to St Vincent ('Hairoun,' as they called it) after their home islands were conquered – it was the Caribs' last stand. On the island, Caribs intermarried with Africans who had escaped from slavery, and the new mixed generation split along ethnic lines as 'Black Caribs' and 'Yellow Caribs.'

In 1783, after a century of competing claims between the British and French, the Treaty of Paris placed St Vincent under British control. Indigenous rebellions followed and British troops rounded up the 'insurgents,' forcibly repatriating around 5000 Black Caribs to Roatán island, Honduras. With the native opposition gone, the planters capitalized on the fertile volcanic soil and achieved the success that had eluded them. However, it didn't last long: two eruptions of La Soufrière, the abolition of slavery in 1834 and a few powerful hurricanes stood in the way of their colonial dreams. For the remainder of the British rule the economy stagnated; plantations were eventually broken up and land redistributed to small-scale farmers.

In 1969, in association with the British, St Vincent became a self-governing state, and on October 27, 1979, St Vincent was cobbled together with the Grenadines as an independent member of the Commonwealth. Tourism, for all its good and bad, has helped to reinvigorate the once flagging economy, although unemployment is still a major issue.

THE CULTURE

Vincy culture is superficially conservative, formal and a bit macho, but is warm and relaxed below the surface. The people live in one of the most beautiful places in the world, but do not necessarily fit the stereotype of residents of paradise. They are concerned with many of the quotidian stresses and anxieties of life in any developing country – particularly how to make ends meet and how to create a more secure future for their children. Culture varies a bit from island to island, but Vincentians generally work in the tourism industry, or labor in fishing, boat transportation, small-scale agriculture or other traditional trades. Foreigners are looked upon with a degree of suspicion – undoubtedly the legacy of generations of foreign profiteering and colonialism. There is a significant generational schism, as the youth are a bit more cosmopolitan and savvy in their relations with outsiders. The older generation tends to view the younger generation as lazy and opportunistic.

If you are able to move beyond the curtain of typical tourist/local relations, you will find a very friendly and unique culture. Once you are a friend, you are practically family and will be treated as such. It is true that many locals like to lie around and smoke spliffs on the beach, but Vincy culture runs much deeper than stale Caribbean stereotypes. For example, people gathered under a shady tree are more often than not debating the merits of Caribbean politics, international affairs or wide-ranging current events.

ST VINCENT & THE GRENADINES

0 ——— 10 km
0 ——— 6 miles

St Vincent Passage

La Soufrière ▲ (4048ft)

St Vincent

Chateaubelair
Georgetown

Barrouallie

KINGSTOWN

CARIBBEAN SEA

Bequia

Port Elizabeth

The Grenadines

Mustique

Canouan

Mayreau   Tobago Cays

Union Island   Clifton
           Palm Island

GRENADA

Carriacou

Petit St Vincent

Petit Martinique

Mushroom Island

RELIGION

Most people – especially of the older generation – take religion seriously. Locals dress up for church and strictly observe the Sabbath, so don't plan to get much done on a Sunday.

The majority of islanders are Protestant, with Anglicans representing the largest denomination. Other religions include Methodist, Seventh Day Adventist, Jehovah's Witness, Baptist, Streams of Power and Baha'i. About 20% of Vincentians are Roman Catholic.

The trappings of Rastafarianism are popular expressions of fashion and West Indian identity, but few participate in its religious elements.

ARTS

Reggae, soca, calypso and steel-band music are popular throughout the Grenadines, although most of the younger generation listens to Jamaican dancehall and American hip-hop.

Boat building, both full-scale and models, is an island art form, particularly in Bequia. Some of the best miniature boats sell to collectors for more money than real boats.

Scrimshaw, the art of etching of traditional scenes on whale bone, is experiencing a renaissance in Bequia (see p613). There are also a good number of locally famous landscape painters, who generally work with oil, pastel and watercolors. Lennox 'Dinks' Johnson's paintings of the Tobago Cays are ubiquitous.

ENVIRONMENT
The Land

St Vincent is a high volcanic island, forming the northernmost point of the volcanic ridge that runs from Grenada in the south up through the Grenadine islands. It is markedly hilly, and its rich volcanic soil is very productive – St Vincent is often called the 'garden of the Grenadines.' It has a rugged interior of tropical rainforest, and lowlands thick with coconut trees and banana estates. The valley region around Mesopotamia, northeast of Kingstown, has some of the best farmland and luxuriant landscapes.

The island of St Vincent makes up 133 sq miles (344 sq km) of the nation's 150 sq miles (388 sq km). The other 17 sq miles (44 sq km) are spread across 31 islands and cays, fewer than a dozen of which are populated. The largest of these islands are Bequia, Mustique, Canouan, Mayreau and Union Island. The larger Grenadine islands are hilly, but relatively low-lying, and most have no source of freshwater other than rainfall. All have stunning white-sand beaches and abundant (although dwindling) sea life.

Wildlife

SVG is known more for its sea life than island wildlife, although there are a few land animals of note. The national bird is the endangered St Vincent parrot, a beautiful multihued bird that lives in the interior rainforests. The jungle also provides a habitat for *manicou* (opossum) and *agouti*

(a rabbitlike rodent). Agouti roam freely on Young Island, where they are easy to spot.

St Vincent harbors Congo snakes (tree snakes), and two terrestrial species, the black snake and the white snake – all three are harmless.

Spotted eagle rays, sharks, giant sea turtles, octopi, moray eels, drummer fish and parrot fish are just a few of the hundreds of sea species that attract divers, snorkelers and fishing enthusiasts to the area.

Environmental Issues

The most pressing environmental issues in SVG exist below the water's surface. Overfishing, water pollution and reef death caused by too much human and boat traffic are altering the unique ecosystems of the islands. Never touch or collect corals or other sea life, and do not anchor above a reef.

Freshwater for local consumption and waste disposal (both on land and from passenger ships) are issues that cause political frictions on the islands. Unfortunately there are no comprehensive solutions at this point. Be conservative with tap and shower water, and never litter on land or sea.

FOOD & DRINK

Vincentian cuisine is similar to most West Indian food, although the fertile volcanic soil of St Vincent provides fresh locally grown produce that is not always available in other parts of the Caribbean. In fact, St Vincent produces most of the fruit and vegetables sold throughout the Grenadines and much of what is for offer in Barbados. Seafood is abundant and fresh, with conch, fish, shrimp and lobster on most menus.

Common West Indian foods include callaloo soup, pumpkin soup, saltfish, pigfoot *souse* (broth with vegetables, spices and meat) and various breadfruit dishes. A popular St Vincent dish is *bul jol*, which is made of roasted breadfruit and saltfish with tomatoes and onions. Prepared meals with chicken or fish, including roti, are rarely deboned, so take a close look before taking a big bite. Many restaurants will offer a 'boneless' version of a dish for a slightly higher price.

St Vincent's tap water comes from mountain reserves and is chlorinated; it's safe to drink, but can have a chemical taste. On the Grenadines water comes from the sky, but bottled water is a safer bet.

St Vincent Brewery, in Kingstown, makes the crisp Vincy lager Hairoun (high-rone). It also produces the region's Guinness stout and some refreshing soft drinks, like Bitter Lemon.

ST VINCENT

pop 105,000

For most visitors the island of St Vincent is a portal to the Grenadines, more than a destination in itself.

Its beaches are plain and uninspiring, and there is high population density around the main city of Kingstown. While St Vincent disappoints some visitors, others like the fact that it is a window into normal Vincy life – unlike the contrived 'steel drum and rum punch' atmosphere found at resorts and some of the more 'desirable' destinations.

The island is lush and green, with deep valleys cultivated with bananas, coconuts and arrowroot, and a mountainous interior that peaks at the spectacular 4048ft (1233m) La Soufrière volcano. The majority of travelers enter SVG at the ET Joshua Airport near Kingstown. If you are short on time, it's advisable to move on to the smaller islands. If you have more time on your hands, there are some attractive bays, waterfalls and smaller towns to explore beyond Kingstown.

Getting There & Away

The runway at ET Joshua Airport receives regular flights (with connections further afield) to/from Barbados, St Lucia, Grenada and Trinidad.

There are also intracountry flights to Bequia, Canoun, Mustique and Union Island. Ferries will take you to Barbados, through all of the Grenadines, where you can continue on to Grenada.

For details on the cargo/passenger mailboat ferries that ply the waters between St Vincent and Union Island, see p623.

Fantasea Tours (☎ 457-4477; www.fantasea.com; Villa) arranges sailing day tours from St Vincent to the Grenadine islands. One goes to Mustique and Bequia for US$70 per person, and another takes in Canouan, Mayreau and the Tobago Cays for US$90 per person.

Getting Around

See individual sections for information on travel around the island.

Sam's Taxi Tours (☎ 458-4338; sams-taxi-tours@carib surf.com) offers day-tours that take in the sights of either St Vincent's west coast or east coast for around US$100 for up to two people.

Hiking trips to La Soufrière cost US$100 for up to six people.

For information on tours to the Falls of Baleine, see p611.

KINGSTOWN

pop 30,000

Kingstown – a sweaty city of winding streets and boxy cement structures – is the capital and commercial center of SVG. The city doesn't go out of its way to cater to tourists, but has everything one might need: banks, shops, restaurants, Internet cafés and a tourist office. Many Vincys from other islands visit Kingstown to stock up on provisions that are not for sale on the smaller islands.

Most hotel and guesthouse options for foreigners are located in Indian Bay and Villa, a couple of miles southeast of Kingstown on the far side of the airport. The area begins at Villa Point and runs along Indian Bay and Villa Beach, and past Young Island Cut, a narrow channel that separates Young Island from the St Vincent mainland.

Orientation

The city is hemmed in by the island's hilly topography, and the center consists of only about a dozen dense blocks. Ferries from the Grenadines arrive at the jetty just south of the city center. Note that Upper and Lower Middle St is more properly called Upper and Lower Long Lane, although people use these names interchangeably.

MAPS

You'll find basic maps of Kingstown in pamphlets and maps of the Grenadines that are distributed through the Tourist Office (p607) and various travel agencies.

Information
BOOKSTORES

R&M Adams Books (☎ 457-5174; Cruise Ship Terminal) The best selection of Caribbean and international books.

EMERGENCY

Police station (☎ 999; cnr Upper Bay & Hillsborough Sts)

INTERNET ACCESS

Office Essentials (☎ 457-2235; oel@caribsurf.com;
Bonadie Plaza, Upper Middle St, per hr EC$6)
MSA Internet Cafe (☎ 457-1131;
internetcafé@vincysurf.com; Upper Middle St;
per hr EC$6; ☻ 8am-11pm) Located on the 3rd floor
of the office building across from the Public
Library.

LAUNDRY

MagiKleen (☎ 457-1514; Lower Bay St; per pound
wash & dry EC$2.50; ☻ 7:30am-5pm Mon-Fri, 7:30am-
2pm Sat)

MEDICAL SERVICES

Kingstown General Hospital (☎ 456-1185) On the
Leeward Hwy, west of Victoria Park. For serious illness or

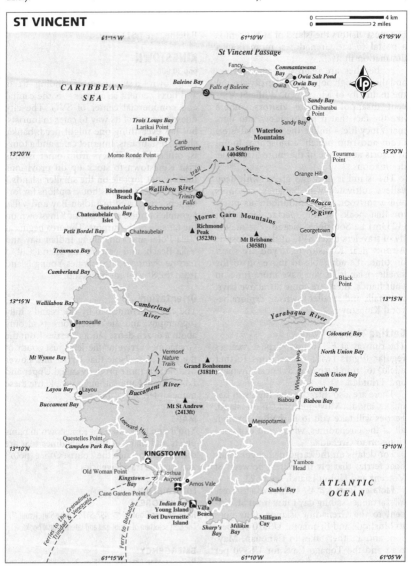

ST VINCENT

decompression sickness from diving you will be sent to the Queen Elizabeth Hospital in Bridgetown, Barbados (p630).

MONEY
All the following banks have 24-hour ATMs.

Barclays Bank (☎ 456-1706; Halifax St; 8am-3pm Mon-Thu, 8am-5pm Fri) Opposite the LIAT office.

National Commercial Bank (☎ 457-1844; cnr Bedford & Grenville Sts; 8am-3pm Mon-Thu, 8am-5pm Fri)

Scotiabank (☎ 457-1601; Halifax St; 8am-2pm Mon-Thu, 8am-5pm Fri)

POST
General post office (☎ 456-1111; Halifax St; 8:30am-3pm Mon-Fri, 8:30-11:30am Sat) Also offers telephone service.

TELEPHONE & FAX
Cable & Wireless (☎ 457-1901; Halifax St; 7am-7pm Mon-Sat, 8-10am & 6-8pm Sun)

TOURIST INFORMATION
Tourist Office (☎ 457-1502; www.svgtourism.com; Cruise Ship Terminal; 8am-noon & 1-4:15pm Mon-Fri)

TRAVEL AGENCIES
Fantasea Tours (☎ 457-4477; www.fantaseatours .com; Villa; 9am-5pm) A one-stop shop for all travel needs; inbound, outbound and all around the islands.

Sights & Activities
FORTRESSES
Just offshore from Villa is a blunt rocky column that protrudes some 250ft (76m) out of the sea. At the top is **Fort Duvernette Island** (24hr), which was originally commissioned to defend against Napoleon's navy. Hike up the crumbling steps to the old fort's cannons and a gorgeous view of the Grenadines. Take extreme care on the crumbling lower reaches of the climb and don't mess with it at night.

Fort Charlotte (daylight hours), on a 660ft (201m) ridge north of the city, provides a panoramic view of Kingstown and the Grenadines to the south.

The fort, named after King George III's wife, was built in 1806 to fend off the French navy, and in its prime housed 600 troops and 34 cannons. Public buses can drop you off nearby on the main road, from where it's a 10-minute uphill walk – ask at the bus station.

> **BREADFRUIT BOUNTY**
>
> Near the St Vincent Botanic Gardens is a breadfruit tree that was grown from one of the original saplings brought to St Vincent from Tahiti in 1793 by Captain William Bligh. The gardens were the original destination of Bligh and the *Bounty* when the famous mutiny occurred in 1789. It was not until Bligh's second voyage that he managed to complete his mission of bringing breadfruit as a source of cheap food for the slave population.

BOTANIC GARDENS
The **St Vincent Botanic Gardens** (☎ 457-1003; Montrose; 6am-6pm) are the oldest botanical gardens in the western hemisphere. Lovingly tended, they are an oasis of calm amid the frenzy of Kingstown. Originally established in 1762 to propagate spices and medicinal plants, the gardens now comprise a neatly landscaped 20-acre (8-hectare) park with lots of flowering bushes and tall trees. There's a small **aviary** that is intermittently home to some of the island's remaining 500 endangered St Vincent parrots. Guided tours are available for US$2 per person.

BEACHES
Indian Bay Beach and **Villa Beach** are mediocre by Caribbean standards. There's decent snorkeling just offshore, however, and any water taxi will take you out for a negotiated low fee (around EC$20).

Festivals & Events
The big event on St Vincent is the carnival **Vincy Mas**, which takes place at the end of June or early July. The calypso and soca competitions culminate in a street party in Kingstown with steel bands, dancers and drinks. For more festivals and events, see p621.

Sleeping
Very few people stay in central Kingstown, instead preferring to spend the night in the city's suburbs of Indian Bay and Villa. It is a good idea to stay near the airport in Arnos Vale if you have to catch a particularly early flight, or in central Kingstown if you are leaving early on a boat, although the accommodations are usually of lesser quality.

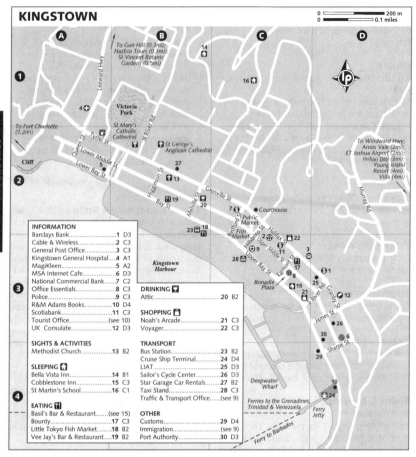

KINGSTOWN

BUDGET

Skyblue Apartments (☎ 457-4394; skyblue@caribsurf .com; Indian Bay; s/d US$55/65; ⊠) Nothing exciting in terms of ambience, but good value, with eight large apartments, each with kitchen and cable TV. A short walk from Villa Beach and popular with long-term guests, including a few American medical students.

Bella Vista Inn (☎ 457-2757; s/d US$45/75) This guesthouse in a private residence has a simple charm. Most rooms have two single beds and upright fans, and some have a private bath. It's a 10-minute walk from the city center; take the steep footpath leading uphill opposite St Martin's School.

Adam's Apartments (☎ 458-4656; abel@caribsurf .com; Arnos Vale; s/d from US$25/30) Adam's is across

the parking lot from the airport and has the lowest rates around, but only stay here if you are on a tight budget and/or need to catch a very early flight.

MIDRANGE

Cobblestone Inn (☎ 456-1937; www.thecobblestone inn.com; Upper Bay St; d/tr US$65/75; ⊠ 🖳) An atmospheric hotel in a renovated 1814 Georgian-style cobblestone warehouse. It has old-world character, wooden floors and cobblestone walls. It's popular with business travelers, and the well-liked Basil's Bar & Restaurant (opposite) is located below.

Beachcombers Hotel (☎ 458-4283; www.beach combershotel.com; Villa; s US$65-125, d US$90-150, incl continental breakfast; 🖳 🖭) On the west side of

Villa Beach, this is a friendly family-run operation. Its dozen rooms vary in size and decor, but the price is right for the beach-side location.

TOP END

Young Island Resort (☎ 458-4826, in USA 800-223-1108; www.youngisland.com; Young Island; d incl meals US$485-745; 🖳 🖳) Once the residence of a Carib chief, Young Island, just 200yd (185m) off Villa Beach, is now an upscale resort. Pleasant stone cottages open to surrounding gardens, and some have private pools. The beach is a relaxed and well-manicured stretch of sand, with full service from the hotel.

Villa Lodge Hotel (☎ 458-4641; villalodge@caribsurf.com; Indian Bay; s/d/tr from US$110/125/140; 🖳 🖳) Popular with visiting Caribbean politicians and business travelers, Villa Lodge offers excellent value for a top-end hotel. There are 10 attractive rooms with all the amenities; rooms seven through 10 have splendid views. There are lush gardens, and the staff are friendly.

Eating & Drinking

BUDGET

Bounty (☎ 456-1776; Egmont St; meals from EC$10) Run by a Canadian couple, this friendly 2nd-floor place, with a balcony view overlooking the street, serves affordable local fare, including rotis, macaroni cheese pie, and fish or chicken with chips.

Vee Jay's Bar & Restaurant (☎ 457-2845; Lower Bay St; 🕑 until late) This is a good local place for West Indian food and frosty Hairoun beers. Sports are televised, and there is karaoke on the rooftop on every Wednesday and Friday. There are three other Vee Jay's, including one by airport.

MIDRANGE

Slick's (☎ 457-5783; Villa; mains from EC$30) This highly recommended Creole and seafood restaurant/bar has a pleasant atmosphere, with terrific service. It also offers a range of West Indian, Italian and French fare, and there's a respectable wine list. Main courses include lobster, shrimp and steak dishes. There's a small play area for children.

Basil's Bar & Restaurant (☎ 457-2713; Upper Bay St; mains from EC$30) If you aren't insanely wealthy enough to hang out in Mustique and party at the original Basil's, you can visit this St Vincent sibling. Serious business types meet here to make deals over a mix of international and West Indian dishes. The weekday lunch buffet (noon to 2pm) is popular.

Lime 'n' Pub (☎ 458-4227; Villa; pub food from EC$25, mains from EC$40) Near Young Island Cut, this easygoing bar serves inexpensive pub food – bangers and chips, flying fish and salad – and also has a more upmarket restaurant with an à la carte menu that specializes in West Indian seafood dishes. There's an extensive wine list.

Attic (☎ 457-2559; Melville St; cover EC$10-15; 🕑 5pm-late) A chilled 2nd-floor club in an old stone building, the Attic has live jazz a few nights a week and sometimes soca bands on Saturday.

TOP END

French Restaurant (☎ 458-4972; Villa Beach; mains from US$18) Regarded as the best restaurant in St Vincent, French food and seafood with a West Indian accent is served here. There are lunchtime sandwiches, and simple fish and chicken dishes. In the evening starters include a superb onion soup, and mains include seafood and beef dishes.

Young Island Resort (lunch EC$60, dinner EC$120; 🕑 lunch 11am-2pm, dinner 7:30-9:30pm) This fancy resort (left) serves lunches and a succulent five-course dinner with more West Indian and Continental choices than you can imagine. All meals are open to nonguests, but reservations are required. Collared shirts and pants are obligatory for dinner.

Shopping

Noah's Arcade (☎ 456-1513; Upper Bay St) Noah's is an excellent little arts-and-crafts shop that sells everything from cheap souvenirs to local art, books, maps, oil-drum art, gourmet coffee and spices, and West Indian dolls.

Voyager (☎ 456-1686; Halifax St) This modern duty-free store stocks the standard range of cosmetics and jewelry, as well as a vast range of trashy souvenirs.

Getting There & Away

Kingstown is the transportation hub of SVG. If you arrive in St Vincent by boat, you will disembark in Kingstown; if you arrive by plane, you will land in the nearby suburb of Arnos Vale. There are numerous boats and airlines that service St Vincent (see p623).

For boats to Bequia, see opposite.

The Cruise Ship Terminal at the south end of Kingstown Harbour receives international cruise ships and has tourist facilities, including information and shops.

The bus station is near the Little Tokyo Fish Market on Bay St, although buses can also be hailed along the road. For details of travel to other parts of St Vincent, see the appropriate sections following.

Getting Around

There are an abundance of taxis and minivan buses to shuttle you around town, but it is easy to walk around Kingstown, which is surprisingly small. A taxi from the airport in Arnos Vale to Kingstown costs EC$20.

WINDWARD HIGHWAY

The windward (east) coast of St Vincent is raw and jagged, with Atlantic surf lashing its shoreline. The Windward Hwy runs up and down the coast, passing black-sand beaches, banana plantations and deep valleys thickly planted with coconut trees. Small villages of rickety wooden houses and simple cement rooms intermittently appear along the roadside.

Buses from Kingstown to Georgetown are fairly regular (except on Sunday) and cost EC$5. Buses driving north from Georgetown are irregular, so get information from the Kingstown bus station before heading off.

La Soufrière & Beyond

Heading north, the land becomes more rugged and less developed. The active volcano of La Soufrière looms overhead, giving the forested region a primeval feel. A mile (1.6km) north of Georgetown, the road goes over the **Rabacca Dry River**, a one-time stream that is now a hardened lava flow after filling with lava during La Soufrière's violent 1902 eruption.

North of the dry river a 4WD road heads inland, through coconut and banana plantations, toward the volcano and the beginning of the 3.25 mile (5km) **hiking trail** to La Soufrière's crater. The route passes through banana estates and rainforest, up past the tree line to the volcano's barren summit, where, weather permitting, hikers are rewarded with views down into the crater lake and out over St Vincent. The

easiest access is from the island's east side, but even that is a strenuous 7-mile (11km) round-trip hike. As the trailhead is 1.5 miles (2km) west of the Windward Hwy and the nearest bus stop, the easiest way to do the hike is to join a tour (see p622). Most who do the hike go with a group from Kingstown, or just negotiate a trip with a taxi driver (prices vary, but are usually over US$100 from Kingstown).

Continuing north you will hit **Sandy Bay**, a sizable village that has the island's largest concentration of Black Caribs. North of Sandy Bay is Owia Bay and the village of **Owia**, where you'll find the **Salt Pond**, tidal pools protected from the crashing Atlantic by a massive stone shield. This is a popular swimming hole with crystal-clear waters and a view of St Lucia to the north. There are thatched shelters, picnic tables and restrooms here.

LEEWARD HIGHWAY

The Leeward Highway runs north of Kingstown along St Vincent's west coast for 25 miles (40km), ending at Richmond Beach. Offering some lovely scenery, the road climbs into the mountains as it leaves Kingstown, and then winds through the hillside and back down to deeply cut coastal valleys that open to coconut plantations, fishing villages and bays lined with black-sand beaches.

About a 15-minute drive north of Kingstown is a sign along the Leeward Highway, pointing east to the **Vermont Nature Trails**, 3.5 miles (5.5km) inland. Here you'll find the Parrot Lookout Trail, a 1.75-mile (2.8km) loop trail (two hours) that passes through the southwestern tip of the **St Vincent Parrot Reserve**.

The drive from Kingstown all the way to the gorgeous black-sand **Richmond Beach** takes about 1½ hours. There are fairly frequent weekday buses from Kingstown to Barrouallie (EC$4, 45 minutes). From there it is a 15-minute walk to Wallilabou Bay, and about four buses per day continue north to Richmond.

Wallilabou Bay & Falls

Port Royal, the town in the beginning of the Hollywood blockbuster *Pirates of the Caribbean – The Curse of the Black Pearl*, was filmed here in Wallilabou (with a few computer-generated additions). Part of the sequel was filmed here too. Wallilabou is a calm bay, lined with a black-sand beach and surrounded by high cliffs and a rock arch at its northern end.

Wallilabou Falls are near the inland side of the main road, about a mile (1.6km) north of Wallilabou Bay. Although only 13ft (4m) high, the falls are beautiful and drop into a waist-deep bathing pool.

Wallilabou Anchorage (☎ 458-7270; wallanch@ caribsurf.com; PO Box 851, Wallilabou) runs the mooring facilities, and has a pleasant bayside restaurant and bar. Adjacent to the restaurant is its small **hotel** (r from US$50), with seafront accommodations.

Falls of Baleine

The 60ft (18m) Falls of Baleine, at the isolated northwestern tip of the island, are accessible only by boat. These scenic falls, which cascade down a fern-draped rock face into a wide pool, are a few minutes' walk from the beach where the boats anchor.

Most tour operators charge around US$50 for the day tour and require at least three people to make the trip. **Sea Breeze Nature Tours** (☎ 458-4969) has both a 36ft (11m) sloop and a powerboat. It charges US$40 per person.

BEQUIA

pop 5000

Bequia (beck-way) arguably has the most to offer of any island in SVG, from beaches to nightlife, fine restaurants, diving, shopping, local charm and art. This northernmost and most populous of the Grenadines boasts all of these activities without losing its small and intimate feel. While Bequia doesn't have many options for budget travelers, it is still more reasonable than its sibling islands.

Although the island is only 7 sq miles (18 sq km) in size, there are a number of areas to visit outside of the main town of Port Elizabeth, including more remote bays and beaches on the far side of the island. Bequia is an easy ferry trip from St Vincent, and its Admiralty Bay is packed with visiting yachters from all over the world.

Getting There & Away

AIR

Bequia's airport is near Paget Farm, at the southwest end of the island, and is served

by LIAT, Mustique Air, SVG Air and TIA. For details, see p623.

SEA

Ferry

The **Bequia Express** (☎ 458-3472; bequiaexpress@ caribsurf.com) ferry between Bequia and St Vincent is cheaper than flying and is much more convenient.

The docks are located in the center of Port Elizabeth. The ferries are generally punctual and serve basic food and drink, and the crossing takes only one hour. Tickets are sold upon entry; the fare is EC$15/25 one way/round-trip.

Boats leave Bequia at 6:30am, 8:30am, 2pm and 4:30pm Monday to Friday; at 6:30am, 10:15am and 5pm Saturday; and at 7:30am and 5pm Sunday. Departures from St Vincent are at 9:30am, 11:30am, 4:30pm and 7pm Monday to Friday; 9am, 12:30pm and 7pm Saturday; and 9am and 7pm Sunday.

Tours

A handful of boats offer cruises through the Grenadines. You can usually find a few options posted on the notice board at Mac's Pizzeria, the tourist office and the bigger hotels. Sailing schedules are usually a bit flexible, and boats generally don't sail if there aren't enough passengers to make it worthwhile.

The 80ft (24m) **Friendship Rose** (☎ 458-3202; ⏰ 8am-5pm) is a Bequian-built wooden schooner that once served as the mail boat between Bequia and St Vincent. The schedule varies, but each week there are typically day trips from Bequia to Mustique for US$70, and others to Canouan or the Tobago Cays for US$90. Tours vary in length from 8½ to 11 hours.

The 60ft (18m) catamaran **Passion** (☎ 458-3884; passion.bequia.net; ⏰ variable Tue-Fri & Sun) covers most of the popular spots in the Grenadines on its different day trips (which vary from day to day). It can carry up to 45 people and tours cost US$60 to $75 per person, depending on the trip.

Yacht

Port Elizabeth is a port of entry for SVG. Customs and immigration, opposite the ferry dock, are open 9am to 3pm. There are a couple of well-stocked supply stores in Port

Elizabeth, and water, fuel, bottled gas, ice and nautical charts are readily available.

Getting Around

As the island is small, many places are accessible on foot from Port Elizabeth. Everything else is a quick trip by bus, taxi or other motorized transportation.

BUS

Port Elizabeth is full of 'dollar cabs,' which are shared taxis that will take you on short trips for EC$1 and longer trips for EC$2. The busiest route is from Port Elizabeth to Paget Sound. They sometimes get crowded, so they're not the best option if you're carrying luggage.

CAR, MOTORCYCLE & BICYCLE

Opposite the waterfront in Port Elizabeth, **Handy Andy's** (☎ 458-3722) rents out mountain bikes (per day US$18), motor scooters (US$25), Honda 250cc motorcycles (US$55) and Jeep Wranglers (US$75).

TAXI

Taxis commonly come in the form of open-air pickup trucks with bench-type seats in the back. Taxis charge set fees, and are generally distinguished from dollar cabs by a 'taxi service' sign.

From Port Elizabeth it costs EC$18 to Lower Bay or Friendship Bay, and EC$30 to the airport. Taxis meet flights at the airport and there is a glut of them near the docks in Port Elizabeth.

PORT ELIZABETH

pop 2500

Port Elizabeth, built along the curve of Admiralty Bay, is an appealing seaside community with a busy port (by Grenadines' standards), and a number of grocery stores and other places to shop.

The town has an international flavor, and many restaurants and shops are operated by expats – mostly yachters who can't bear to leave.

Orientation

A narrow sidewalk along the shoreline at the south side of Port Elizabeth – known as the Belmont Walkway – provides the main access to many of the town's restaurants and accommodations.

Information

BOOKSTORES

Bequia Bookshop (☎ 458-3905; Front St; 🕙 8:30am-5pm Mon-Fri, 8:30am-12:30pm Sat & Sun) The best bookstore in the Grenadines stocks everything from charts and survey maps to yachting books, flora and fauna guides, and West Indian, North American and European literature.

INTERNET ACCESS

Lenroc (☎ 457-3440; www.lenroc.com; per hr EC$20; 🕙 9am-noon & 1-9pm Mon-Fri) Located below Julie's Guesthouse on Front St, and there are discounts for the guesthouse's guests. It also has the best rates on the island for calling cards (per minute EC$1 to most countries).
Surf 'n' Send (☎ 458-3577; www.surfnsend.com; Belmont Walkway; per hr EC$15; 🕙 8:30am-6pm Mon-Fri, 8:30am-2pm Sat) Located under the Gingerbread Restaurant. Worth the rate just to enjoy the powerful air-con.

LAUNDRY

Guesthouses and hotels that don't do laundry onsite can recommend locals that will do it for a negotiated fee.
Lighthouse Yacht Services (☎ 457-3187; per load EC$20) Behind St Mary's Cathedral.

MONEY

The following banks have a 24-hour ATM:
National Commercial Bank (☎ 458-3700; Front St; 🕙 8am-1pm Mon-Thu, 8am-1pm & 3-5pm Fri)
RBTT (☎ 458-3845; Front St; 🕙 8am-2pm Mon-Thu, 8am-5pm Friday)

POST

Port Elizabeth post office (☎ 458-3350; 🕙 9am-noon & 1-3pm Mon-Fri, 9-11:30am Sat) Opposite the ferry dock on Front St.

TELEPHONE

Coin and card phones are located in front of the post office on Front St.

TOURIST INFORMATION

Bequia Tourism Association (☎ 458-3286; www.bequiatourism.com; 🕙 9am-noon & 1:30-4pm Mon-Fri, 9am-noon Sat) Located in the small building on the ferry dock, this place has a number of flyers and tourist material about Bequia, helpful staff and maintains a good website.

Dangers & Annoyances

Beware of manchineel trees around Lower Bay Beach as they can cause a rash. There are reports of a rare scorpion around the island – check inside your shoes before putting them on.

Sights & Activities
BEACHES
The nicest beach in the Port Elizabeth area, **Princess Margaret Beach**, is a secluded swath of golden sand surrounded by bushland. To get there, take the shoreline walkway to its end, and then the dirt path that climbs over Princess Point and down to the beach, some 10 minutes' walk away.

Friendship Bay is a deep, beautiful bay with a long golden-sand beach, a few minutes' walk from the Port Elizabeth–Paget Farm road.

Petit Nevis is an uninhabited island that lies about a mile (1.6km) south of Friendship Bay. It's the site of a deserted whaling station and old whalebones still lie about. The island has good snorkeling and water taxis can be arranged through hotels at Friendship Bay or on the beach.

Hope Bay is another of the island's top beaches.

DIVING
There are some fantastic diving sites right along the edges of Admiralty Bay and at other points around the island. There are two excellent dive shops in Port Elizabeth (see p620) and others run by hotels in Friendship Bay.

Sleeping
BUDGET
Julie's Guesthouse (☎ 458-3304; fax 458-3812; julies @caribsurf.com; Front St; front r with breakfast EC$90) The old wooden boarding house out back is less expensive, but the newer rooms on the main street are still well worth the price, and have hot water and good ceiling fans. The veranda is a tranquil spot to observe the action at the port below and get a feel for the workings of Port Elizabeth. The family that owns the place is friendly and helpful, and can cook quite a Caribbean meal.

L'Auberge des Grenadines (☎ 458-3201; www .caribrestaurant.com; d US$40-60) This delightful guesthouse, right on the water, has good budget rooms and also houses a quality restaurant (run by the former owner of St Vincent's chic French Restaurant), with excellent lobster dishes.

MIDRANGE
Frangipani Hotel (☎ 458-3255; www.frangipanibequia .com; Belmont Walkway; s US$130-150, d US$150-175, s/d with shared bath US$40/55) Owned by the family of the former prime minister James Mitchell, who was born here in room No 1, Frangipani was converted into an inn and is now one of the most well-known spots on the island. The 2nd floor of the wooden-shingled house has pleasantly simple rooms. Out back are the modern garden units, with stone walls and harbor-view sundecks. The restaurant and bar are popular in the evening.

Gingerbread Apartments (☎ 458-3800; www.gin gerbreadhotel.com; Belmont Walkway; d US$110-185) This ornate hotel in the middle of the action has nine rooms, six of which are fancier suites with four-poster beds, kitchens, covered terraces and dining areas. It has a good restaurant, a café and an onsite travel agency.

SCRIMSHAW

In the days of sailing ships and wooden harpoons, hunting whales took time – lots and lots of time. While sitting aboard the whaling boats in search of their elusive prey, men did all sorts of things to pass the hours. Most of these things were best left onboard, but the art of scrimshaw – fine, razor-thin etching into whale ivory (bone and teeth) – is a pastime that has endured. It was President John F Kennedy, an enthusiastic collector, who actually brought scrimshaw into mainstream culture.

Sam McDowell, generally regarded as the world's best scrimhander, lives and works in Bequia. Rumored to have taught art at Princeton University, he was introduced to scrimshaw by JFK himself in 1955. He has revitalized the art form on the island and is passing it along to future generations.

These days it is not particularly couth to kill a whale, even for the sake of art. Therefore scrimhanders work with pre-embargo ivory (ivory purchased prior to whaling bans), hippo ivory (supposedly taken from legal hippo kills), fossilized ivory (ivory found in the ground, often belonging to ancient walruses and mastodons) or nonivory alternatives, including camel bones, deer antlers, nut palms and micarta plastic.

Sam's **Banana Patch Studio** (☎ 458-3865; Paget Farm) is open by appointment.

TOP END

Spring on Bequia (☎ 458-3414; www.springonbequia
.com; s US$100-175, d US$130-220; ❄ closed Jun-Nov; ⚡)
This inn is a family-run affair situated in a
plantation over 225-years-old. Overlooking
Port Elizabeth, the buildings are made of
hand-cut stone and receive a cooling wind
that rises up from the sea. The view is unbeatable, and the gardens still grow tropical
fruits and delicious vegetables. This place is
incredibly tranquil, yet only minutes' walk
up the hill from Port Elizabeth.

Eating & Drinking

Frangipani Restaurant & Bar (☎ 458-3255; Belmont
Walkway; lunch EC$12-30, dinner from EC$35; ❄ 7:30am-
9pm) This popular seaside bar-restaurant offers sandwiches, burgers, salads, omelettes
and fresh fish dishes until 5pm, and then
seafood and West Indian fare is served at
dinner. There's live music on Thursday and
occasionally on other nights. This place can
really jump – by Grenadines standards.

Green Boley (☎ 457-3625; Belmont Walkway; boneless chicken roti EC$8, chicken dinner EC$20) This tiny
bar-restaurant has a casual Bequian feel to
it, although it's smack in the middle of a
strip of touristy restaurants. A good place to
grab a drink and mix with locals, it serves
inexpensive rotis and callaloo soup, along
with full dinners of chicken or fish.

Gingerbread Restaurant (☎ 458-3800; lunch EC$12-
25, dinner from EC$35; ❄ 8am-9:30pm) This 2nd-floor
restaurant is a popular dining spot, with
high ceilings, gingerbread trim and a fine
harbor view. At lunch it serves sandwiches,
omelettes and pasta dishes. Dinner features
international and West Indian food with a
seafood slant. There's live music on Sunday
evening.

Gingerbread Cafe (❄ 7:30am-6:30pm) At the
south side of Gingerbread Restaurant, this
café serves cake, ice cream, coffee, iced coffee
(which is rare in the Grenadines) and cappuccino. The staff is supremely friendly.

Mac's Pizzeria (☎ 458-3474; Belmont Walkway;
sandwiches from EC$12, pizza EC$24-80; ❄ 11am-10pm)
Mac's is a venerable pizzeria, with porch-
side dining overlooking Admiralty Bay. It
has pizza, whole-wheat or pita-bread sandwiches, quiches and pasta dishes.

Shopping

Several artisans sell the model boats for
which Bequia is famous. The island is also

known for scrimshaw (see p613). There is a
souvenir market at the port, where you can
buy T-shirts, handmade dolls, jewelry and
other islands crafts (hours vary).

Sargeant Brothers (☎ 458-43312; Front St) This
is one of the better-known studios to shop
for Bequian model boats. You can even
order a replica of your own boat for a negotiated price.

Mauvin (☎ 458-3344; Front St) This is a top
choice to look for model boats, selling in
the US$50 range.

Bequia Market (❄ vegetable market 7am-6pm Mon-
Sat, 7am-4pm Sun) The area along the shoreline,
near the fisherman's wharf houses, not only
the vegetable market, but the fish market
also (hours are not fixed, but they blow a
conch-shell horn when there is fresh fish for
sale). Market boutiques surround a small
courtyard on the beach, where you can sit
on benches under the almond trees, have a
drink and gaze out to sea.

The Bequia Bookshop (p612) stocks a
fine selection of locally made scrimshaw
pieces for sale.

LOWER BAY

pop 500

Lower Bay is a little beachside community
at the southern end of Admiralty Bay. It's
fronted by a delightful golden-sand beach
and clear turquoise water. It's more low key
than Port Elizabeth (not that Port Elizabeth is exactly wild), and has a few guesthouses.

It is a clearly marked out 10-minute walk
from the Lower Bay bus stop on the Port
Elizabeth–Paget Farm road, or you can take
the footpath over from Princess Margaret
Beach.

Sleeping & Eating

Keegan's (☎ 458-3530; keegansbequia@yahoo.com;
Lower Bay; d without meals US$50-60, d incl breakfast &
dinner US$80-90; ⚡) Right across from Lower
Bay Beach, Keegan's has attractive rooms –
Nos 8 and 9 are particularly nice – with
good views. It's a comfortable place and is
not only closer to the beach, but less expensive than similar options in Port Elizabeth.
Dinner is by reservation only and usually
features fresh seafood.

Fernando's Hideaway (☎ 458-3758; dinner from
EC$60; ❄ 6pm-late) In the village center, this
local spot serves very good West Indian

food. The owner, Fernando, also catches much of the fresh fish that is served here. Reservations are advised.

FRIENDSHIP BAY
On the south side of the island, this attractive bay is one of the more sedate parts of Bequia that has hotels and restaurants.

Sleeping & Eating
Blue Tropic Hotel (☎ 458-3573; www.bluetropic.de; s/d with breakfast US$55/75) On the main road just above Friendship Bay, Blue Tropic is the more affordable option on this side of the island. It has 10 clean, modern rooms with kitchenettes, as well as a good restaurant. It can also help to arrange diving trips with the island's dive shops.

Friendship Bay Hotel (☎ 458-3222; www.friend shipbayhotel.com; s US$125-375, d US$165-375) A pleasant Swedish-run beachfront hotel decked out with all sorts of bright Caribbean artwork. The hotel has a tennis court, a dive shop, a jetty, a restaurant with a splendid view, and a beach bar.

MUSTIQUE

pop 3000
Mustique, the Rolls-Royce of the Grenadines, is a privately owned island that has been developed into an exclusive haven for the rich and famous. This well-manicured retreat is only 5 miles (8km) long. Most of its residents work in tourism.

Colin Tennant (now Lord Glenconnor), an eccentric Scotsman, purchased the island in 1958 to turn it into a destination for his aristocratic friends. Today there are over 70 privately owned villas on the island belonging to people of wealth and fame, like Mick Jagger, David Bowie and Tommy Hilfiger.

The island is managed by the Mustique Company, which is responsible for everything from operating the medical clinic and desalination plant to providing accommodations for the Britannia Bay fishermen who still live on Mustique. It is supposedly the largest single employer in SVG, after the government.

The island has an irregular coastline richly indented with bays and coves, most of which harbor fine, sandy beaches. There's good swimming and snorkeling along the west coast, including at Britannia Bay. There are no towns on the island, but the Mustique Company, opposite the airport terminal, can arrange anything you need – so long as you can afford it.

Sleeping
Firefly Mustique (☎ 488-8414; www.mustiquefirefly .com; r incl meals & transportation US$725-825;) Set on a steep cliffside overlooking Britannia Bay, each of the four supremely well-appointed rooms has a private bath, ocean view and unique styling. Although it is pricey, Firefly is not stuffy and is a popular hangout in the evenings. It's a first-rate option for a honeymoon, and has special weekly rates.

Mustique Company (☎ 448-8000, in USA 212-758-8800, in UK 0162-858-3517; www.mustique-island. com; villas for 7 night minimum US$8000-35,000) The Mustique Company, which owns and manages the island, can arrange weekly or seasonal rentals of privately owned villas. The size, decor and amenities vary, but each comes with a cook/housekeeper and transportation, and most have a pool. Yes, you could send your kid to university for a year for the same price, but hey, you're in Mustique.

Eating & Drinking
Basil's Bar & Restaurant (☎ 488-8350; www.basilsbar .com; dinner from EC$70; 9am-late) Famous Basil's is a delightful open-air thatch-and-bamboo restaurant that extends out into Britannia Bay, and is the place to eat, drink and meet up with others in Mustique. On Wednesday night it has a lively jump-up with a steel band and barbecue buffet for EC$75. The bar also hosts the Mustique Blues Festival in late January each year.

You can pick up groceries at the general store near Basil's.

Getting There & Away
Mustique's airport is served by Mustique Airways, SVG Air and TIA. For details, see p623. Britannia Bay is Mustique's port of entry and the only suitable anchorage for visiting yachts; immigration and customs can be cleared at the airport. It is also possible to hop on one of the tour ships from Bequia (see p611) to get to the other Grenadines.

CANOUAN

pop 1250

Canouan (cahn-oo-ahn), midway through the Grenadine chain, was until recently the least developed of the larger islands. During the mid-1990s there was a messy scheme by an Italian business group, Carenage, to construct a mega-resort on the north end of the island. Friction over the privatization of the beaches led to the posting of Israeli mercenaries to keep Canouanians out. The project underwent some changes and was reopened in 2004 as Raffles Resort Canouan Island, with private beaches, an 18-hole golf course, luxury villas, four restaurants and a Donald Trump–managed casino.

Although there is the obvious benefit of employment from the resort, Carenage little more for the local population. During the dry season, as the resort's sprinkler system battles to keep the golf course green, locals are hard-pressed to get fresh drinking water. Thankfully there are a few other places to stay on this long, hook-shaped island.

Canouan's main attractions are its lovely, lengthy beaches, several of which are reef-protected and good for swimming, snorkeling and diving. The main anchorage is in Grand Bay, where the jetty is located, while the airport is about a mile (1.6km) to the west.

Sleeping & Eating

Ocean View Inn (☎ 482-0477; www.oceanview-can.com; Charlestown Bay; s/d from US$105/125; ✿) This is one of the places on the island that keeps the local flavor going. It's clean and simple, with friendly management and prices that are unbeatable value on Canouan.

Casa del Mar (☎ 482-0639, in the US 510-658-3203; www.adonalfoyle.com/afe_casa_del_mar.shtml; ste US$250-600, deals for longer rentals) Owned by the 6ft 10in (207cm) Canouanian Adonal Foyle (aspiring poet, democracy activist and NBA star for the Golden State Warriors), this classy villa has five luxurious and comfortable suites. The recently constructed two-story building is close to the sea, and has a patio with a bar and great views.

Hill Top Restaurant & Bar (☎ 458-8264; meals from EC$40) This well-known restaurant is family-owned and -run. It serves West Indian seafood and other dishes, including tasty vegetarian options, and has a good variety of wines. It will also deliver full meals to hotels and yachts.

Pompey's Restaurant & Bar (☎ 482-0037; Retreat Village; meals from EC$30) This island standout specializes in cakes and West Indian favorites. Reservations are recommended.

Getting There & Away

The airport is served by Mustique Airways, SVG Air, TIA and LIAT. For international flight links to Canouan and interisland air travel, see p623. The mail boat and some ferries from St Vincent connect Canouan with the other Grenadine islands (see p623).

MAYREAU

pop 500

Mayreau is a smallish, lightly populated island west of the Tobago Cays. There's no airport and only a couple of roads, which run from the dock at Saline Bay through the island's sole village and over to Saltwhistle Bay. The town is supremely relaxed, with a few restaurants, nice views and not much else. The pace of the island picks up considerably when cruise ships are in dock, but quickly returns to normal once they leave. The stone church, at the top of the hill above town, has stunning views of the Tobago Cays.

Saltwhistle Bay is protected by a long, narrow arm of sand, which at its thinnest is just a few yards wide. Saltwhistle, which appears on postcards sold throughout the Grenadines, has calm clear waters, beautiful white sands and a protected anchorage for visiting yachts. Closer to town, Saline Bay also has a decent beach, which sometimes hosts barbecues and parties from passing ships.

Sleeping

There are only two hotels on the island, but it is also possible to rent a room or a house, sometimes for a better nightly rate. Ask around at restaurants such as Robert Righteous & De Youths (opposite).

Dennis' Hideaway (☎ 458-8594; www.dennis-hideaway.com; d US$65) The original and only locally owned hotel on Mayreau, Dennis' still gets a stream of career yachtsmen and Caribbean characters. It has five large, clean and basic rooms, some with high ceilings and all with ocean-view balconies. Dennis, a former yacht captain himself, now spends part of the year in the UK, but appears from time to time to serenade you with a CD of his soca band. The hotel has a very good, albeit pricey, restaurant on the 3rd-floor terrace.

Saltwhistle Bay Club (☎ 458-8444; www.saltwhistle bay.com; s/d incl breakfast & dinner US$390/540; ⊙ closed Sep & Oct) German-owned, this tasteful minimalist-style beachside resort has spacious bunga-lows. The rooms vary, but all have ceiling fans, patios and king-size beds. Guests get picked up at the airport in Union Island and shuttled by boat to Mayreau.

Eating

Combination Café (fish sandwich EC$18) A casual two-story spot right on the edge of town, this bar-restaurant has friendly manage-ment, an excellent fish sandwich called the 'Beachcomber' and a good variety of other local dishes. It's a good place to meet and converse with locals, and it also has Internet access (per hour EC$20). The views from the upstairs bar are not impeded by electric-al wires like most outlooks from town.

Bushman (☎ 527-8357, ask for Bushman; barbecue US$30) Bushman (a man, not a restaurant) lives down at the west end of Saltwhistle

Bay. With a couple of hours' notice, he can arrange succulent beach barbecues of lob-ster, fish, conch and chicken. It's a much better Caribbean experience than eating at the overpriced Saltwhistle Bay Club right down the beach.

Robert Righteous & De Youths (☎ 458-8203; lunch EC$35-50, dinner EC$45-65) Up the hill in town, this Rastafarian-themed restaurant serves decidedly un-Rastafarian fare, such as pork chops (EC$50) and Long Island Iced Teas (EC$12). The kitchen is slow even by May-reau standards, but the fish dishes are worth the wait. The decor ranges from pictures of Rasta icons Bob Marley and Marcus Garvey to the odd Michael Jordan poster.

Getting There & Away

For information on ferries connecting May-reau with the other Grenadine islands, see p623. When leaving Mayreau talk with the management at Dennis' Hideaway, who can check the variable boat schedule for you.

The **Captain Yannis** (☎ 458-8513; yannis@caribsurf .com; Yacht Club, Union Island) catamaran tours from Union Island can drop passengers off at Mayreau and pick them up the following day for the usual cost of its day tour (EC$150). For details, see p618.

NEW PIRATES OF THE CARIBBEAN

The islands that comprise St Vincent & the Grenadines (SVG) were once the trawling grounds of pirates and rogues. Indeed, it was here in 1717 that Blackbeard made his name by taking the French slave ship *La Concorde* and marooning its crew on Bequia. These days eye patches and swords only belong to buccaneers of the movie sort (*Pirates of the Caribbean: The Curse of the Black Pearl* and its upcoming sequel were filmed in St Vincent and the Tobago Cays). However, SVG is still a smuggler's paradise, complete with a smattering of international fugitives and money launderers. The islands are not a dangerous place – these folks are just part of the mix of ran-dom eccentrics and shady characters that live the laissez-faire lifestyle that has defined SVG.

The remote and dispersed nature of the islands, coupled with a tiny police force, makes law enforcement a difficult task. St Vincent is the Eastern Caribbean's largest producer and ex-porter of marijuana (mainly to Grenada and Barbados), and drug traffickers use the islands as a trans-shipment and storage point for cocaine from South America to North America and Europe. Most of the drugs slip through nonchalantly in small cargo ships, the occasional propeller plane and private yachts (hey, the upkeep on those things gets expensive).

As money and drugs go hand in hand, SVG has had problems with both money launder-ing and unregulated banking. Until 2003 the country was on the Financial Action Task Force's blacklist of states that were not cooperative with efforts to stop money laundering. Since the post–9/11 crackdown on the murky world of offshore banking, its shaped up, and now only deals in regulated and reputable murky offshore banking. The country also allows foreign nationals to purchase citizenship. Thereby, international criminals can use their Vincentian citi-zenship to set up front companies to wash money in SVG and also avoid extradition to certain countries – that is, if anyone finds them here in the first place.

UNION ISLAND

pop 3000

Union Island is the anchor of the Grenadine chain, just a short boat ride from Carriacou, Grenada. Its main town, Clifton, is a tangle of streets and concrete buildings with more energy than any other spot between Kingstown, St Vincent, and St George's, Grenada. Although many tourists pass through Clifton – from the airport to boats traveling to the Tobago Cays or to Palm Island and back – few stay the night.

The transient nature of the visitors has had a strange effect on the town, which can feel built-up and touristy, yet empty and local all at once. Many people from other Grenadines to the north and Carriacou to the south also stop by Union Island to purchase provisions, or drink and dance at the famous Eagle's Nest dancehall on Friday night.

There are a few nice beaches at the northern end of the island, and the town of Ashton, towards the middle of Union, is a calm alternative to Clifton.

Information

Internet Café (☎ 485-8258; youngbuffalo@yahoo .com; Clifton; per hr EC$20; 🕒 8am-4:30pm Mon-Fri, 8am-noon Sun)

National Commercial Bank (🕒 8am-1pm Mon-Thu, 8am-1pm & 3-5pm Fri) Towards the airport. Has a 24-hour ATM.

Union Island Tourist Bureau (☎ 458-8350; 🕒 9am-noon & 1-4pm) In front of the ferry dock.

Sleeping & Eating

Clifton Beach Hotel (☎ 458-8235; Clifton; s/d from US$31/50; 🍽️) This ever-expanding hotel has some 30 rooms and a couple of private cottages. It's an affordable and pleasant choice (when it is not doing construction), with a decent seafood restaurant and bar right on the water. The staff are friendly and helpful.

Anchorage Yacht Club Hotel (☎ 458-8221; d from US$120; 🍽️) Near the airport, this is one of Union's more upmarket options. The comfortable rooms with ocean views are popular with French tourists and visiting sailors. The restaurant is highly regarded, and the bar serves baguette sandwiches, pizza, pastries and croissants at reasonable prices.

Lambi's Guesthouse (☎ 458-8395; Clifton; s/d US$19/28) Above Lambi's restaurant, hardware and grocery store, this guesthouse has a dozen dim rooms. The building is a little dilapidated, but it's a fine budget option if you are just passing through for the night. Lambi, who is usually hanging out in the store, is a jovial guy who can answer most local travel questions.

Olivia's Family Restaurant (☎ 458-8319; Clifton; lunch EC$12-15) A cavernous dancehall, which serves up good, well-priced West Indian lunches during the day and doubles as the Eagle's Nest dancehall at night. It can get pretty raucous on Friday nights, with DJs and bands playing dancehall, reggae and hip-hop.

Getting There & Away

AIR

SVG Air, LIAT, TIA and Mustique Airways have flights to Union Island. For details, see p623 and p623.

SEA

For details on the MV *Barracuda*, which connects Union Island with St Vincent's other main islands, see p623. For details of boat service between Union Island and Carriacou, see p623.

TOURS

Captain Yannis (☎ 458-8513; Yacht Club; yannis@carib surf.com) has three 60ft (18m) sailboats – the catamarans *Cyclone*, *Typhoon* and *Tornado* – which account for most of the daytime sailing business from Union Island. The cruise (EC$150) includes a stop on Palm Island, a few hours in the Tobago Cays for lunch and snorkeling, and an hour on Mayreau before returning to Union in the late afternoon. There's a good buffet lunch, and an open bar of rum punch and beer. The boats leave Clifton around 9am, but schedules are flexible.

YACHT

Midway between the airport and central Clifton, **Anchorage Bay Yacht Club** (☎ 458-8221) has stern-to berths for 15 boats, ice, water, fuel, showers and laundry facilities.

Other popular anchorages are at Chatham Bay, on Union Island's west coast, and the west sides of Frigate Island and Palm Island.

Getting Around

The island is small enough to explore on foot. It's less than 10 minutes' walk from the airport to the center of Clifton, and 30 minutes' walk from Clifton to Ashton. There are a few pickup trucks that serve as buses.

OTHER ISLANDS

TOBAGO CAYS

The Tobago Cays are considered the crown jewels of the Grenadines. They are comprised of five small, deserted islands surrounded by coral reefs and splendidly clear turquoise waters.

The islands, which are rocky and studded with cactus, have tiny coves and beaches of powdery white sand.

The Tobago Cays have been set aside as a national park. Several measures have been taken to protect the area, including the installation of moorings and prohibitions against the taking of marine life. Perhaps the biggest danger to the cays is their popularity, as the water often gets crowded with visiting yachts.

The Tobago Cays offer great snorkeling and diving, especially on Horseshoe Reef. For information on day trips to the cays, see opposite.

PALM ISLAND

Once called Prune Island, the now more attractively titled Palm Island is just a 10-minute boat ride southeast of Clifton, Union Island. It's a small, whale-shaped isle dominated by a private resort. **Casuarina Beach** has long been a popular anchorage with yachters, and is a stopover on many day tours between Union Island and the Tobago Cays.

The very plush **Palm Island Beach Club** (☎ 458-8824, in the US 800-858-4618; www.palmisland resorts.com; s/d/tr from US$620/700/850; ❄ ▣) has 40 bungalows on a 135-acre (55-hectare) property. Rooms are airy, with screened, louvered windows, a ceiling fan and sliding glass doors that open onto a patio. Rates include meals, and use of windsurfing gear and Sunfish boats. The resort also rents a handful of villas and apartments. A convivial beachside bar and restaurant welcomes day-trippers.

PETIT ST VINCENT

In late 2004 *Outside* magazine rated Petit St Vincent (PSV) as one of the best private islands in the world. The southernmost and smallest of the inhabited Grenadines, it's fringed by white-sand beaches, coral reefs and crystalline waters. While not necessarily more attractive than the other islands, it is definitely less visited and more secluded. The island has been developed into a single-resort 'hideaway' destination.

The **Petit St Vincent Resort** (☎ 954-963-7401, in USA 800-654-9326; www.psvresort.com; s & d US$720-910; ▣) is your only accommodations option on PSV. The bungalows have tropical decor and pleasant sundecks. Each cottage has a bamboo flagpole, from which you hoist a colored flag to 'call' room service. The all-inclusive resort is considered one of the best in the Grenadines, although some guests have complained that wine and food items are in short supply, and that the hotel might need a few light repairs. The resort organizes transportation to the island.

DIRECTORY

ACCOMMODATIONS

There are a handful of exclusive resorts in SVG. Most are casual, although some spots on Palm Island and Mustique require collared shirts, pants and shoes at dinner. Hotels of all categories are small-scale operations – few have more than a couple of dozen rooms and you will find no high-rises here. Many hotels have the same rates year-round, although most hike their prices during the popular winter season. The rates listed in this chapter do not include the 7% hotel tax or the 10% service charge that are frequently tacked on to bills (it is always smart to ask ahead about these fees). Prices are in either EC$ or US$, depending on the hotel. Some of the fancier hotels offer discount air vouchers to customers who

> **EMERGENCY NUMBERS**
>
> **Police, Fire, Ambulance, Coast Guard** (☎ 999)
> **Hospital** (St Vincent ☎ 456-1955, Bequia ☎ 458-3794)

PRACTICALITIES

- **Newspapers & Magazines** There are two local weekly newspapers: the *Vincentian* and the *News*. *Cross Country* comes out midweek and the *Herald* is a daily paper that covers international news. You can buy international news magazines at the airport. The *Caribbean Compass* is an excellent monthly paper that covers marine news and travel issues. Two useful (and free) tourist magazines are *Ins and Outs* and the smaller *Life in St Vincent and the Grenadines*.

- **Radio & TV** The one local AM radio station, NBCSVG, broadcasts at 705kHz. Three stations broadcast on the FM band: NICE FM 6.3, HITZ FM107.3 and WE FM99.9. St Vincent has one broadcast TV station, SVGBC, on channel 9, and two local cable TV broadcasters. Additionally, most hotels pick up US cable.

- **Electricity** The electric current is 220V to 240V (50 cycles). British-style three-pin plugs are used.

- **Weights & Measures** Imperial system.

---

stay for a longer period of time (say, a week or more).

There are no campgrounds on SVG, and camping is not encouraged.

ACTIVITIES
Beaches & Swimming
The exceptional white-sand beaches of the Grenadines are some of the best in the world. They are generally uncrowded and uncommercialized, and the waves are weak. For details on specific beaches, see the individual island sections.

Diving
Off virtually all the islands you will find world-class dive sites with 60ft to 80ft (18m to 24m) of visibility, 78° to 82°F (26° to 28°C) water and extensive coral reefs. The sea have black coral, colorful sponges, soft corals, great stands of elkhorn coral, branching gorgonian, a few sunken wrecks, iridescent fish, sea turtles, rays, sharks, eels and other sea life. There's a range of dives

suitable for any level of experience, from calm, shallow dives to wall dives and drift dives. Spearfishing is prohibited.

The going rates are around US$50 for a single dive, US$90 for a two-tank dive and US$60 for a night dive. A 'resort course' for beginners that includes a couple of hours of instruction and a shallow dive is available for around US$70. Dive prices come down considerably for larger packages.

Many dive shops also offer complete certification courses. Dive St Vincent (below), one of the best-regarded shops on the islands, charges US$435, and offers Professional Association of Diving Instructors (PADI), NAUI or CMAS accreditation.

For more on SVG diving, see p56.

DIVE SHOPS
All of the major islands have a dive shop, except for Mayreau (however, Grenadines Dive on Union Island services Mayreau). Dive shops in SVG include the following:
Bequia Dive Adventures (☎ 458-3826; www.bequia diveadventures.com; Belmont, Port Elizabeth, Bequia)
Dive Bequia (☎ 458-3504; www.dive-bequia.com; Belmont, Port Elizabeth, Bequia)
Dive Canouan (☎ 458-8044; www.tamarind.us; Canouan) Located at the Raffles resort.
Dive St Vincent (☎ 457-4714; www.divestvincent.com; Young Island Dock, St Vincent) There is a 5% surcharge for credit-card payments.
Grenadines Dive (☎ 458-8138; www.grenadines dive.com; Clifton, Union Island) The owner, Glenroy, will pick you up on PSV, Palm Island or Mayreau. This is your best choice for diving in the Tobago Cays or surrounding islets.

Hiking
Hiking trails are not well developed on St Vincent, and access to them can be difficult. The most popular walking area is the Vermont Nature Trails (p610), a series of short walking tracks 3.5 miles (5.5km) inland from the Leeward Highway. The most challenging and most rewarding hike in the country is La Soufrière volcano (see p610).

Other Water Sports
The trade winds that blow across the Grenadines create some fine sailing and windsurfing conditions. Many resorts rent or loan (to guests) windsurfing gear, Hobie Cats and Sunfish boats. There are watersports huts on many of the more-developed

tourist beaches that rent similar equipment for widely varying and always negotiable prices.

Most of the dive shops (opposite) also offer snorkeling trips, or simply rent out the gear. Water taxis will also take snorkelers out for the day and are less expensive. However, if you are not a strong and experienced swimmer/snorkeler it is better to stick to the dive shops, as they tend to follow more of the standard precautions.

BOOKS

Although there are a slew of pirate books, SVG is not known for its literature. There are a couple of classic works, like *Ruler in Hiroona* (1972, out of print) by Vincentian GCH Thomas. This darkly humorous and wise tale tells of labor movements and politics as the Eastern Caribbean islands struggled for independence from England. The most famous Vincy poem, considered 'the Caribbean's first epic poem' is 'Hiroona' by Horatio Nelson Huggins. It recounts the Black Carib War against the English in St Vincent at the end of the 18th century. Although it was published in 1937, evidence suggests that it was composed around 1885.

St Vincent appears from time to time in contemporary literature. For example, it is the setting of much of Anthony Doerr's enchanting 2004 novel *About Grace*.

CHILDREN

While there are few accommodations or restaurants in SVG that go out of their way to cater to families with children, some of the more tranquil islands are great for relaxed family time. Most resorts allow children, but you should always check ahead.

EMBASSIES & CONSULATES

St Vincent & the Grenadines Embassies & Consulates

Belgium (☎ 02-513-8724; 24 Ave de la Toison d'Or, 1050 Brussels)
UK (☎ 020-7565-2874; 10 Kensington Ct, London W85DL)
USA (☎ 202-364-6730; 3216 New Mexico Ave NW, Washington, DC 20016)

Embassies & Consulates in St Vincent & the Grenadines

Only the **UK** (☎ 457-1701; Granby St, PO Box 132, Kingstown) has representation in SVG. For the

US and other countries, see the consulate in Barbados, p647.

FESTIVALS & EVENTS

The carnival, called Vincy Mas (supposedly short for St Vincent Masquerade, although there are a few competing theories), is the main cultural event of the year.

Blessing of the Whaleboats (last Sunday in January) On Bequia.
National Heroes' Day (March 14)
Easter Regatta (Bequia) Around Easter, this is SVG's main sailing event.
Easterval (Union Island) Around Easter, a three-day music and costume festival.
May Day (May 1)
Canouan Regatta (May) Five days of sailing and events.
Vincy Mas (end of June or early July) This carnival lasts for 12 days.
Nine Mornings Festival (December) Carolers and steel bands take to the streets, with parties every day from December 16 through Christmas.

GAY & LESBIAN TRAVELERS

If you take a closer listen to the dancehall music that is dominant in this region, you will hear violent, sometimes brutal homophobia in the lyrics.

There is little or no tolerance for male homosexuality – use discretion outside of resort areas.

HOLIDAYS

SVG has the following public holidays:
New Year's Day January 1
St Vincent & the Grenadines Day January 22
Good Friday Late March/early April
Easter Monday Late March/early April
Labour Day First Monday in May
Whit Monday Eighth Monday after Easter
Caricom Day Second Monday in July
Carnival Tuesday Usually second Tuesday in mid-July
Emancipation Day First Monday in August
Independence Day October 27
Christmas Day December 25
Boxing Day December 26

INTERNET ACCESS

All of the populated islands have Internet access, either in cafés or in larger hotels. Connection speeds, computer quality and prices vary from island to island. For more details, see Internet Access in specific island sections.

ST VINCENT & THE GRENADINES

INTERNET RESOURCES

Following are some of the better sites regarding SVG:

www.bequiasweet.com This site looks a little dated, but has all of the Bequia information that you might need, and is good for checking up on events, activities and other island happenings.

www.bequiatourism.com The official site of the Bequia Tourism Association, this is your best place to learn more about Bequia and to search for accommodations.

www.caribbeanchoice.com A clearinghouse site on Caribbean information, with almost too much going on.

www.heraldsvg.com This is the site of one of the Vincentian newspapers, the *Herald*. You must have Acrobat on your computer to read the daily issue, which is in PDF format. The first few pages are usually international news, but are followed by Caribbean affairs.

www.hwcn.org/~aa462/svgref.html This site is maintained by a part-time resident of SVG. It gathers Vincy-related information from other pertinent sites and will link you to them.

www.scubasvg.com Primarily a site for diving and water-sports information, this has some good historical, cultural and hotel information, too.

www.svgtourism.com This official site is a good source of tourism information, but there are no critical reviews.

LANGUAGE

English is the official language. The oldest island generations also speak a French patois, but this language is rapidly dying out. A good number of tourism professionals speak some French, German or Spanish to cater to the high number of European visitors.

MONEY

The Eastern Caribbean dollar (EC$ or XCD) is the local currency. Major credit cards are accepted at most hotels, car-rental agencies, dive shops and some of the larger restaurants. All of the major islands, except for Mayreau, have a bank and 24-hour ATMs (which usually accept international cards).

A 7% government tax and a 10% service charge is added to most hotel and restaurant bills, in which case no further tipping is necessary.

TELEPHONE

St Vincent phone numbers have seven digits. When calling from North America, dial ☎ 1-784 followed by the local number. From elsewhere, dial your country's international access code, followed by ☎ 784 and the local number. We have included only the seven-digit local number in SVG listings in this chapter.

Both coin and card phones can be found on the major islands. Phonecards can be purchased at Cable & Wireless offices or from vendors near the phones. It costs EC$0.25 to make a local call. For more information on card phones and making international calls, see p767. Many individuals and businesses now use cell (mobile) phones. Some Internet cafés, restaurants, hotels and other businesses will let you make a local call on their cell phone for a reasonable fee.

TOURIST INFORMATION
Local Tourist Offices

The main **Department of Tourism St Vincent & the Grenadines** (☎ 457-1502; www.svgtourism.com; Cruise Ship Terminal, Kingstown) is on St Vincent. In addition, there's a tourist information desk at St Vincent's ET Joshua Airport, and branch tourist offices in Bequia and Union Island.

Tourist Offices Abroad

Overseas offices of the SVG Department of Tourism include the following:

Canada (☎ 416-633-3100; 333 Wilson Ave, Suite 601, Toronto M3H 1T2)

Germany (☎ 70-3180-1033; Karibik Pur, Wurmberg Strasse 26, D-7032 Sindelfinger)

UK (☎ 0207-937-6570; 10 Kensington Ct, London W8 5DL)

USA (☎ 212-687-4981, 800-729-1726; 801 Second Ave, 21st fl, New York, NY 10017)

TOURS

HazEco Tours (☎ 457-8634; www.hazecotours.com; Gun Hill, Kingstown) Concentrates on St Vincent's natural-history tours, although it also does land, scenic and boat trips. A half-day outing to the Vermont Nature Trails is US$30 per person, or a hiking trip to the summit of La Soufrière is US$100 for up to two people.

Sailor's Cycle Centre (☎ 457-1274; modernp@ caribsurf.com; Upper Middle St, Kingstown) Offers various mountain-bike outings from US$18 per person, with a four-person minimum. You can ride/hike to La Soufrière's summit for US$60 per person.

SVG Tours (☎ 458-4534; svgtours@caribsurf.com) Run by a trained agronomist, these tours give an intimate understanding of agricultural land usage, as well as St Vincent's wildlife and wilderness areas.

WOMEN TRAVELERS

Women traveling in SVG needn't expect any hassles unique to this country. Normal precautions are sensible, especially after dark. Drunken European sailors in the port towns are probably the greatest potential threat – although they, too, are usually well behaved.

TRANSPORTATION

GETTING THERE & AWAY

Entering the Islands

All visitors should carry a valid passport with them; US citizens see the boxed text, p772. A round-trip or onward ticket is officially required.

Immigration is both reasonably efficient and lax. Passengers arriving on Union Island from Carriacou must pay EC$10 to Customs for entry. Passengers departing Carriacou pay EC$1 to Immigration.

It is up to you to register at the island's customs office, located at the ferry dock and the airport in Clifton.

If you fail to do this you may, or may not, have problems leaving the country. It all depends on the temperament of the customs official.

Air

There are no direct flights to SVG from outside the Caribbean, as the runway is too small to land jet aircraft. International passengers first fly into a neighboring island and then switch to a prop plane for the final leg of their journey. Bequia, Mustique, Canouan and Union Island all have small airports, and Palm Island has a small private airfield.

The following airlines fly to and from SVG from within the Caribbean:

British West Indies Air (BWIA; ☎ 800-538-2942; www.bwee.com; hub Trinidad & Tobago)
Caribbean Star (☎ 800-744-7827, outside the Caribbean 866-864-6272; www.flycaribbeanstar.com; hub Antigua)
LIAT (☎ 457-1821; www.liatairline.com; Halifax St, Kingstown; hub Antigua)
Mustique Airways (☎ 458-4380; www.mustique.com; hub SVG)
SVG Air (☎ 457-5124; www.svgair.com; hub SVG)
TIA (☎ 246-418-1650; www.tia2000.com; hub Barbados)

Sea

A new boat service runs between Union Island and Carriacou, Grenada, every Tuesday and Friday. The boat (US$30, 30 minutes) departs Union at 10:30am and Carriacou at 11:30am. A ferry (EC$15, one hour) departs Union every Monday and Thursday at 7:30am for Carriacou. It returns at 12:30pm on the same days. For information on entry requirements, see left.

You could also try hopping on one of the various commercial ships that haul goods back and forth between Union Island and Carriacou or Petit Martinique, Grenada, or pay a water taxi (EC$100 to EC$150) for the bumpy 40-minute ride.

GETTING AROUND

Air

Mustique Airways (☎ 458-4380; www.mustique.com) Interisland flights connecting various Grenadine islands with St Vincent.
SVG Air (☎ 457-5124; www.svgair.com) Flies twice daily each way from St Vincent to Canouan and Union Island, and five times to Mustique. Flies once daily from Canouan to Union Island and Bequia. It will charter between any of the islands.
TIA (☎ 246-418-1650; www.tia2000.com) This charter airline runs a circuit flight that begins at 8:30am in Barbados and works its way through all of the Grenadines (including Carriacou, but not St Vincent). It returns to Barbados by 1:45pm. Fares vary from island to island.

Bicycle

Bikes are not as available as one might hope, but there are a few options on the major islands.

Sailor's Cycle Centre (☎ 457-1274; modernp@carib surf.com; Upper Middle St), in Kingstown, rents road bikes and mountain bikes from EC$25 per day.

Boat

For details on the **Bequia Express** (☎ 458-3472; bequiaexpress@caribsurf.com) ferry service which operates between Bequia and Kingstown, see p611.

Fares from St Vincent are EC$15 to Bequia, EC$20 to Canouan, EC$25 to Mayreau and EC$30 to Union Island. The schedule is a bit flexible; it's always a good idea to check around the port for updates on the progress of a boat.

The mail boat MV *Barracuda* carries passengers and cargo five times weekly between

St Vincent, Bequia, Canouan, Mayreau and Union Island. On Monday and Thursday it leaves St Vincent at 10:30am, Bequia at 11:45am, Canouan at 2pm and Mayreau at 3:25pm, and arrives finally at Union Island at 3:45pm. On Tuesday and Friday it leaves Union Island at 6:30am, Mayreau at 7:30am, Canouan at 8:45am and Bequia at 11am, and arrives in St Vincent at noon. On Saturday the boat skips Bequia, leaving St Vincent at 10am, Canouan at 2:30pm and Mayreau at 3:30pm, arriving at Union Island at 4pm, and then departing Union at 5:30pm finally arriving back in St Vincent at 10:30pm.

The MV *Gem Star* leaves Kingstown on Tuesday and Friday at 11am, stops in Canouan and arrives in Union Island when it feels like it. On Wednesday and Saturday it does the reverse route, departing Union Island at 7:30am. Sometimes it stops in Mayreau.

The MV *Rita* (aka the *Slow Boat*) leaves Kingstown on Wednesday and Saturday at 10:30am, and supposedly arrives at Union Island at 4:30pm. On Monday and Thursday it leaves Union Island at noon and gets to Kingstown around 3:30pm. It sometimes stops in Canouan and Mayreau.

See the Getting There & Away sections earlier for information on boat tours between the islands.

Bus

Buses in St Vincent are privately owned minivans that can cram in a good 20 people (or more if necessary). Destinations are usually posted on the front windshield. There's a 'conductor' on board who collects fares (EC$1 to EC$5); you pay during the ride or as you get off. Many buses have sound systems, and the music is all part of the experience. Buses are a reliable and cheap way to travel, and a good way to mix with locals.

There are also buses on Bequia and Union Island; see those island sections for details.

Car

RENTAL

Rentals typically cost from US$50 a day for a car and from US$65 for a 4WD. Seventy-five free miles (121km) are commonly allowed, and a fee of EC$1 is charged for each additional mile (1.6km) driven. Note that collision-damage insurance is not a common concept, and if you get into an accident you're likely to be liable for damages.

Car-rental agencies in St Vincent include **Star Garage** (☎ 456-1743; Grenville St), in Kingstown, and **Ben's Auto Rental** (☎ 456-2907) and **Unico Auto Rentals** (☎ 456-5744), which are both at the airport. Most will deliver cars to your hotel.

Most of the Grenadine islands have no car rentals at all. On some islands there are no roads.

ROAD RULES

Driving is on the left-hand side. To drive within SVG you must purchase a local license (EC$40). In Kingstown, licenses can be obtained at the **Traffic & Transport office** (☼ 24hr), inside the police station.

Taxi

On St Vincent, taxis are available at the airport and at a couple of stands in central Kingstown. They are abundant on most islands and affordable for shorter trips. Agree on a fare before departure.

Barbados

There is a simple reason why Barbados is the Eastern Caribbean's most popular destination: the beaches are impossibly beautiful. They embody the white-sand-and-turquoise-water ideal of tropical paradise. However, Barbados is hardly a Robinson Crusoe islet: the beaches are attached to a densely populated and heavily developed country. As the more intrepid visitor will discover, there are many facets to Barbados, and this well-oiled tourist machine has deeper cultural, historical and natural attractions.

A lone coral island on the fringe of the Caribbean and the Atlantic Ocean, Barbados sits nearly 99 miles (160km) east of its closest neighbor. The country's distant position kept it beyond the brutal colonial rivalries that marred the history of the Caribbean, and it experienced almost 350 years of unbroken British rule. While there remains an undeniable British influence, the often-hyped 'little England' analogy is superficial at best. Barbados is West Indian to its core, with its own quirks and characteristics. The country is the source of classic calypso rhythms, a cuisine of breadfruit and flying fish, and world-famous rums.

The long connection to Britain ensured that Barbados didn't become insular and Barbadians have long been open to interacting with foreigners. For visitors, Barbados is a comfortable mix of the familiar and enough local flavor to feel exotic. That said, you have to make an effort to get beyond the trappings of package tourism and, facing costs among the highest in the Caribbean, budget travelers may want to seek out other destinations.

BARBADOS

FAST FACTS

- **Area** 167 sq miles (432 sq km)
- **Capital** Bridgetown
- **Country code** ☎ 246
- **Departure tax** B$25 for stays over 24 hours
- **Famous for** Beaches, rum, flying-fish sandwiches
- **Language** English
- **Money** Barbados dollar (B$ or BBD); B$1 = US$0.50 = €0.42 = UK£0.29
- **People** Barbadian (formal), Bajan (colloquial)
- **Phrases** Workin' up (dancing)
- **Population** 280,000
- **Visa** Not necessary for stays under one to six months, depending on nationality (see p649).

HIGHLIGHTS

- **White-sand beaches** (p634) Unwind on the blissful beaches that fringe the west and south coasts.
- **Bajan sports** (p644) Join the raucous crowd at a cricket match or a Saturday horse race. For a more tranquil experience, try your hand at beach cricket.
- **Tropical gardens** (p641 and p642) Experience earthly paradise, of the tropical sort, at Welchman Hall Gully and the Andromeda Botanic Gardens.
- **Flying-fish sandwiches** (p629) Sample Barbados' most popular dish: inexpensive, fresh and always delicious.
- **Rum shops** (p629) Knock back a drink or three and banter with Bajans at one of the island's 1600 colorful rum shops.

ITINERARIES

- **One week** Depending on budget, stay on the mid-priced south coast or the fancier west coast, go diving or snorkeling and spend an afternoon in Bridgetown.
- **Ten days** Take a trip from the beaches to see natural and cultural landmarks in the interior. Go to a weekend cricket match and stay for a couple of nights in underdeveloped Bathsheba.
- **Two to three weeks** Make your way around the island, sampling the lively south coast, the rugged east coast and the idyllic west coast. Venture into the country's interior to see colonial sites and lush tropical gardens.

CLIMATE & WHEN TO GO

The climate in Barbados tends to be nice year-round: in January, the average daily high temperature is 83°F (28°C), while the low average is 70°F (21°C). In July, the average daily high is 86°F (30°C), while the average low is 74°F (23°C). February to May are the driest months (April averages only seven days of rain), while July is the wettest month with some 18 days of rain.

The tourist high season runs from mid-December through mid-April. June through October is the hurricane season: September and October are the most humid months and have the highest hurricane risk.

HISTORY

The original inhabitants of Barbados were Arawak Indians, who were driven off the

---

HOW MUCH?

- **Taxi from the airport to Bridgetown** B$30
- **Day trip around Central Barbados** B$150-200
- **Day of diving on the west coast** B$150
- **Meal of fresh fish in a touristy restaurant** B$25
- **Meal of fresh fish in a local restaurant** B$14

LONELY PLANET INDEX

- **Liter of gas** B$2.16
- **Liter of bottled water** B$2
- **Bottle of Banks beer** B$2
- **Souvenir T-shirt** B$20
- **Street snack: roti** B$8

---

island around AD 1200 by invading Caribs from South America. The Caribs, in turn, abandoned (or fled) Barbados close to the arrival of the first Europeans. The Portuguese visited the island in 1536, but Barbados was uninhabited by the time Captain John Powell claimed it for England in 1625. Two years later, a group of settlers established the island's first European settlement, Jamestown, in present-day Holetown. Within a few years, the colonists had cleared much of the forest, planting tobacco and cotton fields. In the 1640s, they switched to sugarcane. The new sugar plantations were labor intensive, and the landowners, who had previously relied upon indentured servants, began to import large numbers of African slaves. These large sugar plantations – some of the first in the Caribbean – proved immensely profitable, and gave rise to a wealthy colonial class.

The sugar industry boomed during the next century, and continued to prosper after the abolition of slavery in 1834. As the planters owned all of the best land, there was little choice for the freed slaves other than to stay on at the cane fields for a pittance.

Social tensions flared during the Depression in the 1930s, and Barbados' Black majority gradually gained more access to the political process. The economy was

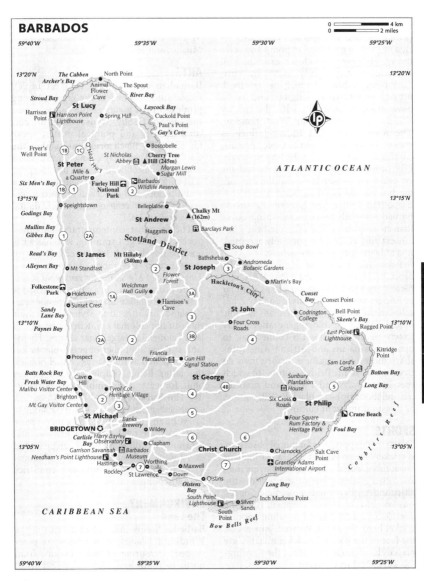

diversified through the international tourism boom and gave more islanders the opportunity for economic success and self-determination. England granted Barbados internal self-government in 1961 and it became an independent nation on November 30, 1966, with Errol Barrow as its first prime minister. While not politically

flawless, Barbados has remained a stable and growing democracy.

THE CULTURE

Bajan culture displays some trappings of British life: cricket, polo and horse racing are popular pastimes, business is performed in a highly organized fashion, gardens are lovingly tended, older women often wear prim little hats and special events are carried out with a great deal of pomp and ceremony. However, on closer examination, Barbados is very deeply rooted in Afro-Caribbean tradition. Family life, art, food, music, architecture, religion and dress have more in common with the nearby Windward Islands than West London. The African and East Indian influences are especially apparent in the spicy cuisine, rhythmic music and pulsating festivals. Like other Caribbean cultures, Barbadians are relatively conservative and the men are macho, but the ongoing bond with a cosmopolitan center like London has made Barbados slightly more socially progressive than its neighbors. For example, while homosexuality is far from generally accepted, it is at least open to some debate.

Bajan youth are now within the media orbit of North America. The NBA and New York hip-hop fashion are as popular in Bridgetown as in Brooklyn, and Jay Z has eclipsed the likes of Prince William as a role model. While the older generations may frown on the growing US connection, in many ways Bajans and African-Americans share more of a common history than do Bajans with White British culture (to which they have always had a tense and subordinate relationship) – or Black British culture, as it is an immigrant culture.

SPORTS

The national sport, if not national obsession, is cricket (see p644). Per capita, Barbadians boast more world-class cricket players than any other nation. One of the world's top all-rounders, Bajan native Garfield Sobers, was knighted by Queen Elizabeth II during her 1975 visit to Barbados, while another cricket hero, Sir Frank Worrell, appears on the face of the B$5 bill. Cricket matches are played throughout the year at the Kensington Park Oval in Garrison.

Horse races and polo are traditionally watched, while windsurfing, surfing and soccer are popular participatory sports.

RELIGION

The majority of the population is Anglican. Other Christian denominations on Barbados include Methodist, Moravian, Roman Catholic, Pentecostal, Baptist, First Church of Christ Scientist, Jehovah's Witness and Seventh Day Adventist; there are also Baha'i, Muslim and Jewish adherents.

ARTS

Barbadian contributions to West Indian music are renowned in the region, having produced such greats as the calypso artist the Mighty Gabby, whose songs on cultural identity and political protest speak for emerging Black pride throughout the Caribbean. These days, Bajan music leans toward the faster beats of soca (an energetic offspring of calypso), *rapso* (a fusion of soca and hip-hop) and dancehall (a contemporary offshoot of reggae with faster, digital beats and an MC).

The foremost contemporary Barbadian novelist is George Lamming, who has written six novels and several collections of short fiction. His most acclaimed novel, *The Castle of My Skin,* portrays what it was like to grow up Black in a colonial Barbados that was struggling toward independence.

Island architectural styles have their roots in the colonial era, when virtually all land belonged to large sugar estates. The island still has a number of grand plantation homes as well as numerous chattel homes, the latter being simple wooden homes built for easy disassembly and portability. The **Barbados National Trust** (☎ 436-9033; natrust@sunbeach.net; house visit B$15; ⏱ 2:30-5:30pm Sun) runs an Open House program offering visits to some of the island's grander private homes. A different house can be visited every week and members of the National Trust in other Commonwealth countries get a discounted price.

ENVIRONMENT
The Land

Barbados lies 99 miles (160km) east of the Windward Islands. It is somewhat pear-shaped, measuring 21 miles (34km) from north to south and 13.5 miles (22km) at its widest. The island is composed largely of coral accumulations built on sedimentary rocks. Water permeates the soft coral cap, creating underground streams, springs and limestone caverns, the most notable of which, Harrison's Cave (p641), is one of the island's leading attractions. Most of the island's terrain is relatively flat, rising to low, gentle hills in the interior. However, the

---

A HAIRY ENCOUNTER

The Portuguese explorer Pedro a Campos stopped on Barbados in 1536 en route to Brazil. He had no interest is settling the island, but it was he who named the island Los Barbados (Bearded Ones) – presumably after the island's fig trees (*Ficus citrofolia*), whose long, hanging aerial roots resemble beards.

---

northeastern part of the island, known as the Scotland District, rises to a relatively lofty 1115ft (340m) at Barbados' highest point, Mt Hillaby. The west coast has white-sand beaches and calm turquoise waters, while the east side of the island has turbulent Atlantic waters and a coastline punctuated by cliffs. Coral reefs surround most of the island and contribute to the fine white sands on the western and southern beaches.

Wildlife

The majority of Barbados' indigenous wildlife was overwhelmed by agriculture and competition with introduced species. Found only on Barbados is the harmless and elusive grass snake. The island also shelters a species of small, nonpoisonous, blind snake; whistling frogs; lizards; red-footed tortoises; and eight species of bat. Hawksbill turtles regularly come ashore to lay their eggs, as does the occasional leatherback turtle. Some of the introduced mammals found in the wild are green monkeys, mongooses, European hares, mice and rats.

More than 180 species of bird have been sighted on Barbados. Most of them are migrating shorebirds and waders that breed in North America and stop over in Barbados en route to winter feeding grounds in South America. Only 28 species nest on Barbados; these include wood doves, blackbirds, bananaquits, guinea fowl, cattle egrets, herons, finches and three kinds of hummingbird.

Environmental Issues

The forests that once covered Barbados were long ago felled by the British planters. One of the knock-on effects is that the country now has a problem with soil erosion. This loose dirt, along with pollution from ships and illegally dumped solid wastes, threatens to contaminate the aquifers that supply the island's drinking water.

FOOD & DRINK

Bajan food is similar to other West Indian cuisines, in that it has African and East Indian influences, but it also has unique ingredients and variations. Make sure to try the ubiquitous flying fish, which is served fried in delicious sandwiches all over the country. Some of the local dishes include *conkies* (a mixture of cornmeal, coconut, pumpkin, sweet potato, raisins and spices, steamed in a plantain leaf), *cou-cou* (a creamy cornmeal and okra mash), *cutters* (meat or fish sandwiches in a salt bread roll), *jug-jug* (a mixture of Guinea cornmeal, green peas and salted meat), roti (a curry filling rolled inside flat bread), pumpkin fritters and pudding, and *souse* (a dish made out of pickled pig's head and belly, spices and a few vegetables).

The tourism industry has brought Barbados a range of international fare, from American fast food and Thai restaurants to fine continental cuisine and even a few vegetarian spots. It is advisable to make reservations at the more upscale restaurants. The grocery stores are well stocked and more international foods and ingredients are available in Barbados than in other Eastern Caribbean islands.

Those who have been stuck with instant coffee in the Windward Islands will welcome a good range of real coffees in Barbados. Tap water is safe to drink; it comes from underground reservoirs that are naturally filtered. For those who prefer something a little harder, Barbadian rum is considered some of the finest in the Caribbean, with Mount Gay being the best-known label. The island beer, Banks, is refreshing after a day in the hot sun.

Distillery & Brewery Tours

Tours can be made of four rum distilleries on the island. Rates are about the same at each, with a basic 30- to 45-minute tour explaining the distilling operation and capping off with a rum tasting for B$15.
Banks Beer Brewery (☎ 228-6486; www.banksbeer .com; tours B$10; ☺ 3 tours daily, call for times) This is the island's largest and most famous brewery, about 2 miles (3km) east of Bridgetown in Wildey. Call ahead for reservations. The St Patrick's bus also passes here.

BARBADOS

Heritage Park & Foursquare Rum Distillery
(☎ 420-1977; tours B$15; ⊗ 9am-5pm) Near Six Cross Roads in St Philip. Although it's set in an old sugar mill, Heritage Park has some of the most modern equipment. It's as much a theme park as a distillery, and the standard tour includes access to the museum and craft shops. You can take a St Patrick's bus from the Fairchild St Bus Terminal or River Bus Terminal in Bridgetown.

Malibu Beach Club & Visitor Centre (☎ 425-9393; Brighton, Black Rock, St Michael; tours B$18; ⊗ 9-11am & noon-4pm Mon-Fri) Coconut-flavored Malibu is more of an export product for American spring-breakers and sororities than a Bajan drink, but the company has a popular tour at the beachfront distillery. There are more expensive packages, including a buffet lunch, unlimited drinks, hotel transfer, and rented beach chair and umbrella with prices up to B$75.

Mount Gay Rum Visitors Centre (☎ 425-8757; www.mountgay.com; Spring Garden Hwy; tours B$12, lunch tour with transportation B$55; ⊗ 9am-3:45pm Mon-Fri) The aged rums here are some of Barbados' best – the visitors centre is about a kilometer north of Bridgetown Harbour. The original refinery in **St Lucy** (☎ 439-8812), at the north end of the island, has free tours if you make reservations.

BRIDGETOWN

pop 80,000

Barbados' bustling capital, Bridgetown is the island's only city and is situated on its only natural harbor. Most of the main streets are modern and businesslike in appearance, but there is also a handful of nicely restored colonial buildings, as well as side streets that lead off into residential neighborhoods scattered with rum shops and chattel houses.

Bridgetown doesn't boast a lot of essential sights, but it is worth checking out to get a feel for Barbados beyond the tourism facade. There are some good shopping opportunities, especially at the Broad St duty-free stores and on pedestrian-only Swan St, which is thick with vendors selling jewelry, clothes, sandals and fruit.

ORIENTATION

Bridgetown sits on attractive Carlisle Bay on the southwest corner of Barbados. The city is developed around an inlet from the bay known as the Careenage, and connects directly to most highways across the island.

Maps

Bridgetown is not very large and the map in this book will suffice for most navigational needs. Tourist maps are available everywhere and will cover basic road trips in and out of the city.

INFORMATION

Bookstores

Cave Shepherd (☎ 431-2121; Broad St) This department store has a wide selection of Caribbean and international literature.

Cloister Bookstore (☎ 426-2662; Hincks St) Cloister carries local, regional and international literature and guidebooks.

Internet Access

Connect (☎ 228-8648; Shop 9, 27 Broad St; per hr B$12; ⊗ 9am-5pm Mon-Fri, 9am-2pm Sat) Upstairs in the Galleria Mall behind Nelson's Arms (enter from Lancaster Lane). There are discounts for students with ID.

Net2Serve (☎ 228-6382; 10 James Fort Bldg, Hincks St; ⊗ 9am-5pm Mon-Fri, 9am-2pm Sat) Next to the LIAT office.

Libraries

National Library (☎ 426-3981; Coleridge St; ⊗ 9am-5pm Mon-Sat) To check out books here you'll pay a refundable deposit of B$20. The deposit is valid also at Holetown, Speightstown and Oistins branches.

Medical Services

Queen Barbados Hospital (☎ 436-6450, ☎ ambulance 511; Martindale's Rd)

Money

Banks are generally open 8am to 3pm Monday to Thursday and 8am to 5pm Friday, and most have 24-hour ATM access.

Barbados National Bank (☎ 431-5700; Broad St) At the west end. There's a branch on Fairchild St.

First Caribbean International Bank (☎ 431-5151; Broad St) Near National Heroes Sq.

Royal Bank of Canada (☎ 429-4923; Broad St) Near National Heroes Sq.

Scotiabank (☎ 426-7000; Broad St) At the west end. There's also a branch on Fairchild St.

Post

Post office (Cheapside; ⊗ 7:30am-5pm Mon-Fri)

Telephone & Fax

Telephone office (Hincks St; ⊗ 8am-4:30pm Mon-Fri) Here you can make international calls, and send faxes and telegrams.

BRIDGETOWN

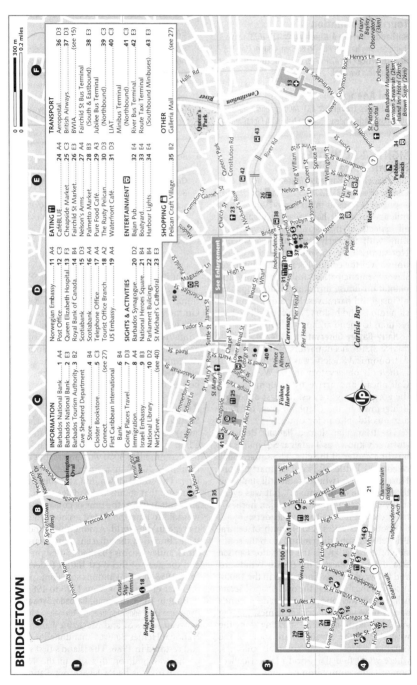

INFORMATION
Barbados National Bank.........**1** A4	
Barbados National Bank.........**2** E3	
Barbados Tourism Authority...**3** B2	
Cave Shepherd Department	
Store.......................**4** B4	
Cloister Bookstore.............**5** C3	
Connect...................(see 27)	
First Caribbean International	
Bank........................**6** B4	
Going Places Travel............**7** D3	
Immigration..................**8** A4	
Israeli Embassy................**9** B3	
National Library..............**10** D2	
Net2Serve...................(see 40)	

Norwegian Embassy...........**11** A4	
Post Office....................**12** C3	
Queen Elizabeth Hospital.....**13** F3	
Royal Bank of Canada.........**14** B4	
Scotiabank...................**15** D3	
Scotiabank...................**16** A4	
Telephone Office..............**17** A4	
Tourist Office Branch..........**18** A2	
US Embassy...................**19** A4	

SIGHTS & ACTIVITIES
Barbados Synagogue...........**20** D2	
National Heroes Square.......**21** B4	
Parliament Buildings...........**22** B4	
St Michael's Cathedral.........**23** E3	

EATING 🍴
CaféBLUE...................**24** A4	
Cheapside Market.............**25** C3	
Fairchild St Market............**26** E3	
Nelson's Arms................**27** A4	
Palmetto Market..............**28** B3	
Pure Food Café...............**29** A3	
The Rusty Pelican............**30** D3	
Waterfront Café...............**31** D3	

ENTERTAINMENT 🎭
Bajan Pub....................**32** E4	
Boatyard...................**33** E4	
Harbour Lights...............**34** E4	

SHOPPING 🛍
Pelican Craft Village..........**35** B2	

TRANSPORT
Aeropostal..................**36** D3	
British Airways...............**37** D3	
BWIA.....................(see 15)	
Fairchild St Bus Terminal	
(South & Eastbound).......**38** E3	
Jubilee Bus Terminal	
(Northbound)..............**39** C3	
LIAT......................**40** C3	
Minibus Terminal	
(Northbound)..............**41** C3	
River Bus Terminal...........**42** E3	
Route Taxi Terminal	
(Southbound Minibuses).....**43** E3	

OTHER
Galleria Mall................(see 27)	

BARBADOS

Tourist Information

Barbados Tourism Authority (☎ 427-2623; www
.barbados.org; Harbour Rd; ⏱ 8:15am-4:30pm Mon-Fri)
Branch office (☎ 426-1718) Inside the customs area at
the cruise ship terminal.

Travel Agencies

Going Places Travel (☎ 431-2400; ground fl, Speed-
bird House, Independence Sq) Can help with flights and
most travel needs.

SIGHTS & ACTIVITIES
Historical Sites

The excellent **Barbados Museum** (☎ 427-0201;
Garrison; adult/child B$11.50/5.75; ⏱ 9am-5pm Mon-Sat,
2-6pm Sun) is housed in an early-19th-century
military prison. It has engaging displays on
all aspects of the island's history, beginning with its early indigenous residents.
Not surprisingly, the most extensive collections cover the colonial era, with exhibits on
slavery, emancipation, military history and
plantation-house furniture, all accompanied
by insightful narratives. For a quick immersion into island history, you couldn't do better than to spend an hour or two here.

Harry Bayley Observatory (☎ 426-1317; adult/
child B$8/5), the headquarters of the Barbados
Astronomical Society, was built in 1963 and
is the only observatory in the West Indies.
Call ahead and arrive by 8:30pm to view
the gorgeous night skies. It's east of central
Bridgetown in the Clapham area, off Rendezvous Rd; phone for times.

The triangular-shaped **National Heroes Sq**
(formerly known as Trafalgar Sq) marks the
bustling center of the city. The square once
celebrated Battle of Trafalgar martyr Lord
Horatio Nelson (whose statue still stands on
the west side of the square), but was eventually changed to honor 10 Bajan heroes –
from cricket heroes to slave leaders.

About 1.25 miles (2km) south of central
Bridgetown, spreading inland from the south
side of Carlisle Bay, is the Barbados **Garrison
area**, the home base of the British Windward
and Leeward Islands Command in the 1800s.
A central focal point is the oval-shaped **Savannah**, which was once large parade grounds
and is now used for cricket games, jogging
and Saturday horse races. Standing along the
west side of the Savannah are some of the
Garrison's more ornate colonial buildings,
where you'll find the world's largest collection of 17th-century iron cannons.

The **Parliament Buildings** (☎ 427-2019; ⏱ tours
10am & 2pm Mon-Fri) on the north side of National Heroes Sq are two stone-block, neo-
Gothic-style buildings constructed in 1871.
The west-side building with the clock tower
contains public offices; the building on the
east side houses the Senate and House of
Assembly and is adorned with stained-glass
windows depicting British monarchs. It is
best to call ahead for tours.

Religious Sites

St Michael's Cathedral (St Michael's Row; admission
free; ⏱ 9am-4pm) is the island's Anglican cathedral. It was originally completed in 1665
to accommodate 3000 worshipers, but came
tumbling down in a hurricane a century
later. The scaled-down, but still substantial,
structure that stands today dates from 1789
and seats 1600. At the time of construction it
was said to have the widest arched ceiling of
its type in the world. Among the island notables buried in the adjacent churchyard are
Sir Grantley Adams (Barbados' first premier
and the head of the West Indies Federation
from 1958 to 1962) and his son Tom (prime
minister of Barbados from 1976 to 1985).

Built in 1833, the small **Barbados Synagogue**
(Synagogue Lane; admission free; ⏱ 10am-4pm Mon-Fri),
between James St and Magazine Lane, near
National Heroes Sq, was abandoned in 1929
and restored in 1986. The island's first synagogue was built on this site in the 1600s,
when Barbados had a Jewish population of

more than 800. Many were refugees who had fled Portuguese oppression in South America. They brought with them the important knowledge of sugarcane cultivation.

SLEEPING

Almost no foreign visitors stay in Bridgetown and there are few accommodations available. Aquatic Gap, just south of town, is the first spot with any hotels to speak of; however, it is recommended that you head the few minutes further to Hastings, Rockley, Worthing, St Lawrence Gap or beyond (see p634).

Island Inn Hotel (☎ 436-6393; www.funbarbados.com/lodgings/islandinn.cfm; s/d from US$75/105; P ☒ ☒) Toward the water off Bay St, this hotel is partially built in a restored 1804 garrison building that was originally a military rum store. It is close to town and has all-inclusive rate options.

EATING

Rusty Pelican (☎ 436-7778; Bridge House, Cavans Lane; lunch B$22-30, dinner B$35-50; ☒ 10am until late) This is one of Bridgetown's most pleasant places to dine. Sample the coconut shrimp or some flying fish while sitting on the 2nd-floor balcony and looking out over the Careenage.

Waterfront Café (☎ 427-0093; Careenage; weekday buffet B$45, meals from B$30; ☒ noon-3pm & 6-10pm Mon-Sat, 6-10pm Sun) This café prepares tasty sandwiches and specialty salads or fish of the day. On Tuesday there's a Caribbean buffet with steel-pan music(the steel pan is an instrument made from oil drums). Ask for an outdoor waterside table.

Pure Food Café (☎ 436-4537; Chapel St; lunch from B$14; ☒ 8am-5pm Mon-Fri, 8am-2pm Sat) It's all in the name. This restaurant serves healthy and affordable dishes with a good selection of vegetarian options.

Nelson's Arms (☎ 431-0602; Galeria Mall, 27 Broad St; meals B$15-25; ☒ 11am-4pm Mon-Fri, 10am-3pm Sat) This well-known lunch spot has balcony dining and a relaxed pub atmosphere. Here you can accompany a few beers with baguette sandwiches or specials such as lasagna or Cajun chicken.

Brown Sugar (☎ 426-7684; lunch buffet B$35, dinner B$42-75; ☒ noon-2:30pm Sun-Fri, 6-10pm daily) The renowned Brown Sugar, next to the Island Inn Hotel at Aquatic Gap, is a veritable greenhouse of hanging plants, complete with a waterfall and whistling frogs.

It has an excellent West Indian buffet and is also open for dinner served à la carte, with the likes of shrimp Creole and lobster. Reservations are advised.

The best places at which to buy fruits and vegetables are at the **Palmetto Market** (Swan St), at the east end, and at the public markets on Fairchild St and Cheapside, which are open from 7am to late afternoon Monday to Saturday.

ENTERTAINMENT

While visitors are welcome in Bridgetown's many rum shops, the watering holes do not make any effort to cater to foreigners, and a distinct local character prevails. Along Baxters Rd, just north of the center, you'll find a concentration of these bars, where alcohol flows and fish is fried up until late at night. Although women will not be turned away, be warned that rum shops are predominantly a masculine haunt.

Bajan Pub (☎ 436-1664; Ray St) For a more tame, but rum shop–style experience, check out Bajan Pub, where there's live music on occasion.

Harbour Lights (☎ 436-7225; Bay St; cover varies; ☒ 9pm-3am) This open-air nightclub at the south end of Bridgetown has dancing and live bands most nights. Friday is the liveliest, and Monday night there's a beach party. While it's not gay-oriented, it is more gay-friendly than other spots. Harbour Lights and the Boatyard are generally considered the best clubs in the whole Bridgetown/south coast area and both get a good mix of foreigners and locals.

Boatyard (☎ 436-2622; Bay St; ☒ 6pm-1am) The Boatyard always has something going on, whether it's live bands, DJs, unlimited drinks with a B$25 cover, or the Friday-night fish fry. Sunday afternoon it is a popular hangout spot for locals, especially couples.

The Waterfront Café (left) offers free live music from 8pm to 11pm Tuesday to Saturday.

SHOPPING

Pelican Craft Village (Princess Alice Hwy) This ever-evolving complex of craft stores and workshops, between downtown and the cruise ship terminal, features pottery, leather, wood and fabric designs and makes for easy souvenir and art shopping. You also have the opportunity to watch the artists at work.

GETTING THERE & AWAY

As most people stay along the southern coast they will arrive and depart in vans from the route-taxi terminal along the river. A little closer in toward the center of town is the River Bus Terminal, which sends minibuses along central and eastern routes.

Public buses going south and east leave from the **Fairchild St Bus Terminal** (Bridge St), north of Fairchild. Public buses going north up the west coast leave from the **Jubilee (Lower Green) Terminal** (Lower Broad St), at the west end. Minibuses going north up the west coast leave from near the general post office on Cheapside.

GETTING AROUND

Bridgetown is easily covered on foot, although taxis can be flagged on the street, if necessary.

SOUTH COAST

The south coast is the island's tourism epicenter, with most of the budget-to-midrange accommodations along its fine white-sand beaches. This virtually uninterrupted stretch of development runs from the outskirts of Bridgetown all the way to the airport.

Getting There & Away

There are frequent No 11 minibuses from the route-taxi terminal in Bridgetown that run along Main Rd (Hwy 7) on the southern coast and link the south-coast villages. Private taxis are relatively easy to find in the main tourist areas (prices to the airport and Bridgetown are negotiable and depend on the driver and time of day).

HASTINGS & ROCKLEY

pop 20,000

Just a 15-minute bus ride from Bridgetown are the first major tourist areas of Hastings and Rockley. They are home to a lot of midrange hotels and some attractive, popular beaches, the largest being Accra Beach. The zone behind the beach is generally overdeveloped and blighted by strip malls. The center of activity is Rockley Beach, a roadside white-sand beach with shade trees, snack kiosks and clothing vendors. About halfway between Bridgetown

and Rockley is Hastings Rock, a nice spot to enjoy views of the ocean. On weekends, community groups set up flea markets and hold activities around the gazebo in the small park above the water.

Information

There are a number of banks along the main road. Most have 24-hour ATMs.

A&R Computer Service (☎ 435-8608; arcomputers@sunbeach.net; per hr B$15; 🕑 8:30am-5:30pm Mon-Fri, 9am-3pm Sat) You'll find this place across the street from Hastings Plaza.

Queen's Laundromat (☎ 228-4731; cnr Hastings & Hart Gap Rds; per load B$12) Near Coconut Court Hotel.

Royal Bank of Canada (☎ 431-6650; Main Rd, Hastings)

Sleeping

Abbeville Hotel (☎ 435-7924; abbeville@sunbeach.net; Main Rd, Rockley; r from US$55; **P** 🔀 🖳) This former plantation house has 19 straightforward rooms with private bathroom and is good value considering its proximity to Rockley Beach. Bert's Bar, beside the hotel's pool, is a popular local eating and drinking spot.

Coconut Court Beach Resort (☎ 427-1655; www.coconut-court.com; Main Rd, Hastings; r from US$149; 🔀 🖳) Coconut Court is a five-story beachfront hotel popular with British package tourists and good for visiting families – they even have in-house baby-sitters. While not luxurious, it is a solid midrange choice and has many amenities for the price range.

Tree Haven Beach Apartments (☎ 435-6673; arturoolaya@caribsurf.com; Main Rd, Rockley; apt from US$50; 🔀) This affordable, laid-back option has three spacious units just across the road from the beach. The owner is friendly and Tree Haven has many satisfied repeat guests.

Eating

Champers (☎ 435-6644; Keswick Centre; dinners from B$50; 🕑 11:30am-midnight Mon-Sat) This highly regarded spot has a romantic sea-view restaurant on the 2nd floor with a surfside bar below. It makes excellent sauces to go with the fresh seafood and meat dishes, including a succulent ginger-and-coconut sauce and blueberry sauce. It also has a wide selection of imported champagne and wine.

Trini Hot Shop (☎ 435-7981; Hastings Plaza; meals from B$6; 🕑 8am-3pm Mon-Thu, 8am-5pm Fri, 9am-3pm

Sat) In the center of Hastings, the Hot Shop serves inexpensive Trinidadian delicacies including rotis and doubles (a chickpea curry, sometimes with fish, wrapped in thin tortilla-like bread). It's known for its Trinidadian version of the Indian paratha with curried chicken or beef.

Ryanne's Restaurant (☎ 436-1177; dishes from B$12; ☺ 8am-5pm) This casual, breezy restaurant on the eastern edge of Hastings Rock is popular with locals and foreigners. It serves Bajan breakfasts of saltfish with breadfruit, and traditional dishes like *cou-cou* and fish throughout the day. Soups, salads and sandwiches are also available, and there's a small bar.

Shak Shak (☎ 435-1234; Main Rd, Hastings; mains from B$40; ☺ noon-11pm Mon-Fri, 5-11pm Sat) In a Mediterranean-style setting overlooking the ocean, Shak Shak offers an international menu of fish, chicken and beef, or a bistro and pizzeria menu in the bar. Friday night there's live music.

WORTHING
pop 7500
Worthing sits between the developed tourist areas of Hastings/Rockley and St Lawrence Gap and can make a nice base, particularly if you're on a tight budget but still want to be near all the excitement. It has relatively inexpensive places at which to eat and a handful of lower-priced guesthouses that are either on the beach or just steps from it. Sandy Beach, which fronts Worthing, is a nice strip of powdery sand.

It is a short walk to the nightlife in St Lawrence, but do take care as the road is narrow, sidewalks are narrower and the cars move rather quickly.

Information
First Caribbean International Bank (☎ 431-3830; Rendezvous Rd) Has a 24-hour ATM.
Southshore Laundromat (Main Rd; per load from B$8; ☺ 8am-4pm Mon-Fri, 8am-2pm Sat)
Worthing post office (Main Rd; ☺ 8am-3pm Mon-Fri) North of the First Caribbean bank.

Sleeping
Heindrun Rice of **Karibik Tours** (☎ 428-1035; karibik@sunbeach.net), manager of House Cleverdale, has information about several places with inexpensive rooms on the south coast and other parts of the island.

House Cleverdale (☎ 428-1035; 3rd Ave; r from US$25) Set back just a bit from the beach, this large wooden home is popular with backpackers. Rooms have mosquito net and fan. Baths and a large kitchen are shared.

Maraval Guest House (☎ 435-7437; 3rd Ave; s & d US$30) Across the street from Cleverdale, Maraval has attractive, simple rooms with shared bath and in-room sinks. There's access to a well-equipped kitchen and a pleasant living room with TV and stereo. This friendly and comfortable place is good for longer stays.

Shell's Guest House (☎ 435-7253; 1st Ave; s/d incl continental breakfast US$25/38, with private bath US$28/40; ✗) Shell's Scandinavian-run guesthouse is also popular with budget travelers and is gay-friendly. There are seven nonsmoking rooms, each with a ceiling fan, sink, small dresser and lamp. Four rooms have private bath, while three rooms share two baths. Credit cards are accepted.

Eating
Worthing has some good inexpensive dining choices and a few garish midrange themed restaurants. For a nicer meal you are better off heading down the road to St Lawrence.

Roti Hut (☎ 435-7362; Hwy 7; rotis B$4-9, lunch specials B$8.95; ☺ 11am-10pm Mon-Thu, later Fri & Sat) This place is a favorite with locals and travelers alike. There is a variety of delicious and affordable rotis and the lunch specials are hearty. The ambience is a bit utilitarian, but it is a good place to grab a Banks and have an inexpensive meal before wasting the rest of your money at the bars.

Carib Beach Bar & Restaurant (☎ 435-8540; 2nd Ave; lunch B$12-16, dinner B$24; ☺ kitchen 11am-10pm) This open-air eatery right on Sandy Beach has a variety of seafood dishes and bar-type food. The flying-fish sandwich can be a touch dry, but this is a congenial spot, with friendly service. It gets crowded and the bar stays open later than the kitchen.

CaféBLUE (☎ 435-7699; Hwy 7; sandwiches B$10.50, espressos B$3.50; ☺ 7am-10pm Mon-Sat) This popular Bajan take on a California-style café has made-to-order sandwiches and paninis, good teas and coffees (including elusive iced coffee), fruit smoothies with all important vitamin supplements, salads and baked goods. There are a few vegetarian options. There is a second branch on Broad St in Bridgetown.

ST LAWRENCE & DOVER BEACH

pop 25,000

St Lawrence has the south coast's most active nightlife as well as numerous mid-range and top-end restaurants and places at which to stay, many of which front the ocean. The western end of St Lawrence is at the junction of Little Bay and Hwy 7, but most of the village lies along St Lawrence Coast Rd, in the area known as the Gap – the whole area has been developed into a tidy tourist mall of sorts. Dover Beach, near the middle of the coastal road, is a nice, broad white-sand beach that attracts swimmers, bodysurfers and windsurfers.

Information

ICS Internet Café (☎ 428-1513; Lower St, Lawrence Gap; per hr B$18; ⏱ 8:30am-10pm)

Royal Bank of Canada (☎ 431-6565; St Lawrence Coast Rd) Beside Ship Inn (right).

Sleeping

BUDGET

Rio Guest House (☎ 428-1546; riogh@hotmail.com; Dover Beach; r from US$40) A travelers haunt with seven unpretentious fan-cooled rooms, Rio features a fully-equipped kitchen and friendly Swiss-Bajan managers who speak French and German. It's a tranquil location, off the main drag but just minutes from the beach and all of the nightlife.

MIDRANGE

Gallery (☎ 435-9756; www.barbados.org/rest/davids/gallery.htm; St Lawrence Coast Rd; studio from US$65; ✗) Formerly a Canadian artist's space, this is now a very pleasant guesthouse with a woodsy touch to the decor. The Gallery has a certain alternative charm that is absent in most of the nearby choices.

St Lawrence Apartments (☎ 435-6950; St Lawrence Coast Rd; studios from US$70; ✗ ✕) Comprised of two hotels with a total of 75 units, St Lawrence West has big studios with ceiling fans and St Lawrence East has essentially the same facilities, but its rooms are smaller and more basic. This is a dependable option that is close to the action.

Salt Ash Apartment Hotel (☎ 428-8753; Dover Beach; apt US$70; ✗) This small, family-run operation caters to both overseas and Caribbean travelers. While certainly not fancy, it's good value considering the proximity to the beach.

TOP END

Casuarina Beach Club (☎ 428-3600; www.casuarina.com; Dover Beach; r from $145; ✗ ▢ ✕) Popular with package-tour groups and families, this hotel is surrounded by coconut and casuarina trees. The pleasant grounds contain 129 rooms, tennis courts, a restaurant, a bar and other amenities.

Dover Beach Hotel (☎ 428-8076; www.doverbeach.com; s/d from US$105/120; ✗ ▢ ✕) Though it doesn't have as much of a following as the nearby Casuarina, the Dover Beach Hotel is better value. The 39 studios and one-bedroom apartments have private patios or balconies. It's on the beach and there's a restaurant, TV lounge and bar.

Eating

MIDRANGE

Ship Inn (☎ 435-6961; St Lawrence Coast Rd; meals from B$20; ⏱ 11:30am-11pm) This seafaring-themed restaurant and bar at the west end of the road has been a fixture in the area since 1974. It has a couple of dining spots under one roof. Captain's Carvery, the main restaurant, is pleasant enough, but the food, served buffet-style, is unremarkable. The adjacent **Ship Inn Bar** (meals around B$30) has a pub menu, with chicken-and-mushroom pie or steak and chips. There is entertainment seven days a week.

McBride's Pub & Cookhouse (☎ 435-6352; St Lawrence Coast Rd; meals B$30; ⏱ 6:30-11pm, bar until 2am or later) Also at the west end of the road, McBride's pseudo-Irish pub is a popular restaurant and late-night bar. It serves hearty Irish stew, steak-and-Guinness pie, or bangers and mash. Kids' meals are available and the bar has a pool table and televised international sports. There is also live music nightly.

B4 Blues (☎ 435-6560; meals B$15; ⏱ noon-11pm Mon-Sat) For something a little calmer, except for the waves crashing below, this is a well-recommended bistro serving lunch and dinner. There are lots of shrimp options as well as fresh fish, moussaka and 'shepherdess pie.' The blues and jazz start at 8pm Tuesday and Friday. Wednesday is the night for acoustic rock and Friday is reggae, blues and rock classics.

TOP-END

David's Place (☎ 435-9755; mains from B$50; ⏱ 6-10pm Tue-Sun) This Canadian-Bajan–owned waterfront restaurant has a classy veranda covered in hanging ferns. The nearby lights of St Lawrence glitter across Little Bay and diners are serenaded by classical music. David's caters to couples, serving upscale versions of standard Bajan fare like a delectable macaroni pie alongside fresh barracuda and other seafood dishes. It's on the main road at the entrance to the Gap.

Pisces (☎ 435-6564; St Lawrence Coast Rd; meals B$70; ⊗ 6pm-10pm) Pisces is an open-air restaurant that has candlelight dining to the tune of crashing waves. It is a great place to watch the sunset. While the atmosphere is indeed special, the food (standard fish dishes, seafood fettuccini and lobster) can be hit or miss. It is, nonetheless, always a good bet for a romantic glass of wine and an appetizer.

Entertainment

There's always something happening in St Lawrence Gap – just follow the crowds. Several popular venues keep things hopping with live bands and DJs. Most have a cover charge, sometimes up to B$30 and sometimes partially redeemable in drinks or food. The nightlife here is pretty touristy. Consider starting off in St Lawrence Gap and then heading out to Harbour Lights or the Boatyard in Bridgetown (see p633) or nearby Oistins (below) on weekend nights for a wilder and more Bajan experience.

Both the Ship Inn and McBride's (opposite) are also solid nightspots where there is sure to be some movement.

After Dark (☎ 435-6547; St Lawrence Gap; cover varies; ⊗ 10pm-3am) This big bar is good for late-night mingling with both locals and foreigners. It sometimes stays open until 6am and is at its best on Friday and Saturday. Although it's not dressy, pants and shoes are recommended.

Reggae Lounge (☎ 435-6462; St Lawrence Gap; cover varies; ⊗ 9pm-late) The Reggae Lounge not only plays classic reggae, but dancehall, hip-hop and some incongruous '90s rock. This is a fun option for drinking and dancing, but the B$30 weekend cover charge is robbery.

OISTINS
pop 15,000

This decidedly local town, a few miles down the road from St Lawrence, is best known as the center of the island's fishing industry. Oistins' heart is the large, bustling seaside fish market, which on Friday and Saturday hosts the island's best party, with soca, reggae, pop and country music, vendors selling barbecued fish, and plenty of rum drinking. It's roughly 80% locals, 20% tourists, and makes a fun scene, whether you're out for partying or just getting a solid local meal at a fair price. The height of the action is between 10pm and 2am Friday and Saturday.

SILVER SANDS
pop 10,000

At the southernmost tip of the island, between Oistins and the airport, is the breezy Silver Sands area. It is a good place to stay if you have an early flight, although the area is dominated by some characterless larger resorts. The main redeeming quality is that it is a mecca for kitesurfers and windsurfers. In January and February, everything fills up for the Windsurfing Championship, an event worth watching. Most of the No 11 route taxis continue to Silver Sands from Oistins.

Sleeping & Eating

In addition to the following listings, there are a number of private places in the Silver Sands area that can be rented by the week. Many windsurfers stay a night or two in a hotel and then through word of mouth find a shared house or apartment nearby.

Peach and Quiet Hotel (☎ 428-5682; www.barbados.org/hotels/h48.htm; Inch Marlow; d from US$89) Although it's not on the main windsurfing beach (it's 3 miles/5km from the airport), kitschy-titled Peach and Quiet is a very appealing place with 22 airy rooms with seaview patios. There's an oceanside bar and a restaurant, which offers a new menu every day and gladly caters to special diets.

Round Rock Apartments (☎ 428-7500; www.barbados.org/apt/a40.htm; Silver Sands; d from US$77) Just off the beach, husband-and-wife-run Round Rock has seven self-catering units. A pleasant ocean-view restaurant serves a full breakfast for B$10.50 and hamburgers and tasty *cutters* for around B$5.

Ocean Bliss Apartments (☎ 428-7259; www.barbados.org/apt/oceanbliss; apt US$70) A bit further down the road, east of Silver Sands, tranquil Ocean Bliss has ocean-view studios for up to four people. All apartments have balconies and hammocks, plus there's a storeroom for sailboards and a laundry room. It can connect you with kitesurfing and windsurfing gear and classes.

SOUTHEAST

St Philip, the diamond-shaped parish east of the airport, is sparsely populated, with a scattering of small villages. Along the coast are a couple of resort hotels, while inland, just north of Six Cross Roads, is one of the oldest and most interesting plantation houses on the island.

Getting There & Away
Bus No 11 continues into the southeast of Barbados after heading south from Bridgetown; see p634.

CRANE BEACH
Crane Beach, situated 4.5 miles (7km) northeast of the airport, is a broad swath of sand backed by cliffs and fronted by aqua blue waters. It is generally regarded as one of the best beaches on the island. Public access to the beach can be found along the side roads north of the Crane Beach Hotel.

The most spectacular viewpoint is from the hotel, which sits high on a cliff at the south end of the beach. So scenic is the setting that the hotel has managed to turn itself into a bit of a tourist attraction, charging B$5 to tour the grounds.

Crane Beach Hotel (☎ 423-6220; www.thecrane.com; r from US$105; P ⊠ ⊠) occupies an 18th-century mansion, and has 18 spacious rooms and suites with mahogany furnishings and hardwood floors. The rooms are some of the most distinctive on the island. As with the rest of the hotel, the dining room has a fine view out over the beach. Sunday features a brunch buffet serenaded by a gospel choir for B$40.

SUNBURY PLANTATION HOUSE
Built between 1660 and 1670, the handsome **Sunbury Plantation House** (☎ 423-6270; www.barbadosgreathouse.com; tours adult/child B$13.80/6.90; ⊙ 10am-4:30pm) was painstakingly restored after a fire in 1995. The house has 2ft-thick (60cm) walls made from local coral blocks and ballast stones, the latter coming from the ships that set sail from England to pick

up Barbadian sugar. The interior retains its plantation-era ambience and is furnished in antiques – many made from Barbadian mahogany. In the area behind the house there is a collection of horse-drawn carriages.

Tours are given by guides well versed in local history. Have lunch or tea at the Courtyard restaurant, or a five-course dinner served on Sunbury's 200-year-old mahogany dining table.

WEST COAST

Barbados' west coast has lovely tranquil beaches and the majority of the island's luxury hotels. In colonial times, the area was a popular holiday retreat for the upper crust of British society. These days, the villas that haven't been converted to resorts are owned by wealthy and famous people from all over the world (keep an eye out for Oprah).

Hwy 1, the two-lane road that runs north from Bridgetown to Speightstown, is bordered much of the way by a close mix of tourist facilities and residential areas.

Getting There & Away
Minibuses going north up the west coast leave from near the general post office on Cheapside in Bridgetown and run along Hwy 1.

PAYNES BAY
Fringed by a fine stretch of white sand, gently curving Paynes Bay, in St James, is perhaps the west coast's most popular spot for swimming and snorkeling. Beach access walkways are clearly marked by roadside signs. The main public beach site at the southern end of the bay has picnic tables, rest rooms and a laid-back Friday-night fish fry.

Sleeping
Treasure Beach Hotel (☎ 432-1346; www.treasurebeachhotel.com; r from US$190; P ⊠ ⊠) Right on the beach at Paynes Bay, this personable, yet tasteful, place books heavily with repeat guests. Its 30 rooms have all of the standard high-end amenities. There is a pricey restaurant and stunning views throughout the hotel. This is a top choice for the west coast, without exorbitant prices.

Angler Apartments (☎ /fax 432-0817; www.bar badosahoy.com/angler/online.htm; Clarke's Rd 1, Derricks; r from US$120; **P** ✗) Angler is an unpretentious place with 13 older but clean apartments. Studios in an adjacent old plantation house are similar but smaller. There's a little patio bar and restaurant and the hotel arranges yoga classes.

Eating & Drinking
Bomba's (☎ 432-0569; Prospect; meals about B$30; ☺ 11am-10pm) This is the place in Paynes Bay in which to hang out and have a drink. The sunset is excellent, and it serves casual West Indian fare, including some vegetarian choices.

Crocodile's Den (☎ 432-7625; Paynes Bay; ☺ 4pm-3am) The Crocodile's Den is a good option for an evening fish *cutter* to accompany a cold Banks and a game of pool. There's frequently a live band and it's open late, sometimes with salsa music.

HOLETOWN
pop 30,000
The first English settlers to Barbados landed at Holetown in 1627. An obelisk **monument** along the main road in the town center commemorates the event – although the date on the monument, which reads 'July 1605,' is off by two decades.

Despite being the oldest town on the island, Holetown is a rather bustling place that's more modern than traditional in appearance.

The coastal area north and south of Holetown is designated as the **Barbados Marine Reserve** and is an attempt to safeguard the beaches and offshore sea life.

Sleeping
Coral Reef Club (☎ 422-2372; www.coralreefbarbados .com; Holetown; r from US$420; **P** ✗ ☲) This family-owned luxury hotel has gorgeous landscaped grounds and comfortable rooms. It is close to the beach, and while far from inexpensive it is good value relative to other choices in this area. There is a restaurant and evening entertainment at the hotel.

Glitter Bay (☎ 422-4555; www.fairmont.com/glitter bay; Porters; r from US$500; **P** ✗ ☲) The site was once the home of British tycoon Sir Edward Cunard, a member of the Cunard cruise-line family. Now owned by the Fairmont luxury-hotel group, the handsome 70-room complex has accommodations in three- and four-story Mediterranean-style buildings. The hotel offers good options for families and diversions for kids, without sacrificing its classy, romantic appeal. It's 0.6 miles (1km) from Holetown.

Eating & Drinking
Surfside Beach Bar (☎ 432-2105; lunch special B$10, dinner from B$25; ☺ 9am-midnight) For casual dining with a beach view, check out Surfside, behind the police station. It has West Indian and international bar fare with happy hour and televised sports. There's music and a beachside barbecue on Sundays.

Sitar (☎ 432-2248; 2nd St; dinner from B$55; ☺ 7pm-midnight) This Indian spot has a tandoori oven, a Delhi-born chef and, of course, a waterfall. It serves some quality meat and vegetarian dishes and is known for its *aloo gobi* (potato and cauliflower).

NORTH OF HOLETOWN
Mt Standfast
Mt Standfast is home to hawksbill turtles that feed on sea grasses just off its shore. Most snorkeling tours make a stop here to offer fish to the turtles and to allow customers to swim among them. Without a tour, the beach is accessible by **Dive Blue Reef** (☎ 422-3133; www.divebluereef.com). The Blue Reef can direct you toward the turtles as well as rent you snorkeling gear. If you come at noon, when the tour boats bring lunch to the turtles, you'll be sure to see them.

Lone Star (☎ 419-0598; www.thelonestar.com; meals from B$50, r from US$350; ☺ 7:30am-1am) This fancy hotel and restaurant has smart rooms and serves appetizing meals for equally fancy prices. It can try a bit too hard to be hip, but is nice just the same.

Alternatively, there are a few decent and better-value places (including some vegetarian options) up the road toward the village.

Mullins Beach
Mullins is a popular beach along Hwy 1 between Holetown and Speightstown. The waters are usually calm and good for swimming and snorkeling. It is ideal for a day with the family as the surf is safe for children. There is ample parking, and there are a few upscale hotels in the area.

After a day in the sun playing volleyball or trying some water sports, enjoy cocktails or dinner at the famous **Mullins Beach Bar & Restaurant** (☎ 422-1878; www.baje-intl.com/links /mullins.htm; meals from $B75; ❂ 11am-3pm & 6:30-9:30pm).

SPEIGHTSTOWN

pop 40,000

During the sugarcane boom, Speightstown was a thriving port and the main shipping line ran directly from here to Bristol, England. Since tourism has overtaken sugar, Speightstown has come down a peg and these days it is a relaxed and decidedly Bajan town.

The side streets are thick with older wooden buildings and overhanging galleries. There's more of a genuine town feel here than anywhere else along the west coast, and the waterfront is worth a stroll along to soak up the town's character.

Information

The Fisherman's Pub (right) has a credit card–operated Internet station.

First Caribbean International Bank (☎ 419-8422)

Wish 'N Wash Laundromat (per wash/dry B$5/4, plus for full service B$3; ❂ variable Mon-Sat) In front of Jordan's Supermarket.

Sleeping

If you are interested in staying on here for a longer period of time, apartment and house rentals can be arranged for reasonable rates (from around US$40 per night) through the amiable Clement 'Junior' Armstrong, who manages the Fisherman's Pub (right).

Sunset Sands Apartments (☎ 438-1096; www .sunsetsands.com; Sand St; ste from US$85; ❄) Just north of the town center across from the beach, the Sunset Sands has four attractive suites (ask about discounts for extended stays). The upstairs apartments have stunning ocean views, and there's a secluded garden.

Cobblers Cove (☎ 422-2291; www.cobblerscove .com; s/d from US$475/620; P ❄ ☒) To the south of town, Cobblers Cove is elegant in a relaxed Bajan manner. The nearby beach is small so the pool seems to be the main attraction. It gets many repeat guests and has a very good and very expensive French restaurant on site.

Eating & Drinking

Fisherman's Pub (☎ 422-2703; Queen's St; meals B$12; ❂ 11am-1am Mon-Tue, Thu & Sat, 11am-3am Wed & Fri, noon-midnight Sun) On the waterfront, this spirited place has inexpensive local food and a lot of character. Essentially an oversized beach shack, it is the town's most popular eating and drinking spot. Around 7pm Wednesday, locals and visitors come for dinner and live steel-pan music. As the evening wears on, the scene gets more Bajan. Try the national dish of *cou-cou* and flying fish here.

Mango's by the Sea (☎ 422-0704; Main Rd; mains B$55; ❂ 6-10pm Sun-Fri) A fancier dinner option in the town center, Mango's will even pick you up from your hotel for free. Main dishes include mango chicken and seafood crepes and starters include shrimp cocktail and smoked salmon. The restaurant is renowned for its wide variety of fresh seafood.

CENTRAL BARBADOS

From Bridgetown, a series of highways fan out into the interior. Any one of these can make a nice drive, and scores of secondary roads add still more possibilities for exploration. Many of the island's historical, cultural and natural sights lie in the interior, but the area is thin on restaurants, and accommodations are nonexistent in places. Much of the area can be toured by bus or taxi.

Sights & Activities

HISTORICAL SIGHTS

The **Morgan Lewis Sugar Mill** (☎ 422-7429; adult/ child B$10/5; ❂ 9am-5pm Mon-Fri), 1.25 miles (2km) southeast of Cherry Tree Hill, claims to be the largest intact sugar windmill surviving in the Caribbean. The recently restored interior has a simple display of historic photos, a few artifacts of the plantation era and the original gears, shaft and grinding wheel. A stairway leads up around the works to the top, where you can get a bit of a view of the surrounding area.

St Nicholas Abbey (☎ 422-8725; admission B$10; ❂ 10am-3:30pm Mon-Fri), a Jacobean-style mansion 820yd (750m) west of Cherry Tree Hill, is one of the oldest plantation houses in the Caribbean. One of its early owners, Sir John Yeamans, led a 1663 expedition that colonized Carolina; he went on to

---

EXPLORING THE INTERIOR

The most popular touring route, which takes in some of the island's finest scenery and many of the leading attractions, starts along Hwy 2 and runs northeast from Bridgetown. As you reach the edge of the city you first pass Tyrol Cot Heritage Village. From there the suburbs soon give way to small villages, sugarcane fields and scrubby pastureland. About 6 miles (10km) out of the city the road leads to Welchman Hall Gully, Harrison's Cave and the Flower Forest. Hwy 2 continues through the hilly Scotland District and then turns westward, leading to a scenic loop drive that takes in the Morgan Lewis Sugar Mill, the vista at Cherry Tree Hill, St Nicholas Abbey, Farley Hill National Park and the Barbados Wildlife Reserve. From here, it's possible to head down the east coast to Bathsheba and return to Bridgetown via Gun Hill Signal Station, with a detour to the Francia Plantation.

---

become governor of that North American colony. Visitors can tour the ground floor of the mansion, which has a fine collection of 19th-century Barbadian and English furnishings. One peculiar feature of the house is the inclusion of fireplaces, apparently the result of strict adherence to an English design that didn't give consideration to Barbados' tropical climate.

About 235yd (215m) off Hwy 3B, **Gun Hill** (☎ 429-1358; Fusilier Rd; adult/child B$10/5; ✆ 9am-5pm Mon-Sat) is a hilltop signal tower that has an impressive view of the surrounding valleys and the southwest coast. The island was once connected by six such signal towers that used flags and lanterns to relay messages. The official function of the towers was to keep watch for approaching enemy ships, but they also signaled colonial authorities in the event of a slave revolt.

Just south of Gun Hill, **Francia Plantation** (☎ 429-0474; adult/child incl drink B$10/5; ✆ 10am-4pm Mon-Fri) has an elegant plantation house with an interior of rich woods and period furnishings, and an interesting collection of antique maps and prints. On the grounds are pleasant formal gardens out back, and some surrounding fields of vegetable crops. The plantation was built in the early 20th century and is still occupied by descendants of the original French owner.

Tyrol Cot Heritage Village (☎ 424-2074; Codrington Hill; adult/child B$11.50/5.75; ✆ 9am-5pm Mon-Fri) is a somewhat contrived traditional Bajan village centered on the former home of Sir Grantley Adams, first premier of Barbados, and of his son Tom Adams, the second prime minister. The site, on Hwy 2 just north of Bridgetown, is complete with chattel houses where artists work on their crafts and where there's a working black-

smith. The stables have been converted into a restaurant, and sandwiches are available in a replica rum shop. It's managed by the Barbados National Trust.

NATURAL SIGHTS
Welchman Hall Gully (☎ 438-6671; Hwy 2, Welchman Hall; adult/child B$11.50/5.75; ✆ 9am-5pm Mon-Sat) is a thickly wooded ravine with a walking track that leads you through nearly 200 species of tropical plants. Gullies like this were virtually the only places planters were unable to cultivate crops, and they thus represent an unspoiled slice of forest similar to what once covered much of the island. By public transport, take a 'Sturdges' minibus from the Cheapside station in Bridgetown.

Actually a network of limestone caves, **Harrison's Cave** (☎ 438-6640; www.harrisonscave.com; Hwy 2, Welchman Hall; tours adult/child US$16/7; ✆ tours every half-hour 8:30am-4pm) has dripping stalactites, stalagmites and subterranean streams and waterfalls. A tram goes down into the cave, stopping en route to let passengers get out and closely examine some of the more impressive sites. These include the Great Hall – a huge domed-shaped cavern – and the Cascade Pool – an impressive body of crystal-clear water 55yd (50m) beneath the cave entrance level.

Flower Forest of Barbados (☎ 433-8152; Hwy 2; adult/child B$14/7; ✆ 9am-5pm), about 2 miles (3km) north of Harrison's Cave at the western edge of the Scotland District, is a 50-acre (20-hectare) botanical garden on the site of a former sugar estate. Paths meander through the grounds, which are now planted with virtually every plant found on Barbados, including lots of flowering species. The gardens retain the estate's mature citrus and breadfruit trees. Plaques display

---

MONEY FOR MONKEYS

There are some 7000 green monkeys *(Cercopithecus aethiops sabaeus)* who consider Barbados to be home. Introduced as pets from West Africa around 350 years ago, the monkeys found their way into the wild and with no natural predators, they thrived – no natural predators except for humans, that is.

They are shy and live mainly in forested gullies, traveling in groups of up to a dozen. Indeed, because monkeys have many of the same food preferences as humans, they are considered a pest by Bajan farmers, who can lose as much as a third of their banana, mango and papaya crops to the pesky primates.

Consequently, the government has long encouraged the hunting of monkeys. The first bounties were introduced in the late 1600s: the princely sum of five shillings for each monkey head delivered to the parish church. In 1975, the Ministry of Agriculture introduced a new bounty of B$5 in exchange for each monkey tail, and after the Barbados Primate Research Centre was founded in 1982, it began to offer a more enticing B$50 reward for each monkey captured alive and delivered unharmed. As a result, many farmers now trap rather than shoot the monkeys – although the animal's eventual fate may be far worse than shooting. It is rumored that some 1500 monkeys pass through the Centre each year and many are resold abroad for US$1500 a piece.

---

both the English and Latin names of flowers and trees, making this a particularly nice place to come if you want to identify flora you've seen around the island. Many of the trails are wheelchair accessible.

The well-landscaped **Farley Hill National Park** (☎ 422-3555; Hwy 2; per car B$3; ⏰ 8:30am-6pm) is a 17-acre (6.8-hectare) property with stunning views out over the Atlantic. As well as being a popular picnic spot for Barbadians, Farley Hill is one of the venues of the Barbados Jazz Festival. It is a great place to stop while on a trip over to the eastern side of the island.

Barbados Wildlife Reserve (☎ 422-8826; adult/child under 12 B$23/11.50; ⏰ 10am-5pm) is a walk-through zoo opposite Farley Hill, with short paths that meander through a mahogany forest of scurrying green monkeys, sluggish red-footed turtles and a caiman pond. Other creatures that may be spotted include brocket deer, iguanas and agoutis. There's a small aviary with macaws and cockatoos, as well as some caged parrots and uncaged peacocks and pelicans. To top it off, there's an orchid display and an iguana sanctuary.

Getting There & Away

From most destinations, it's possible to negotiate a taxi to stop at various points on a day trip. You can also catch buses from the River Bus Terminal in Bridgetown – let the driver know where you want to visit so that you can be let off at the proper spot.

EASTERN BARBADOS

The Atlantic-facing east coast has a predominantly rugged shoreline, turbulent seas and an unspoiled rural character. The salty air corrodes the buildings along the shore and has prevented large-scale development. The East Coast Rd, which connects Hwy 2 with Bathsheba, is the only coastal road of any length on this side of the island.

BATHSHEBA
pop 5000
Bathsheba is the main destination on the east coast and its rocky beach is pictured on postcards sold throughout the country. It's a sedate place, strung along the back of the beach. There's no clear center to the town and there are few facilities. It attracts surfers and those who want to escape the standard tourism hustle that dominates much of the rest of Barbados.

Sights & Activities
ANDROMEDA BOTANIC GARDENS
At the top of the southern entrance to Bathsheba, the splendid **Andromeda Botanic Gardens** (☎ 433-9261; andromeda.cavehill.uwi.edu; Hwy 3; adult/child B$12/6; ⏰ 9am-5pm, no admission after 4:30pm) cover 6 acres (2.4 hectares) and have a wide collection of introduced tropical plants, including orchids, ferns, water lilies, bougainvillea, cacti and palms. Boulders of

coral are strewn across the property, which has breathtaking views out to the ocean. A walk through these gardens is sure to be a highlight of a visit to Barbados. Entry includes booklets that identify the plants on self-guided trails. Buses that run to and from Bathsheba stop just below the entrance.

SURFING
The world-famous reef break known as **Soup Bowl** is right off the beach in northern Bathsheba. It is one of the best waves in the Caribbean Islands. Don't underestimate the break just because the region is not known for powerful surf – Soup Bowl gets big. Moreover, the reef is shallow and covered in parts by spiny sea urchins. This is not a spot for beginners. Soup Bowl hosts the world's top surfers in international surf competitions in November when the Atlantic is at its strongest. Any of the hotels can give you updates on competition dates.

Sleeping & Eating
Sea-U! Guest House (☎ 433-9450; www.seaubarbados .com; Tent Bay, Bathsheba; r from US$90; P) Right up the hill from Atlantis Hotel, Sea-U is a tidy, modern choice and a supremely relaxing spot. A balcony circles the upper level of the wooden house, affording excellent views of the garden and sea. Breakfast and dinner can be served in the garden and Internet access is available for guests.

Edgewater Inn (☎ 433-9900; www.newedgewater .com; r US$110; P) This refurbished and fully upgraded hotel in north Bathsheba is one of the largest and fanciest options on the east coast. It is more affordable than similar-level accommodations in this area. It is airy and spacious with well-maintained grounds. The restaurant deck runs along a bluff above the ocean and the views are stellar. Rooms 212, 218 and 221 are the most requested rooms because they have the best views of the coast. There are two Internet stations that are open to non-guests (per hour B$20).

Atlantis Hotel (☎ 433-9445; www.atlantisbarbados .com; Tent Bay, Bathsheba; s/d from US$85/105; P) Just south of Bathsheba, Atlantis was the original hotel in town and is a traditional place to stop for the Sunday West Indian buffet (B$40). It is a salty old place, with a noble faded glory and a strong local flavor. While the rooms are not luxurious, they are clean

and those facing the water are as close as you can stay to the ocean. The sound of the breaking waves will soothe you to sleep.

Roundhouse Restaurant (☎ 433-9678; meals B$40; breakfast, lunch & dinner) This popular touristy restaurant has customers throughout the day who sit around, sip cocktails and savor the views. Tempting starters such as baked rum nut brie lead into a variety of fish and meat dishes. The staff is friendly and the bar is a good place to strike up a conversation.

Getting There & Away
A taxi can be negotiated for B$35 to B$40 from Bridgetown or the south coast, or, if you have some time on your hands, catch a bus from the River Bus Terminal in Bridgetown.

DIRECTORY

ACCOMMODATIONS
Though prices for lodging tend to be excessive, a handful of relatively inexpensive guesthouses and midrange hotels can be found. The guesthouses are often small rooms in a wooden house with a shared bathroom. While not truly budget places, they're good value by Caribbean standards. Midrange hotels vary greatly, but the less expensive ones tend to be drab boxy places with little or no character located along the highway.

Most of the upscale resorts are along the west coast, in the parish of St James, a relatively quiet and subdued area. The south coast, which generally attracts a more boisterous crowd, has most of the low-end and midrange accommodations. There's a light scattering of places to stay elsewhere on the island, including a few secluded options on the east and southeast coasts.

EMERGENCY NUMBERS

Ambulance (☎ 511)
Coast Guard Defense Force (☎ emergencies 427-8819; nonemergencies 436-6185) For boating issues or decompression-related diving illness.
Fire (☎ 311)
Police (☎ 211, 436-6600 for routine police matters)

PRACTICALITIES

- **Newspapers & Magazines** Barbados has two daily newspapers, the *Barbados Advocate* and the *Nation*. Two free tourist publications are the weekly *Visitor* and the bimonthly *Sunseeker*.

- **Radio & TV** The government-owned TV station CBC broadcasts on Channel 8; CNN, ESPN and TNT are picked up by satellite. Local radio is on FM 92.9 and 98.1 or AM 790 and 900; soca music on FM 95.3; and gospel on FM 102.1.

- **Electricity** The current used is 110V, 50 cycles, with a flat two-pronged plug; many hotels have 240V converter outlets in the bathrooms.

- **Weights & Measures** Barbados uses the metric system; however, many islanders still give directions in feet and miles and sell produce by the pound.

Many hotels charge the same rate for single and double occupancy. Some places have three rate schedules: a low rate for the summer, a marginally more expensive spring and autumn rate and a high rate for the winter.

A list of accommodations, with links to many, can be found at www.barbados.org.

If you arrive without a reservation, the tourist office at the airport can book you a room.

There's no charge for the service, and it can almost always come up with something in every price range. The tourist office also keeps a short list of families that rent out bedrooms in their homes, from about US$20 per person per night. During the high season, it is best to make arrangements in advance. Camping is generally not allowed on Barbados.

Most hotels add a 7.5% government tax plus a 10% service charge. And many have a minimum stay, so be sure to check.

ACTIVITIES

Barbados has a plethora of activities classes and groups from flower arranging to diving to transcendental meditation. Groups and classes are listed in the *Sunseeker* and *Visitor* tourist publications.

Beaches & Swimming

Some of the island's prettiest beaches and calmest waters are along the west coast. Top spots include Paynes Bay and Mullins Bay – all lovely white-sand beaches that are easily accessible.

The southwest side of the island also has some fine beaches, including Sandy Beach in Worthing, Rockley Beach and Dover Beach. On the southeast side is Crane Beach, a scenic stretch of pink-tinged sand that's popular with bodysurfers but rough for swimming.

Around Bridgetown, the locally popular Pebbles Beach on Carlisle Bay and the area around the Malibu rum distillery are frequented by visitors as well.

The east coast has dangerous water conditions, including shallow reefs and strong currents, and only the most confident swimmers and surfers should take to the waters. The Bathsheba area, in particular, has been the scene of a number of visitor drownings.

Cricket

In Barbados, you can catch an international Test Match, a heated local First Division match or even just a friendly game on the beach or grassy field. Thousands of Bajans

BEST BAJAN BEACHES

- **Crane Beach** (p638) This remote beach with pinkish fluffy sands is a tranquil paradise.
- **Mullins Beach** (p639) Close to Speightstown, it is attractive with a famous beach bar.
- **Paynes Bay Beach** (p638) North of Bridgetown, this calm, sandy bay is a family favorite.
- **Accra Beach** (p634) Near Rockley, this is the biggest and most popular beach on the south coast.
- **Bathsheba Beach** (p642) This rugged coastline is gorgeous to see and gnarly to surf.

and other West Indians pour into the world-class matches at **Kensington Oval** (☎ 436-1397; ☺ 9am-4pm), at Fontabelle, outside Bridgetown. The **Barbados Tourism Authority** (www.barbados.org/evncrick.htm) keeps an online schedule of upcoming cricket matches and related events. The sports sections of the local papers also have listings.

For tickets, contact the **Barbados Cricket Association** (☎ 436-1397, 800-744-4263; theoffice@bca.org.bb).

Deep-Sea Fishing

For those who want to catch their own tuna, barracuda or kingfish for dinner, the **Billfisher II** (☎ 431-0741) and **Blue Jay Charters** (☎ 429-2326) have group and private fishing trips. A half-day with a group is B$200 per person including hotel pickup. For a whole day, you must charter the boat. Both are located in Bridgetown; call ahead for arrangements.

Diving & Snorkeling

The west coast of Barbados has reef dives with soft corals, gorgonians and colorful sponges. There are also about a dozen shipwrecks. The largest and most popular, the 364ft (111m) freighter *Stavronikita*, sits upright off the central west coast in 138ft (42m) of water, with the rigging reaching to within 20ft (6m) of the surface. In Bridgetown's Carlisle Bay, the coral-encrusted tug *Berwyn* lies in only 23ft (7m) of water and makes for good snorkeling as well as diving.

One-tank dives with gear average B$110, and two-tank dives B$150. For beginners, most dive companies offer a brief resort course and a shallow dive for B$90 to B$140. Many also offer full Professional Association of Diving Instructors (PADI) or National Association of Underwater Instructors (NAUI) certification courses for B$700 to B$800. Rates often include free transportation from your hotel. Check out the **Barbados Tourism Authority** (www.barbados.org/diveops.htm) for the most complete list of diving information. Better-known Barbadian dive shops:

Bubbles Galore Incorporated (☎ 430-0354; www.barbados.org/diving/bubbles/dive.html; Sandy Beach Island Resort, Worthing)

Carib Ocean Divers Incorporated (☎ 422-4414; www.funbarbados.com/activities/caribocean.cfm; Pemberton Princess Hotels, St James)

Dive Blue Reef (☎ 422-3133; www.divebluereef.com; Mt Standfast)

Dive Shop (☎ 426-9947; www.barbados.org/diving/diveshop/diveshop.html; Bay St, Aquatic Gap)

Exploresub Barbados (☎ 435-6542; www.skyviews.com/x-sub; St Lawrence Gap)

Hightide Watersports (☎ 432-0931; www.divehightide.com; Coral Reef Club, St James)

West Side Scuba Centre Inc (☎ 432-2558; www.skyviews.com/westsidescuba; Baku Beach, Holetown)

Snorkeling sets can be rented for about B$20 per day at beach water-sports huts, dive shops and some hotels and restaurants. Several companies offer one- to two-hour snorkeling tours. Two of the best options include snorkeling at the *Berwyn* in Carlisle Bay or swimming with the hawksbill turtles on the west coast.

Hiking

The **Barbados National Trust** (☎ 436-9033) leads guided hikes in the countryside. Hike leaders share insights into local history, geology and wildlife. Locations vary, but all hikes end where they start, last around three hours and cover about 5 miles (8km). Once a month, a moonlight hike replaces the afternoon hike. There is no fee. Schedule information can be found in the free tourist publications and is also available by calling the trust.

Adrian Loveridge at the Peach and Quiet Hotel (p671) near Silver Sands, leads nature hikes during the high season.

A nice hike to do on your own is along the old railroad bed that runs along the east coast from Belleplaine to St Martin's Bay. The whole walk is about 12.5 miles (20km), but it can be broken into shorter stretches.

Surfing

Barbados has some surprisingly good waves for the Caribbean. The biggest swells hit the east coast, with prime surfing at the Soup Bowl (p643), off Bathsheba, and another spot called Duppies, up the coast. South Point and Rockley Beach on the south coast are sometimes surfable, although they don't compare to Bathsheba. **Barbados Surfing Association** (☎ 433-9247; BDF Hospital Bldg, Bathsheba) has good information on upcoming events and other surfing information. The **Edgewater Inn website** (www.edgewaterinn.com/surf.html) has a comprehensive list of the better waves on the island.

There are local guys renting out boards on the beach at most of the popular surf spots. Prices are negotiable depending on the quality of the board, but even the nicest board should never be over B$15 to B$20 per hour. **Dread or Dead** (☎ 228-4785; dreadordeadsurf@yahoo .com; Main Rd, Hastings) is a first-rate surf shop that rents out boogie boards for B$20 a day and surfboards for B$40 a day, each requiring a B$100 deposit. Unfortunately, you'll have to travel a little way from Hastings to find any good surf.

Horse Races & Horse Riding

Horse races are held at the Garrison Savannah on Saturday afternoons throughout the year, except April and September. Admission to the grandstand is B$20, but for no charge you can also watch the races from benches under the trees around the outside of the track – you can also place a bet at booths on the south or west side. **Barbados Turf Club** (☎ 426-3980; www.barbadosturfclub.com) offers three packages with reserved seating in the grandstand, a racing program, a betting voucher and either a snack or lunch in the track-view restaurant. Packages start at B$60 for adults and B$40 for children.

If you are more of a participant than spectator, **Wilcox Riding Stable** (☎ 428-3610) near the airport offers one-hour rides twice daily. The trails are in Long Beach on the southeast coast, and cost around B$90, including hotel pickup.

Windsurfing & Kitesurfing

Barbados has good windsurfing and kitesurfing, with the best winds from December to June. Silver Sands, at the southern tip of the island, has excellent conditions for advanced boarders, while Maxwell, just to the west, is better for intermediates. Most beginners also take lessons in Silver Sands.

Club Mistral (☎ 428-7277; www.clubmistralbados.com; Maxwell Main Rd) rents out windsurfing gear in Oistins and windsurfing and kitesurfing equipment in Silver Sands. Sailboards start at US$150 for a three-day rental, while a week's rental of a kiteboard and kite will set you back US$250 (you must be level 5 to rent, meaning you have to prove that you know how to kitesurf upwind). Club Mistral gives lessons to beginners starting at US$150 for windsurfing and US$205 for kitesurfing. There are special group rates and many other options, so check the website.

Equipment can be rented at various smaller operations around the island, including **Dread or Dead** (☎ 228-4785; dreadordead surf@yahoo.com; Main Rd, Hastings) or **Charles Watersports** (☎ 428-9550; Dover Beach).

BOOKS

The most common type of book on Barbados is the coffee-table photograph book. *Barbados: Portrait of an Island,* by Dick Scoones, is one of the better choices. Numerous books cover Barbadian history and sights: *The Barbados Garrison and its Buildings,* by Warren Alleyne and Jill Sheppard, is a well-written little volume describing the many historic buildings that comprise the Garrison area; *Treasures of Barbados* (which surveys island architecture), by Henry Fraser, president of the Barbados National Trust; and books on Barbadian political figures, including *Tom Adams: A Biography* and *Grantley Adams and the Social Revolution,* both by local historian FA Hoyos. Those interested in natural features of Barbados may enjoy *Geology of Barbados,* by Hans Machel, or *A Naturalist's Year in Barbados,* by Maurice Batemman Hutt. *The Barbadian Rum Shop: The Other Watering Hole,* by Peter Laurie, is an overview of the history of the rum shop and the role that it has played in Barbadian life. A variety of Bajan cookbooks can also be found at most bookstores.

BUSINESS HOURS

Most banks are open from 8am to 3pm Monday to Thursday, and until 5pm on Friday. A few branches are also open Saturday morning. Most stores are open from 8am to 5pm Monday to Friday and until noon Saturday. Larger supermarkets stay open until at least 8pm.

CHILDREN

Barbadian tourism has gone to great lengths to make sure the island is a family-friendly destination. Most hotels – even the fanciest ones – accept children. Some limit children under the age of 12 or have restrictions during the high season, so check ahead. A number of resorts have organized children's activities or in-house daycare/baby-sitting.

Most beaches are safe for children to play on and many of the south- and west-coast beaches are calm enough for younger swimmers. The east-coast surf is too powerful for novice swimmers.

DANGERS & ANNOYANCES

Crime, including assaults on tourists, is not unknown on Barbados. Most crimes, however, are simple tourist scams – normal precautions should suffice.

Beware of pickpockets in Bridgetown – keep your valuables secure around the bustling center on Swan and Broad Sts. There are some slick hustlers who hang out at the entrance to St Lawrence Gap and also around south coast nightlife venues. Steer clear unless you want to invest in someone's habit.

Crack has been a major problem on the island for a number of years.

Sidewalks are narrow or nonexistent and roads are curvy, so use the utmost caution while walking along even more-quiet streets.

Portuguese man-of-war jellyfish are occasionally encountered in Barbadian waters (although they are large, slow and usually easy to spot), and poisonous manchineel trees grow along some beaches.

Truth be told, the greatest risk is a bad sunburn.

EMBASSIES & CONSULATES
Barbadian Embassies & Consulates
Australia (☎ 02-9327 7009; 4 Warren Rd, Double Bay, NSW 2028)
France (☎ 01-42-65-13-04; 64 rue des Mathurins, 75008 Paris)
UK (☎ 0207-7631 4975; 1 Great Russell St, London WC1 B3JY)
USA (☎ 202-939-9200; 2144 Wyoming Ave NW, Washington, DC 20008)

Embassies & Consulates in Barbados
Australia (☎ 435-2834; Bishop's Court Hill, St Michael)
Belgium (☎ 435-7704; 609 Rockley Resort & Country Club, Christ Church)
Canada (☎ 429-3550; Bishop's Court Hill, St Michael)
China (☎ 435-6607; 17 Golf View Terrace, Golf Club Rd, Rockley, Christ Church)
Colombia (☎ 429-6821; Dayrell's Rd, Rockley, Christ Church)
Costa Rica (☎ 431-0250; Dayrell's Court Business Centre, Dayrell's Rd, Rockley, Christ Church)
Cuba (☎ 435 2769; Erin Court, Collymore Rock, St Michael)

Denmark (☎ 424-4995; Grazettes Industrial Park, St Michael)
France (☎ 435-6847; Bulkeley Great House, Bulkeley, St George)
Germany (☎ 427-1876; Dayrell's Rd, Pleasant Hall, Christ Church)
Haiti (☎ 436-6144; Salters, St George)
Israel (☎ 426-4764; Palmetto St, Bridgetown)
Italy (☎ 437-1228; Bannatyne, Christ Church)
Netherlands (☎ 418-8074; Balls Plantation, Christ Church)
Norway (☎ 429-7286; Nile St, Bridgetown)
Sweden (☎ 427-4358; Brancker's Complex Fontabelle, St Michael)
UK (☎ 430-7800; Lower Collymore Rock, St Michael)
USA (☎ 436-4950; CIBC Bldg, Broad St, Bridgetown)
Venezuela (☎ 435-7619; Hastings)

FESTIVALS & EVENTS

The official list of Barbados' festivals and events is posted on the **Barbados Tourism Authority website** (www.barbados.org/eventcd.htm).
Holetown Festival (February) This festival celebrates the February 17, 1627, arrival of the first English settlers on Barbados. Holetown's weeklong festivities include street fairs, a music festival at the historic parish church and a road race.
Oistins Fish Festival (Easter weekend) Commemorates the signing of the Charter of Barbados and celebrates the skills of local fishermen. It's a seaside festivity with events focusing on boat races, fish-deboning competitions, local foods, crafts and dancing.
Congaline Carnival (late April) This is a big street party with music and arts. The focus of the event is an all-day band parade and conga line that winds its way from Bridgetown to St Lawrence Gap.
Gospel Fest (late May) The Fest celebrates Barbadians' love of gospel music with major performers from the US, UK and Caribbean.
Crop-Over Festival (mid-July) The island's top event. It originated in colonial times as a celebration to mark the end of the sugarcane harvest. Festivities stretch over a three-week period beginning in mid-July with spirited calypso competitions, fairs and other activities around the island. The festival culminates with a Carnival-like costume parade and fireworks on Kadooment Day, a national holiday, in August.
National Independence Festival of Creative Arts (November) Features talent contests in dance, drama, singing and the like. Performances by the finalists are held on Independence Day (November 30).

There is also a handful of international sporting events, including the Barbados Windsurfing World Cup, in January; the Caribbean

BARBADOS

Surfing Championship, in November; Banks Field Hockey Festival, in late August; and the early December marathon, Run Barbados.

GAY & LESBIAN TRAVELERS

Barbados is a conservative, religious and macho place that is generally opposed to homosexuality, particularly among males. That said, it is a bit more progressive than the rest of the Eastern Caribbean and there are a few openly homosexual Bajan couples (although they still tend to be discreet) and even the rare transvestite.

Homosexual visitors to Barbados will need to be judicious outside of international resorts and especially in smaller, more traditional towns.

HOLIDAYS

Public holidays:

New Year's Day January 1
Errol Barrow Day January 21
Good Friday late March/early April
Easter Monday late March/early April
Heroes' Day April 28
Labour Day May 1
Whit Monday eighth Monday after Easter
Kadooment Day first Monday in August
UN Day first Monday in October
Independence Day November 30
Christmas Day December 25
Boxing Day December 26

INTERNET ACCESS

There are Internet cafés and service centers in Bridgetown, most of the tourist centers and larger towns. In more-remote areas, hotels often allow guests access to one of their computers for shorter periods of time.

INTERNET RESOURCES

www.barbados.org Barbados Tourism Authority maintains the official, and best overall, site about the island.
www.bhta.org The Barbados Hotel and Tourism Association is a great resource for accommodation needs.
www.funbarbados.com Fun Barbados is a general travel information site with links to offers and hotels.
www.insandoutsofbarbados.com The engaging and comprehensive tourist magazine *Ins & Outs* now has an online version.
www.nationnews.com *National News* is Barbados' daily newspaper.
www.yellowpages-caribbean.com/Countries /Barbados/index.cfm Here you'll find a searchable version of the Barbados *Yellow Pages*.

MONEY

You'll certainly want some Barbados dollars on hand, but larger payments can be made in US dollars, frequently with a major credit card. Hotels and guesthouses quote rates in US dollars (as do many dive shops and some fancier restaurants), although you can use either US or Barbadian currency to settle the account.

The common street exchange rate is B$2 to US$1 for traveler's checks or cash, although true rates can fluctuate a couple of cents either way.

Banks are easy to find in larger towns and major tourist areas. Credit- and debit-card holders can obtain cash from 24-hour ATMs at many branches of the Royal Bank of Canada, Scotiabank, Caribbean Commercial Bank, First Caribbean and Barbados National Bank, most of which are on the Cirrus and Plus networks. There's are a few ATMs at the airport. Notes come in B$2 (blue), B$5 (green), B$10 (brown), B$20 (purple), B$50 (orange) and B$100 (gray) denominations.

TELEPHONE & FAX

The area code for Barbados is ☎ 246. To call from North America, dial ☎ 1-246 + the local seven-digit number. From elsewhere, dial your country's international access code + ☎ 246 + the local number. We have included only the seven-digit local number for Barbados listings in this chapter.

Barbados public phones accept both coins and cards. You'll get three minutes' calling time to anywhere on the island for each B$0.25 cents; 5c, 10c and 25c coins are accepted. Phone cards, available in B$10, B$20, B$40 and B$60 denominations, are sold at the airport, phone company offices, convenience stores and supermarkets. They can also be used in most other parts of the Eastern Caribbean.

Faxes and telegrams can be sent from 8am to 3:30pm Monday to Friday at the telephone company office on Hincks St in Bridgetown.

For more information on phone cards and making long-distance calls, see p767.

TOURIST INFORMATION

Information on restaurants, tours, museums and other sights can be found in tourist-brochure racks in many restaurants and hotels, and most all-inclusive hotels have an activities office to help with any plans.

Barbados Hotel & Tourism Association (☎ 426-5041, 429-2845; www.bhta.org; 4th Ave, Belleville, St Michael; ☽ 8am-5pm Mon-Sat)

Barbados Tourism Authority (www.barbados.org); Bridgetown (☎ 427-2623; Harbour Rd; ☽ 8am-8pm); Grantley Adams International Airport (☎ 428-5570; ☽ 8am-10pm or until the last flight arrives); Cruise ship terminal (☎ 426-1718; ☽ when ships are in docks)

VISAS

Visas are not required for stays of up to six months for citizens of the US, Canada, Australia, Japan and most Western European countries except Sweden, Switzerland and Portugal, who are limited to stays of 28 days without a visa. Visas are not required for passengers on cruise ships, with the exception of citizens of the CIS, Eastern European countries, China, Taiwan, South Africa and Korea. Visa requirements and periods of stay vary for other nationalities.

To obtain or extend a visa while in Barbados, contact the **Immigration Department** (☎ 426-1011; Careenage House, The Wharf, Bridgetown). The fee for a single-entry visa is B$50, and a multiple-entry visa is B$60.

TRANSPORTATION

GETTING THERE & AWAY
Entering Barbados

Nearly all visitors will enter the country through Grantley Adams International Airport or through Bridgetown's cruise ship terminal. Those who enter by yacht or ferry should visit the Immigration Department (see above) or risk difficulty leaving the country. All foreigners entering Barbados should be in possession of a valid passport (US citizens see the boxed text, p772) and a return or onward ticket. Cruise-ship passengers who are in transit and stay less than 24 hours are not required to carry a valid passport.

Air
AIRPORT

Grantley Adams International Airport (BGI; ☎ 428-7101) is on the island's southeast corner, about 10 miles (16km) from Bridgetown. As of 2005, it was still undergoing renovation and transforming into what will be the largest airport in the Eastern Caribbean and the major point of entry for the region, with 20 immigration counters, 12 customs stations and five new baggage carousels.

The friendly **Barbados Tourism Authority** (☎ 428-5570; ☽ 8am-10pm or until the last flight arrives) booth can help you book a room and is a good place to pick up tourist brochures. There are a number of ATMs in the departures area of the airport. The airport also has phones that accept both cards and coins; a post office; a sit-down restaurant; and a few stalls selling drinks, food and souvenirs. The departure lounge has shops selling duty-free liquor, watches and jewelry, as well as a money-exchange window.

AIRLINES

Most airlines have offices in Bridgetown, though some only have desks at the airport. Tickets purchased in Barbados for flights originating in-country will add on a 15% tax.

The following airlines fly to and from Barbados from within the Caribbean:

Aeropostal (☎ 426-5640; www.aeropostal.com; Indian River Mall, Hincks St, Bridgetown)

Air Jamaica (☎ 800-523-5585, 228-6625; www.airjamaica.com; Bayside Plaza, Bridgetown)

American Eagle (☎ 428-4170; www.aa.com; Grantley Adams International Airport)

British West Indies Air (BWIA; ☎ 426-2111, 428-1650; www.bwee.com; cnr Fairchild & Probyn Sts, Bridgetown)

Caribbean Star (☎ 800-744-7827, 431-0540; www.flycaribbeanstar.com; Bayshore Complex, Bay St, Bridgetown)

LIAT (☎ 434-5428, ☎ airport 428-0986; www.liatair line.com; Hincks St, Bridgetown)

Mustique Airways (☎ 428-1638; www.mustique.com; Grantley Adams International Airport)

Surinam Airways (☎ 436-1858; www.surinamairways.net; Lower Bay St, Bridgetown)

SVG Air (☎ 800-744-5777, 784-457-5124; www.svgair.com; St Vincent)

Trans Island Air (☎ 418-1654; www.tia2000.com; Grantley Adams International Airport)

Sea
CRUISE SHIP

About 450,000 cruise-ship passengers arrive in Barbados each year. Ships dock at Bridgetown Harbour, about 0.6 miles (1km) west of the city center. The port has the usual duty-free shops and a branch office of the **Barbados Tourism Authority** (☎ 426-1718; ☽ when ships are in docks).

BARBADOS

YACHT

Because of Barbados' easterly position and challenging sailing conditions, it is well off the main track for most sailors and there is no yacht charter industry on the island.

Tours

The most popular interisland day tour from Barbados is to the Grenadines. The day starts with a morning snack, followed by a flight to Union Island (p618) and a sail in a catamaran around the spectacular Tobago Cays (p619), Palm Island (p619) and Mayreau (p616). The tour includes lunch, complimentary drinks and a bit of beach and snorkeling time, returning to Barbados at around 6:30pm. Prices start at B$590. You can add Mustique (p615) for B$200 more.

There are various other day tours to Grenada, St Lucia, Martinique, Dominica, St Vincent and Tobago for about the same price. Two- and three-day tours with accommodations in charming island guesthouses are also available.

Following are two of the largest interisland tour companies:

Caribbean Safari Tours (☎ 427-5100; www.carib -safari.com; Ship Inn Complex, St Lawrence Gap)

Chantours (☎ 432-5591; chan@caribsurf.com; Sunset Crest Plaza No 2, St James)

GETTING AROUND
To/From the Airport

If you're traveling light, it's possible to walk out of the airport to the road and wait for a passing bus. Look for buses marked 'Sam Lord's Castle' (or just 'Castle') if you're going east, 'Bridgetown' if you're going to the south coast. For the west coast, occasional buses run to Speightstown, bypassing the capital; alternatively, take a bus to Bridgetown, where you'll have to hike across town to the west-coast terminal.

Make sure the bus driver knows your destination.

You will find a line of taxis outside the arrival lounge and there is a helpful dispatcher that gets you into a car.

Bicycle

Barbados is predominantly flat and is good for riding. Most shops require a credit card or B$100 deposit for rentals.

Express Rent-a-Car (☎ 428-7845; St Lawrence Gap; per day B$25)

Flex Bicycle Rentals (☎ 424-0321; flexbikes@barb ados.org; per day B$40) Based in Speightstown, this bike shop is the most professional of the lot. It will deliver the bike to you and it also leads custom bike tours. There are discounts for longer rentals.

Rob's Bike Hire (☎ 437-3404; per day/week B$20/100) At the Dread or Dead Surf Shop in Hastings.

Bus

It's possible to get to virtually any place on the island by public bus. There are three kinds of buses: government-operated public buses, which are blue with a yellow stripe; privately operated minibuses, which are intermediate-size buses painted yellow with a blue stripe; and route taxis, which are white, individually owned minivans that have 'ZR' on their license plates and ply shorter, heavily traveled routes. All three types of buses charge the same fare: B$1.50 to any place on the island. You should have exact change when you board the government bus, but minibuses and route taxis will make change.

Most buses transit through Bridgetown, although a few north–south buses bypass the city. Buses to the southeast part of the island generally transit through Oistins. To get to the east coast, you can catch one of the hourly direct buses between Bridgetown and Bathsheba. There's also bus service between Speightstown and Bathsheba; these leave Speightstown on odd-numbered hours (9am, 11am etc) and return from Bathsheba on the even hour.

Bus stops around the island are marked with red-and-white signs printed with the direction in which the bus is heading ('To City' or 'Out of City'). Buses usually have their destinations posted on or above the front windshield.

Buses along the main routes, such as Bridgetown to Oistins or Speightstown, are frequent, running from dawn to around midnight. You can get schedule information on any route by calling the **Transport Board** (☎ 436-6820).

For the locations of terminals in Bridgetown, see p634.

Car & Motorcycle
RENTAL

Barbados doesn't have any car-rental agents affiliated with major international rental chains. There are, instead, scores of independent car-rental companies, some so small that they are based out of private homes. You simply call to book a car and someone will swing by your hotel to pick you up.

Despite the number of companies, prices don't seem to vary much. The going rate for a small car is about B$150 a day including unlimited mileage and insurance. Most companies rent out small convertible buggies called 'mokes,' which are usually cheapest. Rental cars are marked with an 'H' on the license plate.

While most car-rental companies don't have booths at the airport, there are a number of nearby agencies that will pick you up there. Inquire at the airport tourist office about the nearest options.

Corbins Car Rentals (☎ 427-9531; rentals@corbins cars.com; Collymore Rock, St Michael)

Courtesy Rent-A-Car (☎ 418-2500; fax 429-6387; Grantley Adams International Airport)

Direct Rentals (☎ 420-6372; direct@sunbeach.net; Enterprise, Christ Church)

Express Rent a Car (☎ 428-7845; fax 428-1593; St Lawrence Gap)

Rayside Car Rental (☎ 428-0264; Charnocks, Christ Church)

Sunny Isle Car Rentals (☎ 435-7979; Worthing)

Sunset Crest Car Rentals (☎ 432-2222; fax 422-1966; Sunset Crest, St James)

Caribbean Scooters (☎ 436-8522; codc@caribsurf.com) rents out scooters with helmets for B$60/80 per day for one-/two-seaters.

ROAD CONDITIONS

Highways are not very well marked, although landmarks are clearly labeled, as are key roundabouts (traffic circles) and major intersections. The most consistent highway markings are often the low yellow cement posts at the side of the road; they show the highway number and below that the number of kilometers from Bridgetown.

All primary and main secondary roads are paved, although some are a bit narrow. There are lots of gas stations around the island, including one outside the airport. Some stations in the Bridgetown area are open 24 hours.

ROAD RULES

In Barbados, you drive on the left. At intersections and narrow passages, drivers may flash their lights to indicate that you should

proceed. At roundabouts, if taking the first left exit, stay in the left lane. Otherwise, keep right to continue around. Temporary driving permits are required; they cost B$10 and can be obtained through your car-rental agency.

Hitchhiking

Hitchhiking is tolerated, but the practice is not widespread, in part because buses are cheap and frequent. All the usual safety precautions apply.

Taxi

Taxis have a 'Z' on the license plate and usually a 'taxi' sign on the roof. They're easy to find and often wait at the side of the road in popular tourist areas.

Although fares are fixed by the government, taxis are not metered, and you will have to haggle for a fair price. The rate per kilometer is about B$1.50, and the flat hourly rate B$35. The 'official' prices from the airport to most of the island's main destinations are: north of Speightstown B$55, Speightstown B$48, Bathsheba B$48, Holetown B$38, Prospect B$34, Harrison's Cave B$34, Bridgetown Harbour B$30, Garrison B$24 and Crane B$20.

Tours

BOAT & SUBMARINE CRUISES

Day cruises are a popular way to explore the island. Many of the larger boats are floating parties, while the smaller operations tend to be more tranquil. For those who want the scuba experience without getting wet, there are submarine cruises.

Atlantis (☎ 436-8929; www.atlantisadventures.com) Operating in most of the Caribbean's major destinations, the *Atlantis* is a 28-seat submarine lined with portholes. This underwater vessel departs from Bridgetown and takes visitors on tours of the coral reef off the island's west coast for US$89 (there is a US$13 discount for online reservations).

El Tigre (☎ 417-7245; www.eltigrecruises.com) El Tigre offers a three-hour cruise with two snorkeling stops for B$100, or a day trip for B$140. The cruises are a good choice if you want to see turtles.

Harbour Master (☎ 430-0900; www.tallshipscruises .com) This is a four-deck party vessel with a huge water slide attached. The B$123 fee includes transfers, snorkeling equipment, lunch and unlimited drinks. On Thursday evening, B$130 will get you a moonlight cruise with dinner, a live band and a floor show.

BARBADOS

Jolly Roger (☎ 436-6424; www.tallshipscruises.com) This pirate-themed party boat offers a four-hour excursion from Bridgetown that includes lunch, an open bar and snorkeling off of Holetown for B$123.

Some of the smaller and more relaxed sailboat cruises include **Limbo Lady** (☎ 420-5418) and **Secret Love** (☎ 432-1972).

SIGHTSEEING TOURS

Most tour companies offer a variety of half- and full-day options that either provide an overview with stops at key sites or emphasize special interests such as nature and gardens.

Adventureland 4x4 Tours (☎ 429-3687; www .adventurelandbarbados.com; Wotton Plantation) These 4WD adventures depart at 8:30am, and while not exactly trailblazing, they let you see more remote parts of the island – and get you drunk in the process.

Bajan Tours (☎ 437-9389; bajan@caribnet.net; Erin Court, Bishop's Court Hill; half-/full-day tours US$56/40; 9am-5pm) This Bajan family–owned company does eight different tours by luxury bus. It's a reputable outfit that allows you to customize your trip to include historical sites, ecotourism and/or cultural exhibitions. It's known for its knowledgeable guides.

Barbados Transit Authority's Sunday Scenic Rides (☎ 436-6820; adult/child B$15/10; tours 2-7pm Sun) More oriented toward local tourism, this bus caravan covers a different area of the island each week, departing from Independence Sq in Bridgetown. While not very personalized, it's affordable and doubles as a good cultural experience. Tickets are available at the Fairchild St and Jubilee terminals. Entrance fees are additional, but there is usually a discount for tour participants. Bring your own food and drink.

Island Safari (☎ 429-5337; safari@barbadostraveler .com; Bush Hall Main Rd, St Michael) Same as Adventureland, Island Safari takes 4WD trucks to many of the usual sights, but also ventures off-road to lesser-known places.

LE Williams Tour Co (☎ 427-6007; Hastings; tours with lunch US$50; 8:30am-end of tour Mon-Sat) LE Williams is a well-established bus tourism operator that will take you to see all of the main attractions. Buses pick you up at your hotel and drive you all over the island in about seven hours. The tours are wheelchair accessible.

The going rate for custom tours by taxi drivers is B$40 an hour, but you can usually negotiate with individual drivers to work out your own deal. **Eugene Belle** (☎ 239-2864) is a pleasant guy who owns a good car and will give you a fair price for a trip anywhere on the island.

Grenada

No, it's not a city in southern Spain and, yes, it is that island that was invaded by the US back in 1983. Grenada (gren-*ay*-duh), the smallest independent country in the western hemisphere, is made up of several islands, with Grenada island the largest.

The islands are a heady mix of idyllic tropical landscapes – there are fecund valleys, rainforested mountains, rivers and waterfalls that lead out to craggy cliffs over white-sand beaches. Grenada island's busy capital, St George's, is graced with the Carenage, an attractive harbor with 19th-century buildings that rise up the steep hillsides and into the surrounding greenery. It is arguably the most beautiful urban waterfront in the Caribbean.

The tourism juggernaut is smaller and quieter in Grenada than in the more famous Caribbean destinations. The arrival of cruise ships quickens the island's pulse, but Grenada is otherwise relaxed and personable. There is little or no tourism hustle, and drugs and panhandling are rare.

While Grenada Island accounts for 90% of the nation's land and people, the country's smaller islands are definitely worth a visit too. Carriacou gets a handful of overnight visitors and a few more day-trippers, while Petit Martinique is one step further off the beaten track. Both are just a short boat ride away from Grenada island and offer comfortable lodgings, beaches and a sublime laid-back tempo.

GRENADA

FAST FACTS

- **Area** 132 sq miles (344 sq km)
- **Capital** St George's
- **Country Code** ☎ 473
- **Departure tax** EC$50 (US$20), half-price for children aged five to 10
- **Famous for** Nutmeg and the 1983 US invasion
- **Language** English
- **Money** Eastern Caribbean dollar (EC$); EC$1 = US$0.37 = €0.31 = UK£0.21
- **People** Grenadians
- **Phrases** Goin up de road (you're busy and heading somewhere)
- **Population** 100,000
- **Visa** Not required

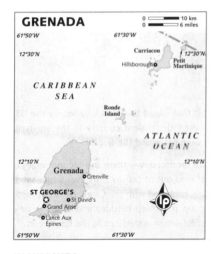

HIGHLIGHTS

- **Carriacou** (p666) Enjoy the scenic ferry ride out to the island and take in the slow pace, vibrant culture and warm waters.
- **Beaches** (p662) and (p663) Head for white sands and turquoise seas of Grand Anse and Morne Rouge, just minutes from the city of St George's.
- **Grand Etang National Park** (p665) Hike along through the rainforest on the park's trails for excellent views out over the island.
- **Petit Martinique** (p670) Walk around this small island, taking time to savor the tranquility.
- **Riding the reggae buses** (p675) Participate in local life by riding in Grenada's crowded minibuses, particularly around busy St George's – always with a bit of reggae and contemporary island music thumping.

ITINERARIES

- **Three days** Explore the southern sights on the island: St George's, Grand Anse, Morne Rouge, Annandale Falls and Grand Etang National Park.
- **One week** After the south, visit the attractive smaller towns of Gouyave, Sauteurs or Grenville, and spend a few nights on Carriacou.
- **Two weeks** Follow the one-week itinerary, then take your time to enjoy the different towns on Carriacou (you may prefer it to Grenada) and visit Petit Martinique.

CLIMATE & WHEN TO GO

Although the climate is tropical and hot, it's tempered by the northeast trade winds. In St George's, the average daily high temperature in January is 84°F (29°C) and the average low is 75°F (24°C). In July the average daily high temperature is 86°F (30°C) and the low is 77°F (25°C).

During the rainy season – from June to November – rain falls an average of 22 days per month in St George's. In the driest months, January to April, there's measurable rainfall for 12 days a month; this is the best time to visit. Hurricane season runs from June to November.

HISTORY
Colonial Competition

In 1498 Christopher Columbus became the first European to sight the island of Grenada, during his third voyage to the New World. It wasn't until 1609, however, that English tobacco planters attempted to settle on the island and, within a year, most were killed by Carib Indians. Some 40 years later, the French 'purchased' the island from the Caribs for a few hatchets, some glass beads and two bottles of brandy. Not all Caribs were pleased with the land deal and skirmishes continued until French troops chased the last of them

---

HOW MUCH?

- **Taxi from the airport to St George's**
Daytime EC$30, nighttime EC$40

- **Day trip around Grenada island**
EC$270

- **Day of diving, with half tank**
US$40/75

- **Meal of fresh fish in a touristy restaurant** EC$30

- **Meal of fresh fish in a local restaurant** EC$20

LONELY PLANET INDEX

- **Gallon (imperial) of gas** EC$7.50

- **Liter of bottled water** EC$4

- **Bottle of Carib beer** EC$4

- **Souvenir T-shirt** EC$40

- **Street snack: chicken roti** EC$8

to Sauteurs Bay at the north end of the island. Rather than submitting to the colonists, the remaining Caribs – men, women and children – jumped to their deaths off the rugged coastal cliffs.

French planters established crops that provided indigo, tobacco, coffee, cocoa and sugar, and imported thousands of African slaves to tend to the fields. Grenada remained under French control until 1762, when Britain first recaptured the island. Over the next two decades, colonial control of the land shifted back and forth between Britain and France – until 1783, when the French ceded Grenada to the British under the Treaty of Paris.

In 1877 Grenada became a crown colony, and in 1967 it converted to an associated state within the British Commonwealth. Grenada, Carriacou and Petit Martinique adopted a constitution in 1973 and gained collective independence on February 7, 1974.

Independence

One-time trade unionist Eric Gairy rose to prominence after organizing a successful labor strike in 1950, and was a leading voice in both the independence and labor movements. Gairy established ties with the British government and monarchy and was groomed to become the island's first prime minister when Britain relinquished some of its Caribbean colonies. After independence Gairy's Grenada United Labour Party (GULP) swept to power.

Gairy made early political missteps, such as using his first opportunity to speak in front of the UN to plead for more research into UFOs and the Bermuda Triangle. There were rumors of corruption, of ties with the notorious General Augusto Pinochet of Chile and of the use of a group of thugs (called the Mongoose Gang) to intimidate and eliminate adversaries. Power went to Gairy's head and this former labor leader was soon referring to his political opposition as 'sweaty men in the streets.'

Revolutions, Coups & Invasions

Before dawn on March 13, 1979, while Gairy was overseas, a band of armed rebels supported by the opposition New Jewel Movement (NJM) party led a bloodless coup. Maurice Bishop, a young, charismatic, London-trained lawyer and head of

the NJM, became prime minister of the new People's Revolutionary Government (PRG) regime.

As the head of a Communist movement in the backyard of the US, Bishop tried to walk a very fine line. He had ties with Cuba and the USSR, but attempted to preserve private enterprise in Grenada. A schism developed between Bishop and hardliners in the government who felt that he was incompetent and was stonewalling the advance of true Communism. The ministers voted that Bishop should share power with the hardline mastermind (and Bishop's childhood friend) Bernard Coard. Bishop refused and was placed under house arrest. While Coard had the support of the majority of the government and the military, Bishop had support of the vast majority of the public.

On October 19, 1983, thousands of supporters spontaneously freed Bishop from house arrest and marched with him and other sympathetic government ministers to Fort George. The army was unmoved by the display and Bishop, his pregnant girlfriend (Minister of Education Jacqueline Creft) and several of his followers were taken prisoner and executed by a firing squad in the courtyard. To this day, it is unclear if the order came directly from Coard – although most believe that it did.

FEDON'S REBELLION

Animosity between the new British colonists and the remaining French settlers persisted after the Treaty of Paris. In 1795 a group of French Catholics, encouraged by the French Revolution and supported by comrades in Martinique, armed themselves for rebellion. Led by Julien Fedon, an African-French planter from Grenada's central mountains, they attacked the British at Grenville. They captured the British governor and executed him along with other hostages. Fedon's guerrillas, who controlled much of the island for more than a year, were finally overcome by the British navy. Fedon was never captured – he likely escaped to Martinique, or drowned attempting to get there, though some islanders believe he lived out his days hiding in Grenada's mountainous jungles.

Six days later, 12,000 US marines, along with a few soldiers from half a dozen Caribbean countries, were on Grenadian shores. Seventy Cubans, 42 Americans and 170 Grenadians were killed in the fighting. Most of the US forces withdrew in December 1983, although a joint Caribbean force and 300 US support troops remained on the island for two more years. The US sunk millions of dollars into establishing a new court system to try Coard and 16 of his closest collaborators.

Fourteen people, including Coard and his wife, were sentenced to death for the murder of Bishop. Although the death sentences were commuted to life in prison in 1991, the most recent appeal for full clemency and release from prison was rejected in February 2005.

The New Era

After the US invasion (or 'intervention' or 'rescue mission' – depending on one's political perspective), elections were reinstituted in December 1985, and Herbert Blaize, with his New National Party, won handily. Many PRG members reinvented themselves politically and found jobs in the new administration. From 1989 to 1995, different political parties jockeyed for control and a few short-term leaders came and went, but all within the democratic process.

In 1995 Dr Keith Mitchell became prime minister and has steadily held the position until the time of this book's printing. Although Mitchell had success building the tourism economy, his term has been plagued by accusations of corruption and financial misdealing. He has also been criticized for a weak initial response to the devastation of 2004's Hurricane Ivan (see the boxed text, p658).

THE CULTURE

Grenadian culture is a proud mix of British, French, African and East and West Indian influences. Overall, it is a nation of fairly conservative people who tend to be religious and don't approve of skimpy clothing in town, or topless sunbathing. Unlike some Caribbean islands, open consumption of marijuana is not accepted and there is a general emphasis on the rule of law. That said, Grenadians are friendly and humorous, and most males have a

(sometimes embarrassing) nickname (such as the politician and businessman who is still saddled with his life-long nickname of Devil Child). Grenadians are politically savvy because many have first-hand experience with political history, and the average Grenadian knows a lot more about global politics and international affairs than does the average American.

There is a strong emphasis on education and almost all young Grenadians attend school. Many young adults spend a period of time working or studying abroad, usually in Brooklyn, Toronto or London.

Music and sport are unifying factors in the country. Pan (steel-band) and calypso music are still popular, while reggae, hip-hop and dancehall (a contemporary offshoot of reggae with an MC 'toasting' over rapid digital beats) are the most widespread types of music.

Cricket, sailing and soccer are the best liked sports, while basketball is gaining some popularity.

RELIGION

Almost 60% of all Grenadians are Roman Catholic. There are also Anglicans, Seventh Day Adventists, Methodists, Christian Scientists, Presbyterians, Scots Kirk, Baptists, Baha'i and an increasing number of Jehovah's Witnesses.

ENVIRONMENT
The Land

Grenada island, Carriacou and Petit Martinique comprise a total land area of 133 sq miles (344 sq km). Grenada island, at 121 sq miles (313 sq km), measures 12 miles (19km) wide by 21 miles (34km) long. The island is volcanic, though part of the northern end is coral limestone. Grenada's rainy interior is rugged, thickly forested and dissected by valleys and streams. The island rises to 2757ft (840m) at Mt St Catherine, an extinct volcano in the northern interior. Grenada's indented southern coastline has jutting peninsulas, deep bays and small nearshore islands, making it a favorite haunt for yachters.

Carriacou, at just under 5 sq miles (13 sq km), is the largest of the Grenadine islands that lie between Grenada and St Vincent. Most of the others are uninhabited pinnacles or sandbars in the ocean.

Wildlife

Grenada has a varied ecosystem of rainforests, montane thickets, woodlands and lowland dry forests. Breadfruit, immortelle, flamboyant and palms are some of the more prominent trees.

Mona monkeys, introduced from West Africa centuries ago, live in Grenada's wooded areas. Other mammals include the nine-banded armadillo, opossum and mongoose. Bird life features the hummingbird, pelican, brown booby, osprey hawk, endangered hook-billed kite and hooded tanager.

There are no poisonous snakes, but Grenada does have tree boas. These nocturnal serpents spend the day wound around branches high above the ground, and human contact is quite unusual.

Sea turtles nest along some of Grenada's sandy beaches. Although all sea turtles are endangered, their shells are still used to make many of the souvenirs that tourists buy, and they also appear on the menus of a few island restaurants.

FOOD & DRINK

Oil down is the national dish of Grenada and is served at households and in many West Indian restaurants. It consists of vegetables and meat boiled down in a pot with coconut milk. Other local dishes revolve around callaloo (a spinachlike green, originally from Africa), fresh fish and fish stews, curried *lambi* (conch) and rotis (curried potato, sauce and a choice of meats or vegetables wrapped in a roti skin – a flat Indian-style bread). The inexpensive roti is perhaps the world's best version of fast food. Pigeon peas and rice, flour dumplings, plantains, yams and callaloo soup are common side dishes.

Grenada has a number of restaurants that cater to visitors, serving Italian, Mexican, Chinese and French food. There are also restaurants specializing in pizza, sandwiches or seafood.

Tap water is generally safe to drink but bottled water is readily available and is a safer bet. Carib beer is a decent, if watery, brew that's made on Grenada. Rum is also made locally using imported sugar; Westerhall and Clarke's Court are a couple of favorite brands. Local nutmeg and other spices are incorporated into some very drinkable cocktails that pack quite a punch. Good nonalcoholic fruit juices are available, as are the locally famous *mauby* (a bittersweet drink made from the bark of the rhamnaceous tree) and ginger beer.

GRENADA ISLAND

pop 90,000

For information on getting to, from and around the island, see p674.

ST GEORGE'S

pop 30,500

Quaint but bustling St George's lines the curve of a deep horseshoe-shaped harbor called the Carenage. The colorful old colonial buildings, forts and churches wind around a maze of narrow, hilly streets, giving the town a pleasant character. The center of the city is on the far side of the hill from the Carenage and is a dense urbanized area radiating out from the market. Most tourist amenities are located in the Carenage area, while the local shops and services tend to be in the city center.

Orientation

To get from the Carenage to the city center one must walk up and over the hill on Young or Lucas Sts, or cut through the narrow Sendel Tunnel on Monckton St (be sure to walk along the west side of the tunnel, where cars make room for walkers).

Further south from the Carenage, the road sweeps around another inlet, called the Lagoon, on its way to the resort precinct at Grand Anse. At the time of writing, a new cruise-ship terminal – along with parking and a new bus station – was being constructed just off the city center, on the waterfront.

Information

BOOKSTORES

Fedon Books (☎ 435-2665; Blaize St) Located inside a law office, Fedon has all the best Grenadian and West Indian books.

Sea Change Bookshop (☎ 440-3402; the Carenage) Below the Nutmeg restaurant, you'll find trashy novels, magazines and lots of postcards here.

INTERNET ACCESS

Compu-Data (☎ 443-0505; St John's St; per hr EC$6; ⏰ 9am-5pm Mon-Fri, 9am-3pm Sat) Best price in town.

Javakool (☎ 453 3506; the Carenage; per hr EC$8; ⏰ 9am-7pm Mon-Sat)

MEDICAL SERVICES

St George's General Hospital (☎ 440-2051; Fort George Point) The island's main medical facility.

MONEY

RBTT (☎ 440-3521; cnr Cross & Halifax Sts; ☉ 8am-3pm Mon-Thu, 8am-5pm Fri) Has a 24-hour ATM.

Scotiabank (☎ 440-3274; Halifax St; ☉ 8am-3pm Mon-Thu, 8am-5pm Fri) Has a 24-hour ATM.

POST

Main post office (☎ 440-2526; Lagoon Rd; ☉ 8am-3:30pm Mon-Fri)

TELEPHONE & FAX

Cable & Wireless (☎ 440-1000; www.candw.gd; the Carenage; ☉ 7:30am-6pm Mon-Fri, 7:30am-1pm Sat, 10am-noon Sun)

TOURIST INFORMATION

Grenada Tourist Board (☎ 440-6637; www.grenada .org; ☉ 8am-4pm Mon-Fri) At the old cruise-ship dock.

TRAVEL AGENCIES

Joy's Travel Service (☎ 440-5720; the Carenage; ☉ 8am-4:30pm Mon-Fri) Joy's can help with international and regional flight arrangements.

Sights

GRENADA NATIONAL MUSEUM

This **museum** (cnr Young & Monckton Sts; adult/child EC$5/1; ☉ 9am-4:30pm Mon-Fri, 10am-1:30pm Sat) has a rather sad little display of colonial and other artifacts. There's also an exhibit on the events leading to the execution of Maurice Bishop, and the US invasion that followed.

FORTRESSES

Fort George (Church St; admission free; ☉ 6am-5pm), Grenada's oldest fort, was established by the French in 1705. It has stunning views of the harbor, the Lagoon and down toward Grande Anse. The national police occupy many of the fort buildings, but the grounds are open to the public and it's well worth the steep climb up from town. In the inner fort is the courtyard where Maurice Bishop was executed.

Fort Frederick (admission US$1; ☉ 8am-4pm), constructed by the French in 1779, was soon used – paradoxically – by the British to defend against the French. It now provides a striking panoramic view that includes Quarantine Point, Point Salines and

---

A LOW BLOW

On the night of September 6, 2004, Hurricane Ivan headed toward Barbados. Grenadians hunkered down in case they experienced some of the hurricane's side storms. The island was generally considered to be below the hurricane belt and had not been hit by a major storm since Hurricane Janet in 1955. At midnight, Ivan's eye unexpectedly dropped three degrees and set itself on a collision course with Grenada.

September 7 started like any other day – the weather was calm and the arrival of a hurricane seemed impossibly surreal. However, the skies turned by noon, and within three hours, 120mph (193km/h) winds were slamming Grenada from the south. The storm crashed directly into Grenada's most heavily populated southern parishes of St George's and St David's, ripping roofs off homes, downing trees and electrical lines, and tearing some structures from their foundations.

Thirty-nine Grenadians died, and many public buildings and some 90% of homes were damaged. The Catholic Cathedral and the Anglican church lost their roofs and the cricket stadium at Queen's Park was smashed to pieces. Nutmeg, cocoa, banana and other cash crops were devastated. The hurricane was followed by waves of desperate looting and vandalism. Many residents spent months without roofs or electricity and with only limited access to running water.

Life is now returning to normal in Grenada. The country received massive support from other Caribbean nations, especially Trinidad & Tobago (who sent in troops to maintain order) and Cuba (who sent in armies of workers to fix electrical and other infrastructural problems). The reconstruction effort has been heartening and, although there were problems in the early stages after the hurricane, things are now improving rapidly. The devastated Queens Park is slated to be rebuilt for the 2007 Cricket World Cup, but at the time of publication plans were tangled in insurance and construction issues.

The best way to help is to visit Grenada and thereby contribute toward getting the important tourism industry back on its feet.

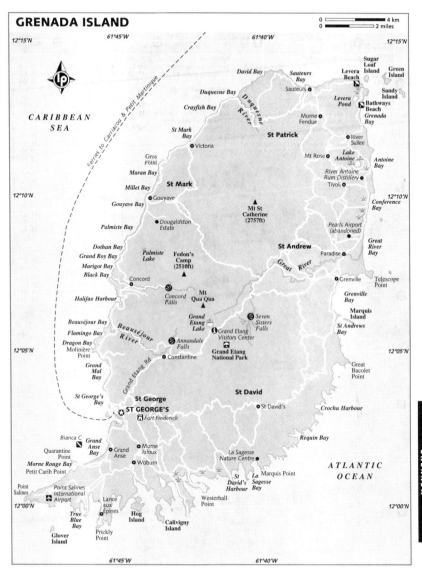

GRENADA ISLAND

CARIBBEAN
SEA

ATLANTIC
OCEAN

Grover Island. You'll find it atop Richmond Hill, 1.25 miles (2km) east of St George's.

CHURCHES

St George's has a number of 19th-century churches. Most were heavily damaged by Hurricane Ivan in 2004 (see the boxed text, opposite) and a number lost their roofs.

Erected in 1825, **St George's Anglican Church** (Church St; admission free; ☻ variable hours) features a four-sided clock tower that serves as the town timepiece.

A marble tablet commemorates the English colonists killed in the 1795 French-inspired Fedon uprising (see the boxed text, p655).

ST GEORGE'S

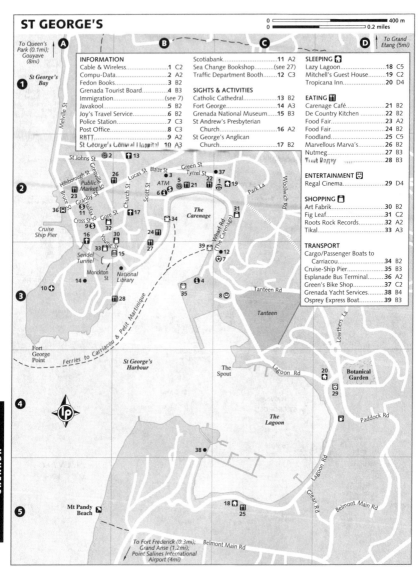

To Queen's Park (0.1mi); Gouyave (8mi)

St George's Bay

To Grand Etang (5mi)

The **Catholic Cathedral** (Church St; admission free; variable hours) is the largest church on the island. It has a brightly painted interior and took a real beating in the hurricane of 2004.

The yellow-brick **St Andrew's Presbyterian Church** (Church St; admission free; variable hours), immediately north of Fort George, dates from 1833 and has a spired four-sided clock tower.

Sleeping

Mitchell's Guest House (☎ 440-2803; Tyrrel St; r US$30) Mitchell's is the only budget option in the Carenage. It is a standard guesthouse and an agreeable place, although dogs and roosters in the street can be a bit noisy. The upstairs rooms get better light, but are often occupied by long-term guests. Baths are communal.

Tropicana Inn (☎ 440-1586; tropicana@caribsurf .com; Lagoon Rd; s/d US$65/77; ☷) Just down the road from the yacht club, Tropicana made it through Ivan practically unscathed The rooms, with all midrange amenities, are good value and the popular West Indian/ Chinese restaurant and bar gets a steady stream of locals and visitors. Tropicana would be a more relaxed spot if not for the traffic on the street out front.

Eating

BUDGET

Marvellous Marva's (Grenville St; rotis EC$8; ☷ 10:30am-8pm Mon-Sat) This famous local restaurant overlooking the market serves fresh lunch meals, rotis and fish wraps. Marva's rotis are considered by Grenadians to be among the best in the city. Unfortunately, the food goes fast and after 2pm the selection is thin. There is also a kitschy bar in the back.

De Country Kitchen (the Carenage; sandwiches EC$4) The corner spot has inexpensive local food to go, including saltfish sandwiches and chicken sandwiches. Try the star-fruit juice.

Carenage Café (☎ 440-8701; the Carenage; roti EC$12, pizza EC$35; ☷ 8am-11pm Mon-Sat) Although it can be a bit touristy, this centrally located café is a good choice to escape the afternoon heat and unwind with a drink, sandwich or roti. Don't bother with the pizza unless you have a good tolerance for grease.

Foodland (☎ 440-1991; Lagoon Rd; ☷ 9am-7pm Mon-Thu, 9am-8pm Fri, 9am-9pm Sat) Almost totally

reconstructed after Ivan and the subsequent looting, Foodland is Grenada's largest supermarket and the best place to find imported foods.

Food Fair (☎ 440-2588; the Carenage; ☷ 8am-5pm Mon-Thu, 8am-5:30pm Fri, 8am-3pm Sat) This grocery store is a good place to pick up a cold drink or an ice cream in the Carenage for a reasonable price. There's a second, much busier branch over on Halifax St.

MIDRANGE

Nutmeg (☎ 440-2539; the Carenage; mains EC$12-30; ☷ 8am-11pm Mon-Sat, 5-11pm Sun) The harborview tables upstairs at the Nutmeg are positively serene. The restaurant can get packed with small groups of tourists, but still caters to local couples. It is a good place to have a drink and read during the day or to take a date for a romantic meal at night. Specialties include fish and shrimp dishes and there is also lighter fare, such as sandwiches and rotis.

Tout Bagay (☎ 440-1500; the Carenage; mains EC$48-70; ☷ 10am-10pm Mon-Sat, 10am-5pm Sun) This large, airy restaurant at the end of the Carenage is a relaxing choice for a meal on the waterfront. There is a good variety of dishes, including Mexican, Italian, French and, of course, West Indian. It has a good callaloo soup.

Entertainment

Regal Cinema (☎ 440-2403; Paddock Rd; tickets EC$10) For a quiet evening, check out the (mainly Hollywood) films at this small theatre.

Shopping

Art Fabrik (☎ 440-0568; Young St) This longestablished shop sells batik wall hangings and clothing that is made on site.

Tikal (☎ 440-2310; Young St) Across the street from Art Fabrik, Tikal has a collection of local handicrafts, batiks and wood carvings.

Fig Leaf (☎ 440-9771; the Carenage; ☷ 9am-5pm Mon-Fri, 9am-2pm Sat) This souvenir shop stocks a pleasing selection of local goods and artworks.

Roots Rock Record Shop (☎ 440-8423; Gore St; CDs EC$25-30; ☷ 7:30am-6pm Mon-Fri) This small specialist reggae and Jamaican music store is stacked with classics and new compilations on vinyl and CD. The staff is friendly and helpful.

GRENADA

Getting There & Away

Buses (which are really just vans) leave St George's from the Esplanade bus terminal and charge EC$1.50 for all local points and more for those further afield. Although larger destinations are posted on the front of the bus, you may need to ask the conductor or driver which bus is best to get to smaller places outside town. There are stops along all the major routes, and you can flag down a bus pretty much anywhere.

Taxis are available throughout town and will take you to any destination on the island for a negotiated price.

Getting Around

St George's is best (and most efficiently) explored on foot, although you can flag down any bus along Lagoon Rd to get you to the far end of town (EC$1.50).

A taxi to/from the airport costs EC$30 (EC$40 at night) and takes around 20 or 30 minutes.

GRAND ANSE

pop 22,000

Grenada's main resort area is along Grand Anse Beach, a long, broad sweep of whitish sand fronted by aqua blue Caribbean water. There were numerous midrange and higher-end places at which to eat and stay around Grand Anse, but the area took a direct hit during Hurricane Ivan and many places are currently under reconstruction. There is no real center – the area runs along the beach and expands back into the hills.

Information

There is a 24-hour ATM at the Grand Anse Shopping Centre and there are a few banks behind the roundabout on Lagoon Rd.

Sleeping

Wave Crest Apartments (☎ 444-4116; www.grenadawavecrest.com; s/d apt US$68/98; ❄) About five minutes' walk from the beach, Wave Crest offers clean, attractive, well-appointed one-bedroom singles/doubles. It is not exactly fancy, but the place is definitely good value and has a good location. Ask for a room with an ocean view.

Coyaba Beach Resort (☎ 444-4129; www.coyaba.com; s/d US$155/210; ❄ ⓡ) This resort, full of tropical gardens, took a hard hit from Hurricane Ivan, but will reopen in late 2005.

The 80-room hotel leads right onto Grand Anse beach. Rooms are comfortable, with modern conveniences, and most have at least a partial ocean view.

Flamboyant Hotel (☎ 444-4247; www.flamboyant.com; r US$145-550; ❄ ⓡ) Located on the hillside along the west end of Grand Anse beach, Flamboyant is generally recognized as one of the best top-end options in the area. There's a variety of accommodations, mostly in buildings of two to four units, and all with ocean-facing terraces. It also has a restaurant, a minimart, car rental and pretty much everything else that you may need.

Cinnamon Hill & Beach Club (☎ 444-4301; www.grenadaexplorer.com/cinnamon; r from US$165-200; ❄ ⓡ) This two-story Spanish-style villa houses 26 large rooms with kitchens and big balconies. The spacious accommodations are a good choice for families with children. The 2nd-floor apartments have exposed beam ceilings and ocean views. At the time of writing some of the rooms were still undergoing repairs for hurricane damage.

Eating

Grand Anse has no real town center and is basically a series of large hotels. Therefore, although there's a sprinkling of independent budget eateries, most midrange and top-end restaurants are located in the larger hotels. Almost all hotel restaurants accept nonguests for dining.

St George's University Restaurant (mains from EC$8; ⏰ 9:30am-11pm) This large, informal, open-air restaurant, right on Grand Anse beach, caters to St George's medical-school students (it's located next to the school), tourists and locals. The different cooks – Sonia, Thomas and Julie – all serve different menus, including rotis, sandwiches, pizza, macaroni pie, chicken or fish-and-chips, and seafood dishes.

Beachside Terrace (☎ 444-4247; mains from EC$40; ⏰ 7:30am-10:30pm) Flamboyant Hotel's open-air restaurant has an expansive view and a menu to match. Fish-and-chips, rotis or fresh tuna salad are available through the day. At dinner, main dishes include fish and lobster.

Southside Restaurant and Bar (☎ 444-1975; roti EC$9; ⏰ 8am-8pm) Also known as D Green Grocer, this small West Indian take-out place on the main road by the roundabout is recognizable by the large Carlsberg beer logos on the roof and front. It has one of the better boneless chicken rotis of any fast-food shop on the island.

La Dolce Vita (☎ 444-3456; starters EC$16, mains from EC$40; ※ 7am-11pm Tue-Sun) Upscale Italian food is prepared at La Dolce Vita, at the Cinnamon Hill & Beach Club (opposite). Tables and chairs are set up on a veranda cooled by evening breezes. The Italian chef makes his own pasta and combines traditional Italian dishes with the abundant local seafood.

MORNE ROUGE BAY
pop 12,000

Morne Rouge is a lovely beach-lined bay, just over the little peninsula past Grande Anse beach. Except for when the *Rhum Runner* party boat vomits its drunken passengers onto the shore, it is quieter and less trafficked than Grand Anse. The swimming at Morne Rouge beach is delicious – sparkling water, white sands and green hills all around. There's good snorkeling, with sea fans and coral, around Petit Carib Point at the south end of the bay.

Sleeping & Eating

Mariposa Beach Resort (☎ 444-3171; www.mariposa resort.com; r from US$100; P ☒ ☒) Mariposa overlooks Morne Rouge and has a stellar pool area on the hillside above the beach. The rooms are smallish, but tidy, and have high ceilings. Only the upstairs rooms have views.

Sur La Mer Restaurant (☎ 444-2288; www.gem beachresort.com; mains from EC$30; ※ breakfast, lunch & dinner) Right on the beach with a water view, Sur La Mer serves dishes with an emphasis on seafood and West Indian flavors. There's often live music, and sometimes a bit of a show.

AUTHOR'S CHOICE

Laluna (☎ 439-0001; www.laluna.com; cottages from US$610; P ☐ ☒) These gorgeous Balinese-style cottages look out over the ocean and the hotel's private beach. Each bamboo cottage has its own small pool and deck. This is an excellent romantic choice, combining a rustic, tropical, get-away feel with the highest standards of service and comfort (as it should be for the price). Be sure to dine at the hotel's remarkable Italian restaurant.

Entertainment

Fantazia 2001 (☎ 444-2288; ※ 10pm-late Wed-Sat) This is the most popular nightclub on the island. It is a relaxed and safe venue that gets packed with locals but is also welcoming to foreigners – it's your best bet for a big night out.

POINT SALINES & TRUE BLUE BAY
pop 16,000

The Point Salines area, around the airport, is a dry and scrubby place. St George's Medical School, a private school serving foreign students, occupies much of the surrounding area. Ronald Reagan cited the risk to safety of students at this small American-run facility as a justification for the 1983 invasion of Grenada.

True Blue is an area between Point Salines and Lance aux Épines. It has yacht moorings and a few higher-end hotels and restaurants, while remaining more chilled than other tourist areas.

Sleeping & Eating

True Blue Bay Resort & Marina (☎ 433-8783; www.truebluebay.com; True Blue Bay; r US$160-420; P ☒ ☐ ☒) This delightful, family-owned resort is a true highlight on the island. It is quaint and stylish with a waterfront pool, Horizon Yacht Charters (p672), Aquanauts dive shop (see p671) and an attractive waterfront bar and restaurant serving some Mexican dishes. True Blue's attractively furnished rooms deliver the comfort and relaxation of a resort, while not sacrificing character.

Fox Inn (☎ 444-4123; Point Salines; s & d US$72; ☒) Although it isn't a great deal, Fox Inn is still your cheapest option near the airport. Occupying an odd spot just off the main road, it has comfortable rooms, a decent restaurant and a spacious pool area. Fox Inn is a smart choice if you have an overnight layover at the airport and just want to sleep – otherwise, you can find better scenery on the beaches or in town.

Bananas Restaurant & Bar (☎ 439-4369; www .bananasgrenada.com; True Blue Rd; mains from EC$30; ※ 9am-late) Bananas always seems to have a crowd, whether it be medical-school students at the bar, locals partying late at night in the backroom club or tourists dining on fresh fish and garlic mashed potatoes. We think the food is overpriced, but it's still pretty good. Bananas boasts a solid menu of cocktails and frequently has music and dancing at night, including latin dancing. It also has ladies' nights.

LANCE AUX ÉPINES
pop 9100

Lance aux Épines (lance-a-peen) is the peninsula that forms the southernmost point of Grenada.

It's an affluent and quiet area with charming coastal views, some good places to stay and clean, attractive beaches. While it's supremely relaxing, it has a bit of a colonial air and it would be possible to spend a week in Lance aux Épines and only meet Grenadian hotel staff.

Information

There's a customs and immigration office on the full marina of **Spice Island Marine Services** (☎ 444-4257; www.spiceislandmarine.com), on Prickly Bay.

Sleeping

Lance aux Épines Cottages (☎ 444-4565; www .laecottages.com; r US$145-320) Catch memorable sunset views from these large duplex cottages, with full kitchens, screened windows and ceiling fans. The cottages sit on a lovely tree-shaded beach. They're good value and popular with return visitors, so stick around and check out the deals for extended stays.

Calabash Hotel (☎ 444-4334, www.calabashhotel .com; r from US$385; ☒ ☒) This upmarket resort hotel occupies a significant part of the main beach in Lance aux Épines. The grounds are well manicured, the service is impeccable and the restaurants and rooms are world-class.

Eating

Boatyard (☎ 444-4662; mains from EC$20 ☒ 8am-11pm Mon-Sat) Situated at the Spice Island Marine Services marina, Boatyard offers dependable burgers and fries, and fish or chicken dishes. A Friday-evening steel band makes for an enjoyable atmosphere.

Red Crab (☎ 444-4424; mains EC$30-50; ☒ 11am-2pm & 6-11pm Mon-Sat) Red Crab's front patio dining has a following of locals and visitors. The cuisine is imaginative, the seafood is good value and the steaks are delicious. Dinner is à la carte, and a 'light bites' menu is offered along with other main dishes.

LA SAGESSE NATURE CENTRE

Sitting along a coconut tree–lined bay with protected swimming and a network of hiking trails, **La Sagesse Nature Centre** (☎ 444-6458; lsnature@caribsurf.com; tours US$32) occupies the former estate of the late Lord Brownlow, a cousin of Queen Elizabeth II. His beachside estate house, built in 1968, has been turned into a small inn.

La Sagesse is about a 25-minute drive from St George's on the Eastern Main Rd. The entrance is opposite an old abandoned rum distillery. Buses bound for the province of St David can also drop you here (EC$2.50).

The **manor house** (☎ 444-6458; www.lasagesse .com; manor r US$150) at La Sagesse Nature Centre features lots of character and history and has 12 airy rooms with double beds. There is now a new building with five additional rooms and three suites. The beachside **restaurant** (☒ 8am-1pm) has fish sandwiches and burgers for EC$18.

GRAND ETANG ROAD

The Grand Etang Rd cuts across the mountainous center of the island, through the Grand Etang National Park. Annandale Falls and a number of forest trails are easily accessible from the road. Take River Rd or Sans Souci Rd out of St George's, and when you reach the Mt Gay traffic circle, take the road north.

It's a lovely, if sometimes difficult, drive through the rainforest.

The area is thick and verdant with ferns, bamboo groves, heliconia and buttressed kapok trees, as well as roadside plantations of nutmeg, cocoa and bananas.

Annandale Falls

An idyllic waterfall with a 30ft (9m) drop, Annandale Falls is surrounded by a grotto of lush vegetation. There's a pool beneath the falls where you can take a refreshing swim. Unfortunately, it can get packed with tourists when cruise ships are in port.

In the village of Constantine, 3.5 miles (5.6km) northeast of St George's, turn left on the road that leads downhill immediately past the yellow Methodist church. After three-quarters of a mile (1.2km) you'll reach the **Annandale Falls visitors center** (admission free; ☒ 8am-4pm Mon-Fri). The falls are just a two-minute walk from the center.

Grand Etang National Park

Two and a half miles (4.1km) northeast of Constantine, after the road winds steeply up to an elevation of 1900ft (579m), a road-side sign welcomes visitors to Grand Etang National Park.

Half a mile (0.8km) past the roadsign, the visitors center sits to the side of the road overlooking Grand Etang Lake – a crater lake that forms the centerpiece of the park. The **Grand Etang visitors center** (☎ 440-6160; ◷ 8:30am-4pm Mon-Fri, Sat & Sun if cruise ships are in) was badly damaged in Hurricane Ivan and was partially closed at the time of writing. Near the parking lot are a couple of stalls selling soft drinks and souvenirs.

PARK TRAILS

Concord Falls Serious hikers branch off shortly before the end of the Mt Qua Qua Trail to pick up this five-hour trek (one way from the visitors center) to Concord Falls. From the falls, you can walk another 1.5 miles (2.4km) to the village of Concord on the west coast and take a bus back to St George's.

Fedon's Camp A long, arduous hike that leads deep into the forested interior, to the site where Julien Fedon, a rebel French plantation owner, hid out after his 1795 rebellion (see p655).

Grand Etang Shoreline This 1½-hour loop walk around Grand Etang Lake is gentle, but it can get muddy and doesn't offer the same sort of views as the higher trails.

Morne La Baye This easy walk starts behind the visitors center and takes in a few viewpoints, passing native vegetation along the way.

Mt Qua Qua This is a moderately difficult three-hour round-trip hike that leads to the top of a ridge, offering some of the best views of the interior forest.

Seven Sisters Falls The hike to this series of seven waterfalls in the rainforest east of the Grand Etang Rd is considered the best hike in Grenada. The main track starts from the tin shed used by the banana association, 1.25 miles (2km) north of the visitors center on the right side of the Grand Etang Rd. The hike takes only about two hours round-trip; a small fee is sometimes charged.

GRENVILLE

pop 15,600

Grenada's second-largest town, Grenville, is the main port on the east coast and a regional center for cocoa, nutmeg and other crops. The town is enjoyable to walk around and feels less touristy and busy than St George's. The defunct Pearls Airport, 2 miles (3.2km) north of town, was once the island's main runway. The airport still has a Russian biplane and a rusting Cubana air-craft, abandoned during the US invasion. Nowadays the most action the runway sees is local hot-rod drag racing.

Artist **Maureen St Clair** (☎ 442-8296, www.maureenstclair.com; Harford Village) produces culturally inspired paintings celebrating movements through dance and drum. She sells original paintings, prints, notecards and T-shirts. Ten percent of sales go to Under One Roof, a community-based project focusing on edu-cation and participation through commun-ity arts and crafts programs. By the end of 2005, Under One Roof will sell 100% local arts and crafts through its artisan collective.

Grenville is fairly easy to get to by the No 6 or 9 bus (EC$5, about 40 minutes) from St George's, along scenic Grand Etang Rd.

Eating

Ebony Restaurant (☎ 440-4778; Victoria St; ◷ 6:30-11pm Mon-Sat, 10:30am-6pm Sun) This classic Gren-ville spot has a high, vaulted wooden ceiling and a lax island feel. Traditional local food, including crab and callaloo, is on the menu, along with chicken and fish dishes.

My Place (Ben Jones St; rotis EC$6-8) This is the place to go in Grenville to grab a quick roti or double (a chickpea curry, sometimes with fish, wrapped in thin tortilla-like bread). It is standing room only, but the West Indian fast food is worth sticking around for.

Good Food (Convent Hill; meals EC$7-12) The name, although not the most imaginative, really does sum it up. Good Food is a wonder-ful choice for trying local cuisine – chicken, beef or fish – and is a top spot to sample the Grenadian national dish, *oil down*. Chase your food down with one of the delicious fresh fruit juices.

NORTH OF GRENVILLE

The **River Antoine Rum Distillery** (☎ 442-7109; tours EC$5; ◷ 8am-4pm Mon-Fri) has produced rum since 1785 and claims to have the old-est working water mill in the Caribbean. It is south of Lake Antoine and most easily accessed from Tivoli (bus EC$5, 1½ to 2 hours).

Lake Antoine, a crater lake in an extinct volcano, is a mile (1.6km) south of River Sallee. This shallow crater lake is host to a large variety of wildlife. The lake's perim-eter trail makes for a beautiful walk, and it's excellent for bird-watchers.

GRENADA

BATHWAYS BEACH & AROUND

From River Sallee, a road leads to Bathways Beach, a stretch of coral sands. At the north end, a rock shelf parallels the shoreline, creating a very long, 30ft-wide (9m) sheltered pool that's great for swimming.

Sandy Island is one of three small islands that sit off the coast of Bathways Beach. It is uninhabited and home to crystal-clear waters; there's also a beautiful beach on the leeward side that offers fine swimming and snorkeling. It's possible to arrange for a boat to take you from Sauteurs to Sandy Island; make inquiries with the fishermen on Sauteurs beach. Expect to pay about EC$150 per boat, round-trip.

LEVERA BEACH

Backed by eroding sea cliffs, Levera Beach is a wild, beautiful sweep of sand. Just offshore is the high, pointed Sugar Loaf Island (also called Levera Island), while the Grenadine Islands dot the horizon to the north. The beach, the mangrove swamp and the nearby pond have been incorporated into Grenada's national-park system and are an important waterfowl habitat and sea-turtle nesting site.

The road north from Bathways Beach to Levera Beach is usually passable in a vehicle, but it can be rough, so most visitors end up hiking. The walk from Bathways Beach takes about 30 minutes; stick to the road, as sea cliffs and rough surf make it impossible to walk along the coast between the two beaches.

SAUTEURS

pop 15,000

The largest town on the north side of Grenada, Sauteurs takes its name from the French word for 'jump.' This is because in 1651 Carib families jumped to their deaths here in their final retreat from approaching French soldiers. Today, these 130ft-high (39m) coastal cliffs are called Caribs' Leap. The cliffs are on the north side of the cemetery, behind St Patrick's church. Sauteurs is pleasant and is a good place to experience West Indian life away from the tourist centers.

VICTORIA

pop 2640

The west-coast road can be a bit hairraising – some sections are along eroded cliffs that occasionally release falling rocks. One of the larger fishing villages that dot the west coast is Victoria, which has churches, schools, a post office, a market, a police station and a health clinic. Buses to St George's cost EC$3.50.

GOUYAVE

pop 14,700

Gouyave, between Victoria and Concord, is a supremely attractive fishing village with a warm small town feel. It is well worth spending an afternoon or longer here, just walking around, relaxing, having a drink and taking in the ambience.

On the town's main road is a large **nutmeg processing station** (admission US$1; 🕒 8am-4pm Mon-Fri). A worker will take visitors on a tour through fragrant vats of curing nuts and various sorting operations for the admission fee, plus a small tip. Just south of the bridge, on the south side of Gouyave, a road leads inland 0.5 miles (0.8km) along the river to the **Dougaldston Estate**, where cocoa and spices are processed.

CONCORD FALLS

There are a couple of scenic waterfalls along the Concord River. The lowest, a picturesque 100ft (30m) cascade, can be viewed by driving to the end of Concord Mountain Rd, a side road leading 1.5 miles (2.4km) inland from the village of Concord. These falls are on private property and the owner charges US$1 to visit them.

The 0.5-mile (0.8km) trail to the upper falls begins at the end of the road. Because of a history of muggings, the tourist office now provides a uniformed security guard, who will, on request, accompany visitors on the walk to the upper falls for no charge (available at the trail head). The Concord Falls are also accessible by a five-hour hiking trail from the Grand Etang National Park; see p665 for details.

CARRIACOU

pop 9000

Carriacou (carry-a-cou) is gorgeous and hospitable, yet it remains somewhat off the mass tourism trail. The great majority of the accommodations and hotels are locally owned. No cruise ships dock on the islands and many people will tell you that Carriacou is one of the last places in the Caribbean to experience unsullied West Indian life. After the buzz of St George's and Grenada, you'll find sleepy Carriacou a laid-back delight and an idyllic place to spend some time.

It's a hilly island, about 7 miles (11km) long and a third as wide. It gets a few day-trippers who have bought round-trip ferry tickets from St George's, and the island's low-key character and natural harbor attract yachters. Locals are friendly and once you get to know someone, you are practically considered family.

Getting There & Away
AIR
Carriacou's Lauriston airport is a modest affair with a single ticket counter for all flights. **Prime Travel** (☎ 443-7362) has a desk at the airport and can help with ticket sales, car rentals and other travel essentials.

SVG Air (☎ 444-3549; www.svgair.com; Paterson St, Hillsborough) is a small airline with four or five daily flights (depending on the day) each way to and from Grenada and Carriacou. The first flight leaves Grenada at 7:50am, and the latest return from Carriacou is 4:50pm. Fares are US$37 one way (20 to 25 minutes) and US$73 round-trip. There are also daily flights from Carriacou to Union Island (in the Grenadine Islands) for US$34 each way (15 minutes).

Sometimes, if all flights are fully booked, it is possible to organize a group and split the cost of a charter flight to/from Carriacou (EC$150 to EC$200 per person). Contact Prime Travel for details.

BOAT
There are two types of boats plying between Grenada and Carriacou. You can either hop on an old-fashioned cargo boat that takes four hours, or ride on the *Osprey*, an ex-press catamaran that takes half as long and costs twice as much. The *Osprey* departs from the east side of the Carenage.

Cargo/Passenger Boats
Any attempt to publish a schedule of the cargo ships would be crazy; much depends on when the boat gets enough items loaded to make the trip worthwhile. On Grenada island it's best to go to the large boats on the north side of the Carenage in St George's

and ask on board. On Carriacou they can be found at Hillsborough's town pier or some-times in Tyrrel Bay. Any hotel owner will be able to track down the latest information for you. Expect departure to be at least an hour after the reported time – but never count on it. The fare on the larger boats is EC$20 one way; buy your ticket on board.

Catamaran
Osprey (☎ 440-8126; www.ospreylines.com), based in Petit Martinique, runs a 144-seat motorized catamaran that connects Grenada's three populated islands in less than two hours (per person one way/round-trip Grenada to Carriacou EC$50/90, Carriacou to Petit Martinique EC$15/30). You can call for a reservation, although it's much easier to show up dockside 30 minutes before sailing time. It rarely sells out unless it's a holiday.

The *Osprey* schedule:
Carriacou to Grenada Departs 6am and 3:30pm Monday to Saturday, and 3:30pm Sunday.
Carriacou to Petit Martinique Departs 10:30am and 7pm Monday to Friday, 10:30am and 3pm Saturday, and 9:30am and 7pm Sunday.
Grenada to Carriacou & Petit Martinique Departs 9am and 5:30pm Monday to Friday, 9am Saturday, and 8am and 5:30pm Sunday.
Petit Martinique to Carriacou & Grenada Departs 5:30am and 3pm Monday to Saturday, and 3pm Sunday.

Water Taxi
Privately hired water taxis can take you up to Union Island. **Scooby** (☎ 443-6622; fare US$75) runs an organized operation, but Zion (ask for him at the north end of Main St, Hillsborough, at the Rasta shops) will give you a better deal. Water taxis can also take you around Carriacou and to Sandy Island, White Island and Petit Martinique for negotiated prices.

Getting Around
TO/FROM THE AIRPORT
It is best to get to and from the airport by taxi – a ride from the airport to Hillsborough is EC$15, while a trip to Tyrrel Bay or Bogles is EC$20.

BUS & TAXI
Buses (privately owned minivans) charge EC$2.50 to go anywhere on the island, or EC$1 if the distance is less than a mile. The two main routes run from Hillsborough –

one south to Tyrrel Bay, the other north to Windward. Minibuses start at around 7am and stop at around sunset.

Some minibuses double as taxis, and usually you can count on a couple of them swinging by the airport when a flight comes in (they will charge taxi rates from the airport).

CAR
There are a few of places to rent vehicles on Carriacou, with rates typically around US$50 per day. **Quality Jeep Rental** (☎ 443-8307; ajrental@caribsurf.com; rental per day US$40), in L'Esterre, southwest of the airport, has good prices. There is a gas station on Patterson St in Hillsborough.

TOURS
You can hire a taxi for a 2½-hour island tour, costing EC$150 for up to five people, or you can tour just the northern half of the island, which only takes half as long and costs EC$75.

HILLSBOROUGH
pop 5000
The main town on Carriacou, Hillsborough is an unhurried place – a mix of colorful wooden shops, cement buildings and a lot of folks chillin' out on the sidewalks. Town activity is centered on the pier, where the ferries dock. After the long sandy sweeps of Grand Anse and Morne Rouge, Hillsborough's beach seems a little plain, but the sunsets are spectacular.

Information
Ade's Dream Guest House (☎ 443-7317; adesdea@caribsurf.com; Main St; per hr EC$10) Reasonably fast Internet connection. Be careful: if you go even five minutes over one hour, they may charge you for two hours.
Cable & Wireless (☎ 443-7000; Patterson St; ⊗ 7:30am-6pm Mon-Fri, 7:30am-1pm Sat)
Grenadines.net (☎ 443-8207; webmaster@grenadines.net; Main St; per 30min EC$10 with complimentary drink) Above the Grenada General Insurance office. As well as Internet access this place also has paperback books to trade.
National Commercial Bank (☎ 443-7289; Main St) Has a 24-hour ATM.
Post office (☎ 443-6014; Main St; ⊗ 8am-3pm Mon-Fri) Located at the pier.
Princess Royal Hospital (☎ 443-7400) Located outside of Hillsborough in Belair.
Tourist office (☎ 443-7948; Main St; ⊗ 8am-noon & 1-4pm Mon-Fri) Located across from the pier.

Sights
The small, community-run **Carriacou Museum** (☎ 443-8288; Patterson St; admission EC$5; ⊗ 9:30am-3:45pm Mon-Fri) has an interesting collection of Native American artifacts, a display about African heritage and paintings by local artists. There is also an odd collection of colonial-era objects, including an old urinal.

Sleeping
John's Unique Guest House (☎ 443-8345; johnresort@grenadines.net; Main St; r from US$20; ❄) Turtles on the front lawn and views of verdant forested hills out the back – John's Unique is a large, clean guesthouse and is the best value in town. The restaurant is one of the few places that serves food on Sunday. The 2nd-floor rooms at the back have better sunlight and views. Some rooms have air-con. You'll find it 200m up the road towards Bogles.

Ade's Dream Guest House (☎ 443-7317; adesdea@caribsurf.com; Main St; r from US$25; ❄ 💻) Need to use the Internet? Buy a bicycle? Stock up on rum and ice cream? You can do it all at Ade's, right in the middle of town. It has a range of tidy rooms, some with private kitchenettes. The hotel is clean and well maintained but lacks good communal areas and staff are not keen on negotiating better rates for longer stays.

Peace Haven Guest House (☎ 443-7475; Main St; s/d with shared bath from US$21/45, apt US$38) Peace Haven has comfortable rooms and apartments with full kitchens. It is a little older than Ade's and John's Unique, but room Nos 1 and 2 have oceanfront balconies and views of Sandy Island.

Eating
Callaloo Restaurant (☎ 443-8004; callaloo@grenadines.net; lunch EC$10-15.50, dinner EC$35-70; ⊗ 10am-2pm & 6-10pm Mon-Sat) This well-known restaurant serves excellent West Indian dishes on the beachfront. The menu runs from lamb to *lambi* and, of course, callaloo soup. The service is slow, but if you're in a rush, you're not really experiencing Carriacou. Try the *oil down* when it's on the menu.

Butterfly Bar & Pizza Hut (Main St; pizzas from EC$25; ⊗ 9am-6pm Mon, Tue & Thu, 9am-10pm Wed, Fri & Sat) At the west end of town, this is a sunny, low-key place for snacks, drinks and light meals. The pizza (no connection to the American fast-food chain) is pretty good and the fish cakes are delectable.

Garden Restaurant (☎ 443-7979; www.the gardencarriacou.com; Main St, 3-course meal EC$55; ☺ dinner Sun-Tue & Thu-Sat) Run by the New York–trained chef who once made the Round House restaurant in Bogles (right) famous, this is the best place to eat on the island. It's in a gorgeous lavender-colored, flower-filled house, with a garden-view deck. Dinner is by reservation only and is sure to please, with the best fruits, vegetables and fresh seafood available on the island. The soups, salads and fish dishes are memorable. Don't miss this one.

NORTH OF HILLSBOROUGH

The northern region of Carriacou has some of the island's prettiest scenery, a couple of secluded beaches and agricultural areas that were formerly sugarcane plantations.

The hilltop **hospital**, just north of Hillsborough, has a magnificent view of the bay and offshore islands. Take Belair Rd, about a third of a mile (0.5km) north of Silver Beach Resort, and follow it uphill for half a mile (0.8km), then bear right on the side road that leads to the hospital.

Continuing north from the hospital, the road traverses the crest of **Belvedere Hill**, providing sweeping views of the east coast and the islands of Petit St Vincent and Petit Martinique. There are also the remains of an **old stone sugar mill** just before the Belvedere Crossroads. From here, the route northeast (called the High Rd) leads down to **Windward**, a small, windy village backed by gentle hills.

The road from Windward leads another mile (1.6km) to **Petit Carenage Bay**, at Carriacou's northeastern tip. There's a good beach and views of the northern Grenadines from here.

If, instead, you go west from the Belvedere Crossroads, you'll soon come upon the village of **Bogles**. Just to the north is one of the best (if not *the* best) beaches in Grenada, at **Anse La Roche**. Buses from Hillsborough can drop you at Bogles (EC$2.50, 15 minutes) and it's about a mile (1.6km) to the beach. Red markers along the path help direct the way.

Sleeping & Eating

Bayaleau Point Cottages (☎ 443-7984; www.carria coucottages.com; Windward; per week per 2 adults US$345) These cottages are ideal for couples or families on longer stays. Each cottage is different, but all are comfortable, private and stylish. Bayaleau Cottages are a perfect escape and are highly recommended.

Round House (☎ 443-7841; roundhouse@grenad ines.net; Bogles; dinner from US$65) This used to be one of the best restaurants on the island. Now it is more of a venue for dinner parties and events. It is still good for meals, but not what it once was. The building is a giant, circular structure, which sits upon the hillside and has commanding views.

SOUTH OF HILLSBOROUGH

L'Esterre is a small village southwest of the airport that retains a bit of French influence, which is manifested most noticeably in the French patois that some of village elders still speak. **Paradise Beach** just outside of L'Esterre is the best beach close to Hillsborough.

Near the beach, **Paradise Inn** (☎ 443-8406; www.paradise-inn-carriacou.com; Paradise Beach; s/d from US$30/45) is a good-value retreat with six large rooms all with ceiling fans, rattan furnishings, verandas and top-notch views. If you want to stay on the beach in Carriacou, this is your best option. Moderately priced meals are served at the beachside bar. Staff can also arrange 4WD rentals.

TYRREL BAY & THE NEARSHORE ISLANDS

Tyrrel Bay (population 750) is a deep, protected bay with a sandy (although somewhat dirty) beach. It is a popular anchorage for visiting yachters and hosts a number of regattas throughout the year. A new commercial dock in Tyrrel Bay was opened in 2005, so it is receiving more boat traffic. There are a few sleeping and eating options in town. Buses run with some frequency to Hillsborough (EC$2, 15 minutes).

Sandy Island, off the west side of Hillsborough Bay, is a favorite daytime destination for snorkelers and yachters. It's a tiny postcard-perfect reef island of glistening sands surrounded by turquoise waters. Snorkelers take to the shallow waters fronting Sandy Island, while the deeper waters on the far side are popular for diving. Water taxis (EC$50 to EC$75 return) run from Tyrrel Bay (20 minutes) or Hillsborough (15 minutes). Be clear about when you want to be picked up – as the island takes only a couple of minutes to walk around, a whole afternoon can tick by very slowly.

White Island makes for a nice day trip. It has a good, sandy beach and a pristine reef for snorkeling. White Island is about one mile (1.6km) off the southern tip of Carriacou. Water taxis run from Tyrrel Bay (about EC$75 return, 30 minutes).

PETIT MARTINIQUE

pop 1000

The near-circular isle of Petit Martinique is 3 miles (4.8km) northeast of Carriacou. It's about one mile (1.6km) in diameter and has a volcanic cone rising to 738ft (221m). There are a couple of schools, a restaurant and a few stores. A road wanders up the west coast; otherwise, people get about on foot, and it's a serene place to go for a stroll.

Most of the 900 islanders make their living from the sea, either in fishing or as mariners working the region's ships. The *Osprey* express ferry (see p667) is owned by a family in Petit Martinique and the service is based out of the island. The islanders have a close-knit community, sharing some half-dozen surnames. The people are devoutly Catholic, which makes for very quiet Sundays.

Sleeping & Eating

Melodies Guest House (☎ 443-9052; www.spiceisle .com/melodies; r US$30-50) Melodies has simple rooms, some with balconies facing the impossibly blue ocean. It is worth the couple of extra dollars for an ocean-view room. The downstairs restaurant and bar serves good local food and stiff cocktails – sometimes followed by a round of drunken karaoke.

Seaside View Holiday Cottages (☎ 443-9007; www.grenadines.net/petitmartinique/loganhomepage .htm; cottages US$25-35; 🐾) Seaside's quaint, self-contained cottages seem to have been concocted as the antidote for a stressful lifestyle. They are no-frills, with good light and ocean views and not much more to do than read a book and relax. There is a supermarket out front and the owners can arrange transfers to/from Carriacou.

THE GRENADIAN FLAG

Curious about the significance of Grenada's unique flag? It is red, green and gold with seven stars and a stylized nutmeg on the left side.

- **Red** is for the courage of the people
- **Gold** is for the wisdom and warmth of the people
- **Green** signifies the land and its lush vegetation
- **Seven stars** represent the seven parishes of Grenada
- **Nutmeg** is Grenada's main commodity (along with tourism) – the bounty of the island

---

Getting There & Away

The *Osprey* catamaran ferries passengers between Grenada, Carriacou and Petit Martinique daily (see the schedule on p667).

A water taxi can take you from Carriacou to Petit Martinique. They are cheaper from Windward (EC$120, about one hour) than from Hillsborough.

DIRECTORY

ACCOMMODATIONS

Although St George's is the center of the action in Grenada, the main tourist precincts are Grand Anse and Lance aux Épines, and both are at the upper end, price wise. Grand Anse was pretty 'licked up' (as Grenadians would say) by Hurricane Ivan and a number of the hotels are being reconstructed. Lance aux Épines is very neat and tidy but is somewhat isolated from the rest of the island. If you are looking to interact more with local culture, consider staying in or around St George's while on Grenada. Carriacou and Petit Martinique also have a number of good accommodations.

It is worth noting that budget guesthouses in Grenada, catering mostly to locals, rarely

---

EMERGENCY NUMBERS

Ambulance, fire & police ☎ 911

charge the 8% tax or the 10% service charge, which results in considerable savings on the cost of a room.

Camping

Camping is allowed in Grand Etang National Park, but there are no established facilities and the park is in one of the rainiest parts of the island. Arrangements can be made through the park **visitors center** (☎ 440-6160; ☺ 8:30am-4pm Mon-Fri, Sat & Sun if cruise ships are in), if it is actually open. There is a modest camping fee.

ACTIVITIES
Beaches & Swimming

Grenada's most popular beach, Grand Anse, is justifiably famous – it's broad and long, a beautiful sweep of fine white sands. Morne Rouge Bay, on the other side of Quarantine Point, has a lovely secluded beach that's much quieter than Grand Anse. The calm Caribbean water is warm and clear, and a delight for swimmers

There are also quality beaches along the Lance aux Épines peninsula, on the northern portions of the island at Levera and Bathways Beaches, and on the islands of Carriacou and Petit Martinique.

PRACTICALITIES

- **Newspapers & Magazines** The weekly *Grenada Today* and *Grenadian Voice* are the island's two main weekly papers. International newspapers, including *USA Today*, can be found in large grocery stores. The tourist office issues *Discover Grenada*, a glossy magazine with general information on Grenada, Carriacou and Petit Martinique.

- **Radio & TV** Grenada has three local TV stations and four radio stations. Most larger hotels also have satellite or cable TV, which pick up major US network broadcasts.

- **Electricity** The electrical current is 220V, 50 cycles. British-style three-pin plugs are used.

- **Weights & Measures** Grenada uses the imperial system of feet, miles, pounds and gallons.

Cycling

For those who are fairly fit, bicycles are an excellent way to explore hilly Grenada island. Try **Green's Bike Shop** (☎ 435-1089; Tyrell St; rental per day EC$40; ☺ 8am-4:30pm Mon-Fri, 8am-2pm Sat) in St George's for bike rental.

Diving & Snorkeling

The waters around Grenada have extensive reefs and a wide variety of corals, fish, turtles and other marine life. One popular dive is the wreck of the *Bianca C* ocean liner, off Grenada's southwest coast. Strong currents and a depth of more than 100ft (30m) make it strictly for experienced divers only.

Molinière Point, north of St George's, has some of the best snorkeling around Grenada, though land access is difficult. Most dive shops will take snorkelers along with divers to check out spots like Molinière Point.

DIVE SHOPS
Grenada

The following are some of the better dive shops in Grenada. Always check to see if a shop is Professional Association of Diving Instructors (PADI) or National Association of Underwater Instructors (NAUI) certified, or proceed at your own risk.

Aquanauts Grenada (☎ 444-1126; www.aquanautsgrenada.com) Aquanauts, at Grand Anse and True Blue Bay, is the dive-shop juggernaut on the island. It has it all, from the boats to the gear to an army of staff. Open-water courses cost US$394.

Dive Grenada (☎ 444-1092; www.divegrenada.net) Located at the Flamboyant Hotel (p662) at Grand Anse beach, Dive Grenada is a smaller, more personal operation than Aquanauts. It can tailor special dive trips, and two-tank dives cost US$80.

ScubaTech (☎ 439-4346; www.scubatech-grenada.com) This small shop on the beach in Lance aux Épine (based at Calabash Hotel – see p664) is well organized and delivers good wreck dives.

Carriacou

The first and still the best shop on Carriacou, **Carriacou Silver Diving** (☎ 443-7882; www.scubamax.com; Hillsborough) has two-tank dives for US$88.

Hiking

Grenada's most popular hiking area is the Grand Etang rainforest, where trails wind through a forest of mahogany and ferns,

GRENADA

leading to a crater lake, waterfalls and mountain ridges. For details on specific trails, see p665.

Sailing

Sailing is definitely the best way to experience Grenada and its surrounding islands. **Horizon Yacht Charters** (☎ 439-1000; www.horizonyachtcharters.com; True Blue Bay Marina) can put you on a beautiful, well-maintained yacht, with excellent service at a fair price. Staff can tailor your itinerary to numerous gorgeous destinations, fitting them with your interests. Whether you opt for a crewed yacht or decide to be your own captain, this is a unique way to see the region and it's an unforgettable adventure.

BOOKS

There are few bookstores around the islands. Books can be found for loan or trade in some guesthouses and many Grenadians are willing to share books from their homes.

A good book about geology, flora and fauna is *A Natural History of the Island of Grenada,* by John R Groome, a past president of the Grenada National Trust. *The Mermaid Wakes: Paintings of a Caribbean Isle* is a hardcover book featuring paintings by Carriacou artist Canute Calliste; the text, by Lora Berg, is about island life.

Grenada 1983, by Lee Russell, and *Urgent Fury: The Battle for Grenada,* by Mark Adkin, are detailed accounts of the events that surrounded US President Ronald Reagan's invasion of Grenada in 1983. While both books are rather pro-US, they shouldn't be dismissed as propaganda – they do show some of the complexities from both sides. *Revolution in Reverse,* by James Ferguson, presents a critical account of Grenada's development since the US invasion.

Lorna McDaniel's *The Big Drum Ritual of Carriacou: Praisesongs for Rememory of Flight* explores the Big Drum rituals, as practiced in Carriacou, that call ancestors as part of an Afro-Caribbean religious experience. Performed since the early 1700s, it is the only ceremony of its type that has survived in the Caribbean.

Grenada: A History of its People, written by University of the West Indies senior lecturer Beverley Steele, follows the history of the island people from the early days of Arawak settlement to 2003.

CHILDREN

While Grenada is not specifically a family destination, it has many areas where children can have some free range, such as Carriacou, Lance aux Épines and Morne Rouge.

DANGERS & ANNOYANCES

St George's is a city (by Eastern Caribbean standards) and all normal city precautions should be taken, especially after dark. Hikers (women in particular) should double-check with a tourism professional (even a taxi driver) that their guide is to be trusted. That said, Grenada has a pretty low crime rate.

EMBASSIES & CONSULATES
Grenadian Embassies & Consulates

UK (☎ 020-7631-4277; 5 Chandos Street, London W1G 9DG)

USA (☎ 202-265-2561; 1701 New Hampshire Ave NW, Washington DC 20009)

Embassies & Consulates in Grenada

UK (☎ 440-3536; 14 Church St, St George's)

USA (☎ 444-1173; Lance aux Épines)

FESTIVALS & EVENTS

The **Grenada Board of Tourism** (www.grenada.org) can provide all details on yearly festivals and events.

Carriacou Carnival (usually early March)

Easter Regatta (Easter) Petit Martinique holds a regatta that includes a swimming relay, rowboat races, kite flying, music and a beer-drinking competition.

Carriacou Maroon Jazz Festival (mid-June)

Carriacou Regatta (late July or early August) This major sailing event features races to Grenada, Union Island and Bequia. Beyond sailing races there are also beauty pageants, music, parties and various sporting events.

Grenada Carnival (second weekend in August) The big annual event. The celebration is spirited and includes calypso and steel-band competitions, costumed revelers, pageants and a big grand-finale jump-up on Tuesday.

GAY & LESBIAN TRAVELERS

Attitudes to same-sex couples in Grenada (and the Caribbean generally) are not modern or tolerant. Gay and lesbian couples should be discreet in public to avoid hassles.

HOLIDAYS

New Year's Day January 1
Independence Day February 7
Good Friday Late March/early April
Easter Monday Late March/early April

GRENADA

Labour Day May 1
Whitmonday Eighth Monday after Easter
Corpus Christi Ninth Thursday after Easter
Emancipation Days First Monday & Tuesday in August
Thanksgiving Day October 25
Christmas Day December 25
Boxing Day December 26

INTERNET ACCESS

St George's has a growing number of Internet cafés. Some hotels provide Internet access and there are a few cafés on Carriacou. Rates runs from EC$6 to EC$12 per hour.

INTERNET RESOURCES

www.grenada.org This is the official site of the Grenada Board of Tourism, and features links to masses of excellent information. Unfortunately, some of the hotel and restaurant information is out of date.

www.grenadaexplorer.com This is an online tourist guide with information in English and German.

www.grenadaguide.com This is a site with tourist information, real estate and hotel links.

www.grenadahotelsinfo.com The Grenada Hotel & Tourism Association maintains this site, from which you can book accommodations online.

www.spiceisle.com Spiceisle.com hosts many of Grenada's commercial web pages. It also maintains a good links page.

www.travelgrenada.com This site is similar to grenadaguide.com, but has more background articles.

LANGUAGE

The official language is English. A French-African patois is spoken by a few elderly people.

MONEY

The official currency is the Eastern Caribbean dollar (EC$ or XCD). There are a growing number of 24-hour ATMs all over Grenada, that dispense Easter Caribbean dollar. Most hotels, shops and restaurants will accept US dollars, but you'll get a better exchange rate by changing to Eastern Caribbean dollars at a bank and using local currency. Major credit cards are accepted by most hotels, top-end restaurants, dive shops and car-rental agencies. Be clear about whether prices are being quoted in Eastern Caribbean or US dollars, particularly with taxi drivers.

An 8% tax and 10% service charge is added to many hotel and restaurant bills. If no service charge is added at restaurants, a 10% tip is generally expected. Prices quoted in this chapter do not include the 18% tax and charge.

POST

Grenada's main post office is in St George's, and there are smaller post offices in many villages and on Carriacou. Mail service is pretty slow and packages are expensive. Postcards to anywhere are reasonable, though.

TELEPHONE & FAX

When calling from within Grenada, you only need to dial the seven-digit local phone number. When calling from North America, dial ☎ 1-473 + the local number. From elsewhere, dial your country's international access code + ☎ 473 + the local number. We have included only the seven-digit local number for Grenada listings in this chapter.

Grenada has coin-operated and card phones. Coin phones take 25-cent coins (either EC or US) or EC$1 coins. Card phones accept the same Caribbean phone card used on other Eastern Caribbean islands; cards are sold at the airport and numerous shops.

You can make international phone calls and send faxes from the often-crowded Cable & Wireless office at the Carenage in St George's (p658).

TOURIST INFORMATION
Local Tourist Offices

There's a tourist office booth at Point Salines International Airport, just before immigration, where you can pick up tourist brochures; the staff can also help you book a room.
Grenada Board of Tourism (☎ 440-2279; www .grenada.org; the Carenage, St George's, Grenada island)
Grenada Board of Tourism – Carriacou (☎ 443-7948; www.grenada.org; Main St, Hillsborough, Carriacou)

Tourist Offices Abroad

Canada (☎ 416-595-1339; fax 416-595-8278; tourism@grenadaconsulate.com; 439 University Ave, Suite 920, Toronto, Ontario M5G 1Y8)
Germany (☎ 6112-67-67-20; grenada@discover-fra .com; Schenkendorfstrasse 1, 65187, Wiesbaden)
UK (☎ 0207-71-7016; fax 0207-71-7016; grenada@cibgroup.co.uk; 1 Battersea Church Rd, London SW11 3LY)
USA (☎ 212 687 9554, 800-927-9554; fax 212-573-9731; noel@rfcp.com; 317 Madison Ave, New York, NY 10017)

GRENADA

TOURS

The following tours are for Grenada island; for information on taxi tours of Carriacou, see p668.

Adventure Tours (☎ 444-5337; www.grenadajeep tours.com) This reputable operator has full-day tours that take in all of the major sights and also can hook you up with mountain-biking tours through affiliated Trailblazers.

Caribbean Horizons (☎ 444-1555; www.caribbean horizons.com) Has a range of excursions and self-drive options that can include hiking, sailing and fishing, and moonlight tours of the rainforest at Grand Etang. The options are many, and full-day outings include lunch.

Henry's Safari Tours (☎ 444-5313; www.travelgre nada.com/safari.htm) Various treks into the interior are offered by this company, which specializes in hiking tours. Lunch and drinks are included. Try the five-hour tour that includes a hike to the Seven Sisters Falls.

Lester 'Greenface' DeSouze (☎ 405-0117) Many taxi drivers offer tours, some with fancier cars or minivans, but visiting Grenada island with Greenface is a unique experience. He has lived the island's history and was directly involved in many of the major events – including working with Maurice Bishop in the early stages of the revolution and then spending many years as a political prisoner when the revolution shifted gears. If you want to hear some good stories and learn about Grenadian history, this is the man for the job.

Mandoo Tours (☎ 440-1428; www.grenadatours .com) Offers full- and half-day tours of the island and can be tailored for historical or photographic interests. It has quality vehicles with air-conditioning.

WOMEN TRAVELERS

It's unusual for local women to travel alone at night, and as such, female travelers are likely to attract attention. However, taking care if you're out after dark is prudent for both sexes. Otherwise, women needn't expect too many hassles.

TRANSPORTATION

GETTING THERE & AWAY
Entering Grenada

All visitors should present a valid passport; US citizens see the boxed text, p772.

Air

Point Salines International Airport (GND; ☎ 444-4101, 444-4555; fax 444-4838) has car-rental offices, an ATM, pay phones and a restaurant. A tourist office booth is in the arrivals section before you reach immigration.

For information on flying from outside the Caribbean to (and from) Grenada, see p775. The following airlines fly to/from Grenada from within the Caribbean:

Air Jamaica (☎ 800-523-5585; www.airjamaica.com)
American Eagle (☎ 444-2222; www.aa.com)
British West Indies Air (BWIA; ☎ 444-1221; www .bwee.com)
Caribbean Star (☎ 800-744-7827; www.flycarib beanstar.com)
SVG Air (☎ 800-744-5777; www.svgair.com)
LIAT (☎ 440 5420; www.liatairline.com)

Sea

For information on boats between Carriacou and Union Island, see p618. For boats between Grenada and Carriacou, see p667.

CRUISE SHIP

Grenada is a port of call for numerous cruise ships, which dock on the southeast side of St George's harbor, the Carenage, or at the new dock off of the city center. For more on cruises, see p777.

FERRY

A new boat service (US$30, 30 minutes) now runs between Carriacou and Union Island in the Grenadines. It departs Union Island at 10:30am Tuesday and Friday and departs Carriacou at 11:30am. A ferry (EC$15, one hour) departs Union every Monday and Thursday at 7:30am for Carriacou and departs Carriacou at 12:30pm on the same days. Passengers departing Carriacou pay EC$1 to Immigration, while those arriving on Union Island must pay EC$10 to Customs for entry (see p623).

YACHT

Customs and immigration (open 8am to 3:45pm Monday to Friday) can be cleared on Grenada island at **Spice Island Marine Services** (☎ 444-4342) on Prickly Bay, or at **Grenada Yacht Services** (☎ 440-2508) in St George's. Most yachts anchor in St George's in the nearby lagoon. If for some reason you decide not to clear immigration at one of the marinas, you can get all of the necessary stamps at the police station in St George's.

On Carriacou, clearance can be made in Hillsborough.

The most frequented anchorages are along the southwest side of Grenada, including

Prickly Bay, Mt Hartman Bay, Hog Island and True Blue Bay.

Horizon Yacht Charters (☎ 439-1000; www.horizonyachtcharters.com) is the place to go in True Blue Bay. **Moorings** (☎ 444-4439) bases its yacht-charter operation at Secret Harbour, and **Sea Breeze Yacht Charters** (☎ 444-4924) is at Spice Island Marine Services – both at Lance aux Épines.

GETTING AROUND

This section describes options for getting around Grenada island. For information on getting around Carriacou, see p667.

Bus

Buses on Grenada are privately operated minivans. Catching the bus is a good way to rub shoulders with locals and to experience the rhythms of daily life on Grenada.

A local bus ride is a spirited event, as the driver steers his van around the skinny, hilly streets, in and around the traffic, dropping and collecting passengers on the roadside, and using the horn to signal to friends, all at breakneck speed.

For the location of the bus terminal in St George's, see p662. Fares in the greater St George's area and to Grande Anse are EC$1.50. From St George's, fares are EC$3 to La Sagesse, EC$3.50 to Gouyave or Grand Etang, and EC$5 to Grenville or Sauteurs. Depending on passengers, it takes about 45 minutes from St George's to Grenville and 1½ hours to Sauteurs.

Buses run frequently all day from around 7am. They start getting hard to catch after 6pm, so head home early enough so as not to get stuck. A few buses run on Sunday, though they are much more infrequent.

To be let off the bus, knock on the metal interior a few times right before your destination.

Car & Motorcycle

DRIVER'S LICENSE

To drive a vehicle you need to purchase a Grenadian driving license (EC$30). You can get it from most car-rental companies, police stations or the **Traffic Department booth**

(☎ 440-2267) at the fire station on the east side of the Carenage in St George's. Grenada's larger towns, including Grenville, Sauteurs and Victoria, have gas stations.

RENTAL

There are numerous rental agencies on Grenada island: local agencies can to offer you a better deal on prices, but the international chains have better insurance deals. Cars cost from around US$65 a day; 4WDs US$80. Optional Collision Damage Waiver (CDW) insurance, which limits your liability in the event of an accident, starts at an additional US$8 per day.

Grenadian agencies:

Budget (☎ 444-2877; Point Salines International Airport)

Dollar (☎ 444-4786; Point Salines International Airport)

McIntyre Bros (☎ 444-1555; True Blue Rd) Affiliated with Caribbean Horizons (see opposite).

Thomas & Sons (☎ 444-4384; True Blue Rd)

Y&R Car Rentals (☎ 444-4448; Point Salines International Airport)

ROAD RULES

Drive on the left-hand side of the road. The roads are very narrow and curvy and the bus drivers are pretty daring. For safety, slow down when approaching blind curves and use your horn liberally. There are few road signs on the island, so a road map and a measure of caution are useful when driving.

Taxi

Taxi fares are supposedly regulated by the government, although sometimes you have to negotiate a bit. From the airport to Grand Anse or Lance aux Épines costs EC$25; to St George's EC$30. From central St George's it costs EC$8 to other parts of the city, EC$25 to Grand Anse or Morne Rouge and EC$35 to Lance aux Épines.

Elsewhere, taxis charge EC$4 per mile up to 10 miles (16km) and EC$3 per mile after that. The waiting charge is EC$15 per hour. Taxis can be hired for a flat EC$40-per-hour rate for sightseeing. A EC$10 surcharge is added to fares between 6pm and 6am.

GRENADA

Trinidad & Tobago

While it has all the Caribbean accoutrements – beaches, seafood, rum cocktails – the dual-island nation of Trinidad & Tobago rocks to its own steel-pan drum. It's as multihued as its people and sunsets, and embraces a national identity intensified by isolation, a patchwork history, politics and the ubiquitous beat of the music.

With a booming oil and gas industry, Trinidad & Tobago hasn't had to rely on tourism to pay the bills. As a result, the country's tourism infrastructure wobbles like a fawn: sometimes it falls down and other times it charms with wide-eyed innocence.

There are no pretences on Trinidad; whether you navigate the vibrant streets of Port of Spain, visit the rainforest or play mas during Carnival, as long as you're ready to jump in, Trinidadians will welcome you with open arms. On Tobago, tourism is more developed, though still rustic enough to feel genuine. The tiny island's fantastic beaches and amazing offshore reefs beckon sun-worshipers and divers. Resorts are plentiful, but you never lose the valuable, endangered experience of cultural interaction.

Whether you come for the bird-watching, beach, Carnival or cultural bounty, come now, before the rest of the world catches on.

FAST FACTS

- **Area** Total: 13,281 sq miles (5128 sq km); Trinidad: 12,504 sq miles (4828 sq km), Tobago: 777 sq miles (300 sq km)
- **Capital** Port of Spain, Trinidad
- **Country code** ☎ 868
- **Departure tax** TT$100 (see also p720)
- **Famous for** Carnival, calypso, soca and steel-pan music
- **Languages** English, Hindi, Creole, Spanish
- **Money** Trinidad & Tobago dollar (TT$); TT$10 = US$1.59 = €1.32 = UK£0.90
- **Official name** Republic of Trinidad & Tobago, West Indies
- **Phrases** Where you liming tonight? (Where are you going to party tonight?)
- **People** Trinidadian or Tobagonian (formal); Trini or Trinbagonian (colloquial)
- **Population** 1.3 million
- **Visa** Not necessary for US, UK, Canadian and most EU citizens; others see p719

HIGHLIGHTS

- **Port of Spain** (p685) Trinidad's bustling big city grooves to a permanent beat, with live music and the world's hottest Carnival.
- **Asa Wright Nature Centre** (p697) and **Caroni Bird Sanctuary** (p699) Grab your binoculars to spot Trinidad's 433 bird species at Asa Wright, or to watch flocks of scarlet ibis at Caroni Bird Sanctuary.
- **Diving** (p705) Explore underwater canyons and shallow coral gardens in Tobago's crystal-clear waters.
- **Paria Falls** (p698) and **Argyle Falls** (p713) Work up a sweat hiking lush rain forest trails and then shower under these gushing cascades.
- **Leatherback turtles** (p702) Head up to Trinidad's northeast coast to see these giant turtles nesting in the sand.

ITINERARIES

- **One week** Spend a couple of days exploring Trinidad, then fly to Tobago for sun and fun.
- **Two weeks** Spend four days in Port of Spain, take a day trip to Pitch Lake and Caroni Bird Sanctuary, spend a day at Maracas Bay, spend two days in Manzanilla Bay, then head to Tobago for a week of diving, snorkeling and hiking.
- **Three weeks** As for the two-week itinerary, while you're on Trinidad add a day trip to Asa Wright Nature Centre. Head to Tobago, do all the beachy stuff and then chill for a few days in the quiet fishing village of Charlotteville.

CLIMATE & WHEN TO GO

Because of Trinidad's southerly location, temperatures are equable year-round. Its average daily temperature is 80°F (27°C). For temperatures in Port of Spain, see the climate chart on p762. Average humidity hovers around 75%.

The only real seasons are the rainy season (June to November) and the not-rainy season (December to May). The high season is January to March, with a noticeable peak in February when Carnival draws hordes of visitors and the cost of hotel rooms skyrockets. Booking ahead is essential.

Accommodations are cheaper and crowds almost nonexistent in the shoulder seasons – October to December and April to June –

HOW MUCH?

- **Taxi from Trinidad's airport to Port of Spain** US$20
- **Day of diving on Tobago (gear included)** US$75-100
- **Fresh coconut juice** TT$3
- **Meal of fresh fish in a touristy restaurant** US$25
- **Meal of fresh fish in a local restaurant** US$7

LONELY PLANET INDEX

- **Liter of gas** TT$2.75
- **Liter of bottled water** TT$2
- **Bottle of Carib or Stag** TT$7
- **Souvenir T-shirt** US$10
- **Street snack: curried beef roti** TT$12

---

though you should do a little dance to keep the rain lords from weeping on your beach blanket.

Trinidad and Tobago sit outside the central hurricane belt and generally don't experience the severe storms that hit the more northerly islands.

HISTORY
Early History

Carib and Arawak Indians lived alone on Trinidad until 1498, when Columbus arrived and christened the island La Isla de la Trinidad, for the Holy Trinity.

The Spanish who followed in Columbus' wake enslaved many of Trinidad's Native American inhabitants, taking them to toil in the new South American colonies. Spain, in its rush for gold, gave only scant attention to the potential of Trinidad's land, which lacked precious minerals. It took until 1592 for the Spanish to establish their first settlement, San Josef, just east of present-day Port of Spain. Over the next two centuries the Spanish and French imported slaves from West Africa to cultivate tobacco and cacao plantations.

British forces took the island from the Spanish in 1797. With the abolishment of slavery in 1834, slaves abandoned

TRINIDAD & TOBAGO

plantations; this prompted the British to import thousands of indentured workers, mostly from India, to work in the cane fields and service the colony. The indentured labor system remained in place for over 100 years.

Tobago's early history stands separate from neighboring Trinidad's. Also sighted by Columbus, Tobago was claimed by the Spanish, but they didn't attempt to colonize it. In 1628, Charles I of England decided to charter the island to the Earl of Pembroke. In response, a handful of nations took an immediate interest in colonizing Tobago.

During the 17th century, Tobago changed hands numerous times as the English, French, Dutch and even Courlanders (present-day Latvians) wrestled for control. In 1704 it was declared a neutral territory, which left room for pirates to use the island as a base for raiding ships in the Caribbean. The British established a colonial administration on Tobago in 1763, and within two decades slaves helped establish the island's sugar, cotton and indigo plantations.

Tobago's plantation economy slid into decline after the abolition of slavery but sugar and rum production continued until 1884, when the London firm that controlled finances for the island's plantations went bankrupt. Plantation owners unable to sell their sugar or rum, quickly sold or abandoned their land, leaving the economy in a shambles.

A Free Colony

In 1889, Tobago was joined with Trinidad as a British Crown Colony. Trinidad & Tobago's demand for greater autonomy grew, as did anticolonial sentiment. Though the British granted universal suffrage in 1946, they didn't hand over the keys until 1956, when the People's National Movement (PNM), led by Oxford-educated historian Dr Eric Williams, took measures to institute self government. The country became an independent member of the Commonwealth in August 1962, and became a republic within the Commonwealth in August 1976.

Frustration with the colonial structure led to the 'Black Power' movement, which created a political crisis and an army mutiny, but ultimately led to stronger country identity. Bankrupt and without prospects, the country's luck changed in 1970 with the discovery of oil, which brought instant wealth and prosperity. During the 1980s, when oil prices plummeted, Trinidad & Tobago found itself in recession and the seeds of political unrest grew. Accusations that the PNM was mired in corruption and had failed to appeal to the East Indian community led to the party's defeat in 1986 by the National Alliance for Reconstruction (NAR).

More corruption developed as a result of a judicial system bogged down with a backlog of drugs-related trials (the country is a stopover in the South American drug trade). In July 1990, members of a minority Muslim group attempted a coup. They stormed parliament and took 45 hostages, including Prime Minister ANR Robinson, who was shot in the leg after refusing to resign. Though the coup was unsuccessful, it managed to undermine the government, and the PNM returned to power.

Vast petroleum and natural gas reserves were discovered in the late 1990s, which helped stabilize the economy. In 1995, Basdeo Panday of the United National Congress (UNC) beat the PNM's Patrick Manning in a controversial election that saw Panday become the first prime minister of Indian descent. A hung parliament meant the political process was mired in uncertainty for most of 2002, until October elections gave the PNM a majority and Manning once again became prime minister. The prime minister is the head of government, while the president (George Maxwell Richards) is the head of state.

Today, political parties are largely divided along ethnic lines, with the PNM being the predominant party of Afro-Trinidadians and the UNC representing the interests of the East Indian community. Local government is divided into three municipalities, eight counties and the island of Tobago. Tobago has its own legislative assembly and since 1987 has exercised an extended measure of internal self-government in an effort to protect itself from becoming co-opted by more-dominant political forces on Trinidad.

THE CULTURE

Trinidadians and Tobagonians love to party and take every opportunity to shamelessly sing, dance and lime (hang out) whenever the whim hits. Official and unofficial celebrations are plentiful and most revolve around calypso (a popular Caribbean music developed from slave songs) or steel pan (music produced on oil drums), great food and large amounts of rum. Like other Caribbean destinations, things here move at a slower pace. Though their energy is bountiful, Trinis see no need to rush, and stress is thought to be entirely unnecessary. Residents laugh easily and often, taking time to visit with one another and discuss everything from politics to the lyrics of the new soca (the energetic offspring of calypso) tune that's dominating the airwaves.

The National Psyche

Much discussion these days focuses on Vision 2020, Prime Minister Patrick Manning's plan for Trinidad & Tobago to reach 'developed country' status by the year 2020. It's an ambitious agenda, calling for dramatic reform of everything from education and employment to health care and poverty-reduction. Vision 2020's mission statement says:

> By the year 2020, we will be a united, resilient, productive, innovative and prosperous nation with a disciplined, caring, fun loving society comprising healthy, happy and well educated people and built on the enduring attributes of self-reliance, respect, tolerance, equity and integrity…

It's a tall order. Over the past decade, Trinidad & Tobago has grown steadily every year, thanks especially to foreign investment and growth in Trinidad's oil and gas industry. But government officials know that Vision 2020 demands more than economic growth; it requires a total shift in mindset at a basic level. It sounds idyllic in the prime minister's speeches, and many locals support the plan. However, others think it's an overzealous program that will entice foreign investment but ultimately deepen economic disparity. While politicians shake hands with CEOs over cocktails and garlic shrimp, many Trinbagonians work long hours for little pay, wondering how to put food on the table.

Lifestyle

While business in the energy sector is booming, Trinidad & Tobago's government continues to grapple with strengthening the social infrastructure. Some 22% of the population lives in poverty, and many people live without easy access to potable water, adequate housing or quality health care. Working with the UN Development Programme (UNDP), the government aims to halve the number of people living in poverty by 2015.

The average home in Trinidad & Tobago is a friendly place where hot stew simmers on the stove and cheery conversation pours onto the street. Traditional roles still dominate and women cook, clean and take care of the kids. Children dress in colorful, pressed uniforms before flagging down a ride to school.

The inequality between women and men remains depressingly stone age. While women generally receive a higher level of education and fill about half the professional and management jobs, they earn about 50% less than men in equitable roles. In 2002, for example, professional women earned an average annual income of about US$5500, while men at the same professional level earned US$12,400.

Single women are very often considered 'washed up' at 30, while men stay 'on the market' into old age. Many men think it's natural for a man to 'stray' from a committed relationship, but they'd think it an unforgivable sin if a woman were to do the same. Things are slowly changing, however, as women gain more vital roles in government and join forces to demand better equality.

TRINIDAD & TOBAGO

Population

Of the country's 1.3 million inhabitants, just 51,000 live on Tobago. Trinidad has one of the most ethnically diverse populations in the Caribbean, a legacy of its checkered colonial history. The majority is of East Indian (40.3%) and African (39.5%) descent.

The remaining 20% of islanders are of mixed ancestry, but there are also notable minorities of European, Chinese, Syrian and Lebanese people. In addition, a community of a few hundred native Caribs lives in the Arima area.

SPORTS
Cricket

Introduced by the British in the 19th century, cricket is not just a sport in Trinidad & Tobago, it's a cultural obsession. It's a necessity, like oxygen or rum. International cricket star Brian Lara – the 'Prince of Port of Spain' – hails from Trinidad and his popularity ranks up there with Jesus. When the West Indies team sweeps in for a test match, everything grinds to a halt as people park themselves in front of their TVs to capture the action.

The main venue for cricket is the Queen's Park Oval, home to the **Queen's Park Cricket Club** (☎ 622-4325; www.qpcc.com; 94 Tragarete Rd), a few blocks west of the Queen's Park Savannah in Port of Spain. The Oval, originally built in 1896, is the site of both regional and international matches and will be one of eight Caribbean venues hosting the much-anticipated **ICC Cricket World Cup** (www.icc -cricket.com) in 2007. The pavilion holds 25,000 spectators and has the northern hills as a spectacular backdrop. Call the cricket club for ticket information.

Soccer

Referred to as football in this British-influenced country, soccer is second only to cricket in the minds of spectators who cheer endlessly for the national team, the **Soca Warriors** (www.socawarriors.net). The team plays at several venues on Trinidad, including **Arima Municipal Stadium** (☎ 667-3508) in Arima and **Ato Boldon Stadium** (☎ 623-0304), a 30-minute drive south of Port of Spain in Couva. For information about games and local leagues, contact **Trinidad & Tobago Football Federation** (☎ 623-7312).

Cycling

Velodromes at Queen's Park Oval, the Arima Velodrome, and Skinner Park in San Fernando host cycling meets and sponsor road races. For information on cycling events contact the **Trinidad & Tobago Cycling Federation** (☎ 624-0384).

RELIGION

Roughly a third of all islanders are Roman Catholic. Another 25% are Hindu, 11% are Anglican, 13% are made up of various other Protestant denominations, and 6% are Muslim. Traditional African beliefs also remain strong in some areas, as does Rastafarianism.

ARTS
Literature

Trinidad boasts a number of acclaimed writers, among them Samuel Selvon, Earl Lovelace, CLR James and, most notably, the Naipaul brothers – Vidiadhar Surajprasad (VS) and Shiva (see the boxed text, opposite). VS' *A House for Mr Biswas* and Shiva's *The Chip Chip Gatherers* both create a vivid portrait of East Indian life on Trinidad. St Lucian native Derek Walcott, the 1992 Nobel Prize winner in literature, has lived on Trinidad for much of his adult life.

Music

Stop for a moment on the streets of Trinidad & Tobago and listen. You'll likely hear the fast beat of soca playing on a maxi-taxi radio, or kids drumming on metal garbage cans, or a woman singing as she walks home from work. Often festive, sometimes political or melancholy, music digs down deep to the core of island life. It is from there, in that space of truth and emotion, that Trinbagonians feel life's rhythm.

Although Carnival happens in February, there's always plenty of great live music, especially in the months leading up to Carnival. Every day in Trinidad & Tobago, music brings people together, regardless of age or race.

In bars and outdoor venues, it's common to see young kids, teenagers and grandparents partying together.

CALYPSO

A medium for political and social satire, calypso hearkens back to the days when

---

VOICE OF COLONIALISM

Sir Vidiadhar Surajprasad (VS) Naipaul is Trinidad's foremost literary figure. His writing has been both widely praised for its artistic merit and harshly criticized for its unflattering view of post-colonial societies. Despite his international stature, Naipaul's controversial views have been coolly received in his native Trinidad, a country he has not inhabited for many years.

VS Naipaul was born in Chaguanas, Trinidad, in 1932, the son of a prominent Trinidadian journalist. The young Naipaul had his primary education in Port of Spain, graduating from Queen's Royal College in 1950. He left Trinidad at 17 to attend Oxford on an island scholarship. His debut novel, *The Mystic Masseur,* was published in 1957. It is a satirical story set amid the chaos of Trinidad's first parliamentary elections.

Naipaul's prodigious literary output – he has written over 20 books – takes multiple forms, from fiction to straightforward history to richly nuanced travel writing. The author's writings generally take a critical view of the effects of colonial rule on the societies that once came under its sway.

Naipaul has earned disapproval for his barbed observations on Third World societies, in which critics detect racist overtones. He emerges as an intolerant – and rather cranky – figure from *Sir Vidia's Shadow,* Paul Theroux's account of his decades-long but ultimately aborted friendship with VS. Although nurtured as a writer by Naipaul, Theroux depicts his Trinidadian mentor as a difficult companion who made unreasonable demands on his friends and held his peers in disdain.

As a product of the very societies he has denounced – one more colonial cast-off cut off from his own heritage – Naipaul has lamented his own difficulties in defining himself. Theroux and others savored the irony of Naipaul's being knighted (in 1989) by the country he had once so forcefully condemned.

Whatever his inconsistencies, VS Naipaul remains an articulate voice of the dispossessed, an extraordinarily knowledgeable interpreter of the colonial experience and an author of undeniable depth and power.

The novels of Shiva Naipaul, VS Naipaul's younger brother, also deserve to be read for their sharply drawn depictions of Indian family life on Trinidad, among them *Fireflies* and *Beyond the Dragon's Mouth.*

---

slaves – unable to chat when working – would sing in patois, sharing gossip and news while mocking their colonial masters. Mighty Sparrow, long acknowledged the king of calypso, has voiced popular concerns and social consciousness since the 1950s. Another famous calypsonian, David Rudder, helped revive the musical form in the mid-1980s by adding experimental rhythms and reminding listeners of both the cultural importance and flexibility of calypso.

SOCA

The energetic teenage offspring of calypso, soca was born in the 1970s. Soca uses the same basic beat but speeds things up, favoring danceable rhythms and risqué lyrics over pointed social commentary and verbal wordplay. Soca dominates the nightclub scene and the most popular soca tunes rule the radio airwaves.

STEEL BAND/STEEL PAN

Rhythm and percussion are the beating heart behind Carnival. Traditionally, percussionists banged together bamboo cut in various lengths, or simply drummed on wherever they could – the road, sides of buildings, their knees. When African drums were banned during WWII, drummers turned to biscuit tins, then oil drums discarded by US troops. Today, drums come in a variety of sizes and each drum produces a unique note. Heard together, they become individual drops in a cascading waterfall of sound. During Carnival, bands of up to 130 members are transported on flatbed trucks along the parade route. All bands aim to win Panorama, the national competition that runs throughout Carnival season.

PARANG

Heard mostly at Christmas time, *parang* originated in Venezuela. Lyrics are sung in

Spanish and accompanied by guitars and maracas. At first heard only in rural areas inhabited by Hispanic Trinis, *parang* has evolved into a nationwide phenomenon. At Christmastime, groups of *parang* carolers wander through neighborhoods, and appreciative audiences serve them food and booze.

CHUTNEY

This up-tempo, rhythmic music is accompanied by the *dholak* (Northern India folk drum) and the *dhantal* (a metal rod played with a metal striker). *Chutney* songs celebrate social situations – everything from women witnessing a birth to men partying at a bar. It's a fusion of musical styles, combining classical Hindu music with more contemporary sounds.

ENVIRONMENT

The Land

Geographically, boot-shaped Trinidad was once part of the South American mainland. Over time, a channel developed, separating Trinidad from present-day Venezuela. The connection to South America is readily visible in Trinidad's lofty Northern Range, a continuation of the Andes, and in its abundant oil and gas reserves, which are concentrated on the southwestern side of the island.

The Northern Range spreads east to west, forming a scenic backdrop to Port of Spain. The rest of the island is given to plains, undulating hills and mangrove swamps. Trinidad's numerous rivers include the 31-mile (50km) Ortoire River, and the 25-mile (40km) Caroni River, which empties into the Caroni Swamp.

Tobago, 12 miles (19km) northeast of Trinidad, has a central mountain range that reaches almost 2000ft (610m) at its highest point. Deep, fertile valleys run from the ridge down toward the coast, which is indented with bays and sandy beaches.

Wildlife

Because of its proximity to the South American continent, Trinidad & Tobago has the widest variety of plant and animal life in the Caribbean. There are more than 430 species of bird, 600 species of butterfly, 70 kinds of reptiles and 100 types of mammals, including red howler monkeys, anteaters, agouti and armadillos.

Plant life is equally diverse, with more than 700 orchid species and 1600 other types of flowering plants. Both islands have luxuriant rainforests, and Trinidad also features elfin forests, savannas and both freshwater and brackish mangrove swamps.

Environmental Issues

Water pollution is by far the biggest environmental concern on Trinidad & Tobago. Agricultural chemicals, industrial waste and raw sewage seep into groundwater and follow rivers and streams to the ocean. Reef damage continues to be a problem, due mostly to overuse and pollution.

Tourism puts a lot of pressure on the water supply, especially in Tobago, where resorts are plentiful and the freshwater supply limited. Be sure to conserve water. Tobago is small enough that a resort filled with people taking extra-long showers can deplete the local freshwater supply.

Deforestation and soil erosion due to development are also problems. Sand erosion is a special concern on the northeast coast of Trinidad, where leatherback turtles lay eggs.

Environmental Management Authority (☎ 628-8042; www.ema.co.tt) is charged with monitoring the country's environmental issues but, as in other developing countries, the pressure of 'progress' often wins over preservation.

FOOD & DRINK

Trinidad & Tobago have West Indian, Creole, Chinese and Continental restaurants. East Indian influence prevails in the roti, a Trinidadian variation found throughout the Caribbean, and a similar fast food called 'doubles,' a sandwich of curried chickpeas wrapped in a soft, flat bread. Curried meats and seafood are common main dishes, often served with a side of *pelau* (rice mixed with peas, meat and coconut).

Another popular Trinidadian fast food is 'shark & bake.' This sandwich, made with a slab of fresh, grilled or fried shark and deep-fried, pita-style bread, is the standard at informal beachside eateries. Fried flying fish-and-chips is another inexpensive local favorite.

Because of the large East Indian population and a sizable number of Seventh Day Adventists, vegetarian food is easy to come by on both Trinidad and Tobago.

Tap water is safe to drink on Trinidad & Tobago. The Caribbean's premium beer, Carib, hails from Trinidad. Another local beer, Stag, is promoted as 'a man's beer' because it has a slightly higher alcohol level than Carib. The island also produces a number of rums, including Vat 19 and Royal Oak. Fresh-fruit juices and drinks are common, especially ginger beer and the juices of sorrel and *mauby* (made from the bark of the rhamnaceous tree).

TRINIDAD

Unlike Tobago, which attracts visitors to its silky sand beaches and coral reefs, Trinidad draws visitors who seek cultural immersion. Adventurers of all types come to explore the tropical bird–filled rainforests, to hike amid nature or to partake in Carnival and the lively music scene.

Despite its size, Trinidad is one of the least 'touristy' islands in the Caribbean – it lacks the sort of resorts that attract crowds of vacationers, and its capital city, Port of Spain, has more bustle than charm. What makes Trinidad such a worthwhile destination is its ethnic diversity. You'll find Anglican and Spanish churches beside Hindu temples and Muslim mosques, and festivals throughout the year reflect the mix of cultures. Trinidad has the Caribbean's most festive Carnival – Port of Spain turns into one huge street party, attended by thousands of revelers from around the world.

Traveling around Trinidad requires resilience, creativity and adaptability. Directions to understanding the island don't show up on any shiny brochures or flashing signposts; travel here requires you to jump in with both feet – to touch, feel, smell and taste. It's an incredibly inviting place where the genuine, friendly people share with pride their country's treasures.

Orientation

Virtually the shape of a molar tooth sitting on its side, Trinidad is surrounded by four bodies of water – the Caribbean (north), Atlantic Ocean (east), Gulf of Paria (west) and the Columbus Channel (south). This watery mix makes each coast of the country a little different. Port of Spain, the country's bustling capital, sits along a wide bay on the Gulf, and most of the country's better-known attractions are within an hour's drive of the city. Driving, you could get from one side of the country to the other in less than three hours, maybe less if you're a pro at bumpy, winding roads.

West of the capital, a peninsula pointing toward Venezuela leads to Chaguaramas – one of the Caribbean's chief yachting centers. North of Port of Spain, the Saddle Rd becomes the North Coast Rd that leads to Trinidad's popular north-coast beaches. East of Port of Spain is Piarco International Airport, and the key northern towns of Arima and Sangre Grande. Along the desolate east coast lie endless palm-fringed beaches. To the northeast is the remote Northern Range and the turtle nesting areas of Grande Rivière and Matura. To the south of Port of Spain are Chaguanas – the heart of East Indian Trinidad – and San Fernando – the industrial center of the country.

MAPS
The tourist office distributes free, reasonably good maps of both Trinidad and Tobago. Still, if you're going to be doing a lot of exploring, the best resources are the government's Lands & Surveys Division maps of Tobago and Trinidad (TT$23 each), sold in Port of Spain at the **Lands & Surveys office** (Frederick St) and at Trinidad Book World (p687). They're also available at the airport tourist office in Tobago.

Getting There & Around
AIR
Trinidad's only airport, **Piarco International Airport** (POS; ☎ 669-8047; www.tntairports.com), is 15.5 miles (25km) east of Port of Spain. There's a tourist office, duty-free shops, car-rental booths, ATMs and fast-food restaurants near the ticketing area. There is also a place to store luggage (see p687). A currency exchange office inside the terminal is open 6am to 10pm. For details of flights to and from Port of Spain, see p720.

To/From the Airport
The established fare for a taxi from the airport to Port of Spain is US$20 (TT$120), and it is by far the easiest way to get to town. Alternatively, take an Arouca route taxi (found to the left just outside the terminal) and get off at the Eastern Main Rd

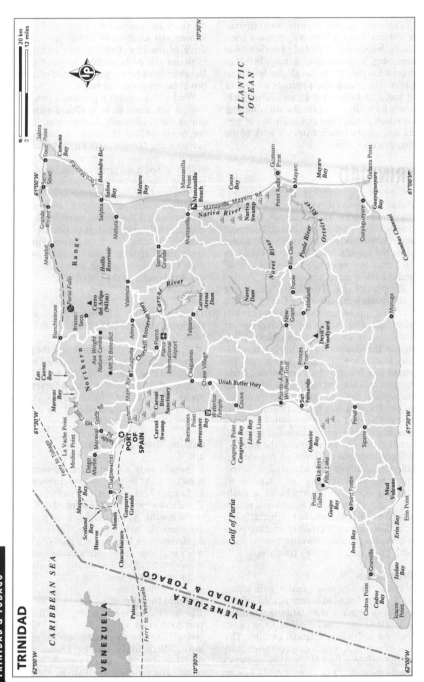

TRINIDAD & TOBAGO

TRINIDAD

(TT$2); from here, catch a red-striped maxi-taxi to the capital (TT$4). Heading from the airport to Maraval will cost you TT$150, and to San Fernando TT$186.

BOAT
Ferries run daily between Port of Spain on Trinidad and Scarborough on Tobago. See p720 for more information.

BUS
The main bus terminal is in Port of Spain; see p695 for details of services available around Trinidad.

CAR
A number of small, reliable car-rental companies operate on Trinidad. Prices average about TT$300 a day including insurance and unlimited mileage. Discounts are usually offered for weekly rentals. The following have offices in Port of Spain, as well as booths at Piarco International Airport:

Econo-Car Rentals (www.econocarrentalsltd.com); Airport (☎ 669-2342); Port of Spain (☎ 622-8074; 191-193 Western Main Rd), Has reliable cars and the cheapest rates (TT$200 to TT$250 a day).

Kalloo's Auto Rentals (www.kalloos.com); Airport (☎ 669-5673); Port of Spain (☎ 669-4868; 31 French St) Also runs a taxi service (p696).

Singh's Auto Rentals (www.singhs.com) Airport (☎ 669-5417); Port of Spain (☎ 623-0150; 7-9 Wrightson Rd)

Thrifty (☎ 669-0602; www.thrifty.com) Does not have an office in Port of Spain, but can make pickup arrangements beyond the airport.

TAXI
For details on getting around the island by taxi, see p695.

TOURS
See p719 for a list of ecotours operating on the island.

You can arrange island tours with individual taxi drivers. For an all-day round-the-island tour, drivers will generally ask about TT$1000, though you should be able to negotiate that down by about 25%.

PTSC Know Your Country Tours (☎ 624-9839) Started in 2002 as a way for locals to learn more about their country, the Public Transport Service runs weekend-only minibus tours of Trinidad. The day-long tours leave from City Gate at 8:30am, last about eight to 10 hours and cost TT$30 to TT$80. You need to book a few days in advance.

Trinidad & Tobago Sightseeing Tours (☎ 628-1051; www.trintours.com; 12 Western Main Rd, St James, Port of Spain) Serves cruise-ship passengers and other groups and offers a variety of full-day driving tours in air-con minivans. Guides can conduct tours in English, Spanish, French, German and Italian. A perimeter tour of Trinidad costs US$75, while a three-hour Port of Spain city tour is US$30. It also organizes day trips to Tobago for US$168 (including flight).

PORT OF SPAIN
pop 50,500

Not designed for tourists, Port of Spain, the country's capital and commercial center, is a bustling metropolitan hub. Crowds fill the streets, drivers disregard lanes and honk frivolously, and streets suffer poor signage. Add hot, muggy air and a confusing public transit system, and navigating the city can be a nerve-fraying experience. The best way to approach Port of Spain is to ride it like a wave or a roller-coaster. Go for the experience and trust that the tracks beneath the train will keep you from flying away.

The city is a lively place with a variety of good restaurants and clubs. The downtown architecture mimics the multicultural mishmash that forms the population. A sprinkling of modern office buildings pops up amid old corrugated tin stalls and 19th-century colonial buildings. Streets are packed with food stalls, air-conditioned indoor malls and labyrinthine pedestrian arcades. Vendors hawk fruit, candy, jewelry and bootleg recordings, often playing at maximum volume from scratchy boom boxes.

Port of Spain is at its best and brightest during Carnival and the months leading up to it, starting as early as September. While here, be sure to take a look into some of the mas camps (headquarters for the parading bands), where artists create colorful costumes, and visit the panyards, where local steel bands diligently practice their rhythms for the upcoming festivities.

Orientation
Port of Spain lies about 15.5 miles (25km) northwest of Piarco International Airport. Downtown is an area about 140 square blocks between Park St on the north side, Wrightson Rd to the west, St Ann's River to the east and the Gulf of Paria to the south The 'center' of town is along Independence Sq, not really a square but two one-way

TRINIDAD & TOBAGO

PORT OF SPAIN

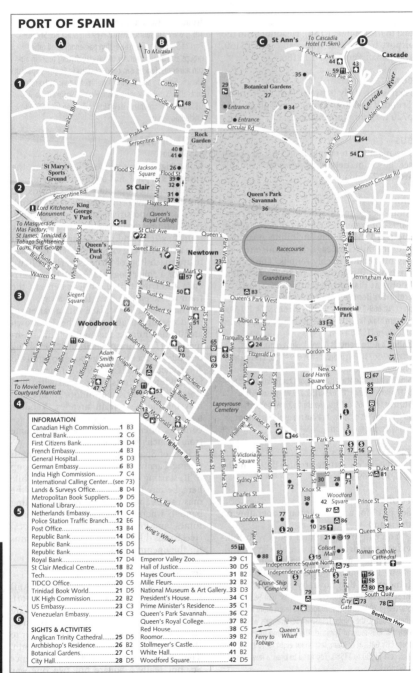

SLEEPING 🏠
Alicia's House..............................**43** D1
Chancellor Hotel & Conference
  Center...................................**44** D1
Coblentz Inn...............................**45** E1
Copper Kettle.............................**46** C4
Gingerbread House......................**47** A4
Kapok Hotel................................**48** B1
La Calypso.................................**49** B3
Par-May-La's Inn.........................**50** B3
Sundeck Suites...........................**51** B3
Tourist Villa................................**52** B4
Trinbago....................................**53** B4
Trinidad Hilton............................**54** D2

EATING 🍴
Apsara..................................(see 61)
Battimamzelle.......................(see 45)
Breakfast Shed...........................**55** C5
Food Court..............................(see 9)
Hosein's Roti Shop.....................**56** D6
Hott Shoppe..............................**57** B3
Jenny's on the Boulevard........(see 63)
Najin Fastfoods..........................**58** D6
Solimar....................................**59** D1
Sweet Lime...............................**60** B4
Tamnak Thai..............................**61** D2
Tiki Village..............................(see 48)
Veni Mangé...............................**62** A3

DRINKING 🍷
Carnival Bar...........................(see 54)
Cellar......................................**63** C4
Pelican Inn................................**64** D2

ENTERTAINMENT 🎭
Fifty One Degrees.......................**65** C3
Legacy Mas Camp.......................**66** B3
Mas Camp Pub........................(see 60)
Rampage Mas Camp....................**67** D4
Renegades Panyard.....................**68** D4
Silver Stars Panyard....................**69** C4
Woodbrook Playboyz Panyard...**70** B4

SHOPPING 🛍
Cleve's One Stop Music Shop....**71** D5

TRANSPORT
BWIA.......................................**72** C5
City Gate...................................**73** D6
Ferries to Tobago.......................**74** C6
Independence Square Taxi
  Stand....................................**75** D6
Kalloo's Taxi Service...................**76** D4
LIAT...**77** C5
Maxi Taxi Terminal (Eastbound)..**78** D6
Maxi taxis to Chaguaramas..........**79** C6
Maxi taxis to Laventill, Arima &
  Sangre Grande........................**80** D6
Maxi taxis to Maraval, Maracas &
  Blanchisseuse.........................**81** D5
Parking....................................**82** C5
Queen's Park Savannah Taxi
  Stand....................................**83** C3
Route Taxis to Chaguanas...........**84** D6
Route Taxis to Maraval................**85** D4
Route Taxis to St Ann's..............**86** D5
Route Taxis to St James..............**87** D5
Route Taxis to San Fernando....(see 79)
Singh's Auto Rentals...................**88** C5

streets running along a narrow pedestrian strip. Here you can pick up a route taxi and find travel agents, banks and cheap food. The south end of Frederick St is the central shopping area.

North of downtown, the fabulous Queen's Park Savannah pulsates with cricket and soccer matches, live music and cultural events, and sits within the 2.3-mile (3.7km) Circular Rd. The northern neighborhoods of St Ann's, Cascade and Maraval have excellent accommodations options. West of downtown, the lively areas of Woodbrook (where you'll find good restaurants along Ariapita Ave) and St James (entered through an arch at the west end of Tragarete Rd), offer up the best nightlife. East of downtown and St Ann's River is the Central Market. Further east are the poorer neighborhoods of Laventille (the birthplace of pan music) and Barataria.

Information
BOOKSTORES
Metropolitan Book Suppliers (☎ 623-3462; 13 Frederick St; ⏰ 9am-5:30pm Mon-Thu, 8:30am-5:30pm Fri, 9am-1pm Sat) Upstairs in the Colsort Mall, with a great selection of Caribbeana.
Trinidad Book World (☎ 623-4316; cnr Queen & Chacon Sts; ⏰ 8:30am-4:30pm Mon-Thu, 8:30am-5:30pm Fri, 8am-1pm Sat) Good general bookstore that also sells maps and local literature. You'll find it opposite the cathedral.

INTERNET ACCESS
International Calling Center (City Gate, South Quay; per hr TT$10; ⏰ 6am-11pm) You'll find many centers like this downtown along Independence Sq.
Tech (☎ 623-2397; 86 Frederick St; per hr TT$15; ⏰ 8:30am-5pm Mon-Fri, 8:30am-12:30pm Sat) Found at the corner of Queen St.

LAUNDRY
Because Trinidad is not a tourist-oriented city, public laundries are scarce, but many hotels and guesthouses have facilities. If the don't, they can arrange to have it done for you.

LEFT LUGGAGE
You can store your luggage at the airport for TT$5 per piece of luggage per day.

LIBRARIES
National Library (☎ 623-6962; www.nalis.gov.tt; cnr Hart & Abercromby Sts; ⏰ 8am-6pm Mon-Fri, 8:30am-noon Sat)

MEDICAL SERVICES
General Hospital (☎ 623-2951; 56-57 Charlotte St) A large, full-service hospital.
St Clair Medical Centre (☎ 628-1451; 18 Elizabeth St) A private hospital preferred by expatriates. There are also smaller hospitals in the towns of Arima, San Fernando and Mt Hope, the latter near Tunapuna.

MONEY
The major banks – Central Bank, Republic Bank, Royal Bank and First Citizens Bank – have branches on Park St east of Frederick St and on Independence Sq. Most are open 8am to 2pm Monday to Thursday and 8am to 1pm and 3pm to 5pm Friday, and have 24-hour ATMs.

POST
Main post office (☎ 800-7678; Wrightson Rd; ☯ 8am-4pm Mon-Fri) TT Post has outlets all over town, including this main office.

TELEPHONE
International Calling Center (City Gate, South Quay; ☯ 6am-11pm) This center has private calling booths for making international calls (per minute TT$1 to the USA, Canada, UK and Europe).

TOURIST INFORMATION
Tourism and Industrial Development Company of Trinidad & Tobago (Tidco; ☎ 675-7034; www.visittnt .com) Has a helpful outlet at **Piarco International Airport** (☎ 669-5196; ☯ 8am-11pm) and another office **downtown** (☎ 624-5082; cnr Queen & Edward Sts; ☯ 8am-4pm Mon-Fri).

Dangers & Annoyances
Port of Spain has a reputation for high crime and, although some of it is hype, some of it is valid. Robberies and kidnappings are increasingly common. Anyone traveling alone should not walk solo at night, especially around Nelson St and the east side of downtown. If you stick to the suburbs of St Ann's and St James, you'll be fine, though women might find the intense attention a little threatening.

If you're renting a car, beware when you park downtown. The street signs can be confusing and the police often tow cars away. You're better off using a public parking lot (usually TT$5 per hour). If you do get towed, you can bail out your car at the police station traffic branch on Piccadilly St on South Quay. The fine is TT$100.

Sights
QUEEN'S PARK SAVANNAH
The city's crowning jewel, 'The Savannah' was once part of a sugar plantation and is now a public park. Throughout the year, residents play soccer and cricket and fly kites in the park's expansive grassy field. It's a great place to go for a jog, walk or simply hang out and people-watch, especially in the early evening when the scorching heat subsides a bit. Food stalls serve treats like fresh coconut juice, rotis and shark & bake. In the park's northwest corner there's a small **rock garden** with a lily pond and benches. Concerts and Carnival events take place on the **grandstand** at the south side of the park. The 2.3-mile (3.7km) road circling the park has one-way traffic flowing in a clockwise direction; locals call it the world's largest roundabout.

MAGNIFICENT SEVEN
Along the west side of the Queen's Park Savannah along Maraval Rd are the Magnificent Seven, a line of seven eccentric and ornate colonial buildings constructed in the early 20th century. From south to north, they are the Germanic Renaissance **Queen's Royal College** (a boys' high school); **Hayes Court** (the Anglican bishop's residence); **Mille Fleurs** (headquarters for the Law Association); **Roomor** (a private residence); the Catholic **Archbishop's Residence**; stately **White Hall** (the prime minister's office); and **Stollmeyer's Castle**, built to resemble a Scottish castle, complete with turrets. Unfortunately, these buildings are not open to the public, but it's worth passing by for a look.

EMPEROR VALLEY ZOO
Just north of Queen's Park Savannah is the 6.2-acre (2.5-hectare) **Emperor Valley Zoo** (☎ 628-9177; www.trinizoo.com; adult/child TT$4/2; ☯ 9:30am-5:30pm), which opened in 1947. Though small, the zoo has an interesting collection of more than 220 animals, including many indigenous creatures like red howler monkeys, scarlet ibis, agoutis and various snakes. Several cats such as ocelots (called a 'tiger cat' by locals) prowl around in cages, and you can get very close to a skinny and hot-looking Siberian lion.

East of the zoo is the entrance to the **Botanical Gardens** (admission free; ☯ 6am-6:30pm), which date from 1818 and have grand trees and attractive strolling paths, plus pavilions containing orchids and anthuriums. The **President's House** (not open to the public), a mansion originally built as the governor's residence in 1875, is adjacent to the gardens, as is the **prime minister's residence** (not open to the public).

NATIONAL MUSEUM & ART GALLERY
Housed in a classic colonial building, the **museum** (☎ 623-5941; cnr Frederick & Keate Sts; admission free; ☺ 10am-6pm Tue-Sat, 2-6pm Sun) contains interesting historical exhibits, from early Native American settlers to African slaves, and the indentured Indians who followed. There are also simple displays of rocks, shells, colonial agriculture and the technology behind oil exploration. One room is devoted to Carnival, with a nice exhibit on the evolution of steel-pan instruments, a photo gallery of calypso greats and videos of mas bands in action. There's also a room full of dusty costumes.

INDEPENDENCE SQUARE
The hustle and bustle of downtown culminates along Independence Sq, two parallel streets that flank a promenade that features benches, chess tables and food kiosks. The west end of the promenade is marked by the towering buildings of the Central Bank, and the east end is marked by the commanding 1836 Roman Catholic Cathedral.

South of the promenade is imposing **City Gate**, a huge Victorian building that was formerly the city's train station. Today it's a transportation hub, the terminus for all buses and maxi-taxis. West of City Gate is **King's Wharf**, the landing point for anyone arriving by boat. It's also where you catch the ferry to Tobago. Nearby is the **Cruise Ship Complex**, where overpriced souvenir stalls come to life when the big boats exhale their passengers.

WOODFORD SQUARE
Sometimes referred to as the University of Woodford Sq because of its occasional use by soapbox speakers and gospel preachers, this public park marks the symbolic center of downtown. Dr Eric Williams, Trinidad & Tobago's first prime minister, lectured to the masses here about the importance of sovereignty, which later led to the country's independence from Britain. Woodford Sq

remains a 'speakers corner' where people can express opinions. Upcoming discussion topics are posted on a chalkboard on the southeast corner of the square.

Surrounding the park are some interesting edifices, including **Red House**, the imposing red Renaissance-style parliament building constructed in 1906; and the contemporary steel-and-concrete **Hall of Justice** and **City Hall**. Opposite the square's southwest corner is the **National Library** (p687).

The majestic, Gothic-designed **Anglican Trinity Cathedral** at the south side of Woodford Sq dates from 1818 and seats 1200. Its impressive ceiling is supported by an elaborate system of mahogany beams, a design modeled on London's Westminster Hall. Stained-glass windows open to the breeze, and there's a marble monument to Sir Ralph Woodford, the British governor responsible for the church's construction.

Sleeping
When people stay in Port of Spain they are generally here for cricket, Carnival, birdwatching or business. The average hotel guest isn't here to chill out on vacation (you'd go to the beaches or Tobago for that), so many hotels offer efficient if slightly uninspired lodgings.

Most hotels have security gates that are guarded 24/7. Be cautious when walking from your hotel, especially at night. Nothing says 'I'm a tourist, rob me' like walking out of a lobby freshly showered and jingling your room key.

Rates listed below are high-season rates. Anticipate that an extra 10% service charge and 15% VAT will be added to your bill.

BUDGET
Alicia's House (☎ 623-2802; www.aliciashousetrinidad .com; 7 Coblentz Gardens; r US$48-58; ✄ ▨ ▣) You feel as though you're staying in a West Indian local's home at this friendly modern guesthouse. It's just north of Queen's Park Savannah, and there are 21 tidy, simple rooms, five with shared bath. Some rooms overlook the pool/Jacuzzi area. Meals are served in the small **restaurant** (breakfast US$8, lunch & dinner mains US$6-10).

Sundeck Suites (☎ 628-2008; www.sundeck.co.tt; 42-44 Picton St; s/d/tr apt US$49/68/84, 10-night Carnival packages from US$1200; ▨) In a good location walking distance from Queen's Park Oval,

---

CARNIVAL – PREPARE TO PARTY

Several ideas float around about the birth of Carnival. Some say it's a spin-off of ancient Greece's Bacchus celebrations; others suggest Carnival was used by African slaves as a means of mimicking colonial authority, while paying homage to African mythology and music. The majority of celebrants say Carnival (meaning 'farewell to the flesh') marks the approach of Lent, the ultimate indulgence before the upcoming sober disciplines. Whatever the origin, Carnival is an important embracing of culture that's celebrated throughout the Caribbean.

The king of all Caribbean Carnivals is unmistakably Trinidad's. Many Trinidadians prepare for Carnival with a near-consuming devotion. Starting as early as September (Carnival is in February), activities swing into full gear as people prepare to 'play mas' (participate in the masquerade). At mas camps, costume designers work late into the evenings. The panyards (practice venues) are full of steel-band performers tuning up their rhythms, and soca and calypso music blasts through the night at pre-Carnival fetes. A week before Carnival, preliminary competitions for the king and queen contenders get under way.

Carnival festivities begin on Monday morning, two days before Ash Wednesday, with the predawn J'ouvert (dirty mas), when revelers take to the streets smeared in mud and grease and dressed in scary costumes. As the day proceeds, masquerade bands hit the streets for 'pretty mas,' with members of each troupe wearing identical costumes. Tens of thousands parade and dance throughout the night, accompanied by steel bands, brass bands, and soca trucks with DJs, and the event becomes a massive street party. On Tuesday, the activities culminate with Panorama, the final competition for the Band of the Year, and by midnight Carnival is officially over.

Most of the larger events take place at the Queen's Park Savannah in the center of Port of Spain, including the major steel-band and calypso competitions.

Information on upcoming Carnival events is available from the **National Carnival Commission of Trinidad & Tobago** (☎ 627-1350; www.ncctt.org).

Carnival Calendar

- **Saturday two weeks prior to Carnival** Panorama preliminaries, where steel bands begin competing for the national title of best band. The competition culminates in Panorama, the final competition that takes place on the last night of Carnival.

- **Saturday prior** Red Cross children's parade of the bands; Calypso Monarch semifinals

- **Carnival Friday** National Single Pan Bands Final; International Soca Monarch Finals; Carnival King and Queen semifinals

---

the Savannah and Woodbrook, this no-frills, all-suite inn offers city and mountain views from atop its broad 1400-sq-ft (130-sq-meter) rooftop deck. The 15 apartments each have two or three beds, a kitchenette and a small veranda. It's a good place to meet other travelers. The same goes for **Par-May-La's Inn** (☎ 628-2008; www.parmaylas.com; 53 Picton St; s/d US$40/60; 🔀), which is a block away and run by the same owners. Prices at both places include tax.

Gingerbread House (☎ 625-6841; www.trinidad gingerbreadhouse.com; 8 Carlos St; r US$35, during Carnival US$50; 🔀 🔀) This 1920s host home was recently renovated and is a true find for anyone wanting an immersed cultural experience at great value. The comfortable rooms (there

are only three) come with private baths and TV, and there are several communal areas. Friendly hosts Rosemary and Bernard McKay help guests plan day trips.

Several ultrabudget guesthouses compete for in-town business. The following are simple but clean and offer air-con private rooms for about US$35 to US$40. Try the bustling **Copper Kettle** (☎ 625-4381; 66 Edward St) or **Tourist Villa** (☎ 627-5423; 7 Methuen St), the latter on a quiet street with lots of balconies and a small pool. Nearby, on a busier street, with access to Tourist Villa's pool, **Trinbago** (☎ 627-7114; 37 Ariapita Ave) has six rooms. In the heart of Woodbrook's entertainment zone, **La Calypso** (☎ 622-4077; 46 French St) is a homey place with 18 rooms.

- **Carnival Saturday** National Panorama finals (at Queen's Park Savannah); Junior parade of bands
- **Carnival Sunday** Dimanche Gras: crowning of Carnival King and Queen; Calypso Monarch finals (at Queen's Park Savannah)
- **Monday morning** J'ouvert
- **Monday & Tuesday** Parade of the bands; crowning of King of de Road
- **Tuesday** Last lap
- **Saturday after** Carnival champs in concert (at Queen's Park Savannah)

Carnival Glossary

- **Bands** Refers not to musical bands but to large groups of costumed masqueraders
- **Big Yard** The competition stage at Queen's Park Savannah
- **Chip** To shuffle along behind a steel band
- **Calypso Tents** Venues for Calypso performances
- **Carnival** Literal translation means 'farewell to the flesh' and marks the approach of Lent
- **Dimanche Gras** A big show on Carnival Sunday night, where the winners are determined
- **Fetes** Giant outdoor parties held throughout Carnival season
- **J'ouvert** Carnival's opening day
- **Mas Camp** Headquarters for the various parading bands, where costumes are designed and produced
- **Panorama** The National Steel Band Competition
- **Panyard** Rehearsal space for large steel bands; visitors can watch bands practice and there's usually a bar stocked with rum and cold Carib
- **Playing Mas** To 'play mas' means to be part of a masquerade band. You'll often hear people ask 'you playin' mas?'
- **The Drag** The warm-up area where performers gather prior to their performance at the Queen's Park Savannah
- **Road March** The calypso song most played by the band during the two days of Carnival
- **Wining** The hip-gyrating move done while dancing to soca music

MIDRANGE

Monique's Guesthouse (☎ 628-3334; www.moniques trinidad.com; 114 Saddle Rd; s/d/tr/q US$55/60/65/70, with kitchen extra US$10, 5-night Carnival rate US$900; P ✕ 🕱) In Maraval, 1.8 miles (3km) north of Queen's Park Savannah, Monique's has 10 pleasant rooms with two single or double beds, private bath, air-con and TV. A hillside annex has 10 large studios with cooking facilities and balconies from which you can sometimes spot parrots in the treetops. Friendly owners, Michael and Monica Charbonne, organize nature tours for guests.

Carnetta's House (☎ 628-2732; carnetta@trinidad .net; 99 Saddle Rd; s/d/tr US$65/75/90, with kitchenette extra US$6; P ✕ 🕱) Also in Maraval, Carnet-ta's is comprised of two separate buildings. Five rooms are at the home of Winston and Carnetta Borrell, in a quiet neighborhood alongside the Maraval River. Six newer units, most with kitchenettes, are on Saddle Rd, opposite Monique's Guesthouse. All rooms include air-con, cable TV, phones and private bath. Carnetta's riverside bar serves Creole-style meals (US$8 to US$15). Winston, a former tourist-board director, enjoys helping guests plan their daily outings.

Chancellor Hotel & Conference Center (☎ 623-0883; www.thechancellor.com; 5 St Ann's Ave; s/d US$95/110; P ✕ 🕱 🖳 🕱) The 22-room hacienda-style Chancellor offers the service and efficiency of a business hotel with the ease and decor of a small inn. Each bright room is

---

EARLY FLIGHT?

If you have an early flight at Piarco International Airport the next morning and need to stay near the airport, you have a couple of options.

Airport View Guesthouse (☎ 669-4186; s/d US$30/35; ☒) This guesthouse sits in a nondescript building over a supermarket, just a few minutes from the airport. The 17 large, clean though simple rooms have TVs and the helpful management offers courtesy airport transfers.

Bel Air International Airport Hotel (☎ 669-4771; www.belairairporthotel.com; Golden Grove Rd; s/d US$62/74; P ☒ ☒ ☒) More upscale than Airport View, the Bel Air has 56 rooms and is just outside the airport perimeter. There's an outdoor pool, bar and restaurant, plus free transfers to the airport.

---

decorated in West Indies style, comes with queen-size beds and has high-speed Internet access. The pool, bar and restaurant offer ample refreshment.

Courtyard Marriott (☎ 627-5555; www.marriott .com; Audrey Jeffers Hwy; r from US$130; P ☒ ☒ ☒ ☒) Opened in late 2004, this 116-room Marriott is a new addition to the growing list of the city's business hotels. It's next door to MovieTowne, across from the Hasley Crawford Stadium at Invaders Bay.

TOP END

Kapok Hotel (☎ 622-5765; www.kapokhotel.com; 16-18 Cotton Hill; s/d from US$130/145, with kitchenette extra US$7; P ☒ ☒ ☒ ☒) A popular business hotel toward the south end of Saddle Rd and a two-minute walk to Queen's Park Savannah, the Kapok boasts an authentic

Caribbean vibe. Its 94 rooms are decked out with rattan furnishings, TV, phones and high-speed Internet. The outdoor pool lures sweaty travelers, as does the self-service launderette. There are two restaurants here, including the popular Polynesian-themed Tiki Village (see opposite).

Trinidad Hilton (☎ 624-3111, 800-321-3232; www .hiltoncaribbean.com/trinidad; Lady Young Rd; r from US$200; P ☒ ☒ ☒ ☒) The 394-room Hilton sits on 25 acres (10 hectares). Its hillside setting affords a sweeping city view across Queen's Park Savannah and the Gulf of Paria.

When local companies or politicians hold conferences they gather here, in boardrooms or over cocktails, making the Hilton a hub of mover-and-shaker activity. The full-service hotel offers large, modern rooms (most with balconies), two restaurants and three bars, including the lively Carnival Bar (see p695). Tennis courts, a large pool, spa, shops, banks and a fitness center round out the amenities. Rates vary widely, depending on occupancy levels.

Eating

Pickup trucks piled high with chilled drinking coconuts (TT$3) and other snacks can be found around Queen's Park Savannah. In the evening, the neighborhood of St James is the best place to go for a street snack. Street vendors dish out delicious Jamaican jerk chicken, Indian food, seafood stews and other yummy delights. Vendors adhere to strict health codes, so you needn't worry about sanitation.

BUDGET

Hosein's Roti Shop (☎ 627-2357; cnr Independence Sq South & Henry St; mains TT$6-12; ☺ lunch & dinner) On the south side of town, this is a hugely

---

AUTHOR'S CHOICE

Coblentz Inn (☎ 624-0541; www.coblentzinn.com; 44 Coblentz Ave; s/d US$105/108; P ☒ ☒) Reminiscent of a European boutique hotel, the 16-room Coblentz Inn is a peaceful haven that feels far away from the city chaos even though it's just minutes from the Savannah. Each brightly colored and immaculate room captures feng shui ideologies, a harmoniousness that makes you feel as though you've just popped a muscle relaxant. Sip a cocktail on the cool rooftop bar, or read a book on the waterfall garden terrace. Amenities include a small gym, a reading library, a computer station where you can get online, and room service and laundry service. With ultrafriendly staff and a free continental breakfast at the adjoining Battimamzelle restaurant (see p694), the Coblentz offers perhaps the best value in town.

popular carryout for mini-rotis and dhal *puri* (a type of roti stuffed with split peas).

Najin Fastfoods (☎ 627-7613; 6 Henry St; mains TT$15-20; ☺ lunch & dinner) Around the corner from Hosein's, this little hole-in-the-wall serves good, cheap Chinese food, including an excellent, filling wonton and bok choy soup, and plates of vegetables and rice.

Breakfast Shed (Wrightson Rd; mains TT$15; ☺ breakfast & lunch) Located in front of the cruise-ship complex, this place is literally a tin shed. It's a good place to rub shoulders with locals and to try local delicacies. Island women in stalls around the perimeter of the shed make everything from scratch. You can have a big meal of Trinidadian fare, including fish, dasheen (a type of taro), plantains and rice.

Hott Shoppe (☎ 622-2858; 52 Maraval Rd; roti TT$3.50-9.50; ☺ lunch & dinner) Found near the Savannah, the Hott Shoppe is bright and clean and offers a wide choice of roti fillings, including vegetarian minis. Fresh orange and grapefruit juice are also available.

The **food courts** (lunch TT$15; ☺ 10am-6pm Mon-Fri, 10am-2pm Sat) in the malls along Frederick St are handy spots for a quick sit-down lunch. Local and international fast-food places abound around Independence Sq.

MIDRANGE

Sweet Lime (☎ 624-9983; cnr Ariapita Ave & French St; mains TT$40-65; ☺ lunch & dinner) Attached to Mas Camp Pub (p694) on Ariapita Ave, this casual sidewalk restaurant/bar has an open-air kitchen. The menu includes salads, grilled meats and fish, vegetarian options and a few exotic specialties, such as Viagra broth (a spicy fish soup).

Tamnak Thai (☎ 625-0647; 13 Queen's Park East; mains US$8-22; ☺ lunch Tue-Fri, dinner daily; ☒) A sensual experience, from the latticed, tropical-wood tables to the lily-pad pond to the spicy Thai curries. Dishes include lemongrass-infused soups; seafood salad; vegetable, lamb and shrimp curries; and spicy tofu with vegetables.

Apsara (☎ 623-7659; 13 Queen's Park East; mains US$12-30; ☺ lunch & dinner Mon-Sat; ☒) Specializing in North Indian cuisine, Apsara is named after the dancers of the court of Indra, who, it's said, could move freely between heaven and earth. Well, you're here on terra firma, but your mouth just may make it to the heavenly gates. Favorites like

tandoori, curry and biryani dishes will melt in your mouth. Vegetarians will also find many options here. Apsara is in the same building as Tamnak Thai.

Jenny's on the Boulevard (☎ 625-1807; Cipriani Blvd; mains US$15-25; ☺ lunch & dinner Mon-Sat; ☒) In a colonial house, Jenny's sighs under the weight of its Victorian antiques, but the vivacious crowd keeps coming for American-style steaks and authentic Cantonese cuisine. Downstairs, the Cellar (p695) is a good place to have a drink before or after dinner.

TOP END

Tiki Village (☎ 622-5765; 16-18 Cotton Hill; mains US$12-30; ☒ ☒ ☒) The Kapok Hotel's Tiki Village is a worthwhile choice, with its great views of the Savannah and downtown, a swanky Polynesian-slash-Asian ambience and a menu stocked with Chinese favorites that are infused with Polynesian and Trini flavors. Come for the lunch buffet served Monday to Friday, or the delicious dim sum on Sunday.

Solimar (☎ 624-6267; 6 Nook Ave; mains US$12-30; ☺ dinner Mon-Sat; ☒ ☒) This innovative restaurant is run by an Englishman, Joe Brown, a well-traveled former chef for the Hilton chain. On any given night the menu may include Asian, Indian and Italian food. It's a mellow place, with low lights and a relaxed vibe. Cigar aficionados will want to check out the humidor, which boasts an excellent collection of stogies.

Battimamzelle (☎ 621-0541; 44 Coblentz Ave; breakfast & lunch US$8-15, dinner US$20-30; ⊙ closed Sun; ☒ ☒) Brainchild of chef Khalid Mohammed, Battimamzelle (the local word for butterfly) appeals to more than just your salivary glands. A feast for the eyes, the vibrant decor mimics the colors of tropical birds, with yellow, green and red walls and splashes of color throughout. Nestled in the fabulous Coblentz Inn (p692), the small restaurant boasts a creative menu featuring meats, seafood or whatever the chef wants to create. Mohammed adds his artistic touch to food presentation; you'll enjoy a delicious and beautiful meal.

Drinking & Entertainment

Port of Spain's nightlife rocks continuously. Locals love to lime and listen to live music and you can always find a bit of both. Wednesday night is popular for live music; people tend to lime on Friday; and steel bands play on Saturday. Some bars have a cover charge (up to TT$50), depending on who's playing.

BARS & NIGHTCLUBS

Mas Camp Pub (☎ 627-8449; cnr Ariapita Ave & French St; occasional cover charge TT$50) For a variety of live music and DJs, this super popular pub has something going on most evenings. Odds are you'll catch calypso, Latin or soca, and, at Christmas, a *parang* party. An adjoining sports room has pool tables and slot machines. Pick up a weekly program at the door.

Pelican Inn (☎ 624-7486; 2-4 Coblentz Ave; ⊙ 11am-11pm; ☒) North of the Hilton, this English-style pub is popular with expats, though folks

---

PANYARDS & MAS CAMPS

Panyards are little more than vacant lots, where steel bands store their instruments for much of the year. Come Carnival season, panyards become lively rehearsal spaces, pulsating with energy and magnificent sound. Here, you can see the underbelly of one of the most important and sacred parts of Trinidad's urban landscape. You feel the music, and you begin to understand it, relate to it and love it. Band members span gender and age; you could see an eight-year-old girl drumming alongside her great-grandfather.

Steel bands start gearing up for Carnival as early as late September, sometimes rehearsing and performing throughout the year. The best way to find out about practice and performance schedules is by asking around. You can also contact **Pan TrinBago** (☎ 623-4486; www.pan trinbago.co.tt).

Some popular panyards that welcome visitors:

- **Desperadoes** (☎ 752-2742; Upper Laventille Rd, Laventille) An authentic experience but note that this panyard is in a sketchier part of town and is less accustomed to visitors. You'd be best to take a taxi and go with a group.
- **Renegades** (☎ 624-3348; 138 Charlotte St)
- **Silver Stars** (☎ 633-4733; 56 Tragarete Rd)
- **Woodbrook Playboyz** (☎ 628-0320; 27 Tragarete Rd)

Visiting a mas camp is another worthwhile way to glimpse Carnival life. Headquarters for the various groups 'playing mas,' (part of the masquerade) mas camps are workshops where respected designers create intricate and lavish Carnival costumes. They are busy months before the main event, often designing for Carnivals all over the world. They become buzzing hives of energy in the weeks leading up to Carnival. The thrill is so addictive, you may find yourself shopping for a costume and signing up to play mas.

If you would like to visit a mas camp or join a mas band for Carnival, here are some good choices:

- **Legacy** (☎ 622-7466; www.legacycarnival.com; 88 Robert St)
- **Mas Factory** (☎ 785-5088; 7 Dengue St)
- **Masquerade** (☎ 623-2161; www.masquerade.co.tt; 19 De Vertueil St)
- **Rampage Mas Camp** (☎ 627-9408; 127 Charlotte St)

have grumbled in recent years about the inflated beer prices. Still, live music on Wednesday night makes it one of the liveliest places in town, and it's popular for after-work liming on Friday night.

Cellar (☎ 625-1807; 6 Cipriani Blvd; 🌠) A more mature crowd limes around the mahogany bar at this cool, smoke-filled lounge, downstairs from Jenny's on the Boulevard (p693).

Carnival Bar (☎ 624-3211; Trinidad Hilton, Lady Young Rd; 🌠) A fun place for drinks and a snack, the Hilton's bar has a weekly parade of events. Catch Latin night on Tuesday, Reggae Wednesday, Karaoke Thursday, the Friday Night Lime or Saturday Classics & Oldies.

Fifty One Degrees (☎ 627-0051; 51 Cipriani Blvd; weekend cover charge TT$50; 🕑 7pm-very late Tue-Sat; 🌠) Beautiful people crowd into this hip and happening dance club. They come to boogie to every genre of popular dance music, from up-tempo reggae, to soca, to Top-40 tunes. Expect queues on the weekend.

The suburb of St James, just west of central Port of Spain, becomes a hub of activity almost any evening. Rub shoulders with politicians, cricket stars or just about anyone at **Smokey & Bunty's** (97 Western Main Rd), a hole-in-the wall watering hole and the center of St James action.

If you'd like someone to accompany you on your first night on the town, contact Gunda Harewood for an **Evening Entertainment Tour** (☎ 625-2410; cell 756-9677; gunda@wow .net). Gunda knows what's going on around town and she'll plan activities around your interests. An evening out might include visits to a couple of panyards, a local live band, and guidance in choosing the best street snacks. About three hours of fun and transportation costs US$40 per person. It's a safe, informative and fun way to see Trini nightlife.

CINEMAS
MovieTowne (☎ 627-8277; www.movietowne.com; Audrey Jeffers Hwy, Invaders Bay; tickets adult/child TT$35/25; 🅿 🌠 🌠) Trinis just about blew their minds when this giant megaplex opened in 2002. Besides 10 wide-screen movie theaters, there's also a shopping mall, restaurants, video arcades, a rock climbing wall and even a babysitting service. It is across from Hasely Crawford Stadium.

Shopping
The central area of Port of Spain, especially around Independence Sq, Queen St and Frederick St, is filled with malls and arcades selling everything from spices to fabric by the yard. Music is the best souvenir to shop for in Port of Spain. You can pick up bootleg recordings from street vendors, or get originals of the latest tunes at **Crosby's Music Centre** (☎ 622-7622; 54 Western Main Rd), which is in St James opposite Smokey & Bunty's, or at **Cleve's One Stop Music Shop** (☎ 624-0827; 58 Frederick St), in a small shopping center downtown, northeast of Woodford Sq. You can also pick up recordings at the airport.

Getting There & Around
BUS
Most buses traveling around Trinidad originate from the City Gate terminal on South Quay in Port of Spain. Bus service tends to be slow and inconsistent, with schedules changing often and without notice, but buses can be an affordable way to get around if you're not in a rush. The red, white and black Express Commuter Service (ECS) buses are faster, more reliable and air-conditioned. They are geared toward commuters, so they run most frequently in the morning and afternoon. Check ahead of time for schedules at the **information/ticket booth** (☎ 623-7872; 🕑 7am-7pm Mon-Fri, 7am-noon Sat) on the west side of the bus platform.

Buses from City Gate terminal are:

Destination	Fare	Duration
Blanchisseuse	TT$8	1½hr
Chaguanas	TT$4	30min
Chaguaramas	TT$3	1hr
Maracas Bay	TT$4	45min
San Fernando	TT$7	1hr

CAR
See p685 for details of car-rental companies located in Port of Spain.

TAXI
For more information on the following taxi types, see p721.

Maxi-taxi
The main maxi-taxi terminal for southbound and eastbound buses is on South Quay, adjacent to City Gate. Figuring out

which maxi to catch can be a little confusing, so don't hesitate to call the **Trinidad & Tobago Unified Maxi Taxi Association** (☎ 624-3505).

The maxi-taxi color-coding system:

Green-band maxis Serve areas south of Port of Spain, including Chaguanas and San Fernando (from San Fernando, maxi-taxis connecting to outlying areas have black or brown stripes), leaving from City Gate.

Red-band maxis Serve areas east of Port of Spain, including Laventille, Arima and Sangre Grande, leaving from South Quay, near City Gate.

Yellow-band maxis Serve Port of Spain's western and northern suburbs. Maxis to Chaguaramas via St James leave from the corner of South Quay and St Vincent St; maxis traveling to Blanchisseuse via Maraval leave from the corner of Duke and Charlotte Sts.

Regular Taxi

Between 10pm and 6am there's a 50% surcharge on regular taxis. To call for a taxi, dial ☎ 669-1689 (airport), or ☎ 625-3032 (Independence Sq taxi stand).

Kalloo's Taxi Service (☎ 622-9073; 31 French St; ☼ 24hr) has an office less than a block north of Ariapita Ave and is convenient after an evening of liming at the Mas Camp pub.

Route Taxi

Within Port of Spain, the route taxi is the predominant mode of public transportation. Outside the city center, route taxis can be hailed along the route. Occasionally, drivers of private vehicles (with 'P' on the license plate) also offer route-taxi service, though be wary of these unofficial vehicles.

Port of Spain route taxi pickup points:

Route Taxis to Chaguanas Corner South Quay and Charlotte St (east side).

Route Taxis to Maraval (circling the Savannah) On the corner of Oxford and Charlotte Sts.

Route Taxis to St Ann's (circling the Savannah) Corner Hart and Frederick Sts (south side).

Route Taxis to St James (via Tragarete Rd) Corner Hart and Frederick Sts (north side).

Route Taxis to San Fernando Corner South Quay and St Vincent St.

AROUND PORT OF SPAIN
Chaguaramas

A 25-minute drive from the capital, Chaguaramas (sha-guah-*ra*-mas) was the site of a major US military installation during WWII. It now hosts traveling sailors and yacht owners at its ever-expanding marine

facilities. Yachties come here for safe harbor, because Trinidad sits safely out of the hurricane belt. Inexpensive teak from local forests also attracts boaters, as do comparatively inexpensive marina and dry-docking facilities. Oil and gas companies use the peninsula as a jumping-off point to access offshore oil rigs. Definitely geared toward the marina set, it's a nice place to come for a sunset dinner or to enjoy the weekend party scene.

The almost 15,000-acre (6000-hectare) Chaguaramas peninsula is a designated national park, lush with rain forest. The town of Chaguaramas is the launching point for tours to a chain of five offshore islands. Other attractions include a nine-hole golf course and the interesting **Chaguaramas Military History & Aerospace Museum** (☎ 634-4391; adult/child TT$10/7; ☼ 9am-5pm), which depicts Trinidad & Tobago's complex military history.

Hiking, swimming, history and boating tours arranged by appointment with the **Chaguaramas Development Authority** (☎ 634-2052/4048; www.chagdev.com) are the best way to see the area. Popular tours include the boat trip out to **Gasparee Grande** (US$20, three hours), at the south side of Chaguaramas Bay, where you can swim in tidal pools and visit caves that drip with stalactites.

The most distant island, 900-acre (360-hectare) **Chacachacare**, was once a leper colony; camping is permitted on the now-deserted isle, which is replete with beaches and stunning cliff views of Venezuela. **Scotland Bay**, on the western edge of the peninsula, has a pleasant beach that's accessible only by boat. Arrange independent boat trips with boatmen at the Island Property Owners' jetty, on the west side of Chaguaramas. Expect to pay about TT$120 per person for Gasparee Grande or Scotland Bay.

SLEEPING

Bight (☎ 634-4839; www.peakeyachts.com; 5 Western Main Rd; s/d US$70/80; P X ☒) Simple, tidy rooms overlooking the bay make the Bight great value at these prices. Its **restaurant** (mains US$8-20; ☼ breakfast, lunch & dinner) has terrace dining and is a fun, casual sports bar with a pool table, darts and big-screen TVs.

CrewsInn Hotel & Yachting Center (☎ 634-4384; www.crewsinn.com; Point Gourde; s/d US$130/140; P X ☒ ☐ ☒) This busy, 46-room hotel has bright rooms, all with patios and refrigerators. This hotel-and-marina complex is home to the open-air upscale **Lighthouse Restaurant** (mains US$8-30; ☼ breakfast, lunch & dinner), which sits on a covered deck overlooking the marina and serves up seafood and superb sunsets.

EATING & DRINKING

Most of the marinas have restaurants and bars where you can munch seafood and sip a Carib while the sun goes down.

Anchorage (☎ 634-4334; Hart's Cut, Western Main Rd; ☼ 11am-2am) Live bands often play here, especially during Carnival season. On Sunday in July and August, the Anchorage holds a pop music competition, where the best local bands come to compete. It also serves lunch and dinner overlooking the waterfront.

MoBS 2 (☎ 634-2255; ☼ noon-3am) Features a large open-air amphitheater and hosts Carnival launches for mas bands. Lunch and dinner are available from the grill.

Pier One (☎ 634-4426; Western Main Rd; ☼ 9pm-3am Wed-Sun) Dance the night away under starry skies at this popular club. The dance floor is a long, wooded dock that makes you feel like you're dancing on the sea. For those returning to Port of Spain, maxi-taxis often wait on the Western Main Rd near the entrance to the clubs.

Base (☎ 634-4004; ☼ 9pm-4am Fri & Sat) Designed to evoke the atmosphere of a 1940s military-base club, the Base is a DJ-driven dance club geared toward the young, affluent and beautiful.

Mt St Benedict

A Benedictine **monastery** sits on 600 acres (240 hectares) on a hillside north of Tunapuna, 8 miles (13km) east of Port of Spain. Though not a major sight in itself, the monastery attracts people who want to stay or eat at its secluded guesthouse, bird-watch or walk in the rain forest. Today, the monastery is home to just 12 aging monks who live peacefully inside the giant walls.

A hikers' haven, the thickly wooded hills behind the monastery are home to hawks, owls and numerous colorful forest birds, as well as the occasional monkey. A favorite **hike** is the Donkey Trail, which offers good birding and takes just a couple of hours to walk (round-trip) from the guesthouse.

Pax Guest House (☎ 662-4084; www.paxguesthouse .com; s/d US$55/85; P ☒ ☒) is a restored colonial house that is owned by the monastery, Pax welcomes visitors from all over the world who come to do research at the University of the West Indies in Port of Spain, write poetry or study the amazing variety of butterflies and birds. Hosts Gerard and Oda (he from Trinidad, she from Holland) welcome visitors as though they're family, and bend over backwards to arrange day trips, transportation and bird-watching hikes.

This relaxed place is a good choice for anyone seeking a peaceful retreat. The 18 rooms feature teak floorboards, washbasins and fine views, but no TVs or telephones. Some rooms have two twin beds, others antique four-poster queen-size beds; most have private baths. Unless you have a car, you're pretty much stuck here (although you could call for a taxi or tour guide to come get you), so rates include a full breakfast and a healthy multicourse dinner.

Nonguests can come for dinner or a delightful afternoon tea with scones or Trinidadian sweet bread (dessert cakes or rolls). Reservations are essential for meals but not necessary for tea (served from 3:30pm to 6pm).

To arrive at Mt St Benedict from Port of Spain, take St John's Rd north 2 miles (3.3km) from Eastern Main Rd. During the day there's bus service roughly every 30 minutes from the turn-off at the Eastern Main Rd.

Asa Wright Nature Centre

A former cocoa and coffee plantation transformed into a 198-acre (80-hectare) nature reserve, the **Asa Wright Nature Centre** (☎ 667-4655; www.asawright.org; adult/child US$10/6) blows the minds of bird-watchers and makes a worthwhile trip, even if you can't tell a parrot from a parakeet. The center has won a number of ecotourism awards, and in 1999 *Audubon Magazine* called it one of the 'world's ultimate outposts.'

Located amid the rain forest of the Northern Range, the center has attracted naturalists from around the world since its founding in 1967. The property has a lodge catering to birding tour groups, a research station for biologists and a series of hiking trails.

A varied range of bird species inhabits the area, including blue-crowned motmots, chestnut woodpeckers, channel-billed toucans, blue-headed parrots, 10 species of hummingbird and numerous raptors. The sanctuary encompasses Dunston Cave, which is home to a breeding colony of the elusive nocturnal guacharo (oilbird). To protect the oilbirds, access is limited. Guests staying at the center's lodge for a minimum of three nights can view them for free; nonguests must pay an additional TT$150.

The trail network starts at the main house and branches out through the property. Day visitors join guided tours along the center's trails (10:30am and 1:30pm); reservations should be made at least 24 hours in advance.

The center's accommodations is a 24-room **lodge** (☎ 667-4655, in the USA 800-426-7781; s/d summer US$120/180, winter US$185/280; P ✗ ✗), with some rooms in the weathered main house and others in nearby cottages; all are quite simple but do have private baths. Rates are high but include three ample meals a day, afternoon tea, rum punch each evening, tax and a service charge. A minimum stay of three days includes a guided tour of the grounds and the oilbird cave. Airport transfers can be arranged for US$45 per person, round-trip. Nonguests can eat at the lodge, but reservations must be made 48 hours in advance.

Asa Wright Nature Centre is about a 1½-hour drive from Port of Spain. At Arima, 16 miles (26km) from Port of Spain, head north on Blanchisseuse Rd, turning left into the center after the 7½-mile marker (look for the sign). A taxi to Asa that would take you there and back (essentially an all-day affair) costs about TT$800.

NORTH COAST

If you follow the Saddle Rd north out of Port of Spain past Maraval, the road becomes the North Coast Rd. It climbs up over the mountains through a forest that's decorated with tall trees, ferns and bamboo while hugging the Caribbean coastline. Just east of Maracas Bay, you'll come across quieter and less commercial **Las Cuevas Bay**, a beautiful U-shaped bay; there's surfing at its west end and calmer conditions at its center. Finally, you'll hit the settlement of Blanchisseuse (right) before the road passes a small suspension bridge and narrows into impassability.

Maxi-taxis and route taxis travel to Maracas Bay, but to explore the rest of the north coast it's best to have a rental car or a prearranged taxi driver.

Maracas Bay

Just 40 minutes' drive from Port of Spain, Maracas Bay has Trinidad's most popular beach. The wide, white-sand beach thick with palm trees contrasting against the backdrop of verdant mountains remains an irresistible lure for both locals and travelers.

In summer, the water is mostly flat, but at other times, the bay serves up good waves for bodysurfing. There's a lifeguard, changing rooms (TT$1, open 10am to 6pm), showers, picnic shelters and huts selling cold Caribs and the best shark & bake on Trinidad. You can also rent beach chairs, hammocks and umbrellas. On weekends, the beach gets pretty crowded, but the rest of the week it can feel almost deserted.

Maracas Bay Hotel (☎ 669-1914; www.maracasbay .com; Maracas Bay; r US$70; P ✗ ✗ ▢ ▣) is right on the bay, and rightly calling itself 'Trinidad's only beach hotel,' with 30 rooms that all face the ocean and have private baths and balconies. The hotel's **Bandanya** (mains TT$60-150) restaurant sits in an open-air dining room under a giant pagoda and has a large menu of local and international cuisine.

Blanchisseuse

The road narrows east of Maracas Bay, crossing several small wooden bridges, ending up at the tiny village of Blanchisseuse (*blon*-she-suhze), where some of Port of Spain's wealthy own weekend homes. The village's three beaches aren't the best for swimming, especially in the fall and winter, but the surfing is usually good and the scenery is lovely.

Laundry inspired the town's name. Village women who washed their clothes in the nearby Marianne River were called 'washerwomen' and this was translated to *blanchisseuse*, the French word for 'launderer,' during the French occupation.

Blanchisseuse makes a great base for hiking, especially the good day hike to **Paria Falls**. The trailhead starts just past the suspension bridge that spans the Marianne River, just before the end of the North Coast Rd. The Paria River begins in the foothills of the

Northern Range. About two hours each way, the hike winds through the forest, over the Jordan River to the spectacular waterfalls, where you're greeted with a clear, refreshing bathing pool. Parts of the trail aren't well marked and in the past there have been warnings of assaults on foreigners, so it's best to go with a local guide (about US$25 per person). **Eric Blackman** (☎ 669-3995) has a good reputation as a guide and he can also arrange kayaking trips.

SLEEPING & EATING

Almond Brook (☎ 678-0822; Lamp Post 16, Paria Main Rd; s/d US$30/50; P ✕) Casual and comfortable, this B&B has three pleasant, clean rooms – two with queen-size beds – and a view on the inland side to the center of the village. Rates include breakfast, tax and a service charge. There's a large shared kitchen and sitting area.

Surf's Country Inn (☎ 669-2475; North Coast Rd; r US$60; P ✕) Three rooms perch on the hillside overlooking dense tropical forest and the cove beach below. Rooms lack air-con but ceiling fans and the sea breeze do the trick. The rate includes breakfast, tax and a service charge. Local lunches and dinners are also available here, for US$10 to US$20.

Laguna Mar (☎ 669-2963; www.lagunamar.com; 65½-mile marker, Paria Main Rd; r US$80; P ✕) The most comfortable place in the area, Laguna Mar comprises a pair of two-story, six-room buildings on the hillside at the end of the road, plus a four-bedroom cottage. Rooms have private baths and ceiling fans (no air-con), and upstairs rooms have balconies.

BLANCHISSEUSE–ARIMA ROAD

If you have a rental car and are looking for a little excitement, you'll definitely want to drive the 24-mile (39km) cut-off road that traverses the mountains from Blanchisseuse (opposite) to Arima. The windy drive on mostly single-lane roads is not for the faint of heart, but will reward hardy travelers with total immersion in the lush tropical rainforest. The road passes by the Asa Wright Nature Centre before twisting down toward Arima. There, you can pick up the Eastern Main Rd heading west back to Port of Spain.

Meals are available at Los Cocos, a small, cozy place near the end of the road and under the same ownership as Laguna Mar. Double-decker sandwiches with a huge side of potato salad run around TT$30; a fresh fish or chicken platter is TT$60 to TT$80.

If you are planning to stay in Blanchisseuse for a while, do shop for provisions before coming, as shops are almost nonexistent here.

WEST COAST
Caroni Bird Sanctuary

Caroni Bird Sanctuary is the roosting site for thousands of scarlet ibis, the national bird of Trinidad & Tobago. At sunset, the birds fly in to roost in the swamp's mangroves, giving the trees the appearance of being abloom with brilliant scarlet blossoms. Even if you're not an avid birdwatcher, the sight of the ibis flying over the swamp, glowing almost fluorescent red in the final rays of the evening sun, is not to be missed.

Long, flat-bottomed motorboats, holding up to 30 passengers, pass slowly through the swamp's channels. To avoid disturbing the birds, the boats keep a fair distance from the roosting sites, so bring along a pair of binoculars. You can also expect to see lots of herons and egrets, predominant among the swamp's 150 bird species. Note that during the summer months very few ibis are sighted, but the trip is still worthwhile.

The main swamp tour companies are **David Ramsahai** (☎ 663-4767), **Nanan's Bird Sanctuary Tours** (☎ 645-1305; nantour@tstt.net.tt) & **James Madoo Tours** (☎ 662-7356). All offer 2½-hour tours starting at 4pm daily, for US$10 per person. Reservations are recommended, but if you just show up you'll probably be able to find space on one of the boats. If your main interest is photography, the light is more favorable in the morning. Morning tours, which leave at 4:30am, can be arranged through David Ramsahai.

The sanctuary is off the Uriah Butler Hwy, 8.7 miles (14km) south of Port of Spain; the turn-off is marked. If you don't have your own vehicle, Nanan's Bird Sanctuary Tours will combine transportation from Port of Spain with the tour for about US$35 per person. You can also arrange trips to Caroni through guesthouses and hotels in Port of Spain.

Chaguanas

pop 73,000

Birthplace of the Nobel Prize–winning writer VS Naipaul (for more on Naipaul see the boxed text, p681), Chaguanas (sha-*gwon*-as) represents the heart of Trinidad's Indian population. Largely descendants of indentured East Indians brought to work the plantations after the abolition of slavery, today's Indian population owns much of the land around south-central Trinidad, amid undulating hills planted with citrus, coffee, cocoa and bananas. The towns have a decidedly East Indian appearance, from the style of the homes to the roadside temples.

Chaguanas is a sprawling collection of communities that come alive during the annual festivals of Phagwa and Divali (see p718), which celebrate Hindu traditions. The most interesting stop for visitors is south of Chaguanas, in the village of Edinburg (near Chase Village). It's here that potters make **Chaguanas pottery**, including *deya* (tiny earthenware lamps) and other ceramic items in traditional styles, using traditional methods. Several large pottery workshops are on the main road.

Waterloo Temple

This tranquil, almost surreal Hindu **temple** (7am-7pm Sat & Sun) sits at the end of a causeway jutting 98yd (90m) off the central west coast. Its formal name is Siewdass Sadhu Shiv Mandir, after its spiritual creator. Grateful for his safe return from India through the WWI-embattled waters of the Pacific, Sadhu committed himself to building a temple. Construction began in 1947 on state-owned land. When the state demolished his efforts, Sadhu began building out in the sea, carrying each foundation stone on his bicycle to the water's edge. When he died in 1970, his work was still incomplete. In 1994, the Hindu community completed the temple. It is accessed through the Waterloo Bay Recreation Park, where prayer flags and seabirds add to the sense of serenity. The grounds are open daily, but the temple is only open on weekends. Visitors are welcome, with no admission charge.

To get to Waterloo, travel south from Port of Spain on the Uriah Butler Hwy to Chaguanas, then 5.3 miles (8.5km) on the Southern Main Rd to St Mary's. Turn west

on the Waterloo Rd until you reach the temple. Alternatively, take a maxi-taxi to Chaguanas (TT$6), then another to St Mary's (TT$2), from where you can get a route taxi (TT$3) to the temple.

Pointe-à-Pierre Wildfowl Trust

This is a special place. Despite being in the midst of the island's sprawling oil refinery a few miles north of San Fernando, **Pointe-à-Pierre Wildfowl Trust** (658-4200, ext 2512; adult/teen/child TT$8/5/3; 8am-5pm Mon-Fri, 10am-4pm Sat & Sun), a wetland sanctuary, has an abundance of bird life in a highly concentrated 64.2 acres (26 hectares). There are about 90 bird species, both wild and in cages, including endangered waterfowl, colorful songbirds, ibis, herons and other wading birds. In a 20-minute stroll around the grounds you can easily spot a few dozen species.

A nonprofit organization, the trust is an environmental education center that rehabilitates and breeds endangered species. The birds are released into the wild, where they bolster natural populations. The visitors center has small exhibits and a gift shop.

Reservations should be made a day in advance, just so that the refinery guards know you're coming. Several entrances lead into the surrounding PetroTrin Oil Refinery, and gate access to the sanctuary occasionally changes, so get directions when you make reservations.

San Fernando

pop 75,250

Trinidad's second-largest city, San Fernando, is also the center of the island's gas and oil industries. Oddly shaped San Fernando Hill, a spot once sacred to Native Americans and now a popular spot for picnicking families, dominates the town. The hill is oddly shaped, a consequence of earlier excavations that have since halted. Anyone looking for real cultural immersion would enjoy San Fernando, as few tourists come through the town. Most of the action happens at shops and stands around the Harris Promenade.

San Fernando is the transportation hub for the region. Maxi-taxis and route taxis run regularly to Port of Spain and other outlying areas. Most of the town's hotels cater to visiting oil and gas types who are in town on business.

Tradewinds Hotel (☎ 652-9463; www.tradewinds hotel.net; 36-38 London St; s/d US$79/89, ste incl kitchen US$99/109; **P** ⊠ 🐾 🖳 🖳) is a full-service hotel with outdoor pool, bar, restaurant, spa and gym, the 40-room, family-owned Tradewinds offers a good value, whether you're here on business or not. Four different room configurations range from the small standard room to the deluxe suite with kitchen and sitting area.

The hotel's **Treehouse Restaurant** (mains US$7-15; ✍ 5am-midnight) serves up good breakfasts, sandwiches, seafood and meat dishes and offers views of the city from its tree-house patio.

Pitch Lake

Some 35.4 miles (22km) southwest of San Fernando near the town of La Brea, **Pitch Lake** (☎ 648-7697; tours TT$30; ✍ 9am-5pm) is perhaps Trinidad's greatest oddity. This 99-acre (40-hectare) expanse of asphalt is 295ft (90m) deep at its center, where hot bitumen is continuously replenished from a subterranean fault. The lake, one of only three asphalt lakes in the world, has the single largest supply of natural bitumen, and as much as 300 tons are extracted daily. The surface of Pitch Lake looks like a clay tennis court covered with wrinkled elephantlike skin. On the tour, you can walk across it, so wear comfortable, flat-soled shoes. Call ahead to book a tour.

EAST COAST

Trinidad's east coast is wild and rural, a mix of lonely beaches with rough Atlantic waters, mangrove swamps and coconut plantations that create some of the most dramatic scenery in the country. Deserted most of the year, the area sees big crowds after Carnival, when it becomes the post-festivities beach destination.

Long, wide and windswept, **Manzanilla Beach**, the main beach, has caramel-colored sand, palm trees and white beach morning glory. The strong winds and tempestuous waters make swimming a challenge, but the post-Carnival crowd comes in droves to play in the surf and sun. During the nonpeak seasons, Manzanilla becomes almost deserted. A public beach facility at the northern end has changing rooms, snacks and lifeguards.

The Manzanilla–Mayaro Rd, along the east coast, is narrow but traffic is light. Cows and water buffalo roam freely, coconut palms and orange heliconia line the roadside and you can easily spot vultures, egrets and herons along the way.

The road continues south, skirting the freshwater **Nariva Swamp**, an international Ramsar-protected site with more than 14,820 acres (6000 hectares) of wetlands of 'international importance.' A few tour guides offer boat trips through the swamp but tours must be arranged ahead of time. Winston Nanan of **Nanan's Bird Sanctuary Tours** (☎ 645-1305; nantour@tstt.net.tt; tours per person US$75, minimum 2 people) is the best choice. His day-long trip includes lunch and transportation from Port of Spain. If you have a group of five or more, the cost is US$60 per person.

After crossing the **Ortoire River**, Trinidad's longest, you'll encounter a couple of small settlements with simple wooden houses on stilts before reaching the town of **Mayaro**, where a sign points west to San Fernando, 34.7 miles (56km) away. At Mayaro is a small, minimally maintained beach facility. Flags are posted to alert swimmers of safety conditions.

Sleeping & Eating

Few hotels operate on the east coast, but the few that do offer clean, friendly accommodations. Rates listed here are for the high season (January to May). Expect to pay up to half-price in the off-season.

Hotel Carries on the Bay (☎ 668-5711; r US$65; **P** ⊠ 🐾) Built in 2002, this immaculate 16-room hotel sits right on the main road as you approach Manzanilla Beach. Just steps from the beach, with bright, spacious rooms that come equipped with TVs, queen beds and a small sitting area, Hotel Carries has the nicest rooms around. The restaurant here serves three meals (TT$12 to TT$40) a day.

Calypso Inn (☎ 691-5939; r US$58; **P** ⊠ 🐾) Friendly owners Anil and Sunil Maharaj welcome visitors to their modern two-level hotel on the north end of the beach. All 12 spacious rooms have private baths and private decks overlooking the beach (but no TVs). Six rooms have queen beds; the other six have two twin beds. The indoor/outdoor restaurant serves breakfast, lunch and dinner (meals TT$45 to TT$75).

Amelia's on the Beach (☎ 668-5308; r US$50; **P** 🐾) Falling into disrepair, Amelia's, just south of the Calypso, has five rooms with refrigerators, TVs, queen-size beds and pull-out futons. Cracked walls and some junk in the yard make it a bit of an eyesore, but the simple, clean rooms come with fresh towels and flowers, so at least they're trying.

Several houses further south are available for rent to primarily local families, who bring their own bedding, food and cleaning supplies. If you're traveling with friends, these can be quite a good deal for a peaceful stay. **BBS Beach Resort** (☎ 653-3158; house US$50) has two five-bedroom houses with full kitchens.

NORTHEAST COAST

The northeast coast is an extension of the rugged Maracas-Blanchisseuse coastline, but you may see more sea turtles than tourists. Inaccessible by road from Blanchisseuse, the quiet, arrowhead-shaped region is bounded by Matelot in the north and Matura in the southeast. The area is accessed via Arima or Sangre Grande, where the Eastern Main Rd forks and the Toco Main Rd extends northeast along the coast, skirting some wild beaches and pleasant bays.

At **Matura Bay**, near Salybia, and further north at **Grande Rivière**, giant leatherback turtles nest on the almost-deserted beaches between March and August. Rounding the northeast corner, the village of **Toco** has a small folk museum. A lighthouse marks **Galera Point**, which offers fantastic views of the dramatic coastline.

Sleeping & Eating

Mt Plaisir Estate Hotel & Spa (☎ 670-8381; www .mtplaisir.com; Grande Rivière; s/d incl breakfast US$90/ 120, incl 3 meals US$130/210, extra per person US$50; P X X) Arguably the best place to stay on Trinidad, this nature-embracing eco-resort offers an array of guided activities, from rain forest hikes to turtle-nesting walks and environmental education. The beach-side lofts and suites feature teak floors and handcrafted furnishings. Suites sleep four to six people. The hotel offers shuttles to Piarco International Airport, 54.5 miles (88km) away, for US$95/170 one way/round-trip. Mt Plaisir's restaurant (mains US$10 to US$25) serves fresh seafood, organic fruits and vegetables and homemade bread.

Salybia Nature Resort & Spa (☎ 668-5959; www .salybiaresort.com; 13.75-mile post, Toco Main Rd, Saly-bia; villa r US$160, deluxe r US$175, Jacuzzi ste US$330;

P X X 🖵 🖵) Many Trinidadian companies hold conferences or weekend retreats at this lovely resort that overlooks Saline Bay, which could explain the high rates. The grounds are lovely, with lush tropical landscaping, an outdoor pool and a waterfall. You can walk and sunbathe on the rugged beach, but the surf is too dangerous for swimming. Matura, the turtle-nesting beach, is just around the bend. Guests eat at the so-so hotel restaurant (mains US$10 to US$35).

TOBAGO

If the tiny island of Tobago was a cocktail, it would be delicious – refreshing but decidedly uncomplicated. It may get its own tiny umbrella, but the joy would be in the taste, not in how fancy it had dressed itself up. Tobago is delightfully relaxed. Locals riding by on their bicycles will wave hello or stop for a chat. They'll tell you about the good beaches, the best snorkeling and diving spots and where to get a good snack. Options for excellent bird-watching and hiking juxtapose against lazy days at the beach. The island is small, just 777 sq miles (300 sq km), so seeing the whole island is rewarding and easy.

When Hurricane Flora ripped by in 1963, she basically blew away the agro-based plantation economy. The government then turned its rebuilding efforts to tourism. It's been a slow, controlled process and there's just enough tourism to make visiting Tobago easy, but not so much that the island feels overrun – yet. No longer the sleeper it was just a few years ago, Tobago is still one of the most overlooked and best-value destinations in the Caribbean: get here while it lasts.

Most of the white-sand beaches and tourist development are centered on the southwestern side of Tobago, starting at Crown Point and running along a string of bays up to Arnos Vale. The lowlands that predominate in the southwest extend to Tobago's only large town, Scarborough. The coast beyond is dotted with small fishing villages and the interior is ruggedly mountainous, with thick rain forest. Divers and snorkelers and those seeking mellow days visit the easternmost villages of Speyside and Charlotteville. The nearby uninhabited islets of

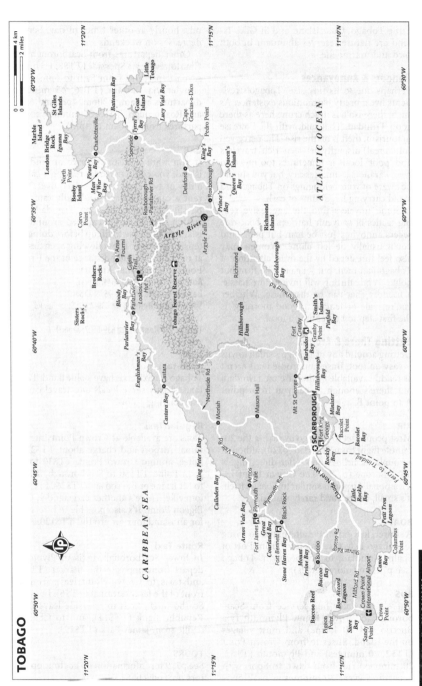

TOBAGO

0 ——— 4 km
0 ——— 2 miles

CARIBBEAN SEA

ATLANTIC OCEAN

Little Tobago

St Giles Islands

Marble Island

London Bridge Rock

Iguana Island

Booby Island

North Point

Pirate's Bay

Man of War Bay

Charlotteville

Speyside

Cape Gracias-a-Dios

Pedro Point

Batteaux Bay

Goat Island

Lucy Vale Bay

Tyrrel's Bay

King's Bay

Queen's Island

Queen's Bay

Corvo Point

L'Anse Fourmi

Gilpin Trail

Delaford

Roxborough–Parlatuvier Rd

Prince's Bay

Roxborough

Argyle River

Argyle Falls

Parlatuvier

Lookout Hut

Richmond Island

Brothers Rocks

Bloody Bay

Parlatuvier Bay

Tobago Forest Reserve

Richmond

Goldsborough Bay

Sisters Rocks

Englishman's Bay

Castara

Castara Bay

Northside Rd

Moriah

Hillsborough Dam

Windward Rd

Smith's Island

Pinfold Bay

Fort Granby

Granby Point

Barbados Bay

Hillsborough Bay

King Peter's Bay

Amos Vale Rd

Mason Hall

Mt St George

Culloden Bay

Arnos Vale

Plymouth Rd

Plymouth

Black Rock

Fort King George

SCARBOROUGH

Minister Bay

Bacolet Point

Bacolet Bay

Rockly Bay

Ferry to Trinidad

Arnos Vale Bay

Fort James

Great Courland Bay

Fort Bennett

Stone Haven Bay

Mount Irvine Bay

Buccoo

Buccoo Bay

Shirvan Rd

Claude Noel Hwy

Little Rockly Bay

Petit Trou Lagoon

Buccoo Rd

Canoe Bay

Columbus Point

Buccoo Reef

Pigeon Point

Bon Accord Lagoon

Milford Rd

Crown Point International Airport

Crown Point

Sandy Point

Store Bay

TRINIDAD & TOBAGO

Little Tobago, Goat Island and St Giles Island are nature reserves abundant in both bird and marine life.

Dangers & Annoyances

Perhaps due to its tiny size, Tobago's residents live a pretty harmonious existence. As such, there isn't as much crime here as there is on Trinidad. That said, with the increase in tourism, theft is on the rise. The perceived (often real) disparity between 'rich' travelers and 'poor' locals is sometimes too much to bear. Paranoia is unnecessary, but you should be aware of your belongings on Tobago, and avoid carrying large sums of cash.

Some travelers find the aggressive selling tactics of souvenir hawkers or boat-ride sellers annoying. Just be firm but polite and you'll usually be left alone. Women may also feel threatened by the overt attention of Tobagonian men, but – again – be firm but polite. While flirting will invite more hassle, a friendly chat can be disarming. Whether you're male or female, a 'good morning' is the first step to befriending a local.

Getting There & Around

Getting around any of Tobago's small towns is easy on foot. Buses and route taxis aren't as readily available as they are on Trinidad, but there's enough to get you from point A to point B.

AIR

Most people get to Tobago by taking the 20-minute flight from Trinidad (p720), although a couple of airlines now offer direct flights from Europe (p777). The Crown Point International Airport is similar to Tobago itself: it's small, relaxed and rarely rushed.

BOAT

A slower, less expensive alternative to flying to Tobago is to take the ferry from Port of Spain, Trinidad, to Scarborough, Tobago (see p720 for more details).

BUS

There's a regular bus service from Scarborough to Crown Point, Plymouth (via Buccoo and Mt Irvine) and most villages on the island. Buses to/from Crown Point (TT$2, 20 minutes) and Plymouth (TT$2, 20 minutes) run from dawn to 8pm, with departures every 30 minutes at peak peri-

ods, hourly at other times of day. Service decreases on weekends.

Other departures from Scarborough are: Charlotteville via Speyside (TT$8, 1½ hours, seven departures from 5am to 6pm), Parlatuvier via Castara (TT$6, 45 minutes, departures at 6am, 2:30pm, 4pm and 6pm) and Roxborough (TT$5, 30 minutes, six departures from 6:30am to 4pm).

CAR

If you want a leisurely drive around the island, you could consider renting a car for a day or two. You must be aged over 25 to rent a car on Tobago, and daily rates can be slightly higher than on Trinidad. Gas stations are sparsely scattered around the island, so it's wise to fill up before doing extensive touring. The following agencies are at or within walking distance of the Crown Point International Airport:

Auto Rentals (☎ 639-0644; airport)

Baird's Rentals (☎ 639-2528; airport)

Spence's Car Rental (☎ 639-7611; Store Bay Rd, Crown Point)

Thrifty Car Rental (☎ 639-8507; airport)

TAXI

Maxi-taxi

Tobago's maxi-taxis have a blue band. These taxis mostly serve locals and travel can be excruciatingly slow.

Regular Taxi

Taxis are available at Crown Point International Airport and charge about TT$25 to hotels around Crown Point, TT$30 to Pigeon Point, TT$50 to Scarborough, TT$60 to Mt Irvine or Buccoo and TT$260 to Charlotteville. There's another taxi stand at Club Pigeon Point. It's also possible to hire a taxi for an island tour for around TT$120.

Route Taxi

In lower Scarborough, taxis to Plymouth depart from opposite the market (TT$4), and taxis to Crown Point leave from in front of the ferry terminal (TT$6). In upper Scarborough, taxis to Speyside leave from Republic Bank (TT$11), and to Charlotteville from James Park (TT$12).

TOURS

See p719 for information on ecotour operators on Tobago.

CROWN POINT

Growing every year, the dusty little town of Crown Point on Tobago's southwest tip has a good range of accommodations and restaurants and is fast becoming a sprawling holiday zone. The island's airport – Crown Point International Airport – is in the middle of the resort area; hotels, restaurants and the beach are all within a few minutes' walk of the terminal.

Foreign visitors are fairly evenly divided between Europeans and North Americans, all drawn to the area's attractive beaches. However, anyone wanting to appreciate Tobago's cultural charms should plan to push eastward to explore other parts of the island.

Information

INTERNET ACCESS

Clothes Wash Café (☎ 639-0007; Lot 7, Store Bay Rd; per hr TT$10; ◔ 8am-9pm) Check your email during the spin cycle at this Internet café-slash-laundry.

LAUNDRY

Clothes Wash Café (☎ 639-0007; Lot 7, Store Bay Rd; ◔ 8am-9pm) You can use the coin-operated washers and dryers (about TT$23 each load) here, or drop it off and they'll do it for you (TT$40).

MEDICAL SERVICES

Anyone needing medical services should head to the hospital, a 15-minute drive away, in Scarborough (p712).

MONEY

In Crown Point, Republic Bank, at the airport, and Royal Bank, next to the Clothes Wash Café, have ATMs available 24 hours a day. You'll also find banks and ATMs in Scarborough. Be advised that there are no ATMs or banking facilities in Castara, Charlotteville or Speyside.

TOURIST INFORMATION

Tourist office (☎ 639-0509; Crown Point International Airport; ◔ 8am-10pm) This office is unaffiliated with Tidco but is the best place to get island information. The staff here can help you book a room, and they stock a list of hiking and bird-watching tour guides.

Sights & Activities

In Crown Point, it's all about the beach and the water, and a couple of great beaches fit the bill. Other sights include the remains of **Fort Milford**, a crumbling coral-stone fort built by the British in 1777. Today, it's a small park, but a bit of the old fort walls and half a dozen cannons remain. It's a five-minute walk southwest of Store Bay.

BEACHES

Store Bay

You'll find white sands and good year-round swimming at Store Bay, the body of water on the west side of Crown Point. It's a center of activity where vendors sell souvenirs and hawkers push glass-bottom boat tours of Buccoo Reef. The facilities include a clean rest room (TT$1) and lockers (TT$10). Several food huts here serve up delicious local food (see p708). The beach's upside is that it's just a five-minute walk from the airport and there's no admission fee. The downside is that the glass-bottom boat pushers can get a little aggressive.

Pigeon Point

You have to pay to get access to **Club Pigeon Point** (admission TT$18, weekly pass TT$60; ◔ 9am-7pm), whose facilities are harmoniously landscaped, with bars and snack bars, toilets and showers spread out along plenty of beachfront. The postcard-perfect, palm-fringed beach has powdery white sands and clear aqua water. It's just 1 mile (1.6km) north of Store Bay, about a 15-minute walk from the airport. The complex also has a dive shop, and you can rent windsurfing gear or kayaks from **World of Watersports** (☎ 631-5150; windsurf boards per hr TT$250, kayaks per hr TT$100; ◔ 9am-5pm) at the northernmost end. Several glass-bottom boat tours of Buccoo Reef (see the boxed text, p706) depart from the jetty. Vendors rent out beach chairs for TT$10 per day.

DIVING

Stupendous water clarity, giant shoals of tropical fish, stunning corals, a variety of dive sites and excellent operators make diving on Tobago some of the best in the Caribbean. Whether you want to do mellow coral-seeing dives or current-zipping drift dives past huge turtles and sharks, Tobago's got it all. Although serious divers head up to Speyside and Charlotteville to dive on the northeast coast, dive operators in Crown Point can run trips all over the island. There is one recompression chamber on the island, in the east-coast village of Roxborough.

TRINIDAD & TOBAGO

BUCCOO REEF

Stretching offshore between Pigeon Point and Buccoo Bay, the extensive Buccoo Reef was designated as a marine park in 1973. The fringing reef boasts five reef flats separated by deep channels. The sheer array of flora and fauna – dazzling sponges, hard corals and tropical fish – makes marine biologists giddy.

Glass-bottom boat reef tours give both experienced and novice reef explorers an opportunity to explore Tobago's incredible treasure. Tours leave from Store Bay, Pigeon Point and the village of Buccoo (p709). Most operators charge US$15 per person for a two-hour trip. The boats pass over the reef (much of which is just a yard or two beneath the surface), stop for snorkeling and end with a swim in the **Nylon Pool**, a calm, shallow area with a sandy bottom and clear turquoise waters. **Johnson & Sons** (☎ 639-8519; tours TT$90; ⏱ 7½hr) runs a good tour, leaving from Buccoo village's pier. Unlike most boats, which go out at 11am every day, Johnson goes out when the tide is low (and the snorkeling best), leaving between 9am and 2pm.

Despite efforts of conservation groups like the **Buccoo Reef Trust** (www.buccooreeftrust.org), Buccoo Reef has been battered by too much use and not enough protection. In addition to anchor damage, reef walking and overfishing, polluted run-off from sewage, construction and agricultural activities floods the water and smothers the reef. Like all living things, reefs die without oxygen.

Tourists can do their part by never walking on or touching coral and by discouraging others from doing so. Never buy products made from coral or marine species (like turtle shell jewelry) and, most importantly, remember that a reef is a living organism. Treat it gently.

Several dive operators vie for your business here. With diving, you often get what you pay for, so be wary of operators offering cheap trips – it can mean shoddy equipment and unprofessional divemasters. We recommend the operators at the Hilton and Coco Beach hotels, as well as the following:

Extra Divers Tobago (☎ 639-7424; extradivers@ tstt.net.tt; Surfside Hotel, Pigeon Point Rd) Staff here are all National Association of Underwater Instructors (NAUI) and Professional Association of Diving Instructors (PADI) trained – they use top-quality equipment and offer everything from dive training and refresher classes to advanced and divemaster. A two-tank dive with full equipment costs US$100, or US$75 without equipment. Beginners become fully certified in three to four days for US$380.

R&Sea Divers (☎ 639-8120; www.rseadivers.com; Toucan Inn, Store Bay Local Rd) Safe, professional and friendly, R&Sea is a PADI facility that's been around for a long time. It offers similar dives and gear as Extra Divers, at a slightly lower cost. Staff will pick up divers at any hotel.

Sleeping

Crown Point has it all, from inexpensive guesthouses to luxury resorts.

Unless otherwise indicated, all accommodations are less than a 1-mile (1.6km) walk to the airport and to the Store Bay beach.

BUDGET

Bananaquit (☎ 639-9733; www.bananaquit.com; Store Bay Local Rd; d US$55, 6-person ste US$90-110) Whether you're on a tight budget or just looking for a more personal travel experience, the friendly Bananaquit can't be beat. You'll feel more like you're living in Tobago than vacationing when you unpack your stuff into one of the 14 apartments that overlook a garden courtyard. Each spacious room has its own kitchenette and small veranda. Downstairs rooms are for one or two people, while the bigger upstairs suites sleep four to six. Guests can use the pool at neighboring Store Bay Resort. It's a five-minute walk to the airport or Store Bay beach, and about 20 minutes' walk to Pigeon Point.

Surfside Hotel (☎ 639-0614; Pigeon Point Rd; s/d/tr US$26/40/60; P ☒ ☒) This budget hotel seems like some kind of hide-out you'd run to after a crime spree in the 1950s. A place where you could change your name and no one would ever find you. It's a great deal because each of the 34 rooms has a small kitchen, sitting area and little veranda. There's also a pool in the parking lot. It's a good place to meet people who are traveling on the cheap.

Coral Inn Guesthouse (☎ 639-0967; John Gorman Trace; s/d US$25/50; P ☒ ☒) A short walk from Store Bay Rd and peacefully located amid fields and grazing goats, this four-room guesthouse makes a good budget option. The recently renovated apartments have kitchens, baths and two bedrooms each (with double beds). The friendly owner, Veda Gopaul, lives upstairs. Rates are basically US$25 per person, but are negotiable for longer stays.

Douglas Apartments (☎ 639-7723; dougapp@tstt .net.tt; cnr Milford Rd & John Gorman Trace; d/q US$50/90; P ☒) All five rooms in this tidy, friendly guesthouse have kitchens and either one or two separate bedrooms. The air-con is in the bedrooms only.

House of Pancakes (☎ 639-9866; kittycat@tstt.net .tt; cnr Milford Rd & John Gorman Trace; s/d US$25/37.50; P ☒ ▣) These accommodations are in the home of a friendly couple who operate an informal restaurant and rent out three rooms. The rooms are simple, with shared or private bath. Guests can use shared kitchen facilities.

Mike's Holiday Resort (☎ 639-8050; Store Bay Rd; 1-/2-bedroom apt US$35/70; P ☒) A two-minute walk north of the airport, Mike's has 12 clean, modern apartments with large kitchens. Each bedroom has one double bed. Most units have TVs.

Store Bay Resort (☎ 639-8810; sbaymair@cablenett .net; units US$40-55, high season US$60-75; P ☒ ▣) A five-minute walk east of the airport, next to the Kariwak Hotel, this recommended family-run place has 20 self-contained units. Most are studio and one-bedroom apartments. Attractive upper-level decks overlook a swimming pool.

MIDRANGE

Rainbow Resorts (☎ 639-9940; Milford Rd; d/tr/q US$55/60/75; P ☒ ☒ ▣) This pleasant two-story building consists of 20 spotless and well-maintained modern apartments. Each has a fully equipped kitchen, a separate bedroom with two comfortable queen-size beds, cable TV and a private balcony or patio facing the pool. A couple of rooms are wheelchair accessible.

Crown Point Beach Hotel (☎ 639-8781; www .crownpointbeachhotel.com; d studio US$90, cabana US$100, 1-bedroom apt US$130; P ☒ ☒ ▣) Although it's seen better days and the staff could use some happy pills, this 77-room hotel has a good beachfront location next to Fort Milford and the Royalton Casino. All rooms have kitchenettes and views of the ocean. There's also a nice pool, tennis courts and a restaurant.

Sandy Point Beach Club (☎ 639-0820; www.sandy pointbeachclub.com; Sandy Point; apt US$82-130; P ☒ ☒ ▣) A great-value option for families or bigger groups, this resort is next to Fort Milford and mostly rents its 46 apartments for week-long stays. The apartments range in size from studios for up to four people, and three-bedroom units that sleep eight. They all have full kitchens. The resort, which is also a timeshare, has a nice slice of beach, pool, beach volleyball and a fitness center. It's also home to the Steak & Lobster Grill (p708) and the Deep (p709).

AUTHOR'S CHOICE

Toucan Inn (☎ 639-7173; www.toucan-inn .com; Store Bay Rd; d summer/winter US$60/80; P ☒ ☒ ▣) Unquestionably one of the best-designed places in Crown Point and perhaps the best value, the 20-room Toucan features four circular duplex cabins arranged around a pool and a section of rooms that wraps around a lush garden. Suitably simple, rooms have tiled floors, teak furnishings, comfortable beds and private baths. Also on the grounds is the popular Bonkers (p708) veranda bar-restaurant. It's about a 10-minute walk to the airport. Rates include tax.

TOP END

Tropikist Beach Hotel (☎ 639-8512; www.tropikist .com; d/ste US$100/135; P ☒ ☒ ▣) At the west end of the airport runway, the 54-room Tropikist attracts vacationers looking for comfortable rooms and plenty of resort amenities. You'll find a great pool with a swim-up bar, two on-site restaurants, a lively bar and lots of activities, like cricket and volleyball.

Canoe Bay Beach Resort (☎ 685-4785; www.find -us.net/canoebay; Cove Estate, Lowlands; d/q US$100/150; P ☒) Accessed by a dirt road a few miles east of Crown Point, Canoe Bay is a beautiful shallow bay that's popular with picnicking families. This 44-acre (17.6-hectare) resort is a quiet, low-key place featuring 18 apartment-style villas, a bar, restaurant and several huts along the beach.

Kariwak Village Holistic Haven & Hotel (☎ 639-8442; www.kariwak.co.tt; summer/winter d US$108/150; P ☒ ☒ ▣) Off Store Bay Rd, just a two-minute walk from the airport, Kariwak sits shrouded in lush landscaping. Two dozen rooms in duplex cabanas are nestled among paths that lead through the property's tropical gardens. It's both rustic and refreshing. There's an herb garden, two pools (one with waterfall) and free classes in yoga and tai chi. The restaurant serves some of Tobago's freshest, tastiest food.

Coco Reef Resort (☎ 639-8572; www.cocoreef.com; r from US$300; P ☒ ☒ ☐ ☒) Simply stunning, Coco Reef pays elegant homage to luxurious colonial architecture. A palm-lined drive leads to the hotel, whose 135 rooms overlook pretty Coconut Bay. Guests enjoy top-tier amenities and excellent service. The resort is just next to the Store Bay parking lot off Milford Rd, about five minutes' walk from the airport.

Hilton Tobago Golf & Spa Resort (☎ 660-8500; www.tobago.hilton.com; r/ste from US$300/400; P ☒ ☒ ☐ ☒) The 200-room Hilton occupies 20 acres (8 hectares) of the Lowlands area about 3 miles (5km) east of Crown Point, including its own protected mangrove forest. You'll find an 18-hole golf course, tennis courts, a gorgeous seaside pool, several restaurants and bars, shops and a dive shop.

Eating
BUDGET

The best place to each lunch is at the row of food huts opposite the beach at Store Bay. Several huts lovingly run by local women offer delicious local dishes like rotis, shark & bake, crab & dumplin' and simple plate lunches for TT$8 to TT$25. Miss Jean's and Miss Esmie's are favorite stalls, but all are good. Wash it all down with a drinking coconut (TT$3), which you can pick up from beachside vendors.

Crystal's (☎ 639-7648; cnr Store Bay & Milford Rds; mains TT$30-40; ☒ breakfast, lunch & dinner) Stop by this popular local's hangout for an evening beer or cheap local food. It has fruit juices, shark & bake, flying fish and heaping supper plates.

House of Pancakes (☎ 639-9866; cnr Milford Rd & John Gorman Trace; mains TT$36-75; ☒ breakfast) Breakfast is served until noon here on a pleasant wooden deck, often shared by aggressively hungry grackles. Dishes include buttermilk cakes, eggs and fresh fruit.

Triple B Burger (burgers TT$14) Located where Milford Rd curves east, this is a good, busy roadside stand. Beef, chicken and fish burgers are prepared on the grill. It may be the only place in Tobago where you can find a T-bone steak for TT$35, served with some fine potato wedges. Though it's primarily a carryout operation, there are a few indoor and outdoor picnic tables.

Backyard (☎ 639-7264; Milford Rd; mains TT$30-60; ☒ lunch & dinner) Come to this clean and relaxed roadside restaurant, next to Triple B Burger, for a fresh-squeezed fruit juice (TT$12) or a healthy sandwich or veggie pasta dish. A great spot to pick up a picnic lunch.

Vie de France (☎ 631-8088; mains TT$20-40; ☒ from 6:30am) Just across from the airport on Store Bay Rd, this open-air café makes a great place to kill time while waiting for a flight. Try the breakfast omelette, or lunchtime sandwiches. Another option just across from the airport terminal, Royal Castle, the local fast-food favorite, serves up fried chicken and burgers.

Several minimarts on Store Bay Rd sell basics, but if you're looking to do a big grocery shop you should head east of Crown Point to **Pennysaver's** (Milford Rd) near the community of Canaan.

MIDRANGE & TOP END

Bonkers (☎ 639-7173; Toucan Inn, Store Bay Rd; breakfast & lunch mains TT$25-35; dinner mains TT$75-130; ☒ breakfast, lunch & dinner) This favorite liming spot is run by a pair of English expats. The open-air restaurant and bar (the latter open until midnight) serves breakfast, sandwiches, salads and fish-and-chips. There's a 'lime table' Monday, Tuesday, Thursday, Friday and Saturday from 8pm, with live steel pan or African dancing.

Kariwak Village (☎ 639-8442; Kariwak Village Hotel; mains TT$40-90; ☒ breakfast, lunch & dinner) Beneath the thatched roofs and coral stone walls of this open-air restaurant, the Kariwak chefs create masterpieces of Caribbean and Creole cuisine using fresh ingredients including herbs and from the garden. Breakfast includes a healthy bowl of fresh fruit, eggs or granola and homemade toast. At lunch and dinner, you can do no wrong with the specials, usually featuring grilled fish and seafood. There are plenty of vegetarian options too.

Steak & Lobster Grill (☎ 639-0820; Sandy Point Beach Club, Sandy Point; breakfast & lunch mains US$7-10, dinner mains US$10-16; P) With gorgeous views overlooking Sandy Point, and luscious sea breezes, this is a great place for a romantic

---

AUTHOR'S CHOICE

Café Coco (☎ 639-0996; Old Store Bay Rd; mains TT$30-90; ☻ dinner from 4pm) You walk into this giant open-air restaurant and notice the clicking of your sandals on the tile floor, the mellow candle-light, the splendid breeze from the overhead fans. You're greeted by a friendly staff, which seems to be composed of the most beautiful women on Tobago. You saunter up to the wide welcom-ing bar and sip a fabulous cocktail then settle into a table for scrumptious meal of fresh grilled fish, rotisserie chicken or the Parlatuvier Bay peppered fish salad. There's also a kids' menu (TT$50) and a good selection of pizzas, burgers and sub sandwiches. Truly a treat, the restaurant is located on Old Store Bay Rd, the first left off Pigeon Point Rd. You can also get here by cutting through the driveway between the bank and Clothes Wash Café.

---

dinner. Come too for the fresh snapper, grouper or well-prepared steaks, or to see live steel-pan music on Saturday night. No shorts or sleeveless shirts.

Shirvan Watermill (☎ 639-0000; starters from TT$20, mains TT$75-180; ☻ dinner from 6pm) On Shirvan Rd between Crown Point and Buc-coo Bay, this longtime popular restaurant sits under a coral-columned gazebo beside the mill of a former sugar estate. The restau-rant has pleasant outdoor dining and some of the island's best food, such as delicate soups and salads, meats, chicken Creole and lobster.

Entertainment

Café Iguana (☎ 631-8205; cnr Store Bay & Milford Rds; ☻ 6-10pm, Thu-Tue) This cool space across from Crystal's (opposite) is a stylish, casual hangout serving up good cocktails and live jazz-inspired tunes. The menu offers good local cuisine, but most folks come for the Friday and Saturday night jazz or Sunday Latin music.

Golden Star (☎ 639-0873; cnr Milford & Pigeon Point Rds; occasional cover charge TT$30) A locally popu-lar club with a sizable dance floor, open nightly. Wednesday night there are live steel bands; Friday features Afterwork Lime with DJs, dancing and, occasionally, local bands. Golden Star's restaurant serves pass-able food.

Deep (Sandy Point Beach Club, Sandy Point; ☻ 9pm-dawn Fri & Sat) DJs spin soca, salsa and merengue at this dance destination. It's only open in the high-season months and it gets packed.

Diver's Den (☎ 639-0287; 14 Roberts St, Bon Ac-cord; ☻ 6pm-late) A dining, drinking, dancing on tables kind of place just east of Crown Point.

Royalton Casino (☎ 631-8500; next to Crown Point Beach Hotel; ☻ 4pm-3am) Has roulette and craps tables, blackjack and slots. It also offers free shuttle to and from area hotels.

BUCCOO

The narrow brown-sand beach of Buccoo Bay doesn't compete with the generous white sands of Store Bay, and swimming here isn't recommended because of pollution from new developments inland. But tiny Buccoo offers glimpses of village life and breathtak-ing sunsets over the bay. Besides, it boasts a high-spirited weekly fiesta and the craziest annual event on Trinidad & Tobago.

Festivals & Events

Sunday School Lacking any religious affiliation and having absolutely nothing to do with the Lord's Prayer, 'Sunday School' is the sly title for a weekly street party held in Buccoo every Sunday night. Locals and tourists alike pour themselves onto the village streets, boogying away to live steel-pan music. It starts at about 9pm, and later on, DJs spin everything from reggae to soca and the libation-sipping scene turns into a pickup party. Snack on corn soup, *souse* (a dish made out of a pickled pig's head and belly) and plates of meat salad and rice sold from various stalls; there's also plenty of rum and beer.

Easter Weekend One of the largest events in Tobago happens over the Easter weekend when everyone flocks to Buccoo for a series of open-air parties, massive feasts and – the highlight of it all – goat racing. Taken very seriously, goat racing draws more bets than a Las Vegas casino. The competing goats get pampered like beauty contestants and the eventual champion is forever revered. The partying stretches throughout the weekend and the big races happen on Tuesday. Also look out for the live crab races, certainly less high-profile but equally bizarre.

Sleeping & Eating

Seaside Garden Guesthouse (☎ 639-0682; www.toba go-guesthouse.com; Buccoo; d TT$180-270, q apt TT$510-600; ☒ ☒) One of the nicest small guest-houses in Tobago and barely a stumbling distance from Sunday School celebrations. Four guest rooms sleep up to four people (TT$60 per extra person) and two apartments sleep up to six. All rooms have mosquito nets, fans, air-con and private baths. A tastefully decorated sitting room with a bay window enhances the serenity of the place. A fruit-filled breakfast is available for TT$35 and dinner is TT$70; alternatively, you can use the kitchen.

Teaside Pizza House (☎ 639-8437; Battery St; pizza from TT$30) Found 218yd (200m) north of the beach, the pizza here is good and comes with a choice of seven toppings. You can order meat or vegetarian, whole-wheat or white crust. Teaside also has fruit juices and desserts.

La Tartaruga (☎ 639-0940; Buccoo Bay Main Rd; mains US$65-165; ❤ dinner, closed Sun) Let the breeze tickle your skin while you eat excellent, authentic Italian cuisine alfresco on the candlelit patio. An extensive wine list complements homemade pasta and seafood dishes, and there are several good vegetarian options.

LEEWARD ROAD

The stretch of coastline from Mt Irvine Bay to Plymouth is a rather exclusive area replete with a golf course, elegant guest villas and several resort hotels, each hugging its own bay.

A roadside public recreation facility at **Mt Irvine Beach**, 218yd (200m) north of Mt Irvine Bay Hotel, has sheltered picnic tables and changing rooms, plus a good beachside restaurant (see Surfer's Restaurant & Bar, right) and a decent craft shop. This beach attracts surfers from December to March.

On a rocky hill at the north side of Stone Haven Bay is **Fort Bennett**, about 545yd (500m) west of a marked turn-off on the main road. The British built the fort in 1778 to defend against US enemy ships. Little remains of it other than a couple of cannons, but there's a good view of the coast.

Sleeping

Resorts and rental villas dominate on this stretch of coastline.

Mount Irvine Bay Hotel & Golf Club (☎ 639-8871, in the USA 800-448-8355; www.mtirvine.com; Mt Irvine Bay; r US$195-460; P X X Q) Built upon a former sugar plantation, this luxurious resort hotel has its own world-class 18-hole

golf course, 105 guest rooms, three restaurants and six bars.

Le Grand Courlan Resort & Spa (☎ 639-9667, in the USA 800-655-1214; www.legrandcourlan-resort .com;Stone Haven Bay, Black Rock; r US$270-440; P X X Q) This exclusive, all-inclusive resort has 83 rooms overlooking Stone Haven Bay. Amenities include two restaurants, tennis, gym, pool and spa. Rates include drinks and all meals.

Grafton Beach Resort (☎ 639-0191, in the USA 800-223 6510; www.grafton-resort.com; Stone Haven Bay, Black Rock; garden-view/ocean-view d US$152/162; P X X Q) Next door to Le Grand Courlan and with the same owners, this is a much cheaper all-inclusive that shares some amenities with its sister resort. Rooms are wheelchair-accessible.

Seahorse Inn (☎ 639-0686; www.seahorseinntoba go.com; Stone Haven Bay; r incl breakfast summer/winter US$95/125; P X X) A nice contrast to the big resorts, this lovely guesthouse, just below the Grafton Beach Resort, is a low-key establishment with four spacious rooms with teak floors and broad balconies facing Stone Haven Bay. Rates include taxes and breakfast.

Several companies rent out villas, which can be a great value for families or groups who plan on staying longer than a few days. Costs for four people range from US$350 to US$650 per night. Recommended companies include **Plantation Beach Villas** (☎ 639-9377; www.plantationbeachvillas.com) and **Villas at Stonehaven** (☎ 639-0361; www.stonehavenvillas.com).

Eating

Surfer's Restaurant & Bar (☎ 639-8407; Mt Irvine Beach) This casual spot serves up delicious fish stew, fish & bake and sandwiches.

Seahorse Inn Restaurant & Bar (Seahorse Inn, Stone Haven Bay; lunch TT$50-70, dinner TT$80-140) Sitting alfresco amid a tropical setting overlooking the water, with the sound of waves crashing below, this special restaurant specializes in gourmet Creole cuisine.

PLYMOUTH

Although it's the largest town on the west coast, Plymouth is home to just a few thousand inhabitants and is not a major destination. At the end of Shelbourne St is the **Mystery Tombstone** of Betty Stiven, who died in 1783, presumably during childbirth. Her tombstone reads, rather cryptically, 'She was a mother without knowing it, and a wife without letting her husband know it, except by her kind indulgences to him.'

Plymouth was the first British capital of Tobago, and it was here that the British built **Fort James** in 1811, the remains of which stand 218yd (200m) west of the tombstone. Affording extraordinary views of Great Courland Bay, this small hilltop fortification remains largely intact.

Coming back from Fort James, turn right after the bus stop and continue 163yd (150m) to reach the **Great Courland Bay Monument**, an odd concrete creation honoring the early Courlander colonists who settled the area in the 17th century.

CASTARA & AROUND

About an hour's drive from Plymouth, Castara is a pleasant fishing village that has become popular with independent-minded travelers. They're attracted by its wide, sandy beach, relaxed atmosphere and picturesque setting. A few bars face the harbor, where a fleet of modest fishing boats moors. Snorkeling is good in the calm inlet to the right of the main beach.

North of Castara, the road winds past a stretch of coast that's punctuated by pretty beaches and villages, unhurried places with kids playing cricket on the road. At **Englishman's Bay**, a superb, undeveloped beach shaded by stands of bamboos and coconut palms draws snorkelers to its gentle waters – a coral reef lies 66ft (20m) offshore. A snack bar and latrine serve the handful of visitors who make it up here. Further on, at Bloody Bay, you can catch the Roxborough–Parlatuvier Rd through the Tobago Forest Reserve (see the boxed text, p713). Just west of Bloody Bay, **Parlatuvier** is a tiny fishing village on a striking circular bay.

Sleeping & Eating

Sandcastles (☎ 635-0933; sandcastles@tstt.net.tt; r US$60-125; P ✗ ⊠) Several Lonely Planet readers have told us about this friendly place, which is just a few minutes' walk from the beach. We agree: it's great value, with two self-contained apartments with private baths. Owners Adam and Rea are friendly and helpful. Rates include taxes and breakfast.

Sea Level Guesthouse (☎ 660-7311; Castara; d/q US$35/45; P ⊠) Although it lacks an ocean view, this guesthouse sits peacefully amid

woods and is just minutes from the beach. Eight spacious rooms have balconies or patios; all come with kitchenettes, baths, fans, air-con and handcrafted beds.

Naturalist Beach Resort (☎ 639-5901; natural@ trinidad.net; d apt US$30-50; ⊠) This cheerful, family-run place is at beach level, and its cozy apartments include kitchens, TVs, fans, air-con and reading lamps. The apartments are all different; some have water views, others don't. The newer 'Blue Marlin Suite' (US$160) sits right on the beach. Airport transfers can be arranged for US$30.

Blue Mango Cottages (☎ 639-2060; www.blue-mango.com; d from US$90) Touted as a private retreat for writers, artists or anyone wishing privacy, the Blue Mango's seven rustic but comfortable cottages offer spectacular views from their hillside perch. Of varying size, the cottages offer private baths with running water, kitchens and mosquito nets. The most spectacular 'Sea Steps' cabin, at US$350, takes maximum advantage of its cliff setting. While the location is lovely, we've heard complaints over the years that the cottages are overpriced.

Margarite's, in the center of the village on the main road, offers delicious local food at incredibly low prices. At the beachfront, L&H Restaurant is a small kitchen serving full plates of chicken or fish with beans, rice and coleslaw (TT$45). CasCreole Bar is the beachfront gathering place, with simple wood tables under a palm-frond roof, and an adjoining sunset deck on the sand. It serves a hearty kingfish platter with potato salad and other provisions (TT$55). It's lively most nights, but there's live music Friday night.

SCARBOROUGH

pop 16,800

Located 15 minutes' drive east of Crown Point, Scarborough is the island's administrative center, a crowded port with bustling one-way streets and congested traffic. Largely commercial in character, it's Tobago's only real town to speak of. Tobagonians come here to bank, pay bills or send packages. Some 30 cruise ships nestle alongside the docks every year and the passengers often shuttle to Crown Point beaches. Those who stay in Scarborough browse through the town's underwhelming shops and public market. Independent travelers arriving by ferry after dark may want to spend a night, but others will want to push onward.

Information

J-Puter Tech (☎ 639-3393; 20 Burnett St; per hr TT$10; ⊙ 9:15am-2pm Mon-Sat) Head here for Internet access or to make international calls.

Scarborough General Hospital (☎ 639-2551; Calder Hall Rd; ⊙ 24hr) Handles most emergencies and serious medical issues on Tobago. It is just before the entrance to Fort King George.

MONEY

There are branches of Republic Bank and Scotiabank just east of the docks, both equipped with ATMs. There's another ATM right outside the ferry terminal. If you are heading to Speyside or Charlotteville, do your banking in Scarborough first, as there are no banks on the east end of Tobago.

POST

Post office (Post Office St; ⊙ 7:30am-6pm Mon-Fri, 9am-1pm Sat) There's a TT Post postal outlet in the ferry terminal too.

TOURIST INFORMATION

Tidco (☎ 639-4333; Sangster Hill Rd; ⊙ 8am-4pm Mon-Fri) Tobago's Tidco administrative office is upstairs in the bright yellow building off Sangster Hill Rd, about 218yd (200m) west of the cruise-ship complex.

Sights & Activities

The **Botanical Gardens** (admission free; ⊙ daylight hr) occupies the 18 acres (7.2 hectares) of a former sugar estate. It's a pretty place, with a variety of flowering trees and shrubs, including flamboyants, African tulips and orchids (in an orchid house).

Immediately beyond the hospital, **Fort King George** (admission TT$5; ⊙ 9am-5pm Mon-Fri) sits on a hill at the end of Fort St. Built by the British between 1777 and 1779, it's the only substantial colonial fortification remaining in Tobago, and is worth a visit for its history and fine coastal view. Benches under enormous trees allow you to gape at the harbor and observe exotic birds darting about. At the edge of the grounds, a small Tobago-shaped hedge is cleverly labeled to indicate the locations of the island's other forts.

Cannons line the fort's stone walls. A small museum displays Native American artifacts and a shop in the old powder magazine sells locally made handicrafts. The lighthouse

features a lead crystal lens that can throw a beam 31 miles (50km) out to sea.

Sleeping

Those arriving on the evening ferry will find a couple of cheap guesthouses a walkable distance from the waterfront.

Hope Cottage (☎ 639-2179; hopecottage100@hotmail .com; Calder Hall Rd; s without/with bath TT$55/88, d TT$165; ⊠) Scarborough's best budget option, Hope Cottage is found near Fort King George, an arduous half-hour walk uphill from the dock (a taxi ride is TT$10). Located in the former home of a 19th-century governor (James Henry Keens, acting governor from 1856–57, is buried in the backyard), it's a great place to hang out or meet other travelers. There are 12 rooms, most with shared baths. Guests can order breakfast (TT$25) or whip up their own meals in the big group kitchen. Other communal areas include a TV room, dining room, big backyard and front porch.

Federal Villa (☎ 639-3926; maredwards@hotmail .com; 1-3 Crooks River; s/d US$15/25) This cozy B&B has five pleasant wood-floor rooms, two with private baths. Owner Miriam Edwards is director of the Tobago Bed & Breakfast Association and is a valuable source of area information.

Sandy's Bed & Breakfast (☎ 639-2737; cnr Robinson & Main Sts; s/d incl breakfast US$35/60; ⊠) At the back of the Blue Crab Restaurant (see opposite), friendly owners Ken and Alison Sardinha rent out three rooms in their home. Set off a bit for privacy, the rooms are pleasantly simple, with pine floors, private baths and views overlooking Rockly Bay.

A few more reasonably priced options hug the coast along the Windward Rd on its way out to Bacolet Bay. Perched on a hillside overlooking the bay, **Sea View Guesthouse** (☎ 639-5613) and **Della Maria Guesthouse** (☎ 639-2531; r US$35-60) offer inexpensive rooms with private baths.

Blue Haven Hotel (☎ 660-7400; www.bluehaven hotel.com; Bacolet Bay; low/high season d US$180/238, ste US$270/355; P ⊠ ⊠ ⊠) According to Daniel Defoe's novel, Robinson Crusoe was stranded at this beach in 1659. Today, it's home to the Blue Haven, a romantic, beautifully landscaped resort hotel. Amenities here include a beachside pool, tennis courts and spa services, and each of the 55 rooms has an ocean-front balcony. Visitors can purchase meal plans that range from continental breakfast only (US$9) to all-inclusive (US$99).

Eating

Blue Crab Restaurant (☎ 639-2737; cnr Main & Robinson Sts; lunch mains TT$45, dinner mains TT$85-165; ☺ lunch Mon-Fri, dinner by reservation) A family-run restaurant with pleasant alfresco seating and good West Indian food. You'll have a choice of main dishes such as Creole chicken, flying fish or garlic shrimp, all served with rice and vegetables. Call a day ahead for dinner.

Ciao Cafe (☎ 639-3001; Burnett St; mains TT$25-45; ☺ lunch & dinner Mon-Sat, lunch only Sun; ⊞) Cool air blasts through this pleasant, clean café that serves up lasagna, pizza and Italian ice cream.

Phyllis' (☎ 639-3606; cnr Dutch Fort & Milford Rds; mains TT$25-45; ☺ 'any day, any time') Another first-rate Caribbean kitchen and an island of calm in the hectic market area, Phyllis' serves large lunch platters of steamed fish and all the 'provisions.'

Ma King's Dinette (Wilson Rd; mains TT$35-65; ☺ 9am-8pm Mon-Sat) Opposite the market, this locally popular snack shed offers stick-to-your-ribs breakfasts like smoked herring & bake (TT$40), with fresh-squeezed orange juice and the best coffee around.

For cheap fast food, Pizza Boys and Roti Boys, across from the ferry terminal, stay open late.

WINDWARD ROAD

Just east of Scarborough, the landscape turns mountainous and rural. The Windward Rd, which connects Scarborough with Speyside, winds past scattered villages, jungly valleys and dark-sand beaches. The further east you go, the more ruggedly beautiful the scenery becomes. Although much of the road is potholed, narrow and curvy, it's drivable in a standard vehicle. If you were to drive straight through from Scarborough to Speyside, it would take about 1½ hours.

Five miles (8km) east of Scarborough is Granby Point, a jut of land separating Barbados Bay from Pinfold Bay. In 1764, the British established a temporary capital on the east side of Barbados Bay and built **Fort Granby** at the tip of the point. Little remains other than a solitary soldier's gravestone, but day-trippers will find a couple of hilltop picnic tables, a nice view and a brown-sand beach with changing rooms.

The triple-tiered **Argyle Falls** (admission TT$20; ☺ 7am-5:30pm) are on the Argyle River, just west of Roxborough; the entrance to the

---

TOBAGO FOREST RESERVE

The paved Roxborough–Parlatuvier Rd crosses the island from Roxborough to Bloody Bay following a narrow, curving squiggle through the rain forest. The 30-minute drive to completely undeveloped jungle passes pretty valleys and mountain views, making it the best drive on the island.

The road passes through the Tobago Forest Reserve, which was established in 1765 – this makes it the oldest forest reserve in the Caribbean. A number of trailheads lead off the main road into the rain forest. There's excellent bird-watching in this area, and it's common to hear squawking parrots and to see hummingbirds, cocricos, woodpeckers, hawks and blue-crowned motmots.

Three-quarters of the way from Roxborough, the **Gilpin Trail** branches northeast to Bloody Bay, a 3-mile (5km) walk through the rain forest. Authorized guides at the trailhead charge TT$100 per person to take you down to a waterfall, or TT$300 for a two-hour hike through the forest to the Main Ridge lookout hut, a bit further down the road. Rubber boots, walking sticks and rain gear are provided for managing the muddy trails. The lookout hut affords scenic views of Bloody Bay and the offshore Sisters Rocks. On a clear day you can see Grenada, 75 miles (120km) away. Local women sell homemade cakes and natural fruit drinks here, and other guides offer their services. Reputable guides include Castara-based David Williams of **King David Tours** (☎ 660-7906; www.kingdavidtobago.com).

From the lookout hut, it's just a five-minute drive down to Bloody Bay, which takes its name from a fierce battle that occurred here between the Dutch, French and British in the 1600s. From Bloody Bay, the road heads south to the village of Castara (p711).

site is 654yd (600m) north of the Windward
Rd. In addition to the admission fee, you
must pay an authorized guide TT$15 to
lead you on the 20-minute hike up to the
falls. Guides gather at the entrance; official
guides wear khaki uniforms and carry ID.
At 177ft (54m), this is Tobago's highest waterfall and is also easily accessible on well-
defined trails. The falls cascade down four
distinct levels, and each level has its own
pool of spring water – perfect for a refreshing dip. **Roxborough** has a gas station and a
few stores where you can pick up snacks.

SPEYSIDE

The small fishing village of Speyside fronts
Tyrrel's Bay, and attracts divers and birders. It's the jumping-off point for excursions to uninhabited offshore islands,
including Little Tobago (see below), a bird
sanctuary 1.2 miles (2km) offshore, and St
Giles Island. Protected waters, high visibility, abundant coral and diverse marine life
make for choice diving. Nondivers can take
glass-bottom boat tours. Several small hotels, guesthouses and restaurants nestle together along the bay. There's a public beach
with facilities at the south end of the bay.

Information

Speyside has a **tourist office** (☎ 660-6012; ☷ 9am-
5pm Mon-Fri Nov-Mar) at the point where the
Windward Rd meets the waterfront. There
are no banks or ATMs in Speyside.

Little Tobago

Also known as Bird of Paradise Island, Little
Tobago was the site of a cotton plantation
during the late 1800s. In 1909, Englishman
Sir William Ingram imported 50 greater
birds of paradise from the Aru Islands, off
New Guinea, and established a sanctuary
to protect the endangered bird. In 1963,
Hurricane Flora devastated the habitat and
decimated the flock.

Now managed by the government, Little
Tobago remains an important seabird sanctuary, nonetheless. Red-billed tropic birds,
magnificent frigate birds, brown boobies,
Audubon's shearwaters, laughing gulls and
sooty terns are some of the species found
here. For those who want to hike, the hilly,
arid island, which averages just 0.9 miles
(1.5km) in width, has a couple of short
trails. Be sure to bring something to drink.

Several operators run glass-bottom boat
tours, but the best is **Frank's** (☎ 660-5438; tours
US$20; ☷ 10am & 2pm), based at Blue Waters Inn
(below) or Birdwatcher's Restaurant & Bar
(opposite). The trip to Little Tobago island, a
15-minute crossing, includes bird-watching
on Little Tobago and snorkeling at Angel
Reef. Masks and fins are provided. Other
reputable operators include **Top Ranking Tours**
(☎ 660-4904) and **Fear Not** (☎ 660-4654), both of
which depart from the beach near Jemma's
restaurant (opposite).

Sleeping

Blue Waters Inn (☎ 660-2583; www.bluewatersinn
.com; Batteaux Bay; s/d US$140/160, 1-/2-bedroom with
kitchen US$190/330; ℗ ☷) The most upscale
place to stay and also geared to divers,
Blue Waters sits on quiet, pretty Batteaux
Bay, just 0.62 miles (1km) from the main
road. The beachside resort's 38 rooms all
have patios and great views. Guests get use
of tennis courts, beach chairs and kayaks.
There's also a restaurant, bar, spa services
and Aquamarine Dive, a full-service PADI
dive center.

Manta Lodge (☎ 660-5268; in the USA 800-544-
7631; www.mantalodge.com; s/d with ceiling fan US$95/
115, air-con US$115/135; ☷ ☷) Geared toward
divers, this is a modern, plantation-style
house fronting the beach. Its 22 airy rooms
have wicker furniture, private baths and
ocean-view balconies. The ground-level
bar-restaurant opens onto the small pool.
Breakfast is included and you can purchase a meal plan (lunch and dinner) for
US$35 per person. The hotel is also home
to the reliable Tobago Dive Experience
dive shop.

Top Ranking Hill View Guest House (☎ 660-
4904; www.caribinfo.com/toprank; s/d US$35/40; ☷)
Reached via a series of steps from Top
Hill St, about a 10-minute walk from the
beach, this guesthouse has five handsomely
furnished rooms with one or two double
beds. Wraparound balconies provide excellent views of both the ocean and rainforest.
Top Ranking also runs boat tours and has a
minimart (at the bottom of the steps).

Seacrest Guesthouse (☎ 660-6642; r US$25; ☷)
This rustic-looking guesthouse on the left
before you get to the main village has a
downstairs bar. There are five small but tidy
rooms with baths and patios that overlook
the sea across the street.

Eating

Dining choices are slim in Speyside, but the following seaside restaurants clustered together along the main road offer good choices for breakfast, lunch and dinner.

Jemma's (☎ 660-4066; mains from TT$60; ♒ breakfast, lunch & dinner Sun-Thu, breakfast & lunch Fri) Nestled in a tree house setting and blessed by a soft sea breeze, Jemma's has the best atmosphere and food in Speyside. The cuisine features fresh local food, including fish, chicken and shrimp dishes. Prices can be at the upper end (TT$140 for shrimp), but portions are huge, the service friendly and the setting lovely. Jemma is a Seventh-Day Adventist, which means the restaurant does not serve booze (however, you are welcome to bring your own).

Birdwatchers Restaurant & Bar (☎ 660-5438; mains TT$70; ♒ lunch & dinner) Kick back on the candlelit deck and enjoy fresh seafood and cold beers at this friendly place. The menu changes with the catch of the day.

Redman's (mains TT$50; ♒ lunch & dinner) Another raised-deck affair, Redman's, a local hangout, is cheaper and less refined than Jemma's and Birdwatchers.

CHARLOTTEVILLE

There are about 2.5 winding miles (4km) over the mountains from Speyside to Charlotteville, a delightful little fishing village. Sleepy and secluded, and with an earthy simplicity, it has the appearance of some long-forgotten outpost. In the winter, the

hillsides behind the village are bright with the orange blossoms of immortelle trees, which were introduced from Martinique in colonial times to shade cocoa plantations.

Sights & Acivities

A palm-studded brown-sand beach good for swimming edges **Man of War Bay**, the large, horseshoe-shaped harbor that fronts the village. When it's calm, there's excellent snorkeling and fantastic beach-chillin' at **Pirate's Bay**, 0.5 miles (800m) across the point at the north side of Charlotteville, and good snorkeling around **Booby Island**, just southwest of the village.

Scuba divers should contact **Man Friday Diving** (☎ 660-4676; www.manfridaydiving.com), housed in a small shop along the main road. This full-service dive center rents out full gear and offers a variety of dive trips and certification. It also rents out kayaks (US$20/35 for a half-/full day).

If you are up for some exploring on dry land, take a walk to the site of the old **Fort Campbelton**, on the west side of the bay, which offers a good coastal view; or take a more substantial hike up **Flagstaff Hill**, a popular spot for sunset picnics, and a good place to watch the birds circling St Giles' Island.

Sleeping

There are several small, unofficial guesthouses in Charlotteville and you'll rarely have a problem getting a room.

Top River Pearl (☎ 660-6011; www.topriver.com; 32-34 Spring St; d apt US$60, house US$120; ✗ ☒) Although it's not on the beach, this guesthouse, just 200yd (182m) up Spring St from the waterfront, is truly a treat. With furnishings built from local teak, red-tiled floors and private baths, each of the three immaculate apartments has a balcony with ocean views, plus a minikitchen. A separate rental house is excellent value for a family or small group.

Belle Aire Inn (☎ 660-5984; 16 Belle Aire Rd; s/d US$30/40; ℙ ☒) Reach this attractive wooden home by climbing a steep street at the north end of the village. Affable owner Gifford Neptune offers straightforward rooms with sunken bathroom and minibar. Guests are welcome to use the kitchen and relax in the gazebo.

Cholson Chalets (☎ 639 8553; 74 Bay St, 1-/2-person studio US$25, 2-bedroom apt with kitchen & bath

US$60, per extra person US$12; P ∷) A clean, friendly place just steps from the beach. It has nine units of varying size, some in the main house and others in a newer annex.

Man-O-War Bay Cottages (☎ 660-4327; www .man-o-warbaycottages.com; Charlotteville Main Rd; 1-/4-bedroom cottage US$65/135; P) The grounds here are like a little botanical garden, with lots of tropical trees, ferns and flowering plants. Ten simple cottages with private baths, kitchens and screened, louvered windows open to the breeze and the sound of the surf. Pat Turpin, who leads nature tours around Tobago, owns the cottages – you'll find them on the beach, about five minutes' walk south of the village.

Eating

There are a couple of minimarts in town. Along the waterfront are several small huts selling rotis, baked goods and even meals.

Gail's (☎ 660-4316; mains from TT$50; ⏲ from 8:30am for breakfast, 7pm for dinner, closed lunch & all day Sun) At the northern end of the waterfront, Gail's serves up freshly caught fish with rice and greens.

Sharon's & Pheb's (☎ 660-5717; mains TT$40-60; ⏲ lunch & dinner) Doing amazing things with fresh fish, beef, chicken and vegetables, all of which grow nearby, chef Sharon cooks up excellent local cuisine. At lunch, expect a single-dish meal, such as curry or stew; at dinner, full meals come with soup or salad. There's indoor or outdoor seating.

Banana Boat Beachfront Bar (☎ 660-5176; 6 Mac's Lane; mains from TT$40; ⏲ breakfast, lunch & dinner) A festive place to kick back – come here to lime with locals and other travelers, especially at the Friday night barbecue or the daily 5pm to 6pm happy hour. You can also rent rooms here (US$30 per person).

Top River Pearl Cappuccino Cafe (☎ 660-6011; 32-34 Spring St; sandwiches TT$15; ⏲ 8:30am-6:30pm Mon-Sat) Located at its eponymous guesthouse, this comfortable outdoor café whips up espresso, milkshakes, breakfast, burgers and fish sandwiches.

A handful of family-run restaurants offer good food at honest prices (meals TT$45 to TT$65); all are open for lunch and dinner, except during the rainy season, when hours become more sporadic. Jane's Quality Kitchen provides seating in the shade of an almond tree with excellent views of the bay. Eastman's, an open-air eatery by the waterfront, serves fish dinners with rice, steamed veggies and salad. At the beach facility, there are rest rooms and the Charlotteville Beach Bar & Restaurant, which dishes up all the local favorites, as well as cocktails, daily.

DIRECTORY

ACCOMMODATIONS

Both islands have good-value guesthouses and small hotels. If you arrive without reservations, the airport tourist offices can help you book a room. Finding a room on Trinidad & Tobago is seldom a problem, but during Carnival season reservations on Trinidad should be made far in advance – also be aware that rates increase dramatically.

Trinidad & Tobago is less expensive than many places in the Caribbean, so budget options abound, especially in the low or shoulder seasons when hotels dramatically drop rates.

Each year, **Tidco** (☎ 675-7034; www.visittnt.com) publishes a small *Accommodation Guide* and it also features updated listings of B&Bs, guesthouses and hotels on its website. **Trinidad & Tobago Bed & Breakfast Co-Operative Society** (☎ /fax 663-4413) can help you find host-home and B&B accommodations on both islands. On Tobago, try the helpful **Tobago Bed & Breakfast Association** (☎ 639-3926; 1-3 Crooks River).

Beware of taxes! A 10% hotel room tax, 10% service charge, *plus* the government's 15% value-added tax (VAT) can add 35% more to your bill. Some accommodations rates include the tax and service charge, so be sure to ask first.

BOOKS

For bird-watchers, in addition to James Bond's well-regarded *Field Guide to Birds of the West Indies,* there's Richard ffrench's comprehensive *A Guide to the Birds of Trinidad and Tobago* and William L Mur-

---

EMERGENCY NUMBERS

Ambulance & police (☎ 999)
Fire (☎ 990)
Roadside Assistance (☎ 800-4826)

phy's 125-page *A Birder's Guide to Trinidad and Tobago. The Trinidad and Tobago Field Naturalists Club Trail Guide* describes hiking trails on the islands, complete with sketch maps.

For more details on Carnival and the music associated with it, grab a copy of Peter Mason's *Bacchanal* or Peter van Koningsbruggen's *Trinidad Carnival: Quest for a National Identity*. And for those interested in food, *Callaloo, Calypso & Carnival: the Cuisine of Trinidad & Tobago,* by Dave deWitt and Mary Jane Wilan, has recipes, and tidbits on the country's exotic flavors.

BUSINESS HOURS

Government and business offices are usually open from 8am to 4pm Monday to Friday. Retail hours are generally 8am to 4pm Monday to Wednesday, 8am to 6pm Thursday and Friday, and 8am to noon Saturday; however, most malls are open later and all day Saturday. Banks are open 8am to 2pm Monday to Thursday, and 8am to noon and 3pm to 5pm Friday.

DANGERS & ANNOYANCES

Tobagonians warn of rampant lawlessness in Trinidad, and Trinidadians say crime has reached epidemic proportions in Tobago. While such claims indicate a real concern over rising levels of crime in Trinidad & Tobago, they tend to exaggerate the dangers of travel on the islands. At night, it is best to avoid walking around dark areas, particularly in Port of Spain. Theft can be a problem, especially in touristy parts of Tobago, so be sure to keep an eye on your valuables.

Like most Caribbean islands, Trinidad & Tobago gets its share of no-see-ums (tiny fleas that munch on your skin), especially in the afternoon and early evening. Mosquitoes in the rain forest can also be a bother. A good strong bug spray will make you a much happier person.

If you've traveled around other Caribbean islands you may have encountered a lax attitude toward drugs. Beware – smoking pot in Trinidad & Tobago is a serious offense and getting caught can quickly ruin your holiday.

EMBASSIES & CONSULATES
Trinidadian & Tobagonian Embassies & Consulates

Belgium (☎ 32-2-762-9400; 14 Ave de la Faisanderie, 1150 Brussels)
Canada (☎ 416-495-9442; 2005 Sheppard Ave E, Suite 303, Willowdale, Ontario M2J 5B4)
India (☎ 01-911-1-461-8186; 131 Jor Bagh, New Delhi 110003)
UK (☎ 0207-245-9351; 42 Belgrave Sq, London SW1 X8NT)
USA (☎ 202-467-6490; 1708 Massachusetts Ave NW, Washington, DC 20036)

Embassies & Consulates in Trinidad & Tobago

All of the following are located in Port of Spain:

Canada (☎ 622-6232; Maple Bldg, 3-3A Sweet Briar Rd)
France (☎ 622-7446; Tatil Bldg, 11 Maraval Rd)
Germany (☎ 628-1630; 7-9 Marli St)
India (☎ 627-7480; 6 Victoria Ave)
Netherlands (☎ 625-1201; Life of Barbados Bldg, 69-71 Edward St)
UK (☎ 622-2748; 19 St Clair Ave)
USA (☎ 622-6371; 15 Queen's Park West)
Venezuela (☎ 627-9821; 16 Victoria Ave)

FESTIVALS & EVENTS

Trinidadians and Tobagonians love to celebrate life, and this is reflected in the many events held throughout the year. Trinidad's main annual event is Carnival (see the boxed text, p690), which formally begins two days before Ash Wednesday, in early February.

Several East Indian festivals, primarily in Trinidad, whose dates vary with the lunar calendar, draw large crowds.

Phagwa (March) A Hindu festival celebrating spring and harvest, with lots of dancing, singing of Hindi folk songs and the lighting of a big bonfire. It all culminates when participants are sprayed with *abeer*, a lavender-colored water. The main events take place in Chaguanas (p700), on Trinidad.

Hosay (March/April) This three-night Muslim celebration commemorates the martyrdom of the prophet's grandsons. Key events include the parading of brightly decorated replicas of the martyrs' tomb, and the Moon Dance, in which a dancing duo cavorts through the streets to the driving rhythms of tassa drums.

Easter Tuesday (April) The entire village of Buccoo (p709), on Tobago, celebrates Easter with this event, which features goat and crab races.

Pan Ramajay (May) A competition of small steel bands.

Tobago Heritage Festival (July) Tobago celebrates traditional culture, food and lifestyle in this two-week outpouring of creativity. Each village has its own celebration.

Emancipation Day (August 1) This public holiday celebrates the abolishment of slavery in 1834. Several cultural events take place, as well as a power-boat race from Trinidad to Tobago.

Caribbean Latin Jazz Festival (September)

National Pan Chutney Competition (November)

World Steel Band Festival (October)

Divali (November) This is the Hindu festival of lights, when elaborate towers are constructed of thousands of *deya* (tiny earthenware lamps). Festivities take place in and around Chaguanas (p700), on Trinidad.

National Parang Competition (December)

HOLIDAYS

Carnival Monday and Tuesday, and some religious festival days, are unofficial holidays, with banks and most businesses closed.

New Year's Day January 1
Good Friday Late March/early April
Easter Monday Late March/early April
Spiritual Baptist/Shouter Liberation Day March 30
Indian Arrival Day May 30
Corpus Christi Ninth Thursday after Easter
Labour Day June 19
Emancipation Day August 1

Independence Day August 31
Republic Day September 24
Christmas Day December 25
Boxing Day December 26
Eid Ul Fitr (Muslim New Year) Late December/January

INTERNET ACCESS

Internet service is available at or near the airports, as well as in several shopping malls in downtown Port of Spain. Some smaller towns also have Internet cafés. The rate is about TT$10 per hour.

INTERNET RESOURCES

www.insandoutstt.com Good information on restaurants, bars and entertainment.

www.mytobago.info Has tourism information plus a forum for visitors and locals to exchange ideas and information.

www.visittnt.com Tidco's website, with good information on hotels, transportation and current events.

MONEY

The official currency is the Trinidad & Tobago dollar (TT$). Banks will exchange a number of foreign currencies, but you'll generally get better rates for US dollars. In this book, we quote rates as they are given in Trinidad & Tobago. For instance, most hotels quote rates in US dollars, while local restaurants or tour guides charge in TT dollars.

POST

Postcards and letters of up to 0.7oz (20g) cost TT$2.50 to send to other Caribbean countries, TT$3.75 to the USA or Canada, TT$4.50 to the UK or Europe and TT$5.25 to Australia, or anywhere else in the world.

TELEPHONE

The country's area code is ☎ 868. When calling from North America, dial ☎ 1-868 + the local number. From elsewhere dial your country's international access code + ☎ 868 + the local number. When you are in Trinidad & Tobago, you just need to dial the seven-digit local number, which is what we have included in this chapter.

Public phones are numerous in Trinidad and Tobago, but few are functional. Those that do work are either coin- or card-operated, and even local calls are charged by duration. Your best bet is to purchase a Telecommunications Services of Trinidad &

Tobago (TSTT) phone card. Purchase them at airports, shopping malls and small shops.

TOURIST INFORMATION
Local Tourist Offices
Tourism and Industrial Development Company of Trinidad & Tobago (Tidco; ☎ 675-7034; www.visittnt .com) has offices at the airports on Trinidad and Tobago, on Edward St in Port of Spain, and in Scarborough. When requesting information by mail, write to: Tidco, PO Box 222, Level 1 Maritime Center, No 29 Tenth Ave, Barataria, Trinidad, West Indies.

Tourist Offices Abroad
Overseas representatives of Tidco:
Canada (☎ 416-485-8724; fax 416-485-8256; RMR Group, Taurus House, 512 Duplex Ave, Toronto, Ontario M4R 2E3)
UK (☎ 0208-350 1009; fax 0208 350 1011; Morris Kevan International, Mitre House, 66 Abbey Rd, Bush Hill Park, Middlesex EN1 2QE, UK)
USA (☎ 305-444-4033; fax 305-447-0415; Cheryl Andrews Marketing, 331 Almeria Ave, Coral Gables, FL 33134)
Venezuela (☎ /fax 58-212-284-6517; Caribbean Adventures; 7ma transversal de Altamira, con Ave San Felipe, La Castellana, Caracas 1060)

TOURS
Those wanting to piece together an organized 'ecotour,' whether it be bird-watching, rain-forest hikes or just general environmental and cultural appreciation outings, will find a number of excellent tour guides on Trinidad and Tobago.

Tobago
David Rooks Nature Tours (☎ 756-8594; www.rooks tobago.com) is operated by perhaps the most renowned naturalist in the country. David Rooks is the former president of the **Trinidad & Tobago Field Naturalist Club (** ☎ 624-8017; www .wow.net/ttfnc) and has worked on BBC and PBS nature programs. He lives in Charlotteville and leads three-hour bird-watching trips on the island, starting at US$50 per person. You will need to book at least a week in advance.

Other well-regarded ecotourism operators on Tobago include **Pat Turpin (** ☎ 660-4327) and **Hubert 'Renson' Jack (** ☎ 660-5175).

Trinidad
Courtenay Rooks (☎ 622-8826; www.pariasprings .com) David Rooks' son runs this outfit, specializing in bird ing and natural-history hikes on Trinidad's north coast.

Island Experiences (☎ 625-2410, 756-9677; gunda@wow.net; 11 E Hill, Port of Spain) Highly recommended. Gunda Harewood and her staff offer excellent half- and full-day 'eco-cultural tours.' German-born Gunda aims to give her clients a good view of the country's underbelly, and is happy to impart local knowledge and lore. Her half-day trips (US$35 to US$40) include the Caroni Bird Sanctuary, a Port of Spain city tour, a trip to Maracas Bay, or the excellent Evening Entertainment Tour (p695). Full-day trips include the Leatherback Turtle Adventure (US$85) and the Coastal Tour (US$65).
Nanan's Bird Sanctuary Tours (☎ 645-1305; nantour@tstt.net.tt; 38 Bamboo Grove, Port of Spain) Highly regarded as one of the best tour companies for visiting Trinidad's Caroni Bird Sanctuary, Asa Wright Nature Centre and Nariva Swamp. Costs vary, depending on the length of the tour and the number of participants.
PathMaster (☎ 621-0255; www.thepathmaster.com; 13 Idlewild Rd, Port of Spain) An excellent ecotourism company that leads single- and multiday nature-oriented camping, cycling, hiking and kayaking tours. Participants can choose from a range of skill levels. Tours are booked via phone or website.

From March through midsummer, most ecotour operators offer an overnight turtle observation expedition. This takes you for a stroll along the beach at Grand Rivière, on Trinidad's north coast, to search for nesting leatherbacks.

VISAS
Visas are not necessary for citizens of the US, Canada, the UK or most European countries for stays of less than three months.

Visas are required by citizens of Australia, New Zealand, South Africa and India, and some other Commonwealth countries (including Nigeria, Papua New Guinea, Sri Lanka, Tanzania and Uganda). In most countries, visas are obtained through the British embassy, or you can pay TT$100 upon arrival.

WOMEN TRAVELERS
A woman traveling alone, especially on Trinidad, is about as common as snow. Men will stare at you. They'll make kissy noises, hiss, offer to be anything from your protector to your sex slave. Says one Trini woman, 'Trini men feel compelled to let women know they are noticed and appreciated.' While your reaction may be more annoyance than appreciation, most men are harmless. Most, in fact, would actually be courteous and friendly

if you were to stop and talk to them. The constant staring, lewd comments and hissing, however, can wear on your nerves. You're best bet is to smile politely, or ignore it altogether and move on.

TRANSPORTATION

GETTING THERE & AWAY
Entering the Islands
Provided that you have a valid passport (US citizens see the boxed text, p772), you'll have little trouble coming and going from Trinidad & Tobago. When you arrive, you'll fill out an Immigration Arrival Card. It's straightforward, but one line on the card asks for your intended address in Trinidad & Tobago. Customs officials require that you fill this out – if you don't know where you're staying yet, just list the name, address and phone number of any local hotel.

Air
Airports in both Trinidad and Tobago handle international air traffic, but the bulk of international flights arrive and depart from Trinidad. For information on international flights to Trinidad & Tobago, see p777.
Crown Point International Airport (☎ 639-8457; www.tntairports.com) Located in Crown Point, 7 miles (11km) southwest of Scarborough, on Tobago.
Piarco International Airport (☎ 669-8047; www.piarcoairport.com) Located 15.5 miles (25km) east of Port of Spain, on Trinidad.

Airlines flying to Trinidad & Tobago from within the Caribbean are:
American Eagle (☎ 669-4661, 800-433-7300; www.aa.com)
British West Indies Air (BWIA; ☎ 627-2942; www.bwee.com; 30 Edward St, Port of Spain) This airline was founded in Trinidad & Tobago in 1940.
Caribbean Star (☎ 623-8243, 800-744-7827; www.flycaribbeanstar.com)
LIAT (☎ Trinidad 627-6274, Tobago 639-0324; www.flyliat.com; 9-11 Edward St, Port of Spain)

Sea
CRUISE SHIP
Cruise ships dock on the south side of Port of Spain. The large cruise-ship complex contains a customs hall, souvenir and clothing shops, car-rental agencies, taxis and a couple of local eateries. There's a smaller cruise-ship

---

DEPARTURE TAX

A TT$75 departure tax and a TT$25 security fee (TT$100 total) must be paid upon departure, payable in TT or US dollars (about US$16). The departure tax for the ferry to Venezuela is TT$75. There's no departure tax when flying between Trinidad and Tobago. At the Trinidad airport, the fee can be paid via a special ATM machine. You'll be asked to show the ATM receipt, or pay the tax, as you enter the departure security area.

---

facility in central Scarborough on Tobago. See p777 for more information on cruises.

YACHT
Trinidad & Tobago is beyond the main sweep of most hurricanes, making it a safe haven for yachters. Trinidad's Chaguaramas Bay has the primary mooring and marina facilities as well as immigration and the customs office for yachters. Tidco publishes a print and online **Boater's Directory** (www.boatersenterprise.com), with an array of information for yacht travelers.

GETTING AROUND
Air
Flying between Trinidad and Tobago is easy, inexpensive and fast. The 20-minute flight between the islands costs TT$100 per person, each way (round-trip tickets cost double). The checked baggage weight allowance is 44.2lb (20kg). You should be at the airport an hour ahead of time. While it's wise to book in advance, it is often possible to buy tickets at the airport on the day of departure. Two companies offer similar service for these flights:
BWIA (☎ Trinidad 627-2942, Tobago 660-2942; www.bwee.com)
Tobago Express (☎ 627-5160; www.tobagoexpress.com)

Boat
Until very recently, the only way to travel by sea between the islands was to take the five-hour ferry between Queen's Wharf in Port of Spain (Trinidad) and the main ferry dock in Scarborough (Tobago). The journey costs TT$25 each way for economy-class tickets. Tourist class (TT$30) supposedly

assures you a reclining seat, but, in reality, seating is minimally controlled. Cabins are available for TT$80. It's a cheap way to travel, but the journey is long and often rough, which prompted the government's decision in 2004 to lease a fast ferry that makes the journey in 2½ hours and costs just TT$25/50 one way/round-trip.

The slow ferry departs Port of Spain at 2pm Monday to Friday, with an extra sailing at 11pm Tuesday to Thursday. On Saturday and Sunday, the ferry departs at 11am. From Scarborough, the ferry leaves daily at 11pm, and at 11am Tuesday to Friday. Tickets are sold at Port of Spain's ferry terminal from 7am to 4pm Monday to Friday. Be sure to arrive at least two hours before sailing or your ticket can be resold.

The fast ferry sails once a day each way, departing Queen's Wharf at 4pm and returning from Scarborough at 6:30am. Extra sailings are added during holidays and other peak periods.

For more information, call the **Port Authority** (☎ Trinidad 625-3055, Tobago 639-2417).

Bus

Buses on both islands provide a substantial means of transportation for locals. Many people take buses to and from work in neighboring towns, and children depend on buses to get to and from school. Buses offer travelers an inexpensive way to get around, especially on longer cross-island trips, but beware that bus service is often painfully slow. For shorter distances, travelers are better off taking maxi-taxis or route taxis. Check the bus information for Trinidad (p685) and Tobago (p704).

Car

RENTAL

Driving yourself can be a great way of getting around the islands. Car rentals start at about TT$300, and include insurance and unlimited mileage. See the Getting There & Around sections for Trinidad (p685) and Tobago (p704) for more information.

ROAD RULES

Cars drive on the left on Trinidad and Tobago, and the car's steering column is on the right (as in the UK). Your home driver's license is valid for stays of up to three months.

Twisting, narrow roads and fast, horn-happy drivers can make driving on the islands an adventure; in Port of Spain, traffic, complicated roads and poor signage can make driving a white-knuckle experience. Your best bet is to study a map before you get in the car, take a deep breath and practice Zen-like patience. You will get the hang of it, and you'll find driving much easier if you simply relax a little and follow the flow. Be aware that fellow road users will stop suddenly to drop off a friend, say 'Hi' to a neighbor or pick up a cold Carib. Sometimes they'll simply stop, while other times they'll wave an arm up and down to signal they are about to do something.

The speed limit on highways is 50mph (80km/h), and 30mph to 35mph (50km/h to 55km/h) on city streets. All gas stations are National (NP), a state-owned network. Gas is at a fixed price of TT$2.75 a liter for regular and TT$3.20 for super throughout Trinidad & Tobago. It'll cost about TT$100 to fill up a tank.

Hitchhiking

Hitching a ride is very common with islanders, especially with children, who hitch to and from school, and with workers trying to get home at night. However, hitching is not a safe mode of transportation for foreign visitors, especially women (your want of a ride will be misconstrued for a want of other things).

Taxi

For island-specific taxi information, see p695 (Trinidad) and p704 (Tobago).

MAXI-TAXI

Maxi-taxis are 12- to 25-passenger minibuses that travel a fixed route within a specific zone. They're color-coded by route and often depict the personality of the driver – you may hop on a bus blazoned with 'Jah Mon' and booming with Rasta music, or catch a ride on a bus dedicated to Jesus. Regardless, maxis run 24 hours, are very cheap and are heavily used by the locals; catching one can be a great cultural experience. Rides cost TT$2 to TT$12, depending on how far you go. You can flag a maxi at any point along its route, or hop on at the appropriate taxi stand. Keep in mind that, due to frequent stops, maxis take a long time to get from A to B.

On Trinidad, many maxi-taxis operate out of the maxi-taxi terminal adjacent to City Gate. For information on Trinidad's maxi-taxi color-coding system, see p695. On Tobago, all maxis have a blue band.

For information about maxi-taxi routes, contact **Trinidad & Tobago Unified Maxi Taxi Association** (☎ 624-3505).

REGULAR TAXI

Regular taxis, locally called 'tourist taxis,' are readily available at the airport, the cruise ship complex and hotels. These large, often left-hand-drive vehicles are unmetered, but follow rates established by the government; hotel desks and the airport tourist office have a list of fares. Make sure you have established the rate before riding off.

ROUTE TAXI

These taxis are shared cars that travel along a prescribed route and can drop you anywhere along the way.

Registered route taxis look like regular cars, except that their license plates start with an 'H' (for 'hire').

Aruba, Bonaire & Curaçao

Aruba, Bonaire and Curaçao may be close to South America – Aruba is only 15 miles (24km) from Venezuela – but they are little like the continent to the south. In fact, they are unlike anywhere else, really. Colonized first by the Spanish, then by the Dutch and populated by thousands of African slaves, the ABCs, as they are known, have blended those cultures and picked up influences of many more. The islands have always been on the trade routes and have prospered by buying and selling goods, some produced locally, others from far away.

Today it's goods from afar, in the form of tourists, that bring wealth, lured by the warm, dry weather, and the deep blue water. But the attractions of the ABCs aren't as closely related as their initials in the alphabet: each of the islands has a distinct personality. Broadly, Aruba offers great beaches and comfortable accommodations; Bonaire has pristine reefs for divers; and Curaçao mixes rich history with local urban culture and rural escapes.

Visit all of the ABCs and you'll truly feel like you've been to three unique places.

FAST FACTS

- **Area** Aruba: 70 sq miles (181 sq km); Bonaire: 110 sq miles (285 sq km); Curaçao: 182 sq miles (471 sq km)

- **Capital** Aruba: Oranjestad; Bonaire: Kralendijk; Curaçao: Willemstad

- **Country code** Aruba: ☎ 297; Bonaire: ☎ 599; Curaçao: ☎ 599-9

- **Departure tax** Aruba: included in ticket; Bonaire: international US$20, interisland US$6; Curaçao: international US$22, interisland US$7

- **Famous for** Aruba: beaches; Bonaire: diving; Curaçao: city and rural charm

- **Languages** Dutch, Spanish, English and Papiamento (a mix of the first three)

- **Money** Aruba: Aruban florins (Afl); Bonaire & Curaçao: Netherlands Antillean guilders (NAf). US$1 = €0.82 = UK£0.55 =Afl1.77 = NAf1.77

- **People** (formal) Arubans, Bonairians, Curaçaoans

- **Population** Aruba: 71,000; Bonaire: 14,500; Curaçao: 132,000

- **Visa** Most nationalities do not need a visa for a 90-day stay on each of the islands

HIGHLIGHTS

- **Bonaire's Reefs** (p743) Unesco-recognized natural beauty that offers perfect diving conditions.
- **Eagle Beach** (p735) Just one of many seemingly endless expanses of gorgeous white sand on Aruba.
- **Willemstad** (p745) Unesco-recognized Dutch colonial heritage with superb museums that are seasoned by Curaçao's urban grit.
- **Kralendijk** (p740) Bonaire's small and relaxed main town has great nightlife to match.
- **Arikok National Wildlife Park** (p736) Aruba's pristine celebration of the natural life and land of the ABCs.

ITINERARIES

- **Three Days** Pick one of the ABCs and stay there, as this is the minimum time required to enjoy any of the three islands.
- **One Week** Either have a very relaxing time on one island or try two, depending on your taste.
- **Two Weeks** Plenty of time to see all three islands and have time to lounge on the beach.

CLIMATE & WHEN TO GO

Average temperature for the ABCs year-round is a perfect 82°F (28°C). High noon is a bit warmer and at night it can get breezy, but mostly you'll be fine in shorts and

---

HOW MUCH?

- **One-tank dive** US$25 to US$40
- **Daily 4WD rental** US$40 to US$70
- **Beaches** Free
- **Fresh garlic shrimp** US$12
- **Silly fruity drink** US$4

LONELY PLANET INDEX

- **Liter of gas** US$0.90
- **Liter of bottled water** US$1
- **Bottle of Heineken beer** US$2
- **Souvenir T-shirt** US$10
- **Street snack: empanas** (meat fritter) US$1

T-shirt. The islands are fairly dry, averaging a little over 1in (2.5cm) of rain per month. Much of this falls from September to early December. The islands usually avoid the Caribbean hurricane season, although in 2004 the tail of Ivan churned up beaches and damaged trees, and 1999's Lenny was unkind to some offshore reefs.

The high season for cruise ships runs October to April. Outside of these times the port towns can be almost sleepy.

THE CULTURE

If Aruba, Bonaire and Curaçao were named, say, Moe, Larry and Curley and their initials were MLC, it might be easier for outsiders not to link them so closely. For despite their proximity geographically and alphabetically, the cultures of the three islands have many differences, mainly due to their history after colonization.

Bonaire was populated with a few thousand African slaves who worked the salt flats. After slavery ended their descendents lived quiet lives farming and raising animals, largely ignored by the world. Not until the explosion of postwar tourism and scuba diving did the island open itself to the outside. The result is a large island with a small population of African-Caribbeans rooted in traditional ways, yet welcoming the opportunity brought by travelers from around the world.

Curaçao was also populated by African slaves, but its superb port drove its economy after slavery ended and the cultural roots today are a mix of African-Caribbean, Latin American and European. Willemstad is at times relaxed, frenetic and buttoned-down. The population is growing and there's money to be made. Out in the country – increasingly the home of commuters – traditional ways of life are fading.

Aruba had neither resources to exploit nor any geographic advantage, so it was large ignored during the colonial era. Here the indigenous population survived, and were later joined by immigrants from Latin America looking for work in the refinery and Dutch people who were simply looking for sun. It feels new and it largely is, with wealth coming from the one million visitors who arrive each year. Still there is a bit of island culture to be found and locals love a good gossip session fueled by rum.

Because of these differences, the ABCs have never been close. Politically they were linked within the Netherlands Antilles, but like siblings in a large family, as they have matured they've each looked to chart their own path. Aruba was first out the door. In 1986 it took its wealth and separated ties with its neighbors, while maintaining a mostly symbolic link to the Netherlands. Twenty years later, Curaçao is now ready to do the same. In contrast, Bonaire, with its small population and one-trick-pony economy, plans to move closer to the benevolent largess of its past colonial master. It hopes to return to direct rule by the Netherlands.

ARTS

The main form of art on the ABCs is music. Here it takes on a vibrant mix of European, African and new forms. No style is sacred and improvisation is the rule. At times you'll hear Creole, blues, jazz, rock, pop, rap and more. Some songs combine all of these elements and more. Making music is popular, and many people on the islands play in small groups with friends and relatives. No social gathering of any significance is complete without some live music.

The best architecture on the islands is the Caribbean-colored old Dutch colonial styles, with their thick walls defending against the heat. Modern buildings tend to be utilitarian or serve the needs of tourists.

ENVIRONMENT

The ABCs are primarily arid, with cacti and other hardy plants that can make do with the minimal rainfall each year. Reptiles – especially huge iguanas – are the main creatures native to the land. However, each island has mangroves in some parts and these attract more birds than the islands do tourists. Some of the species are quite spectacular, from Bonaire's flamingos to the brightly colored parrots found everywhere.

In the water is where the ABCs are truly rich in life. Coral reefs grow in profusion along the lee coasts of all three islands, especially Bonaire. Hundreds of species of fish and dozens of corals thrive in the clear, warm waters. Sharks, dolphins and rays are among the larger creatures swimming about.

For information on local plants common across the ABCs, see Arikok National Wildlife Park (p736).

For information on environmental issues in the ABCs, look to the relevant sections for Aruba (p728), Bonaire (p737) and Curaçao (p745).

FOOD & DRINK

Because of the arid conditions, local food in the ABCs has always been hearty. Thick stews made with meats, like goat and chicken, and vegetables, like okra and squash, have been predominate. Given the repetitive nature of the food, spices were used to give things variety. The Dutch brought a love of cheese, but dishes made with this have mostly always been a special treat.

Even today most fruits and vegetables on the islands are imported. Seafood, however, is common and good, especially shellfish, like shrimp and lobsters. While a huge array of foods is available in places geared toward visitors, locals have been quick to forsake goat stew and an appetite for fast food has exploded. Traditional food is not always easy for travelers to find.

Dutch and American brands dominate the ABC suds market. However Balashi, an Aruban brew that began production in the late 1990s, can be found throughout the island where it is popular because it is *not* Dutch or American, but rather local. You will at times see it on Bonaire and Curaçao as well. It is a typically light lager.

ARUBA

Aruba is the most touristed of the ABCs, a not surprising fact given that it has miles of the best beaches, plenty of resorts, and a compact and cute main town, Oranjestad, which is ideally suited for the two-hour strolls favored by day-tripping cruise-ship voyagers. Scores of visitors never get far from their beachside loungers, except for the odd foray to one of the modest casinos or good restaurants. Judging from the accents in the airport, you may think you are in New York.

The island does offer diversions for those who venture away from the hotels. The extreme ends offer rugged, windswept vistas and uncrowded beaches. Arikok National Wildlife Park is an alien landscape of cacti, twisted divi-divi trees and abandoned gold mines. Mostly, however, Aruba is a place to

ARUBA

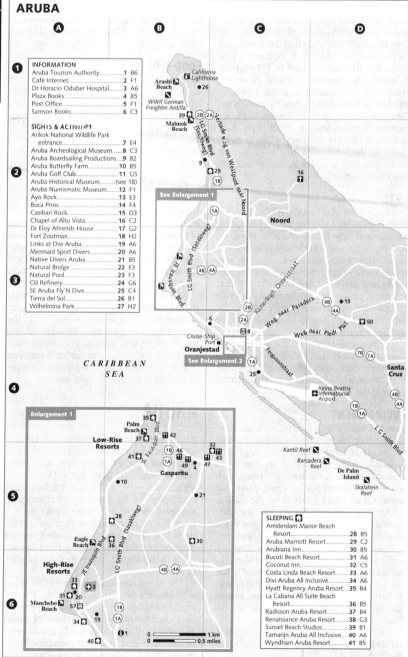

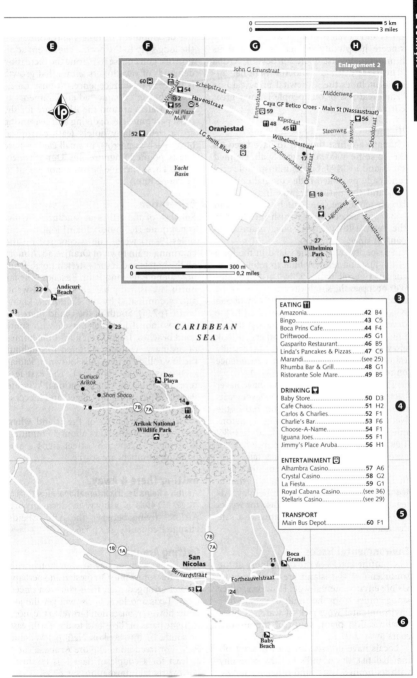

0 — 5 km
0 — 3 miles

Enlargement 2

John G Emanstraat

60 ▣
12
Schelpstraat
▣ 54
Havenstraat
55 ⊙ 2
5
Royal Plaza
Mall
52 ▣
LG Smith Blvd

Middenweg

Caya GF Betico Croes - Main St (Nassaustraat)
59
Klipstraat
48   45 ▣
Steenweg

56 ▣

Oranjestad

Wilhelminastraat
58 ▣
Zoutmanstraat
17

Schoolstraat
Kruisweg

Yacht Basin

▥ 18
51

27
Wilhelmina Park
▨ 38

Zoutmanstraat
Lagoenweg
Julianastraat

0 — 300 m
0 — 0.2 miles

22 ● **Andicuri Beach**

13 ●

23 ●

CARIBBEAN SEA

Cunucu Arikok
● *Shoti Shoco*

7 ●

Dos Playa

14
▣
44

(7B) (7A)

Arikok National Wildlife Park

(1B) (1A)

(7B)
(7A)

San Nicolas
Bernardstraat
53 ▣
24

Boca Grandi
11

Fortheauvelstraat

Baby Beach

EATING 🍽
Amazonia.........................**42** B4
Bingo...............................**43** C5
Boca Prins Cafe................**44** F4
Driftwood........................**45** G1
Gasparito Restaurant........**46** B5
Linda's Pancakes & Pizzas...**47** C5
Marandi.........................(see 25)
Rhumba Bar & Grill...........**48** G1
Ristorante Sole Mare.........**49** B5

DRINKING 🍷
Baby Store.......................**50** D3
Cafe Chaos......................**51** H2
Carlos & Charlies..............**52** F1
Charlie's Bar....................**53** F6
Choose-A-Name................**54** F1
Iguana Joes......................**55** F1
Jimmy's Place Aruba..........**56** H1

ENTERTAINMENT 🎭
Alhambra Casino...............**57** A6
Crystal Casino..................**58** G2
La Fiesta.........................**59** G1
Royal Cabana Casino........(see 36)
Stellaris Casino................(see 29)

TRANSPORT
Main Bus Depot.................**60** F1

unwind, sip a tropical drink, page through a novel and develop a tan. It wears its mostly sincere hospitality on its sleeve (and its bumpers): license plates proclaim Aruba 'The Happy Island' and the national anthem includes the somewhat unlyrical line 'The greatness of our people is their great cordiality.'

History

Humans are first thought to have lived on Aruba some 4000 years ago. Spain claimed the island in 1499, but its inhospitable arid landscape provoked little colonial enthusiasm and the native Arawak Indians were largely left alone. The Dutch took claim in 1636, and except for a British interlude in the early 19th century, have maintained control since.

Prosperity came to the island in the form of the huge oil refinery built to refine Venezuelan crude oil in the 1920s. This large complex occupies the southwestern end of Aruba and dominates the blue-collar town of San Nicolas. Jobs at the plant contributed to the development of a local middle class. Automation meant a necessity for workers to look elsewhere, and the island has successfully transferred its economy from dependence on refining oil to relaxing tourists.

The three islands of the ABCs have never been palsy, and Aruba was able to leverage its affluence to break away from the rest of the Netherlands Antilles and become an autonomous entity within the Netherlands in 1986. Talk of achieving full independence has not become anything more than that: talk.

Aruba made an unwanted media splash in the US during 2005 when an Atlanta teenager disappeared while on holiday. Allegations swirled around the case for weeks and tarnished the island's status as a safe destination.

Environmental Issues

The puffing stacks of the oil refinery at the south end of the island are Aruba's most visible environmental woe. However, other smog comes from the result of yet another environmental woe: lack of water. A huge desalinization plant, south of the airport, roars away 24/7.

Locals have pressed for growth controls that balance the island's healthy economy with its limited water and other resources.

This has slowed but by no means stopped the development of hotels and condos on the long strip to the north. The recent addition of a golf course to placate the recreation demands of vacationers shows that growth is likely to take precedence. At busy times, roads through Oranjestad are jammed.

The waters around the island are for the most part quite clean; diving and swimming are a treat. Many hotels feature tropical birds, such as parrots, in small cages where guests pointedly ignore the 'Don't Touch' signs. These sociable birds are not meant to be cooped up.

Orientation

Smallest of the ABCs in landmass, Aruba is not quite 18.5 miles (30km) long and 5.5 miles (9km) wide. Life is centered on the charming main town of Oranjestad. Almost all the hotels and resorts stretch north from here along Eagle and Palm Beaches. The far north is classically barren and windswept, and is dominated by the California Lighthouse (p735). South of the island there are various industries interspersed with some good beaches. Inland you'll find the homes of ordinary Arubans scattered throughout the low rolling brown hills known in Papiamento as *cunucu* (country). The east features the wilds of Arikok National Wildlife Park (p736) and much rugged and inaccessible shoreline.

Driving the length of the island when there is little traffic takes about 35 minutes. Road signs – especially street signs – and building numbers are scarce.

Getting There & Away

Aruba's **Reina Beatrix International Airport** (AUA; ☎ 297-582-4800) is a busy, modern airport. Airlines flying between the ABC islands change frequently; see p756.

Getting Around

If you just want to stay at your hotel, with only a few forays into Oranjestad and perhaps a hotel-arranged tour, then you won't need a car. Taxis and local buses will get the job done; however, buses don't travel to the more extreme parts of the island to the north, east or south, or into Arikok National Wildlife Park. For freedom to explore Aruba, a car – at least for a couple of days – is essential. For car-rental information, see p735.

WARNING FOR PASSENGERS TO THE US

Passengers flying to the US absolutely must take heed of their airline's warning to check in three hours before flight time. Actually four hours might be better because the US government has decided to have all passengers clear US customs and immigration *before* they leave Aruba. Most flights back to the US leave during a small timeslot in the afternoon and the US-staffed immigration facilities are not up to the task. Passengers are stuck in lines snaking through the terminal; waits of two hours or more are common. Cleverly, the airport has lined the lengthy route with duty-free shops. One gives out free samples of beer – ask for two. Meanwhile, the good vibes built up over a week of sunny relaxation are erased as stressed-out families immolate around you.

ORANJESTAD & THE NORTH

Oranjestad is a large island town that manages to – mostly – radiate a serene charm, except when hordes of cruise-ship day-trippers run into hordes of tourists down from the beachside resorts. At these times, the streets are jammed and you're better off at the beach. At other times, there's an appealing mix of old and new structures intermingled with scads of shops, bars and restaurants. At night when the boats have reabsorbed their passengers, the town is rather quiet.

Almost all of Aruba's hotels and resorts are northwest of town. This area has wide roads, lush landscaping and excellent beaches. It's really a world unto itself, similar to beachside developments found the world over.

Orientation

It's hard to get anywhere on Aruba without passing along Lloyd G Smith Blvd, Oranjestad's main street and the central island artery linking the tourist resorts of the north with the airport to the south. Little in Oranjestad is more than a 10-minute walk from the Yacht Basin in the town center.

Large tourist developments begin less than 1.85 miles (3km) north of Oranjestad's center. Both conveniently and accurately, the hotels and condos along Eagle Beach are known as the Low-Rise Resorts. An undeveloped area stretching for about 0.9 miles (1.5km) leads to the High-Rise Resorts along Palm Beach. This area – about 3.7 miles (6km) north of the Yacht Basin – is also where you'll find many restaurants and shops.

Information
BOOKSTORES

Like the rest of the ABCs, bookstores on Aruba are more like stationery stores. Supplies of books where the pages are already filled with text are often meager. Hotel shops usually have selections limited to hackneyed potboilers; if your reading aspirations go beyond Sheldon or Clancy, bring books from home.

Plaza Books (☎ 297-586-4267; Noord; ⏰ 8:30am-6:30pm Mon-Sat) Small selection of local guidebooks.

Samson Books (☎ 297-582-3434; Lloyd G Smith Blvd; ⏰ 8am-6:30pm Mon-Sat, 9am-1pm Sun) Bestsellers and a few local books.

INTERNET ACCESS

Café Internet (☎ 297-582-4500; Royal Plaza Mall 8, Lloyd G Smith Blvd; per hr US$5; ⏰ 9am-9pm Mon-Sat, 11am-6pm Sun) Full services, including wi-fi, and cheap international phone calls.

MEDICAL SERVICES

Dr Horacio Oduber Hospital (☎ 297-587-4300; Sasakiweg; ⏰ 24hr) Near the Low-Rise Resorts, a large and well-equipped hospital.

MONEY

ATMs are easily found across the island. Hotels and banks change money at average rates.

POST

Post office (Royal Plaza Mall; ⏰ 8am-3:15pm Mon-Fri) Near the cruise-ship port, adept at international mail.

TOURIST INFORMATION

Aruba Tourism Authority (☎ 297-582-3777; Lloyd G Smith Blvd; ⏰ 7:30am-noon & 1-4:30pm Mon-Fri) Helpful staff can answer questions. Otherwise there's not much here you won't find in racks in hotel lobbies.

Sights

Oranjestad is a good place to walk around, It lacks any real must-see sight, rather it's best to just stroll and enjoy the scores of small Dutch colonial buildings painted in a profusion of colors.

Fort Zoutman (Oranjestraat) is not much to look at, but what's left dates from the 18th century. Best-preserved is the **Willem III Tower**, built to warn of approaching pirates. Fortunately, at that time Aruba was seen as having little in the booty department and pirates usually gave the island a pass.

In the base of the tower is the **Aruba Historical Museum** (297-502 6009; Fort Zoutman 4; admission US$1.75; 10am-noon & 1:30-4:30pm Mon-Fri). It's a good place to see how a mélange of cultures (African, European, Caribbean and indigenous) have combined to create the island's unique character.

Nearby, note **Dr Eloy Ahrends House** (Oranjestraat), an elegant, thick-walled 1922 house, which is now part of the city-council complex. At night it's lit up like an emerald. Across Lloyd G Smith Blvd by the Yacht Basin, **Wilhelmina Park** is a shady refuge replete with lush tropical gardens.

The **Aruba Numismatic Museum** (297-582-8831; Zuidstraat 7; admission US$5; 9am-3pm) doesn't just have displays of Aruba's unusual currency past and present (at one time a coin shortage forced locals to cut up coins like pies), but it also has thousands of items used as money worldwide from the 3rd century BC to the present. A bunch of beads once got you Manhattan.

Stone tools found on Aruba dating from 4000 BC are the dusty stars of the **Aruba Archeological Museum** (297-582-8979; Irausquinplein 2A; admission free; 8am-noon & 1-4pm Mon-Fri). Some 3000 years later locals were making tools and pots from ceramics, which are also on display.

Located near the hotels, the touristy **Aruba Butterfly Farm** (297-586-3656; JE Irausquin Blvd; adult/child US$12/6; 9am-4pm) has hundreds of butterflies from around the world living in an enclosed and lovely, albeit very un-Aruban, tropical garden.

Activities

Brochure racks in hotels are jammed with offers of a myriad of activities on Aruba. Most are concocted to divert those already bored after a day or two spent by the beach or pool.

But activities in the water are another matter, and the island is a destination for serious divers from around the world.

DIVING & SNORKELING

While it is not quite Bonaire, Aruba has some world-class diving around its shores. One of the most popular spots is the wreck of the large WWII German freighter *Antilla,* which is close to shore and at times is visible above the surface. It lies between Arashi and Malmok Beaches.

Visibility is often upwards of 98ft (30m), which makes for excellent fish-spotting and photography. Reefs are plentiful with many right off De Palm Island, the barrier island off the southwest coast. Kantil Reef here has a steep drop-off, and it's easy to spot perky parrotfish, bitchy barracudas and spiny lobsters. Other noted nearby reefs include Skalahein and Barcadera.

Costs for diving and snorkeling are competitive. Daily snorkeling gear rental is about US$15, two-tank dives with all equipment about US$70 and week-long Professional Association of Diving Instructors (PADI) open-water courses about US$350.

Most hotels have a close relationship with at least one dive operator. Recommended dive shops include:

Mermaid Sport Divers (297-587-4103; www.scubadivers-aruba.com; JE Irausquin Blvd) A long-established operation offering a range of tours and services.

Native Divers Aruba (297-586-4763; www.nativedivers.com; Washington 19, Noord) A well-established outfit.

SE Aruba Fly'N Dive (297-588-1150; Lloyd G Smith Blvd 1A) A large PADI operation, with a range of courses and dives on the noted reefs off the southeast coast.

GOLF

For a real novelty, try the nine holes at the **Aruba Golf Club** (297-584-2006; Golfweg 82; greens fee US$10) on the far southeast coast. Greens are oiled and rolled sand, while hazards are provided by wandering goats and stationary cactus.

For pretension and beauty, **Tierra del Sol** (297-586-0978; www.tierradelsol.com; greens fee US$70-137) is a hole in one. The championship 18-hole course designed by Robert Trent Jones Jr weaves in and out of lavish vacation homes, with excellent views to the sea. While in the gracious clubhouse, be sure to charge your drinks to the Underhill account.

The **Links at Divi Aruba** (297-586-1357; JE Irausquin Blvd; greens fee US$55) is a new nine-hole addition to the Divi resort empire in the Low-Rise Resorts area. Fees include the use of a cart –

even for nine holes you won't get so worn out that you can't make the all-you-can-eat buffet.

HORSEBACK RIDING

Herds of companies offer tours of the island via horse. **Rancho del Campo** (☎ 297-585-0290; www.ranchodelcampo.com) is one of the better outfits and offers rides to the Natural Pool (p736) and the Natural Bridge (p736) on the rugged northeast coast. Tours cost from US$60. Certainly riding a four-legged critter to these attractions is better than tearing across the landscape in a 4WD – as many operators promote.

SPAS

Day spas are popular on Aruba. Many of the resorts feature world-class services, including Aveda spas at the Costa Linda Beach Resort (p732) and the Aruba Marriott Resort (p733), and one of the most favored on the island at the Wyndham Aruba Resort (p733).

WINDSURFING

Aruba Boardsailing Productions (☎ 297-586-3940; www.visitaruba.com/arubaboardsailing) is a friendly yet feisty operator right on the beach at Fishermen's Huts, a prime bit of windsurfing water just south of Malmok Beach. Rentals start at US$55 per day, and there are a variety of lessons available.

Tours

Scores of companies offer day trips on sailboats and yachts. Many are pegged to the sunset. Other outfits organize pub crawls aboard colorfully decorated school buses. These adventures invariably end up at the ubiquitous Carlos & Charlies (p734) and feature much organized levity.

De Palm Tours (☎ 297-582-4400; www.depalm.com) has a near lock on organized tours of Aruba. Each day its dozens of buses crisscross the island taking vacationers on a dizzying variety of trips. Options range from a basic three-hour sightseeing tour (US$29) to an eight-hour 4WD odyssey (US$78) that may seem like a forced march before it is over. Many tours include an endless buffet at De Palm's private beach. Prices include one child under 12 for each adult, and there is a De Palm booking desk in almost every hotel.

Popular with kids and adults alike, the **Atlantis Submarine** (☎ 297-588-6881; www.atlantisadventures.com; adult/child US$84/34) is the local edition of this attraction found at islands through the Caribbean and Hawaii. In an hour-long tour, you submerge over 98ft (30m) and see various aquatic delights.

Festivals & Events

Every Tuesday night, the **Bon Bini Festival** (admission US$3; 🕑 6:30-8:30pm) is staged at Fort Zoutman by a local tourism association. The event attracts some top folkloric talent from around the island, and local foods and handicrafts are sold.

Sleeping

Accommodations on Aruba are ideally suited to the sort of mass-market tourism the island targets. The two main clusters of resorts – the descriptively named Low-Rise Resorts and High-Rise Resorts – are all fairly large three- and four-star properties. This is not the island for little boutique inns or the kinds of luxury properties that attract fawning articles in glossy magazines.

For the beachside resorts, troll through online booking services, as huge deals are legion and no one pays rack rates, although 20% tax and service charges are common. With various deals – particularly in low season – the difference in price between midrange and top-end places can be minute. Avoid the high-rise Holiday Inn Sunspree Resort and the Aruba Grand Beach Resort until they complete their renovations.

BUDGET

Lower-priced places on Aruba tend to be inland away from the beaches, although the drive/walk can be fairly short. Most have a certain utilitarian charm and are good choices for divers or others planning all-day activities where the joys of a beachfront resort would not be appreciated.

Coconut Inn (☎ 297-586-6288, 1-866-978-4952; www.coconutinn.com; Noord 31; r US$55-95; P ✖ 💻 🏊) Near the collection of restaurants in Noord, just inland from the High-Rise Resorts, the Coconut has a few of the eponymous trees in its simple grounds. Rooms are large and well equipped with cable TVs and other niceties.

Sunset Beach Studios (☎ 297-586-3940, 1-800-813-6540; www.aruba-sunsetblvds.com; Lloyd G Smith Blvd 486; r US$70-115; P ✖ 💻 🏊) Close to

Malmok Beach, this friendly place is popular with windsurfers. The large rooms have kitchenettes and cable TV. The pretty grounds include a Jacuzzi. Larger villas are also available.

Arubiana Inn (☎ 297-587-7700; www.arubianainn .com; Bubali 74; r US$55-85; **P** 🍴 🖵 🕹) About a 15-minute walk east from Eagle Beach, the fairly simple Arubiana has 16 basic but sizable rooms, with kitchenettes and cable TV. The pool area is shaded and attractive.

MIDRANGE

The bulk of Aruba's accommodations are midrange in price. For this you get a room on the beach with usual hotel amenities, like cable TV. Condo-type units can be the best value, as they come with fully equipped kitchens that allow you to prepare your own meals.

Bucuti Beach Resort (☎ 297-583-1100; www.bucuti .com; Lloyd G Smith Blvd 55B; r US$150-300; **P** 🍴 🖵 🕹) One of the best choices among the Manchebo Beach low-rise brigade, the immaculate and adult-oriented 63-room Bucuti has a vaguely Spanish feel. Guest rooms are large, with wi-fi, kitchenettes and deep balconies, many with ocean views. The new Tara wing is quite luxurious. There is a café in a replica pirate ship – perfect for an aye-ce cream.

Costa Linda Beach Resort (☎ 297-583-8000; www .costalinda-aruba.com; JE Irausquin Blvd 59; r US$150-350; **P** 🍴 🖵 🕹) There's nothing flashy about the low-rise Costa Linda, an older timeshare property. But the rooms are very large, have kitchens and balconies, and overlook a huge pool. Its frontage on Manchebo Beach is sweeping. It also has an Aveda Spa.

AUTHOR'S CHOICE

Amsterdam Manor Beach Resort (☎ 297-587-1492; www.amsterdammanor.com; JE Irausquin Blvd 252; r US$130-200; **P** 🍴 🖵 🕹) At the quiet north end of beautiful Eagle Beach, this 71-unit resort mimics a Dutch village and pulls it off. Rooms and buildings come in a variety of shapes and sizes – all laid out in an intriguing manner. Some rooms have sizable balconies or terraces with beach umbrellas and views. The kitchenettes in each unit are quite cheery, and there is a good free Internet area. It's all pretty low-key, but that's the charm.

Divi Aruba All Inclusive (☎ 297-525-5200; www .diviaruba.com; JE Irausquin Blvd 45; d incl drinks & meals US$225-400; **P** 🍴 🖵 🕹) The ever-expanding Divi empire on Aruba has two low-rise all-inclusive properties: this one and the Tamarijn (below). The Divi Aruba is an older property with mature palm trees that give it a relaxed Polynesian feel. There is a large section of units in one-story blocks euphemistically called 'casitas' that have a retro concrete-block charm. These actually have good ocean frontage. Like many all-inclusive resorts, the endless piles of food emphasize quantity over quality, and many guests start swilling the free drinks when most people would be thinking about a second cup of coffee. Still, the beachfront bar is delightful.

Tamarijn Aruba All Inclusive (☎ 297-525-5200; www.tamarijnaruba.com; JE Irausquin Blvd 41; d incl drinks & meals US$300-600; **P** 🍴 🖵 🕹) Guests can enjoy the facilities of both this resort and the Divi Aruba (above). The units are fairly modern and the property received a major revamp in 2004. Some beachfront rooms are a mere 32yd (30m) from the surf. Its pools are better than the Divi Aruba.

La Cabana All Suite Beach Resort (☎ 297-587-9000, 1-800-835-7193; www.lacabana.com/resort; Sasakiweg; r US$140-350; **P** 🍴 🖵 🕹) The Graf Zeppelin of Aruba's Low-Rise Resorts, La Cabana has over 600 rooms in huge blocks. Kitchenettes and balconies are standard, and many have ocean views. There are extensive facilities, including three pools, but there is no real design panache here; this is group city.

TOP END

Most of the High-Rise Resorts fit into the top-end category. These are large complexes that have oodles of restaurants, bars and facilities. In high season their hundreds of rooms are filled and they are anything but secluded retreats. Note that rooms at this level may not have any kitchen facilities at all. Call room service.

Radisson Aruba Resort (☎ 297-586-6555; www .radisson.com/aruba; JE Irausquin Blvd 81; r US$230-500; **P** 🍴 🍴 🖵 🕹) This 358-unit high-rise should win an award for its renovation. The well-run older property now boasts lush tropical grounds highlighted by two fine pools. The frontage on Palm Beach is spacious. The attractive rooms have a classic tropical decor, high-speed Internet access, and balconies or patios. This is the pick of the high-rises.

Hyatt Regency Aruba Resort (☎ 297-586-1234; www.aruba.hyatt.com; JE Irausquin Blvd 85; r US$160-550; (P ✕ ✕ 🖳 🏊) The public spaces at this 360-unit high-rise resort have a lavish and elegant Moorish look. The lush grounds feature waterfalls, and there's a great bar on a pier as well as one by the shuffleboard courts. Rooms are large with decent balconies, but are otherwise fairly standard. There's a good kids' club.

Aruba Marriott Resort (☎ 297-586-9000; www .marriottaruba.com; Lloyd G Smith Blvd 101; r US$150-400; (P ✕ ✕ 🖳 🏊) Anchoring the north end of high-rise land, the Marriott is part of an expanding empire that includes several time-share complexes (if you get bored on the beach, staff will gladly treat you to a sales pitch). The 413 rooms in the imposing U-shaped main building have large balconies and high-speed Internet access. However, don't look for kitchenettes. The pool area is OK. It also has an Aveda Spa.

Wyndham Aruba Resort (☎ 297-586-4466; www .wyndham.com; JE Irausquin Blvd 77; r US$180-430; (P ✕ ✕ 🖳 🏊) There's a good pool on narrow grounds at this 481-room high-rise, which has a 1970s feel. Rooms are pretty standard, but most have decent views from the balconies. The hotel spa is one of the best on Aruba.

Renaissance Aruba Resort (☎ 297-583-6000; www .renaissancearuba.com; Lloyd G Smith Blvd 82; r US$150-400; (P ✕ ✕ 🖳 🏊) The Renaissance is in Oranjestad and is a bifurcated resort: a large complex with 119 rooms, a casino and shopping mall in the heart of town, and a lush tropical complex out by the water. The two are linked by little shuttle boats that leave from a watery atrium in the city complex and both are linked by boat to a third facility: a small island offshore with a beach. The comfortable rooms span the gamut, but be sure to avoid the gloomy ones overlooking the indoor atrium.

Eating

Aruba has the best line-up of restaurants on the ABCs. Outside of the resorts there are numerous restaurants catering to locals, as well as those aimed for visitors. The **Aruba Gastronomic Association** (www.arubadining.com) has several meal plans that offer visitors savings at some of the island's better restaurants.

There are good places in town and in a loose cluster east of the high-rises.

BUDGET

Snack trucks are an island institution. Look for these spotless trucks in the parking lots near the Yacht Basin serving up a range of ultra-fresh food from sunset well into the wee hours. Locals debate who sells the best conch sandwich, but you'll likely enjoy any variation you encounter. Recommended dishes include anything with curry and the sinfully tender ribs. Most of the dishes are under US$5.

Linda's Pancakes & Pizzas (☎ 297-586-3378; Palm Beach 6D; meals Afl7-12; ☺ lunch & dinner Tue-Sun) In a little strip mall just east of the high-rises, Linda's has a vast array of sweet and savory pancakes popular with locals and travelers (especially Dutch ones) alike. Pizza and sandwiches are also good.

MIDRANGE

Many of the drinking options (p734) also have good modestly priced menus.

Rhumba Bar & Grill (☎ 297-588-7900; Havenstraat 4; mains US$6-25; ☺ lunch & dinner Mon-Sat) This open-air restaurant is both stylish and simple, with an attractive vibe that goes with the good food. Coconut shrimp is popular, as are the lunchtime salads. Outdoor tables are ideal for viewing local action.

Ristorante Sole Mare (☎ 297-586-0077; Palm Beach 23; mains US$18-25; ☺ dinner; ✕) Always busy; be sure to book ahead for a table at Sole Mare, a good Italian seafood place east of the high-rises. Popular dishes include *spaghetti alle vongole* and the live lobster (ask for extra garlic). Service is cheery, and there's a short list of Italian wines.

Marandi (☎ 297-582-0157; Lloyd G Smith Blvd 1; mains US$20; ☺ dinner Tue-Sun) A great place to watch the sunsets over a drink and it's not in a hotel! On its own beach on the south side of Oranjestad, open-air Marandi is a classic Caribbean eatery that actually delivers something more than a sandy cliché. The changing lunch and dinner menu is inventive and has an island vibe.

Bingo (☎ 297-586-2818; Palm Beach 6D; meals Afl12-28; ☺ dinner; ✕) Near Linda's, this is a fun local café, with a comforting menu of burgers, salads and steaks. Tables inside and out are good for meeting folks, and the bar stays open until 2am.

TOP END

Gasparito Restaurant (☎ 297-586-7044; Gasparito 3; mains US$17-30; ☺ dinner; ✗ ✗) One of the best places on the island, Gasparito has fine dining inside a classic old country house or outside on the candlelit patio. Many of the recipes are old Aruban, such as the tasty Keshi Yena – Dutch cheese filled with spiced fish and chicken. There's a gallery with fine works of local art.

Driftwood (☎ 297-583-2515; Klipstraat 12; mains US$18-32; ☺ dinner Wed-Mon; ✗) A supper club right out of the 1960s, the fisherman owner, his pals and employees hang out at the bar shooting the sea bass while loads of happy diners chow down on the freshest seafood in town.

Amazonia (☎ 297-586-4444; JE Irausquin Blvd 374; meals from US$27; ☺ dinner; ✗) Meat lovers dining at Amazonia will think they have died and gone to heaven – an outcome made more likely since they can gorge themselves on 15 kinds of meat served in unlimited quantities. Roving servers bring out a steady stream of skewers of grilled meats (the garlic tenderloin and parmesan pork are standouts). It's up to you to say 'stop!' The salad bar is surprisingly good.

Drinking

Many bars on Aruba serve a full menu of burgers, nachos and the like. Others feature live music on sporadic schedules.

Choose-A-Name (☎ 297-588-6200; Havenstraat 6; ☺ 5pm-late Wed-Sat) Popular with locals, this open-air, 2nd-floor joint avoids the cruise-ship mobs. Friday happy hours with all-you-can-drink specials for US$10 are wildly popular. This is the place to hear the local gossip. There's occasional live music.

Cafe Chaos (☎ 297-588-5547; Lloyd G Smith Blvd 60; ☺ 7pm-2am Sun-Fri, 7pm-4am Sat) The place to go if you don't want an umbrella in your drink. Sinatra is often crooning from the jukebox at this smallish place popular with local professionals. Saturday and some other nights feature live jazz, blues or rock.

Iguana Joes (☎ 297-583-9373; upper level, Royal Plaza Mall, Lloyd G Smith Blvd; ☺ 11am-midnight) Get liquored up at this open-air bar and watch your cruise ship leave port without you. High above the mobs, you can watch Oranjestad action while quaffing decent drinks.

Jimmy's Place Aruba (☎ 297-582-2550; Kruisweg 15; ☺ 4pm-2am Sun-Thu, 4pm-4am Fri & Sat) A friendly and low-key bar popular with gay and lesbian visitors. Watch for live music and themed dance parties.

Carlos & Charlies (☎ 297-582-0355; Weststraat 3A; ☺ 11am-1am Sun-Thu, 11am-3am Fri & Sat; ✗) Thanks to enormous T-shirt sales, this black hole for cruise-ship passengers claims to be 'world famous.' The menu features drinks 'by the yard,' a gimmick that gets the easily entertained chuckling – and leaves them sober thanks to glasses barely 4.5in (11cm) in diameter.

Entertainment

CASINOS

Almost every high-rise resort has a casino, many of which are quite small. Slot machines are by far the most common game, and facilities at even the flashiest places are not comparable to anything in Las Vegas. Slot machines are typically open 10am to 4am, tables 6pm to 4am.

Stellaris Casino (☎ 297-586-9000; Aruba Marriott Beach Resort, Lloyd G Smith Blvd; ✗) One of the largest casinos, always busy and a bit flashy.

Alhambra Casino (☎ 297-583-5000; Alhambra Bazaar; ✗) Penny slots attract the punters to this bustling place, which has live magic and comedy shows (US$28) many nights.

Crystal Casino (☎ 297-583-6000; Renaissance Aruba Beach Resort, Lloyd G Smith Blvd; ✗) Closest to the cruise-ship port, the Crystal is upstairs and is medium-sized.

Royal Cabana Casino (☎ 297-587-9000; La Cabana All-Suite Beach Resort, Sasakiweg; ✗) Large and unattractive, this heavily promoted place is the Wal-Mart of casinos.

CLUBS

La Fiesta (☎ 297-583-5874; Havenstraat 4; ☺ 9pm-2am Sun-Thu, 9pm-4am Fri & Sat) You'll see this 2nd-floor, open-air place, you'll hear the seductive mix of salsa, reggae, disco and more, but you'll be stumped trying to find the door. That's because this huge place spans two buildings via a bridge (with some very comfy wicker chairs for chilling) and the entrance is in the quiet building. Big with locals and tourists alike.

Shopping

The words 'duty-free' inspire a mad consumer lust in many and Aruba profits heavily from shopping-crazed visitors who throng the shops of Oranjestad and the

BEACHES

Aruba has the best beaches of the ABCs; most are along the south and west coast. Here are some you won't want to miss, going counterclockwise from the north.

Arashi Beach Near the island's northwest tip is a favorite with locals and popular with families. There is good body surfing, some shade and just a few rocks right offshore.

Malmok Beach Shallow waters extending far out from shore make this a popular spot for windsurfers. Nearby are some of the most expensive homes on the island.

Palm Beach Classic white-sand beauty, but only for those who enjoy meeting lots of people as it fronts the array of High-Rise Resorts.

Eagle Beach Fronting a stretch of the Low-Rise Resorts just northwest of Oranjestad, Eagle is a long stretch of white sand that's much less crowded at the north end, away from the development. The best all-around choice for everyone, from singles to couples to families with kids.

Manchebo Beach Just south of Eagle, this large beach reaches out to a point. Popular with topless sunbathers.

Baby Beach Nice curve of sand in the uncrowded south. The waters are calm. Nearby Coco's Beach is almost as nice, except for the view of the refinery.

Boca Grandi Reached by a rough road, this small cove is often deserted but for a few windsurfers. As is typical of windward beaches, conditions here are often hazardous, albeit dramatic.

Andicuri Beach A hidden gem on the isolated east coast, this black-pebble beach is often the scene of photo shoots. Near the Natural Bridge, the beach is reached by a road that demands 4WD. Take care as the beach can be hazardous, with some strong rips.

---

resorts. But 'duty-free' does not necessarily mean 'bargain,' and if you really want to save money, check prices at home because those on Aruba are often similar. Numerous shopping malls cluster around Lloyd G Smith Blvd and the cruise-ship port. Most international luxury brands are amply represented. Bargaining is not encouraged.

Getting There & Around
BUS

The **Main Bus Depot** (Lloyd G Smith Blvd) is right in the center of town. **Arubus** (☎ 297-588-0616) bus Nos 10, 10A and 10B serve the hotel areas from Oranjestad. Buses run every 15 to 30 minutes from 6am to 11:30pm, and cost US$1.15/2 one way/round-trip. Bus Nos 1, 2, 2A and 8 link Oranjestad to the airport every 30 to 60 minutes.

Buses do not go to the rugged parts of the island to the north, east or south, or into Arikok National Wildlife Park.

CAR

You'll know the tourists not only by the V-registrations of their rental cars but also by their use of turn signals. All the major car-rental companies have offices at the airport. It's worth comparing prices with local outfits, such as **Economy Car Rental** (☎ 297-583-0200; www.economyaruba.com) and **Optima Rent-A-Car** (☎ 297-582-4828; www.optimarentacar.com).

TAXI

Taxis are easy to come by at hotels and resorts. Fares are set for fixed distances. From the airport to the High-Rise Resorts costs US$20, for example. Extra passengers cost US$2, and you can charter a taxi for touring for US$40 per hour. **Best Taxi** (☎ 297-588-3232) is one of several companies.

AROUND ARUBA
Northeast Coast

Near Arashi Beach is a road leading to the **California Lighthouse**, on the island's northern tip. This tall sentinel is named for an old shipwreck named *California*, which is *not* the ship of the same name that stood by ineffectually while the *Titanic* sank (despite much local lore to the contrary). The views over the flat land extend in all directions, and when it's especially clear you can see all the way to Oranjestad. The surf is always pounding and dunes extend far inland. If the views are not enough to excite you, there's a nearby office where you can enjoy a spiel for a timeshare. The unobstructed vistas may not last forever.

On the opposite side of Aruba from the high-rises, **Chapel of Alto Vista** is a remote 1950s church built on the site of one dating to 1750. The road to salvation here is lined with small crosses, starting in temptation at the Alto Vista Rum Shop, east of Noord.

RUM SHOPS

Throughout Aruba's hinterlands you will see rum shops. These island institutions are part bar, part café and part social center. Here's where you'll meet anyone from gardeners to bankers. Although there are dozens and they come in all sizes, it's not hard to identify them as they invariably say 'Rum Shop' somewhere on the sign. The rum itself is often locally produced.

The rules are simple: you stand, drink rum – or beer – have a snack and unburden yourself to whoever is nearby. On Friday after work, crowds spill out into the streets. A good place to sample this culture is **Baby Store** (☎ 297-585-0839; ⓨ 6:30am-8:30pm), which is on the main road 2 miles (3km) north of Santa Cruz near the Piedra Plat Church. Beers cost Afl3 and a *frekedel* (a Dutch-derived meatball made with plantain) is Afl2.

Further south along the northeast coast are two popular natural attractions. **Natural Bridge** is one of several on Aruba, but this one comes with a decent (and well-signed!) road and a gift shop. Wave action hollowed out a limestone cave on the sea cliffs that later collapsed, leaving the 'bridge.' Mobs descend when cruise ships are in port, but other times it's a moody and windswept spot.

A detour back inland takes you to the **Natural Pool**, a depression behind a limestone ridge that often fills with sea water thanks to wave action. Given the rough swimming conditions on this side of Aruba, this is a good spot for a dip. Again, your enjoyment may depend on the number of day-trippers with the same goal. The road out here passes by **Ayo Rock**, a smooth-sided geologic wonder popular with rock climbers. It also has some ancient drawings.

If you get off on rocks, you should also visit **Casibari Rock**, about 0.9 miles (1.5km) west of Ayo Rock. Steps lead to the top where there are good views across the island.

Arikok National Wildlife Park

Arikok National Wildlife Park comprises 20% of the island. It's arid, rugged and can easily occupy a full day of exploring. The **park entrance hut** (admission free; ⓨ office 7am-5pm, park 24hr) has useful maps and other information. To get here, follow the marked roads east from the busy *cunucu* town of Santa Cruz.

Two gardens inside the park entrance are worth visiting. **Cunucu Arikok** and **Shon Shoco** have short trails with signs and labels describing the many native plants. More than 70% of the types of plants here are used in traditional medicine.

Roads are a test for typical rental cars, but a simple circuit allowing you to see the scruffy land and remnants of old gold mines built long ago by Europeans and slaves is possible. A 4WD vehicle will let you enjoy tracks off the main circuit that include sand dunes, rocky coves, caves and remote hiking trails. Watch out for the many iguanas as you drive. Numerous hiking trails lead across the hilly terrain. Bring water and ask for recommendations at the entrance hut.

The principal road to the coast is 3.7 miles (6km) long and, although slow going, is doable in your budget Toyota rental. Look for the park's three main types of trees: the iconic and bizarrely twisted divi-divi; the Kwihi, with its tasty sweet-sour long yellow beans; and the Hubada, which has sharp, tough thorns. Spiky aloe plants abound – see how many of the 70 varieties of cactus you can find.

Near the coast you will see a small creek, which is the only natural supply of water on Aruba. It flows into a large mangrove by the ocean. Here you can also see vast **sand dunes**. At **Boca Prins** on the coast there is a dramatic and dangerous beach in a narrow cove that forms explosive surf. Nearby, **Boca Prins Cafe** (☎ 297-584-5455; burgers US$7; ⓨ 10am-6pm) is a cheery place that is totally open to the trade winds. There is no other development here.

For safer swimming, a really bad road leads north to **Dos Playa**, which as the name implies is two beaches. Otherwise, from Boca Prins you can head south along the coast and end up in San Nicolas.

San Nicolas

A small town near the island's ill-placed **oil refinery**, San Nicolas preserves Aruba's former rough-and-ready character long since scrubbed away from Oranjestad. Prostitution is legal here and a string of bars in the 'Red Zone' grind into action nightly. Most of the women are from Colombia. It's all tightly regulated and the streets are pretty safe.

Charlie's Bar (☎ 297-584-5086; Zeppenfeldstraat 56; meals US$6-20; ⏰ 10am-10pm) is one of those classic old joints that has become an attraction in and of itself. There's a mix of crusty characters and partying tourists enjoying cheap beers and trading yarns. The walls are covered in flotsam, jetsam and junk. The Creole food is good and spicy.

South of San Nicolas and the oil refinery are dramatic vistas and cliffs.

BONAIRE

Diving, diving, diving (and maybe some snorkeling). Bonaire's worldwide appeal is its amazing reef-lined coast, all of which is a national park. But while no pilgrim will be disappointed underwater, Bonaire also has much to offer above the surface. Although the beaches are mostly slivers of rocky sand, several take on a pink hue from ground coral washed ashore. Also in the pink are the flamingos found throughout the salt flats and mangroves of the south.

Bonaire has a real community feel: your innkeeper may be your divemaster by day or your waiter at a friend's restaurant at night.

Much of the infrastructure on the island supports diving: where else can you find a hotel with a drive-through air-tank refilling station? However, there are some good restaurants, and the main town of Kralendijk has a modest but enjoyable nightlife. If you're not a diver – or an avid reader – you may not find much to fill a week on Bonaire, but a few days will pass delightfully. And just in case you forget why most people come, check out the license plate of the car in front of you, it says: 'Diver's Paradise.'

History

The Arawak Indians lived on Bonaire for thousands of years before Spain laid claim

---

BONAIRE: NOT FRENCH AT ALL

Contrary to popular myth, Bonaire does not get its name from some variation of French for 'good air' (although the air is nice), rather it derives from an Arawak Indian word that means 'low country.'

---

in 1499. A mere 20 years later there were none left as the Spanish sent all the natives to work in mines elsewhere in the empire. The only reminder that the Arawaks once lived on Bonaire are a few inscriptions in remote caves. No one knows what they mean.

The depopulated Bonaire stayed pretty quiet until 1634, when the Dutch took control. Soon the Dutch looked to the flat land in the south and saw a future in salt production. Thousands of slaves were imported to work in horrific conditions. You can see a few surviving huts at the south end of the island (p744). When slavery was abolished in the 19th century, the salt factories closed. The population, a mix of ex-slaves, Dutch and people from South America, lived pretty simple lives until after WWII, when the reopening of the salt ponds (this time with machines doing the hard work) coupled with the postwar booms in tourism and diving gave a real boost to the economy.

Meanwhile relations with Curaçao, capital of the Netherlands Antilles, slowly turned frosty. Locals felt ignored by their wealthier neighbor. In 2005, Bonaire, along with Saba, decided it would split from the Netherlands Antilles (and Curaçao) and return to being governed directly by the Hague.

Environmental Issues

Bonaire has few major environmental concerns. Possibly the most pressing is the ongoing shortage of freshwater, which mostly comes from desalinization plants. Protections of the marine park are strict and any environmental damage from the salt ponds is limited mostly to the ponds themselves. The beach-ringed arid island of Klein Bonaire off Kralendijk is uninhabited and protected by the government.

Orientation

Bonaire is the second largest of the ABCs at 110 sq miles (285 sq km). The main town of Kralendijk is just north of the airport. Major roads loop north midway up the island to Rincon and south past Lac Bay, the southern tip and the salt pans. Rough secondary roads circle the far north and Washington-Slagbaai National Park and reach parts of the remote east coast. You can drive the main roads in half a day.

Almost all hotels and other businesses are in or near Kralendijk.

ARUBA, BONAIRE
& CURAÇAO

BONAIRE

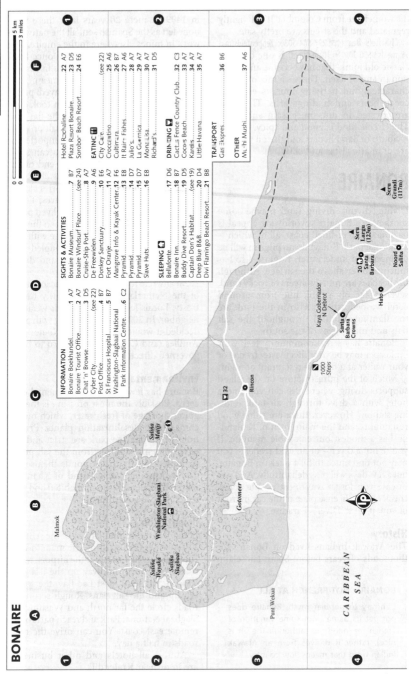

0   5 km
0   3 miles

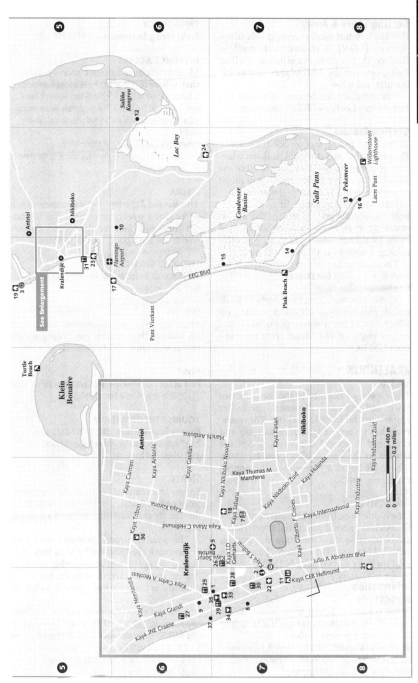

Getting There & Away

Bonaire's whimsically named Flamingo Airport (BON) is immediately south of Kralendijk. It's small but efficient. Airlines flying between the ABC islands change frequently; see p756.

Car ferry service to/from Curaçao is a Davy Jones Locker of failed operators.

Getting Around

There is no public bus service on Bonaire. However, dive operators will haul you wherever you need to go. You can see all of the island in two days of driving, so you might consider renting a car for just that period.

International car-rental firms at the airport include **Budget** (599-717-4700). **AB Carrental** (☎ 599-717-8980; www.abcarrental.com) is the main local firm. Many places to stay offer packages with a car thrown in cheap.

There are a couple of gas stations in Kralendijk, including **Gas Ekspres** (599-717-7171; Kaya Tribon; 7am-10pm).

Taxis from the airport to hotels in Kralendijk cost US$7 to US$15 depending on which end of town you're going to. A taxi to any place on the island costs no more than US$20.

KRALENDIJK

pop 3000

The capital of Bonaire is also its principal town, and you can walk around the center and waterfront in under an hour. The waterfront has several delightful restaurants and bars, and is good for a stroll. Shops are limited to the basics, plus a few for those who can't go on a trip without buying an expensive watch.

Orientation

One block back from the waterfront, Kaya Grandi is the main commercial street. Hotels can be found south of the cruise-ship port on Julio A Abraham Blvd and north past the sea inlet on Kaya Gobernador N Debrot.

Information

BOOKSTORES

Bring reading material from home, as it's easier to spot a manta ray off the reef than it is to find a decent book.

Bonaire Boekhandel (☎ 599-717-8499; Kaya Grandi 50; 8am-noon & 2-6pm Mon-Sat) A few local titles, international magazines and stationery.

EMERGENCY

Scuba Diving Emergencies (☎ 599-717-8187)

INTERNET ACCESS

Most hotels have Internet access points.

Chat 'n' Browse (☎ 599-717-2281; Kaya Gobernador N Debrot 79; per hr US$8; 9am-8pm Mon-Fri, 9am-6pm Sat & Sun) Top choice. The gregarious owner stocks Cuban cigars, ice cream and a good selection of Bonaire guidebooks.

Cyber City (Kaya Grandi; per 15min NAf5; 9am-11pm) Located in the town center, in the Hotel Rochaline (opposite).

MEDIA

The **Bonaire Reporter** (www.bonairereporter.com) is a free glossy weekly newspaper that is a fascinating read. *Bonaire Affair* and *Bonaire Nights* are both good tourist freebies.

MEDICAL SERVICES

St Franciscus Hospital (☎ 599-717-8900; Kaya Soeur Bartola 2; 24hr)

MONEY

Prices are given in local currency more often on Bonaire than Aruba, but US dollars are just as welcome. ATMs abound.

POST

Post office (☎ 599-717-8508; Kaya Simon Bolivar 11; 7:30am-noon & 1:30-5pm Mon-Fri)

TOURIST INFORMATION

Bonaire Tourist Office (☎ 599-717-8322; Kaya Grandi 2; 9am-5pm Mon-Fri) Answers questions and has a good selection of brochures.

Sights

Follow the cannons south along the waterfront to **Fort Oranje**, a small bastion built by the Dutch and modified often through the years.

The small one-room **museum** (admission free; 8am-noon & 1:30-4:30pm Mon-Fri) has a good display of vintage photos among other displays. Behind an unmarked door to the left of the museum are the cleanest public toilets in town.

A bit out from the town center, the **Bonaire Museum** (☎ 599-717-8898; Kaya J Ree 7; adult/child NAf1.50/1; 8am-noon & 2-5pm Mon-Fri) is in an 1885 house filled with folklore displays. Look for the detailed paintings of local mythology by Winifred Dania.

Activities

For details on kayaking and windsurfing on Lac Bay, see p744.

CYCLING

Roads to the south end of the island with its windswept flat expanses and Lac Bay are ideal for cycling.

De Freewielen (☎ 599-717-8545; Kaya Grandi 61; ☼ 8:30am-5:30pm Mon-Fri, 8:30am-12:30pm Sat) is a friendly outfit run by a Dutch cyclist, with rentals per day from NAf12.50.

DIVING & SNORKELING

For details of the Bonaire Marine Park, see the boxed text, p743.

Tours

Karel's (☎ 599-790-8330) This waterfront bar (p742) runs daily boats (US$10 to US$18 per person) to Turtle Beach on Klein Bonaire. It also has a pirate-themed sunset cruise (US$40), with an open bar guaranteed to knock you off your peg leg.

Mushi Mushi (☎ 599-790-5399; Bonaire Nautico Pier) Runs sailing, snorkeling and sunset trips, with cruises from US$35. You can also get a shuttle boat (adult/child US$14/7) to the Klein Bonaire beaches from the same location.

Sleeping

Bonaire has an interesting and varied selection of places to stay. Unlike other Caribbean islands it doesn't have much in the way of large resorts, rather the places tend to be smaller and more personal. Ask about a pool and managers usually point to the ocean; at many you can go diving right off the back deck. Prices are lower on average than the other ABCs. Taxes and service charges can add 20% to rates.

BUDGET

Hotel Rochaline (☎ 599-717-8286; www.mainstreet bonaire.com; Kaya Grandi; r US$45-80; ✄ 🖳 🐾) Right in the center of town, the hotel runs the popular City Cafe (p742). Rooms come in two varieties: budget (Spartan) and economy (basic but with views). It's all clean and the vibe is relaxed and friendly.

Bonaire Inn (☎ 599-717-3948; www.bonaireinn .com; Plasa Fraternan da Tilburg 2; d from US$35; ✄) Just east of the town center, this charming inn is in a restored 1913 friar's house. The 17 rooms are very basic, but who can argue at these rates. The plaza outside is leafy.

MIDRANGE & TOP END

Wide variations in rooms mean that you have numerous choices at most places to match your budget.

Buddy Dive Resort (☎ 599-717-5080; www.buddy dive.com; Kaya Gobernador N Debrot 85; r US$125-130, apt US$165-330; ✄ 🖳 🐾) The reef is right off the deck and there's a drive-through air-tank refill station out front. Obviously this is a great place for divers, and the 70 apartments offer good respite from the deep. All apartments have kitchens and views. Request a view for your hotel room at no extra charge.

Captain Don's Habitat (☎ 599-717-8290; www.habit atbonaire.com; Kaya Gobernador N Debrot; units US$147-210; ✄ 🖳 🐾) The captain tries to promote a renegade image through his pirate flag bearing a skull impaled by a sword, but in reality this is really a rather posh resort. The 85 units on the spacious grounds range from large to very large and are very comfortable. Air tanks are available 24 hours a day.

Deep Blue B&B (☎ 599-717-8073; www.deepbluc view.com; Kaya Diamanta 50; d per 3 nights US$570-645; ✄ 🐾) On a hill just north of the town center in the Santa Barbara neighborhood, this spotless B&B has great views. Run by two delightful women, this is a very restful place, with whirlpools, a refrigerator full of drinks and no TVs.

Bellafonte (☎ 599-717-3333; www.bellafontebon aire.com; EEG Blvd 10; r US$95-180; ✄) A modern and very comfortable place south of town just past the airport, Bellafonte has 20 luxurious units in a vaguely Mediterranean building. Units vary in size, and feature balconies or terraces, kitchens and cable TV. There's a pier for divers.

Divi Flamingo Beach Resort (☎ 599-717-8285; www.diviresorts.com; Julio A Abraham Blvd 40; r US$120-200; ✄ 🖳 🐾) This hodge-podge of a resort has standard rooms in all shapes and sizes – some in largish blocks, others hutlike. The latter are better. There is a minute beach and a pier for divers. The diminutive casino is the one on Bonaire.

Plaza Resort Bonaire (☎ 599-717-2500; www .plazavillas.com; Julio A Abraham Blvd 80; units US$120-300; ✄ 🖳 🐾) This timeshare resort has 200 units on a large site between the edge of town and its center; in fact you can easily walk from one end to the other. You can choose between a range of large units, which all have kitchens, balconies or patios, and views of the lagoon or ocean. However, it all feels a bit generic; restaurants have hackneyed resort names, like Tipsy Seagull and Conch Corner.

Eating

The small population means that Bonaire hasn't appeared on the chain restaurant radar – yet. There are several good places to eat, all seasoned with varying degrees of eccentricity.

BUDGET

Julio's (cnr Kaya Grandi & Kaya LD Gerharts; meals NAf3-18; 8am-3am) Enjoy classic Bonaire fast food in the center of town. It's totally open-air, and the high-protein menu combines beef, ham, cheese and fish in a myriad of ways.

City Cafe (599-717-8286; Kaya Grandi 7; meals US$5-15; breakfast, lunch & dinner;) On the waterfront side of the Hotel Rochaline, this busy open-air place is good for a drink or a meal. The bar is open until 2am. Sit here long enough and you might just see everyone in town.

Cultimara (599-717-8278; Kaya LD Gerharts 13; 7:30am-7pm Mon-Sat, 8am-2pm Sun) The best supermarket, with a large selection.

MIDRANGE & TOP END

Mona Lisa (599-717-8718; Kaya Grandi 15; mains NAf30-40; dinner Mon-Sat) This local institution is a faithful version of a traditional Dutch brown café. There's a lively mix of locals and travelers, and an extensive beer selection. Excellent food from a changing menu is served from a kitchen that cooks with color and flair. Steaks and seafood are superb, and garlic abounds.

It Rains Fishes (599-717 8780; Kaya Jan NE Craane 24; mains NAf30-40; dinner Mon-Sat) Succulent fresh seafood is served in a relaxed setting at the quiet end of the waterfront. The garlic shrimp are so good, you'll book another table before you leave.

La Guernica (599-717-5022; Kaya Bonaire 4C; small dishes NAf8-14; dinner Thu-Tue) There's a real Spanish feel at this waterfront tapas place in an old home with wide verandas. Wash down the grilled shrimp with one of the many red wines on offer.

Richard's (599-717-5263; Julio A Abraham Blvd 60; mains NAf30-35; dinner Tue-Sun) The mood of casual elegance at the open-air tables on the water is set by the white tablecloths accented by blue napkins. The changing menu focuses on fresh fish; try the garlic shrimp.

Croccantino (599-717-5025; Kaya Grandi 48; mains US$20-25; dinner Tue-Sun;) Take a table outside on the plant-filled, engagingly lit veranda and enjoy fine Italian food. Inside it's cute as heck and the menu, which includes seven kinds of vegetarian pasta, is excellent.

AUTHOR'S CHOICE

Little Havana (599-786-0717; Kaya Bonaire 4; 5pm-2am Sun-Fri) A classic atmospheric bar in a historic whitewashed building. Walk through the open doors and you pass back many decades in time. Settle into a leather couch and order a mojito (rum cocktail with mint, sugar, seltzer and fresh lime juice) – if the boat bringing the ingredients from Curaçao hasn't been blown off course. Or sit at the rich wooden bar and enjoy a fine Cuban cigar. There's live jazz many nights.

Drinking

Several of the places listed under Eating are also good for a drink.

Coco's Beach (599-717-8434; Kaya Bonaire; 11am-midnight) Lots of tropical plants set the mood at this lively outdoor bar on the waterfront. On Saturday a steel-drum band plays at 7pm.

Karel's (599-790-8330; Waterfront; 10am-2am) Two bars set on a concrete pier over the water. Ponder people passing while you enjoy a US$2 beer during happy hour (5pm to 7pm).

NORTH OF KRALENDIJK

The road north along the coast is like a roller-coaster, but in good shape. There are great vistas of the rocky seashore and frequent pullouts for the marked dive sites. About 3 miles (5km) north of Kralendijk the road becomes one way, north, so you are committed at this point.

Rincon is a small town about 8.6 miles (14km) north of the capital. It's the oldest town on the island, and was built so as to be hidden from pirates prowling the shore. A very quiet place, most of the residents are descended from slaves. Homes have a classic Caribbean look and are painted in a myriad of pastels.

Washington-Slagbaai National Park

Covering the northwest portion of the island and comprising almost 20% of the land, Washington-Slagbaai National Park is a great place to explore. Roads are rough and all-but-impassable after a rain, but are well worth the effort. The terrain is mostly tropical desert, and there is a proliferation of cacti and birds. Look for flamingos in the lowlands and parrots perched on shrubs. Large bright green iguanas are just one of the many reptile species you might find. You'll also see lingering evidence of the aloe plantation and goat ranch that used to be here – don't run over any wild descendents of the latter.

From the excellent **information center** (☎ 599-717-8444; www.bonairenature.com/washingtonpark; adult/child US$10/2; ☒ 8am-5pm, last entry at 2:45pm) and museum at the entrance you can take one of two drives: a five-hour 20-mile (33km) route or a five-hour 14.8-mile (24km) route. Regular cars are discouraged but not banned. There are picnic, dive and swimming stops along the way.

The park entrance is at the end of a good 2.4-mile (4km) concrete road from Rincon. Along the way you'll pass the **Cactus Fence Country Club** (☎ 599-568-9613; ☒ from 11am Sun), which true to its name is surrounded by one of the living cactus fences common on Bonaire. There's no golf here, but there is good music, a barbecue and a friendly crowd.

EAST OF KRALENDIJK

The road from Kralendijk to Lac Bay is a highlight. Off the main road, a branch goes around the north side of the water. At first you drive through groves of cactus so thick that it's like driving through someone's crew cut. Close to the water there are dense mangroves and flocks of flamingos. It's a popular ride for cyclists.

Along this road, the **Mangrove Info & Kayak Center** (☎ 599-790-5353; www.mangrovecenter.com; ☒ Mon-Sat) has kayak tours (from US$25) and information about the protected Lac Bay mangroves. About 3.4 miles (5.5km) from the turn-off the road ends at Lac Cai, a sandy point with a small beach, snack stand,

---

DIVING IN BONAIRE

Bonaire's dive sites are strung along the west side of the island. The closeness of the reefs and the clarity of the waters make for unparalleled access for divers. You can reach more than half of the identified dive sites from shore (or your hotel!). The range of fish species is amazing, and diving goes on around the clock.

For all of its fame as a diving location, Bonaire doesn't slouch in the organization department. The Unesco World Heritage **Bonaire Marine Park** (☎ 599-717-8444; www.bmp.org) covers the entire coast of the island to a depth of 18ft (60m). There are almost 90 identified dive sites and they are numbered using a system adopted by all the dive operators on the island. Most maps show the sites and as you are driving along coastal roads you'll see painted yellow rocks identifying the sites. See the Diving & Snorkeling chapter for information on diving off Klein Bonaire, p54.

Conservation is taken seriously and all divers must purchase a tag (US$10) from any dive operator with the proceeds going to infrastructure maintenance. Additionally, first-timers to Bonaire must take a mandatory orientation dive with an operator. It goes without saying: don't touch or collect anything.

The park website is an excellent resource. Additionally, the widely distributed and free *Bonaire Dive Guide* has basic descriptions and a map of all the sites. One of the most famous is **1000 Steps** on the west coast. It's named not for the 72 steps from the road down to the water but the way the climb feels when you return. A myriad of coral here supports turtles, eels and many other fish.

A good guide to Bonaire's waters is *New Guide to the Bonaire Marine Park* by Tom van't Hof.

Every place to stay has a relationship with a dive operator; additionally Buddy Dive Resort (p741) and Captain Don's Habitat (p741) have their own large operations.

With so many sites accessible from land, snorkelers also find Bonaire a very rewarding destination. **Renee Snorkel Trips** (☎ 599-785-0771; www.infobonaire.com/reneesnorkeltrips) offers good-value tours by day and night (from US$20). Equipment and lessons are included

and literally mountains of huge pearly white and pink conch shells. On Sunday bands play and locals party.

Lac Bay itself is one of the world's premier windsurfing destinations. At the end of the main road on the south side, **Bonaire Windsurf Place** (☎ 599-717-2288; www.bonairewindsurf place.com; ☼ 10am-6pm) rents equipment (from US$35), gives lessons and has a good café. The view from the deck here is stunning, let alone the action on the windswept, shallow waters.

Nearby, an impenetrable green fence surrounds **Sorobon Beach Resort** (☎ 599-717-8080; www.sorobonbeachresort.com; chalets from US$155; Ⓟ ☒). This 28-room complex is for nudists and is set on one of the island's best beaches. Units are comfortable in a very modest way, and each comes with a kitchen. One thing is soon apparent: no matter what your age, nudists look like your parents.

South of Lac Bay, a good road follows the flat windward coast, which has pounding surf, and you'll see nary another human.

SOUTH OF KRALENDIJK

The south end of Bonaire is flat and arid, and you can see for many miles in all directions. Salt pans where ocean water evaporates to produce salt dominate the landscape. Metal windmills are used to transfer water out of the ponds. As evaporation progresses, the water takes on a vibrant pink color from tiny sea organisms. The color complements the flamingos, which live in a sanctuary and feed in the ponds.

Along the coast you will see the legacy of a vile chapter in Bonaire's past: tiny restored **slave huts**. Living conditions in these miniscule shelters are hard to imagine now, but they were home to hundreds of slaves working in the salt ponds through the 19th century. Three different-colored 33ft (10m) **pyramids** are another legacy of the Dutch colonial era. Colored flags matching one of the pyramids were flown to tell ships where they should drop anchor to load salt.

Just north of the slave huts, **Pink Beach** is a long sliver of sand that takes its color from pink coral washed ashore. It's pretty rough and you'll want a thick pad for sunbathing, but the swimming (not to mention the diving and snorkeling) is good.

On the south side of the airport runway, the nonprofit **Donkey Sanctuary** (☎ 599-560-7607; admission free; ☼ 10am-4pm Mon-Sat) is home to offspring of donkeys left to wander the island when slave-era salt production ceased. About 400 are still wild, others live here after they get sick, injured or, as the staff say, just get lonely. Even Republicans will find these donkeys cute as hell.

CURAÇAO

More than either of its neighbors, Curaçao feels like a real place. It doesn't suck up to tourism like Aruba or live off its idyllic beauty like Bonaire. It has numerous pluses and minuses, many connected to the urban fabric of the capital of Willemstad.

On the plus side, it has a rich history dating back to the 16th century. Willemstad is filled with fascinating old buildings and boasts some excellent museums. Remnants of plantations dot the countryside and some are now parks. The coast along the west side of the island has many beautiful little beaches, as well as some excellent dive sites.

On the minus side, Curaçao has a lot of economic activity beyond tourism, which means that Willemstad, apart from its historical core, has factories, many humdrum neighborhoods and at times bad traffic. With a few notable exceptions there are not as many good places to stay or eat as you'd expect.

Still, Curaçao is the most balanced of the islands. Here, you can combine urban pleasures with natural charms.

The website Curacao.com is an excellent resource for local information on culture, shops and more.

History

Like Aruba and Bonaire, Curaçao was home to the Arawak Indians until the Spanish laid claim in 1499. Origins of the island's name are lost with one story linking it to the name of an Arawak tribe, while another more improbably says that it derives from the Spanish *curación* (cure) in honor of several sailors who were cured of illness on the island.

Either way, the arrival of the Spanish proved the opposite of a cure for the locals, who were soon carted off to work elsewhere in the empire or killed. The Dutch West India Company arrived in 1634, and so did slavery, commerce and trade. Half the slaves destined for the Caribbean passed through the markets of Curaçao.

The end of slavery and colonialism sent Curaçao into a 19th-century economic decline. Subsistence aloe and orange farming provided a meager living for most. Oil refineries to process Venezuelan oil were built in the early 20th century and this fuelled the economy. Relative affluence and Dutch political stability have made Curaçao a regional center for commerce and banking. Tourism and a growing expat population provide additional income. Agreements reached in 2004 should allow Curaçao to cast off its role as capital of the Netherlands Antilles and become an independent entity within the Netherlands, just like its rich and envied neighbor Aruba.

Environmental Issues
One only has to glimpse the *Mad Max*–like array of blazing pipes and belching stacks to know that the number one environmental issue on Curaçao is air and water pollution from the oil refinery and other industry built on the inner harbor (Schottegat) of Willemstad. Given the importance of these installations to the local economy, efforts to control their negative effects are modest at best.

Like the other ABCs, water is in short supply and primarily comes from desalinization plants.

Orientation
Curaçao is the largest of the ABCs at 182 sq miles (471 sq km). Willemstad is home to almost two-thirds of the population and surrounds Schottegat, one of the world's finest deep-water ports. The coast on both sides of Willemstad is where most of the large resorts are found. The lower third of the island is arid, rugged and little visited. Half of the island is northwest of the capital. It's pretty, at times verdant and perfect for diving on the lee side. A good road loops around the area. At the northwest tip is the little town of Westpunt.

Getting There & Around
Curaçao's **Hato International Airport** (CUR; ☎ 599-9-839-3201) is getting some much-needed renovations. Airlines flying between the ABC islands change frequently; see p756.

See p751 for details on getting around the island from Willemstad.

WILLEMSTAD
pop 70,000
The capital of the Netherlands Antilles, Willemstad is both a big city and small town. Residents live in the hills surrounding Schottegat and much of the city is rather mundane. But this changes radically in the old town. Here colonial Dutch heritage collides with modern Curaçao for an energetic mix that has an almost cosmopolitan feel. Wandering the old town and its excellent museums can occupy a couple of days. The Queen Emma Bridge regularly swings open to let huge ships pass through the channel, a sight in itself, and these interruptions 'force' you to take one of the enjoyable water ferries.

Orientation
The old town of Curaçao is split by Sint Annabaai, which is really a channel to Schottegat. On the north side is Otrobanda, an old workers neighborhood, which still has shops popular with the masses and a mixture of beautifully restored buildings and areas rough around the edges. South of the water – and linked by the swinging Queen Emma Bridge – is Punda, the commercial center of town, and home to the best stores, offices and markets. North across the Queen Wilhelmina Bridge is the old port and warehouse neighborhood of Scharloo.

Arching over all is the 17ft tall (56m) Queen Juliana Bridge, which allows even the largest ships to pass underneath. (In case more bridges need to be built, the Netherlands may need to come up with more queens.)

Information
On Sunday when cruise ships are in port many places open that are normally closed for business.

BOOKSTORES
Bring books you really want to read from home. Finding good titles on Curaçao can be hit or miss.
Vandorp-Eddine (☎ 599-9-461-8133; Breedestraat; ☒ 8:30am-12:30pm & 2-6pm Mon-Fri, 8:30am-6pm Sat) Lots of international magazines, local guidebooks and a few bestsellers.

CURAÇAO

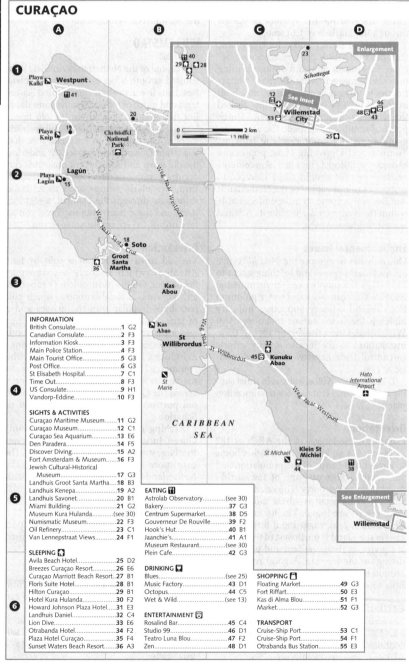

INFORMATION
British Consulate.........................1 G2
Canadian Consulate...................2 F3
Information Kiosk........................3 F3
Main Police Station....................4 F3
Main Tourist Office.....................5 G3
Post Office..................................6 G3
St Elisabeth Hospital..................7 C1
Time Out.....................................8 F3
US Consulate...............................9 H1
Vandorp-Eddine........................10 F3

SIGHTS & ACTIVITIES
Curaçao Maritime Museum.......11 G2
Curaçao Museum.......................12 C1
Curaçao Sea Aquarium..............13 E6
Den Paradera.............................14 F5
Discover Diving..........................15 A2
Fort Amsterdam & Museum.....16 F3
Jewish Cultural-Historical
    Museum.................................17 G3
Landhuis Groot Santa Martha...18 B3
Landhuis Kenepa.......................19 A2
Landhuis Savonet......................20 B1
Miami Building...........................21 G2
Museum Kura Hulanda........(see 30)
Numismatic Museum.................22 F3
Oil Refinery................................23 C1
Van Lennepstraat Views............24 F1

SLEEPING
Avila Beach Hotel.......................25 D2
Breezes Curaçao Resort.............26 E6
Curaçao Marriott Beach Resort...27 B1
Floris Suite Hotel.......................28 B1
Hilton Curaçao...........................29 B1
Hotel Kura Hulanda...................30 F2
Howard Johnson Plaza Hotel.....31 E3
Landhuis Daniel.........................32 C4
Lion Dive...................................33 E6
Otrabanda Hotel........................34 F2
Plaza Hotel Curaçao..................35 F4
Sunset Waters Beach Resort......36 A3

EATING
Astrolab Observatory.............(see 30)
Bakery.......................................37 G3
Centrum Supermarket...............38 D5
Gouverneur De Rouville............39 F2
Hook's Hut................................40 B1
Jaanchie's..................................41 A1
Museum Restaurant...............(see 30)
Plein Cafe..................................42 G3

DRINKING
Blues.....................................(see 25)
Music Factory............................43 D1
Octopus....................................44 C5
Wet & Wild...........................(see 13)

ENTERTAINMENT
Rosalind Bar..............................45 C4
Studio 99...................................46 D1
Teatro Luna Blou.......................47 F2
Zen...48 D1

SHOPPING
Floating Market.........................49 G3
Fort Riffart................................50 E3
Kas di Alma Blou.......................51 F1
Market.......................................52 G3

TRANSPORT
Cruise-Ship Port........................53 C1
Cruise-Ship Port........................54 F1
Otrabanda Bus Station..............55 E3

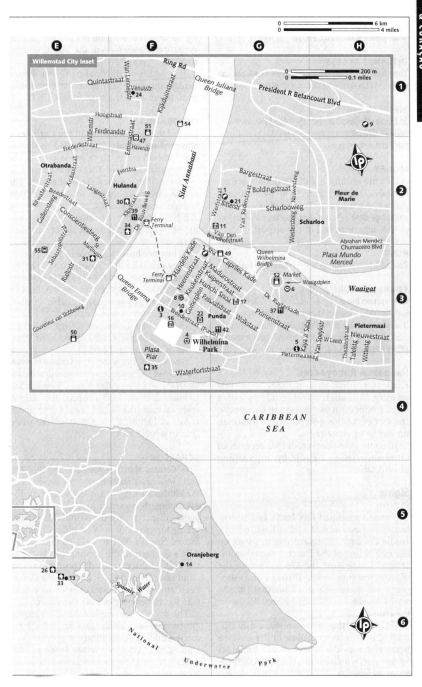

0 —————— 6 km
0 —————— 4 miles

Willemstad City Inset

0 —————— 200 m
0 —————— 0.1 miles

Quintastraat

Van Lenepstr
Venusstr
24

Ring Rd

Queen Juliana
Bridge

President R Betancourt Blvd

Kijkduinstraat

Hoogstraat

9

Willemstr
Ferdinandstr

51
47

Frederikstraat

Emmastraat
Havenstr

54

Otrabanda

Iserstra

Sint Annabaai

Bargestraat

Nieuwesteeg
Boldingstraat

Rif Waterstraat
Breedestraat
Ariadastraat
Langestraat

Hulanda

30

Werfstraat
1

Radestraat
Van

Scharlooweg

Westersteeg

**Fleur de
Marie**

Galleriestraat
Gasthuisstraat
Conscientiestraat

Klipstraat

39

Bitterstr
21

Scharloo

Sebastopolstra
St
Marinustr

Rialtostr
31

34

De Rouvilleweg

Ferry
Terminal

11
Van Den
Brandhofstraat

Queen
Wilhelmina
Bridge

Abrahan Mendez
Chumaceiro Blvd

*Plasa Mundo
Merced*

55

Handels Kade

2
49

Queen Emma
Bridge

Ferry
Terminal

Heerenstraat
Keukenstraat
Kuiperstraat

Madurostraat
Caprileskade

52 Market
6
Waaigatplein

De Ruyterkade

Waaigat

Gouverneur van Slobbeweg

50

8
10
3
16

Gomezplein
Hanchi Snoa
Prinsestraat

Breedestraat
(Punda)

22

Punda

17

Wolkstraat

Prinsenstraat

37

Pietermaai

Kaya Jr Salas

Van Speykstr
W Leestr
Nieuwestraat

42

Theaterstraat
Tafelstg
Wittestg

35

**Wilhelmina
Park**

4

5

*Plasa
Piar*

Waterfortstraat

Pietermaaiweg

*CARIBBEAN
SEA*

Oranjeberg
14

26
13
33

Spaanse Water

National

Underwater Park

EMERGENCY
Main police station (☎ 911; Wilhelminaplein; ⊙ 24hr)

INTERNET ACCESS
Time Out (☎ 599-9-524-5071; Keukenstraat 8; per 5min US$1; ⊙ 8am-6pm) Cute café on a small restful square.

MEDICAL SERVICES
St Elisabeth Hospital (☎ 599-9-462-5100; www .stelisabethhospital.com; Breedestraat 193; ⊙ 24hr) Large and well equipped

MONEY
ATMs are common and US dollars are accepted everywhere. Banks will change money during usual hours. There's also a **foreign-exchange desk** (⊙ 8am-7pm Mon-Sat, 8am-4pm Sun) in the departure hall of the airport.

POST
Post office (Waaigatplein 1; ⊙ 7:30am-5pm Mon-Fri)

TOURIST INFORMATION
Information kiosk (⊙ 8am-6pm Mon-Fri, 8am-5pm Sat) The Curaçao Tourism Board runs this kiosk by the Queen Emma Bridge on the Punda side. It has a wealth of information and is everything the unhelpful **main tourist office** (☎ 599-9-434-8200; Pietermaai 19) is not.

Dangers & Annoyances
Curaçao's urban mix includes some real poverty. Although street crime is not a huge problem, it is important to exercise the sort of caution you may have forgotten on Aruba or Bonaire.

In some of the darker, deeper recesses of Otrobanda, drugs are sold by thugs sitting at card tables.

Sights
PUNDA
The much modified **Fort Amsterdam** is now home to government and official offices. Inside the large courtyard you can soak up the rich colors of the Dutch colonial architecture dating from the 1760s. Parts of the old battlements weave through the complex, and there is a small **museum** (☎ 599-9-461-1139; admission US$3; ⊙ 9am-noon Mon-Fri) in the church.

Since 1651 the oldest continuously operating Jewish congregation in the western hemisphere is the Mikvé Israel Emanuel Synagogue, which houses the **Jewish Cultural-Historical Museum** (☎ 599-9-461-1633; Hanchi Snoa

29; admission US$5; ⊙ 9-11:45am & 2:30-4:45pm Mon-Fri). Items from the long history of the congregation are displayed; the building dates to 1732.

For details on the floating Queen Emma Bridge and ferry service across Sint Anna-baai, the inlet to the harbor, see p751.

OTROBANDA
One of the best museums in the Caribbean, **Museum Kura Hulanda** (☎ 599-9-434-7765; Klipstraat 9; adult/child US$6/3; ⊙ 10am-5pm) is part of the sensational hotel of the same name and is inside 19th-century slave quarters. The brutal history of slavery in the Caribbean is documented here in superb and extensive exhibits. Look for the unflinching account by John Gabriel Stedman of slavery in 1700s Suriname.

When not burning a hole in your pocket, money can tell a fascinating story. The **Numismatic Museum** (☎ 599-9-434-5500; De Rouvilleweg 7; admission free; ⊙ 8:30am-noon Mon, Tue, Thu & Fri, 1-4:30pm Mon-Fri) has many valuable exhibits and a guide written in English.

Follow Van Lennepstraat uphill into a safe and historic neighborhood for great **views** of the city and harbor.

Away from the water, the **Curaçao Museum** (☎ 599-9-462-3873; Van Leeuwenhoekstraat; adult/child US$3/1.75; ⊙ 8:30am-4:30pm Mon-Fri, 10am-4pm Sun) is housed in an 1853 hospital for yellow-fever victims. Inside the beautiful verandas is lots of historical stuff, sort of like you'd find in a huge attic.

SCHARLOO
The **Curaçao Maritime Museum** (☎ 599-9-465-2327; www.curacaomaritime.com; Van Brandhofstraat 7; adult/child NAf10/6; ⊙ 9am-4pm Mon-Sat) is the other superb museum in Willemstad. Engaging displays trace the island's history detailing how the Dutch West India Company kicked Spain's butt to gain control of the ABCs through to the commercial boom of the 20th century, when the port was where commerce from the US, Europe, the Caribbean and Latin America met. A nice little café has tables overlooking the water.

The docks in the neighborhood are mostly closed, but wander around and you'll see many building restorations in progress, including the Art Deco **Miami Building** (Bitterstraat 3-9). At night a counter across the street serves beer to cheery locals.

Activities
DIVING & SNORKELING
Curaçao's reefs are home to almost 60 species of coral, much of it the hard varieties. That coupled with the 98ft (30m) visibility and the warm water make the island very popular with divers, especially locals.

The main areas for diving are from Westpunt south to St Marie, central Curaçao up and down the coast from St Michael, and the south, beginning at the Curaçao Sea Aquarium.

The latter coast and reefs have been protected as part of the **National Underwater Park**. There are hundreds of species of fish, including reef octopus, trumpetfish, bridled burrfish and yellow goatfish.

Dive operators on Curaçao are often located in hotels. For more information on diving in Curaçao, pick up a copy of the tourism board–produced *Take the Plunge*. The proximity of the reefs to shore attracts many snorkelers as well.

GUIDED WALKS
Several local historians offer tours of the Unesco World Heritage–listed old town. They cost US$10 to US$20 per person and booking is essential.

Old City Tours (☎ 599-9-461-3554) Architect Anko van der Woude focuses on the buildings of Otrobanda during a weekly walk (5:15pm on Thursday).

Otrobanda Tours (☎ 599-9-767-3798) Jopi Hart is well known for his walks through the historic working-class neighborhood. They take place at 5:15pm on Wednesday.

Talk of the Town Tour (☎ 599-9-747-4349; evanarkel@hotmail.com) Custom walks of Punda led by Eveline van Arkel (by appointment).

Sleeping
With the exception of Avila Beach Hotel (right) and Hotel Kura Hulanda (p750), accommodations in Willemstad are not terribly exciting.

BUDGET
Curaçao is not blessed with a great variety of decent budget accommodations.

Howard Johnson Plaza Hotel (☎ 599-9-462-7800; www.howardjohnson.com; Bionplein; r US$85-120; P 🗙 🔀 🔲 🗩) A new place in Otrobanda, get a room with a view of the water – the ones at the back get the butt-end of the views. Rooms are fairly generic, although they have high-speed Internet access. Re-

grettably, there are no balconies. Shuttles run to a private beach.

Otrobanda Hotel (☎ 599-9-462-7400; www.otrobandahotel.com; cnr Breedestraat & De Rouvilleweg; r US$80-100; 🔀 🗩) Be sure to get a good deal here. Despite the premier position on the water, this hotel has seen better days and is nowhere near old enough to be called a 'classic.' Still if the uninspired rooms and daggy pool area (again with great views!) don't put you off, you can't beat the location.

MIDRANGE & TOP END
Avila Beach Hotel (☎ 599-9-461-4377; www.avilahotel.com; Penstraat 130; r US$180-250; P 🔀 🔲 🗩) A fascinating mix of old and new, the Avila Beach has classic rooms in its original building, which was the 18th-century home of the Dutch governor. More upmarket accommodations are available in a newish wing nearby. The grounds are elegant and the entire place radiates class. The beach is a fine crescent of sand. There is even a small museum dedicated to revolutionary Simón Bolívar, who stayed here plotting his assault on the Spanish.

Floris Suite Hotel (☎ 599-9-462-6111; www.florissuitehotel.com; John F Kennedy Blvd; ste US$160-255; P 🔀 🔲 🗩) The Floris' striking and minimalist design makes up for not being right on the beach. The rooms – more like suites – are large and look out onto the lush grounds with the Piscadera Bay beyond. Accents are provided by strange lamps in the bar and some quite good artwork by members of staff.

Curaçao Marriott Beach Resort (☎ 599-9-736-8800; www.marriott.com; John F Kennedy Blvd; r US$170-250; P 🗙 🔀 🔲 🗩) This 247-room resort is attractive with a tropical motif accented by traditional touches. Rooms have decent-sized balconies, and most have views of the large pool and Piscadera Bay. There's wi-fi and high-speed Internet access.

Hilton Curaçao (☎ 599-9-462-5000; www.hiltoncaribbean.com; John F Kennedy Blvd; r US$140-240; P 🗙 🔀 🔲 🗩) The address is fitting, as Kennedy was president about the time this 1960s classic was envisioned. It has vast grounds that include the 17th-century remains of Fort Piscadera and two rather old-fashioned pools. Half the rooms have views of Piscadera Bay, the other half see the power plant and town. Balconies are good-sized.

ARUBA, BONAIRE & CURAÇAO

AUTHOR'S CHOICE

Hotel Kura Hulanda (☎ 599-9-434-7700; www.kurahulanda.com; Langestraat 8; r US$180-500; P 🚫 💻 🛒) One of the Caribbean's finest hotels is also a major attraction in itself. Entrepreneur Jacob Gelt Dekker took a run-down workers neighborhood in Otrobanda and created an amazing hotel that is really a village of restaurants, cafés and rooms. And what rooms! All 80 are unique and decorated with a sumptuous traditional tropical feel. You'll think you're a 1920s millionaire – until you turn on the air-con. Besides the museum (p748) and restaurants (right), there are gardens, two pools and more. Look for specials online that make the experience affordable.

Plaza Hotel Curaçao (☎ 599-9-461-2500; www .plazahotelcuracao.com; Plasa Pier; r US$80-180; P 🚫 🛒) Desperately needed renovations began in 2004 at this prominent hotel at the entrance to the harbor. Most of the average rooms in the 14-story tower lack balconies, but the views of ship traffic from the mezzanine-level pool are superb. Part of the hotel is built into old battlements and if the renovations are done well, the hotel could regain its former superior status.

Eating

The string of cafés along the Punda side of Sint Annabaai are not particularly inspired, despite the great views.

BUDGET

Plein Cafe (☎ 599-9-461-9666; Wilhelminaplein 19-23; sandwiches NAf8; 🕙 9am-11pm Mon-Sat) This Dutch café is so authentic that if it were 30°F (minus 1°C) and raining, you'd think you were in Amsterdam. The outside tables are enormously popular with locals and travelers alike. There's 15 varieties of beer from the Netherlands and Belgium.

Bakery (cnr Bakkerstraat & De Ruyterkade; snacks NAf2; 🕙 7am-7pm Mon-Sat, 7am-4pm Sun) It doesn't get much simpler than the name of this literal hotspot or the food sold within. Filled croissants are a treat.

Centrum Supermarket (☎ 599-9-869-6222; cnr Weg Naar Westpunt & Weg Naar Bullenbaai; 🕙 8am-7:30pm Mon-Sat, 8am-1pm Sun) Popular with expats, this large supermarket has a bakery and a deli.

MIDRANGE & TOP END

Willemstad has some excellent restaurants, but beware of some mediocre places by the water that serve OK food at extraordinary prices.

Astrolab Observatory (☎ 599-9-434-7700; Hotel Kura Hulanda, Langestraat 8; mains US$23-38; 🕙 breakfast & dinner; 🚫) The top restaurant in the Kura Hulanda is set in a fantasy of little fountains and gardens. Inside, the refined elegance is accented by antique astrological instruments. The food changes daily, reflecting both what's in season and the whim of the chef to create a fusion of French, Caribbean and nouvelle cuisine.

Museum Restaurant (☎ 599-9-434-7700; Hotel Kura Hulanda, Langestraat 8; mains US$10-23; 🕙 lunch & dinner; 🚫 🚫) Another of the several restaurants in the Kura Hulanda, this is the casual one and is mostly set outside in gardens and under trees. The menu is eclectic – from pasta to sandwiches – with regional touches, like banana cream soup from Cuba. Service is superb.

Gouverneur De Rouville (☎ 599-9-462-5999; De Rouvilleweg 9; mains US$15-25; 🕙 lunch & dinner, bar until 1am) Excellent Caribbean food is served in this restored colonial building. Try the Yeshi Yena, a local treat of stuffed cheese, or the fish stew on leeks. Tables on the breezy veranda have good views of Punda and the waterfront. There's a secluded courtyard and a fine bar.

Hook's Hut (☎ 599-9-462-6575; Piscaderabaai; mains US$8-20; 🕙 lunch & dinner, bar until 1am) A classic beach café on lovely Piscadera Bay, the rough edges have been smoothed away so as to appeal to guests at the nearby resorts. Lounge at tables on the sand while enjoying sandwiches and seafood to the beat of a steel-drum band. Several far more humble and nameless joints nearby cater to beach-going locals with a thirst for beer.

Drinking

Yes, you can drink curaçao here, but note that the namesake booze of the island is now a generic term for liquor flavored with bitter oranges. For obscure reasons the concoction is often dyed blue. While duty-free shops burst with stuff from numerous distillers, locals prefer rot-gut rum and beer – in that order.

Music Factory (☎ 599-9-461-0631; Salina 131; 🕙 8pm-2am Mon-Wed, 8pm-3am Thu, 8pm-4am Fri &

Sat) A great bar near the clubs, this place is about as friendly as they come, and you can imbibe at the tables outside or enjoy the DJ music inside. Wednesday is karaoke night.

Blues (☎ 599-9-461-4377; Avila Beach Hotel, Penstraat 130; ⏰ 5pm-midnight Tue-Sun) On a pier over the water, this cool bar has live jazz Thursday and Saturday and happy hours nightly. There's a good tapas menu.

Among the places listed earlier that are great for just a drink are the Gouverneur De Rouville, the Astrolab Observatory and the Plein Cafe (opposite).

Entertainment

CASINOS

Curaçao's casinos are no great shake of the dice. They tend to be small and designed to meet the basic needs of the hotel gamblers who use them.

CLUBS

Willemstad has several clubs catering to the local love of music and dancing. Places come and go, so check out the free weekly *K-Pasa,* which lists entertainment around the island.

Zen (☎ 599-9-599-9-461-4443; Salina 129; admission NAf10; ⏰ 11pm-4am Thu-Sat; ⛄) A high-concept nightclub with a stark decor, Zen is easily the most posh choice in town.

Studio 99 (☎ 599-9-465-5555; Lindberghweg; admission NAf10; ⏰ 9pm-1am Tue-Thu, 10pm-4am Fri & Sat) A huge and popular place, with karaoke and DJs during the week and local bands on weekends.

THEATER

Teatro Luna Blou (☎ 599-9-462-2209; www.lunablou .org; Havenstraat 2-4) Offers a varying schedule of offbeat films and live theater. Many of the programs are gay-themed.

Shopping

Breedestraat in Punda has the best stores of the conventional variety, but you can buy much the same stuff at home.

Floating Market (Sha Caprileskade) A colorful place to see piles of papayas, melons, tomatoes and much more. The vendors sail their boats the 43.5 miles (70km) from Venezuela every morning.

Market (Waaigatplein; ⏰ 7am-2pm Mon-Sat) Near the Floating Market, this large UFO-shaped market sells cheap household goods, snacks and more.

Kas di Alma Blou (☎ 599-9-462-8896; De Rouvilleweg 67; ⏰ 9am-12:30pm & 2-5:30pm Mon-Sat) Located in Otrobanda, this place has a name that means 'Home of the Blue Soul.' The store in the brilliant blue 19th-century house sells excellent local artworks, as well as handicrafts, books about Curaçao and more.

Heavily hyped, Fort Riffart is a shadow of its former solid self. The walls have been punched out for gift shops, and when the cruise ships are away, the bored employees turn the courtyard into a playground.

Getting There & Around

Watching the long Queen Emma Bridge move ponderously aside for passage of a huge ship is one of the simple pleasures of Willemstad. There's always someone literally leaping onto the end as it swings away from Punda. If the bridge is open, look for flags by the pilot's cabin: orange means it has been open less than 30 minutes, blue means it has been open longer and *may* soon close. When the bridge is open, two old free public ferries nearby cruise into action. The four-minute ride on these is a treat in itself.

BUS

The bus network is designed to transport the local commuter, but a couple of routes are useful for visitors: No 4B links the airport to Otrobanda (20 minutes, departs hourly) and No 9A follows the coastal road to Westpunt (one hour, every two hours). The **bus stations** (☎ Punda 599-9-465-0201, Otrobanda 599-9-462-8359) are near the post office in Punda and near the base of Arubastraat in Otrobanda. Fares are NAf1.25 to NAf1.75 depending on distance; buses run from about 7am to 9pm.

CAR

One of the greatest challenges to getting around Willemstad (and the rest of Curaçao) is the lack of road signs. Where they do exist, they're fading into oblivion by the sun. Fortunately, locals are happy to help.

Because attractions are so spread out, you may choose to rent a car. All the major international car-rental agencies have desks at the airport.

TAXI

Plans call for the installation of meters in taxis, meanwhile fares are fixed. From the airport to most hotels and Willemstad costs

US$12 to US$15. Taxis hang around hotels, otherwise order one from **central dispatch** (☎ 599-9-869-0747).

SOUTH OF WILLEMSTAD

Residential neighborhoods make up much of the land immediately south of the center of Willemstad. Spaanse Water, a large enclosed bay to rival Schottegat, is shedding its role supporting the offshore oil-drilling industry, and is becoming an upscale area that is sure to grow as people take advantage of the beaches and sheltered waters. There's little further south to the tip of Curaçao except arid scrub. Offshore is some of the island's best diving.

Sights

Following the coast south from Punda for a little over 2.5 miles (4km) you get to the **Curaçao Sea Aquarium** (☎ 599-9-461-6666; www.cura cao-sea-aquarium.com; Bapor Kibra; adult/child US$15/7.50; ❉ 8:30am-5:30pm). This large facility anchors a whole area of development that includes hotels, bars and artificial beaches.

The Seaquarium, as it's known, is home to over 600 marine species, the loudest of which are the sea lions whose barking you can hear as you get out of your car. Most of the creatures are native to the ABCs, and there's informative and helpful displays. There's also no end of opportunities to upgrade your visit through extra-fee activities, including diving, snorkeling, and the chance to pet a porpoise and stroke a sea lion.

Inland near Oranjeberg, **Den Paradera** (☎ 599-9-767-5608; Seru Grandi Kavel 105A, Bandi Riva; admission US$4; ❉ 9am-6pm Mon-Sat) is a labor of love of Dinah Veeris, who is single-handedly preserving and celebrating traditional Caribbean herbal medicine. Hundreds of herbs and plants are grown organically in this fascinating garden, with signs explaining what's growing. Call in advance to arrange a tour led by Veeris herself.

Sleeping

Condos are multiplying like turtles after a hatching. **Royal Resorts** (☎ 599-9-465-6699; www .royalresorts.com) offers rental details. Rates for multiroom units begin at about US$300 a night.

Lions Dive (☎ 599-9-434-8888; www.lionsdive.com; Bapor Kibra; r US$120-190; ⓟ 🛇 🕱) This low-key place reflects tropical resorts of old with its wood-and-metal roof design. Diving is obviously the main feature, but rooms are decent with good balconies or patios. However, only a few have kitchenettes. The beach is OK and protected by barriers.

Breezes Curaçao Resort (☎ 599-9-736-7888; www .superclubs.com; Martin Luther King Jr Blvd; r per 2 nights US$470-700; ⓟ 🛇 🕱) An all-inclusive resort near the aquarium, Breezes claims to be a family resort, but pushes its casino, unlimited premium drinks and toga parties. Everything is inclusive from the unlimited chow to the myriad of activities on the long white beach. Facilities, however, feel a bit dated and rooms are just standard.

Eating & Drinking

Wet & Wild (☎ 599-9-561-2477; Curaçao Sea Aquarium, Bapor Kibra; snacks US$2-10; ❉ 9am-6pm Mon-Thu, 9-3am or later Fri-Sun) One of several beachfront bars that you can wander between according to the happy-hour schedule. On weekends it becomes a real scene with locals and visitors partying on the sand until nearly dawn.

NORTH OF WILLEMSTAD

There is much to explore along both coasts going north. Parks, villages and beaches all hold appeal. You can make an easy loop of this half of the island by car in a day. The main roads are all in good condition.

West Coast

About 3.7 miles (6km) from Otrobanda, **Kleine St Michiel** is a traditional fishing village on a tiny bay. The small ruins of a 17th-century Dutch fort are on the cliffs above the water.

There are a few simple beachfront cafés. The best is **Octopus** (☎ 599-9-888-4414; meals NAf4-10; ❉ café 10am-10pm, club some nights until 3am), which literally has a great vibe thanks to the saxophonist Michael Anthony on Tuesday

---

CURAÇAO'S BEACHES

Like the island itself, Curaçao's beaches fall midway between those of Aruba and Bonaire. There are not endless expanses of beach, but there are some very nice coves and bays with crescents of fine white sand. The best, **Playa Kalki**, **Playa Knip**, **Playa Lagún** and **Kas Abou** (opposite), are on the far northwest coast.

nights, and local bands on Friday and Sunday nights. The music is often a heady mix of Curaçaoan Creole and the place gets jammed. The café also has a dive shop offering a full range of courses and trips.

To head to the north end of the island via the northwest coast, take the main road, Weg Naar Westpunt (literally, 'road to Westpunt'), 5 miles (8km) from Willemstad to Kunuku Abao, where you turn left or west onto the Weg Naar St Willibrordo. For 11 miles (18km) you drive through some of the most lush countryside in the ABCs. At some points huge trees form canopies over the road.

About 2.5 miles (4km) after the turn-off, look for signs to the beautiful beach **Kas Abou**. It's another 2.5 miles (4km) down a side road to get there, but the reward is worth it, with turquoise waters, good snorkeling, full facilities and rentable loungers.

Passing through the hamlet of Groot Santa Martha, there are a couple of stores where you can stop for a cold drink and **Landhuis Groot Santa Martha** (☎ 599-9-864-2969; admission NAf5; ⊗ 7:30am-4pm Mon-Fri). This is one of the best preserved of the dozens of Dutch colonial houses that dot the island. Here a sugarcane plantation was started in the 17th century to supply the rum and molasses trade. The main house dates from 1700 and is part of a large complex of relics from the era. Recent restorations have worked wonders, and the complex is now a vocational school for mentally and physically challenged people. Some produce beautiful handicrafts which are for sale.

A 2-mile (3km) side road from Groot Santa Martha twists through the hills to the coast and the **Sunset Waters Beach Resort** (☎ 599-9-864-1233; www.sunsetwaters.com; r US$120-200; P ✗ ⌨ ☎). This very secluded low-key complex is built on the side of a hill above the beach. Rooms are comfortable and have balconies; larger ones feature kitchens.

At Lagún the road nears the coast and the first of many fabulous beaches. **Playa Lagún** is a narrow and secluded beach situated on a tiny cove. There's shade and a snack bar. Just back from the sand, **Discover Diving** (☎ 599-9-864-1652; www.discoverdiving.nl; d from US$60; P ✗) has basic but nice apartments, with simple kitchens. It has a pleasant little café, and offers well-priced diving services

(from 9am to 5pm Tuesday to Sunday), including PADI open-water certificates for US$243.

About 1.25 miles (2km) on from Lagún is **Landhuis Kenepa**, the main house of another 17th-century plantation. The hilltop site is stunning, but the real importance here is that this was where a slave rebellion started in 1795. Several dozen torched their miserable huts and joined up with hundreds of others who were refusing to work. Eventually the plantation owners regained control and killed the leaders, but the event set in motion protests that continued for decades.

Down the hill from the plantation, **Playa Knip** is really two beaches. Groot Knip is long, while Klein Knip is, well, small. Both have brilliant white sand, shady shelters, azure waters and snack bars. Avoid weekends when half the island shows up for a dip.

In the small village of Westpunt, **Playa Kalki** has parking, lockers and kayak rental. On the main road you'll have a tough time missing **Jaanchie's** (☎ 599-9-864-0126; mains US$6-14; ⊗ noon-8pm), a local institution where you can sample a full menu of island delicacies, like okra soup and goat stew. Some of the meats are rather exotic but fear not: it all tastes like chicken. The open-air dining room is very comfortable and there are uncaged songbirds flying about.

From here the road turns east and crosses the island to the northeast coast.

East Coast

The windward side of the island is rugged and little developed. To take this route stay on Weg Naar Westpunt past the junction at Kunuku Abao.

Just beyond the turn look east for the entrance to **Landhuis Daniel** (☎ 599-9-864-8400; www.landhuisdaniel.com; r US$35-60; P ✗ ⌨ ☎), a rambling lodge and restaurant run by a Dutch family. Rooms are basic, but the pool and gardens have a rural charm. The real lure is its **restaurant** (mains US$8-20; ⊗ breakfast, lunch & dinner), which has a changing menu of local, Creole and French dishes all prepared with ingredients from the organic kitchen garden. Kids are well catered for here: there are 25 types of pancakes on offer.

Nearby and just off the main road, **Rosalind Bar** (⊗ evening Thu-Sat) is a very friendly local hangout in an old pastel green building.

Sip rum, beer or whiskey, and enjoy the local bands playing island music.

About 15.5 miles (25km) north of Willemstad lies **Christoffel National Park** (☎ 599-9-864-0363; adult/child US$15/3; ☺ 8am-4pm Mon-Sat, 6am-3pm Sun), a 4446-acre (1800-hectare) preserve formed from three old plantations. The main house for one of the plantations, **Landhuis Savonet**, is at the entrance to the park. It was built in 1662 by a director of the Dutch West India Company.

The park has two driving routes over 19.8 miles (32km) of dirt roads, and sights include cacti, orchids, iguanas, deer, and caves with ancient drawings. At the entrance is an excellent museum and café. You can also make arrangements to tour the park by horse. Call ☎ 599-9-697-8709 for details.

The road after the park follows the windswept northeast coast to Westpunt.

DIRECTORY

Information listed in this directory is specific to the ABCs. For information pertaining to the entire region, check the book's main directory (p757).

ACCOMMODATIONS

All three islands have beach resorts, with Aruba having by far the most. Curaçao has the most varied range of places to stay, with some interesting nonbeach choices in Willemstad. Camping is uncommon. High-season prices usually run mid-December to mid-April. Rates – and crowds – fall by a third or more during other times.

ACTIVITIES

Diving is the number one activity on the ABCs, with the azure waters and pristine reefs of Bonaire being a destination of dreams for many. Snorkeling is also ideal, and the waters around the islands never

---

PRACTICALITIES

- **Newspapers & Magazines** Each of the islands has English-language news papers aimed at tourists that combine oodles of boosterism with dollops of news. Newspapers from the US are surprisingly hard to find. International magazines are widely available.

- **Radio & TV** Most hotels have at least a few satellite TV channels in English. This islands have numerous FM and AM radio stations. 89.9FM on Aruba features the hyper-boosterish Dick Miller Show between 7pm and 8pm.

- **Video Systems** NTSC, the standard used in North America.

- **Electricity** 110AC to 130AC (50 to 60 cycles).

- **Weights & Measures** Metric system.

---

get below a comfy 70°F (21°C). Swimming is popular, but remember that the best beaches are on Aruba. Bonaire is a hot destination for windsurfers, who find near ideal conditions on Lac Bay.

Away from the water, activities are less common. Besides the thrills of resort pursuits as diverse as tennis and shuffleboard, there is golf on Aruba. All three islands have extensive national parks that make for good exploring, but the arid terrain gets hot and at noon you will understand what it means to be a lizard. Hiking in these areas is best done early and late in the day when you can also enjoy sunrises and sunsets respectively.

CHILDREN

The ABCs are good destinations for families. Almost all resorts have activities for kids – some quite extensive. In addition, the famous reefs protect the beaches from really nasty surf, although the windward sides of the islands can get rough. However, note that Bonaire and Curaçao are not overstocked with sights specifically aimed at kids, like amusement parks or themed attractions.

EMBASSIES & CONSULATES

Visa-free travel to the ABCs means that most people will not need diplomatic assistance prior to traveling. Most nations have

---

EMERGENCY NUMBERS

Ambulance Aruba (☎ 911); Bonaire (☎ 114); Curaçao (☎ 912)

Fire Aruba (☎ 911); Bonaire (☎ 191); Curaçao (☎ 911)

Police Aruba (☎ 911); Bonaire (☎ 911); Curaçao (☎ 911)

official dealings with the islands through the Netherlands. There are a few very small consulates in Curaçao. For general information on embassies and consulates in the Caribbean, see p763.

Consulates in Curaçao

Canada (☎ 599-9-466-1115; Plaza JoJo Correa 2-4, Willemstad)
UK (☎ 599-9-747-3322; Werfstraat 6, Willemstad)
USA (☎ 599-9-461-3066; JB Gorsiraweg 1, Willemstad)

FESTIVALS & EVENTS

Carnival (January) This is a big deal on the islands, especially Curaçao where a packed schedule of fun begins right after New Year's Day. Aruba is known for staging elaborate parades.
Simadan (Early April) Bonaire's harvest festival is usually held in the small town of Rincon, and celebrates traditional dance and food.
Séu Parade Curaçao's 'Feast of the Harvest' features a parade replete with lots of folk music and dancing on Easter Monday.
Aruba Music Festival (October) Aruba's annual two-day international concert attracts international and local talent.

HOLIDAYS

The ABCs observe the following holidays:
New Year's Day January 1
Good Friday Friday before Easter
Easter Monday Monday after Easter
Queen's Birthday April 30
Labour Day May 1
Ascension Day Sixth Thursday after Easter
Christmas Day December 25
Boxing Day December 26

In addition to the above, each island has its own holidays:
Aruba GF (Betico) Croes Day (January 25); Carnival Monday (Monday before Ash Wednesday); National Day (March 18)
Bonaire Carnival Rest Day (usually in January); Bonaire Day (September 6); Antillean Day (October 21)
Curaçao Carnival Monday (Monday before Ash Wednesday); Flag Day (July 2); Antillean Day (October 21)

MONEY

You can pay for just about everything in US dollars on the ABCs. Sometimes you will get change back in US currency, other times you will receive it in Aruba florins (Afl) or Netherlands Antillean guilders (NAf) on Bonaire and Curaçao. Both currencies are divided into units of 100. Some of the coins are

quite charming such as the square Aruban 50-cent piece. Most ATMs let you withdraw currency in US dollars.

TELEPHONE

Telephone service on the ABCs is reliable. On Bonaire all the seven-digit local numbers begin with 7; numbers beginning with another digit are cell (mobile) phones registered elsewhere. On Curaçao, a 9 has been added in front of all the seven-digit numbers. You must always dial this calling from abroad in addition to the country code of ☎ 599. Cell phones are common. Country codes have been included in the ABC listings in this chapter.

All the usual warnings about pirates posing as phones in hotel rooms apply on the ABCs. Your international dial-home services may or may not work, which means you will probably have to pay extortionate hotel rates. Worse are scores of private pay phones that have signs touting the ease of calling home, but less disclosure when it comes to the rates, which cost US$2 to US$3 per minute.

TOURIST INFORMATION

Local Tourist Offices

Aruba Tourism Authority (☎ 297-582-3777; www .aruba.com) A well-funded entity, with a comprehensive and useful website. See p729 for the office in Oranjestad.
Curaçao Tourism Board (www.curacao-tourism.com) Offers a mixed bag of services. The website could be a lot better, and many once-useful guides to the island are out of print. For the equally mixed quality of personal assistance offered on the island, see Willemstad's tourist information (p748).
Tourism Corporation Bonaire (www.infobonaire.com) Does a good job of promoting the island and answering questions. See p740 for the office in Kralendijk.

Tourist Offices Abroad

Aruba has the following overseas tourist offices:
Canada (☎ 1-800-268-3042; 5875 Hwy No 7, Ste 201, Woodbridge, Ontario L4L 1T9)
UK (☎ 020-7928-1600; the Copperfields, 25 Copperfield St, London, SE1 0EN)
USA (☎ 1-800-862-7822; 1200 Harbor Blvd, Weehawken, NJ 07087)

VISAS

Travelers from most countries can visit the ABCs without a visa for up to 90 days.

TRANSPORTATION

GETTING THERE & AWAY
Entering the ABCs

All visitors need a passport and a return or onward ticket to enter the islands; US citizens see the boxed text, p772.

Air

Aruba is the main entry point for the ABCs, with extensive service from North America and the Caribbean. Recently, Continental Airlines announced a weekly nonstop service from Houston, USA, to Bonaire starting mid-December, 2005. Both Bonaire and Curaçao have service from Europe, as well as regional Caribbean service. For details of international air service to the islands, see p772.

Airlines flying to Aruba, Bonaire and Curaçao from within the Caribbean include the following:

Air Jamaica (www.airjamaica.com); Bonaire (☏ 599-717-7447); Curaçao (☏ 599-9-888-2300) Flies to Bonaire and Curaçao only.
American Eagle (www.aa.com); Aruba (☎ 297-582-2700); Bonaire (☎ 599-717-2004); Curaçao (☎ 599-9-869-5707) Flies to all three islands.

Sea

Cruise ships flock to Aruba and Curaçao, with an increasing number calling on Bonaire as well. However, these are not for independent travelers and passengers are expected to be back onboard after a few hours ashore quaffing sugary drinks and buying souvenirs of dubious origin. See p777 for more on cruises.

GETTING AROUND

The only way to get between the ABCs is by air. On the islands, many travelers opt for a rental car for all or part of their visit. Public transportation outside of the core of Aruba is limited, although taxis are common.

Air

Although there is no other option, inter-island service in the ABCs has a checkered past. The routes are busy, but have not proved profitable for airlines. Operators come and go with such frequency that the best advice we can offer is to check with a travel agent, online booking service or your accommodations on the island to find out who is presently flying between the ABCs.

Bicycle

Although there are no bike lanes on the ABCs, many people enjoy riding along the many flat roads on each of the islands, especially Bonaire. You can rent bikes at many resorts and bike shops.

Bus

Aruba (p735) and Curaçao (p751) each have limited networks of local buses.

Car & Motorcycle

Major car-rental companies can be found at each of the ABC airports. In addition, there are numerous reliable local firms that offer competitive rates. See p735 (Aruba), p740 (Bonaire) and p751 (Curaçao) for details.

Main roads are generally in pretty good condition on all the islands; however, roads in national parks and other remote spots can be quite rough.

Consider renting a 4WD or other vehicle with high-ground clearance if you want to go exploring. Driving is on the right-hand side, seat belts are required and motorcyclists must use helmets. Gasoline is very easily found.

Road signs are sporadic. Outside of well-marked resort areas, you will soon discover just how friendly the locals are as you stop often for directions.

Taxi

Taxis are available on all the islands; see the relevant Getting Around sections.

Caribbean Islands Directory

CONTENTS

This chapter gives you the lowdown on all things practical in the Caribbean Islands. It is a broad overview that is meant to complement the individual chapters. This book covers hundreds of islands, so the information given here is based on collective generalizations to give you a sense of the region as a whole, and to help you plan your trip. Start your search here (subjects are listed alphabetically) then turn to the individual chapter directories for more specific details.

ACCOMMODATIONS

A wide range of accommodations awaits travelers in the Caribbean, from inexpensive guesthouses and good-value efficiency apartments – which have refrigerators and partial kitchens – to elaborate villas and luxury beachside resorts. The bulk of our listings fall somewhere in between.

In this book the phrase 'in summer' refers to the low season (mid-April to December) and 'in winter' to the high season (December to mid-April). Throughout the book we've listed high-season rates unless otherwise noted. Keep in mind that hotel rates can be up to 30% cheaper in the low season and, in most places, they'll fluctuate with tourist traffic.

The price structure we have followed applies to most of the islands. However, not all islands have rooms in all price categories – many have no budget accommodations at all, while other islands are less expensive across the board. The individual chapters outline any deviations but, in general, 'budget' means US$75 or less, 'midrange' means US$76 to US$195 and 'top end' means US$196 and up.

Some hotels close for a month or so in late summer, usually around September. If business doesn't look promising, some of the smaller hotels and guesthouses might even close down for the entire summer.

'Private bath' in this book means the room has its own toilet and shower – it does not necessarily mean that it has a bathtub, and in most cases it will not. If having a TV or telephone is important to you, call ahead, as many hotel rooms don't come equipped – although this is changing with the advent of satellite service.

Camping

Camping is limited in the Caribbean, and on some islands freelance camping is either illegal or discouraged – usually to protect nature or because of crime. This is certainly not the rule everywhere, however, and it's best to check with the local tourist office for rules and regulations.

There are a number of camping possibilities on St John in the US Virgin Islands (USVI), and there is established camping at a handful of small, private campgrounds on Guadeloupe and Martinique. At the Grand Etang National Park in Grenada, and on St Eustatius (Statia) and St Kitts & Nevis,

---

PRACTICALITIES

- **Newspapers** Most Caribbean islands have their own newspapers and these are well worth reading to gain insight into local politics and culture. Foreign newspapers, such as the *International Herald Tribune* and *USA Today*, are usually available as well. **Caribbean Travel & Life** (www.caribbeantravelmag.com) is an excellent, glossy monthly magazine with feature stories and information on the entire Caribbean.

- **Radio & TV** Most islands have their own radio stations, which is a great way to tune in to the latest calypso, reggae, soca and steel-band music. Local TV stations offer mostly news while satellite TVs show CNN and foreign shows.

- **Video Systems** The local system is NTSC, but videotapes are sold in various formats.

- **Electricity** The electric current varies in the islands. On many the current is 110V, 60 cycles (as in the US), but others have 220V, 50 cycles (as in Europe). Adapters are widely available at shops and hotels. Check the Practicalities boxes in the individual chapters.

- **Weights & Measures** Some Caribbean islands use the metric system, while others use the imperial system, and a few use a confusing combo of both; check the individual chapters. All weights and measures in this book are listed in imperial with the metric equivalent in brackets.

---

camping is officially permitted but there are no facilities. Cuba has its *campismos*, which are actually concrete cabins set in the wilderness (see p172).

Guesthouses

The closest thing the Caribbean has to hostels, guesthouses are usually great value. Often in the middle of a town or village, and rarely alongside a beach, they offer good opportunities for cultural immersion. Rooms usually have a bed and private bath, and some have communal kitchens and living rooms. In some areas you can arrange private homestays, where you stay in the home of a local family. These are most readily available in Cuba (p172).

Hotels

Looking at the Caribbean as a whole, you'll see that hotel rooms can range from flea-ridden hovels to massive 1000-room resorts, to glorious villas hovering over the sea. Prices run the gamut as well. Look a little closer and you realize that on the islands themselves the hotel options seem in short supply. On one island, for example, there will be a lot of budget accommodations but few 'nicer' hotels; elsewhere, you'll see dozens of top-end resorts but not a budget hotel in sight. If you're trying to plan a trip, it's a good idea to read through the Accommodations listings in each chapter to find out the range of hotels available on each island.

The **Caribbean Hotel Association** (www.caribbean hotels.com) has helpful links that connect to the individual islands' hotel associations.

ALL-INCLUSIVE RESORTS

Born in Jamaica, and now prevalent across the Caribbean, all-inclusive resorts allow you to pay a set price and then nothing more once you set foot inside the resort. You usually get a wristband that allows you free access to the hotel or resort's restaurants, bars and water-sports equipment. Many properties have jumped onto the 'all-inclusive' bandwagon, but don't necessarily supply the goods. Be sure to find out exactly what 'all-inclusive' includes, the variety and quality of food available, whether or not all drinks are included and if there are any hidden charges.

Rental Accommodations

If you're traveling with your family or a large group, you might want to look into renting a villa. Villas are great because you have room to stretch out, do your own cooking, and enjoy plenty of privacy. Rentals cost anywhere from US$600 per week, for a basic villa with bedrooms, a kitchen and living space, to US$15,000 per night for the beachside mansion George Clooney rented last time he stopped by for a Caribbean tan. Agencies on the individual islands rent properties; the following rent villas throughout the region:

Caribbean Way (☎ 514-393-3003, 877-953-7400; www.caribbeanway.com) A Montreal-based company with villa rentals in Anguilla, Antigua, Aruba, Bahamas, Barbados, Cayman Islands, Dominican Republic, Grenada, Jamaica, Mustique, Nevis, St Barth, St Lucia, St Martin, Tobago and the USVI and British Virgin Islands (BVI).

Island Hideaways (☎ 212-663-9222, 800-832-2302; www.islandhideaways.com) This US-based company rents villas in Barbados, BVI, the Caymans, Jamaica, St Lucia, St Martin and USVI.

Owners Syndicate (☎ 020-7801-9801; www .ownerssyndicate.com) This London-based company has worldwide villa rentals in Anguilla, Antigua, Barbados, BVI, Grenada, the Grenadines, Jamaica, Mustique, St Kitts & Nevis, St Lucia, Tobago and USVI.

West Indies Management Company (Wimco; www .wimcovillas.com); USA (☎ 401-849-8012, 800-449-1553, fax 401-847-6290); UK (☎ 0870-850-1144) Wimco's extensive listings include villas on Barbados, Mustique, Nevis, Saba, St Barth, St Martin and Turks & Caicos.

ACTIVITIES

As unlikely as it sounds, hanging out and sipping rum cocktails on the beach can get tiring. For anyone sun-scorched, or simply tired of lazing around, the islands have plenty to offer and, with water everywhere, it's no wonder that aquatic sports dominate the activity roster for most vacationers.

Diving & Snorkeling

Undoubtedly graced with several of the world's best diving, the Caribbean offers plenty of underwater fun for everyone, from first-time snorkelers and novice divers to salty sea hounds. Check out the special Diving & Snorkeling chapter (p51) for more information.

Fishing

There's reasonably good deep-sea fishing in the Caribbean, with marlin, tuna, wahoo and barracuda among the prime catches. Charter fishing-boat rentals are available on a number of islands. Expect a half-day of fishing for four to six people to run to about US$400. Charter boats are usually individually owned and consequently the list of available skippers tends to fluctuate; local tourist offices and activity desks can provide the latest information on availability.

Golf

The Caribbean has some of the world's most beautiful and challenging golf courses, where both major and local tournaments are held throughout the year. Green fees vary greatly, from around US$30 at smaller courses to US$150, plus caddy and cart, at the ultrafamous courses. Most places offer club rentals, but serious golfers tend to bring their own. Some of the best golf courses are found on Jamaica, Nevis and Aruba, and in the Bahamas, the Dominican Republic and the Cayman Islands.

While it's lovely to swing away at your favorite course, be aware that the building of golf courses often comes at a huge environmental cost, including habitat destruction and massive water waste. Still, golf is a big moneymaker for the islands. Two new courses being constructed in Antigua, for example, gave impetus to that island's new airport.

Hiking

Verdant peaks rise high above dramatic valleys, volcanoes simmer and waterfalls rumble in the distance. Rainforests resonate to a chorus of birdsong and reveal more green than you've ever imagined. Most people come to the Caribbean for the beaches, but many islands draw hikers seeking rugged terrain and stunning mountain vistas.

If you're looking to get your legs moving on mountain trails, you'll want to head to the higher, rainforested islands. On lofty Dominica you can hike to a variety of waterfalls, take an easy rainforest loop trail through a parrot sanctuary or hire a guide for an arduous trek. Or, explore smoldering volcanoes on Guadeloupe and Martinique. St Lucia's trails lead to the world-famous Pitons and trek-filled national parks surround the Dominican Republic's impressive Pico Duarte. A couple of national parks offer excellent hiking on Haiti. In USVI, the forested island of St John is mostly protected parkland, filled with hiking trails that lead to sand-swept beaches. The small but steep island of Saba has some good easy-access hiking, including a lightly trodden network of footpaths that once connected Saba's villages, before the introduction of paved roads and cars just a few decades ago. Jamaica, Grenada, Bonaire and Aruba also have good hiking trails.

On many of the smaller low-lying islands there are few, if any, established trails, but, as cars are also scarce the dirt roads that connect villages can make for good walking.

HIKING PRECAUTIONS

Some rainforest hiking trails take you into steep, narrow valleys with gullies that require stream crossings. The capital rule here is that if the water begins to rise it is not safe to cross, as a flash flood may be imminent. Instead, head for higher ground and wait it out.

On island hikes, long pants will protect your legs from sharp saw grass on overgrown sections of trails. Sturdy footwear with good traction is advisable on most hikes. Mosquitoes can get downright aggressive, so be sure to have good bug repellant with you.

Most experienced hikers know what to bring, but here's a quick reminder:

- a flashlight (island trails are not a good place to be caught unprepared in the dark)
- lots of fresh drinking water
- a snack
- a trail map or a compass
- rain gear (especially on long hikes)
- bug repellant

On several islands, especially in the Bahamas and Turks & Caicos, the only hiking you'll do is walking along a sandy beach. For more detailed information on hiking see the individual island chapters.

Horseback Riding

Horseback riding can be a fun way to explore a place. On several islands outfitters offer guided rides along mountain trails and quiet valleys, or trips along remote beaches. A few combine both in a single outing. Specific information on horseback riding can be found in the individual island chapters.

Sailing

The Caribbean is a first-rate sailing destination, and boats and rum-sipping, salty-skinned sailors are everywhere. On many public beaches and at resorts, water-sports huts rent out Hobiecats or other small sailboats for near-shore exploring. Many sailboat charter companies run day excursions to other islands, and offer party trips aboard tall ships or sunset cruises on catamarans (usually complete with champagne or rum cocktails). Boat rentals abound for experienced sailors and there are plenty of crewed charters for those just finding their sea legs.

Due to island proximity, calmer waters and plenty of protected bays, USVI and BVI offer some of the best sailing and charter opportunities in the Caribbean. For information on renting your own bareboat sailboat or chartering a crewed yacht, check out the boxed text, p398.

Surfing

Except for Barbados, which is situated further out into the open Atlantic, the islands of the Eastern Caribbean aren't really great for surfing. Once you head north and west, however, you can find particularly surfable swells on Puerto Rico's west coast, Jamaica's north and east coasts, the north coasts of USVI and BVI, and the north and south coasts of the Dominican Republic.

In late summer, swells made by tropical storms off the African coast begin to race toward Barbados, creating the Caribbean's highest waves and finest surfing conditions. The most reliable time for catching good, high, surfable waves is September, October and November. Bathsheba, on Barbados' east coast, is the center of activity, attracting wave action from the north, south and east.

Surfing is also possible at times in Guadeloupe, Trinidad & Tobago and St Martin.

Windsurfing

Favorable trade winds and good water conditions throughout the area have boosted the popularity of windsurfing, or sailboarding, in recent years. Public beach facilities rent out windsurfing equipment and offer lessons to first-timers, and some resorts offer the use of windsurfing gear free to guests.

BOOKS

A discussion of pertinent books from or about each destination is included in its Directory section.

BUSINESS HOURS

Business hours vary from island to island, but there are a few general rules that we've followed in this book. On most islands, business offices are open 8am or 9am to 4pm or 5pm weekdays. Most tourist information centers are open 8am to 4pm weekdays, and 9am to noon on Saturday.

OPEN UP

It's important to remember that this is the Caribbean and life moves at a slow, loosely regimented pace. You'll often see signs in front of shops, bars and restaurants that say 'open all day, every day' and this can mean several things; the place could truly be open all day every day of the week, but don't count on it. If business is slow, a restaurant, shop or attraction might simply close. If a bar is hopping and the owner's having fun, it could stay open until the wee hours of morning. If the rainy season is lasting too long, a hotel or restaurant might simply close for a month. If a shop owner has a hangover, doctor's appointment or date, or simply needs a day off – hey mon, store's closed. In other words, be aware that hard and fast rules about opening times are hard to come by. The only consistent rule is that Sundays are sacred and 'open every day' generally translates to 'open every day except Sunday.'

Shops are open 9am to 5pm Monday to Saturday (malls stay open later), and 9am to noon on Sunday. Post offices are generally open 8am to 3pm weekdays, and banking hours are normally 8am to 3pm Monday to Thursday, or 8am to 5pm on Friday.

Restaurants are usually open from 11am to 11pm daily, though many also serve breakfast and open earlier. Bars are often open from noon to midnight, although in some party-zone bars stay open until the last person leaves.

Where opening and closing hours veer from these general guidelines, we've noted this in individual listings or in the chapter directories.

CHILDREN

Children in the Caribbean are encouraged to talk, sing, dance, think, dream and play. They are integrated into all parts of society: you see them at concerts, restaurants, churches and parties. Most families can't afford baby-sitters, so parents bring their kids everywhere. As a result children are a vibrant part of the cultural fabric, and if you travel with children you'll find this embracing attitude extends to your kids too.

Children often seem more independent in the islands. You'll notice that kids playing in the streets are rarely supervised. By culture and imperative, children are taught to look out for each other. The concept of 'it takes a village to raise a child' is alive and well in the Caribbean; there's an unspoken cultural understanding that adults look out for kids, whether they are family or not. Exposing your kids to the Caribbean way of life can be a great learning experience for all involved.

The Caribbean is a huge family destination and many hotels offer extensive kids' activities, baby-sitting services, children's meals in restaurants and rental equipment like strollers, car seats and extra cots. Most major cruise lines also offer special services and activities for children, some extensive enough to keep their parents free (and children happy) for much of the trip. **Premier Cruise Lines** (☎ in the US 800-992-4299; www.premier cruises.com) specializes in family cruises.

Successful travel with young children requires planning and effort, however. Avoid overpacking – both your suitcase and your itinerary. Include children in the trip planning: if they've helped to plan, they'll be much more interested when they get there. Where possible, encourage cultural immersion by eating local cuisine and taking part in local customs. Your kids will more likely remember eating johnnycakes (corn-flour griddle cakes) for the first time than eating a burger in the resort restaurant.

Finding diapers, baby wipes and formula can be difficult and is usually expensive, so it's wise to bring the bulk of what you need from home.

Popular family destinations include the Bahamas, Turks & Caicos, the Cayman Islands, Cuba, the USVI, Barbados, St Martin, Guadeloupe and the ABC islands. Some islands are better for kids than others, so check in the regional directories for more information.

For vacationers with children, Lonely Planet's *Travel with Children,* by Cathy Lanigan, has lots of valuable tips and interesting anecdotes. Another experienced mother and world traveler, Claire Tristram, provides some great all-around survival strategies for getaways with the younger set, focusing on infants and young children, in her book *Have Kid, Will Travel.*

CLIMATE CHARTS

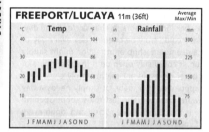

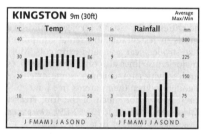

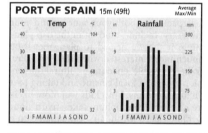

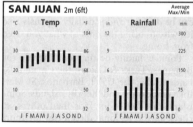

CUSTOMS

All the Caribbean islands allow a reasonable amount of personal items to be brought in duty-free, as well as an allowance of liquor and tobacco. Determining what you can take home depends on where you're vacationing and your country of origin. Check with your country's customs agency for clarification.

Spear guns are prohibited in the waters around many islands, so divers interested in spear fishing should make advance inquiries. Most islands prohibit unregistered firearms; travelers arriving by boat who have guns on board should declare them on entry. Some islands are free of rabies and have strict rules on the importation of animals; this is mainly of interest to sailors, who might not be allowed to bring their pets onto land.

DANGERS & ANNOYANCES
Crime

In terms of individual safety and crime, the situation is quite varied in the Caribbean. It's hard to imagine a more tranquil area than Saba, where most people don't even have locks on their doors, whereas walking the streets of Port of Spain (Trinidad) or Fort-de-France (Martinique) after dark can certainly be a risky venture, especially for women (see p769).

In most areas there is a huge disparity between the income of locals and the (real or perceived) wealth of visitors. If you venture beyond the borders of your resort or tourist area, you'll likely observe populations devastated by poverty, a lack of medical supplies and no clean water. Add to this drug production and trafficking and you can see why crime is a problem in some areas.

Theft can occur, so it's best to keep your valuables close to you at all times and it's a good idea to never flaunt wealth. If you've got a car, you'll want to lock belongings in the trunk, but be mindful that car theft is also a problem. Most resorts and hotels have gated security or guards to keep non-guests out. Still, where possible, lock your valuables in the hotel safe.

There is no need for paranoia and most visitors will enjoy their Caribbean trip without incident, but being aware of your surroundings can go a long way. Of course, the precautions you should take depend on which island you're visiting. For a better grasp of the situation, see the individual island chapters.

Manchineel Trees

Manchineel trees grow on beaches throughout the Caribbean. The fruit of the manchineel, which looks like a small green apple, is poisonous. The milky sap given off by the fruit and leaves can cause severe skin blisters, similar to the reaction caused by poison oak. If the sap gets in your eyes, it can result in temporary blindness. Never take shelter under the trees during a rainstorm, as the sap can be washed off the tree and onto anyone sitting below.

Manchineel trees can grow as high as 40ft (12m) with branches that spread widely. The leaves are green, shiny and elliptical in shape. On some of the more visited beaches, trees will be marked with warning signs or bands of red paint. Manchineel is called *mancenillier* on the French islands and *anjenelle* on Trinidad & Tobago.

Pesky Creatures

Although some people groove to the music of nature, others do not. Squawking roosters and croaking frogs often begin their chorus in the predawn hours, so light sleepers may want to bring along earplugs. You can expect to find mosquitoes and sand flies throughout the region, both of which can be quite voracious; arming yourself with insect repellent is an excellent idea. In addition, a few of the islands have chiggers and centipedes.

DISABLED TRAVELERS

Unfortunately, travel in the Caribbean is not particularly easy for those with physical disabilities. Overall there is little or no consciousness of the need for easier access onto planes, buses or rental vehicles. One exception is Puerto Rico, where good compliance with the Americans with Disabilities Act means many sights and hotels have wheelchair accessibility.

Visitors with special needs should inquire directly to prospective hotels for information on their facilities. The larger, more modern resorts are most likely to have the greatest accessibility, with elevators, wider doorways and wheelchair-accessible baths.

While land travel may present some obstacles, cruises are often a good option for the disabled in the Caribbean. Many cruise lines can coordinate shore-based excursions in wheelchair-accessible tour buses.

Resources & Organizations

Disabled travelers might want to get in touch with national support organizations in their home country. These groups commonly have general information and tips

on travel and are able to supply a list of travel agents specializing in tours for the disabled. Here are some resources:

Access-Able Travel Source (☎ 303-232-2979; www .access-able.com) A US-based organization with an excellent website that has links to international disability sites, travel newsletters, guidebooks, travel tips and information on cruise operators.

Accessible Journeys (☎ 610-521-0339, 800-846-4537; www.accessibletravel.com) A US-based organization that arranges group trips and cruises and has resources like villa rentals for independent travelers.

Royal Association for Disability & Rehabilitation (☎ 0207-250 3222; www.radar.org.uk) A UK-based advocacy organization providing general information on overseas travel.

Society for Accessible Travel and Hospitality (☎ 212-447-7284, 800-513-1126; www.sath.org) This advocacy group and resource publishes a quarterly magazine and has various free information sheets on travel for the disabled.

EMBASSIES & CONSULATES

It's important to realize what your own embassy – the embassy of the country of which you are a citizen – can and can't do to help you if you get into trouble. Generally speaking, it won't be much help in emergencies if the trouble you're in is remotely your own fault. Remember that you are bound by the laws of the country you are visiting. Your embassy will not be sympathetic if you end up in jail after committing a crime locally, even if such actions are legal in your own country.

In genuine emergencies you might get some assistance, but only if other channels have been exhausted. For example, if you need to get home urgently, a free ticket is exceedingly unlikely – the embassy would expect you to have insurance. If you have all your money and documents stolen, it might assist with getting a new passport, but a loan for onward travel is out of the question.

Not all Caribbean nations have diplomatic representation. See the individual chapter directories for a list of foreign embassies in each region, and island representation abroad.

FESTIVALS & EVENTS

Specific information on festivals and special events, which vary throughout the region, is found in the Directory sections of the individual island chapters.

GAY & LESBIAN TRAVELERS

Taken as a whole the Caribbean is not a particularly gay-friendly destination, and on many of the islands an element of overt homophobia and machismo is prevalent.

In the late 1990s several Caribbean governments made news by refusing gay cruise ships the right to land on their islands. Under the threat of boycotts by several cruise lines, the governments relented publicly, while continuing to campaign at home against outside influences of 'immorality.' Today several gay cruises ply the Caribbean waters (see p780), but the welcome is still rather tepid.

The situation for gay men and lesbians is a low-profile one on all the islands, and public hand-holding, kissing and other outward signs of affection are not commonplace. Still, there are several niches for gay travelers. Particularly friendly islands include Cuba, Dominican Republic, Puerto Rico and USVI. The low-key Dutch attitude makes the ABC islands warmer to gay travelers and the French influence on St Martin, Guadeloupe and Martinique makes them reasonably tolerant. Saba is a gay-friendly little island, although there's not a lot happening, but neighboring St Barth offers a welcome attitude and nightlife aplenty.

Islands where gay travelers will likely feel uncomfortable at best, and physically threatened at worst, include Jamaica, St Vincent & the Grenadines and Barbados. Outward affection on most of the former British islands is also not recommended. The comments here are general, and each region of each island is different. For a better idea on the gay climate of each island, turn to the chapter directories.

Resources & Organizations

Good websites with information on gay and lesbian travel as well as links to tour operators:

- gaytravel.com
- gaytravel.co.uk
- www.outandabout.com

The following organizations can recommend travel agents, tour companies and cruises that book gay-friendly travel:

Gay & Lesbian Tourism Australia (☎ 08-8379 7498; www.galta.com.au)

International Gay & Lesbian Travel Association (☎ 800-448-8550; www.iglta.org)
Out & About Travel (☎ 800-842-4753; www.outand abouttravel.com)

Ferrari International Publishing (☎ 602-863-2408; www.ferrariguides.com) produces several travel guides for gay men and lesbians. **Odysseus: The International Gay Travel Planner** (☎ 516-944-5330; www.odyusa.com) is another useful resource.

HOLIDAYS

A useful list of public holidays, which vary throughout the region, is found in the Directory sections of the individual island chapters.

INSURANCE

Travel insurance covering theft, loss and medical problems is a wise idea. At the very least it will bring you piece of mind and at best it could save you thousands of dollars. Before opting for a policy think about the coverage you require. There are a wide variety of policies, and you'll want one to suit your itinerary. Check the fine print as some policies exclude 'dangerous activities' such as diving, motorcycling, rock climbing and even hiking. Check to see whether you have coverage through your credit-card company, and find out about any penalties involved if you need to cancel flights or rebook hotels. Finally, as with all travel documents, make a couple of extra copies – one to leave at home and one to pack in your carry-on bag.

INTERNET ACCESS

Most of the Caribbean is riding the telecommunications wave and Internet services are rapidly expanding on many islands. Internet cafés are common in heavily touristed areas and many hotels offer free Internet service to guests – often a solitary computer shared by all guests.

For those traveling with a laptop, a few of the more modern and expensive hotels have separate lines for modem hookup, but high-speed and wireless connections are rare. If you plan to bring a laptop, be sure to call ahead to your hotel or resort to find out if hookup is available.

Also note that the power supply voltage in the Caribbean might differ from yours at home, which can sometimes mess up your equipment. If you bring along an international AC adaptor you can plug it in anywhere and not risk frying your computer's insides.

If you access your Internet account at home through one of the smaller ISPs, or through your office or school network, your best bet is to either open an account with a global ISP, like **AOL** (www.aol.com). Most travelers make use of free Web-based email though **Yahoo** (www.yahoo.com) or **Hotmail** (www.hotmail.com).

LANGUAGE

Spanish is the official language in Cuba, the Dominican Republic and Puerto Rico. French is spoken on Haiti, Guadeloupe, Martinique, St Barth and St Martin. They speak Dutch on Sint Maarten, St Eustatius, Aruba, Bonaire and Curaçao. English is the official language everywhere else, where the lovely lilt of each regional patois makes it sound like a brilliant foreign language.

LEGAL MATTERS

Due to the widespread stereotype that everyone in the Caribbean is a pot-smoking Rasta, some visitors take a casual attitude about sampling island drugs. When in Rome, right? Well, be forewarned that drug-trafficking is a serious problem throughout the Caribbean and most officials have little to no tolerance of visitors who come in and assume it's OK to partake. Penalties vary throughout the islands, but getting caught smoking or possessing marijuana (or any illegal drug for that matter) can send you to jail in a hurry.

While it's not strictly enforced, the legal drinking age ranges from 16 (Antigua) to 21 (USVI), but on most of the islands it is 18 years. In many places you must be at least 25 years to rent a car.

MAPS

Island tourist offices typically provide free tourist maps that will suffice for most visitor needs. Travelers who intend to explore an island thoroughly, however, may want something more detailed. On the former British islands, British Ordnance Survey maps are generally the best available, although they're not always up to date. On the French islands, the Institut Géographique National (IGN) maps are very detailed and updated frequently.

Blue Water Books & Charts (☎ 800-942-2583; www.bluewaterweb.com) A Florida-based company and one of the world's best resources for nautical charts, electronic charts and books.

IGN (☎ in Paris 01-43-98-80-00; www.ign.fr) A Paris-based map seller with maps of the French West Indies.

International Travel Maps & Books (☎ 604-879-3621; www.itmb.com) A Vancouver-based company that publishes maps for both popular and obscure destinations.

Map Link (☎ 805-692-6777, 800-962-1394; www.maplink.com) A California-based distributor that sells maps from hundreds of different publishers.

Stanfords (☎ 020-7836 1321; www.stanfords.co.uk) A UK-based map specialty store, with outlets in London, Manchester and Bristol, which sells British Ordnance Surveys, maps and nautical charts.

MONEY

There are 13 official currencies in the Caribbean, which can make things a bit confusing if you're jumping back and forth between islands. Fortunately, the US dollar (US$) is accepted on virtually all of the islands (Cuba being the obvious exception). A number of hotels, restaurants and car-rental places quote prices and car rentals in US dollars. However, for most transactions you'll be better off exchanging your money into the local currency. Banks can usually exchange British pounds sterling (UK£) and Canadian dollars (C$), both of which are not commonly accepted by businesses.

Countries whose official currency is the US dollar include Turks & Caicos, Puerto Rico, USVI and BVI. Countries with their own dollars include Bahamas (BS$), Cayman Islands (CI$), Barbados (B$), Jamaica (J$) and Trinidad & Tobago (TT$). Cuba has the Cuban Convertible Peso (CUC) and the Dominican Republic uses Dominican Pesos (RD$). Haiti uses the gourde, though US dollars are widely used.

The Eastern Caribbean dollar (EC$) is the official currency of Anguilla, Antigua & Barbuda, Dominica, Grenada, Montserrat, St Kitts & Nevis, St Lucia and St Vincent & the Grenadines.

The Netherlands Antilles islands of Saba, St Eustatius, Sint Maarten, Bonaire and Curaçao use the Antillean florin (written 'NAf' at banks and 'Fls' in stores, and also known as the 'guilder'), and Aruba uses the Aruba florin (Afl). The French West Indies islands of St Martin, Guadeloupe, Martinique and St Barth use the euro (€).

ATMs & Credit Cards

ATMs are found on most islands throughout the region. Major credit cards are widely accepted, most commonly Visa and MasterCard, followed by American Express. Note that on some islands, hotels may add a surcharge for credit-card payments, so you might want to inquire in advance.

Cash

As the US dollar is accepted almost everywhere, it's handy to carry some for when you first arrive. Many airports have banks or currency exchange booths where you can pick up local cash, so it's not necessary to have local currency before you arrive. Generally, it's best to carry smaller denominations to pay for taxis, street snacks or tips.

Tipping

The tipping situation varies. On some islands it's automatically added to your restaurant bill as a service charge, while on other islands you're expected to add a tip of about 15% to the bill.

Traveler's Checks

Traveler's checks in US dollars are widely accepted. However, if you come from a country other than the US, you might find changing your local currency into US traveler's checks an expensive way to go, as fees add up each time you exchange. With ATMs prevalent on most islands, many travelers find cash withdrawals more convenient.

PHOTOGRAPHY & VIDEO

The Caribbean Islands create the perfect backdrop for any photographer's dream shots. Succulent sunsets give color a whole new meaning; tropical flowers burst with pink and orange and yellow; green peaks sit at impossible angles; turquoise water seems to dance along the white-sand beaches; your family and friends have tans and sun-kissed hair; the local people wear colorful clothing and eat marvelously strange delights. Incredible photos are just a click away.

Film & Equipment

Print film is available on the main islands, but it's often expensive. Slide film? Forget it. There are same-day photo processing centers on the larger islands, but they can be quite expensive, so you might want to consider processing at home.

Travelers with digital cameras will want to bring along extra memory sticks. Some of the more savvy Internet cafés will have connections to download photos, but these are few and far between.

The availability of camera gear varies from island to island. In terms of camera and video equipment, videotapes and camera accessories, it's a basic rule of thumb that wherever there is a cruise-ship dock, there will also be a photo store, but elsewhere camera stores are few in number and poorly stocked. In virtually all cases, you can expect to pay more than you would at home.

EXCHANGE RATES (JULY 2005)

Local Currency	US$1	C$1	€1	UK£1
Aruba florin	Afl1.77	Afl1.40	Afl2.23	Afl3.23
Bahamas dollar	B$$1	B$$0.82	B$$1.21	B$$1.76
Barbados dollar	B$1.99	B$1.63	B$2.40	B$3.49
Cayman Islands dollar	CI$0.80	CI$0.67	CI$0.99	CI$1.44
Cuban Convertible Peso (CUC$)	$1.08	$0.73	$1.17	$1.70
Dominican Republic peso	RD$28.85	RD$23.65	RD$34.77	RD$50.59
Eastern Caribbean dollar	EC$2.67	EC$2.19	EC$3.22	EC$4.68
Euro	€0.83	€0.68	€1.00	€1.45
Haiti gourde	HTG40.59	HTG33.26	HTG48.88	HTG71.12
Jamaica dollar	J$61.91	J$63.34	J$74.59	J$108.51
Netherlands Antilles florin	NAf1.77	NAf1.40	NAf2.23	NAf3.23
Trinidad & Tobago dollar	TT$6.27	TT$5.14	TT$7.56	TT$10.99

For current exchange rates see www.xe.com.

Photographing People

It's common courtesy to ask permission before taking photos of people. Occasionally those who have their pictures taken without permission will become quite upset and may demand money. In some places, kids have realized the income potential in this and will offer to pose for you and then expect payment. As a general rule, adults are much more reluctant to have their pictures taken, unless there's been some social interaction.

Technical Tips

Beware that the high air temperatures in the tropics, coupled with high humidity, greatly accelerate the deterioration of film; store your exposed film in a dark, cool place. Don't leave your film or digital camera in direct sunshine any longer than necessary. It's a good idea to bring along extra Ziploc bags for storing your camera in when you're at the beach or on a boat trip.

Remember that sand and water are intense reflectors and in bright light they'll often leave foreground subjects shadowy. You can try attaching a polarizing filter, but the most effective technique is to take photos in the gentler light of early morning and late afternoon.

POST

Postal systems vary greatly in the Caribbean. Specific information on island post offices is given in the individual island directories.

SOLO TRAVELERS

Though traditionally a destination for lovers, honeymooners, families and groups, the Caribbean is a terrific place to travel alone. Solo travelers find that they can mosey up to any beach bar and find a cold Carib and good conversation. Single sojourners will also get closer to the local population. Whether out of necessity or curiosity, you're more apt to chat with a local fisherman or make friends with a taxi driver when you're going it alone. Most hotels, however, assume double occupancy and charge rates per room. Women traveling alone will want to be careful and aware that they'll get lots of extra attention (see p769).

TELEPHONE

Overall, the telephone systems work relatively well throughout the Caribbean. You can make both local and long-distance calls from virtually all public phones, but coin-operated phones are becoming a thing of the past and you'll find most islands favor phone cards. If you're making a lot of calls you'll be better off using a public phone, as most hotels charge per-call connection rates above and beyond the cost of the call.

Avoid the credit-card phones found at the airport and in some hotel lobbies, as they charge a steep US$2 per minute for local calls, US$4 to other Caribbean islands or the US, and as much as US$8 per minute to elsewhere.

Cell (Mobile) Phones

The use of cell phones is quite widespread throughout the Caribbean and most islands have their own network. You'll be able to use your cell on some islands, but on others you may need to purchase a separate SIM card. Before you bring your phone be sure to contact your provider; often the prohibitive cost of roaming far exceeds the convenience.

Phone Cards

If you're going to be doing much calling in the Caribbean, you'd be wise to purchase a public phone card, as these are widely used throughout the Caribbean.

Phone cards, the size of a credit card, are either inserted into the phone or have a private code that you dial before each call. Each card has an original value, and the cost of each call is deducted automatically as you talk. You discard it when the initial value of the card runs out.

It's a good idea to buy cards in smaller denominations, as the per-unit cost is virtually the same on all cards and you won't get a refund for unused minutes. Each island has its own system, shared only by other islands with the same national affiliation. If you're island hopping, the card you buy in St Thomas will work on the other USVI, but it won't, for example, work on St Barth.

Phone Codes

For Caribbean Island country codes, see inside the front cover as well as the Fast Facts box at the beginning of each individual island chapter.

In this book we have only included the local number in the listings in each regional chapter, unless the country code needs to be dialed for local calls or for interisland calls, in which case we have included the country code in the listings.

Some Caribbean nations are members of the North America Numbering Plan (NANP) and share the same country code (1) as the US and Canada in addition to their own country/area code. Anyone dialing from within North America just dials ☎ 1 + the three-digit country code + the local number. When calling these islands from outside North America, dial the access code of the country you're calling from + the island country code + the local number. For clarification, see the Telephone section in the individual regional directories.

Nations outside of the NANP include Aruba, Bonaire, Curaçao, Saba, St Eustatius and the Dutch side of Sint Maarten, which all have a country code of ☎ 599 and no area code. To call these islands from overseas, dial the access code of the country you're calling from + ☎ 599 + the local number. The French islands of St Martin, St Barth, Guadeloupe and Martinique are also outside the NANP. On these islands, the six-digit local number is preceded by a three-digit area code and a three-digit French West Indies country code (confusingly, these numbers have the same digits). To call Guadeloupe direct from the US, for example, dial ☎ 011 + 590 + 590 + the local number. To call other islands within the French phone system, omit the first country code and add a zero, thus: 0590-11-22-33.

Cuba is another exception and has a phone system all its own. See p175 for information.

TIME

The Bahamas, Turks & Caicos, Jamaica, the Cayman Islands, Cuba, Haiti and the Dominican Republic are on Eastern Standard Time (EST), five hours behind Greenwich Mean Time (GMT) and the same time as New York. All the other islands are on Atlantic Standard Time (AST), four hours behind GMT and an hour ahead of New York. Only the Bahamas and Turks & Caicos observe Daylight Savings Time; Cuba once did, but the practice was suspended in 2004. To check the time in relation to your city of origin, check www.timeanddate.com.

TOURIST INFORMATION

Tourism makes the world go round in most of the Caribbean. As a result, travel information is often excellent and easy to come by. Most islands have a tourist information center in the main town and several have satellite offices at the airport. Check the regional directories for local offices. The following are the phone numbers (main local and US toll-free where possible) and websites for the island tourism authorities.

Anguilla (☎ 264-497-2759, 800-553-4939; www.anguilla-vacation.com)
Antigua & Barbuda (☎ 268-462-0480, 888-268-4227; www.antigua-barbuda.com)
Aruba (☎ 297-582-3777, 800-862-7822; www.aruba.com)
Bahamas (☎ 242-302-2000, 800-224-3681; www.bahamas.com)
Barbados (☎ 246-427-2623; fax 246-426-4080; www.barbados.org)
Bonaire (☎ 599-7-8322, 800-266-2473; www.bonaire.org)
BVI (☎ 284-494-3134, 800-835-8530; www.bvitourism.com)
Cayman Islands (☎ 345-949-0623; www.caymanislands.ky)
Cuba (☎ 7-863-6884; www.infotur.cu)
Curacao (☎ 599-434-8200, 800-328-7222; www.curacao-tourism.com)
Dominica (☎ 767-448-2045; www.dominica.dm)
Dominican Republic (☎ 809-221-4660; www.dominicana.com.do)
Grenada (☎ 473-440-2279, 800-927-9554; www.grenada.org)
Guadeloupe (☎ 590-590-82-09-30; www.lesilesdeguadeloupe.com)
Haiti (☎ 509-222-8896; www.haititourisme.com)
Jamaica (☎ 876-929-9200, 800-233-4582; www.visitjamaica.com)
Martinique (☎ 596-596-63-79-60, 800-391-4909; www.martinique.org)
Montserrat (☎ 664-491-2230; www.visitmontserrat.com)
Nevis (☎ 866-556-3847; www.nevisisland.com)
Puerto Rico (☎ 787-721-2400, 800-223-6530; www.prtourism.com)
Saba (☎ 599-416-2231; www.sabatourism.com)
St Barth (☎ 590-590-27-87-27; www.st-barths.com)
St Eustatius (☎ 599-318-2433; www.statiatourism.com)
St Kitts (☎ 869-465-4040; www.stkitts-tourism.com)
St Lucia (☎ 758-452-4094, 800-456-3984; www.stlucia.org)

VOLUNTEER OPPORTUNITIES IN THE CARIBBEAN

Caribbean Volunteer Expeditions (www.cvexp.org) A US-based organization that sends volunteers to work on archaeology projects, artifact restoration and environmental preservation projects throughout the Caribbean. Fees typically cost about US$800 per week, including accommodations, food and land transportation, but not airfare.

Earthwatch (www.earthwatch.org) This organization sends volunteers to work on scientific and conservation projects, including rainforest conservation in Puerto Rico, turtle protection in Barbados and Trinidad, and crocodile studies in Cuba. Rates for two-week courses range from US$700 to US$4000, including meals, accommodations and airfare.

Greenforce Conservation Expeditions (www.greenforce.org) A UK-based organization that specializes in wildlife conservation expeditions for gap-year and university students who work with scientists to study the Andros reef system in the Bahamas. Cost is around £2300 for 10 weeks, including room and board, interisland flights but not the international flight to the Bahamas.

Habitat for Humanity (www.habitat.org) An international nonprofit, ecumenical Christian housing organization where volunteers build simple, decent, affordable housing for people in need. Costs vary, depending on the size and scope of the project.

Healing Hands for Haiti (www.healinghandsforhaiti.org) A foundation dedicated to bringing rehabilitation medicine to Haiti. You don't need a medical background to join a 10-day medical mission, which costs about US$1500, not including airfare.

St Martin (☎ 590-590-87-57-23, 877-956-1234; www.st-martin.org)

St Vincent & the Grenadines (☎ 784-457-1502, 800-729-1726; www.svgtourism.com)

Sint Maarten (☎ 599-542-2337, 800-786-2278; www.st-maarten.com)

Trinidad & Tobago (☎ 868-675-7034; www.visittnt.com)

Turks & Caicos (☎ 649-946-2321, 800-241-0824; www.turksandcaicostourism.com)

USVI (☎ 340-774-8784, 800-372-8784; www.usvitourism.vi)

VISAS

Passport and visa requirements vary from island to island; specific information is given in the individual island directories. There are new passport regulations for US citizens traveling from the Caribbean back into the US; see the boxed text, p772.

WOMEN TRAVELERS

Although the situation varies between islands, male machismo is alive and well in the Caribbean and women need to take precautions. Men can get aggressive, especially with women traveling alone. They rarely have qualms about catcalling, hissing, whistling, sucking their teeth or making kissy sounds to get your attention. While much of this is simply annoying, it can make women feel unsafe and vulnerable.

Like it or not, you'll feel so much safer traveling with a male companion. For women who love traveling alone, just be sensible and careful. Avoid walking alone after dark, heading off into the wilderness on your own, hitching or picking up male hitchhikers. Generally try to avoid any situation where you're isolated and vulnerable. Don't wear skimpy clothing when you're not on the beach – it will just garner you a lot of unwanted attention. Also note that 'harmless flirtation' at home can be misconstrued as a serious come-on in the Caribbean.

WORK

The Caribbean has high unemployment rates and low wages, as well as strict immigration policies aimed at preventing foreign visitors from taking up work.

Generally the best bet for working is to crew with a boat. As boat-hands aren't usually working on any one island in particular, the work situation is more flexible and it's easier to avoid hassles with immigration. Marinas are a good place to look for jobs on yachts; check the bulletin-board notices, strike up conversations with skippers or ask around at the nearest bar. You can also look for jobs with a crew placement agency like Florida-based www.crewfinders.com or UK-based www.crewseekers.co.uk.

Transportation in the Caribbean Islands

CONTENTS

THINGS CHANGE...

The information in this chapter is particularly vulnerable to change. Check directly with the airline or a travel agent to make sure you understand how a fare (and ticket you may buy) works and be aware of the security requirements for international travel. Shop carefully. The details given in this chapter should be regarded as pointers and are not a substitute for your own careful, up-to-date research.

GETTING THERE & AWAY

This chapter explains how to reach the Caribbean Islands from other parts of the world. For details on interisland travel within the Caribbean, see p780 and the Transportation sections in the relevant destination chapters.

ENTRY REQUIREMENTS

Upon arrival at many islands, the immigration officer will ask how long you're staying and stamp that exact number of days in your passport or on your entry card. Give yourself plenty of leeway, so that if you stay longer than originally planned you won't need to make a special trip to the immigration office or the police station for an extension. Another question commonly asked by immigration officers is where you will be staying; always have the name of a hotel in mind, even if you don't end up staying there.

One more thing to keep in mind as you travel throughout the region is that many islands require visitors to be in possession of either an onward or round-trip ticket. As part of this policy Leeward Island Air Transport (known only as LIAT) and other regional airlines often won't allow you to board a flight to an island unless you're also in possession of an onward ticket off the island.

Visa and document requirements vary throughout the Caribbean. For specific information, turn to the Directory sections at the end of each regional chapter.

AIR

It doesn't matter which island you fly into, touching down on Caribbean land is always a thrilling experience. Some islands, like Saba or St Eustatius, have tiny runways, where regional jumper planes miraculously land on airstrips that don't look much longer than Band-Aids. When you fly into the Bahamas you feel like you're surely going to land in the ocean. Other islands look like vague colonial outposts, surrounded by cane fields, dusty roads or mountains. Regardless, excitement and anticipation build as you look out the window and see heat shimmering on the runway.

Almost every major airline in the US offers service to the Caribbean and many European airlines have daily flights, either direct or through the US. There are no direct flights to the Caribbean from Australia, New Zealand or Asia – travelers fly via Europe or the US. Many airlines utilize the regional hubs. Puerto Rico is a major hub for flights from the US. Likewise, Sint

ONWARD & UPWARD?

While some islands may be lax about enforcing the onward-ticket requirement for entry, we've had reports of travelers enduring substantial frustration over this matter, ranging from fines to threats of imprisonment. It's best to make sure that you have proof of onward passage (or sufficient funds to pay for an onward ticket on the spot) before entering any of the islands.

Maarten, Antigua and Barbados act as hubs for European flights.

Many Caribbean countries have national airlines (Air Jamaica, Cayman Islands Airways, Bahamasair, Cubana) that often have the least expensive flights as long as you come and go from their scheduled cities. Many airlines have multiple scheduled flights to the Caribbean Islands from New York and Miami, so flights from those cities tend to be cheaper.

An extensive network of regional carriers operates between the islands. See p780 for more information on interisland flights.

Airlines

The following international airlines fly to the Caribbean. The ☎ 800 and ☎ 888 numbers are toll-free calls from the US, Canada, Mexico and the Caribbean.

Aerocaribe (☎ 998-884-2000; www.aerocaribe .com; hub Cancún, Mexico)

Aeropostal (☎ 888-802-8466; www.aeropostal .com; hub Caracas, Venezuela)

Air Canada (☎ 888-247-2262; www.aircanada.ca; hub Toronto, Canada)

Air Caraïbes (☎ 877-772-1005; www.aircaraibes .com; hub Guadeloupe)

Air Europa (☎ 902-401-501; www.air-europa.com; hub Madrid, Spain)

Air France (☎ 800-237-2747; www.airfrance.com; hub Paris, France)

Air Jamaica (☎ 800-523-5585; www.airjamaica .com; hub Montego Bay, Jamaica)

Air Sunshine (☎ 800-327-8900; www.airsunshine .com; hub Fort Lauderdale, USA)

Air Transat (☎ 866-847-1112; www.airtransat.com; hub Montreal, Canada)

American Airlines/American Eagle (☎ 800-433-7300; www.aa.com; hub Chicago, USA)

Bahamasair (☎ 800-222-4262; www.bahamasair .com; hub Nassau, Bahamas)

British Airways (☎ 800-247-9297, 800-744-2997; www.british-airways.com; hubs London-Heathrow & London-Gatwick, UK)

British West Indies Air International (BWIA; ☎ 800-538-2942; www.bwee.com; hub Trinidad & Tobago)

Cayman Airways (☎ 800-422-9626; www.caymanair ways.com; hub Nassau, Bahamas)

Chalks Ocean Airways (☎ 800-424-2557; www.fly chalks.com; hubs Nassau, Bahamas and Fort Lauderdale & Miami, USA)

Condor (☎ in North America 800-524-6975, in Europe 1805-707-202; www.condoramericas.com; hub Frankfurt, Germany)

Continental Airlines (☎ 800-523-3273; www.continental.com; hub Newark, USA)

Copa Airlines (☎ 800-234-3672; www.copaair .com; hub Panama City, Panama)

Cubana de Aviación (☎ in Havana 7-834-4949; www.cubana.cu; hub Havana, Cuba)

Delta (☎ 800-241-4141, 800-354-9822; www.delta .com; hub Atlanta, USA)

Gulfstream International (☎ 800-688-7225; www.gulfstreamair.com; hub Miami, USA)

Iberia (☎ in Puerto Rico 787-725-7000; www.iberia .com; hub Madrid, Spain)

Island Express (☎ 954-359-0380; www .abacotoday.com/islandexpress; hub Fort Lauderdale, USA)

JetBlue Airways (☎ 800-538-2583; www.jetblue .com; hub Salt Lake City, USA)

KLM (☎ 800-374-7747; www.klm.com; hub Amsterdam, the Netherlands)

LanChile (☎ 866-435-9526; www.lanchile.com; hub Santiago de Chile, Chile)

Lasca/Grupo Taca (☎ 800-400-8222; www.taca .com; hub San Salvador, El Salvador)

LTU International Airways (☎ 866-266-5588; www.ltu.com; hub Düsseldorf, Germany)

Martinair (☎ in the US 561-391-6165; www.martinair .com; hub Amsterdam, the Netherlands)

Mexicana de Aviación (☎ 800-531-7921; www .mexicana.com.mx; hub Mexico City, Mexico)

Northwest Airlines (☎ 800-447-4747; www.nwa .com; hub Detroit & Minneapolis/St Paul, USA)

Spirit Airlines (NK; ☎ 800-772-7117; www.spiritair .com; Fort Lauderdale, USA)

Surinam Airways (☎ 597-465700; www.surinamair ways.net; hub Paramaribo, Surinam)

United Airlines (☎ 800-538-2929; www.ual.com; hub Chicago, USA)

US Airways/US Air Express (☎ 800-622-1015; www.usair.com; hub Charlotte, USA)

Virgin Atlantic (☎ 800-744-7477; www.virgin-atlantic .com; hub London-Gatwick, UK)

Tickets

The cost of plane tickets to the Caribbean varies widely, depending on such variables as the time of year, weather conditions and traffic in the region. Airlines often run special fares to their destinations, so it's worth checking their websites or calling directly. Before you book, compare ticket prices on travel sites online. Here are some we recommend:

- www.cheaptickets.com
- www.expedia.com
- www.itn.net
- www.lowestfare.com
- www.orbitz.com
- www.sta.com
- www.travelocity.com

CHARTERS

Charter flights from the US, Canada, UK and Europe offer another option for getting to the islands. Fares are often cheaper than on regularly scheduled commercial airlines, but you usually have to depart and return on specific flights, and you'll probably have no flexibility to extend your stay.

In the high season, charters often operate with such frequency that they carry more passengers than the scheduled airlines.

Although charter companies do most of their business booking package tours that include both accommodations and airfare, they commonly find themselves with a few empty seats on planes that they've chartered. Some companies will then sell these empty seats for bargain prices a week or two prior to departure.

In the US you can sometimes find these seats advertised in the travel pages of larger Sunday newspapers, such as the *New York Times* and the *Boston Globe*. Travel agents

---

NEW US TRAVEL LAW

As part of the Western Hemisphere Travel Initiative, which aims to tighten US border controls, the US has announced that, effective December 31, 2005, all US citizens traveling to the Caribbean will need a passport, or other secure document, to re-enter the US. Don't leave home without it! The new law does not affect the US state territories of Puerto Rico and the US Virgin Islands, which will continue to be able to use established forms of identification.

---

who specialize in discount travel can also be helpful.

Anguilla

Anguilla's **Wallblake Airport** (AXA; ☎ 264-497-2514) is undergoing massive expansion that will transform it from a regional airport to a hub for jets coming from the US. At the moment, international travelers usually connect through Sint Maarten or San Juan. See p411 for more details.

Antigua & Barbuda

Flights to Antigua & Barbuda fly into Antigua's **VC Bird International Airport** (ANU; ☎ 268-462-0358). Most flights from the US connect through San Juan or Sint Maarten.

Air Canada Flies to Antigua from Montreal and Toronto.
Air Sunshine Serves Antigua from Montreal and Toronto.
British Airways Flies to Antigua from London.
Continental Airlines Flies to Antigua direct from Newark.
Delta Flies to Antigua from New York–JFK, New York–La Guardia and Newark.
US Airways Flies to Antigua from Charlotte and Philadelphia.
Virgin Atlantic Flies to Antigua from London.

Aruba, Bonaire & Curaçao

The majority of international flights to the ABC Islands arrive at Aruba's **Reina Beatrix International Airport** (AUA; ☎ 292-582-4800)

EUROPE

KLM is the only airline with direct flights from Europe; otherwise travelers from Europe have to change planes at a gateway airport such as New York–JFK or Miami, and this often entails an overnight stay.

Air France Offers service from Paris to Aruba and Curaçao.
BWIA International Flies to Curaçao via Trinidad.
KLM Flies daily from Amsterdam to each of the islands.

NORTH AMERICA

Air Canada Flies from Toronto and Montreal to Aruba, via Miami.
American Airlines Flies to Aruba from Boston, Miami and New York–JFK. It also flies to Curaçao from Miami.
Continental Airlines Flies from Houston and Newark to Aruba, and from mid-December, 2005, flies direct from Houston to Bonaire.
Delta Flies to Aruba from Atlanta and New York–JFK.
United Airlines Flies to Aruba from Chicago and Washington-Dulles.
US Airways Flies to Aruba from Boston, Charlotte and New York–La Guardia.

SOUTH AMERICA

Aerolinas Argentinas Flies from Buenos Aires via Caracas.

Aeropostal Flies from Caracas to Aruba and Curaçao.

Avianca Flies to Aruba and Curaçao from Bogota and Santiago.

Surinam Airways Flies from Paramaribo to Aruba.

Bahamas

The Bahamas has six international airports, including two major hubs: **Nassau International Airport** (NAS; ☎ 242-377-7281; Nassau, New Providence) and **Freeport International Airport** (FPO; ☎ 242-352-6020; Freeport, Grand Bahama).

NORTH AMERICA

The Bahamas is well served by flights from North America. Its proximity to Florida means regular, relatively inexpensive flights from Miami, Fort Lauderdale and Orlando, as well as other East Coast gateways. Nassau is less than three hours' flying time from northeast USA and about 30 minutes by jet from Miami.

Air Canada Flies direct from Toronto to Nassau and has connections from other Canadian cities.

Air Sunshine Serves Nassau and the outer Bahamian islands from Fort Lauderdale.

American Eagle Flies direct from Miami to Nassau.

Bahamasair Flies direct from eastern US cities, including Boston, Charlotte, Fort Lauderdale, Miami, New Orleans and Washington DC.

Chalks Ocean Airways Serves Nassau and the outer Bahamian islands from Fort Lauderdale.

Delta Flies direct from Atlanta and New York to Nassau.

Gulfstream Air Flies between Florida cities and Nassau, Freeport, Abaco, Andros, Eleuthera, Exumas and Cat Islands.

Island Express Serves Nassau and the outer Bahamian islands from Fort Lauderdale.

Spirit Airlines Flies to Nassau from New York, Washington DC and Fort Lauderdale.

US Airways Flies to both Nassau and Freeport from Charlotte and New York, and to Nassau from Philadelphia.

UK & EUROPE

British Airways has direct flights to Nassau from London-Heathrow. Virgin Atlantic, American Airlines, United, Delta and Continental Airlines have flights from the UK to the Bahamas with connections in Miami, Atlanta, Orlando or New York.

Barbados

Barbados' **Grantley Adams International Airport** (BGI; ☎ 246-428-7101) is having extensive renovations. On completion it will be the main point of entry to the south and southeastern Caribbean, especially for flights from Europe.

NORTH AMERICA

Air Canada Flies from Toronto and Montreal to Barbados.

Air Jamaica Delta's affiliate operates from several US cities to Barbados.

Air Sunshine Flies direct from Toronto and Montreal to Barbados.

American Airlines Serves Barbados from New York, Miami and St Louis.

Continental Airlines Flies from Newark to Barbados.

US Airways Flies to Barbados from Charlotte and Philadelphia.

UK & EUROPE

British Airways Flies direct from London-Gatwick to Barbados.

BWIA International Flies to Barbados from London-Gatwick.

Condor Flies to Barbados from its Frankfurt hub.

Virgin Atlantic Flies to Barbados from London-Gatwick.

British Virgin Islands

Terrence B Lettsome Airport (EIS; ☎ 284-494-3701) is on Beef Island, which is connected by bridge to Tortola. The airport does not receive flights from the US, Canada or Europe. Most travelers coming to the British Virgin Islands (BVI) need to transfer to Tortola through regional hubs, such as San Juan, Sint Maarten and Antigua. See p400 for more details.

Cayman Islands

The main passenger airport in the Cayman Islands, **Owen Roberts International Airport** (GCM; ☎ 345-949-5252), is on Grand Cayman. Several airlines have direct flights to the Caymans from US cities, with 28 of the island's 55 weekly flights coming from Miami.

Air Canada Flies direct from Toronto to the Caymans.

American Airlines Has daily flights from Miami to the Caymans.

British Airways Offers direct flights from London-Heathrow to the Caymans.

Cayman Airways The country's national airline serves the islands from Miami, Fort Lauderdale, Tampa, Houston, Chicago and Boston.

Continental Airlines Flies to the Cayman Islands from Newark.

Delta Flies from Atlanta to the Caymans.

Northwest Airlines Flies daily from Memphis to the Caymans.

US Airways Flies daily from Charlotte and Philadelphia to the Caymans.

Cuba

Cuba has 11 international airports. Mostly, travelers fly into Havana's **Aeropuerto Internacional José Martí** (HAV; ☎ 7-266-4133), Veradero's **Aeropuerto Juan Gualberto Gómez** (VRA; ☎ 45-24-70-15) or Santiago de Cuba's **Aeropuerto Antonio Maceo** (SCU; ☎ 22-69-10-14). The national airline, Cubana de Aviación, has the most international flights to the island.

The US embargo on Cuba means there are no direct flights from the US. Anyone wishing to travel to Cuba from the US must connect through a 'gateway' country, such as Canada or Mexico. Since US citizens can't buy tickets to Cuba using US-based airlines, travel agents or Internet sites, many agencies in Mexico, Canada and the Caribbean specialize in air-only deals – though they sometimes don't sell the flight from the US to the gateway country, for fear of embargo-related repercussions. These agencies should arrange the mandatory tourist card (see p176).

Except during peak holiday seasons, you can usually arrive in the gateway country and buy your round-trip ticket to Cuba there. US travelers with a license to travel to Cuba should contact **Marazul Charters, Inc** (☎ 201-319-3900; 305-644-0255, toll free 877-756-1433; www.marazul charters.com), which runs daily charter flights from Miami to Havana. For more details on the US travel ban, see the boxed text, p177.

CANADA

Air Canada Charter flights to almost all of Cuba's airports leave from several Canadian cities.
Air Transat Charters flights similar to Air Canada.
Cubana de Aviación Flies to Havana direct from Montreal (one per week) and Toronto (three per week).
Lasca Operated by Grupo TACA, Costa Rica's national carrier has three flights a week to Cuba from Toronto.
Mexicana de Aviación Flies daily to Havana from Vancouver.

CENTRAL & SOUTH AMERICA

Air Caribbean Flies between Havana and Managua in Nicaragua.
Copa Airlines Flies to Havana from its hub in Panama.
Cubana de Aviación Flies to Havana from several Central and South American cities, including Cancún, Mexico City, Panama City, Guatemala City, Bogota, Caracas, Buenos Aires and Sao Paulo.
LanChile Flies to Havana from Santiago.
Mexicana de Aviación Flies daily to Havana from Cancún and Mexico City, and has frequent flights from another dozen cities including Mérida and Tijuana.

UK & EUROPE

Air Europa Flies daily to Havana, with connections in Milan, Rome, Paris, Frankfurt and Copenhagen.
Air France Flies to Havana from Paris.
Cubana de Aviación Flies to Havana from Madrid, Barcelona, Canary Islands, London, Milan, Rome and Moscow.
Iberia Flies to Havana from Dusseldorf, Amsterdam, Barcelona, Brussels, Canary Islands, Geneva, Lyon, Lisbon, Madrid, Milan, Munich, Paris, Rome and Zurich.
LTU International Airways Flies from several German cities to Havana and Veradero.
Martinair Flies from Amsterdam to Havana, Varadero and Holguín.

Dominica

There are no direct flights available from Europe or the US into Dominica, so overseas visitors fly to a gateway island. See p556 for details.

Dominican Republic

Seven international airports operate in the Dominican Republic, but the majority of flights land at Santo Domingo's **Las Américas International Jose Francisco Peña Gomez Airport** (SDQ; ☎ 809-549-0081), Puerto Plata's **Aeropuerto Internacional Gregorio Luperón** (POP; ☎ 809-586-1992) and, to a lesser degree, **Aeropuerto Internacional Punta Cana** (PUJ; ☎ 809-959-2473) and Santiago's **Aeropuerto Internacional Cibao** (STI; ☎ 809-581-8072).

NORTH AMERICA

The easiest (and cheapest) way to get to the Domincan Republic is through New York–JFK or Miami.
Air Transat Charter flights to the Dominican Republic leave from several Canadian cities, including Montreal, Toronto, Vancouver, Calgary and Edmonton.
American Airlines Runs at least eight daily flights from New York–JFK and Miami to Santo Domingo and daily flights to Puerto Plata. Less frequent flights leave from Boston, Fort Lauderdale and Tampa to Santo Domingo.
Continental Airlines Flies direct from Newark to Santo Domingo, Puerto Plata and Santiago.
Delta Flies to Santo Domingo and Santiago direct from New York–JFK, New York–La Guardia and Newark.
JetBlue Airways Has a twice-daily service from New York–JFK to Santo Domingo and Santiago.
Spirit Airlines Flies to Santo Domingo from New York–La Guardia and Washington-Reagan through Fort Lauderdale.
US Airways Flies to Santo Domingo from Fort Lauderdale, and to Punta Cana from Charlotte.

SOUTH AMERICA

Copa Airlines Has daily flights between Santo Domingo and Panama City.

LanChile Flies from Lima.

UK & EUROPE

There are no direct flights to the Dominican Republic from the UK.

Most British travelers come via package charter flights that route through Miami or New York.

Air Europa Has a scheduled service between Santo Domingo and Madrid.

Air France Flies daily to Santo Domingo from Paris.

Condor Flies to Punta Cana and Puerto Plata from Dusseldorf, Frankfurt, Hamburg and Berlin.

Iberia Flies between Santo Domingo and Madrid.

LTU Flies from Dusseldorf and Munich.

Martinair Flies from Amsterdam to Santo Domingo and Puerto Plata.

Grenada

Flights to Grenada land at **Point Salines International Airport** (GND; ☎ 473-444-4101, 473-444-4555; fax 473-444-4838) on the southwestern tip of the island.

There are few direct flights into Grenada from North America or Europe as most connect through Bridgetown, Barbados (BGI), San Juan, Puerto Rico (SJU), Port of Spain, Trinidad (POS), Tobago (TAB) or Antigua & Barbuda (ANU).

Air Jamaica Delta's affiliate flies to Grenada from several US cities via Montego Bay.

American Airlines Serves Grenada from the US via Puerto Rico.

British Airways Flies direct from London-Gatwick to Grenada.

BWIA International Serves Grenada via Barbados, Port of Spain or Tobago.

Condor Flies to Grenada via Barbados from its Frankfurt hub.

Virgin Atlantic Serves Grenada via Barbados, Port of Spain or Tobago.

Guadeloupe

Guadeloupe's airport is **Pole Caraïbes Airport** (PTP; ☎ 590-590-21-14-72) in Point-á-Pitre.

Most US travelers fly into Miami, Sint Maarten or San Juan and then connect to Guadeloupe on American Eagle or Air Caraïbes. International carriers offering nonstop flights to Guadeloupe include Air Caraïbes, Air France (from Paris) and Air Canada (from Montreal).

Haiti

Haiti's main international airport is officially called **Guy Malary International Airport** (PAP; ☎ 509-246-4105) but is better known as Port-au-Prince International.

Air Canada Flies from Montreal and Toronto to Haiti.

Air France Has a Paris–London–Port-au-Prince route.

Air Transat Has flights from Montreal to Haiti.

American Airlines Operates the majority of flights from the US to Haiti, with direct flights from Fort Lauderdale, Miami, New Orleans and New York. It also flies from London and Paris.

Jamaica

Jamaica has two international airports. The majority of the flights arrive at Montego Bay's **Donald Sangster International Airport** (MBJ; ☎ 876-952-5530; www.sangster-airport.com.jm) but several carriers also serve Kingston's **Norman Manley International Airport** (KIN; ☎ 876-924-8546; www.manley-airport.com.jm).

NORTH AMERICA

Air Canada Flies to Montego Bay and Kingston from Toronto, Montreal, Halifax and Winnipeg.

Air Jamaica The country's national airline operates direct flights from many US cities, including Atlanta, Miami, Los Angeles, Chicago, Boston, Baltimore, Houston, Newark and Washington. It also has regular flights from Toronto.

Air Transat Has a regular service to Montego Bay from Toronto and Montreal.

American Airlines Flies to Kingston and Montego Bay from Miami, New York and Boston.

Continental Airlines Flies to Kingston and Montego Bay from Newark.

Delta Flies to Montego Bay from Atlanta.

Northwest Airlines Flies to Montego Bay from Detroit, Minneapolis and Memphis.

US Airways Flies to Montego Bay from Charlotte and Philadelphia.

UK & EUROPE

Air Jamaica Flies to Kingston and Montego Bay from London-Heathrow and Manchester.

British Airways Flies to Kingston and Montego Bay from London-Gatwick.

Condor Serves Montego Bay from Frankfurt.

Iberia Flies to Montego Bay from Vienna, Dusseldorf, Munich, Stuttgart, Frankfurt and Hamburg.

Martinair Operates a regular service from Amsterdam to Montego Bay.

Martinique

The modern **Lamentin International Airport** (FDF; ☎ 08-36-68-43-14) in Fort de France, receives some international flights, but mainly just connections from nearby hubs. Most flights from the US and Europe connect to Martinique through Puerto Rico or Miami.

Air Caraïbes Flies to Martinique direct from Paris.

Air France Has daily direct flights direct from Paris to Martinique.

Air Transat Flies direct from Montreal to Martinique.

American Airlines Flies to Martinique from New York, Newark and other US cities.

BWIA International Flies daily from New York–JFK, with connections in Antigua or Barbados.

Puerto Rico

International flights arrive at and depart from San Juan's **Aeropuerto Internacional de Luis Muñoz Marín** (SJU; ☎ 787-749-5050). A major hub, San Juan sees almost half of the Caribbean's flight traffic passing through en route to other Caribbean Islands.

NORTH AMERICA

Air Canada Has daily direct service from Toronto and Montreal to San Juan.

American Airlines Has a base in San Juan and more than a dozen daily direct flights from US cities, including Miami, Los Angeles, New York–JFK, Chicago, Dallas/Fort Worth, Hartford and Boston.

Continental Airlines Flies from Newark and Houston to San Juan.

Delta Has daily direct flights to San Juan from Atlanta, Boston, Orlando and New York–JFK.

JetBlue Has daily service from New York–JFK to San Juan and Aguadilla.

Northwest Airlines Flies from Detroit, Memphis and Minneapolis.

Spirit Airlines Flies to San Juan from New York, Washington DC and Fort Lauderdale.

US Airways Serves San Juan from Washington-Dulles, Charlotte, Philadelphia, Boston and Pittsburgh.

UK & EUROPE

As well as those listed below, several other airlines feed through Miami and Fort Lauderdale from the UK, including American Airlines, Delta and Virgin Atlantic.

British Airways Offers a daily connecting service to San Juan through Miami.

Condor Flies direct to San Juan from Frankfurt.

Iberia flies direct to San Juan from Madrid.

St Barth, Saba & St Eustatius

The tiny airports in St Barth, Saba and St Eustatius can only receive regional flights. International travelers must first fly into a

regional hub, such as Sint Maarten or Antigua, then catch a prop plane to the islands. See the island chapters for more information.

St Kitts & Nevis

Travelers to St Kitts & Nevis arrive at St Kitts's **Robert Llewellyn Bradshaw Airport** (SKM; ☎ 869-465-8121). Most international flights to St Kitts connect through Antigua, St Croix, St Thomas, Sint Maarten or Puerto Rico.

American Airlines Has flights from Miami, New York and Boston, with connections in Puerto Rico.

BWIA International Flies to St Kitts from Toronto and from London-Heathrow.

United Airlines Flies to St Kitts from Chicago and Denver.

US Airways Offers direct flights from Charlotte and Philadelphia to St Kitts.

St Lucia

St Lucia's airport, **Hewanorra International Airport** (UVF; ☎ 768-454-6355), receives several international flights daily.

NORTH AMERICA

As well as those listed below, other airlines serve St Lucia through connections in San Juan.

American Airlines Offers daily service into St Lucia from Miami and Washington DC.

Air Canada Flies from Toronto to St Lucia.

Air Jamaica Delta's affiliate flies to St Lucia from several US cities.

Air Sunshine Flies from Toronto to St Lucia.

Delta Flies from Atlanta to St Lucia.

UK & EUROPE

British Airways Flies to St Lucia from London-Heathrow.

BWIA International Flies to St Lucia from London-Heathrow.

Condor Has seasonal flights to St Lucia from Frankfurt.

Virgin Atlantic Offers service to St Lucia from London-Gatwick.

St Martin/Sint Maarten

International travelers arriving to this dual-nation island land at Sint Maarten's **Juliana Airport** (SXM; ☎ 599-545-2060; www.pjiae.com), a major hub where regional flights connect to smaller Eastern Caribbean islands.

EUROPE

Air France Run direct flights to Sint Maarten from Paris.

KLM Operate flights to Sint Maarten from Amsterdam.

Martinair Have direct flights from Amsterdam to Sint Maarten.

NORTH AMERICA
Air Canada Flies direct from Toronto to Sint Maarten.
Air Transat Flies from Toronto, Montreal, Vancouver, Calgary and Halifax to Sint Maarten.
American Airlines Flies direct to Sint Maarten from New York, Miami and San Juan.
Continental Airlines Flies from Newark to Sint Maarten.
Delta Flies from Atlanta to Sint Maarten.
United Airlines Flies direct to Sint Maarten from Chicago.
US Airways Flies from Philadelphia and Charlotte to Sint Maarten.

St Vincent & the Grenadines
International flights cannot fly direct to St Vincent & the Grenadines; instead, international passengers fly into a neighboring island and then switch to a prop plane for the final leg of their journey. See p623 for more information.

Trinidad & Tobago
Trinidad & Tobago is home to two international airports: the **Piarco International Airport** (POS; ☎ 868-669-8047; www.piarcoairport.com) on Trinidad and the **Crown Point International Airport** (TAB; ☎ 868-639-8547; www.tntairports.com) on Tobago.

NORTH AMERICA
Air Canada Flies to Trinidad from Toronto and Montreal.
Air Sunshine Flies to Trinidad from Toronto and Montreal.
American Airlines Flies to Trinidad from Baltimore and Miami.
BWIA International Flies to Trinidad from Miami, New York, Toronto and Washington DC.
Continental Airlines Flies from Houston and Newark to Trinidad.

SOUTH AMERICA
Surinam Airways Flies to Trinidad from Paramaribo, Suriname.

UK & EUROPE
British Airways Flies from London-Gatwick to Tobago.
BWIA International Flies to Trinidad from London-Heathrow, via Barbados, St Lucia or Antigua, and from Manchester via Barbados.
Caledonian Airways Flies from London-Gatwick to Tobago.
Condor Airlines Serves Tobago from Frankfurt.
Martinair Flies to Tobago from Amsterdam.
Virgin Atlantic Flies from London-Gatwick to Tobago.

Turks & Caicos
Three international airports handle traffic to the Turks & Caicos islands, but most international flights arrive at Provo's **Providenciales International Airport** (PLS; ☎ 649-941-5670).

A few carriers offer direct flights to Turks & Caicos, but most fly through Miami or Nassau.
American Airlines Flies daily from Miami and weekly from New York and Boston.
British Airways Weekly flights from London-Heathrow.
US Airways Flies direct from Charlotte and Philadelphia.

US Virgin Islands
The USVI has two international airports: **Cyril E King Airport** (STT; ☎ 340-774-5100; www.viport.com/aviation.html) on St Thomas and **Henry E Rohlsen Airport** (STX; ☎ 340-778-0589; www.viport.com/aviation.html) on St Croix.

There are no direct flights from Europe.
American Airlines Run direct service from Miami to both islands, and to St Thomas from New York–JFK and Boston.
Continental Airlines Flies to St Thomas from Newark.
Delta Serves both islands direct from Atlanta.
United Airlines Flies to St Thomas from Washington DC and Chicago.
US Airways Have direct flights to St Thomas from Philadelphia, Charlotte and New York–La Guardia, and from Charlotte to St Croix.

SEA
Cruises
More than two million cruise-ship passengers sail the Caribbean annually, making it the world's largest cruise-ship destination. While the ships get bigger the amenities also grow, and today your ship can have everything from climbing walls and an inline skating rink, to nightclubs and waterfalls. Most ships hit four or five ports of call, sometimes spending a night, other times only a few hours.

The typical cruise-ship holiday is the ultimate package tour. Other than the effort involved in selecting a cruise, it requires minimal planning – just pay and show up – and for many people this is a large part of the appeal.

For the most part, the smaller, 'nontraditional' ships put greater emphasis on the local aspects of their cruises, both in terms of the time spent on land and the degree of interaction with islanders and their environment. While the majority of mainstream cruises take in fine scenery along the way, the time on the islands is generally quite limited, and the opportunities to experience a sense of island life are more restricted.

Because travel in the Eastern Caribbean can be expensive and because cruises cover rooms, meals, entertainment and transportation in one all-inclusive price, cruises can also be comparatively economical.

COST

The cost of a cruise can vary widely, depending on the season and vacancies. While it will save you money to book early, keep in mind that cruise lines want to sail full, so many will offer excellent last-minute discounts, sometimes up to 50% off the full fare.

You'll pay less for a smaller room, but beware that the really cheap rooms are often claustrophobic and poorly located (be sure to ask before booking). Some cruise lines provide free or discounted airfares to and from the port of embarkation (or will provide a rebate if you make your own transportation arrangements), while others do not.

Meals, which are typically frequent and elaborate, are included in the cruise price. Alcoholic drinks are usually not included and are at bars prices. Guided land tours are almost always offered at each port of call, generally for about US$35 to US$100 each.

Most cruises end up costing US$200 to US$400 per person, per day, including airfare from a major US gateway city.

Port charges and government taxes typically add on about US$150 per cruise. Be sure to check the fine print about deposits, cancellation and refund policies, and travel insurance.

BOOKING A CRUISE

When it comes to figuring out what cruise to take, read whatever you can, ask around for referrals, and then call some travel agents. Agents most knowledgeable about cruises are apt to belong to **Cruise Lines International Association** (CLIA; www.cruising.org), an organization of cruise lines that works with about 20,000 North American travel agencies. You could also find a travel agent who subscribes to the *Official Cruise Guide,* which is a good source of information on cruise lines, listing schedules and facilities for virtually all ships.

Useful websites include **Cruise Critic** (www .cruisecritic.com), which gives ship profiles, reviews

of different cruise-ship companies, and details of bargains and special deals. **First Cruise Tips** (www.firstcruisetips.com) is geared toward first-time cruisers and gives great advice about the advantages and pitfalls of cruising.

For travelers with physical limitations, **Flying Wheels Travel** (☎ 507-451-5005, 800-535-6790; www.flyingwheelstravel.com) specializes in booking disabled-accessible Caribbean cruises.

Several agencies in the US deal specifically in booking Caribbean cruises and can be a great source of information on special deals. A few we recommend:

Cruise411 (☎ 800-553-7090; www.cruise411.com)
Cruise.com (☎ 888-999-2783; www.cruise.com)
Cruise Outlet (☎ 800-775-1884; www.thecruise outlet.com)
Cruise Web (☎ 800-377-9383; www.cruiseweb.com)
Cruises at Cost (☎ 800-274-3866; www.cruisesat cost.com)
World Wide Cruises (☎ 800-882-9000; www .wwcruises.com)

TRADITIONAL CRUISES

The following cruise lines sail to one or more of the Caribbean Islands.

American Canadian Caribbean Line (☎ 800-556-7450; www.accl-smallships.com) Specializes in smaller ships with a maximum capacity of 100 passengers. Trips include the Bahamas; Turks & Caicos; Virgin Islands; Antigua and Grenada; and Sint Maarten and Antigua.

Carnival Cruise Lines (☎ 800-327-2058; www .carnival.com) Long known for its glitzy bigger-is-better cruises, Carnival has 21 ships, from 'boutique' boats to mega yachts, most holding about 2000 passengers. It hits ports of call throughout the Caribbean.

Celebrity Cruises (☎ 800-892-6019; www.celebrity -cruises.com) Plying the waters since 1989, Celebrity offers plenty of flash on its nine ships. Its Millennium-class ships can take up to 2500 passengers and offer ultramodern amenities and decor, from glass elevators to Internet cafés, martini bars and super spas.

Cunard Line (☎ 800-728-6273; www.cunardline .com) Owner of the *Queen Mary II, Queen Elizabeth II* and forthcoming *Queen Victoria* (due in 2007), Cunard offers wintertime cruises in the Caribbean before its ships cross the Atlantic to cruise the Mediterranean, Baltics or Canary Islands. The focus is on 'classic luxury' and the ships hold up to 2600 passengers.

Disney Cruise Line (☎ 800-511-1333; www.disney .com/disneycruise) The ultimate family cruise line, Disney's ships are like floating theme parks, with special features like movie theaters, children's programs and family-sized staterooms. Disney currently has two ships that sail from Florida through the Bahamas.

Holland America (☎ 877-724-5425; www.holland america.com) With 13 ships plying the waters between seven continents, Holland America is one of the world's biggest operators. Its Vista-class ships offer the most modern amenities and most staterooms have ocean views and verandas. They offer classic touches like afternoon tea, art-nouveau decor and wireless Internet.

Norwegian Cruise Line (NCL; ☎ 305-436-4000, 800-343-0098; www.ncl.com) With the most US ports of embarkation, NCL attracts a lot of American passengers who come aboard for the variety of restaurants and full-menu entertainment, from full-scale Broadway musicals and casinos, to piano bars and pulsing discos.

Princess Cruises (☎ 800-568-3262; www.princess .com) The 14 ships range in size and style, but you get the ultimate in organized activities on a Princess cruise.

Radisson Seven Seas Cruises (☎ 877-505-5370; explore.rssc.com) Every stateroom is a suite on these ships that offer luxury and less regimented itineraries. Ships carry a maximum of 700 passengers, so the cruises feel more intimate than the big 2000-passenger ships.

Royal Caribbean Cruise Line (RBC; ☎ 800-398-9819; www.royalcaribbean.com) In operation since 1969, RBC has the largest cruise ships in the Caribbean, offering the whole gamut, from shuffleboard to rock-climbing walls, multiple pools, and a variety of restaurants and bars.

NONTRADITIONAL CRUISES

Clipper Cruise Line (☎ 800-325-0010; www.clip percruise.com) While it's a conventional cruise ship, the *Yorktown Clipper* carries only 138 passengers and has a shallow draft, enabling it to navigate secluded waterways. In summer, it cruises the Pacific Inside Passage to Alaska. In winter, it returns to the Caribbean to tour through the USVI and BVI, as well as the Grenadines and other Eastern Caribbean islands.

Club Med (☎ 800-258-2633; www.clubmed.com) The luxurious *Club Med II* is one of the largest sailing ships

in the world. It has computerized sails and a high-tech design, holds 386 passengers and operates much like any other all-inclusive Club Med resort, except that it's at sea. The ship has a distinctive European atmosphere, with the majority of the crew coming from Europe. Itineraries vary, but ports of call include St Kitts, Nevis, St Martin, Dominica, St Barth and Antigua.

Sea Cloud (☎ 888-732-2568; www.seacloud.com) This four-mast, 360ft-long (110m) ship was once owned by cereal heiress Majorie Merriweather Post, whose husband built it for her in 1931. It has luxury accommodations in 34 staterooms. The company also runs a few other sailing ships, which tour the BVI, the French and Dutch islands, as well as Trinidad & Tobago.

Star Clippers (☎ 800-442-0551; www.starclippers.com) These modern four-masted clipper ships have tall-ship designs and carry 180 passengers. Ports of call include St Martin, Dominica, Guadeloupe, Martinique, St Barth, St Lucia, St Vincent, Tortola, Jost Van Dyke, Bequia, Union Island and the Tobago Cays.

Windjammer Barefoot Cruises (☎ 800-327-2601; www.windjammer.com) The fleet consists of a restored four-mast, 282ft (86m) stay-sail rigged schooner and other tall sailing ships, carrying 65 to 128 passengers. They tend to attract a younger, more active and budget-minded crowd. Some cruises are geared for singles only. Boats depart from several locations including Aruba, Freeport, Antigua, Grenada, St Martin and Tortola. There are several different trips available, including a tour of the ABC islands, BVI, the Bahamas, the French West Indies and St Vincent & the Grenadines.

Windstar Cruises (☎ 800-258-7245; www.wind starcruises.com) These luxury four-mast, 440ft (134m) boats have high-tech, computer-operated sails and take 148 or 312 passengers. The company has three ships that focus on great cuisine, relaxation and few organized activities. Trips travel throughout the Windward and Leeward Islands.

OFF THE BOAT

Cruise-ship passengers who show interest in the local culture and put money directly into the hands of small merchants are more appreciated by islanders than those who stay wrapped in the cocoon of organized land tours or see nothing beyond the duty-free shops.

While the cruise line's optional land tours are conveniently packaged to take in many of the islands' sightseeing highlights, they also move quickly and tend to shield visitors from interaction with the local people. In addition, a fair percentage of the money paid for these tours stays with the organizers rather than going into the local economy.

If you venture out on your own you're likely to enjoy a richer cultural experience. If you want to really see an island consider hiring a local taxi driver, who will likely shed light on local issues and give you a more colorful tour. Wander the streets of the main town, poke into little shops, eat at local restaurants and buy souvenirs from street vendors, or veer off the beaten track. Visit small businesses and chat with the owners, buy local rums and other souvenirs in small shops instead of on board – you'll help fuel the local economy and likely save money in the process.

GAY & LESBIAN CRUISES

The following US-based companies organise gay-friendly cruises to the Eastern Caribbean:

Atlantis Events (☎ 800-628-5268; www.atlantisevents .com) Specializes in booking all-gay resort trips and cruises aboard a variety of ships, with a serious focus on fun.

Gay Cruise Vacations (☎ 888-367-9398; www.gay cruisevacations.com) These popular all-gay vacations on giant cruise ships travel throughout the Caribbean on mostly seven-day trips.

Journeys By Sea, Inc (☎ 800-825-3632; www.journey sbysea.com) Offers relaxed, gay-only charters on small yachts in the Virgin Islands, and the Leeward and Windward Islands. Trips typically last seven days.

RSVP Vacations (☎ 800-328-7787; www.rsvp vacations.com) Good for active travelers, RSVP has trips on both large cruise ships and smaller yachts.

Ferry

Once a week, a passenger ferry travels between Chaguaramas, Trinidad and Guiria, Venezuela, offering an alternative for people traveling to/from South America. Service is operated by **Pier 1 Marine** (☎ 868-643-4472; Pier 1 Chaguaramas). The boat leaves Trinidad Wednesday mornings at 9am, but passengers should get there at 7am for early boarding (one way/ return TT$290/580, children under 12 half-price; 3½ hours). All passengers must pay a TT$75 departure tax. From Venezuela, the boat leaves at 3pm, and passengers must pay a US$23 departure tax. All passengers arriving in Venezuela must have a valid passport, a visa if applicable (check your consulate) and proof of yellow-fever shots. Those arriving in Trinidad must have a valid passport, a visa if applicable, and a valid plane ticket back to their country of origin.

GETTING AROUND

AIR
Airlines in the Caribbean

Several regional airlines jump between the islands. LIAT is a major carrier, as is Caribbean Star. A certain level of patience and understanding is required when you island hop. Schedules can change at a moment's notice, the flights can be bumpy and the airplanes old and jittery. For the number of flights that happen daily in the Caribbean, there are very few accidents, so your best bet is to relax and enjoy the ride.

Regional planes are sometimes like old buses, seemingly stopping at every possible corner to pick up passengers. You'll sometimes get stuck on what we like to call the 'LIAT shuffle' – where your plane touches down and takes off again from several different airports. For example, if you're flying from St Thomas to Trinidad, you might stop in Antigua, St Lucia and St Vincent before making it to Trinidad. This can easily turn a short flight into half a day. Again, it's best just to enjoy the ride.

For the most part, regional transportation is convenient and necessary. Flights individually are reasonably priced, but if you're doing a lot of traveling around, they can quickly add up. It's a good idea to plan ahead carefully. **Caribbean Connections** (☎ 888-255-6889; www.islandhoppingexperts.com) specializes in helping travelers plan island-hopping trips. They'll help you figure out an itinerary, no matter what your budget.

REGIONAL AIRLINES

For more detailed interisland flight information, turn to the individual chapters. These are the main regional airlines flying between islands.

Aerocaribbean (☎ 7-870-4965, 7-879-7524; www .aero-caribbean.com; hub Havana, Cuba) This small airline flies within Cuba, and links it to the Cayman Islands and Central American destinations.

Air Jamaica (☎ 800-523-5585; www.airjamaica.com; hub Montego Bay, Jamaica) Flies from Montego Bay and Kingston to Antigua, Bahamas, Barbados, Bonaire, Cuba, Curaçao, Dominican Republic, Grand Cayman, Grenada, Haiti, Puerto Rico, St Lucia and Turks & Caicos.

Air Antilles Express (☎ 890-648-648; www.airantilles .com; hub Guadeloupe) Flies between Martinique, Guadeloupe, Sint Maarten and St Barth and Dominican Republic.

Air Caraïbes (☎ 877-772-1005; www.aircaraibes.com; hub Guadeloupe) Flies between Guadeloupe, Martinique, St Barth, Sint Maarten, Dominica, Dominican Republic and Haiti.

Air St Thomas (☎ 800-522-3084; www.airstthomas .com; hub St Thomas) This regional carrier flies between USVI, BVI and Puerto Rico.

Air Sunshine (☎ 800-327-8900; www.airsunshine .com; hub San Juan, Puerto Rico) In addition to its service between Florida and the Bahamas, this regional carrier flies between San Juan and Vieques and St Thomas, St Croix, Tortola and Virgin Gorda.

American Eagle (☎ 800-433-7300; www.aa.com; hub San Juan, Puerto Rico) American Airlines' regional carrier flies to Anguilla, Antigua, Bahamas, Barbados, BVI,

Dominica, Dominican Republic, Jamaica, Montserrat, Nevis, St Croix, St Kitts, St Thomas and Trinidad & Tobago.

BWIA (☎ 800-538-2942; www.bwee.com; hub Port of Spain, Trinidad) This Trinidad-based carrier flies between several islands including Antigua, Barbados, Grenada, Jamaica, St Kitts, St Lucia, Sint Maarten, St Vincent and Trinidad & Tobago.

Caribbean Star (☎ 866-864-6272; www.flycarib beanstar.com; hub Antigua) This major regional airline flies between Anguilla, Antigua, Barbados, Dominica, Grenada, St Croix, St Kitts, St Lucia, Sint Maarten, St Thomas, St Vincent and Trinidad & Tobago.

Caribbean Sun (☎ 866-864-6272; www.flycsa.com; hub San Juan, Puerto Rico) Flies from Puerto Rico to Antigua, St Croix, St Kitts, Sint Maarten, St Thomas and Tortola.

Cape Air (☎ 800-352-0714; www.flycapeair.com; hub San Juan, Puerto Rico) Flies from San Juan and Vieques to St Croix, St Thomas and Tortola.

LIAT (☎ 888-844-5428; www.liatairline.com; hub Antigua) As the major carrier to several Caribbean islands, LIAT provides regular service between Anguilla, Antigua & Barbuda, Aruba, Bahamas, Barbados, BVI, Dominica, Dominican Republic, Grenada, Guadeloupe, Jamaica, Martinique, Nevis, St Croix, St Kitts, St Lucia, Sint Maarten, St Thomas and Trinidad & Tobago.

Winair (☎ 877-255-6889; www.fly-winair.com; hub Sint Maarten) Flies between the Windward Islands of Anguilla, Nevis, Saba, St Barth, St Eustatius, St Kitts, Sint Maarten & Tortola.

Air Passes
AIR JAMAICA
The Caribbean Hopper Program enables travelers flying Air Jamaica from a US city to visit three or more islands (economy US$399; first class US$699) within their Caribbean and Central American network, which includes anywhere in Jamaica, Turks & Caicos (Providenciales), Grand Cayman, the Bahamas, Cuba, Panama City (Panama), Bonaire, Barbados, Grenada and St Lucia. The minimum stay is three days and the maximum is 30 days. No backtracking allowed.

BRITISH WEST INDIES AIR (BWIA)
Port of Spain–based BWIA offers a Caribbean Travelers Air Pass to anyone flying into the Caribbean on a BWIA international flight. The pass (economy US$399; first class US$599) lets passengers travel within 30 days to any of the airline's Caribbean destinations. The itinerary must be set in advance and there's a US$20 charge to make changes. Each destination can be visited only once, other than for connecting flights.

CARIBBEAN STAR
The Caribbean Star Starpass allows passengers to make up to four flights for US$299. The pass can be used on any of the airline's destinations. The pass must be purchased through a travel agent in conjunction with an international return ticket.

LIAT
Antigua-based LIAT offers three passes, all of which require advanced booking, with no open returns and no backtracking. Flights must be operated by LIAT (not an affiliate). You can change dates only, for a fee of US$15.

Airpass (per sector US$98) European travelers who buy an air pass in conjunction with their international flight can get three to six stopovers for US$98 per sector. Travel must be completed within 21 days.

Caribbean Super Explorer (US$575) Gives you unlimited travel to any of LIAT's destinations within 30 days.

Explorer (US$300) Travelers can have a maximum of three stopovers in 21 days, returning to the originating destination to connect with the international flight.

BICYCLE
The popularity of cycling in the Caribbean depends on where you go. Several islands are prohibitively hilly, with narrow roads that make cycling difficult. On others, such as Cuba, cycling is a great way to get around. Some of the islands have bicycles for rent; for details see the island chapters. If you want to do any serious riding, consider bringing your own bike, but be prepared to fix your own flats and broken chains. Bike shops are virtually nonexistent. Most ferries will let you bring bikes on board at no extra charge; regional airlines will likely charge you a hefty fee, so it's best to check ahead if you're going to island-hop with your bike.

BOAT
Ferry
For a place surrounded by water, the Caribbean Islands don't have as many ferries as you'd think. However, microregional ferries do travel between several island groups. An extensive and inexpensive ferry network connects the USVI and BVI islands. Ferry services are also available between the following islands: Anguilla and St Martin; St Martin, Saba and St Barth; St Kitts and Nevis; St Vincent and Bequia; Grenada and Carriacou; and Trinidad and Tobago.

Ferries also run between Guadeloupe, Martinique and the outlying islands of Terre-de-Haut, Marie-Galante and La Désirade. High-speed catamaran ferries connect the islands of Guadeloupe, Dominica, Martinique and St Lucia. Catamarans also sail between St Martin and St Barth for day trips. In the Bahamas, a high-speed ferry links Nassau to outlying islands.

Details on all these boats are in the relevant individual island chapters.

Yacht

The Caribbean is one of the world's prime yachting locales, offering diversity, warm weather and fine scenery. The many small islands grouped closely together are not only fun to explore but also form a barrier, providing relatively calm sailing waters.

The major yachting bases are in the BVI, St Martin, Antigua, Guadeloupe, Martinique, St Lucia, St Vincent and Grenada.

It's easiest to sail down-island, from north to south, as on the reverse trip boats must beat back into the wind. Because of this, several yacht charter companies only allow sailors to take the boats in one direction, arranging for their own crews to bring the boats back to home base later.

Information on ports and marinas can be found in the individual island chapters.

YACHT CHARTERS

You can choose from two basic types of yacht charters: bareboat (sail it yourself) and crewed (you relax, someone else sails). Some yacht-charter companies offer everything from live-aboard sailing courses to full luxury living.

With a bareboat charter you rent just the boat. You are the captain and you sail where you want, when you want. You must be an experienced sailor to charter the boat. Bareboat yachts generally come stocked with linen, kitchen supplies, fuel, water, a dinghy, an outboard, charts, cruising guides, a cellular phone and other gear. Provisioning (stocking the boat with food) is not included, although sometimes it is provided for an additional fee.

With a crewed charter the yacht comes with a captain, crew, cook and provisions. You don't have to know how to sail, or anything else about boats. You can either make your own detailed itinerary or provide a vague idea

of the kind of places you'd like to visit and let the captain decide where to anchor.

Costs vary greatly. The more established companies generally charge more than small, little-known operators, and large ritzy yachts of course cost more than smaller, less luxurious boats. For more details on yacht charters, see the boxed text, p398.

The following charter companies offer both bareboat and crewed yacht charters in the Caribbean:

Catamaran Company (☎ 800-262-0308; www.catamarans.com)

Horizon Yacht Charters (☎ 877-494-8787; www.horizonyachtcharters.com)

Moorings (☎ 888-952-8420; www.moorings.com)

Sunsail (☎ 800-327-2276; www.sunsail.com)

TMM Bareboat Vacations (☎ 800-633-0155; www.sailtmm.com)

CHARTER BROKERS

For those who don't want to be bothered shopping around, charter-yacht brokers can help. Brokers work on commission, like travel agents, with no charge to the customer – you tell them your budget and requirements and they help make a match.

A few of the better-known charter-yacht brokers are:

Ed Hamilton & Co (☎ 800-621-7855; www.ed-hamilton.com)

Lynn Jachney Charters (☎ 800-223-2050; www.lynnjachneycharters.com)

Nicholson Yacht Charters (☎ 800-662-6066; www.yachtvacations.com)

BUS

Inexpensive bus service is available on most islands, although the word 'bus' has different meanings in different places. Some islands have full-size buses, while on others a 'bus' is simply a pickup truck with wooden benches in the back.

Buses are often the primary means of commuting to work or school and thus are most frequent in the early mornings and from mid- to late afternoon. There's generally a good bus service on Saturday mornings, but Sunday service is often nonexistent.

Buses can get crowded. As more and more people get on, children move onto their parents' laps, school kids share seats, people squeeze together and everyone generally accepts the cramped conditions with good humor. Whenever someone gets off

WHICH SIDE?

What side of the road to drive on depends on the island, and this can prove particularly confusing if you're island-hopping and renting cars on each island. Adding to the confusion, some cars have steering columns on the opposite side of the car. As a rule, drivers stick to the following:

Left Side of the Road (like the UK)

Anguilla, Antigua & Barbuda, Bahamas, Barbados, British Virgin Islands, Cayman Islands, Dominica, Grenada, Jamaica, St Kitts & Nevis, St Lucia, St Vincent, Trinidad & Tobago, Turks & Caicos, US Virgin Islands.

Right Side of the Road (like the US)

Aruba, Bonaire, Cuba, Curaçao, Dominican Republic, Guadeloupe, Haiti, Martinique, Puerto Rico, Saba, St Barth, St Eustatius (Statia), St Martin/Sint Maarten.

the back of a crowded minivan, it takes on the element of a human Rubik's Cube, with seats folding up and down and everyone shuffling; on some buses there's actually a conductor to direct the seating.

CAR & MOTORCYCLE

Driving in the Caribbean Islands can rock your world, rattle your brains and fray your nerves. At first. Soon, you'll get used to the chickens, goats, stray dogs and cows wandering the roadways. You'll get the hang of swerving like a maniac, of slowing for no reason, of using your horn to communicate everything from 'Hey, I'm turning right!' to 'Hey, you're cute!' to 'Hey, [expletive] you!'

It often seems like the only time island residents rush is when they get in their cars. For no apparent reason, many islanders like to haul ass through traffic, roar around twisting roads and use highways to test just how fast their cars will go. Truly, you will get used to all this. Just beware, if you rent a car in the islands, it might change your driving for good!

Driver's License

You'll need your driver's license in order to rent a car. On most of the former British islands, you'll also need to purchase a local driver's license when you rent a car, but you can do that simply by showing your home license and dishing out the appropriate fee. If you're going to St Lucia, having an International Driving Permit (IDP) will save you the price of a local license, but on the other islands there's no benefit to having an IDP in addition to your home license.

Rental

Car rentals are available on nearly all of the islands, with a few exceptions (usually because they lack roads). On most islands there are affiliates of the international chains, but the local rental agencies are often just as good, and usually have lower prices. Always purchase insurance; it's usually cheap and the unique driving conditions up the likelihood of getting in an accident.

During the busy winter season, some islands simply run out of rental cars, so it's a good idea to book one in advance. On many islands you need to be 25 years old to rent a car. Check the Transportation section of each chapter for specific details.

HITCHHIKING

Hitchhiking is an essential mode of travel on most islands, though the practice among foreign visitors isn't as common.

If you want to hitch a ride, stand by the side of the road and put your hand out. Be aware that this is also how locals flag taxis and since many private cars look like taxis, this can be confusing (note that most taxis have the letter 'H' – for Hire – on their front license plate). Foreign women traveling alone should not hitchhike – your want for a ride could be misconstrued as a want for something else. Men traveling alone should also be cautious. Though most drivers will happily give you a ride, others might see you as a target, especially if you're carrying around expensive luggage or camera equipment.

If you're driving a rental car, giving locals a lift can be a great form of cultural interaction. Again, be cautious and obey your instincts.

Health David Goldberg MD

CONTENTS

Prevention is the key to remaining healthy while abroad. Travelers who receive the recommended vaccines and follow common-sense precautions usually come away with nothing more than a little diarrhea.

From the medical standpoint, the Caribbean is generally safe as long as you're reasonably careful about what you eat and drink. The most common travel-related diseases, such as dysentery and hepatitis, are acquired by consumption of contaminated food and water. Mosquito-borne illnesses aren't a significant concern on most of the islands, except during outbreaks of dengue fever.

BEFORE YOU GO

Bring medications in their original containers, clearly labeled. A signed, dated letter from your physician describing all medical conditions and medications, including generic names, is also a good idea. If carrying syringes or needles, be sure to have a physician's letter documenting their medical necessity.

INSURANCE

If your health insurance does not cover you for medical expenses abroad, consider supplemental insurance. US travelers can find a list of medical-evacuation and travel-insurance companies at the website of the **US State Department** (www.travel.state.gov/medical .html). Find out in advance if your insurance plan will make payments directly to providers or reimburse you later for overseas health expenditures.

RECOMMENDED VACCINATIONS

Since most vaccines don't produce immunity until at least two weeks after they're given, visit a physician four to eight weeks before departure. Ask your doctor for an international certificate of vaccination (also known as the 'yellow booklet'), which will list all the vaccinations you've received. This is mandatory for countries that require proof of yellow-fever vaccination upon entry, but it's a good idea to carry it wherever you travel.

MEDICAL CHECKLIST

- acetaminophen/paracetamol (eg Tylenol) or aspirin
- adhesive or paper tape
- antibacterial ointment (eg Bactroban) for cuts and abrasions
- antibiotics
- antidiarrheal drugs (eg loperamide)
- antihistamines (for hay fever and allergic reactions)
- anti-inflammatory drugs (eg ibuprofen)
- bandages, gauze and gauze rolls
- DEET-containing insect repellent for the skin
- iodine tablets (for water purification)
- oral rehydration salts
- permethrin-containing insect spray for clothing, tents and bed nets
- pocketknife
- scissors, safety pins and tweezers
- steroid cream or cortisone (for poison ivy and other allergic rashes)
- sunblock
- syringes and sterile needles
- thermometer

INTERNET RESOURCES

There is a wealth of online travel-health advice. **LonelyPlanet.com** (www.lonelyplanet.com) is a

REQUIRED & RECOMMENDED VACCINATIONS

Vaccine	Recommended for	Dosage	Side effects
chickenpox	travelers who've never had chickenpox	2 doses, 1 month apart	fever; mild case of chickenpox
hepatitis A	all travelers	1 dose before trip; booster 6-12 months later	soreness at injection site; headaches; body aches
hepatitis B	long-term travelers in close contact with local population	3 doses over 6 months	soreness at injection site; low-grade fever
measles	travelers born after 1956 who've had only 1 measles vaccination	1 dose	fever; rash; joint pains; allergic reactions
rabies	travelers who may have contact with animals and may not have access to medical care	3 doses over 3-4 weeks	soreness at injection site; headaches; body aches
tetanus-diphtheria	all travelers who haven't had booster within 10 years	1 dose lasts 10 years	soreness at injection site
typhoid	all travelers to Haiti, and for extended stays in rural areas on other islands	4 capsules by mouth, 1 taken every other day	abdominal pain; nausea; rash
yellow fever	travelers to rural areas in Trinidad & Tobago	1 dose lasts 10 years	headaches; body aches; severe reactions rare

good place to start. The **World Health Organization** (www.who.int/ith/) publishes a superb book called *International Travel & Health*, which is revised annually and is available on its website at no cost. Another website of general interest is **MD Travel Health** (www.mdtravelhealth.com), which provides complete travel-health recommendations for every country, updated daily, also at no cost.

It's usually a good idea to consult your government's travel-health website before departure, if one is available.

Australia (www.smartraveller.gov.au)
Canada (www.hc-sc.gc.ca/english)
UK (www.doh.gov.uk/traveladvice)
USA (www.cdc.gov/travel)

FURTHER READING

If you're traveling with children, Lonely Planet's *Travel with Children,* by Cathy Lanigan, is useful. *ABC of Healthy Travel,* by E Walker et al, and *Medicine for the Outdoors,* by Paul S Auerbach, are other valuable resources.

IN TRANSIT

DEEP VEIN THROMBOSIS (DVT)

Blood clots may form in the legs during plane flights, chiefly because of prolonged immobility. Note that the longer the flight, the greater the risk. Though most blood clots are reabsorbed uneventfully, some may break off and travel through the blood vessels to the lungs, where they could cause life-threatening complications.

The chief symptom of DVT is swelling or pain in the foot, ankle or calf, usually but not always on just one side. When a blood clot travels to the lungs, it may cause chest pain and difficulty in breathing. Travelers with any of these symptoms should immediately seek medical attention.

To prevent the development of DVT on long flights, you should walk about the cabin, perform isometric compressions of the leg muscles (ie contract the leg muscles while sitting), drink plenty of fluids, and avoid alcohol and tobacco.

JET LAG & MOTION SICKNESS

Jet lag is common when crossing more than five time zones, and is characterized by insomnia, fatigue, malaise or nausea. To avoid jet lag, try drinking plenty of fluids (nonalcoholic) and eating light meals. Upon arrival, get exposure to natural sunlight and readjust your schedule (for meals, sleep etc) as soon as possible.

Antihistamines like dimenhydrinate (Dramamine) and meclizine (Antivert, Bonine)

HEALTH

are usually the first choice for treating motion sickness. Their main side effect is drowsiness. A herbal alternative is ginger, which works like a charm for some people.

IN THE CARIBBEAN ISLANDS

AVAILABILITY & COST OF HEALTH CARE

Acceptable health care is available in most major cities throughout the Caribbean, but may be hard to locate in rural areas. In general, the quality of health care will not be comparable to that in your home country. To find a good local doctor, your best bet is to ask the management of the hotel where you are staying or contact your local embassy. In many countries, the US embassy posts a list of English-speaking physicians on its website.

Many doctors and hospitals expect payment in cash, regardless of whether you have travel-health insurance. If you develop a life-threatening medical problem, you'll probably want to be evacuated to a country with state-of-the-art medical care. Since this may cost tens of thousands of dollars, be sure you have insurance to cover this before you depart (see p784).

Many pharmacies are well supplied, but important medications may not be consistently available. Be sure to bring along adequate supplies of all prescription drugs.

INFECTIOUS DISEASES

Bancroftian Filariasis

Otherwise known as elephantiasis, bancroftian filariasis occurs in Haiti, the Dominican Republic and some other islands. The disease is carried from person to person by mosquitoes. In severe cases, filariasis may cause enlargement of the entire leg or arm, as well as the genitals and breasts. Most cases occur in longtime residents, but travelers should be aware of the risks and should follow insect protection measures, as outlined on p789.

Dengue Fever

Dengue fever is a viral infection common throughout the Caribbean. Dengue is transmitted by Aedes mosquitoes, which bite mostly during the daytime and are usually found close to human habitations, often indoors. They breed primarily in artificial water containers, such as jars, barrels, cans, cisterns, metal drums, plastic containers and discarded tires. As a result, dengue is especially common in densely populated, urban environments.

Dengue usually causes flulike symptoms, including fever, muscle aches, joint pains, headaches, nausea and vomiting, often followed by a rash. The body aches may be quite uncomfortable, but most cases resolve uneventfully in a few days. Severe cases usually occur in children under age 15 who are experiencing their second dengue infection.

There is no treatment for dengue fever except to take analgesics such as acetaminophen or paracetamol (Tylenol) and drink plenty of fluids. Severe cases may require hospitalization for intravenous fluids and supportive care. There is no vaccine. The cornerstone of prevention is insect protection measures; see p789.

Fascioliasis

This is a parasitic infection that is typically acquired by eating contaminated watercress grown in sheep-raising areas, especially in Cuba. Early symptoms of fascioliasis include fever, nausea, vomiting and painful enlargement of the liver.

Hepatitis A

Hepatitis A is the second-most common travel-related infection (after traveler's diarrhea). It occurs throughout the Caribbean, particularly in the northern islands. Hepatitis A is a viral infection of the liver that is usually acquired by ingestion of contaminated water, food or ice, though it may also be acquired by direct contact with infected persons. The illness occurs throughout the world, but the incidence is higher in developing nations. Symptoms may include fever, malaise, jaundice, nausea, vomiting and abdominal pain. Most cases resolve without complications, though hepatitis A occasionally causes severe liver damage. There is no treatment.

The vaccine for hepatitis A is extremely safe and highly effective. If you get a booster six to 12 months later, it lasts for at least 10 years. You should get it before you go to any developing nation. Because the safety of hepatitis A vaccine has not been established for pregnant women or children under age two, they should instead be given a gammaglobulin injection.

Hepatitis B

Like hepatitis A, hepatitis B is a liver infection that occurs worldwide but is more common in developing nations. Unlike hepatitis A, the disease is usually acquired by sexual contact or by exposure to infected blood, generally through blood transfusions or contaminated needles. In the Caribbean the risk is greatest in Haiti and the Dominican Republic. The vaccine is recommended only for long-term travelers (on the road more than six months) who expect to live in rural areas or have close physical contact with locals. Additionally, the vaccine is recommended for anyone who anticipates sexual contact with the local inhabitants or a possible need for medical, dental or other treatments (especially if transfusions or injections are involved) while abroad.

Hepatitis B vaccine is safe and highly effective. However, a total of three injections are necessary to establish full immunity. Several countries added hepatitis B vaccine to the list of routine childhood immunizations in the 1980s, so many young adults are already protected.

HIV/AIDS

HIV/AIDS has been reported in all Caribbean countries. More than 2% of all adults in the Caribbean carry HIV, which makes it the second-worst-affected region in the world, after sub-Saharan Africa. The highest prevalence is reported from the Bahamas, Haiti and Trinidad & Tobago. In the Caribbean most cases are related to heterosexual contacts, especially with sex workers. The exception is Puerto Rico, where the most common cause of infection is intravenous drug use. Be sure to use condoms for all sexual encounters. If you think you might visit a piercing or tattoo parlor, or if you have a medical condition that might require an injection, bring along your own sterile needles.

Leishmaniasis

Reported in the eastern part of the Dominican Republic, leishmaniasis is transmitted by sandflies, which are about one-third the size of mosquitoes. The most common form of the disease is manifested by skin ulcers on exposed parts of the body, developing over weeks or months. Involvement may be either limited or widespread. Leishmaniasis may be particularly severe in those with HIV. There is no vaccine. To protect yourself from sandflies, follow the same precautions as for mosquitoes (see p789), except that netting must be a finer mesh – at least 18 holes to the linear inch (or seven holes to the linear centimeter).

Malaria

In the Caribbean malaria occurs only in Haiti and certain parts of the Dominican Republic. For those areas, the first-choice malaria pill is chloroquine, taken once weekly in a dosage of 500mg, starting one to two weeks before arrival, continuing through the trip and for four weeks after departure. Chloroquine is safe, inexpensive and highly effective. Side effects are typically mild and may include nausea, abdominal discomfort, headache, dizziness, blurred vision or itching. Severe reactions are uncommon.

Protecting yourself against mosquito bites (see p789) is just as important as taking malaria pills, since pills are never 100% effective.

If you may not have access to medical care while traveling, you should bring along additional pills for emergency self-treatment, which you should undergo if you can't reach a doctor and you develop symptoms that suggest malaria, such as high-spiking fevers. One option is to take four tablets of Malarone once daily for three days. If you self-treat for malaria, it may also be appropriate to start a broad-spectrum antibiotic to cover typhoid fever and other bacterial infections. The drug of choice is usually a quinolone antibiotic such as ciprofloxacin (Cipro) or levofloxacin (Levaquin). If you start self-medication, you should try to see a doctor at the earliest possible opportunity.

If you end up with a fever after returning home, see a physician, as malaria symptoms may not occur for months.

Rabies

Rabies is a viral infection of the brain and spinal cord that is almost always fatal. The rabies virus is carried in the saliva of infected animals and is typically transmitted through an animal bite, though contamination of any break in the skin with infected

HEALTH

saliva may result in rabies. Animal rabies occurs on several of the Caribbean islands, particularly in the small Indian mongoose.

Rabies vaccine is safe, but a full series requires three injections and is quite expensive. Those at high risk for rabies, such as animal handlers and spelunkers (cave explorers), should certainly get the vaccine. In addition, those at lower risk for animal bites should consider asking for the vaccine if they are traveling to remote areas and might not have access to appropriate medical care if needed. The treatment for a possibly rabid bite consists of rabies vaccine with rabies-immune globulin. It's effective, but must be given promptly. Most travelers don't need rabies vaccine.

All animal bites and scratches must be promptly and thoroughly cleansed with large amounts of soap and water, and local health authorities should be contacted to determine whether or not further treatment is necessary.

Schistosomiasis

A parasitic infection that is carried by snails and acquired by exposure of skin to contaminated freshwater, schistosomiasis is reported in parts of the Dominican Republic, Guadeloupe, Martinique, Puerto Rico, Antigua & Barbuda, Montserrat and St Lucia. To find out whether or not schistosomiasis is present in the areas you'll be visiting, go to the World Health Organization's **Global Schistosomiasis Atlas** (www.who. int/wormcontrol/documents/maps/country/en/).

Early symptoms may include fever, loss of appetite, weight loss, abdominal pain, weakness, headaches, joint and muscle pains, diarrhea, nausea and cough, but most infections are asymptomatic at first. Long-term complications may include kidney failure, enlargement of the liver and spleen, engorgement of the esophageal blood vessels and accumulation of fluid in the abdominal cavity. Occasionally, eggs may be deposited in the brain or spinal cord, leading to seizures or paralysis.

When traveling in areas where schistosomiasis occurs, you should avoid swimming, wading, bathing or washing in bodies of freshwater, including lakes, ponds, streams and rivers. Toweling yourself dry after exposure to contaminated water may reduce your chance of getting infected, but

does not eliminate it. Saltwater and chlorinated pools carry no risk of schistosomiasis.

Typhoid

Typhoid is uncommon on most of the Caribbean islands, except Haiti, which has reported a number of typhoid outbreaks.

Typhoid fever is caused by ingestion of food or water contaminated by a species of salmonella known as *Salmonella typhi*. Fever occurs in virtually all cases. Other symptoms may include headache, malaise, muscle aches, dizziness, loss of appetite, nausea and abdominal pain, diarrhea or constipation. Possible complications include intestinal perforation, intestinal bleeding, confusion, delirium and (rarely) coma.

Typhoid vaccine is recommended for all travelers to Haiti, and for travelers to the other islands who expect to stay in rural areas for an extended period or who may consume potentially contaminated food or water. Typhoid vaccine is usually given orally, but is also available as an injection. Neither vaccine is approved for use in children under age two. If you get typhoid fever, the drug of choice is usually a quinolone antibiotic such as ciprofloxacin (Cipro) or levofloxacin (Levaquin), which many travelers carry for treatment of traveler's diarrhea.

Yellow Fever

Yellow fever occurs among animals on Trinidad & Tobago, but has not been reported among humans there in recent years. However, yellow-fever vaccine is strongly recommended for travelers going outside urban areas in Trinidad & Tobago.

There's no yellow fever on the other Caribbean islands, but the following require proof of yellow-fever vaccination if you're arriving from a yellow fever–infected country in Africa or the Americas: Anguilla, Antigua & Barbuda, Bahamas, Barbados, Dominica, Grenada, Guadeloupe, Haiti, Jamaica, Montserrat, Netherlands Antilles, St Kitts & Nevis, St Lucia, St Vincent & the Grenadines, Trinidad & Tobago.

Yellow-fever vaccine is given only in approved yellow-fever vaccination centers, which provide validated international certificates of vaccination (yellow booklets). The vaccine should be given at least 10 days before any potential exposure to yellow fever and remains effective for approximately 10 years. Reactions to the vaccine are generally mild and may include headaches, muscle aches, low-grade fevers or discomfort at the injection site. Severe, life-threatening reactions have been described but are extremely rare. In general, the risk of becoming ill from the vaccine is far less than the risk of becoming ill from yellow fever, and you're strongly encouraged to get the vaccine.

The yellow-fever vaccine is not recommended for pregnant women or children less than nine months old. These travelers, if arriving from a country with yellow fever, should obtain a waiver letter, preferably written on letterhead stationary and bearing the stamp used by official immunization centers to validate the international certificate of vaccination.

TRAVELER'S DIARRHEA
To prevent diarrhea, avoid tap water unless it has been boiled, filtered or chemically disinfected (with iodine tablets); eat fresh fruits or vegetables only if cooked or peeled; be wary of dairy products that might contain unpasteurized milk; and be highly selective when eating food from street vendors.

If you develop diarrhea, be sure to drink plenty of fluid, preferably an oral rehydration solution containing lots of salt and sugar. A few loose stools don't require treatment, but if you start having more than four or five stools a day, you should start taking an antibiotic (usually a quinolone drug) and an antidiarrheal agent (such as loperamide). If diarrhea is bloody, persists for more than 72 hours or is accompanied by fever, shaking chills or severe abdominal pain, you should seek medical attention.

ENVIRONMENTAL HAZARDS
Bites & Stings
Do not attempt to pet, handle or feed any animal, with the exception of domestic animals known to be free of any infectious disease. Most injuries from animals are directly related to a person's attempt to touch or feed the animal.

Any bite or scratch by a mammal, including bats, should be promptly and thoroughly cleansed with large amounts of soap and water, then an antiseptic such as iodine or alcohol should be applied. The local health authorities should be contacted immediately regarding possible postexposure rabies treat-

ment, whether or not you've been immunized against rabies. It may also be advisable to start an antibiotic, since wounds caused by animal bites and scratches frequently become infected. One of the newer quinolones, such as levofloxacin (Levaquin), which many travelers carry in case of diarrhea, would be an appropriate choice.

MOSQUITO BITES
To prevent mosquito bites, wear long sleeves, long pants, a hat and shoes (rather than sandals). Bring along a good insect repellent, preferably one containing DEET, and apply to exposed skin and clothing, but not to eyes, mouth, cuts, wounds or irritated skin. In general, adults and children over 12 should use preparations containing 25% to 35% DEET, which usually lasts about six hours. Children between two and 12 years of age should use preparations containing no more than 10% DEET, applied sparingly, which will usually last about three hours. Products containing lower concentrations of DEET are as effective, but for shorter periods of time. Neurological toxicity has been reported from DEET, especially in children, but appears to be extremely uncommon and generally related to overuse. Compounds containing DEET should not be used on children under the age of two.

Insect repellents containing certain botanical products, including eucalyptus oil and soybean oil, are effective but last only 1½ to two hours. Repellents containing DEET are preferable for areas where there is a high risk of malaria or yellow fever. Products based on citronella are not effective.

For additional protection you can apply permethrin to clothing, shoes, tents and bed nets. Permethrin treatments are safe and remain effective for at least two weeks, even when items are laundered. Permethrin should not be applied directly to skin.

Don't sleep with the window open unless there is a screen. If sleeping outdoors or in accommodations that allow entry of mosquitoes, use a bed net, preferably treated with permethrin, with edges tucked in under the mattress. The mesh size should be less than 0.06in (1.5mm). If the sleeping area is not otherwise protected, use a mosquito coil, which will fill the room with insecticide through the night. Wristbands impregnated with repellent are not effective.

HEALTH

SEA STINGERS

Spiny sea urchins and coelenterates (coral and jellyfish) are a hazard in some areas. If stung by a coelenterate, apply dilute vinegar or baking soda. Remove tentacles carefully, and not with bare hands. If stung by a stinging fish, such as a stingray, immerse the limb in water at about 115°F (45°C).

SNAKE BITES

Snakes are a hazard on some of the Caribbean islands. The fer-de-lance, which is the most lethal, has been spotted on Martinique and St Lucia. It generally doesn't attack without provocation, but may bite humans who accidentally come too close as it lies camouflaged on the forest floor. The fer-de-lance is usually 5ft to 6ft long (1.5m to 1.8m), but may reach up to 9ft (2.7m). Its coloration is gray or brown, with light stripes, dark diamond markings and a yellow throat.

The bushmaster, which is the world's largest pit viper, may be found on Trinidad. Like other pit vipers, the bushmaster has a heat-sensing pit between the eye and nostril on each side of its head, which it uses to detect the presence of warm-blooded prey.

Coral snakes, which are somewhat retiring and tend not to bite humans, are reported in Trinidad as well as other islands.

If a venomous snake bite occurs, place the victim at rest, keep the bitten area immobilized and move the victim immediately to the nearest medical centre. Avoid tourniquets, which are no longer recommended.

Heatstroke

To protect yourself from excessive sun exposure, stay out of the midday sun, wear sunglasses and a wide-brimmed sun hat, and apply sunscreen with SPF15 or higher, plus UVA and UVB protection. Sunscreen should be generously applied to all exposed parts of the body about 30 minutes before sun exposure, and reapplied after swimming or vigorous activity. Travelers should also drink plenty of fluids and avoid strenuous exercise when the temperature is high.

Water

Tap water is safe to drink on some of the islands, but not on others. Unless you're certain that the local water is not contaminated, you shouldn't drink it.

Vigorous boiling for one minute is the most effective means of water purification. At altitudes greater than 6500ft (1980m), boil for three minutes.

Another option is disinfecting water with iodine pills. Instructions are usually enclosed and should be carefully followed. Or you can add 2% tincture of iodine to 4½ cups (1L) of water (five drops to clear water, 10 drops to cloudy water) and let it stand for 30 minutes. If the water is cold, longer times may be required. The taste of iodinated water may be improved by adding vitamin C (ascorbic acid). Iodinated water should not be consumed for more than a few weeks. Pregnant women, those with a history of thyroid disease and those allergic to iodine should not drink iodinated water.

A good number of water filters are on the market. Those with smaller pores (reverse osmosis filters) provide the broadest protection, but they are relatively large and are readily plugged by debris. Those with somewhat larger pores (microstrainer filters) are ineffective against viruses, although they remove other organisms. Manufacturers' instructions must be carefully followed.

TRAVELING WITH CHILDREN

In general, it's safe to take children to the Caribbean. However, because some of the vaccines listed in this chapter are not approved for use in children, you should be particularly careful to avoid giving kids tap water or any questionable food or beverage. Make sure children are up to date on all routine immunizations. It's sometimes appropriate to give children some of their vaccines a little early before visiting a developing nation. You should discuss this with your pediatrician.

HEALTH

Language

CONTENTS

The rich and colorful language environment of the greater Caribbean is testament to the diverse array of people that have come to call its many shores home.

From a colonial past that saw the annihilation of virtually all traces of indigenous culture (and language) there is the legacy of Dutch, English, French, Portuguese and Spanish. Stir in a blend of elements from a veritable Babylon of other tongues, and you begin to understand why almost every part of every island has its own peculiar linguistic offering.

Outside the predominant colonial languages, perhaps the most notable influences can be traced back to the slaves brought to the islands from West Africa to be exploited by the colonial masters. European tongues, creoles, patois (pa-twa), local accents and pidgins all go into the melting pot to create a linguistic symphony as rich and diverse as the region's enchanting musical offerings.

WHO SPEAKS WHAT WHERE?

Bahamas

English is the official language of the Bahamas and it is used in all facets of daily life. It's spoken by everyone but a handful of Haitian immigrants, who speak their own creole.

'True-true' Bahamanians, mostly Black, usually speak both Bahamian Standard English (BSE) and their own distinct island patois, a musical Caribbean dialect with its own rhythm and cadence. Though there are variances among the islands and between Blacks and Whites, all sectors of Bahamian society understand patois, the language of the street. Even educated Bahamians, who tend to speak in a lilting Queen's or Oxford English, will sometimes lapse into patois at unguarded moments.

Cuba

Spanish is the official language of Cuba. Away from the hotels and tourist centers, few people speak English and then only very poorly. Despite this, many Cubans have some knowledge of English, since it's taught in primary school from grade six.

Cuban Spanish is rich, varied and astoundingly distinct. Slang and *dichos* (sayings) so dominate daily conversation, even native Spanish speakers sometimes get lost in the mix. Borrowing words from African languages, bastardizing English terms (Spanglish) and adopting language from movies, marketing and sports, Cuban Spanish is constantly evolving, with new, invented words surfacing all the time.

Eastern Caribbean

English is the main language spoken on all the islands except for the French West Indies (Guadeloupe, Martinique, St Barts and the French side of St Martin), where French is the primary language. See p793 for some useful French words and phrases.

English speakers can travel throughout the Eastern Caribbean without problems,

LANGUAGE

and the difficulty of getting around the French West Indies for people who don't speak French is generally exaggerated. Although many people outside the hotel and tourism industry don't speak English, as long as you have a phrasebook and a reasonable English-French dictionary – and a measure of patience and a sense of humor – you should be able to get by.

Dutch is spoken on the islands of Saba, St Eustatius and Dutch Sint Maarten (the southern half of St Martin). While it remains the official language of government and is taught in schools, for most practical purposes it is a secondary language after English. See the boxed text on p793 for some basic Dutch words and phrases.

On many Eastern Caribbean islands the local language is Creole, a complex patois of French, English, and West African languages with remnants of Carib, the language of the indigenous people of the same name who once thrived in the region. In addition, Hindi is spoken among family members on islands with sizable Indian populations, most notably on Trinidad.

Dominican Republic & Haiti

Spanish is the country's official language and the language of everday communication. Some English and German are also spoken within the tourist business.

Any traveler to the region who doesn't already speak some Spanish and is intending to do some independent travel in the Dominican Republic outside Santo Domingo or Puerto Plata is well advised to learn a little Spanish and carry a Spanish-English dictionary. See p796 for some useful Spanish words and phrases.

Jamaica

Officially, English is the spoken language. In reality, Jamaica is a bilingual country, and English is far more widely understood than spoken. The unofficial lingo, the main spoken language of poor Jamaicans, is called patois, a musical dialect with a staccato rhythm and cadence, laced with salty idioms and wonderfully and wittily compressed proverbs.

Patois evolved from Creole English and a twisted alchemy of the mother tongue peppered with African, Portuguese, and Spanish terms and, in this century, Rastafarian slang.

Patois is deepest in rural areas, where many people don't know much standard English. Although it's mostly the lingua franca (linking language) of the poor, all sectors of Jamaica understand patois, and even polite, educated Jamaicans lapse into patois at unguarded moments. Most Jamaicans will vary the degree of their patois according to whom they're speaking.

Puerto Rico

Every Puerto Rican learns to speak Standard Modern Spanish in school, and this is the language you'll hear from hotel and restaurant staff if you address them in Spanish. However, many seasoned Spanish speakers find themselves a little off balance when they first hear Spanish in Puerto Rico. The Spanish you hear on the streets is Antillian Spanish or, as it's known locally, Boricua (the language of Borinquen). For a number of reasons, an ear accustomed to Castillian, Mexican or South American dialects of Spanish can take a little time to get used to the rhythm and sound of spoken Boricua.

Travelers hoping to submerge themselves in the island's rich culture need to have some command of basic Spanish, as well as some sense of the distinctions between Puerto Rican and other kinds of Spanish. However, even if you speak Spanish well, you can expect Puerto Ricans, proud of their hard-earned English skills, to address you in English. One of the great rewards for many travelers to Puerto Rico is remaining long enough at a destination to hear the locals address them in Spanish.

Turks & Caicos

The official language of Turks & Caicos is English. The local islanders' distinct dialect bears much resemblance to the dialect of the Bahamas. The Haitians speak their own French-based creole patois, which foreigners may find difficult to follow. However, rarely is it as incomprehensible as it can be in Jamaica, for example.

Virgin Islands

English is the main language spoken throughout the Virgin Islands, although you'll hear quite a bit of Spanish if you visit St Croix

Hello.		
Dag/Hallo.	dakh/ha·*loa*	
Goodbye.		
Dag.	dakh	
Yes.		
Ja.	yaa	
No.		
Nee.	nay	
Please.		
Alstublieft. (pol)	als·tu·*bleeft*	
Alsjeblieft. (inf)	a·shə·*bleeft*	
Thanks.		
Bedankt. (pol or inf)	bə·*dangt*	
That's fine/You're welcome.		
Graag gedaan.	khraakh khə·*daan*	
Excuse me.		
Pardon or	par·*don*	
Excuseer mij.	eks·ku·*zayr* may	
I'm sorry.		
Sorry/Excuses.	so·ree/eks·ku·zəs	
How are you?		
Hoe gaat het met u/jou? (pol/inf)	hoo khaat hət met u/yow	
I'm fine, thanks.		
Goed, bedankt.	khoot, bə·*dangt*	
What's your name?		
Hoe heet u? (pol)	hoo hayt u	
Hoe heet je? (inf)	hoo hayt yə	
My name is ...		
Ik heet ...	ik hayt ...	

(see p296 for Spanish words and phrases). For the most part, islanders speak Standard English, but color it with an accent that is lyrical and euphonious. This distinctive accent derives from the traditional dialect of the islands, the so-called Creole, Calypso or West Indian, which blends West African grammar and speech patterns with colonial English, Danish, French and Dutch. Creole varies significantly from island to island, each displaying its own particular brand of local slang.

Creole is easy to understand when spoken slowly, but sometimes islanders use their language as code when they speak to each other quickly and sprinkle in a strong dose of slang. *Doan worry. Dem jus' limin' and fowl bus'ness no cockroacy.* (Don't worry. They are just relaxing, and it's best to mind your own business.)

PHRASEBOOKS & DICTIONARIES

An excellent resource to facilitate your hopping around the French-speaking islands is Lonely Planet's *French Phrasebook*. It's lightweight and compact, and it'll provide you with all the basics you need to get around and make new friends. There are also a number of good French-English/English-French pocket dictionaries, such as those published by Langenscheidt, Larousse and Oxford Hachette.

On the Spanish-speaking islands, Lonely Planet's *Latin-American Spanish Phrasebook* is the perfect companion. Another recommended resource is the compact and surprisingly comprehensive University of Chicago *Spanish-English, English-Spanish Dictionary*.

FRENCH

The French used in the Caribbean reflects hundreds of years of intermingling with English as well as West African languages. In addition to borrowing words freely from these other tongues, it's flatter in intonation, with less of the traditional French lilting cadence. Also, speakers of Creole pay less attention to gender; anything or anyone can be *il*. Nevertheless, in the following phrases both masculine and feminine forms have been indicated where necessary. The masculine form comes first and is separated from the feminine by a slash.

In general, you'll find that francophones in the Caribbean are very forgiving of your efforts to speak French, no matter how faltering those efforts may be.

ACCOMMODATIONS

I'm looking for a ...	*Je cherche ...*	zher shersh ...
campground	*un camping*	un kom·*peeng*
guesthouse	*une pension (de famille)*	ewn pon·*syon* (der fa·mee·ler)

hotel	*un hôtel*	un o·tel
youth hostel	*une auberge*	ewn o·berzh
	de jeunesse	der zher·nes

Do you have any rooms available?
Est-ce que vous avez des chambres libres?
e·sker voo·za·vay day shom·brer lee·brer
May I see it?
Est-ce que je peux voir la chambre?
es·ker zher per vwa la shom·brer

I'd like ...	*Je voudrais ...*	zher voo·dray ...
a single room	*une chambre à*	ewn shom·brer
	un lit	a un lee
a double-bed	*une chambre*	ewn shom·brer
room	*avec un grand*	a·vek un gron
	lit	lee
a twin room	*une chambre*	ewn shom·brer
with two beds	*avec des lits*	a·vek day lee
	jumeaux	zhew·mo

How much is it ...?	*Quel est le prix ...?*	kel e ler pree ...
per night	*par nuit*	par nwee
per person	*par personne*	par per·son

CONVERSATION & ESSENTIALS

Hello.	*Bonjour.*	bon·zhoor
Goodbye.	*Au revoir.*	o·rer·vwa
Yes.	*Oui.*	wee
No.	*Non.*	no
Please.	*S'il vous plaît.*	seel voo play
Thank you.	*Merci.*	mair·see
You're welcome.	*Je vous en prie.*	zher voo·zon pree
	De rien. (inf)	der ree·en
Excuse me.	*Excuse-moi.*	ek·skew·zay·mwa
I'm sorry.	*Pardon.*	par·don

What's your name?
Comment vous ko·mon voo·za·pay·lay voo
appelez-vous? (pol)
Comment tu ko·mon tew ta·pel
t'appelles? (inf)
My name is ...
Je m'appelle ... zher ma·pel ...
Where are you from?
De quel pays êtes-vous? der kel pay·ee et·voo
De quel pays es-tu? (inf) der kel pay·ee e·tew
I'm from ...
Je viens de ... zher vyen der ...
I like ...
J'aime ... zhem ...
I don't like ...
Je n'aime pas ... zher nem pa ...

SIGNS

Entrée	Entrance
Sortie	Exit
Renseignements	Information
Ouvert	Open
Fermé	Closed
Interdit	Prohibited
Toilettes/WC	Toilets
Hommes	Men
Femmes	Women

DIRECTIONS

Where is ...?
Où est ...? oo e ...
Go straight ahead.
Continuez tout droit. kon·teen·way too drwa
Turn left.
Tournez à gauche. toor·nay a gosh
Turn right.
Tournez à droite. toor·nay a drwat
at the corner
au coin o kwun
at the traffic lights
aux feux o fer
far (from)
loin (de) lwun (der)
near (to)
près (de) pray (der)

EMERGENCIES

Help!
Au secours! o skoor
There's been an accident!
Il y a eu un accident! eel ya ew un ak·see·don
I'm lost.
Je me suis égaré/e. (m/f) zhe me swee·zay·ga·ray
Leave me alone!
Fichez-moi la paix! fee·shay·mwa la pay

Call ...!	*Appelez ...!*	a·play ...
a doctor	*un médecin*	un mayd·sun
the police	*la police*	la po·lees

HEALTH

I'm ill.	*Je suis malade.*	zher swee ma·lad
It hurts here.	*J'ai une douleur*	zhay ewn doo·ler
	ici.	ee·see

I'm ...	*Je suis ...*	zher swee ...
asthmatic	*asthmatique*	(z)as·ma·teek
diabetic	*diabétique*	dee·a·bay·teek
epileptic	*épileptique*	(z)ay·pee·lep·teek

I'm allergic	Je suis	zher swee
to ...	allergique ...	za·lair·zheek ...
antibiotics	aux antibiotiques	o zon·tee·byo·teek
nuts	aux noix	o nwa
peanuts	aux cacahuètes	o ka·ka·wet
penicillin	à la pénicilline	a la pay·nee·see·leen

| diarrhea | la diarrhée | la dya·ray |
| nausea | la nausée | la no·zay |

LANGUAGE DIFFICULTIES

Do you speak English?
Parlez-vous anglais?   par·lay·voo ong·lay
Does anyone here speak English?
Y a-t-il quelqu'un qui   ya·teel kel·kung kee
parle anglais?   par long·glay
I understand.
Je comprends.   zher kom·pron
I don't understand.
Je ne comprends pas.   zher ner kom·pron pa

NUMBERS

0	zero	zay·ro
1	un	un
2	deux	der
3	trois	trwa
4	quatre	ka·trer
5	cinq	sungk
6	six	sees
7	sept	set
8	huit	weet
9	neuf	nerf
10	dix	dees
11	onze	onz
12	douze	dooz
13	treize	trez
14	quatorze	ka·torz
15	quinze	kunz
16	seize	sez
17	dix-sept	dee·set
18	dix-huit	dee·zweet
19	dix-neuf	deez·nerf
20	vingt	vung
21	vingt et un	vung tay un
22	vingt-deux	vung·der
30	trente	tront
40	quarante	ka·ront
50	cinquante	sung·kont
60	soixante	swa·sont
70	soixante-dix	swa·son·dees
80	quatre-vingts	ka·trer·vung
90	quatre-vingt-dix	ka·trer·vung·dees
100	cent	son
1000	mille	meel

SHOPPING & SERVICES

I'd like to buy ...
Je voudrais acheter ...   zher voo·dray ash·tay ...
How much is it?
C'est combien?   say kom·byun

Can I pay by ...?
Est-ce que je peux payer avec ...?
es·ker zher per pay·yay a·vek ...

credit card		
ma carte de crédit		ma kart der kray·dee
traveler's checks		
des chèques de voyage		day shek der vwa·yazh

more	plus	plew
less	moins	mwa
smaller	plus petit	plew per·tee
bigger	plus grand	plew gron

I'm looking	Je cherche ...	zhe shersh ...
for ...		
a bank	une banque	ewn bonk
the hospital	l'hôpital	lo·pee·tal
the market	le marché	ler mar·shay
the police	la police	la po·lees
the post office	le bureau de	ler bew·ro der
	poste	post
a public phone	une cabine	ewn ka·been
	téléphonique	tay·lay·fo·neek
a public toilet	les toilettes	lay twa·let
the telephone	la centrale	la son·tral
centre	téléphonique	tay·lay·fo·neek

TIME & DATES

What time is it?	Quelle heure est-il?	kel er e til
It's (8) o'clock.	Il est (huit) heures.	il e (weet) er
It's half past ...	Il est (...) heures et	il e (...) er e
	demie.	day·mee
today	aujourd'hui	o·zhoor·dwee
tomorrow	demain	der·mun
yesterday	hier	yair

Monday	lundi	lun·dee
Tuesday	mardi	mar·dee
Wednesday	mercredi	mair·krer·dee
Thursday	jeudi	zher·dee
Friday	vendredi	von·drer·dee
Saturday	samedi	sam·dee
Sunday	dimanche	dee·monsh

January	janvier	zhon·vyay
February	février	fayv·ryay
March	mars	mars
April	avril	a·vreel
May	mai	may

LANGUAGE

June	*juin*	zhwun
July	*juillet*	zhwee·yay
August	*août*	oot
September	*septembre*	sep·tom·brer
October	*octobre*	ok·to·brer
November	*novembre*	no·vom·brer
December	*décembre*	day·som·brer

TRANSPORTATION
Public Transportation

What time does	*À quelle heure*	a kel er
... leave/arrive?	*part/arrive ...?*	par/a·reev ...
boat	*le bateau*	ler ba·to
bus	*le bus*	ler bews
plane	*l'avion*	la·vyon
train	*le train*	ler trun

I'd like a ...	*Je voudrais*	zher voo·dray
ticket.	*un billet ...*	un bee·yay ...
one-way	*simple*	sum·pler
round trip	*aller et retour*	a·lay ay rer·toor

I want to go	*Je voudrais aller*	zher voo·dray a·lay
to ...	*à ...*	a ...
ticket office	*le guichet*	ler gee·shay
timetable	*l'horaire*	lo·rair

Private Transportation
I'd like to hire ...

Je voudrais louer ...   zher voo·dray loo·way ...

a car

une voiture   ewn vwa·tewr

a bicycle

un vélo   un vay·lo

Is this the road to ...?

C'est la route pour ...?   say la root poor ...

Where's a gas/petrol station?

Où est-ce qu'il y a une   oo es·keel ya ewn
station-service?   sta·syon·ser·vees

Please fill it up.

Le plein, s'il vous plaît.   ler plun seel voo play

I'd like ... liters.

Je voudrais ... litres.   zher voo·dray ... lee·trer

SPANISH

In Spanish, nouns are either masculine or feminine, and there are rules to help determine gender (with exceptions, of course!). Where both masculine and feminine forms are included in this language guide, they are separated by a slash, with the masculine form first, eg *perdido/a* (lost).

ACCOMMODATIONS

I'm looking for ...

Estoy buscando ...   e·stoy boos·kan·do ...

Where is ...?

¿Dónde hay ...?   don·de ai ...

a hotel	*un hotel*	oon o·*tel*
a boarding	*una pensión*	oo·na pen·*syon*
house		
a youth hostel	*un albergue*	oon al·*ber*·ge
	juvenil	khoo·ve·*neel*

Are there any rooms available?

¿Hay habitaciones libres?
ay a·bee·ta·*syon*·es *lee*·bres

May I see the room?

¿Puedo ver la habitación?
pwe·do ver la a·bee·ta·*syon*

I'd like a ...	*Quisiera una*	kee·*sye*·ra *oo*·na
room.	*habitación ...*	a·bee·ta·*syon* ...
single	*individual*	een·dee·bee·*dwal*
double	*doble*	*do*·ble
twin	*con dos camas*	kon dos *ka*·mas

How much is it	*¿Cuánto cuesta*	*kwan*·to *kwes*·ta
per ...?	*por ...?*	por ...
night	*noche*	*no*·che
person	*persona*	per·*so*·na

CONVERSATION & ESSENTIALS

Hello.	*Hola.*	*o*·la
	Saludos.	sa·*loo*·dos
Good morning.	*Buenos días.*	*bwe*·nos *dee*·as
Good afternoon.	*Buenas tardes.*	*bwe*·nas *tar*·des
Good evening/	*Buenas noches.*	*bwe*·nas *no*·ches
night.		
Bye.	*Hasta luego.*	*as*·ta *lwe*·go
Yes.	*Sí.*	see
No.	*No.*	no
Please.	*Por favor.*	por fa·*vor*
Thank you.	*Gracias.*	*gra*·syas
Many thanks.	*Muchas gracias.*	*moo*·chas *gra*·syas
You're welcome.	*De nada.*	de *na*·da
Pardon me.	*Perdón.*	per·*don*
Excuse me.	*Permiso.*	per·*mee*·so
(used when asking permission)		
Forgive me.	*Disculpe.*	dees·*kool*·pe
(used when apologizing)		

How are you?

| *¿Cómo está usted?* (pol) | *ko*·mo es·*ta* oos·*ted* |
| *¿Cómo estás?* (inf) | *ko*·mo es·*tas* |

What's your name?

| *¿Cómo se llama?* (pol) | *ko*·mo se *ya*·ma |
| *¿Cómo te llamas?* (inf) | *ko*·mo te *ya*·mas |

My name is ...
Me llamo ...   me *ya*·mo ...
Where are you from?
¿De dónde es? (pol)   de *don*·de es
¿De dónde eres? (inf)   de *don*·de e·res
I'm from ...
Soy de ...   soy de ...

DIRECTIONS
How do I get to ...?
¿Cómo puedo llegar   ko·mo *pwe*·do ye·*gar*
a ...?   a ...
Is it far?
¿Está lejos?   es·*ta* le·khos
Go straight ahead.
Siga derecho.   *see*·ga de·*re*·cho
Turn left.
Voltée a la izquierda.   vol·*te*·e a la ees·*kyer*·da
Turn right.
Voltée a la derecha.   vol·*te*·e a la de·*re*·cha
Can you show me (on the map)?
¿Me lo podría indicar   me lo po·*dree*·a een·dee·*kar*
(en el mapa)?   (en el *ma*·pa)

EMERGENCIES
Help!   *¡Socorro!*   so·*ko*·ro
Go away!   *¡Déjeme!*   *de*·khe·me

Call ...!   *¡Llame a ...!*   *ya*·me a
an ambulance *una ambulancia* oo·na am·boo·*lan*·sya
a doctor   *un médico*   oon *me*·dee·ko
the police   *la policía*   la po·lee·*see*·a

It's an emergency.
Es una emergencia.   es oo·na e·mer·*khen*·sya
Could you help me, please?
¿Me puede ayudar,   me *pwe*·de a·yoo·*dar*
por favor?   por fa·*vor*
I'm lost.
Estoy perdido/a. (m/f)   es·*toy* per·*dee*·do/a

HEALTH
I'm sick.
Estoy enfermo/a.   es·*toy* en·*fer*·mo/a
Where's the hospital?
¿Dónde está el hospital? *don*·de es·*ta* el os·pee·*tal*

I'm allergic *Soy alérgico/a* soy a·*ler*·khee·ko/a
to ...   *a ...*   a ...
antibiotics   *los antibióticos* los an·tee·*byo*·tee·kos
nuts   *las fruta secas* las *froo*·tas se·kas
penicillin   *la penicilina* la pe·nee·see·*lee*·na

I'm ...   *Soy ...*   soy ...
asthmatic   *asmático/a*   as·*ma*·tee·ko/a
diabetic   *diabético/a*   dee·ya·*be*·tee·ko/a
epileptic   *epiléptico/a*   e·pee·*lep*·tee·ko/a

I have ...   *Tengo ...*   *ten*·go ...
diarrhea   *diarrea*   dya·*re*·a
nausea   *náusea*   *now*·se·a

SIGNS	
Entrada	Entrance
Salida	Exit
Información	Information
Abierto	Open
Cerrado	Closed
Prohibido	Prohibited
Servicios/Baños	Toilets
Hombres/Varones	Men
Mujeres/Damas	Women

LANGUAGE DIFFICULTIES
Does anyone here speak English?
¿Hay alguien que hable   ai al·*gyen* ke *a*·ble
inglés?   een·*gles*
Do you speak (English)?
¿Habla (inglés)?   *a*·bla (een·*gles*)
I (don't) understand.
(No) Entiendo.   (no) en·*tyen*·do
What does ... mean?
¿Qué quiere decir ...?   ke *kye*·re de·*seer* ...

NUMBERS
0	*cero*	*ce*·ro
1	*uno/a* (m/f)	*oo*·no/a
2	*dos*	dos
3	*tres*	tres
4	*cuatro*	*kwa*·tro
5	*cinco*	*seen*·ko
6	*seis*	seys
7	*siete*	*sye*·te
8	*ocho*	*o*·cho
9	*nueve*	*nwe*·ve
10	*diez*	dyes
11	*once*	*on*·se
12	*doce*	*do*·se
13	*trece*	*tre*·se
14	*catorce*	ka·*tor*·se
15	*quince*	*keen*·se
16	*dieciséis*	dye·see·*seys*
17	*diecisiete*	dye·see·*sye*·te
18	*dieciocho*	dye·see·*o*·cho
19	*diecinueve*	dye·see·*nwe*·ve
20	*veinte*	*vayn*·te

LANGUAGE

21	*veintiuno*	vayn·tee·*oo*·no
30	*treinta*	*trayn*·ta
31	*treinta y uno*	*trayn*·tai oo·no
40	*cuarenta*	kwa·*ren*·ta
50	*cincuenta*	seen·*kwen*·ta
60	*sesenta*	se·*sen*·ta
70	*setenta*	se·*ten*·ta
80	*ochenta*	o·*chen*·ta
90	*noventa*	no·*ven*·ta
100	*cien*	syen
200	*doscientos*	do·*syen*·tos
1000	*mil*	meel

SHOPPING & SERVICES

I'd like to buy ...
  Quisiera comprar ...   kee·*sye*·ra kom·*prar* ...
How much is it?
  ¿Cuánto cuesta?   *kwan*·to *kwes*·ta
What time does it open/close?
  ¿A qué hora abre/cierra?   a ke *o*·ra *a*·bre/*sye*·ra

Do you accept ...?
  ¿Aceptan ...?   a·sep·*tan* ...
  credit cards
  tarjetas de crédito   tar·*khe*·tas de *kre*·dee·to
  traveler's checks
  cheques de viajero   *che*·kes de vya·*khe*·ro

I'm looking   *Estoy buscando ...*   es·*toy* boos·*kan*·do ...
for the ...
  ATM   *el cajero*   el ka·*khe*·ro
     automático   ow·to·ma·tee·ko
  bank   *el banco*   el *ban*·ko
  exchange office   *la casa de*   la *ka*·sa de
     cambio   *kam*·byo
  market   *el mercado*   el mer·*ka*·do
  pharmacy   *la farmacia*   la far·*ma*·sya
  post office   *los correos*   los ko·*re*·os
  telephone   *el centro*   el *sen*·tro
   centre   *telefónico*   te·le·*fo*·nee·ko
  tourist office   *la oficina de*   la o·fee·*see*·na de
     turismo   too·*rees*·mo

TIME & DATES

When?   *¿Cuándo?*   *kwan*·do
What time is it?   *¿Qué hora es?*   ke *o*·ra es
It's (one) o'clock.   *Es la (una).*   es la (*oo*·na)
It's (seven)   *Son las (siete).*   son las (*sye*·te)
 o'clock.
half past (two)   *(dos) y media*   (dos) ee *me*·dya
today   *hoy*   oy
tonight   *esta noche*   es·ta *no*·che
tomorrow   *mañana*   ma·*nya*·na
yesterday   *ayer*   a·*yer*

Monday	*lunes*	*loo*·nes
Tuesday	*martes*	*mar*·tes
Wednesday	*miércoles*	*myer*·ko·les
Thursday	*jueves*	*khwe*·ves
Friday	*viernes*	*vyer*·nes
Saturday	*sábado*	*sa*·ba·do
Sunday	*domingo*	do·*meen*·go

January	*enero*	e·*ne*·ro
February	*febrero*	fe·*bre*·ro
March	*marzo*	*mar*·so
April	*abril*	a·*breel*
May	*mayo*	*ma*·yo
June	*junio*	*khoo*·nyo
July	*julio*	*khoo*·lyo
August	*agosto*	a·*gos*·to
September	*septiembre*	sep·*tyem*·bre
October	*octubre*	ok·*too*·bre
November	*noviembre*	no·*vyem*·bre
December	*diciembre*	dee·*syem*·bre

TRANSPORTATION
Public Transportion

What time does   *¿A qué hora ...*   a ke *o*·ra ...
... leave/arrive?   *sale/llega?*   *sa*·le/*ye*·ga
  the boat   *el barco*   el *bar*·ko
  the bus   *el autobus*   el ow·to·*boos*
  the plane   *el avión*   el a·*vyon*
  the ship   *el barco*   el *bar*·ko

a ticket to ...   *un boleto a ...*   bo·*le*·to a ...
one way   *ida*   *ee*·da
return   *ida y vuelta*   *ee*·da ee *vwel*·ta
bus station   *la estación de*   la es·ta·*syon* de
     autobuses   ow·to·*boo*·ses
ticket office   *la boletería*   la bo·le·te·*ree*·a

Private Transportation

I'd like to hire a/an ...
Quisiera alquilar ...   kee·*sye*·ra al·kee·*lar* ...
  bicycle
  una bicicleta   *oo*·na bee·see·*kle*·ta
  car
  un auto/un coche   oon *ow*·to/oon *ko*·che

Is this the road to ...?
  ¿Se va a ... por esta   se va a ... por *es*·ta
  carretera?   ka·re·*te*·ra
Where's a gas/petrol station?
  ¿Dónde hay una bomba?   *don*·de ai *oo*·na *bom*·ba
Please fill it up.
  Lleno, por favor.   *ye*·no por fa·*vor*
I'd like ... liters.
  Quiero ... litros.   *kye*·ro ... *lee*·tros

Glossary

accra – a fried mixture of okra, black-eyed peas, pepper and salt

agouti – a short-haired rabbitlike rodent resembling a guinea pig with short ears and long legs, which has a fondness for sugarcane

Arawak – linguistically related Indian tribes that inhabited most of the Caribbean islands and northern South America

asson – sacred rattle that is used in *Vodou* ceremonies

back time – a *Creole* expression meaning 'good old days'

bake – a sandwich made with fried bread and usually filled with shark or fish

bareboat – a sail-it-yourself charter yacht usually rented by the week or longer

biguine – also spelled 'beguine,' an Afro-French dance music with a bolero rhythm that originated in Martinique in the 1930s

bomba – musical form and dance inspired by African rhythms and characterized by call-and-response dialogues between musicians and interpreted by dancers; often considered as a unit with *plena*, as in *'bomba y plena'*

boula – drum used in *Vodou* ceremonies providing an even rhythm holding all the others together

breadfruit – a large, round, green fruit; a Caribbean staple comparable to potatoes in its carbohydrate content and prepared in much the same way

bul jol – roasted *breadfruit* and saltfish made with tomatoes and onions

bush tea – tea made from the islands' leaves, roots and herbs; each tea, with names like 'sorrel,' 'tamarind,' 'worry vine,' 'worm grass' and 'Spanish needle,' cures a specific illness, such as gas, menstrual pain, colds or insomnia

callaloo – also spelled kallaloo; a spinachlike green, originally from Africa; callaloo soup is the quintessential Caribbean soup, made with dasheen leaves and often coconut milk, resembling a creamy spinach soup

calypso – a popular Caribbean music developed from slave songs; lyrics reflect political opinions, social views and commentary on current events

campismo – national network of 82 camping installations in Cuba

carambola – star fruit; a green-to-yellow fruit with a star-shaped cross section that has a crisp, juicy pulp and can be eaten without being peeled

Carnival/Carnaval – the major Caribbean festival that originated as a pre-Lenten festivity but is now observed at various times throughout the year on different islands

cassareep – a molasseslike sauce used in local recipes, made of *cassava*, water, sugar and spices

cassava – also called yucca or manioc; a root used since precolonial times as a staple of island diets, whether steamed, baked or grated into a flour for bread

cay – an Arawak word meaning 'small island'

cayo – a coral key (Spanish)

chattel house – a type of simple wooden dwelling placed upon cement or stone blocks so it can be easily moved; often erected on rented land

christophene – a common pear-shaped vegetable, like a cross between a potato and a cucumber, that is eaten raw in salads or cooked like a squash

chutney – an up-tempo, rhythmic music used in celebrations of various social situations in Trinidad's Indian communities

colombo – a spicy, east Indian–influenced dish that resembles curry

compas – traditional Haitian music; a fusion of dance band and merengue beats

conch – also called *lambi*; a large gastropod; common throughout the Caribbean, the chewy meat of the *conch* is often prepared in a spicy *Creole* sauce. Due to overfishing, the *conch* is headed for the endangered-species list.

conkies – a mixture of cornmeal, coconut, pumpkin, sweet potatoes, raisins and spice, steamed in a *plantain* leaf

cou-cou – a creamy cornmeal and okra mash, commonly served with saltfish

Creole – people: a person of mixed Black and European ancestry; language: local pidgin that's predominantly a combination of French and African; food: a cuisine characterized by spicy, full-flavored sauces and a heavy use of green peppers and onions

dancehall – a contemporary off-shoot of reggae with faster, digital beats and an MC

dasheen – a type of taro; the leaves are known as 'callaloo' and cooked much like spinach or turnip leaves, and the starchy tuberous root is boiled and eaten like a potato

daube meat – a pot roast seasoned with vinegar, native seasonings, onion, garlic, tomato, thyme, parsley and celery

dolphin – both a marine mammal found in Caribbean waters and a common type of white-meat fish (also called *mahimahi*); the two are not related, and 'dolphin' on any menu always refers to the fish

down island – a *Creole* expression referring to the islands of the Lesser Antilles

duppy – a ghost or spirit; also called a *jumbie*

flying fish – a gray-meat fish named for its ability to skim above the water, particularly plentiful in Barbados
fungi – a semihard cornmeal pudding similar to Italian polenta, added to soups and used as a side dish; also a *Creole* name for the music made by local scratch bands

gade – Danish for 'street'
gîte – small family-run accommodations (French)
gneps – a fruit the size of a large marble that yields a sweet, orange flesh
goat water – a spicy goat-meat stew often flavored with cloves and rum
gommier – a large native gum tree found in Caribbean rainforests
ground provisions – roots used for cooking
guagua – local bus (*gua-gua* in Dominican Republic)

houmfor – *Vodou* temple or ceremonial altar
houngan – *Vodou* priest

I-tal – a natural style of vegetarian cooking practiced by Rastafarians
irie – alright, groovy, used to indicate that all is well

jambalaya – a *Creole* dish usually consisting of rice cooked with ham, chicken or shellfish, spices, tomatoes, onions and peppers
jinetero/a – 'jockey'; a tout or prostitute
johnnycake – a corn-flour griddle cake
jug-jug – a mixture of Guinea cornmeal, green peas and salted meat
jumbie – a ghost or spirit; also called a *duppy*
jump-up – a nighttime street party that usually involves dancing and plenty of rum drinking

kónet – trumpet made from hammered zinc, ending in a flared horn

lambi – Caribbean name for *conch*
limin' – from the *Creole* verb 'to lime,' meaning to hang out, relax, chill

mahimahi – see *dolphin*
mairie – town hall (French)
manchineel – a common tree on Caribbean beaches whose poisonous fruit sap can cause a severe skin rash; called *mancenillier* on the French islands and *anjenelle* on Trinidad & Tobago
manicou – opossum, a small marsupial
mas camps – short for 'masquerade camps,' workshops where artists prepare Carnival costumes
mash up – a wreck, a car accident or a street riot
mauby – a bittersweet drink made from the bark of the rhamnaceous tree, sweetened with sugar and spices
mento – folk *calypso* music

mocko jumbies – costumed stilt walkers representing spirits of the dead, seen in carnivals
mojito a cocktail made from rum, mint, sugar, seltzer and fresh lime juice
mountain chicken – the legs of the crapaud, a type of frog found in Dominica

native seasoning – homemade mixtures of salt, ground hot pepper, cloves, garlic, mace, nutmeg, celery and parsley
négritude – a Black Pride philosophical and political movement that emerged in Martinique in the 1930s

obeah – a system of ancestral worship related to *Vodou* and rooted in West African religions
oil down – a mix of breadfruit, pork, callaloo and coconut milk; national dish of Grenada
out islands – islands or cays that lie across the water from the main islands of an island group

Painkiller – a popular alcoholic drink made with two parts rum, one part orange juice, four parts pineapple juice, one part coconut cream and a sprinkle of nutmeg and cinnamon
paladar – privately owned restaurant in Cuba serving reliable, inexpensive meals
panyards – the places where steel-pan bands practice their music in the months leading up to Carnival
parang – a type of music sung in Spanish and accompanied by guitars and maracas and played at Christmastime in some Caribbean countries; originated in Venezuela
pate – a fried pastry of *cassava* or plantain dough stuffed with spiced goat, pork, chicken, *conch*, lobster or fish
pepperpot – a spicy stew made with various meats, accompanied by peppers and *cassareep* (extract of *cassava*)
pigeon peas – the brown, pealike seeds of a tropical shrub that are cooked like peas and served mixed with rice
plantain – a starchy fruit of the banana family, usually fried or grilled like a vegetable
Planters punch – also known as Planteur, a punch mixing rum and fruit juice
playa – beach (Spanish)
plena – form of traditional Puerto Rican dance and song that unfolds to distinctly African rhythms beat out with maracas, tambourines and other traditional percussion instruments; often associated with *bomba*
público – collective taxis (*publique* in Haiti)

quelbe – blend of jigs, quadrilles, military fife and African drum music

rapso – a fusion of *soca* and hip-hop
reguettón – Spanish-speaking dancehall
roti – West Indian fast food of curry filling (often potatoes and chicken) rolled inside flat bread

rumba – an Afro-Cuban dance form that originated among plantation slaves during the 19th century; during the 1920s and '30s, the term 'rumba' was adopted in North America and Europe for a ballroom dance in 4/4 time; in Cuba today, 'to rumba' simply means 'to party'

salsa – Cuban music based on *son*

Santería – Afro-Caribbean religion representing the syncretism of Catholic and African beliefs, based on the worship of Catholic saints and their associated Yoruba deities

scratch band – a West Indian band that uses homemade percussion instruments such as washboards, ribbed gourds and *conch* shells to accompany a singer and melody played on a recorder or flute

snowbirds – North Americans, usually retired, who come to the Caribbean for its warm winters

soca – the energetic offspring of calypso, soca uses danceable rhythms and risqué lyrics to convey pointed social commentary

son – Cuba's basic form of popular music that jelled from African and Spanish elements in the late 19th century

sorrel juice – a lightly tart, bright-red drink rich in vitamin C made from the flowers of the sorrel plant

souse – a dish made out of pickled pig's head and belly, spices and a few vegetables, commonly served with a pig-blood sausage called 'pudding'

steel pan – also called 'steel drum,' an instrument made from oil drums or the music it produces

Taino – a settled, Arawak-speaking tribe that inhabited much of the Caribbean prior to the Spanish conquest; the word itself means 'we the good people'

tamarind – the pod of a large tropical tree of the legume family; the juicy, acidic pulp of the tamarind seeds is used in beverages

taptap – local Haitian bus

timba – contemporary *salsa*

Vodou – a religion practised in Haiti that is a synthesis of West African animist spirit religions and residual rituals of the Taino Indians

Vodouisants – adherents of *Vodou*, many of whom are also Roman Catholics

zouk – popular French West Indies music that draws from the biguine, cadence and other French Caribbean folk forms

Behind the Scenes

THIS BOOK

This fourth edition of *Caribbean Islands* was written by Debra Miller, Ginger Adams Otis, Conner Gorry, Michael Kohn, Thomas Kohnstamm, Alex Leviton, Oda O'Carroll, Gary Prado Chandler, Liza Prado Chandler, Michael Read and Ryan Ver Berkmoes. Ned Friary and Glenda Bendure coordinated the second edition (formerly known as *Eastern Caribbean*) and Kevin Anglin coordinated the third. Material from *Puerto Rico* 2 and *Virgin Islands* 1 (both by Randall Pfeffer), *Jamaica* 3, *Bahamas, Turks & Caicos* 2 (both by Christopher P Baker) and *Dominican Republic & Haiti* 2 (by Scott Doggett and Joyce Connolly) was used as base text for this title. Dr David Goldberg MD contributed the Health chapter.

THANKS from the Authors

Debra Miller A book this size and scope requires a tremendous amount of teamwork and I must extend a mighty toast to my fellow authors for their ideas, enthusiasm and incredibly good cheer. At the helm, Alex Hershey was a fearless leader who kept us on course and kept me sane when I was drowning in details. A special thanks also goes to Heather Dickson, Erin Corrigan and Alison Lyall. A mighty ho ho ho and a bottle of rum to friend and colleague Randy Pfeffer whose text and good advice helped me enormously. A very special nod of appreciation to tourism folks who made my life so much easier, especially Kelly Clarke, Nicole Mahoney and Janelle James. To Gunda Harewood in Trini: what a great way to meet a friend. To Gerard and Oda at Pax Guest House:

you cleared my vision and helped so much. To Mat & Jeremy: thank you for making me laugh. To all the incredible islanders I've met on my way, you have my gratitude for imparting your local knowledge, friendly conversation and honest ideas. Thanks for the sails, the scuba dives, the drinks and the hospitality. Finally, I would be lost adrift on a rolling sea without my cocaptain Rob, who always makes home such a great place to return to. Clink.

Ginger Adams Otis Thanks to Marta and everyone at the Puerto Rico Tourism Company for their friendly support, Frances Borden and Edelman Public Relations in New York, Michael in Culebra, Peter and the marvelous staff in El Convento, the many islanders who helped me along the way (especially the crew in San Juan along Calle Fortaleza) and my friends and family for all the much-needed assistance through the project. Thanks also to Debra Miller for being the most patient, accessible and well-informed Coordinating Author ever, and to the Caribbean coauthors for sharing information so openly. Thanks to Commissioning Editors Alex Hershey and Erin Corrigan for their enthusiasm and dedication to the project, and the editorial and cartography team in Oz.

Conner Gorry *No es fácil*, writing an LP guide, and many people have come to my aid and rescue along the way. *Muchísimas gracias* to the CMMLK family, especially Ariel Moriyón, Muro (*¡por los tabacos sobre todo!*), Alicia, Ramoncito and the IT team; Teresita, Gisella and Giselle in Boyeros; Bernardo,

---

THE LONELY PLANET STORY

The story begins with a classic travel adventure: Tony and Maureen Wheeler's 1972 journey across Europe and Asia to Australia. There was no useful information about the overland trail then, so Tony and Maureen published the first Lonely Planet guidebook to meet a growing need.

From a kitchen table, Lonely Planet has grown to become the largest independent travel publisher in the world, with offices in Melbourne (Australia), Oakland (USA) and London (UK). Today Lonely Planet guidebooks cover the globe. There is an ever-growing list of books and information in a variety of media. Some things haven't changed. The main aim is still to make it possible for adventurous travelers to get out there – to explore and better understand the world.

At Lonely Planet we believe travelers can make a positive contribution to the countries they visit – if they respect their host communities and spend their money wisely. Every year 5% of company profit is donated to charities around the world.

Sarahi, Aracely and Juan Carlos in Trinidad; Abbie Jenks and the WFP cabal; and the entire Caribbean Islands team, especially Deb Miller, who crafted this book *con tremendo* swing – the mojitos are on me! A special thanks to my Mom and Carolyn who make it all possible and to my husband Joel Suárez, *'el coordinador de mi vida,'* who makes it all worth it.

Jill Kirby Firstly, my thanks go to Christopher P Baker whose excellent work on the first editions of the *Bahamas, Turks & Caicos* guide was inspiring and more than helpful. My appreciation also goes to Commissioning Editors Alex Hershey and Heather Dickson, Managing Cartographer Alison Lyall, and Coordinating Author Debra Miller for their cheerful support and leadership.

Members of the Turks & Caicos Hotel & Tourism Association and the Bahamian Ministry of Tourism were helpful along the way, as was the enthusiastic Renea Knowles of the Nassau & Paradise Island Promotions Board – much gratitude to you all. Also my warm thanks to Jean Pierce and Kris Newman of Reel Divers, Dinesh Rampersaud and Shaun Deane of J&B Tours, Godfrey Minns, Alvin Demeritte and Kay Turnquest of Bahama Houseboats and Paolo Garzaroli of Graycliff.

For helping me throughout my time in Nassau, Long Island and Caicos, respectively, my great thanks to Vernetta Roker and the helpful staff of Nassau's Holiday Inn Junkanoo, Lucy Wells of Seaview Lodge, and Wayne Garland and the fabulous employees of Provo's Comfort Suites.

My greatest support and companion on and off the road is John Allen, who makes my life a joy: thank you.

Michael Kohn Many thanks to the people of Haiti and the expats living there who offered tips, suggestions and information on all things Haitian. Many thanks to Kevan Higgins, David Reimer and Sara Luther of the US embassy in Port-au-Prince. Thanks to Genie and Wilhelm Lemke. At Lonely Planet, thanks to Alex Hershey and my fellow *Caribbean Island* authors. Back home in California, thanks for continued support to my friends, family and most of all to Baigal.

Thomas Kohnstamm Thanks to the indomitable Greenface de Souze along with Joyce and Brikeeta for their hospitality and friendship. Bogo and Norman de Souza for their help and incredible stories, not to mention Ray-Ray for all the connections. Also a debt of gratitude is owed to Jacqui Pascall for her generosity, Rod Thompson for Mayreau

expertise and Kelly Mahoney for St Vincent guidance (sorry that Chateaubelair was cut). Stateside, Kalidas and Wolfie deserve a heartfelt thanks for predeparture logistics. Thank you also to Erin Corrigan for making my second Grenada trip possible and Laila Taji for invaluabe research assistance on that return. Thanks to Deb Miller, Heather Dickson and Alex Hershey for making this happen, and last but not least, thanks to Fionnuala Twomey and the whole Australia crew for pulling it all together in the end.

Alex Leviton As always, enormous thanks go to Len Amaral, my travel partner and driver, who transported carrot cake across national boundaries for this book. Mark Bimson: you are my St Kittitian hero. On St Barth, Rosemond (and Ellen) Gréaux, Peter O'Keefe, Marielle Gréaux and Catherine Charneau – *merci!* Also, a huge debt of gratitude goes to Charanell Jackman on Anguilla; Oliver, Angelika, James, Zuleika and Suzanne on Saba; Devon and Maaike on Statia; and to Steven and the tourist office of Nevis. And thanks to the thieves of St Martin, who graciously relieved me of my wallet and driver's license, letting me discover the joys of hitchhiking through the Leewards. And thanks back home to Greg DeWitt for providing an office and some normalcy.

Oda O'Carroll Thanks to Heather Dickson and Alex Hershey who steered this project so efficiently and patiently and especially to Deb Miller, coordinator extraordinaire, without whose wit, support and good sense I may have lost a few more fingernails and hair follicles than I can afford. Thanks also to Etain and Joe Costello in Antigua for his local insight and the coffee. A big thanks to Ashling for keeping my young fairies Esa and Mella off my lap during write-up and to my lovable 'cultured individual' Eoin for accompanying me to Guadeloupe. Ginormous thanks to my sister Lisa who drove our battered chick-mobile, tuned the radio, commented and quaffed beer with me on the road so tirelessly.

Gary & Liza Prado Chandler Thank you to the hundreds of Dominicans and expats whose friendly assistance and sound advice enriched this book immeasurably, as well as our experience researching and writing it. We are especially grateful to Doña Agustina for her warm Valentine's Day welcome in Santo Domingo, Andy from samanaonline .com in Las Galeras, Rosanna Selman de León from Paraiso Caño Hondo at Parque Los Haitises and the staff at the tourist offices in Jarabacoa.

At Lonely Planet, thank you (and good luck apple-picking) to Alex Hershey who got us started, to Erin Corrigan and Fionnuala Twomey who saw us through to the end, to Alison Lyall, Bonnie Wintle and everyone in cartography, and to coordinating author Deb Miller.

We are blessed with loving and supportive families. Thank you to Mom and Dad Chandler, Ellen, Elyse, Joey, Sue, Katy and Kyle, and to Mom and Dad Prado, who visited us in Bávaro and opened our eyes to ocean aerobics and the joys of the hotel lobby bar. Thanks also to Javier, Deb, Sammy, Owen and David; along with our friends, they make coming home one of the best parts of traveling abroad.

Michael Read First and foremost, thanks to Lonely Planet's energetic and talented publishing mavens Heather Dickson, Alex Hershey and Debra Miller for nurturing this title as it went from the brief phase to production. A warm thank-you also to my beleaguered coauthors who provided a sense of community and bonhomie along the way. Rebecca Ellis-Owen of Financial Dynamics provided extremely valuable tactical support for my journey to Jamaica, as did Joanne Gammage and Becky Addley of the Cayman Islands Department of Tourism. Paul Kahn graciously offered office space in Paris during the months of research and write-up, asking only for tiny cups of espresso in return. In San Francisco, Paul Catasus gave me shelter during the dark final days of writing and forgave me for nearly burning down his house. In Jamaica, special thanks to Kingstonians Valerie Dean and her partner Calvin for their warm welcome, and to Jason Henzell in Treasure Beach for everything that he does for his beautiful community. Above all, thanks to Irene Rietschel for her amazing tolerance and support. May we travel deep and blissfully into the Great Morass.

Ryan Ver Berkmoes Thanks to all the people of the ABCs who charmed me during my visit. Special thanks include: on Aruba, Francis Jacobs was music to my ears and was never early and never late; on Bonaire Rolando Martin left his flooded mother's basement and forded the floods themselves to answer a long list of questions with grace and humor; on Curaçao, Genevieve de Palm was simply brilliant and made me almost forget about the deficiencies of the tourist office. And to Deb Miller for being a fine coordinator, and the many LP folks like Heather Dickson, Alex Hershey, David Zingarelli, Allison Lyall and more. Of course Erin Corrigan is always my favorite beach babe.

CREDITS

Commissioning Editors: Alex Hershey, Erin Corrigan and Heather Dickson
Coordinating Editor: Fionnuala Twomey
Coordinating Cartographer: Bonnie Wintle
Coordinating Layout Designer: Pablo Gastar
Managing Cartographer: Alison Lyall
Assisting Editors: Monique Choy, Kate Evans, Kyla Gilizan, Paul Harding, Charlotte Harrison, Helen Koehne, Pat Kinsella, Katie Lynch, Kristin Odijk, Anne Mulvaney, Joanne Newell and Julia Taylor
Assisting Cartographers: David Connolly, Corey Hutchinson, Laurie Mikkelsen, Anthony Phelan, Jolyon Philcox, Herman So and Simon Tillema
Assisting Layout Designers: Kaitlin Beckett and Jacqui Saunders
Cover Designer: Marika Kozak
Indexers: Adrienne Costanzo and Stephanie Pearson
Project Manager: Eoin Dunlevy
Language Content Coordinator: Quentin Frayne

Thanks to: Yvonne Bischofberger, Sally Darmody, Trent Holden, Martin Heng, Laura Jane, Rebecca Lalor, Adriana Mammarella, John Shippick, Nick Stebbing, David Zingarelli

THANKS from Lonely Planet

Many thanks to the following travelers who used the last edition and wrote to us with helpful hints, useful advice and interesting anecdotes.

A John A Adams, Skip Albertson, Donald & Ileens Allen, Paul Alper, Jorge Alvar Villegas, Bruce Anderson, Fabian Andersson, Paul Aquilina, Maria Archuleta, Juha Asikainen, Arne Augedal **B** Ingvar Backeus, Hauke Baeumel, David Baker, Emilio Baldi, Reimar Banis, Andy Banner, Gabriele Bapst, Claudia Barchiesi, Tamara Barr, Jeff Barton, Gordon Bass, Dyanne Bax, Rosemary Beattie, Johannes Beck, Philippe Bélisle, Robyn Belzner, Silke Bender, Jorg Beyeler, Leander Bindewald, Linda Gray Biok, Stephen Blythe, Suzana Boavida, Ruth Bolton, Nic Boulton, Tom Brailsford, Harvey Brant, Beau & Priscilla Brendler, Barbara Brendley, Dan Broockmann, Doug Browne, Gemma Brunton, Heather Buck, Rollo Burgess, Susan Butler, Mandy Byrnes **C** Andrew & Barb Campbell, Robert Carbo, Paola Carnevale, Bonnie Carpenter, Olivia Carrescia, Chris Cecapel, Robert Chaleff, Martha Chapman, Karen Cheung, George & Shelly Chilton, David Church, Ann Cleary, James Cocks, Jeffrey Cohen, Nikki Collins, Elizabeth M Corrie, Alistair Crawford, H Crighton, Michael Critchley, Toni Crow, Margaret Cunningham, Peter Currie **D** Edward William Dadswell, Jane & Walter Dal Bo, Linda Daniele, Robert D'Avanzo, Susan Davis, Bart de Blende, Chad de Groot, Katrien de Schrijver, Andrew Dean, Ronald Dekker, Luis Di Criscio, Kate Dickens, Ruud Dirksen, Jonathan Distad, Daniel Dolan, Robert F Domagala Jr, Faye Donnaway, Joseph Dragon, Jean Duggleby, Sheila Duncan, Ljiljana Duplanic **E** Frank Ehrlicher, Dimos Ermoupolis, Ana Escorbort, Nils Elvemo, Rhian Evans **F** Maria Falgoust, Jim Ferrier, Hanne

Finholt, Angela Fischer, Angelika Fischer-Krischik, Jude Raymond Fish, Patricia Fobare Erickson, Pavel Fochler, Rolf Forster, Muriel Foucher, Eric Franco, Claire Frank, Elena Frazzoni, Joseph & Laura Frey, Jonathon Frisbee **G** Jean Marc Gaude, Joanna Gaughan, Mordechai Gemer, Hilde Gerlofs, Mylene Gibbs, Mark Ginsburg, Jeffrey Glazer, Stephan Gorthner, John Grant, Sally Gray, Maarten Gresnigt, Sam Griffiths, Sonia Grillo **H** Bart Haarsma, Ronald Hakenberg, David Hall, Sanford Halperin, Jean-Lou Hamelin, Chris Hastings, Virginia Haynes, Bob Helkowski, Charles Hergenroeder, Christophe Hervet, Carolyn Hill, Thomas Hill, Melissa Hinkle, Damien Home, Coleman Hookaylo, Karen Hookaylo, Caroline Houde, JE Hovens, Paul Hover, Frans Huber, Eleanor Humphreys, Olivia Hung, Maggie Hurchalla, Hannes Hutzelmeyer **I** John Ide **J** Ellen James, Volkmar E Janicke, Jan Jasiewicz, Greg Jennings, Fausto Jimenez, Neysha Jimenez, Joey Johnson, Patty Johnston, Erin Jones **K** Janne & Sanna Kalliola, Leena Karkkainen, Linda Karlbom, Karen Keane, Kevin Keller, John Kenyon, Ebru Keskine, Zia Asad Khan, Lisa Kirkman, Toni Klein, Peggie Klekotka, Anja Kohler, Cara & Sam Kolb, Carla Koretsky, Peter Korfits, Richard Kowalczyk, Kryn Krautheim, Jack Kravitz, Martin Kreiner, T Gopal Krishna Murthy, Dennis Kroeger, Irina Kuha **L** Andy Lam, Sharon Lans, Terry Larcombe, Cheryl Laufle, Jeff Laufle, Brian Lema, Jeff Lester, Michelle Lewis, Richard Lewis, Heidi Leyhourne, Rebecca Lidstone, David Lockwood, Charlott Loebsack, Brice Lorenzi, Bart W Lorijnen, Paul Luchessa, Paul Lucock, Larry Ludmer, Kelsi Luhnow, Kirsten Lund Andersen **M** Fulvio Maccarone, Julia Mackenzie, Julien Magerel, Harold Mahabir, Andre Marcil, Anna Marfitt, Judit Marothy, Amy Martin, Volker Maschmann, David Mason, Sara Mason, Nick Massey, David Maufe, Michael Mayan, Kara McCaffrey, Theresa McDonald, John McEnroe, Jeanette McGarry, Liam McKnight, Patrik Mertens, Iris Metawi, Clemens Meyer, Harvey Meyer, Alexandros Mikropoulos, Pete Miller, Ryan Miller, Brian Mills, Helen Miner, Riz & Nina Mithani, Landon M Modien, Denise Molina, Dennis Mooij, Jim Murray **N** Akanksha Naik, Peter Necas, Jorg Neher, Margaret Nelson, Leah Nichols, Vivian Nielsen, Elisabetta Niero, Gunda & Howard A Nollenberger, Cathrine Nordal, Jean Norris, Anne Nothof, Sally Nowlan, Keith Nuthall **O** Marielle Ogor, Ed & Shirley O'Keefe, Alexander Olaoye, Grant O'Neill, Rob Ostrowski, Ingrid Oudman, Todd Owens **P** Rolf Palmberg, Wolfgang Pannocha, Alessandra Passerini, Carlos Paz-Soldan, Enrico Pere, Muriel Michele Peretti, Cory Perez, Paula Peterman, Katja Philipp, Veronica Piekosz, Johnathan Pierce, Melissa Pike, Tom Pisula, William Plowden, Sonya N Plowman, Jan Poole, Sergio Prescivali, S Proeschel, Sylvie Proidl, Peter Puranen **Q** Johanna Quigley **R** Ian Ramsden, Helen Rankin, Claudia Rantes, Beverly Raymond, Ken Reed, Charles Regnier, Myka Reinsch, Karin Rengefors, Riikka Reunanen, Eddie Reynoso, Thomas Riis, John Riley, Pierluigi Rizzini, Jodi Roan, Angus Robinson, Antoinette & Dey Rose, Raymond Rose, Bruce Rumoga **S** Norman Sadler, Loeve Saint-Ourens, Michelle Salazar, Francesca Salvemini, Sara Sande, Molly Saudek, Gabriele Schenk, Beate Schmahl, Carolyn Schneider, Mark Schuler, Alexis Seccombe, Sheila Sedgwick, Brigitte Seidel, Nancy Sellers, Anne Sey, Anne Shanley, Don Shanley, Karina Shaw, Nigel Shepherd, Stephanie Sherony, Malin Skarin, Charles Skinner, Bronwyn Smith, Gregory E Smith, Travis Smith, Karen Söderberg, Ioannis Sofilos, Carol Sookhoo, Kim Sowers, Zoe Spyvee, Claudia Stanzani, Erik Stark, Doug Steinburg, Beverley Stell, JE Stellingwerf, Gordon Stewart, Margaret Stock, Pat Stockdale, Louie Strano, Jon Strom, Ben Stubenberg, Rena Sumbera, Erik Svane, David Swabey, Michael & Lee Sylva, Michael Szonyi **T** Gerard Tarly, Erin Taylor, Mary Taylor, Helen Temple, Suzanne Teune, Rosalie Thanh, Peter Theglev, Betty R Theriault, Heather Thoreau, David Thornton, Armin Timmerer, Marc Tolud, Anne Dallen Touchin, Patrick Traynor, Monika & Martin Treipl, SP Tschinkel, John Tucker, Leo Tucker, Geoff Tuckwell, Jack Tyler **V** Adrie van Sorgen, Monika Vetsch, Eric Viel, NR Virgallito, Anne & Uli Vorderbruegge **W** Eunice Walaska, Rainer Waldmann, Clive Walker, Morgan Walker, Richard Walton, Garth Ward, Trish Ward, Wolfgang Weitlaner, Wayne West, Mark Whiffin, Uwe & Sandra Wietzel, Doug Wilkins, Clifford Williams, Matthew Williams, David Wilson, E Winmill, Ruth Wise, Swiatoslaw Wojtkowiak, Aaron Wronko, Ute Wronn **Y** Douglas Yeo, Elaine Yong, Andrew Young, Catherine Gina Young, L Young **Z** Karen Zabawa, Cristina Zaganelli, Harald Zahn, Ondrej Zapletal, Dirk Zeiler, Baerbel Zimmer, Marshall Zipper, John Zubatiuk

ACKNOWLEDGMENTS

Many thanks to the following for the use of their content:

Globe on back cover © Mountain High Maps 1993 Digital Wisdom, Inc.

SEND US YOUR FEEDBACK

We love to hear from travelers – your comments keep us on our toes and help make our books better. Our well-traveled team reads every word on what you loved or loathed about this book. Although we cannot reply individually to postal submissions, we always guarantee that your feedback goes straight to the appropriate authors, in time for the next edition. Each person who sends us information is thanked in the next edition – and the most useful submissions are rewarded with a free book.

To send us your updates – and find out about Lonely Planet events, newsletters and travel news – visit our award-winning website: **www.lonelyplanet.com/feedback**.

Note: we may edit, reproduce and incorporate your comments in Lonely Planet products such as guidebooks, websites and digital products, so let us know if you don't want your comments reproduced or your name acknowledged. For a copy of our privacy policy visit www.lonelyplanet.com/privacy.

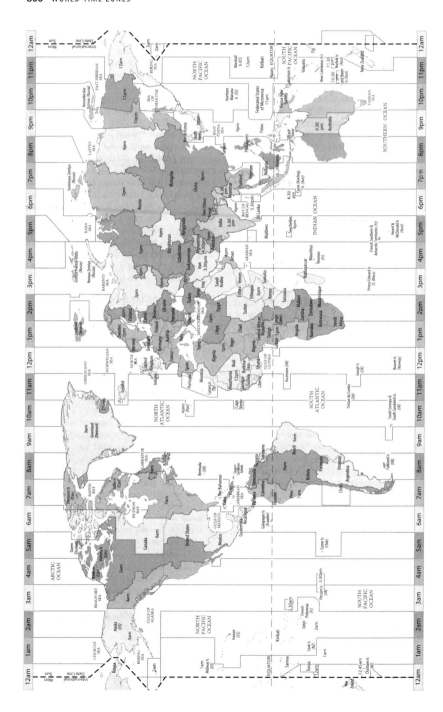

Index

INDEX

INDEX

MAP LEGEND

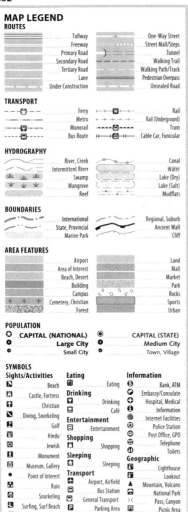

ROUTES

Tollway	One-Way Street
Freeway	Street Mall/Steps
Primary Road	Tunnel
Secondary Road	Walking Trail
Tertiary Road	Walking Path/Track
Lane	Pedestrian Overpass
Under Construction	Unsealed Road

TRANSPORT

Ferry	Rail
Metro	Rail (Underground)
Monorail	Tram
Bus Route	Cable Car, Funicular

HYDROGRAPHY

River, Creek	Canal
Intermittent River	Water
Swamp	Lake (Dry)
Mangrove	Lake (Salt)
Reef	Mudflats

BOUNDARIES

International	Regional, Suburb
State, Provincial	Ancient Wall
Marine Park	Cliff

AREA FEATURES

Airport	Land
Area of Interest	Mall
Beach, Desert	Market
Building	Park
Campus	Rocks
Cemetery, Christian	Sports
Forest	Urban

POPULATION

⊕ CAPITAL (NATIONAL)	◉ CAPITAL (STATE)
● Large City	● Medium City
● Small City	○ Town, Village

SYMBOLS

Sights/Activities
- Beach
- Castle, Fortress
- Christian
- Diving, Snorkeling
- Golf
- Hindu
- Jewish
- Monument
- Museum, Gallery
- Point of Interest
- Ruin
- Snorkeling
- Surfing, Surf Beach
- Windsurfing
- Zoo, Bird Sanctuary

Eating
- Eating

Drinking
- Drinking
- Café

Entertainment
- Entertainment

Shopping
- Shopping

Sleeping
- Sleeping

Transport
- Airport, Airfield
- Bus Station
- General Transport
- Parking Area
- Gas Station
- Taxi Rank

Information
- Bank, ATM
- Embassy/Consulate
- Hospital, Medical
- Information
- Internet Facilities
- Police Station
- Post Office, GPO
- Telephone
- Toilets

Geographic
- Lighthouse
- Lookout
- Mountain, Volcano
- National Park
- Pass, Canyon
- Picnic Area
- Shelter, Hut
- Waterfall

LONELY PLANET OFFICES

Australia
Head Office
Locked Bag 1, Footscray, Victoria 3011
☎ 03 8379 8000, fax 03 8379 8111
talk2us@lonelyplanet.com.au

USA
150 Linden St, Oakland, CA 94607
☎ 510 893 8555, toll free 800 275 8555
fax 510 893 8572, info@lonelyplanet.com

UK
72–82 Rosebery Ave,
Clerkenwell, London EC1R 4RW
☎ 020 7841 9000, fax 020 7841 9001
go@lonelyplanet.co.uk

Published by Lonely Planet Publications Pty Ltd
ABN 36 005 607 983

© Lonely Planet 2005

© photographers as indicated 2005

Cover photograph: Female folklore dancers, Trinidad, Cuba, Torino/Photolibrary (front); Wharf at dive resort, María la Gorda, Cuba, Simon Foale/Lonely Planet Images (back). Many of the images in this guide are available for licensing from Lonely Planet Images: www.lonelyplanetimages.com.

Although the authors and Lonely Planet have taken all reasonable care in preparing this book, we make no warranty about the accuracy or completeness of its content and, to the maximum extent permitted, disclaim all liability arising from its use.